The Psychology of Gender
Volume I

The International Library of Critical Writings in Psychology

Series Editors: A.J. Chapman
Professor of Psychology
University of Leeds
N.P. Sheehy
Professor of Psychology
School of Psychology
The Queen's University of Belfast
Leo Goldberger
Professor of Psychology
New York University

Industrial and Organizational Psychology (Volumes I and II)
Edited by Cary L. Cooper
The Psychology of Gender (Volumes I, II, III and IV)
Edited by Carol Nagy Jacklin
Social Psychology (Volumes I, II and III)
Edited by Elliot Aronson and Anthony R. Pratkanis

Future titles will include:
Memory
Edited by Peter E. Morris and Martin Conway
Developmental Psychology
Edited by Peter E. Bryant
Ageing
Edited by Patrick Rabbitt
Cognitive Science
Edited by Noel P. Sheehy and Antony J. Chapman
Attention
Edited by Geoffrey Underwood
Ergonomics and Human Factors
Edited by David Oborne
Mathematical and Statistical Psychology
Edited by Philip Levy
Physiological Psychology
Neuropsychology
Perception
Learning
Emotion
Language
Motivation
Personality
Psychodiagnostics
Psychoanalysis and Psychotherapy

The Psychology of Gender
Volume I

Edited by
Carol Nagy Jacklin
Professor of Psychology
University of Southern California

A New York University Press Reference Collection

© Carol Nagy Jacklin 1992. For copyright of individual articles please refer to the Acknowledgements.

All rights reserved.

First published in the U.S.A. in 1992 by
NEW YORK UNIVERSITY PRESS
Washington Square
New York, N.Y. 10003

Library of Congress Cataloging in Publication Data
The Psychology of gender/edited by Carol Nagy Jacklin.
    p. cm. – (International library of critical writings in psychology)
"New York University Press reference collection".
Includes index.
ISBN 0–8147–4185–1 (v.1). – ISBN 0–8147–4186–X (v.2).
ISBN 0–8147–4187–8 (v.3). – ISBN 0–8147–4188–6 (v.4).
ISBN 0–8147–4184–3 (set)
  1. Sex differences (Psychology) I. Jacklin, Carol Nagy.
II. Series.
  [DNLM: 1. Gender Identity. 2. Sex Behavior–psychology.
3. Sex Characteristics. BF 692 P9743]
BF 692.2.P764 1992
155.3'3–dc20
DNLM/DLC
for Library of Congress   92–16187
                                                                                        CIP

Manufactured in Great Britain

Contents

Acknowledgements ix
Introduction xiii

PART I   HISTORICAL ISSUES

1. Leta Stetter Hollingworth (1914), 'Variability as Related to Sex Differences in Achievement: A Critique', *American Journal of Sociology*, **19**, 510–30   3
2. Leta S. Hollingworth (1916), 'Sex Differences in Mental Traits', *Psychological Bulletin*, **XIII** (10), 377–84   24
3. Leta S. Hollingworth (1918), 'Comparison of the Sexes in Mental Traits', *Psychological Bulletin*, **XV** (12), 427–32   32
4. Helen Thompson Woolley (1910), 'A Review of the Recent Literature on the Psychology of Sex', *Psychological Bulletin*, **VII**, 335–42   38
5. Helen Thompson Woolley (1914), 'The Psychology of Sex', *Psychological Bulletin*, **XI** (10), 353–79   46
6. Anne Anastasi (1981), 'Sex Differences: Historical Perspectives and Methodological Implications', *Developmental Review*, **1**, 187–206   73
7. Janice Haaken (1988), 'Field Dependence Research: A Historical Analysis of a Psychological Construct', *Signs: Journal of Women in Culture and Society*, **13** (2), 311–30   93

PART II   NEONATAL AND INFANCY PERIODS

8. Elizabeth J. Aries and Rose R. Olver (1985), 'Sex Differences in the Development of a Separate Sense of Self During Infancy: Directions for Future Research', *Psychology of Women Quarterly*, **9**, 515–31   115
9. Thomas Gualtieri and Robert E. Hicks (1985), 'An Immunoreactive Theory of Selective Male Affliction', *The Behavioral and Brain Sciences*, **8** (3), September, 427–41   132
10. 'Open Peer Commentary on Thomas Gualtieri and Robert E. Hicks' (1985), *The Behavioral and Brain Sciences*, **8** (3), September, 441–77   147
11. Carol Nagy Jacklin and Eleanor M. Maccoby (1982), 'Length of Labor and Sex of Offspring', *Journal of Pediatric Psychology*, **7** (4), 355–60   184
12. Anneliese F. Korner (1969), 'Neonatal Startles, Smiles, Erections, and Reflex Sucks as Related to State, Sex, and Individuality', *Child Development*, **40** (4), December, 1039–53   190

13. Anneliese F. Korner, Byron W. Brown, Jr., Elaine P. Reade, David K. Stevenson, Stephen A. Fernbach and Valerie A. Thom (1988), 'State Behavior of Preterm Infants as a Function of Development, Individual and Sex Differences', *Infant Behavior and Development*, **11**, 111–24   205
14. Helena C. Kraemer, Anneliese Korner, Thomas Anders, Carol Nagy Jacklin and Sue Dimiceli (1985), 'Obstetric Drugs and Infant Behavior: A Reevaluation', *Journal of Pediatric Psychology*, **10** (3), 345–53   219
15. Marilyn M. McMillen (1979), 'Differential Mortality by Sex in Fetal and Neonatal Deaths', *Science*, **204** (6), April, 89–91   228

PART III BRAIN ORGANIZATION AND BRAIN INJURY

16. William Kerr Hahn (1987), 'Cerebral Lateralization of Function: From Infancy Through Childhood', *Psychological Bulletin*, **101** (3), May, 376–92   233
17. Andrew Kertesz and Thomas Benke (1989), 'Sex Equality in Intrahemispheric Language Organization', *Brain and Language*, **37**, 401–8   250
18. Doreen Kimura (1987), 'Are Men's and Women's Brains Really Different?', *Canadian Psychology*, **28** (2), 133–47   259
19. Richard S. Lewis and Lois Christiansen (1989), 'Intrahemispheric Sex Differences in the Functional Representation of Language and Praxic Functions in Normal Individuals', *Brain and Cognition*, **9**, 238–43   275
20. Jeannette McGlone (1980), 'Sex Differences in Human Brain Asymmetry: A Critical Survey', *The Behavioral and Brain Sciences*, **3** (2), June 215–27   281
21. Parley W. Newman, Karin Bunderson and Robert H. Brey (1985), 'Brain Stem Electrical Responses of Stutterers and Normals by Sex, Ears, and Recovery', *Journal of Fluency Disorders*, **10**, 59–67   294
22. L. Pizzamiglio, A. Mammucari and C. Razzano (1985), 'Evidence for Sex Differences in Brain Organization in Recovery in Aphasia', *Brain and Language*, **25**, 213–23   303
23. Martha Taylor Sarno, Antonia Buonaguro and Eric Levita (1985), 'Gender and Recovery from Aphasia after Stroke', *The Journal of Nervous and Mental Disease*, **173** (10), October, 605–9   314
24. Mirna I. Vrbancic and James L. Mosley (1988), 'Sex-Related Differences in Hemispheric Lateralization: A Function of Physical Maturation', *Developmental Neuropsychology*, **4** (2), 151–67   319

PART IV MATURATION AND MOTOR DEVELOPMENT

25. Peter H. Buschang, Robert M. Baume and G. Gisela Nass (1983), 'A Craniofacial Growth Maturity Gradient for Males and Females Between 4 and 16 Years of Age', *American Journal of Physical Anthropology*, **61**, 373–81   339
26. Rachel K. Clifton, Jane Gwiazda, Joseph A. Bauer, Marsha G. Clarkson and Richard M. Held (1988), 'Growth in Head Size During Infancy: Implications for Sound Localization', *Developmental Psychology*, **24** (4), July, 477–83   348
27. Jerry R. Thomas and Karen E. French (1985), 'Gender Differences Across Age in Motor Performance: A Meta-Analysis', *Psychological Bulletin*, **98** (2), September, 260–82   355
28. Frank L. Smoll and Robert W. Schutz (1990), 'Quantifying Gender Differences in Physical Performance: A Developmental Perspective', *Developmental Psychology*, **26** (3), 360–69   378
29. Warren O. Eaton and Lesley Reid Enns (1986), 'Sex Differences in Human Motor Activity Level', *Psychological Bulletin*, **100** (1), July, 19–28   388
30. Paula M. Duke, J. Merrill Carlsmith, Dennis Jennings, John A. Martin, Sanford M. Dornbusch, Ruth T. Gross and Bryna Siegel-Gorelick (1982), 'Educational Correlates of Early and Late Sexual Maturation in Adolescence', *The Journal of Pediatrics*, **100** (4), 633–7   398
31. Lloyd G. Humphreys, Timothy C. Davey and Randolph K. Park (1985), 'Longitudinal Correlation Analysis of Standing Height and Intelligence', *Child Development*, **56** (6), December, 1465–78   403
32. Paula Rantakallio, L. von Wendt and Helena Mäkinen (1985), 'Influence of Social Background on Psychomotor Development in the First Year of Life and its Correlation with Later Intellectual Capacity: A Prospective Cohort Study', *Early Human Development*, **11** (2), July, 141–8   417
33. Deborah P. Waber, Madeline B. Mann, James Merola and Patricia M. Moylan (1985), 'Physical Maturation Rate and Cognitive Performance in Early Adolescence: A Longitudinal Examination', *Developmental Psychology*, **21** (4), July, 666–81   425

PART V HORMONES AND BEHAVIOUR

34. Jo-Anne Finegan, Betty Bartleman and P.Y. Wong (1989), 'A Window for the Study of Prenatal Sex Hormone Influences on Postnatal Development', *The Journal of Genetic Psychology*, **150** (1), March, 101–12   443

35. Anke A. Ehrhardt (1985), 'The Psychobiology of Gender' in A.S. Rossi (ed.), *Gender and the Life Course*, Hawthorne, NY: Aldine Publishing Co., 81–96   455
36. Carol Nagy Jacklin, Karen Thompson Wilcox and Eleanor E. Maccoby (1988), 'Neonatal Sex-Steroid Hormones and Cognitive Abilities at Six Years', *Developmental Psychobiology*, **21** (6), 567–74   471
37. Elizabeth J. Susman, Gale Inoff-Germain, Editha D. Nottelmann, D. Lynn Loriaux, Gordon B. Cutler, Jr., and George P. Chrousos (1987), 'Hormones, Emotional Dispositions, and Aggressive Attributes in Young Adolescents', *Child Development*, **58**, 1114–34   479
38. E.J. Susman, E.D. Nottelmann, G.E. Inoff-Germain, L.D. Dorn, G.B. Cutler, Jr., D.L. Loriaux and G.P. Chrousos (1985), 'The Relation of Relative Hormonal Levels and Physical Development, and Social-Emotional Behavior in Young Adolescents', *Journal of Youth and Adolescence*, **14** (3), 245–64   500
39. J. Brooks-Gunn and Michelle P. Warren (1989), 'Biological and Social Contributions to Negative Affect in Young Adolescent Girls', *Child Development*, **60**, 40–55   520
40. Michelle P. Warren and J. Brooks-Gunn (1989), 'Mood and Behavior at Adolescence: Evidence for Hormonal Factors', *Journal of Clinical Endocrinology and Metabolism*, **69** (1), July, 77–83   536
41. William R. Hazzard (1986), 'Biological Basis of the Sex Differential in Longevity', *Journal of the American Geriatrics Society*, **34** (6), June, 455–71   543

Name Index   561

Acknowledgements

The editor and publishers wish to thank the following who have kindly given permission for the use of copyright material.

Ablex Publishing Corporation for article: Anneliese F. Korner, Byron W. Brown, Jr., Elaine P. Reade, David K. Stevenson, Stephen A. Fernbach and Valerie A. Thom (1988), 'State Behavior of Preterm Infants as a Function of Development, Individual and Sex Differences', *Infant Behavior and Development*, **11**, 111–24.

Academic Press, Inc. for articles: Richard S. Lewis and Lois Christiansen (1989), 'Intrahemispheric Sex Differnces in the Functional Representation of Language and Praxic Functions in Normal Individuals', *Brain and Cognition*, **9**, 238–43; L. Pizzamiglio, A. Mammucari and C. Razzano (1985), 'Evidence for Sex Differences in Brain Organization in Recovery in Aphasia', *Brain and Language*, **25**, 213–23; Andrew Kertesz and Thomas Benke (1989), 'Sex Equality in Intrahemispheric Language Organization', *Brain and Language*, **37**, 401–8; Anne Anastasi (1981), 'Sex Differences: Historical Perspectives and Methodological Implications', *Developmental Review*, **1**, 187–206; Paula Rantakallio, L. von Wendt and Helena Mäkinen (1985), 'Influence of Social Background on Psychomotor Development in the First Year of Life and its Correlation with Later Intellectual Capacity: A Prospective Cohort Study', *Early Human Development*, **11** (2), 141–8.

American Association for the Advancement of Science: Marilyn M. McMillen (1979), 'Differential Mortality by Sex in Fetal and Neonatal Deaths', *Science*, **204** (6), 89–91.

American Geriatrics Society for article: William R. Hazzard (1986), 'Biological Basis of the Sex Differential in Longevity', *Journal of American Geriatrics Society*, **34** (6), 455–71.

American Psychological Association for articles: Deborah P. Waber, Madeline B. Mann, James Merola and Patricia M. Moylan (1985), 'Physical Maturation Rate and Cognitive Performance in Early Adolescence: A Longitudinal Examination', *Developmental Psychology*, **21** (4), 666–81; Rachel K. Clifton, Jane Gwiazda, Joseph A. Bauer, Marsha G. Clarkson and Richard M. Held (1988), 'Growth in Head Size During Infancy: Implications for Sound Localization', *Developmental Psychology*, **24** (4), 477–83; Frank L. Smoll and Robert W. Schutz (1990), 'Quantifying Gender Differences in Physical Performance: A Developmental Perspective', *Developmental Psychology*, **26** (3), 360–69; Helen Thompson Woolley (1910), 'A Review of the Recent Literature on the Psychology of Sex', *Psychological Bulletin*, **VII**, 335–42; Helen Thompson Woolley (1914), 'The Psychology of Sex', *Psychological Bulletin*, **XI** (10), 353–79; Leta S. Hollingworth (1916), 'Sex Differences in Mental Traits', *Psychological Bulletin*, **XIII** (10), 377–84; Leta S. Hollingworth (1918), 'Comparison of the Sexes in Mental Traits', *Psychological Bulletin*, **XV** (12), 427–32; Jerry R. Thomas and Karen E. French (1985), 'Gender Differences Across Age in Motor Performance: A Meta-Analysis', *Psychological Bulletin*, **98** (2), 260–82; Warren O. Eaton and Lesley Reid Enns (1986), 'Sex Differences in Human Motor Activity Level', *Psychological Bulletin*, **100** (1), 19–28; William Kerr Hahn (1987), 'Cerebral Lateralization of Function: From Infancy Through Childhood', *Psychological Bulletin*, **101** (3), 376–92.

American Sociological Association for excerpt: Anke A. Ehrhardt (1985), 'The Psychobiology of Gender' in A.S. Rossi (ed.), *Gender and the Life Course*, 81–96.

Cambridge University Press for articles: Elizabeth J. Aries and Rose R. Olver (1985), 'Sex Differences in the Development of a Separate Sense of Self During Infancy: Directions for Future Research', *Psychology of Women Quarterly*, **9**, 515–31; Jeannette McGlone (1980), 'Sex Differences in Human Brain Asymmetry: A Critical Survey', *The Behavioral and Brain Sciences*, **3** (2), 215–27; Thomas Gualtieri and Robert E. Hicks (1985), 'An Immunoreactive Theory of Selective Male Affliction', *The Behavioral and Brain Sciences*, **8** (3), 427–41; 'Open Peer Commentary on Thomas Gualtieri and Robert E. Hicks' (1985), *The Behavioral and Brain Sciences*, **8** (3), 441–77.

Canadian Psychological Association for article: Doreen Kimura (1987), 'Are Men's and Women's Brains Really Different?', *Canadian Psychology*, **28** (2), 133–47.

Elsevier Science Publishing Co., Inc. for article: Parley W. Newman, Karin Bunderson and Robert H. Brey (1985), 'Brain Stem Electrical Responses of Stutterers and Normals by Sex, Ears, and Recovery', *Journal of Fluency Disorders*, **10**, 59–67.

Heldref Publications for article: Jo-Anne Finegan, Betty Bartleman and P.Y. Wong (1989), 'A Window for the Study of Prenatal Sex Hormone Influences on Postnatal Development', *The Journal of Genetic Psychology*, **150** (1), 101–12.

John Wiley & Sons, Inc. for articles: Peter H. Buschang, Robert M. Baume and G. Gisela Nass (1983), 'A Craniofacial Growth Maturity Gradient for Males and Females Between 4 and 16 Years of Age', *American Journal of Physical Anthropology*, **61**, 373–81; Carol Nagy Jacklin, Karen Thompson Wilcox and Eleanor E. Maccoby (1988), 'Neonatal Sex-Steroid Hormones and Cognitive Abilities at Six Years', *Developmental Psychobiology*, **21** (6), 567–74.

Lawrence Erlbaum Associates, Inc. for article: Mirna I. Vrbancic and James L. Mosley (1988), 'Sex-Related Differences in Hemispheric Lateralization: A Function of Physical Maturation', *Developmental Neuropsychology*, **4** (2), 151–67.

Mosby Year Book Inc. for article: Paula M. Duke, J. Merrill Carlsmith, Dennis Jennings, John A. Martin, Sanford M. Dornbusch, Ruth T. Gross and Bryna Siegel-Gorelick, 'Educational Correlates of Early and Late Sexual Maturation in Adolescence', *The Journal of Pediatrics*, **100** (4), 633–7.

Plenum Publishing Corporation for articles: Carol Nagy Jacklin and Eleanor M. Maccoby (1982), 'Length of Labor and Sex of Offspring', *Journal of Pediatric Psychology*, **7** (4), 355–60; Helena C. Kraemer, Anneliese Korner, Thomas Anders, Carol Nagy Jacklin and Sue Dimiceli (1985), 'Obstetric Drugs and Infant Behavior: A Reevaluation', *Journal of Pediatric Psychology*, **10** (3), 345–53; E.J. Susman, E.D. Nottelmann, G.E. Inoff-Germain, L.D. Dorn, G.B. Cutler, Jr., D.L. Loriaux and G.P. Chrousos (1985), 'The Relation of Relative Hormonal Levels and Physical Development and Social-Emotional Behavior in Young Adolescents', *Journal of Youth and Adolescence*, **14** (3), 245–64.

Society for Research in Child Development, Inc. for articles: Anneliese F. Korner (1969), 'Neonatal Startles, Smiles, Erections, and Reflex Sucks as Related to State, Sex, and Individuality', *Child Development*, **40** (4), 1039–53; Lloyd G. Humphreys, Timothy C. Davey and Randolph K. Park (1985), 'Longitudinal Correlation Analysis of Standing Height and Intelligence', *Child Development*, **56** (6), 1465–78; Elizabeth J. Susman, Gale Inoff-Germain, Editha D. Nottelmann, D. Lynn Loriaux, Gordon B. Cutler, Jr., and George P. Chrousos (1987), 'Hormones, Emotional Dispositions, and Aggressive Attributes in Young Adolescents, *Child Development*, **58**, 1114–34; J. Brooks-Gunn and Michelle P. Warren (1989), 'Biological and Social Contributions to Negative Affect in Young Adolescent Girls', *Child Development*, **60**, 40–55.

University of Chicago Press for articles: Leta Stetter Hollingworth (1914), 'Variability as Related to Sex Differences in Achievement: A Critique', *American Journal of Sociology*, **19**, 510–30; Janice Haaken (1988), 'Field Dependence Research: A Historical Analysis of a Psychological Construct', *Signs: Journal of Women in Culture and Society*, **13** (2), 311–30.

Williams and Wilkins for articles: Michelle P. Warren and J. Brooks-Gunn (1989), 'Mood and Behavior at Adolescence: Evidence for Hormonal Factors', *Journal of Clinical Endocrinology and Metabolism*, **69** (1), 77–83; Martha Taylor Sarno, Antonia Buonaguro and Eric Levita (1985), 'Gender and Recovery from Aphasia after Stroke', *The Journal of Nervous and Mental Disease*, **173** (10), 605–9.

Every effort has been made to trace all the copyright holders but if any have been inadvertently overlooked the publishers will be pleased to make the necessary arrangement at the first opportunity.

In addition the publishers wish to thank the library of the London School of Economics and Political Science, Tom Chao and Rebecca Custodio, assistants to Professor Jacklin, and many of the authors for their assistance in obtaining these articles.

Introduction

THE GENDERING OF PSYCHOLOGY

'Gender' is a relatively new word in Psychology which no doubt provides a key to current thinking about this topic. Historically other terms have been used for comparisons of females and males. Included in Part I of this volume, 'Historical Issues', are some of the earliest psychology papers comparing behavioural traits of women and men. These were written under the rubrics of 'the psychology of sex' (Woolley, 1910, 1914)[1] and 'sex differences' (Hollingworth, 1914, 1916, 1918). The 'psychology of sex' label was relatively short-lived, possibly because it could be confused with sexuality. Havelock Ellis published the sixth volume of his study of sexuality, *Studies in the Psychology of Sex*, in the same year as Woolley's first review (1910). The term 'sex differences' continued to be used through the intervening decades (for instance in Miles, 1935) and into the 1960s and 1970s. Towards the end of the 1970s the labelling of this topic of inquiry, the comparison of females and males, changed. 'Sex-related differences' was a term widely used for a time (see for example Wittig and Petersen, 1979).

There are differing implications of these terms. The words 'sex differences' imply that the divergences being discussed are closely attached to the condition of being a female or of being a male. 'Sex differences' imply a natural or biological attachment. The newer term, 'sex-related' difference, is more neutral, suggesting that a trait may or may not be naturally (biologically) attached to the condition of being a member of one or other sex.

But times have continued to change and 'sex-related' is no longer used to denote this field of inquiry. Instead 'gender' has become the rubric of choice (although the latter is sometimes still used interchangeably with 'sex' as in Ruble, 1988.) Also, specific behaviours and particular areas of inquiry seem to be associated with the use of one or other label. Infancy research, for example, continues to use the term 'sex differences' while work with older children is more likely to use 'gender differences'.

The word 'gender' would seem to imply that the psychological traits being discussed are more socially and less biologically derived. Perhaps that is why infancy research continues to use 'sex differences'; one presumes that the infant is more influenced by biology since it has not yet been exposed to the environmental input of the older child. Yet studies using 'gender' terminology often concern biological issues. And in many discussions of social behaviour, biological variables are prominent. This seeming paradox is one of the topics we shall discuss. Suffice to note here that the difference in terminology gives us a clue to some of the subtler aspects of the subject at hand.

This introduction has four objectives. First, I will try to show that the changing of labels discussed above has not been an arbitrary matter, but related to changes in psychology's

---

[1] I will follow the convention of underlining dates of those articles that are reprinted in the present volume.

understanding of behaviour. In part, developing new labels has reflected the general view of the extent to which biology, as opposed to the social environment, accounts for human behaviour. I will first describe the nature-nurture controversy as it exists in psychology. Second, I will briefly outline the systematic comparison of females and males in pre-empirical work and in the empirical work on which this volume is based. Third, I will show that the interest in comparing females and males in psychology depends on the social position of women in society. Finally, I will describe the specific papers in this volume and provide the context of each contribution.

Before we begin, a warning: there is a bias towards positive results in the field of gender studies. That is, only studies that find actual differences between women and men or girls and boys get published. Researchers are likely to have file drawers full of studies finding no differences or close similarities between females and males. In fact, the 'file drawer phenomenon' (Rosenthal, 1979) is now a recognized problem in trying to ascertain actual gender or any other differences between groups. Reports of no differences do rarely get published (usually by being connected to findings of differences), but they are not easy to find. Similarities do not gain entry in the psychological abstracts or social science indexes and are also unlikely to get publicized by the media. These similarities, then, are under-represented in the literature, in review articles and in our general understanding of what females and males are like. We will discuss this problem again in the section of 'Methodological Issues' in Volume II. However, I must emphasize that we are exacerbating the problem. By selecting portions of an already biased literature, the very existence of the present four volumes perpetuates the bias to our understanding!

Biological vs. Social-Environmental Explanations

The nature-nurture controversy has been a part of psychology for most of its history. Yet the understanding of the controversy and the arenas in which it applies continue to change. We are obviously limited by our biological characteristics, as each species is limited. And although we humans closely resemble each other when compared to other species, we vary greatly in relation to other humans. How much of that variability, that difference between individuals, is due to our genetic makeup (nature) and how much is due to social-environmental influences (nurture)? A full analysis of this conundrum could take up an entire volume. But some believe such a discussion would be fruitless because it addresses the wrong question. The right question is what are the processes or the ways that biology influences behaviour and what are the processes by which the social environment influences behaviour? There is a second reason which makes the nature-nurture question seem wrongheaded. That is, we cannot do anything about the biological contributions to behaviour, but we can do something about the environmental ones. Summarizing this problem, Lewis Lipsitt writes (1990): '... the genes are all finished once you're born ... they're set for life'.

The nature-nurture question in studies of gender is more specialized. Are nature or nurture more important to females or to males? That is, do the influences of biology or the environment differentially affect females or males? Is one sex influenced by biology or the environment in different degrees than the other sex? Before one can answer this, a prior question arises. Are there more differences between females as a group or between males as a group in relation to any one characteristic?

Many have proposed that females have more similarities with each other regarding psychological and biological characteristics, while males have more within-group differences. Investigating any characteristic, can we find more variation in groups of males than in groups of females? The issue of whether females or males are more variable has been empirically investigated from the earliest psychological papers (Hollingworth, 1914), but no difference in variability has ever been demonstrated. (see Maccoby and Jacklin, 1974, for a review).

Given no gender differences in variability, we can return to the original question: does nature or nurture have a greater influence on males or females? Again, the answer is that after decades of study – using methods ranging from family similarity correlations to the sophisticated behavioural genetics of today – no differential effects of nature or nurture on males or females have ever been demonstrated.

We will discuss specific papers that address the nature-nurture question in several volumes of this series on gender. In this volume, two articles in the 'Maturation and Motor Development' section, Part IV, examine the nature-nurture issue. Generally, however, the papers chosen attempt to understand mechanisms that explain behaviour, rather than what portion of the explanation is due to nature and what portion is due to nurture. Sometimes these mechanisms are biological and sometimes environmental. In the articles that follow, both kinds of mechanisms of explanation are well represented.

Historical Comparisons of Females and Males

In the psychological literature, the earliest papers comparing females and males were by Woolley and Hollingworth (from 1910) some of which are reprinted in this volume. Little work was done for the next decade. In 1927 and 1930 two summary articles appeared in *Psychological Bulletin* written by C. Allen. The wide variety of variables covered in these reviews offers a glimpse of the kinds of topics studied by psychology in the 1920s. Allen covers both physical and psychological characteristics; many references cited in these papers are not empirical.

In 1935, a remarkable comprehensive review was written. Catharine Cox Miles published a chapter on the literature of sex differences for the *Handbook of Social Psychology*. In that chapter, she traces Biblical, philosophical and medical comparisons of females and males. She puts the study of these issues in perspective by suggesting that four trends shaped the 'psychological problems of sex' of her day. (1) The development of child psychology and the study of children, often both girls and boys. (2) The study of other cultures, which included marriage and sexual practices and women's and men's behaviour. (3) The medical study of 'normal' sexual behaviour and 'deviations' including what we would now call sex roles. (4) Freud and psychoanalysis and its emphasis on childhood sexuality. After an exhaustive review of the empirical literature, Miles concludes that, given the social circumstances of her day, social comparisons are unfair.

> Social tradition encourages man to achievement. ... It now permits woman to achieve in the same domains far more than ever before in history. ... But given the present economic pressures and humanity's deep prejudices progress can hardly go rapidly in the direction of a wisely ordered exploitation of women's good mental powers' (p. 781).

The Study of Gender and the Social Position of Women

In the classic articles reprinted in this volume from the early 1900s, Woolley and Hollingworth point out the relationship of their inquiries to the position of women, to the feminist movement and to the women's suffrage movement. After the flurry of these early articles, very little was published for several decades. In the late 1960s and the 1970s, a widespread revival of interest in gender issues matched the revival of the feminist movement of that time. The relationship of the first and second waves of the feminist movement to gender scholarship in psychology is not surprising in light of two historic conditions. First, the work on gender is largely carried out by professionally trained women (Rosenberg, 1982). Second, women have only been professionally trained in large numbers in parallel with these two waves of feminism. (See Rosenberg, 1982, for a full discussion of the historical issues relating to feminism in psychology.)

This volume has five parts which I will describe in turn. Aside from the logic of beginning with the historical section, the order in which these five areas are presented is somewhat arbitrary.

Historical Issues

Part I contains classic examples of papers by the earliest empirical psychologists, Woolley and Hollingworth, on the comparisons of females and males. Both of these writers were important members of the new experimental psychology of the early 1900s.

Helen Thompson Woolley was one of the first presidents of the American Psychological Association and one of the very few women presidents until the last 15 years. In 1910, she wrote one of the earliest summaries of other researchers' findings on the 'psychology of sex' as she called it. The materials she consolidated largely related to mental abilities.

Leta S. Hollingworth was also a prolific writer, publishing many books which became standard texts (such as on adolescents, on gifted children and on variability). But the passion inspiring much of her work was to refute the 'armchair scribbling' and 'armchair dogma' written by men about women (Hollingworth, 1990). Beginning with her dissertation (which became the 1914 article reprinted here), she systematically studied many of the allegations of differences between the sexes. It is interesting to note that, after all of this early empirical work establishing unequivocally that no differences exist between females and males, the stereotypes have changed so little.

A summary paper by Anne Anastasi, 'Sex Differences: Historical Perspectives and Methodological Implications', was chosen both for its author and its content. Anastasi was one of the few scholars to have continued work on gender issues for decades, being almost a lone voice in the 1950s and 1960s. This is in part because her field was psychological testing much of which has been conducted in schools on both boys and girls. In fact, psychological testing has remained an exception in psychology in that both sexes have been studied. (We will discuss the issue of the sex of subjects in the 'Methodological' section of Volume II.) The paper by Anastasi is a summary of research and an analysis of methodological issues that plague gender research and all research comparing group differences. No historical section would be complete without the recognition of Anne Anastasi's work.

The final paper in Part I is a contemporary one by Janice Haaken describing the history of one psychological construct – 'field dependence-independence'. This construct is particularly interesting because it stood out as a recognized gender difference from the 1940s into the 1970s. Haaken shows how differences can be conceptualized and labelled and how values matter to any conceptualization. She demonstrates the bias in scientific concepts and how bias in gender studies relates to the value of females and males in the larger society.

Neonatal and Infancy Periods

The papers in Part II contain both theoretical and empirical examples of this very extensive field.

One of the facts about prenatal life is the vulnerability of the male fetus. Indeed, from conception the male may be more vulnerable. Chapter 15 by McMillen (1979) gives some of the data on mortality rate by sex before birth and at birth.

The many issues associated with differential mortality by sex are interrelated. For example, labour length at birth may be related to mortality rates at birth. Chapter 11 by Jacklin and Maccoby (1982) shows that there is a difference in length of labour by sex of offspring. After controlling for related variables, male offspring necessitate longer labours. Another connection is that between length of labour and the amounts and types of obstetric drugs administered. This complex issue is described in Chapter 14 by Kraemer, Korner, Anders, Jacklin and Dimiceli (1985). Labour length and not obstetric drug usage is associated with differences in infant behaviour.

But why are male offspring more vulnerable? In an influential paper, Gualtieri and Hicks (1985) postulate their theory of 'selective male affliction'. Simply stated, they propose that a male body (embryo and fetus) carried in a female body (the mother) stimulates activity within the immune system of the mother to fight the 'foreign [male] body'. This immune reaction is not set up by the female embryo and fetus. Although an interesting and much-cited theory, the many peer commentaries published with the article (and reprinted here in Chapter 10) take issue with a number of aspects of the Gualtieri and Hicks contention.

Part II also includes three papers on infant behaviour. These were chosen as exemplars of the very different kinds of work currently being undertaken in infancy research. The article by Korner, Brown, Reade, Stevenson, Fernbach and Thom (1988) is a typical example of traditional research regarding infancy. The state of the infant (whether asleep or awake, calm or agitated) is related to other indicators of development. This work grows out of the tradition that extended experimental psychology work on animals to newborn humans. The classic paper by Korner (1969) is another example of this line of research. Here, Korner counts startles, smiles, erections and reflexive sucking and relates these variables to the state of the infant and its sex, demonstrating individual differences.

The paper by Aries and Olver (1985) is differently motivated. It looks at early mother-infant interaction to try to support the hypothesis that the sense of self one has in adulthood is developed in different ways for girls than for boys. We will look at other examples of differential socialization in the section called 'Socialization' in Volume II of this series.

Brain Organization and Brain Injury

Part III includes papers which are quite recent, half being published in the last five years. This field is changing rapidly largely because of improvements in the technology used in the research.

The question most of these papers address is stated clearly by the title of the article by Kimura (1987): 'Are men's and women's brains really different?' The simple answer is yes. Hahn (1987), Lewis and Christiansen (1989) and McGlone (1980) all show ways in which female and male brains do differ. The main finding is that there is somewhat different hemispheric specialization in females when compared to males. However, both Kertesz and Benke (1989) and Vrbancic and Mosley (1989) show that simply accepting that differences exist may be oversimplifying a complicated process. There are certainly structural differences, but do these lead to functional differences? Difference has often implied deficit. Is there evidence for deficits by sex? Here the answer is not clear.

Another method of trying to understand brain function in humans is to study the effects of brain injury and recovery from brain injury. Three articles are included that investigate brain injury. Newman, Bunderson and Brey (1985) report on brain stem electrical responses of stutterers and normals; Pizzamiglio, Mammucari and Razzano (1985) document recovery in aphasia, while Sarno, Buonaguro and Levita (1985) describe recovery from aphasia after strokes.

As the technology for conducting research on the human brain continues to improve, we will further extend our understanding of how the brain works. We will then be better equipped to answer the questions of how and in what ways female and male brains are structurally different. And we will be able to tackle the more important questions of how and in what ways structural differences relate to functional differences.

Maturation and Motor Development

Two papers included in Part IV report common physiological measures of maturation: craniofacial growth and head size. Craniofacial growth patterns are given for females and males from age 4 to age 16 in the article by Buschang, Baume and Nass, who thus exemplify how physiological growth can be quantified and measured. The authors find small differences between the sexes and between their French-Canadian and American samples, but in all cases they report a similar 'unfolding' growth process. This study does not link physiological growth to psychological functioning.

Clifton and her colleagues (Gwiazda, Bauer, Clarkson and Held) report physiological growth, as measured by head size, and show its integral relation to the psychological processes of sound localization (Chapter 26). These investigators measured head size between birth and 22 weeks. They found that the average size of the head is slightly larger in boys than in girls, but that growth rates for all infants is very similar. They then demonstrate the psychological consequences of these growth changes.

Three chapters consider motor or physical performance. Thomas and French investigate motor performance across age; Smoll and Schutz study physical performance as a function of gender and body type, and Eaton and Enns describe motor activity level.

Thomas and French (1985) have a physical education perspective. In an attempt to understand differences in girls' and boys' performance in relation to several motor tasks, they conducted meta-analysis, a statistical technique which allows the researcher to compare many studies. (Meta-analyses are discussed in detail in several chapters of Volume II.) Thomas and French compared various kinds of motor performance as a function of age across childhood and adolescence. They discovered that the performance of some tasks (such as vertical jump and grip strength) changes after puberty and probably is related to biological development. But they did not find a uniform development of gender differences in motor performance, concluding that most gender differences are related to differential teaching, coaching and practice of girls as opposed to boys.

Smoll and Schutz (1990) take this line of inquiry one step further. They studied 2,142 children from 9 to 17 years old, measuring height, weight and body fat in relation to many kinds of physical performance. They found that most of the differences between girls' and boys' performance, as well as the largest predictor of performance for all children, was percent of body fat. Girls had more body fat than boys and thus showed poorer performance. With the body fat of each equated, gender differences disappeared. At older ages, bodily variables contributed less and less to gender differences. The authors concluded that 'with advancing age gender differences may become increasingly more a function of environmental factors'.

Gender differences in activity level, or energy expenditure through movement, were investigated by Eaton and Enns in another meta-analysis. They concluded that situational factors and age were important variables in understanding activity levels. They also found a small but consistent effect: boys have higher activity levels than girls.

The remaining four papers in this section compare maturation and some measure of cognitive function. Duke, Carlsmith, Jennings, Martin, Dornbusch, Gross and Siegel-Gorelick (1982) relate educational variables with early and late sexual maturity in adolescence. Humphreys, Davey and Park (1985) correlate height and intelligence. Rantakallio, von Wendt and Mäkinen compare motor development in the first year with later intellectual ability. Finally, Waber, Mann, Merola and Moylan (1985) relate physical maturation rate and intellectual performance.

The results of these four studies have some commonality but some differences as well. Duke et al. found that sexual maturation is not related to educational success in girls, whereas early maturing boys received higher scores in all of their educational categories. Humphreys et al. found height to be related to intellectual ability for girls, but less so for boys. Rantakallio and her colleagues concluded that fast learners in the first year were superior to others in educational capacity at age 14, though maturational differences were less predictive. Waber and her colleagues (1985) found maturation rate unrelated to performance either on cognitive-ability or on dichotic measures of laterality (which we will not describe here).

A fuller presentation of gender and cognitive abilities appears in Volume II. In the present context of maturation and cognitive ability, we must conclude that more work is required before we can even partially understand how the two are connected.

Hormones and Behaviour

In the last section in this volume we consider how, and on what behaviours, hormones affect humans. Most of the chapters describe some relationship between sex-steroid hormones and behaviour. Although other kinds of hormones are being studied, sex-steroid hormones are thought to be the best candidates for understanding differences between females and males.

Two ways in which sex-steroid hormones are believed to influence human behaviour are by sensitizing and by activating. Sensitizing refers to changes in the body (probably mostly the brain) in the developing embryo and fetus caused by hormones. For example, three months post-conception, there are large concentrations of the male sex-steroid hormone testosterone circulating in the fetal bloodstream. It is believed that differing amounts of testosterone within males, for example, sensitize or change the brain in relation to such subtle individual differences as thickness of beard growth. The brain of the fetus has been sensitized even though differences in beard growth will not be apparent for about 15 years. Activating effects refer to changes in the body or in behaviour caused by hormones present at the time. In the example of beard growth, beard thickness will thus depend both on the sensitizing of testosterone on the fetus as well as on the activating effect of the amount of testosterone present in the post-puberty male.

The first paper by Finegan, Bartleman and Wong (1989) describes how prenatal sex hormones can be studied in order to understand their influence on postnatal development. The second paper by Ehrhardt (1985) further describes the theory of sensitization and activation, supplying some of the data which supports the theory.

One example is given of sensitization effects seen in childhood. Jacklin, Wilcox and Maccoby (1988) measured five sex-steroid hormones at birth (as the best estimate of the hormone measures of the developing fetus). We found, in this and other studies, different effects of the same sex-steroid hormones on girls than on boys. In the article reprinted here, we found no relationship for boys between sex-steroid hormones at birth and intellectual abilities at six years, but we did find effects for girls. Girls with low amounts of male hormone at birth had higher intellectual abilities at six years.

The two papers by Susman and her colleagues (1985 and 1987) studied activating effects in adolescents. Both papers find evidence of a relationship between concurrent hormones and behaviour. Similarly, Brooks-Gunn and Warren find evidence for the activating effects of concurrent hormones and moods and behaviour in adolescents.

Finally, at the other end of the life span, Hazzard (1986) summarizes the information available on the biological basis of the sex differential in longevity.

References

Allen, C.N. (1927), 'Studies in sex differences', *Psychological Bulletin*, **24**, 294–304.
Allen, C.N. (1930), 'Recent studies in sex differences', *Psychological Bulletin*, **27**, 394–407.
Hollingworth, H.L. (1990), *Leta Stetter Hollingworth: A Biography*. Bolton, MA: Anker Publishing Co.
Hollingworth, L.S. and Lowie, R.H. (1916), 'Science and feminism', *The Scientific Monthly*, **3**, 277–84.
Lipsitt, L. (1990), 'Science directions', *A.P.A. Monitor* (December), 13.
Maccoby, E.E. and Jacklin, C.N. (1974), *The Psychology of Sex Differences*, Stanford, CA: Stanford University Press.
Miles, C. (1935), 'Sex in social psychology' in C. Murchinson (ed.), *Handbook of Social Psychology*, Worcester, MA: Clark University Press.

Rosenberg, R. (1982), *Separate Spheres: Intellectual Roots of Modern Feminism*, New Haven, CT: Yale University Press.

Rosenthal, R. (1979), 'The "File Drawer Problem" and tolerance for null results', *Psychological Bulletin*, **86**, 638–41.

Ruble, D.N. (1988), 'Sex-role development' in M. Bornstein and M. Lamb (eds), *Developmental Psychology: An Advanced Textbook*, Hillsdale, NJ: Lawrence Erlbaum Associates.

Wittig, M.A. and Petersen, A.C. (1979), *Sex-Related Differences in Cognitive Functioning*, New York: Academic Press.

Part I
Historical Issues

[1]

VARIABILITY AS RELATED TO SEX DIFFERENCES IN ACHIEVEMENT

A CRITIQUE

LETA STETTER HOLLINGWORTH
New York City

This paper is the outcome of prolonged reflection on the doctrine of greater male variability. It comprises an attempt to assemble and review briefly data at present accessible as to the comparative variability of the sexes in mental traits, and to discuss critically the hypothesis that the great difference between the sexes in intellectual achievement and eminence is due to the inherently greater variability of the males. This hypothesis is stated clearly and concisely by Thorndike[1] thus:

The trivial difference between the central tendency of men and that of women which is the common finding of psychological tests and school experience may seem at variance with the patent fact that in the great achievements of the world in science, art, invention, and management, women have been far excelled by men. One who accepts the equality of typical (i.e., modal) representatives of the two sexes, must assume the burden of explaining this great difference in the high ranges of achievement.

The probably true explanation is to be sought in the greater variability within the male sex. . . . .

In particular, if men differ in intelligence and energy by wider extremes than do women, eminence in and leadership of the world's affairs of whatever sort will inevitably belong oftener to men. They will oftener deserve it.

It is at once evident how important are the implications here stated for those who hope much from the present tendency to remove all disabilities of law, custom, and prejudice from women. If the explanation of women's failure to achieve significant things in the fields named by Thorndike is really to be found in the inherently greater variability of males, then complete liberation of women from excessive maternity and from all the consequent customs and legal disabilities that have developed, will result

[1] E. L. Thorndike, *Educational Psychology* (1910), p. 35.

only in raising the *average* intelligence and happiness of the race. We shall not expect any increase from this source in the number of eminent individuals, nor in achievement of that high order which forces knowledge and wisdom farther.

Thorndike[1] states the implications for pedagogy thus:

This one fundamental difference in variability is more important than all the differences between the average male and female capacities . . . . a slight excess of male variability would mean that of the hundred most gifted individuals in this country not two would be women, and of the thousand most gifted, not one in twenty. . . . . Women may and doubtless will be scientists and engineers, but the Joseph Henry, the Rowland, and the Edison of the future will be men; even should all women vote, they would play a small part in the Senate. . . . . Not only the probability and the desirability of marriage and the training of children as an essential feature of woman's career, *but also the restriction of women to the mediocre grades of ability and achievement should be reckoned with by our educational systems.* The education of women for such professions as administration, statesmanship, philosophy, or scientific research, where a very few gifted individuals are what society requires, is far less needed than education for such professions as nursing, teaching, medicine, or architecture, where the average level is the essential. . . . . Postgraduate instruction, to which women are flocking in large numbers is, at least in its higher reaches, a far more remunerative investment in the case of men.[2]

The first discussion of the comparative variability of the sexes bore on anatomical traits, and began about a century ago. The anatomist Meckel[3] concluded on pathological grounds that the human female showed greater variability than the human male, "and he thought that since man is the superior animal and variation a sign of inferiority, the conclusion was justified." Later, when anatomists and naturalists arrived at the conclusion that the male is more variable, variability came to be regarded as an advantage, a characteristic affording the greatest hope for progress, and finally as the probable explanation of the fact that all the world's greatest deeds of intellect have been the deeds of men. This latter view obtains at present among men of science, though not without exceptions, the most notable of whom is Karl Pearson.[4]

[1] E. L. Thorndike, "Sex in Education," *The Bookman*, XXIII, 213.

[2] The italics here are mine.

[3] Meckel, *Manual of Descriptive and Pathological Anatomy* (see Ellis, *Man and Woman* [1909], p. 410).

[4] Karl Pearson, *Chances of Death* (1897).

It will be well at this point to consider not only the social and biological significance of variability, but also the connotation of the term itself, and whether every author who discusses variability means the same thing. There is, in fact, complaint among authors that the term is indefinite. Even in their controversial matter,[1] Ellis and Pearson complain of each other that there is failure to define the word. Theoretically greater variability always implies *greater range*, if the trait distributed conforms to the Gauss curve of probability. Empirical data, however, are not yet forthcoming to demonstrate that mental traits conform to the theoretical curve; and there is at present no conclusive empirical evidence to show that in cases where the coefficient of variation is greater for one sex than for the other, this greater variability consists in *greater range*. If we neglect theory and confine ourselves to facts as demonstrated, greater variability is found to consist in any or all of three typical conditions:

1. Greater range (Series B as compared with Series A).

2. Equal range for both groups, but greater frequency at the extremes for one group (Series C as compared with Series A).

3. Smaller range for the more variable group, with slight flattening at the top of the curve of distribution (Series D as compared with Series A).

A fourth condition is found in the work of Bonser, where the males are seen to be more variable than the females, though the *range* for the sexes is equal, and the *frequency at both extremes* is nearly twice as great for the females. This case will be taken up later in connection with other results from Bonser.

Let us now consider a hypothetical case. Table I gives four possible distributions of the same trait, including the same number of cases. This trait may be, for example, ability to perform an amount of work in a specified time, this ability being indicated by units varying from 1 to 15. Let Series A be a group of 1,000 women, and let Series B, C, and D be groups of 1,000 men each. It is seen that these Series all show greater variability on the part of the males (reference to Table I will show just how much greater is the *A.D.* in each case), but the social implications differ widely.

[1] H. Ellis, *Man and Woman* (Appendix).

In Series B the greater variability of the males consists in greater *range*. It is on this Series that we might base the explanation of the fact that *all* the world's greatest deeds of ntellect have been the deeds of men; for here no women equal the best men.

In Series C the greater variability of the males consists in greater frequency at the extremes, *the range being equal*. On this Series might be based an explanation of the fact that *more* men than women have reached the *same* degree of eminence. It would not explain why no women have reached the greatest eminence.

In Series D the greater variability of the males consists in a flattening at the top of the curve of distribution, the *range* for the men being actually *less* than for the women.

Now it is clear that if social significance is to be attached to greater variability, not only the coefficient of variation must be stated, but also *what form the distribution takes*. Obviously a greater male variability like that shown in Series D would have no validity at all in explaining why the greatest deeds of intellect have been the deeds of men. If greater male variability takes this form, all the greatest deeds will be those of *women*.

In his discussions of greater male variability and its implications for pedagogy, Thorndike[1] theoretically means greater range: "Though the central tendencies were the same, there would still be two men of the hundred who were better than the best woman and two men who were worse than the worst woman." This condition would be represented under Series B. But, in discussing certain statistics regarding third-year high-school classes see Table I, p. 514.

This condition would be that of Series C. The range for the sexes is equal, but the frequency at the extremes is greater for males. Such cases of greater variability do not suggest an explanation of the fact that no women have achieved the greatest intellectual eminence. They would only explain the condition in which twice as many men as women achieved the *same* intellectual eminence. But our chief problem is to explain why no women have equaled the best men.

Havelock Ellis,[2] in a chapter on "The Variational Tendency

[1] E. L. Thorndike, *op. cit.*, p. 42.   [2] H. Ellis, *op. cit.*, p. 412.

of Men," discusses certain anatomical and pathological data which show, on the whole, the greater variability of the male. Karl Pearson, in a polemical article, undertook to disprove the conclusions of Ellis, stigmatizing them as "scientific superstition." This controversy between Ellis and Pearson is very familiar to students of social science, and each of us may weigh the evidence for himself, since we have here two authorities, of perhaps equal competence, in diametrical disagreement.

TABLE I

Degree or Amount of the Trait Measured	Frequency Series A	Frequency Series B	Frequency Series C	Frequency Series D
1	0	1	0	0
2	0	3	0	0
3	1	7	6	0
4	10	14	18	11
5	45	42	60	57
6	117	115	112	130
7	205	200	197	190
8	244	236	214	224
9	205	200	197	190
10	117	115	112	130
11	45	42	60	57
12	10	14	18	11
13	1	7	6	0
14	0	3	0	0
15	0	1	0	0

(Standard group)	Series A Women	Series B Men	Series C Men	Series D Men
Number	=1,000	=1,000	=1,000	=1,000
Central Tendency	=8	=8	=8	=8
Average Deviation	=1.238	=1.544	=1.406	=1.330

On the whole boys are twice as frequent as girls in the youngest and oldest age, and about one and one-half times as frequent at ages fourteen and nineteen.

But if it were definitely proved that there is greater male variability in anatomical measurements, it would only suggest, not prove, that there is greater male variability in *mental* traits also. Very, very little precise evidence has been adduced as to the comparative variability of the sexes in mental traits. Such general evidence as that previously brought forward, for instance by Ellis, that the great geniuses of the world have been men, and that there are at the same time more idiots among men, is obviously fallacious. For the geniuses on the one hand may be accounted for by the fact that woman's biological function of reproduction has so conditioned her that eminence in the fields where mental energy is publicly recognized has been extremely improbable; and we should expect statisticians to find more idiots and feeble-minded individuals among men, because they take their data from institutions, where defective men are more likely to be admitted than women of the same degree of defectiveness. Women have been and are a dependent and non-competitive class, and when defective can more easily survive outside of institutions, since they do not have to compete *mentally* with normal individuals, as men do, to maintain themselves in the social *milieu*. This conclusion is well confirmed by the records of the Clearing-House for Mental Defectives at the Post-Graduate Hospital in New York City. Among 1,000 consecutive cases of mental defect (including idiocy, imbecility, and feeble-mindedness), taken from all cases diagnosed at this Clearing-House during the years 1912 and 1913, there were 568 males and 432 females. But of individuals *over sixteen years of age* there were only 78 males, while there were 159 females; and of individuals *over 30 years of age* there were 9 males and 28 females. A detailed account of this study may be found in an article recently published.[1] At present it suffices to point out that the fact that females escape the Clearing-House till beyond the age of thirty years three times as frequently as males, fits very well with the fact that more males than females are brought to the Clearing-House, on the whole. The boy who cannot compete mentally is found out, becomes at an early age an object of concern to relatives, is brought to the Clearing-House, and directed toward an institution. The girl who cannot compete mentally is not so often recognized as definitely defective, since it is not unnatural for her to drop into the isolation of the home, where she can "take care of" small children, peel potatoes, scrub, etc. If physically passable, as is often the case, she may marry,

[1] L. S. Hollingworth, "The Frequency of Amentia as Related to Sex," *Medical Record*, 1913.

thus fastening herself to economic support; or she may become a prostitute, to which economic pursuit feeble mentality is no barrier. Thus they survive *outside of institutions*. The writer has frequently questioned those who accompany these feeble-minded women over thirty years of age to the Clearing-House. Their tardy appearance there is usually accounted for by the fact that some accident has at last happened: "her husband has just died"; "she has rheumatism, and can scrub no more"; "an illegitimate pregnancy has again befallen, to the distraction of relatives"; "she was a prostitute, but physical illness has driven her in from the street." No one can doubt that there are scores of feeble-minded women at large, to whom these accidents have not happened.

It will be well at this point to survey and compare precise data already at hand to show sex differences in mental variability. Such data have been assembled here from scattered sources. Thorndike[1] gives precise data tending to show greater mental variability in men and boys. He calculated as well as might be from data given, the variability for each sex in the traits tested by Helen Bradford Thompson.[2] His results show that men are about one-twentieth more variable than women, in these experiments. He also concludes from certain measurements of reaction time, spelling, arithmetical ability, etc., that "it is extremely probable that, except in the two years nearest the age of puberty for girls, the male sex is slightly more variable."

Wissler's results with college students show female variability to be in general about nine-tenths that of males. The number of women measured was, however, only 42, and the ratio of female variability differed greatly in the different traits, so that the nine-tenths would, by itself alone, be of no great reliability.[3]

Thorndike deplores the fact that there is so little precise data at hand, but leaves us to suppose that he considers what is available as sufficient to lend a very, very high degree of probability to the conclusion which he states, and which was quoted at the outset. Several articles and monographs, however, have appeared

[1] E. L. Thorndike, *op. cit.*, pp. 33–43.
[2] H. B. Thompson, *The Mental Traits of Sex* (1906).   [3] Thompson, *op. cit.*

since 1910 which are in disagreement with the results cited by this author.

Wells[1] in a study of "Sex Differences in the Tapping Test" reached the conclusion that men are more variable than women. He had, however, only ten subjects, five women and five men—too small a number on which to generalize. In another study including five women and five men this author concludes:

> The groups of subjects are perhaps too small to expect any special sex differences to be illustrated. . . . . In the addition test the performance of the women is much more variable than that of the men, in the number-checking test it is much less so.

H. L. Hollingworth[2] made a study of judgments of persuasiveness, using advertisements as material. He had as subjects 20 Juniors in Barnard College and 20 Juniors in Columbia College. Among his conclusions he states: "Men correlate with their group average about 25 per cent more closely than women," and "the range of variability in the above coefficient is for the men only 43 per cent as large as for women." In the course of discussion this author says:

> Another set of measurements of interest is found in the figures which show the approximation of the individual's judgments to the average judgment of his group. . . . . The coefficients for the women range between —0.13 and 0.66, thus giving a total range of 0.79, with the average at 0.48. For the men the coefficients cover a much narrower range, varying between 0.40 and 0.74, thus giving a total range of only 0.34, a range only 43 per cent as large as that of the women. The average for the men is 0.59, the median is 0.61, being thus about 25 per cent higher than the same for the women. Only four women exceed the median for men, while all the men but four exceed the median for women.
>
> Both of these facts—that of higher correlation and that of narrower range—point in the same direction, that is, toward the greater homogeneity of the group of men. The high coefficients indicate that any one man selected at random will be a better example of the characteristics of his group than will a similarly selected woman of her group. And the narrow range again indicates the tendency of the men, not only to depart but slightly from the type, but also to depart in approximately equal degrees from it. Whether

---

[1] F. L. Wells, "Sex Differences in the Tapping Test," *American Journal of Psychology*, 1909.

[2] H. L. Hollingworth, "Judgments of Persuasiveness," *Psychological Review* XXVIII (1911), 4.

these facts point to a greater general variability of women as compared with men, or only to the particular composition of the two groups taking part in this experiment, one cannot say. But the present method seems to indicate a concrete and interesting way of studying this much disputed question of the relative variability of the sexes, in what may be called the higher mental processes.

E. K. Strong, Jr.,[1] in a study of the merits of advertisements by the method of relative position, had twenty-five subjects—fifteen men and ten women. Among his conclusions he states the following:

> An inspection of the diagram of Table I shows that the range of judgments for the men is much less than for the women, i.e., from $+0.84$ to 0 for the men, and from $+0.75$ to -0.43 for the women. Both have 55 per cent of the entire range below the median judgment. But the average $A.D.$ of the medians of the individual judgments for each advertisement for the women is 69 per cent greater than for the men. This is the more striking, as the women would apparently be a more homogeneous group than the men, as they were all Juniors or Seniors in Barnard College, and within a very few years of each other in age, while the men included graduate students and professors and vary at least twenty years in age. . . . . A comparison of the two groups shows us that the $P.E.$ of the women averages 69.7 per cent greater than that of the men.

In the arrangements of another series of advertisements, where a greater number of subjects was used, this author found the women to be less variable than the men. He remarks upon these contradictory findings as follows:

> It is true that the methods employed in the two chapters are different. But if different methods can give exactly opposite results as to variability, they can be of little value as to its determination. Personally I believe that the situation is this. The results of chap. vii show that when women are given an equal opportunity with men to rate appeals (advertisements) they are able to classify their dislikes as readily as their preferences, which the men do not do. Such a condition naturally results in a greater total range where methods of experimentation similar to those in this chapter are used, and consequently in a seemingly greater variability. A careful analysis of the data will not really show greater variability of judgment among the women. What it does show is that women have more and greater dislikes and are surer of them.

Hollingworth, however, used the method employed by Strong in chap. vi, and his results show women to be more variable than men by this very method. It is also true that to say that the

[1] E. K. Strong, Jr., *Relative Merits of Advertisements* (1911), pp. 78, 79.

women varied more *because* "they have more and greater dislikes, and are surer of them" is not to conclude that "a careful analysis of the figures will not show greater variability of judgment among the women." It is only to restate the fact that women *do* vary more in this case than men do, *in affective processes*.

Table XVI in Strong's monograph gives details from which he concluded that men are more variable. These figures show that the group of women does not differ as much from the first group of men in variability as the first group of men differs from the second group of men. For the group of women $Q=3.5$; for the first group of men $Q=4.0$; for the second group of men $Q=5.0$. Thus the group of women differs from the first group of men by .5, and from the second group of men by 1.5. Averaging these we get $d=1.00$. For the two groups of men $d=1.00$. On page 59 of his monograph Strong explains the great variability of the second group of men ($Q=5.0$) on the ground that the group is composed of uneducated persons who were possibly unable to differentiate complex appeals. Thus he explains a difference in variability between two groups of men on incidental grounds, but describes the same amount of difference in variability between a group of men and a group of women as a sex difference!

Gertrude Kuper[1] studied children of various ages and classes in their responses to a series of appeals. "The children numbered over 200, 10 boys and 10 girls for each year's age from 6.5 to 16.5. They were almost entirely attendants of the public schools of New York City, and came from quite varied sections of the city." This author draws the following conclusion:

A great sex difference was found in the variability measures as calculated for the various ages, appeals, social classes, and nationalities. In every case but two the girls exceeded the boys in their *P.E.*, and in these two exceptions the boys' *P.E.* was once greater than the girls' by 5 per cent, and another time exactly equal to the girls' *P.E.* . . . . The girls' average *P.E.* was 1.66; that for the boys was 1.36.

A monograph just published by Garry C. Meyers[2] offers an opportunity to note sex differences in variability, and is more

[1] Gertrude Kuper, "Group Differences in the Interests of Children," *Journal of Philosophy, Psychology, and Scientific Methods* (1912), p. 377.

[2] Garry C. Meyers, *Incidental Memory* (1913).

valuable from our point of view than any of the studies already cited, because he investigated a much greater number of subjects. His study of incidental memory of objects of common experience—bills, coins, and stamps—comprises 704 subjects—337 males and 367 females. Meyers classified these subjects into groups, and these groups range from third-grade pupils to college students, teachers, merchants, and bankers. The tables in which he gives the data for these groups separately have been studied and from them have been tabulated the number of groups of males showing greater variability than the corresponding group of females, and the number of groups of females showing greater variability than the corresponding group of males. The total number of groups is 182. Of this number 65 groups show greater variability for the males; 107 groups show greater variability for the females; 10 groups show exactly equal variability for both sexes. On the basis of these figures one might infer that females are much more variable than males. In his general conclusions about incidental memory for these objects Meyers himself says:

The amount of overestimation and underestimation of the sizes of the one dollar bill, stamp, and coins decreases as age and experience increases, and is as a rule greater for the females than for the males. Generally the males are better performers than the females, and less variable.

Meyers also studied incidental memory for words, using 1,663 subjects—773 males and 890 females. He states among his general conclusions:

The females are markedly superior to the males for average number of words remembered and for average efficiency; they have a high central tendency, vary more in the high schools and fourth grades; but in the fifth, sixth, seventh, and eighth grades they vary less than the males.

It must be noted here that the finding scarcely agrees with the exception previously quoted, i.e., that girls are more variable at the years nearest puberty, for on the average it seems likely that these two years would fall in the seventh and eighth grades, rather than in the fourth grade and the high school.

William Brown[1] in a study of *The Correlation of Mental Abilities* found that in groups of about equal homogeneity with respect

[1] W. Brown, "Correlation of Mental Abilities," *British Journal of Psychology* (1910), 296.

to age, training, etc., females are more variable in crossing out E, R; males are more variable in crossing out A, N, O, S; the sexes are equally variable in motor performance; males are more variable in the addition test, in speed, and females in accuracy; in the Müller-Lyer Illusion the male children are more variable, and the female adults are more variable.

Fox and Thorndike[1] studied arithmetical abilities of school children, using as subjects 28 boys and 49 girls. As to variability they conclude that in addition girls are only 93 per cent as variable as boys, and in multiplication only 96 per cent as variable.

Stone[2] also studied arithmetical abilities of school children in various school systems, using as subjects 250 girls and 250 boys. Six tests were given in four systems. Out of the 24 groups thus yielded, 9 show a greater variability for the boys, 14 show a greater variability for the girls, and 1 shows the same variability for both sexes. If we average the coefficients of variation for all groups, a procedure for which there seems to be little justification though not infrequently employed, the boys are found to be only 99.5 per cent as variable as the girls. Stone himself says:

> This table shows that for the first two systems—the boys are somewhat more variable, and in systems 8 and 14 about the same amount less variable. This is interesting, and points to a need for further investigation, for the common opinion is that men are more variable than women; and supposedly boys more so than girls. But as seen by the averages for these four systems, so far as these 250 boys and 250 girls show the true tendency, there are no more exceptionally bright or exceptionally dull pupils among the boys than among the girls at this age.

Bonser[3] in a study of arithmetical abilities of school children had a greater number of subjects than Stone and a much greater number than Fox and Thorndike. He tested 757 pupils—385 boys and 372 girls. He found that in arithmetical ability boys are only 66 per cent as variable as girls.

Bonser studied the reasoning ability of these 757 pupils with the result that in controlled association girls are once more variable

---

[1] Fox and Thorndike, "Sex Differences in Arithmetical Ability," *Columbia Contributions to Philosophy, Psychology, and Education*, XI.

[2] Stone, *Arithmetical Abilities* (1908), p. 36.

[3] Bonser, *The Reasoning Ability of Children* (1910), p. 20.

and once less variable than boys; in selective judgment the girls are once more variable and once less variable than the boys; in arithmetical ability, as noted above, the girls are much more variable than the boys; in literary interpretation the boys are more variable; in spelling the boys are slightly more variable. Bonser's final conclusion regarding sex differences in variability in reasoning processes is as follows:

> Taking the totals of all, the boys are slightly higher, the ratio being 1.047. The fluctuations are so numerous, and the differences so slight, that it seems unsound to make any general statement to the effect that the boys of these grades are more variable than the girls, in so far as these tests have shown.

Bonser's study affords a case[1] which illustrates very well the prime importance of considering the *whole table of frequencies* when we wish to infer social consequences. He distributed his subjects as to age, sex, and grade, and the medians and quartiles show much greater variability in age on the part of boys. Bonser states this fact as follows:

> The variability in age is seen to be much greater among the boys than among the girls, as shown by a comparison of the Q's.

But fortunately for our purpose, Bonser gives the complete table of frequencies. From this we are able to see *in what* the greater male variability consists. We see that *the range* for the sexes is *equal*. At the *oldest extreme* we find 1.04 per cent of the boys and 1.88 per cent of the girls, while at the *youngest extreme* we find 0.51 per cent of the boys and 1.06 per cent of the girls. *The boys are more variable, but the highest achievements are more than twice as frequent, and the lowest achievements are nearly twice as frequent, on the part of girls.* The social significance would be the *exact opposite* of what greater male variability is ordinarily supposed to imply.

None of these studies was made for the chief purpose of studying sex differences in variability. The variations were calculated and stated more or less incidentally. There has been no attempt to select for reference here studies which found greater female variability. All studies known and accessible to the present writer,

---

[1] Bonser, *op. cit.*, p. 20.

where the variability of the sexes in mental traits has been computed, have been noted. In view of the facts that in many of the cases the conclusions are based on a small number of subjects, and that the evidence is conflicting, it seems necessary to conclude that the comparative variability of the sexes in mental traits has not been determined experimentally. If the evidence can be said to point in one direction rather than another, a greater female variability seems actually to be indicated in experiments so far made on the higher mental processes.

But even if it were determined that men *actually do* vary more in mental traits than women do, still nothing would be proved regarding their *inherent* variability. In order to establish the greater native variability of either sex it is necessary to show (1) that in the trait being distributed the opportunity and training of the sexes have been exactly equal, and (2) that in neither group has variability had more or less survival value than in the other group.

Under these conditions the only measurements of the sexes that may properly be compared with respect to variability are the measurements of infants at birth and for a short period thereafter. These are limited to anatomical traits, and objections are made to the validity of even these data. No measurements, especially mental measurements, of adults under the social customs which have obtained in the world of men and women fulfil either of our two necessary conditions. Men and women have devoted themselves to different activities because of the very different parts they play in the reproduction of the species. Women are under the biological necessity of bearing and rearing the children, and in the present almost as invariably as in the past, childbearing has implied and compelled as a consequence the one occupation of housekeeping. Thus intellectual variability had no survival value for women, but rather the opposite. Women married, or were married by their parents, at an early age. They bore children—and *many* of them, since until the present century the very existence of a nation depended on the increase in its numbers of fighting men. All the influences of social pressure, religious precept, and even of the legal restriction of knowledge have been brought to bear on women to the end that there might be enough increase in the population to offset the wastage of war and disease. Physiological facts made it natural, and consequent public expectation made it well nigh imperative, that women should contribute to the care of these numerous children by *housekeeping*. This was formerly almost absolutely the case, and even in this century the cases of women who have found a way to vary from the modal occupation and status, and yet procreate, are rare indeed. Individual prejudice hinders, poverty forbids, or society enacts legal measures against it, as in the case of a New York City teacher, which was recently given much publicity in the daily press. But men, except slave men, could always procreate and at the same time be as diverse in occupation, trade, and inclination as possible.

Thus (1) the opportunity and exercise of the two sexes in the traits which make for intellectual achievement have been very dissimilar in kind and amount, and (2) for one sex variability has had survival value; for the other sex it has had no survival value—this by virtue of the different parts played by the sexes in perpetuating the race. Darwin[1] says:

> With respect to the causes of variability we are in all cases very ignorant, but we can see that in man, as in the lower animals, they stand in some relation to the conditions to which each species has been exposed during several generations. . . . . We see the influence of diversified conditions in the more civilized nations; for the members, belonging to different grades of rank, and following different occupations, present a greater range of character than do the members of barbarous nations. . . . .

This statement by Darwin involves, of course, a fallacy. For we do not know whether the civilized nations are more variable because they are civilized, or civilized because they are more variable. We can, however, paraphrase this statement and apply it to the situation of the two sexes. Men have been influenced by diversified conditions; they have followed the greatest possible range of occupations, and have at the same time procreated unhindered. Women have been limited to *one* set of activities, *because* of the part they play in the perpetuation of the species.

Men of science studying the ever-interesting subject of genius and leadership have pointed out women's inferiority to men in

[1] Charles Darwin, *Descent of Man* (1871), p. 44.

art, science, war, politics, and invention. They have diligently sought to explain the causes of this failure on the part of women. Ellis finds the causes in the greater primitiveness, less variability, and greater affectability of women. Lafitte finds the cause in the fact that women's minds are concrete and incapable of abstraction. Upton finds it in the fact that woman "is emotional by temperament and nature, and cannot project herself outwardly." Thorndike finds it chiefly in the greater variability of the male, and partly in the fact that women lack the fighting instinct. Countless men have found it in the "less ability" of women. None, so far as I know, has announced that he finds it in the conditioning influence of woman's biological function, the inescapable fact that she bears and rears the children. Frederic Harrison among general writers, in an essay on "The Future of Woman," recognizes the great influence that excessive maternity has had on woman's achievement:

We look to the good feeling of the future to relieve women from the agonizing wear and tear of families far too large to be reared by one mother—a burden which crushes down the best years of life for so many mothers, sisters, and daughters—a burden which, while it exists, makes all expectation of superior education or greater moral elevation in the masses of women mere idle talk.

Yet Harrison ends by forgetting this entirely, finding the final causes of woman's inferior achievement in "slighter nervous organization," "smaller cerebral mass," and in the fact that she is subject to the catamenial function and men are not.

J. McK. Cattell[1] in his study of the thousand most eminent persons of history says:

I have spoken throughtout of eminent men as we lack in English words including both men and women, but as a matter of fact women do not have an important place on the list. They have in all 32 representatives in the thousand. . . . . Belles lettres and fiction—the only department in which women have accomplished much—give ten names. . . . . Women have not excelled in poetry or art. Yet these are the departments . . . . in which the environment has been, perhaps, as favorable for women as for men. Women depart less from the normal than men—a fact that usually holds throughout the animal series. . . . . The distribution of women is represented by a narrower, bell-shaped curve.

[1] J. McK. Cattell, "Statistical Study of Eminent Men," *Popular Science Monthly*, LXII.

It is interesting to notice that the "only department in which women have accomplished much" is one in which work could be carried on more or less successfully in conjunction with the modal occupation—providing there was wealth enough to hire servants for the actual drudgery. Cattell does not say explicitly what he means by the implied unfavorableness of the environment for women in lines other than art and poetry. He is not entirely certain that the environment has been as favorable for them as for men even in art and poetry, since he qualifies his statement by "perhaps." But it is clearly implied that this author recognizes an *environmental* condition unfavorable to women.

It seems indubitable that great numbers of women of intellectual gifts, confronted with the necessity of choosing a "career" or "domestic happiness," have chosen, either consciously or unconsciously the latter. And it must be remembered that even the possibility of a *choice* has existed only in recent times; that throughout almost the whole course of history women were predestined to their work of housekeeping. It is not and cannot be known how much nor what grade of potential leadership has thus been turned into energy-absorbing channels where eminence is impossible. Housekeeping and the rearing of children, though much commended to women as proper fields for the exploitation of their talents, are, unfortunately for their fame, not fields in which eminence can be attained. No one knows, for instance, who at present is the best housekeeper in America, nor who has borne and reared the largest and finest family of children. It is not known how much intellectual acumen is being brought to bear on these ends. Eminent housekeepers and eminent mothers *as such* do not exist. Yet to say that women of great intellectual gifts have not thus expended their energies is to affirm either (1) that there are no women of intellectual gifts, an affirmation now *passé* in the scientific world, (2) that intellect is unattractive to men, and that thus the most intelligent women are left unmarried, (3) that the most intelligent women will not marry, or (4) that the bearing and rearing of children, and the performance of household tasks at present coincident therewith constitute no handicap to the highest attainment in the fields where eminence is possible.

Such statements as these are very likely to be construed as an attack on maternity as such. It is certain, however, that no such attack is intended. The whole and the sole purpose of this paper is to criticize the hypothesis that inherently greater male variability is the cause of woman's failure to attain intellectual eminence. Such a criticism involves the unsentimental statement of biological facts, and of their social consequences. Men of science, seeking the cause of woman's failure, have not sufficiently recognized these facts and consequences, or else they have deemed it unpedagogical to announce them. We do not need, even, to look to the high ranges of achievement for light on our thesis. We need only to take the grade of intellectual attainment represented by the Ph.D. degree. It is proposed soon to make a comprehensive study of the percentage of women who have taken this degree after becoming mothers, as compared with the percentage of men who have taken it after becoming fathers. It is likely that any person of academic experience would forecast the result that few or no women have taken this degree after becoming mothers.

Cora Sutton Castle[1] in her study of eminent women has attempted to determine why women have not played a greater part in the history of intellectual progress. She has treated eminent women with respect to their matrimonial relations, occupations, ages, nationalities, and epochs. But she has not yet determined *the number of children* borne by those women who attained eminence through *their intellectual labor*, as compared with the birth rate among women in general during the time when these women lived. Castle implies that woman's failure may be due to lack of educational opportunities, but we have farther to seek than that. For how did it come about that woman lacked educational opportunities? What was the genesis of this situation, since in the beginning there was no "educational opportunity" for either sex?

Thorndike has gone farther than almost any other man of science in declaring that woman's failure may to some extent be due to a difference in instincts *connected with reproduction*. He declares also that "We should first exhaust the known physical causes"

[1] Cora Sutton Castle, *Statistical Study of Eminent Women* (1913).

before we proceed to any assumption of mental inferiority in explaining woman's lack of achievement. But have these "known physical causes" been exhausted if we end with the conclusion that "the probably true explanation is to be found in the greater variability within the male sex"? Surely we should consider *first* the established, obvious, inescapable, physical fact that women bear and rear the children, and that this has always meant and still means that *nearly 100 per cent of their energy is expended in the performance and supervision of domestic and allied tasks, a field where eminence is impossible.* Only when we had exhausted this fact as an explanation should we pass on to the question of comparative variability, or of differences in intellect or instinct. Men of science who discuss at all the matter of woman's failure should thus seek the cause of failure in the most obvious facts, and announce the conclusion consequent upon such search. Otherwise their discussion is futile scientifically.

Undoubtedly one of the most difficult and fundamental problems that today confront thinking women is how to secure for themselves the chance to vary from the mode of their sex, and at the same time to procreate, in a social order that has been built up on the assumption that there is and can be little or no variation in tastes, interests, and abilities within the female sex. It is a problem that has never confronted men. At times it seems wellnigh insoluble. But to affirm that it is insoluble is at the same time to affirm that there will always be a hard choice confronting women whose tastes vary from the mode; that there will be restlessness, unhappiness, and strife with the social order on the part of these individuals; and that society must tend to lose the work of its intellectual women or else lose their children.

Briefly our thesis may be summed up thus:

1. The greater variability of males in anatomical traits is not established, but is debated by authorities of perhaps equal competence.

2. But even if it were established, it would only suggest, not prove, that men are more variable in mental traits also. The empirical data at present available on this point are inadequate and contradictory, and if they point either way, actually indicate greater female variability.

3. But even if it were established that there *actually* is greater male variability in mental traits, it would only suggest, not prove, that there is greater *inherent* variability. For (a) the opportunity and exercise of the sexes have been dissimilar and unequal; (b) intellectual variability has had survival value for men, but for women it has had little or none—this by virtue of the different parts played by the sexes in the perpetuation of the species.

4. It must be remembered that variability in and of itself does not have social significance, unless it is known *in what* the variability consists—whether in greater range, greater frequency at the extremes, or in flattening at the top of the curve of distribution.

5. It is undesirable to seek for the cause of sex differences in eminence in ultimate and obscure affective and intellectual differences until we have exhausted as a cause the known, obvious, and inescapable fact that women bear and rear the children, and that this has had as an inevitable sequel the occupation of housekeeping, a field where eminence is not possible.

As a corollary it may be added that

6. It is desirable, for both the enrichment of society and the peace of individuals, that women may find a way to vary from their mode as men do, and yet procreate. Such a course is at present hindered by individual prejudice, poverty, and the enactment of legal measures. But public expectation will slowly change, as the conditions that generated that expectation have already changed, and in another century the solution to this problem will have been found.

BIBLIOGRAPHY CONSULTED

Bonser, *Reasoning Ability of Children* (1910).
Brown, W., "Correlation of Mental Abilities," *British Journal of Psychology* (1910).
Castle, Cora S., *Statistical Study of Eminent Women* (1913).
Cattell, J. McK., "Statistical Study of Eminent Men," *Popular Science Monthly*, 62.
Darwin, Charles, *Descent of Man* (1871).
Dubois, H., *Les gros enfants au point de vue obstetrical.* Thèse de Paris (1897).
Ellis, H., *Man and Woman* (1909).
Fox and Thorndike, "Sex Differences in Arithmetical Ability," *Columbia Contributions to Philosophy, Psychology, and Education*, II.
Harrison, F., *Realities and Ideals* (1908).

Hollingworth, H. L., "Judgments of Persuasiveness," *Psychological Review*, XXVIII (1911), 4.
Hollingworth, L. S., "The Frequency of Amentia as Related to Sex," *Medical Record* (1913).
Hrdlicka, A., *Anthropological Investigation of One Thousand Children* (1899).
Kuper, G., "Group Differences in the Interests of Children," *Journal of Philosophy, Psychology, and Scientific Method* (1912).
Meyers, G. C., *Incidental Memory* (1913).
Pearson, K., *Chances of Death* (1897).
Scripture, E. W., "Arithmetical Prodigies," *American Journal of Psychology* (1891).
Stone, *Arithmetical Abilities* (1908).
Strong, E. K., Jr., *Relative Merits of Advertisements* (1911).
Thorndike, E. L., *Educational Psychology* (1910).
Thorndike, E. L., "Sex in Education," *The Bookman*, XXIII, 213.
Wells, F. L., "Sex Differences in the Tapping Test," *American Journal of Psychology* (1909).
Wells, F. L., "Relation of Practice to Individual Differences," *American Journal of Psychology* (1912).

THE PSYCHOLOGICAL BULLETIN

GENERAL REVIEWS AND SUMMARIES

SEX DIFFERENCES IN MENTAL TRAITS

BY LETA S. HOLLINGWORTH

Teachers College, Columbia University

Since the very complete and painstaking review of the literature of sex differences which appeared in the BULLETIN in October, 1914 (11), there have been few studies undertaken with the chief aim of investigating sex differences in mental traits. Such results as have been published in the last two years are derived chiefly as incidental matter from studies prosecuted with some other main problem in view. In this field, as in other scientific fields, little has come from abroad. The few articles and monographs which have appeared in Europe under titles which would imply that they contain data on sex differences have not been accessible to the present reviewer, and it is doubtful if they are at all accessible in this country.

Researches undertaken for the purpose of obtaining developmental norms have yielded interesting data on sex differences. In the standardization of their Point Scale for measuring intelligence, Yerkes and Bridges (14) report that in their English-speaking groups girls attain higher scores than boys between the ages of five and seven; that they then tend to fall below the averages for the boys, with minor variations up to the age of eleven, when they again for a year or two surpass the boys, only to drop below once more from fourteen onward. The authors interpret this crossing and recrossing of the curves of the sexes to be a revelation of actual and reliable sex differences. As a result of their research they are "fully convinced that the accurate determination of norms for the sexes is eminently desirable," and they "suspect that at certain ages serious injustice will be done to individuals by evaluating their scores in the light of norms which do not take account of sex differences."

Terman (9) in his experiments with 1,000 unselected children, in revising the Binet-Simon Intelligence Scale, finds a small but fairly constant superiority of the girls up to the age of thirteen years. At fourteen years the curve for the girls drops below that for the boys. The apparent superiority of boys at the age of fourteen years is, however, fully accounted for by the more frequent elimination of fourteen-year-old girls from the grades by promotion to the high school. "The superiority of girls over boys is so slight that for practical purposes it would seem negligible." Terman offers "no support to the opinion expressed by Yerkes and Bridges that 'at certain ages serious injustice will be done individuals by evaluating their scores in the light of norms which do not take account of sex differences.'" Apart from the very slight superiority of girls, Terman finds the distribution of intelligence in the two sexes to be the same. The supposed greater variability of boys is not found. "Girls do not group themselves around the median more closely than do boys."

Terman suggests that the fact that so few women have attained eminence "may be due to wholly extraneous factors," the most important of which are (1) that the occupations in which it is possible to achieve eminence are for the most part only now beginning to open their doors to women, homemaking, the traditional occupation of women, being a field in which eminence is impossible; (2) that even of the small number of women who embark upon a professional career, a majority marry and devote a large amount of their time and energy to perpetuating the species; (3) that both the training given to girls and the atmosphere in which they grow up are unfavorable to the inculcation of the professional point of view. The author also notes the possibility that the affective traits of women may be such as to favor the development of sentiment at the expense of intellectual ability.

Trabue (10) in standardizing his Completion Test Language Scales finds that on the whole boys make a somewhat lower median score than girls in the same grade, although the difference is small, and the amount of overlapping is enormous. His figures for 1,590 boys and 883 girls show that according to the quartiles there is no sex difference in variability.

Woolley and Fisher (12) report in full, in monograph form, their mental and physical measurements of working children in Cincinnati. The children were tested at fourteen years when they came to the work-certificate office to obtain certificates, and again, one year later. The physical tests applied were of height, weight, visual acuity, auditory acuity, vital capacity, steadiness of hand, strength of hand, rapidity of movement, and accuracy of movement. The mental tests included cancellation, memory, substitution, completion of sentences, association by opposites, and the puzzle-box test. Except for height at fifteen years, in which the two sexes are about the same, the girls excel the boys in height, weight, steadiness, and card-sorting, while the boys excel in strength, rapidity of movement and vital capacity. Boys excel in performances where strength is the chief factor, and girls in those where coordination and a fine control of muscles is most prominent. In the mental tests the only large sex difference in the entire series is that of the great superiority of the boys in the opening of the puzzle box. The authors feel that this test is unfairly selected on the ground of sex, as boys are more encouraged to take an active interest in mechanical construction, and accordingly understand more about how many things are made, and what the simple mechanical devices are. This would give the boys an unfair advantage on the ground of training, just as tying a bow-knot (in which Terman found girls superior to boys) would give an unfair advantage to girls.

In the preparation of a scale for the measurement of fourteen- and fifteen-year-old adolescents, Woolley (13) reports with respect to variability, that "if variability is measured by the difference between the five and ninety-five percentiles, the differences between the two sexes are small and not entirely consistent. In the physical tests the boys are a trifle more variable at fourteen, and decidedly so at fifteen. In the mental tests the boys are a little more variable at fourteen, while there is a somewhat greater difference in favor of the girls at fifteen." One fact with regard to variability holds for all series. The girls show a wider variation below the median than above it. The research covers 750 fourteen-year-olds and 680 of the same children at fifteen years of age, all being school children who were dropping out of school to go to work.

E. K. Strong, Jr. (8), publishes the results of an experiment with fragments of advertisements. Strong first exposed the advertisements to the subjects (forty women students, and a group of forty men composed of college students, instructors and professors) at the rate of one per second. When fragments of the original advertisements were studied by these subjects, the women remembered 51 per cent. more details than did the men. The investigator then allowed the subjects to inspect another series at their leisure, giving unlimited time to look over the material. Under these conditions the women remembered 53 per cent. more details than did the men. Strong concludes that a genuine sex difference is disclosed in this experiment, but does not attempt to determine whether the difference is due to inherent capacities or to differences in training. He ascribes the more pronounced emotional response of women to advertisements, which he noted in a previous study, to their superior ability to note detail.

Among the investigations which have been undertaken for the explicit purpose of studying sex differences is Boring's experiment on capacity to report on moving pictures. Boring (1) experimented with both children and adults of both sexes, in order to make comparisons of the reliability of testimony as conditioned by sex and age. Forty-four subjects were used: thirteen women, the majority of them being undergraduates in Cornell University; eleven men, the majority of whom were graduate students of psychology or professors of psychology; twelve boys and eight girls, taken from a single class in the Ithaca public schools, and having an average age of 12.3 years.

A scene from a photo-play was presented. The subjects were not told what the purpose of the experiment was, but those who were students or professors of psychology suspected from the conditions and instructions that the test was to be one of ability to report. The traits scored were (1) range of report, (2) spontaneity of report, (3) range of knowledge, (4) accuracy of report, (5) assurance, (6) reliability of assurance, (7) warranted assurance, (8) assured accuracy, (9) tendency to oath, (10) warranted tendency to oath, (11) unwarranted tendency to oath, (12) reliability of oath.

The author concludes from the results of his experiment that "There is evidence that the boys exceed the girls in range of report, in tendency to oath, and also in unwarranted tendency to oath, and that the girls exceed the boys in reliability of oath. The significance of none of these coefficients is very high, although the last is undoubtedly reliable. With men and women the differences are more marked. The greatest difference occurs in the unwarranted tendency to oath, in which the women exceed the men. The men exceed the women in range of report, range of knowledge, assurance, warranted assurance, assured accuracy, and reliability of oath."

"It appears, then, that there is little difference apparent, with the material used, between boys and girls, whereas there is quite a marked superiority of the men over the women with respect to six (perhaps seven) coefficients. This conclusion accords with the general psychological principle that even those mental sex differences which are large in adults are relatively slight in childhood." The author notes the fact that there is a source of error in the circumstance that the group of women was otherwise constituted than was the group of men. He nevertheless accepts the difference which he finds between the men and the women as a sex difference, although it coincides with what would be expected *a priori* from differences in age, training and preliminary knowledge of the experiment, quite apart from sex. In the group of children, where none of these factors was present, no reliable sex differences were found, except that the girls showed much greater caution in taking oath than did boys.

Gates (3) reports tests on a large number of school children of both sexes, conducted with the purpose of determining variations in diurnal efficiency. He finds no sex difference in the variations of diurnal efficiency; the records of both sexes may be combined in platting the course of the daily rhythm. The correlations of the various tests with each other also failed to reveal any sex difference. The average scores of boys and girls when compared revealed the following sex differences: "(1) In addition and multiplication the girls appear to be somewhat superior, although such is not invariably the case. (2) In the drawing test the girls appear to follow the method of emphasizing accuracy rather than speed, and the boys speed rather than accuracy. That one sex is actually capable of excelling the other in either speed or accuracy cannot be said with certainty. . . . With respect to accuracy, there is a small amount of evidence favoring the superiority of boys. (3) In the completion test the girls show a distinct superiority. (4) The girls are decidedly more efficient in cancellation. . . . (5) The girls excel without exception in money for auditory and visual digits, and in recognition of nonsense syllables. (6) Excluding the tests for speed and accuracy of movement, in which results, as far as ability is concerned, are uncertain, out of forty-two comparisons (six classes in seven tests) the girls excel in thirty-eight, and the boys in four."

Gates (4) also reports tests on 197 students of elementary psychology, for memory of visual and auditory digits, memory of verbal sense material, recognition of geometrical forms, and learning in a substitution test. The separate correlations for the sexes are very similar. The results of the memory tests are "in harmony with the generally accepted belief that women excel in this kind of work." The men excel slightly in the substitution test, but the difference is not great.

L. S. Hollingworth (5) presents a series of tests on twenty-five subjects to determine whether any relation can be established between the mental and motor efficiency of women and the catamenial period. Twenty-three women were subjected to the tests, and two men were tested at the same time as controls. The traits tested were speed and accuracy of perception, controlled association, speed of voluntary movement, steadiness, rate of learning and muscular fatiguability. The results of the experiment are negative. No influence of menstruation upon the processes tested can be demonstrated from the data thus collected.

Pittinger (7) has made a study of the choices of occupation, the scholarship, etc., of high-school graduates in five north central states. Fewer females than males undertake courses of advanced training. Variety of training or employment is less among females than among males. Various differences in occupations selected are indicated. The most scholarly of both sexes go on to take advanced training.

Jastrow (6) has added to the general discussion of sex differences in his chapter on the psychology of group traits. He has made no systematic attempt to cite sources of authority or data. Many of the traditional views about sex differences, which were advanced before experimental data were sought, are rehearsed. The author points out that "men and women are organically different," from which he derives the conclusion that a contrasted psychology is involved. Pathology is appealed to as furnishing valuable clues to innate sex differences. For instance, "Among the typically masculine insanities is general paralysis. Its early stages parallel the symptoms of alcoholic intoxication: tremor of speech and movement; coarseness of expression; uncertainty of sensory action; and free indulgence of expansive thought. It develops quickly to the later stages with paralytic symptoms, illusions of grandeur, loss of control, and a generally disordered excessive functioning—throughout a picture of exaggerated masculine psychology." The author seems here to imply that the greater frequency of general paralysis in men is a clue to the existence of some innate sex difference in neural functioning. In such instances the appeal to pathology fails, as the etiological factor in general paralysis of the insane is not psychological but organic. It occurs more frequently among men because syphilis occurs more frequently among them.

Brown (2) and his co-workers have carried out a series of careful experiments to investigate individual and sex differences in suggestibility. As the experiments were numerous and the technique detailed, no brief summary can be successfully presented. Those who wish to consult the data in detail must be referred to the original monograph. Brown concludes that "a general review of the entire series of twenty-six experiments reveals a very distinct difference between the sexes. In thirteen of the experiments there is a clear difference between the sexes, and in only one of these experiments are the men more suggestible. There are only four experiments in which no sex difference can be made out. . . . The difference between the sexes is more distinct in some of the groups of experiments than in other groups. There can be little doubt that women are more suggestible in tests which involve an imagined sensation, a series of progressive changes, distortion of memory, and estimation of magnitude. The tests with illusion do not give clear differences between the sexes, and the tests with aesthetic judgments give contradictory or indecisive results."

Two considerations have especially impressed the reviewer in going over these recent contributions to the literature of sex differences. The first has to do with method. Investigators seem to have acquired the habit of dividing their subjects automatically into two groups on the basis of sex. Thereupon they proceed to describe all differences found between the two groups as sex differences. As a matter of fact, differences thus found should logically be treated only as group differences, unless the author is able to show that the group of males differs more from the group of females than from other groups of males similarly selected. In general, the investigators here reviewed have not covered this technical point.

The second consideration has to do with the results bearing on the question of the comparative variability of the sexes. Terman, Trabue, and Woolley present variability figures on hundreds of boys and girls with the uniform result that neither sex is found to be more variable than the other. This is in accord with the result derived from the researches of Courtis and Goddard, previously reviewed in the BULLETIN. More extensive and reliable data have been made available on this point in the last five years than in all time preceding.

REFERENCES

1. BORING, E. G. Capacity to Report upon Moving Pictures, as Conditioned by Sex and Age. *J. of Crim. Law & Criminol.*, 1916.
2. BROWN, W. Individual and Sex Differences in Suggestibility. *Univ. of Cal. Pub. in Psychol.*, 1916, 2, 291–430.
3. GATES, A. I. Variations in Efficiency During the Day, Together with Practice Effects, Sex Differences and Correlations. *Univ. of Cal. Pub. in Psychol.*, 1916, 2, 1–156.
4. GATES, A. I. Correlations and Sex Differences in Memory and Substitution. *Univ. of Cal. Pub. in Psychol.*, 1916, 1, 345–350.
5. HOLLINGWORTH, L. S. *Functional Periodicity.* New York: Teachers College, 1914. Pp. 101.
6. JASTROW, J. *Character and Temperament.* New York: Appleton, 1915. Pp. xviii + 596.
7. PITTINGER, B. F. The Distribution of High School Graduates in Five North Central States. *Sch. and Soc.*, 1916, 3.
8. STRONG, E. K., JR. An Interesting Sex Difference. *Ped. Sem.*, 1915, 22, 521–528.
9. TERMAN, L. M. *The Measurement of Intelligence.* Boston: Houghton, Mifflin, 1916. Pp. 362.
10. TRABUE, M. R. *Completion Test Language Scales.* New York: Teachers College, 1916.
11. WOOLLEY, H. T. The Psychology of Sex. *Psychol. Bull.*, 1914, 11, 353–379.
12. WOOLLEY, H. T., & FISHER, C. R. Mental and Physical Measurements of Working Children. *Psychol. Monog.*, 1914, 18, (No. 77). Pp. 247.
13. WOOLLEY, H. T. A New Scale of Mental and Physical Measurements for Adolescents. *J. of Educ. Psychol.*, 1915, 6, 521–550.
14. YERKES, R. M., BRIDGES, J. W., & HARDWICK, R. S. *A Point Scale for Measuring Mental Ability.* Baltimore: Warwick & York, 1915. Pp. viii + 218.

GENERAL REVIEWS AND SUMMARIES.

COMPARISON OF THE SEXES IN MENTAL TRAITS

BY LETA S. HOLLINGWORTH
Teachers College, Columbia University

To give this review a satisfactory title has not been altogether easy. It is the custom of the BULLETIN to publish from time to time summaries showing the results of experimental investigations in which the sexes are compared in mental traits, and the present review is intended to perpetuate this custom for the years 1916–1918. To entitle it "Sex Differences in Mental Traits" would lead the reader falsely to infer that all or most of the comparisons have shown differences. To call it "The Mental Traits of Sex" would imply that it discloses mental traits which are sex-limited. On the other hand, a title like "Sex Identity in Mental Traits" would be unfair, especially to such expressions of opinion as are to be included, which take the time-honored view that there are, and must be notable, inherent psychological differences between the sexes. Simply to adopt for a title "The Psychology of Sex" would give the erroneous impression that the review treats of literature pertaining to the sexual instinct. The title finally chosen seems to circumvent most of these difficulties.

From the standpoint of the experimental behaviorist no conclusions should be noted in a review under this title, except such as were based on the quantitative study of large numbers of both sexes, selected at random, or on exactly the same basis. And any difference found between the two groups thus selected and studied, could be announced as a sex difference only if it reliably exceeded the probable error of the average or median; or, being within the probable error, was found constantly to occur in a large number of comparisons of similar groups with each other. Furthermore, a reliable difference thus found could be called an *inherent* sex difference only if it were shown to be present when the training and environment of both groups had been similar. The only point in pausing thus to state the obvious is that investigators sometimes neglect these principles of scientific method, and announce any difference found between two groups, arbitrarily segregated on the basis of sex, as a "sex difference." They forget that a chance difference would be found if the individuals composing the groups were re-segregated on the basis of any incidental factor—say eye-color or presence and absence of freckles.

The reviewer who would confine himself exclusively to results gained by the experimental method outlined above would, however, automatically tend to do himself out of his review. He would have very little to report. It was formerly a kind of convention among psychologists to include in the summary of results of a study where both male and female subjects participated, a paragraph on "sex differences." There seems now to be a growing tendency among those who have studied individual differences most extensively to omit this customary paragraph. For instance, Pintner and Paterson (14) make no reference to sex differences in their recent standardization of performance tests. On the basis of the extensive data from which his *Mental Survey* is derived, Pintner (16) states merely that "sex differences in these tests are too slight to justify separate norms for boys and girls." In the standardization of the picture completion test, Pintner and Anderson (15) say, "the test is equally well adapted to boys and to girls." Pressey and Pressey (17) postpone discussion of sex differences for a later paper.

Two comparisons of the sexes in memory tests have come to notice: E. F. Mulhall (13) tested 285 boys and 353 girls for recall and recognition, with various kinds of materials. She found that "for memory of words and syllables the averages are slightly higher for the girls, for forms slightly higher for boys," and that "there appears to be no marked sex difference in variability." A. I. Gates (5) from tests of adults concludes that women show slightly better performance than men in memory, and that men are slightly superior to women in reasoning. The amount of overlapping and the reliability measures are not given.

Marsh (11) presents results on two individuals, a man and a woman, who subjected themselves to a long fast, during which mental tests were administered in order to detect possible changes in performance and feeling. "The sensory and passive sides of the self are not greatly affected, generally speaking, but sexually show male sensitivity for pain and perceptivity for dots increased, and for touch decreased; while for the female the reverse is true. Some improvement for both sexes is shown in mental clearness and accuracy, though not decisively; and a most pronounced effect upon the memory, disadvantageous for the male subject, and advantageous for the feminine. The feelings, usually acute for several days, and then usually apathetic for a time, were on the whole ambiguous indices of the grades of objective performance, less so for the male than for the female." What justification there could be for entitling such a study "sex differences" is hard to see, since it includes but one man and one woman, each of whom might easily differ as much or more from others of the same sex, as from each other.

The experiments of Berliner (3) with æsthetic judgments of school children, made on 180 girls and 180 boys of grammar school ages, show that "the ranking of a group of pictures is to a high degree the same for both sexes"; that "different groups of girls agree more closely in their æsthetic judgments than groups of boys"; that "the average positions of the pictures differ more from one another in groups of girls than in groups of boys"; that "inside the group the girls agree more closely in their æsthetic judgment than boys"; that "boys agree more closely in their dislikes than in their likes; girls agree more in their likes than in their dislikes,"—a result contradictory to results previously announced by H. L. Hollingworth and by E. K. Strong, Jr.; and that "the variability between the extreme and middle pictures tends to be greater in groups of girls than in groups of boys."

Rosanoff, Martin and Rosanoff (19) in extending the studies of free association previously undertaken by Kent and Rosanoff and by Rosanoff and Rosanoff, have made special comments in comparison of the sexes. They state that "all conditions being approximately equal, no difference is found in the showings of the two sexes, as regards our most significant measure —the sum of 'high standard' values; but male subjects show very consistently a tendency to give either individual reactions or common reactions having no 'high standard' value, where female subjects furnish failure of reaction instead." They state also that "a tendency to give individual reactions or common reactions without 'high standard' value, where normal subjects fail of reaction, seems to characterize neuropathic subjects, independently of sex."

Terman (21) and his collaborators have now published in monograph form the data from which The Stanford Revision of The Binet-Simon Scale is derived. Here the curves representing the performance of the two sexes are seen to be practically identical. No sex differences in variability appear. The conclusion of the authors is that the norms for general intelligence apply equally to both sexes.

Elizabeth E. Farrell (4) reports statistics from a survey of certain ungraded classes for children of exceptionally low mentality, in New York City. In these classes there were 258 boys and 103 girls. The investigator comments as follows: "The fact that more boys than girls are found in these ungraded classes permits of explanations other than that of greater variability in males. One of these is based on the fact that boys have greater freedom, are less restrained. Because of this they come into conflict with their school environment. This maladjustment makes it imperative that some notice be given to them, and some explanation sought." Race (17) selecting pupils for an ungraded class of superior children in a city school system, found 10 boys and 11 girls who were eligible on the basis of exceptionally high intelligence, and physical fitness.

In the field of animal psychology Bagg (2) has contributed a quantitative study of individual differences in the performance of white rats, which reveals no sex differences.

Turning from conclusions based on quantitative data, we wish to note recent expressions of theory and opinion, bearing on the behavior of the sexes. These are mainly discussions of the psychological considerations involved in the changing social status of women. Hull (7) has published an article pointing out the implications of psychoanalytic concepts in the study of the behavior of women and girls. The concept of hysterical and irrational reaction as the result of chronic blocking of strong, fundamental conations, by taboo, social suppression, economic nonentity, and the like, is brought to the attention of those who would understand the efforts of women to find another "place." In this same vein are chapters of Adler's work (1), published some years ago, but not translated into English until recently.

Moxcey (12) has written a readable book, based with discrimination on the data of psychology, and intended for those whose work has to do with the guidance of adolescent girls. L. S. Hollingworth

(6) has advanced the theorem that the traditional division of labor between the sexes implies no sex difference in mental traits; that it is to be explained solely on the basis of sex difference in the physiological function of reproduction, which has always bound the female to the house and offspring, leaving the male relatively free vocationally; that the traditional division of labor is what we should expect to find, even though there were no sex differences in mental traits.

Russell (20) expresses the belief that the concept of maternal instinct has been greatly overworked, in the service of social control, and that women will become increasingly resistant to exaggeration of its importance as a determinant of their careers. Jastrow (8) is convinced that "the feminine mind" is a type, different qualitatively and quantitatively from "the masculine mind," and has again presented his opinions in a chapter of his recent volume, *The Psychology of Conviction*. Wells (22) occasionally implies the existence of sex differences in instinctive equipment, as when he discusses work trends and mastery trends in connection with the masculine pronoun, and parental trends in connection with the feminine pronoun. On the whole, however, the reader is left to infer that the mechanisms of adjustment work independently of sex.

It is quite certain that not all the literature which compares the sexes in mental traits, and which would deserve comment, has been seen by the present reviewer. For example, publications have appeared under titles which would imply that they contain such comparisons, by Lipmann (9) and by Lombroso-Ferraro (10) respectively, but they have not been accessible to the reviewer. Now that the war is finished, foreign contributions will doubtless begin to become available once more. They are conspicuously absent from this report.

REFERENCES

1. ADLER, A. *The Neurotic Constitution*. New York: Moffat, Yard, 1917.
2. BAGG, H. J., Individual Differences and Family Resemblances in Animal Behavior. *Amer. Natur.*, 1916.
3. BERLINER, A. Æsthetic Judgments of School Children. *J. of Appl. Psychol.*, 1918, 229–242.
4. FARRELL, E. E. *Nineteenth Annual Report of The Superintendent of Schools*. New York City. 1916–1917.
5. GATES, A. I. Experiments on the Relative Efficiency of Men and Women in Memory and Reasoning. *Psychol. Rev.*, 1917. 24, 139–146.
6. HOLLINGWORTH, L. S. The Vocational Aptitudes of Women. (Chapter in *Vocational Psychology*, by H. L. Hollingworth.) New York: Appleton, 1916.

7. HULL, H. The Long Handicap. *Psychoan. Rev.*, Oct., 1917.
8. JASTROW, J. The Feminine Mind. (Chapter in *The Psychology of Conviction*.) New York: Houghton Mifflin, 1918.
9. LIPMANN, F., *Psychische Geschlectsunterschiede*. Leipzig: Barth.
10. LOMBROSO-FERRARO, G. Importanza del l'abbigliamento per la Psiche Feminile. *Riv. di Psicol.* 1917, 3, 305–307.
11. MARSH, H. D. Individual and Sex Differences Brought out by Fasting. *Psychol. Rev.*, 1916, 23, 6.
12. MOXCEY, M. E. *Girlhood and Character*. New York: Abington Press, 1916.
13. MULHALL, E. F. Tests of the Memories of School Children. *J. of Educ. Psychol.*, 1917.
14. PINTNER, R., & PATERSON, D. G. *A Scale of Performance Tests*. New York: Appleton, 1917.
15. PINTNER, R., & ANDERSON, M. M. The Picture Completion Test. *Educ. Psychol. Monog.*, No. 20. Baltimore: Warwick and York, 1917.
16. PINTNER, R. *The Mental Survey*. New York: Appleton, 1918.
17. PRESSEY, S. L., & PRESSEY, L. W. A Group Scale of Intelligence, with First Norms from 1,100 School Children. *J. of Appl. Psychol.*, 1918.
18. RACE, H. V. A Study of a Class of Children of Superior Intelligence. *J. of Educ. Psychol.*, 1918, 9, p. 91–97.
19. ROSANOFF, A. J., MARTIN, H. E., & ROSANOFF, I. R. A Higher Scale of Mental Measurement and Its Application to Cases of Insanity. *Psych. Monog.*, 1918, 25, No. 3.
20. RUSSELL, B. Marriage and The Population Question. (Chapter in *Why Men Fight*.) New York: Century, 1917.
21. TERMAN, L. M., & OTHERS. *The Stanford Revision and Extension of the Binet-Simon Scale for Measuring Intelligence*. Warwick and York: Baltimore, 1917.
22. WELLS, F. L. *Mental Adjustments*. New York: Appleton, 1916.

[4]
PSYCHOLOGICAL LITERATURE.
A REVIEW OF THE RECENT LITERATURE ON THE PSYCHOLOGY OF SEX.

Although the past few years have witnessed the appearance of a number of comprehensive and even encyclopedic works on various aspects of the problem of sex, there has been comparatively little advance in knowledge of the mental characteristics of sex. The few positive contributions in the literature of anatomy and experimental psychology I will review first, and will then deal briefly with the more pretentious treatises which are summaries and theoretical discussions.

The most important single contribution to our knowledge of the facts of the case is to be found in Dr. Franklin P. Mall's paper ' On Several Anatomical Characters of the Human Brain Said to Vary According to Race and Sex, with Especial Reference to the Weight of the Frontal Lobe' (*Am. J. of Anat.*, IX., p. 1, 1909). Dr. Mall's general conclusion is that there is as yet no reliable evidence for the variation of anatomical characters with either race or sex. The belief that the brains of females differ from those of males has been widely accepted, and has been thought to be conclusive evidence of the permanent inferiority of the female mind. The points in which the female brain has been said to be inferior to the male are: (1) total weight; (2) proportionate weight of the frontal lobe indicated by (*a*) actual weighings, and (*b*) determinations of the position of the central sulcus; (3) the area of the corpus callosum; (4) the complexity of gyri and sulci; (5) the conformation of gyri and sulci; and (6) the rate of development of the cortex in the fœtus. Dr. Mall's paper gives a critical review of the literature of the subject to date, and adds important new data.

It is now a generally accepted belief that the smaller gross weight of the female brain has no significance other than that of the smaller average size of the female. With regard to the other anatomical characters enumerated, Dr. Mall shows that those observers who have found differences characteristic of sex have been guilty of serious errors in scientific procedure. They have based conclusions on too small a series of observations, have used methods too crude to make anything but large and constant differences (which they did not obtain) significant, have made their determinations *with a knowledge of the sex of*

THE PSYCHOLOGY OF SEX.

the brain under consideration, and have even, in some cases, drawn conclusions not justified by their own data. Those observers who have avoided these errors have found no differences characteristic of sex. Dr. Mall himself finds none, and is inclined to believe that they do not exist. The only exception to this statement is that he finds some evidence of a greater tendency of the male brain to vary from the normal conformation of gyri and sulci.

Waldeyer in his paper 'Ueber Gehirne menschlicher Zwillings- und Drillingsfrüchte verschiedenen Geschlechts' (*Zeit. f. Ethnol.*, 1908, Bd. 40, S. 262–272) agrees with Dr. Mall that it is by no means a general law that the male brain in twin fœtuses of different sex is further advanced in the formation of convolutions than the female. The male fœtus is frequently, though not always, larger than the female; and in case it is larger, usually has a more developed cortex.

Experimental psychology has yielded a few scattered researches bearing on the psychology of sex. They deal with (1) motor functions, (2) sensory processes, and (3) intellectual processes. Wells, 'Sex Differences in the Tapping Test' (*Amer. J. of Psychol.*, 1909, pp. 354–363) carried out a series of experiments in tapping on a telegraph key, in which he used ten men and ten women, attendants in an insane asylum, as subjects. He found the men somewhat superior to the women in the rate of tapping, but detected no difference between them in fatigue — a fact probably explained by the very slight amount of fatigue involved. (See Thompson, *Mental Traits of Sex*, p. 14, where the test involved much more intense fatigue.) He found a greater difference in the efficiency of the two hands in women than in men. (Compare below, Schuyten.) The women Wells found on the whole more variable than the men — a heresy which he attributes to their greater affectability. Schuyten, 'Bijdrage tot de Kennis der Rechts- en Linkshandigheid van de onderste ledematen (*Paedologisch. Jaarboek*, 10, S. 42–51, 1908), found that in both sexes the left leg preponderates over the right in length and in development, but the difference is greater in men than in women, greater in women than in children. Miss Downey, 'Judgments on the Sex of Handwriting' (PSYCHOL. REV., XVII., p. 205, 1910), investigated sex differences in the complicated function of handwriting. Her method was to collect 200 envelopes addressed by educated men and women, 100 by each sex. These were sorted according to sex by thirteen people. The percentage of right judgments was about the same as in Binet's tests. It ranged from 60 to 77 per cent. If only those judgments are recorded of which the observer felt certain, the percentage is raised materially. The characteristics of handwriting on which judgments of sex were based were that the typical feminine hand is colorless, conventional, neat, and small, and frequently shows signs of unaccustomedness; while the typical male hand is 'bold, or careless, or experienced, above all individual.' In the case of ten men and seventeen women there was an inversion of the sex signs, leading to constant false judgments. Of the ten men, at least two had done very little writing, and four others were teachers — a profession which fosters a conventional hand. Of the seventeen women, at least half had been accustomed to more than a usual amount of writing. Miss Downey concludes that the sex signs of handwriting are of social rather than psychophysiological origin. They are largely determined by (1) the amount of writing done, (2) age and (3) professional requirements.

The only contribution I have been able to find dealing with any phase of sensory processes in relation to sex is the article by Winch on 'Colour Preferences of School Children' (*British J. of Psychol.*, III, p. 42, 1909). His method was to ask each of 2,000 school children to write the four primary colors, black and white in the order of preference. The results were then tabulated according to age, sex and position in school. Winch found constant differences correlated with sex which he considers characteristic, but he makes no attempt to interpret them. An examination of his tables shows that the like points between the two sexes are far more striking than their differences. In both cases blue ranks first and red second, while black is last. The sexual differences are that very young boys sometimes rank red first, while girls never do. White is somewhat more popular with girls than with boys, while green and yellow are a trifle more popular with boys than with girls. It is at least a very plausible guess that white gains its greater popularity among the girls by virtue of white dresses, their gala attire. The trifling displacements of green and yellow in the girls' records as compared with the boys may easily be explained by the higher rank of white. To speak of genuine sexual differences in color preference on the basis of these tests seems farfetched.

In the realm of intellectual processes recent experimentation has dealt only with association. Of the two studies of association, I will deal first with the more detailed, though it was published later. Wrenschner, 'Die Reproduction und Association von Vorstellungen' (*Zeit. f. Psychol.*, Erganzb. III, 1907–1909) makes elaborate comparisons between men and women, the cultured and the uncultured, and children and adults—all on results obtained from twenty-two individuals. He examined two children, two servant maids, three working men, five educated women, and ten educated men. Although generalizations based on such an exceedingly small number of subjects, and frequently on trifling differences in the data, seem of very doubtful value, I will state briefly his conclusions with regard to sex. He found that men have a shorter reaction time for association than women. There are, as far as I know, no other tests made by the reaction time method. Tests made by requiring the subject to write a series of associations to a given word (see Thompson, *l. c.*, p. 131) have yielded contradictory results. With regard to qualitative differences in association, he makes the following statements. Men preponderate in the number of symmetrical reactions, mediate associations, multiple associations, associations by content, tendency to visualize, experience of emotional coloring, tendency to use previous stimulus words in reacting, number of unintended answers, and reduction with practice of the tendency to repeat the stimulus word. Women preponderate in the number of formal associations, the number of long reaction words, the variety of answers to a given stimulus word, the number of failures to react, the number of mistakes in the apprehension of the stimulus, the tendency to individualize, to reject answers because of emotional coloring, and to experience a rivalry in answers. From these characteristics Wrenschner draws the following formidable set of conclusions with regard to the process of association in the sexes. Women as compared with men show abnormality of reaction, meager presentations, a less active flow of ideas, less variety in ideas, a greater frequency of formal associations, imperfect adaptation to the conditions of the experiment, a more concrete form of response, a more subjective attitude, more indecision, and a less active attitude toward the experiment. It would be a simple matter to take Wrenschner's own data and derive quite a different set of generalizations which would have at least as much value as those he has drawn. Emma Fürst, 'Statistische Untersuchungen über Wortassoziationen und über familiäre Übereinstimmungen im Reactionstypus bei Ungebildeten' (*J. f. Psychol. und Neurol.*, IX., S. 243, 1907), carried out association tests on 100 individuals, men, women, and children, with the purpose of examining family likenesses in the type of association. She, like several previous observers, found that women have a greater tendency than men to the predicative type of association—a statement with which Wrenschner does not agree. She found men more given to outer and women to inner associations, and that men preponderate in the definition type of association. Like Wrenschner, she detects a more personal attitude in the women. She found more uniformity among the ideas of related women than among those of related men. If her table of results is formulated according to formal associations and associations by content, the result accords with Wrenschner's statement, though the difference between the sexes is too slight to be really significant. The two sets of results agree, then, in finding formal associations more frequent among women, and associations by content among men, and in detecting a more personal attitude on the part of women. With regard to the other topics discussed, either they disagree, or the two sets of results are not comparable.

Though there is no very recent experimentation on memory as correlated with sex, Max Offner, in his book *Das Gedächtnis* (Berlin, 1909), devotes a brief section to a summary of the experimental material. For the sake of the value of the book as a whole, one hopes that his account of experimentation on other phases of the memory problem is more accurate than that of this section. By means of omissions and misrepresentations he gives quite a wrong impression of the general trend of experimentation on the subject. He seems to have singled out the few cases in which males were shown to excel in some phase of memory, and ignored many of the cases in which the reverse was true. In quoting Lobsien's results he states the fact that boys were slightly more accurate in reproducing the exact order of a series, and omits to mention the fact that the general range of memory was shown to be decidedly better in girls. He also misrepresents Miss Thompson's results. She found memory distinctly better in women for both visual and auditory material, instead of a *geringe Ueberlegenheit der Mädchen auf visuellem Gebiete*, and is entirely innocent of the *stärkeres Abschweifen der Reproduction vom Gegenstand* on the part of the women with which she is credited.

In an article in the *American Journal of Psychology* (XXI., p. 114, 1910) on 'Spontaneous Constructions and Primitive Activities of Children Analogous to those of Primitive Man,' Acher draws some comparisons between the activities of boys and girls, based on the answers to a questionnaire. He says that boys are more interested than girls in points and edges because of their use of knives and sticking instruments; both sexes collect string, but they use it for different purposes — boys to tie hard knots, fish, and fly kites; girls to tie decorative knots, crochet, and make ornaments; girls are more apt than boys to attempt to modify bodily form; boys show a much greater interest than girls in the use of the whip and in throwing. The interpretation of such observations is obviously sociological rather than psychological.

The most important of the comprehensive discussions of the question of sex are those of Iwan Bloch, *The Sexual Life of our Times; its Relation to Modern Civilization* (London: Rebman, 1909), and the work entitled *Mann und Weib. Ihre Beziehung zu einander und zum Kulturleben der Gegenwart* (Stuttgart: Union, 1908) edited by R. Kossmann and J. Weiss, and written by a dozen or more authors. Havelock Ellis makes another contribution to the field in the volume called *Studies in the Psychology of Sex*, Vol. VI., *Sex in Relation to Society* (Philadelphia: Davis, 1910). None of these works are to be considered important from the point of view of psychology, except for the fact that they and similar works contain the only psychological accounts of the sexual impulse itself which we possess. Such material is difficult to obtain and difficult to evaluate, and it will probably be a long time before it has much scientific value. The chief point of agreement among these writers is that the sexual impulse is much less intense in women than in men. Aside from this discussion, these works contain no original psychological data. Although it is impossible to discuss the problems of sexual physiology and hygiene, sexual ethics, the theory and practice of marriage, and prostitution, without at times adopting the psychological point of view, it is not the dominant one in any of these books. They belong rather in the field of sociology. The work of Kisch, *The Sexual Life of Women* (New York: Rebman, 1910), and of Mertens, *Das sexuelle Problem und seine moderne Krise* (München: Kupferschmid, 1910), are written exclusively from the physiological standpoint. They deal with problems of sexual hygiene, sexual disease, and, as a corollary, sexual education. It is well worth while in passing to remark that all of the group of books under discussion advocate more instruction for children in matters of sex. Most of them agree that such instruction should begin not later than the sixth year. There is a difference of opinion as to whether it should form part of the curriculum of the public schools. In addition to these larger works, there is the usual crop of magazine articles on various phases of the psychology of sex.

The general impression produced by a survey of this motley mass of material is first, that the literature of the subject is improving in tone. There is perhaps no field aspiring to be scientific where flagrant personal bias, logic martyred in the cause of supporting a prejudice, unfounded assertions, and even sentimental rot and drivel, have run riot to such an extent as here. It is very significant to note the importance ascribed by Dr. Mall to the personal equation in so tangible and definite a problem as that of comparing the anatomical characters of the brains of the sexes. The outcome of problems where personal opinion has a still larger scope should be received with far more critical caution than heretofore. The signs in the literature of greater moderation in tone and more respect for evidence are in the direction of a much needed reform.

As to content, there seems to be a general trend toward the opinion that mind is probably not a secondary sexual character—in other words that there are probably few if any psychological differences of sex which are of biological origin—a statement which I think holds true in spite of the continued popularity of such books as Möbius' *Physiologischer Schwachsinn des Weibes* and Weininger's *Geschlecht und Character*. The tendency to minimize sexual differences is most marked with regard to intellectual processes, the field where most of the experimental work has been done, and in which the practical educational tests have been made. Even the time-honored belief that men are more capable of independent and creative work is beginning to give way in view of the successful competition of women in graduate work and in obtaining the doctorate (see Marion Talbot's *The Education of Women*, p. 21). The fundamental importance of sexual differences in affective processes and in standards of conduct still commands a larger measure of credence. The world at large is quite agreed that women are to a greater extent than men dominated by emotions, though the only direct experimental evidence does not support this view (see Thompson, *l. c.*, p. 137), and it is hard to reconcile with the attributes of patience, self-control, and power to endure pain, and with the much smaller share in the grand passion which are also ascribed to women.

The belief that there are fundamental differences in standards of conduct is less wide spread, and shows no such unanimity. It seems to part of the world quite certain that women have ethical disabilities consisting chiefly in an innate tendency to lie (Havelock Ellis, Weininger. See a refutation of the latter's arguments by M. Jörges, 'Geschlecht und Character,' *Zeitschr. f. Philos. u. philos. Kritik*, Bd. 135, S. 200, which takes them more seriously than they deserve), while to a long series of equally competent observers it seems quite certain that women are ethically superior to men, and that they may be counted upon to raise the moral tone of society! (For a recent exponent of this view see Wells, 'Some Questions Concerning the Higher Education of Women,' *Amer. J. of Sociol.*, 1909, p. 731).

Finally, one might characterize the drift of recent discussion as a shift of emphasis from a biological to a sociological interpretation of the mental characteristics of sex. The very small amount of difference between the sexes in those functions open to experimentation, the contradictory results obtained from different series of investigations, and the nature of the differences which prove to be most constant, have led to the belief that the psychological differences of sex are of sociological rather than of biological origin. (See Densmore, *Sex Equality*, New York: Funk and Wagnalls, 1907; Alsberg, 'Die geistige Leistungsfähigkeit des Weibes im Lichte der neueren Forschung,' *Arch. f. Rassen- u. Gesell. Biol.*, IV., p. 476, 1907; Pelletier, 'La prétendue infériorité psychologique des femmes,' *Rev. socialiste*, XXIV., p. 45, 1908.)

Those who feel opposed to allowing women full opportunity of mental development have accordingly shifted the stress of their argument from the personal to the social standpoint. The cry is no longer that woman will injure herself by the mental and physical over-strain involved in the higher intellectual training, but that she will injure society by reducing her own reproductive activity (later marriages, fewer marriages, fewer children, opposition between intellectual and sexual functions), and thus lessen the chances of the best element to perpetuate itself (Alsberg, Wells, *l. c.*). The conclusion seems to be that it is the highest duty of woman to refrain voluntarily from developing her own intellectual capacities for fear of injuring society — a form of asceticism to which it is hard to subscribe. It seems possible that the higher education of women is being saddled with sins which belong by right to other phases of modern society, though this is not the place to discuss so complicated and difficult a problem.

HELEN THOMPSON WOOLLEY.

CINCINNATI, OHIO.

THE PSYCHOLOGICAL BULLETIN

GENERAL REVIEWS AND SUMMARIES

THE PSYCHOLOGY OF SEX

BY HELEN THOMPSON WOOLLEY

Cincinnati, Ohio

During the four years since my last review of the literature of the psychology of sex (PSYCHOL. BULL., October, 1910) the number of experimental investigations in the field has increased to such an extent that whereas it was difficult at that time to find anything to review, it is now impossible to review all I could find. The number of books and essays devoted to general discussions of the subject has also increased and their quality has improved very markedly. The emphasis placed on sex by the Freudian school and the interest in sex education, to say nothing of the whole feminist and woman's suffrage movement, have swelled the dimensions of the literature aside from experimental contributions to such an extent that no brief review could pretend to deal with it. Confronted by such a dilemma I have chosen the course of attempting a summary in the field of experimental psychology as complete as time and library facilities would allow, and a very brief mention of what seem to me the most important contributions to the other phases of the subject.[1]

I. EXPERIMENTAL AND STATISTICAL STUDIES

There have been two extended series of tests applied for the purpose of measuring sex differences, one by Burt and Moore (19),

---

[1] I am indebted to Mr. Charles A. Reed, librarian of the University of Cincinnati, for special library privileges and for assistance in borrowing books and periodicals from libraries at a distance, without which it would have been impossible to prepare this review in Cincinnati.

in England, summarized by Jones (46), and one by Cohn and Dieffenbacher (22) in Germany. A third one by Pyle (69) in the United States, less comprehensive in scope, but representing a larger number of individuals, has sex as one basis of formulation. Other experimental papers either deal with only a few phases of the sex problem, or are formulated primarily from some other point of view. I will make the summary by topics, referring to the parts of the special investigations under the various headings.

(a) *Heredity.*—The present status of the theory of sex inheritance is very clearly and concisely summed up by Morgan (59). So far as a layman can see, there is little if anything in the theory which applies to the psychological problem. The ancient idea that the female is essentially an undeveloped male seems to be finally disproved by the fact that it requires more determiners—usually one more chromosome, or a larger sex chromosome—to produce a female than a male. When the additional sex chromosome was first discovered the assumption was that it determined maleness, doubtless because of the idea that the male was a more highly developed type. If there were any sense at all in such a formulation—which there probably is not—it would now have to be reversed. It seems certain that sex is determined at the moment of fertilization, and its determination is quite independent of environmental factors. Morgan believes that both the primary and the secondary characters of sex follow the laws of Mendelian inheritance, though not all biologists agree with him (Meijere, 55).

Secondary sexual characters are in some instances—chiefly in insects—determined independently of the sex glands. In the higher animals they are to a great extent dependent on the action of the sex glands, so much so that successful transplantation of the sex glands in the guinea pig carries with it a development of the secondary sexual characters of the opposite sex, even to the extent of producing secretion of milk in the milk glands of the male. The mechanism by which this is brought about is that of hormones given off to the body fluids by the sex glands.

The part played by sexual selection in evolution Morgan considers very small. There is little evidence that it takes place at all in animals. Even when consciously practised it is incapable of originating modifications of species, or producing steady change in any direction. It merely serves to develop in pure strain traits which have become mixed. Modifications of species always arise as mutations, for the appearance of which no explanation can at present be offered. Mutations when they arise may be inherited as sex-linked traits of the type of color-blindness, which are found predominating in one sex, though in certain combinations they may be inherited by the other.

Both Morgan and Tandler and Gross (77), point out that it is impossible to find any single secondary character which belongs exclusively to either sex throughout the animal kingdom. For instance, superior size and brilliant plumage in some species belong to the female, while even the instinct for incubating eggs is assigned in some species to the male. Tandler and Gross interpret all secondary sexual characters as modifications of characters belonging to the species as such. They believe that the reason the sexes resemble one another after castration is merely that under those circumstances both sexes tend to revert to the original species type, an assumption which makes it unnecessary to assume the presence in each sex of the determiners of the other sex.

The theory of heredity, then, seems incapable of throwing light on the question as to what systems of the body carry sex-linked factors. Conceivably any of them, including the nervous system, might. It merely describes the machinery by means of which any mutation which arises may be inherited as a sex-linked trait.

(b) *Physical Development.*—Under this head I shall report a few papers which are of interest from a psychological point of view. Beik (9), instead of measuring children in absolute amounts, as most previous observers have done, measured a series of 6½-year old children in terms of the proportion to adult standards for each sex. On this basis, he found girls more advanced than boys in height, weight, dentition, brain weight, and probably in the development of the skeleton. Measured in absolute terms boys are ahead in most of these respects. Hertz, in the report of the Danish Anthropological Society (26) gives a series of measurements kept for the last 27 years which show that during that time girls have gained considerably in height and weight, while boys have been at a standstill. Burgerstein (17) in reporting European statistics, states that girls show a much greater susceptibility to disease than boys.

(c) *Motor Ability.*—Beik (9) found that at 6½ years, girls, measured in terms of proportion to adult attainment, were ahead of boys in motor control. In simple reaction time and in rate of tapping, boys and men—as in previous tests—have shown themselves superior (Burt and Moore 19). In card dealing, Burt and Moore found the boys quicker, while Calfee (20) found girls quicker. In card sorting and in alphabet sorting, girls were found decidedly superior by Calfee and by Burt and Moore. Culler (25) also found women faster on first trials of card sorting, though his group was small (17 of each sex) and he was not primarily interested in that point. In mirror drawing Calfee found the girls—college freshmen —faster than the boys throughout six successive trials. This agrees with previous work. Burt and Moore found the boys superior, but they do not consider their own test very reliable because of a change of method.

Mead (54) gives a small but reliable set of statistics supporting the popular opinion that girls learn to walk and talk earlier than boys. Starch (72) measured the handwriting of the entire school system of Madison, Wisconsin, and found the girls superior to the boys in speed, legibility, and form. The sex difference was greatest in form. Burt and Moore found the same difference with regard to speed. Cohn and Dieffenbacher (22) found that girls read faster than boys, a result also obtained by Burt and Moore in reading and in counting for speed.

Ballard (7) found a relation between left-handedness and stammering, both of which are more prevalent among males. He tries to show that while the greater frequency of left-handedness is characteristic of the male sex, the greater frequency of stammering among boys is an artificial condition brought about by attempting to force left-handed individuals to write with the right hand. Statistics show that stammering is far more frequent among the left-handed who have been forced to write with the right hand than among those who were allowed to write with the left hand. He offers no explanation of how the result is brought about.

The tentative generalizations which may be drawn from this series of facts are (1) that girls develop faster than boys from infancy; (2) that boys are superior to girls in rapidity of movement under conditions in which the direction of attention remains fixed, as in reaction time and tapping; and (3) that girls are superior to boys in rapidity of motion in types of activity in which the direction of attention is constantly shifting—activities which involve rapid adaptations—such as card sorting, mirror drawing, reading and writing.

(*d*) *Sensation and Perception.*—(1) *Skin and Muscle Sense.* Bobertag (11) found that boys of 8, 9, and 10 years are more accurate in the Binet-Simon test for discrimination of weights than girls. Burt and Moore (19) confirm this result for both children and adults. They also found the space threshold of females, child and adult, very much finer than that of males. These sex differences are in accord with previous investigations. (2) *Hearing.* Hentschel (38), who tested 250 children of each sex in Germany, found that boys discriminate pitch better than girls both when a musical interval is employed, and when much smaller differences of vibration rate are made the basis of comparison. The boys are from 2 to 7 per cent. ahead in the several series. Burt and Moore, like previous investigators, found females a little better in pitch discrimination than males. (3) *Vision.* Burt and Moore found females superior in fineness of color discrimination. Monroe (58) in giving the Binet-Simon tests to 300 boys and 300 girls, of from three to six years, found that the girls excel the boys in color perception and in color naming. Burt and Moore found the boys superior in judging visual space. These results also agree with previous work. (4) *Perception.* The group of tests which belong most distinctly under this head are tests of the cancellation type, which involve both perception and motor reaction. In these tests females of all ages are uniformly better than males (Haggerty and Kempf (36), Woodworth and Wells (86), Pyle (68, 69)).

The possible generalizations in this field are (1) females have a finer spatial threshold on the skin, better color vision, and more rapid motor responses to changing perceptions than males; and (2) males are superior to females in the discrimination of weights and visual areas. The results with regard to pitch discrimination are contradictory.

(*e*) *Memory.*—There have been two sorts of experiments which may be included under this head, the rote memory experiments and those in "Aussage" or report. Under the first head there have been tests by Aall (1) using objects, by Burt and Moore (19) material not stated, by Myers (64) using words and letters in testing incidental memory, by Vertes (79) using words, by Cohn and Dieffenbacher (22) using digits, by Pyle (69) using words, and by Winch (85) using consonants. All of these workers found females superior except Cohn and Dieffenbacher, and Pyle, who found no difference of sex. These results are in accord with most previous investigations.

The experiments in the psychology of report have been carried on chiefly in Germany, Holland and Norway, and are published in

German. The term *Bericht* refers to the spontaneous account given by the subject of the picture, story, or series of events presented to him, while *Verhör* refers to the results of an examination which he subsequently undergoes on the subject matter. These words I shall translate *report* and *examination*. The trustworthiness (*Treue*) is estimated by finding the proportion of correct statements to the total number of statements made, both correct and false. Spontaneity is measured by finding the proportion of correct statements in the report to the total number of correct statements in both report and examination. Some of the questions used in the examination are distinctly suggestive, which gives an opportunity to measure suggestibility. Finally it is possible to classify the kind of items reported by each sex, for qualitative differences of memory.

With regard to the extent of memory displayed by the sexes in these experiments, the results are somewhat contradictory. In view of the small number of individuals represented in many of the series (from 15, or even less of each sex, to 30) contradictions are not surprising. Aall reports two tests, one with adults (2) and one with school children (1). In both cases he followed the plan of asking for a second reproduction of the story without warning. In some groups a mental attitude of expecting an immediate reproduction had been induced, while in others the expectation was that the reproduction would be deferred. In all variations of the experiment he found the extent of immediate memory greater in the female. With adults the same difference held for the second reproduction, but the school boys were better in the second reproduction than the girls. Aall is inclined to lay great stress on the latter result. The same type of test was tried by Lem (49) with school children with exactly the reverse result. His boys displayed a greater extent of memory in the immediate reproduction than the girls, while in subsequent ones, asked for without warning, the girls caught up with and at last a bit surpassed the boys. Breukink (15) and Schramm (71) both compared groups of university students. Breukink used pictures and Schramm a story. Breukink found the extent of memory a bit greater in men, while Schramm found it greater in women. Cohn and Dieffenbacher (22), and Pyle (69), whose test of logical memory belongs here, both found school girls superior to boys at all ages. With regard to trustworthiness, Breukink, Schramm, and if I understand him correctly, Aall, found women superior, Lem found boys superior, and Cohn and Dieffenbacher found no difference of sex. The latter authors report that girls have a decidedly greater degree of spontaneity.

Aall lays great stress on the qualitative differences in the reports as distinctive of sex. These analyses have been carried to too great length to be reported here. The chief point of agreement among them is that females report visual elements and particularly colors more frequently than men. Several of them also find that males report space relations more accurately than females, a fact corroborated by Myers (64) in his study of incidental memory.

Memory of dreams can be considered a special case of the psychology of report. In an Italian kindergarten in which the children take a nap every day, they were questioned immediately on waking with regard to what they had dreamed. Doglia and Banchieri (27) made records for 100 children at three years of age. The girls remembered more dreams and remembered them more fully than the boys. Two years later Banchieri (8) reexamined a large portion of the same group, and found that the same sex difference persisted.

To sum up then, females are superior to males in memory at all ages. The difference is clear and very uniform with regard to rote memory. In experiments in report sometimes one sex and sometimes the other has shown itself quantitatively superior, but on the whole the advantage is with the females.

(f) *The Effect of Drill.*—Closely allied to memory are the investigations on the effect of drill. Brown (16) and F. M. Phillips (67) both tested elementary school children with respect to the efficacy of drill work in arithmetic. Brown found no difference in this respect between the sexes, while Phillips found that the boys gained more than the girls. Wells has two papers which touch on the subject, but in both instances the sex groups are too small to be significant. In one (83) he found a progressive improvement of endurance with practice which was greater in women than in men. In the other (82) he found no difference in the gains made by practising addition and number checking. Yoakum and Calfee (88) report that their freshmen boys gained more in practising mirror drawing than the girls, though they did not catch up with them. Culler (25) observed that the men of his comparable group (only 7 of each sex) gained with practice in card sorting enough faster than the women to surpass them, particularly after an interference due to a rearrangement of the system of sorting. These investigations have been very different in type, and most of them represent small groups, so that generalizations are not safe, but there have been more of them which report a faster rate of improvement with drill in boys than in girls. It is interesting to notice that these tests have been carried out with processes in which females are at the start faster.

(g) *Association.*—Huber (45) carried out, with soldiers in training, the same series of free associations that Reinhold had previously tried with the girls of an advanced school. Though he states that differences of sex exist, the specific differences which he finds, such as greater uniformity in the associations of the girls, and more predicate, adjective and definition reactions on the part of the soldiers, he explains as due not to sex, but to the amount of education in the two groups Free association tests consisting in recording the number of words which could be written in a given length of time are reported by Burt and Moore (19) as showing boys faster, and by Pyle (69) and Lobsien (51) as showing girls faster. The latter found the difference marked from 9 to 11 years, but insignificant in older children. Since girls write faster than boys, such a test cannot throw much light on the rapidity of the thought process. Free associations in which the reaction time for each word has been measured, have been very uniformly found faster in men than in women. Haggerty and Kempf (36) and Wells (81) confirmed this result. Controlled association of the type represented by fundamentals in arithmetic (addition, etc.) is usually faster in females. Burt and Moore found boys faster, but Courtis (24) with his enormous series of New York school children, Phillips with a smaller number of school children, and Haggerty and Kempf with university students found girls and women faster. In controlled association of the opposite type girls are also apt to be superior (Burt and Moore, Pyle, Bonser, (15)), though in this case correctness of idea is a larger factor in estimating results than time of association. Haggerty and Kempf, considering speed alone, found men faster. The Ebbinghaus completion test has been used as a measure of sex difference by Cohn and Dieffenbacher (22), Burt and Moore, and Bonser. Burt and Moore, who call the test "completion of argument" because of the nature of the text used, found no sex difference, while the other two found boys superior. In a substitution test, Pyle found the girls faster at all ages, while in the number of associations suggested by an ink blot (called a test in imagination) boys were superior.

The generalization which is suggested by these results is that males are faster in free associations, while females are faster in practised systems of associations.

Both Wells and Haggerty and Kempf discuss the reasons for the more rapid free associations of men. Both papers take the view that the lengthened time of the women is due to a greater tendency to interference and suppression of ideas. This means, as Wells points out, that the associations of women are really controlled associations—controlled by the self for various reasons—to a greater extent than those of men. He thinks it possible that this result may be due merely to the fact that men have tested women, and that a woman testing men might obtain reverse results. Haggerty and Kempf are inclined to think that this tendency to be "on guard" against embarrassment is characteristic of the female sex. Apparently the Freudian school would find this interpretation in harmony with their theory of hysteria, which they explain exclusively on the basis of the suppression and substitution of sex impulses and ideas, and which is so much more prevalent among women.

With regard to types of reproduction within the associative process, Wells (81) and Lobsien (51) give results. The only decided difference of sex observed by Wells was the greater frequency of predicate associations in women, and of coordinate associations in men, a difference which had been previously noted. Among children Lobsien found the vast majority of associations belonging to the type in which no connection was evident. He calls them "springende" reproductions. The next largest class was the co-ordinates, while verbal and predicate associations were very few. The sex differences were small. Taking the entire group from 7 to 15 years, he found a few more "springende" associations for girls, and a few more of each of the other three types for boys. He also, then finds coordinate associations a bit more frequent for boys, though he fails to find predicate associations more frequent for girls. However differences of method make a comparison of results of doubtful value.

(h) *Attention.*—Cohn and Dieffenbacher (22) measured attention in terms of the distraction involved in simultaneous reading and writing, in which the girls suffered less from distraction than the boys. Burt and Moore (19) used two tests, one a test of the scope of attention called the spot pattern test, a tachistoscopic test in which a pattern composed of spots is reproduced, and one called irregular dotting which consists in tapping as rapidly as possible when each tap must hit one of an irregular series of dots. In both tests they found the boys superior, though in the second one the girls were better if the time interval was short. Heymans (39) lays stress on the narrower range of consciousness of the female, which he thinks can be deduced from her greater emotionality, and which is corroborated by the greater prevalence of hysteria in women. These two tests of the scope of attention give contradictory results.

(i) *Judgment and Reasoning.*—Breukink (15) tested judgments of time and space in men and women, and found men more accurate with regard to time, but no sex difference with regard to space. In judging space from memory, Myers (64) found males more accurate. Cohn and Dieffenbacher (22) thought the boys showed better judgment in their series of tests in several respects. They judged better the additional time required to learn the long series of digits than did the girls, though they came out with no better result in the end. He found that the boys had more questioned judgments in their tests of report, and that they were more trustworthy than the girls on the most essential points of the picture, though not in the report as a whole. In the logical arrangement of themes of the two sexes they found no difference. Burt and Moore (19) found boys better than girls in solving mechanical puzzles, but observed no difference in the sexes in respect to reasoning power tested by a group of tests consisting of the completion of an argument, the completion of analogies, constructing sentences, opposites, and the correction of syllogisms. Bonser (14) who made a particularly careful and many-sided investigation of a large group of children in the fourth, fifth, and sixth grades, found the boys a little ahead in the median for the series, seven tests in all. In details there were more marked differences. The boys were ahead in reasoning out problems, in selecting correct reasons for statements, and a bit so in a completion test. The girls were ahead in opposites, in selecting correct definitions, and particularly in the interpretation of literature. With regard to age, he found the boys ahead up to twelve years, and the girls ahead above twelve years.

The other tests which I have been able to find deal with reasoning as displayed in the solution of problems in arithmetic. F. M. Phillips (67) using the Stone tests, and Courtis (24) using his own tests found the boys better than the girls in tests of correct reasoning. Fox and Thorndike (31) report that in their group of high school pupils, girls surpassed boys in arithmetical ability, but they believe that the girls in that community were a more selected set than the boys.

On the whole, then, males have stood better than females in tests of judgment and reasoning.

(*j*) *General Intelligence.*—Under this head there have been (1) several investigations of school marks in the United States and Europe, and statistics with regard to the number of advanced and retarded children in school systems, (2) Binet-Simon tests, (3) groups of selected tests, and (4) some single tests which can be more conveniently classified here than elsewhere.

(1) The instability of school marks as a measure of ability has been strikingly brought out by Starch and Elliot, who sent an examination paper to 180 head mathematics teachers to be marked, and received grades all the way from 25 to 90! However, taken in the mass they doubtless have some significance. Baldwin (5) studied school marks in the fourth and fifths grades of a city school. He found that the girls maintained a higher standard of scholarship than the boys. In accord with this was the fact that there were more repeaters among the boys and more girls who skipped grades. Miles (57) made a study of the marks in both elementary school and high school for a group of 106 children for whom he had continuous records. The girls were consistently ahead in every grade, and in every subject except arithmetic, where there was no sex difference. Klinkenberg (47) studied school marks in a school system in Holland which was partly coeducational and partly segregated. Boys were ahead in mathematics, physical sciences, history, and geography, subjects, he remarks, in which an analytic process of thought is uppermost. Girls were ahead in literary studies and languages. He states that girls do not stand examinations as well as boys, but do better in class work than one would expect from their examinations. Girls were further behind boys in geometry than in algebra, which is due, he says, to their well-known disinclination to constructive thought. Cohn (see Bobertag, 13), in the "Dritter deutscher Kongress für Jugendbildung und Jugendkunde" gave a report on school marks in a coeducational school in Baden. Taken as a whole, he found no sex difference, but in grouping the subjects he also found boys better in science and mathematics, and girls in the language group. Forsyth (30) reports that the mean college grade of women in the University of Illinois is a little higher than that of the men. Heymans (39) collected statistics on this point from the universities of Holland, and found that the women rank higher than the men. The fact is so well established in this country that it has given rise to the

witticism that university professors who used to object to admitting women to their classes on the ground that it would lower the standards of scholarship, now object because the women do so much better class work that the men become discouraged and refuse to compete in the game.

The number of advanced and retarded children in large school systems in the United States have been tabulated by Bevard (10) in Washington, D. C., by Hill (41) in New Orleans, by B. A. Phillips (66) in Philadelphia, and by Lurton (52) for fifty-five towns in Minnesota. In every instance there were more retarded boys than girls, and more accelerated girls than boys.

(2) The Binet-Simon tests have been made the basis of sex comparison in the United States by Goddard (35), A. C. Strong (75), and Monroe (58), and in Europe by Bobertag (11) and Wiersma (84). Monroe dealt only with children from three to six years of age. He tested 300 of each sex, and found no sex difference on the whole, though there were small differences in the various years. Goddard's results represent the largest number of children tested by the Binet-Simon scale under one director, 2,000 children. His table shows no clear difference of sex. Reduced to percents on the basis of the proportion of each sex who are two years or more retarded, or two years or more advanced—a procedure which he did not himself carry out—it appears that there is no sex difference in retardation (boys 18.4 per cent., girls 18.6 per cent.), but the girls have a slightly greater proportion of accelerated individuals (boys 3.7 per cent., girls 4.8 per cent.). Strong in tests of 225 white children found on the same basis a similar state of affairs, though the differences were larger—retarded, boys 9.6 per cent., girls 10.7 per cent.; accelerated, boys 3.2 per cent., girls 6.9 per cent. The European results rest on much smaller numbers. Wiersma, who tested 68 boys and 73 girls, found the girls ahead on the whole, while the boys had larger groups both of retarded and of accelerated individuals. Bobertag alone found boys superior to girls. His results are stated in terms of years and fractions of years for each sex at each age. The boys were superior at each age by amounts varying from 0.06 to 0.20 of a year. Bobertag is quite too scientific to regard this result as conclusive, since it rests on about fifteen of each sex at each age, but he remarks that if it is substantiated it would be in accord with other experimental findings. That it does not agree with the general trend of Binet-Simon tests so far is evident. It is quite possible, however, that results in the co-

educational school systems of Holland and the United States may prove to be different from those in the segregated schools of Germany.

(3) Cohn and Dieffenbacher (22), Burt and Moore (19), and Pyle (69) carried out series of tests on comparable groups of the two sexes. The subjects of Cohn and Dieffenbacher varied in age from 7 to 19 years. They were selected as representatives of the better and the poorer sections of their school classes. There were about 100 of them in all. Burt and Moore tested about 140 children of $12\frac{1}{2}$ to $13\frac{1}{2}$ years, and about 100 university students. These two series agree in finding no sex differences as a whole. Specific differences which they report have been mentioned under the appropriate headings. Pyle, testing school children in this country, found the girls superior, but his tests were not as varied in type as the other series.

(4) Two investigations, those of Libby and his coworkers (50) and that of Franken (32), were made by means of questions on general information. Franken, though he had a considerable number of subjects, had only small comparable sex groups. The younger girls were superior to the boys, but there were no differences among the older children. Libby and his associates tested grade children from the fourth to the eighth grade, and first year high school students. They report boys superior in all age groups. The girls were more cautious in their replies, and not so likely to guess if they did not know. Ash (4) tried giving school children the choice of two kinds of tasks, one of which required original observations, and the other compilations from books. He found no sex difference on the whole, but the boys were most numerous in the group who selected all their tasks from one type, while the girls were more likely to divide the choice. With regard to mental fatigue, which should, I suppose, be regarded as an element in general intelligence, Offner (65) reports that no sex difference has been observed.

On the whole, then girls have stood better than boys in measures of general intelligence. So far as I know, no one has drawn the conclusion that girls have greater native ability than boys. One is tempted to indulge in idle speculation as to whether this admirable restraint from hasty generalization would have been equally marked had the sex findings been reversed! The usual explanation of the result offered is that girls are more docile and industrious than boys. The greater industry of girls has been turned to account by Lipmann in a novel argument for the inherent superiority of the boys. In his summary of the evidence on variability (see Bobertag, 13) he states that there are a larger number of series of measures in which the boys proved to be the more variable sex in the sense that there were more boys in the extreme quartiles of the range of values, and more girls in the two middle quartiles. He argues that the greater industry of the girls would be capable of raising them from the lowest quartile to a higher one, but would not suffice to overcome their lesser native ability to the extent of raising them from a lower to the highest quartile. To limit the effects of industry so much as to make it inoperative through a whole quarter of the range of a measure seems a bit extreme.

The writers who explain the results just quoted on the ground of the greater industry of girls are also those who emphasize their greater emotionality and rapid changes of mood. They seem to find no contradiction in the fact that the sex which is most dominated by emotions and moods is also the one which has the greatest capacity for plugging away at a task whether it is interesting or not. Another explanation quite as reasonable as that of the greater industry of girls might be sought in the fact that girls develop somewhat faster than boys. In the case of university students it may be, as Thorndike points out, that the sexes are selected on a different basis.

(*k*) *Affective Processes, Tastes and Ideals.*—The only direct experimental investigation of affective processes is that of Burt and Moore (19) in which they measured the psychogalvanic reflex in adults under stimulation of various sorts, and found the deflection in response to emotional disturbances greater in women than in men. It would be interesting to find out whether the same difference obtains when a woman instead of a man does the testing of the two groups. Under those conditions the plethysmograph and respirator—which to be sure are not very safe measures—gave opposite results in my own tests. Burt and Moore believe that an analysis of the content of association reactions revealed a difference of sex in emotionality at an early age, and that the difference increases with years.

Heymans (39) attacked the question of the relative emotionality of the sexes by the questionnaire method. A large number of intelligent people in Holland filled out the blanks, and a tabulation of results showed that a larger number of women than men were classed as emotional. Moreover the traits that were assigned predominantly to women were also those assigned to emotional men. (For a discussion of the scientific value of this method see Thorndike, 78.)

There have been a few bits of experimental evidence bearing on other phases of affective life than degree of affectability. E. K. Strong (76) found that women have more and greater dislikes than men and are better able to classify them. H. L. Hollingworth (42) suggests the generalization, which he says needs further confirmation, that men resemble one another more clearly in their preferences, while women are more alike in their aversions. Kuper (48) confirmed for children Strong's statement that women have more dislikes than men. Her method was to ask 200 children, evenly divided as to sex and varying in age from 6½ to 16½ years, to arrange three series of pictures in the order of preference. All three series represented the same nine subjects. It is interesting to notice how nearly alike the order was for the two sexes. For girls it was religion, patriotism, children, pathos, animals, sentiment, landscape, heroism, and action. The only change in the order for boys was that the positions of children and of heroism and action together were reversed, bringing children last and heroism and action third and fourth in the boys' lists.

Ballard (6) classified preferences in the themes of free drawings made by London school children. The themes of boys in order of preference were ships, miscellaneous drawings, plant life, houses, human beings, vehicles, animals, weapons, and landscapes, while for girls the order was plant life, houses, miscellaneous drawings, human beings, animals, ships, vehicles, weapons, and landscapes. Here again the order is very similar. The chief difference is that boys show a much greater liking for ships and girls for plant life. Stockton (74) tried to measure preference by means of the choice of one of a pair of words. He found far more resemblance than difference. Both boys and girls choose time words a bit more frequently than space words, words for food rather than words for dress, and adjectives rather than verbs. For words of activity boys showed a small preference, while girls choose words of passivity a little more frequently. He found that preference based on the idea of the word increased with age, and more markedly so in the case of boys than in that of girls, but neither sex based the choice on meaning to as great an extent as upon mere position.

There have been three investigations which consisted in asking each of a large number of children to state what person, whether acquaintance, historical character, or character of fiction he would most like to resemble. Brandall, reported by Gilbertson (34) worked with Swedish children, Hill (40) with American children, and Hoesch-Ernst (see Bobertag, 13) also with American children. They all agree that girls choose personal acquaintances oftener than boys, and that boys choose more public and historical characters. Brandall and Hill found that girls choose ideals from the opposite sex many times as often as boys. In the Swedish study boys choose characters from fiction more frequently than girls, while in this country the reverse was true. Brandall recorded also the reasons assigned by the children for their choices. He found that girls name moral, intellectual and artistic qualities more frequently than boys, while boys name material advantages, honor, and social position more frequently.

Anderson (3) gives the result of a questionnaire on the kind and amount of reading done by school children. She found no difference of sex with regard to amount, though girls read more books and boys more magazine articles. The girls used libraries more than boys. The preferences for kinds of literature were for boys, (1) stories of adventure, (2) detective stories, (3) and (4) war and love stories; for girls (1) love stories, (2) stories of adventure, (3) detective stories, and (4) travel and biography. Anderson also found that girls displayed a greater range in their reading, received more advice about it, and talked more about what they read than boys. The boys were more independent and original in choice.

Scheifler (70) has a paper on the tastes of boys and girls in games, based on a questionnaire given to 5,000 children. He divided plays into four classes, imitation plays (dolls, soldier, etc.), plays of bodily movement and contest (ball, tag, etc.), plays of intellectual activity and contest (building, checkers, chess, etc.), and occupation plays (sewing, reading, collecting, etc.). His general result is that girls give a greater preference to imitation plays, and boys to plays of bodily movement and contest, while there is no sex difference in the other two groups of plays. However when he picked out a set of plays which he designates as constructive— such as drawing, building and chess—the boys predominate. Scheifler is much relieved to note that coeducation shows no tendency to make the plays of boys and girls alike. If it did he thinks it would be a sufficient reason for doing away with coeducation. "Freuen wir uns vielmehr der schönen Eigenart der Geschlechter und pflegen wir sie! Unser Volk braucht immer noch beides: Männer die da wägen und wagen, Frauen die im kleinsten Kreise unendlich Grosses wirken."

Melville (56) asked each member of the four high school classes to write down all the slang phrases he knew. He then selected 100 papers, evenly divided between the sexes, from each class. The boys were ahead of the girls in the number of expressions by amounts increasing from 18.7 per cent. to 40.0 per cent. in the four classes.

(*l*) *Creative Ability in Art and Letters.*—There have been several studies of children's drawings published. Cohn and Dieffenbacher (22) and Wagner (80) both followed the method of asking large groups of children to draw, under experimental conditions, illustrations for Hans Sach's poem "Schlaraffenland." They both classified the drawings as Kerschensteiner had done, on the basis of representations of space, from the entire spacelessness of primitive drawings through linear and group arrangements to well-developed perspective. They agree that the primitive spacelessness is more characteristic of girls' drawings than of boys', and that girls take more pains than boys with decorative details. Cohn and Dieffenbacher found that girls treated a greater number of themes than boys, while Wagner found the reverse. Wagner noticed more elaboration of details in the drawings of the boys, and found them superior in inventiveness, in the representations of humor, and of motion. On the whole Wagner considers the boys very superior. The girls in his group excelled only in details which had to do with feminine interests. Cohn and Dieffenbacher noticed that the drawings of the boys were larger than those of the girls, and more characterized by heavy lines and strong colors, whereas the girls preferred delicate lines and soft colors. This difference in color preference had been previously noted in Kirkpatrick's monograph on "Studies in Development and Learning."

Muth (63) asked children from the first to the seventh years in school to decorate the outline of a plate and of a shield. She agrees with the two reports just quoted that girls prefer fine lines and a smaller more delicate type of drawing. She found that the sense of rhythm is earlier developed in girls and is stronger than in boys. The girls showed a better sense of proportion between the filled and the blank spaces of the surfaces. From the point of view of mere decorative effect, then, girls were superior, though she found the boys excelling in the expression of humor and in the originality of their drawings.

The generalization suggested by these pieces of work is that boys excel in perspective drawing and girls in decorative drawing.

Within the years with which I am dealing, I have found but one attempt to measure the relative merits of literary productions in the sexes. Cohn and Dieffenbacher (22) asked their group of children to write a theme on experiences at the local railroad station. They found the themes of the girls superior in most of the measures which they applied. Their themes were longer, both in words and in statements, their sentences were longer, they used more figures of speech, and a greater number of unusual expressions. Their themes were richer in content, and better in literary style. Analyzed for content they found that the boys mentioned more objects, more definite numbers and spaces than the girls. The girls' themes were richer in feeling, and more subjective. The sexes differed in the kind of feeling expressed. With girls sentimental and comic moods predominated, and with the boys the loyal and ethical sentiments. Though it does not belong in my period, it seems worth while to mention the fact that Giese (33) arrives at generalizations opposed to most of those just quoted! His monograph is an extended study of the free literary productions of boys and girls from the ages of five to twenty. The material he collected from all sorts of sources, chiefly from the public press. He criticizes Cohn and Dieffenbacher for passing judgment on a question of personal opinion like literary style, but does not seem to feel that his own work is open to the same criticism with reference to his selection of material, and his judgments of originality and value. He finds that boys write more poetry than girls, and do it much better, that their compositions are longer, more philosophic, and of higher artistic quality. The monograph contains very detailed comparisons of a large number of factors, and is half devoted to a collection of literary productions representative of the various ages.

(*m*) *Suggestibility.*—Two of the papers on the psychology of report (Aussage) contain measures of suggestibility. Breukink (15) in his group of adults found the women more suggestible than the men. They answered more of the suggestive questions both wrongly and correctly than the men did. Cohn and Dieffenbacher (22) in their group of school children found no sex difference in suggestibility, measured in the same way.

(*n*) *Variability.*—Several of the experimental series to which we have referred have been formulated in terms of variability, but most of the groups have been too small to be significant unless there was wide agreement, which there has not been. The results dealing with the largest number of individuals, those of Goddard (35) on Binet-Simon tests and of Courtis (24) on tests in arithmetic fail to show any sex difference in variability. There have been two papers which sum up experimental evidence on the subject, one by L. S. Hollingworth (44) and one by Lipmann (see Bobertag, 13). Hollingworth sums up her review by saying, "If the evidence can be said to point in one direction rather than another, a greater female variability seems actually to be indicated in experiments so far made on the higher mental processes." Unfortunately I have not seen Lipmann's original paper, but only the abstract of it in the report of the congress at which it was delivered. He says that he worked over all the available statistics on variability in the sexes, and found that in 53 per cent. of the series of measures males were more variable, in 37 per cent. females were more variable, and in 10 per cent. there was no difference. Thorndike (78) selected a set of measures of various traits which he thinks most reliable as a basis for estimating variability, and concludes that they indicate somewhat greater variability of the male. He is convinced that greater variability of the male must be the explanation of the great preponderance of male geniuses. The amount of the sex difference in genius is most vividly brought out by comparing Cattell's former study of eminent men with that of Castle (21) on eminent women, and is of course not brought into question by sketches of the contributions to science made by women, such as those by Mozans (60), interesting as they may be.

Hollingworth questions the genuineness both of the greater number of male geniuses and of the greater number of male deficients, facts which have usually been thought to be proofs of male variability. She points out (43) that most of the evidence for the greater number of male deficients rests on statistics from institutions for the feeble-minded, which she and others consider unreliable because it is easier for feeble-minded women to maintain themselves outside of institutions than for feeble-minded men, since the former may earn their way either as household drudges or as prostitutes. As evidence of the truth of this assumption she reports a series of 1,000 consecutive cases passing through the New York clearing house for mental defectives, in which she found the females much more numerous than the males in the older group, showing that they had been able to maintain themselves longer in society than the corresponding males. The Binet-Simon tests confirmed this by showing that of those individuals who tested at a given mental age, the women were older than the men. She concludes that if social pressure bore equally on the sexes, there would be as many females as males in institutions for the feeble-minded. The statistics from a social survey of the number of the feeble-minded outside of institutions, which gives more males than females, Hollingworth considers unreliable, though Thorndike apparently accepts them. With regard to genius (44) she makes the very pertinent suggestion that no one who has discussed the question has given sufficient weight to the fact that most women have devoted the greater portion of their time to occupations connected with bearing and rearing children, and in maintaining a home—occupations in which eminence is impossible though genius is not. No one can tell, she says, how much genius of a high order may have gone into these tasks where recognition in terms of fame is out of the question. She concludes that there is little ground for explaining the lesser scientific and artistic achievements of women on the ground of greater male variability. Finot (28, 29) makes much the same point in stating that in proportion to the number of women devoting themselves to scientific and artistic pursuits, the number of persons of eminence has compared favorably with males.

II. General Discussions

The general discussions of the psychology of sex, whether by psychologists or by sociologists show such a wide diversity of points of view that one feels that the truest thing to be said at present is that scientific evidence plays very little part in producing convictions. As Coolidge puts it: "In our present stage, the conclusions as to the permanence or significance of any feminine peculiarity at which any observer will arrive are in accordance usually with his anti- or pro-feminine bias." Hartley expresses the same idea. Among psychologists Burt and Moore (19), Stern (73), Heymans (39), Wreschner (87), and Thorndike (78) have expressed opinions with regard to the facts of the psychology of sex, based on the experimental evidence. The generalization at which Burt and Moore arrive is that sex differences are most marked in the simpler functions of sensation and motion and decrease as one rises to the higher levels of mental activity, until in the most complicated functions no difference is to be observed. Stern arrives at exactly the opposite generalization! The simpler and more easily measured functions show no significant difference of sex, he says, while we may be certain that as we penetrate further with experimental methods into the more complex mental functions, the significant differences will appear. Heymans, basing his opinion largely on the returns from the questionnaires which he and Wiersma sent out, though he considers experimental results also, derives a differential psychology of sex from two fundamental factors, first the greater emotionality of women, and second their greater activity, in the sense of readiness to act. The differences in intellectual capacity he explains in terms of interest and attention, which are ultimately determined by emotionality. Heymans's book is exceedingly readable, but not altogether convincing. His principle fails to work at a very vital point. The fact that women are in many respects poorer observers than men, he explains on the ground that their emotionality limits their interests, so that they observe well only that which has emotional value for them. When it comes to accounting for the better rank of women in academic work, he finds that while men put effort chiefly on that which interests them, women are industrious and conscientious in all tasks, whether they find them interesting or not. This contradiction he attempts to resolve on the ground that women are more readily spurred to action than men. Wreschner's book is in the nature of a popular lecture summarizing experimental studies of sex. He gives no references, and no indication of the strength of the evidence underlying his generalizations. The source of his material is easily recognized by any one familiar with the field. As a matter of fact some of his statements rest on evidence so contradictory or so meagre that they are worth no more than a personal opinion. In his conclusions he agrees with Heymans in assigning to women a stronger emotional nature, and a smaller participation in abstract intellectual processes, but takes the opposite point of view with regard to activity, which he regards as distinctly greater in men. Thorndike (78) regards the differences between the sexes of the type revealed by experimental psychology as too small, in view of the large variations within each sex, to be considered significant except with regard to the greater variability of the male. So far as central tendencies in various abilities are concerned, he assumes no difference of sex. He is inclined to agree with the others that women are more emotional than men, and thinks it probable that the chief difference of sex aside from variability is to be found in the fighting instinct of the male and the nursing instinct of the female, instincts which affect lines of conduct.

One element in the success of men in scientific, artistic or social fields is their love of getting ahead of the other fellow, while women have less of a desire to win, and a more pronounced humanitarian tendency.

All of this group of men, in spite of their wide differences of opinion as to the nature of the psychological characteristics of sex, are convinced that they are inherent and are not to be explained by environmental influences during the life of the individual. Burt and Moore base their conviction on the fact that the sex differences which they found in English children and adults were similar in kind and amount to those of my series of American university students. Differences which remain constant at different ages and in different countries must, they think, be inherent in sex itself. They do not seem to have considered whether or not there are factors in the social environment of sex which remain constant in all modern civilized countries. Stern believes that sex differences have been found in processes which are not influenced by social environment, such as spontaneous drawings. Wreschner holds that some of the traits most characteristic of women, notably emotionality, are of a nature to be repressed rather than fostered by the social environment of women. Heymans points out with much justice that much of the argumentation with regard to what effect the social milieu would have on given traits is very inconclusive. It is no difficult matter to get up fairly plausible arguments to prove either that social conditions tend to foster emotionality in women (Finot) or that they tend to repress it (Wreschner). Heymans thinks it quite as reasonable to suppose that differences in traits determined the differences in environment as vice-versa. Finally Wreschner inquires somewhat peevishly how in the world we are to know what is inherited and what socially acquired, and calls upon all good citizens to help along the course of evolution, whose direction he is confident he perceives, by cherishing our present valuable distinctions of sex instead of subversively trying to overthrow them. However none of these men, except perhaps Stern, believes that the nature or amount of the psychological difference of sex is a sufficient ground for separate systems of education for the two.

There are a few points in the literature of experimental psychology which point to the importance of social influences. The sex difference in size, whose hereditary origin has seldom been questioned, is decreasing with the change in the educational regime of girls. The Danish Anthropological Society (26) has found that within the last generation girls have made large gains in height and weight, while boys have not changed. It is interesting to notice, too, that in Germany, where the tradition of the mental inferiority of women is still strong, and the girls' schools are even yet inferior (Münsterberg, 62) experimental results are more likely than in other countries to show differences of sex, and to find them in the direction of male superiority. In the tests conducted by Cohn and Dieffenbacher in one of the few coeducational schools of high school rank in Germany, they found the girls superior not only to the segregated girls, but to the boys in the same school. They were a small group, and German psychologists explain their high rank on the ground that they were to a greater extent than the boys selected on a basis of ability. It is also significant that differences between the cultured and the uncultured in experimental results are usually far larger than those between the sexes (Breukink, 15).

When one turns to the books written more largely from the historical and sociological point of view, the trend of opinion is that mental differences of sex are of social origin. There are four scholarly and exceedingly interesting books of this type, Coolidge (23), Hartley (37), Finot (28, 29), and Müller-Lyer (61), coming respectively from the United States, England, France, and Germany. The last three all contain historical sketches of the position of women from primitive times to modern. Hartley and Finot also discuss the question of sex in animals, and its bearing on human problems. Coolidge's book is particularly interesting to American readers because it is written with immediate reference to the social position of women in the United States during the last few generations. They all lay stress on the view that social conditions account for most of the traits ordinarily considered feminine, and particularly for the limited accomplishment of women in art and science. Coolidge gives a vivid sketch of the way traditional domesticity limited and determined the intellectual life of women. The same point is effectively brought out from the German standpoint by Maurenbrecher (53).

References

1. AALL, A. Ein neues Gedächtnisgesetz? *Zsch. f. Psychol.*, 1913, 66, 1–51.
2. AALL, A. Zur Psychologie der Wiedererzählung. *Zsch. f. angw. Psychol.*, 1913, 7, 185–210.
3. ANDERSON, R. E. A Preliminary Study of the Reading Tastes of High School Pupils. *Ped. Sem.*, 1912, 19, 438–460.

4. Ash, I. E. The Correlates and Conditions of Mental Inertia. *Ped. Sem.*, 1912, 19, 425-437.
5. Baldwin, B. T. A Psycho-Educational Study of the Fourth and Fifth School Grades. *J. of Educ. Psychol.*, 1913, 4, 364-365.
6. Ballard, P. B. What London Children Like to Draw. *J. of Exp. Ped.*, 1912, 1, 186-197.
7. Ballard, P. B. Sinistrality and Speech. *J. of Exp. Ped.*, 1912, 1, 289-310.
8. Banchieri, F. I sogni dei bambini di cinque anni. *Riv. di psychol.*, 1912, 8, 325-330.
9. Beik, A. K. Physiological Age and School Entrance. *Ped. Sem.*, 1913, 20, 277-321.
10. Bevard, K. H. Progress of the Repeaters of the Class of 1912 of the Public Schools of Washington, D. C. *Psychol. Clinic*, 1913, 7, 68-83.
11. Bobertag, O. Ueber Intelligenzprüfungen (nach der Methode von Binet und Simon). *Zsch. f. angew. Psychol.*, 1911, 5, 105-203.
12. Bobertag, O. Ueber Intelligenzprüfungen (nach der Methode von Binet und Simon). *Zsch. f. angew. Psychol.*, 1912, 6, 495-538.
13. Bobertag, O. Dritter deutscher Kongress fur Jugendbildung und Jugendkunde zu Breslau von 4 bis 6 Oktober, 1913. *Zsch. f. angew. Psychol.*, 1913, 8, 345-353.
14. Bonser, F. G. *The Reasoning Ability of Children of the Fourth, Fifth and Sixth School Grades.* New York: Teacher's College, 1910. Pp. 133.
15. Breukink, H. Ueber die Erziehbarkeit der Aussage. *Zsch. f. angew. Psychol.*, 1910, 3, 32-87.
16. Brown, J. C. An Investigation of the Value of Drill Work in the Fundamental Operations of Arithmetic. *J. of Educ. Psychol.*, 1912, 3, 485-492, 562-570.
17. Burgerstein, L. Coeducation and Hygiene with Special Reference to European Experience and Views. *Ped. Sem.*, 1910, 17, 1-15.
18. Burt, C. Experimental Tests of Higher Mental Processes and their Relation to General Intelligence. *J. of Exp. Ped.*, 1911, 1, 93-112.
19. Burt, C. and Moore, R. C. The Mental Differences between the Sexes. *J. of Exp. Ped.*, 1912, 1, 273-284, 355-388.
20. Calfee, M. College Freshmen and Four General Intelligence Tests. *J. of Educ. Psychol.*, 1913, 4, 223-231.
21. Castle, C. S. A Statistical Study of Eminent Women. *Arch. of Psychol.*, 1913, No. 27. Pp. vii + 90.
22. Cohn, J. and Dieffenbacher, J. *Untersuchungen über Geschlechts-, Alters-, und Begabungs- Unterschiede bei Schulern.* Leipzig: Barth, 1911. Pp. vi + 213.
23. Coolidge, M. R. *Why Women are So.* New York: Holt, 1912. Pp. 371.
24. Courtis, S. A. Report on the Courtis Tests in Arithmetic. *New York Committee on School Inquiry*, 1911, 1, 391-546.
25. Culler, A. J. Interference and Adaptability. An Experimental Study of their Relation with Special Reference to Individual Differences. *Arch. of Psychol.*, 1912, No. 24. Pp. 80.
26. Danish Anthropological Society. Middelelser am Danmarks Antropologi. Reviewed in *Ped. Sem.* 1913, 20, 544.
27. Doglia, S. and Banchieri, F. I sogni dei bambini di tre anni. L'inizio dell' attivita onirica. *Cont. d. lab. psicol. d. univer. d. Roma*, 1910, 1, 9.
28. Finot, J. *Préjugé et problème des sexes.* Paris: Alcan, 1912. Pp. 520.
29. Finot, J. *Problems of the Sexes.* (Trans.) New York: Putnam, 1913. Pp. xiv + 408.

30. FORSYTH, C. H. Correlation between Ages and Grades. *J. of Educ. Psychol.*, 1912, 3, 164.
31. FOX, W. A. and THORNDIKE, E. L. Relations between the Different Abilities Involved in the Study of Arithmetic: Sex Differences in Arithmetical Ability. Colum. Univ. Cont. to Phil., Psychol. and Educ., 1911, 2, 32–40.
32. FRANKEN, A. Aussageversuche nach der Methode der Entscheidungs- und Bestimmungsfrage bei Erwachsenen und Kindern. *Zsch. f. angew. Psychol.*, 1912, 6, 174–253.
33. GIESE, F. *Das freie literarische Schaffen bei Kindern und Jugendlichen.* Leipzig: Barth, 1914. Pp. xiv + 220; iv + 242.
34. GILBERTSON, A. N. A Swedish Study in Children's Ideals. *Ped. Sem.*, 1913, 20, 100–106.
35. GODDARD, H. H. Two Thousand Normal Children Measured by the Binet Measuring Scale of Intelligence. *Amer. J. of Psychol.*, 1911, 18, 232–259.
36. HAGGERTY, M. E. and KEMPF, E. J. Suppression and Substitution as a Factor in Sex Differences. *Amer. J. of Psychol.*, 1913, 24, 414–425.
37. HARTLEY, C. G. (Mrs. W. M. Gallichan). *The Truth about Women.* New York: Dodd, Mead & Co., 1913. Pp. xiv + 404.
38. HENTSCHEL, M. Zwei experimentelle Untersuchungen an Kindern aus dem Gebiete der Tonpsychologie. *Zsch. f. angew. Psychol.*, 1913, 7, 55–69; 211–222.
39. HEYMANS, G. *Die Psychologie der Frauen.* Heidelberg: Winter, 1910. Pp. viii + 308.
40. HILL, D. S. Comparative Study of Children's Ideals. *Ped. Sem.*, 1911, 18, 219–231.
41. HILL, D. S. *Exceptional Children in the Public Schools of New Orleans.* A Report of the Committee of the Public School Alliance. New Orleans: 1913. Pp. 36.
42. HOLLINGWORTH, H. L. Experimental Studies in Judgment. *Arch. of Psychol.*, 1913, No. 29. Pp. vi + 119.
43. HOLLINGWORTH, L. S. The Frequency of Amentia as Related to Sex. *Med. Record*, 1913.
44. HOLLINGWORTH, L. S. Variability as Related to Sex Differences in Achievement. *Amer. J. of Sociol.*, 1914, 19, 510–530.
45. HUBER, E. Associationsversuche an Soldaten. *Zsch. f. Psychol.*, 1911, 59, 241–272.
46. JONES, G. E. Mental Differences between the Sexes. *Ped. Sem.*, 1913, 20, 401–404.
47. KLINKENBERG, L. M. Ableitung von Geschlechtsunterschieden aus Zensurenstatistiken. *Zsch. f. angew. Psychol.*, 1913, 8, 228–266.
48. KUPER, G. Group Differences in the Interests of Children. *J. of Phil., Psychol., etc.*, 1912, 9, 376–379.
49. LEM, M. H. Kinderaufsätze und Zuverlässigkeit der Zeugenaussagen. *Zsch. f. angew. Psychol.*, 1911, 4, 347–363.
50. LIBBY, W., COWLES, H., etc. The Contents of Children's Minds. *Ped. Sem.*, 1910, 17, 242–272.
51. LOBSIEN, M. Ueber den Vorstellungstypus der Schulkinder. *Päd. Mäg.*, 457 H., 1911. Pp. iii + 67.
52. LURTON, F. E. Retardation in Fifty-five Western Towns. *J. of Educ. Psychol.*, 1912, 3, 326–330.
53. MAURENBRECHER, H. *Das Allzuweibliche. Ein Buch von neuer Erziehung und Lebensgestaltung.* München, 1912.

54. MEAD, C. D. The Age of Walking and Talking in Relation to General Intelligence. *Ped. Sem.*, 1913, 20, 460-484.
55. MEIJERE, J. C. H. Zur Vererbung des Geschlechtsmerkmale und secundärer Geschlechtsmerkmale. *Arch. f. Rassen und Gesell. Biol.*, 1913, 10, 1-36.
56. MELVILLE, A. H. An Investigation of the Function and Use of Slang. *Ped. Sem.*, 1912, 19, 93-100.
57. MILES, W. R. A Comparison of Elementary and High School Grades. *Ped. Sem.*, 1910, 17, 429-450.
58. MONROE, W. S. Intelligence of 600 Young Children. *Psychol. Rev.*, 10, 74-75.
59. MORGAN, T. H. *Heredity and Sex*. New York: Columbia University Press, 1913. Pp. 282.
60. MOZANS, H. J. *Woman in Science*. New York: Appleton, 1913. Pp. xiii + 452.
61. MÜLLER-LYER, F. *Phasen der Liebe. Eine Sociologie des Verhältnisses der Geschlechter*. München: Langen, 1913. Pp. xv + 254.
62. MÜNSTERBERG, H. The German Woman. *Atlantic Mo.*, 1912, 109, 457-467.
63. MUTH, G. Ueber Alters-, Geschlechts- und Individualunterschiede in der Zierkunst des Kindes. *Zsch. f. angew. Psychol.*, 1913, 8, 507-548.
64. MYERS, G. C. A Study in Incidental Memory. *Arch. of Psychol.*, 1913, No. 26. Pp. 108.
65. OFFNER, M. *Mental Fatigue*. Baltimore: Warwick and York, 1911. Pp. viii + 133.
66. PHILLIPS, B. A. Retardation in the Elementary Schools of Philadelphia. *Psychol. Clinic*, 1912, 6, 79-90, 107-121.
67. PHILLIPS, F. M. Value of Daily Drill in Arithmetic. *J. of Educ. Psychol.*, 1913, 4, 159-163.
68. PYLE, W. H. Standards of Mental Efficiency. *J. of Educ. Psychol.*, 1913, 4, 61-70.
69. PYLE, W. H. *The Examination of School Children; a Manual of Directions and Norms*. New York: Macmillan, 1913. Pp. 70.
70. SCHEIFLER, H. Zur Psychologie der Geschlechter: Spielinteressen des Schulalters. *Zsch. f. angew. Psychol.*, 1913, 8, 124-144.
71. SCHRAMM, F. Zur Aussagetreue der Geschlechter. *Zsch. f. angew. Psychol.*, 1911, 5, 355-357.
72. STARCH, D. The Measurement of Handwriting. *J. of Educ. Psychol.*, 1913, 4, 445-464.
73. STERN, W. Abstracts of Lectures on the Psychology of Testimony and on the Study of Individuality. *Amer. J. of Psychol.*, 1910, 21, 270-282.
74. STOCKTON, M. I. Some Preferences by Boys and Girls as Shown in their Choice of Words. *Psychol. Rev.*, 1911, 18, 347-373.
75. STRONG, A. C. Three Hundred Fifty White and Colored Children Measured by the Binet-Simon Measuring Scale of Intelligence. A Comparative Study. *Ped. Sem.*, 1913, 20, 485-515.
76. STRONG, E. K. The Relative Merits of Advertisements. *Arch. of Psychol.*, 1911, No. 17. Pp. 81.
77. TANDLER, J. and GROSS, S. *Die biologishen Grundlagen der secundären Geschlechtscharactere*. Berlin: Springer, 1913. Pp. iv + 169.
78. THORNDIKE, E. L. *Educational Psychology*. Vol. III. New York: Teacher's College, Columbia University, 1914.
79. VERTES, J. Das Wortgedächtnis im Schulkindesalter. *Zsch. f. Psychol.*, 1913, 63, 19-128.

80. WAGNER, P. A. Das freie Zeichnen von Volkschulkindern. *Zsch. f. angew. Psychol.*, 1913, 8, 1–70.
81. WELLS, F. L. Some Properties of the Free Association Time. *Psychol. Rev.*, 1911, 18, 1–23.
82. WELLS, F. L. The Relation of Practice to Individual Differences. *Amer. J. of Psychol.*, 1912, 23, 75–100.
83. WELLS, F. L. Practise and the Work-Curve. *Amer. J. of Psychol.*, 1913, 24, 35–51.
84. WIERSMA, E. D. Intelligenzprüfungen nach Binet und Simon, und ein Versuch zur Auffindung neuer Tests. *Zsch. f. angew. Psychol.*, 1913, 8, 267–275.
85. WINCH, W. H. A Motor Factor in Perception and Memory. *J. of Exp. Ped.*, 1912, 1, 261–273.
86. WOODWORTH, R. S. and WELLS, F. L. Association Tests. *Psychol. Monog.*, 1911, No. 57. Pp. 85.
87. WRESCHNER, A. *Vergleichende Psychologie der Geschlechter*. Zürich: Art. Inst. Orell. Füssli, 1912. Pp. 40.
88. YOAKUM, C. S. and CALFEE, M. An Analysis of the Mirror Drawing Experiment. *J. of Educ. Psychol.*, 1913, 4, 282–292.

Sex Differences: Historical Perspectives and Methodological Implications

ANNE ANASTASI

Fordham University

Apart from its historical interest, early psychological research on sex differences provides methodological and interpretive insights and permits the comparison of sex differences under different societal conditions. Conclusions about sex differences from published studies should consider sample size, differential selection, overlapping of distributions, psychometric properties of the measuring instruments, and nature of the constructs employed as a basis for sex comparisons. In order to advance from a description of sex differences to an understanding of the operation of biological and cultural factors in their etiology, male and female differences in both cognitive and personality variables should be investigated under changing cultural conditions. Examples of etiological hypotheses that can be tested through such an approach are followed by some illustrative findings on changing sex differences over time. The need for well-designed cohort studies spanning critical periods of societal change is indicated.

According to Boring (1929, p. vii), it was Ebbinghaus who first remarked that psychology has a long past, but only a short history. To trace the origins and development of psychological research on any given topic, one does not need to go back very far in time. For psychological studies of sex differences, I have accordingly chosen to concentrate on the first 60 years of the 20th century, with occasional minor excursions into immediately preceding or following years. It was in the 1960s that, stimulated by the women's movement, research on sex differences assumed fresh vigor and began to explore some new directions. That decade thus provides a convenient marker to separate "then" from "now," to differentiate the historical background from the modern scene.

CONTRIBUTIONS OF EARLY STUDIES

Why should we re-examine this early research? One reason can certainly be found in the mounting interest in all aspects of the history of psychology. This interest is evidenced in recent writings not only by psychologists (e.g., Benjamin, 1977; Shields, 1975a, b; Wolf, 1973) but also by historians (e.g., Cravens, 1978; Sokal, 1973, 1980, 1981). The two articles by Shields (1975a) are especially relevant to the early research on

---

This article is an expanded version of a portion of a Master Lecture given at the 1979 Convention of the American Psychological Association, as part of the APA Continuing Education Program. Requests for reprints should be sent to Anne Anastasi, Psychology Department, Fordham University, Bronx, NY 10458.

sex differences. The book by Cravens (1978) provides a lucid and comprehensive picture of the social and scientific climate in which research on individual and group differences as a whole was conducted in America during the first 4 decades of the 20th century.

When dealing with sex differences, however (as when dealing with any other group or individual differences), we can identify more compelling reasons for studying the research of earlier decades. First, an analysis of earlier studies can sensitize us to the methodological and interpretive pitfalls that beset this field of research. We can learn both from the investigators who were misled by weak methodology and inadequate data, and from those research pioneers who designed ingenious ways of coping with methodological hazards.

Second, in research on group differences, if we want to go beyond description to an understanding of the causes of differences, we should not limit ourselves to one time period. We need cohort studies of psychological sex differences within a changing social context. We can think of this approach as the longitudinal study of populations (Anastasi, 1958a; pp. 209–211; 1982, Chap. 12). It is illustrated by comparisons of the test performance of cohorts of the same chronological age examined 10 or 20 or 30 years apart. A classic example is provided by the Scottish surveys (Scottish Council for Research in Education, 1949), in which the same intelligence test was administered to nearly all 11-year-old Scottish children in 1932 and to a similar sample of 11-year-olds in 1947. The findings of such a study can be used to test hypotheses about what is happening to a particular population over time; and they can be related to relevant societal changes occurring over the interval.

When observations on sex differences are limited to a relatively uniform and unchanging societal context, the findings are likely to remain at a descriptive level. We can tell only how the behavior of females and that of males compare under the existing conditions. For obvious ethical and practical reasons, research on human subjects cannot expose individuals to drastic and long-lasting variations in living conditions. In comparison, societal changes are likely to provide differences in experiential variables that are more extreme in degree, of longer duration, and more pervasive in their influence on psychological development than could be achieved by experimental manipulation. Hence cohort studies spanning one or more decades, during which significant social changes were under way, represent a valuable natural experiment—or at least a quasi-experiment. This type of study helps in analyzing the relation between cultural and behavioral variables. A comparison of findings obtained in the last quarter of this century with the published findings of earlier studies should contribute to an understanding of the origins of psychological sex differences.

The data obtained in the earlier studies are irreplaceable, insofar as the societal conditions under which they were collected cannot be reproduced. A fundamental approach of differential psychology as a whole is to study a behavioral characteristic under differing cultural conditions. Such an approach contributes to an understanding of the operation of heredity and environment in the etiology of behavior in general. The method is essentially the same whether the source of variation is horizontal (across contemporary cultures or subcultures) or vertical (across time periods within a single culture). There have been scattered attempts to investigate sex differences in different cultures, from the early work of Mead (1930, 1935) in New Guinea and other studies in primitive societies (Berry, 1966; Schlegel, 1977) to the more recent surveys conducted in Israeli kibbutzim (Mednick, 1975, 1981; Spiro, 1979; Tiger & Shepher, 1975), in the Soviet Union (Lapidus, 1978), in the People's Republic of China (Tavris & Offir, 1977, Chap. 9; Wolf & Witke, 1975), in Scandinavian countries (Tavris & Offir, 1977, Chap. 9), and in Morocco (D. H. Dwyer, 1978). It is noteworthy that these cross-cultural studies provide meager objective, quantitative data on either aptitudes or personality characteristics. In general, cross-cultural studies present special methodological problems; and comparisons of results across widely different cultures are difficult. For these reasons, cohort studies across time would seem to be more productive.

To summarize, early psychological research on sex differences is of interest for at least three reasons: (1) it has historical significance; (2) it can provide methodological and interpretive insights; and (3) it permits comparisons between sex differences that develop under different societal conditions. The implications of the third point are twofold. In order to advance beyond mere description toward an understanding of the causes of observed sex differences, we should: (1) preserve and utilize the irreplaceable early data on sex differences; and (2) conduct systematic cohort studies of sex differences in the future, as the delayed effects of gradual societal changes in sex roles and status become manifest.

METHODOLOGICAL AND INTERPRETIVE INSIGHTS

We may now turn to some examples of methodological and interpretive insights that can be gleaned from the early literature on sex differences. Such insights pertain not only to the way research is conducted, but also to the way research literature is surveyed (see, e.g., Block, 1976a, b; Maccoby & Jacklin, 1974). How should the results of independent studies, with their many procedural differences, be integrated, in the effort to draw general conclusions from their findings? An examination of early studies on sex differences highlights several procedural variables to which the student of group differences should be alerted. The illustrations to be discussed have been grouped into three categories: sampling problems, the overlapping of distributions, and the nature of measuring instruments.

Sampling Problems

Statistical significance. With regard to sampling problems, we have all learned to look for statistically significant differences. That is because we want to be able to generalize from the sex difference found in the tested sample to the difference expected in the specified population that this sample represents. If the difference is *not* significant, it may indicate that there is no mean sex difference in the measured variable in the population (or the difference may be in the opposite direction). It may also indicate, however, that the sample was too small to demonstrate the difference. On the other hand, if the difference is statistically significant, it could mean that the sample is large enough to yield statistical significance even for a very small difference. The implication is that we should not draw conclusions by simply tallying the number of studies that yielded significant or insignificant differences. We need to look also at the magnitude of the differences—in terms of the scale of measurement, the size of the standard deviations, the practical meaning of a difference of such magnitude, or any other standard appropriate to the context. In comparing results from studies conducted at different time periods, or from studies using group tests with those using individual tests, large discrepancies in number of cases are likely to be found. It is particularly important under those conditions to take sample size into account in combining or comparing such studies.

Differential selection. Another methodological pitfall associated with sampling pertains to the differential operation of selective factors for males and females. Under these circumstances, the two sex samples are not equally representative of their respective populations and hence not comparable. Suppose that, because of some accident of availability, the men in a study come from the upper end of their distribution in the trait in question, while the women come from the lower end of theirs. The results would undoubtedly show a statistically significant mean difference in favor of the men; but this would not be a difference associated with sex, nor would it hold for the general population.

The effect of differential selective bias was illustrated by two early studies in which the same group intelligence test was administered to a sample of over 2500 elementary school pupils (Pressey, 1918) and to approximately 6000 high school students (Book & Meadows, 1928). In the elementary school sample, the girls excelled the boys in mean score at all ages; but among the high school seniors, the boys excelled. At the time these data were obtained, a favorite interpretation was that, since girls develop faster than boys physically, they are also accelerated in their mental development; and this acceleration would account for their temporary superiority during the elementary school years. By the time they reach the high school senior years, it was argued, boys have caught up developmentally, and they accordingly excel girls in intelligence test performance.

An alternative explanation emerged, however, when the rate of high school dropouts was compared for the two sexes. The boys not only dropped out in much larger numbers than did the girls, but the dropouts also came largely from the low end of the distribution of academic achievement. Superficially, it would seem that samples of high school boys and girls attending the same classes should be comparable. The obtained score difference, however, resulted from a selective bias which acted differentially for the two sexes.

Another classical example of the unsuspected operation of differential sampling bias pertains to the hypothesis of sex differences in variability. Early writers on sex differences, including especially Ellis (1894/1934), Cattell (1903), and Thorndike (1914), maintained that, while men and women might have the same mean intelligence, the male sex showed wider variability. The evidence adduced in support of this hypothesis included the greater number of men in institutions for the mentally retarded, at one end of the distribution, and the greater incidence of eminent men in published directories, at the other end. In reference to the latter, critics of the hypothesis were quick to point out the conspicuous differences in opportunities available to men and women for attaining eminence (Hollingworth, 1914; Woolley, 1914).

The discrepancy at the low end of the scale was more difficult to explain and was widely attributed to a fundamental biological difference, possibly related to the greater frequency of sex-linked defects in the male. It now seems doubtful, however, that such defects could account for sizable discrepancies in the incidence of mental retardation in the two sexes. An alternative explanation can be found in the operation of selective bias in the institutionalization of mental retardates. The operation of this bias was first clearly demonstrated in a study by Hollingworth (1922). Essentially, this study showed that, while there were more mentally retarded males in institutions, there were more mentally retarded females outside. Among persons referred for mental examination, the females as a group were older and had lower IQs than the males. Both of these discrepancies were even greater when the cases actually committed were compared. A survey of the previous occupations and case histories of the subjects indicated that the probable explanation of these differences lay in the less demanding nature of the occupations and life patterns open to the mentally retarded females. Such a female could survive outside an institution by remaining at home with her family, or by turning to domestic service, prostitution, or marriage. Males, on the other hand, were more likely to be pushed into competitive industrial work at a relatively early age, where their mental retardation was soon revealed.

These two examples, one with high school seniors and one with mental retardates, point up the importance of investigating the possible operation of differential selection in any study of sex differences.

Overlapping Distributions

When Samuel Johnson was asked which is more intelligent, man or woman, he is said to have replied, "Which man, which woman?" This is a succinct way of expressing the wide individual differences found within each sex, with the resulting overlapping of their distributions. Since in any psychological trait women differ widely from one another, and men likewise vary widely among themselves, any relationship found between group means will not necessarily hold for individuals. Even when one group excels the other by a large and statistically significant amount, individuals can be found in the lower-scoring group who surpass certain individuals in the higher-scoring group. Because of the large extent of individual differences within any one group as contrasted to the relatively small difference between group means, a person's membership in a given group provides little or no information about his or her status in most traits.

Most published reports of sex differences focus on means or other group parameters. For a complete picture of the relative standing of the two groups, however, some index of the extent of overlapping should be included. The best procedure would be to reproduce the entire frequency distributions of the two groups. A simpler alternative, in the case of normally distributed samples, is to report the percentage of persons in one group who reach or exceed the median of the other. In terms of this index, complete overlapping is indicated when 50% of one group reach or exceed the median of the other and the ranges are the same. This is understandable when we remember that, within any one group, 50% of its own members reach or exceed its own median.

When more than 50% of Group A reach or exceed the median of Group B, then Group A is to that extent superior to Group B. When less than 50% of A reach or exceed the median of B, Group A is inferior to Group B. It should be borne in mind that overlapping is typically expressed with reference to the *median* of one group, not with reference to the *lowest* score. Thus even if 0% of Group A reaches or exceeds the median of Group B, there are still some individuals in Group A who equal or exceed the performance of certain individuals in Group B. Moreover, in distributions that deviate substantially from the normal curve, it is possible for the ranges to be identical even when the percentage of one group reaching or exceeding the median of the other falls considerably below 50.

In my *Differential Psychology* text (Anastasi, 1958a, p. 455) I reproduced a graph from an early study (Schiller, 1934), showing the complete distribution curves of 189 boys and 206 girls in the third and fourth elementary school grades on a test of arithmetic reasoning. The mean difference in favor of the boys was substantial, amounting to 4.6 points out of a total of 60 points. This difference, significant at the .01 level, was equivalent to more than half a standard deviation of either group. In terms of the usual index of overlapping, only 28% of the girls reached or exceeded the boys' median. Yet the ranges of the two groups were virtually identical. In fact, the range of the boys' scores extended from 10 to 55, that of the girls from 13 to 55. The data about overlapping distributions provide a sort of empirical, statistically respectable underpinning for the current efforts to regard women, as well as men, as individuals. These data should serve as a corrective against the traditional tendency to "homogenize" women into narrowly defined sex roles—to use a very apt term introduced by Sandra and Daryl Bem (1970, p. 94).

Nature of Measuring Instruments

The third category concerns characteristics of the measuring instruments employed to compare the sexes. In drawing conclusions from any one study—and especially in pulling together the results of different studies to summarize what is known about sex differences—we need to examine carefully the particular tests or other observational procedures used by each investigator. Many features of the assessment techniques are obviously relevant to an evaluation of the findings. For example, when ratings are employed, the probable influence of social stereotypes on raters' judgments must be considered. The reliability of instruments (whether ratings or objective tests) must surely be looked into.

Item-selection procedures. Certain questions regarding the construction of instruments are also especially pertinent. For instance, were items selected with reference to sex differences in responses? If so, were they chosen so as to minimize or maximize sex differences? There are examples of both practices in published tests. The Stanford–Binet illustrates the former, while all the early masculinity–femininity (M–F) scales illustrate the latter (Constantinople, 1973; Terman & Miles, 1936). Among the best known examples of these early M–F scales are those incorporated in the following inventories: Strong Vocational Interest Blank, Minnesota Multiphasic Personality Inventory, California Psychological Inventory, and Guilford–Zimmerman Temperament Survey. The implications of these item-selection procedures is that neither type of instrument is appropriate for assessing sex differences in the variables it measures. The Stanford–Binet was constructed so as to obliterate sex differences in performance; the M–F scales were constructed so as to exaggerate sex differences in responses, since any items that failed to yield significant sex differences in the standardization sample were rejected. It should be noted that these comments are not intended as criticisms of the test-construction procedures employed. In both cases, the procedures were appropriate for the purposes for which the instruments were designed. But failure to take these procedures into account could lead to misuses of the tests and misinterpretation of the results.

Global scores. A related interpretive problem arises from the use of global scores on any heterogeneous test, however constructed. Shortly after the development of the first intelligence tests, there was a flurry of studies comparing the sexes in "general intelligence." The resulting sex differences, whether reported as an IQ on an individual scale such as the Binet or as some other global score on group tests, were difficult to interpret. The direction and amount of sex difference depended in part on the extent to which test items were drawn from different content domains, such as verbal, numerical, or spatial. Since the early, traditional intelligence tests were quite heterogeneous in their content coverage, the resulting composite scores tended to blur or wipe out sex differences in performance. Apparently it was partly because of the failure of traditional intelligence tests to reveal large sex differences that some early investigators turned to the hypothesis of sex differences in variability.

With the development and widespread application of factor analysis, intellectual functions were sorted into distinct group factors or aptitudes (see Anastasi, 1982, Chap. 13). The most influential findings on the identification of such aptitudes undoubtedly stem from the research of Thurstone, which yielded a dozen or so primary mental abilities (Thurstone, 1938; Thurstone & Thurstone, 1941), and that of Guilford, which yielded over 100 abilities organized into his structure-of-intellect model (Guilford, 1967; Guilford & Hoepfner, 1971). It is certainly more fruitful to investigate sex differences in terms of these more clearly defined traits than in terms of the composite of diverse functions sampled by traditional intelligence tests. Both test development and studies of sex differences have made increasing use of the traits identified through factor-analytic research.

Broad group factors. Nevertheless, there are two questions that remain to be considered in assessing available sex-difference research. The first pertains to the breadth of group factors investigated in the comparison of male and female performances. If the categories into which intellectual functions are grouped are too broad, we may obtain the same canceling out or blurring effect found with the early intelligence tests. This blurring may occur within individual studies, if comparisons are limited to total scores in such broad areas as verbal, numerical, or spatial aptitudes. It is even more likely to occur, however, in surveys of different studies. Here, for example, the results obtained with many different kinds of numerical tests may be combined and a conclusion drawn about sex differences in a

SEX DIFFERENCES 195

broad area, which is labeled "quantitative aptitude" simply because all the tests involved numbers. Yet even in Thurstone's research, which yielded a relatively small number of abilities, separate factors were identified for number computation and for quantitative reasoning. There were also at least two factors in the verbal domain, including verbal comprehension and word fluency. The spatial-perception domain has shown evidence of several identifiable factors, including perceptual speed and accuracy, spatial orientation, and the manipulation of spatial relations, among others.

It is noteworthy that several studies have found sex differences in opposite directions within these content domains. For instance, while males excelled in quantitative reasoning, females excelled in numerical computation. Females excelled in word fluency and in language usage; but verbal comprehension tests yielded either no sex difference or a difference in favor of males, especially at the older age levels. Females excelled in perceptual speed and accuracy, while males excelled in most other spatial tests. These findings are still tentative and are themselves influenced by other concomitant variables such as age and educational level. But they recurred often enough in studies conducted before 1970 to merit careful scrutiny and further investigation (Anastasi, 1958a, Chap. 14; Garai & Scheinfeld, 1968, Chap. 7; Tyler, 1965, Chap. 10).

Trait organization. The second question is more basic. It concerns the actual organization of abilities and the identification of factors in males and females (Anastasi, 1970; Hyde, Geiringer, & Yen, 1975). There is an increasing body of data indicating the role of experiential conditions in the very formation of group factors. It is not only the level of performance in different abilities, but also the way performance is organized into distinct traits, that is influenced by experiential background. Differences in factor patterns have been found to be associated not only with sex but also with different cultures or subcultures, socioeconomic levels, age, amount of education, and types of school curricula (Anastasi, 1970). In general, there is evidence to suggest that greater differentiation of abilities into more specialized factors occurs in those domains in which the particular group excels. For example, several differentiated verbal factors may be identified in the female, but only one in the male; similarly, several spatial factors may emerge for males, but only one for females.

The factorial composition of the same objective task may differ among individuals with diverse experiential backgrounds (Anastasi, 1982, Chap. 13; Burns, 1980; Frederiksen, 1969; French, 1965). One reason for these individual differences may be found in the use of different methods to carry out the same task. Individuals with highly developed verbal abilities, for example, are likely to utilize verbal mediators to solve a mechanical or spatial problem; those whose experiences have been predominantly mechanical, on the other hand, are likely to follow a perceptual or spatial approach in solving the same problem.

The examples cited thus far have been limited to the cognitive domain. But the same two questions regarding excessive breadth of trait categories and sex differences in trait organization can and should also be raised about personality variables. Moreover, in the personality domain, it is often necessary to get down to the item level in research on both group differences and trait organization. In an early study of sex differences in introversion–extroversion, for example, Heidbreder (1927) found no significant sex differences in total scores; but she did find a significant difference when items were regrouped into those interfering with interpersonal relations and those interfering with efficient work. It should be noted that several recent examples of such behavioral specificity—and of the resulting need for caution in combining sex-difference results from different personality studies—can be found in an excellent article by Block (1976b).

When dealing with personality variables, we also have to consider the problem of situational specificity (Anastasi, 1982, Chap. 17; Mischel, 1968, 1969, 1973, 1979). While not a major concern in the assessment of aptitudes, the variability in an individual's behavior from one situational context to another has been receiving increasing attention in research on personality. And it is quite likely that situational context interacts with sex in the personality domain.

Conjoint Analysis of Procedural Variables and Reported Sex Differences

In concluding this discussion of methodological and interpretive insights that can be gained from early research, we may consider how published studies might be most effectively utilized. It is apparent that a box score or a simple tallying of studies that found a significant sex difference and those that did not is inappropriate. A better approach is the systematic analysis of the significance and magnitude of reported sex differences in relation to certain major procedural features of each study. For the purpose of this analysis, the sex difference can be treated as the dependent variable, while the independent variables are the relevant characteristics of each study. The latter could include such variables as number of cases; age, education, occupation, socioeconomic level, and ethnic background of subjects; date when behavior was assessed; reliability and construct validity of instruments employed; and degree of specificity of behavioral assessment (e.g., analysis of subtest scores, item responses, situational context).

This approach is quite similar to what Glass calls "meta-analysis" (Glass, 1976, 1977; Johnson, Maruyama, Johnson, Nelson, & Skon, 1981; Kulik, Kulik, & Cohen, 1979; Smith & Glass, 1977). To be sure, available published research on sex differences may not permit extensive application of the precise statistical procedures of meta-analysis described by Glass. For one thing, much of the information on sex differences was obtained incidentally in studies designed for other purposes. Procedures are quite diverse, and any ordering of studies in terms of procedural variables would probably be too crude for quantitative analyses. Nevertheless, at this stage we can at least be guided by the general orientation of meta-analysis in evaluating and utilizing the findings of particular studies.

SEX DIFFERENCES IN RELATION TO SOCIETAL CHANGES

If we want to advance beyond the description of existing sex differences to an explanation of the origins of these differences, we need to consider the operation of what has been variously designated as heredity and environment, or nature and nurture, or biology and culture. During the first half of the 20th century, the changing model of the heredity–environment relation led to heated controversies, first in terms of *which behaviors* were inherited and which acquired, and more recently in the effort to estimate how much of the variance of particular traits was attributable to heredity and how much to environment (Cravens, 1978). In the 1950s, I suggested that a more fruitful approach was provided by the question "How?" (Anastasi, 1958b). What can be learned about the actual *modus operandi* of specific hereditary and environmental factors in the development of behavioral differences? What is the chain of events whereby hereditary and environmental variables interact in the etiology of a particular behavioral outcome? The study of sex differences offers some promising opportunities to explore such etiological mechanisms.

Examples of Proposed Etiological Hypotheses

A consideration of biological sex differences suggests some intriguing possibilities regarding the role that such physical differences may play in the development of aptitude and personality differences within particular cultural contexts. Some of these possible etiological mechanisms were proposed in early surveys of sex differences (Scheinfeld, 1943; Seward, 1946). The operation of such mechanisms in turn suggests changes in trait differences between the sexes that may occur as societal conditions change.

One example is provided by the developmental acceleration of the female, a well-established sex difference that begins before birth and extends to maturity (Anastasi, 1958a; Garai & Scheinfeld, 1968; Tyler, 1965). The psychological effects of this difference in developmental rate probably vary widely from trait to trait. For instance, the developmental acceleration of girls in infancy has been repeatedly proposed as a significant factor in their more rapid progress in the acquisition of language, which may give them a head start in verbal development as a whole. Another possible implication of developmental acceleration is a social one. Because of their physical acceleration, adolescent girls have traditionally tended to associate socially with boys older than themselves (Scheinfeld, 1943). This probably accounts also for the common age discrepancy in marriage. Since the girl was generally younger than the boys she dated—and younger than the man she married—she was surpassed by most of her male associates in amount of education and general experience. The resulting age differences in knowledge and information may have been perceived and fostered as a sex difference and could thus be at the root of many social attitudes and sex stereotypes. With the sharp increase in coeducation over the decades, the resulting daily contact with age peers of the opposite sex may serve as a corrective for this traditional misperception and may eventually be reflected in an equalization of expectations, attitudes, and self-concepts.

Another conspicuous set of biological sex differences pertains to general body size, muscular strength, and speed and coordination of gross bodily movements, in all of which males excel (Anastasi, 1958a; Garai & Scheinfeld, 1968; Tyler, 1965). Of course, in this case as in all other traits, we must not lose sight of the overlapping of distributions. But the *mean* sex differences in these physical characteristics are certainly large and consistent. Sex differences in gross motor coordination, for example, have been noted from infancy and tend to increase throughout childhood (Gesell et al., 1940).

In addition to the probable contribution of these physical differences to the development of aggressiveness, in which sex differences have been consistently reported (Anastasi, 1958a; Garai & Scheinfeld, 1968; Maccoby & Jacklin, 1974; Tyler, 1965), some early writers discussed their implications for occupational specialization. Surveys of the occupational distribution of males and females in contemporary primitive cultures, as well as historical records, support the relation between the physical demands of occupational roles and their frequency among males and females (Murdock, 1937; Scheinfeld, 1943; Seward, 1946). The authors of these surveys, among others, further observed that in the more advanced cultures, the physical demands of occupations have steadily decreased following the introduction of machinery. In modern technological societies, occupational achievement and success show a progressively diminishing dependence on sex-related physical skills. What will be the effect of such a change in occupational criteria on the psychological concepts that men and women have about themselves and others? This suggests another area for comparative exploration over time.

From a different angle, one could also investigate changes in male and

SEX DIFFERENCES

female scores on the traits of aggressiveness and dominance as assessed by self-report inventories, in relation to a diminishing societal tolerance for violent methods of conflict resolution. A plausible hypothesis would be that male means in aggressiveness should drop and female means in dominance rise, with a consequent decrease in the sex difference in both traits.

Another type of relationship that may be reflected in sex differences is that between motivational, emotional, and attitudinal variables on the one hand and aptitudes and achievement on the other. As the former alter under the impact of societal changes, they may lead eventually to corresponding modifications in the latter. That not only immediate achievement but also the long-term development of aptitudes is influenced by the individual's motivation and related noncognitive variables has been repeatedly demonstrated, notably in the continuing research of Atkinson and his associates (Atkinson, 1974; Atkinson & Birch, 1978, Chap. 4; Atkinson, O'Malley, & Lens, 1976; see also Anastasi, 1982, Chap. 12). According to Atkinson's schema, motivation affects both the efficiency with which a task is performed and the time the individual devotes to the task (e.g., studying different subjects, carrying out a job-related activity). The final achievement or product shows the combined effects of level of performance and time spent on task. An important consequent of level of performance × time spent on task is the lasting cumulative effects of this activity or experience on the individual's own cognitive and noncognitive development.

With particular reference to sex differences, several investigations have yielded suggestive data on the relationship between motivational or attitudinal variables and test performance. For example, an early study on sex-role identification and problem-solving ability (Milton, 1957) found that total problem-solving scores correlated significantly with Terman–Miles masculinity–femininity scores, not only in the combined-sex group but also within each sex. In other words, the women with the more masculine scores on the M–F scale were better problem solvers than were those with the more feminine scores; and the same relation held among the men.

More recent studies have contributed further data on the relation between the individual's attitudes, sex-role standards, and sex-role identification and such variables as academic achievement in reading and arithmetic. The procedures of these studies are extremely varied; and the results are scattered and disparate, but they nevertheless provide provocative leads. For instance, in a study of schoolchildren from the 2nd to the 12th grade, reading and arithmetic scores on standardized achievement batteries proved to be more a function of the child's perception of these areas as sex-appropriate or sex-inappropriate than of the child's own sex, individual preference for masculine or feminine sex role, or personal liking or disliking for reading or arithmetic (C. A. Dwyer, 1974). In another study (Fitzpatrick, 1978), the achievement of bright 10th-grade girls in mathematics, as assessed by both grades and standardized tests, was found to be significantly related to the students' attitudes toward various aspects of the female role. Those girls showing a more liberal orientation on the women's role scale performed better in mathematics than did those with a more traditional orientation. It would thus seem desirable to investigate also aptitude changes over time, since these changes may be the indirect result of socially instigated attitudinal and motivational shifts.

Some Scattered Comparisons of Sex Differences over Time

A few investigators have followed a retrospective approach by gathering sex-difference data that were roughly comparable to available earlier data. For instance, children's preferences for play activities surveyed in the 1950s were compared with the findings of a similar survey conducted in 1926 (Rosenberg & Sutton-Smith, 1960). In the later study, the girls retained their interest in most of the female play activities of the earlier study, but in addition showed an increased preference for some traditional male activities. Boys' preferences, however, revealed no such broadening, but actually had become somewhat more confined. The authors interpreted the results as consistent with an expansion in the girls' role concept to include more traditional masculine activities, without a corresponding change in the boys' role perception.

In the early 1970s, Spence (1974) used TAT-like stories, followed by a structured questionnaire, to investigate women's attitudes toward achievement. The results were compared with those obtained a decade earlier by Horner with the same TAT-like stories (see Horner, 1972). The more recent findings suggested that the so-called fear of success, or motive to avoid success, was not so prevalent in the 1970s as in the 1960s.

A third example is from the cognitive domain (Cunningham & Birren, 1976). Although the number of cases employed in this study is small, the experimental design is well controlled and the findings are suggestive. Essentially, the study involved a three-way comparison of 32 cases. Out of a sample of 485 undergraduates tested in 1944, 32 were identified and retested in 1972. In addition, the same test was administered in 1972 to 32 undergraduates individually matched with the original 32 in sex and in total standard score within their own cohort. Although the test used was the Army Alpha, performance was analyzed in terms of a verbal factor, a highly speeded relations factor, and a number factor. Only the number factor showed a different developmental pattern for the sexes. In this factor, the female scores were 1 SD higher for the 1972 cohort than for the 1944 cohort, while those of the males showed no significant difference.

Neither males nor females showed any significant change in the number factor when the 1944 cohort was retested in 1972. The authors suggest that the cohort difference in the females may reflect a decline in "traditional stereotypes regarding female occupational roles, with a consequent shift in patterns of education" (p. 82).

The study just described utilized a simplified version of a sophisticated experimental design first fully described by Schaie (1965). Designated as the cross-sequential method, it involves the testing of a representative sample of different age groups on two or more occasions. This permits *cross-sectional* comparisons of different age groups tested at one time period, *longitudinal* comparisons of the same individuals tested at two or more time periods, and *time-lag* comparisons of samples of equal age drawn from different cohorts tested at the different time periods—for instance, 30-year-olds tested in 1950 could be compared with 30-year-olds tested in 1960. The last comparison is similar to what was described earlier in this paper as the longitudinal study of populations.

A large-scale pioneer application of the cross-sequential model is illustrated in an investigation by Schaie and his co-workers (Schaie & Labouvie-Vief, 1974; Schaie, Labouvie, & Buech, 1973; Schaie & Strother, 1968). The study began in 1956 with the administration of the SRA Primary Mental Abilities test and Schaie's Test of Behavioral Rigidity to a stratified-random sample of 500 adults. The population from which this sample was drawn consisted of approximately 18,000 members of a prepaid medical plan, whose membership was fairly representative of the census figures for a large metropolitan area. The sample included 25 men and 25 women at each 5-year age interval from 20 to 70. All the original participants who could be located 7 years later were contacted and 302 of them were given the same tests again. A second 7-year retest was administered in 1970 to 161 of the original participants (Schaie & Labouvie-Vief, 1974). In addition, the same tests were given to three independent age-stratified samples drawn from the same population in 1956, 1963, and 1970 (Schaie et al., 1973).

Although the principal object of this study was to analyze age changes, data were also available on sex differences in each cohort. The results revealed virtually no significant change in the relative performance of the sexes either across age or across cohorts. The pattern of sex differences followed the traditional results. For example, the most conspicuous sex differences were in spatial aptitude in favor of males and in verbal fluency in favor of females. The authors themselves suggest that their findings are consistent with the hypothesis that sex differences in cognitive functions "are either genetically determined or established by early imprinting and when thus established are maintained throughout life" (Schaie et al., 1973, p. 164).

In connection with the "early imprinting," it is relevant to note that the mean birth dates of the cohorts covered by this study ranged for 1889 to 1945. The participants were therefore reared during periods when changes in sex roles were minor relative to the changes characteristic of the late 1960s and the 1970s. It would be of particular interest to investigate sex differences in cohorts born between 1945 and 1965. In their discussion of age and cohort differences, Schaie and his associates point to the need for research involving a conjoint analysis of environmental and behavioral change (Schaie et al., 1973; Schaie & Labouvie-Vief, 1974). This is the type of analysis that would be especially appropriate in the assessment of sex differences during a period when relevant societal attitudes and opportunities were undergoing conspicuous change.

More recent work by some investigators following the general cross-sequential approach was focused more directly on sex-role changes. Urberg and Labouvie-Vief (1976) administered the Adjective Check List (Gough & Heilbrun, 1965) to 40 males and 40 females in each of three groups: 7th-grade students, 12th-grade students, and students in adult education classes (ages 20 to 74). In a balanced design, half of the females and half of the males in each of the three groups were instructed to check the adjectives describing their concept of an ideal female; the other half were asked to do the same for an ideal male. The study was replicated with an independent sample 2 years later (Urberg, 1979). With only a few significant exceptions, the results showed the pervasiveness of traditional sex-role stereotypes across all age groups; nor was any change in the prevalence of these stereotypes found in the 2-year follow-up. In the self-descriptions, which were obtained only in the follow-up, however, the male descriptions did not differ significantly from the female descriptions (with a single minor exception). As for the lack of change in the ideal descriptions, it should be noted that 2 years represents a very short period over which to investigate cohort changes.

Cohort Studies and Societal Change: Future Prospects

If we wish to investigate the effects of a changing societal context on sex differences in behavior, we ought to compare cohorts assessed by equivalent procedures at different historical periods. Nor need this approach be limited to sex differences. Large-scale cohort studies, with representative samples and well-designed instruments, could serve a useful function in providing *psychological indicators*. They could show what is happening to the attitudes, interests, values, and psychological well-being of a population over time.

We have become accustomed to economic indicators, which record changes in the gross national product, the consumer price index, and other measures of the economic health of the nation. We are beginning to witness the emergence of social indicators, concerned with the quality of life and the general well-being of the population (Sheldon, 1976; Strumpel, 1976), and educational indicators, concerned with the state of the nation's educational system and the knowledge that young people have acquired in selected subject-matter areas (Gooler, 1976; Womer, 1970). Perhaps the addition of psychological indicators to this list would help to unify and add meaning to the other indicators, insofar as what happens to societal variables is both a result and a cause of what happens to the behavioral variables of the constituent individuals.

REFERENCES

Anastasi, A. *Differential psychology* (3rd ed.). New York: Macmillan, 1958. (a)

Anastasi, A. Heredity, environment, and the question "How?" *Psychological Review*, 1958, 65, 197–208. (b)

Anastasi, A. On the formation of psychological traits. *American Psychologist*, 1970, 25, 899–910.

Anastasi, A. *Psychological testing* (5th ed.). New York: Macmillan, 1982.

Atkinson, J. W. Motivational determinants of intellective performance and cumulative achievement. In J. W. Atkinson & J. O. Raynor, *Motivation and achievement*. Washington, D.C.: Winston, 1974. Chap. 20.

Atkinson, J. W., & Birch, D. *An introduction to motivation* (2nd ed.). New York: Van Nostrand, 1978.

Atkinson, J. W., O'Malley, P. M., & Lens, W. Motivation and ability: Interactive psychological determinants of intellective performance, educational achievement, and each other. In W. H. Sewell, R. M. Hauser, & D. L. Featherman (Eds.), *Schooling and achievement in American society*. New York: Academic Press, 1976. Chap. 8.

Bem, S. L., & Bem, D. J. Case study of a nonconscious ideology: Training the woman to know her place. In D. J. Bem, *Beliefs, attitudes, and human affairs*. Belmont, Calif.: Brooks/Cole, 1970. Pp. 89–99.

Benjamin, L. T., Jr. The psychological round table: Revolution of 1936. *American Psychologist*, 1977, 32, 542–549.

Berry, J. W. Temne and Eskimo perceptual skills. *International Journal of Psychology*, 1966, 1, 207–229.

Block, J. H. Debatable conclusions about sex differences: Review of E. E. Maccoby & C. N. Jacklin, *The psychology of sex differences*. *Contemporary Psychology*, 1976, 21, 517–522. (a)

Block, J. H. Issues, problems, and pitfalls in assessing sex differences: A critical review of *The psychology of sex differences*. *Merill-Palmer Quarterly*, 1976, 22, 283–308. (b)

Book, W. F., & Meadows, J. L. Sex differences in 5925 high school seniors in ten psychological tests. *Journal of Applied Psychology*, 1928, 12, 56–81.

Boring, E. G. *A history of experimental psychology*. New York: Century, 1929.

Burns, R. B. Relation of aptitudes to learning at different points in time during instruction. *Journal of Educational Psychology*, 1980, 72, 785–795.

Cattell, J. McK. A statistical study of eminent men. *Popular Science Monthly*, 1903, 62, 359–377.

Constantinople, A. Masculinity-femininity: An exception to a famous dictum? *Psychological Bulletin*, 1973, 80, 389–407.

Cravens, H. *The triumph of evolution: American scientists and the heredity-environment controversy, 1900–1941*. Philadelphia: Univ. of Pennsylvania Press, 1978.

Cunningham, W. R., & Birren, J. E. Age changes in human abilities: A 28-year longitudinal study. *Developmental Psychology*, 1976, 12, 81–82.

Dwyer, C. A. Influence of children's sex role standards on reading and arithmetic achievement. *Journal of Educational Psychology*, 1974, 66, 811–816.

Dwyer, D. H. *Images and self-images: Male and female in Morocco.* New York: Columbia Univ. Press, 1978.

Ellis, H. *Man and woman, a study of secondary and tertiary sexual characteristics* (8th rev. ed.). London: Heinemann, 1934. (1st ed., 1894.)

Fitzpatrick, J. L. Academic underachievement, other-direction, and attitudes toward women's roles in bright adolescent females. *Journal of Educational Psychology*, 1978, 70, 645–650.

Frederiksen, C. H. Abilities, transfer, and information retrieval in verbal learning. *Multivariate Behavioral Research Monographs*, 1969, No. 69-2.

French, J. W. The relationship of problem-solving styles to the factor composition of tests. *Educational and Psychological Measurement*, 1965, 25, 9–28.

Garai, J. E., & Scheinfeld, A. Sex differences in mental and behavioral traits. *Genetic Psychology Monographs*, 1968, 77, 169–299.

Gesell, A., et al. *The first five years of life.* New York: Harper, 1940.

Glass, G. V. Primary, secondary, and meta-analysis of research. *The Educational Researcher*, 1976, 10, 3–8.

Glass, G. V. Integrating findings: The meta-analysis of research. In L. Schulman (Ed.), *Review of research in education.* Itasca, Ill.: Peacock, 1977.

Gooler, D. D. The development and use of educational indicators. *Proceedings of the 1975 ETS Invitational Conference.* Princeton, N.J.: Educational Testing Service, 1976. Pp. 11–27.

Gough, H. G., & Heilbrun, A. B. *The Adjective Check List manual.* Palo Alto, Calif.: Consulting Psychologists Press, 1965.

Guilford, J. P. *The nature of human intelligence.* New York: McGraw–Hill, 1967.

Guilford, J. P., & Hoepfner, R. *The analysis of intelligence.* New York: McGraw–Hill, 1971.

Heidbreder, E. Introversion and extroversion in men and women. *Journal of Abnormal and Social Psychology*, 1927, 22, 52–61.

Hollingworth, L. S. Variability as related to sex differences in achievement. *American Journal of Sociology*, 1914, 19, 510–530.

Hollingworth, L. S. Differential action upon the sexes of forces which tend to segregate the feebleminded. *Journal of Abnormal and Social Psychology*, 1922, 17, 35–57.

Horner, M. S. The motive to avoid success and changing aspirations of college women. In J. M. Bardwick (Ed.), *Readings on the psychology of women.* New York: Harper & Row, 1972. Pp. 62–67.

Hyde, J. S., Geiringer, E. R., & Yen, W. M. On the empirical relation between spatial ability and sex differences in other aspects of cognitive performance. *Multivariate Behavioral Research*, 1975, 10, 289–307.

Johnson, D. W., Maruyama, G., Johnson, R., Nelson, D., & Skon, L. Effects of cooperative, competitive, and individualistic goal structures on achievement: A meta-analysis. *Psychological Bulletin*, 1981, 89, 47–62.

Kulik, J. A., Kulik, C-L. C., & Cohen, P. A. A meta-analysis of outcome studies of Keller's personalized system of instruction. *American Psychologist*, 1979, 34, 307–318.

Lapidus, G. W. *Women in Soviet society: Equality, development, and social change.* Berkeley: Univ. of California Press, 1978.

Maccoby, E. E., & Jacklin, C. N. *The psychology of sex differences.* Stanford, Calif.: Stanford Univ. Press, 1974.

Mead, M. *Growing up in New Guinea.* New York: Morrow, 1930.

Mead, M. *Sex and temperament in three primitive societies.* New York: Morrow, 1935.

Mednick, M. T. S. Social change and sex-role inertia: The case of the kibbutz. In M. T. S. Mednick, S. S. Tangri, & L. W. Hoffman (Eds.), *Women and achievement: Social and motivational analyses.* New York: Halsted Press, 1975. Pp. 85-103.

Mednick, M. T. S. The revolution that never was: Review of M. E. Spiro, *Gender and culture: Kibbutz women revisited. Contemporary Psychology,* 1981, **26,** 101-102.

Milton, G. A. The effects of sex-role identification upon problem-solving skills. *Journal of Abnormal and Social Psychology,* 1957, **55,** 208-212.

Mischel, W. *Personality and assessment.* New York: Wiley, 1968.

Mischel, W. Continuity and change in personality. *American Psychologist,* 1969, **24,** 1012-1018.

Mischel, W. Toward a cognitive social learning reconceptualization of personality. *Psychological Review,* 1973, **80,** 252-283.

Mischel, W. On the interface of cognition and personality: Beyond the person-situation debate. *American Psychologist,* 1979, **34,** 740-754.

Murdock, G. P. Comparative data on the division of labor by sex. *Social Forces,* 1937, **15,** 551-553.

Pressey, L. W. Sex differences shown by 2544 schoolchildren on a group scale of intelligence, with special reference to variability. *Journal of Applied Psychology,* 1918, **2,** 323-340.

Rosenberg, B. G., & Sutton-Smith, B. A revised conception of masculine-feminine differences in play activities. *Journal of Genetic Psychology,* 1960, **96,** 165-170.

Schaie, K. W. A general model for the study of developmental problems. *Psychological Bulletin,* 1965, **64,** 92-107.

Schaie, K. W., Labouvie, G. V., & Buech, B. U. Generational and cohort-specific differences in adult cognitive functioning: A fourteen-year study of independent samples. *Developmental Psychology,* 1973, **9,** 151-166.

Schaie, K. W., & Labouvie-Vief, G. Generational versus ontogenetic components of change in cognitive behavior: A fourteen-year cross-sequential study. *Developmental Psychology,* 1974, **10,** 305-320.

Schaie, K. W., & Strother, C. R. A cross-sequential study of age changes in cognitive behavior. *Psychological Bulletin,* 1968, **70,** 671-680.

Scheinfeld, A. *Women and men.* New York: Harcourt, Brace, 1943.

Schiller, B. Verbal, numerical, and spatial abilities of young children. *Archives of Psychology,* 1934, No. 161.

Schlegel, A. (Ed.). *Sexual stratification: A cross-cultural view.* New York: Columbia Univ. Press, 1977.

Scottish Council for Research in Education. *The trend of Scottish intelligence.* London: Univ. of London Press, 1949.

Seward, G. H. *Sex and the social order.* New York: McGraw-Hill, 1946.

Sheldon, E. B. The social indicators movement. *Proceedings of the 1975 ETS Invitational Conference.* Princeton, N.J.: Educational Testing Service, 1976. Pp. 3-10.

Shields, S. A. Functionalism, Darwinism, and the psychology of women: A study in social myth. *American Psychologist,* 1975, **30,** 739-754. (a)

Shields, S. A. Ms. Pilgrim's progress: The contributions of Leta Stetter Hollingworth to the psychology of women. *American Psychologist,* 1975, **30,** 852-857. (b)

Smith, M. L., & Glass, G. V. Meta-analysis of psychotherapy outcome studies. *American Psychologist,* 1977, **32,** 752-760.

Sokal, M. M. APA's first publication: *Proceedings of the American Psychological Association, 1892-1893. American Psychologist,* 1973, **28,** 277-292.

Sokal, M. M. *Science* and James McKeen Cattell, 1894 to 1945. *Science,* 1980, **209,** 43-52.

Sokal, M. M. (Ed.). *An education in psychology: James McKeen Cattell's journal and letters from Germany and England, 1880–1888.* Cambridge, Mass.: MIT Press, 1981.

Spence, J. T. The Thematic Apperception Test and attitudes toward achievement in women; A new look at the motive to avoid success and a new method of measurement. *Journal of Consulting and Clinical Psychology,* 1974, 42, 427–437.

Spiro, M. E. *Gender and culture: Kibbutz women revisited.* Durham, N.C.: Duke Univ. Press, 1979.

Strumpel, B. (Ed.). *Economic means for human needs: Social indicators of well-being and discontent.* Ann Arbor, Mich.: Institute for Social Research, 1976.

Tavris, C., & Offir, C. *The longest war: Sex differences in perspective.* New York: Harcourt Brace Jovanovich, 1977.

Terman, L. M., & Miles, C. C. *Sex and personality: Studies in masculinity and femininity.* New York: McGraw–Hill, 1936.

Thorndike, E. L. *Educational psychology* (Vol. 3). New York: Teachers College, Columbia University, 1914.

Thurstone, L. L. Primary mental abilities. *Psychometric Monographs,* 1938, No. 1.

Thurstone, L. L., & Thurstone, T. G. Factorial studies of intelligence. *Psychometric Monographs,* 1941, No. 2.

Tiger, L., & Shepher, J. *Women in the kibbutz.* New York: Harcourt Brace Jovanovich, 1975.

Tyler, L. E. *The psychology of human differences* (3rd ed.). New York: Appleton–Century–Crofts, 1965.

Urberg, K. A. Sex role conceptualization in adolescents and adults. *Developmental Psychology,* 1979, 15, 90–92.

Urberg, K. A., & Labouvie-Vief, G. Conceptualizations of sex roles: A life span developmental study. *Developmental Psychology,* 1976, 12, 15–23.

Wolf, M., & Witke, R. (Eds.). *Women in Chinese society.* Stanford, Calif.: Stanford Univ. Press, 1975.

Wolf, T. H. *Alfred Binet.* Chicago: Univ. of Chicago Press, 1973.

Womer, F. B. *What is National Assessment?* Ann Arbor, Mich.: National Assessment of Educational Progress, 1970.

Woolley, H. T. The psychology of sex. *Psychological Bulletin,* 1914, 11, 353–379.

RECEIVED: November 17, 1980; REVISED April 7, 1981

[7]
FIELD DEPENDENCE RESEARCH:
A HISTORICAL ANALYSIS OF A PSYCHOLOGICAL CONSTRUCT

JANICE HAAKEN

Analyses of cultural and political bias in social science inquiry can tell us not only about the limits of our work but also about competing visions of human capabilities and society that underlie theory and research. In psychology, such analyses are often constrained by conceptions of what constitutes ideal social scientific science. The term "bias" carries a pejorative meaning—as a failure to maintain an objective, scientific stance—and its presence is viewed primarily as a methodological problem. The aim in mainstream psychology is to adopt methodological procedures that enable researchers to overcome sources of bias and to achieve impartial, value-neutral representations of reality. Challenges to this ideal that come from the study of the sociology of knowledge, for example, that knowledge is tied to specific social interests and ideologies and to historically problematic questions, have had relatively little impact on psychological inquiry. However, in recent years, a still small group of psychologists is cultivating an interest in the social and historical basis of psychological knowledge.[1]

I would like to thank Johanna Brenner, Norman Diamond, Nona Glazer, Cathleen Smith, and the readers for *Signs* for their helpful comments on earlier drafts of this manuscript.

[1] A. R. Buss, "The Emerging Field of the Sociology of Knowledge," in *Psychology in Social Context*, by A. R. Buss (New York: Irvington Publishers, 1979), 1–24.

Haaken / FIELD DEPENDENCE RESEARCH

I focus here on Herman Witkin. Key historical and social influences shaped Witkin's research on sex differences in field dependence-independence and shaped the extent to which it has been absorbed into psychology's corpus. Witkin was the first researcher to extend the study of psychological sex differences into the area of human perception. His findings, beginning in the late 1940s, that women were more field dependent than men—that is, they were more dependent on the external stimulus field in interpreting visual stimuli—are considered by many contemporary psychologists to be among the most stable findings concerning psychological sex differences in adulthood.[2] Witkin's field dependence-independence work is an attempt to use experimental methods to legitimize, on scientific grounds, the prevailing psychoanalytic theory of his time. By subjecting that theory to experimental verification, Witkin's research seemed to offer more definitive evidence of psychoanalytic ideas concerning gender development than the existing impression-based clinical accounts could offer.

My analysis, then, focuses on experimental psychology and how social and historical developments have influenced the construction of experimental problems, here, in particular, the study of gender and perceptual abilities. I offer Witkin's work—which began in the 1940s and extended over a period of over thirty years—as a case study in the social formation of a construct and its acceptance among professionals in psychology. Witkin's study of the role of context in perceptual abilities illustrates not only the limitations of experimental research in the behavioral sciences but also the ways in which research method becomes reified by its own findings. For instance, "decontextualization," to field-dependence theorists, means the perceptual ability to focus on a discrete stimulus while overcoming or ignoring the background context. I use the term to describe this tendency in positivist research at large, and I discuss the field-dependence literature as an example of the positivist rendering of a construct. To me, decontextualization means breaking down social reality into small units and focusing on a limited set of discrete interactions while ignoring the social context. It is what Parlee calls "context stripping."[3] That is, positivist research often omits a broad-based view of how everyday social experience influences the phenomenon under investigation. Such research typically lacks an analysis of how collective experiences (e.g., historical, ideological, and economic) shape individual experience—including the formation of research questions and constructs by scientists.

Ruth Bleier points out that the affinity for positivism in the social sciences has been particularly pronounced in psychology, where feminist

[2] E. Maccoby and L. Jacklin, *The Psychology of Sex Differences* (Stanford, Calif.: Stanford University Press, 1974), 351; C. Tavris and C. Offir, *The Longest War: Sex Differences in Perspective* (New York: Harcourt Brace Jovanovich, 1984).

[3] Mary Brown Parlee, "Psychology and Women," *Signs: Journal of Women in Culture and Society* 5, no. 1 (1979): 121–33, esp. 131.

scholarship and sociology of knowledge debates have had minimal impact.[4] In part, this emphasis on decontextualization is due to psychology's longstanding epistemological commitment to the experimental method, "directed toward finding and elucidating universal *laws* of human behavior by lifting behaviors out of the context within which they occur and subjecting them to scrutiny under 'controlled' laboratory conditions."[5]

I make a distinction here between the objectification of human experience that is present in all social science constructs and reification. Constructs involve more than simply naming phenomena; they point to a set of connections or underlying relationships. The construct of field dependence, for example, suggests a pattern that characterizes the organization of perceptual experiences and that connects the inner world and outer reality. The most useful constructs are those guided by a theoretical framework that explains how and why particular phenomena are related. What is interesting about Witkin's field-dependence construct is that it is more than a simple typology; it is guided by a body of theory that is also anchored in concrete empirical observations.

Reification is closely related to the problem of ideological and social domination in science. By approaching scientific constructs as metaphor, some have attempted to "de-reify" science by emphasizing the forms of social domination that underlie claims of scientific neutrality.[6] Constructs that are dissociated from the social reality that informs them can become reified in ongoing theoretical usage. In Witkin's case, key historical and ideological factors influenced his interest and interpretations of perceptual phenomena, which came to be understood as gender based.

The historical context

The term "field dependence-independence," introduced into psychology by Witkin in 1954, achieved wide currency in subsequent years. Based on a series of experiments in visual perception reported first by Witkin and Solomon Asch,[7] the construct referred to a subject's ability to separate a stimulus from its embedding context. Operationally, one of the main procedures involved placing subjects in a darkened room and asking them to place a luminous rod, suspended within a tilted frame, into a vertical

[4] Ruth Bleier, *Science and Gender* (New York: Pergamon Press, 1984), 68–69.
[5] Ibid., 69.
[6] See ibid.; Lynda Birke, *Women, Feminism and Biology* (New York: Methuen, 1986); Elizabeth Fee, "Women's Nature and Scientific Objectivity," in *Woman's Nature: Rationalizations of Inequality*, ed. M. Lowe and R. Hubbard (New York: Pergamon Press, 1983).
[7] H. A. Witkin and S. E. Asch, "Studies in Space Orientation, Part III: Perception of the Upright in the Absence of a Visual Field," *Journal of Experimental Psychology* 38 (December 1948): 603–14.

position. Subjects who did not or were unable to place the rod in a vertical position, relying more on the frame than on their own bodily and postural cues in positioning the rod, were labeled "field dependent." Witkin concluded that field dependence indicated a global, less differentiated mode of perception, whereas field independence was a more analytical approach that overcame misleading background cues in the stimulus field. Most significant was the apparent difference between men and women, with women tending to be significantly more field dependent than men.[8]

Considerable controversy surrounds Witkin's claim that field dependence is related to a larger constellation of personality attributes and analytical abilities.[9] Personality traits such as passivity, dependence, and conformity have been linked to field dependence as a perceptual style.[10] The empirical basis of these links has been recently reexamined by researchers in the psychology of women.[11] Most of the controversy focuses on the social significance of small but statistically significant sex differences and on Witkin's claims of a relationship between spatial abilities and other personality attributes and analytical abilities. The critiques of his work are limited, for the most part, to methodological problems, for example, construct validity and generalization from specific findings. Although Helen Block Lewis, a coinvestigator of Witkin's, has offered a feminist interpretation of sex differences in perception, that is, social explanations for women's greater field dependence,[12] she does not challenge the premises of Witkin's research nor his specific findings.[13]

---

[8] H. A. Witkin, "Sex Differences in Perception," *Transactions of New York Academy of Science* 12, no. 1 (November 1949): 25; H. A. Witkin, H. B. Lewis, M. Hertzman, K. Machover, P. B. Meissner, and S. Wagner, *Personality through Perception* (New York: John Wiley & Sons, 1954), 154.

[9] Maccoby and Jacklin, 104; J. Sherman, *Sex-related Cognitive Differences* (Springfield, Ill.: C. C. Thomas, 1978).

[10] H. Young, "A Test of Witkin's Field-Dependence Hypothesis," *Journal of Abnormal Social Psychology* 59 (September 1959): 188–92; Witkin et al., *Psychological Differentiation* (New York: John Wiley and Sons, 1962); C. Pitblado, "Orientation Bias in the Rod-and-Frame Test," *Perceptual and Motor Skills* 44 (June 1977): 891–900.

[11] Maccoby and Jacklin, 129; J. Levy, "Yes, Virginia, There Is a Difference: Sex Differences in Human Brain Assymetry and in Psychology," *L.S.B. Leakey Foundation News* 20 (Fall 1981): 3, 12–13.

[12] Helen B. Lewis, *Psychic War in Men and Women* (New York: New York University Press, 1976).

[13] Ibid. Lewis places the problem of sex roles and sex differences in psychological differentiation in the context of changing modes of production. She argues that capitalism promotes the division between an affective, private world of family life where dependency needs are permissably gratified and an objectified, exploitive world of work. The former world, with which women are primarily identified, propels women toward field dependence; the latter world, into which men are more consistently drawn, promotes field independence. Lewis also presents a persuasive analysis of the interdependence of internal processes, i.e., perceptual, cognitive, and emotional functioning, on the one hand, and internal and external reality, on the other. But she overstates the congruities within and between these various

Gender emerged as a specific theme of Witkin's research during the late 1940s and 1950s, but his early perceptual research did not explicitly focus on sex differences. His early studies, undertaken in 1942 and supported by a grant from the Civil Aeronautics Administration, were designed to identify problems of spatial orientation and visual perception in the training of airplane pilots. Thus, there was a practical aim relevant to the war effort that guided these early studies. Witkin and coinvestigator Asch shared a philosophical interest, however, in the dependency of the "ego" or "self" on the perceptual field. They were interested in challenging the notion that the self was an autonomous agent, inherently in opposition to the social world. In summarizing, retrospectively, the philosophical intent behind the early perceptual research, Asch states: "The usual way of explaining the limited operation of self-centeredness is to refer to the restrictions imposed by social demands or to the curbing of the egocentrism of each by the ego-centrism of all. We have attempted to show that *the ego is not fundamentally ego-centered.* The ego is not dedicated solely to its own enhancement. It needs and wants to be concerned with its surroundings, to bind itself to others, and to work with them."[14]

While the term "field dependence" was not introduced into the literature until 1954, Asch's description of this perceptual phenomenon suggests that, in the early research, a positive value was placed on "field dependence" or, in Asch's terms, field "relatedness." However, during the postwar years, Witkin moved away from Asch in his theoretical interests, and his interpretations of perceptual phenomena took on a more conservative cast than those of Asch. Witkin turned away from the issue of the field's problematic nature and from the Gestalt emphasis on general human tendencies to *depend* on the field to focus instead on personality factors and individual differences in the ability to overcome the field and to perceive the "upright position."

In this new postwar emphasis on personality factors in perception, gender emerged as a central theme in Witkin's research. In the 1947–53 studies, reported in detail in *Personality through Perception*, Witkin pursued the relationship between personality differences and perceptual abilities. Among other research questions, he asked: "In what ways do men and women differ in perception, and are those differences related to differences in personality? Are the perceptual characteristics of women and men related to personality characteristics more commonly found within each

---

dimensions of experience. It is important to recognize differentiating tendencies in male and female personality development which correspond to the structure of the social world without overstating or reifying these tendencies. Women are not wholly dependent, along all dimensions of experience, nor are men wholly independent.

[14] S. E. Asch, *Social Psychology* (New York: Prentice-Hall, Inc., 1952), 320.

sex? Are there sex differences in perception at all ages or are these differences first manifested at a particular stage of development?"[15]

Witkin's new focus on sex differences during the late 1940s and 1950s took place during an important watershed in American history, one which shaped the content and growing influence of his work. During World War II, prior to Witkin's research on sex differences, large numbers of married women entered the American labor force. In 1943, the War Manpower Commission campaigned to draw women into traditionally male occupations such as welding, riveting, inspecting, and other industrial work.[16] Researchers and policymakers agreed that, when services such as child care were provided, women were as effective in these jobs as men.[17] But even though the war effort redefined and expanded job opportunities for women, propaganda all throughout World War II emphasized that women were working only temporarily, until the war was won, after which a more natural division of labor between the sexes would be restored.[18]

This belief in natural sex differences became increasingly important in the United States in the postwar period as public support for women in the work force shifted to support for the "domestic mystique."[19] As men returned from the war to resume their jobs and women workers were displaced, a renewed emphasis on enduring and essential differences between the sexes appeared in popular literature.[20] The contradiction between the belief in biological sex difference and the presence of women in traditionally men's jobs during the war could be reconciled with the caveat that, though one might learn to overcome natural differences, those differences were deeply fixed and enduring. This conflict—between the recognition of variability in women's roles and the assertion of polarized natural differences between men and women—also appears in Witkin's work.

Witkin was the first investigator to study sex differences in perception, emphasizing "the importance of knowing about sex differences in this area."[21] Though his initial research on sex differences in perception in 1949 was limited to technical aspects of perception, his results nonetheless provided a scientific rationale for the exclusion of women from industrial

---

[15] Witkin et al., 12.

[16] R. Baxandall, L. Gordon, and S. Riverby, *America's Working Women* (New York: Vintage Books, 1976), 284.

[17] Ibid., 291.

[18] K. Anderson, *Wartime Women: Sex Roles, Family Relations and the Status of Women during World War II* (Westport, Conn.: Greenwood Press, 1981), 59, 161; S. M. Hartmann, *The Home Front and Beyond: American Women in the 1940s* (Boston: Twayne Press, 1982), 23.

[19] B. Friedan, *The Feminine Mystique* (New York: W. W. Norton & Co., 1963), 44.

[20] B. Ehrenreich and D. English, *For Her Own Good* (New York: Doubleday & Co., 1978), 220–21; Hartmann, 169.

[21] Witkin (n. 8 above), 25.

jobs after the war because perceptual abilities are closely related to technical job skills.

Witkin did not necessarily condone this social application of field-dependence research, however. Coinvestigator Lewis maintains that Witkin did not believe initially that males and females would differ significantly in their performance.[22] She says that she and other members of the research team were concerned about the possible political uses of their findings, fearful of reporting sex differences that could be used politically against women in the postwar period. Witkin's emphasis on learned behavior and adaptation in his initial reporting of sex differences in 1949 may have been a concession to their concerns: "With continued testing under this condition, however, women became adapted to the unstable field and, in time, were able to do considerably better. Thus, when confronted with unstable surroundings, women are initially made much more unsteady than men, although they are eventually able to come to terms with this instability."[23]

In reporting findings of the studies undertaken from 1947 to 1953, Witkin noted women's capacity for adaptation, but the central theoretical focus was on passive submission and active coping as bipolar traits (i.e., the more the presence of one tendency, the less the capacity for the opposing tendency) associated with sex differences. Active coping, the central personality characteristic associated with males, meant the ability to function with "relatively little support from the environment."[24] Witkin concluded that "women, more often than men, passively accept a new visual framework 'as is,' without any effort or active analysis of it"[25] and, at the same time, women tend to give more variable performances than do men under different conditions.[26]

More recently, researchers have countered that Witkin's method resulted in overstating the frequency of field dependence by labeling as field dependent both those persons who respond consistently to the frame as a cue and those who respond inconsistently.[27] Some critics of trait theories have argued that individuals who are highly variable in their responses may have a "highly refined discriminative facility" in the ability to respond to subtle differences in situations.[28] These findings suggest that women's variable responses could have been interpreted differently by Witkin,

---

[22] H. B. Lewis, personal communication, May 1984.
[23] Witkin, 25.
[24] Witkin et al. (n. 8 above), 467.
[25] Ibid., 482.
[26] Ibid., 465.
[27] H. Nyborg and B. Isaksen, "A Method for Analyzing Performance in the Rod-and-Frame Test," *Scandinavian Journal of Psychology* 15, no. 2 (1974): 124–26.
[28] D. Bem and A. Allen, "On Predicting Some of the People Some of the Time: The Search for Cross-situational Consistencies in Behavior," *Psychological Review* 81 (November 1974): 517.

Haaken / FIELD DEPENDENCE RESEARCH

who concluded that "as a general rule" women are more field dependent than men.

I would suggest that Witkin overinterpreted his findings in a direction that was consistent with prevailing stereotypes of women during a postwar shift in ideas about essential differences between the sexes. Congruent with this shift, Witkin began to emphasize "enduring sets" (personality traits) in the structuring of perceptual tasks in contrast to the work of previous Gestalt theorists who stressed situational or transitory factors. Men, according to Witkin, consistently and enduringly exert control over the perceptual field, whereas women respond in a more variable and task-dependent way and so must have greater field dependence than men.[29] While Witkin concluded that "awareness of the body as a separate entity, independent of the surroundings, has progressed further in men than women," he noted that "when the situation makes it easy or necessary to utilize bodily experiences in performing the required task, they (women) are able to do so about as effectively as men."[30] In other words, men more readily drew on internal bodily cues to orient themselves in a destabilizing perceptual situation, but women could also draw on bodily cues when the task *required* them to do so. Historical disjunctures in what was "required" of women by social organizations, then, were reconciled with presumed substrative differences between the sexes.

The social assumptions that were embedded in Witkin's research are also evident in the naming of the phenomenon. In a society that valued independence and individual autonomy, field dependence had negative connotations. The phrase "inability to separate a stimulus from its embedding context" could have been interpreted positively to mean that women have greater sensitivity to the embedding context as they make judgments about a stimulus. During the postwar years, as women's productive capabilities were devalued and as exaggerated sex roles gained importance, field independence emerged as a masculine virtue, a decisively more desirable trait than field dependence. Then, in the 1970s, when the values attached to gender differences were called into question by feminists, Witkin began to stress the positive capabilities associated with field dependence, that is, that field-dependent individuals have a greater capacity for interpreting social cues than do field-independent individuals.[31]

The ideological context of Witkin's research extended, too, to Witkin's Gestalt predecessors, who fled Germany to escape political persecution and derived their research questions from their attempts to understand the rise of authoritarianism. In contrast, American psychologists pursued re-

---

[29] Witkin et al., 465.
[30] Ibid., 169, 171.
[31] H. A. Witkin, D. R. Goodenough, and P. K. Oltman, "Psychological Differentiation: Current Status," *Journal of Personality and Social Psychology* 37 (July 1979): 1127–45.

search problems related to U.S. military activity during and after World War II.³² Perceptual research throughout the war was tied to military needs, for example, to problems of detecting camouflage or evaluating a terrain upon which a landing must be made.³³ During the postwar years, Witkin continued his research with funding from the Office of Naval Research. Like so many psychologists whose research activities were sponsored by military-related programs,³⁴ Witkin was influenced by program policies that encouraged quantitative, clinically based research and refinement of assessment tools. The military funded research, for instance, to develop scales for selecting recruits for specific kinds of military training.³⁵ The emphasis on testing and measurement gave psychology greater scientific and social legitimacy as a part of the effort to prepare the armed forces for the defense of American interests abroad and for maintaining peace at home.

While psychologists may not have endorsed these applications of testing, there was a heady confidence after the war in the predictive power and social utility of psychological tests. As Zigler noted in his 1963 review of Witkin's research, the promise was great: "If valid, such a typology (field dependence/independence) would be of great value. It would be marvelously efficient to administer a few simple perceptual tests and then be able to predict with a respectable degree of confidence, problem-solving behavior, impulse control, major psychological defenses and cognitive controls, activity level, attitudes towards and interactions with other persons, as well as the types of pathology to which [an individual] is susceptible."³⁶

Governmental funding of training programs and research did not dictate specific research findings, but it did restrict the kinds of questions that could be pursued and the scope of the inquiry, that is, how much social reality could be called into question. Even though Witkin expanded the focus of his early research on visual perception to include a broader range of psychological factors, he was predominantly concerned with the organization of the internal psychological world. While recognizing the importance of the content of human experience as a source of variance within his typological groups—what people "wanted, were in conflict about, became angry over, believed in, as well as the life themes that ran through their histories"³⁷—he never focused on this as important to his research in-

---

³² D. Bernstein and M. Nietzel, *Introduction to Clinical Psychology* (New York: McGraw-Hill Book Co., 1980), 50–51.
³³ G. Murphy, "Introduction," in Witkin et al., *Personality through Perception* (n. 8 above), xvii.
³⁴ Birke (n. 6 above), 91–92.
³⁵ Bernstein and Nietzel, 50–51.
³⁶ Edward Zigler, "A Measure in Search of a Theory?" *Contemporary Psychology* 8 (1963): 133.
³⁷ Witkin et al., *Personality through Perception*, 8.

terests. This dissociation of personality structure from the content of lived experience contributed to the reification of both the field dependence-independence construct and psychological sex differences because the dissociation precludes recognition of the active, motivated subject and the dynamic tension between an inner world and an outer reality.

In a general way, Witkin's studies were concerned with problems of orientation and control in a disorienting world. In the experimental setting, the extent to which people could overcome the disorientation created by the tilted field—remaining faithful to internal cues that determined the upright position—was of central importance. The experiment itself, then, is a metaphor for the disorientation of the postwar period—a disorientation or confusion experienced with particular acuity by the socialists and left-wing intellectuals with whom Witkin associated.

A number of historians have described the public's preoccupation with stability following the destabilizing decades of the Depression and World War II.[38] But the combined impact of the Holocaust and Hiroshima created a particular despair and confusion for radicals as the political involvement of the Left declined.[39] Dorothy Dinnerstein, who worked closely with members of Witkin's research group, described it as a state of moral shock and "anesthesia" that radicals of her generation experienced after the war and into the 1950s. Many withdrew from large-scale social concerns and turned to more narrowly defined, psychological realities. According to Dinnerstein, "in these people, whose adolescence and youth had spanned the mid-thirties to mid-forties, capacities for connectedness—which in the preceding period had embraced historic considerations and a temporally and spatially extended human scene—were now focused on a world recreated in miniature."[40]

Witkin's research emphasized that it was possible to assert individual control over a confusing world. The field-independent person accomplished this by not "yielding" to distracting and regressive external cues. Witkin's interest in the individual's resources, and the implicit devaluing of relatedness, represented a very different stance from Asch's more pessimistic view of the possibilities for individual control over a disorienting world. Asch believed that the "contradictory and threatening world" in which people find themselves "takes a toll on the individual's very ability to establish and maintain contact with reality."[41]

---

[38] See discussion of this theme in Linda Gordon, *Woman's Body, Woman's Right* (New York: Penguin Books, 1977), 356–62; Stuart Ewen, *Captains of Consciousness* (New York: McGraw-Hill Book Co., 1976), 206; Stanley Aronowitz, *False Promises* (New York: McGraw-Hill Book Co., 1973), chap. 7.

[39] Christopher Lasch, *The Minimal Self* (New York: W. W. Norton & Co., 1984), chap. 7.

[40] Dorothy Dinnerstein, *The Mermaid and the Minotaur* (New York: Harper & Row, 1976), 258–62, esp. 261.

[41] Asch (n. 14 above), 604.

In contrast to Witkin, Asch saw the experiments as a metaphor for the individual's struggles in the social world.

Gestalt influences

Asch maintained his intellectual and political commitment to those issues that had informed and motivated the research base from which Witkin's work diverged. While Witkin's Gestalt predecessors did not focus on sex differences, their work suggests an interpretation of field dependence that emphasizes the social relational basis of perception.

Max Wertheimer, the intellectual leader of the German Gestalt movement, whose work guided Witkin's initial thinking, also conducted military-sponsored research early in his career. During World War I, his research in Germany focused on listening devices for submarines and harbor fortifications.[42] Unlike Witkin, whose research ties to the military continued harmoniously beyond the war years, Wertheimer had to carry on his research in a country suffering from postwar economic and political instability. Indeed, Wertheimer and Wolfgang Köhler, two of the major Gestalt theorists, came into growing conflict with the Nazi government and fled to the United States during the 1930s.[43]

Wertheimer's early experimental interest in "apparent motion" or illusions of movement—beginning in 1912—was congruent with his critique of industrial society. He was deeply concerned about prevailing notions of the nature and possibilities of human freedom and, in particular, about liberal thinkers who equated rapid change with progress and confused "freedom of business enterprise" with "real mutual freedom."[44] In the classic mirror experiment on which Witkin's work was based, Wertheimer concluded that people tended initially to "perceive the scene as tilted, but with continued inspection came gradually to regard it as upright and to see everything within it as normal."[45] This early perceptual research, then, focused on problematic aspects of perception, specifically the tendency to adapt to or perceive as "normal" a skewed world.

As important figures in left-wing German academia, Wertheimer and Kohler were aware of the politically conservative implications of restricting psychological research to observable phenomena.[46] Their own research

---

[42] Duane Schultz, *A History of Modern Psychology* (New York: Academic Press, 1969), 245.

[43] Ibid.

[44] M. Wertheimer, "On the Concept of Democracy" (1937), in *Documents of Gestalt Psychology*, ed. M. Henle (Berkeley: University of California Press, 1961), 50.

[45] Witkin et al., *Personality through Perception* (n. 8 above), 4.

[46] M. Leichtman, "Gestalt Theory and the Revolt against Positivism," in Buss, ed. (n. 1 above), 59.

examined the human capabilities that were restricted or diminished under particular social conditions. The capacity of human beings to recover meaning and coherence in a fragmenting, destabilizing environment was central to their philosophical and experimental interests. Human beings, they claimed, are bound by the requirements of existing conditions yet are capable of envisioning new possibilities and new meanings within a given reality.[47]

While he was influenced directly by Wertheimer's work on organizing factors in perception, Witkin was part of the "New Look" movement in experimental psychology. This approach attempted to demonstrate the importance of personality factors and unconscious processes in structuring the perceptual field.[48] Witkin was critical of the Gestalt theorists' exclusive concern with field factors and their neglect of developmental and motivational processes in structuring perception. "The individual is not 'subservient' to the field to the extent conceived in Gestalt theory; he is not a passive mirror-like recorder upon whom the field impresses itself, but an active agent who contributes to the progress and outcome of the act of perceiving."[49]

Witkin's conception of the self as active agent was an important corrective to theoretical tendencies within psychology to view humans as entirely governed by situational factors. But he attempted to resolve the conflict between subjective and objective factors by turning to psychoanalytic theory and its emphasis on the individual and early childhood as the primary context for understanding subjective experience. Indeed, his conception of the perceptual field was a narrowly defined configuration of stimuli, dissociated from social meaning.

While Witkin moved toward psychoanalysis in the 1950s, focusing on the primacy of the internal world in structuring outer reality, his early coinvestigator, Solomon Asch, pursued the relationship between independence, conformity, and the social world. Asch argued that relations with others are the basis of ego development and independence, not an inherent constraint on these capacities. This was the premise behind his critiques of classical psychoanalysis—which posited a fundamental opposition between the individual and society—and of bourgeois individualism and capitalism as an economic system.[50]

---

[47] See M. Wertheimer, "Some Problems in the Theory of Ethics" (1935), in Henle, ed. (n. 44 above), 39; and "On the Concept of Democracy," 51; W. Köhler, *The Place of Value in a World of Facts* (New York: Liveright Publishing Corp., 1938), 40.

[48] D. Goodenough, "History of the Field Dependence Construct," in *Field Dependence in Psychological Theory, Research and Application*, ed. M. Bertini, L. Pizzamiglio, and S. Wagner (Hillsdale, N.J.: Lawrence Erlbaum Associates, 1986), 6.

[49] Witkin et al., *Personality through Perception*, 497.

[50] Asch (n. 14 above), 313–16.

In discussing the social basis of psychological phenomena, Asch used examples from perceptual research to explain how people respond defensively to social conflict. For example, he pointed out that some individuals respond to social movements that call for equality (e.g., the early civil rights movement) with "efforts to keep parts of the field out of awareness or out of focus." Other individuals withdraw altogether from social conflict, reasserting conservative views of the past in order to "maintain clear lines in the field," avoiding "the danger of disorientation by clinging to the frame of reference [they] happen to have and resisting any change."[51]

Asch stressed the possibilities for human resistance to the prevailing socially constructed field, asserting that psychology "has almost exclusively stressed the slavish submission of individuals to group forces, has neglected to inquire into their possibilities for independence and for productive relations with the human environment, and has virtually denied the capacity of men under certain conditions to rise above group passion and prejudice."[52] If individualism meant that self-realization was achieved in contradistinction and opposition to the group, then, alternately, to "submerge" oneself in the group was to regress. In challenging a view of independence and conformity based on fear of group forces, Asch focused on social relational processes, emphasizing the importance of allies in resisting group pressures. The solitary individual was more likely than the social one to yield to an "oppressive majority."[53] Asch's work suggests that the individual is most vulnerable to persuasion when her or his independence is based on social isolation. Because we are by nature social beings, true autonomy and independence can be sustained only in a social context that supports and nurtures those capacities.

Witkin's asocial conception of field independence is in sharp contrast to the concepts of the individual's relationship to social context that were held by his Gestalt predecessors and his early coinvestigator. For Witkin, field independence became a stable, cross-situational human trait, the result of a psychology that had itself dissociated from the real world of political struggle. Asch's critical analysis of social psychology could have provided a basis for interpretations of sex differences in field-dependence research that challenged, rather than reinforced, normative assumptions about gender and dependence. One implication of Asch's analysis, for instance, is that field independence is not so much a masculine trait as it is a masculine illusion. Contemporary feminist psychoanalytic theorists observe that men often experience dependency longings as frightening and overwhelming

---

[51] Ibid., 604–5.
[52] S. E. Asch, "Group Pressure and Modification of Judgements" (1951), in Henle, ed. (n. 44 above), 233.
[53] Ibid., 213.

and, consequently, develop defensively a kind of pseudo-independence based on maintaining emotional distance from others.[54]

Psychoanalytic theory and the research field

The studies undertaken by Witkin from 1947 to 1953 were ambitious. In his theoretical formulations, Witkin combined psychoanalytic assumptions about motivational processes and Gestalt ideas about perceptual organization. He attempted to demonstrate the consistency of human perception and that personality dynamics determined perceptions of physical properties of the world just as they determined social situations.[55] Hence, he turned to the concept of differentiation to formulate a metapsychological bridge from Gestalt theory to psychoanalytic theory.[56]

Psychoanalytic theory posited that human development is a process of differentiation. According to Freud, the human infant exists in an undifferentiated state in which no boundaries are experienced between the self and others, between inner and outer reality.[57] External stimuli are assimilated into the internal rhythms of the infant's world. This is the stage of primary narcissism during which the infant is one with the object of its dependency. As the infant develops the conceptual capacity to differentiate between "me" and "not me," she or he experiences the ontological anxiety associated with separateness. This experience of anxiety stimulates ego development, however, as the child progressively internalizes the regulatory functions of caretakers. The ego emerges as an integrative, self-regulating capacity within the self.

For Witkin, field-independence experiments provided operational criteria for assessing ego strength. To make this link, subjects' scores on spatial orientation tasks were correlated with various measures of personality organization. The latter included projective tests (Rorschach and Thematic Apperception Test) and ratings based on clinical interviews.

The reliance on internal bodily cues in overcoming a distorted perceptual field indicated highly differentiated body image and ego boundaries. Joined to this conception of ego boundaries was Witkin's emphasis on the capacity for regression, defined as the ability to defend against distracting external and internal stimuli.

---

[54] See Nancy Chodorow, *The Reproduction of Mothering* (Berkeley: University of California Press, 1978); and Dinnerstein.

[55] Witkin et al., *Personality through Perception*, 502.

[56] I have limited the scope of my treatment of psychoanalysis since the social history of psychoanalysis has been more extensively documented and discussed than that of Gestalt theory.

[57] S. Freud, "On Narcissism: An Introduction," in *Standard Edition* (1914; 1937), 14:67–102; and *New Introductory Lectures on Psychoanalysis* (New York: W. W. Norton & Co., 1933), 93.

Witkin's conception of field independence had specific political implications. Field independence was presented as the higher form of development, indicating higher levels of differentiation between self and environment. Independence represented a reliance on "internal frames of reference" and a concomitant freedom from environmental influence. Field-dependent people, in contrast, "tend to be submissive to authority, to require environmental support, to deny inner events—a mechanism of defense especially characteristic of children—to have difficulty in impulse control and to make childish drawings of the human figure. The presence of such characteristics seems to suggest an 'arrest' in progress toward emotional maturity."[58]

In a period of repressive anticommunism, Witkin could argue to a receptive audience that it was more mature to be self-reliant and emotionally distant from the group. Of course, defending independent thought was an important emphasis of academics and intellectuals during the McCarthy era, particularly for the Leftists with whom Witkin associated. But Witkin's emphasis on independence as an individual trait and his assumption that the individual and the collective were inherent opposites made it possible for his work to be easily assimilated into conventional thought.

It was in this context, then, that Witkin's clinical data were collected. Inconsistencies and overinterpreted materials are evident in his psychoanalytically derived clinical data, that is, responses to projective tests and interview questions. The assumptions embedded in the research procedures, as well as the complexity of the phenomena under investigation, are especially apparent in the clinical data. They are more effectively concealed in the scientific or experimental data and in Witkin's final conclusions. The clinical data, by their phenomenological nature, offer fuller descriptive accounts of human experience than do the scientific data and so offer more opportunity to identify biases in clinical interpretation.

One area of ambiguity in Witkin's clinical data concerns the defensive nature of field independence. The case histories reported in 1954 suggest that field-independent subjects exhibited no less conflict in relation to dependency issues than did field-dependent subjects.[59] The primary difference was in the capacity for repression, mastery, and control. Outer reality was treated by Witkin as a projective field, that is, as a vehicle for the expression of internal conflict rather than as a source of such conflict for both independent and dependent subjects. Witkin did not ask what about the nature of the social world contributed to the apparent pervasiveness of dependence-independence conflicts.

Witkin's interpretation of his clinical data was also influenced by what

---

[58] Witkin et al., *Personality through Perception* (n. 8 above), 470.
[59] Ibid., 312–24.

Haaken / FIELD DEPENDENCE RESEARCH

we now see as problematic views of gender. Accepting the psychoanalytic account of gender development current in the 1950s, Witkin interpreted male and female strivings differently. In the clinical examples Witkin published, the field-independent female subject's attempts at control were described less favorably than those of her male counterpart. While the field-independent male was able to "maintain integration and control while undergoing great struggles,"[60] the field-independent female was described as self-assured, narcissistic, with "sadistic tendencies—especially toward men."[61] She took "considerable pleasure in exerting her power" while being "not at all aware of how deeply frightened she is of the 'surrender' of power which accepting a man represented to her."[62] The female field-dependent subject exhibited conflicts similar to those shown by males, but she defended herself against them less effectively: "Her penis envy seems only to increase her sexual confusion and guilt." Responses to Thematic Apperception Test (TAT) cards revealed that "the sexual scene was conceived of in terms of rape and death." The response to another TAT card: "The wife feels immobilized and must accept punishment, which, in this scene, is a form of blackmail."[63]

Once again, the outer world is conceived of largely as a projective field. Witkin did acknowledge the influence of socially constructed "sexual roles" in the acquisition of field dependence, concluding that "the more protected existence that is socially acceptable for women obviously places fewer demands on their functioning."[64] A more plausible interpretation of the clinical accounts described above would be that the women felt victimized, not protected, by men.

While acknowledging that cultural factors did influence gender development, Witkin emphasized biological factors in sex differences and personality development. He treated "penis envy" as an inevitable developmental "disappointment" for females that resulted in a "permanent sense of inferiority" and a diminished capacity for active mastery over the environment.[65] A stance more consistent with Freud's general methodology (the pursuit of the conflictual experiences that underlie symbolic representations) would have been that the phallus symbolizes domination and male privilege in patriarchal societies. Women both envy and resent what the phallus socially signifies. This stance, articulated by a few leading psychoanalysts in the 1940s and 1950s such as Clara Thompson,[66] had very

[60] Ibid., 287.
[61] Ibid., 298.
[62] Ibid., 299.
[63] Ibid., 296.
[64] Ibid., 487.
[65] Ibid., 489.
[66] C. Thompson, "Cultural Pressures in the Psychology of Women," *Psychiatry* 5, no. 3 (August 1942): 331–39, and "Penis Envy in Women," *Psychiatry* 6, no. 2 (May 1943): 123–25

little impact on psychoanalytic thought in the postwar period. The reworking of psychoanalysis to take into account the social construction of gender and gender-based inequality emerged with more force and cohesion as a response to the women's movement in the 1970s.

The experimental context

Field independence, as a concept, idealizes individuality and the possibilities for individual control—particularly male control—over the environment. Specifically, it privileges the ability to attend to and control discrete events while ignoring or overcoming the context. Relatedly, field independence also describes the experimenter's self-conception and epistemological approach to the world. His or her research world is divided into discrete independent and dependent variables that can be studied apart from the context in which they occur normally. In the classical model of experimental design, the background of individual experience is viewed as something to be overcome—as a source of error variance. The relationship between the observer-scientist and the subject is understood in terms of the ability of the former to control the conditions of the latter's responses. At the same time, there has been a strong tendency in experimental psychology to deny evidence that the experimenter does influence her or his subject beyond the specific variables under investigation.[67] While Robert Rosenthal's research in the 1960s, demonstrating the effects of the experimenter's unconscious bias on research outcomes, casts doubt on the notion of experimental objectivity,[68] experimental psychologists have generally viewed such effects as idiosyncratic and as simply requiring more careful attention to technical aspects of research design.

Obviously, Witkin could not, years earlier, have known about these findings, but he was aware of the role of ego defenses in field independence, though he did not extend this understanding to the experimental field, that is, the psychodynamic meaning of the experiment and the experimenter's relation to the subject. Witkin viewed field independence as a higher-level response, developmentally, than field dependence, but he also acknowledged that some extremely field-independent people distorted reality in the use of defensive operations.[69] Certain cues were recognized by field-independent subjects while others were denied—particularly social and emotional cues. In emphasizing the problematic

---

[67] H. Gadlin and G. Ingle, "Through the One-Way Mirror: The Limits of Experimental Self-Reflection," *American Psychologist* 10 (October 1975): 1003–9.
[68] R. Rosenthal, *Experimenter Bias in Behavioral Research* (New York: Appleton-Century-Crofts, 1966).
[69] Witkin et al., *Personality through Perception*, 470.

aspects of masculine personality tendencies, coinvestigator Lewis[70] has more recently stressed the commonalities between field independence and obsessive compulsive neurosis and paranoia. Defenses such as emotional isolation, obsessive attention to detail, and overvaluation of control dominate responses to the world in both field independence and these psychopathological conditions.

In the design and interpretations of the research setting, Witkin became a perpetuator of his own field-independent ideology by not attending to the social and emotional properties of the experimental field. Given his psychoanalytic perspective, one would expect the phenomenology of the field to include transference and countertransference dimensions (i.e., the emotional connections between experimenter and subject) of the experimental setting as well as of the symbolic meaning of the stimulus materials. For the rod-and-frame test, which Witkin concluded to be the most reliable measure of field dependence, the subject enters a totally darkened room with the experimenter and is asked to sit in a reclining or upright position. She or he is then asked to make judgments in a perceptual task, that is, to locate the vertical position of an illuminated rod placed in a tilted illuminated frame. All of this takes place in the dark with the subject in a somewhat vulnerable position with a stranger.

While Witkin "ran subjects" himself, along with his male and female colleagues,[71] the sex of the experimenters is perhaps less crucial, psychoanalytically, than their shared belief in the predictive value of these experiments and their failure to recognize the ramifications of subjects' unconscious associations with the configuration of stimuli as a whole. This particular experimental situation could have evocative social meaning for female subjects. The experimental setting might have elicited associations with potential danger (the completely darkened room) and loss of control, and responses to the rod-and-frame task would be mediated by such social meaning. The stimulus materials and experimental task could have suggested, on an unconscious level, a reenactment of women's position in a patriarchal society; they were asked to orient themselves in relation to the phallus, the illuminated rod.

It has been demonstrated that anxiety and stress do influence responses to the rod-and-frame task,[72] a finding anticipated by Karen Machover, one of Witkin's coinvestigators. Machover suggested during the 1947–53 studies that a "dark room effect" might mediate the sex differences in their

---

[70] Lewis (n. 12 above), 184.
[71] H. B. Lewis, personal communication, March 1986.
[72] F. Gross, "The Role of Set in Perception of the Upright," *Journal of Personality* 27 (March 1959): 95–103; P. Quinlan and S. Blatt, "Field Articulation and Performance under Stress: Differential Predictions in Surgical and Psychiatric Nursing Training," *Journal of Consulting and Clinical Psychology* 39 (December 1972): 517.

findings.[73] However, Lewis said that this hypothesis was not pursued because it did not account for the correlations of the rod-and-frame scores with scores from other perceptual tests.[74] Continued exploration of field factors, beyond technical properties of the immediate task, was clearly not part of the research plan.

The dissociation of the task from its representational correspondence to the external world is a direct result of this field-independent orientation. Some critics of the experimental method have raised questions about whether laboratory conditions really do correspond to the conditions of "real life."[75] Others have argued that experimental tasks sometimes elicit different responses in males and females because of the sex role dimensions of the task rather than the inferred psychological attribute.[76] For example, Sheridan Fenwick Naditch found that when female subjects were told that the experiment was a test of empathy and a human figure was substituted for the rod, they scored significantly higher on field independence than when they were asked to judge a rod.[77] This is consistent with Lewis's thesis that, in capitalist societies, men are encouraged to be more "thing-oriented" and to view people and objects interchangeably, while women are more "people-oriented."[78] Witkin's claim that the physical properties of the world are perceived essentially in the same manner as social situations is consistent with this male point of view.

There is some evidence that Witkin was sensitive to the tendency in experimental psychology to overobjectify and oversimplify human phenomena. In the final chapter of *Personality through Perception*, he issues a caveat concerning the conclusions to be drawn from the reported findings: "While simplification of conditions is necessary, great care must be exercised in applying to nature itself in generalizing from these findings. The omission of critical elements of lived experience may result in misrepresenting phenomena."[79]

Throughout the course of his extensive research career, Witkin was not so much overinvested in a methodological stance as he was overinvested in his construct. Witkin did move from the narrowly circumscribed problems of experimental comparative (animal) psychology in the 1930s, that is,

[73] H. B. Lewis, personal communication, March 1986.
[74] Lewis was referring here to the Tilting-Room-Tilting-Chair Test and the Embedded-Figure Test, both tests of visual perception that were included in the studies published in 1954.
[75] Gadlin and Ingle (n. 67 above), 1003.
[76] I. Frieze, J. Parsons, P. Johnson, D. Ruble, and G. Zellman, *Women and Sex Roles: A Social Psychological Perspective* (New York: W. W. Norton & Co., 1975), 19.
[77] S. Sheridan Fenwick Naditch, "Effect of Experimental Artifact on Sex Differences in Field Dependence," (Ph.D. diss., Cornell University, 1975).
[78] Lewis (n. 12 above), 105.
[79] Witkin et al., *Personality through Perception* (n. 8 above), 507.

maze learning in rats, to increasingly broader domains of human phenomena and applied research in the 1960s and 1970s, that is, cross-cultural and ecological factors in the acquisition of field dependence. But as he cast his net further and further in search of theoretical and empirical links to field dependence, this construct continued to be the lens through which he organized the phenomenal world and upon which he built his career in psychology. This preoccupation with validating experimentally the field-dependence construct diminished his capacity to understand the meaning of the research for the subjects.

Once Witkin adopted it as a trait, field dependence lost much of its original theoretical meaning and descriptive power. For the early Gestalt theorists, who were the primary influence on Witkin's work, the perceptual field represented both an experimental problem and a metaphorical vehicle for a critique of society. For these theorists, human subjectivity was bound by the "requirements" of the field but contained the potential for conceiving of new possibilities and new arrangements in the field of experience.

Witkin took the most conservative and asocial premise shared by Gestalt theory and psychoanalysis—the idea that human development is a process of progressive differentiation of the self—and elaborated a construct that stressed individual autonomy and the primacy of the internal world in structuring outer reality. In attempting to demonstrate the merits of Gestalt theory and psychoanalysis on this narrowly defined empirical ground, he lost the self-critical and self-conscious dimensions of both perspectives as well as the possibility for broad-based social theorizing in field-dependence research.

Department of Psychology
Portland State University

Part II
Neonatal and Infancy Periods

SEX DIFFERENCES IN THE DEVELOPMENT OF A SEPARATE SENSE OF SELF DURING INFANCY: DIRECTIONS FOR FUTURE RESEARCH

Elizabeth J. Aries and Rose R. Olver
Amherst College

Women have been characterized as having more difficulty than men in developing a separate sense of self. This sex difference is held to have its origins in infancy in the differential response of mothers to sons and daughters. While there is clinical evidence for this sex difference, as yet there is no clear support for it in the experimental literature. In this paper we provide a foundation for future experimental research on the origins in mother-infant interaction of sex differences in the development of a separate sense of self. Using Mahler's description of the separation-individuation process as a general framework, we specify behavioral indicators of differential progress in the development of a separate sense of self at each subphase of separation-individuation and define the particular maternal behaviors relevant to that progress. An examination of existing experimental studies that employ these measures suggests that sex differences in the experience of a separate sense of self begin to emerge in early infancy and that mothers engage in different types of contact with sons and daughters in ways that facilitate the achievement of separation more for boys than for girls. The implications of these findings for future research are discussed.

Societal norms and clinical judgments place high positive value on the ability to function autonomously and objectively (Broverman, Broverman, Clarkson, Rosenkrantz, & Vogel, 1970) yet the establishment of this separate sense of self is more easily achieved by men than by women. Self-definition for adult women has been characterized as embedded in relationships and the emotional responses of others, while self-definition for adult men has been characterized as having more distinct boundaries between self and others (Bardwick, 1971; Douvan, 1972; Douvan & Adelson, 1966; Gilligan,

1977; Gutmann, 1970; Hoffman, 1972). Women tend to experience greater difficulty than men in knowing what they genuinely want or feel apart from what others expect or approve (Wolowitz, 1972). In addition, women depend on the responses of others in developing criteria of worth and competence, while men rely on their own internal standards of judgment (Bardwick & Douvan, 1972; Hoffman, 1972). As a consequence, however, women also have a greater capacity for relatedness, emotional closeness, and boundary flexibility (Surrey, 1983), because their sense of self is "organized around being able to make and then to maintain affiliations and relationships" (Miller, 1976, p. 83). As with most sex differences, what is noted here is not an absolute difference between men and women, but rather overlapping distributions such that, on the average, women have more difficulty than men in experiencing a separate sense of self.

Some provocative arguments have been put forth that this sex difference, manifested in adulthood, has its origins in early infancy in the differential responses of mothers to their sons and daughters.[1] From a psychoanalytic perspective, it has been argued that mothers experience daughters as "more like, and continuous with, themselves" (Chodorow, 1978, p. 166); that they experience "affectively-tuned empathy" more readily with daughters (Jordan, 1983, p. 4); and that there is "a more effortless identification, a smoother communication" with daughters than sons (Dinnerstein, 1976, p. 68). Sons are experienced as a "male opposite," a "sexual other" (Chodorow, 1978, p. 110); with sons there is more "difference and separateness, more of a barrier to be bridged" (Dinnerstein, 1976, p. 68). As a result, girls remain more involved in issues of merging and separation, while boys are pushed out and so develop a "more defensive firming of ego boundaries" (Chodorow, 1978, p. 167).

A second line of argument, emphasizing cognitive factors, is found in the literature on sex role stereotyping. Here it is suggested that noting the child's sex causes a mother to organize "her perceptions of the infant with regard to a wide variety of attributes—ranging from its size to its activity, attractiveness, even its future potential" (Rubin, Provenzano, & Luria, 1974, p. 512). Rubin et al. found that within the first 24 hours postpartum parents make distinctions between newborn male and female infants in keeping with cultural stereotypes of masculinity and femininity even though the sample of male and female infants did not differ in birth length, weight, or Apgar scores. Given the positive value placed on the acquisition of sex role-appropriate behavior (i.e., independence for men, attachment and interpersonal relations for women), it is argued that mothers will modulate their interactions with their children in light of these assumed characteristics and will reinforce differentially the behavior of sons and daughters. It is important to note here that while the psychoanalytic and cognitive arguments derive from different psychological traditions, both suggest the same outcome: differential maternal behavior toward sons and daughters that can be expected to facilitate the separation and individuation of sons and make it more difficult for daughters.[2] Mothers' behavior may result from the simultaneous and consistent influence of both types of factors.

While the psychoanalytic and cognitive arguments for the origins of sex differences in the development of a separate sense of self are intuitively compelling, there is as yet no clear support for these differences in the experimental literature. The widely cited comprehensive review of psychological sex differences by Maccoby and Jacklin (1974), for example, indicates that overall there are few consistent findings about the differential treatment of boys and girls in the early years, or of sex differences in areas of behavior such as attachment and dependency that appear relevant to the development of a separate sense of self. One response to this lack of consistent findings is to argue, as Chodorow (1978) does, that because this literature involves studies which document observable behavior that can be reliably coded and counted, more subtle differences in "nuance, tone and quality" may have been missed. We believe, however, that the problem may not lie in subtlety of behavioral expression, but rather in failure to conceptualize appropriately the sequential nature of the development of a separate sense of self and to specify appropriate child and mother behaviors for measurement within this developmental sequence.

Mahler's work (Mahler, Pine, & Bergman, 1975) on what she terms "the separation-individuation process" is particularly helpful in this regard. While her focus is not on sex differences, both her general description of the behavioral indicators of the sequence of stages in the separation-individuation process and her argument that successful progress through these stages is dependent upon the appropriateness of the mother's behavior at each stage provide a framework within which sex differences can be examined.

The purpose of this paper is to provide a foundation for future experimental research on the origins in mother-infant interaction of sex differences in the development of a separate sense of self.[3] Using Mahler's characterization of the separation-individuation process as a general framework, we will first specify the behaviors of the child at each stage that might serve as indicators of differential progress in the development of a separate sense of self, and second specify the particular maternal behaviors at each stage relevant to that progress. We will discuss the results of experimental studies that employed the behavioral indicators we have defined and that examined subjects whose age range is within a single subphase of the separation-individuation process. This review will enable us to determine the extent of existing experimental support for sex differences during infancy in the development of a separate sense of self and for differential maternal treatment of sons and daughters. Our intent, then, is not to provide a complete review of the literature on sex differences in infancy, but rather to use Mahler's conceptual framework to focus solely on those behaviors of mothers and children that are relevant to the development of a separate sense of self.

INFANT SEX DIFFERENCES IN THE DEVELOPMENT OF A SEPARATE SENSE OF SELF

Mahler holds that the intrapsychic development of self is accompanied by changes in the child's observable behavior. She divides the separation-individuation process into four subphases (differentiation, practicing, rapprochement, and "on the way to libidinal object constancy") "in accordance with the repeatedly observable behavioral referents of that process" (Mahler et al., 1975, p. 39).[4] Mahler thus provides us with a behaviorally referenced description of the development of the sense of self, a framework within which sex differences in the development of a separate sense of self can be considered. We will begin by specifying the behaviors indicative of differential progress in the development of a separate sense of self at each subphase of the separation-individuation process and examining experimental studies that have measured those behaviors.

Differentiation

In Mahler's view, the development of a separate sense of self begins at about 4–5 months, when the child begins to differentiate him/herself from the mother—"from the undifferentiated dual unity within one common boundary" (Mahler, 1975, p. 44) of the preceding symbiotic stage. This differentiation of the child's own from the mother's body is marked at about 6–7 months by the infant's distancing from the mother's body rather than molding to it when held and by engaging in manual, tactile, and visual exploration of her/his own and the mother's face and body.

Mahler's description of infant behavior at differentiation enables us to specify two possible behavioral indicators for sex differences in the experience of a separate sense of self at this subphase. These measures are defined such that a high score is indicative of a greater degree of separateness:

1. amount of distancing initiated by child from mother's body when held
2. amount and intensity of resistance to being closely held.

We have found no studies of children at this stage that use these measures, but Mahler's observation that boys are "more stiffly resistant to hugging and kissing, beyond and even during differentiation" (Mahler et al., 1975, p. 104) suggests that such studies might prove useful in providing evidence for a more separate sense of self in males than in females.

Practicing

The practicing subphase is initiated by the increased locomotor capacity that both permits the child to have a more active role in determining closeness

Separate Sense of Self

and distance to the mother and widens his/her experience of the physical environment. The early practicing phase (7–10 months) begins with the infant's first ability to move physically away from the mother by crawling, paddling, climbing, etc., and the practicing period proper (from 10–12 to 16–18 months) is marked by the ability to walk freely with upright posture. As Mahler sees it, it is not the development of motor skills per se, but rather "the elated investment in the exercise of the autonomous functions, especially motility, to the near exclusion of apparent interest in the mother at times" (Mahler et al., 1975, p. 69) that is the central feature of the practicing period. However, Mahler notes that "during the entire practicing subphase mother continues to be needed as a stable point, a 'home base' to fulfill the need for refueling through physical contact" (Mahler et al., 1975, p. 69), which the child accomplishes by approaching and touching the mother, perhaps leaning against her, or by making contact from a distance through seeing and hearing.

Again, Mahler's description of infant behavior at practicing enables us to specify behavioral indicators for sex differences in the experience of a separate sense of self at this subphase. The first set of measures is defined such that a high score is indicative of greater degrees of separateness:

1. geographic distance from mother while playing
2. amount and intensity of resistance to being closely held and to expressions of physical affection unless self-initiated.

The second set of measures is defined such that a high score is indicative of a lack of separateness:

1. amount of interaction initiated with mother
2. requests for mother's help without previous attempts to solve problem oneself
3. frequency of "refueling"

Several of these measures have been useful in experimental studies with children in the age range of the practicing subphase. An examination of the results of these studies reveals evidence that sex differences in the experience of a separate sense of self begin to emerge at practicing. At both 9 and 12 months, girls initiated more interactions with mothers even though mothers were not differentially reinforcing their initiations (Gunnar & Donahue, 1980). At approximately one year, girls stayed in closer proximity to their mothers than boys (Brooks & Lewis, 1974a; Goldberg & Lewis, 1969; Klein & Durefee, 1978); girls showed a greater frequency of returns to their mothers during free play (Goldberg & Lewis, 1969; Messer & Lewis, 1972); girls showed more positive involvement with mothers (Clarke-Stewart, 1973); and girls showed a greater frequency of touching and looking at their mothers (Brooks & Lewis, 1974a; Goldberg & Lewis, 1969; Messer & Lewis, 1972). While all these studies did not report sex differences on all measures, a consistent pattern does emerge.

There are also studies which found no sex differences in proximity to the mother during the practicing subphase when the child is in a low-stress free play situation (Ainsworth & Bell, 1970; Coates, Anderson, & Hartup, 1972; Maccoby & Jacklin, 1973; Rheingold & Eckerman, 1969; Rheingold & Samuels, 1969). These findings may be due to the fact that the observation times of free play (unconfounded by the stress produced by presence of a stranger or separation from the mother) used in these studies were too short for sex differences to have emerged in the subjects' behavior. Brooks and Lewis (1974b) found that while there were no sex differences in the first three minutes of play in maintaining proximity and looking at the mother, sex differences did increase over time, and became significant over a 15-minute period. There is also evidence (Goldberg and Lewis, 1969) that at 13 months girls cry and motion for help when faced with a barrier while boys make a more active attempt to get around the barrier, suggesting that at this age boys may have greater self-reliance or confidence in their ability to solve problems on their own.

Rapprochement

The rapprochement subphase (16-24 months) begins with a shift from a relative lack of concern about the mother's presence characteristic of the practicing subphase to seemingly constant concern with the mother's whereabouts and active approach behaviors. The toddler "seems to have an increased need, a wish for mother to share with him every one of his new skills and experiences, as well as a great need for the object's love" (Mahler et al., 1975, pp. 76-77). The most important behavioral sign of this new relating is "the toddler's continual bringing of things to the mother, filling her lap with objects that he has found in his expanding world" indicating "by words, sounds or gestures that he wished her to be interested in his 'findings' and to participate with him in enjoying them" (Mahler et al., 1975, p. 90).

Yet the child is ambivalent, both wishing for reunion with the love object and fearing re-engulfment by it, as is indicated by two patterns of behavior characteristic of this subphase: "shadowing" of mother (incessant watching and following every move of the mother) and darting away from her with the expectation of being chased and swept into her arms. Mahler notes "a more distinct awareness in the child of his own body and its relation to other persons' bodies" (Mahler et al., 1975, p. 91), behaviorally indicated by not liking to be "handled"—resistance to being held in a passive position while being dressed or diapered, and not liking to be hugged or kissed—"unless he was ready for it." Children would want "to 'go see' mother, but not with the intention of staying with her; rather they would pass by her, veer away, and then return to their own occupations" (Mahler et al., 1975, p. 92).

Separate Sense of Self

Mahler's description of behavior at rapprochement suggests a variety of behavioral indicators for sex differences in the experience of a separate sense of self at this subphase. The first set of behavioral indicators is defined such that a high score is indicative of a lack of separateness:

1. amount of "shadowing" of the mother (watching and following every move of the mother)
2. frequency of returns to the mother for physical contact and assistance (which were characteristic of the practicing subphase).

The second set of behavioral indicators is defined such that a high score is indicative of a greater degree of separateness:

1. amount and intensity of resistance to being closely held and to expressions of physical affection unless self-initiated
2. amount of "darting" behavior
3. frequency of soliciting mother's interest in child's findings.

Mahler herself notes the emergence of sex differences during rapprochement, commenting that "the task of becoming a separate individual seemed at this point to be generally more difficult for girls than for boys . . ." (Mahler et al., 1975, p. 106). "In our comparatively small sample of cases, the boys, if given a reasonable chance, showed a tendency to disengage themselves from mother and to enjoy their functioning in the widening world . . . , the girls, on the other hand, seemed to become more engrossed with mother in her presence; they demanded greater closeness and were more persistently enmeshed in the ambivalent aspects of the relationship" (Mahler et al., 1975, p. 102). She finds, for example, that claims to the body's autonomy (not liking to be handled) and veering away from mother rather than staying with her are more prominent in boys than in girls. It has also been reported that girls have a higher level of interaction with mothers (Clarke-Stewart, VanderStoep & Killian, 1979), and ask for help from their mothers more than boys do (Fagot, 1974). Maccoby and Feldman (1972) report no sex differences in staying close to mother during free play, but their observation time of six minutes, as noted above, may have been too short for sex differences to have emerged.

Mahler attributes this sex difference in the development of a separate sense of self to different responses of boys and girls to their realization of anatomical sex differences during the rapprochement subphase, claiming that " . . . the girls, upon the discovery of the sexual difference, tended to turn back to mother, to blame her, to demand from her, to be disappointed in her, and still to be ambivalently tied to her" (Mahler et al., 1975, p. 106), while boys are better able to turn to the outside world or their own bodies for pleasure and satisfaction and to fathers as someone with whom to identify.

The evidence we have just summarized, however, indicates sex differences in the development of a separate sense of self even prior to rapprochement, which suggests that it is necessary to look beyond the discovery of anatomical sex differences to account for the origin of sex difference in the development of a separate sense of self.

In the first portion of this paper, we have suggested behavioral indicators for sex differences in the development of a separate sense of self at each subphase of the separation-individuation process. Indeed, our review of such experimental studies as exist which employ these measures reveals initial support at both practicing and rapprochement for this sex difference.[5] The psychoanalytic and cognitive arguments presented above hold that this sex difference in a separate sense of self derives from the differential maternal treatment of sons and daughters. In the second portion of this paper we will specify the types of maternal behavior that facilitate or hinder the process of separation and individuation and will examine existing experimental studies that measure those behaviors.

Sex Differences in Maternal Treatment of Sons and Daughters

In order to establish behavioral indicators of the promotion by mothers of a separate sense of self, one needs to pay particular attention to types of behavior that indicate a willingness to let go, to give a gentle push when needed, and to provide a sense of security in being on one's own in the context of the child's developing capabilities. Mahler's description of child behavior at each subphase of the separation-individuation process provides a framework for defining a variety of maternal behaviors at each stage that would help facilitate or hinder the child's development of a separate sense of self. In the following listing of maternal behaviors, a high score on the items marked (F) indicates facilitation of separateness; a high score on the items marked (D) indicates discouragement of separateness.

At Differentiation

1. amount of distancing allowed or encouraged when child is held (F)

At Practicing

1. number of interruptions of child's play to give advice (D)
2. number of interruptions of child's play to offer assistance (D)
3. amount of fearfulness and apprehension expressed regarding bodily harm to the child (D)
4. number of expressions of confidence in child's judgment and ability (F)
5. amount of criticism expressed about child's judgment and ability (D)
6. number of initiations of physical closeness not requested by the child (D)

Separate Sense of Self 523

At Rapprochement

1. discouragement of shadowing (F)
2. amount of sharing of child's interests in his/her findings (F)
3. number of expressions of confidence in child's judgment or ability (F)
4. encouragement of shadowing (D)
5. offers of physical contact and assistance not specifically requested by child (D)
6. amount of fearfulness and apprehension expressed regarding bodily harm to the child (D)
7. amount of criticism expressed about child's judgment and ability (D)

A number of the behavioral indicators we have suggested involve the nature and extent of physical closeness that mothers initiate with children. Since the majority of experimental studies of differential maternal behavior towards infants center on physical contact, there are a variety of studies that employ measures related to the ones we have defined. There is evidence practically from birth that mothers engage in different types of physical contact with their male and female infants and that this does not result from sex differences in infant behavior. Lewis and Weinraub (1979) argue that

> the greater incidence of sex differences in adult behavior relative to sex differences in infant behavior suggests that sex-differentiated parental behavior may be more a cause than a result of sex differences in infant behavior. Recent studies designed to tease out the effects of infant sex and adult expectations regarding infant sex suggest that sex differences in certain adult behaviors, particularly touching, may depend more on adult expectations than real infant sex difference (Frankel & Weinraub, 1977; Seavey, Katz, & Zalk, 1975). (p. 141)

Studies have found that during the first six months of life boys receive more proximal contact and stimulation than girls. Mothers of newborns 6–48 hours old touch sons more than daughters (Parke, O'Leary & West, 1972). Boys receive more affectionate contact than girls (Leiderman, Leifer, Seashore, Barnett, & Grabstein, 1973), are more stimulated/aroused (Moss, 1967, 1974), receive more intensive proximal social stimulation (Kelly, 1976), are touched, held and rocked more than girls (Lewis, 1972) and have more physical contact with their mothers (Landerholm & Scriven, 1981). This pattern,[6] however, begins to reverse itself at the beginning of the child's separation-individuation process. At 6 months, Goldberg and Lewis (1969) found that mothers touch daughters more than sons. At 1 year, Ban and Lewis (1974) report equal physical contact for sons and daughters while Messer and Lewis (1972) report less physical contact between mothers and sons. Clarke-Stewart and Hevey (1981) report that at 1 year mother-initiated contact with sons was still higher than with daughters, but that there was a sharp decline in mother-son contact from 12 to 18 months, while the amount of mother-daughter physical contact remained constant. Thus mothers maintain a closer physical relationship with daughters while physically distancing sons during the separation-individuation process. It is this change in physical contact for sons that may encourage the development of separateness.

At rapprochement mothers leave boys more often to play on their own while criticizing girls more (Fagot, 1974). In addition, Minton, Kagan, and Levine's (1971) findings with older children (age 27 months) that mothers were more concerned about physical danger to their daughters than to their sons suggest that an investigation at an earlier age of another one of the measures we defined (i.e., mothers' fearfulness and apprehension regarding bodily harm) might reveal this differential maternal behavior to occur earlier in infancy as well.

In sum, there is evidence in the existing experimental literature suggesting that mothers treat their sons and daughters differently in ways that would facilitate the process of separation and individuation for boys more than for girls. Based on the studies reviewed above, however, there is no evidence that differential maternal treatment of sons and daughters *causes* sex differences in the development of a separate sense of self. The psychoanalytic and cognitive arguments suggest that mothers' experiences of greater "difference and separateness" vs. "continuity" with infants and mothers' sex-stereotypic attributions are crucial factors that contribute to this differential response. We have found no studies that directly investigate the relationship between mothers' behavior toward their children and these mediating variables. There are parallel trends in mother and child behavior that may be causally related, but such a relationship needs to be investigated experimentally.

There have been several studies which have investigated parental sex role stereotyping of children's behavior, reporting combined data for mothers and fathers. These studies demonstrate that parents do hold sex stereotyped views of children's behavior (Fagot, 1974; Segal, 1981; Smith & Daglish, 1977). Segal did not relate these stereotypes to the actual behavior of parents or children, while Fagot and Smith and Daglish found only low correlations between parental stereotypes and the degree of sex typing in either parents' or children's behavior. Unfortunately, most of the behaviors examined in these studies were not indicators of the child's developing separate sense of self or of parental encouragement of its development. Further experimental investigations such as these which examine both mothers' sex-stereotypic attributions and their experiences of "continuity" are clearly called for. The intercorrelations must then be examined between these mediating variables, the maternal behaviors defined above as relevant to the facilitation or hindering of the child's separation-individuation process, and the child behaviors defined above as indicative of differential progress in the development of a separate sense of self.

The literature on mother-child variables involved in the separation-

Separate Sense of Self

individuation process reveals failures of replication (e.g., Birns, 1976; Clarke-Stewart, VanderStoep, & Killian, 1979; Maccoby & Jacklin, 1974; Moss, 1974). Some of these inconsistencies may be attributed to differences in the length of the observation period used, the social class and birth order of the subjects, the size and equipment present in the room where the observation took place, and the presence or absence of stress (Brooks & Lewis, 1974b; Lewis & Weinraub, 1974; Moss, 1974). Where sex differences have been found, there is certainly a great deal of overlap in the male and female distributions. Moss (1974), summarizing 10 years of work on mother-infant behavior, suggests that these sex differences may indeed be "fairly fragile phenomena" (p. 152) that reflect "an existing phenomenon that may be evident only when certain external conditions occur" (p. 162).[7] However, he also reports that his studies reveal "fairly cohesive and distinct trends in infant behavior and parental treatment for the respective sexes" (p. 151). It is trends such as these to which we are drawing attention in the present paper. We are suggesting that there is some evidence already existing in the experimental literature which provides support for recent conceptual work on the origins in the mother-child relationship of sex differences in the development of a separate sense of self and that this evidence is sufficient to warrant a more direct and thorough experimental investigation of this phenomenon.

The Contribution of Biology

Given the diversity and inconsistency among the findings of empirical studies of infant sex differences in behavior, sensory functions, attention, and temperament, it is difficult to assess the contribution that biologically based sex differences might make to differential maternal responses to male and female infants or to the infant behaviors we suggest indicate differential progress in the development of a separate sense of self. While there are conflicting reports in the literature, sex differences have been noted in a variety of behaviors and characteristics in very early infancy prior to extensive opportunity for modification by social interaction. Female infants are reported to exceed male infants in such characteristics as rate of maturation (Engel & Benson, 1968; Garai & Scheinfeld, 1968; Roche, 1968), tactile sensitivity (Bell & Costello, 1964; Lipsitt & Levy, 1959; Wolff, 1969), responsiveness to auditory stimulation (Friedman & Jacobs, 1981), period of alertness (Berg, Adkinson, & Strock, 1973), responsiveness to sweet taste (Nisbett & Gurwitz, 1970), recovery of attention following habituation (Friedman, Bruno, & Vietze, 1974), level of heart rate variability (Stamps & Porges, 1975), reflex smiles and rhythmical mouthing (Korner, 1969), mouth domination of hand-to-mouth approach (Korner, 1973), time spent in sleep (Moss, 1967), and vocalization to faces (Kagan, 1971). Male infants are reported to exceed female infants in such characteristics as size and weight (Garai & Scheinfeld, 1968), grip strength (Jacklin, Snow, & Maccoby, 1981), degree of startle response (Korner, 1969), irritability (Moss, 1967; Phillips, King, & DuBois, 1978), and incidence of pregnancy and birth complication and neonatal abnormalities (Bell, Weller, & Waldrop, 1971; Parmalee & Stern, 1972; Singer, Westphal, & Niswander, 1968). These discrepant findings lead some of those who have reviewed the literature to conclude that "there are probably not very many initial biologically based behavioral differences... strong enough to elicit differential reactions from caretakers" (Maccoby & Jacklin, 1974, p. 343), and that using behavioral characteristics to label newborns as male and female "would be extremely difficult if not entirely impossible" (Birns, 1976, p. 236). Others argue, however, that "the current state of knowledge on infant characteristics leaves unanswered the question of biological determinants of sex differences" (Frieze, Parsons, Johnson, Ruble, & Zellman, 1978, p. 78) or go as far as to suggest that behavioral sex differences "do exist in the newborn" (Korner, 1973, p. 23) and that it is the "cumulative evidence of these studies rather than the results of any single study" (Korner, 1974, p. 198) that supports acceptance of these differences as valid.

There may indeed be some biologically based sex differences that contribute to the growth of a more separate sense of self in males than in females. It is unlikely, however, that biologically based sex differences can fully account for differential maternal responses to male and female infants, since such differential maternal responses occur as early as the first days after birth (Parke, O'Leary & West, 1972; Thoman, Leiderman, & Olson, 1972) and differential adult responses are noted in studies that hold infant behavior constant (e.g. Frankel & Weinraub, 1977; Lewis & Weinraub, 1979; Seavey, Katz, & Zalk, 1975) or attempt to control for relevant characteristics of the infant such as state (Moss, 1967), and "objective" physical characteristics (Rubin et al., 1974).

CONCLUSION

The arguments that sex differences in the development of a separate sense of self derive from differential maternal treatment of sons and daughters in infancy have received much attention, despite the lack of confirming experimental evidence. In this paper, we have drawn on Mahler's general description of the separation-individuation process to specify both the child and maternal behaviors that need to be measured in an experimental investigation of these arguments. We have thus provided the foundation for future experimental research linking the mediating variables of mothers' experiences of continuity and sex-stereotypic attributions with mothers' differential behavior towards sons and daughters and tracing the consequences of that differential behavior for sex differences in the development of a separate sense of self.

Understanding the dynamics that produce this sex difference in infancy and tracing its development through childhood and adolescence are important because, in their extreme form, existing sex differences in the experience of a separate sense of self pose difficulties for both men and women. Many adult women find their autonomy severely undermined and their needs sacrificed because their self-definition and appraisal remain so tied to the emotional responses of others. "Many women do not develop dependable self-empathy because the pull of empathy for the other is so strong, because women are conditioned to attend to the needs of others first" (Jordan, 1983, p. 3). However, at the other extreme, many adult men find themselves unable to experience real empathy or connectedness with others. "Males tend to have more difficulty with the essential and necessary surrender to affect and momentary joining with the other" (Jordan, 1983, p. 3). Further research of the nature we have suggested would help mothers and other caretakers to understand the ways in which they might foster a healthy degree of separateness through interaction with infants.

NOTES

1. This perspective thus places the origin of sex differences at an earlier period than the traditional theoretical perspectives, i.e. cognitive-developmental (Kohlberg, 1966), social learning (Mischel, 1966), and psychoanalytic (Freud, 1925), which suggest that sex differences begin to emerge with the acquisition of gender identity at around age two and become more fully apparent during the oedipal period.
2. We recognize that, regardless of the sex of their children, there will be some mothers whose personalities and needs cause them to maintain a symbiotic relationship that makes it difficult for their children to differentiate and to establish a sense of their own boundaries and will (Balint, 1963; Fliess, 1971; Olden, 1958). Both sons and daughters reared by such a mother are likely to have an indistinct sense of self. We are arguing, however, that within the range of "normal" mothering, mothers will facilitate the process of individuation for sons to a greater extent than they do for daughters.
3. Our discussion of sex differences in the separation-individuation process focuses on the relationship between the mother and the infant, because traditionally mothers have been the primary caretakers of infants and fathers have played a minor role in the early months. We believe that specifying the relationship between the behavior of the caretaker and the development of a separate sense of self will provide the basis for understanding the consequences of fathers' increased involvement in early child care.
4. Since we are concerned with developments that occur in infancy, our focus will be limited to the first three subphases of the separation-individuation process.
5. Our review has focused on studies directly relevant to the development of a *separate* sense of self and thus has not included the more general studies of self-reference, self-recognition, self-awareness, or self-performance. These self indicators do not necessarily reflect the degree to which the intrapsychic self is differentiated from the mother. The connections among these various aspects of self need to be explained.
6. The greater degree of maternal proximal behavior to sons than daughters before differentiation is intriguing. It has been argued that "This cross-sex maternal attachment behavior is perhaps a precursor of the more intense oedipal relationships that have been observed clinically in 3-to-5-year-old children" (Leiderman et al., 1973, p. 169).

7. For example, studies of attachment frequently use stressful situations such as presence of an adult stranger or separation from mother. Brooks and Lewis (1974b) suggest that "under stress sex differences which would normally appear are washed out" (p. 315). Boys appear to be more upset by the stress of separation episodes and seek close proximity to parents in this situation (Feldman & Ingham, 1975). In addition, our concern is with "normal individuation-separation, in contrast to situations of traumatic separation, and it takes place in the presence of the mother" (Mahler, 1963, p. 308).

REFERENCES

Ainsworth, M. D. S., & Bell, S. M. (1970). Attachment, exploration, and separation: Illustrated by the behavior of one-year-olds in a strange situation. *Child Development, 41*, 49–67.

Balint, E. (1963). On being empty of oneself. *International Journal of Psycho-Analysis, 44*, 470–480.

Ban, P., & Lewis, M. (1974). Mothers and fathers, girls and boys: Attachment behavior in the one-year-old. *Merrill-Palmer Quarterly, 20*, 195–204.

Bardwick, J. (1971). *Psychology of women: A study of bio-cultural conflicts*. New York: Harper & Row.

Bardwick, J., & Douvan, E. (1972) Ambivalence: The socialization of women. In J. Bardwick (Ed.), *Readings on the psychology of women* (pp. 52–58). New York: Harper & Row.

Bell, R. Q., & Costello, N. (1964). Three tests for sex differences in tactile sensitivity in the newborn. *Biologia Neonatorum, 7*, 335–347.

Bell, R. Q., & Darling, J. F. (1965). The prone head reaction in the human neonate: Relation with sex and tactile sensitivity. *Child Development, 36*, 943–949.

Bell, R. Q., Weller, G. M., & Waldrop, M. F. (1971). Newborn and preschooler: Organization of behavior and relations between periods. *Monographs of the Society for Research in Child Development, 36* (1–2, Serial No. 142).

Berg, W. K., Adkinson, C. D., & Strock, B. D. (1973). Duration and frequency of periods of alertness in neonates. *Developmental Psychology, 9*, 434.

Birns, B. (1976). The emergence and socialization of sex differences in the earliest years. *Merrill-Palmer Quarterly, 22*, 229–254.

Brooks, J., & Lewis, M. (1974a). Attachment behavior in thirteen-month-old, opposite-sex twins. *Child Development, 45*, 243–247.

Brooks, J., & Lewis, M. (1974b). The effect of time on attachment as measured in a free play situation. *Child Development, 45*, 311–316.

Broverman, I. K., Broverman, D. M., Clarkson, F. E., Rosenkrantz, P. S., and Vogel, S. (1970). Sex-role stereotypes and clinical judgments of mental health. *Journal of Consulting and Clinical Psychology, 34*, 1–7.

Chodorow, N. (1978). *The reproduction of mothering: Psychoanalysis and the sociology of gender*. Berkeley: University of California Press.

Clarke-Stewart, K. A. (1973). Interactions between mothers and their young children: Characteristics and consequences. *Monographs of the Society for Research in Child Development, 38* (6–7, Serial No. 153).

Clarke-Stewart, K. A., & Hevey, C. M. (1981). Longitudinal relations in repeated observations of mother-child interaction from one to two and one-half years. *Developmental Psychology, 17*, 127–145.

Clarke-Stewart, K. A., VanderStoep, L. P., & Killian, G. A. (1979). Analysis and replication of mother-child relations at two years of age. *Child Development, 50*, 777–793.

Coates, B., Anderson, E. P., & Hartup, W. W. (1972). Interrelations in the attachment behavior of human infants. *Developmental Psychology, 6*, 218–230.

Dinnerstein, D. (1976). *The mermaid and the minotaur*. New York: Harper & Row.

Douvan, E. (1972). Sex differences in adolescent character processes. In J. Bardwick (Ed.), *Readings on the psychology of women* (pp. 44–48). New York: Harper & Row.

Douvan, E., & Adelson, J. (1966). *The adolescent experience*. New York: Wiley.

Engel, R., & Benson, R. C. (1968). Estimate of conceptional age by evoked response activity. *Biologia Neonatorum, 12,* 201-213.

Fagot, B. I. (1974). Sex differences in toddler's behavior and parental reaction. *Developmental Psychology, 10,* 554-558.

Feldman, S. S., & Ingham, M. E. (1975). Attachment behavior: A validation study of two age groups. *Child Development, 46,* 319-330.

Fliess, R. (1971). *Ego and body ego: Contributions to their psychoanalytic psychology*. New York: International Universities Press.

Frankel, J., & Weinraub, M. (1977, May). Adult-infant interaction: Effects of infant real sex, infant labeled sex, and adult sex. Paper presented at the Southeastern Psychological Association meetings, Miami.

Freud, S. (1925). Some physical consequences of the anatomical distinction between the sexes. *Standard edition of the complete psychological works* (Vol. 19, pp. 243-258). London: Hogarth Press and Institute of Psycho-Analysis.

Friedman, S., Bruno, L. A., & Vietze, P. (1974). Newborn habituation to visual stimuli: A sex difference in novelty detection. *Journal of Experimental Child Psychology, 18,* 242-251.

Friedman, S. L., & Jacobs, B. S. (1981). Sex differences in neonates' behavioral responsiveness to repeated auditory stimulation. *Infant Behavior and Development, 4,* 175-183.

Frieze, I. H., Parsons, J. E., Johnson, P. B., Ruble, D. N., & Zellman, G. L. (1978) *Women and Sex Roles*. New York: Norton.

Garai, J. E., & Scheinfeld, A. (1968). Sex differences in mental and behavioral traits. *Genetic Psychology Monographs, 77,* 169-299.

Gilligan, C. (1977). In a different voice: Women's conceptions of self and of morality. *Harvard Educational Review, 47,* 481-517.

Goldberg, S., & Lewis, M. (1969). Play behavior in the year-old infant: Early sex differences. *Child Development, 40,* 21-31.

Gunnar, M. G., & Donahue, M. (1980). Sex differences in social responsiveness between six months and twelve months. *Child Development, 51,* 262-265.

Gutmann, D. (1970). Female ego styles and generational conflict. In J. Bardwick, E. Douvan, M. Horner, and D. Gutmann, *Feminine personality and conflict* (pp. 76-96). Belmont, CA: Brooks/Cole.

Hoffman, L. W. (1972). Early childhood experiences and women's achievement motives. *Journal of Social Issues, 28* (2), 129-155.

Jacklin, C. N., Snow, M. E., & Maccoby, E. E. (1981). Tactile sensitivity and muscle strength in newborn boys and girls. *Infant Behavior and Development, 4,* 261-268.

Jordan, J. V. (1983). Empathy and mother-daughter relationship. *Work in Progress* (Report No. 82-02). Wellesley, MA: Stone Center for Developmental Services and Studies (Wellesley College).

Kagan, J. (1971). *Change and continuity in infancy*. New York: Wiley.

Kelly, P. (1976). The relation of infant's temperament and mother's psychopathology to interactions in early infancy. In K. F. Riegal and J. A. Meacham (Eds.), *The developing individual in a changing world* (Vol. II, pp. 664-675). Chicago: Aldine.

Klein, R. P., & Durefee, J. J. (1978). Effects of sex and birth order on infant social behavior. *Infant Behavior and Development, 1,* 106-117.

Kohlberg, L. A. (1966). A cognitive-developmental analysis of children's sex-role concepts and attitudes. In E. E. Maccoby (Ed.), *The development of sex differences* (pp. 82-173). Stanford, CA: Stanford University Press.

Korner, A. F. (1969). Neonatal startles, smiles, erections, and reflex sucks as related to state, sex, and individuality. *Child Development, 40,* 1039-1053.

Korner, A. F. (1973). Sex differences in newborns with special reference to differences in the organization of oral behavior. *Journal of Child Psychology and Psychiatry, 14,* 19-29.

Korner, A. F. (1974). Methodological considerations in studying sex differences in the behavioral functioning of newborns. In R. C. Friedman, R. M. Richart, & R. L. Vande Wiele (Eds.), *Sex Differences in Behavior* (pp. 197–208). New York: Wiley.

Landerholm, E., & Scriven, G. A. (1981). A comparison of mother and father interaction with their six-month-old male and female infants. *Early Child Development and Care, 7*, 317–328.

Leiderman, P. H., Leifer, A. D., Seashore, M. J., Barnett, C. R., & Grabstein, R. (1973) Mother-infant interaction: Effects of early deprivation, prior experience and sex of infant. *Association for Research in Nervous and Mental Disease Research Publication, 51*, 154–175.

Lewis, M. (1972). State as an infant-environment interaction: An analysis of mother-infant interaction as a function of sex. *Merrill-Palmer Quarterly, 18*, 95–121.

Lewis, M., & Weinraub, M. (1974). Sex of parent × sex of child: Socio-emotional development. In R. C. Freeman, R. M. Richart, & R. L. Vande Wiele (Eds.), *Sex differences in behavior* (pp. 165–189). New York: Wiley.

Lewis, M., & Weinraub, M. (1979). Origins of early sex-role development. *Sex Roles, 5*, 135–153.

Lipsitt, L. P. and Levy, N. (1959). Electrotactual threshold in the neonate. *Child Development, 30*, 547–554.

Maccoby, E. E., & Feldman, S. S. (1972). Mother-attachment and stranger-reactions in the third year of life. *Monographs of the Society for Research in Child Development, 37* (1, Serial No. 146).

Maccoby, E. E., & Jacklin, C. N. (1973). Stress, anxiety and proximity seeking: Sex differences in the year-old child. *Child Development, 44*, 34–42.

Maccoby, E. E., & Jacklin, C. N. (1974). *The psychology of sex differences*. Stanford, CA: Stanford University Press.

Mahler, M. (1963). Thoughts about development and individuation. *Psychoanalytic Study of the Child, 18*, 307–324.

Mahler, M., Pine, F., & Bergman, A. (1975). *The psychological birth of the human infant.* New York: Basic Books.

Messer, S., & Lewis, M. (1972). Social class and sex difference in the attachment and play behavior of the year-old infant. *Merrill-Palmer Quarterly, 18*, 295–306.

Miller, J. B. (1976). *Toward a new psychology of women.* Boston: Beacon.

Minton, C., Kagan, J., & Levine, J. (1971). Maternal control and obedience in the two-year-old. *Child Development, 42*, 1873–1894.

Mischel, W. (1966). A social-learning view of sex differences in behavior. In E. E. Maccoby (Ed.), *The development of sex differences* (pp. 56–81). Stanford, CA: Stanford University Press.

Moss, H. A. (1967). Sex, age, and state as determinants of mother-infant interaction. *Merrill-Palmer Quarterly, 13*, 19–36.

Moss, H. (1974). Early sex differences and mother-infant interaction. In R. Friedman, R. Richart, & R. Vande Wiele (Eds.), *Sex differences in behavior* (pp. 149–163). New York: Wiley.

Nisbett, R. E., & Gurwitz, S. B. (1970). Weight, sex and eating behavior of human newborns. *Journal of Comparative and Physiological Psychology, 73*, 245–253.

Olden, C. (1958). Notes on the development of empathy. *Psychoanalytic Study of the Child, 13*, 505–518.

Parke, R. D., O'Leary, S. E., & West, S. (1972). Mother-father-newborn interaction: Effects of maternal medication, labor, and sex of infant. *Proceedings of the Annual Convention of the American Psychological Association, 7* (pt. 1), 85–86.

Parmalee, A. H., Jr., & Stern, E. (1972). Development of states in infants. In C. D. Clemente, D. P. Purpura, & F. E. Mayer (Eds.), *Sleep and the maturing nervous system* (pp. 199–228). New York: Academic Press.

Phillips, S., King, S. & DuBois, L. (1978). Spontaneous activities of female versus male newborns. *Child Development, 49*, 590–597.

Separate Sense of Self

Rheingold, H. L., & Eckerman, C. O. (1969). The infant's free entry into a new environment. *Journal of Experimental Child Psychology, 8,* 271–283.

Rheingold, H., & Samuels, H. (1969). Maintaining the positive behavior of infants by increased stimulation. *Developmental Psychology, 1,* 520–527.

Roche, A. F. (1968). Sex-associated differences in skeletal maturity. *Acta Anatomica, 71,* 321–340.

Rubin, J. Z., Provenzano, F. J., & Luria, Z. (1974). The eye of the beholder: Parents' views on sex of newborns. *American Journal of Orthopsychiatry, 44,* 512–519.

Seavey, C. A., Katz, P. A., & Zalk, S. R. (1975). Baby X. The effect of gender label on adult responses to infants. *Sex Roles, 2,* 103–109.

Segal, J. (1981). Age of infants and parental sex-role perception. *Journal of Psychology, 107,* 267–272.

Singer, J. E., Westphal, M., & Niswander, K. R. (1968). Sex differences in the incidence of neonatal abnormalities and abnormal performance in early childhood. *Child Development, 39,* 103–112.

Smith, P. K., & Daglish, L. (1977). Sex differences in parent and infant behavior in the home. *Child Development, 48,* 1250–1254.

Stamps, L. E., & Porges, S. W. (1975). Heart rate conditioning in newborn infants: Relationships among conditionability, heart rate variability, and sex. *Developmental Psychology, 11,* 424–431.

Surrey, J. L. (1983). The relational self in women: Clinical implications. *Work in Progress* (No. 82-02, pp. 6–11). Wellesley, MA: Stone Center for Developmental Services and Studies (Wellesley College).

Thoman, E. B., Leiderman, P. H., and Olson, J. P. (1972). Neonate-mother interaction during breast-feeding. *Developmental Psychology, 6,* 110–118.

Wolff, P. H. (1969). The natural history of crying and other vocalizations in early infancy. In B. M. Foss (Ed.), *Determinants of infant behavior* (Vol. 3, pp. 113–138) London: Metheun.

Wolowitz, H. (1972). Hysterical character and feminine identity. In J. Bardwick (Ed.), *Readings on the psychology of women* (pp. 307–314). New York: Harper & Row.

An immunoreactive theory of selective male affliction

Thomas Gualtieri and Robert E. Hicks
Department of Psychiatry and Biological Sciences Research Science Center, University of North Carolina, Chapel Hill, N.C. 27514

Abstract: Males are selectively afflicted with the neurodevelopmental and psychiatric disorders of childhood, a broad and virtually ubiquitous phenomenon that has not received proper attention in the biological study of sex differences. The previous literature has alluded to psychosocial differences, genetic factors and elements pertaining to male "complexity" and relative immaturity, but these are not deemed an adequate explanation for selective male affliction. The structure of sex differences in neurodevelopmental disorders is hypothesized to contain these elements: (1) Males are more frequently afflicted, females more severely; (2) disorders arising in females are largely mediated by the genotype; in males, by a genotype by environment interaction; (3) complications of pregnancy and delivery occur more frequently with male births; such complications are decisive and influence subsequent development. We hypothesize that there is something about the male fetus that evokes an inhospitable uterine environment. This "evocative principle" is hypothesized to relate to the relative antigenicity of the male fetus, which may induce a state of maternal immunoreactivity, leading either directly or indirectly to fetal damage. The immunoreactive theory (IMRT) thus constructed is borrowed from studies of sex ratios and is the only explanation consistent with negative parity effects in the occurrence of pregnancy complications and certain neurodevelopmental disorders. Although the theory is necessarily speculative, it is heuristic and hypotheses derived from it are proposed; some are confirmed in the existing literature and by the authors' research.

Keywords: birth order; developmental disorder; embryology; immunology; parity effects; sex differences

Males are selectively afflicted with virtually every neurologic, psychiatric, and developmental disorder of childhood (see Table 1). There are conditions, of course, like anencephaly and dysraphism, which are commoner in females (Glucksmann 1978; Nakano 1973); but for the most important neurodevelopmental disorders – mental retardation, autism, hyperactivity, dyslexia, epilepsy, dysphasia, cerebral palsy, and conduct disorders – the sex differential works unequivocally to male disadvantage (Butler & Bonham 1963; Nichols & Chen 1981; Rutter 1970). This phenomenon is largely unexplained. Though the biology and psychology of sex differences has been an attractive area of recent scientific concern, the issue of selective male affliction seems to have generated neither broad interest nor systematic research.

In its ubiquity and breadth, the phenomenon compels an explanation that is couched, somehow, in the biology of sex differences. Although it is not unlikely that sex differences in parental handling or societal attitudes may have a role in the development or identification of at least some of the behavioral and emotional disorders of childhood (Rutter 1970), the role sex differences in adult perceptions of children, referral and labeling processes, and tolerance of deviant behaviors may actually play in the development of psychiatric disorders in children with normal brain development has yet to be determined. Boys are believed to be more vulnerable than girls to certain kinds of family disharmony (Rutter 1970) and other psychosocial stressors (Cadoret & Cain 1980), but the reason for this is not understood. However, psychosocial theories are hardly germane to the problem of selective male affliction with severe neurodevelopmental disorders like epilepsy, autism, and mental retardation.

It has been suggested that the genetic endowment of the male comprises sufficient cause for male "inferiority" (Childs 1965; Ounsted & Taylor 1972; Rutter 1970). The Y chromosome is considerably smaller than the X and also relatively inert, thus giving the female a "4–5% quantitative superiority in genetic material" (Childs 1965). This disparity means that the homogametic sex (female) is diploid with respect to many loci, whereas the heterogametic sex (male) must always be haploid. Because there are loci on the X chromosome that control functions apart from reproductive sex, males are necessarily the victims of whatever uncompensated dosage effects may exist (Childs 1965). X linkage has been proposed to account for greater male variability for virtually all biological traits, including mental functioning (Lehrke 1978). Untoward X-linked recessive genes will be expressed in males but not in heterozygous females, and the occurrence of X-linked disorders of development is not infrequent. However, they are not sufficiently frequent to account for the breadth and ubiquity of the phenomenon of selective affliction. Most of the conditions in Table 1 are not X linked, and the large majority do not show a pattern of inheritance that characterizes specific chromosomal abnormalities.

The effect of the Y-chromosome message has been

Gualtieri & Hicks: Immunoreactive theory

Table 1. *Male–female differences in developmental neuropsychiatry and obstetrics*

Disorder	Sex ratio	Reference
A. *Pediatric psychiatry*		
Hyperkinetic syndrome	300	(Butler & Bonham 1963; Trites et al. 1979)
Conduct disorders	270	(Rutter 1970; Trites et al. 1979)
	200–900	(Zerssen & Weyerer 1982)
Childhood schizophrenia	170	(Kramer 1978)
Early onset schizophrenia	160	(Samuels 1979; Flor-Henry 1974)
Process schizophrenia	150	(Flor-Henry 1974; Allon 1971)
Suicide		(Schaffer & Fisher 1981)
Referrals to child psychiatry clinics	200	(Taylor & Ounsted 1972)
Admission to child psychiatric service	213	(Gualtieri 1983)
B. *Pediatric neurology*		
Seizure disorders		
All ages	120	(Taylor & Ounsted 1972)
Neonatal convulsions	116	(Taylor & Ounsted 1972)
Childhood seizures	140	(Taylor & Ounsted 1972)
Infantile spasms	210	(Taylor & Ounsted 1972)
Temporal lobe epilepsy	132	(Taylor & Ounsted 1972)
Febrile seizures	140	(Taylor & Ounsted 1972)
In mentally retarded children	170	(Corbett, Hannis & Robinson 1975)
Cerebral palsy	150–260	(Wing 1981; Taylor & Ounsted 1972)
Subacute schlerosing panencephalitis	220	(Taylor & Ounsted 1972)
Encephalitis (echo type 9)	220	(Sabin, Krombiegel & Wigand 1958)
Abnormal neurological exam at one year of age	114	(Singer et al. 1968)
C. *Developmental disorders*		
Severe mental retardation	130	(Abramowicz et al. 1975)
Down's syndrome	128–260	(Tsai & Beisler 1983; Burgio et al. 1981)
Speech and language disorders	260	(Ingram 1959)
Stuttering	400	(Reinisch et al. 1979)
Learning difficulties	219	(Nichols & Chen 1981)
Dyslexia	430	(McKinney & Feagans 1983)
Autism	400	(Ingram 1964)
D. *Obstetrics perinatal*		
Spontaneous abortion	120–140	(McMillen 1979)
Toxemia	109–171	(Toivanen & Hirvonen 1970)
Placenta praevia	120	(Ounsted 1972)
Abruptio placentae	206	(Ounsted 1972)
Anteparium hemmorhage	140–210	(Rhodes 1965)
Intra-partum anoxia	130	(Butler & Bonham 1963)
Pulmonary infection	250	(Butler & Bonham 1963)
Hyaline membrane disease	180	(Butler & Bonham 1963)
Pulmonary hemorrhage	210	(Butler & Bonham 1963)
Cerebral birth trauma	180	(Butler & Bonham 1963)
Apgar 6	130	(Singer et al. 1968)

The sex ratio is expressed, by convention, as the number of males divided by the number of females, multiplied by one hundred, or $(N_m/N_f)100$.

described by Ounsted and Taylor (1972, p. 257) as catalytic; that is, it serves to "modify any genome." Females express neither the fullest advantages nor the worst disadvantages of their genome. Their characteristics are said to be "less scattered," whereas males suffer the "extremes of viable disadvantage and the greatest advantage" (Ounsted & Taylor 1972, p. 258). Thus, male inferiority is said to be the consequence of greater genetic variability for "the majority of measurable characteristics" (Wing 1981).

According to Ounsted and Taylor, the increased variability expressed in males is at least in part a consequence of the function of the Y chromosome in regulating the pace of development. "Transcription of expressed genomic information in males occurs at a slower ontogenetic pace; the operation of the Y chromosome is to allow more genomic information to be transcribed" (Ounsted & Taylor 1972, p. 245). Whether or not the pace of development is regulated by the Y chromosome – there is, to the author's knowledge, no direct evidence that it is – it is an incontestable fact that development and maturation occurs more slowly in males (Taylor, 1969). At every developmental stage, the male is less mature than the female (D. C. Taylor 1969). A newborn girl is the physiological equivalent of a 4-to-6-week old boy, and physiological maturity is achieved two years later in boys than in girls (Hutt 1972). In general, immature organisms are more susceptible to damage than mature ones (Rutter 1970), and the developing male is more susceptible to the information he extracts from his genome and the environment (Taylor & Ounsted 1972). Thus, relative immaturity means that males are more vulnerable to environmental factors for a longer period of time; these may be intrauterine, peri- or postnatal, psychosocial, or biologic. The classical and often cited example of the untoward clinical sequelae of prolonged immaturity was reported by Taylor and Ounsted (1971). The interval of susceptibility to convulsive seizures originating in the temporal lobe as a consequence of cerebral injury is considerably longer in the male infant.

The complement to prolonged maturation is increased complexity; the male human is said to be a more complex organism than the female and his brain is a more complex organ. The male brain is more completely lateralized (McGlone 1980), it is heavier (Dekaban & Sadowsky 1978), its oxygen requirements are higher (Hutt 1972), and it is an androgenized female brain (Reinisch, Gandelman & Spiegel 1979). If male brain development is more complicated and prolonged, "there are likely to be more opportunities for errors to occur" (Reinisch et al. 1979, p. 221). However, it is not explicit precisely how these errors come about, or precisely what they are, at least on a physiologic basis. By the same token, the immaturity hypothesis fails to describe any specifics about the information the developing child extracts from his genome or his environment, or how this process unfolds.

Male vulnerability is, of course, hardly limited to congenital disorders, and no review of the topic can afford to overlook the general pattern of male vulnerability at every age to accident and disease. (The notable exceptions are the autoimmune diseases and, of course, diseases of the female reproductive organs [Rutter 1970; Vessey 1972].) The higher mortality of males is reflected in the sex ratio ((male/females) × 100). Although the primary sex ratio (i.e. at conception) is probably around 120 (estimated range 110 – 170), male fetuses are more prone to spontaneous abortion and stillbirth, and by the end of gestation the (secondary) sex ratio falls to about 105 (McMillen 1979). By the end of childhood, the sex ratio drops to unity, a consequence of increased male mortality from accidents and childhood diseases (Reinisch et al. 1979). The relative vulnerability of males is a lifelong phenomenon, and overall the population of the United States is 51% female (Reinisch et al. 1979).

It is not likely, however, that this general, lifelong pattern of male vulnerability can be molded to accommodate a single, parsimonious, and unifying theory, or at least one that would make sense or generate testable hypotheses. The range of problems to which males succumb is simply too broad; each is probably the consequence of a host of different intervening variables. The specific area of concern here, the neurodevelopmental disorders of childhood, also encompasses a broad and diverse range of problems, but the topic is more tractable, and one that may well be open to intelligent theory.

It is fair to say that most of the foregoing ideas about selective male affliction may succeed as explanations or as seminal ideas, but they fail as theories; their capacity to generate testable hypotheses seems to have been extremely limited. Like Butler, we conclude that "the explanation for most of these striking [sex] differences is not understood" (Butler & Bonham 1963, p. 268). Many of the ideas have merit and are incorporated into the theory that is developed herein. However, by themselves, they leave an "unexplained residue . . . of staggering proportions" (Medawar 1963, p. 321).

The structure of sex differences

In general, the morbific processes, mild and grave, attack the females with greater intensity than the males (Ciocco 1940, p. 204)

While females are less prone to affliction with neurodevelopmental problems, when such conditions do arise in the female, a severer form is usually manifest (Taylor & Ounsted 1972). This principle appears to hold for most of the pathologic conditions in which it has been tested. For example, although males are more frequently found to be mentally retarded, at the lowest levels of IQ the proportion of females is relatively higher (Taylor & Ounsted 1972). Autistic children are more commonly males, but at the lowest IQ levels the number of autistic females is proportionately higher (Lord, Schopler, & Revicki 1982; Lotter 1974; Tsai & Beisler 1983; Tsai, Stewart, & August 1981; Wing 1981). The mortality rate of institutionalized retardates (Forssman & Akesson 1970) and of Down's children (Fabia & Drolette 1970) is higher in females and the mortality rate of females with cerebral palsy is also higher (Ingram 1964; Schlesinger, Alaway & Peltin 1959). Females are less prone to epilepsy, but they are more prone to the morbid sequelae of febrile seizures (Taylor & Ounsted 1972) and to the development of epileptic psychosis (Flor-Henry 1969; Slater, Beard & Glithero 1963; D. C. Taylor 1969; Taylor & Ounsted 1972). In order to understand why this is important, it is essential to consider the structure of male–female differences as they relate to the disorders in question, and especially as they relate to the occurrence of perinatal problems.

In the neurodevelopmental disorders, sex differences cause a dissociation between the elements of frequency, or incidence, and intensity, or severity. As a general rule, males are more frequently afflicted and females more severely impaired when they are afflicted. An additional sex-based dissociation is that the occurrence of neurodevelopmental disorders in females seems to be mediated primarily through genetic channels, and that their disorders may be, as a consequence, more specific, whereas in males, the disorders are mediated largely through the occurrence of perinatal problems, and are less specific and more diverse in their manifestation. There is strong evidence suggesting this.

The occurrence of pure type dyslexia is more frequent in girls (Pennington & Smith 1983) and it is possible to fit a genetic model to learning disabilities in girls but not boys (Lewitter, DeFries & Elston 1980). The clinical picture of autistic children with positive family histories of developmental dysfunction is more homogeneous than that of those with negative family histories (August, Stewart & Tsai 1981). The range of IQ in autistic males is wider

Gualtieri & Hicks: Immunoreactive theory

(Wing 1981). Autistic girls are more likely than boys to have family histories of cognitive and language dysfunction (Tsai & Beisler 1983) and members of the families of dyslexic girls (Decker & DeFries 1980) and of girls with conduct disorders (Robins 1966) are more frequently afflicted. The clinical presentation of a disorder that is largely mediated by the genotype is likely to be more specific, whereas the behavioral and developmental sequelae of early brain damage are known to be relatively nonspecific (Graham & Rutter 1968).

The same pattern is suggested by studies of the genetics of schizophrenia. For example, the concordance for schizophrenia in monozygous (MZ) twins is higher for females than males (Rosenthal 1962). Schizophrenic mothers of children who become schizophrenic tend themselves to have had an earlier onset of the disorder than mothers of children who do not become schizophrenic (Mednick 1970), and the births of their children are characterized by relative difficulty (Mednick 1970; Mednick, Mura, Schulsinger & Mednick 1971). However, severity of the maternal illness is associated with the level of schizophrenia only in high-risk daughters and not in sons (Gardner 1967; Sobel 1961); perinatal complications, on the other hand, are more likely in high risk sons than in daughters (Mednick, Schulsinger, Teasdale, Schulsinger, Venables & Rock 1978). There is a significant relation between perinatal complications and the later development of schizophrenia in high-risk boys but not in girls (Mednick, Schulsinger, Teasdale, Schulsinger, Venables & Rock, 1977). The daughters of schizophrenic mothers are likely to be schizophrenic if they have any disorder at all, whereas the sons exhibit a more diverse range of psychopathology, especially sociopathy and criminal behavior (Mednick et al. 1978). What this suggests is that "schizophrenia in females is more genetically determined and that schizophrenia in males has a heavier environmental weight" (Mednick et al. 1977, p. 181). When the high risk daughters of schizophrenic mothers develop schizophrenia, it is largely (though not entirely) determined by their genotype; the sons develop schizophrenia or other severe psychiatric disorders, and this is mediated by a genotype by environment interaction. The environmental effect is keenly felt by male fetuses during pregnancy and parturition.

Schizophrenia is not properly counted among the neurodevelopmental disorders, although a cogent case could probably be made that it ought to be, especially the form of schizophrenia with early onset, which occurs more commonly in males, responds poorly to treatment, is often associated with demonstrable neuropathic changes, and follows a dementing course (Weinberger, Cannon-Spoor, Potkin & Wyatt 1980).

We have recently described a similar structure in the sex differences that occur in developmentally handicapped children (Hicks & Gualtieri 1984). In a retrospective review of 223 developmentally handicapped children referred for evaluation at the University of North Carolina within a given year, the majority of patients were, as expected, male (78%). In terms of IQ and SQ (social quotient), however, females were more severely impaired (Table 2A). For both males and females, there was found to be a positive linear relationship between the occurrence of newborn problems (e.g., hypoxia, jaundice) and IQ (F_{linear} [1,166] = 5.255,

Table 2. *The structure of sex differences*

A. Females are more severely impaired than males

		Males	Females
IQ	Mean	55.3	41.2
	S.D.	±23.7	±21.5
	N	139	35
	$F(1,172) = 10.18, P = .002$		
		Males	Females
SQ	Mean	63.0	52.9
	S.D.	±24.2	±18.9
	N	154	40
	$F(1,192) = 6.0, P = .015$		

B. Proportion of each sex classified by number of problems in pregnancy

	Pregnancy problems			
	None	One	More than one	N
Boys	.058	.234	.708	171
Girls	.283	.130	.587	46
				217

Pearson $\chi^2 = 19.785, P = .0001$

C. Proportion of each sex classified by family history of neurodevelopmental disorders

	Relatives affected	Relatives not affected	
Male proband	21	146	167
Female proband	11	31	42
	32	177	209

Pearson $\chi^2 = 4.798, P = .05$

$P = .025$) and SQ (F_{linear} [1,185] = 4.715, $P = .025$), and between the occurrence of neurological problems in the first year of life (e.g., seizures, dystonia) and IQ (F_{linear} [1,168] = 11.907, $P = .001$) and SQ (F_{linear} [1,188] = 10.713, $P = .001$). Newborn problems and first-year neurological problems were associated (Pearson $\chi^2 = 24.295, P = .0001$). There was a positive relationship between newborn problems and low birthweight (F_{linear} [1,204] = 8.087, $P = .005$) as well as with delivery complications (Pearson $\chi^2 = 21.7, P = .0002$). Both newborn problems (F_{linear} [1,172] = 8.521, $P < .01$) and neurological problems were associated with pregnancy complications (F_{linear} [1,174] = 15.147, $P < .001$). However, pregnancy complications were significantly more common with male fetuses (Table 2B). On the other hand, a family history of neurodevelopmental disorders was more frequent in females (Table 2C). The severity of affliction was worse for females, and their genetic background was loaded. Male fetuses were more frequently afflicted, they experienced a higher rate of pregnancy complications, and their genetic background was less decisive (Hicks & Gualtieri 1984).

The structure of sex differences occurring in the neurodevelopmental disorders of childhood consists of four elements: Males are more commonly afflicted. When females are afflicted, the manifestation of the condition is more severe. In females, such disorders are largely influenced by the genotype and as a consequence, the manifestation is more specific. In males, the occurrence of neurodevelopmental disorders is mediated by a genotype by environment interaction; pre- and perinatal problems play a more important role and their manifestation is more diverse.

Such a pattern is consistent with a model that posits a spectrum or a continuum of liability. Liability to a neurodevelopmental disorder is a function of a number of genes acting in concert, and these polygenes are presumed to be normally distributed within the population (Carter 1965). The essential part of this model is a differential threshold for expression of the phenotype for males and females. For females, a substantial genetic load is required for expression; for males a lower quantity of untoward genes is required. This threshold of liability model was originally proposed by Carter to account for sex differences in the occurrence of certain congenital malformations (Carter 1965) and the model has also been advanced with respect to dyslexia (Lewitter, DeFries & Elston 1980) conduct disorder and sociopathy (Cloninger, Christiansen, Reich & Gottesman 1978), stuttering (Garside & Kay 1964), left handedness (Hicks & Kinsbourne 1981), autism (Tsai & Beisler 1983), pyloric stenosis (Carter 1965), and cleft lip and palate (Woolf 1971).

The threshold for expression of neurodevelopmental problems in males may be lower by virtue of their proclivity to encounter serious and damaging pre- and perinatal difficulties. It is not necessary to postulate an increased level of vulnerability to such difficulties for males, although this may be the case, simply because the very occurrence of pregnancy complications in male fetuses is substantially more frequent (Butler & Bonham 1963; Nichols & Chen 1981; Singer, Westphal & Niswander 1968). The male fetus is much more likely to encounter intrauterine difficulties like toxemia (Toivanen & Hirvonen 1970b), abruptio placentae (Rhodes 1965), placenta praevia (Ounsted 1972), prematurity (Niswander & Gordon 1972), and miscarriage (McMillen 1979). It is well known that severe pre- and perinatal problems may cause or aggravate developmental problems, and that less severe gestational events like occasional bleeding are significantly associated with subsequent neurological, behavioral, and developmental problems (Nichols & Chen 1981). The increased frequency with which males encounter an inhospitable uterine environment or a difficult passage compromises brain development and lowers their threshold of liability to neurodevelopmental problems.

The natural question here is why male fetuses are more prone to pre- and perinatal difficulties. Males are heavier in utero and at birth (Butler & Bonham 1963), and larger fetuses are more prone to certain kinds of obstetrical and perinatal problems, but when birth weight is controlled, such problems are still more common in males (Singer et al. 1968). There seems to be something about the male fetus that evokes an untoward uterine environment.

Maternal insufficiency and negative parity effects

Selective male affliction is hypothesized to arise as a consequence of a lower threshold for expression of a deviant phenotype, and the threshold is lowered through the mediation of complications during pregnancy and delivery. These occur more frequently with male fetuses, and "the female conceptus is better adapted to survive in the maternal uterine environment than the male" (Loke 1978, p. 164). An evocative principle is called for: What is it about the male fetus that causes such trouble? Fetal size is not a suitable answer, but what may be?

There are two plausible alternatives: an endocrine effect or an antigenic effect. The former is a compelling idea, because a male fetus causes intermittent elevation of maternal levels of testicular androgens (Mizuno, Lobotsky, Lloyd, Kobayashi & Murasawa 1968), and the balance among androgenic, progestational, and estrogenic hormones is known to affect fetal brain development (Maccoby, Doering, Jacklin & Kraemer 1979) and the gestational health of the mother (Siiteri, Febres, Clemens, Chang, Gondos & Stites 1977). The endocrine aspects of pregnancy and fetal brain development, however, are extraordinarily complex, even ambiguous, and the state of the science is not amenable, in our opinion, to a ready explanation of the phenomenon of selective affliction. In addition, immediately below, we describe data that are incompatible, in our opinion, with an endocrinologic viewpoint.

The idea of male antigenicity is also interesting and is considered at greater length below. It is necessary, first, to turn to two additional areas of study that have important bearing on the occurrence of perinatal complications; these are the issues of maternal insufficiency, and the existence of parity effects in disorders of development. Together, they suggest that successive pregnancies are not independent events, but that there exists a kind of "memory" in the phenomenon of reproduction. The fate of one pregnancy influences, even predicts, the outcome of the next.

The terms "maternal insufficiency" (Costeff, Cohen, Weller & Kleckner 1981), "uterine inadequacy" (Ahern & Johnson 1973), and "reduced optimality" (Gillberg & Gillberg 1983) refer to the tendency of some mothers to experience an unusual degree of pre- and perinatal complications, including bleeding, toxemia, prematurity, difficult delivery, miscarriage, and perinatal death. As described above, the adequacy of a child's intrauterine environment exercises a substantial long-term influence on his neurological and cognitive development (Joffe 1969). Maternal insufficiency is an important risk factor in developmental disorders like autism (Aarkrog 1968; Gillberg & Gillberg 1983; Tsai & Beisler 1983; Tsai et al. 1981), mental retardation, mild and severe (Costeff, Cohen & Weller 1983; Drillien 1968; Hagberg, Hagberg, Lewerth & Linberg 1981; Lilienfield & Pasamanick 1956), minimal brain dysfunction (MBD) (Nichols & Chen 1981; Gillberg & Rasmussen 1982), and childhood psychoses (Funderburk, Carter, Tanguay, Freeman & Westlake 1983), among others. There may be a dosage effect because signs of uterine inadequacy occur more frequently and in greater number in severer disorders like autism than in MBD. It is also interesting that the signs of uterine inadequacy associated with certain disorders such as autism are not necessarily those that directly induce cerebral hypoxia (Gillberg & Gillberg 1983).

Central to the concept of maternal insufficiency is the idea of tendency. Although any woman can have an isolated bad pregnancy, there are some who are unusually prone to bad pregnancies. This tendency is at least in part genetically determined; for example, the tendency to give birth prematurely is familial (Keller

Gualtieri & Hicks: Immunoreactive theory

1981), there is a maternal genetic effect on the birth weight of cousins (Robson 1955), and the aunts and sisters of mentally retarded children have more mental retardation, miscarriage, stillbirth and neonatal death in their families than the uncles and brothers of mentally retarded children have in theirs (Ahern & Johnson 1973). Daughters from toxemic pregnancies are affected themselves with toxemia more often than those from control groups (Chesley, Annito & Cosgrove 1968).

Because of familial uterine inadequacy, a troubled pregnancy does not occur as an independent event. The nature of one pregnancy is capable of predicting the nature of another. The low birth weight of the first child is the most powerful predictor of low birth weight in the second (Bakketeig 1977), the percentage of premature infants increases with the previous number of premature births (Placek 1977), previous fetal, peri- or neonatal deaths predict similar deaths in subsequent pregnancies (Niswander & Gordon 1972). And there is, again, an element of nonspecificity, since previous fetal loss predicts prematurity, and previous prematurity predicts fetal loss (Niswander & Gordon 1972; Placek 1977). The first factor that operates here is the mother's constitutional insufficiency, which is genetic and probably speaks to a common underlying mechanism; the second factor is pre- or perinatal damage, and the effects of this on the fetus are nonspecific.

A demonstration of how reproductive inefficiency of mothers of developmentally impaired children may be related to fetal antigenicity is provided by Costeff, Cohen, Weller, and Kleckner (1981) who compare the incidence of complications of pregnancy, labor, and infancy in 87 mentally retarded children ("undifferentiated phenotype") of consanguinous matings with 161 (idiopathic) mentally retarded children of nonconsanguinous matings. Complications were significantly more common in the latter group. Consanguinous matings, in which antigenic differences are minimized, were not associated with obstetrical or perinatal complications. The authors speculated that "maternal [reproductive] inefficiency [i.e., obstetrical difficulties] may well reflect some so far unidentified factor [which also causes] fetal brain damage" (Costeff et al. 1981, p. 489).

Beyond the genetic memory of inherited uterine inadequacy is another kind of memory that is expressed in the parity effect. The parity effect refers to systematic change in some measurable characteristic of offspring with increasing birth order or pregnancy order. Here again, there is a common pattern: the incidence of the complications of pregnancy and delivery, prematurity, miscarriage, fetal and neonatal deaths increases with birth order; later born are at greater risk (Niswander & Gordon 1972). Parity effects are also observed in at least some of the neurodevelopmental disorders, for example, mental retardation (Belmont, Stein & Wittes 1976), MBD (Badian 1984; Nichols & Chen 1981; Schrag 1973) and autism (see below, "The primiparity effect"). A retarded, hyperactive, or learning disabled child is more frequently later born.

Maternal insufficiency has a predictable negative effect on pregnancies occurring within an extended family. The effects of maternal insufficiency within a family seem to be mediated however, by the parity effect, with an increasingly negative impact on successive pregnancies. This incremental phenomenon is a form of nongenetic memory. It suggests an immunologic aspect; some kind of sensitisation process is at work. What could be inherited as maternal insufficiency is, in fact, a genetic proclivity to react immunologically to fetal antigen. The ensuing maternal immune attack against the fetus would appear to the clinician as a complication of pregnancy and as a sign of an inadequate uterine environment.

Selective male affliction, or at least a portion of it, is mediated through complications of pregnancy and childbirth, which occur more frequently in male offspring. An evocative principle was postulated to characterize the male fetus and to render the occurrence of such complications more likely. The phenomenon of maternal insufficiency suggests a genetic element at play on the mother's side. The existence of negative parity effects is compatible with an antigenic but not an endocrine explanation of the phenomenon on the fetal side. The evocative principle, therefore, is deduced to be the unique antigenic character of the male fetus.

The existence of an evocative principle: The antigenic character of the male fetus

The identification of a male-specific antigen, termed H-Y, was originally made in connection with the Eichwald-Silmser effect (see below, "The primiparity effect"). The expression of H-Y antigen probably derives from a monomorphic gene locus (Ohno 1979). The original hypothesis was that H-Y antigen is specified by a gene located on the Y chromosome (Goodfellow & Andrews 1982), but Wolf (1981) presented evidence to suggest that the structural gene for H-Y antigen is autosomal and that its expression is regulated by an X-linked repressor and a Y-linked inducer. Whatever the genetic origin of H-Y antigen, there is no disagreement over issues of ubiquity or specificity. H-Y antigen has been shown to be conserved to the extreme throughout vertebrate evolution (Ohno 1979). Having performed an extensive series of H-Y antibody absorption tests, Wachtel, Koo, and Boyse (1975) demonstrated that male cells of all mammalian species tested, including man, absorbed out the male-specific cytotoxicity of H-Y antibody, whereas no cross reacting materials were found on female cells. H-Y antigen is ubiquitously expressed in every somatic cell type of the mammalian male (Ohno 1979). It is first expressed in preimplantation male embryos at the eight cell stage (Krco & Goldberg 1976). An exact and invariant function seems to have been assigned by evolution to H-Y antigen, and as far as mammals are concerned, it is believed to lie in the determination of primary (gonodal) sex; H-Y is an absolute prerequisite, though it is not necessarily sufficient, for testicular organization (Ohno 1979).

Although H-Y is the prime candidate to account for the hypothesized antigenicity of the male fetus, it is a minor histocompatibility antigen, and its effects may be exercised in clinically important ways only through a cumulative effect with other antigens, including those of the ABO (Toivanen & Hirvonen 1970a), Rh (Renkonen & Timonen 1967; Scott & Beer 1973) and human lymphocytotoxic antigen (HLA) systems (Goulmy, Termijtelen, Bradley & van Rood 1977; Johansen, Festenstein & Burke 1974; Loke, 1978). Alternatively, maternal-fetal immunoreactivity could be mediated in males whose mothers are sensitized to other antigens but not to H-Y, or in females, who do not express H-Y antigen, by virtue of an X-linked antigenic system (e.g. H-X, Xg^a) (Berryman & Silvers 1979; Loke 1978) that may have clinical importance.

Sex differences in antigenicity were first described in the so called Eichwald–Silmser effect: male skin grafts survive less well in female animals than do male-to-male, female-to-male, or female-to-female allografts (Eichwald & Silmser 1955). Trophoblast grafts from female concepti survive longer than male trophoblasts (Borland, Loke & Oldersnaw 1970); most choriocarcinomas arise from female concepti (Scott 1976) and those which arise from male concepti are notably less aggressive (Loke 1978).

There is clinical evidence that male fetuses are more antigenic than females. Immune complexes are found more frequently in the cord blood of male newborns (Farber, Cambiaso & Masson 1981); runt disease and Rh disease occur more commonly in males (Beer & Billingham 1973; Scott & Beer 1966); toxemia, which is probably an autoimmune disorder, is more common when the fetus is male, and the sex ratio increases proportionately with the severity of the disease (Toivanen & Hirvonen 1970b) (see Figure 1).

Antigenic differences between zygote and mother are thought to confer an implantation advantage (Kirby, McWhirter, Teitelbaum & Darlington 1967). Trophoblastic invasion of the uterine decidua may be more extensive if the fetus is antigenically dissimilar to the mother, a mechanism that seems to promote genetic diversity. The male zygote, by virtue of its greater antigenic dissimilarity, is the beneficiary of this putative implantation advantage (Brent 1971). Thus, the special antigenic character of the male fetus was first studied in connection with studies of the sex ratio. The secondary sex ratio, or sex ratio at birth, favors males in every human society that has been studied; the mean value for the United States is about 105 (Novitski 1977). The primary sex ratio, that is the sex ratio at conception, although difficult to measure, is even more favorable: around 120 (McMillen 1979). As if to compensate for selective male affliction, nature has produced an excess of boys to begin with. The implantation advantage of antigenic dissimilarity has been proposed to account for this initial male advantage. Thus, the advantage enjoyed by males in the primary and secondary sex ratio has been attributed to their unique possession of H-Y antigen.

Sex differences in antigenicity may confer a growth advantage as well as an implantation advantage (Clarke & Kirby 1966; Ounsted & Ounsted 1970). Fetuses which are antigenically dissimilar to their mothers are likely to be larger (Clarke & Kirby 1966), and the greater the antigenic dissimilarity, the greater the fetal growth rate (Ounsted & Ounsted 1970). Male embryos, of course, grow faster than females; a baby boy is about 150 grams heavier than a girl at term. The sex ratio of large-for-dates infants is 150 whereas that of small-for-dates infants is 63 (Ounsted 1972).

Placental weight is correlated with birth weight (Sedlis, Berendes, Kim, Stone, Weiss, Deutschberger & Jackson 1967), and mammalian placentation also seems to be under some sort of immunologic control (Jones 1968). In animal studies, antigenic dissimilarity is often found to promote placental growth (D. A. James 1965). The placental size of male fetuses is larger (Ounsted 1972). Interesting also in light of the presumed autoimmune origin of the disorder is the fact that increased placental size is associated with the development of toxemia (Gleicher & Siegel 1980).

Just as understanding the structure of sex differences influences one's appreciation of how males and females come to be afflicted by different pathways, so the sex ratio itself may influence one's respect for antigenicity as a causative agent in males, for at least some neurodevelopmental disorders. A telling example is the fact that the sex ratio decreases with parity; with increasing birth order, fewer boys are born (Novitski & Sandler 1956). There is a parallel between the sex ratio and selective affliction because in both there is a male preponderance, and in both parity effects are observed, and in both an argument in favor of male antigenicity and maternal immunoreactivity is raised.

An antigenic explanation for the secondary sex ratio, implantation, placentation, and fetal growth suggests that maternal sensitization to male antigens occurs and affects subsequent pregnancies. The sex ratio decreases with parity, whereas birth weight and placental size increase (Niswander & Gordon 1972; Novitski & Sandler 1956; Vernier 1975; Warburton & Naylor 1971). There is a nice balance here: the original implantation advantage enjoyed by the male zygote may be offset in subsequent pregnancies by the development of humoral antibodies or cell-mediated immune response in the mother. HLA antibodies, for example, develop in some mothers in response to pregnancy; with successive pregnancies, the number of HLA positive mothers increases (a ceiling seems to be reached at parity three or four) (Burke & Johansen 1974; Doughty & Gelsthorpe 1976). The sex ratio declines with parity in HLA positive mothers; in mothers who fail to develop HLA titres, the sex ratio actually increases with parity (Johansen & Burke 1974). (See Figure 2.) The model has a certain elegance: an early positive effect of immunoreactivity, which serves to promote genetic diversity, is balanced by a later negative

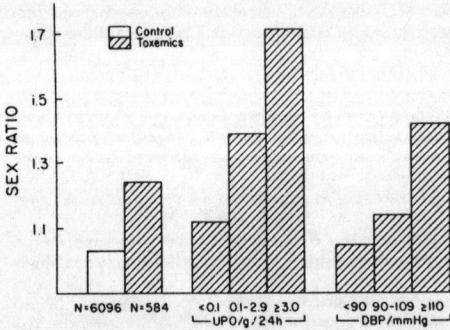

Figure 1. Preponderance of males in toxemia of pregnancy, from Toivanen & Hirvonen (1970b). UPO refers to urinary protein output; DBP to diastolic blood pressure; both are measures of the severity of toxemia, which increases with the sex ratio, on the ordinate.

Gualtieri & Hicks: Immunoreactive theory

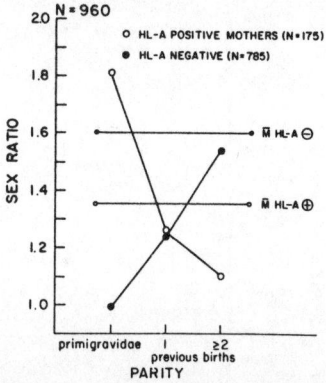

Figure 2. Sex ratio and maternal HLA antibodies, from Johansen, Festenstein & Burke (1974). In mothers who develop HLA antibodies, the sex ratio declines with parity; the opposite is true of HLA negative mothers. The mean (M) sex ratio of HLA positive mothers is lower than that of HLA negative mothers (horizontal lines).

effect which seems to favor in large sibships the birth of the less expensive (female) sex.

If male fetuses are more antigenic, they should be more likely to sensitize mothers, and the impact of this should be felt in subsequent pregnancies in changes in placentation and the sex ratio. In fact, predictions based on the antecedent brother effect seem to hold up. Placental size increases with parity in all male sibships but not in all female sibships; mixed sibships fall in between (Vernier 1975). The sex ratio declines with parity if all antecedent siblings are male; it increases if all antecedent siblings are all female (Gualtieri, Hicks & Mayo 1984b; Renkonen, Mäkelä & Lehtovaara 1962) (See Figure 3).

It appears the parity effect on the sex ratio is mediated through an antecedent brother effect. This effect has also been observed with respect to the occurrence of pregnancy complications in the past history of autistic children.

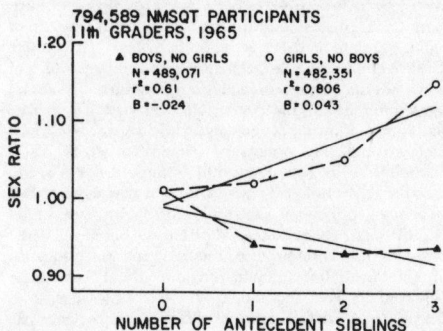

Figure 3. Sex ratio by sex of antecedent siblings, from Gualtieri, Hicks & Mayo's (1984b) reanalysis of Breland's (1974) data.

Table 3. *Antecedent brother effect on complications of pregnancy, 167 autistic boys*

		Antecedent brothers		
		None	One	
Complications of pregnancy	none	12	2	14
	one	31	8	39
	more than one	71	43	114
		114	53	167

χ^2 for linear trend = 5.815, P = .015

		Antecedent sisters		
		None	One	
Complications of pregnancy	none	8	6	14
	one	32	7	39
	more than one	79	35	114
		119	48	167

χ^2 for linear trend = 0.005, N.S.

We have reviewed the medical records of 209 autistic children evaluated at the Medical School at the University of North Carolina. In 167 autistic boys, there was a significant relationship between the occurrence of pregnancy complications and the antecedent birth of brothers but not of sisters (see Table 3). Pregnancy complications were more common in autistic boys who had older brothers, but not in autistic boys who had older sisters. The number of autistic girls was too small to permit a complementary analysis, however.

Maternal immune attack

> The concurrent evolution of viviparity and the ability to render an immunologic response to foreign antigens raised certain problems for the fetus. (Medawar 1963, p. 324)

> Pregnancy is associated with the development of circulating maternal antibodies directed against the histocompatability antigens of the fetus simultaneously with the specific inhibition of immune reactivity against the fetus as a graft. (Simmons 1971, p. 407)

The mechanisms by which the fetus is protected against the circulating antibodies and effector lymphocytes of the mother have been of considerable interest to transplantation biologists, oncologists, and other scientists, who have reviewed the topic (Bernard 1977; Billingham 1964; Simmons 1971). It is sufficient here to say that the mechanisms by which the fetus as an allograft is protected from maternal immune attack are still imperfectly understood (Simmons 1971); when they are, someday, they will doubtless prove to be marvels of biology. But they do not always work. The system, whatever it is, can break down. Fetal antigens and cells enter the maternal circulation and maternal antibodies and effector lymphocytes enter the fetal circulation (Adinolfi 1976; Adinolfi, Beck, Haddad & Seller 1976; Barnes & Tuffrey 1971). A cell-mediated immune response can develop in mothers during pregnancy; it may increase in intensity with gestation and increase even more so with succeeding pregnancies (Burke & Johansen 1974; Doughty & Gelsthorpe 1976; Johansen & Burke 1974; Terasaki, Mickey, Yamazaki & Vredevoe 1970).

For HLA, maternal lymphocytotoxic antibody production increases with the first three or four pregnancies and then levels off (Doughty & Gelsthorpe 1976). It has been hypothesized that if certain kinds of cytotoxic antibodies reach critical levels in the maternal circulation, they will exceed the number of available binding sites on the placenta and enter the fetal circulation (Doughty & Gelsthorpe 1974). Other fetal antigens may also play a role; for example, the ABO system may also contribute to maternal immune sensitivity, and ABO incompatibility between mother and fetus is known to contribute to increased fetal wastage (Cohen & Mellitts 1971).

In the British Perinatal Study (Butler & Bonham 1963), perinatal mortality data relative to maternal ABO typing was available for 14,730 pregnancies. As predicted by the IMRT, perinatal mortality increased more sharply with parity in O type mothers, who are more likely to react to fetal red blood cell antigens than A, B, or AB mothers. The slope of the perinatal mortality–parity regression line was significantly steeper for O mothers: O = 16.9, A = 13.2, B = 12.7, AB = 12.9 (Gualtieri, Hicks & Mayo 1984a). (See Figure 4.) Thus, ABO antigens as well as sex-linked antigens may induce maternal immunoreactivity.

There appears to be substantial interindividual variation in the maternal immune response (Lawler, Ukaejoofo & Reeves 1975). In one study, only 15% of pregnancies were characterized by the development of maternal HLA antibodies (Doughty & Gelsthorpe 1974). Medawar has shown that antigenic incompatibility is necessary but not sufficent to cause Rh disease. Rh disease is also more likely to afflict males (Loke 1978; Medawar 1963); isoimmunization is necessary, but not sufficient, to produce hemolytic anemia in the newborn (Medawar 1963). Figure 5 captures the wide range of reactivity that may exist between maternal and fetal lymphocytes (Lawler et al. 1975). Maternal immunoreactivity is more likely in some women and it is more likely when the fetus is male. In light of the genetic nature of maternal insufficiency, it would be interesting to know whether maternal–fetal immunoreactivity follows a similar genetic pattern.

There are known pathologic consequences of maternal immune attack on the fetus, for example, Rh disease and

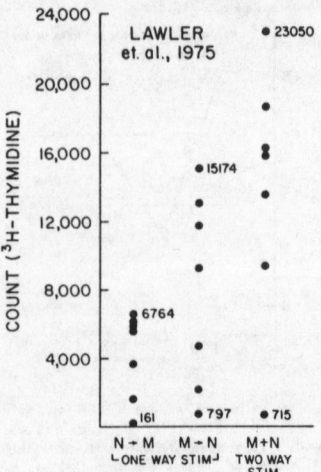

Figure 5. Maternal/neonatal cell interactions in mixed lymphocyte cultures, from Lawler, Ukaejoofo & Reeves (1975). One-way stimulation refers to live neonatal (N) cells admixed with killed maternal (M) cells, and vice-versa. Two-way stimulation (M + N) refers to two populations of live cells.

runt disease, as mentioned above. ABO incompatibility between mother and fetus is associated with an increased perinatal mortality (Cohen & Mellitts 1971). Other examples include autoimmune thrombocytopenia and autoimmune hemolytic anemia, myasthenia gravis, thyroiditis, and the lupus erythematosis (LE) phenomenon and cardiomyopathy in children of mothers with systemic lupus erythematosis (SLE) (Beer & Billingham 1973; Brent 1971; Bresnihan, Grigor, Oliver, Leiskomia & Hughes 1977; Kitzmiller 1978). In the latter condition, transplacental transfer of antinuclear antibody from mother to fetus occurs (Beck & Rowell 1963).

The autoimmune diseases are extremely interesting to consider in this context, because they are the only diseases to which both sexes are vulnerable that are more common in females; they are characteristically diseases of young women in their reproductive years (Kitzmiller 1978). Autoimmune disorders are also good examples of how maternal immunoreactivity can afflict the fetus. Some autoimmune disorders, like rheumatoid arthritis, tend to remit during pregnancy, while others, like SLE, often arise during pregnancy (Bresnihan et al. 1977; Kitzmiller 1978). In autoimmune hemolytic anemia, the disorder may remit post partum, only to arise again with a subsequent pregnancy (Kitzmiller 1978). Increased fetal loss through spontaneous abortion is seen in SLE, scleroderma, autoimmune hemolytic anemia, and autoimmune thrombocytopenic purpura. Fetal wastage is increased in SLE mothers even before the disease is clinically manifest (Kitzmiller 1978). Lymphocytotoxic antibody titres are higher in SLE mothers who have had spontaneous abortions than in mothers who had normal live births (Bresnihan et al. 1977). Toxemia is more common in mothers with SLE (Kitzmiller 1978). And,

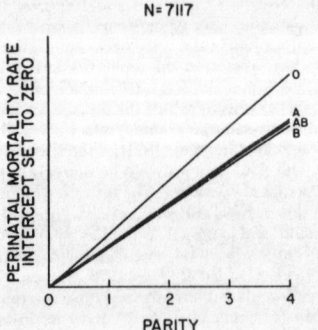

Figure 4. Perinatal mortality and maternal blood groups from Butler & Bonham (1963). See also Gualtieri, Hicks & Mayo (1984b).

based on our review of an admittedly sparse literature, more girls than boys are born to mothers with SLE.

Brain as the target of immune attack

The brain may be an immunologically privileged site in some respects, but immune attack on nervous tissue does occur in conditions like multiple sclerosis, polyneuropathy and spongiform encephalopathy (Abramsky, Lisalc, Silberger & Pleasure 1977; Dalakas & Engel 1981; Hauser, Dawson, Lehrich, Beal, Kevy, Propper, Mills & Weiner 1983; Sotelo, Gibbs & Gadjusek 1980). The heyday of taraxein is over (McPherson 1970), but neurobiologists continue to pursue the possibility of autoimmune mechanisms in the genesis of some forms of schizophrenia (Abramsky & Litvin 1978).

Brain tissue is antigenic (Foster & Archer 1979). It shares antigens with other tissues, including histocompatibility antigens, organ specific antigens, and antigens present on tissue cells (Foster & Archer 1979; Roszkowski, Plaut & Lichtenstein 1977). There are brain antigens specific to neurons and oligodendroglia (Poduslo, McFarland & McKahanon 1977); there are antigens specific to cells in functional groups (Williams & Schupf 1977) or anatomic areas (Blessing, Costa, Gefen & Rush 1977); there are antigens specific to subcellular components of neural tissue (Sotelo et al. 1980). Antibodies to brain antigens can act as teratogens when injected into pregnant animals (Brent 1971). Rats and guinea pigs immunized to nerve growth factor (NGF) develop anti-NGF antibodies which attack fetal nervous tissue in utero when the animals are bred (Johnson, Gorin, Brandeis & Pearson 1980). The immature blood–brain barrier is not capable of protecting the developing brain from damage by maternal antibodies or effector lymphocytes (Adinolfi 1976; Adinolfi et al 1976).

It is not our purpose to review the vast research areas having to do with the immunoprotection of pregnancy or the immunopathology of the brain. Nor can we describe the precise immunopathic mechanisms that mediate maternal attack and induce neuropathic changes in the fetus. Nor can we specify whether H-Y antigen alone is involved, or whether there are other important antigens in the male at particular points in time during gestation, nor whether incompatibility in other antigen systems, like HLA and ABO, may also play a role, and if so, whether the reaction that ensues is additive or multiplicative. These are grounds for speculation and basic research. Sufficient to guide the argument are these conclusions, which are fair and conservative: fetal immunoprotection is not invariant or complete; breakdowns in the system do occur, with occasional pathologic consequences to the fetus, occurring along a continuum of severity; the brain, especially the fetal brain, is not invulnerable to immune attack; and in laboratory animals at least, maternal antibodies can damage the developing nervous tissue of the fetus.

The idea that male antigenicity or maternal immunoreactivity may exert a negative influence on the neurological development of children has been suggested on previous occasions by Adinolfi (1976), Foster and Archer (1979), Loke (1978), Rubenstein (1982), and Singer, Westphal, and Niswander (1968). The hypothesis has usually been advanced on the basis of indirect evidence, to explain, for example, the prevalence of pregnancy complications in males (Singer et al. 1968) or the negative parity effect on IQ (Foster & Archer 1979). Adinolfi based his argument on the immaturity of the fetal blood–brain barrier (Adinolfi et al. 1976), the detection of maternal specific antibodies in the cerebro-spinal fluid (CSF) of infants tested during the first week of life (Thorley, Holmes, Kaplan, McCracken & Sanford 1975), and supporting data from preclinical experiments (Adinolfi 1976). There is additional direct evidence, but not much.

Bonner, Terasaki, Thompson, Holve, Wilson, Ebbin, and Slavkin, 1978 reported cytotoxic antibodies in the sera of 574 parous women; 25% had cytotoxins after their first pregnancy and 50% after the sixth. Children with congenital anomalies are more likely to be born to mothers who have developed cytotoxic antibodies. Harris and Lordon (1976) reported that mothers with lymphocytotoxic antibodies were more likely to show signs of maternal insufficiency (pre-eclampsia, fetal distress, carbohydrate intolerance, unexplained fetal death, intrauterine growth retardation, congenital anomaly and premature labor) than mothers with no lymphocytotoxic antibodies. Bardawil et al. (1962) reported that a group of 20 women with repeated miscarriage manifested rapid rejection of skin grafts from husbands four times more frequently than grafts that were made from unrelated donors (Loke 1978). In a mixed lymphocyte reaction paradigm, the percentage of transformed cells was discovered to be lower in normal fertile couples and higher in infertile couples; a dosage effect was observed in women who had had repeated miscarriage (Halbrecht & Komlos 1976; Omaha & Kadotani 1971). Finally, in two papers from the Soviet Union, it was reported that mothers with "antibrain antibodies" were more likely to give birth to children with developmental or neurological disorders (Burbaeva 1972; Kolyaskina, Boehme, Buravlev & Faktor 1977).

The immunoreactive theory

Selective male affliction with the neurodevelopmental disorders may be related to male vulnerability to environmental stressors, to the genetic endowment of the male, or to his complexity and relative immaturity. In our opinion, these hypotheses are strong and compelling but insufficient. They do not explain the male fetus's proclivity to encounter complications in pregnancy and childbirth. It is argued, with some support, that pregnancy complications mediate the occurrence of neurodevelopmental disorders more strongly in male offspring. The incidence of such complications in males leads to the postulation of an evocative principle, which may be hormonal or antigenic. The first alternative is extremely attractive but it is not consistent with the occurrence of parity effects in fetal loss and in at least some developmental disorders.

The antigenicity of the male fetus is consistent with the negative parity effect. The proposition that the male is especially antigenic and that some mothers are immunoreactors finds convincing support in the literature. The antigenicity of the male is probably related to the sex-linked H-Y antigen, although the contribution of other antigen systems cannot be discounted.

Maternal immune attack on the fetus is well known in a number of pathologic conditions and when it occurs, it is the male who is more severely afflicted. Brain tissue is antigenic, the immature blood–brain barrier affords only slight protection from maternal immune attack, and maternal antibodies are sometimes found in the infant's CSF. Congenital anomalies, infertility, and complications of pregnancy may occur in mothers with elevated antibody titres more frequently than in mothers with low or absent titres.

The argument is based on indirect evidence for the most part, although there is some direct supporting evidence. The relative paucity of direct support is not surprising. Although the theory of maternal–fetal immunoreactivity was first applied to studies of the sex ratio by Renkonen, Makela, and Lehtovaara in 1962, only a few scientists have even raised the question with respect to selective male affliction. Furthermore, the argument presented above relies heavily on the structure of sex differences in the occurrence of schizophrenia, and this dimorphic pattern has not been widely tested in clinical samples of developmentally handicapped children. When we did test the idea, it held up (see above, "Structure of sex differences"). Finally, it is unfortunate that most scientists who undertake studies of pregnancy complications and developmental disorders do not analyze their data taking sex of the proband into consideration.

The fundamental premise of the immunoreactive theory is that pregnancy is an immunological phenomenon characterized by a state of maternal tolerance. But fetal immunoprotection is relative, not absolute, and the system can break down. There is substantial interindividual variation in maternal–fetal immunoreactivity, but on the average, male fetuses are more antigenic than females, and maternal attack on the male embryo is more likely, especially if the mother has been sensitized by previous male pregnancies. Finally, maternal immunologic attack can be directed against fetal brain antigens.

Immunoreactivity is by no means a global explanation for all of the neuropathic disorders of childhood. The phenomenon may be robust but at the same time relatively weak and difficult to discern, especially in small clinical samples. Furthermore, the precise nature of the immunologic reaction cannot be described: whether it involves cell-mediated or humoral antibodies, whether a specific antigen, like H-Y, is responsible, or whether a number of fetal antigens or a combination thereof may be involved. Some fetal antigens may be short-lived and impossible to detect postnatally.

We are aware that there is disagreement surrounding at least some of the facts upon which the theory is based. Parity estimates can be inaccurate, for example, since early abortions are easily missed (Metrakos & Metrakos 1963). Not every investigator has agreed that placentation is promoted by antigenic similarity (Jones 1968), or that the sex ratio decreases with antecedent brothers (McLaren 1962), or that toxemia is an autoimmune disorder (Gleicher & Siegel 1980). H-Y antigen is a fascinating new development in the study of sexual differentiation, but it is very difficult to measure (Goodfellow & Andrews 1982); nor is there any direct evidence that H-Y antigen is present on neural cell membranes in humans (Johnson, Bailey & Mobraaten 1981). There are, not surprisingly, alternative (and occasionally credible) explanations for virtually every natural or clinical phenomenon that has been described thus far or is described below. Still, it is our opinion that the theory has an appeal, and perhaps also a certain usefulness.

Hypotheses engendered by the theory

The immunoreactive theory and the structure of sex differences on which it is based are particularly interesting in light of the hypotheses they engender. It is likely that many of the hypotheses presented below can be tested in existing data sets.

Parity effects. The immunoreactive theory is derived, in part, from the demonstration of negative parity effects in at least some of the developmental disorders. But it does not require, nor does it predict that parity effects will be found for all psychiatric, neurologic, and developmental disorders. The birth order–parity literature with respect to specific psychiatric and neurologic disorders (e.g. schizophrenia, epilepsy, alcoholism) is extensive but inconsistent, and there are serious methodological difficulties in executing a definitive parity study in clinical populations.

Because birth order effects are relatively slight, large numbers of subjects are required to detect them (Birtchnell 1971). Birth order studies rarely compare their findings to a general population control group, and the statistical analysis that is most often used, the Greenwood–Yule method, is not without its critics (McKeown & Record 1956). Birth order effects are sensitive to changes in the birth rate, numbers of marriages, and family size in the general population; a decrease in family size, for example, may lead to an overrepresentation of early birth ranks in small sibships and an increase in later birth ranks in large sibships (Price & Hare 1969). To consider sibling position irrespective of the size or composition of the sibship in which it occurs is probably unjustifiable (Birtchnell 1971). Additional sources of bias that can compromise the findings of a birth order study include the analysis of incomplete sibships, differential survival by birth rank, differential migration to sources of ascertainment of patients (i.e., places such as clinics where patients are identified) (Hare & Price 1969) and the fact that birth order is not necessarily the same as pregnancy order (Metrakos & Metrakos 1963). Parity studies of psychiatric disorders may be compromised by the fact that death, divorce, separation or other causes of early parental loss cannot prevent the conception of the last child in a family. Accordingly, the likelihood of parental deprivation having occurred during early childhood will always be greater for later born than for earlier born persons (Delint 1966).

The primiparity effect. The deleterious effects of primiparity may obscure a birth order effect. Primiparas are more prone to obstetrical complications, such as dystocia and toxemia. Subfertile women will be overrepresented among primiparas. A woman whose first child is defective has a number of strong reasons to limit the size of her family. Congenital rubella and infantile autism are examples of disorders in which relative risk is greatest for first

Gualtieri & Hicks: Immunoreactive theory

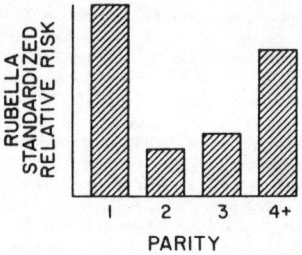

Figure 6. Rubella and parity effects, from Schoenbaum, Biano & Mack (1975).

borns (Deykin & MacMahon 1980; Schoenbaum, Biano & Mack 1975); thereafter, however, a parity effect appears to emerge. A U-shaped distribution of pathologic events with parity has also been described in association with fetal loss after 20 weeks gestation, stillbirths, and neonatal death (Ernst & Angst 1983).

In Figures 6 and 7, the relative risk of rubella and autism is plotted against birth order. First borns are at greatest risk, but for ensuing birth orders there is a clear parity effect. One way to measure the relationship between parity and risk for these disorders is orthogonal polynominal analysis of variance. When this method is applied to the data contained in Deykin & MacMahon (1980) and Schoenbaum et al. (1975), it is found that the quadratic relation (i.e. risk declines from birth order 1 to 2; increases thereafter) captures substantially more of the variance in the sample than the linear relation. (Rubella: r^2 [linear] = 0.04, F [1,106] = 143.5; r^2 [quadratic] = 0.93, F [1,106] = 1423.3; analysis of difference between slopes by Fischer's r to z transform, z = 13.04 [150]. Autism: r^2 [linear] = 0.05, F [1,455] = 45.86; r^2 [quadratic] = 0.46, F [1,455] = 417.3; difference, zRR = 4.07 [151].) The proper analysis of a birth order effect has to take this primiparity effect into consideration.

Sex differences in parity effects. Parity effects are more interesting to examine with an eye to specific hypotheses (Ernst & Angst 1983). If, for example, the question has to do with relative male vulnerability to a negative birth order effect, study of parity effects is enlightening. For

Figure 7. Autism and parity effects, from Deykin and MacMahon (1980).

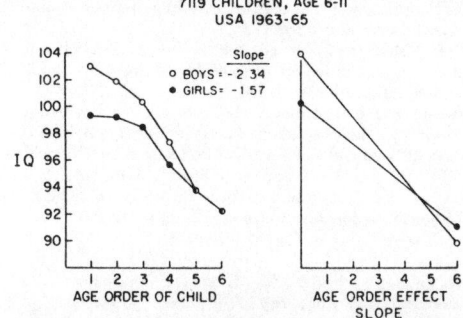

Figure 8. Parity effects on IQ by sex of proband, from the National Health Survey, USA, 1963-65.

example, the authors' reanalysis of data from the Second National Health Survey, 1963-65 (Roberts & Engel 1974), shows that males are more vulnerable to parity effects than females. The National Health Survey was an epidemiologically sophisticated population survey of 7,119 American children age 6-9 (Roberts & Engel 1974). One part of the survey was an IQ estimate derived from vocabulary and block design subtests of the Wechsler Intelligence Scale for Children. In this survey, clear parity effects on IQ were found; however, the parity effect was felt more sharply by boys than girls (see Figure 8). The slope of the regression line of IQ on birth orders is −2.34 for boys and −1.57 for girls. (Orthogonal polynominal regression analysis, sex × birth order [linear], F [1,7117] = 239.13, $p < .005$. After we had made this analysis, Steelman and Mercy published the same data set using multiple regression analysis, and demonstrated the same effect [Steelman & Mercy 1983].)

Our reanalysis of IQ data published in two additional studies confirms the relative susceptibility of male offspring to negative birth order effects. In 1965, Reed and Reed published *Mental retardation. A family study*, an extraordinary and unique collection of pedigree analyses on 289 residents of an institution for the mentally retarded in Minnesota. Actual IQ scores were available for 258 probands, 118 boys and 140 girls. These were regressed against birth order. The correlation between IQ and birth order for boys was negative ($r = −0.45$, $p < .001$, slope = −1.5) whereas for girls the correlation was actually positive ($r = 0.48$, $p < .001$, slope = 1.4) (difference between slopes, F [1,256] = 37.075, $p < .0005$).

The data are even more striking in a more homogeneous group of mentally retarded children who had all been born prematurely. These data were reanalyzed from Moore's 1965 study of 137 mentally retarded residents of the Arizona Children's Colony. The correlation between birth order and degree of retardation was again negative for boys ($N = 63$, $r = −0.85$, p .001, slope = −0.74) and positive for girls ($N = 71$, $r = 0.93$, $p < .001$, slope +0.30) (F [1,126] = 11.22, $p < .001$).

It is clear that there is more to parity effects than a simple birth order analysis yields. The sex of the proband is a relevant variable, but it is not usually considered in birth order studies of cognitive development or of neuropsychiatric disorders.

If parity effects are greater on the male fetus, one should expect to see the birth of developmentally handicapped boys earlier in the sibship. The data of Reed and Reed (1965) and of Moore (1965) provide at least some support for this prediction. The mean birth rank for 137 boys in Reed and Reed was 3.3 (±2.4) and for 152 girls, 3.7 (±2.5). In Moore, the mean birth rank for boys ($N = 63$) was 3.1 (±3.0) and for girls ($N = 71$) 3.3 (±2.5). Although neither result was significant at the 0.05 level, both were in the predicted direction.

Another way to look at parity effects is to examine the sex ratio–parity interaction in special populations. Sex ratio decreases with parity in the general population, but the decrement is very small (slope = -0.001 [Novitski & Sandler 1956]). The IMRT predicts that the sex ratio–parity regression line will be steeper in developmentally impaired populations because of increased occurrence of maternal immunoreactivity. A comparison of sex ratio–parity lines is given in Figure 9 for three populations: the general population from the 1946–52 U.S. vital statistics (Novitski & Sandler 1956), a sample of 496 patients with congenital cleft lip–palate (Woolf 1971), and 880 siblings and probands from Reed and Reed's MR study (1965). The regression lines are substantially steeper, by a factor of 30, in the two disordered samples.

Yet another way to analyze parity effects in light of the IMRT is to test the hypothesis that with increasing birth order, offspring should increasingly come to resemble their mothers. Having been sensitized by several previous pregnancies, mothers ought to "prefer" antigenically similar zygotes. This hypothesis is guided, of course, by the fact that the sex ratio decreases with parity; that is, relatively more girls are born later in the sibship. Judging from the very small sex-ratio effect, however, we think that only a very large data base will yield a proper answer to this question.

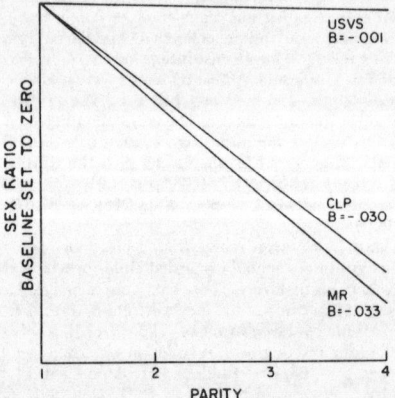

Figure 9. Sex ratio and parity, normal and handicapped populations from Novitski & Sandler (1956); Reed & Reed (1965); and Woolf (1971). USVS = United States Vital Statistics, i.e., census data. CLP = cleft lip and palate; MR = mentally retarded.

An atheoretical approach to parity effects in psychiatric illness or neurodevelopmental disorders, executed in relatively small and possibly biased samples, is not likely to yield useful information. Within the context of a specific hypothesis, however, such as relative male–female vulnerability or the IMRT, the study of birth order effects can be both interesting and enlightening.

Parity effects and IQ. In 1874 Francis Galton noted a disproportionate number of firstborn children among fellows of the Royal Society. Galton was the first modern scientist to suggest that primogeniture conferred a unique and selective advantage on intellectual development. The modern variant is found in studies of parity or birth order effects on intelligence. It is reasonably well established that IQ scores of first borns are higher, and that IQ decreases with birth order (Belmont & Marolla 1973), even when maternal age is controlled. This finding has usually been explained in psychosocial terms: parents spend more time with first-born children, they play with them more, they talk to them more, they expect more of them (Altus 1966; Galton 1874; Zajonc 1976). The family environment of later borns is necessarily shared and diminished. This is an intuitive explanation, and one that is given to empirical examination; however, attempts to confirm the hypothesis have not been notably successful (Ernst & Angst 1983; Grotevant, Scarr & Weinberg 1977). For example, socioeconomic advantage and early stimulation mitigates, but does not abolish parity effects on IQ (Zajonc 1983). The family–environment argument, or confluence model, (Zajonc 1976) predicts that closer spacing of siblings will compound the parity effect; in fact, spacing effects on intellectual development have not been found to exist in developed countries, where close spacing does not lead to maternal undernutrition (Belmont, Stein & Zybert 1978; Grotevant et al. 1977).

Negative parity effects are found not only for IQ and academic achievement, which may be amenable to psychosocial explanation, but also for specific learning disabilities (Badian 1984; Schrag 1973), mental retardation (Belmont, Stein & Wittes 1976), perinatal mortality (Niswander & Gordon 1972), and height (Belmont, Stein & Susser 1975) which clearly are not. Parity effects have even been observed in newborns (Waldrop & Bell 1966). The IMRT represents an alternative, biological explanation for negative parity effects in general, and it is particularly germane to parity effects on intellectual development.

The antecedent brother effect. The IMRT predicts that parity effects on later born boys will be greater if antecedent siblings are boys. In such cases, mothers may be sensitized to H-Y antigen, or to other sex-linked antigens. This sensitization can compromise the development of subsequent male fetuses. The idea is borrowed from studies of the sex ratio and of placentation relative to antecedent brothers. The antecedent brother hypothesis can be tested by comparing relative parity effects on any neurodevelopmental measure in males with antecedent brothers against males with antecedent sisters. Crossed comparisons can also be made with females who have antecedent brothers or sisters.

In a study of college entrance examination scores in 1013 students, secondborn males were found to score

Gualtieri & Hicks: Immunoreactive theory

lower than firstborn males, whereas secondborn females scored the same as or higher than firstborn females. Boys with older sisters scored higher than boys with older brothers. The data in this paper, however, were not sufficient to allow a statistical reanalysis (Rosenberg & Sutton-Smith 1969).

Additional statistical support for the antecedent brother hypothesis is available, however, in Breland's study of 794,589 eleventh grade students who took the National Merit Scholarship Qualifying Test in 1965 (Breland 1974). In our reanalysis of these data, four family configurations were compared: males with antecedent brothers, males with antecedent sisters, females with antecedent brothers, and females with antecedent sisters. Negative parity effects are seen for all four groups, but the sharpest negative parity effect is observed in boys with antecedent brothers (Gualtieri, Hicks & Mayo 1984b).

These two data sets contain selected populations, college bound high-school students and college freshmen, who are not representative of the population as a whole. The fact that these students were at least 16 years old means that psychosocial factors may have played a role in the development of younger children from same sexed sibships, but we are not aware of a convincing psychosocial explanation for such an effect.

The antecedent brother hypothesis could conceivably be tested in large populations relative to any intellectual, developmental, or neuropathic measure. It could also be tested in deviant populations: In mentally retarded children, for example, the hypothesis predicts that increased severity or retardation will occur in males who have antecedent brothers compared to males who have antecedent sisters. The antecedent brother effect may also play a role in some other hypotheses derived from the IMRT.

Subfertility. If maternal immunoreactivity is related to development disorders, one may expect to see relative infertility in the families of developmentally disabled children. Relative infertility can be measured indirectly by family size or directly by the length of time required for unprotected mothers to conceive. In fact, relative infertility has been found in mothers of children with mental retardation (Wallace 1974), Down's syndrome and cerebral palsy (Tips, Smith & Mayer 1964), epilepsy and congenital anomalies (Drillien 1968), learning problems (Nichols & Chen 1981), and low birth weight (Wilson, Parmelee & Huggins 1963). This effect is even more pronounced when the disordered child is male (Wallace 1974). There is, as a rule, a longer period of relative infertility after the birth of male children (Wyshak 1969).

The IMRT predicts not only that relative infertility should characterize mothers of developmentally disabled children, but also that the phenomenon should be more apparent when the disabled child is a male. This prediction is supported by at least one study of children with febrile seizures (Bernard 1977). A reanalysis of Reed and Reed (1965) reveals that mentally retarded males tend to come from smaller families (males, mean family size 6.1, females 7.0, $t = 2.12$, $P = 0.02$, one-tailed test). Maternal immunoreactivity may contribute to the birth of a fetus who is developmentally retarded and may also lower fertility thereafter.

Studies of maternal subfertility and reproductive inefficiency support the IMRT, but further studies with much larger samples ought to be done.

Additional hypotheses. The IMRT predicts that antigenic dissimilarity would increase the likelihood of maternal immune attack upon the fetus. When a developmentally handicapped child is born into a large sibship, it is hypothesized that he will be more likely to differ from his mother in measurable antigenic characteristics such as HLA or ABO. It is also predicted that there will be a tendency for later born sibs to resemble their mothers more closely in terms of the same antigenic characteristics. It is also proposed that antigenically dissimilar matings will be prone to produce female offspring. These hypotheses are based, of course, on the premise that H-Y and other antigen systems exercise an additive effect. They could conceivably be tested in the data banks that are maintained by tissue transplant services when typing records are maintained on families.

The IMRT is premised on the idea of an immunoreactive subgroup of mothers. It predicts that such immunoreactive mothers will exhibit an increased incidence of infertility and maternal insufficiency. It is possible that such women may be identified by the presence of allergic or autoimmune disorders. The occurrence of maternal insufficiency in women with autoimmune disease has been reviewed above. We propose that allergic and autoimmune disorders will occur more commonly in the mothers of developmentally handicapped children, in their families, and in the children themselves.

In fact, parents of developmentally disabled children frequently complain of their children's proneness to allergies. Although this has never received much attention from clinicians or researchers, recent studies have shown patterns of abnormal immunoresponsivity in children with infantile autism and Down's syndrome (Fialkow 1966; Stubbs 1976; Stubbs & Crawford 1977; Weizman, Weizman, Szekely, Wijsenbeek & Levni 1982). The IMRT predicts that mothers of such children would include a substantial number of immunoreactive individuals, and this factor could contribute to their children's disabilities. In support, abnormal levels of immunoreactivity have been reported in the families of children with Down's syndrome (Fialkow 1966). Geschwind's recent report of an increased occurrence of autoimmune disorders in left handers and their families is also consistent with this line of thinking, although in that study no distinction was made between familial and pathological sinistrals (Geschwind & Behan 1982). The latter would be expected to exhibit the trait more strongly. It is not unreasonable to suggest that a genetic disposition to autoimmune or allergic disorders might be associated with heightened maternal immunoreactivity, and non-right handedness may simply be one more clinical consequence thereof.

Clinicians who work with developmentally handicapped children occasionally come upon families who exhibit this pattern: the first child is normal, the second, learning disabled, and the third, retarded or autistic. Such families represent an ideal immunoreactive subgroup for further investigation. Mothers whose children follow such a pattern would be expected to be especially immunoreactive and might also be expected to have strong family histories of immunoreactive disorders. Hypotheses concerning specific kinds of immune activity connected with maternal-fetal attack would best be tested in such a subgroup.

Finally, a farfetched idea, but one which is intriguing and irresistible to us in light of the foregoing: there appears to be a unique and truly remarkable association between the sex of the fetus and schizophrenia occurring in pregnancy. In 1967, Shearer, Davidson, and Finch reported that only female children were born to women who conceived within one month before or after an acute schizophrenic episode. This finding was later confirmed by M. A. Taylor (1969) who also reported four stillbirths (all males), two perinatal deaths (both male) and six severe birth defects (five of six male) in mothers who became psychotic during the second or third month of pregnancy. It was suggested that there is a factor in acutely psychotic mothers that is especially toxic to the male embryo (Shearer et al. 1967). This element could be hormonal, but, in light of some recent autoimmune theories of schizophrenia, it could also be immunologic. Perhaps the element is the initiation of an acute hyperimmune state provoked by the fetus, leading to maternal attack not only against fetal tissue, but also against her own brain tissue. Of course there is no direct evidence to support the idea. But it is not outlandish to suggest that hypotheses germane to the IMRT might be profitably tested in schizophrenics, at least in schizophrenics with early onset or evidence of neuropathic damage.

Summary

The IMRT draws from a diverse array of sources to present a possible etiology for many cases of neurodevelopmental impairment. It is concerned with the problems of selective male affliction, maternal insufficiency, the structure of sex differences, and negative parity effects on intellectual development. The strongest appeal of the theory lies neither in its internal consistency nor in its success in bringing together obscure and seemingly unrelated findings, but in its ability to engender testable hypotheses. Many of these are affirmed in the literature or by preliminary investigations derived from existing data. The theory suggests two interesting routes for further investigation: the antecedent brother effect and the study of immunoreactive subgroups. We strongly suggest that studies of parity effects, pre- and perinatal complications, maternal insufficiency, and family genetic background relative to intellectual development take the following elements into considerations: the sex of the proband and of antecedent siblings, and the family proclivity to autoimmune and to allergic disorders.

If the theory were supported by research along the lines suggested above, hypotheses concerning specific immunologic mechanisms might be developed. Such research might yield strategies for the prevention of some of the neurodevelopmental disorders of childhood.

ACKNOWLEDGMENTS
The authors wish to acknowledge the contributions of the following to the preparation of this manuscript: Susan Council, Sue Ellis, Morris Lipton, James Mayo, and Debra Patterson. Work was supported in part by grants from the National Institute of Child Health and Human Development (HD 07201) and from the National Institute of Mental Health (MH 33127).

Commentary/Gualtieri & Hicks: Immunoreactive theory

Open Peer Commentary

Commentaries submitted by the qualified professional readership of this journal will be considered for publication in a later issue as Continuing Commentary on this article. Integrative overviews and syntheses are especially encouraged.

Immunoselection and male diseases

Matteo Adinolfi
Paediatric Research Unit, Prince Philip Research Laboratories, Guy's Hospital Medical School, London SE1 9RT, England

On the whole, I think it is unlikely that Gualtieri & Hicks (G & H) can convince a large number of readers that maternal imunoreactivity to fetal, male-specific antigens is responsible for the higher frequency and severity of diseases in males than in females. Although they cite a very long list of presumptive evidence to support their hypothesis, they provide little critical analysis of the data mentioned.

For example, much emphasis is given to the theory, first put forward by Kirby and collaborators (Kirby 1967; Kirby, McWhirter, Testelhaum & Darlington 1967) that antigenic differences between zygote and mother confer implantation advantages. Yet in 1975 McLaren reanalyzed these studies and concluded that "the experimental foundations on which the hypothesis was originally based are no longer secure and much evidence points to the opposite direction" (p. 270).

Again, when G & H attribute "the advantage enjoyed by males in the primary and secondary sex ratio . . . to their unique possession of the H-Y antigen," they do not cite the many studies showing that maternal H-Y antibodies do not induce an immunoselection against Y-bearing sperm or male blastocysts (Hoppe & Koo 1984; McLaren 1962).

G & H also often cite studies by Renkonen and collaborators (Renkonen, Mäkelä & Lehtovaara 1962; Renkonen & Timonen 1967). These suggest that in humans the sex ratio at birth becomes progressively lower with increasing parity and that this can be attributed to maternal immunization against male antigens. However, a careful analysis of the published data does not support an immunological interpretation, first because the variations of the sex ratios were only marginal, and second because the sex ratios of the fourth or fifth child after three or four previous male infants were not lower than those observed at the end of the first pregnancy.

When G & H, in order to support their theory, stress that "toxemia, which is probably an autoimmune disorder, is more common when the fetus is male," they overlook more recent investigations which have not confirmed a higher incidence of male than female conceptuses (Juberg, Gaar, Humphries, Cenac & Zambie 1976; Redman, Bodmer, Bodmer, Berlin & Bonnar 1978).

Readers actively working in the field of immunology of reproduction will also find it disturbing to see so many papers miscited. For example Loke (1978) is often mentioned in the text to imply that he supports certain findings and conclusions. Yet these findings are only cited critically in his book on the immunology and immunopathology of human fetal–maternal interaction. My own work is miscited, first, because I have not shown transfer of lymphocytes across the placenta – on the contrary, I maintain that there is little or no traffic of these cells between mother and fetus – and second because the references reported in the text deal with a different topic. In describing the results of the studies of Lawler, Ukaejoofo & Reeves (1975) on maternal–newborn cell interaction G & H imply that the maternal immunoreactivity was more likely when the fetus was male. Yet the entire investigation was performed using families with male infants.

Commentary/Gualtieri & Hicks: Immunoreactive theory

The hypothesis reproposed by G & H is very interesting and it may explain why in certain disorders males are more severely affected than females, but in expounding and supporting a theory still surrounded by controversy, G & H should be presenting a more balanced account of the experimental data.

Testing the immunoreactive theory

William W. Beatty[a], Patricia A. Beatty[a], and Donald E. Goodkin[b]
[a]*Department of Psychology, North Dakota State University, Fargo, N. Dak. 58105 and* [b]*Neuropsychiatric Institute, Fargo, N. Dak. 58103*

The principal attraction of the immunoreactive theory (IMRT) is the prospect that its central concept can unify hitherto unrelated findings concerning gender differences in a variety of neurological, psychiatric, pediatric, and behavioral disorders of childhood within a framework that can also encompass parity effects on the viability and cognitive development of normal males and females. Given the enormity of this goal it is not surprising that the empirical basis of support for the IMRT, at least at present, is less than secure. Furthermore, Gualtieri & Hicks (G & H) interpret some of their own data in a way we regard as overly enthusiastic. For example, consider the data reported in Table 2. Examination of IQ and SQ (social quotient) scores for developmentally disabled children indicates that, on average, males are less severely impaired than females, but there are roughly three times as many impaired males as females. Ostensibly these data support the view advanced by G & H that the occurrence of neurodevelopmental disorders in females is "largely influenced by the genotype" whereas in males "the occurrence of neurodevelopmental disorders is mediated by a genotype by environment interaction; pre- and perinatal problems play a more important role *and their manifestation is more diverse*" (emphasis added). In statistical terms this means that on any index of development the variability in the scores of handicapped males ought to be greater than the variability in the scores of handicapped females. Inspection of the standard deviations in Table 2 offers only modest support for this prediction.

To provide stronger support for the IMRT, data of the sort collected by Hicks and Gualtieri (1984) would have to reveal that: (1) The frequency of profoundly disturbed males is at least as great as the frequency of profoundly disturbed females. This follows from the assumption that the most devastating departures from normal development are primarily the results of genetic influences. If this is true for females, it must also be true for males. (Whether there should be an equal number of severely disturbed males or females or a slight preponderance of males depends on whether or not one assumes that the important genes are located only on autosomes or on autosomes and the X chromosome.) (2) There is a marked preponderance of moderately disturbed males because of the presumably greater tendency of antigens produced by the male fetus to provoke an immunological counterattack by its host-mother. As the data of Hicks and Gualtieri (1984) are presented, however, one cannot judge how well they fit the more precise predictions of the theory.

The major drawback of the immunoreactive theory is that there is simply no serological or pathological evidence to support an argument for an immunological attack on the child's central nervous system or the mother's uterus or placenta in any of the conditions listed by G & H. (It is also noteworthy that many of the "developmental disorders" listed in their Table 1 are not truly developmental; several are postinfectious, inflammatory, metabolic, vascular, or postanoxic.) Immunologically mediated conditions leave pathological calling cards which are clearly definable and reproducible in animal models. Serological abnormalities are also present in such conditions and are definable, reproducible, and even fluctuate measurably with disease activity. An immunoreactive theory not taking these aspects of basic clinical immunology into account is open to serious question and criticism. Even if this theory is statistically supported, one should remain skeptical as to whether a significant primary immunological mechanism is etiologic. It is obvious that "maleness" can affect a patient's response to a variety of insults without implicating an immunological process. The theory proposed reaches conclusions without having properly dealt with the potentially potent effects of other factors such as hormone levels.

Intellectually gifted students also suffer from immune disorders

Camilla Persson Benbow
Study of Mathematically Precocious Youth, Department of Psychology, Johns Hopkins University, Baltimore, Md. 21218

Gualtieri & Hicks (G & H) present an intriguing immunoreactive theory of selective male affliction. From this theory they predict that "allergic and autoimmune disorders will occur more commonly in the mothers of developmentally handicapped children, in their families, and in the children themselves." Geschwind and Behan (1982) and Behan (in press) have found such a relationship. Some new findings from my work with intellectually talented students also bear on this issue, but may be difficult to reconcile with the theory.

My study involved over 400 highly precocious students who had been tested earlier than usual with the Scholastic Aptitude Test (SAT) – Mathematics and Verbal – in a talent search and *before age 13* had scored at least 700 on SAT-M and/or 630 on SAT-V. Such students are estimated to represent at least the top 1 in 10,000 of their age group. Among such students I found a high frequency (over 50%) of allergies or other immune disorders (Benbow 1984). This was much higher than in the general population (10–20%) and in a much less able but gifted comparison group (35%). Moreover, the parents and siblings of these extremely precocious students were also more likely to suffer from such disorders (Benbow 1984). Although it seems plausible that maternal immunological attack against fetal brain antigens can cause learning disabilities or neurological impairment, it is not exactly clear to me how it can cause extreme intellectual giftedness. My training is not in this specific area, however.

There are well-documented sex differences favoring males in several specific abilities, such as high mathematical reasoning ability (Benbow & Stanley, 1980; 1983). Such differences may not be the sole result of environmental factors. It would be interesting if a theory dealing with selective male affliction could also account for selective male advantage. It is, of course, conceivable that they are independent.

In conclusion, I find the immunoreactive theory appealing and hope G & H can address the above concerns.

Male antigenicity and parity

Carl-Gustaf Berglin
Parkgatan 12, S 411 38 Gothenburg, Sweden

In their target article Gualtieri & Hicks (G & H) point out that many of the findings they refer to may have alternative explanations. Their theory, however, finds strong support in the overrepresentation of congenital disorders in males. This phenomenon had already been observed in the 1860s by Mitchell (1866), who found a sex ratio of 1.27 among 1,345 mentally retarded. W. H. James (1975) stated that the interval between a male and a female (MF) pregnancy is longer than in MM and FF cases and that the average FM interval is especially short. Among early-born schizophrenics more men than women become hospitalized (Schooler 1964). One should not forget, however, that women are much more prone to affective psychoses. The findings of Juret, Couette, Delozier, Leplat, Mandard & Vernhes (1978) – that mothers who many years after the birth of a firstborn boy developed a breast cancer with axillary node involvement had a much better prognosis than mothers with a female first pregnancy ($\chi^2 = 11.08$, $p < .001$) – are highly suggestive of immunoreaction.

The occurrence of obstetrical complications in mentally retarded offspring or in boys who later develop autism (Table 3) is suggestive but should be compared with complications in pregnancies in which the offspring are not disturbed in order to clarify the connection between male sex and disorder. Parity, too, plays a marked role in Table 3. Provided there are no mixed cases (with two antecedent siblings), a combination of the two subtables into one 2×3 cell table leads to a χ^2 of 10.96, $p < .005$, clearly indicating that antecedent sisters contribute to the complications, a parity effect.

Control groups from the general population are crucial in all birth order studies. Cobb stressed this as early as 1914 in a criticism of the fallacious Greenwood-Yule model that later exerted a disastrous influence on birth order research for half a century. Weinberg (1913) had shown that sibship size must be taken into account before estimating any birth order effect; a trait that is more common in large sibships will elude a seeming overrepresentation of late ranks which are lacking in small sibships. The works of Hare and Price (1969) and of Birtchnell (1971) started a new era in international birth order research. Changes in birth cohort size, family size and length of intersibling interval produce an excess of late or early borns that is accessible to accurate calculation (Berglin 1981). It is now possible to predict the variation of birth ranks even in five-year cohorts of the general population fairly exactly (Berglin 1982).

In connection with G & H's reanalysis of the Reed and Reed (1965) study I find myself obliged to show (for the first time in literature, actually) how mean rank can be computed.

In a family of five, the sibling with rank III occupies the space from 2.00 to 2.99 around a mean point of 2.5. As the middle child, it occupies the middle position of its sibship: $2.5/5 = .5$. A person with rank r among s siblings can be regarded as having the position $p = (r - \frac{1}{2})/s$.

If a sample is distributed with only children in one row, probands from two-child families in a second row, probands from three-child families in a third row, and so on, as in Table 1, we can record the number of probands in a certain row in an n-column so that Σn is the total number of probands. After dividing each n-value by its corresponding s-value we arrange a column of (n/s)-expressions. This column describes the relative distribution of families within $\Sigma(n/s)$ families in that population from which the probands were chosen. The mean size of such families is $\Sigma n/\Sigma(n/s)$, as Greenwood and Yule correctly demonstrated in 1914.

Now to the new formula, that of mean rank: The mean position of a sample is the sum of positions divided by the number of positions: $\bar{p} = \Sigma p/\Sigma n$. The mean point of any complete sibship is $.5 \times s$, for instance, $.5 \times 5 = 2.5$. The mean rank is registered half a space higher: $2.5 + \frac{1}{2} =$ rank III. With mean rank $\bar{r}$, mean size $\bar{s}$, and mean position $\bar{p}$, we have $\bar{p} = (\bar{r} - \frac{1}{2})/\bar{s}$, or $\bar{r} = \bar{p}\bar{s} + \frac{1}{2}$. The analysis above allows us to simplify: $\bar{r} = \Sigma p/\Sigma n \times \Sigma n/\Sigma(n/s) + \frac{1}{2}$, that is, mean rank of a sample: $\bar{r} = \Sigma p/\Sigma(n/s) + \frac{1}{2}$.

Table 1 is chosen for its simplicity and taken from the pedigree charts of Reed and Reed: 19 males in the primarily environmental category. A fourth column of ns-values has been added, giving the sum of all members of the probands' sibships. One cannot simply divide this sum by the sum of sibships represented ($\Sigma(ns)/\Sigma n$) in order to compute a sort of mean sibship size; that would be a coarse overestimation because large sibships are overrepresented. $\Sigma(ns)$ is needed for calculating the variance of $\bar{s}$: $\Sigma(ns)/\Sigma(n/s) - \bar{s}^2$. This variance divided by $(\Sigma(n/s) - 1)$ gives the squared error of $\bar{s}$ (Berglin 1981, p. 57).

If one treats the total male sample of Reed and Reed (136, not 137, boys, for case KMD 276 was wrongly described as a male) in this way, one arrives at a mean sibship size of $4.17 \pm .54$ and a mean rank of 2.4. The 153 females have a mean sibship size of $5.43 \pm .56$ and a mean rank of 3.0.

Most authors writing on birth order influences have until now made the same mistakes, but no doubt the new methods will slowly penetrate. Of course this formal flaw does not in the least detract from the interest evoked by G & H's stimulating synopsis and theory.

Table 1. (Berglin). *Arrangement of birth order data for calculating mean sibship size $\bar{s}$, mean sibling position $\bar{p}$, and mean sibling rank $\bar{r}$.*

	Birth order									
s	I	II	III	IV	V	VI	n	n/s	Σp	ns
1	1						1	1	.5	1
2	1						1	.5	.25	2
3		1	2				3	1	2.17	9
4	1	2		1			4	1	1.75	16
5	1			1			2	.4	.8	10
6							—	—	—	—
7	1		1		1		3	.43	1.5	21
8	1						1	.12	.06	8
9	1				1		2	.22	.78	18
10	1						1	.1	.15	10
⋮							⋮			
14				1			1	.07	.32	14
							19	4.84	8.28	109

Note: $\bar{s} = 19/4.84 = 3.92$; $\bar{p} = 8.28/19 = .44$; $\bar{r} = 8.28/4.84 + .5 = 2.21$; $\text{var}_{\bar{s}} = 109/4.84 - 3.92^2 = 7.15$; $\text{error}_{\bar{s}} = (7.15/3.84)^{\frac{1}{2}} = 1.36$.

The sex ratio at conception: Male biased or 100?

Ray H. Bixler
Department of Psychology, University of Louisville, Louisville, Ky. 40292

Gualtieri & Hicks's (G & H's) target article is a substantial heuristic contribution to both practice and theory. It should hasten our understanding of the effects of the interaction of birth (and pregnancy) order with the sex of the child. It will certainly stimulate prenatal sex differences research. It might even encourage those many investigators who study embryos without regard to sex to identify conceptuses as female or male. It has been obvious for some time that momentous physiological events early in gestation play a crucial role in sex differences in morphology and behavior. Nevertheless, much embryological research has ignored sex as a dimension.

G & H's reference to the strong male bias of sex ratios at conception is the focus of my comments. The primary sex ratio is central to any theory or analysis of selective male affliction. The immunoreactive theory (IMRT) is strengthened by the widely held belief that the conception ratio is 110 or higher (Daly & Wilson 1983; Kellokumpu-Lehtinen & Pelliniemi 1984; McMillen 1979; Ounsted & Taylor 1972; Yamamoto 1977). If,

Commentary/Gualtieri & Hicks: Immunoreactive theory

however, those who have found evidence to support a sex ratio approaching 100 are right (Allan 1975; Mikamo 1969; Sasaki, Ikeuchi, Obara, Hayata, Mori & Kohno 1971) a theoretical adjustment to account for a disproportionate early loss of female embryos is essential.

I think we simply do not know enough to embrace either position at present. Kellokumpu-Lehtinen and Pelliniemi (1984) and Yamamoto (1977) appear to have developed more adequate methods of determining the sex of embryos and fetuses than the investigators who found a sex ratio approaching parity (also see Mikamo 1969 for additional discussion of the intricate problems associated with embryonic sex determination).

Yet there is provocative evidence that a ratio of 100 may be correct. Some other mammals approach parity at conception (Fechheimer & Beatty 1974; W. H. James 1982; Kaufman 1973). If parity is widespread at conception in mammals, it would be unlikely that our species would have evolved a different reproduction pattern (but see Clutton-Brock 1982 for a discussion of secondary sex ratio in a variety of species; also Spector 1956, Table 440). The sex difference, which is found in several disorders that probably develop during the embryonic period, also supports the belief that the ratio may be lower at conception. Anencephaly, spina bifida, cleft palate, and some congenital heart disorders are more common in female neonates (Hay 1971; Moore 1982). If – and it is a big if – these sex differences reflect a much greater female susceptibility to spontaneous malformation during the early and mid-embryonic period, it seems reasonable to assume that spontaneous female abortion would also be much more frequent during this period. Of course, it is possible that these afflictions are actually visited equally on the sexes and that affected males, faced with a less friendly intrauterine environment, are aborted in greater numbers.

Since the issue can be resolved only by examination of zygotes, animal studies are the essential first step. The human conceptuses available for determination of the early sex ratio are clinically aborted fetuses. Since many zygotes and embryos have been spontaneously aborted before these clinical specimens are obtained, no valid data regarding the sex ratio at conception can be collected. Definite conclusions about our species will have to await our developing relevant technology.

The sex ratio at conception is a theoretical issue which does not detract at all from the clinical significance of G & H's article. However, parity at conception would certainly prove heuristic for natural selection theory. What are the ramifications of a reproductive strategy – if it exists – that rapidly rejects atypical female embryos but follows a much more deliberate course with male conceptuses? Some evolutionists have speculated that, especially in polygamous species, a conservative reproductive "policy" is best suited to selection of female offspring but that the payoff from unique male progeny might produce a greater tolerance of diversity in that sex.

Undistributed middle term in the logic of Gualtieri & Hicks's immunoreactive model

Charles E. Boklage
Laboratory of Behavioral and Developmental Genetics, Genetics Program, East Carolina University School of Medicine, Greenville, N.C. 27834

Does the immunoreactivity model generate testable hypotheses? Yes, but I question the specificity and stringency of those offered.

Concentration of complications in a subgroup should cause more concern than it seems to; are there not, for example, genetic reasons why some mothers develop HLA antibodies quickly, others never? Could allergy-proneness in affected children be due to the same immunoreactivity (IMR) genes?

Correlation may suggest, but can never imply, causation.

Even the correlations discussed here have not been sufficiently questioned: Are mothers of neurodevelopmentally disabled (NDD) males indeed excessively immunoreactive compared to mothers of normal children or of NDD girls? This could be directly tested. Negative results would be evidence against any causal relationship between IMR and sex and NDD. If reproductive competence is really reduced in the affected families, can causes, and not just correlations, be found among immune functions?

Gualtieri and Hicks (G & H) consider parity and antecedent brother effects their best evidence against nonimmunological alternative interpretations. But isn't an NDD child more likely to be the last, especially if there is already a son? And wouldn't the likelihood of an affected child being last increase with the number of previous children? How can the reduced reproductive competence proposed for these families be reconciled with proposed parity effects?

The primiparity effect is said to be crucial, then averaged out of subsequent discussion. Least likely to have an immune basis, primiparity is a negative factor in reproductive competence, with known endocrine correlates. Wouldn't the NDD child be more of a problem for new parents, and more likely to reduce further reproduction? Aren't parity effects as likely to be mediated behaviorally as biologically?

Effects of maternal age have not been addressed. Increasing maternal age changes the hormonal dynamics of pregnancy, reduces reproductive competence, and alters immunoreproductive relationships (Holinka 1981). Aging of oocytes, directly, and as a result of coital frequency decreasing with age or parity, increases sex ratio and the probabilities of overripe gamete fertilization and abnormal development (Guerrero 1974; Guerrero & Rojas 1975; Harlap 1980; Lanman 1968; reviewed in Boklage, submitted). Potential for statistical confounding with parity effects is high indeed, and must be addressed.

The autism–parity results of Deykin and MacMahon (1980) are crucial to the argument, but do not make the stated point. If I include 20 autistic children left out because they had no sibs (the omission of which inflates all parities of two or more) and still reluctantly omit nine families with two autistic children each because their birth orders were not published, then all parities greater than one are deficient among the autistic children compared to their normal siblings. (In parity six plus, there are four cases instead of the expected three.) Compared to total live births (North Carolina Vital Statistics 1977), there are among these autistic children six cases more than the expected 21 of fourth and higher parities ($\chi^2 = 1.701$, 3 d.f.) This is far from significant and easily explained by sampling biased toward larger families. (Ideally, the comparison should be made with total live birth parities in the same races, cities and years.) According to Deykin and MacMahon themselves, their results, even without the above changes, "cannot be construed to indicate an excess risk for children who are the youngest of several siblings" (1980, p. 861). I have to agree.

Rubella results (Schoenbaum, Biano & Mack 1975) used by G & H to corroborate the autism results show only an excess of younger mothers among rubella cases compared to controls. Schoenbaum et al. state: "Not only is there no increased risk for multiparae, but there is clearly an excess of primiparae among the mothers with rubella" (p. 154). Table 2 of Schoenbaum et al. shows every parity but the first deficient among rubella cases compared to controls.

G & H's Figure 9 shows the male fraction of mental retardation declining as parity increases. If one imagines that the primary sex ratio is stable to parity and age, then the normal slight decline of the secondary sex ratio would mean reduced male survival to term (because of IMR?). Since the IMR hypothesis equates causes of male excess NDD with those of poor male survival, the fraction of males among retardates should rise with parity to satisfy the model. It falls. If instead, as it seems, the primary sex ratio and developmental anomalies increase with gamete aging (due in part to coital frequency decreasing with age or parity), upward pressure would be even greater. Differential survival to term is a major unaddressed issue.

Sex differences are presumed by G & H to be mediated by histocompatibility differences, not necessarily limited to effects of minor antigens made in response to sex-determining genes on the Y chromosome. But sex affects the outcome of major sex-independent incompatibility (Scott & Beer 1973). We might therefore suppose that compatibility itself, regardless of the antigens in question, is of minor import. Antigenic maleness is present or absent, but for even the highest sex ratios in Table 1, 10–20% of those affected are female. There have to be other determinants, and interactions. Several X-linked genes, for example, affect control of the immune system or surface antigens (McKusick 1983: #30030, 30040, 30823–25, 31345–46, 31470, 31485, 31490).

Steroid hormones modify immunoreproductive relationships (Holinka 1981). The fertile female-preponderant expression of autoimmune disease can be hormonally altered (Smolen & Steinberg 1981). Prospects of endocrine bases for observed sex differences have been too readily dismissed, given known immunoendocrine interactions. Development of the thymus, as with most of the endocrine system, depends on neural crest derivatives (Bockman & Kirby 1984). Which is more sex-dependent?

Since sex differences have long been at issue in studies of usual and unusual brain laterality and NDDs represent anomalies of lateralization or lateralized function as well as of sex ratio, eventual resolution of these questions may be aided by adding laterality to the complexity of the present situation.

Parental nonrighthandedness (NRH) is associated with increased miscarriage and stillbirth and decreased family size (Fraser & Rex 1984). In Rife's (1940) data, families with either parent NRH averaged 15% fewer children, 72% as many sons, and 106% as many daughters, as families with both parents dextral (χ^2 = 5.78, 1 d.f.). Nonrighthandedness is excessive in the parents of twins (Boklage 1981) and in the parents of children with neural tube defects, orofacial clefts, or congenital heart defects, raising prospects of shared genetic neural crest involvement (Boklage & Fraser 1984; Boklage & Fraser, in preparation; Fraser 1983). Autoimmune and allergic disorders are excessive in nonrighthandeders (Geschwind & Behan 1982; 1984) as well as among fertile females, and neuroendocrine relationships are lateralized (Gerendai 1984). A common feature of all these anomalies and relationships is the involvement of cell surface interactions.

An obvious component of sex differences lies in tissue specific growth rates. Genes on both X and Y are involved (Alvesalo & Portin 1980; Alvesalo & Tammisalo 1981; Alvesalo & Varrela 1980) as well as steroid hormones. Such sex and tissue-specific growth has been plausibly implicated in sex differences of both laterality and immune response (Geschwind & Behan 1984).

NDD children and male children have more birth problems. Some birth problems are caused by maternal IMR. It has not been shown that the excess of birth problems is greater in NDD males than in other males, it does not follow that maternal immunoreactivity causes either, and the proposed tests will not fill in the middle. Other tests might, with (in my opinion) a high likelihood of different conclusions.

Possible involvement of maternal alloreactivity in negative parity effects

Antonín Bukovský and Jiří Presl
Institute for the Care of Mother and Child, Prague, Podolí, CS 147 10, Czechoslovakia

Gualtieri & Hicks (G & H) have advanced the idea of selective male affliction by maternal immunoreactivity. However, males are selectively afflicted not only in mammals with the XY male phenotype but also in nonmammalian vertebrates (for instance, male aves have phenotype XX), and even in dimorphic plants (Geodakjan 1983). During the past 20 years Geodakjan has elaborated on an attractive hypothesis concerning the role of sexual dimorphism during evolution (Geodakjan 1982). Sexual dualism may ensure two basic principles of any adaptive system. The female sex represents the conservative genetic aspect ensuring the transmission of the genetic pool from one generation to the other whereas the male sex performs a progressive ecological function by introducing new information from the environment into the system (Geodakjan 1982; 1983). This proposed sexual specialization localizes all advantages and failures in the male subsystem, whereas females ensure the selection of "male experiences" and the transmission of progressive trends into the genetic pool. Females are less phenotypically dispersed and more adaptive during ontogeny, but more stable during phylogeny; the evolutionary changes during ontogeny more easily afflict the male sex, which is depleted in adaptability but favored in variability (Geodakjan 1983).

Nevertheless, particularly in *Placentalia*, the contribution of maternal immunoreactivity to fetal development during intrauterine development cannot be overlooked, transmission of maternal immune influence is even possible during breast feeding (Beer & Billingham 1976; Freier & Eidelman 1980). Such maternal immunoreactivity could be either beneficial or deleterious to the fetus and infant. G & H have suggested that Rh isoimmunization, which is clearly of immunological origin and in which minimal risk of affliction to the first Rh+ proband can be expected in Rh− unsensitized mothers (Rote 1982), represents an analogy to negative parity effects on male affliction by maternal immunoreactivity and that the male brain is the most frequently afflicted tissue. Negative parity effects on IQ have been reported in all four possible groups of family configurations of students tested (also in females with antecedent sisters), but the sharpest negative parity effect is observed in boys with antecedent brothers; G & H find no convincing psychosocial explanation for such an effect. One concludes that there is some negative imprint of antecedent pregnancy on the subsequent progeny and that greater male affliction could be related either to higher male sensitivity to the same deleterious effect or to some antigenic substance present in the brain of male fetuses. Until the latter is tested it is difficult to decide between these possibilities. Unfortunately, the mechanisms responsible for selective male affliction by the maternal immune system have not been analyzed in more detail; nor are the mechanisms responsible for survival of fetal allografts yet understood.

If there is some negative effect of parity on brain development, it should be interesting to determine whether a brain organizational process is afflicted or whether it is the organized brain tissue itself which is the target of maternal immunoreactivity. Mental function starts to develop after birth, and in the newborn the brain hemispheres are unmyelinated (Lecours 1975; Yakovlev & Lecours 1967). The organizational process is most vulnerable during its most rapid stage; whereas during the initial stages recovery is possible, with no effect once organization is complete; damage of stable organized tissue can never be recovered from (Scott 1979). The cortex is histologically immature at birth compared to the nuclei of the central gray and brain stem (Trevarthen 1979). The speed of the organizational process may be related to incremental rates in DNA content in the human brain, which exhibit two peaks, one reflecting neuron multiplication in the midgestational period (20th week), and a second corresponding to glial multiplication associated with increased brain weight, dendrite development and synaptogenesis, and peaking in the 12th postnatal week (Dobbing 1971). The organizational process for sensorimotor function, which is already developed to some extent in the newborn, may be more vulnerable during intrauterine life, whereas the organizational process for higher mental function may still be highly

Commentary/Gualtieri & Hicks: Immunoreactive theory

vulnerable during the first postnatal months. DNA incremental rates are lower before term and thus the organizational process may be less active, that is, less vulnerable during parturitional stress; nonetheless, the hitherto organized brain tissue can still be irreversibly afflicted by serious perinatal complications.

In view of the high vulnerability of the organizational process for mental function during the first postnatal months one may wonder how maternal immunoreactivity can postnatally affect subsequent progeny sharing the genetic background of their older sibships. Human colostrum and milk have been shown to possess immunoglobulins of which only low quantities can be absorbed a few days after birth (Ogra, Fishaut & Theodore 1980). There are, however, a considerable number of maternal immunocytes (macrophages, T-cells, B lymphocytes and plasma cells) and polymorphs, whose entry or nonentry into the breast-fed infant's tissues is still an open question. Nevertheless, studies of prolonged breast feeding by tuberculin positive mothers have suggested that there is transient transfer of tuberculin specific T-cell reactivity up to 10 to 12 weeks after birth (Ogra, Fishaut & Theodore 1980). The question can be raised whether or not the prolonged breast feeding of an infant having antecedent sibling can be correlated with lower IQ.

The mechanisms by which the maternal immunocytes may exert a deleterious effect on the developmental organization of the brain or on organized infant brain tissues are as yet highly speculative. We have recently suggested that there are specialized cellular mechanisms controlling cellular differentiation. The functional ability of most proliferating adult tissues may be dependent on a supply of committed Thy-1 glycoprotein released by specialized Thy-1+ cells; a role for Ia+ cells, macrophages, and lymphocyte subsets in the control of tissue growth has also been suggested (Bukovský & Presl 1984; Bukovský, Presl & Holub 1984). Some of these cells (macrophages, lymphocyte subsets) clearly belong to the immune system (IS) and it has been proposed that the IS plays a dual role in the tissues: the first, positive, stimulating cellular proliferation; the second, negative, eliminating superfluous or afunctional cells (Bukovský, Presl & Holub 1984). The other cells participating in the control of tissue growth (Thy-1+ dendritic cells associated with vessels, Ia+ cells of dendritic type) have been hypothesized to belong to a specialized tissue control system (TCS), cooperating with the immune, endocrine, and nervous system in the control of tissue function (Bukovský, Presl & Holub 1984). One of the most complex roles of IS and TCS may be to control the survival of an allogeneic fetus in the mammalian female (Bukovský & Presl 1984; 1985; Bukovský, Presl & Židovský 1984).

We agree that maternal lymphoid cells are unable to invade (allogeneic) fetal tissues during intrauterine life but, as mentioned above, they may enter the infant via breast feeding. The adult brain of various species (including man) has been found not to express class I MHC molecules (for data and review see Ponder, Wilkinson, Wood & Westwood 1983; Williams 1982). In our investigation of the brain development of 20-week-old human fetuses we have found that the maturation of brain cells proliferating from membrana limitans is associated with the interaction of the same control cells of the IS and TCS as described or expected within adult rat tissues, that is, macrophages, lymphocytes, Thy-1+ pericytes, and Ia+ dendritic cells (Bukovský & Presl, unpublished data). Moreover, the developing fetal neuronal cells bordering the "mature" Thy-1+ brain cells exhibit class I MHC molecules in addition to some differentiation antigen (DA) of lymphocytes on their surface, that is, leukocyte common antigen (Bukovský & Presl, unpublished data). Thus the maternal lymphoid cells entering the tissues of a breastfed infant could interfere with the organization of brain development for mental function, which perhaps peaks during the 12th postnatal week. Maternal lymphocytes may react by means of dual recognition (reviewed in Klein 1982), that is, against species-specific DA present on both maternal lymphocytes and fetal lymphoid cells and brain, and against sensitizing allogeneic class I MHC molecules of fetal lymphoid cells or a particular layer of developing neuronal brain cells. Such reactivity simulates the well-known mixed lymphocyte reaction in tissue cultures and is called DA restriction (Bukovský & Presl 1984; 1985). The infant's targets may also be its lymphoid cells participating in the organizational process for postnatal brain development, or the particular layer of still-developing brain tissue. The resulting effect can be either transient interruption or definitive termination of development and the maturation of additional neuronal cells with subsequently lowered brain capacity. As an alternative to the transfer of maternal lymphoid cells from milk, large quantities could enter the fetal tissues via maternofetal "blood transfusions" due to insufficiencies of the fetal placental barrier associated with degenerative changes of the placenta during late stages of pregnancy. Moreover, maternal blood lymphoid cells have been reported to exhibit substantially higher reactivity than milk T-cells against alloantigens (reviewed in Ogra, Fishaut & Theodore 1980). Thus the absolute benefit of therapeutic intrafetal blood transfusions containing viable alloreactive lymphoid cells in Rh isoimmunizations is questionable. It is interesting that retarded, hyperactive, and learning disabled children more frequently tend to be laterborn.

As to possible disadvantages of breast feeding, it has been reported of animals that milk can produce fatal graft-versus-host disease if the progeny of one inbred strain is nursed by the foster mother of another strain with different MHC specificity (Head & Beer 1979). This suggests that an infant should be breast fed only by his own mother. However, subsequent pregnancies could function as booster immunizations against the same father's genetic background, similar to enhanced anti-Rh reactivities in repeatedly sensitized mothers. Breast feeding is greatly beneficial to the infant, however, particularly because of the well-known induction of resistance to negative influences of the environment it produces. It is also tempting to speculate that the introduction of allogeneic MHC molecules into the infant's tissues via maternal milk lymphoid cells could enhance the antiallogeneic reactivity of the infant's IS, the phenomenon considered important in defense against cancer (Bukovský & Presl 1984; 1985).

In conclusion, we suggest that negative parity effects may be related to maternal alloreactivity increasing with birth order. The psychosocial effects among siblings could play an additional role in the mental development of an infant. The selective affliction of males could be in part related to the higher vulnerability of the male sex throughout evolution; possible involvement of male-specific antigen(s) cannot be rejected at present. The only way to minimize negative effects of parity is to avoid prolonging pregnancy or even to deliver shortly before term (38th week of pregnancy), particularly in later pregnancies. In view of the benefits of the biological mother's milk for the newborn, we suggest that the negative effects of longer-lasting breast feeding on the mental development of subsequent progeny with the same genetic background be viewed with suspicion.

Is the H-Y antigen a malefactor?

Hanan Costeff
Loewenstein Hospital and Tel Aviv University School of Medicine, Raanana, Israel

Gualtieri & Hicks's (G & H's) immunoreactive theory contains one central, ambitious, and stimulating idea which, for its own good, should be isolated from the remainder of their essay: the proposition that maternal reactivity to the H-Y antigen damages some male fetuses and thus contributes to the surplus of males in fetal wastage and in early-onset psychiatric, neurologic, and developmental disorders. Like any original thought, the theory's appeal is inseparable from the risk it runs. It is elegant, testable, and therefore unlikely to be confirmed. In my opinion there is no need to wed it to such postulated mechanisms as brain antibodies, ABO and HLA incompatibility, or maternal allergic and autoimmune disease, all of which fail to explain selective male vulnerability. In fact, to invoke brain antibodies is not only unnecessary but positively harmful. Should an H-Y stimulated maternal immune attack on the male fetus be confirmed, it could conceivably operate through nonneuroimmunologic mechanisms, explaining the male preponderance in nonneurologic, postnatal morbidity (Winter 1972). How brain antibodies could mediate these phenomena is difficult to imagine.

The hypotheses arising from this theory include the following:
1. In the population:
   a. Male intelligence will show a lower mean and a larger variance than female.
   b. Male intelligence will negatively correlate with numbers ($n \geq 1$) of elder brothers when social class is held constant, whereas female intelligence will not. Similar but weaker correlations will obtain with birth order and family size.
2. In brain-damaged groups:
   a. More complications of pregnancy will occur with male fetuses than with females. ("Complications" include a mother who tends to abort.)
   b. Proportion of male fetuses with complications of pregnancy will positively correlate with number of elder brothers, and less strongly with birth order and family size, when allowance is made for social class. Females will show no such phenomenon; pooled males and females will show it to an intermediate degree.

The population data so far adduced are equivocal. Birth order, when rendered independent of family size or social class, shows the expected effect on Raven scores of 19-year-old males in Holland (Belmont & Marolla 1973), but not on IQs of Scottish and French schoolchildren (Zajonc 1976). The expected birth-order effect is seen in all National Merit Scholarship Qualifying Test (NMSQT) scores among gifted American college applicants, but the same data show a male superiority, against expectations (Zajonc 1976). Since the theory attempts to explain a minority brain damage phenomenon, gifted groups may not be appropriate for testing the hypothesis. In that case, however, the observed American birth-order effect would not be relevant to the theory. At least one report (Altus 1966) suggests that in the U.S. this birth-order effect is indeed seen in bright college candidates but not in high-school graduates as a whole.

No brain-damaged populations have yet been analyzed to test the above hypotheses, with the exception of G & H's data on autistic children. After reading their target article I reviewed the raw data on Israeli mental retardates who were the subject of previous reports (Costeff, Cohen & Weller 1983a; 1983b). Among nonspecific retardates of nonconsanguineous parents the sex ratio was about 3 to 2 as in other series. Complications of pregnancy and delivery were seen in 58.2% of the males and 61.5% of the females. Fewer complications in males would suggest a genetic X-linked factor rather than immune attack. The difference is not significant, but even equality would go against the immune hypothesis.

Number of elder brothers and birth order are not readily available, but number of siblings at time of assessment is at hand. I analyzed the data separately for mildly and severely retarded probands and found the same trend in both. The overall association between family size, sex, and proportion of cases with complications of pregnancy and/or delivery is seen in Table 1. The trend, observed equally in both sexes, is for complications to be associated with smaller families, and presumably with lower birth order. The trend is statistically signifi-

Table 1 (Costeff). *Proportions of retardates with complications of pregnancy or delivery*

	Sibship size			
Sex	1–2	3–4	≥5	Total
Male	47/70	44/68	26/63	117/201
Female	32/38	23/47	28/50	83/135

cant, and it is against the hypothesis. One possible explanation for this finding could be that an insidious maternal immune attack on the fetal brain is parity related and is not associated with bleeding, toxemia, or other complications. This would be consistent with Adinolfi's (1976) suggestions, but not with the immunoreactive theory as stated by G & H. Since the trend holds for both sexes, it also allows no significant role for the H-Y antigen.

Two other reported findings seem intuitively to conflict with the immunoreactive theory. One would expect an increasing preponderance of male fetal loss toward the end of pregnancy, but this seems not to occur (McMillen 1979; Ounsted 1972). Similarly, one would expect cases of congenital cerebral palsy to show a higher sex ratio than cases of postnatal cause, but they likewise do not (Stanley & Blair 1984).

These observations lessen the likelihood that the immunoreactive theory will be confirmed, but they do not completely refute it. In view of its attractiveness, the theory deserves further testing on its own terms. What this means is that sex and order of all pregnancies in the family have become relevant data for those of us who collect statistics on intelligence and on varieties of childhood brain dysfunction.

A possible role of sex steroid hormones in determining immune deficiency differences between the sexes

Marian C. Diamond
Department of Physiology-Anatomy, University of California, Berkeley, Calif. 94720

Gualtieri & Hicks (G & H) offer strong support for a most reasonable theory that male fetal antigenicity may induce a state of maternal immunoreactivity. They also mention that endocrine effects may be a plausible alternative. Perhaps both an endocrine effect and an antigenic effect play a role. Not being an immunologist, I respect the authors' well documented proposal, but I offer some thoughts about a possible role of the sex steroid hormones in determining immune deficiency differences between the sexes.

My reasoning is as follows: Estrogen receptors are present in both the female and male rat cerebral cortex for about the first three weeks of life (MacLusky, Chaptal & McEwen 1979). In the male at birth, the right hemisphere is significantly thicker than the left, although there are areas where this is not true. The female left cortex is in general thicker than the right, but not significantly so (Diamond, Dowling & Johnson 1981). We found that the addition of exogenous estrogen to the sexually mature female, which had been ovariectomized at birth, decreases her cortical thickness (Pappas, Diamond & Johnson 1979). After removing the gonads at birth and examining changes in asymmetrical patterns in the adult cortex, we also found that sex steroid hormones play a role in laterality (Diamond et al. 1981).

With this knowledge, Sandhu, Cook & Diamond (unpublished) from our laboratory have hypothesized that cortical

Commentary/Gualtieri & Hicks: Immunoreactive theory

laterality may be induced by estrogen and that therefore the left cortex in the male would have more estrogen receptors during the early weeks of the animal's life. If this is true for the male, then the opposite is true for the female. With their recent data Sandhu et al. have shown that the male does indeed have more estrogen receptors in his left cortex during the first weeks of life and the female possesses the opposite. The estrogen receptors are no longer present after the first few weeks of life, as has been reported by others (MacLusky et al. 1979). The high levels of testosterone in the early stage of the male rodents' life may be responsible, when converted to estrogen, for determining the pattern of laterality.

The knowledge that male rats have a thinner left cortex and females in most cases a thinner right proved of value in the next series of experiments when we had learned that lesions in the left cortex of female mice reduced natural killer lymphocytes. Lesions in the right cortex did not (Renoux, Biziere, Renoux & Guillaumin 1980). Here was evidence that the left cerebral cortex could alter immune functions. We ask now a major question: is the left or right hemisphere associated with mediating immune responses in the male? We are presently measuring the cortical thickness in the male and female nude mouse and have found that in the female the frontal lobes and area 2 are significantly thinner than in a BALBc (mouse strain) control. The nude female mouse's area 18 in the left cortex is also significantly thinner than in the right. The measurements of the male are not as yet complete, although shortly we will have the answers from them as well. If the left cortex is thinner than the right in the male nude as well as in the BALBc control, then the evidence collected so far points to the left cortex as being related to immune functions in both males and females. These two experiments begin to shed light on factors which can control cortical laterality and may in turn relate to immune deficiency patterns between the sexes.

Short and sweet: The classic male life?

Mark W. J. Ferguson
Department of Basic Dental Sciences, University of Manchester, Turner Dental School, Manchester M15 6FH, England

That selective affliction of male *Homo sapiens* has a long evolutionary history is evidenced by the male-biased sex ratio at birth and the more rapid senescence of adult males. Indeed, numerous other mammals (elephant seals [LeBoeuf 1972; 1974]; Soay sheep [Grubb 1974]; deer [Robinette, Gashweiler, Low & Jones 1957]; and nonmammals (grackle [Selander 1966]) exhibit marked differential mortality of males. Such a widespread phenomenon demands a general explanation, but Gualtieri & Hicks's (G & H's) immunoreactive theory fails in this regard.

The starting problems arise when considering egg-laying species in which immunoreactivity between mother and offspring would not occur. Moreover, in birds the mechanism of sex determination is opposite that in mammals: males are homogametic (ZZ) and females heterogametic (ZW). Nevertheless in many species the mortality of males exceeds that of females, for example, the great-tailed grackle (Selander 1966). Even in freshwater crocodiles, whose sex is environmentally determined, there is differential mortality of eggs containing male and female embryos (Webb & Smith 1984). The common features of both invertebrate and vertebrate species exhibiting differential male affliction and mortality are polygynous breeding strategies and male competition for mating opportunities (Daly & Wilson 1983). It is among these features that we must search for the underlying causes of selective male affliction.

In man, as in many other animals, males compete with one another for the opportunity to inseminate females (who usually choose the mating partners). The intensive nurture that females bestow on offspring is a resource for which males pay a substantial competitive price; for the male who wins the right to inseminate a female also wins for his progeny a share of the female's parental investment. However, in many cases the very qualities that permit males to compete for mating opportunities also commit them to greater risks and resultant mortality. Darwin (1871) addressed such potentially maladaptive features in his theory of sexual selection and emphasized that sexual selection could, in principle, act in opposition to natural selection and so explain such burdensome characteristics as oversized antlers. These sexually selected features may expose males to higher mortalities not only through external factors such as risky behavior (Daly & Wilson 1983) but also through internal factors such as androgen secretion.

The most extreme case of increased male mortality due to internal factors is seen in marsupial mice of the genus *Antechinus* who exhibit a semelparous life history characterized by "big bang" or "kamikaze" reproduction (J. M. Diamond 1982; Lee, Bradley & Braithwaite 1977). In *A. stuartii* there is a brief mating season in the late Australian winter (August); pregnancy lasts about a month and all births in a population occur within a two-week period. The offspring never see their fathers, however, because within three weeks of the onset of mating all the males in the population die (J. M. Diamond 1982; Lee et al. 1977). In nature death is often caused by predation or fighting but even under controlled laboratory conditions male *A. stuartii* self-destruct with atrophy of the reproductive system, hepatic necrosis, anaemia, gastric and duodenal hemorrhages, hypertrophied adrenals, elevated corticosteroid levels, and suppression of the immune system (J. M. Diamond 1982; Lee et al. 1977). This physiological collapse is related to dramatic antecedent changes in behavior during the brief mating season including increased aggression, activity day and night, and repeated copulations of several hours duration. Even if captured prior to the mating season and isolated from cohorts, male *A. stuartii* still die. Although they sometimes survive for a few extra weeks, they never live to the next breeding season. Male *A. stuartii* is obligatorily semelparous, although a female may live for another two or three breeding seasons.

In man, androgens not only induce males to violent and risky behavior but probably also hasten degeneration and senescence. Hamilton and Mestler (1969) found that the mean age attained by a group of castrated males was 69.3 years whereas a comparable intact group averaged only 55.7 years. (Experimentally castrated cats also live longer [Hamilton, Hamilton & Mestler 1969].) One theory of senescence suggests that some attributes enhance fitness and hence by increasing reproductive success early in the life cycle are selected for, even though the same attributes have degenerative consequences later in life history (W. D. Hamilton 1966). It is not life span that selection maximizes but rather fitness (as measured by the number of offspring).

Such ideas may apply with equal vigor early in life. Given that females choose their mates and that males compete with each other for this prize, it is obvious that there is some advantage in having a higher degree of variation in males on which natural selection can operate. This greater degree of variation may reflect a higher mutation rate from whatever cause – transposed DNA segments, errors in controlling genes, and so forth. This in turn is likely to produce a higher degree of male affliction for a number of diseases and conditions. Such a mechanism would operate independent of whether the male was homogametic or heterogametic. An interesting common feature of homogametic, heterogametic, environmentally determined, oviparous or viviparous males is developmental rate during embryonic life. In general, males develop faster than females (Burdi & Silvey 1969a; 1969b; Ferguson & Joanen 1983; Mittwoch 1983; Mittwoch & Mahadevaiah 1980a; 1980b). A faster developmental rate, means that any upset (either environmental or genetic) is likely to have more serious sequelae, particularly relating to

Commentary/Gualtieri & Hicks: Immunoreactive theory

the coordination of developmental events following compensatory growth (Snow & Tam 1979; Tam & Snow 1981). Such desychronization can lead to subtle behavioral and structural malformations of the central nervous and reproductive systems which do not manifest themselves until later life (Snow & Tam 1979; Tam & Snow 1981). These may contribute to selective male affliction.

Other factors influencing differential male affliction include circumstances in which individual parents might profit by biasing the sex of their offspring (Trivers & Willard 1973). Evidence for this comes from a study of the Florida packrat (McClure 1981). Well-fed females invested equal amounts of energy in sons and daughters, reared them in equal numbers, and weaned them at the same weight, whereas mothers who were food deprived during lactation channeled 68% of "transferred energy" into daughters and only 32% into sons. Thus many male pups died and those that survived grew more slowly and were weaned at lighter weights than their sisters. According to Trivers and Willard (1973), extra investment in a son of good quality may yield greater returns (in terms of numbers of future offspring) than comparable investment in a daughter of good quality. Thus a mother may prefer to produce sons when she has the resources necessary to give them a better than average competitive ability and daughters when she does not. Maternal physiology and nutrition may thus provide an alternative explanation for the "sex ratio according to birth order" data presented by G & H. However, if mothers could detect the nonpreferred sex (males when the maternal environment is poor) early and abort at low cost in time and energy then Trivers and Willard's (1973) theory would be in accord with the immunoreactive one. Clearly the multifactorial issue of selective male affliction is ripe for further investigation.

The immunoreactive theory: One for all?

Christopher Gillberg
Department of Child and Youth Psychiatry and Institute of Handicap Research, University of Göteborg, S-402 35 Göteborg, Sweden

The intriguing immunoreactive theory (IMRT) put forward by Gualtieri & Hicks (G & H) to account for selective male affliction in a vast number of neurodevelopmental disorders deserves very careful consideration. G & H's case seems to be strong enough and there is – as G & H point out – certainly considerable attractiveness in the theory's ability to generate testable hypotheses. Ever since Adinolfi's (1976) paper in which it was suggested that neurological abnormality in children might result from cross-placental transfer of maternal antibodies to the fetal central nervous system, the idea that certain kinds of brain dysfunction in childhood might result from mechanisms similar to those occurring in Rh-disease has been kept alive, albeit at a low level. The principal merit of G & H's target article resides in its forceful and rather comprehensive argument for reviving the Adinolfi idea.

However, I think some pros and cons should be highlighted. First, the main weakness of the argument, namely its failure to explain any of the great phenotypical variation in children with neurodevelopmental disorders, is toned down and assigned a very obscure and nonspecific statement to the effect that the IMRT is not "put forth as a global explanation for all neuropathic disorders of childhood." It would have been interesting to know G & H's opinion about how such clinically extremely different conditions as Down's syndrome and the autistic syndrome might result from unitary pathogenetic mechanisms. Not having discussed this variation at all, the whole IMRT argument risks the fate of claims for universal explanations for other well-known dichotomies, such as overweight versus underweight, namely that of being discarded at once because of its lack of general credibility.

I am not yet sure whether the IMRT can stand up to such criticism. There are, of course, different ways in which immunological attacks on the fetus might be achieved. G & H propose greater antigenic differences in male than in female fetuses when compared with the mother. Depending on the kind of differences and "the allergic state" of the mother, I suppose it is conceivable that different parts of the developing nervous system, or, for that matter, different chromosomes, may be injured.

However, in the case of Down's syndrome, for instance, is it not more probable that the chromosomal nondisjunction (trisomy 21) is primary, and not produced by a mother–fetus attack? By G & H's argument, Down's syndrome children, regardless of sex, might be more antigenic because of their different chromosomal makeup and therefore more prone to brain damage. Furthermore, boys would be more vulnerable than girls (IMRT prediction). Wouldn't this lead to either (1) an increased rate of abortion in Down's syndrome boys or (2) to brain damage and mental retardation being more severe in boys than in girls with Down's syndrome? Certainly it would not lead to an excess of live boys with Down's syndrome. Down's syndrome may be a bad example since experts differ in their views on sex ratios; for example Ratcliffe, Stewart, Melville & Jacobs (1970) state that males are equal to females. Nonetheless, G & H use Down's syndrome as an example in their first table; in any case my argument can be extended to include other chromosomal abnormalities with male excess.

The fragile-X syndrome in autism (Brown, Jenkins, Friedman, Brooks, Wisniewski, Raguthu & French 1982) represents another puzzling disorder in the realm of IMRT. Obviously, in the clearcut sex-linked cases, this chromosomal abnormality accounts for a substantial minority of the excess male cases with autistic syndromes. Possibly these cases too are more liable to additional brain damage than chromosomally normal children. There is in fact growing evidence that this may be the case (Gillberg & Wahlström 1984). There are, however, several autism–fragile-X cases that appear to be new mutations. Are these viewed by G & H as resulting from a maternal immunological attack?

Obviously, among such heterogeneous syndrome groups as "autism," and "stuttering," there are bound to be a variety of reasons accounting for male excess, and IMRT is able to explain only a fraction of them. Although it is theoretically attractive to hypothesize that the IMRT could account for a variety of developmental *abnormalities*, other theories, such as the immaturity model proposed by Ounsted and Taylor (1972), might be able to explain another fraction, namely some of the developmental delays (enuresis, language delays, some cases of dyslexia).

Another important and related point is that the IMRT may be relevant only in some of the neurodevelopmental disorders of childhood. G & H rely heavily on data from studies on autistic children, making generalization about other conditions hazardous.

In the case of autism, however, I think their argument is really suggestive. It would be most interesting to know, for instance, whether or not the antecedent brother effect has been observed in conditions like infantile spasms, the hyperkinetic syndrome, and the like. In preliminary analyses of a total population-based sample of children with minimal brain damage (MBD) (with perceptual, motor and attentional deficits) and controls, Gillberg, Rasmussen, Carlström, Svenson & Waldenström 1982) found no differences across the groups. However, in a population-based group of autistic children and controls (Gillberg 1984), autistic boys tended to have older brothers more often than controls (Table 1), even though the numbers involved were small, and statistical significance was not achieved. There was a clear trend toward boys (especially in the autistic group) with elder brothers having occasioned pregnancy

Commentary/Gualtieri & Hicks: Immunoreactive theory

Table 1 (Gillberg). *Antecedent brother effect on complications of pregnancy. Results from a pouplation-based study of 19 autistic boys (A) and 19 age-, sex-, and maternity-clinic-matched controls (C).*

	Antecedent brothers	
	None	One
	n	n
Complications of pregnancy	A,C	A,C
None	1,4	0,0
One	2,3	1,3
More than one	5,5	10,4

	Antecedent sisters	
	None	One
	n	n
Complications of pregnancy	A,C	A,C
None	1,0	0,4
One	2,4	1,2
More than one	13,9	2,0

complications more often than boys without elder brothers. On the other hand, there was no tendency toward an excess of firstborn males.

Studies indicative of links between high maternal age and neurodevelopmental disorders, like autism (Gillberg 1980), might, if analyzed in detail, provide additional support for the IMRT. Coleman and Gillberg (1984) and Funderburk, Carter, Tanguay, Freeman and Westlake (1983) have suggested that abortions are common in the preconception histories of autistic children.

Stubbs, Ritvo, and Mason-Brothers (1984) recently performed a very interesting study which might prove pertinent to the future elaboration of the IMRT. They examined 52 pairs of parents of autistic children and 83 pairs of parents of normal children and found that 77% of the former group shared at least one HLA antigen compared with 22% of the latter group ($p < .0001$). Studies on HLA in parents and children with autism comparing boys with girls might prove fruitful.

Inferential clues and suggestions for future scientific testing of the IMRT might also be provided by some data from another recent study. In a population-based study of infantile autism in Gothenburg, Sweden, 1 out of 40 boys (2.5%) and 2 out of 6 girls (33%) with infantile autism showed fragile sites on the sixth chromosome. The major histocompatibility complex, exercising control over susceptibility to autoimmunity and other immunological reactions, is located on the sixth chromosome.

Having read G & H's target article, I analyzed some more of my own data on children with MBD and children with left-handedness with a special view to finding evidence of autoimmune and allergic disorders in subgroups of these children. There was no excess of atopic disease (asthma, eczema or allergic rhinitis) in the population-based group of seven-year-olds with MBD (Rasmussen & Gillberg 1983). Among population-representative ten-year-olds with left-handedness (Gillberg, Waldenström & Rasmussen 1984), allergies were not more pronounced in cases with pathological left-handedness (i.e., those showing a very poor performance with the nonpreferred hand; Bishop 1980) from those with "normal" left-handedness. However, as in Geschwind's study (Geschwind & Behan 1982), allergies and autoimmune diseases tend to be common in the undifferentiated group of left-handers. To provide support for

the IMRT, the pathological handers (i.e., those who are presumed to have sustained brain damage) would have to have the highest rate of allergies.

In summary I would say that the vast bulk of the scientific evidence reviewed by Gualtieri & Hicks does indeed favor the IMRT, but that the theorists would do well to refrain from overgeneral statements about the applicability of their model.

Does maternal–fetal incompatibility lead to neurodevelopmental impairment?

Reginald M. Gorczynski
Division of Biological Research, Ontario Cancer Institute, Toronto, Ontario, Canada M4X 1K9

The basic premise laid out in Gualtieri & Hicks's (G & H's) target article is a provocative one – namely that the underlying etiology in a significant number of cases of neurodevelopmental impairment is to be found in an immune response on the part of a subgroup of immunoreactive mothers directed against antigenic disparities encountered more frequently with a male fetus. G & H interpret the structure of the sex differences seen in neurodevelopmentally impaired offspring (in general, afflicted males outnumber females, though the female impairments tend to be more severe) as suggestive of a predominantly genotypic effect for females and a genotype-environmental interaction effect for males.

There is evidence that a maternal genetic principle or principles underlie the phenomenon of maternal insufficiency. In addition, G & H cite work suggesting that negative parity effects operate primarily against males as a result of genetic incompatibility (in part at least associated with an H-Y antigen). Both phenomena are consistent with G & H's hypothesis. Thus, for instance, the primary sex ratio (at fertilization) exceeds the secondary sex ratio (120:105). G & H report that implantation is favored by antigenic disparity between mother and fetus; placental size and birth size increase with parity, but predominantly only in male fetuses. Interestingly, the sex ratio decreases in mothers who develop an immune response to the fetus (characterized by HLA antibodies, see G & H's Figure 2) and in parous women with antecedent male children (Figure 3). The sex ratio actually increases if antecedents are female. It would be of interest to know the composition of anti-HLA+ mothers in the data in Figure 3. The reader must be alert, as G & H indicate, to the myriad other incompatibilities that may contribute to these effects, ABO blood group disparities for instance (Figure 4).

In keeping with Popper's views on what constitutes a good theory, G & H are concerned to point out the falsifiability of their hypotheses. In their analysis of the data shown in Table 3, for instance, if the negative parity effect is indeed mediated by immunoreaction against antecedent males, there should be less correlation – or none – between pregnancy complications and antecedent brothers–sisters where autistic females (or females=males with other neurodevelopmental impairments) are studied. The number of autistic girls was unfortunately too small for this particular analysis. However, a more recent study cited (submitted in 1984c), using Breland's examiation of 794,589 eleventh grade students taking the National Merit Scholarship Qualifying Test in 1965, suggests that of the four family configurations possible the greatest negative parity effect was seen in boys with antecedent brothers. This is again in keeping with G & H's hypothesis.

The concept of a familial tendency towards immunoregulatory disorders in mothers of neurodevelopmentally impaired offspring is purely speculative. There are to my knowledge no data suggesting an increased frequency of impairments in males or females born to mothers exhibiting classical autoimmune-type disorders. Moreover, there is good evidence for a psychoneuroendocrine axis in the latter disorders (Solomon 1983). Thus we must consider the likelihood that in these cases any hostile uterine environment may reflect a neuroendocrine effect and not one induced by fetal histoincompatibility antigens. Any additional bias in favor of greater frequency of impairment in the male fetus could presumably reflect alterations in fetal brain development as a result of changes in the balance of androgens, estrogens, and progestational hormones (caused even by elevation of androgens of fetal origin).

The effect of sex hormones on immune responsiveness per se is well established (e.g., the ability of castration to promote immunocompetence in male mice, particularly cellular immunity). Moreover, there are a number of reports that suggest that deliberate pertubation of hormonal balance during pregnancy may have long-term effects on subsequent offspring (Bakke, Lawrence, Bennett & Robinson 1975). G & H might be interested to note that a case has been made for an X-linked immunoregulatory gene contributing to the overall superior immunological performance of females (Purtilo & Sullivan 1979).

The evidence that in outbred matings, male antigens are more antigenic than female and thus more likely to evoke an immunological attack is not established. The first major evidence that maternal–fetal incompatibility might lead to fetal loss came from analyzing blood groups and not from minor histocompatibility, that is, H-Y antigens. Hirfeld and Zborowski reported a deficiency in the number of expected type A offspring born to matings of mothers of type O and fathers of type A. In contrast, they found the anticipated concordance of expected and observed frequencies when mothers were type A and fathers type O (Mourent, Kopec & Domaniewski-Sobczak 1978). This observation contributed to the later analysis of the etiology of hemolytic disease of the newborn.

In an outbred population the major antigenic disparity evoking immunological rejection phenomena are those of the major histocompatibility complex. Exactly how the fetus, a highly successful allograft, survives is as yet an unsolved problem. Attempts to explain the phenomena range from the notion of the trophoblast as a barrier to allograft rejection; to the now probably abandoned idea of diminished alloantigen expression on trophoblast tissue; to the concept of a role for active suppression of maternal antifetal immunity in fetal graft survival (Beer & Billingham 1976). It is worthy of note that the immunity developed by the mother to a fetal allograft is not typical of the response to an organ allograft in general. In particular, a state of hyporeactivity is the norm; "blocking" rather than "cytotoxic" antibodies are produced and there is general failure to evoke antigraft specific cytotoxic killer cells. Nor should it be forgotten that the fetus itself is a source of a great many agents known to have immunosuppresive potential, for example alpha-feto protein (which gains access to the maternal–fetal circulation), fetal suppressor cells, and the like.

That immune responses to H-Y antigen can occur in pregnancy has been established using inbred groups of experimental animals. In fact it was inferred from early studies by Eichwald and Silmser (1955) on skin grafting in mice. The natural biological function of the product of the H-Y locus on the cell surface, however, seems to be to provide the signal for testicular differentiation from an undifferentiated gonad. Indeed, Wachtel, Hall, Muller and Chaganti (1980) reported that the transformation of the freemartin gonad in bisexual twins in cattle is itself probably due to H-Y antigen secreted by the fetal bull, which passes into the common circulation. I know of no evidence that this particular antigenic system of the developing fetus is expressed to any significant degree in the developing neuronal tissue. This particular argument seems to be a prerequisite if one postulates that neuronal tissue is an important site of the immune system-mediated damage occurring as a result of maternal anti-H-Y immune activity.

What is in fact the evidence that immunoreaction on the part of the female is detrimental; particularly to the male conceptus in parous women? G & H cite older data from Bardawil (1962) suggesting that women with repeated miscarriages are more likely to reject grafts of their husband's skin than that of third-party donors. It is also known that over 20% of all spontaneous abortions are chromosomally normal. Similarly, mixed leukocyte reactivity is allegedly lower in fertile than in infertile couples. However, the relationship of the types of immune response measured in any of these studies to the critical reaction in monitoring in situ the maternal–fetal interaction is unknown. Judging from animal studies, I believe that a reaction of maternal cells to fetal antigens, especially as expressed on the trophoblast, is critical to survival and growth of the fetus, especially for a histoincompatible conceptus. That maternal reactivity produces increased vascularity at the site of implantation is a possible mechanism. Interestingly, there are reports that women with histories of abortion have demonstrable antipaternal, cell-mediated immunity, but lack serum "blocking" antibodies to counter this activity, unlike the serum of women with normal pregnancies. Finally, of note are claims that treating women with a history of spontaneous abortion and with low levels of incompatibility with paternal cellular antigens with a mixture of foreign lymphocytes leads to the birth of healthy children (Komlos & Halbrecht 1979; Taylor & Faulk 1981).

The subject G & H address is unquestionably very complex, dealing with little-understood immunological and neurodevelopmental problems. It has been noted that if all of the immunological factors of maternal antifetal type we can measure were of physiological significance, the mammalian world would not exist (Sio & Beer 1982). G & H's hypothesis certainly seems open to test. Unlike the authors, however, I would anticipate that the explanation for the paradoxical overrepresentation of males in neurodevelopmentally impaired children is not likely to be found in studies which view the female conceptus as "immunologically privileged," but may indeed reflect a complex interplay of neuroendocrine and immune phenomena. (Hirfeld & Zborowski is cited in Beer & Billingham 1976.]

Some implications of the immunoreactive theory for evolution and sex ratios

Katharine Blick Hoyenga
Psychology Department, Western Illinois University, Macomb, Ill. 61455

Are the sex ratios in human mortality and morbidity always in the direction predicted by the immunoreactive theory? Is the greater "maternal attack" on male than on female an evolutionary accident, or can it serve some selective function? If birth order and H-Y antigen are important to the male-specific maternal attack, then similar sex ratios should be observed in lower species. Humans with greater H-Y antigen levels should have an even greater frequency of the male-typical childhood diseases listed by Gualtieri & Hicks (G & H). This commentary will address these implications along with some problems and alternative explanations.

Sex ratios in human morbidity and mortality. It is not always true that male children suffer more often from various childhood disorders and that when female children have the disorder, they often express a more severe form of that disorder. Throughout life, men typically suffer more often from the life-threatening disorders, whereas women more often suffer from chronically disabling disorders (Gove 1984; Hoyenga & Hoyenga 1979). Even during childhood, in some disorders such as sickle cell disease (Phebus, Gloninger & Maciak 1984) and retardation (Abramowicz & Richardson 1975; Clements, Van Arsdale & Hafer 1974; LaVeck & LaVeck 1977), boys are often more severely affected.

Females with a given disorder may not always have a more

Commentary/Gualtieri & Hicks: Immunoreactive theory

disturbed environment and/or more genetic "load." In Cadoret's work on adoptive children (Cadoret & Cain 1980; Cadoret, Cunningham, Loftus & Edwards 1975; Cunningham, Cadoret, Loftus & Edwards 1975), psychiatric disorders among natural parents were found to be related to antisocial behaviors among boys and to physical disorders among girls. But during adolescence, the genetic load for antisocial behaviors showed no sex differences, and boys were more vulnerable to an unfavorable adoptive environment than girls were.

Dosage compensation more typically refers to X inactivation, which occurs early during fetal development in all mammalian females (Lyon 1972). So even though X-linked disorders appear more often in the genome of females, because of X-inactivation females will often express a less severe form of the disorder than will males who have only the one X (Berg 1979). Examples of this include color blindness (Born, Grützner & Hemminger 1976; Feig & Ropers 1978), disorders of myelination (Skoff & Montgomery 1981), and muscular dystrophy (Gomez, Engel, Dewald & Peterson 1977).

Because of sex differences in brain lateralization, which G & H suggest might be related to "maternal attack," the sexes are also differentially vulnerable to the effects of brain damage. However, contrary to what G & H imply, recent research has found that verbal ability in males is more severely affected by left- than by right-sided lesions, and spatial ability in males is more severely affected by right- than by left-sided lesions. Both types of ability in women are equally impaired by either left- or right-sided lesions (Inglis & Lawson 1981; 1982). Thus, males might be more severely affected in one area, but females might be more often affected by any type of brain damage.

Sex ratios in schizophrenia: Positive versus negative subtypes. Researchers have suggested that schizophrenia might be usefully divided into positive and negative subtypes based on types of symptoms, etiology, and prognosis (see Seidman 1983 for a review). G & H imply that males, having an earlier onset, would dominate the negative subtype, whereas females, with a later onset, would dominate the positive subtype. Males do tend to show not only an earlier onset, but also less affect, a more chronic course, and poorer premorbid functioning (Lewine 1981; Lewine, Burbach & Meltzer 1984). Female schizophrenics show a higher level of a dopamine metabolite in their cerebrospinal fluid (Bowers, Swigar & Jatlow 1983). However, when chronic schizophrenics were divided into positive and negative subtypes independent of gender, there were more males than females in the positive subtype (7 versus 3) and more females than males in the negative subtype (5 versus 3) (Opler, Kay, Rosado & Lindenmayer 1984).

Evolution and variation in sex ratios. Mammalian females may be able to regulate the strength of their maternal attack in order to vary the sex ratio of their offspring according to current conditions. Generally, females produce the most offspring of the gender which has the least competition among its siblings (Charnov 1982).

Did maternal attack evolve as a mechanism to adjust sex ratios? Birds also use H-Y antigen to control gonadal gender (the protein is expressed by females) (Wachtel, Wachtel, Nakamura & Gilmour 1983), and finches can vary the sex ratio of offspring in a clutch of eggs according to the "sexual attractiveness" of the mother and father. For example, attractive females had a greater proportion of female offspring than did unattractive females (Burley 1981). Among rats, stressing the male parent (by confinement prior to fertilization) reduces the sex ratio, whereas stressing the female increases it (Schuster & Schuster 1969). Can the degree of maternal attack be controlled to adjust sex ratios according to differential stress or attractiveness?

Sex ratios of morbidity and mortality in lower animals show some similarity to human sex ratios. The earliest research suggested that females often have a greater life expectancy than males do, though the sex difference was usually attributed to biological effects of sex hormones and to the reproductive roles of males versus females (e.g., intramale combat) (see review in Hoyenga & Hoyenga 1979). In more recent data, similar sex differences in mortality were seen in species as diverse as fruit flies and cats (Bronson 1981; Lints, Bourgois, Delalieuz, Stoll & Lints 1983). Among rats, the body weight of male fetuses is inversely related to the number of fetuses (and thus the number of males and the severity of the maternal attack?) in the ipsilateral uterine horn, but the body weight of females is not affected by the number of other fetuses present (Ward, Karp & Aceto 1977). However, animal data do not always parallel human sex ratios. Among monkeys, the sex ratio of the incidence of hyaline membrane disease is the reverse of the ratio among humans (Truog, Kessler, Palmer, Murphy, Woodrum & Hodson 1981).

Even more important, sex ratios at birth in cattle also show a male preponderance. Furthermore, the sex ratio varies with parity (Gray & Hurt 1979). Just as G & H note for humans, the sex ratio declines with birth order, at least up to the third parity (53.1, 51.42, 48.7). However, contrary to what G & H predict, the sex ratio then again increases for the fourth and fifth parities (54.5, 53.71).

Sex chromosome abnormalities. The level of H-Y antigen is increased over normal levels for the gender in various chromosome abnormalities such as in XYY males (Fraccaro, Mayerovó, Bühler, Gebauer, Gilgenkrantz, Lindsten, Curto, Lo & Ritzén 1982) and in Turner's females (XO mosaics) Müller, Mayerova, Fraccaro, Zuffardi, Mikkelsen & Prader 1983). If H-Y antigen is related to the severity of maternal attack, then XYY males and Turner's females should suffer more often from childhood diseases.

Several of the disorders listed in the target article are reported to have an increased frequency of occurrence in XYY and XO people. These include stuttering, immunological impairments, birth problems, learning disorders, hyperactivity, epilepsy, and schizophrenia (Haberman, Hollingsworth, Falek & Michael 1975; Hakola & Iivanainen 1978; Hier, Atkins & Perlo 1980; Nanko 1979; Ratcliffe, Axworthy & Ginsborg 1979; Ratcliffe, Tierney, Smith & Callan 1981; Robinson, Bender, Borelli, Puck & Salbenblatt 1983; Sørenson & Nielsen 1977). However, sometimes the elevated frequencies of disorders are shared with other chromosome abnormalities that have normal levels of H-Y antigen. For example, increased susceptibility to infection and asthma also occur in XXY males (Ratcliffe, Axworthy & Ginsborg 1979).

Alternative explanations and problems. G & H's support of their theory is marred by some logical problems. For example, when they suggest that "antigenic differences between zygote and mother are thought to confer an implantation advantage," the evidence cited in that paragraph has to do with sex ratios at conception and at birth. A very high sex ratio at conception has little to do with any implantation advantage of males, and the decline in the sex ratio from conception to birth does not suggest that males have any great advantage. G & H's hypothesis can explain why toxemia increases with parity, especially with prior males, but why are primiparas at the greatest risk? G & H rule out psychosocial explanations for negative parity effects by showing that traits such as height also show these effects – even though height is also sensitive to environmental variables.

A critical problem faced by G & H's theory is the greater frequency of immune disorders in females than in males. For example, systemic lupus erythematosis affects ten times as many females as males, and XXY males are more susceptible than are XY males; similar sex differences are seen among mice (Hoyenga & Hoyenga 1979; Siiteri, Jones, Roubinian & Talal 1980).

Factors other than maternal attack can affect sex ratios in childhood disorders. Maternal age, independent of parity, may affect sex ratios (Rostron & James 1977), and the incidence of breast feeding also covaries with parity (Broad & Duganzich 1983). Sex hormone levels at birth vary with parity (Maccoby,

Doering, Jacklin & Kraemer 1979), and at least some of the sex differences in childhood diseases have been attributed to sex differences in prenatal sex hormone levels (Arena & Smith 1978). Geschwind and Behan (1982) attribute the greater frequency of learning disorders, allergies, and autoimmune disorders in left- than in right-handed males to a higher level of fetal testosterone levels.

Thus, G & H's theory can explain some data not presented in their paper, but there are also some areas in which the theory does not successfully predict the observed sex ratios. Nevertheless, more research guided by the theory's predictions would certainly seem productive, regardless of the outcome.

The alleged antecedent brother effect in sex ratio

William H. James
Medical Research Council Mammalian Development Unit, University College London, London NW1 2HE, England

Gualtieri & Hicks (G & H) write that their hypothesis is "borrowed from studies of the sex ratio." They frankly acknowledge that "there is disagreement surrounding at least some of the facts upon which the theory is based.... Not every investigator has agreed that ... sex ratio decreases with antecedent brothers (McLaren 1962)."

In this commentary I urge that indeed the evidence points strongly in the opposite direction, that sex ratio (proportion of boys) *increases* with antecedent brothers (though not as an immediate consequence of them).

The literature. It must be noted that the types of variation to be discussed are small. So, bearing in mind the unanimity of the two largest samples (Ben-Porath & Welch 1976; Malinvaud 1955), nonsignificant data from small samples cannot be regarded as informative. Malinvaud's data (which have since been reprinted in [James 1975]) were on the sexes of nearly four million French births from 1946 to 1950, classified simultaneously by the numbers of prior brothers and prior sisters. Ben-Porath and Welch (1976) offered data from nearly 150,000 U.S. white women in the 1 in 100 Public Use Sample of the U.S. 1970 Census.

In both sets of data, the probability of a male child increases with the number of prior male children and decreases with the number of prior female children. The effect is greater in the U.S. data than in the French data, but the agreement between these studies is striking.

There are two points. First, G & H seem almost certainly wrong in their interpretation of the data here (although that does not necessarily falsify their hypothesis). Second, one wants to know the source of the variation shown in these two large samples.

The sorts of variation that could occur in principle are Poisson variation (variation within couples of p, the probability of a male child), Lexis variation (variation between couples of p), and Markov variation (influence of the sex of one pregnancy upon the sex[es] of subsequent one[s]) or any combination of these three types of variation [Edwards 1960]). Probably no final conclusion about the nature of the observed variation can be reached by statistical means in the absence of a very large sample of data giving the frequencies of sibships by the permutations of the sexes of their members (Crouchley, Davies & Pickles 1984; Pickles, Crouchley & Davies 1982).

However, if statistical manipulation cannot identify the nature of the variation in the data of Malinvaud and of Ben-Porath and Welch, other forms of argument might suggest it. In Western societies, it has usually been found that a large proportion of parents express a preference for families containing one or more representatives of each sex (Adelman & Rosenzweig 1978; Clare & Kiser 1951; Markle & Nam 1971; Sloane & Lee 1983). One effect of this is that parents with n existing children are rather more likely to have another child if the n existing children are all of the same sex than if they contain both sexes. This has the effect of diminishing the variance of the frequency distributions of small completed families of size n with 0, 2, 2 ... n boys. However, the variance of such distributions is usually greater than binomial variance as, for example, in the data examined by Edwards (1958). Hence there is either Lexis variation or Markov variation, or both. Now the sort of Markov variation that could, in principle, be responsible would – from a biological standpoint – be rather odd. If a couple had a boy, that would make them more likely to have further boys; and if they had a girl, that would make them more likely to have further girls. Any tendency of this sort – if it exists – must be rather small; Greenberg and White (1967) could find no relationship between the sexes of consecutive sibs in more than 100,000 sibships. At any rate, if it is accepted that such variation is either nonexistent or minimal, the inference is that there is Lexis variation.

The point of this excursus may now become clear. I have noted that if maternal gonadotrophin levels at the time of conception were partially responsible for the sex of the infant (high levels being associated with females), then almost all of the observed variation in the human sex ratio (including the Lexis variation suggested above) would be explained (W. H. James 1980a). Moreover, pregnancies following ovulation induced by gonadotrophin or clomiphene do indeed contain a significantly high proportion of females (W. H. James 1980b). So it seems that hormones play a part in the determination of sex. Accordingly, one may wonder whether hormone imbalance – rather than antigenic action – is responsible for some of the selective male affliction addressed by the authors. The point is general because a large number of congenital malformations are also disproportionately associated with one sex or the other (Arena & Smith 1978); the possibility that hormone imbalance is responsible here too seems not implausible.

Breland's (1974) data. I now want to explain why I think the support given by the data of Breland (1974) to the antecedent brother hypothesis (in sex ratio) is illusory. G & H specify the sex ratio of nth children when their $(n - 1)$ predecessors were all of the same sex in families of exactly size n. Now as remarked above, there is good evidence that parents want families containing representatives of both sexes. So one would expect that if the first $(n - 1)$ children are all the same sex, then in families of exactly size n, the nth child would be of the sex opposite to that of its predecessors. This would reflect not a biological fact, but a sociological one, namely, that a family in which all the first n children were of the same sex is more likely to have another child (and thus eliminate itself from the category of family size n) than a family in which the first $(n - 1)$ children were of one sex and the nth child was of the other sex.

Accordingly, I suggest that if Breland's data were analysed without the restriction described above, they would show variation of the sort identified in the data of Malinvaud (1955) and Ben-Porath and Welch (1976).

Immunoreactive theory and the genetics of mental ability

Arthur R. Jensen
School of Education, University of California, Berkeley, Calif. 94720

The variety of evidence presented by Gualtieri & Hicks (G & H) consistent with the immunoreactive theory (IMRT) is impressive and convincing, even if one acknowledges the many difficulties in ruling out possible alternative hypotheses that may accommodate many of the phenomena on which the IMRT

Commentary/Gualtieri & Hicks: Immunoreactive theory

has been brought to bear. I suspect that G & H have exposed what may well turn out to be merely the tip of the iceberg of all of the implications and ramifications of the IMRT in general for the understanding of human variation, of which the sex difference in frequency of developmental disorders is only one aspect.

Implications of IMRT in general (not just the heightened antigenicity of the male fetus) for human behavioral genetics, and particularly for the genetics of mental development, seem worth investigating. Two problematic topics in the genetics of intelligence immediately come to mind: (1) the problem of accounting for all of the nongenetic variance in general mental ability, as indexed by IQ, and (2) the problem of the large differences between certain ethnic groups in the rate of what has been termed "reproductive casualty" and its associated developmental behavioral disorders, including mental retardation.

One of the problems in the study of the broad heritability (h^2) of intelligence is the difficulty in accounting for all of the nonerror variance in IQ. The best present estimates of h^2, based on various kinship correlations fitted to polygenic models, fall mostly in the range of .40 to .70, that is, some 40 to 70% of the IQ variance is attributable to genetic factors (Scarr & Carter-Saltzman 1982). Theoretically, then, the nongenetic, or environmental, variance should be $1 - h^2$, or between .30 and .60. But the commonly measured environmental variables – socioeconomic status, styles of child-rearing, and the like – repeatedly fail to account for even as much as 30% of the nongenetic variance. Much more telling is the fact that unrelated children reared together in adoptive homes show such very low correlations for IQ (see Scarr & Carter-Saltzman, Table 13.28) as to make it impossible to account for at most a small percentage – perhaps even less than 10% – of the total IQ variance in terms of differences in family environment. Yet the correlations between full siblings reared apart, and between other kinships, are of a magnitude such that the broad heritability (i.e., proportion of the total variance attributable to genetic factors) of IQ is not much more than about .50. In a review of recent studies on the heritability of intelligence, Plomin and DeFries (1980) state, "we know of no specific environmental influences nor combinations of them that account for as much as 10 percent of the variance in IQ" (p. 21). Yet Plomin and DeFries attribute only about 50% of the IQ variance to genetic factors. What, then, is the source of the remaining variance?

A closely related anomaly in this field is the fact that monozygotic twins reared apart show an IQ correlation of close to .70, which is a direct estimate of h^2, but it is a higher estimate of h^2 than the h^2 derived from other kinship correlations. The difference is not explainable in terms of the possibly correlated environments of the separated MZ twins, and the basis of the discrepancy has remained obscure.

The IMRT may provide at least a partial explanation of these phenomena – phenomena which so far have seemed puzzling. The usual answers, in terms of genetic theory, have invoked the mechanisms of epistasis (interactions between genes at different chromosomal loci) and genotype–environment interaction. But it has been difficult to get an empirical handle on these hypothesized effects. The IMRT may afford one handle, albeit a strictly biological one. Assuming the development of the brain is affected, varying degrees of antigen incompatibility between mother and fetus would tend to reduce the size of all kinship correlations except those of MZ twins, relative to the correlations expected on the basis of polygenic theory. Because MZ twins share exactly the same antigens, they would have the same degree of mother–fetus incompatibility. This effect should constitute, strictly speaking, an environmental enhancement of the degree of phenotypic similarity between MZ twins relative to the phenotypic similarity of other kinships.

Probably the most feasible test of this hypothesis could be made by studying a large number of sibships with respect to antigens such as the ABO, Rh, and HLA systems, as well as H-Y in male siblings. Sibling pairs would be categorized in terms of degree of similarity in a number of antigens and IQ correlations between siblings within each category would be compared. In addition, children's IQs would be looked at as a function of degree of mother–child antigenic compatibility and as a function of father–mother antigenic similarity. Statistically significant effects would definitely implicate the IMRT as an explanatory factor in this domain. Such information could ensure the IMRT explanation for the slight but significant negative effects of parity on mental development.

Another poorly understood phenomenon to which the IMRT would seem to be relevant is the quite different rates of "reproductive casualty" in black, white, and Asian Americans. The rates of fetal loss and of various developmental disabilities that affect mental development and scholastic performance are twice as high in the black American population as in the white and Asian populations, a difference that cannot be accounted for in terms of socioeconomic status. Blacks in general show higher rates for various types of reproductive casualty than the lower fifth of the white population in socioeconomic status. On the other hand, Jews and Asians living in poverty show lower rates than the middle-class white population (see Jensen 1973, chap. 19, for a review of evidence on ethnic differences in reproductive casualty). In addition, consider the following: (1) The sex ratio for live births is lowest in the black and highest in the Asian population, with the white population intermediate; these sex ratios have not changed in the U.S. in the past 50 years. (2) There is considerable evidence that the sex difference (favoring females) in mental abilities is greater among the black than among the white population (Jensen 1971). (3) The American black population is ethnically hybrid; on average, about 20% of the genes of black persons in America come from European–Caucasian ancestors (Reed 1969).

It is a plausible hypothesis that an ethnically hybrid population would be more heterogeneous with respect to antigens and would show a higher rate of mother–fetus antigenic incompatibility than would a more homogeneous population in which natural selection had minimized those specific antigenic factors which have the potential for producing the most deleterious developmental effects of antigenic incompatibility. Bresler (1970) has found that, even within the white population of the northeastern United States, the rate of fetal loss is directly related to the degree of ancestral heterogeneity of the fetus. Fetal loss was found to increase cumulatively by approximately 2.5 to 3% with each additional country of birth in the great-grandparental generation. Increased fetal loss was also found to be related to greater distances between the birth places of the mates within the grandparental generation. Conversely, low fetal loss is encountered with a small number of countries in the background and short distances between the birthplaces of the parents. There is no scientifically established explanation for these findings, but a hypothesis involving the IMRT obviously suggests itself and seems plausible in terms of genetic and evolutionary theory. The possible implications of the IMRT for understanding these various phenomena, after further theoretical consideration, may warrant empirical investigation.

A reproductive immunologist's view on the role of H-Y antigen in neurological disorders

Y. W. Loke
Division of Experimental and Cellular Pathology, Department of Pathology, University of Cambridge, Cambridge CB2 1QP, England

As a reproductive immunologist, I am very pleased to see that our subject has succeeded in attracting the interest of behavioral scientists like Gualtieri & Hicks (G & H). Their immunoreactive theory, propounded to explain the selective male affliction with neuropathic disorders, is certainly most attractive, but I wonder whether it is somewhat premature on evidence presently available. The fundamental premise of the theory – that the male fetus, because of its additional H-Y antigen, is likely to be more immunogenic to the mother than an equivalent female fetus – is not in doubt. But it is debatable whether or not this is actually reflected in any discernible effects on human reproductive performance. G & H have amassed a great deal of evidence from studies on the sex ratio at birth which may be interpreted as indicating that the H-Y antigen, acting either alone or synergistically with some other stronger histocompatibility systems (that is ABO or HLA), can lead to a greater degree of maternal sensitization. However, as G & H have themselves admitted, there is a substantial degree of disagreement surrounding some of the observations on which their theory is based. Several investigators in this field do not believe that the H-Y antigen has any effects on the sex ratio at all. Indeed, some data may even point the other way, that is, that mothers become increasingly tolerant rather than sensitized to H-Y antigen with successive pregnancies. Thus, at the present moment it would be wise to admit that we do not know how the H-Y antigen behaves during mammalian reproduction.

Apart from the particular aspect of H-Y, the whole question of immunoregulation during pregnancy is in the process of reevaluation, so that G & H's concept that "pregnancy is an immunological phenomenon characterized by a state of maternal tolerance" can no longer be taken for granted. Analyses of the HLA phenotypes of women who are habitual aborters have yielded the paradoxical finding that they tend to share more HLA antigens with their husbands than women with normal pregnancies; this implies that too great a degree of histocompatibility rather than histoincompatibility between fetus and mother may be detrimental to fetal survival. Also, the discovery of "blocking" (nondestructive) antibodies in normal pregnancy sera but not in the sera of women with abortions has led to the hypothesis that the immune response of pregnant females is not simply lower or suppressed, rather, it is actually different from the response mounted by nonpregnant individuals, and this special response is in some way important for successful gestation. In other words, immunoregulation during pregnancy is not just a passive phenomenon geared towards producing a state of maternal nonreactivity but an active phenomenon, with the mother producing the kind of protective response mandatory for fetal survival against her allogeneic conceptus. This concept has a certain intellectual appeal in that it offers a possible mechanism whereby reproduction helps in maintaining a degree of antigenic diversity within the population. If this is indeed what happens during pregnancy, then it would be difficult to see how selection against H-Y can be fitted into this immunological framework.

Even if it were to be accepted that the H-Y antigen does lead to "selective male affliction," it is unclear how it could result in neuropathic disorders. G & H admit that "the precise nature of the immunologic reaction cannot be described," but it would be nice to have some kind of working hypothesis to strengthen their argument. I myself cannot offer any. It is easy to visualize the possible synergistic action between H-Y and another alloantigen like Rhesus to produce a distortion of the sex ratio in a disease such as erythroblastosis fetalis, but how incompatibility for H-Y can lead to selective destruction of the nervous system is more problematic. Perhaps the neuropathy is mediated by the deposition of immune complexes, in which case the patients with such disorders would also have other manifestations of this type of hypersensitivity.

In conclusion, I would like to stress that I am very much on the side of Gualtieri and Hicks in thinking that the H-Y antigen could theoretically have some effect on the fetal–maternal interaction. It is just that, with the evidence available at present, I am not at all certain what this effect is in practice. This may be because, as the authors have pointed out, "the phenomenon may be robust but at the same time relatively weak and difficult to discern." It remains to be seen whether or not the immunoreactive theory proves to be correct. It is such an elegant concept that it deserves to succeed.

Selective immunoreaction as an adaptive trait

Wade C. Mackey
Division of Social Sciences, Iowa Wesleyan College, Mt. Pleasant, Iowa 52641

Gualtieri & Hicks (G & H) provide us with a most interesting data base aligned with a cogent, reasonable theory that, in turn, helps make sense of the patterns within that data base. Their efforts lend themselves congenially to complementary data and alternative theories from diverse disciplines.

Without delving into the fine points of G & H's work, let me attempt to fit the immunoreactive theory (IMRT) of selective male affliction into a phylogenetic or Darwinian perspective. First, two levels of analysis should be distinguished: one that G & H use and a second, presented here. The two levels of analysis are a "proximate causation" analysis and an "ultimate causation" analysis.

A proximate causation analysis attempts to isolate and understand the conditions and mechanisms of an organism's environment, whether internal or external, that trigger the responses of that organism (Immelmann, Barlow, Petrinovich & Main 1981; Wilson 1975). In other words, an analysis of proximate causation addresses the question of *how* – how did the behavior of an organism become organized and initiated. G & H's IMRT is an example of a proximate causation analysis.

A separate yet supplementary type of inquiry investigates the ultimate causation of a behavior pattern. An analysis of ultimate causation addresses the conditions or mechanisms in a species' history which render some behavioral traits adaptive and others nonadaptive (Immelmann et al. 1981; Wilson 1975). The adaptive traits become progressively overrepresented in the population and become characteristic or typical of the species. Framed differently, an ultimate causation analysis asks not *how* but *why*. Why do the behaviors in question exist to be emitted at all? I would like to look at the IMRT from this perspective. Why would the selective immunoreaction by gender exist at all?

Briefly, the IMRT suggests that humans have developed the following mosaic: There is a bias on the part of women, especially primiparous women, to conceive and to bear more sons than daughters. For subsequent births, sons rather than daughters are more at developmental risk and the sex ratio progressively decreases. In other words, there is an initial bias toward healthy, viable sons for firstborn and thereafter a progressive bias away from sons and towards daughters.

The data presented by G & H are diverse, and, given the intricacy of human biology, are fairly unambiguous. The question emerges: Why this pattern?

To help address this question, let us look at the kind of being *Homo sapiens* is:

1. K-selected organisms (few offspring per mother, each receiving extensive, intensive parental investment) (Gould 1977).
2. Gender dimorphic with a strong division of labor by gender (Whyte 1978).
3. Mammals in which the female has a relatively heavier

Commentary/Gualtieri & Hicks: Immunoreactive theory

investment in each offspring than the male (Charnov 1982; Clutton-Brock & Albon 1982; Fisher 1930; Trivers 1972; 1974; Trivers & Willard 1973).

4. A "marriage" system (not coterminous with our sexual system) which is somewhere between monogamous and polygynous (van den Berghe 1979), but definitely not polyandrous (Divale & Harris 1976).

5. Compared to females, males have the potential to be much more variable in the number of offspring they may sire (Dawkins 1976).

6. Hypergamy (marrying "up" in rank or status) is more a female prerogative than a male prerogative (Dickemann 1979; cf. Altmann 1980). [See also BBS multiple book review of Symons: *The Evolution of Human Sexuality*, BBS 3(2) 1980.]

Consequently, if the female is confident of resources (for herself and thereby for her children) and secure in her position within her immediate social hierarchy, she would be expected to have a bias toward an initial son. He is expensive, but a good gamble for many grandchildren. If unsure of resources or tenuous in her social position, she would be expected to have a bias away from a son toward a daughter. Daughters are more hypergamous than sons and they are good candidates for some grandchildren (more than zero); yet a daughter does not have nearly as much potential for many grandchildren as does an attractive, well provisioned male (Mackey and Coney, unpublished).

Socially powerful males – with access to resources and to high position – can draw from a large pool of potential mates. Similarly, a low-ranking female can draw upon an equally large pool of potential mates. Because low-ranking males tend not to marry up a social hierarchy and high-ranking females tend not to marry down a social hierarchy, they have restricted categories of mates.

As a result of these conditions, confident females should be expected to have a bias toward firstborn sons – sons who would be a good bet to sire numerous grandchildren. To avoid dilution of power, influence and resources, successive sons in close proximity of birthing intervals would be avoided. Since males and females follow different, if complementary reproductive strategies, a son, followed by a daughter, would not involve direct competition for the same type or amount of resources. Two sons within a close birthing interval would compete for the same type and amount of resources to the probable detriment of both in terms of attractiveness to females.

Low-ranking, uncertain females should be expected to have a bias toward daughters. Their lowborn sons would be poor candidates for attracting mates. Their daughters would be good candidates for some grandchildren – but not too many.

Accordingly, a mechanism that was insensitive to successive daughters but sensitive to sibling gender following the birth of a son would be expected to arise in the species' phylogeny. G & H present just such a mechanism: selective inmmunoreaction.

At this point the proximate causation perspective (how) conjoins rather well with the ultimate causation perspective (why). Over geological time, those women bearing successive sons within close birthing intervals have reaped progressively fewer grandchildren than those women with either successive daughters or with a son followed by a daughter.

The placental and uterine mechanisms affecting and being affected by the fetal–maternal biochemistry have been positively selected for a type of immunoreaction which has been biased against successive sons in close birth intervals. The alleles subserving such mechanisms have been an evolutionary success and are preeminent over alternate alleles generating alternate mechanisms. So in the twentieth century, we find patterns of gender bias within our species as described by Gualtieri & Hicks that are neither random nor capricious. They are structured and represent an adaptive response by a social species to their social environment.

Eve first, then Adam

John Money
Department of Psychiatry and Behavioral Sciences and Department of Pediatrics, Johns Hopkins University and Hospital, Baltimore, Md. 21205

Selective male affliction is but one manifestation of the ubiquitous principle of the male's greater vulnerability. This principle is evident in embryogenesis insofar as the differentiation of Eve takes precedence over that of Adam. The embryo cannot differentiate as a male if it has only a Y chromosome, but no X, because it is nonviable. By contrast, with an X but no Y (Turner's syndrome) it is able to differentiate as a morphologic female, albeit agonadal, with or without one or more of an array of accompanying somatic deformities, and the possibility of specific nonverbal disability.

For the embryonic and fetal differentiation of the male it is imperative that, under the governance of H-Y antigen, the gonads differentiate as testes, and that they secrete fetal testicular hormones: mullerian inhibiting hormone to vestigiate the mullerian ducts, and testosterone (including dihydrotestosterone) to differentiate the male genitalia. If the testes fail to secrete their hormones, then feminine differentiation takes precedence over male. The same thing also happens if the body is unable to utilize its testicular secretions, which is precisely what happens in the androgen-insensitivity syndrome, also known as testicular feminization.

The absolute dependence of the embryo on testicular hormones if it is to develop as a male is very well substantiated in both the animal experimental literature and the clinical literature. It attests to the general principle that to differentiate a male, nature requires that something be added. The stage thereby is set for error: either too much, not enough, or the wrong component may be added. Herein lies the greater vulnerability of the male, which may be traced across the life span.

The source of the error that induces the greater vulnerability of the male does not need to be only hormonal. Some other intervening factor may interfere with either the synthesis, secretion, or utilization of hormones. Prenatally, the origin of such an intervening factor may be within the fetus itself, fetoprotein, for example, or it may be within the mother. It may be something that the mother has ingested, breathed, or had enter her bloodstream. It may be an infectious agent – and it may be one for which the preferred host within the fetus is a male-hormone producing cell, with which it enters into symbiosis. The interfering factor may also be the product of a maternal immune reaction, which may be male-hormone facilitated.

Although all of the foregoing supplements, rather than vitiates Gualtieri & Hicks's immunoreactive theory of selective male affliction, it also shows that G & H become committed to immunology too soon after targeting it as the source of their theory. Theory building is analogous to differential diagnosis. It requires that one seek out and list as many alternative hypotheses as possible. There is no other way to guarantee against becoming too restricted by a single hypothesis.

ACKNOWLEDGMENT
Preparation of this commentary was supported by USPH grant #HD-00325 and grant #83086900, the William T. Grant, Jr. Foundation.

Male-specific antigens and HLA phenotypes

Susumu Ohno
Beckman Research Institute, City of Hope, Duarte, Calif. 91010

Although couched in jargon unfamiliar to readers from nonneurobiological disciplines such as myself, the essentials of the

Commentary/Gualtieri & Hicks: Immunoreactive theory

article by Gualtieri & Hicks (G & H) were clearly understandable. As G & H are well aware of the evidence contrary to the favorable data they cite, my comments will be based on the assumption that their theory is essentially correct.

Genetic differences that separate human males from females reside solely in the hemizygocity of X-linked genes in males and the male-specific occurrence of the Y-chromosome. As far as fetomaternal compatibility is concerned, however, the X-chromosome does not enter the picture, unless one invokes a newly sustained X-linked mutation, for the single X-chromosome of a son is invariably derived from his mother. Thus, the mother should always be compatible with her sons with regard to all X-linked immunogens.

As to the Y-linked immunogens (plasma membrane antigens), a part of the Y-chromosome is homologous to the X. Accordingly, human 12E7 antigen is specified by a gene on the short arm of the Y and by its allele located at the tip of the short arm of the X (Goodfellow, Banting, Sheer, Ropers, Caine, Ferguson-Smith, Povey & Voss 1983). The male-specificity of such antigens depends upon polymorphism and a frequency of crossing-over involving the X-linked and Y-linked alleles. With regard to H-Y antigen, there is a debate as to whether or not serologically detected H-Y antigen and H-Y transplantation antigen are one and the same (Silvers, Gasser & Eicher 1982). Nevertheless, major histocompatibility antigen (MHC) dependence of the cell-mediated immune response (and probably also that of the humoral immune response to H-Y antigen) should certainly be pointed out. In the mouse, in order to evoke the specific cytotoxic T-cell response from the female, H-Y antigen on the male target-cell plasma membrane has to be associated with H-2D^b antigen (Matsunaga & Simpson 1978). In humans even humoral anti-H-Y antibody appears to be HLA dependent. One such antibody is able to lyse male cells only if HLA-A2 antigen was present with H-Y antigen (Goulmy, Bradley, Van Leeuwen, Lansberg, Munro, Termijtelen & van Rood 1977).

Needless to say, H-Y antigen is an extremely weak immunogen; thus, the anti-H-Y response can be observed only if the donor and the recipient (a male fetus and his mother) are MHC (HLA) compatible, which occurs but seldom in human matings. Yet, one of the consequences of altered self-recognition by the cell-mediated immune system (Zinkernagel & Doherty 1974) is rather frequent misidentification of altered self MHC antigens as allogeneic MHC antigens and vice versa. In the mouse, for example, the receptor of female cytotoxic T-cells raised against H-Y + H-2D^b antigen complex of male cells may also react against H-2D^d antigen, indiscriminately lysing male and female target cells bearing H-2D^d antigen (von Boehmer, Hengartner, Nablolz, Lernhardt, Schreier & Haas 1979). What is relevant to G & H's immunoreactive theory is the converse situation. Cytotoxic T-cell receptors and antibodies of a mother bearing HLA-A2 antigen raised against one or the other paternally derived allo-HLA antigen of previous fetuses may react against H-Y + HLA-A2 antigen complex of a subsequent male fetus (Ohno & Stapleton 1981). The hypothesis predicts HLA association in the types of selective male affliction discussed.

The Y chromosome message

Christopher Ounsted
Park Hospital for Children, Oxford OX3 7LQ, England

Gualtieri & Hicks (G & H) generously refer to my writings and those of my colleagues. Perhaps the best way to explain the points of view that we adopted is to recapitulate them. We opened by quoting Sir Peter Medawar (1969), whose brilliant aphorism ended the nature–nurture controversy: "Heredity proposes and development disposes."

Tersely stated, the theory that Taylor and I (Ounsted and Taylor 1972) set out reads thus:
1. The differential ontogenesis of the two sexes depends wholly on the Y chromosome.
2. The Y chromosome transmits no significant information specific to itself.
3. Transcription of the expressed genomic information in males occurs at a slower ontogenetic pace.
4. The operation of the Y chromosome allows more genomic information to be phenotypically transcribed from any given genome.

We thought there were seven sets of questions one might properly ask in relation to the Y chromosome message. These are:
1. What is the formal nature of the message? What kind of laws does it impose on development? What systems are involved?
2. At what point in development is the message delivered? Is it fundamental to the development of the organism? Can the organism survive at all without it? At what stage in development is the presence or absence of the genomic message phenotypically recognisable?
3. Over what period in development does the genetic message endure? Does its phenotypic expression endure for life or is it transient?
4. How is the message translated developmentally? What physiological steps lie between the genetic instruction and its expression?
5. Which contingencies limit, and which promote the expression of a particular message? Do the contingencies reside in the genome or are they dependent upon developmental experience?
6. How frequently and with what consequences does the genetic order go wrong? Is it possible that certain instructions appropriate in one situation are disastrous in another?
7. How does the genetic message relate to the evolution of the particular species? What advantages does it confer? What consequences has it for the ecology of each creature? Are there advantages to the expression of phenotypic variation in specific ecologies that depend upon a single genetic instruction?

Since we formulated these ideas and put some of them to the test a good deal more evidence has come forward.

It seems to me that Gualtieri & Hicks have not taken the full measure of Sir Peter Medawar's dictum. His up-to-date book *Pluto's Republic* (1982) makes most useful reading for those concerned with biological theories.

Immunoreactive theory: A conceptually narrow theory reflecting androcentric bias

Anne C. Petersen and Kathryn E. Hood
Department of Individual and Family Studies, Pennsylvania State University, University Park, Pa. 16802

Gualtieri & Hicks (G & H) propose an intriguing but speculative theory to explain the greater affliction of males with the neurodevelopmental and psychiatric disorders of childhood. Although immune reactions are clearly involved in the development of such disorders, we find the theory conceptually narrow because of both the limited focus on biological mechanisms and the sole focus on male affliction. In addition, the evidence for the theory is often weak and based on selective review or interpretation of prior research.

G & H assume that if biological mechanisms are found to play some role in the development of specific disorders, psychosocial factors are excluded. Such a view of development is naive and not supported by substantial evidence (Lerner 1984; Petersen 1980); most often, psychosocial and biological influences act in concert. For example, stress stimulates changes in an indi-

Commentary/Gualtieri & Hicks: Immunoreactive theory

vidual's immune system (Palmblad 1981); therefore, immunological responses may not be the "cause" of difficulties but rather represent the biological mechanism through which psychosocial factors operate.

The biased focus on biological explanation by G & H is exemplified in their assumption that parity effects seen in data on the National Merit Scholarship Qualifying Test (Figure 3) are explained by cumulative immunological processes in successive pregnancies. First, the n's, r^2's, and B's given for this figure do not make sense (for example, the n's for the two lines are close to but not identical to the total). Second, although there has been much less investigation of psychosocial effects relative to the large body of research examining biological effects on cognition (Petersen 1980), there is evidence for several processes: more intense brother–brother competition and aggression and less brother–brother tutoring and help, to identify just two (Cicirelli 1972; 1973; 1976). G & H's selective bias for biologisms limits the understanding of developmental process.

In addition, an androcentric perspective guides the use of phrases like "uterine inadequacy" and "maternal insufficiency." Whereas G & H note that the fetus itself evokes an "untoward uterine environment," the process is nevertheless labeled as a "maternal immune attack," rather than with more neutral terms such as "maternal immune response." Indeed, the same data could be used to "blame the fetus" and argue for "male fetal pathogenicity." Until there is more compelling evidence one way or the other, however, the mother-fetus *system* should be the focus of investigation rather than presuming that problems may be attributed to the mother.

Even a focus on the mother–fetus system neglects another crucial element in reproduction: the father. Constitutionally "inadequate" mothers (i.e., chronic miscarriers) were four times as likely to reject skin grafts from their husbands compared to those from unrelated sources ("Brain as the Target of Immune Attack" section). Yet the contribution of suitable paternal genetic factors is nowhere integrated into a theory which is otherwise focused on blaming the mother. Complications of pregnancy and delivery constitute a danger to the mother as well as the fetus.

In the broadest perspective, one might ask why females should tolerate the risks associated with producing males. Within evolutionary theory, these issues have been addressed without resolution. The evidence on sex ratios of births among various species is mixed (Clutton-Brock & Albon 1982). Comparative studies do, however, show us sources of individual variation that may be useful in considering this proposal. For example, among baboons observed in the wild, the sex ratio of offspring produced by individual females depends on the mother's social status (Altmann 1980). Dominant females tend to produce daughters, whereas subordinate females produce more sons, showing that in this matrilineal society, sex ratios reflect the effects of the inheritance of social rank by females. In this system, then, biology serves psychosocial functions. (For a review, see Meikle, Tilford & Vessey 1984.) We might well inquire about possible third factors that could cause a relationship between maternal immune responsiveness (presumably partly mediated by social stress) and sex of offspring among humans. We know that sex ratios vary across human cultures and socioeconomic classes (Parkes 1926; Teitelbaum 1970; 1972). It is difficult, however, to obtain accurate estimates of the sex ratio in some Asian cultures, where infant mortality may be 50 times higher than in the U.S. Actual births of female infants are likely to go completely unreported, masking the rate of female infanticide, and invalidating estimates of the sex ratio (Barclay, Coale, Trussel & Stoto 1976). Moreover, in many cultures, accidental mortality and homicide preferentially affect female infants, especially in the first few days of life (World Health Organization 1983).

Finally, the empirical base for the immunoreactive theory is less strong than G & H claim. Their argument is diminished by several instances of incorrect assertion of significance in data presented as well as misattributions of evidence from other research. Perhaps the instances that we have noted are the only ones in the target article. We are concerned, however, that they may equally represent just a sample of more such errors throughout the article.

For example, the theory of maternal immune response is derived from studies of the sex ratio, especially "antecedent brother" effects on sex ratios. On our analysis however, the data presented by G & H show no such effect. (In Table 3, complications of pregnancy are equally predicted by antecedent sisters as by antecedent brothers ($\chi^2 = .82$, $p > .05$).) Furthermore, G & H cite one source which disputes the decrease in sex ratio with antecedent brothers (McLaren 1962). There are other uncited sources that dispute this proposal (Edwards 1966; Greenberg & White 1967). Furthermore, the evidence from other species does not support G & H's contention (Clutton-Brock, Albon & Guinness 1982). Their proposal that the infertile period is longer after the birth of males is not supported in the considerable literature on other species (Clutton-Brock & Albon 1982). Finally, the finding that sex ratios decline or increase, with all male or female antecedent siblings, respectively, simply reflects the differential odds of these combinations.

An example of misattribution may be seen in G & H's claim that "the balance among androgenic, progestational and estrogenic hormones is known to affect fetal brain development." They attribute this finding to Maccoby, Doering, Jacklin, and Kramer (1979), a very interesting study which presents results describing relationships of sex hormone concentrations in umbilical cord blood to sex and birth order of infants; that article does not, however, present data pertaining to fetal brain development.

It is sensible to build a theory based on the possibility that "males and females come to be afflicted by different pathways," especially in a theoretical context that assumes different life histories for each gender. By this view, we should not view males as "selectively afflicted" relative to females, but rather as on a different trajectory, with different forces operating in the course of normal male development. However, the view of the two paths of gender development need not assume antagonism between female and male. Each can be seen as contributing to a cooperative effort of reproduction, in biological, social and cultural evolution (Hartung 1981; Wrangham 1982).

Although we have no doubt that immune reactions play a role in fetal development, the theory proposed is too narrow in its strictly biological focus and androcentric in its sole attention to male affliction and blame placed on the mother. A model that considers the complex interactions among the biological, psychological, and social levels of influence is more explanatory and accurate.

Immunoreactive theory and pathological left-handedness

Alan Searleman
Department of Psychology, St. Lawrence University, Canton, N.Y. 13617

Gualtieri & Hicks (G & H) provide some convincing evidence that pre- and perinatal complications are more frequent in males than in females and that these complications can have a lasting neurodevelopmental effect. As part of the evidence to support their immunoreactive theory they cite the work of Geschwind and Behan (1982), in which it was found that left handers were more likely to have autoimmune disorders than were right handers.

It should be noted, however, that Geschwind and Behan attribute the reported increase in autoimmune disorders in left handers to excess production of testosterone during fetal development. Their hypothesis is that testosterone, which is usually found in greater amounts in male fetuses, slows the growth of the left hemisphere (which they claim can account for the increased incidence of left-handedness often reported in males) and also has a suppressive effect on the thymus gland (an important part of the immune system). Therefore, Geschwind and Behan are invoking a hormonal cause for the increase in autoimmune disorders in left handers rather than an immunoreactive one as do G & H. It is unfortunate that Geschwind and Behan did not report the data for each sex separately. This would have made it possible to determine whether or not the immunoreactive theory IMRT is correct in predicting that left-handed males would be more prone than left-handed females to having the immune disorders.

G & H state that Geschwind and Behan fail to distinguish between familial and pathological sinistrals, and go on to add that "The latter would be expected to exhibit the trait more strongly." It would appear from this that G & H are equating pathological left-handedness with nonfamilial sinistrality (FS−). In my opinion this is a premature and possibly wrong conclusion. For example, although Bradshaw and Taylor (1979) reported that birth complications were more likely in FS− left handers than in FS+ (positive history of familial sinistrality) left handers, Bakan, Dibb, and Reed (1973) found just the opposite. In addition, Searleman, Tsao, and Balzer (1980) examined three different populations of students (high school, community college, and private university) and although they reported that FS was not strongly related to reported birth stress, what little evidence was found of a relationship was confined to the FS+ group. Furthermore, if FS− were synonymous with pathological left-handedness, one might expect to find evidence that individuals with that trait were at a cognitive disadvantage when compared with their FS+ counterparts. However, there is a growing body of evidence that it is the FS+ left handers that are more likely to do worse on cognitive ability–intelligence tests (Bradshaw, Nettleton & Taylor 1981; Briggs, Nebes & Kinsbourne 1976; Burnett, Lane & Dratt 1982; Searleman, Herrmann & Coventry 1984).

There is evidence from the lateral preference literature consistent with the IMRT. For example, specific birth stressors (e.g., premature birth or low birth weight) are correlated with shifts away from the dextral norm (Coren, Searleman & Porac 1982). These shifts are found for all four lateral preferences (hand, foot, eye, and ear) and are particularly evident for males. In fact, a major theme of a paper reviewing the evidence that pre- and perinatal complications can result in a shift from right-sidedness to left-sidedness is that males are much more likely to show this shift than are females (Searleman, Porac & Coren, in preparation). This certainly supports the selective male affliction phenomenon at the core of the IMRT.

The antecedent brother effect proposed by G & H may also prove useful in helping to clarify some controversial issues. For instance, it has long been debated whether or not left-handedness, particularly in males, is related to birth order by a U-shaped distribution. Perhaps by taking into account the sex of preceding siblings some clarity can be achieved in this area. If it is the case that more males with antecedent brothers are left-handed than are males with antecedent sisters, then a useful method for helping to distinguish pathological from natural male left-handers will have been found.

Development rate is the major differentiator between the sexes

David C. Taylor
Royal Manchester Children's Hospital, Manchester M27 1FG, England

But male "affliction" is not limited to neurodevelopmental and psychiatric problems! It persists, with few exceptions, in all health related spheres. Its profound effect upon population structure is such that, in Western societies currently, the male advantage of 105 births per 100 female births is dissipated by the age of 45 and by age 70 there are twice as many females as males (Taylor 1981). An explanation of so ubiquitous a phenomenon which derives from "maleness" itself must have great generality. The best explanation for the precarious nature of maleness comes with the knowledge that, unless persuaded otherwise, the mammalian genome adopts female development. Males are attempting something extra all through life, and, in the sequence of male differentiating mechanisms, the resources of the genome are explored more in males than in females. Consider human height as an example. At whatever level of genetic endowment, the stature of male progeny exceeds that of the females from the same mating dyad. But many environmental and nutritional as well as neural and endocrine factors stand between a genotype and its phenotypic expression. Modification of any one of these factors may diminish the effect of the sex difference.

Similarly, sex differentiation, though genetically contrived, is achieved through a wide variety of mechanisms acting in sequence and in concert and its phenotypic expression can be modified by the degree of expression of its many constituent parts. We (Ounsted & Taylor 1972) referred to this persistent striving for which the words "male" and "maleness" were in danger of being inadequate as "the Y chromosome message." As each component of the male differentiating sequence operates there are consequences, both within the fetus and between the fetus and its environment. The same obtains postnataley from birth to death. Gualtieri & Hicks (G & H) have, perfectly reasonably, selected one such consequence for special treatment (although it has to be said that such antigenic dissimilarity as exists between a woman and her male conceptus is an expression of the action of his Y chromosome in soliciting from the genome something beyond what would otherwise have the same range of choice as a sister's).

We were persuaded by our data, and have since seen no cause to modify our position that the one most persistent theme in male–female differentiation was *pace* difference in the rate of development. If female fetuses, newborns, and children have the advantage of relative maturity, then they have a substantial benefit in terms of developmental disorders. We have suggested that their developmental advantage is perhaps about three weeks at birth to five years by the age of 30. Whether the pace difference is actively maintained in the cells as some aspect of Y-chromosome presence or whether the message is given once only, and is brief and rather dull, is an interesting question. In the 15 years since we proposed that developmental pace would be of profound importance as a differentiating mechanism, considerable supportive evidence has accrued that experiments in embryology can produce changes in morphology which are crucially dependent upon the timing of the intervention but which vary in a precise and predictable way between the sexes (Ferguson 1981). Our theory that the information on the Y chromosome is exceptionally sparse and of a different order from other genetic messages (in relating not to structures but to pace) has been vindicated conceptually by findings in alligators (Ferguson & Joanen 1982) that there is no chromosomal information at all determining sex; rather, sex determination and differentiation is initiated by incubating eggs in nests of different temperatures. With viviparity and a homothermic environment only a very modest intracellular mechanism would be required to unbalance developmental rates. It is likely that the differences will turn out to be due to different rates of DNA turnover in cells.

I would also argue with G & H on certain specific matters.
1. Some handicapped children are born because they are retained in utero rather than being rejected as they might be when their antigenic dissimilarity becomes intolerable; in essence this is a failure of abortion rather than an undue propensity to abort.

Commentary/Gualtieri & Hicks: Immunoreactive theory

2. Maternal insufficiency is an unfortunate term, because a dyad is reproducing by forming a triad (any one of which might be responsible for the reproductive failure). In analysing sex differences one needs to be aware of the very large range of possible effectors which might be responsible for the differences in numbers of males and females.

3. If mothers do develop some antigenic response to their male fetuses it seems unlikely to be a result of the fetuses' "maleness" (which as we have said is not coded structurally – the current status of the H-Y antigens is somewhat confused), but rather more a result of the range of products called into being in the evocation of maleness. Even then the normal effect is to increase birth weight with each male pregnancy, generally a biological advantage rather than disadvantage.

4. It has not been easy to replicate Toivanen's (1970b) results with toxemic mothers.

The sexual strategy of reproduction in humans may do more than set up male and female forms of human being for selection. If the male genome is explored to a greater range of variation, if the slower pace of male development exposes him to greater hazard and to greater advantage, then the *human* gene pool is being carried at different levels of risk between the more conservative female and the more exploratory male genome. The increased hazard this gives to males is offset by his 105 to 100 numerical advantage at birth, an advantage that just about sees him through his reproductive life. (Taylor, in press)

Sex differences in neurodevelopmental and psychiatric disorders: One explanation or many?

Eric Taylor and Michael Rutter
Department of Child and Adolescent Psychiatry, Institute of Psychiatry, London SE5 8AF, England

This immunoreactive theory is an interesting contribution to the explanation of gender differences in childhood disorders. Its theoretical status is rather complex, however. It proposes an additional factor in a domain where many factors are considered to operate; it does not seek to replace any other agents (except perhaps psychosocial influences determining parity effects on IQ). Accordingly, if maternal immune attack upon the male fetus is to be detected epidemiologically, much else must be allowed for or controlled. The hypothesis, while falsifiable in principle, may therefore be difficult in practice to test with precision.

The mediating factor in selective male affliction is, for Gualtieri and Hicks (G & H), a high male prevalence in complications of pregnancy and childbirth. Such complications will need to be rather powerful in their action if they are to account for the very large differences that obtain between the sexes for a large and heterogeneous range of conditions. Furthermore, they must be supposed to operate with power even in children without overt neurological disease or intellectual handicap, because of course most of the difference in rates of psychiatric disorder between the sexes is accounted for by neurologically normal individuals. These requirements are, on the face of it, at odds with much recent research. Most large-scale studies have found that the known complications of pregnancy and childbirth are associated only rather weakly with later impairments of cognition or behaviour, when allowance has been made for social factors (Davie, Butler & Goldstein 1972, Nichols & Chen 1981). Biological disadvantage interacts with social, so that those reared in good psychosocial conditions enjoy considerable protection against later cognitive and psychiatric disorders. The case history data, briefly cited here from an unpublished study by G & H, do not seem to contradict this point: they are taken from a group of intellectually handicapped children and social factors are not controlled. If, then, the effects of the known complications of pregnancy and childbirth are generally present but weak, their ability to engender so great a difference between the sexes is rendered very doubtful. For this reason, the theory is dependent on a new pathogen (namely, direct immune attack on the fetal brain) whose influence is different from that of the recognized complications.

Similar considerations arise with regard to the immunoreactive theory's (IMRT) account of parity effects. They are important for the hypothesis, as its attractiveness over other neuropathological explanations is precisely its ability to account for birth order effects. Plausible psychosocial explanations are equally available, however. Observations of mother–child interactions have shown the presence of systematic differences, dependent upon the birth order of the child, of the kind required to be operative in a psychosocial hypothesis (Rutter 1984). The arguments adduced by G & H against "stimulation" effects do not seem to us to be persuasive. Evidence against Zajonc's "confluence" model is no argument against the role of family relationships, but only against one speculative formulation of that role. Furthermore, we are unable to share G & H's view that psychosocial explanations are "clearly" inapplicable to specific learning disabilities, intellectual retardation, and school failure (Rutter 1984; Rutter and Madge 1976). The hypothesis, then, is able to explain negative parity effects, which already had an explanation. It is not capable of accounting for positive parity effects, which are equally in need of explanation. Later-born children are less prone to some types of emotional disorder and aggression which also show gender differences of the kind that the theory is trying to embrace (Rutter, Tizard & Whitmore 1970).

Some further predictions follow from the immunoreactive hypothesis in this context. There should, for instance, be no parity effect in adoptive sibships; and presumably no parity effect should be discernible when the influence of complications of pregnancy and birth is allowed for. Considering these predictions, however, emphasises the difficulties of testing. The predictions will only apply if the IMRT replaces other causative influences: if the IMRT coexists and interacts with psychosocial effects, then it survives many challenges but at the price of a reduced sharpness of prediction.

It is not easy to see how the immunoreactive hypothesis can account by itself for the particular pattern of sex differences found for different disorders. The sex ratio is lowest (about 1.3 to 1) for neuroepileptic disorders, which show a substantial association with perinatal complications, and highest (about 5 to 1) for psychosocial disturbances such as delinquency which have but a trivial association with perinatal complications. Other conditions, such as autism and specific reading retardation, with a sex ratio of 3 or 4 to 1, often appear to involve a strong association with neurodevelopmental impairment but yet have only modest associations with perinatal complications. It may well be that rather different explanations are necessary for different conditions.

In summary, we have read G & H's proposals with interest as a useful suggestion for the future investigation of the mechanisms of pathogenesis of congenital neuropsychological disorders. We are left rather doubtful about the wider explanatory power of the hypothesis; and even more sceptical of its potential to replace psychosocial factors as a main part of the environmental influence on impairments of cognition and behaviour.

Possible pathogenic effects of maternal anti-Ro (SS-A) autoantibody on the male fetus

Pamela V. Taylor
Department of Obstetrics and Gynaecology, University of Leeds, Leeds LS2 9JT, England

As the existence of a maternal immune response towards fetal antigens is fundamental to Gualtieri & Hicks's immunoreactive hypothesis it is worth remembering that as far as cell-mediated responses are concerned it has been notoriously difficult to demonstrate them at all in normal or pathological pregnancy. With humoral immunity, the development of HLA-related lymphocytotoxic antibody, far from being associated with abnormal pregnancy, may be a part of a wider antibody response, which evoked as a response to some fetal signal and essential for immunological homeostasis between the mother and the fetoplacental unit. It is relevant that failure to develop such antibody has been taken as an indication that women suffering from recurrent spontaneous abortion can be treated with immunotherapy to boost their responsiveness to paternally derived antigens. The correct maternal immune response compatible with successful gestation has been so poorly defined that it is difficult to reconcile the concepts of an obligatory maternal response on the one hand and an aberration and possibly deleterious reaction on the other with a compounding effect of "male antigenicity" in between.

One factor which may tip the balance is the presence in the mother of autoimmune disease which is accompanied by a spectrum of autoantibodies; it may be easier to define the pathological aspect of the maternal immune status by looking at fetal effects in those cases. We have studied a group of women who gave birth to babies with a complete congenital heart block (Scott, Maddison, Taylor, Esscher, Scott & Skinner 1983). The antibody profiles revealed a significant association between the occurrence of the disease and the transplacental passage of anti-Ro (SS-A) antibody from the mother to baby. This antibody, reactive with a nonhistone ribonucleoprotein antigen, also seemed to be associated with other types of pregnancy pathology. It seems to be directly toxic in various tissue culture systems and is reactive with heart and brain cells when these are subjected to environmental factors such as ultraviolet light (Taylor & Griffiths 1984). In this respect it is interesting that Ro (SS-A) antigen has been shown to be ten times more abundant in the heart and brain than in any other body tissues (Wolin & Steitz 1984). Although the sex ratio in the affected babies was 57, this surviving group may be very different from those dying in utero, for whom data were not obtainable. An association with androgen-related effects may be relevant to the G & H's immunoreactive hypothesis. It is of interest that although complement-mediated cytotoxicity of anti-Ro (SS-A) antibody could not be shown on skin cells under normal conditions it was significantly demonstrable on cells derived from sexual skin. These have intracellular testosterone receptors and one can speculate that testosterone binding may interact in some way to influence the susceptibility of the cells to autoantibody damage.

Authors' Response

The immunoreactive theory: What it is, what it is not, what it might be

Thomas Gualtieri and Robert E. Hicks
Department of Psychiatry and Biological Sciences Research Science Center, University of North Carolina, Chapel Hill, N.C. 27514

The immunoreactive theory (IMRT) covers a broad range, and so do the commentaries. To lend coherence to the discussion, we will organize our response in the following manner:

1. We will reiterate what the IMRT is, and what it is not. Some commentators objected to a perceived claim of global significance or of universal inclusiveness. Other commentators have carried the theory well beyond its intended boundaries, impelled by enthusiasm or disapproval. Still others have attributed a degree of exclusiveness to immunoreactivity we never intended and that we tried to eschew.

2. Specific remarks will address questions raised about parity effects, perinatal complications, the sex ratio, and sinistrality.

3. Commentaries from immunologists have expanded on the complexity of the maternal–fetal interaction. These views will be placed in a perspective that supports the theory in its main thrust if not in fine detail.

4. We will try to address certain errors and ambiguities raised by the commentators. We apologize to our readers for the weaknesses in exposition that are, no doubt, responsible for these errors.

What the immunoreactive theory is. The neurodevelopmental disorders of childhood should be of signal concern to medical science by virtue of the frequency and severity such afflictions cause to children and families. Neither the quality of science in the area, nor the general interest in the topic have been commensurate with the importance of the problem. For example, in seven years of publication, *BBS* has never published a target article bearing directly on mental retardation, autism, childhood epilepsy, dyslexia, developmental dysphasia, or hyperactivity. In a similar vein, one of the most striking differences between the sexes, selective male affliction in the neurodevelopmental disorders, has received very little attention in the otherwise expansive and fertile study of psychological sex differences.

That the genesis of *most* cases of developmental handicap is unknown would ordinarily impel scientists to search energetically for new avenues to explore. Selective male affliction with its likely roots in male antigenicity, "male hormones," or both is one such opportunity. We agree that the developmental disorders are so diverse a population that it may be unrealistic to seek any degree of unity therein. But if there is a common facet to this population of grievances, it is – with exceptions as noted – selective male affliction. We hoped with the target article to bring to the topic at least a measure of the attention it deserves.

Selective male affliction has been credibly dealt with from time to time, most notably in the maturational theory of D. C. Taylor and Ounstead, and in the endocrinologic theories summarized in Money's commentary. However, the alternative theories described in our target article and reiterated in many of the commentaries have not been dramatically successful in reducing what Medawar referred to as an "unexplained residue . . . of staggering proportions" (Medawar 1963, p. 324). Furthermore, the relative antigenicity of the male fetus had not been proposed as a factor that might be relevant to the phenomenon. It has not been difficult to discover information in diverse sources to suggest that it might be. A possible immunoreactive origin of neurodevelopmental disorders was last advanced by Adinolfi (1976). His work

Response/Gualtieri & Hicks: Immunoreactive theory

and other developments in the field of reproductive immunology do not yet seem to have had much impact on developmental neuropsychiatry, neuroscience, or the study of sex differences.

The essential concern of the IMRT is the immunologic environment of the developing fetal brain. The theory is concerned with pathology – how the delicate immunological balance of mother and fetus may sometimes go awry and how the pathological consequences of this imbalance may be measured in human beings. The theory's premises are conservative: maternal immune attack may occur, the development of the fetal brain may be hindered by such an attack and there are specific factors rendering maternal immunoreactivity more likely. Some mothers are by virtue of inheritance more immunoreactive; some fetuses are more antigenic than others, and, on balance, male fetuses are more antigenic than females. We do not presume, however, that the simplicity of these assumptions belies or diminishes the complexity of the actual process, or the degree to which it may be obscured by other events in gestation, parturition, or childhood. The theory, as presented, is probably an oversimplification, but it has a certain appeal. We are encouraged by the favorable reception it has received from some of its most important commentators and also by the grudging agreement, from some of its harshest critics, that there may be something to it after all.

What the Immunoreactive theory is not. In light of at least some of the commentaries, it is important to clarify exactly what the IMRT is not, and what it does not pretend to be. Although indirect evidence in support of the theory is drawn from a broad range of divergent areas, we do not presume to have provided a global theory of evolutionary biology, sexual differentiation, or differential morbidity. Although we find commentaries that attempt to lend a wider biological perspective to the theory both interesting and important, we remind the reader that our primary concern is with the specific issue of selective male affliction in the neurodevelopmental disorders.

We are in the peculiar position of having to admonish two of our harshest critics that the connection between maternal immunoreactivity and neurodevelopmental disorders is not an established scientific fact: "Immune reactions are *clearly involved* [our italics] in the development of such disorders" (**Petersen & Hood**); "some birth problems are caused by maternal [immunoreactivity]" (**Boklage**). Neither of these statements is correct. Most of the commentators agree with us that the theory is speculative and that its basis consists almost entirely of indirect evidence.

The IMRT is not globally inclusive. The IMRT is not about differential morbidity and mortality across the life span nor does it pretend to include all the disorders in which humans succumb. It is possible to suppose that the male preponderance in developmental handicap is simply another manifestation of differential male morbidity and mortality, but that view is neither accurate nor heuristic. Differential male morbidity is the sum of myriad factors; immunological, genetic, endocrine, and environmental elements play different kinds of roles depending on the disorder in question. With respect to the congenital disorders, however, the uterine environment of the fetus should be expected to have a special salience, and in the specific study of congenital disorders of brain development, maternal and fetal factors that influence the uterine environment should be of prime concern. Such factors, however, may have no bearing at all on subsequent development or disorders of later life. Likewise, the antigenic nature of the male fetus may be of importance to the intrauterine environment but not to subsequently. The relative immunocompetence of a mother may be crucial in her capacity to support a successful gestation, but it is not necessarily the central element to every pathological condition that may occur during a woman's life.

The IMRT is not intended to be exclusionary. To propose an additional "pathogen" is not to deny the validity of others. It is not quite justified to fault an article concerned with one particular aspect of human development for not giving equal weight or emphasis to all other aspects. A biological theory is not, for example, an argument against psychosocial theories. An immunological theory does not diminish the importance of endocrine effects.

Thus we can allay **Gillberg**'s fears that the IMRT fails because it attempts to be a "universal explanation," reconciling the occurrence of extremely different conditions with one "underlying pathogenetic mechanism." He cites two conditions, trisomy 21 and the fragile-X syndrome on which, we agree, the theory may have no bearing whatever. These conditions do not weaken the theory, they are irrelevant to it. They are chromosomal disorders that lie fairly and squarely in the "explained residue." Our caveat to the reader of the target article that the IMRT "is by no means a global explanation for all of the neuropathic disorders of childhood" is in our opinion neither very obscure nor nonspecific, but common sense.

Hoyenga also introduces an important issue with respect to chromosomal disorders by pointing out that levels of H-Y antigen are higher, for example, in XYY males (Fraccaro et al. 1982) and in XO females (Müller et al. 1983). Since both disorders are associated with higher levels of H-Y antigen as well as with an apparent increase in the incidence of neurodevelopmental disorders, we had at one time thought of citing these data in support of the IMRT. However, the ambiguity of the clinical data alluded to by Hoyenga, weighed against including them. We elected to marshall only evidence sufficient to render the theory credible, not to include every conceivable example that could support it.

Although the theory makes no claim of universality, **Hoyenga** raises the question whether *all* examples of differential morbidity go in the direction predicted by the theory. Not surprisingly, she discovers that they do not. Her discussion of differential vulnerability to chronic disabling conditions such as sickle cell disease, X-linked disorders, antisocial behavior in adolescence, and dopamine metabolites in schizophrenics comprises simply too diverse a collection of phenomena to bring to bear on the IMRT of neurodevelopmental disorders. Two specific remarks are in order, however, on matters that are germane to the theory. Even in samples where males are more frequently afflicted with severe developmental handicaps, the relative proportion of females with severe afflictions is higher than in mild and moderate conditions.

The report Hoyenga cites of more positive symptoms in male schizophrenics is based on a single study of only 18 patients (Opler et al. 1984).

Hoyenga, Mackey and Ferguson attempt to place the IMRT into a broader evolutionary framework; however, this is a highly theoretical issue on which we do not feel qualified to comment. It is not unreasonable to seek antecedents in evolutionary biology for a phenomenon such as the one we describe. If maternal immunoreactivity plays an important role in human development, it must have some kind of adaptive rationale. We prefer to focus on the validity of the theory before we make such a theoretical leap.

We are delighted with Jensen's remark that maternal IMR with respect to the neurodevelopmental disorders may represent only the tip of the iceberg; however, its wider application can be made only with caution. We ourselves would be quite content if the theory were to hold even for only a small group of disorders in our specific realm of endeavor. On the other hand, it is by no means unreasonable to suspect that a mechanism that may account for pathological outcomes in brain development could also influence intellectual development in normal populations.

Our warning that the IMRT is by no means intended to exclude alternative factors in the genesis of the neurodevelopmental disorders was echoed by many of the commentators who pointed to the salience of specific factors or emphasized the importance of a multifactorial point of view. A multifactorial model of selective male affliction has been called for by Beatty, Beatty & Goodkin, Diamond, Ferguson, Gorczynski, Money, Petersen & Hood, E. Taylor & Rutter, and P. Taylor, as well as by our target article. The development of a unified and integrated theory, especially one that embraces such an expanse of data, is a perilous exercise; it requires critical selection among views and data that may be parallel, divergent, or contradictory. Although there is necessarily much that is subjective in this, there is no need to apologize for being selective. Nor is it necessary to apologize for simplifying what is obviously an extraordinarily complex issue or to be defensive for having neglected the relative importance of other dimensions of the problem. It is the mind's inherent bias to seek order in disorder and coherence in noise. Whether in the case of the IMRT this has been a fruitful exercise or simply an artful concoction is an open question.

Money is concerned that we have become committed to immunology too soon and that we have been too restricted by a single hypothesis. Yet it is he who is able to posit a single element – the secretion of testicular hormones – as the central mediator of the entire range of male morbidity across the life span. Gorcyznski has also decided that any hostile uterine environment is the consequence of endocrine factors but not of maternal alloreactivity. These contentions are far more sweeping than any we have made. There is certainly a complex interplay between endocrine and immunological factors, and the relative weight of these elements will vary in different conditions. The reader is referred to the more balanced views of P. V. Taylor and of Diamond.

Parity effects. It may be that E. Taylor and Rutter are skeptical of the potential of the IMRT to replace psycho-social explanations, but the degree to which it may replace, complement, augment, or be irrelevant to psychosocial factors in development is an empirical question best considered with respect to specific issues. Taylor and Rutter find fault with our development of an alternative, biological mechanism for negative parity effects in the occurrence of severe mental handicaps like dyslexia, autism, and mental retardation because there is already an explanation that presumably has as its basis the role of family relationships. Taylor and Rutter fail to expand upon its nature or to give important details. Family relationships play no small role in the lives of handicapped individuals but they do not cause autism, mental retardation, or dyslexia. We are aware of no data that support a psychosocial explanation for negative parity effects in the occurrence of neurodevelopmental disorders.

Parity effects of IQ in normal populations were found in Belmont's study even when social class was controlled (Belmont & Marolla 1973). The effect on IQ was steeper for lower-class families and it also seemed to occur in adopted children. This suggests that psychological factors are germane to the issue. One would expect an even steeper parity–IQ gradient in families in very poor nations (if such research were ever undertaken) implying that in some circumstances maternal nutrition may also play a role in the negative parity effect on IQ. However, the parity–IQ gradient is clearly consistent with an immunoreactive explanation, and the existence of an antecedent-brother effect renders this view cogent indeed. The existence of other elements that may contribute to this gradient is not sufficient reason to discredit an immunoreactive hypothesis.

The question of parity effects on IQ is also raised by Costeff, who may be right in asserting that normal population studies or studies of academically capable students, with whom most such research is conducted, may be irrelevant to the IMRT and its central focus on neurodevelopmental disorders. The parallel between negative parity effects on IQ and the incidence of developmental disabilities, however, is remarkable and at least suggests a common mechanism. Furthermore, we do not agree that the parity–IQ data are as equivocal as Costeff characterizes them. The exquisite Dutch study of Belmont and Marolla (1973) is not of a piece with that of the Scottish Council for Research in Education (1949), which involved only 1100 eleven-year olds, or with the Enquete Nationale (1973), which used only a nonverbal intelligence test. The authors of the latter study in fact felt that certain elements of family structure in their population may have rendered the findings spurious (Ernst & Angst 1983).

We agree with E. Taylor & Rutter that the IMRT does not account for positive parity effects such as those described by Rutter and Graham (1970) in neurotic and what they term "nonsocialized" antisocial children in the Isle of Wight Study (Rutter, Tizard & Whitmore 1970). On the other hand, the opposite trend, a negative parity effect, was reported by the same authors in "socialized" antisocial children. Given the ambiguities of psychiatric diagnosis in children, the sample size (total $N = 109$), and the fact that statistical analysis compared eldest to youngest, one need not give much credence to this purported exception to the rule. (Incidentally, the Isle of Wight

Response/Gualtieri & Hicks: Immunoreactive theory

Study did detect a negative parity effect for mental retardation and dyslexia; Rutter et al. 1970.)

Boklage refers to our examination of the primiparity effect in the data of Deykin and MacMahon (1980) and in Schoenbaum et al. (1975). We had thought that our text and Figures 6 and 7 were clear in demonstrating a preponderance of affected cases in firstborns. The point to be made here is that the unique problems of primiparas may obscure the existence of a parity effect in children born to multiparas. Boklage's subsequent explication of these data is very difficult to understand, but it does not seem to diminish the importance of the primiparity effect.

Boklage interprets Figure 9 and the accompanying text as if it alluded to the "male fraction of mental retardation"; that is, the proportion of mentally retarded males at birth order one, two, three, and so on. In fact, the figure refers to the sex ratio of sibships that included a handicapped individual. The decrease in sex ratio normally observed with parity is sharper in the families of handicapped individuals. If one grants that the decrease in the sex ratio with parity has an immunoreactive basis, and if the families of handicapped individuals are typified by an excess of maternal immunoreactivity, one would expect to see this distortion in the sex ratio–parity regression line.

Parity effects in sex steroid levels in umbilical-cord blood were reported by Maccoby et al. (1979), as noted by **Hoyenga**. However, consistent parity effects were only noted for progesterone and estradiol. The parity effect on testosterone was described by the authors as tentative, and there was no effect for adrostenedione or estrone. The birth-order analysis there, however, compared firstborns to later borns; in fact, a primiparity effect.

Petersen & Hood attribute a "misattribution" to us in citing Maccoby et al. (1979) since the article did not "pertain . . . to fetal brain development." For the record, Maccoby et al. (1979) discussed their findings in light of endocrine effects on brain development, including parity effects on IQ and the effects of progestins on intellectual development, and cited an extensive literature related to these topics.

One vexing aspect of psychosocial arguments is their inexhaustible capacity to provide alternative (and untestable) explanations for virtually every human circumstance. **Boklage** offers an unwitting display of this in his discussion of parity effects on the occurrence of neurodevelopmental disorders. First, the reader is asked to agree that the likelihood of stopping further procreation after the birth of an affected child will increase in proportion to the number of previous children. So far this sounds like a reasonable idea. Then, two paragraphs later, another rhetorical question vis-à-vis the primaparity effect: "Wouldn't the neurodevelopmentally disabled child be more of a problem for new parents and more likely to reduce further reproduction?" Neither proposition is by itself unreasonable, but they appear to be contradictory.

Readers will understand and perhaps sympathize with our decision not to respond to the suggestion that an immunoreactive study of selective male affliction is "androcentric" or that we "assume antagonism between female and male" in any realm beyond the immunological environment of the gravid uterus. Nor do we understand the basis of one question posed by **Petersen & Hood**, "why females should tolerate the risks associated with producing males."

We do not agree with **Berglin** that population controls are always necessary for a proper birth-order analysis. Our analysis was concerned with the interaction between parity effects and sex, which is the contrasting dimension, and a normal population control is not needed here. In his reanalysis of the data from Reed and Reed (1965), Berglin presents an alternative method of analysis that has neither been published nor, to our knowledge, peer-reviewed. It is reassuring that he has strengthened our original observation, but we cannot be sure that his method is valid, or, on the basis of his remarks, that ours is a "mistake."

Neither **Petersen & Hood** nor **Berglin** have understood the statistical analysis of the data in Table 3, which clearly shows an antecedent-brother effect for autistic boys, not an antecedent-sister effect. Both their reanalyses purport to show a nonspecific parity effect. However, the overall parity effect is meaningless because antecedent sisters contribute nothing to it. It only means that the noise sisters contribute to the data is not sufficient to vitiate the brother effect. A reanalysis, comparing antecedent brothers by complications of pregnancy (linear) to antecedent sisters by complications of pregnancy (linear) yields a chi square statistic $= 5.589$, which is highly significant. The antecedent-brother effect is significant and the antecedent-sister effect is nonexistent.

Perinatal problems. The issue of perinatal complications is addressed by **E. Taylor & Rutter** and **Costeff**. Taylor and Rutter appear to have misread our intent, however, in raising the question to begin with. We postulated that perinatal complications are a manifestation of maternal immunoreactivity, not its sole and exclusive mediator. Perinatal problems are a concomitant of maternal immunoreactivity but neither a necessary nor a sufficient condition for its occurrence. Perinatal complications may arise in the absence of maternal immunoreactivity, and maternal immune attack may occur without outward signs of perinatal complications. Taylor and Rutter also impose an interesting but impossible criterion on the IMRT by demanding a kind of dose–response relationship between perinatal complications, sex ratio, and the presumed neuropathic origins of developmental disorders. Such a criterion would only be valid, of course, if one assumed that no other factor but maternal immunoreactivity had a role to play in the genesis of these conditions. It is *argumentum ab extremis*.

In **Costeff**'s data, complications of pregnancy and delivery were found to be equally common in males and females with nonspecific mental retardation. He was not able to control this analysis for sex of antecedent siblings. Thus, it is not a fair test of the IMRT. The same may be said for the cerebral palsy data he cites (Stanley & Blair 1984). His report that perinatal complications are associated with smaller family size is entirely consistent with the IMRT. We have dealt with the putative relationship between maternal insufficiency, neurodevelopmental disorders, and infertility.

Costeff also mentions that the sex ratio of fetal deaths decreases by month of gestation (McMillen 1979), which

Response/Gualtieri & Hicks: Immunoreactive theory

it does, and which is not predicted by the theory. He neglects to mention, however, that it increases again at term (McMillen 1979). This argument, however, would only be valid for primiparas, who can develop fetotoxic antibodies during the course of a first pregnancy. The data reviewed by McMillen (1979) did not distinguish between primiparas and multiparas, however. In any event, the timing of an intrauterine insult is, as Costeff is well aware, extremely important to the outcome of a pregnancy. An early insult can produce a severe disorder or fetal death, whereas a later event has less grave consequences. A pertinent example from the target article is the pregnancies of acutely schizophrenic mothers, where early psychosis is associated with fetal death whereas psychosis occurring later in pregnancy is associated with fetal malformation (M. A. Taylor 1969).

We thank **Gillberg** for reanalyzing his data, which tend to support our finding of an antecedent-brother effect in autistic boys. We agree with him that certain neurodevelopmental disorders may have a more likely immunoreactive explanation than others, and autism may indeed be a prime candidate. To be sure, Gillberg's data on the association of atopic disease with minimal brain dysfunction or with pathological left-handedness are hardly supportive of the IMRT, although his use of the latter term is different from ours (see below). Neither is **Benbow's** stunning report of an increased incidence of atopic disease in intellectually gifted students, but before drawing conclusions about their findings, we would prefer to review the data. It is not unlikely that the complexity of immunological events in pregnancy and thereafter and the complexity of immunoendocrine relationships will influence certain outcomes, like theirs, in ways that are not predicted by the IMRT. A biological mechanism may confer advantage in some circumstances and disadvantage in others.

Sex ratio. Several commentators have dealt with issues pertaining to sex ratios. **Hoyenga** believes that factors other than maternal immunoreactivity may influence the secondary sex ratio and we are inclined to agree, although the examples she cites – maternal age, breast feeding, and sex hormone levels at birth – are not well chosen. A host of factors have been claimed to influence the secondary sex ratio, including paternal age, race and color, paternal baldness, frequency and timing of intercourse, and SES (socioeconomic status) (Teitelbaum 1972). **Teitelbaum** reports a significant negative association between secondary sex ratio and birth order, a significantly lower ratio for blacks than whites, and a significant association with SES. Neither paternal nor maternal age have been convincingly related to secondary sex ratio.

Boklage is concerned that the effects of maternal age on developmental disorders were not addressed, but they have been. In the Perinatal Collaborative Project, for example, parity effects on perinatal mortality are apparent even when maternal age is controlled (Niswander & Gordon 1972).

Hoyenga doubts that an implantation advantage enjoyed by males, presumably by virtue of heightened antigenicity, could influence the sex ratio at conception. In fact, the primary sex ratio in human beings is necessarily an estimate, and it would be more proper to refer to the sex ratio early in pregnancy. A high sex ratio early in pregnancy may mean that more male zygotes are formed at conception and that males and females are implanted with equal frequency or that males and females are conceived at an equal rate but that males are more likely to be implanted (Kirby et al. 1967). In our opinion the weight of the evidence favors the latter. **Bixler** presents an alternative view, suggesting a primary sex ratio of 100, with disproportionate loss of female embryos. We agree with Bixler that estimates of the primary sex ratio are uncertain, although the weight of the evidence once again favors a value that is higher than unity.

James's suggests that maternal gonadotrophin levels at the time of conception may be "responsible for the sex of the infant," although the evidence he cites does not directly confirm this opinion. It is neither demonstrated nor likely to be shown that "almost all of the observed variation in the human sex ratio" is explicable in terms of gonadotrophins. In fact, at least one of his citations (James 1980), which reports the low sex ratio of relatively infertile mothers, is equally amenable to an immunoreactive explanation.

James is right in pointing out that the data of Malinvaud (1955) and of Ben-Porath and Welch (1976) on the sex ratio do not agree with ours, but he overstates the case with a claim of unanimity, countered by data published by Renkonen et al. (1962) and by Gualtieri, Hicks, and Mayo (1984b) from very large samples supporting the existence of a negative antecedent-brother effect on sex ratio. He is not right in attributing this discrepancy to a statistical weakness on our part and he is advised to review our 1984 publication. The analysis there was *not* confined to families with same-sex antecedent siblings, but a second analysis included family configurations with mixed sibships. The association between antecedent brothers and a decline in the secondary sex ratio held in both analyses, and the size of the regression coefficients in both analyses was about equal.

Both **Hoyenga** and **Adinolfi** allude to a purported increase in the secondary sex ratio at parity four and five. We are hard put to explain this increase, since we did not observe such a trend in our research (Gualtieri, Hicks & Mayo 1984b). The relative infrequency of such sibships in humans, however, renders it inadvisable to draw serious conclusions about a definite trend. In any event, it is known that certain types of maternal antibodies will only develop – if at all – at parity one, two, or three, but not thereafter. The occasional development of maternal tolerance to H-Y (or other) antigens, as described by **Loke**, is another conceivable explanation for the phenomenon, if it does indeed exist in humans.

Immunological aspects of pregnancy. The commentaries from immunologists lend a degree of support to a theory that embraces some form of immunological attack on the developing brain. The immunological commentaries did not take serious issue with the idea of relative male antigenicity, although its mediation may be an open question. Perhaps H-Y antigen is the mediating factor, perhaps it is H-Y in concert with other antigen systems, perhaps there is an alternative antigen system that does not involve H-Y. **P. V. Taylor** aptly captures the complexity of the field: "The correct maternal immune response

Response/Gualtieri & Hicks: Immunoreactive theory

compatible with successful gestation has been so poorly defined that it is difficult to reconcile the concepts of an obligatory maternal response on the one hand and an aberration and possibly deleterious reaction on the other...."

Caught in this tangled net are the following ideas:

1. The precise behavior of H-Y antigen with respect to mammalian reproduction is imperfectly understood (**Loke**).

2. There is indirect evidence of the existence of more than one "male antigen" (Silvers, Gasser & Eicher 1982).

3. In some instances tolerance rather than sensitivity to H-Y antigen may develop with successive pregnancies (**Loke**).

4. The development of a certain class of maternal antibodies may be the prerequisite for successful gestation (**P. V. Taylor; Loke**).

5. Some cases of habitual abortion may be treated successfully by enhancing the maternal immune response (**Gorczynski, P. V. Taylor**).

Where H-Y antigen fits into this puzzle is obscure, and we are sympathetic to **Loke**'s suggestion that the attribution of selective male affliction to H-Y antigen may be premature. Although the antigenicity of H-Y is not doubted (**Loke**), it is a comparatively weak immunogen (**Ohno**) and may only work its deleterious effect by acting in concert with other antigen systems. Loke, for example, has suggested that the expression of a weak antigenic system like H-Y "may be dependent on the degree of interaction with other stronger, histocompatibility systems" (Loke 1978, p. 165). Ohno has expressed the belief that the antigenicity of H-Y may be major-histocompatibility-antigen (MHC) dependent, and in at least one preclinical study, male target cells were killed only when they expressed both the H-Y and the HLA-A2 antigen (Goulmy et al. 1977). (We apologize to **Petersen & Hood**, who object to the martial phraseology of immunological science, but such is the *lingua franca*. No amount of wishing will make killer lymphocytes and cytotoxic antibodies cooperate, share, or resonate with their targets.)

Ohno introduces the idea of antigenic "misidentification," which may speak to a specific mechanism by which the expression of a weak immunogen like H-Y may have damaging consequences. **Bukovský & Presl** also present a hypothetical mechanism by which an immunological reaction may exercise a negative effect on brain development. We appreciate their willingness to share unpublished data that suggest that class I MHC-molecules and "differentiation antigens" of lymphocytes may be demonstrated on developing brain cells. These putative mechanisms suggest that the detection of H-Y antigen on developing neuronal tissue may not be a prerequisite for the IMRT, as **Gorczynski** claims it must be.

The relevance of autoimmune disorders is highlighted by the commentary of **P. V. Taylor** and her reference to a study of congenital heart block in the offspring of mothers with connective tissue disease. Maternal antibodies to soluble tissue ribonucleoprotein antigens appeared to cross the placenta and were associated with the development of congenital cardiac abnormalities; extracardiac defects were not the topic of the paper (Scott et al. 1983). It is therefore extraordinary news to discover that anti-Ro (SS-A) antibody is cross-reactive with neural cells in tissue culture and that it is ten times more abundant in heart and brain than in other body tissues. It will be interesting to learn whether the children in this study will be developmentally handicapped, and whether the degree of handicap is related to the strength of the maternal antibody response or to the level of hypoxia experienced by the children in early life.

Although the potential importance of H-Y antigen is not diminished by commentaries of the immunologists, we agree that it would be premature to commit ourselves to a single-antigen system and that maternal–fetal interaction is probably a great deal more complicated than we suggested in our target article. **P. V. Taylor** also alluded to a specific association between complement-mediated cytotoxicity of anti-Ro (SS-A) antibody and androgenic hormones. This affirms the wisdom of suggestions by **Diamond** and others that endocrine factors may not be irrelevant to the study of immunoreactivity and that endocrine and immunological mechanisms may be independent.

Hoyenga believes that the increased incidence of autoimmune disease in females is a critical problem for the IMRT. On the contrary, it is strongly consistent with the theory, which presumes that the mother is immunoreactive whereas the fetus is antigenic. The "superior immuno-competence of females" (Purtilo & Sullivan 1979, p. 1253), presumably related to X-linked genes, may explain the differential vulnerability of males to infectious disease and cancer as well as to the special female vulnerability to autoimmune diseases.

Gorczynski claims to have no knowledge of an increased incidence of developmental disorders in the offspring of mothers with autoimmune disorders. The research has never been done because the appropriate question has not been raised. There is, however, a clear increase in reproductive inefficiency and spontaneous abortion in these disorders, as we have mentioned. We do not agree that there is anything approaching good evidence for a "psychoneuroendocrine axis" in the autoimmune disorders. The reference cited (Solomon 1983) is a philosophical essay, not a scientific paper.

We agree with **Costeff** that maternal alloreactivity might cause damage to the fetal brain via indirect pathways, and that an actual immunological reaction against fetal nervous tissue is not necessary to account for relative failures in development. Direct immune attack against the brain may not be necessary for the occurrence of neuropathic damage, and indirect mechanisms may play a role. Rh incompatibility, erythroblastosis fetalis, and kernicterus are examples of such an indirect effect. However, a direct immunological mechanism is neither harmful to the theory, as Costeff maintains, nor is it unlikely.

The sharpness or predictiveness of the IMRT, about which **E. Taylor & Rutter** are concerned, will depend not so much on its interaction with psychosocial effects but more probably on the identification of specific immunological mechanisms that may be fetotoxic and specific subgroups of immunoreactive individuals.

Adinolfi's critical comments deserve careful scrutiny, first because he is a respected immunologist, and second because his work has in important ways presaged the IMRT: "Are maternal abnormal states, with regard to hormones and immune reactions, responsible for some of the as yet unclassified congenital forms of "global" mental retardation or, possibly, some specific brain defects and selective neurological handicaps?" (Adinolfi 1976, p. 244).

We cannot agree with **Adinolfi** that we have misrepresented his work and that of others and that we have not exercised sufficient critical judgment in our analysis. We have "miscited" his work, he judges, because he has "not shown transfer of lymphocytes across the placenta." In fact, we did not suggest that he had done so; the transplacental transfer of maternal humoral antibodies is sufficient to effect fetal damage. The entry of maternal cells into the fetal circulation *may* occur under certain circumstances, as Adinolfi is aware (Adinolfi & Wood 1969), although the issue is controversial. When he maintains that there is little or no traffic in lymphocytes across the placenta, he seems to be misrepresenting his own work: "Transfer of fetal lymphocytes into the maternal circulation seems to occur in almost all normal pregnancies" (Adinolfi & Wood 1969, p. 50).

Adinolfi also maintains that we misrepresented his views by citing references that dealt with a different topic. The fact is that Adinolfi himself raised a question central to the IMRT in one of his cited papers: "Immune reactions based on the transfer of antibodies [are] slowly emerging as a possible component of the causation of mental retardation" (Adinolfi 1976, p. 245). We might stand fairly accused of borrowing his ideas but not of misrepresenting the thrust of his work.

Nor were the citations from Loke (1978) taken out of context. Adinolfi is referred to **Loke**'s commentary, which is critical of the IMRT but careful and fair. Loke (1978), for example, referring to the work of McLaren (1962), which Adinolfi cites, commented that "it must, however, be remembered that experiments on isogeneic strains of mice may not be directly comparable with the situation in man" (p. 165). One of Loke's conclusions was that "sex-linked antigens do have some influence on the human fetal–maternal interaction, but the exact consequence to the fetus is, at present, unclear" (Loke 1978, p. 166), a conclusion neither inconsistent with the IMRT nor with our own representation of Loke's views.

The Lawler et al. (1975) reference was cited as an illustration of interindividual variability in maternal–fetal immunoreactivity, not to support the increased antigenicity of the male fetus, as **Adinolfi** suggests. Even with male fetuses maternal reactivity is neither inevitable nor inevitably harmful. Adinolfi also claims that "more recent investigations . . . have not confirmed a higher incidence of male than female conceptuses" in toxemia of pregnancy. The study of Juberg et al. (1976), which he cites, involved 373 patients with toxemia, 95% of whom were black; a study that is not, strictly speaking, comparable to the Finnish sample of 1,064 offspring of toxemic women described by Toivanen and Hirvonen (1970b). Juberg et al. themselves wondered whether "some of the patients had chronic hypertension or renovascular disease instead of pre-eclampsia because both of these diseases are more common among blacks than caucasians" (p. 302). The study of Redman et al. (1978), which Adinolfi also cites, involved only 80 pre-eclamptic women, and the sex ratio of the offspring was apparently deemed by the authors of so little importance that it warranted neither analysis nor discussion. Redman's paper strongly supported the idea of toxemia as an immune disorder,

Response/Gualtieri & Hicks: Immunoreactive theory

however, and discussed in some detail "immune attack on fetal tissues by maternal cells" (p. 399). Support for the findings of Toivanen and Hirvonen (1970b) is cited by Loke (1978) and in Salzmann (1955) and Scott, Beer & Stastny (1976). Toivanen and Hirvonen advanced an immunoreactive theory of toxemia based on H-Y antigen, whereas Salzmann favored an endocrine hypothesis based on maternal reaction to male fetal hormones (Loke 1978).

Hoyenga also refers to the issue of toxemia of pregnancy, and wonders whether the fact that primiparas are at greater risk for the disorder is not inconsistent with the IMRT. This may be another example of the primiparity effect, which, as we have said, may obscure a parity effect. What is the subsequent fertility of severely toxemic primiparas? In addition, it is known that maternal antibodies may develop during the course of a first pregnancy. The antecedent-brother effect has not been tested in toxemia of pregnancy.

Beatty, Beatty & Goodkin complain that there is no direct pathological evidence of maternal immune response in the neurodevelopmental disorders. This is perhaps too facile a criticism. They are themselves "overly enthusiastic" about the capacity of neuropathologists to detect immunological "calling cards" or serologic abnormalities years after a transient alloreactive event. **Gorczynski** also alludes to the importance of monitoring the maternal–fetal interaction *in situ*. How direct evidence of this kind can actually be obtained in a prospective fashion in human beings is a practical question that we, as clinical scientists, invite Beatty et al. to expand upon.

Beatty et al. refer to abnormalities that are "clearly definable and reproducible in animal models." We are mystified by their apparent suggestion that there may actually be animal models for the neurodevelopmental disorders at issue. We have, however, alluded to animal models of maternal antibody attack against fetal CNS tissue (Brent 1971; Johnson et al. 1980).

Direct (or indirect) evidence will have to await the development of specific hypotheses concerning fetal antigens and the precise nature of the maternal immune response along the lines of those suggested by **Ohno, P. V. Taylor**, and **Bukovský & Presl**. Beatty et al. fail to understand the purpose of the theory; perhaps **Ounstead** ought to advise *them* to read Medawar's (1982) book. Were direct evidence for immunoreactivity in neurodevelopmental disorders to exist, one would not need to promulgate the theory. The central purpose of the theory is to guide the development of testable hypotheses. Without a theory it is unlikely that scientists would seek either direct or indirect evidence. Remember, we pointed out how research on the association between pregnancy complications and neurodevelopmental disorders has traditionally failed to consider as relevant variables the sex of other proband, birth order, the sex of antecedent siblings, or the family history of maternal insufficiency, allergy, or autoimmune disease. This may be the reason why so much of the work on perinatal complications has been inconclusive (**E. Taylor & Rutter**).

Costeff, who is as skeptical of the theory as we ourselves, agrees that the IMRT guarantees that such factors will be incorporated into future epidemiological studies of developmental handicap. Judging from **Gillberg**'s data,

Response/Gualtieri & Hicks: Immunoreactive theory

we believe that when they do, the results will indeed be interesting. **Jensen** introduces the relevance of immunoreactivity to studies of the heritability of intelligence, an area of vast importance we had not considered, and **Hoyenga** mentions its relevance to XYY and XO syndromes, which we had. The measure of the value of a theory is not, after all, how convincing it is (**Adinolfi**) or how enthusiastically it reaches conclusions (**Beatty et al.**) or even how elegant (**Loke**), intriguing (**Petersen & Hood**), or interesting (**E. Taylor & Rutter**) it may seem to be. The real measure is whether or not it engenders testable hypotheses and productive research.

Beatty et al. have also misconstrued our interpretation of the salience of genetic influences on sex differences in the neurodevelopmental disorders. We have never assumed that the "most devastating departures from normal development are primarily the results of genetic influences." We have simply cited evidence in support of the idea that genetic influences in certain conditions lead to more specific outcomes, whereas mediation via the occurrence of perinatal complications leads to more diverse pathological outcomes. Nor have we assumed that genetic influences are lost on the male conceptus or that perinatal complications are irrelevant to the female. The issue is one of relative weight between the sexes. The relatively lower proportion of the males in the most profoundly handicapped categories may speak simply to this phenomenon: A male with an untoward genetic complement and severe maternal alloreactivity is not likely to survive the gestational period at all.

Beatty et al. also seem to be in error in their belief that the genotype necessarily exercises equivalent effects in males and females. The premise of a dual threshhold model is just the opposite. Males are afflicted by a less severe genotype, whereas females require a higher genetic load for expression of an untoward phenotype. It may also be wrong to seek a statistical parallel to a clinical dimension as Beatty et al. do. We reiterate the finding of Mednick et al. (1977) that there is more clinical diversity in the pathological outcome of sons of schizophrenic mothers compared to daughters. This qualitative diversity is not translatable into statistical variability on a unidimensional scale, as Beatty et al. propose.

Developmental pace. We have tried to give proper attention to alternative theories of selective male affliction, and especially to the maturational theory of **Ounstead** and **D. C. Taylor.** We are pleased that both of these eminent scientists have taken the opportunity to reiterate their ideas in individual commentaries. We regret to find, however, that the only new evidence they adduce in support of their theory is **Ferguson**'s study of sex differences in *Alligator mississippiensis* (Ferguson & Joanen 1983). This work is also described in Ferguson's commentary. It is ironic, though, that Ferguson himself propounds a maturational theory that is the precise opposite of **D. C. Taylor** and **Ounstead**'s. According to Ferguson, the developmental pace of the male organism is faster than that of the female; androgens hasten senescence and degeneration and *this* may account for increased male morbidity and mortality. Perhaps the forms of life Ferguson mentions, intriguing though they are in their own right, are, like isogeneic strains of mice, not germane to the question of neurodevelopmental disorders in human beings. It is nevertheless interesting to learn that packrats feed enriched milk to their daughters but not to their sons and that by incubating eggs at low temperature, one may produce female lizards or, alternatively, male turtles (Ferguson & Joanen 1983).

With respect to **D. C. Taylor** and **Ounstead**'s theory, however, we are familiar with only one clinical study (the relative vulnerability of boys and girls to febrile seizures) that is directly supportive. However convincing their theory may be, it does not seem to have generated much in the way of research although this may be as much the fault of other researchers. It might be reasonable to apply Taylor's and Ounsted's ideas, for example, to studies of autism or schizophrenia, or to other severe neurodevelopmental disorders with a variable age of onset. Perhaps future work from D. C. Taylor and Ounsted will offer some concrete and testable hypotheses based on the theory. We hope so; the idea is too important to lie fallow.

It is important, however, to register a disagreement with **Ounstead**'s contention that "the Y chromosome transmits no significant information specific to itself," since the expression of H-Y antigen is a direct manifestation of the Y chromosome. The significance of this expression is, according to the IMRT, rather high.

Nonright-handedness. In reply to **Searleman**, we do not equate pathological nonright-handedness with nonfamilial sinistrality. A nonfamilial left-hander is not necessarily pathological. Pathological nonright-handers are defined clinically as individuals with developmental impairment. In handicapped populations, the frequency of nonright-handedness is almost always higher than in the population at large. We only suggested that if Geschwind and Behan's (1982) study were to be replicated in such a group, the incidence of allergies and autoimmune diseases would be even higher than in a normal group of nonright-handers. Nor do we agree that family configuration might be used to determine whether an otherwise normal individual came by his sinistrality in a "natural" or a "pathological" way. If handedness is, in fact, a continuously distributed variable, then sinistrality will occur in some individuals in the absence of a clear family history and irrespective of family configuration.

We feel that **Boklage**'s assertions that the neurodevelopmental disorders "represent anomalies of lateralization or lateralized function" or that neuroendocrine relationships are lateralized are unduly sweeping and premature. His discussion of cell-surface interactions and tissue-specific growth rates is obscure, and extremely difficult to appraise since the two salient references (Boklage & Fraser 1984; Boklage & Fraser in preparation) are not available to us.

Conclusion. The IMRT developed out of our curiosity over the problem of selective male affliction. As we expressed on several occasions in the target article, the origin of this puzzling phenomenon is almost certainly multifactorial, but we were dismayed by the clear failure of most "multifactorial models" to pay any heed at all to the potential significance of male antigenicity. The further we delved into this obscure and relatively neglected corner, the more convinced we grew of its potential significance. We also became convinced that a theory based on male antigenicity and maternal sensitization had the potential to generate specific testable hypotheses in many important areas. If any major part of the IMRT were found to be correct, it could influence clinical practice in predicting or preventing at least some of the neurodevelopmental disorders.

If sufficient indirect evidence were to accrue in support of the theory, one might decide to address the question of specific immunological mechanisms that could mediate maternal immune attack and design specific experiments to test the validity of such mechanisms. Considering the expense involved in actually mounting a series of such immunological studies in humans, the technology required and the invasiveness of such research were it conducted in the proper prospective fashion, we deemed it wise to focus initial efforts on the accrual of indirect evidence and to share the results of this endeavor with other members of the scientific community. We have always considered the theory speculative, but the literature of reproductive immunology suggested that it was neither outlandish nor impossible to test.

The generally favorable reaction of the commentators, especially those who have a background in reproductive immunology, seems to support our opinion. The least favorable commentaries seem to have come from proponents of either one specific point of view or from proponents of the "multifactorial model." We feel quite strongly that no one single mechanism will ever suffice to explain the extraordinary phenomenon of selective male affliction or the larger issue of differential male morbidity and mortality. We fault the multifactorial model, however, for having neglected a very important factor in fetal antigenicity.

We have mentioned that the IMRT is capable of generating testable predictions. May we indulge, at this point, in making a few predictions *about* the IMRT:

1. In its current formulation, the IMRT will almost certainly prove to be wrong. Major modifications of the theory will occur as time goes on. In its ultimate embodiment in the archives of medical wisdom, it will be unrecognizable. As it stands, the IMRT is not only speculative but naive, oversimplified, and much too broad. Our present understanding of the immunological and endocrine events that support a successful gestation, the antigenic nature of fetus, and even the nature of the so-called sex-linked antigens is very limited.

2. Nevertheless, the fundamental premise of the theory will hold. The effect of maternal alloreactivity on fetal development, especially brain development, simply must be reckoned with. So must the related issues of selective male affliction and male antigenicity. The application of the theory to issues like sex ratio or to parity effects on IQ could be far-fetched or right on. Its relevance to evolutionary biology may be high or low, but it will occupy an important place in the future of developmental neuropsychiatry.

3. The problem of selective male affliction will obtain at least some measure of the importance it deserves. There are few indisputable facts in the field of developmental neuropsychiatry, but this is one. It will become an important element in the study of sex differences.

4. It will no longer be possible to maintain that environmental effects on fetal development begin at parturition or that maternal nutrition, freedom from infectious disease, and good obstetrical care are the sole determinants of a successful gestation.

5. The immunoreactive theory will affect research in the neurodevelopmental disorders by turning the attention of some developmental scientists to the field of reproductive immunology. The interaction of immunological and endocrine factors in promoting or retarding neural development will be a fertile area for such research. The extraordinary complexity of both domains will prevent any early resolution of the questions we have raised. Scientists will, as usual, succeed in developing more questions than answers.

6. It is an open question whether the fruits of this theory will someday be translated into practices that can improve the human condition or reduce the number of developmentally impaired individuals. This we cannot predict, but we are hopeful.

References

Aarkrog, T. (1968) Organic factors in infantile psychoses: Retrospective study of 46 cases subjected to pneumoencephalography. *Danish Medical Bulletin* 15:283–88. [taTG]

Abramowicz, H. K. & Richardson, S. A. (1975) Epidemiology of severe mental retardation in children: Community studies. *American Journal of Mental Deficiency* 80:18–39. [taTG, KBH]

Abramsky, O., Lisale, R. P., Silberger, D. H. & Pleasure, D. E. (1977) Antibodies to oligodendroglia in patients with multiple sclerosis. *New England Journal of Medicine* 297:1207–11. [taTG]

Abramsky, O. & Litvin, Y. (1978) Autoimmune response to dopamine-receptor as a possible mechanism in the pathogenesis of Parkinson's disease and schizophrenia. *Perspectives in Biology and Medicine* 22:104–14. [taTG]

Adelman, S. & Rosenzweig, S. (1978) Parental predetermination of the sex of offspring. 2. The attitudes of young married couples with high school and with college education. *Journal of Biosocial Science* 10:235–47. [WHJ]

Adinolfi, M. (1976) Neurologic handicap and permeability of the blood CSF barrier during foetal life to maternal antibodies and hormones. *Developmental Medicine and Child Neurology* 18:243–46. [HC, CG, tarTG]

Adinolfi, M., Beck, S. E., Haddad, S. A. & Seller, M. J. (1976) Permeability of the blood-CSF barrier to plasma proteins during foetal and perinatal life. *Nature* 259:140–41. [HC, taTG]

Adinolfi, M. & Wood, C. B. S. (1969) Ontogenesis of immunoglobulins and components of complement in man. In: *Immunology and development*, ed. M. Adinolfi. Spastics International. [rTG]

Ahern, F. M. & Johnson, R. C. (1973) Inherited uterine inadequacy: An alternative explanation for a portion of cases of defect. *Behavior Genetics* 3:1–12. [taTG]

Allan, T. M. (1975) ABO blood groups and human sex ratio at birth. *Journal of Reproductive Fertility* 43:209–19. [RHB]

Allon, R. (1971) Sex, race, socioeconomic status, social mobility, and process-reactive ratings of schizophrenics. *Journal of Nervous and Mental Disease* 153:343–50. [taTG]

Altmann, J. (1980) *Baboon mothers and infants.* Harvard University Press. [WCM, ACP]

Altus, W. D. (1966) Birth order and its sequellae. *Science* 151: 44–49. [HC, taTG]

Alvesalo, L. & Portin, P. (1980) 47, XXY Males: Sex chromosomes and tooth size. *American Journal of Human Genetics* 32:955–59. [CEB]

Alvesalo, L. & Tammisalo, E. (1981) Enamel thickness in 45, X females' permanent teeth. *American Journal of Human Genetics* 33:464–69. [CEB]

Alvesalo, L. & Varrela, J. (1980) Permanent tooth sizes in 46, XY females. *American Journal of Human Genetics* 32.736–42. [CEB]

Arena, J. F. P. & Smith, D. W. (1978) Sex liability to single structural defects. *American Journal of Diseases of Children* 132:970–72. [KBH, WHJ]

References/Gualtieri & Hicks: Immunoreactive theory

August, G. J., Stewart, M. A. & Tsai, L. (1981) The incidence of cognitive disabilities in the siblings of autistic children. *British Journal of Psychiatry* 138:416–22. [taTG]

Badian, N. (1984) Reading disability in an epidemiologic context: Incidence and environmental correlates. *Journal of Learning Disabilities* 17:129–36. [taTG]

Bakan, P., Dibb, G. & Reed, P. (1973) Handedness and birth stress. *Neuropsychologia* 11:363–66. [ARS]

Bakke, J. L., Lawrence, N. L., Bennett, J. & Robinson, S. (1975) Endocrine syndromes produced by neonatal hyperthyroidism, hypothyroidism, or altered nutrition and effects seen in untreated progeny. In: *Perinatal thyroid physiology and disease*, ed. D. A. Fisher & G. N. Burrow. Raven Press. [RMG]

Bakketeig, L. S. (1977) The risk of repeated preterm or low birth weight delivery. In: *The epidemiology of prematurity*, ed. D. M. Reed & F. J. Stanley. Urban and Schwarzenberg. [taTG]

Barclay, G., Coale, A., Trussel, J. & Stoto, M. (1976) A reassessment of the demography of traditional rural China. *Population Index* 42:606–35. [ACP]

Bardawil, W. A., Mitchell, G. W., McKeogh, R. P. & Marchant, D. J. (1962) Behavior of skin homografts in human pregnancy. 1. Habitual abortion. *American Journal of Obstetrics and Gynecology* 84:1283–95. [taTG]

Barnes, R. D. & Tuffrey, M. (1971) Maternal cells in the newborn. *Advances in Biosciences* 6:457–73. [taTG]

Beck, J. S. & Rowell, N. R. (1963) Transplacental passage of antinuclear antibody. *Lancet* 1:134–5. [taTG]

Beer, A. E. & Billingham, R. E. (1973) Maternally acquired runt disease. *Science* 179:240–45. [taTG]

(1976) *The immunobiology of mammalian reproduction*. Prentice-Hall. [AB, RMG]

Behan, P. O. (in press) Laterality, hormones, and immunity. In: *Cerebral dominance: The biological foundations*, ed. N. Geschwind & A. M. Galaburda. Harvard University Press. [CPB]

Belmont, L. & Marolla, F. A. (1973) Birth order, family size and intelligence. *Science* 182:1096–1101. [HC, tarTG]

Belmont, L., Stein, Z. A. & Susser, M. W. (1975) Comparisons of associations of birth order with intelligence test score and height. *Nature* 255:54–55. [taTG]

Belmont, L., Stein, Z. A. & Wittes, J. A. (1976) Birth order, family size and school failure. *Developmental Medicine and Child Neurology* 18:421–30. [taTG]

Belmont, L., Stein, Z. & Zybert, P. (1978) Child spacing and birth order: Effects of intellectual ability in two-child families. *Science* 202:995–96. [taTG]

Benbow, C. P. (1984) Physiological correlates of extreme intellectual precocity. Submitted. [CPB]

Benbow, C. P. & Stanley, J. C. (1980) Sex differences in mathematical ability: Fact or artifact? *Science* 210:1262–64. [CPB]

(1983) Sex differences in mathematical reasoning ability: More facts. *Science* 222:1029–31. [CPB]

Ben-Porath, Y. & Welch, F. (1976) Do sex preferences really matter? *Quarterly Journal of Economics* 90:285–307. [rTG, WHJ]

Berg, K. (1979) Inactivation of one of the X chromosomes in females is a biological phenomenon of clinical importance. *Acta Medica Scandinavica* 206:1–3. [KBH]

Berglin, C.-G. (1981) Regular skewness of birth order distribution. *Scandinavian Journal of Social Medicine* (Suppl. 23):54–66; 77–106. [C, GB]

(1982) Birth order as a quantitative expression of date of birth. *Journal of Epidemiology and Community Health* 36:298–302. [C-GB]

Bernard, O. (1977) Possible protecting role of maternal immunoglobulins on embryonic development in mammals. *Immunogenetics* 5:1–15. [taTG]

Berryman, P. L. & Silvers, W. K. (1979) Studies on the H-X locus of mice. *Immunogenetics* 9:363–67. [taTG]

Billingham, R. E. (1964) Transplantation immunity and the maternal–fetal relationship. *New England Journal of Medicine* 270:667–72. [taTG]

Birtchnell, J. (1971) Mental illness in sibships of two and three. *British Journal of Psychiatry* 119:481–87. [C-GB, taTG]

Bishop, D. V. M. (1980) Handedness, clumsiness and cognitive ability. *Developmental Medicine and Child Neurology* 22:569–79. [CG]

Blessing, W. W., Costa, M., Gefen, L. B. & Rush, R. A. (1977) Immune lesions of noradrenergic neurons in rat central nervous system produced by antibodies to dopamine-B-hydroxylase. *Nature* 167:368–69. [taTG]

Boehmer, H. von., Hengartner, H., Nabholz, M., Lernhardt, W., Schreier, M. H., & Haas, W. (1979) Fine specificity of a continuously growing killer cell clone specific for H-Y antigen. *European Journal of Immunology* 9:592–97. [SO]

Bockman, D. E. & Kirby, M. L. (1984) Dependence of thymus development on derivatives of the neural crest. *Science* 223:498–500. [CEB]

Boklage, C. E. (1981) On the distribution of nonrighthandedness among twins and their families. *Acta Geneticae Medicae et Gemellologiae* 30:167–87. [CEB]

Boklage, C. E. & Fraser, F. C. (1984) Symmetry-related markers of fusion malformation liability. *March of Dimes Birth Defects Conference Abstracts*. [CEB, rTG]

(in preparation) Twinning, handedness, and congenital malformations: Symmetry-related markers of fusion malformation liability. [CEB, rTG]

Bonner, J. J., Terasaki, P. I., Thompson, R., Holve, L. M., Wilson, L., Ebbin, A. J. & Slavkin, H. C. (1978) HLA phenotype frequencies in individuals with cleft lip and/or cleft palate. *Tissue Antigens* 12:228–32. [taTG]

Borland, R., Loke, Y. W. & Oldershaw, P. J. (1970) Sex differences in trophoblast behavior on transplantation. *Nature* 228:572. [taTG]

Born, G., Grützner, P. & Hemminger, H. (1976) Evidenz für eine mosaikstruktur der netzhaut bei konduktorinnen für dichromasie. *Human Genetics* 32:189–96. [KBH]

Bowers, M. B., Jr., Swigar, M. E. & Jatlow, P. I. (1983) Sex differences in plasma homovanillic acid in acute psychosis. *New England Journal of Medicine* 308:845–46. [KBH]

Bradshaw, J. L., Nettleton, N. C. & Taylor, M. J. (1981) Right hemisphere language and cognitive deficit in sinistrals? *Neuropsychologia* 19:113–32. [ARS]

Bradshaw, J. L. & Taylor, M. J. (1979) A word-naming deficit in nonfamilial sinistrals? Laterality effects of vocal responses to tachistoscopically presented letter strings. *Neuropsychologia* 17:21–32. [ARS]

Breland, H. (1974) Birth order, family configuration and verbal achievement. *Child Development* 45:1011–19. [taTG, WHJ]

Brent, L. (1971) The effect of immune reactions on fetal development. *Advances in Biosciences* 6:421–55. [tarTG]

Bresler, J. (1970) Outcrossings in Caucasians and fetal loss. *Social Biology* 17:17–25. [ARJ]

Bresnihan, B., Grigor, R. R., Oliver, M., Leiskomia, R. M. & Hughes, G. R. V. (1977) Immunological mechanism for spontaneous abortion in systemic lupus erythematosis. *Lancet* 5:1025–07. [taTG]

Briggs, G. G., Nebes, R. D. & Kinsbourne, M. (1976) Intellectual differences in relation to personal and family handedness. *Quarterly Journal of Experimental Psychology* 28:591–601. [ARS]

Broad, F. E. & Duganzich, D. M. (1983) The effects of infant feeding, birth order, occupation and socio-economic status on speech in six-year-old children. *New Zealand Medical Journal* 96:483–86. [KBH]

Bronson, R. T. (1981) Age at death of necropsied intact and neutered cats. *American Journal of Veterinary Research* 42:1606–08. [KBH]

Brown, W. T., Jenkins, E. C., Friedman, E., Brooks, J., Wisniewski K., Raguthu, S. & French, J. (1982) Autism is associated with the fragile X syndrome. *Journal of Autism and Developmental Disorders* 12:303–08. [CG]

Bukovský, A. & Presl, J. (1984) Immune system and tissue proliferation, fetal allograft survival, and tumor growth. *Československá Gynekologie* 49:584–99. [AB]

(1985) Allosensitization in tumor therapy and prophylaxis, and in female contraception – a prospect for clinical use. *Medical Hypotheses*. In press. [AB]

Bukovský, A., Presl, J. & Holub, M. (1984) The ovarian follicle as a model for the cell-mediated control of tissue growth. *Cell and Tissue Research* 236:717–24. [AB]

Bukovský, A., Presl, J. & Židovský, J. (1984) Association of some cell surface antigens of lymphoid cells and cell surface differentiation antigens with early rat pregnancy. *Immunology* 52:631–40. [AB]

Burbaeva, G. S. (1972) Antigen characteristics of the human brain. *Soviet Neurology and Psychiatry* 5:110–18. [taTG]

Burdi, A. R. & Silvey, R. G. (1969a) Sexual differences in closure of the human palatal shelves. *Cleft Palate Journal* 6:1–7. [MWJF]

(1969b) The relation of sex associated facial profile reversal and stages of human palatal closure. *Teratology* 2:297–304. [MWJF]

Burgio, G. R., Fraccaro, M., Ticpolo, L. & Wolf, U. (1981) *Trisomy 21*. Springer-Verlag. [taTG]

Burke, J. & Johansen, K. (1974) The formation of HL-A antibodies in pregnancy: The antigenicity of aborted and term fetuses. *Journal of Obstetrics and Gynaecology of the British Commonwealth* 81:222–28. [taTG]

Burley, N. (1981) Sex ratio manipulation and selection for attractiveness. *Science* 211:721–22. [KBH]

Burnett, S. A., Lane, D. M. & Dratt, L. M. (1982) Spatial ability and handedness. *Intelligence* 6:57–68. [ARS]

References/Gualtieri & Hicks: Immunoreactive theory

Butler, N. R. & Bonham, D. G. (1963) *Perinatal mortality.* Livingstone. [taTG]
Cadoret, R. J. & Cain, C. (1980) Sex differences in predictors of antisocial behavior in adoptees. *Archives of General Psychiatry* 37:1171–75. [taTG, KBH]
Cadoret, R. M., Cunningham, L., Loftus, R. & Edwards, J. (1975) Studies of adoptees from psychiatrically disturbed biologic parents: 2. Temperament, hyperactive, antisocial, and developmental variables. *Journal of Pediatrics* 87:301–6. [KBH]
(1976) Studies of adoptees from psychiatrically disturbed biological parents: 3. Medical symptoms and illnesses in childhood and adolescence. *American Journal of Psychiatry* 133:1316–18. [KBH]
Carter, C. O. (1965) The inheritance of common congenital malformations. *Progress in Medical Genetics* 4:59–84. [taTG]
Charnov, E. L. (1982) *The theory of sex allocation.* Princeton University Press. [KBH, WCM]
Chesley, L. C., Annito, J. E. & Cosgrove, R. A. (1968) The familial factor in toxemia of pregnancy. *Obstetrics and Gynecology* 32:303–11. [taTG]
Childs, B. (1965) Genetic origin of some sex differences among human beings. *Pediatrics* 35:798–812. [taTG]
Cicirelli, V. (1972) The effect of sibling relationships on concept learning of young children taught by child teachers. *Child Development* 43:282–87. [ACP]
(1973) Effects of sibling structure and interaction on children's categorization style. *Developmental Psychology* 9:132–39. [ACP]
(1976) Mother-child and sibling-sibling interactions on problem-solving task. *Child Development* 47:588–96. [ACP]
Ciocco, A. (1940) Sex differences in morbidity and mortality. *Quarterly Review of Biology* 15:59–92. [taTG]
Clare, J. E. & Kiser, C. V. (1951) Preference for children of given sex in relation to fertility. *Milbank Memorial Fund Quarterly* 29:440–92. [WHJ]
Clarke, B. & Kirby, D. R. S. (1966) Maintenance of histocompatibility polymorphisms. *Nature* 211:999–1000. [taTG]
Clements, P. R., & Van Arsdale, M. & Hafer, M. (1974) Variability within Down's syndrome (Trisomy-21): Empirically observed sex differences in IQs. Paper presented at Midwestern Psychological Association. [KBH]
Cloninger, C. R., Christiansen, K. O., Reich, T. & Gottesman, I. I. (1978) Implications of sex differences in the prevalences of antisocial personality, alcoholism, and criminality for familial transmission. *Archives of General Psychiatry* 35:941–51. [taTG]
Clutton-Brock, T. H. (1982) Sons and daughters. *Nature* 298:11–13. [RHB]
Clutton-Brock, T. H. & Albon, S. D. (1982) Parental investment in male and female offspring in mammals. In: *Current problems in sociobiology*, ed. King's College Sociobiology Group. Cambridge University Press. [WCM, ACP]
Clutton-Brock, T. H., Albon, S. D., & Guinness, F. E. (1982) Competition between female relatives in a matrilocal mammal. *Nature* 300:178–80. [ACP]
Cobb, J. A. (1914) The alleged inferiority of the first-born. *Eugenics Review* 5:357–59. [C-GB]
Cohen, B. H. & Mellitts, E. D. (1971) Blood group incompatibility and immunoglobulin levels. *Johns Hopkins Medical Journal* 128:318–31. [taTG]
Coleman, M. & Gillberg, C. (1984) *The biology of the autistic syndromes.* Praeger Publishers CBS. In press. [CG]
Corbett, J. A., Harris, R. & Robinson, R. G. (1975) Epilepsy in mental retardation and developmental disorders, vol. 7. Brunner/Mazel. [taTG]
Coren, S., Scarleman, A. & Porac, C. (1982) The effects of specific birth stressors on four indexes of lateral preference. *Canadian Journal of Psychology* 36:478–87. [ARS]
Costeff, H., Cohen, B. E., Weller, L. E. & Kleckner, H. (1981) Pathogenic factors in idiopathic mental retardation. *Developmental Medicine and Child Neurology* 23:484–93. [taTG]
Costeff, H., Cohen, B. E. & Weller, L. E. (1983a) Biological factors in mild mental retardation. *Developmental Medicine and Child Neurology* 25:580–87. [HC, taTG]
(1983b) Relative importance of genetic and nongenetic etiologies in idiopathic mental retardation estimates based on analysis of medical histories. *Annals of Human Genetics* 47:83–93. [HC]
Crouchly, R., Davies, R. B. & Pickles, A. R. (1984) Methods for the identification of Lexian, Poisson and Markovian variations in the secondary sex ratio. *Biometrics* 40:165–75. [WHJ]
Cunningham, L., Cadoret, R. J., Loftus, R. & Edwards, J. E. (1975) Studies of adoptees from psychiatrically disturbed biological parents: Psychiatric conditions in childhood and adolescence. *British Journal of Psychiatry* 126:534–49. [KBH]

Dalakas, M. C. & Engel, W. K. (1981) Chronic relapsing (dysimmune) polyneuropathy: Pathogenesis and treatment. *Annals of Neurology* 9 (Suppl.):134–35. [taTG]
Daly, M. & Wilson, M. (1983) *Sex, evolution, and behaviour.* Willard Grant Press. [MWJF, RHB]
Darwin, C. (1871) *The descent of man, and selection in relation to sex.* 1887 ed. D. Appleton. [MWJF]
Davie, R., Butler, N. & Goldstein, H. (1972) *From birth to seven: A report of the National Child Development Study.* Longman. [ET]
Dawkins, R. (1976) *The selfish gene.* Oxford University Press. [WCM].
Decker, S. N. & DeFries, J. C. (1980) Cognitive abilities in families of reading-disabled children. *Journal of Learning Disabilities* 13:517–522. [taTG]
Dekaban, A. S. & Sadowsky, D. (1978) Changes in brain weights during the span of human life. *Annals of Neurology* 4:345–56. [taTG].
Delint, J. E. E. (1966) The position of early parental loss in the etiology of alcoholism. *Alcoholism Zagreb* 2:56–64. [taTG].
Deykin, E. Y. & MacMahon, B. (1980) Pregnancy, delivery and neonatal complications among autistic children. *American Journal of Diseases of Children* 134:860–64. [CEB, tarTG]
Diamond, J. M. (1982) Big-bang reproduction and ageing in male marsupial mice. *Nature* 298:115–16. [MWJF]
Diamond, M. C., Dowling, G. A. & Johnson, R. E. (1981) Morphologic cerebral cortical asymmetry in male and female rats. *Experimental Neurology* 71:261–68. [MCD]
Dickemann (1979) Female infanticide, reproductive strategies, and social stratification: A preliminary model. In: *Evolutionary biology and human social behavior: An anthropological perspective*, ed. N. Chagnon & W. Irons. Duxbury Press. [WCM]
Divale, W. & Harris, M. (1976) Population, warfare, and the male supremacist complex. *American Anthropologist* 78:521–38. [WCM]
Dobbing, J. (1971) Undernutrition and the developing brain: The use of animal models to elucidate human problem. In: *Normal and abnormal development of brain and behavior*, ed. G. B. A. Stoelinga & J. J. Van der Werffen Bosch. Williams and Wilkins. [AB]
Doughty, R. W. & Gelsthorpe, K. (1974) An initial investigation of lymphocyte antibody activity through pregnancy and in eluates prepared from placental material. *Tissue Antigens* 4:291–98. [taTG]
(1976) Some parameters of lymphocyte antibody activity through pregnancy and further eluates of placental material. *Tissue Antigens* 8:43–48. [taTG]
Drillien, C. M. (1968) Studies in mental handicap. 2. Some obstetric factors of possible aetiological significance. *Archives of Diseases in Childhood* 43:283–94. [taTG]
Edwards, A. W. F. (1958) An analysis of Geissler's data on the human sex ratio. *Annals of Human Genetics* 23.6–15. [WHJ]
(1960) The meaning of binomial distribution. *Nature* 186:1074. [WHJ]
(1966) Sex ratio rate analysed independently of family limitation. *Annals of Human Genetics*, London 29:337–47. [ACP]
Eichwald, E. J. & Silmser, C. R. (1955) *Transplantation Bulletin* 2:148–49. [RMG, taTG]
Ernst, C. & Angst, J. (1983) *Birth order: Its influence on personality.* Springer-Verlag. [tarTG]
Enquete Nationale. (1973) *Sur le niveau intellectuel des enfants d'age scolaire.* Institue National d'etudes demographique. [rTG]
Fabia, J. & Drolette, M. (1970) Life tables up to age 10 for mongols with and without congenital heart disease. *Journal of Mental Deficiency Research* 14:235–42. [taTG]
Farber, C., Cambiaso, C. L. & Masson, P. L. (1981) Immune complexes in cord serum. *Clinical and Experimental Immunology* 44:426–32. [taTG]
Fechheimer, N. S. & Beatty, R. A. (1974). Chromosomal abnormalities and sex ratio in rabbit blastocysts. *Journal of Reproductive Fertility* 37:331–41. [RHB]
Feig, K. & Ropers, H.-H. (1978) On the incidence of unilateral and bilateral colour blindness in heterozygous females. *Human Genetics* 41:313–23. [KBH]
Ferguson, M. W. J. (1981) Review: The value of the American alligator as a model for research in craniofacial development. *Journal of Craniofacial Genetics and Developmental Biology* 1:123–44. [DCT]
Ferguson, M. W. J. & Joanen, T. (1983) Temperature-dependent sex determination in *Alligator mississippiensis. Journal of Zoology* 200:143–77. [MWJF, rTG, DCT]
Fialkow, P. J. (1966) Autoimmunity and chromosomal aberrations. *American Journal of Human Genetics* 18:93–108. [taTG]
Fisher, R. A. (1930) *The genetical theory of natural selection.* Clarendon Press. [WCM]

References/Gualtieri & Hicks: Immunoreactive theory

Flor-Henry, P. (1969) Psychosis and temporal lobe epilepsy – a controlled investigation. *Epilepsia* 10:363–95. [taTG]
(1974) Psychosis, neurosis and epilepsy: Developmental and gender related effects. *British Journal of Psychiatry* 124:144–50. [taTG]
Forssman, H. & Akesson, J. O. (1970) Mortality of the mentally deficient: A study of 12,903 institutionalized subjects. *Journal of Mental Deficiency Research* 14:276–94. [taTG]
Foster, J. W. & Archer, S. J. (1979) Birth order and intelligence: An immunological interpretation. *Perceptual and Motor Skills* 48:79–93. [taTG]
Fraccaro, M., Mayerová, A., Bühler, E., Gebauer, J., Gilgenkrantz, S., Lindsten, J., Curto, F. Lo & Ritzén, E. M. (1982) Correlation between the number of sex chromosomes and the H-Y antigen titer. *Human Genetics* 61:135–40. [rTG, KBH]
Fraser, F. C. (1983) Association of neural tube defects and parental nonrighthandedness. *American Journal of Human Genetics* 35:89A. [CEB]
Fraser, F. C. & Rex, A. (1984) Nonrighthandedness: A manifestation of developmental instability. *American Journal of Human Genetics* 36:51S. [CEB]
Freier, S. & Eidelman, A. I., eds. (1980) *Human milk, its biological and social value*. Excerpta Medica. [AB]
Funderburk, S. J., Carter J., Tanguay, P., Freeman, B. J. & Westlake, J. R. (1983) Parental reproductive problems and gestational hormonal exposure in autistic and schizophrenic children. *Journal of Autism and Developmental Disabilities* 13:325–32. [CG, taTG]
Galton, F. (1874) *English men of science: Their nature and nurture*. MacMillan. [taTG]
Gardner, C. G. (1967) Role of maternal psychopathology in male and female schizophrenics. *Journal of Consulting Psychology* 31:411–13. [taTG]
Garside, R. F. & Kay, D. W. K. (1964) The genetics of stuttering. In: *The syndrome of stuttering*, ed. G. Andrews & M. M. Harris. Heinemann. [taTG]
Geodakjan, V. A. (1982) Sex dimorphism and evolution of duration of ontogenesis and its stages. *Doklady Akademii Nauk SSSR* 263:1475–80. [AB]
(1983) The logic of evolution of sex differentiation and long-term survival. *Priroda* 1:70–80. [AB]
Gerendai, I. (1984) Asymmetry of neuronal structures involved in the control of neuroendocrine functions in rats. *Cerebral dominance: the biological foundations*, ed. N. Geschwind & A. Galaburda. Harvard University Press. [CEB]
Geschwind, N. & Behan, P. (1982) Left-handedness: Association with immune disease, migraine and developmental learning disorder. *Proceedings of the National Academy of Sciences of the United States of America* 79:5097–5100 [CPB, CEB, CG, taTG, KBH, ARS]
(1984) Associations of dominance with immune disease, migraine, and other biological features. In *Biological foundations of cerebral dominance* ed. N. Geschwind & A. Galaburda. Harvard University Press. In press. [CEB]
Gillberg, C. (1980) Maternal age and infantile autism. *Journal of Autism and Developmental Disorders* 10:293–97. [CG]
(1984) Infantile autism and other childhood psychoses in a Swedish urban region: Epidemiological aspects. *Journal of Child Psychology and Psychiatry* 25:35–43. [CG]
Gillberg, C. & Gillberg, I. C. (1983) Infantile autism: A total population study of reduced optimality in the pre- and peri-, and neonatal period. *Journal of Autism and Developmental Disabilities* 13:153–66. [taTG]
Gillberg, C. & Rasmussen, P. (1982) Perceptual, motor and attentional deficits in seven-year-old children: Background factors. *Developmental Medicine and Neurology* 24:752–770. [taTG]
Gillberg, C., Rasmussen, P., Carlström, G., Svenson, B. & Waldenström, E. (1982) Perceptual, motor and attentional deficits in six-year-old children: Epidemiological aspects. *Journal of Child Psychology and Psychiatry* 23:131–44. [CG]
Gillberg, C. & Wahlström, J. (1984) Chromosome abnormalities in infantile autism and other childhood psychoses: A population study of 66 cases. *Developmental Medicine and Child Neurology*. In press. [CG]
Gillberg, C., Waldenström, E. & Rasmussen, P. (1984) Handedness in Swedish 10-year-olds: Some background and associated factors. *Journal of Child Psychology and Psychiatry* 25:421–32. [CG]
Gleicher, N. & Siegel, I. (1980) The immunologic concept of EPH-gestosis. *Mount Sinai Journal of Medicine* 47:442–53. [taTG]
Glucksmann, A. (1978) *Sex determination and sexual dimorphism in mammals*. Wykeham. [taTG]
Gomez, M. R., Engel, A. G., Dewald, G., & Peterson, H. A. (1977) Failure of inactivation of Duchenne dystrophy X-chromosome in one of female identical twins. *Neurology* 27:537–41. [KBH]

Goodfellow, P., Banting, G., Sheer, D., Ropers, H. H., Caine, A., Ferguson-Smith, M. A., Povey, S. & Voss, R. (1983) Genetic evidence that a Y-linked gene in man is homologous to a gene on the X chromosome. *Nature* 302:346–49. [SO]
Goodfellow, P. N. & Andrews, P. W. (1982) Sexual differentiation and H-Y antigen. *Nature* 295:11–13. [taTG]
Gould, S. J. (1977) *Ontogeny and phylogeny*. Harvard University Press. [WCM]
Goulmy, E., Termijtelen, A., Bradley, B. A. & van Rood, J. J. (1977) Y-antigen killing by T cells of women is restricted by HLA. *Nature* 266:544–45. [tarTG, SO]
Gove, W. R. (1984) Gender differences in mental and physical illness: The effects of fixed roles and nurturant roles. *Society of Science and Medicine* 19:77–91. [KBH]
Graham, P. & Rutter, M. (1968) Organic brain dysfunction and child psychiatric disorder. *British Medical Journal* 3:695–700. [taTG]
Gray, E. & Hurt, V. K. (1979) Distribution of sexes in cattle. *Journal of Heredity* 70:273–74. [KBH]
Greenberg, R. A. & White, C. (1967) The sexes of consecutive sibs in human sibships. *Human Biology* 39:374–404. [WHJ, ACP]
Grotevant, H. D., Scarr, S. & Weinberg, R. A. (1977) Intellectual development in family constellations with natural and adopted children: A test of the Zajonc and Markus model. *Child Development* 48:1699–1703. [taTG]
Grubb, P. (1974) Social organization of Soay sheep and the behaviour of ewes and lambs. In: *Island survivors*, ed. P. A. Javill, C. Miller & J. M. Boyd. Athlone Press. [MWJF]
Gualtieri, C. T. (1983) Unpublished data. [taTG]
Gualtieri, C. T., Hicks, R. E. & Mayo, J. P. (1984a) ABO incompatibility and parity effects on perinatal mortality. Submitted. [taTG]
(1984b) Influence of sex of antecedent siblings on human sex ratio. *Life Sciences* 34:1791–94. [taTG]
(1984c) Parity effects on intellectual development are influenced by sex of antecedent siblings. Submitted. [taTG]
Guerrero, R. (1974) Association of the type and time of insemination within the menstrual cycle with the human sex ratio at birth. *New England Journal of Medicine* 291:1056–59. [CEB]
Guerrero, R. & Rojas, O. I. (1975) Spontaneous abortion and aging of human ova and spermatozoa. *New England Journal of Medicine* 293:573–75. [CEB]
Haberman, M., Hollingsworth, F., Falek, A. & Michael, R. P. (1975) Gender identity confusion, schizophrenia and a 47 XYY karyotype: A case report. *Psychoneuroendocrinology* 1:207–9. [KBH]
Hagberg, B., Hagberg, G., Lewerth, A. & Linberg, V. (1981) Mild mental retardation in Swedish school children. 2. Etiologic and pathogenetic aspects. *Acta Paediatrica Scandinavica* 70:445–52. [taTG]
Hakola, H. P. A. & Iivanainen, M. (1978) Pneumoencephalographic and clinical findings of the XYY syndrome. *Acta Psychiatrica Scandinavica* 58:360–70. [KBH]
Halbrecht, I. & Komlos, L. (1976) E-rosette-forming lymphocytes in mother and newborn. *Lancet* 1:544. [taTG]
Hamilton, J. B., Hamilton, R. S. & Mestler, G. E. (1969) Duration of life and causes of death in domestic cats: Influence of sex, gonadectomy and inbreeding. *Journal of Gerontology* 24:427–37. [MWJF]
Hamilton, J. B. & Mestler, G. E. (1969) Mortality and survival: comparison of eunuchs with intact men and women in a mentally retarded population. *Journal of Gerontology* 24:395–411. [MWJF]
Hamilton, W. D. (1966) The moulding of senescence by natural selection. *Journal of Theoretical Biology* 12:12–45. [MWJF]
Hare, E. H. & Price, J. S. (1969) Birth order and family size: Bias caused by changes in birth rate. *British Journal of Psychiatry* 115:647–56. [C-GB, taTG]
Harlap, S. (1980) Twin pregnancies following conceptions on different days of menstrual cycle. *Acta Geneticae Medicae et Gemellogiae* 29(1):40. [CEB]
Harris, R. E. & Lordon, R. E. (1976) The association of maternal lymphocytotoxic antibodies with obstetric complications. *Obstetrics and Gynecology* 48:302–04. [taTG]
Hartung, J. (1981) Genome parliaments and sex with the Red Queen. In: *Natural selection and social behavior*, ed. R. D. Alexander & D. W. Tinkle. Chiron Press. [ACP]
Hauser, S. L., Dawson, D. M., Lehrich, J. R., Beal, M. F., Kevy, S. V., Propper, R. D., Mills, J. A. & Weiner, H. L. (1983) Intensive immunosuppression in progressive multiple sclerosis. *New England Journal of Medicine* 308:173–80. [taTG]
Hay, W. (1971) Sex differences in the incidence of certain congenital malfunctions: A review of the literature and some new data. *Teratology* 4:277–86. [RHB]

References/Gualtieri & Hicks: Immunoreactive theory

Head, J. R. & Beer, A. E. (1979) In vivo and in vitro assessment of the immunologic role of leukocytic cells in milk. In: *Immunology of breast milk*, ed. P. L. Ogra & D. H. Dayton. Raven Press. [AB]

Hicks, R. E. & Gualtieri, C. T. (1984) The structure of sex differences in developmental handicap. Submitted. [taTG]

Hicks, R. E. & Kinsbourne, M. (1981) Fathers and sons, mothers and children: A note on the sex effect on left-handedness. *Journal of Genetic Psychology* 139:305–06. [taTG]

Hier, D. B., Atkins, L. & Perlo, V. P. (1980) Learning disorders and sex chromosome aberrations. *Journal of Mental Deficiency Research* 24:17–26. [KHB]

Holinka, C. F. (1981) Age-related impairments in rodent pregnancy functions in relation to the maternal immune system. *Reproductive immunology, progress in clinical and biological research*, ed. N. Gleicher. Alan R. Liss. [CEB]

Hoppe, P. C. & Koo, G. C. (1984) Reacting mouse sperm with monoclonal H-Y antibodies does not influence sex ratio of eggs fertilised in vitro. *Journal of Reproductive Immunology* 6:1–9. [MA]

Hoyenga, K. B. & Hoyenga, K. T. (1979) *The question of sex differences*. Little Brown. [KBH]

Hutt, C. (1972) Neuroendocrinological, behavioral and intellectual aspects of sexual differentiation in human development. In: *Gender differences: Their ontogeny and significance*, ed. C. Ounsted & D. C. Taylor. Churchill Livingstone. [taTG]

Immelmann, K., Barlow, G. W. Petrinovich, L. & Main, M., ed. (1981) *Behavioral development*. Cambridge University Press. [WCM]

Inglis, J. & Lawson, J. S. (1981) Sex differences in the effects of unilateral brain damage on intelligence. *Science* 212:693–95. [KBH]

(1982) A meta-analysis of sex differences in the effects of unilateral brain damage on intelligence test results. *Canadian Journal of Psychology* 36:670–83. [KBH]

Ingram, T. T. S. (1959) Specific developmental disorders of speech in childhood. *Brain* 82:450–67. [taTG]

(1964) Paediatric aspects of cerebral palsy. Livingstone. [taTG]

James, D. A. (1965) Effects of antigenic dissimilarity between mother and foetus of placental size in mice. *Nature* 205:613–14. [taTG]

James, W. H. (1975) Sex ratio and the sex composition of the existing sibs. *Annals of Human Genetics* 38:371–78. [C-GB, WHJ]

(1980a) Gonadotrophin and the human secondary sex ratio. *British Medical Journal* 281:711–12. [WHJ]

(1980b) Time of fertilisation and sex of infants. *Lancet* 1:1124–26. [rTG, WHJ]

(1982) The sexes of piglets within the uterine horns. *Journal of Heredity* 73:378. [RHB]

Jensen, A. R. (1971) The race × sex × ability interaction. In: *Intelligence: Genetic and environmental influences*, ed. R. Cancro. Grune & Stratton. [ARJ]

(1973) *Educability and group differences*. Harper & Row. [ARJ]

Joffe, J. M. (1964) *Prenatal determinants of behavior*. Pergamon Press. [taTG]

Johansen, K. & Burke, J. (1974) Possible relationships between HL-A antibody formation and fetal sex. *Journal of Obstetrics and Gynaecology of the British Commonwealth* 81:781–85. [taTG]

Johansen, K., Festenstein, H., & Burke, J. (1974) Possible relationships between maternal HL-A antibody formation and fetal sex: Evidence for a sex-linked histocompatibility system in man. *Journal of Obstetrics and Gynaecology of the British Commonwealth* 81:781–85. [taTG]

Johnson, E. M., Gorin, P. D., Brandeis, L. D. & Pearson, J. (1980) Dorsal root ganglion neurons are destroyed by exposure in utero to maternal antibody to nerve growth factor. *Science* 210:916–18. [tarTG]

Johnson, L. L., Bailey, D. W. & Mobraaten, L. E. (1981) Genetics of histocompatibility in mice. 4. Detection of certain minor (non-H2) H antigens in selected organs by the popliteal node test. *Immunogenetics* 14:63–71. [taTG]

Jones, W. R. (1968) Immunologic factors in human placentation. *Nature* 218:480. [taTG]

Juberg, R. R., Gaar, D. G., Humphries, J. R., Cenac, P. L. & Zambie, M. F. (1976) Sex ratio in the progeny of mothers with toxemia of pregnancy. *Journal of Reproductive Medicine* 16:299–302. [MA, rTG]

Juret, P., Couette, J. E., Delozier, T., Leplat, G., Mandard, A. M. & Vernhes, J. C. (1978) Sex of first child as a prognostic factor in breast cancer. *Lancet* 1:415–16. [C-GB]

Kaufman, M. H. (1973) Analysis of the first cleavage division to determine the sex-ratio and incidence of chromosome anomalies at conception in the mouse. *Journal of Reproductive Fertility* 35:67–72. [RHB]

Keller, J. (1981) Epidemiological characteristics of preterm births. In: *Preterm birth and psychological development*, ed. S. L. Friedman & M. Sigman. Academic Press. [taTG]

Kellokumpu-Lehtinen, P. & Pelliniemi, L. S. (1984) Sex ratio of human conceptuses. *Obstetrics and Gynecology* 64:220–22. [RHB]

Kirby, D. R. S. (1970) The egg and immunology. *Proceedings of the Royal Society of Medicine* 63:59–61. [MA]

Kirby, D. R. S., McWhirter, K. G., Teitelbaum, M. S. & Darlington, C. D. (1967) A possible immunological influence on sex ratio. *Lancet* 2:139–40. [MA, tarTG]

Kitzmiller, J. L. (1978) Auto immune disorders: Maternal, fetal and neonatal risks. *Clinical Obstetrics and Gynecology* 21:385–96. [taTG]

Klein, J. (1982) *Immunology: The science of self-nonself discrimination*. John Wiley and Sons. [AB]

Kolyaskina, G. I., Boehme, D. I., Buravlev, V. M. & Faktor, M. I. (1977) Certain aspects of the study of the brain of the human embryo. *Soviet Neurology and Psychiatry* 10:24–31. [taTG]

Komlos, L. & Halbrecht, I. (1979) Repeated abortions and histocompatibility antigens. *Medical Hypotheses* 5:901–8. [RMG]

Kramer, M. (1978) Population changes and schizophrenia, 1970–1985. In: *The nature of schizophrenia: New approaches*, ed. L. Wynne, R. Cromwell & S. Mathysse. Wiley. [taTG]

Krco, C. J. & Goldberg, E. H. (1976) H-Y (male) antigen: Detection in 8-cell embryos. *Science* 193:1134–35. [taTG]

Lanman, J. T. (1968) Delays during reproduction and their effects on the embryo and fetus. *New England Journal of Medicine* 278:993–99. [CEB]

LaVeck, B. & LaVeck, G. D. (1977) Sex differences in development among young children with Down's syndrome. *Journal of Pediatrics* 91:767–69. [KBH]

Lawler, S. D., Ukaejoofo, E. D. & Reeves, B. R. (1975) Interaction between maternal and neonatal cells in mixed-lymphocyte cultures. *Lancet* 2:1185–87. [MA, tarTG]

LeBoeuf, B. J. (1972) Sexual behaviour in the northern elephant seal Mirounga angustirostris. *Behaciour* 41:1–26. [MWJF]

(1974) Male-male competition and reproductive success in elephant seals. *American Zoologist* 14:163–176. [MWJF]

Lecours, A. R. (1975) Myelogenetic correlates of the development of speach and language. In: *Foundations of language development: A multidisciplinary approach*, ed. E. H. Lenneberg & E. Lenneberg. University Publishers. [AB]

Lee, A. K., Bradley, A. J. & Braithwaite, R. W. (1977). Corticosteroid levels and male mortality in Antechinus stuartii. In: *The biology of marsupials*, ed. B. Stonehouse & D. Gilmore. University Park Press. [MWJF]

Lehrke, R. G. (1978) Sex linkage: A biological basis for greater male variability in intelligence. In: *Human cariation*, vol. 1, ed. R. T. Osborne, C. E. Noble & N. Weyl. Academic Press. [taTG]

Lerner, R. M. (1984) *On the nature of human plasticity*. Cambridge University Press. [ACP]

Lewine, R., Burbach, D. & Meltzer, H. Y. (1984) Effect of diagnostic criteria on the ratio of male to female schizophrenic patients. *American Journal of Psychiatry* 141:84–87. [KBH]

Lewine, R. R. J. (1981) Sex differences in schizophrenia: Timing or subtypes? *Psychological Bulletin* 90:432–44. [KBH]

Lewitter, F. I., DeFries, J. C. & Elston, R. C. (1980) Genetic models of reading disability. *Behavior Genetics* 10:9–30. [taTG]

Lilienfield, A. M. & Pasamanick, B. (1956) The association of maternal and fetal factors with the development of mental deficiency. 2. Relationship to maternal age, birth order, previous reproductive loss and degree of maternal deficiency. *American Journal of Mental Deficiency* 60:667–69. [taTG]

Lints, F. A., Bourgois, M., Delalieuz, A., Stoll, J. & Lints, C. V. (1983) Does the female life span exceed that of the male? *Gerontology* 29:336–52. [KBH]

Loke, Y. W. (1978) *Immunology and immunopathology of the human fetal-maternal interaction*. Elsevier. [tarTG]

Lord, C., Schopler, E. & Revicki, D. (1982) Sex differences in autism. *Journal of Autism and Developmental Disabilities* 12:317–30. [taTG]

Lotter, V. (1974) Factors related to outcome in autistic children. *Journal of Autism and Childhood Schizophrenia* 4:263–77. [taTG]

Lyon, M. F. (1972) X-chromosome inactivation and developmental patterns in mammals. *Biological Reviews* 47:1–35. [KBH]

Maccoby, E. E., Doering, C. H., Jacklin, C. N. & Kraemer, H. (1979) Concentrations of sex hormones in umbilical-cord blood: Their relation to sex and birth order of infants. *Child Development* 50:632–42. [tarTG, KBH, ACP]

Mackey, W. C. Coney, N. (unpublished) Human sex ratio as a function of the woman's psychodynamics: A preliminary study. [WCM]

MacLusky, J. J., Chaptal, C. & McEwen, B. S. (1979) The development of estrogen receptor systems in the rat brain and pituitary: Postnatal development. *Brain Research* 178:143–60. [MCD]

Malinvaud, E. (1955) Relations entre la composition des familles et le taux de

References/Gualtieri & Hicks: Immunoreactive theory

masculinité. *Journal de la Société de Statistique de Paris* 96:49. [rTG, WHJ]
Markle, G. E. & Nam, C. B. (1971) Sex predetermination: Its impact on fertility. *Social Biology* 18:73–83. [WHJ]
Matsunaga, T. & Simpson, E. (1978) H-2 complementation in anti-H-Y T cell responses can occur in chimeric mice. *Proceedings of the National Academy of Sciences of the United States of America* 75:6207–10. [SO]
McClure, P. A. (1981) Sex-biased litter reduction food-restricted wood rats (*Neotoma floridana*). *Science* 211:1058–60. [MWJF]
McGlone, J. (1980) Sex differences in human brain asymmetry: A critical survey. *Behavioral and Brain Sciences* 3:215–63. [taTG]
McKee, G. J. & Ferguson, M. W. J. (1984) The effects of mesencephalic neural crest cell extirpation on the development of chicken embryos. *Journal of Anatomy* 139:491–512. [MWJF]
McKeown, T. & Record, R. G. (1956) Maternal age and birth order as indices of environmental influence. *American Journal of Human Genetics* 8:8–23. [taTG]
McKinney, D. & Feagans, L. (1983) Unpublished data. [taTG]
McLaren, A. (1962) Does maternal immunity to make antigen affect the sex ratio of the young? *Nature* 195:1323–24. [MA, tarTG, WHJ, ACP]
(1975) Antigenic disparity: does it affect placental size, implantation or population genetics? In: *Immunobiology of trophoblast*, ed. R. G. Edward, C. W. S. Howe & M. H. Johnson. Cambridge University Press. [MA]
McMillen, M. M. (1979) Differential mortality by sex in fetal and neonatal deaths. *Science* 204:89–91. [RHB, HC, tarTG]
McPherson, C. F. C. (1970) Immunochemical approaches to the study of brain function and psychiatric diseases. *Canadian Psychiatric Journal* 15:641–45. [taTG]
Medawar, P. B. (1963) Some immunological and endocrinological problems raised by the evolution of viviparity in vertebrates. *Symposia of the Society for Experimental Biology*. Academic Press. [tarTG]
(1969) *The art of the soluable*. Penguin Books. [CO]
(1982) *Pluto's republic*. Oxford University Press. [rTG, CO]
Mednick, S. A. (1970) Breakdown in individuals at high risk for schizophrenia: Possible predispositional perinatal factors. *Mental Hygiene* 54:50–63. [taTG]
Mednick, S. A., Mura, E., Schulsinger, F. & Mednick, B. (1971) Perinatal conditions and infant development in children with schizophrenic parents. *Social Biology* 18:103–13. [taTG]
Mednick, S. A., Schulsinger, F., Teasdale, T. W., Schulsinger, H., Venables, P. H. & Rock, D. R. (1977) Schizophrenia in high risk children: Sex differences in predisposing factors. In: *Cognitive defects in the development of mental illness*, ed. G. Serban. Brunner/Mazel. [tarTG]
Meikle, D. B., Tilford, B. L. & Vessey, S. H. (1984) Dominance rank, secondary sex ratio, and reproduction of offspring in polygynous primates. *American Naturalist* 124:173–88. [ACP]
Metrakos, J. D. & Metrakos, K. (1963) Is pregnancy order a factor in epilepsy? *Journal of Neurology, Neurosurgery, and Psychiatry* 26:451–57. [taTG]
Mikamo, K. (1969) Prenatal sex ratio in man. *Obstetrics and Gynecology*. 34:710–16. [RHB]
Mitchell, A. (1866) Some statistics of idiocy. *Edinburgh Medical Journal* 1866:639–45. [C-GB]
Mittwoch, U. (1983) Heterogametic sex chromosomes and the development of the dominant gonad in vertebrates. *American Naturalist* 122:159–180. [MWJF]
Mittwoch, U. & Mahadevaiah, S. (1980a) Additional growth – A link between mammalian testes, avian ovaries, gonadal asymmetry in hermaphrodites and the expression of H-Y antigen. *Growth* 44:287–300. [MWJF]
(1980b) Comparison of development of human fetal gonads and kidneys. *Journal of Reproduction and Fertility* 58:463–67. [MWJF]
Mitchell, A. (1866) Some statistics of idiocy. *Edinburgh Medical Journal*:639–45. [C-GB]
Mizuno, M., Lubotsky, J., Lloyd, C. W., Kobayahsi, T. & Murasawa, Y. (1968) Plasma androstenedione and testosterone during pregnancy and in the newborn. *Journal of Clinical Endocrinology and Metabolism* 28:1113–42. [taTG]
Moore, B. C. (1965) Relationship between prematurity and intelligence in mental retardates. *American Journal of Mental Deficiency* 70:448–53. [taTG]
Moore, K. C. (1982) *The developing human*, 3d ed. W. B. Saunders. [RHB]
Mourant, A. E., Kopec, A. C., & Domaniewska-Sobczak. (1978) *Blood groups and diseases*. Oxford University Press. [RMG]
Müller, U., Mayerova, A., Fraccaro, M., Zuffardi, O., Mikkelsen, M. & Prader, A. (1983) Presence of H-Y antigen in female patients with sex-chromosome mosaics and absence in testicular tissue. *American Journal of Medical Genetics* 15:315–21. [rTG, KBH]

Nakano, K. K. (1973) Anencephaly: A review. *Developmental Medicine and Child Neurology* 15:383–400. [taTG]
Nanko, S. (1979) Personality traits of 47,XYY and 47,XXY males found among juvenile delinquents. *Folia Psychiatrica et Neurologica Japonica* 33:29–34. [KBH]
Nichols, P. L. & Chen, T. C. (1981) *Minimal brain dysfunction: A prospective study*. Erlbaum. [taTG, ET]
Niswander, K. R. & Gordon, M. (1972) *The women and their pregnancies*. Saunders. [tarTG]
Novitski, E. (1977) *Human genetics*. Macmillan. [taTG]
Novitski, E. & Sandler, L. (1956) The relationship between parental age, birth order and the secondary sex ratio in humans. *Annals of Human Genetics* 21:123–31. [taTG]
Ogra, P. L., Fishaut, M. & Theodore, C. (1980) Immunology of breast milk: Maternal neonatal interactions. In: *Human milk, its biological and social value*, ed. S. Freier & A. I. Eidelman. Excerpta Medica. [AB]
Ohama, K. & Kadotani, T. (1971) Lymphocyte reaction in mixed wife-husband leukocyte cultures in relation to infertility. *American Journal of Obstetrics and Gynecology* 109:477–79. [taTG]
Ohno, S. (1979) *Major sex-determining genes*. Springer-Verlag. [taTG]
Ohno, S., & Stapleton, D. W. (1981) Associative recognition of testis-organizing H-Y antigen and immunological confusion. In: *Bioregulators of reproduction*, ed. G. Jagiero. Academic Press. [SO]
Opler, L. A., Kay, S. R., Rosado, V. & Lindenmayer, J.-P. (1984) Positive and negative syndromes in chronic schizophrenic inpatients. *Journal of Nervous and Mental Disease* 172:317–25. [rTG, KBH]
Ounsted, C. & Taylor, D. C. (1972) The Y chromosome message: A point of view. In: *Gender differences: Their ontogeny and significance*, ed. C. Ounsted & D. C. Taylor. Churchill Livingstone. [CG, taTG, CO, DCT]
Ounsted, C. & Taylor, D. C., eds. (1972) *Gender differences: Their ontogeny and significance*. Churchill Livingstone. [RHB]
Ounsted, C. & Ounsted, M. (1970) Effect of Y chromosome on fetal growth rate. *Lancet* 2:857–58. [taTG]
Ounsted, M. (1972) Gender and intrauterine growth. In: *Gender differences: Their ontogeny and significance*, ed. C. Ounsted & D. C. Taylor. Churchill Livingstone. [HC, taTG]
Palmblad, J. (1981) Stress and immunologic competence: Studies in man. In: *Psychoneuroimmunology*, ed. R. Ader. Academic Press. [ACP]
Parkes, A. S. (1926) The mammalian sex-ratio. *Biological Reviews* 2:1–51. [ACP]
Pappas, C. T. E., Diamond, M. C. & Johnson, R. E. (1979) Morphological changes in the cerebral cortex of rats with altered levels of ovarian hormones. *Behavioral Biology* 26:298–310. [MCD]
Pennington, B. F. & Smith, S. D. (1983) Genetic influences of learning disabilities and speech and language disorders. *Child Development* 54:369–87. [taTG]
Petersen, A. C. (1980) Biopsychosocial processes in the development of sex-related differences. In: *The psychobiology of sex differences and sex roles*, ed. J. E. Parsons. McGraw Hill. [ACP]
Phebus, C. K., Gloninger, M. F. & Maciak, B. J. (1984) Growth patterns by age and sex in children with sickle cell disease. *Journal of Pediatrics* 105:28–33. [KBH]
Pickles, A. R., Crouchley, R. & Davies, R. B. (1982) New methods for the analysis of sex ratio data independent of the effects of family limitation. *Annals of Human Genetics* 46:75–81. [WHJ]
Placek, P. (1977) Maternal and infant health factors associated with low infant birth weight: Findings from the 1972 National Natality Survey. In: *The epidemiology of prematurity*, ed. D. M. Reed & F. J. Stanley. Urban and Schwarzenberg. [taTG]
Plomin, R. & DeFries, J. C. (1980) Genetics and intelligence: Recent data. *Intelligence* 4:15–24. [ARJ]
Poduslo, S. E., McFarland, H. F. & McKahanon, G. M. (1977) Antiserums to neurons and to oligodendroglia from mammalian brain. *Science* 197:270–72. [taTG]
Ponder, B. A. J., Wilkinson, M. M., Wood, M. & Westwood, J. H. (1983) Immunohistochemical demonstration of H2 antigens in mouse tissue sections. *Journal of Histochemistry and Cytochemistry* 31:911–19. [AB]
Price, J. S. & Hare, E. H. (1969) Birth order studies: Some sources of bias. *British Journal of Psychiatry* 115:633–46. [taTG]
Purtilo, D. T. & Sullivan, J. L. (1979) Immunological basis for superior survival of females. *American Journal of Diseases of Children* 133:1251–53. [RMG, rTG]
Rasmussen, B. & Gillberg, C. (1983) Perceptual, motor and attentional deficits in seven-year-old children: Paediatric aspects. *Acta Paediatrica Scandinavica* 72:125–30. [CG]
Ratcliffe, C. G., Stewart, A. L., Melville, M. M. & Jacobs, P-A. (1970) Chromosome studies on 3500 newborn male infants. *Lancet* 1:121–22. [CG]

References/Gualtieri & Hicks: Immunoreactive theory

Ratcliffe, S. G., Axworthy, D. & Ginsborg, A. (1979) The Edinburgh study of growth and development in children with sex chromosome abnormalities. *Birth Defects: Original Article Series* 15:243–60. [KBH]

Ratcliffe, S. G., Tierney, I., Smith, L. & Callan, S. (1981) Psychological and educational progress in children with sex chromosome abnormalities in the Edinburgh longitudinal study. In: *Human behavior and genetics*, ed. W. Schmid & J. Nielsen. Elsevier/North Holland Biomedical Press. [KBH]

Redman, C. W. G., Bodmer, J. G., Bodmer, W. F., Berlin, L. J. & Bonnar, J. (1978) HLA antigens in severe pre-eclampsia. *Lancet* 2:397–99. [MA, rTG]

Reed, E. W. & Reed, S. C. (1965) *Mental retardation. A family study.* Saunders. [C-GB, tarTG]

Reed, T. E. (1969) Caucasian genes in American Negroes. *Science* 165:762–68. [ARJ]

Reinisch, J. M., Gandelman, R. & Spiegel, F. S. (1979) Prenatal influences on cognitive abilities: Data from experimental animals and human genetic and endocrine studies. In: *Sex-related differences in cognitive functioning*, ed. M. A. Wittig & A. C. Petersen. Academic Press. [taTG]

Renkonen, K. O., Mäkelä, O. & Lehtovaara, R. (1962) Factors affecting the human sex ratio. *Nature* 194:308–09. [MA, tarTG]

Renkonen, K. O. & Timonen, S. (1967) Factors influencing the immunization of Rh-negative mothers. *Journal of Medical Genetics* 4:166–68. [MA, taTG]

Renoux, G., Biziere, K., Renoux, M. & Guillaumin, J. M. (1980) Le cortex cérébral regle les responses immunes des souris. *Comptes Rendus des Séances de l'Académie.* 290:719–22. [MCD]

Rhodes, P. (1965) Sex of the fetus in antepartum hemorrhage. *Lancet* 2:718–19. [taTG]

Rife, D. C. (1940) Handedness, with special reference to twins. *Genetics* 25:178–86. [CEB]

Roberts, J. & Engel, R. (1974) Family background, early development and intelligence of children 6–11 years. United States Data from the National Health Survey. DHEW Publ. # (HRA) 75–1624, U.S. Department of Health, Education and Welfare, P. H. S., Rockville, Md. [taTG]

Robinette, W. L., Gashwiler, J. S., Low, J. B. & Jones, D. A. (1957) Differential mortality by sex and age among mule deer. *Journal of Wildlife Management* 21:1–16. [MWJF]

Robins, L. (1966) *Deviant children grown up.* Williams and Wilkins. [taTG]

Robinson, A., Bender, B., Borelli, J., Puck, M. & Salbenblatt, J. (1983) Sex chromosomal anomalies: Prospective studies in children. *Behavior Genetics* 13:321–29. [KBH]

Robson, E. B. (1955) Birth weight in cousins. *Annals of Human Genetics* 19:262–68. [taTG]

Rosenberg, B. G. & Sutton-Smith, B. (1969) Sibling age spacing effects upon cognition. *Developmental Psychology* 1:661–68. [taTG]

Rosenthal, D. (1962) Familial concordance by sex with respect to schizophrenia. *Psychological Bulletin* 59:401–21. [taTG]

Rostron, J. & James, W. H. (1977) Maternal age, parity, social class and sex ratio. *Annals of Human Genetics, London* 41:205–17. [KBH]

Roszkowski, W., Plaut, M. & Lichtenstein, L. M. (1977) Selective display of histamine receptors in lymphocytes. *Science* 195:383–85. [taTG]

Rubenstein, A. (1982) An immunologic hypothesis concerning some congenital diseases and malformations. *Medical Hypotheses* 9:417–19. [taTG]

Rutter, M. (1970) Sex differences in children's response to family stress. In: *International yearbook of child psychiatry*, ed. E. J. Anthony & C. Kupernik. Wiley. [taTG]

 (1984) Family and school influences on cognition. *Journal of Child Psychology and Psychiatry.* In press. [ET]

Rutter, M. & Graham, P. (1970) Epidemiology of psychiatric disorder. In: *Education, Health and Behavior*, ed. M. Rutter, J. Tizard & K. Whitmore. Longman. [rTG]

Rutter, M. & Madge, N. (1976) *Cycles of disadvantage.* Heinemann. [ET]

Rutter, M., Tizard, J. & Whitmore, K., eds (1970) *Education, health and behaviour.* Longman. [rTG, ET]

Sabin, A. B., Krumbiegel, E. R. & Wigand, R. (1958) Echo type 9 virus disease. *Journal of Diseases of Children* 96:197–219. [taTG]

Salzmann, K. D. (1955) Do transplacental hormones cause eclampsia? *Lancet* 2:953–56. [rTG]

Samuels, L. (1979) Reply to Lewine. *Schizophrenia Bulletin* 5.5–10. [taTG]

Sasaki, M., Ikeuchi, T., Obara, Y., Hayata, I., Mori, M. & Kohno, S. (1971) Chromosome studies in early embryogenesis. *American Journal of Obstetrics and Gynecology* 111:8–12 [RHB]

Scarr, S & Carter-Saltzman, L. (1982) Genetics and intelligence. In: *Handbook of human intelligence*, ed. R. J. Sternberg. Cambridge University Press. [ARJ]

Schlesinger, E. R., Alaway, N. C. & Peltin, S. (1959) Survivorship in cerebral palsy. *American Journal of Public Health* 49:343–49. [taTG]

Schoenbaum, S., Biano, S. & Mack, T. (1975) Epidemiology of congenital rubella syndrome: The role of maternal parity. *Journal of the American Medical Association* 233:151–55. [CEB, taTG]

Schooler, C. (1964) Birth order and hospitalization for schizophrenia. *Journal of Abnormal and Social Psychology* 69:574–79. [C-GB]

Schrag, H. L. (1973) Program planning for the developmentally disabled: Using survey results. *Mental Retardation* 11:8–10. [taTG]

Schuster, D. H. & Schuster, L. (1969) Theory of stress and sex ratio. *Proceedings, 77th Annual Convention of the American Psychological Association* 223–24. [KBH]

Scott, J. P. (1979) Critical periods in the organizational process. In: *Human growth, vol. 3: Neurobiology and nutrition*, ed. F. Falkner & J. M. Tanner. Baillière Tindall. [AB]

Scott, J. R. (1976) Immunological aspects of trophoblast neoplasia. In: *Immunology of human reproduction*, ed. J. S. Scott & W. K. Jones. Grune & Stratton. [taTG]

Scott, J. R. & Beer, A. E. (1973) Immunologic factors in first pregnancy Rh immunisation. *Lancet* 1:717–18. [CEB, taTG]

Scott, J. R., Beer, A. E. & Stastny, P. (1976) Immunogenetic factors in preeclampsia and eclampsia. *Journal of the American Medical Association* 235:402–04. [rTG]

Scott, J. S., Maddison, P. J., Taylor, P. V., Esscher, E., Scott, O. & Skinner, R. P. (1983) Connective-tissue disease, antibodies to ribonucleoprotein, and congenital heart block. *New England Journal of Medicine* 309:209–12. [rTG, PVT]

Scottish Council for Research in Education. (1949) *The trend of Scottish intelligence.* London University Press. [rTG]

Searleman, A., Herrmann, D. J. & Coventry, A. K. (1984) Cognitive abilities and left-handedness: An interaction between familial sinistrality and strength of handedness. *Intelligence* 8:295–304. [ARS]

Searleman, A., Porac, C. & Coren, S. (in preparation) Pathological left-handedness and birth stress: A review. [ARS]

Searleman, A., Tsao, Y. C. & Balzer, W. (1980) A reexamination of the relationship between birth stress and handedness. *Clinical Neuropsychology* 2(3):124–28. [ARS]

Sedlis, A., Berendes, H., Kim, H. S., Stone, D. F., Weiss, W., Deutschberger, J. & Jackson, E. (1967) The placental weight–birthweight relationship. *Developmental Medicine and Child Neurology* 9:160–71. [taTG]

Seidman, L. J. (1983) Schizophrenia and brain dysfunction: An integration of recent neurodiagnostic findings. *Psychological Bulletin* 94:195–238. [KBH]

Selander, R. K. (1966) Sexual dimorphism and differential niche utilization in birds. *Condor* 68:113–51. [MWJF]

Shaffer, D. & Fisher, P. (1981) Suicide in children and adolescents. *Journal of the American Academy of Child Psychiatry* 20:545–65. [taTG]

Shearer, M. L., Davidson, R. T. & Finch, S. M. (1967) The sex ratio of offspring born to state hospitalized schizophrenic women. *Journal of Psychiatric Research* 5:349–50. [taTG]

Siiteri, P. K., Febres, F., Clemens, L. E., Chang, R. J., Gondos, B. & Stites, D. (1977) Progesterone and maintenance of pregnancy: Is progesterone nature's immunosuppressant? *Annals of the New York Academy of Sciences* 286:384–97. [taTG]

Siiteri, P. K., Jones, L. A., Roubinian, J. & Talal, N. (1980) Sex steroids and the immune system. I. Sex difference in autoimmune disease in NZB/NZW hybrid mice. *Journal of Steroid Biochemistry* 12:425–32. [KBH]

Silvers, W. K., Gasser, D. L., & Eicher, E. M. (1982) H-Y antigen, serologically detectable male antigen and sex determination. *Cell* 28:439–40. [rTG, SO]

Simmons, R. L. (1971) Viviparity, histocompatibility and fetal survival. *Advances in Biosciences* 6:405–19. [taTG]

Singer, J. E., Westphal, M. & Niswander, K. R. (1968) Sex differences in the incidence of neonatal abnormalities and abnormal performance in early childhood. *Child Development* 39:103–12. [taTG]

Sio, J. O., & Beer, A. E. (1982) Placenta as an immunological barrier. *Biology of Reproduction* 26:15–27. [RMG]

Skoff, R. & Montgomery, I. N. (1981) Expression of mosaicism in females heterozygous for Jimpy. *Brain Research* 212.175–81. [KBH]

Slater, E., Beard, A. W. & Glithero, E. (1963) The schizophrenia-like psychoses of epilepsy. *British Journal of Psychiatry* 109:95–112. [taTG]

Sloane, D. M. & Lee, C.-F. (1983) Sex of previous children and intentions for further births in the U.S. 1965–76. *Demography* 20:353–67. [WHJ]

Smolen, J. S. & Steinberg, A. D. (1981) Systemic lupus erythematosus and pregnancy. Clinical immunological and theoretical aspects. In:

References/Gualtieri & Hicks: Immunoreactive theory

Reproductive immunology, progress in clinical and biological research, ed. N. Gleicher. Alan R. Liss. [CEB]

Snow, M. H. L. & Tam, P. P. L. (1979) Is compensatory growth a complicating factor in mouse teratology? *Nature* 279:555–57. [MWJF]

Sobel, D. E. (1961) Children of schizophrenic patients: Preliminary observations on early development. *American Journal of Psychiatry* 118:512–17. [taTG]

Solomon, G. F. (1984) Emotions, immunity and disease: An historical and philosophical perspective. In: *Breakdown in human adaptation to "stress": Towards a multidisciplinary approach*, ed. R. E. Ballieux, J. F. Fielding & A. L'Abbate. Martinus Nijhoff Publisher. [RMG, rTG]

Sørenson, K. & Nielsen, J. (1977) Reactive paranoid psychosis in a 47,XYY male. *Acta Psychiatrica Scandinavica* 55:233–36. [KBH]

Sotelo, J., Gibbs, C. J. & Gadjusek, D. C. (1980) Auto antibodies against axonal neurofilaments in patients with Kuru and Creutzfeld-Jakob disease. *Science* 210:190–93. [taTG]

Spector, W. S., ed. (1956) *Handbook of biological data.* W. B. Saunders. [RHB]

Stanley, F. & Blair, E. (1984) Postnatal risk factors in the cerebral palsies. In: *The epidemiology of the cerebral palsies*, ed. F. Stanley & F. Alberman. Spastics International Medical Publications. [HC, rTG]

Steelman, L. C. & Mercy, J. A. (1983) Sex differences in the impact of the number of older and younger siblings on IQ performance. *Social Psychology Quarterly* 46:157–62. [taTG]

Stubbs, E. G. (1976) Autistic children exhibit undetectable hemagglutination-inhibition antibody titres despite previous rubella vaccination. *Journal of Autism and Childhood Schizophrenia* 6:269–74. [taTG]

Stubbs, E. G., Ritvo, E. R. & Mason-Brothers, A. (1984) Autism and shared parental HLA antigens. *Journal of the American Academy of Child Psychiatry*. In press. [CG]

Stubbs, F. G. & Crawford, M. L. (1977) Depressed lymphocyte responsiveness in autistic children. *Journal of Autism and Childhood Schizophrenia* 7:49–55.

Tam, P. P. L. & Snow, M. H. L. (1981) Proliferation and migration of primordial germ cells during compensatory growth in mouse embryos. *Journal of Embryology and Experimental Morphology* 64:133–47. [MWJF]

Taylor, C. & Faulk, W. P. (1981) Prevention of recurrent abortions with leukocyte transfusions. *Lancet* 2:68–70. [RMG]

Taylor, D. C. (1969) Differential rates of cerebral maturation between sexes and between hemispheres. *Lancet* 2:140–42. [taTG]
(1981) The influence of sexual differentiation on growth, development, and disease. In: *Scientific foundations of paediatrics*, 2d ed., ed. J. Davis & J. Dobbing. Heinemann Medical Books Ltd. [DCT]
(in press) Mechanisms of sex differentiation: Evidence from disease. In: *Human sexual dimorphism*, ed. F. Newcombe, J. Ghesquiere & R. Martin. Taylor and Francis. [DCT]

Taylor, D. C. & Ounsted, C. (1971) Biological mechanisms influencing the outcome of seizures in response to fever. *Epilepsia* 12:33–45. [taTG]
(1972) The nature of gender differences explored through ontogenetic analyses of sex ratios in disease. In: *Gender differences: Their ontogeny and significance*, ed. C. Ounsted & D. C. Taylor. Churchill Livingstone. [taTG]

Taylor, M. A. (1969) Sex ratios of newborns: Associated with prepartum and postpartum schizophrenia. *Science* 164:723–24. [tarTG]

Taylor, P. V. & Griffiths, S. J. (1984) Pathogenic effects of Ro (SS-A) antibody in heart and brain. Presented at the first Rodin Remediation Symposium, St. Andrews, Scotland. [PVT]

Teitelbaum, M. S. (1970) Factors affecting the sex ratio in large populations. *Journal of Biosocial Science, Supplement* 2:61–71. [ACP]
(1972) Factors associated with the sex ratio in human populations. In: *The structure of human populations*, ed. G. H. Harrison & A. J. Boyce. Clarendon Press. [rTG, ACP]

Terasaki, P. I., Mickey, M. R., Yamazaki, J. N. & Vredevoe, D. (1970) Maternal–fetal incompatibility. *Transplantation* 9:538–41. [taTG]

Thorley, J. D., Holmes, R. K., Kaplan, J. M., McCracken, G. H. & Sanford, J. P. K. (1975) Passive transfer of antibodies of maternal origin from blood to cerebrospinal fluid in infants. *Lancet* 1:651–53. [taTG]

Tips, R. L., Smith, G. & Meyer, D. L. (1964) Reproductive failure in families of patients with idiopathic developmental retardation. *Pediatrics* 33:100–05. [taTG]

Toivanen, P. & Hirvonen, T. (1970a) Placental weight in human foeto-maternal incompatibility. *Clinical and Experimental Immunology* 7:533–39. [taTG]
(1970b) Sex ratio of newborns: Preponderance of males in toxemia of pregnancy. *Science* 170:187–88. [tarTG]

Trevarthen, C. (1979) Neuroembryology and the development of perception.
In: *Human growth 3: Neurobiology and nutrition*, ed. F. Falkner & J. M. Tanner. Baillicre Tindall. [AB]

Trites, R. L., Dugas, E., Lynch, G. & Gerguson, H. B. (1979) Prevalence of hyperactivity. *Journal of Pediatric Psychology* 4:179–88. [taTG]

Trivers, R. L. (1972) Parental investment and sexual selection. In: *Sexual selection and the descent of man. 1891–1971*, ed. B. H. Campbell. Aldine. [WCM]
(1974) Parent–offspring conflict. *American Zoologist* 14:249–64. [WCM]

Trivers, R. L. & Willard, D. E. (1973) Natural selection of parental ability to vary the sex ratio. *Science* 179:90–92. [MWJF, WCM]

Truog, W. E., Kessler, D. L., Palmer, S., Murphy, J., Woodrum, D. E. & Hodson, W. A. (1981) Differential effect of sex in experimental hyaline membrane disease in newborn monkeys. *American Reviews of Respiratory Diseases* 124:435–39. [KBH]

Tsai, L. Y. & Beisler, J. M. (1983) The development of sex differences in infantile autism. *British Journal of Psychiatry* 142:373–78. [taTG]

Tsai, L., Stewart, M. A. & August, G. (1981) Implications of sex difference in the familial transmission of infantile autism. *Journal of Autism and Developmental Disorders* 11:165–73. [taTG]

van den Berghe, P. L. (1979) *Human family systems: An evolutionary view.* Elsevier. [WCM]

Vernier, M. C. (1975) Sex-differential placentation. *Biology of the Neonate* 26:76–87. [taTG]

Vessey, M. P. (1972) Gender differences in the epidemiology of non-neurologic disease. In: *Gender differences: Their ontogeny and significance*, ed. C. Ounsted & D. C. Taylor. Churchill Livingston. [taTG]

Wachtel, S. S., Hall, J. L., Muller, U. & Chaganti, R. S. K. (1980) Serum-born H-Y antigen in the fetal bovine freemartin. *Cell* 21:917–26. [RMG]

Wachtel, S. S., Koo, G. C. & Boyse, E. A. (1975) Evolutionary conservation of H-Y (male) antigen. *Nature* 254:270–72. [taTG]

Wachtel, S. S., Wachtel, G. M., Nakamura, D. & Gilmour, D. (1983) H-Y antigen in the chicken. *Differentiation* 23:S107–S115. [KBH]

Waldrop, M. F. & Bell, R. D. (1966) Effects of family size and density on newborn characteristics. *American Journal of Orthopsychiatry* 36:544–50. [taTG]

Wallace, S. J. (1974) The reproductive efficiency of parents whose children convulse when febrile. *Developmental Medicine and Child Neurology* 16:465–74. [taTG]

Warburton, D. & Naylor, F. (1971) The effect of parity on placental weight and birth weight: An immunological phenomenon. *American Journal of Human Genetics* 23:41–54. [taTG]

Ward, W. F., Karp, C. H. & Aceto, H., Jr. (1977) Developmental effects of the uterine environment: Dependence on fetal sex in rats. *Journal of Reproduction and Fertility* 50:269–74. [KBH]

Webb, G. J. W. & Smith, A. M. A. (1984) Sex ratio and survivorship in the Australian freshwater crocodile *Crocodylus johnstoni*. In: *The structure, development and evolution of reptiles*, ed. M. W. J. Ferguson. Academic Press. [MWJF]

Weinberg, W. (1913) Die kinder der tuberkulösen. Hirzel. [C-GB]

Weinberger, D. R., Cannon-Spoor, E., Potkin, S. G. & Wyatt, R. J. (1980) Poor premorbid adjustment and CT scan abnormalities in chronic schizophrenia. *American Journal of Psychiatry* 137:1410–13. [taTG]

Weizman, A., Weizman, R., Szekely, G. A., Wijsenbeek, H. & Levni, E. (1982) Abnormal immune response to brain tissue antigen in the syndrome of autism. *American Journal of Psychiatry* 139:1462–65. [taTG]

Whyte, M. K. (1978) Cross-cultural codes dealing with the relative status of women. *Ethnography* 12:211–37. [WCM]

Williams, A. F. (1982) Surface molecules and cell interaction. *Journal of Theoretical Biology* 98:221–34. [AB]

Williams, C. A. & Schupf, N. (1977) Antigen–antibody reactions in rat brain sites induce transient changes in drinking behavior. *Science* 196:328–30. [taTG]

Wilson, E. O. (1975) *Sociobiology.* Harvard University Press. [WCM]

Wilson, M. G., Parmelee, A. H. & Huggins, M. H. (1963) Prenatal history of infants with birth weights of 1500 grams or less. *Journal of Pediatrics* 63:1140–50. [taTG]

Wing, L. (1981) Sex ratios in early childhood autism and related conditions. *Psychiatry Research* 5:129–37. [taTG]

Winter, S. T. (1972) The male disadvantage in disease acquired in childhood. *Developmental Medicine and Child Neurology* 14:517–20. [HC]

Wolf, V. (1981) Genetic aspects of H-Y antigen. *Human Genetics* 58:25–28. [taTG]

Wolin, S. L. & Steitz, J. A. (1984) The Ro small cytoplasmic ribonucleoproteins: Identification of the antigenic protein and its binding site on the Ro RNAs. *Proceedings of the National Academy of Sciences of the United States of America* 81:1996–2000. [PVT]

Woolf, C. M. (1971) Congenital cleft lip: A genetic study of 496 propositi. *Journal of Medical Genetics* 8:65–84. [taTG]

World Health Organization (1983) World health statistics. *Annual 1983*. WHO. [ACP]

Wrangham, R. W. (1982) Mutualism, kinship, and social evolution. In: *Current problems in sociobiology*, ed. King's College Sociobiology Group. Cambridge University Press. [ACP]

Wyshak, G. (1969) Intervals between births in families containing one set of twins. *Journal of Biological and Social Sciences* 1:337. [taTG]

Yakovlev, P. I. & Lecours, A. R. (1967) The myelogenetic cycles of regional maturation of the brain. In: *Regional development of the brain in early life*, ed. A. Minkowski. Blackwell. [AB]

References/Gualtieri & Hicks: Immunoreactive theory

Yamamoto, M., Ito, T. & Watanabe, G. (1977) Determination of prenatal sex ratio in man. *Human Genetics* 36:265–69. [RHB]

Zajonc, R. B. (1976) Family configuration and intelligence. *Science* 192:227–36. [HC, taTG]

(1983) Validating the confluence model. *Psychological Bulletin* 93:457–80. [taTG]

Zerssen, D. V. & Weyerer, S. (1982) Sex differences in rates of mental disorders. *International Journal of Mental Health* 11:9–45. [taTG]

Zinkernagel, R. M. & Doherty, P. D. (1974) Immunological surveillance against altered self components by sensitized T-lymphocytes in lymphocytic choriomeningitis. *Nature* 251:547–49. [SO]

Length of Labor and Sex of Offspring[1]

Carol Nagy Jacklin[2] and Eleanor M. Maccoby
Stanford University

Length of labor was found to be longer for mothers giving birth to boys than for mothers giving birth to girls in four independent groups born at two hospitals. Birth weight, parity, and hospital also related to labor length. However, when these factors were held constant, sex of newborn remained a predictor of length of labor.

There is evidence that length of labor is related to a child's behavior and development. Labor length has been found to relate to depressed Apgar scores at birth (Friedman, Niswander, Sachtleben, & Naftaly, 1969), to lower scores on the Bayley mental and motor examinations at 8 months of age (Friedman, Niswander, & Sachtleben, 1969), to speech-language-hearing tests at 3 years of age, and IQ scores at 4 years of age (Friedman, Sachtleben, & Breskey, 1977). In most studies, long labor is confounded with greater usage of perinatal medication, and perinatal medication may also affect a child's later behavior. Whether drugs or labor length is the more important variable is difficult to determine (Kraemer, Korner, & Thoman, 1972). In any case, length of labor remains a potentially important variable in predicting subsequent development.

Boys are more vulnerable during gestation and at birth (Manniello & Farrell, 1977; McMillen, 1979). The greater vulnerability of the male to birth injury and congenital malformations not resulting in death is well documented (Arena & Smith, 1978; Beltran, Robertson, & Page, 1979; Hay, 1971).

---

[1] The research reported was supported by National Institutes of Health grant HD-90814-07.
[2] All correspondence should be addressed to Carol Nagy Jacklin, Department of Psychology, Stanford University, Stanford, California 94305.

Studies which have tried to identify the factors contributing to length of labor have not analyzed for effects related to sex-of-offspring (Agboola & Agobe, 1976; Cohen, 1977; Sokol, Stojkov, Chik, & Rosen, 1977). The present paper addresses the issue of whether there is a sex-of-offspring difference in length of labor. The contribution of other factors predicting labor length is also considered, and the degree of their independence from sex-of-offspring examined.

METHOD

Subjects

Four independent groups of infants[3] were recruited to participate in a longitudinal study. Group 1 had 75 infants; Group 2, 65; Group 3, 74; and Group 4, 106. The birth variables used as selection criteria included: no complications of pregnancy and delivery, 1-minute Apgar score of 7 or more, 5-minute Apgar score of 8 or more. Caesarian delivery babies and twins were excluded from the sample. Group 1 infants were born at a large university hospital during July and August 1973. Group 2 infants were born in both the university hospital and a nearby general hospital from January to March 1974. Groups 3 and 4 were born in a general hospital from August through November 1974 and August through November 1975, respectively.

Procedures

Copies were made from the hospital records for each child recruited into the study. These records included labor duration, parity, sex of the child, and drugs administered.

A drug score was calculated by using a modification of the Stechler (1964) Scale. Since Stechler uses only information regarding administration of analgesics, an analogous scale was constructed using analgesics and anesthesia. Scores were given as follows: 1 = no analgesia, no anesthesia; 2 = no analgesia, but pudendal, paracervical, and/or local anesthesia within 30 minutes before delivery; 3 = no analgesia, but epidural, caudal, or spinal anesthesia; 4 = analgesia, but no anesthesia; 5 = analgesia, and pudendal, paracervical, and local anesthesia within 30 minutes before delivery; 6 = analgesia, and epidural, caudal, or spinal anesthesia.

---

[3]Data from Groups 1, 2, and 4, have been reported in Maccoby, Doering, Jacklin, and Kraemer (1979); Group 3 data have been reported in Martin (1981).

Length of Labor

Table I. Mean Length of Labor in Minutes

Variable	In birth of boys		In birth of girls		In birth of boys and girls	
	Mean	n	Mean	n	Mean	n
Firstborns	535.91	79	453.69	70	497.28	149
Later borns	304.14	76	290.05	95	296.32	171
University hospital	496.06	48	436.50	46	466.91	94
General hospital	389.17	107	329.70	119	357.85	226
Totals	422.27	155	359.47	165	389.89	320

RESULTS

Table I presents labor length means (in minutes) for birth order and hospital, separately by sex. The sex difference for combined means reaches statistical significance, $t(308) = 2.33$, $p < .05$.

Several variables which relate to labor length are also correlated with each other, viz., birth order, birth weight, and the hospital at which the child was born. Thus, a multiple regression analysis was done on the combined group data with labor length as the dependent variable and birth order, birth weight, sex, and hospital as independent variables and an interaction term for both order and sex. The resulting beta weights and probability levels for these variables are presented in Table II. Birth order, birth weight, and hospital are significantly related to length of labor, with longer labors for firstborns, larger infants, and infants born at the university hospital. Sex remains a marginally significant predictor ($p < .06$) after these effects are removed, but the interaction of sex and birth order does not reach statistical significance. Still, as can be seen in Table I, second- and later-born boys and girls are very similar in labor length, whereas

Table II. Predicting Length of Labor: Multiple Regression Results

Independent variables	Beta	$F(df = 1, 309)$
Weight	.118	5.37[b]
Birth order (firstborn = 1)		
(later born = 2)	−.392	59.47[c]
Hospital	−.163	10.30[c]
Sex (males = −1; females = +1)	−.314	3.71[a]
Sex × birth order	.254	2.44

[a] $p < .10$.
[b] $p < .05$.
[c] $p < .01$.

firstborn boys and girls differ considerably. A t test for firstborn boys and girls is significant, $t(45) = 1.98, p = .05$.

Drug use is known to relate to length of labor (Kraemer et al., 1972). In the present sample, drug use and labor are correlated. For boys the correlation is $r(151) = .23, p = .005$. For girls the correlation is $r(157) = .15, p = .06$. To determine whether drug usage interacted with sex, a X2 analysis of variance was performed for high and low drug-usage groups with sex of offspring. A median split was done on the combined boys' and girls' scores for the division into high and low drug-usage groups. Table III presents the mean labor length for high and low drug-scored boys and girls.

The analysis yielded a main effect for drug score, $F(1, 316) = 8.01, p = .005$, and a main effect for sex, $F(1, 316) = 5.26, p = .022$. But there was no significant interaction between sex and drug usage. Thus, male sex adds an increment to length of labor, regardless of the amount of medication being used.

In order to improve our understanding of which variables predict high drug usage, a second multiple regression was run with drug score as the dependent variable and labor length, hospital, birth weight, and sex as independent variables. The resulting beta weights and F values for these variables are presented in Table IV. Birth order is the largest contributor to the prediction of drug usage, with more medication being used with firstborns than later borns. Labor length and hospital are also significantly related to drug score. Shorter labor and the university hospital were associated with lower drug use. Weight and sex were not significantly related to drug use.

Since the university hospital was associated with longer labor but lower drug use, additional analyses were carried out to understand the apparent paradox.

No differences were found in number of natural (no drug) childbirths in the two hospitals, but more first births occurred at the university hospital, $t(329) = 2.18, p = .03$. The relationship between drug use and labor length is significant for each hospital (university hospital, $r = 24, n = 92, p = .02$; general hospital, $r = .22, n = 202, p = .001$).

Table III. Mean Length of Labor in Minutes by Drug Usage and Sex of Offspring

	Males		Females	
	Mean	n	Mean	n
High drug-usage	457.89	93	386.86	95
Low drug-usage	368.84	62	322.30	70

Length of Labor

Table IV. Predicting Drug Usage: Multiple Regression Results

Independent variables	Beta	$F(df = 1, 381)$
Weight	−.003	.003
Birth order (firstborn = 1; later born = 2)	−.281	22.60[b]
Hospital	.182	10.95[b]
Labor length	.122	4.09[a]
Sex males = −1; females = +1)	.058	1.12

[a] $p < .05$.
[b] $p < .01$.

DISCUSSION

Labor is longer in the birth of boys than girls. Drug usage too is related to labor length but does not interact with the sex of the offspring. Other variables such as birth order, weight, and hospital the child is born in relate to labor length, but after the predictive values of these effects have been taken out, sex of child remains significantly related to labor length.

Interestingly, drug usage was best predicted by birth order. Mothers delivering for the first time received more drugs than mothers delivering second- and later-born children regardless of length of labor. This may be true because of greater fear of labor the first time. As expected from earlier work (Kraemer et al., 1972), drug usage was also greater when labor was longer. It may be that physicians make a decision to use medication once a given duration of labor has been reached. Alternatively, it may be that high drug-usage slows labor. Hospital was also significantly related to drug usage. There seemed to be a general pattern of drug usage specific to each of the two hospitals studied, with the university hospital generally having much lower drug usage. Interestingly, the university hospital also had longer labors, because more first births occurred at the university hospital.

The sex difference found in length of labor is probably conservatively estimated here. It should be recalled that high selection criteria were used before subjects were recruited into the study. If there were complications of pregnancy or delivery the child was excluded from the sample. Although no records were kept of the sex of the children not recruited into the study, more boys may have been excluded than girls. In any case, in a large representative sample of normal births, boys do have longer labors than girls, particularly firstborn boys.

REFERENCES

Agboola, A., & Agobe, J. T. A reappraisal of the duration of labor. *Obstetrics and Gynecology*, 1976, *48*, 724-726.

Arena, J. F. P., & Smith, D. W. Sex liability to single structural defects. *American Journal of Diseases of Children*, 1978, *132*, 970-972.

Beltran, I. C., Robertson, F. W., & Page, B. M. Human Y chromosome variation in normal and abnormal babies and their fathers. *Annals of Human Genetics*, 1979, *42*, 315-325.

Cohen, W. R. Influence of the duration of second stage labor on perinatal outcome and puerperal morbidity. *Obstetrics and Gynecology*, 1977, *49*, 266-269.

Friedman, E. A., Niswander, K. R., & Sachtleben, M. R. Dysfunctional labor. XI. Neurologic and developmental effects on surviving infants. *Obstetrics and Gynecology*, 1969, *33*, 785-791.

Friedman, E. A., Niswander, K. R., Sachtleben, M. R., & Naftaly, N. Dysfunctional labor. X. Immediate results to infant. *Obstetrics and Gynecology*, 1969, *33*, 776-784.

Friedman, E. A., Sachtleben, M. R., & Breskey, P. A. Dysfunctional labor. XII. Long-term effects on infant. *American Journal of Obstetrics and Gynecology*, 1977, *127*, 779-783.

Hay, S. Sex differences in the incidence of certain congenital malformations: A review of the literature and some new data. *Teratology*, 1971, *4*, 277-286.

Kraemer, H. C., Korner, A. F., & Thoman, E. B. Methodological considerations in evaluating the influence of drugs used during labor and delivery on the behavior of the newborn. *Developmental Psychology*, 1972, *6*, 128-134.

Maccoby, E. E., Doering, C. H., Jacklin, C. N., & Kraemer, H. Concentrations of sex hormones in umbilical-cord blood: Their relation to sex and birth order of infants. *Child Development*, 1979, *50*, 632-642.

Manniello, R. L., & Farrell, P. M. Analysis of United States neonatal mortality statistics from 1968 to 1974, with specific reference to changing trends in major causalities. *American Journal of Obstetrics and Gynecology*, 1977, *129*, 667-674.

Martin, J. A. A longitudinal study of the consequences of early mother-infant interaction: A microanalytic approach. *Monographs of the Society for Research in Child Development*, 1981, *46*(3), 1-58.

McMillen, M. M. Differential mortality by sex in fetal and neonatal deaths. *Science*, 1979, *204*, 89-91.

Sokol, R. J., Stojkov, J., Chik, L., & Rosen, M. G. Normal and abnormal labor progress. I. A quantitative assessment and survey of the literature. *Journal of Reproductive Medicine*, 1977, *18*, 47-53.

Stechler, G. Newborn attention as affected by medication during labor. *Science*, 1964, *144*, 315-317.

[12]

NEONATAL STARTLES, SMILES, ERECTIONS, AND REFLEX SUCKS AS RELATED TO STATE, SEX, AND INDIVIDUALITY

ANNELIESE F. KORNER

Stanford University School of Medicine

Frequencies of startles, reflex smiles, erections, and reflex sucks were recorded in the context of the state in which they occurred in 32, 2- to 3-day-old healthy neonates. States were monitored for each infant during 2 hours and 20 minutes divided in 6 observation periods. Observer agreements ranged from 80 percent to 100 percent on the infants' states and from 93 to 100 percent on the spontaneous behaviors. Results confirm Wolff's findings (1966) that there is a highly significant relation between state and the type and frequency of the spontaneous behaviors. The frequencies are highest during regular sleep when the infant is most deafferented and they diminish in direct proportion to the infant's closeness to wakefulness. Results on sex differences reflect a consistent trend that males startle more in all states and females engage more frequently in reflex smiles and bursts of rhythmical mouthing. Since the mean rate of the spontaneous behaviors is almost identical for males and females when erections are excluded, it appears that females make up in smiles and reflex sucks what they lack in startles. The data also suggest that erections are spontaneous behaviors which occur over and above the other discharge behaviors. Rank correlations showed that individual infants tend to rely heavily on specific discharge channels over states (e.g., .77 for erections, .53 for rhythmical mouthing). The discussion focuses on the possible function of the spontaneous behaviors for providing endogenous afferent stimulation under conditions of deafferentation, during a period when such stimulation may be critical for the developing central nervous system, and on the potential significance of these behaviors for later development.

Spontaneous behaviors in the newborn which occur in the absence of external or known visceral stimuli have been the object of very few systematic investigations. This is particularly surprising, considering the recent

---

This investigation was supported by U. S. Public Health Service grants HD-00825 and HD-03591-01 from the National Institute of Child Health and

CHILD DEVELOPMENT

interest in research with neonates, and in view of the fact that some of these behaviors occur with great regularity in every healthy newborn (e.g., startles) and others occur with great frequency (e.g., smiles, sucks, penile erections). Perhaps the reason for this lack of interest is that little is known about the developmental function, or the significance for later adaptations, of these spontaneous behaviors.

Some of these behaviors were studied before the recent upsurge of neonatal research. For example, Hunt, Clarke, and Hunt (1936) studied the startle in the infant as distinguished from the Moro reflex. Halverson (1940) studied erections in infants. More recently, Wolff (1963), Tcheng and Laroche (1965), and Emde and Koenig (1967) studied neonatal smiling, especially as this relates to the state of the baby. By far the most comprehensive investigation of all these spontaneous behaviors was undertaken by Wolff (1959, 1966). In his monograph, "The Causes, Controls and Organization of Behavior in the Neonate" (1966), he described these behaviors as "motor patterns that are not related to known external or internal visceral excitations, and [which] have a well-circumscribed morphology." The spontaneous behaviors with such a well-circumscribed morphology include startles, sobbing inspirations, facial twitches, rhythmical mouthing, reflex smiles, and erections. Wolff demonstrated that these discharge behaviors occur periodically and in rhythmical sequence, that they can substitute for each other (e.g., sequences of periodic startles are replaced by sequences of rhythmical mouthing), and that the form of discharge behavior is linked to the state of the baby. Thus Wolff showed that spontaneous startles primarily occur in regular (deep) sleep, and less frequently in irregular sleep and drowse. Rhythmical mouthing was mentioned only in the context of regular sleep. Erections are most frequent in irregular sleep, but also occur in regular sleep and drowse. Reflex smiles never occur in regular sleep, occasionally occur in drowse, and are most frequent in irregular sleep. Since no known stimulus evokes these behaviors, Wolff postulated that they represent the discharge of a neural energy potential, which occurs in inverse proportion to the degree of afferent input. He demonstrated quite clearly that the greatest "work output" of spontaneous behaviors occurs during regular sleep, when the threshold to extrinsic stimulation is high, and when the afferent feedback from motor activity is minimal.

Human Development. I wish to thank Dr. Helena Kraemer for the statistical analyses of the data, Mrs. Rose Grobstein for acting as co-observer of the infants, Miss Bernadine Chuck and Miss Soula Dontchos for the film analysis of the data, and Dr. Evelyn Thoman for her valuable suggestions in preparing this manuscript. The helpful cooperation of the nursing staff of the Stanford Hospital and the Department of Pediatrics of the Stanford University School of Medicine made this study possible. Author's address: Department of Psychiatry, Stanford University School of Medicine, Stanford, California 94305.

ANNELIESE F. KORNER

In the course of a study on individual differences in neonates (Korner 1964; Korner & Grobstein 1967), an attempt was made to replicate some of Wolff's observations and to begin to explore the sexual and individual differences in the discharge channels of these spontaneous behaviors. Specifically my observations were geared to the following questions:

1. To what degree does the infant's state and level of activation influence the form and the rate of the spontaneous discharge behaviors?

2. Are there any sex differences in the frequency of the spontaneous behaviors in the various states and in the reliance on specific discharge channels? If the frequency of the spontaneous discharge behaviors is similar for both sexes, do females, lacking erections as a discharge channel, compensate by relying more heavily on the other discharge channels? Or are erections a form of spontaneous behavior which occurs over and above the other discharge behaviors, thus creating a quantitative difference in the frequency of discharge behaviors between the sexes?

3. In the realm of individual differences, do all infants partake in all forms of spontaneous behaviors or are there some neonates who show no discharges in some of the modalities (e.g., never smile or never show erections)? Also, are some infants high "dischargers" across modalities or does the frequent discharge via one channel diminish discharge in another (e.g., do infants who frequently startle in regular sleep also engage in a lot of reflex sucks or is there an inverse relation between two forms of spontaneous behaviors in the same state)? Furthermore, do individual infants show a consistent and strong reliance on specific discharge channels in every state? If this were the case, strong and consistent reliance on reflex sucking or on erections across states might point to congenital differences in psychosexual disposition.

SUBJECTS

The sample consisted of 32 full-term, bottle-fed Caucasian neonates whose ages ranged between 45 and 88 hours (median age 57 hours). Seventeen were male, 15 were female; 14 were firstborn and 18 were born to multiparae. Since the object of the study of individual differences was to assess the behavioral individuality of the neonates, every effort was made to exclude infants whose behavior might have been affected by pre- or postnatal complications. The following were our selection criteria: weight between 6 and 9 pounds; Apgar ratings of 8 or above at 1 minute; delivery spontaneous or through low forceps, vertex presentation; maternal depressant drugs not exceeding 200 mg, 1–6 hours prior to delivery; maternal first and second stage labor no shorter than 1 hour, no longer than 36 hours; no signs of fetal and postnatal anoxia; parents' history free of metabolic or neurological disease; mother not on tranquilizers or stimulants during pregnancy and free of infectious disease at time of delivery; fetal age between

CHILD DEVELOPMENT

38 and 42 weeks; infant judged to be "normal newborn" on physical examination; infant legitimate, of single birth, and RH positive; a minimum of 24 hours elapsed since circumcision of male subjects.

METHOD

The infants were observed in a treatment room adjoining the newborn nursery. Illumination approximated conditions in the nursery. In order to avoid diurnal variations, all babies were seen at the same time of day. The infants were observed in their own bassinets, placed in the supine, dressed only in a shirt and without diapers. The room temperature was kept at 78°F.

Each infant was observed over a span of 9 hours which were interrupted by 1 hour during each of two feedings. Since one of the objects of the larger study (Korner & Grobstein 1967) was to explore the effects of hunger and satiation on neonatal behavior, the most intensive observations were made during two prefeed half-hour periods, one postfeed half-hour period, and a half-hour period at midpoint. Most of the data presented in this paper were obtained during these four half-hour periods. Frequency of the spontaneous behaviors was also recorded during two 10-minute settling-in periods which took place directly after each feeding. The quantitative results reported here are thus based on 2 hours and 20 minutes of observation on each infant, divided into six separate observation periods.

During each of these periods a running record was kept of the infants' changes in state, and of the spontaneous behaviors which occurred within the context of the various states. Wolff's (1966) behavioral criteria were used, with very minor variations, to establish state ratings. By keeping a continuous timed record, it was possible to calculate the rate at which the various spontaneous discharge behaviors occurred within a given state. The total number of each of the spontaneous discharges in a given state was divided by the total durations of that state during the 2 hour, 20 minute period. This calculation provided occurrence rates per minute of each of the spontaneous behaviors in each state which, multiplied by 60, yielded an hourly rate of each behavior per child.

Also recorded were the spontaneous behaviors whenever they occurred during the rest of the time the infant was watched. (This was a total of 4½ hours for each infant.) In each instance, the state in which the spontaneous behavior occurred was identified and recorded. These observations, while noncontributory to the calculations of the hourly discharge rates, added descriptive information about the phenomena under study.

Also used for data collection were 1,000 feet of film of each baby, taken in 16 2¼-minute time samples, spread over the four half-hour periods during which the infants' states and spontaneous behaviors were monitored. For this purpose, light-sensitive film was used. A timer attached to an

Arriflex camera automatically activated the camera. In this way, unselected behavior samples, identical in length and in interval since the last feeding, were taken on each infant. Of relevance to this paper are the infants' scores on the frequencies of motion and of gross mouthing. For a detailed description of the method of film analysis and of the criteria used, see Korner, Chuck, and Dontchos (1968).

Of the spontaneous behaviors, only startles, reflex smiles, erections, and rhythmical mouthing were used for systematic comparisons. Sobbing inspirations and a few other periodic spontaneous behaviors were too few to be included in such a comparison. The following is a description of the spontaneous behaviors. (The criteria used are almost entirely Wolff's. For comparison and a fuller description see Wolff [1966, pp. 13–16].)

Startles.—Spontaneously occurring massive body jerks which resemble the Moro reflex and involve both sudden extensor and flexor motions of the limbs.

Rhythmical mouthing or reflex sucks.—Bursts of a series of rhythmical, shallow sucks which occur at about two sucks per second, separated by intervals of total inactivity.

Erections.—Sustained or brief tumescence of the penis, usually preceded by peristaltic movement in the cremasteric musculature.

Reflex smiling.—Upward and sideward movement of the muscles surrounding the mouth; morphologically similar to later smiling but distinct from it in being unrelated to a social stimulus and in usually not involving the circular muscles surrounding the eyes.

The following were the most salient criteria used for determining the state of the infant. Again, Wolff's (1966) criteria were used, except that no distinction was made between irregular and periodic sleep. This distinction, which was made by Wolff with the help of pneumographic monitoring of respiration, was more difficult to make reliably through observational criteria alone.

Regular sleep.—The infant is at full rest; his muscle tonus is low. He very rarely moves and for the most part is completely still. He does not grimace and his eyelids are still. Respirations are slow and regular.

Irregular sleep.—The infant's eyelids are closed. Motor activity varies from gentle limb movement to general stirring and writhing. Grimaces and other facial expressions are frequent. Respirations are irregular and faster than in regular sleep. Within this state, interspersed and recurrent rapid eye movements (REMs) can be seen through the eyelids. These episodes are associated not only with extremely irregular breathing, but also with periodic bursts of very rapid and shallow respirations.

Drowsiness.—The infant is relatively inactive. The eyes open and close intermittently; they have a dull, glazed appearance. The eyelids appear to be heavy. Respirations are fairly regular, slower than in irregular sleep, but faster than in regular sleep.

CHILD DEVELOPMENT

Alert inactivity.—The infant is relatively inactive; the face is relaxed and does not grimace; the eyes are open and have a "bright, shining appearance." In this state, the infant is capable of making conjugate eye movements in the horizontal and vertical plane.

Waking activity.—In this state, the infant frequently engages in diffuse motor activity involving the whole body. The eyes are open but not alert. The face may be relaxed or in a cry face. Respirations are grossly irregular.

Crying.—This state is characterized by crying vocalizations associated with vigorous, diffuse motor activity.

Indeterminate state.—This category was used in those instances in which the infant's state did not clearly meet the criteria of any of the above states. This category was added not only to avoid misclassifications but also as a variable in its own right. In the study of individual differences, I was interested in identifying those infants who conveyed their internal states most clearly, as well as least clearly.

Observer Reliability

A second observer was present during the last interfeeding cycle, in the cases of 20 infants randomly distributed over the entire sample. In addition to establishing observer reliability on a series of sensory stimulation experiments which were scheduled during this period, the second observer also served to establish observer reliability on the types of behavior which had been monitored and recorded earlier by a single observer. Observer reliability was calculated for each measure on the basis of dividing the number of agreements by the combined number of agreements and disagreements. In the case of state classifications, agreement was scored when the same state was identified within a 15-second interval and when the sequence of the states was the same for both observers.

The observer agreements obtained on the infants' states were: regular sleep, 100 percent; irregular sleep, 92 percent; drowsiness, 100 percent; alert inactivity, 96 percent; waking activity, 100 percent; crying, 100 percent; indeterminate state, 80 percent. Observer agreements of the spontaneous discharge behaviors were: startles, 97 percent; reflex smiling, 95 percent; erections, 100 percent; rhythmical mouthing, 93 percent.

RESULTS

Relation of State to the Frequency of the Spontaneous Discharge Behaviors

When the incidence of the spontaneous behaviors was tabulated in the context of the states in which they occurred, it was clear that their occurrence was so infrequent during the waking states that it precluded their inclusion in the statistical analyses. Table 1 shows the mean hourly

ANNELIESE F. KORNER

TABLE 1
RELATION OF STATE TO MEAN HOURLY DISCHARGE RATES OF THE SPONTANEOUS BEHAVIORS

Spontaneous Behaviors	Regular Sleep	Irregular Sleep	Drowse	p[a]
Startles ($N = 30$)........	31.86	8.76	3.96	.001
Rhythmical mouthing ($N = 30$)............	18.42	3.06	0	.001
Reflex smiles ($N = 30$)............	0	5.88	2.34	.001
Erections ($N = 16$)......	2.22	4.80	0.66	.001
Total without erections............	50.34	17.28	6.42	.001
Total with erections....	51.48	19.80	6.72	.001

[a] By two-way analysis of variance.

rate of each of the spontaneous behaviors during each of the sleep states. Since two infants were not in regular sleep during the 2 hour, 20 minute observation period, the findings are based on 30 infants rather than 32.

Table 1 confirms Wolff's findings (1966) regarding the highly significant influence of state on the type and the distribution of the spontaneous behaviors. By far the greatest incidence of the spontaneous discharge behaviors is seen during regular sleep, when the infant's deafferentation is greatest and when he is most quiescent. The inverse relation between activation and the spontaneous behaviors was confirmed when frequency of motion, as scored from film, was correlated with the frequency of the spontaneous behaviors during regular sleep. The rank correlation between these two variables was −.66, which is significant at the .001 level.

The distribution of the spontaneous behaviors over the states is very similar in Wolff's study and in this study, even though the rates of the discharges differ considerably in the two samples. Wolff did not consider his rates as normative, nor do I consider mine to be. Except for startles in regular sleep, all of Wolff's rates are considerably higher than those shown in table 1. This is not surprising, since the conditions of observation differed radically in the two studies. Wolff observed his subjects in an Armstrong incubator, which isolates the infant from most environmental stimuli, thus promoting deafferentation which, in turn, enhances the frequency of the spontaneous behaviors.

Relation of State to the Type of the Spontaneous Discharge Behaviors

Startles.—Table 1 shows that startle rates differ significantly in the three sleep states. By far the greatest number of startles occur during regular sleep. There are also state-dependent, qualitative differences among startles. During regular sleep, the startles are much more massive and

CHILD DEVELOPMENT

vigorous than during any other sleep state. Startles were weakest during waking states when they were also extremely rare. Of the 883 startles noted, only six occurred during waking. Most of these six startles were seen during crying or during momentary states between crying episodes.

Rhythmical mouthing.—Table 1 also reflects highly significant differences between states in the incidence of rhythmical mouthing. Rhythmical mouthing was limited to regular sleep and irregular sleep, with and without REMs. The large majority of bursts occurred during regular sleep. The observation that rhythmical mouthing *can* occur during irregular sleep, and particularly during irregular sleep with REMs, agrees with Karacan's observations (1966), but differs with those of Wolff, who ascribed this phenomenon exclusively to regular sleep. Qualitatively, there are slight differences between the sucks during regular and irregular sleep. While rhythmical mouthing is characterized by bursts of sucks at about two per second, separated by intervals of total inactivity between bursts in each state in which they occur, the sucks are slightly more shallow during regular sleep than during the other states. From both Wolff's and my own evidence it seems safe to infer that rhythmical mouthing occurs primarily in the most deafferented stages of sleep. This is confirmed by the fact that rhythmical mouthing occurs much less frequently in irregular sleep without REMs than during irregular REM sleep, when thresholds to external stimuli are significantly higher (see Korner 1968).

Of interest for oral drive theory and in need of clarification is the fact that the use of rhythmical mouthing bears no relation to the infant's gross mouthing, sucking, or tonguing. The rank correlation between the frequency of bursts of rhythmical mouthing and gross mouthing as recorded from film was .14. The relation to hunger of these two measures further underscores their basic difference. Gross mouthing increases significantly with time since the last feeding (analysis of variance significant at the .01 level), whereas rhythmical mouthing shows no relation to hunger.

Reflex smiling.—Table 1 shows a highly significant relation between the occurrence of smiles and the infant's state. As has already been noted by others (Tcheng & Laroche 1965; Wolff 1966), reflex smiles never occur during regular sleep. Their most frequent occurrence is during irregular and REM sleep.

There seems to be some question whether infants are capable of smiling while awake during the first postnatal week. Wolff (1966, p. 77) indicated that spontaneous smiles never occur while the infant is fully awake. In an earlier paper (1963) he did mention two infants who, on occasion, responded to visual stimuli with a smile. In this sample of neonates, eight smiles were noted during waking. Seven of these occurred during alert inactivity. Of these seven, three appeared to be spontaneous, two were in response to a visual stimulus, one in response to the camera turning off, and one following a hand-mouth contact. Only four of the 32 infants smiled during alert inactivity and all but one of these were females. Most of the smiles during waking tended to occur shortly after a feeding. The evidence from this study thus suggests that, on very rare occasions, spontaneous smiles do seem to occur during the neonatal period while the infant is alert. Tcheng and Laroche came to the same conclusion in their longitudinal observation of one subject from birth on.

Erections.—Table 1 demonstrates that there is a highly significant relation between the occurrence of erections and the infant's state. They occur most commonly during irregular sleep, and during that state the large majority are seen while the infant is having rapid eye movements. This is an interesting precursor of a later relation between the REM state and erections. Fisher, Gross, and Zuch (1965) noted that, in adult males, 95 percent of all REM periods were associated with penile erections, and that these begin and end in close temporal relation with the onset and termination of REM periods. While neonates neither show the high frequency nor the synchrony of association between REMs and erections, they nevertheless demonstrate the beginnings of such an association. Neonatal erections are usually shorter in duration. Erections were also noted during waking states, particularly during crying. These were brief and in a sense not entirely spontaneous, since the proprioceptive feedback from the diffuse activity associated with crying undoubtedly served as a stimulus.

Other periodic spontaneous behaviors and their state-relatedness.— On a few occasions, spontaneous behaviors were noted which met the criteria of the other spontaneous behaviors (of occurring repetitively in rhythmic periodicity, without the benefit of a known external or internal stimulus). They also met the criterion of being morphologically well-circumscribed. Thus five infants showed intermittent palpebral blinking very similar to the palpebral reflex. In one infant this occurred during regular sleep; in the remaining four, during irregular REM sleep. These blinks were distinct events and qualitatively quite different from the rapid eye movements seen during REM sleep. Twelve infants showed intermittent extensor kicks of one leg. In three infants this occurred during irregular sleep, and in nine infants during irregular REM sleep.

Sex Differences

Table 2 presents the mean hourly rates of startles, bursts of rhythmical mouthing, and reflex smiles in each state separately for males and females. It reflects a clear and consistent trend showing that boys startle more in all states than girls and also shows that, in each state, girls smiled more and engaged more frequently in bursts of rhythmical mouthing. Only the differences in startles and smiles during irregular sleep were on the borderline of statistical significance. (On t tests, the difference between the sexes in smiling had a p level $<.06$; for startles $<.10$.)

CHILD DEVELOPMENT

TABLE 2

MEAN HOURLY RATE OF SPONTANEOUS BEHAVIORS ACCORDING TO SEX

STATES	STARTLES		RHYTHMICAL MOUTHING		REFLEX SMILES	
	Boys	Girls	Boys	Girls	Boys	Girls
Regular sleep.....	36.06	27.12	13.92	23.58	0	0
Irregular sleep....	11.94	6.72	2.28	3.60	3.72	8.28
Drowse..........	6.42	3.36	0	0	2.10	2.64

Table 3 presents a comparison of the total discharges in each state between males and females. (To the left is a comparison of the discharge rates with erections excluded; to the right erections are included.) It shows that the discharge rates are almost identical for males and females when erections are excluded. This was particularly true for regular and irregular sleep, when the spontaneous behaviors occur with the highest frequency.

TABLE 3

COMPARISON OF MEAN HOURLY RATES OF TOTAL DISCHARGES ACCORDING TO SEX

States	Boys (Erections Excluded)	Girls	Boys (Erections Included)	Girls
Regular sleep......	49.98	50.70	52.20	50.70
Irregular sleep.....	18.30	18.60	24.12	18.60
Drowse...........	8.52	6.00	9.12	6.00

From the evidence in table 2, one may infer that girls make up in smiles and rhythmical mouthing what they lack in startles. The almost identical total discharge rates of males and females when erections are excluded would suggest that erections are spontaneous behaviors which occur over and above the other discharge behaviors. Discrepancies in rates, which, on t tests did not reach statistical significance, do appear when erections are included in the comparison between males and females. This discrepancy is particularly marked in irregular sleep, when erections are most frequent. Since females do not compensate for erections by relying more heavily on startles, reflex smiles, and rhythmical mouthing as discharge channels, the question arises whether females, like males, do not also have an additional discharge channel. Possibly, in the female infant there are already traces of periodic vaginal temperature changes associated with venous engorgement, such as are currently being studied during sleep in the adult female (Bokert, Ellman, Fiss, & Klein 1966; Shapiro, Cohen, DiBianco, & Rosen 1968; and Fisher 1968, personal communication).

1048

ANNELIESE F. KORNER

Individual Differences

Individual patterns of the spontaneous behaviors.—Within the time limitations of the observation period used in this study, only the startle in regular sleep emerged as an obligatory discharge for all babies. There were some infants who never engaged in rhythmical mouthing, others who never showed erections or reflex smiles. While it is quite possible that these behaviors might have emerged had the subjects been observed over a longer period of time, their total absence in some infants during 7 hours of observation compared with their frequent occurrence in others suggests that there are marked quantitative variations among infants in the frequency of the various spontaneous behaviors.

Study of individual records revealed interesting, and often self-consistent, sequences in the spontaneous behaviors. For example, some infants during regular sleep startled several times in rapid succession; others showed long intervals between startles. One infant's startles regularly alternated with episodes of rhythmical mouthing; another invariably startled immediately following bursts of rhythmical mouthing. One baby boy showed repeated and rapid sequences of episodes of rhythmical mouthing, startles, and erections.

Statistical exploration through rank correlation suggested that high work output in one modality does not correspond with high work output in another within a given state. Thus, for example, infants who startled a great deal in regular sleep did not necessarily have a great many erections or episodes of rhythmical mouthing. Only a few of these types of correlations were positive and none exceeded .16. This would suggest that it is unlikely that there is a high energy potential which seeks expression in all modalities within a given individual and within a given state. The correlations obtained also did not suggest an inverse or compensatory relation between the various discharges, except in the case of reflex smiles during irregular sleep. The rank correlation between smiles and startles was $-.35$, which is significant at the .05 level, and between smiles and rhythmical mouthing it was $-.31$, significant between the .10 and .05 levels. As can be seen from the small magnitude of these correlations, there is only a mild inverse relation between the frequency of reflex smiles and the other spontaneous behaviors.

Individual reliance on specific discharge channels.—Judging from the rank correlations obtained, infants do tend to rely on specific discharge channels over states. For example, startle rates in regular sleep correlate significantly with startle rates in irregular sleep ($r = .49$, significant at the .01 level). The correlations were even higher in the case of rhythmical mouthing and erections ($r = .53$ between rhythmical mouthing in regular and irregular sleep, significant at the .001 level; $r = .77$ between the rate of erections in regular sleep and irregular sleep, significant at the .001 level).

CHILD DEVELOPMENT

Correlations between regular sleep and drowse, and between irregular sleep and drowse were meaningless because of the sparse data from the state of drowsing. Since reflex smiles never occur in regular sleep, their rates in irregular sleep and drowse were correlated, in spite of the sparsity of data in drowse. That correlation was not significant ($r = .17$). It should be added that while these correlations point to tendencies in the infants to rely heavily on specific discharge channels, this does not occur necessarily at the exclusion of the use of all other discharge channels.

DISCUSSION

The findings of this study represent both confirmations and extensions of previous research. The extensions primarily involve sex differences and individual variations in the spontaneous discharge behaviors. The findings in these areas suggest a wide variety of further meaningful exploration. For example, it would be of interest to assess whether the consistent trend on the part of males to startle more than females, and for females to use reflex smiles and rhythmical mouthing as discharge channels more than males, would become more significant over a longer period of observation. If this were so, it would highlight biological and physiological differences between the sexes, identifiable at birth, which may be developmental precursors of later sex differences. The startle is by far the most vigorous of all the discharges, involving more muscle groups, with greater intensity, than any of the others. Perhaps the male's greater tendency to startle can be taken as an index of greater muscular endowment and vigor, seen also in his greater capacity to lift his head shortly after birth (see Bell & Darling 1965), and certainly in most of his later development. Similarly, the female's greater tendency in the direction of rhythmical mouthing may highlight that, congenitally, she may rely more heavily in her development on the oral mode, as was suggested by Erikson (1950) in his theory of infantile sexuality. Also, if further research were to confirm the sex-specificity of the distribution of the spontaneous behaviors, it would be of interest to follow longitudinally the development of those infant boys who rely heavily on rhythmical mouthing, and of those infant girls who are prolific and vigorous startlers, in order to see whether their development differs in any way from that of other boys and girls. Of course, normative data regarding the discharge rates of each of the spontaneous behaviors would first be required.

Such normative data would also be essential for further explorations of individual differences. For example, it would be extremely interesting to study longitudinally those infants who, during the neonatal period, consistently show very high or very low rates of spontaneous discharges within a given state. Quite possibly, this might be one avenue through which to study individual variations in drive endowment. Through such longitudinal observation, it would also be possible to study the developmental significance and the transformations of these early behaviors in later development.

The finding that infants tend to rely on the same discharge channels over states is also of interest in terms of individual development. If consistent over time, those infants who heavily rely on rhythmical mouthing or on erections as channels of discharge in several states may from the start show a zone preference which may color, intensify, and possibly render certain phases in their psychosexual development more difficult of resolution. This might be particularly true of those infants who rely on one discharge channel almost exclusively.

This study confirms Wolff's findings (1966) that state and deafferentation influence, to a highly significant degree, the type and the distribution of the spontaneous behaviors. The results of both studies very clearly show that the incidence of the spontaneous behaviors is highest during regular sleep, when thresholds to extrinsic stimulation are high and when the afferent feedback from motor activity is minimal. Furthermore, the data presented in table 1 suggest that the incidence of the spontaneous behaviors diminishes in direct proportion to the infant's closeness to wakefulness.

This raises the question of the function of the spontaneous behaviors during deep stages of sleep. Possibly, hypotheses which have been invoked to explain the function of REM sleep might have some relevance for the function of the spontaneous behaviors as well. Ephron and Carrington (1966), after reviewing much of the sleep research literature, postulated that REM sleep may have the homeostatic function of periodically providing endogenous stimulation to offset the deafferentation of the brain associated with deep stages of sleep. The spontaneous discharges could serve such a homeostatic function as well. The REM literature also shows that the younger the organism, the higher the levels of REM sleep. Parmelee, Wenner, Akiyama, Schultz, and Stern (1967), for example, established that premature infants are in REM sleep from 60 percent to 84 percent of the time and that REM levels of infants born at term are about 50 percent. By the age of 3 years, REM levels are comparable to those of the adult (20 percent, according to Roffwarg, Muzio, & Dement 1966). These authors postulated that the great prominence of the REM state during early life serves to assist the process of central nervous system maturation and differentiation through the endogenous afferent stimulation which the REM state provides. As has been suggested in a previous paper (Korner 1968), the endogenous afferent stimulation which attends the REM state may not quite fill the requirements of the neonate for such stimulation. It seems plausible that the spontaneous behaviors described in this paper may have this function also and may be viewed, like REMs, as expressions of neural activity in the service of endogenous afferent stimulation. Like REM levels, the spontaneous behaviors diminish rapidly with age. In fact, they disappear in their original form long before REM levels decrease significantly. Wolff's

CHILD DEVELOPMENT

longitudinal observations (1966) show that the extensor startles and sobbing inspirations gradually disappear over the first month, and that all that remains of spontaneous startles in sleep by the time the infant is 1½ months old are occasional myoclonic twitches. The frequency of spontaneous erections also decreases over the first 2 weeks. Smiling comes increasingly under the influence of external stimulation from the second week on (Wolff 1963). Only rhythmical mouthing persists beyond the first few weeks, remaining unchanged well into the sixth month of life.

This brings up the whole question of the fate of the spontaneous behaviors in later development. Little is known about their fate or their transformations into later forms of behavior. It is nevertheless noteworthy that, with the exception of rhythmical mouthing, each of the spontaneous behaviors involves motor patterns which are morphologically similar to later behaviors. Perhaps with experience and maturation, behavior patterns which at first have primarily a physiological or regulatory function may take on new or additional functions. Just as the REM state may gradually take on the function of dreaming, the reflex smile may change and become a social smile and a vehicle of social interaction. Similarly, erections may gradually become associated with sexual arousal and startles with fright reactions. It would be interesting to study the links between these morphologically similar behavior patterns. This could be most readily done in the case of reflex smiling. For example, one could assess whether those infants who, in Piaget's terms ([1936] 1952) practiced the smiling schema a great deal by engaging in frequent reflex smiles, are also those infants who become the earliest and most frequent social smilers.

REFERENCES

Bell, R. Q., & Darling, J. F. The prone head reaction in the human neonate: relation with sex and tactile sensitivity. *Child Development*, 1965, 36, 943–949.

Bokert, E.; Ellman, S.; Fiss, H.; & Klein, G. S. Temperature changes in the female genital area during sleep. Paper presented at the meeting of the Association for the Psychophysiological Study of Sleep, Gainesville, Fla., 1966.

Emde, R. N., & Koenig, K. L. Neonatal smiling, sucking and rapid eye movements. Paper presented at the biennial meeting of the Society for Research in Child Development, New York, April 1967.

Ephron, H. S., & Carrington, P. Rapid eye movement sleep and cortical homeostasis. *Psychological Review*, 1966, 73, 500–526.

Erikson, E. H. *Childhood and society*. New York: Norton, 1950.

Fisher, C.; Gross, J.; & Zuch, J. A cycle of penile erections synchronous with dreaming (REM) sleep. *Archives of General Psychiatry*, 1965, 12, 29–45.

Halverson, H. M. Genital and sphincter behavior of the male infant. *Journal of Genetic Psychology*, 1940, 56, 95–136.

Hunt, W. A.; Clarke, F. M.; & Hunt, E. B. Studies in the startle pattern, IV: Infants. *Journal of Psychology*, 1936, 2, 339–352.

Karacan, I. Ontogeny of penile erections during sleep in infants. Paper presented at the meeting of the Association for the Psychophysiological Study of Sleep, Gainesville, Fla., 1966.

Korner, A. F. Some hypotheses regarding the significance of individual differences at birth for later development. In, R. S. Eissler, et al. (Eds.), *The psychoanalytic study of the child.* Vol. 19. New York: International Universities Press, 1964. Pp. 58–72.

Korner, A. F. REM organization in neonates. Theoretical implications for development and the biological function of REM. *Archives of General Psychiatry,* 1968, 19, 330–340.

Korner, A. F., & Grobstein, R. Individual differences at birth: implications for mother-infant relationship and later development. *Journal of the American Academy of Child Psychiatry,* 1967, 6, 676–690.

Korner, A. F.; Chuck, B.; & Dontchos, S. Organismic determinants of spontaneous oral behavior in neonates. *Child Development,* 1968, 39, 1145–1157.

Parmelee, A. H.; Wenner, W. H.; Akiyama, Y.; Schultz, M.; & Stern, E. Sleep states in premature infants. *Developmental Medicine and Child Neurology,* 1967, 9, 70–77.

Piaget, J. *The Origins of intelligence in children,* 1936. New York: International Universities Press, 1952.

Roffwarg, H. P.; Muzio, J. N.; & Dement, W. C. Ontogenetic development of the human sleep-dream cycle. *Science,* 1966, 152, 604–619.

Shapiro, A.; Cohen, H.; DiBianco, P.; & Rosen, G. Vaginal blood flow changes during sleep and sexual arousal. *Psychophysiology,* 1968, 4, 394. (Abstract)

Tcheng, F. C. Y., & Laroche, J. Phases de sommeil et sourires spontanés. *Acta Psychologica,* 1965, 24, 1–28.

Wolff, P. H. Observations on newborn infants. *Psychosomatic Medicine,* 1959, 21, 110–118.

Wolff, P. H. Observations on the early development of smiling. In B. M. Foss, (Ed.), *Determinants of Infant Behaviour.* Vol. 2. London: Methuen; New York: Wiley, 1963. Pp. 113–134.

Wolff, P. H. The causes, controls and organization of behavior in the newborn. *Psychological Issues,* 1966, 5 (1, Whole No. 17).

[*Child Development,* 1969, 40, 1039–1053. © 1969 by the Society for Research in Child Development, Inc. All rights reserved.]

State Behavior of Preterm Infants as a Function of Development, Individual and Sex Differences

ANNELIESE F. KORNER, BYRON W. BROWN, JR., ELAINE P. READE, DAVID K. STEVENSON

Stanford University School of Medicine

STEPHEN A. FERNBACH

Kaiser-Permanente Medical Center

VALERIE A. THOM

The Oregon Health Science University,

Behavioral state was rated 22 times in the course of a standard neurobehavioral maturity assessment for preterm infants ranging from 32 weeks postconceptional age to term. The test items were presented in an invariant sequence and weekly changes were assessed in the infants' response to this identical sequence of events. Highly significant age changes were seen: Sleep decreased and awake states increased; crying increased most markedly with consequent decreases in alert inactivity and drowsiness. Even though highly significant age changes occurred in crying, alert inactivity, and drowsiness, infants tended to show highly stable individual differences in these states over time. The number of state changes and the incidence of mixed states were significantly self-consistent but did not change with development. At 34 weeks postconceptional age, significant sex differences were found in four out of six state categories. Females slept less and were awake and in the state of drowsiness more often. Males were more frequently in the state of waking activity.

development of state behavior   preterm infants
individual differences   sex differences

The importance of state in understanding the behavior and the responses of neonates has been stressed in a number of recent studies. These studies of neo-

---

We thank Sue Dimiceli for programming the computer analyses, Nancy Lane for her assistance in recruiting subjects, P. Sunshine and R.L. Ariagno from the Department of Pediatrics, Stanford University School of Medicine, and C. Landon, Department of Pediatrics of the Sequoia Hospital District for their availability to consult with us regarding the infants in this study and for their administrative help. This research was supported by Grant MH 36884 from the National Institute of Mental Health, Prevention Research Branch, Division of Clinical Research and by Grant RR-81 from the General Clinical Research Center's Program of the Division of Human Resources, National Institutes of Health.

Correspondence and requests for reprints should be sent to Anneliese F. Korner, Division of Child Psychiatry and Child Development, Stanford University School of Medicine, 600 Sand Hill Road, Palo Alto, CA 94304.

natal state have focused on a broad spectrum of issues. The organization of states has been used as an index of central nervous system (CNS) intactness (e.g., Becker & Thoman, 1981; Monod & Guidasci, 1976; Prechtl, Theorell, & Blair, 1973; Thoman, Denenberg, Sievel, Zeidner, & Becker, 1981). The ontogeny of states has been extensively studied, especially through polygraphic recordings (e.g., Dreyfus-Brisac, 1970; Parmelee & Stern, 1972; Roffwarg, Muzio, & Dement, 1966). Neonatal state has been described as both an obstacle to and a mediator of infants' responses to stimulation (Korner, 1972). Neonatal states have been described in a variety of studies as the infant's first means of communication with the external world, signaling distress or hunger or the need for sleep. The alteration of infant state has been the object of several intervention studies, particularly in the areas of soothing or making infants more alert (e.g., Korner, Ruppel, & Rho, 1982; Korner, Schneider, & Forrest, 1983; Korner & Thoman, 1970, 1972). States have been made the precondition for testing different functions of newborns in the context of a number of neurological and behavioral assessments (e.g., Brazelton, 1973; Kurtzberg et al., 1979; Prechtl & Beintema, 1964). Conversely, a few studies have systematically investigated the effects of neurobehavioral assessments on the states of neonates (e.g., Aylward, 1981; Kurtzberg et al., 1979; Michaelis, Parmelee, Stern, & Haber, 1972).

The studies by Michaelis et al. (1972) and Aylward (1981) are of special relevance for the present study because these authors addressed the issue of ontogenetic changes in the states of preterm infants in response to a standard neurological examination. In the Michaelis study, an unspecified neurological examination was administered longitudinally at three different ages to seven relatively healthy preterm infants when they were between 31 weeks postconceptional age and term. The infants' activity states were rated 37 times in the course of the standard examination. The same method was used with a comparison group of 14 infants born at term. It was found that the younger preterms were more often judged to be asleep and had lower scores throughout the examination when compared with term-aged infants. Crying occurred significantly more often with increasing age and was most prominent in the infants born at term. In the Aylward study, 58 relatively low-risk, black preterm infants ranging between 29 weeks postconceptional age and term were examined from one to seven times with a modification of the Prechtl and Beintema (1964) neurological examination, and their states were rated in this process. It was found that "both the rapidity of change from lower to higher states and the predominant highest state reached were clearly dependent on conceptional age," (p. 564) with older infants sleeping less and crying more than younger infants.

Because the studies by Michaelis et al. (1972) and Aylward (1981) both showed consistent maturational changes reflected in significant decreases in sleep and increases in crying with age, we included repeated behavioral state ratings in a new neurobehavioral maturity assessment as variables which potentially could show clear developmental changes. In that examination (Korner et al., 1987), the psychometric soundness of the test items was made a *precondi-*

tion for their inclusion into the maturity assessment. Items included were required to have a test-retest reliability on 2 consecutive days of at least .6 to reflect significant developmental changes, and to be nonredundant with all the other items included in the procedure.

In addition to assessing whether or not certain behavioral states met the above psychometric prerequisites for inclusion in the maturity assessment, we used the state data to address a variety of other questions that included: (a) In frequency of occurrence, which behavioral states increase, decrease, or remain the same as preterm infants mature to term? (b) On average, what are the weekly changes in the rate of different states occurring? (c) Can developmental spurts be identified at particular conceptional ages in the frequency of certain behavioral states? (d) Are there developmental changes in the number of mixed states seen as infants grow to term? (This question was prompted by evidence in the polygraphic literature recently summarized by Parmelee and Garbanati, [1986], to the effect that only between 34 and 38 weeks postconceptional age do the various psychophysiological parameters of states coalesce, and that until then, preterm infants do not show clearly identifiable states.) (e) Do the number of state changes during the examination show significant age changes? (f) Do infants, while changing developmentally in their state behavior, nevertheless show self-consistency (e.g., do some infants consistently sleep or cry more than others as they mature)? (g) Are there sex differences in the maturational rates of state behavior?

METHOD

Subjects

Subjects for the study were recruited between February 1983 and September 1985. To generate results that were as generalizable to as many preterm infants as possible, our sample exclusion criteria were kept to an absolute minimum. Infants were excluded if gestational age estimates by the mother's and obstetrician's dates of confinement (EDC), the Ballard (Ballard, Novak & Driver, 1979) assessment, the infant's head circumference, and/or ultrasound examination were discordant with each other by more than 2 weeks. To further reduce potential error in gestational age estimates, the two most commonly available estimates (Ballard and EDC) of the included infants were averaged. The only other infants excluded were those who had diagnoses suggesting CNS damage such as Grade III or IV intraventricular hemorrhages, congenital herpes, severe asphyxia at birth as defined by Apgars of 4 or less at 5 min, seizures, and other such compromising conditions.

The sample consisted of 175 preterm infants on whom 347 examinations were performed. With the exception of four cases who lacked complete state data, the sample overlapped with the one used in the test construction of our neurobehavioral maturity assessment (Korner et al., 1987). Sixty-three percent of the 175 infants were intubated for a mean of 6.8 days (range 1–54). Of the 175 preterm infants, 51 were born young enough to be assessed three or more times at intervals of 1 week. Seventy-five percent of these infants were intubated for a mean of 8.9 days (range 1–54). Table 1 shows additional characteristics of the sample.

Table 2 shows the number of times the infants were tested in weekly intervals.

Table 3 shows the distribution of how many assessments were made at each postconceptional age. As can be seen, the largest number of infants was avail-

TABLE 1
Characteristics of the Total Sample and of the Longitudinally Studied Subgroup

	All Infants (N=175; males: 86, females: 89)			Infants with 3 or More Examinations (n=51, males: 27, females: 24)		
	M	SD	Range	M	SD	Range
Gestational age (weeks)	32.2	2.5	23–38	30.7	2.7	23–36
Birth weight (gms)	1735.7	454.7	620–3120	1410.8	395.3	620–2200
Apgar, 1 min	6.5	2.3	1–10	5.9	2.5	1–9
Apgar, 5 min	8.1	1.2	4–10	7.7	1.3	5–10
No. of examinations	2.0	1.2	1–5	3.6	0.7	3–5
Age at first test (weeks)						
Conceptional	34.4	1.7	32–39	33.9	1.9	32–38
Chronological	2.2	2.0	1–12	3.2	2.7	1–12

Note. Data from each infant were also used in the test construction of the neurobehavioral maturity assessment.

TABLE 2
Sample by Number of Weekly Assessments

Assessments	n of Infants	% of Infants
Once	84	48.0
Twice	40	22.9
3 times	27	15.4
4 times	18	10.3
5 times	6	3.4
Total sample	175	100

TABLE 3
Number of Assessments at Each Postconceptional Age

	Postconceptional Age							
	32	33	34	35	36	37	38	39	40
Total sample	28	56	69	78	39	35	22	14	6
Longitudinal sample	17	26	34	26	23	24	15	12	6

able for testing at 34 and 35 weeks postconceptional age. Before that time, infants either were not yet born or were medically not ready to be tested. From 36 weeks postconceptional age onward, many infants became unavailable for testing as they were discharged from the hospital.

Procedure

The procedure (Korner et al., 1987), which is applicable to infants from 32 weeks conceptional age to term, is designed primarily to measure the relative maturity of functioning of preterm infants at different ages. Because preterm infants have a finite neurobehavioral repertoire, most of the test items in the assessment, of necessity, overlap with those used in many other behavioral examinations. Our procedure is relatively short and gentle and excludes aversive items such as the Moro and pinprick. On average, the assessment takes 30 min, about half of which is spent purely observing the infants without handling them. The assessment differs from other procedures primarily in the developmental rationale underlying the choice and ordering of the items, in the scoring system, and in our approach to the data analysis.

Infants became eligible for testing within a week after birth, when on room air and free of intravenous lines. Permission to include an infant in this study was first obtained from the attending physician and then by informed consent from the infant's parents. Prior to each weekly examination, it was ascertained from the attending nurse that the infant was not only medically stable but did not have any particular problems that day. When this was not the case, inquiries were made again a week later. To control for the infants' prandial condition, examinations were scheduled approximately 1 hour prior to the next feeding. To keep the infants' temperature stable, they were examined either in incubators or in Servo-Controlled Sierracin warmers.

In developing the maturity assessment, we chose to use an invariant sequence of item presentation designed to bring about the kinds of behavioral states that are most likely to elicit the best possible responses from preterm infants. By incorporating into the procedure a standard sequence of rousing, soothing, and alerting items, the opportunity to test various functions in appropriate behavioral states was maximized and the need to intervene with some infants more than others was minimized. This prevented the examination from becoming a different procedure for each infant. This strategy also provided the opportunity to systematically study the age changes in the infants' states in response to a standard sequence of identical events. In the course of the examination, behavioral states were rated 22 times over 3-s intervals each. We found empirically that a 3-s interval was long enough to determine the infants' states and short enough not to interrupt the flow of the assessment. State was rated at the beginning and end of the examination, before and after the infants were dressed or undressed, swaddled or repositioned, and between most of the test maneuvers. Only on rare occasions were several items administered in sequence without interspersing state ratings. This was done so as not to disrupt the flow of the examination. To rouse the infants who, for the most part, were asleep at the beginning of the examination, items like the scarf sign, arm and leg recoil were administered. Items like the popliteal angle, ventral suspension, head lift, and spontaneous crawling could then be administered in more awake states. All infants were then swaddled to calm those who had become irritable. The rotation test was then administered in preparation for the Brazelton (1973) orientation items because we had found earlier (Korner & Thoman, 1970, 1972) that the vestibular-proprioceptive stimulation entailed in moving infants predictably produced alertness.

Definitions of State Behavior

The state definitions used were adapted from Wolff's study (1966) and from those used in our previous studies (Korner, 1969, 1972; Korner et al., 1982).

State 1—Quiet Sleep. The infant's eyes are closed and respirations are regular; there is little or no movement except for occasional startles or jerks. The face is relaxed.

State 2—Active Sleep. The infant's eyelids are mostly closed; respirations are irregular and faster than in quiet sleep. Motor activity varies from slow limb movements, postural adjustments, to generalized body writhing. Grimaces, reflex smiles, and other facial expressions are frequent. Interspersed are recurrent rapid eye movements (REMs) that can be seen either through the eyelids or while the infant's eyes are open and have a glazed appearance.

State 3—Drowsiness. The infant is relatively inactive. The eyes are open but have a dull or glazed appearance; the eyes may open and close intermittently.

State 4—Alert Inactivity. The infant's face is relaxed, does not grimace, and the eyes are open and have a bright and shiny appearance. Body movements, if any, are slow and not vigorous.

State 5—Waking Activity. The infant engages in vigorous or diffuse motor activity, frequently involving the whole body. The eyes may be open or closed. When the eyes are open, they are not alert. Cry-face grimaces may be seen, but cry vocalizations are absent. Respirations are grossly irregular.

State 6—Crying. Characterized by crying vocalizations associated with vigorous, diffuse motor activity. The eyes may be open or closed.

State 7—Unclassifiable. The infant's state does not clearly meet the criteria of any of the above states. For example, state was rated "unclassifiable" when it was not possible to determine whether the infant was awake or asleep. Across all of the assessments, this classification was made only 1.8% of the time. Because the incidence of unclassifiable state was negligible, it was excluded from the calculations of the percentages of all the other states.

Mixed States. In preterm infants, states, even when observed over a 3-s interval, can change and reflect clearly classifiable characteristics of another, though similar, state. For example, infants may show all the characteristics of State 1, except that respirations are slightly irregular. We classified this state as 1.5. Similarly, the infant may show alertness in State 3 or 5 during part of the time. In this case, the state was classified as 3.5 or 4.5, respectively. Or, when the infant moved vigorously and fussed audibly without really crying, the state was rated as 5.5. In accordance with the findings in the polygraphic literature that suggest that states become clearly definable only between 34 and 38 weeks postconceptional age, we hypothesized that the incidence of mixed states would diminish with development. Mixed states as described above were scored only for purposes of testing this hypothesis. In all other analyses, mixed states per se were not considered. Instead, 1.5 was collapsed into State 1, 3.5 and 4.5 into State 4, and 5.5 into State 6.

Changes of State. Using the 22 consecutive state ratings made during the examination, state changes were counted whenever state differed from one rating to the next. Because state may have changed between ratings during a maneuver or an observation period, our method of counting state changes represents a systematic spot check at standard points during the examination rather than a complete account of all the state changes that might have occurred. We hypothesized that the number of state changes would be few at early ages (32–33 weeks conceptional age), that there would be an increase in state changes in infants between 34 and 36 weeks conceptional age, and that state changes would again diminish slightly after 36 weeks.

Data Analysis
Observer reliabilities based on independent, simultaneous scoring of the infants' performance by pairs of observers were obtained on an on-going basis in 30 examinations of infants who were 34 to 35 weeks conceptional age. The test-retest reliability of 30 infants was assessed on 2 consecutive days over which developmental changes were unlikely, when the infants were 34 weeks postconceptional age. Spearman rank correlations were used to calculate both the interobserver and test-retest reliabilities. In assessing both types of reliabilities, the two independent observations were entered into the analysis in random order to include any possible day-to-day inconsistencies or observer biases as one component of potential unreliability (Bartko & Carpenter, 1976).

Most of the data analyses were performed on the longitudinal data obtained from 51 infants who were tested three or more times at intervals of 1 week. In addition, two cross-sectional analyses were done: One assessed sex differences of the infants' states; the other was to test whether or not the weekly changes in states were similar when the longitudinal sample of 51 infants was augmented with infants assessed only once or twice ($N = 175$). In this cross-sectional analysis, data from only one examination (the first) from each child were included in order to prevent some infants from contributing to the data pool more than others.

Next, to determine if there were significant changes with development, the percentage of time in each state was regressed on conceptional age, first using the first observations ($N = 175$) and second using only those infants with three or more observations ($n = 51$). Each infant was allowed its own intercept, but a common slope was fit for measuring the change in percent per week. The slope was tested against zero using a Student t-test.

To test the infants' self-consistency in states over time, three regression models of increasing specificity were fitted to the data. The first model allowed no slope or developmental trend. The second model allowed a common trend or slope for all infants. The third model allowed each infant his or her own slope over the period of observations. The measure of fit for each model was the multiple correlations coefficient, adjusted for the number of parameters in the model (Armitage, 1971).

Sex differences in the state variables were assessed, based on the first observation of each infant. Conceptional age was used as a covariate.

RESULTS

The infants' states were divided into three broad categories: sleep states (States 1 and 2); drowsiness, a transitional state between sleeping and waking (State 3); and awake states (States 4, 5, and 6). Within sleep, the proportions of quiet and active sleep were considered separately. While awake, the proportions of alert inactivity, waking activity, and crying were separately analyzed. Table 4 shows the interobserver and test-retest reliabilities assessed on 30 subjects each for the infants' states, the number of state changes, and mixed states.

As can be seen from Table 4, there was no difficulty in two independent observers agreeing on the state ratings: The interobserver reliabilities all were highly significant, and the correlations were, for all but one of the states, above .9. Interobserver reliabilities for state changes and for mixed states were .76 and .78, respectively.

Of the 30 infants on whom test-retest reliability was assessed on 2 consecutive days, 14 belonged to the longitudinally tested group and 16 were from the group tested only once or twice. Highly significant reliability was found in the percent of sleep and wake states, and in crying. The proportions of States 4 and 5 while awake were somewhat predictable from one day to the next, but the test-retest correlations were not significantly different from zero. Because quiet sleep hardly ever occurred after the infants were touched, it was collapsed into percent of time in sleep for all subsequent analyses. The number of state changes and mixed states seen from one day to the next was not predictable.

TABLE 4
Measures of Reliability of State Ratings

State Variables	Interobserver Reliability n=30 rho	Test–Retest Reliability n=30[a] rho
% Asleep	.96***	.68***
% Quiet sleep	.91***	−.03
% Awake	.92***	.51*
% Drowsiness	.68***	.21
% Alert inactivity	.97***	.31
% Waking activity	.95***	.32
% Crying	.98***	.62*
N of state changes	.76***	−.04
N of mixed states	.78***	.24

[a] n for Quiet Sleep = 28.
* $p < .005$. ** $p < .0005$. *** $p < .0001$.

Table 5 shows which of the state variables changed significantly with age, as well as the direction and average change in percentage per week as reflected in both the longitudinal and cross-sectional analyses.

As can be seen, the percent of time in sleep, awake, in drowsiness, in alert inactivity, and crying while awake changed significantly with age. Sleep decreased significantly with age, and consequently awake states increased. The most dramatic increases occurred in crying coupled with significant, though small, decreases in drowsiness and in alert inactivity. It is noteworthy that even though the results from the longitudinal and cross-sectional samples were very similar, they were, as is generally the case, much more clearly expressed in the

TABLE 5
Developmental Changes per Week

State Variables	Infants with 3 or More Examinations		All Infants	
	N	M % Change[a]	N	M % Change[b]
Sleep	51	−3.94*	175	−0.98
Awake	51	5.32**	175	1.80
Drowsiness	51	−1.19**	175	−0.78*
Alert inactivity	49	−0.05***	171	−0.03*
Waking activity	49	−0.02	171	−0.01
Crying	49	7.76****	171	3.64****
N of state changes	50	0.18	175	−0.01
N of mixed states	51	0.86	175	−0.32

[a] Change estimated by multiple regression with individual intercepts and common slope: significance by t-test for the common slope.
[b] Change estimated by regressing state observations on postconceptional age, using only the first observation on each subject; significance by t-test for resulting slope.
* $p < .02$. ** $p < .002$. *** $p < .0005$. **** $p < .0001$.

longitudinal data. Furthermore, Table 5 shows that the number of state changes during examination did not change with development. Additionally, the infants' tendency to show mixtures of states did not diminish significantly with age, as had been anticipated.

We next plotted graphs of the weekly state changes of the infants with three or more examinations. Other than underscoring the developmental changes of states displayed in Table 5, we could not detect any meaningful patterns of developmental spurts in the infants' states at any particular age.

Table 6 shows the infants' self-consistency in the state variables over 3 or more weeks.

Table 6 shows the results of fitting the three linear models to the data, the first allowing only for individual differences in means, the second adding a common developmental slope, and the third allowing each infant's own slope in the states. It is clear that the individual variation in means alone (Model 1) explained most of the individual differences. However, there was some additional explanatory power in adding a common developmental rate in Model 2 for most of the states that showed significant developmental trends (percent awake, drowsy, alert inactive, and crying). Except for the percent of time in the active awake state, there was little or no increment in explanatory power through the use of individual trend lines (Model 3). Significant self-consistency was also expressed in how much the infants tended to change states and to show mixture of states. Rather than being developmental, as had been anticipated, these aspects of infant behavior tended to express consistent individual differences of the infants.

TABLE 6
Self-Consistency of Infants

State Variables	N	Exams	Model 1 r^a	Model 2 r^a	Model 3 r^a
% Asleep	51	184	.10	.20	.00
% Awake	51	184	.22	.33*	.20
% Drowsiness	51	184	.50***	.55****	.51*
% Alert inactivity	49	181	.54****	.60****	.66***
% Waking activity	49	181	.22	.22	.48*
% Crying	49	181	.62****	.73****	.76***
N of state changes	50	183	.39**	.39**	.49*
N of mixed states	50	183	.33*	.35*	.44*

^{a} Correlations are multiple correlation coefficients, i.e., square roots of ratios of regression sum squares to total sum squares, adjusted for degrees of freedom. For Model 3, the observations for each infant are fit by a separate straight line, and the sums of squares for regression and total are added across infants and adjusted for degrees of freedom to yield the correlation coefficient. P values are computed by F tests for each of the linear models. The F statistics have degrees of freedom in the numerator equal to the number of infants, number of infants plus one, and twice the number of infants, respectively. In the denominators, the degrees of freedom are equal to the number of observations minus the degrees of freedom in the numerators, for each model.

 $\cdot$ $p<.10.$ * $p<.05.$ ** $p<.02.$ *** $p<.001.$ **** $p<.0001.$

Using the data from the first examination of each infant in the total sample, Table 7 shows the means corrected for postconceptional age of males and females for each state and the results of the F tests with conceptional age used as a covariate. The actual mean conceptional ages of males and females at the time of the first examination did not differ significantly (*males:* 34.34 ± 1.78; *females:* 34.45 ± 1.73; $t = 0.42$, n.s.), nor did their gestational ages and health status. At the time of study, none of the male infants had been circumcised.

Significant sex differences were found in four out of six state categories. Females slept less and therefore were awake more during the examinations. Because, in the sample as a whole, sleep during the examination decreased and wakefulness increased with development, the females' tendency to sleep less and to be awake more may reflect earlier maturation of the females in these characteristics. Girls were also significantly more often in the state of drowsiness. Males, on the other hand, were significantly more often in the state of waking activity. No significant sex differences were found in the number of state changes or the number of mixed states.

We next tested whether the sex differences held up when the infants were tested the second and third times. When tested the second time, the females were on average 34.8 and the males 35 weeks postconceptional age ($t = 0.65$, n.s.). On the third examination, the females were on average 35.1 and the males, 36.4 weeks postconceptional age ($t = 1.18$, n.s.). On the whole, the means corrected for postconceptional age followed a fairly similar pattern of sex differences to those displayed in Table 7, but with the smaller sample sizes, all but one of these differences were not statistically significant. On the second examination, females continued to sleep less (24.0% vs. 30.2%) and were awake more (70.2% vs. 64.4%). By the third examination, females continued to sleep a little less (23.1% vs. 24.0%), but males showed a slightly higher percentage of awake time (70.9% vs. 74.0%). Females continued to be in the state of drowsiness more often in the second and third examinations (5.8% vs. 5.4%, 6.0% vs.

TABLE 7
Sex Differences (First Examinations)

State Variables	Females M^a	(n)	Males M^a	(n)	Sex Effect F^a
% Asleep	22.7	(88)	33.3	(86)	7.11***
% Awake	69.9	(88)	61.6	(86)	4.26*
% Drowsiness	7.4	(88)	5.1	(86)	4.78*
% Alert inactivity	49.3	(87)	42.7	(83)	2.69
% Waking activity	32.9	(87)	42.6	(83)	6.53**
% Crying while awake	17.7	(87)	14.7	(83)	1.02
N of state changes	8.4	(88)	8.1	(86)	0.31
N of mixed states	16.1	(88)	13.6	(86)	2.66

^{a} The means were corrected for postconceptional age. Sex effects were tested with postconceptional age as a covariate.
* $p < .05$. ** $p < .02$. *** $p < .01$.

1.96%, $p < .02$, respectively). Females also continued to have higher percentages of alert inactivity at each examination (52.1 vs. 46.2, 50.5 vs. 40.4, respectively). Males continued to have higher percentages of waking activity (31.7 vs. 34.1, 27.3 vs. 31.5, respectively), but the difference was not as great as on the first examination. Males, who had cried less on the first assessment, cried slightly more than the females on the second and third examinations (16.2% vs. 19.6%, 22.3% vs. 28.1%, respectively). This change might indicate that the males made up for the reduced difference in waking activity on the second and third assessments by expressing their high arousal in crying more.

DISCUSSION

In this study, the ontogeny of behavioral states in response to a standard neurobehavioral maturity assessment (Korner et al., 1987) was investigated in preterm infants. The object of most prior studies was to document the ontogeny of states in the unstimulated preterm infant (Dreyfus-Brisac, 1970; Parmelee & Stern, 1972; Roffwarg et al., 1966). Only two prior studies (Aylward, 1981, and Michaelis et al., 1972) have explored the ontogeny of elicited states in preterm infants in response to external stimulation. Clearly, both types of ontogenetic studies are of importance in their own right in that they address different aspects of infant development. Naturalistic observations or polygraphic recordings of spontaneously occurring sleep and wake states have primarily been used to study the maturation of sleep states and to assess the intactness of developing brain mechanisms. Studies like the one reported here document the maturational changes of the preterm infants' growing capacity for dealing with the environment and the stimulation attending the external world, including the experience of being handled in a variety of ways. The ontogenetic changes in both spontaneous and elicited states very likely express different aspects of one developmental process, namely that of the gradually increasing maturity of CNS functioning.

This study demonstrated highly significant developmental changes in the infant's response to an identical sequence of events: Awake states increased markedly as sleep decreased. Crying increased most dramatically over weeks. It is noteworthy that these findings generalize across three studies, even though the methods of examining the preterm infants differed in each (Aylward, 1981; Michaelis et al., 1972; and the present study). In line with our goal to include measures of infant states as part of our neurobehavioral maturity assessment, we found that the significant decreases in sleep and the significant increases in crying met all the psychometric inclusion criteria of the assessment: The test-retest reliability of the measures exceeded .6 (rho of sleep was .68, of crying, .62). Both measures were developmentally valid in that they changed significantly with age. They were not redundant with any of the other measures within the assessment. Even the measures of time asleep and time crying were not the opposite of each other ($rho = -.24$).

Although the states of the infants as a group changed significantly with age, the results showed, nevertheless, significant stability of individual differences over time. In particular, infants who responded to the examination by being irritable, alert, or in the state of drowsiness, tended to respond in this way over 3 or more weeks. By contrast, the general tendency to be asleep or awake during the assessment was not stable over time.

Contrary to our initial hypothesis, neither the number of state changes nor the incidence of mixed states showed significant developmental changes over time. In line with the findings reported in the polygraphic literature (see the recent review by Parmelee & Garbanati, 1986), we anticipated that the admixture of features of different states would diminish and that the specific parameters of different states would become more mutually exclusive with age. Perhaps our failure to find such ontogenetic changes was a function of the brevity of our state ratings, and that such changes might have become more apparent had our observations of the infants' states been more prolonged. We did find, however, significant stability in the infants' tendency to change states and to show mixed states. These tendencies thus appear to express moderately stable individual differences.

Using the first assessment of the total sample of infants and correcting for postconceptional age, we found significant sex differences in four out of six state categories. Three of these differences (percent asleep and awake and percent waking activity) are compatible with developmental theory that suggests that females mature earlier than males. Although our results showed that sleep decreased and awake states increased with development, males, who were tested on average at the same conceptional age as females, slept significantly more and were awake significantly less than females. Males also showed significantly more waking activity than females. Even though waking activity did not change significantly with development during the postconceptional ages our subjects were assessed, waking activity has been described as an immature and undifferentiated state in studies by Becker and Thoman (1982). The means of males and females on the second and third examinations generally supported the above findings, but, with the reduced sample sizes, all except one of the sex differences were not statistically significant.

One may well ask if the sex differences observed were a function of the preterm boys being more impervious to external stimulation than preterm girls. If that were the case, this difference might be based on differences in disposition or on different maturational rates, or both.

REFERENCES

Armitage, P. (1971). *Statistical methods in medical research*. New York: Halsted Press.

Aylward, G.P. (1981). The developmental course of behavioral states in preterm infants: A descriptive study. *Child Development, 52,* 564–568.

Ballard, J.L., Novak, K.K., & Driver, M. (1979). A simplified score for assessment of fetal maturation of newly born infants. *The Journal of Pediatrics, 95,* 769–774.

Bartko, J.J., & Carpenter, W.T. (1976). On the methods and theory of reliability. *The Journal of Nervous and Mental Disease, 163*, 307-317.

Becker, P.T., & Thoman, E.B. (1981). Intense rapid eye movements during active sleep: An index of neurobehavioral instability. *Developmental Psychobiology, 15*, 203-210.

Becker, P.T., & Thoman, E.B. (1982). Waking activity: The neglected state of infancy. *Developmental Brain Research, 4*, 395-400.

Brazelton, T.B. (1973). Neonatal behavioral assessment scale. *Clinics in Developmental Medicine. No. 50.* Philadelphia: J.B. Lippincott.

Dreyfus-Brisac, C. (1970). Ontogenesis of sleep in human prematures after 32 weeks of conceptional age. *Developmental Psychobiology, 3*, 91-121.

Korner, A.F. (1969). Neonatal startles, smiles, erections and reflex sucks as related to state, sex and individuality. *Child Development, 40*, 1039-1053.

Korner, A.F. (1972). State as variable, as obstacle, and as mediator of stimulation in infant research. *Merrill-Palmer Quarterly, 18*, 77-94.

Korner, A.F., Kraemer, H.C., Reade, E.P., Forrest, T., Dimiceli, S., & Thom, V. (1987). A methodological approach to developing an assessment procedure for testing the neurobehavioral maturity of preterm infants. *Child Development, 58*, 1479-1487.

Korner, A.F., Ruppel, E.M., & Rho, J.M. (1982). Effects of waterbeds on the sleep and motility of theophylline-treated preterm infants. *Pediatrics, 70*, 864-869.

Korner, A.F., Schneider, P., & Forrest, T. (1983). Effects of vestibular-proprioceptive stimulation on the neurobehavioral development of preterm infants: A pilot study. *Neuropediatrics, 14*, 170-175.

Korner, A.F., & Thoman, E.B. (1970). Visual alertness in neonates as evoked by maternal care. *Journal of Experimental Child Psychology, 10*, 67-78.

Korner, A.F., & Thoman, E.B. (1972). Relative efficacy of contact and vestibular stimulation in soothing neonates. *Child Development, 43*, 443-453.

Kurtzberg, D., Vaughan, H.G., Jr., Daum, C., Grellong, B.A., Albin, S., & Rotkin, L. (1979). Neurobehavioral performance of low-birth weight infants at 40 weeks conceptional age: Comparison with normal full-term infants. *Developmental Medicine and Child Neurology, 21*, 590-607.

Michaelis, R., Parmelee, A.H., Stern, E., & Haber, A. (1972). Activity states in premature and term infants. *Developmental Psychobiology, 6*, 209-215.

Monod, N., & Guidasci, L. (1976). Sleep and brain malformation in the neonatal period. *Neuropediatrie, 7*, 229-249.

Parmelee, A.H., Jr. & Garbanati, J. (1986, July). *Clinical neurobehavioral aspects of state organization in newborn infants.* Paper presented at the Fifth International Symposium on Developmental Disabilities, Osaka, Japan.

Parmelee, A.H., Jr., & Stern, E. (1972). Development of states in infants. In C.D. Clemente, D.P. Purpura, & F.E. Mayer (Eds.), *Sleep and the maturing nervous system.* New York: Academic.

Prechtl, H.F.R., & Beintema, D. (1964). The neurological examination of the full-term newborn infants. *Clinics in developmental medicine, No. 12.* London: William Heinemann Medical Books Ltd.

Prechtl, H.F., Theorell, K., & Blair, A.W. (1973). Behavioral state cycles in abnormal infants. *Developmental Medicine and Child Neurology, 15*, 606-615.

Roffwarg, H.P., Muzio, J.N., & Dement, W.C. (1966). Ontogenetic development of human sleep-dream cycle. *Science, 152*, 604-619.

Thoman, E.B., Denenberg, V.H., Sievel, J., Zeidner, L.P., & Becker, P. (1981). State organization in neonates: Developmental inconsistency indicates risk for developmental dysfunction. *Neuropediatrie, 12*, 45-54.

Wolff, P.H. (1966). The causes, controls and organization of behavior in the neonate. *Psychological Issues, 5*(1) Monograph 17. New York: International University Press.

14 July 1987; Revised 15 December 1987 ∎

Obstetric Drugs and Infant Behavior: A Reevaluation[1]

Helena C. Kraemer, Anneliese Korner, Thomas Anders, Carol Nagy Jacklin, and Sue Dimiceli
Stanford University

Received June 14, 1984; revised August 1, 1984

Poorly designed and analyzed studies ascribing effects of obstetric drugs on infant behavior may not only have misrepresented facts but may also have rendered well-designed and analyzed studies difficult to execute.

KEY WORDS: obstetric drugs; infant behavior.

Strong claims have been made about adverse effects of obstetric drugs on the behavioral development of children (Brackbill, 1979). In some cases these claims have received wide coverage in the media. Yet there is growing skepticism about these claims (Kolata, 1979). The present paper focuses on two issues underlying skepticism: (a) problems of the confounding of obstetric drugs and various factors and (b) faulty statistical analysis.

---

[1] The studies reported were supported by the William T. Grant Foundation, the Distribution Fund, the National Institute of Child Health and Development (HD 09814-08), the Ford Foundation, the Spencer Foundation, and Grant RR-81 from the General Clinical Research Center's Program of the Division of Human Resources, and the National Institutes of Health. The authors thank E. Maccoby for her careful reading of the paper.

THE PROBLEM OF CONFOUNDING

Obstetric drug decisions are determined by the difficulty of individual labors. Therefore, drug use should be associated with any factor causative of, associated with, or resultant from, difficult labors: the health status or age of mother, parity, length of labor, level of anxiety, pain or tolerance for pain, and possibly socioeconomic status, home environments, etc. Any such factor related to infant behavior function and to use of obstetric drugs induces a correlation between obstetric drug use and infant behavior function. To interpret such a correlation as indicating a causal relationship is an error (Kenny, 1979). In short, infants found to be behaviorally disadvantaged in the group exposed to higher levels of obstetric drugs might have been so disadvantaged whether or not drugs had been used.

In rejoinder to such criticisms (Brackbill, 1979) points out that parity and length of labor have not been found to be significantly related to behavioral development. Thus, it is argued, obstetric drug decisions behave like random decisions with respect to behavioral parameters. Clearly if such decisions were indeed random, no correlations between parity, length of labor, and behavioral outcome would be found. However there are a remarkable number of ways that correlations may be found to be low when decisions are far from random, e.g., (a) The quality of measurement is poor (e.g., length of labor determined from hospital records). (b) Statistical tests are invalid (e.g., the product-moment correlation coefficient used for nonlinear relationships). (c) Important interactive effects are ignored (such as that between parity and length of labor). (d) Important cohort effects are ignored. (e) Sample sizes are too small to have sufficient power to detect associations.

Any or all of these may account for nonsignificant correlations even if the association between obstetric drug decisions and parity or length of labor were quite strong. Therefore, it is only an assumption, and a meager one at that, that obstetric drug decisions behave like random decisions.

In demonstration of this point, Table I presents the results of a study (Jacklin & Maccoby, 1982) conducted in two hospitals. There are significant differences in use of analgesics between hospitals. In each hospital, a firstborn is more likely to be exposed to analgesia than one later born. Within each hospital and within each parity group, those with longer labor (over 8 hr) are more likely to be exposed to analgesia. This same relationship seems to hold with anesthesia at Stanford but not at El Camino. Similar results have been reported previously (Kraemer, Korner, & Thoman, 1972). The indications are clear that the results of any study that does not control (at least) for parity, length of labor, and locale should not be considered valid evidence for or against adverse effects of obstetric drug use.

Table I. Parity,[a] Length of Labor, Hospital, and Their Effect on Use of Analgesia, Anesthesia

	% Use of analgesia						% Use of spinal/caudal anesthesia						
	Stanford (n = 82)			El Camino (n = 205)				Stanford (n = 82)			El Camino (n = 205)		
Labor (hr)	F %	L %	Total %	F %	L %	Total %	Labor (hr)	F %	L %	Total %	F %	L %	Total %
0–4	—	11	23	60	43	46	0–4	—	44	38	60	61	61
4+–8	55	18	38	91	50	68	4–8	50	59	54	65	61	62
8+–12	62	50	58	89	80	86	8–12	69	100	79	48	80	57
12+	88	—	64	75	—	75	12+	75	—	64	58	—	58
Total	62	20	44	83	49	63		57	60	58	58	62	60

[a] F, firstborn; L, later born.

Controlled Versus Noncontrolled Studies

The optimal method of control for such confounding factors in a drug evaluation is a randomized double-blind, controlled clinical trial. Only one such experimental study has been reported (Kron, Stein, & Goodard, 1966) and that study evaluated a drug (a standard dosage of 200 mg of secobarbital sodium 30 min before delivery) used in a way it is seldom used in obstetric drug practice (Kraemer et al., 1972). Currently, the proliferation of poorly controlled studies purporting to demonstrate adverse effects of obstetrical medication have made it nearly impossible to execute further such trials. Those who have reported the results of uncontrolled studies argue in their defense, that, at the very least, their results should motivate execution of more definitive studies. Yet they simultaneously argue (Brackbill, 1979) that "cumulative indications found in their studies make it ethically impossible to conduct randomized trials." Thus the use of results of studies utilizing poor scientific methodology perpetuate what may be invalid scientific conclusions.

An alternative acceptable method of control for such factors is a process of creating subgroups matched post hoc on these factors and assessing the effect of drugs within matched subgroups.

This paper reports the results of attempting such an analysis. The procedure was followed in three independent infant studies, one on strength and tactile sensitivity (Jacklin, Snow, & Maccoby, 1981), one on activity and irritability (Korner, Hutchinson, Koperski, Kraemer, & Schneider, 1981), and one on sleep (Anders, Keener, Bowe, & Shoaff, 1982).

In the reanalysis of each study, the following technique was used: An infant subject was randomly selected. If the infant was exposed to any analgesia, all infants included in the same study of the same sex, born in the same hospital, during the same year, and with lengths of labor within 1.5 hr of that of the target infant but who were *not* exposed to analgesia were identified. From this group, one infant was randomly selected as the match to the analgesia infant. Both target and match were withdrawn from the group. If no match was found, the target was dropped from the comparison. The process was repeated until all infants were either matched or dropped. A matched-pairs *t* test was used to compare varous behaviors observed in that study between analgesia-exposed infants and their matches. (The analogous process was used to effect the Anesthesia Contrast.)

Using this procedure, it was found that 50-70% of subjects could not be matched. In the case of the Anders et al. (1981) study, when the subjects for whom length of labor could not be determined from the hospital record and the subjects for whom the matches could not be found were discarded, there were not enough matched subjects for a valid statistical test. The results of the other two studies appear in Table II.

Table II. Uncontrolled and Controlled Contrasts Relating to the Effect of Analgesia, Anesthesia on Newborn Behavior

	Analgesia contrast				Anesthesia contrast			
	Uncontrolled		Post hoc sample matched[a] loss %		Uncontrolled		Post hoc sample matched[b] loss %	
	n	t^c	n	t^c	n	t^c	n	t^c
Jacklin et al. (1981)								
Tactile								
Insensitivity	196	−0.50	68	0.14	65	163	0.95	48	1.87	71
Prone head raise	202	1.02	68	−0.07	66	167	−0.12	52	0.28	69
Grip strength	188	0.16	62	−0.54	67	155	1.17	42	0.21	73
Korner (1981)								
Cry rate	61	0.83	28	−0.55	54	71	0.14	32	1.12	55
Noncry activity	69	0.10	34	−0.25	51	79	−0.72	42	0.44	47
Noncry style	65	1.16	32	−0.40	51	76	0.28	38	0.52	50
Anders (1982)								
Longest sustained sleep	30	1.09	—	—	—	30	0.28	—	—	—
Percentage quiet sleep	30	0.19	—	—	—	30	1.23	—	—	—
Out-of-crib frequency	30	2.02[a]	—	—	—	30	1.22	—	—	—
Longest quiet sleep	30	0.39	—	—	—	30	0.63	—	—	—

[a] $p = .053$.
[b] Matched by locale, sex, length of labor.
[c] A positive sign indicates a higher mean score for the Analgesia (Anesthesia) group than for the contrast group.

Two results are noteworthy. First, there is no evidence of any drug effect. Second, matching procedures are extremely difficult to implement under retrospective circumstances, since any subgroup that does not contain a reasonable number of patients both for whom drugs were used and for whom drugs were not used tends to be excluded. Since the impact of the noncontrolled studies has been to decrease drug use and to limit use predominantly to patients with long labors, patients with very short labors tend to be excluded (since few are exposed to drugs) and patients with long labors, particularly nulligravida, tend to be excluded, since few are drug-free. One is left with a limited and unrepresentative sample. Once again, the impact of uncontrolled studies reported widely by the media, as some here have been, is to hamper the conduct of better designed studies.

Finally, yet another method to control the confounding factors is by mathematical analytic procedures, e.g., Multiple Regression or Analysis of Covariance (Cohen & Cohen, 1975). The problems noted above in connection with matching procedures, however, cause multicollinearity problems that compromise the statistical validity of these procedures as well. One cannot "correct" for the effects of length or difficulty of labors if those exposed to drugs are primarily those with long or difficult labors, and those not so exposed, primarily those with short, uncomplicated labors. Thus, although these procedures might have once been acceptable, they are becoming less feasible as the impact of uncontrolled studies is increasingly evident.

Two such studies were done in the past and the conclusions of both indicate that the impact of drug use is either not significant or is trivial in comparison to the effects of parity and length of labor (Kraemer et al., 1972; Woodson & da Costa-Woodson, 1980). In short, the results of these studies are consistent with the present results in Table II.

FAULTY STATISTICAL ANALYSIS

The second area of criticism of these studies has been the statistical validity of the conclusions. If statistical significance had not been found in these studies, the issues discussed above would have been moot, since nonsignificant findings are generally not published in scientific journals. (One wonders: How many studies have found no adverse effect of obstetric drugs and have not been reported?) One must further be concerned with the question of whether the significant results reported have been mostly those that have used inadequate statistical methods and have reported false positive findings.

For example, Table II reports the two-sample t test used, as it frequently is, in uncontrolled studies. Here there appears to be a significant difference in out-of-crib frequency (t_{28} = 2.02, $p \sim .05$). This t test is based on the assumption of equal variances. In the analgesia-free group (n = 23), the mean frequency was 2.7 ± 1.4; in the analgesia-exposed group (n = 7), 4.4 ± 3.3. When, as here, a much larger variance appears in the much smaller group, it is known (Scheffé, 1959) that the usual t-test calculations tend to exaggerate the significance of the result. When a more appropriate test is used (a Mann-Whitney test), not only is the test result not statistically significant but it does not even approach significance ($p \sim .3$).

Arguments defending use of such statistical tests as t tests or tests of the product-moment correlation coefficients in circumstances when the assumptions on which the tests are based are violated are based on claims of a certain robustness, i.e., on the belief that the underlying assumption of normality does not matter too much. In fact this claim is correct but avoids the issues, since it is not the normality assumption that causes problems but such assumptions as those of linearity and equal variances (Scheffé, 1959; Kraemer, 1980).

Added to such concerns regarding the accuracy of calculations of significance levels is one related to the fact that each individual study tests not one but a number of behavioral parameters and, in some cases, assesses the same behavioral response separately in different subsamples. With so many tests, 5% or more might be significant by chance alone. Even if the claims of statistical significance on any *one* parameter were valid, many of the reported statistically significant results may be false positive findings (Miller, 1966).

But then, does not the fact that all reported effects are adverse indicate an overall adverse effect, even if not all were "really" significant (Brackbill, 1979)? The difficulty is that what is or is not termed adverse is frequently arbitrary. If drug-exposed infants cry more frequently, this may be interpreted as increased irritability; if less frequently, as increased lethargy. Any difference can be viewed as adverse. Unless there are standards, independent of the study, defining good and bad behavioral outcomes, the word "adverse" has no specific meaning.

CONCLUSION

Restricting unnecessary drug use is clearly desirable. If it were certain that the impact of uncontrolled study results were to restrict only the use of *unnecessary* drugs, whether or not the conclusions were valid substantively or statistically would be of scientific interest only. One would not question the value of their impact on medical practice or policy decisions. Unfortunately, the impact of such studies may have been to restrict *appropri-*

ate drug use and thus to prolong unnecessary pain and discomfort for mothers; to cause distress or guilt in mothers of behaviorally disadvantaged children who elected or allowed drug use; to compromise optimal clinical decision making for labor management by obstetricians and anesthesiologists.

What is therefore of great concern is that the results of poorly designed and analyzed studies not be allowed to preclude or compromise the conduct of carefully controlled studies necessary to establish the limits of safe use of obstetric drugs with respect to infant development.

What then is known of the effects of obstetric drugs from past studies that should form the basis of future studies?

1. From animal studies and a single, randomized clinical trial (Kron et al., 1966), potent drugs administered near the time of birth do have the potential of affecting infant behavior. It is not known which drugs, in which amounts, administered within which time limits, or to which patients, affect which aspects of infant behavior, or for how long. It is important that the possibility of adverse drug effects not be discounted just because the studies to-date documenting the possibility are not convincing.

2. Uncontrolled studies suggest a correlation between factors associated with use of obstetric drugs and behavioral development. To what extent it is the associated factors and not obstetric drug use itself that are implicated is not known. It should be remembered that such associated factors include potent influences such as birth order, maternal age and health, socioeconomic status, length and difficulty of labor, condition and position of the infant *in utero*, etc.

3. The few existing controlled nonexperimental studies have not demonstrated any statistically or clinically significant association between drug use and infant behavior. They include earlier (Kraemer, 1972; Woodson & da Costa-Woodson, 1980) and the three new studies reported here. Since there have been few of these studies, these must not be interpreted as demonstrating the safety of obstetric drug use.

In summary, we suggest that despite the large number of studies relating obstetric drugs to adverse effects on infant behavior, we yet know very little. What little information we have from the few controlled studies tends not to support the contention of adverse effects. Furthermore, very little will ever be known unless the poorly designed, controlled, or analyzed studies of the past are not used to preclude the conduct of better studies in the future.

Members of Use of Human Subjects Committees need be apprised of the situation, for, under the circumstances, randomized controlled trials are not unethical. Editors and reviewers dealing with submitted papers in this area must be very critical of studies at this stage and more willing to give positive consideration to well-designed and executed studies demonstrating no association between obstetric drugs and behavioral outcome. Researchers in this area should be encouraged to pursue this question by executing well-designed and well-controlled studies to resolve the important issues involved.

REFERENCES

Anders, T., Keener, M., Bowe, T., & Shoaff, B. (1982). A longtudinal study of nighttime sleep-wake patterns in infants from birth through one year. In J. Call & E. Galensen (Eds.), *Frontiers in infant psychiatry* (pp. 152-170). New York: Basic Books.

Brackbill, Y. (1979). Obstetrical medication and infant behavior. In J. D. Osofsky (Ed.), *Handbook in infant development* (pp. 76-125). New York: Wiley.

Cohen, J., & Cohen, P. (1975). *Applied multiple regression/correlation analysis for the behavioral sciences*. Hillsdale, NJ: Lawrence Erlbaum.

Jacklin, C. N., & Maccoby, E. E. (1982). Length of labor and sex of offspring. *Journal of Pediatric Psychology, 7,* 4, 355-360.

Jacklin, C. N., Snow, M. E., & Maccoby, E. E. (1981). Tactile sensitivity and muscle strength in newborn boys and girls. *Infant Behavior and Development, 4,* 261-268.

Kenny, D. A. (1979). *Correlation and causality*. New York: Wiley.

Kolata, J. B. (1979). Scientists attack report that obstetrical medications endanger children. *Science, 204,* 391-392.

Korner, A. F., Hutchinson, C. A., Koperski, J. A., Kraemer, H. C., & Schneider, P. A. (1981). Stability of individual differences of neonatal motor and crying patterns. *Child Development, 52,* 83-90.

Kraemer, H. C. (1980). Robustness of the distribution theory of the product moment correlation coefficient. *Journal of Educational Statistics, 2*(5), 115-128.

Kraemer, H. C., Korner, A. F., & Thoman, E. B. (1972). Methodological considerations in evaluating the influence of drugs used during labor and delivery on the behavior of the newborn. *Developmental Psychology, 6*(1), 128-134.

Kron, R. E., Stein, M., & Goodard, K. E. (1966). Newborn sucking behavior affected by obstetric sedation. *Pediatrics, 37,* 1012-1016.

Miller, R. B., Jr. (1966). *Simultaneous statistical inference*. New York: McGraw-Hill.

Scheffé, H. (1959). *The analysis of variance* (Chap. 10). New York: Wiley.

Woodson, R. H., & da Costa-Woodson, E. M. (1980). Covariates of analgesia in a clinical sample and their effect on the relations between analgesia and infant behavior. *Infant Behavior and Development, 3,* 205-213.

[15]

Differential Mortality by Sex in Fetal and Neonatal Deaths

Abstract. *Vital statistics data for the United States from 1922 to 1936 and from 1950 to 1972 were used to analyze fetal and early neonatal mortality. This analysis corroborates the previously established pattern of the sex ratio of fetal deaths — highest from months 3 to 5, lower from months 6 to 7 or 8, and increasing at term. It also indicates a postponement of late fetal deaths into the early infant period. Whereas earlier research reports have described the pattern of the sex ratio of fetal deaths, this report repeats this analysis for a recent national data base. This line of analysis is extended by using the patterns observed in the data to produce an empirical estimate of the primary sex ratio. For 1950 to 1972, this ratio (male to female) is conservatively estimated to be 120:100.*

A sex ratio at conception (primary sex ratio) in excess of the sex ratio at birth (secondary sex ratio) is a necessary condition for differential mortality by sex in utero. Although discussions of the primary sex ratio focus on the existence and extent of sex differential mortality in utero (*1*, *2*), there is no clear-cut consensus on the primary sex ratio. In fact, estimates of the primary sex ratio (males:females) range from 110:100 to 170:100. The variability in these estimates derives in part from the different data under consideration (*3*) and in part from the subjective judgments that result from each reseacher's examination of the data on hand. Despite the discrepancies among these studies, one overriding similarity emerges in the pattern of the sex ratio of fetal deaths by month of gestation; the sex ratio of fetal deaths is reported to be highest between months 3 and 5, lower between months 6 and 7 or 8, and increases at term (*4*).

Cavalli-Sforza and Bodmer (*2*) have contended that vital statistics provide the best data source for analyzing sex-differential mortality in utero, as vital statistics encompass enough cases to assure the significance of the relatively small differences in sex ratio. Thus, I used annual data for the sex ratio of fetal deaths by month of gestation for the United States from 1922 to 1936 and from 1950 to 1972 (*5*) in conjunction with data on early infant mortality (*6*).

The sex ratios were calculated as the ratio of males to females; after a preliminary graphic analysis of the general trend, least-squares and polynomial regression techniques were used to fit second-degree equations to the fetal death data. This analysis was performed on the arithmetic means of the sex ratio of fetal deaths by months (*7*) (Fig. 1).

Analysis of fetal death data for 1922 to 1936 reveals a nonlinear pattern that reflects the patterns reported in earlier studies (*3*). This pattern can be described by the second-order equation (*8*).

$$SR = 7.5637 - 1.7470M + 0.1155M^2 + e$$
$$(0.3370)\quad(0.0256)$$

$$R^2 = .8965$$

where SR = sex ratio of fetal deaths, M = month of gestation, and e = the least-squares residual; the values in parentheses are the standard errors.

The 1950 to 1972 fetal death data are limited to data from months 5 to 10; these data can be described by the second-order equation (*9*).

$$SR = 2.1958 - 0.2295M + 0.0119M^2 + e$$
$$(0.1176)\quad(0.0076)$$

$$R^2 = .9116$$

The nonlinear pattern of the 1950 to 1972 data differs from the pattern of the earlier data. The difference may be attributed to several factors. (i) The pattern observed from months 5 to 7 in the 1922 to 1936 data is present at a lower level in the 1950 to 1972 data. (ii) Available data from spontaneous and induced abortions in the first trimester of gestation support the notion that sex ratios of early fetal loss are higher than subsequent fetal death sex ratios (*10*). (iii) The largest difference occurs among fetal

Table 1. Male stillbirth mortality loss proportions.

	$y_1 = 0.5652$ (130 : 100)				$y_1 = 0.5455$ (120 : 100)			
	$f = 0.2$	$f = 0.3$	$f = 0.4$	$f = 0.5$	$f = 0.2$	$f = 0.3$	$f = 0.4$	$f = 0.5$
			1950 ($y_2 = 0.5131$)					
m	0.3515	0.4325	0.5136	0.5947	0.2976	0.3854	0.4732	0.5610
$m - f$	0.1515	0.1325	0.1136	0.0947	0.0976	0.0854	0.0732	0.0610
			1964 ($y_2 = 0.5115$)					
m	0.3556	0.4361	0.5167	0.5972	0.3021	0.3893	0.4766	0.5638
$m - f$	0.1556	0.1361	0.1167	0.0972	0.1021	0.0893	0.0766	0.0638

deaths between months 8 and term. The data from 1950 to 1972 indicate that the sex ratio of fetal deaths for month 8 to term remains approximately the same as that of months 6 and 7, whereas data from 1922 to 1936 reflect an increase in the sex ratio of fetal deaths from month 7 to term. Teitelbaum (*11*) observed a similar change in his analysis of perinatal mortality data from five Western European countries, from 1901 to 1963 (*12*). He concluded that decreases in the sex ratio of late fetal deaths (deaths occurring from month 7 on) are associated with increases in the sex ratio of early infant deaths (deaths occurring within 7 days of birth). Data from the United States are less clear. In fact, the sex ratio of late fetal deaths declines over time, whereas the sex ratio of early infant deaths shows no clear trend. Close examination of these data reveals that the sex ratio of perinatal deaths declined from 136:100 in 1922 to 127:100 in 1972. Although the sex ratio of early infant deaths does not increase over time, the decline in the sex ratio of late fetal deaths, from 134:100 in 1922 to 109:100 in 1972, results in an increase in the absolute difference between the sex ratio of late fetal deaths and the sex ratio of early infant deaths (2 in 1922 versus 31 in 1972). Thus, there is a trend toward an increasing excess in the sex ratio of the early infant deaths relative to the sex ratio of the late fetal deaths; Teitelbaum's argument that there is a postponement of late fetal deaths into the early infant period is supported.

Cavalli-Sforza and Bodmer (*2*) presented a model that allows us to consider the implications of these mortality differentials relative to the primary sex ratio. This model provides for the computation of the amount of sex-differential mortality in utero necessary to go from a primary sex proportion to a given secondary sex proportion (*13*). More specifically, the product of the proportion of males surviving to term $(1 - m)$ and the proportion of males at conception (y_1) yields a survival index for males; similarly, the product of the proportion of females surviving to term $(1 - f)$ and the proportion of females at conception (x_1) yields a survival index for females. The survival index for males is divided by the sum of these two indices to produce an empirical estimate of the proportion of males at birth (y_2):

$$y_2 = \frac{(1 - m)y_1}{(1 - m)y_1 + (1 - f)x_1}$$

Thus, if we know the male secondary sex proportion (y_2), and if we can make certain assumptions about the proportional female zygote loss (f) we can deduce the associated levels of male zygote loss (m). From this we can deduce the excess male loss $(m - f)$ that would result from specific male primary sex proportions (*14*). We compare these calculations with the observed values of $(m - f)$ to decide on a minimum estimate of the male primary sex proportion.

The 1950 to 1972 data indicate that the observed male proportions of live births ranged from 0.5115 in 1964 (low) to 0.5131 in 1950 (high) (*15*). The female zygote mortality proportions of 0.2, 0.3, 0.4, and 0.5 are based on reported estimates of fetal loss (*16*). These two sets of values are used in conjunction with primary sex ratio estimates of .130 ($y_1 = 0.5652$) and 120 ($y_1 = 0.5455$) to produce the range of possible values of male fetal mortality proportions (Table 1). By way of example, in 1964 the male secondary sex proportion (y_2) was 0.5115. If for that year, we assume that 40 percent of the female zygotes did not survive ($f = 0.4$), under an assumption of a primary sex ratio of 120 ($y_1 = 0.5445$), 47.66 percent of the male zygotes did not survive ($m = 0.4766$). The difference between the mortality proportions $(m - f)$ reflects the proportion of male fetal mortality in excess of female fetal mortality required to meet each set of assumptions. This value is 0.0766 or 7.66 percent excess of male fetal mortality relative to female mortality for the assumptions in our example.

The data in this analysis support the existence of a primary sex ratio of at least 120:100. More specifically, we expect excesses of male fetal mortality over female fetal mortality on the order of 6 to 10 percent; 1950 $(m - f)$ = 0.0610 to 0.0976 and 1964 $(m - f)$ = 0.0638 to 0.1021. Although we do not have specific observed values of the proportion loss of male and female zygotes, we can compute the excess of male loss relative to female loss. The observed proportions of male fetal deaths by month of gestation are on the order of 0.52 to 0.59, with the corresponding female proportions ranging from 0.48 to 0.41. Thus, the observed excesses of 4 to 18 percent support the 6 to 10 percent estimates of excess male fetal mortality predicted by this analysis.

This analysis uses data for mortality sex differentials in utero, the observed proportion of males at birth, and estimates of zygote loss, to produce empirical estimates of the primary sex ratio. The resulting estimate of the primary sex ratio differs from earlier estimates insofar as it is based on an empirical analysis of observed data. The data for the sex ratio of fetal deaths indicate a disproportionately high level of male mortality in utero; the pattern of this mortality differential is systematic and tends to be relatively constant over the 38 years of available data. A primary sex ratio of at least 120:100 is possible. This is a conservative estimate with confirmation of a primary sex ratio greater than 120:100 contingent upon more complete knowledge of the sex ratios of stillbirths in the first two trimesters of gestation.

MARILYN M. MCMILLEN
*Department of Sociology,
University of Illinois, Urbana 61801*

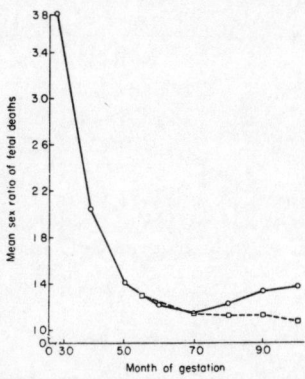

Fig. 1. Mean sex ratio of fetal deaths by month of gestation. ○, 1922 to 1936. □, 1950 to 1972.

References and Notes

1. A. Ciocco, *Hum. Biol.* **10**, 235 (1938); E. Takahashi, *ibid.* **23**, 41 (1951); B. K. Sladen and F. B. Bang, *Biology of Populations* (Elsevier, New York, 1969); A. Scheinfeld, *Heredity in Humans* (Lippincott, New York, 1972).
2. L. L. Cavalli-Sforza and W. F. Bodmer, *The Genetics of Human Populations* (Freeman, San Francisco, 1971).
3. These estimates are based on data from Paris, 1896 to 1902 (from 4 months to term); Washington, D.C., 1874 to 1902 (from 4 months to term); United States, 1922 to 1928 (from 3 months to term); Vienna, 1893 to 1910 (from 3 months to term); Budapest, 1903 to 1907 (from 4 months to term); and Paris, 1901 to 1909 (from 4 months to term).
4. J. B. Nichols, *Am. Anthropol. Assoc.* **1**, 247 (1905-1907); S. J. Holmes and V. P. Mentzer, *Hum. Biol.* **3**, 560 (1931); S. Winston, *ibid.* **4**, 272 (1932); C. Tietze, *ibid.* **20**, 156 (1948); T. McKeown and C. R. Lowe, *ibid.* **23**, 41 (1951).
5. These data provide the most comprehensive record of stillbirths in the United States. Despite the improvement in data collection over the years, the reporting of fetal deaths remains one of the weakest links in the vital statistics system. Within any one year, the coverage is probably best at term and weakest in the earliest months of gestation. There is, however, no reason to assume that there is a disproportionate failure to report male fetal deaths relative to female fetal deaths, or vice versa. In addition to these qualifications, a subset of fetal deaths for which the month of gestation was not reported were excluded from this analysis.
6. Fetal deaths are defined by the World Health Organization as "death prior to the complete expulsion or extraction from its mother of a product of conception, irrespective of the duration of pregnancy." [World Health Organization: Third World Health Assembly, *Official Records of the World Health Organization*, No. 28 (Geneva, December 1950), pp. 16-17.] United States Vital Statistics uses this definition. Data for 1922 to 1936 are from the U.S. Bureau of the Census [*Births, Stillbirths, and Infant Mortality* (Government Printing Office, Washington, D.C., annual)]. Although coverage of birth registrations was not completed until 1933, my analysis uses ratios rather than actual counts; I know of no reason to expect these ratios to change with the inclusion of more states. The data are based on fetal deaths by sex and period of gestation for time intervals less than 3 months and consecutive 1-month intervals to 10 months and more, and infant deaths by sex for the first 6 days of life, under 1 month, 1 month, and 2 months. Data for 1950 to 1972 are from the U.S. Department of Health, Education, and Welfare [*Vital Statistics of the U.S.*, vol. 2, part A, *Mortality* (Government Printing Office, Washington, D.C., annual)]. The data include fetal deaths by sex and period of gestation for months 5 through 10 and more and infant deaths by sex for the first 6 days of life, under 1 month, 1 month, 2 months, and 3 months.
7. Examination of these data by year revealed little annual variability within the years 1922 to 1926 and within the years 1950 to 1972. Thus, for the sake of simplicity the monthly means of each of these groups of years were used in this analysis; this procedure should also yield more robust equations.
8. The linear equation for these data yields a poorer fit, $R^2 = .4760$.
9. The linear equation for these data yields a poorer fit, $R^2 = .8017$.
10. V. Tricomi, D. M. Serr, G. Solish, *Am. J. Obstet. Gynecol.* **79**, 504 (1960); D. Serr and B. Ismajovich, *ibid.* **83**, 63 (1963). These studies report ratios of 135 to 166 males per 100 females.
11. M. S. Teitelbaum, *Demography* **8**, 541 (1971).
12. Perinatal mortality comprises deaths occurring from month 7 of gestation through the first 7 days of life.
13. The sex ratio is defined as the ratio of males to females, whereas the sex proportion reflects the proportion of all individuals who are males.
14. The calculation formula for m is:

$$m = \frac{y_2(1 - x_1 f) - y_1}{y_1 y_2 - y_1}; \quad x_1 = 1 - y_1$$

15. These data are used because the registration system was more complete in the period from 1950 to 1972 than it was for the earlier data (1922 to 1936).
16. M. G. Kerr, *J. Biosoc. Sci.* **3**, 223 (1971).
17. I thank R. Schoen for his help and encouragement at all stages of this research and K. Land, L. Waite, and R. Fagen for their helpful comments. Computer time and facilities were provided by the Social Science Quantitative Laboratory, University of Illinois, Urbana.

31 July 1978; revised 11 October 1978

Part III
Brain Organization and Brain Injury

Cerebral Lateralization of Function: From Infancy Through Childhood

William Kerr Hahn
Purdue University

> This article addresses two fundamental questions concerning cerebral lateralization of functions in normal, right-handed, non-brain-damaged children, namely: Does cerebral specialization develop from an initial bilateral representation to a progressively more focalized specialization, or does it follow an invariant model? And, do sex differences exist? The results from five experimental paradigms were reviewed, including (a) dichotic listening, (b) tachistoscopic viewing, (c) electroencephalography, (d) haptic identification, and (e) somatosensory discrimination. The results from these five paradigms indicated that linguistic functions are localized in the left hemisphere from birth for children of both sexes. The results for functions lateralized in the right hemisphere were less straightforward. Some tasks showed no developmental changes or sex differences, whereas other tasks showed both developmental changes and sex differences. However, factors other than functional brain asymmetries were found to affect the results, challenging the validity of each paradigm. Directions for future research are suggested.

One of the earliest and most consistent findings in neuropsychological research is that the left and right hemispheres of the brain are specialized for different functions. The left hemisphere is specialized for linguistic and sequential functions, whereas the right hemisphere is specialized for nonlinguistic, visuospatial functions. Traditionally, hemispheric asymmetries were considered dichotomous. Today, the generally accepted view is that "there is a continuum of functions between the hemispheres, rather than a rigid dichotomy, the differences being quantitative rather than qualitative" (Bradshaw & Nettleton, 1981, p. 51).

Although differences between the left and right hemisphere exist in the adult brain, it is unclear when these differences first emerge. Two opposing theories have been advanced to account for the development of cerebral asymmetries. The first position, based on the recovery of linguistic functions in brain-damaged children, stresses the importance of maturational processes between infancy and adulthood (Lenneberg, 1967). According to this developmental viewpoint, both hemispheres equally possess the neural substrate capable of subserving linguistic functions during the first 2 years of life. Prior to age 2, damage to either hemisphere is thought to result in little or no long-lasting effects on language acquisition or cognitive functions. As the child develops, a progressive loss in equipotentiality occurs, with the left hemisphere becoming increasingly specialized for the processing of language. By puberty, the adult pattern of hemispheric specialization is established. According to the equipotentiality theory, only after age 2 will left and right brain damage result in unequal language deficits. Lenneberg based many of his conclusions on the work of Basser (1962) who found no differences in the acquisition of single words in children with right or left brain lesions sustained before 2 years of age. More recent proponents of the progressive viewpoint arrived at the same conclusion for non-brain-damaged children (Harris, 1981).

The second theoretical position holds that functional brain asymmetry remains constant, or is invariant, throughout the life span, including childhood (Kinsbourne, 1975). That is, the neural substrate for the development of speech and visual spatial functions is localized in the left and right hemispheres from birth. The invariant lateralization model differs from the progressive model in that it postulates that the neural substrate capable of subserving lateralized functions is focalized in the respective hemispheres from birth. Kinsbourne's invariant model acknowledges that certain lateralized skills may not become apparent until the child reaches a certain age. This differs from the progressive lateralization model, which asserts that functions emerge from an inital bihemispheric base.

Whether cerebral lateralization of functions develops or remains constant through childhood is a major issue in neuropsychological research. A second issue is whether sex differences in cerebral lateralization of function exist. Both theoretical positions make specific predictions regarding sex differences in functional brain asymmetries. Kinsbourne and Hiscock (1977) stated that sex differences do not exist. This position is based on studies that find no Sex × Hemisphere interaction and on methodological criticisms of the ones that do. Harris (1981), however, theorized that in male and female infants both hemispheres are equipotential. As boys mature, they develop hemispheric lateralization for both verbal and nonverbal tasks, whereas for girls, functions are symmetrically distributed.

In her review of cerebral asymmetries in the adult brain, McGlone (1980) concluded that men show a greater degree of hemispheric lateralization of functions than do women. This conclusion is shared by others (e.g., McGee, 1979). However, other authors believe that sex differences in cerebral specialization in adults do not exist (Fairweather, 1980), or they are cautious in their conclusions with regard to which sex shows a greater degree of lateralization for verbal and spatial functions

---

Correspondence concerning this article should be addressed to William Kerr Hahn, Department of Psychological Sciences, Purdue University, West Lafayette, Indiana 47907.

(Bener, 1980; Denenberg, 1980). Research done with children may help explain the discrepant findings in cerebral lateralization of function in adults by identifying whether sex differences develop and whether they appear at different ages for tasks thought to be lateralized in each hemisphere.

This article addresses the two main issues expounded by Kinsbourne and Hiscock (1977) and Harris (1981) concerning cerebral specialization in normal, right-handed children. Both theories relied heavily on the results from dichotic listening experiments. A single task, however, does not fully describe the functional asymmetries of both hemispheres. Therefore, this article reviews the five major paradigms used to investigate cerebral lateralization of function in children. They are (a) dichotic listening of verbal and nonverbal stimuli, (b) tachistoscopic viewing of verbal and nonverbal projections; (c) electrophysiological activity following the presentation of linguistic and nonlinguistic stimuli, (d) manual identification of linguistic and nonlinguistic forms, and (e) identification of somatosensory stimulation. This article does not address studies with brain-damaged children (Hecaen, 1976; Vargha-Khadem & Watters, 1985) nor investigations about anatomical asymmetries (Geschwind & Levitsky, 1968), the relation between information processing and motor performance (Hiscock & Kinsbourne, 1978; Lewkowicz & Turkewitz, 1983), the development of one-handed reaching (Ramsay & Willis, 1984), hand and hemispace effects (Burden, Bradshaw, Nettleton, & Wilson, 1985), the reduction of limb tremors in premature infants following auditory simulation (Segalowitz & Chapman, 1980), or left handedness (Herron, 1980).

Dichotic Listening Task

The dichotic listening technique is the most popular experimental paradigm used to study cerebral lateralization of function in normal children. The technique involves the simultaneous presentation of auditory stimuli to both ears. The anatomical structure of the auditory system ensures that each hemisphere receives a greater amount of information from the contralateral ear (Rosenzweig, 1951). Greater accuracy in reporting the stimuli presented to one ear is interpreted as reflecting the specialization of the hemisphere contralateral to the superior ear. A right-ear advantage (REA) has been found for identifying digits, words, and consonant–vowel syllables, and a left-ear advantage (LEA) has been found for reporting musical notes and environmental sounds. This led several investigators to conclude that the left and right hemispheres are specialized for the processing of verbal and nonverbal stimuli, respectively (Entus, 1977; Geffner & Dorman, 1976; Geffner & Hochberg, 1971; Kimura, 1963; Kraft, 1982).

Findings

Table 1 presents the incidence of a significant REA for verbal materials as a function of age and gender. Kimura (1963) was the first to use the dichotic listening paradigm with children. She examined 120 boys and girls between 4 and 9 years of age. Using free recall of dichotically presented digits as the dependent measure, Kimura found a REA for all children except 7- and 9-year-old girls. Other studies obtained similar results. Kimura (1967) examined children between 5 and 8 years of age. The girls showed a consistent REA, whereas the data for the boys revealed a significant effect by age 6. Knox and Kimura (1970) obtained a consistent REA for both boys and girls 5 to 8 years of age. Although Kimura's results demonstrated an REA for children of both sexes, the inconsistencies in her data suggest that factors other than cerebral asymmetry may influence the dichotic listening task.

Subsequent developmental studies confirmed Kimura's initial findings. An REA for dichotic listening of verbal materials (digits, consonant–vowel syllables, words, and sentences) was found for children as young as 3 years of age (see Table 1). With one exception, no consistent gender differences were observed. The curious exception occurred at age 4. Three of the studies that found no REA for the 4-year-old girls tested a sample of 3-year-old children and found a significant REA for girls, and two studies found the effect for 3-year-old boys (Ingram, 1975; Nagafuchi, 1970; Piazza, 1977). Kinsbourne and Hiscock (1977) examined 150 children between 3 and 12 years of age. They found an REA for boys and girls in every group. Although the sex differences in the 4-year-olds may have been due to idiosyncrasies of the subject samples, the findings are curious and merit further examination in light of the rapid development of linguistic abilities at this age, particularly in girls.

The evidence from dichotic listening studies strongly suggests that the right ear is superior to the left in processing verbal stimuli and that this superiority is present at an early age. However, Porter and Berlin (1975) asserted that most studies failed to find developmental increases in the REA because lateralization of verbal processing occurs prior to age 4 and does not develop thereafter. Porter and Berlin's position, although consonant with a progressive model, differs from Lenneberg's (1967) theory, which viewed progressive lateralization as a process occurring throughout the first decade and up to puberty.

Results from dichotic listening studies with infants are inconsistent. Lokker and Morais (1985) tested 26 children (13 boys and 13 girls) between 21 and 35.5 months of age. Pairs of familiar objects were dichotically presented, and the child was to reach for the object in an array of five objects. They observed a significant REA for children with right-handed parents and a nonsignificant trend toward an LEA for children with at least one left-handed parent. No sex differences were observed. Entus (1977) used the nonnutritive high-amplitude sucking paradigm to the discrimination of novel verbal (consonant–vowel syllables) or nonverbal (musical notes) dichotic stimuli. Infants between 22 and 140 days of age exhibited a significant increase in the rate of sucking when a new syllable was presented to the right ear and when a new musical note was presented to the left ear. No sex or age differences were observed. Vargha-Khadem and Corballis (1979), however, were unable, using verbal stimuli, to replicate these findings in infants 28 to 94 days old. Instead, a recovery of sucking was observed when the novel stimulus was presented to either ear.

Glanville, Best, and Levenson (1977) used a similar procedure, but they measured heart rate instead of sucking. They found a greater recovery of the cardiac orienting response when a new speech stimulus (consonant–vowel syllable) was presented to the right ear as opposed to the left ear in 3-month-old infants. A novel musical note produced a greater response

Table 1
Age and Sex Difference in Right-Ear Superiority for Dichotic Listening of Linguistic Stimuli

Study	Stimulus	3 M	3 F	4 M	4 F	5 M	5 F	6 M	6 F	7 M	7 F	8 M	8 F	9 M	9 F	10 M	10 F	11 M	11 F	12 M	12 F	13 M	13 F	14 M	14 F	15 M	15 F	N
Kimura (1963)	Digits			+	+	+	+	+	+	+	0	+	+	+	0	0	+											120
Kimura (1967)	Digits					+	0	+	+	+	+	+	+															40
Knox & Kimura (1970)	Digits					0	+	+	+	+	+	+	+															120
Bryden (1970)	Digits											+	0															234
Geffner & Hochberg (1971)	Digits			+	+	+	+	+		+	+																	94
Borowy & Goebel (1976)	Digits			+	+	+	+			+	+																	120
Kinsbourne & Hiscock (1977)	Digits	+	+	+	+	+	+	+	+	+	+																	150
Geffen (1978)	Digits													+	+	+	+											48
Bakker, Hoefkens, & Van der Vlugt (1979)	Digits											+	+	+	+	+	+	+	+									27
Geffen & Wale (1979)	Digits									+	+	+	+	+	+	+	+	+	+	+	+							32
Bryden & Allard (1981)	Digits							+	0	+	+																	96
Hiscock & Bergstrom (1982)	Digits									+	+	+	+	+	+													72
G. Berlin, Hughes, Lowell, & Berlin (1973)	CV syllables					+	+			+	+																	150
Hynd & Obrzut (1977)	CV syllables			+	0																							160
Geffner & Dorman (1976)	CV syllables											+	+	+	+	+	+											67
Mirabile, Porter, Hughes, & Berlin (1978)	CV syllables									+	+	+	+	+	+	+	+	+	+			+	+					150
Caplan & Kinsbourne (1981)	CV syllables									0	+															+	+	55
Gordon (1983)	CV syllables													+	+	+	+	+	+	+	+	+	0					138
Pizzamiglio & Checchine (1971)	Words	+	+	+	+	+	+	+	0	+	+	+	+															192
Nagafuchi (1970)	Words	+	+	+	0	0	+																					80
Ingram (1975)	Words	+	+	+	0	+	+																					84
Piazza (1977)	Words	0	+	+	0	+	+																					72
Schulman-Galambos (1977)	Words									+	+	+	+	+	+	+	+	+	+									186
Sexton & Geffen (1979)	Words									+	+							+	+	+	+	+	+					24
Saxby & Bryden (1984)	Sentences					+	+			+	+	+	+	+	+	+	+						+					95
Summary: Significant – right ear		3	4	7	3	10	12	11	10	15	14	11	11	12	11	6	7	8	8	4	4	4	3			1	1	
Total		4	4	7	7	12	12	11	11	16	16	12	12	12	12	7	7	8	8	4	4	4	4			1	1	

Note. M = males; F = females. + = significant right-ear superiority; 0 = nonsignificant ear superiority. CV = consonant–vowel.

recovery when it was presented to the left ear. In a subsequent study, Best, Hoffman, and Glanville (1982) examined 2-, 3-, and 4-month-old infants. They observed developmental changes for the phonetic stimuli only. The 2-month-old infants failed to exhibit ear asymmetries in the orienting response, whereas the 3- and 4-month-old infants showed a right-ear effect for the verbal material. A large orienting response was observed in all three age groups when the novel musical stimulus was presented to the left ear. They concluded that the left hemisphere's linguistic-processing ability develops between 2 and 3 months of age, which is counter to Kinsbourne's model. An alternative explanation is possible. Inspection of the data revealed a floor effect for the 2-month-old infants, suggesting that the nature of the task was insensitive in detecting ear asymmetries for verbal stimuli in very young infants.

The four studies with infants do not provide sufficient data from which to draw firm conclusions. Comparisons between studies are also limited because of their methodological differences. The only two studies that tested infants less than 2 months of age provided inconsistent results. Stronger support for either the progressive or invariant lateralization models will have to come from longitudinal research starting with infants less than 2 months of age. With older infants, the results do suggest that the right ear may process verbal material more effectively than the left ear. The opposite is true for musical stimuli. These results are consistent with the research with older children.

Table 2 presents the results of studies using nonverbal materials (environmental sounds, animal sounds, and different emotional intonations of speech stimuli). The relative paucity of dichotic studies attempting to assess right-hemispheric functioning is striking. The results from these studies provide inconclusive information on the developmental course of the right hemisphere and whether sex differences exist. Knox and Kimura (1970) concluded that boys have a greater right-hemisphere specialization for nonlinguistic stimuli (environmental sounds) than girls do. Their results, however, revealed no significant Sex × Ear interaction. Overall, the left ear was superior to the right ear for 5-to 8-year-olds, but the LEA was statistically significant only for the 6- and 7-year-old girls and the 7- and 8-year-old boys. Subsequent studies failed to replicate Knox and Kimura's initial findings. These inconsistencies challenge the appropriateness of the task in assessing left-ear superiority for nonverbal stimuli.

In summary, on the basis of a wide variety of stimuli and dependent measures, the results from dichotic listening studies support Kinsbourne and Hiscock's (1977) theoretical model that functional brain asymmetry remains constant throughout childhood and that sex differences do not exist. The right ear is more sensitive than the left ear for the processing of verbal material, and this superiority is present in infants. Results from the studies using nonverbal stimuli do not unequivocally support either theory of cerebral lateralization of function in children. However, there is some support for Kinsbourne and Hiscock's model because infants showed an LEA for musical stimuli.

Methodological Criticisms

The results from the dichotic listening studies purposely emphasized ear asymmetries rather than cerebral asymmetries. Other factors such as the reliability of the task, the acoustical properties of the stimulus, attention, and memory seem to influence the direction and magnitude of the ear advantage, challenging the fundamental assumption of the dichotic listening paradigm, namely, that it measures functional brain asymmetries. Each of these factors will be considered individually.

Several authors have examined the reliability of the dichotic listening procedure. The underlying assumption is that if ear asymmetries are due to cerebral asymmetries, the reliability coefficients should be relatively high. A generous test-retest coefficient of 1.00 for a selected group of 10 subjects was reported by Schulman-Galambos (1977). However, more conservative estimates are usually reported. Hiscock and Kinsbourne (1977) obtained a .66 retest coefficient for digits (one pair per trial) over a 2½-week period. It has been demonstrated that the test-retest coefficient depends on the complexity of the task. Bakker, Van der Vlugt, and Claushuis (1978) examined the reliability of two, three, and four pairs of digits per trial over a one-week interval. No consistent age or gender differences were observed, but the coefficients varied greatly (range = .25 to .94).

Split-half reliabilities have also been reported. Using the Spearman–Brown formula, several investigators obtained odd-even coefficients between .89 and .93 (Kraft, 1982; Lewandowski, 1982; Schulman-Galambos, 1977). Springer and Searleman (1978) demonstrated that these coefficients varied according to the data used to compute the ear advantage. The largest coefficient was obtained for the total correct score (.85), whereas the phi, percentage error, and percentage correct scores yielded coefficients of .83, .82, and .72, respectively.

The third approach examined the percentage of subjects who changed ear preference from one testing session to another. Bakker et al. (1978) found that 72.2% of subjects preserved ear consistency for verbal material. Of the subjects reporting an initial right-ear preference, 15.6% showed a left-ear preference on the second test one week later. Approximately 43% of subjects changed preference from the left ear to the right ear. The proportion of subjects preserving an REA varied with age. Although 67% of 3-year-olds preserved an REA, only 50% of the 5-year-olds did so (Hiscock & Kinsbourne, 1977). If the hypothesis that cerebral lateralization develops with age is true, and if REA is a "pure" measure of lateralization, a greater proportion of older subjects, rather than younger ones, would be expected to preserve an REA. Testing a group of adult subjects, Blumstein, Goodglass, and Tartter (1975) found a test-retest coefficient of .74 for consonants, .21 for vowels, and .46 for musical notes. Twenty-nine percent of the subjects reversed ear advantage for consonants, whereas 46% and 19% did so for vowels and musical notes, respectively.

One study reported a reliability index for nonverbal stimuli. Kraft (1982) obtained a split-half reliability of .79 after correcting for attenuation by the Spearman–Brown formula.

The reliability indices for both children and adults strongly suggest that variables other than hemispheric asymmetries affect ear performance in the dichotic listening task. Factors such as the acoustic properties of the stimuli, attentional strategies, and memory appear to influence the results and interpretations of the various dichotic listening studies.

The acoustic properties of the stimuli, such as the intensity and the signal-to-noise ratio, vary from study to study. These

Table 2
Age and Sex Differences in Left-Ear Superiority for Dichotic Listening of Nonlinguistic Stimuli

		Age group and sex																					
		3		4		5		6		7		8		9		10		11		12		13	
Study	Stimulus (sounds)	M	F	M	F	M	F	M	F	M	F	M	F	M	F	M	F	M	F	M	F	M	F	N
Knox & Kimura (1970)	Environmental					0	0	0	+	+	+	+	0											80
	Animal					+	0	+	+	+	+	+	+											120
Piazza (1977)	Environmental	+	+	+	0	+	+																	72
Bryden & Allard (1981)	Environmental									0	0			0	0			0	0					60
Kraft (1982)	Environmental									+	−									+	−			92
Saxby & Bryden (1984)	Emotional intonation					+	+					+	+									+	+	95
Summary: Significant − left ear		1/1		1/1		3/4	2/4	1/2	2/2	3/4	2/4	2/2	1/2	1/1	1/1			0/2	0/2	1/1	0/1	1/1	1/1	
Total																								

Note. M = males; F = females. + = significant left-ear superiority; 0 = nonsignificant ear superiority. − = significant right-ear superiority.

properties are known to affect performance in adults (C. I. Berlin & Cullen, 1977), with the left ear superior to the right in perceiving less audible stimuli. Subtle asymmetries in the intensity and signal-to-noise ratio could be due to slight differences in the earphone channels or in the peripheral auditory system. Many investigators administer gross hearing tests and switch the position of the earphones, but few investigators report the acoustic characteristics of the stimuli to facilitate comparisons between studies.

In the early dichotic listening studies, researchers assumed that attention was divided equally between the ears during stimulus presentation. The purely structural model of ear asymmetry predicts an REA for verbal material regardless of attentional strategies (Kimura, 1967). However, the direction of attention affects ear advantage in adults (Treisman & Geffen, 1968). Bryden and Allard (1981) noticed that in free recall of dichotic stimuli, children tended to report stimuli presented to the right ear first. Statistical control of the first response eliminated the REA. When children attended to and reported stimuli presented to the left ear, the usual REA was significantly attenuated, and this effect persisted for a one-week interval (Hiscock & Bergstrom, 1982). These results suggest that attention has a strong and enduring effect on the direction of the ear advantage.

Geffen and her colleagues have consistently demonstrated that 6- and 7-year-old children cannot effectively attend to left-ear items when told to do so, and consequently, they report a greater number of right-ear items instead (Geffen, 1978; Geffen & Wale, 1979). These effects interact with task complexity. Younger children successfully attended to two pairs of dichotic stimuli presented at a slow rate, but they had difficulty attending to the left ear when the task became more complex (Sexton & Geffen, 1979). Older subjects attended to simple and complex tasks with no difficulty. These results suggest that selective attention, rather than cerebral specialization, develops with increasing age. If attention changes or shifts, the laterality measure will also change, providing misleading information about lateralization differences.

Several investigators have examined the effect of memory in dichotic listening. Using a fixed-recall response procedure, Inglis and Sykes (1967) found a strong memory component, or production deficit, in the dichotic listening of verbal material. Five-to-10-year-old children performed significantly worse on the second half of the items recalled than on the first half. This effect was independent of individual ear performance and age.

Using the free recall of dichotic stimuli as the dependent measure, investigators have noted developmental increases in children's ability to report the items presented to both ears (G. Berlin, Hughes, Lowel-Bell, & Berlin, 1973; Mirabile, Porter, Hughes, & Berlin, 1978; Schulman-Galambos, 1977). These results indicate that memory factors may significantly affect children's performance in dichotic listening experiments. Unless the report order is controlled in the free-recall procedure, the stimuli presented to one ear will remain in memory for a longer period of time than the stimuli presented to the other ear. The development of an REA may result from a shift in reporting items presented to each ear. Bakker, Hoefkens, and Van der Vlugt (1979) observed that changes in ear advantage depended on which ear was reported first, with an increase in left to right shifts with increasing age.

Thus, when children choose, for whatever reason, to report items presented to the right ear first, the subsequent REA will be influenced by structural and nonstructural (attention and memory) asymmetries. The impact of the nonstructural variables seems to vary with age. These results argue against the progressive lateralization model of hemispheric functioning. Younger children resort to involuntary, structural asymmetries when presented with complex dichotic tasks. As children grow older, the ability to attend to and remember more complex stimuli develops.

Although most studies report an REA for verbal material and an LEA for nonverbal stimuli, the results are extremely variable. The uncritical acceptance that the dichotic listening paradigm accurately assesses cerebral lateralization of functions is unwarranted. Factors other than structural asymmetries affect ear performance. That studies with infants have obtained significant right- and left-ear asymmetries for verbal and nonverbal stimuli, respectively, suggests that these effects may be present at birth. If cerebral lateralization develops during childhood, the dichotic listening paradigm may be insensitive to such changes.

Visual Perceptual Asymmetries

In the visual sensory modality, stimuli presented to the visual fields are directed, via the optic track, to the occipital cortex. Each hemisphere receives complete sensory input from the contralateral visual half-field of both eyes. Stimuli presented to the right and left hemifields are transmitted directly to the left and right hemispheres, respectively. In right-handed adults, tachistoscopic presentation of linguistic stimuli (e.g., words) is more efficiently processed when presented to the right visual field (RVF) than when presented to the left visual field (LVF). An LVF superiority usually, but not always, is obtained for nonlinguistic stimuli (Hellige, 1980). During the past decade, an increasing number of studies have focused on developmental issues in cerebral lateralization of function by using the tachistoscopic viewing paradigm. Unfortunately, the results from these studies provide limited information about early hemispheric specialization because most studies examined school-age children.

Findings

Tables 3 and 4 present the results from studies that provided sufficient information concerning age and sex differences to evaluate RVF and LVF superiority for linguistic and nonlinguistic stimuli in normal children. Inspection of Table 3 reveals no consistent pattern of developmental changes or sex differences in RVF superiority for linguistic stimuli. An RVF superiority for linguistic material was obtained for boys and girls by age 7 (Lewandowski, 1982; Marcel & Rajan, 1975). Olson (1973) found a significant overall RVF superiority when the data were collapsed across age and sex. A nonsignificant trend, in the predicted direction, was obtained for boys and girls 7 to 12 years of age.

Several other studies found a progressive development of the RVF effect. However, these studies are in disagreement as to the age at which the RVF advantage first appears. Forgays (1953) examined 7- to 16-year-old boys and girls and found a significant RVF superiority by age 13. Similar results were obtained for a sample of girls (Reynolds & Jeeves, 1978). In contrast, Tomlinson-Keasey, Kelly, and Burton (1978) found an RVF superiority for 13-year-old boys, but not girls, whereas Broman (1978) failed to obtain an RVF effect for 7-, 10-, and 13-year-old boys. Other investigators obtained a significant RVF superiority by age 10 (Carmon, Nachson, & Starinsky, 1976; Miller & Turner, 1973).

In addition, two studies found an LVF superiority (and theoretically a right hemisphere advantage) for the recognition of single letters in 6- and 7-year-olds (Broman, 1978; Carmon et al., 1976). It was suggested that young children used a visual-graphemic (nonverbal) strategy to process single letters because of their relative unfamiliarity with the alphabet. Although it was not explicitly stated, this interpretation assumes that a strict verbal-nonverbal dichotomy accurately characterizes the functioning of each hemisphere. As such, a RVF-left-hemisphere advantage is expected for older children. This prediction was not confirmed. In both studies, no visual field advantage was observed in 8-to-13-year-old children. An LVF advantage has also been observed in adults for letter recognition and for the identification of strings of letters as words (G. J. Bradshaw, Hicks, & Rose, 1979; Hellige, 1980; Pring, 1980). These results suggest that factors other than structural asymmetries influence the results from tachistoscopic studies with children and adults.

Table 4 provides the results from tachistoscopic studies using nonlinguistic stimuli with children as a function of age and sex. As in Table 3, no consistent pattern of developmental changes or sex differences were found. Several studies found no developmental changes or sex differences (Marcel & Rajan, 1975; Turkewitz & Ross-Kossak, 1984; Young & Bion, 1981; Young & Ellis, 1976). These studies obtained an LVF advantage for the recognition of faces in boys and girls between 6 and 13 years of age. When inverted faces were presented as the stimuli, no hemifield preferences were observed (Young & Bion, 1981; Young & Ellis, 1976). This effect was present by age 6 and did not vary with age.

In contrast, sex differences were observed by other authors. Young and Bion (1980) found an LVF advantage for face recognition in 7-, 10-, and 13-year-old boys, but not girls. Jones and Anuza (1982), however, observed a sex difference, but with the reversed laterality effect. An RVF advantage was found in 3- and 4-year-old boys, whereas the girls showed no visual hemifield superiority. Tomlinson-Keasey et al. (1978) observed an RVF superiority in 13-year-old boys, but not girls, in the recognition of line drawings of concrete objects. No visual hemifield asymmetries or sex effects were observed in the 9-year-old age group.

Thus, the studies using linguistic and nonlinguistic stimuli provided an inconsistent picture of visual hemifield asymmetries in children. An RVF and LVF superiority for the processing of linguistic and nonlinguistic stimuli was found in children as young as age 7, but several discrepancies were observed. These discrepancies are difficult to reconcile on the basis of cerebral asymmetries alone. Sergent (1983) suggested that stimulus duration and luminance can have a profound effect on visual hemifield asymmetries by creating stimulus characteristics that disproportionately favor one hemisphere over the other.

Methodological Criticisms

In interpreting the results from tachistoscopic studies, three major issues need to be considered: the reliability of the task, priming effects, and procedural variations associated with stimulus presentation. Only one study examined the reliability of the tachistoscopic viewing task. Lewandowski (1982) found a split-half reliability index of .91 for words presented to the RVF and .85 for slanted lines presented to the LVF for a sample of 48 boys between 7 and 16 years of age. More research is clearly needed, particularly on the stability of the hemifield effect over time.

Only one study examined the role of attention in tachistoscopic studies (Carter & Kinsbourne, 1979). The usual RVF advantage for digits was eliminated when subjects were presented with a geometric prime prior to each trial. This priming procedure induces a spatial mental set that is conceptualized as in-

Table 3
Age and Sex Differences in Right Visual Field (RVF) Superiority for Tachistoscopic Viewing of Linguistic Stimuli

Study	Stimulus	7 M F	8 M F	9 M F	10 M F	11 M F	12 M F	13 M F	14 M F	N
Broman (1978)	Letters	−		0				0		86
Reynolds & Jeeves (1978)	Letters	0 0						+	+	36
Olson (1973)	Words	0 0	0 0	0 0	0 0	0 0				50
Marcel, Katz, & Smith (1974)	Words		+ +	+ +						40
Tomlinson-Keasey, Kelly, & Burton (1978)	Words			0 0				+ 0		154
Yeni-Komshian, Isenberg, & Goldberg (1975)	Words Digits						0 0 0 0			19 19
Summary: Significant − RVF / Total		0/2 0/2	1/2 1/3	1/3 1/3	0/2 0/1	0/1	0/2 0/2	1/2 1/2	1/1	

Note. M = males; F = females. + = significant RVF superiority; 0 = nonsignificant visual superiority. − = significant left visual field superiority.

volving the selective activation of the right hemisphere. The spatial prime produced an LVF-right-hemisphere advantage for the linguistic stimuli. These results suggest that attentional components may affect visual field superiorities.

Procedural variations associated with stimulus presentation may contribute to the inconsistent findings in the tachistoscopic literature. For the stimulus to be projected to only the right or left hemisphere, the stimulus must be presented to the right or left of the central fixation point, and the exposure duration must be brief enough to prevent voluntary lateral eye movements. No standards have been developed for meeting these criteria.

Table 4
Age and Sex Differences in Left Visual Field (LVF) Superiority for Tachistoscopic Viewing of Nonlinguistic Stimuli

Study	Stimulus	3 M F	4 M F	5 M F	6 M F	7 M F	8 M F	9 M F	10 M F	11 M F	12 M F	13 M F	N	Exposure duration (ms)
Young & Ellis (1976)	Faces				+ +		+ +				+ +		42	40–70
Young & Bion (1980)	Upright faces Inverted faces					+ 0 0 0			+ 0 0 0			+ 0 0 0	48 48	150 150
Broman (1978)	Familiar faces					+			+			0	86	100–175
Young & Bion (1981)	Familiar faces Upright faces Inverted faces					+ + 0 0			+ + 0 0				30 30	150 150
Jones & Anuza (1982)	Faces	− 0	− 0										27	200
Turkewitz & Ross-Kossak (1984)	Faces						+ +		+ +			+ +	96	110–140
Witelson (1976)	People									+			156	
Tomlinson-Keasey, Kelly, & Burton (1978)	Objects							0 0				− 0	115	100
Summary: Significant − LVF / Total		0/1 0/1	0/1 0/1		1/1 1/1	3/5 1/4	2/2 2/2	0/1 0/1	2/3 0/2	3/4 2/3	1/1 1/1	2/5 1/4		

Note. M = males; F = females. + = significant LVF superiority; 0 = nonsignificant visual field superiority. − = significant right visual field superiority.

The first criterion is always met, provided the children focus on the fixation point. However, studies have used different degrees of visual angle to present stimuli to the right and left hemiretina. Linguistic materials have been presented at angles of 1 to 6 degrees from the fixation point. Nonlinguistic stimuli have varied from .5 to 6 degrees. A marked decrease in acuity occurs as the stimulus projection moves from a central to a peripheral locus of the retina (Anstis, 1974; Kroon, Rijsdijk, & Van der Wildt, 1980). In adult subjects, a Visual Field × Retinal Locus of Projection interaction has been observed (Sergent, 1983). Although the interaction is confounded with accuracy (task difficulty), the LVF continues to be superior to the RVF for processing degraded information. This effect has not been examined in children.

Inspection of the data, however, suggests that the angle of stimulus presentation may affect visual asymmetries in children. An RVF–left-hemisphere advantage for linguistic stimuli was observed when the visual angle did not exceed 3 degrees (Marcel, Katz, & Smith, 1974; Marcel & Rajan, 1975). Digits presented at 4 degrees of visual angle produced no visual field asymmetries (Yeni-Komshian, Isenberg, & Goldberg, 1975), and letters presented at 3.5 and 6 degrees resulted in an LVF–right-hemisphere advantage (Broman, 1978; Carmon et al., 1976). Similarly, an RVF–left-hemisphere advantage was found for pictures of objects presented at a 2 degree angle from the point of fixation (Tomlinson-Keasey et al., 1978). These results are similar to the findings with adults and suggest that hemifield superiority may depend on the angle of stimulus projection, which in turn affects visual acuity.

The second criterion, a brief exposure duration, is used in tachistoscopic studies to prevent lateral eye movements from exposing the stimulus to both hemispheres. Between-studies differences in exposure duration ranged from 12.5 ms (Carmon et al., 1976) to 200 ms (Jones & Anuza, 1982), and within-studies differences varied up to 130 ms (Marcel et al., 1974). The only explanation given for varying the duration of the exposure time was to correct for performance levels between subjects. The nature of the visual system precludes instantaneous extraction of all the information from the visual display. Information extraction varies as a function of stimulus duration and luminance. Evidence from the adult literature indicates that both hemispheres differ in their ability to process stimuli presented at different levels of energy (Sergent, 1983). At lower energy levels, the right hemisphere is superior to the left, and as the energy level increases, the left hemisphere benefits more than the right. To date, no one has investigated the effects of exposure duration and luminance in children.

Thus, slight variations in methodologies can profoundly affect lateral asymmetries. Stimuli presented at large visual angles, brief exposure durations, and low energy levels are perceived with less acuity than are more centrally projected stimuli presented for longer durations and greater luminance. Hemispheric asymmetries along a linguistic–nonlinguistic dimension do not fully account for all the obtained results. Neither Kinsbourne and Hiscock's (1977) nor Harris's (1981) model was supported by the results from tachistoscopic studies. More research is needed on the effects of selective attention and variables associated with stimulus presentation to determine the nature of the lateral asymmetry measured by the tachistoscopic viewing paradigm.

Electrical Evoked Potentials

Electroencephalography bypasses some of the limitations inherent in behavioral measures of hemispheric specialization by providing a direct measure of the electrical activity of the brain. To detect asymmetrical cortical activity, recordings are taken from electrodes placed in homologous sites across the hemispheres. Measurements have been taken from the parietal, temporal, central, frontal, and occipital regions of both hemispheres.

Two electroencephalograph (EEG) procedures have been used to measure brain activity. Ongoing EEG recordings taken during rest or sleep show no lateral asymmetries from infancy through late adolescence (Benninger, Matthis, & Scheffner, 1984; Peters, Varner, & Ellingson, 1981). The second electrophysiological procedure measures electrical activity following the presentation of repeated stimuli. Average evoked potentials (AEP) are obtained by algebraically summating short portions of the EEG activity time locked with the onset of a stimulus. By using this procedure, the random electrical activity is canceled, whereas the stimulus-specific activity is accumulated (Marsh, 1978). Similar to the dichotic listening and tachistoscopic viewing paradigms, asymmetrical time-locked evoked potentials are evoked by the presentation of stimuli thought to be processed differentially by both hemispheres.

Findings

Table 5 displays the results of studies that examined auditory AEP eliciting greater electrical activity of the left hemisphere. Following the presentation of auditory clicks, syllables, words, and speech, greater electrical activity was localized in the left temporal area than in the homologous area of the right hemisphere (Davis & Wada, 1977; Molfese, 1973, 1977; Molfese, Freeman, & Palermo, 1975). This effect was found in 4-to-11-year-old children and in full-term infants less than 24-hr old. This suggests that from birth, the left hemisphere is sensitive to linguistic stimuli.

Using sophisticated multivariate analysis techniques, Molfese and colleagues found that for children and adults, both hemispheres are involved in processing linguistic stimuli, but each hemisphere is characterized by different components of the AEP (Molfese, 1978; Molfese & Hess, 1978). More important, in full-term infants less than 24-hr old and in preterm infants averaging 35 weeks of conceptional age at the time of testing, the left hemisphere differentiated between synthesized speech syllables within the frequency range common to speech, but not for nonspeech analogues (Molfese & Molfese, 1979, 1980). This confirmed the results from previous studies and provided further support for the hypothesis that the left hemisphere's ability to process linguistic information is present at birth. Molfese and Molfese (1985) demonstrated that at birth, both lateral and bilateral AEP were able to discriminate children who differed in language ability 3 years later. In infants who later exhibited better language performance, the left hemi-

Table 5
Average Evoked Potentials of the Left Hemisphere Following Linguistic Stimuli

Study	Stimulus	Age	N Male	N Female	Results
Davis & Wada (1977)	Clicks	2–10 weeks[a]	11	5	1. Greater coherence of waveform found in the left hemisphere. 2. Greater spectral power found in the left temporal than occipital area, with no temporal-occipital differences in the right hemisphere.
Molfese, Freeman, & Palermo (1975)	Syllables Words	1 week–10 months[b]	4	6	1. Changes in the amplitude of the N_1P_2 wave component were greater in the left hemisphere: (a) in 9 out of 10 infants and (b) in 10 out of 11 children.
Gardiner & Walter (1976)	Speech	6 months	3	1	1. Greater proportion of left hemisphere activity occurred in all infants.
Molfese (1977)	Syllables	<24 hr	4	4	1. All infants showed dishabituation in both hemispheres for changes in the place of articulation. 2. Six out of 8 infants showed dishabituation in both hemispheres for voicing changes crossing a phoneme boundary. 3. All infants showed dishabituation for voicing changes not crossing a phoneme boundary.
Molfese (1977)	Nonspeech	<24 hr	7	7	1. Larger amplitude found in left hemisphere.
Molfese & Hess (1978)	Syllables	3.11–4.11[c]	6	6	1. One factor identified voicing changes between and within phoneme classes in both hemispheres. 2. One factor identified voicing changes crossing a phoneme boundary in the right hemisphere. 3. Sex differences found in right hemisphere.
Molfese & Molfese (1979)	Syllables	<24 hr	8	8	1. Larger amplitude found in left hemisphere for acoustic cues common to speech. 2. Left hemisphere discriminated between consonants with normal formant structure.
Molfese & Molfese (1980)	Syllables	Preterm 32–37 weeks	11		1. One factor differentiated phonetic and nonphonetic syllables in the left hemisphere.
Molfese & Molfese (1985)	Syllables	<36 hr		16[d]	1. Left hemisphere discriminated between vowels. 2. Left hemisphere discriminated between consonant speech sounds among infants who 3 years later demonstrated better language performance.

[a] M = 5 weeks.
[b] M = 5.8 months.
[c] M = 4 years.
[d] Sex of subjects not specified.

sphere differentiated between speech sounds, and the right hemisphere discriminated between nonspeech sounds.

Two studies reported that sex differences were present. One study gave no further information (Molfese & Molfese, 1979), and the other study only mentioned that the sex differences were observed in the right hemisphere (Molfese & Hess, 1978). The nature of the sex differences and the characteristics of the linguistic stimuli processed by the right hemisphere await further research.

Table 6 presents the results from studies assessing the electrical activity of the right hemisphere following the presentation of nonlinguistic stimuli. Brief flashes of light produced longer excursion measures and larger peak-to-trough amplitudes in readings taken over the right hemisphere than in readings taken over the left hemisphere (Bigum, Dustman, & Beck, 1970; Davis & Wada, 1977; Rhodes, Dustman, & Beck, 1969; Richlin, Weisinger, Weinstein, Giannini, & Morganstern, 1971). These results were present from infancy through late adolescence.

Nonlinguistic auditory stimuli also elicited greater electrical activity in the right hemisphere. Molfese et al. (1975) presented repeated noise bursts and musical notes to 10 infants with an average age of 5.8 months and to 11 children with a mean age of 6 years. All 10 infants exhibited greater changes in the amplitude of the N2P3 wave component of the right hemisphere for both the noise burst and musical note. All 11 children showed similar results for the musical note, and 9 children showed similar results for the noise stimuli. Gardiner and Walter (1976), using EEG, observed a greater proportion of right-hemisphere activity in 6-month-old infants following the presentation of

Table 6
Average Evoked Potentials of the Right Hemisphere Following Visual and Nonlinguistic Stimuli

Study	Stimulus	Age	N Male	N Female	Results
Rhodes, Dustman, & Beck (1969)	Flashes	10–11 years	20[d]		1. Larger amplitude in later wave components found in right hemisphere. 2. Larger amplitude found in right hemisphere in boys.
Bigum, Dustman, & Beck (1970)	Flashes	6.8–16.8 years	9	15	1. Larger amplitude found in later wave components in right hemisphere.
Richlin, Weisinger, Weinstein, Giannini, & Morganstern (1971)	Flashes	10.3–16 years	3	3	1. Larger amplitude found in right hemisphere.
Crowell, Jones, Kapuniai, & Nakagawa (1973)	Flashes	Newborns			1. Thirty-six infants showed an increase in spectural power during stimulation. 2. Eighteen infants showed increases in both hemispheres. 3. Sixteen infants showed significantly greater activity in the right hemisphere. 4. Two infants showed significantly greater activity in the left hemisphere.
Molfese, Freeman, & Palermo (1975)	C-Major piano chord	1 week–10 months[a]	4	6	1. Changes in the amplitude of the N_2P_3 wave component were greater in the right hemisphere: (a) in all 10 infants for musical note and noise, (b) in all 11 children for musical note and noise, and (c) in 9 out of 11 children for noise.
	Noise bursts	4–11 years[b]	5	6	
Gardiner & Walter (1976)	Music	6 months	3	1	1. Greater proportion of right hemisphere activity found for all 3 boys.
Molfese (1977)	Nonspeech tones with frequencies similar to speech	<24 hr	7	7	1. Larger amplitude change found in right hemisphere.
Davis & Wada (1977)	Flashes	2–10 weeks[c]	11	5	1. Ten out of 16 showed greater coherence of waveform in the right hemisphere. 2. Greater spectral power in the right occipital than in the right temporal area, with no occipital–temporal differences in the left hemisphere.
Molfese & Molfese (1985)	Syllables	<36 hr	16[d]		1. Right hemisphere discriminated between nonspeech sounds among infants who 3 years later demonstrated better language performance.

[a] M = 5.8 months.
[b] M = 6 years.
[c] M = 5 weeks.
[d] Sex of subjects not specified.

musical stimuli. Using tones outside the frequency for speech as the stimuli, Molfese (1977) obtained greater amplitude changes over the right hemisphere as compared with the left hemisphere in 14 infants less than 24 hr old.

These results suggest that lateral differences in hemispheric specialization for the processing of nonlinguistic information is present at birth. Sex differences in AEPs of the right hemisphere have not been systematically investigated. One study reported sex differences, with boys showing a greater mean amplitude change following visual flashes than did girls (Rhodes et al., 1969).

Methodological Criticisms

To the extent that increased electrical activity is a valid measure of hemispheric processing, the results from AEPs in infants and children indicated that the left and right hemispheres are more active following the presentation of linguistic and nonlinguistic stimuli, respectively. Two comments are in order: First, lateral asymmetries are based on minute differences that are detected by using equipment with a high resolving power, suggesting that both hemispheres are involved in information processing. In fact, Molfese and Molfese (1979, 1985) confirmed that both hemispheres process certain characteristics of linguistic information. Second, as suggested by Molfese and Molfese (1980), subcortical electrical activity interacts with cortical activity in young infants. Thus, AEPs reflect both cortical and subcortical responses, limiting the validity of the AEP as a pure measure of hemispheric activity.

Despite these limitations, AEP yields consistent lateral asymmetries. The reliability coefficients for AEP are within acceptable limits. Test-retest coefficients for 5 min and 2 months range from .97 to .84, respectively (Bigum et al., 1970; Dustman & Beck, 1963; Rhodes et al., 1969). The studies reviewed in this section supported the invariant lateralization model. Newborn infants showed greater electrical activity in the left hemisphere following the presentation of linguistic stimuli and in the right hemisphere following the presentation of noise and musical notes. In cases where within-hemispheres differences were noted, the left hemisphere was more proficient at discriminating between speech sounds, whereas the right hemisphere was better able to discriminate between nonspeech sounds.

Tactile Perceptual Identification

Unlike the dichotic listening, tachistoscopic viewing, and electrophysiological measurement paradigms in which linguistic and nonlinguistic materials are used to examine the functional asymmetry of both cerebral hemispheres, the tactile perceptual identification paradigm, because of its reliance on tactual-spatial information, is used to investigate the specialization of the right hemisphere. Tactile perceptual tasks fall into two broad categories: haptic identification of two- and three-dimensional shapes and tactile somatosensory sensitivity. Similar to the auditory sensory modality, stimuli presented to each hand are conveyed primarily to the contralateral hemisphere. Fine sensory input to the fingers is transmitted solely to the contralateral hemisphere (Brinkman & Kuypers, 1972). Originally, simultaneous, or *dichhaptic,* presentation of different stimuli was thought to produce competition between the hemispheres and more effectively elicit perceptual asymmetries (Witelson, 1974). Flanery and Balling (1979) demonstrated that either simultaneous or successive stimulation produces similar hemispheric asymmetries. A left-hand advantage for identifying forms, dots, and somatosensory stimulation reflects the specialization of the right hemisphere for the processing of tactual-spatial information.

Manual Exploration

The haptic identification task involves blind, manual exploration of forms with the index and middle fingers. Table 7 presents the results of studies assessing hemispheric asymmetries via the tactual modality. A wide variety of stimuli have been used for tactual exploration, including nonsense shapes, shapes of concrete objects, single letters, bigrams, and two-letter words. A left-hand superiority exists for these stimuli, but this superiority appears at different ages for the different stimuli.

Nonsense Shapes

For the nonsense shapes, a left-hand advantage was originally observed by Witelson (1974, 1976) in 6-to-13-year-old boys. Sex differences were observed in 5-year-olds, with boys showing the significant left-hand advantage (Affleck & Joyce, 1979). Other studies found no sex differences. A left-hand advantage was obtained for boys and girls in 7-to-13-year-old children (Coiffi & Kandel, 1979), in 9-year-old children (Klein & Rosenfield, 1980), and in 4-to-5-year-old children (Etaugh & Levy, 1981). A recent study found a left-hand advantage in 2- and 3-year-old boys and girls (Rose, 1984).

The inconsistencies in the observed sex differences in the manual exploration task cannot be attributed to methodological differences. With one exception (Rose, 1984), all studies followed the procedure developed by Witelson (1974). This suggests that the left-hand superiority in the identification of nonsense forms is a relatively fragile effect. The studies investigating manual perceptual asymmetries indicated that a left-hand advantage can be obtained in 2-year-old children of both sexes. In adults, sex differences in the identification of nonsense forms do not exist (McGlone, 1980).

One study found a developmental trend in the left-hand-right-hemisphere specialization for the identification of nonsense tactile stimuli. Flanery and Balling (1979) examined 7-, 9-, and 11-year-old children. A significant left-hand advantage was found only in the 11-year-old group. This effect was significant for boys and girls. Flanery and Balling's study is noteworthy because it used *manual,* as opposed to visual, recognition as the response procedure. This procedure ensures that the stimulus and response materials are initially transmitted to the same hemisphere. One other study used this procedure. Newcombe and Bandura (1983) found a left-hand superiority for the manual recognition of tactually presented nonsense forms in 11-year-old girls. No other age group was investigated. These results suggest that manual recognition may be a particularly sensitive response procedure to examine hemispheric asymmetries in the tactual modality.

Shapes of Concrete Objects

Shapes of concrete objects (i.e., tree, house, cow, etc.) have also been used as stimuli. A left-hand advantage appeared between the ages of 10 and 12 for boys, but not for girls. No hand differences were observed in 8- and 10-year-old children. The results were interpreted as indicating that the right hemisphere's specialization for processing tactile-spatial information develops with age and that this asymmetry develops earlier in boys than in girls (Hatta, Yamamoto, Kawabata, & Tsutui, 1981). The developmental trend observed in this study was similar to those reported by Flanery and Balling (1979). One problem with concrete objects is that they are easily verbalized. Verbal mediation may have interfered with the right hemisphere's superiority for the processing of spatial information. The tactile exploration of linguistic stimuli could help clarify whether verbal mediation interferes with the right hemisphere's processing ability.

Linguistic Stimuli

Linguistic stimuli have been used in tactile identification studies. Originally, it was hypothesized that single letters would be more accurately recognized when presented to the right hand because of the left hemisphere's superiority for the processing of linguistic information (Witelson, 1974). This prediction has not been confirmed. The performance of the right and left hands is equivalent in the manual exploration of single letters (e.g., Klein & Rosefield, 1980; LaBreche, Manning, Goble, & Markman, 1977; Witelson, 1974). Similar to the results ob-

Table 7
Age and Sex Differences in Left-Hand Superiority for Manual Exploration of Shapes

Study	Stimulus (shapes)	Age group and sex																									N
		1		2		3		4		5		6		7		8		9		10		11		12		13	
		M	F	M	F	M	F	M	F	M	F	M	F	M	F	M	F	M	F	M	F	M	F	M	F	M	F	
Witelson (1974)	Nonsense													+				+						+				47
	Letters													0				0						0				47
Witelson (1976)	Nonsense									+	0			+	0			+	0			+	0					200
Flanery & Balling (1979)	Nonsense													0	0			0	0			+	+					64
Coiffi & Kandel (1979)	Nonsense													+	+			+	+			+	+			+	+	112
	Words													−	−			−	−			−	−			−	−	112
	Bigrams													+	0			+	0			+	0			+	−	112
Affleck & Joyce (1979)	Nonsense									+	0																	31
Klein & Rosenfield (1980)	Nonsense																	+	+									30
	Letters																	0	0									30
Etaugh & Levy (1981)	Nonsense							+	+	+	+																	46
Newcombe & Bandura (1983)	Nonsense																					+						85
Hatta, Yamamoto, Kawabata, & Tsutui (1981)	Concrete objects															0	0			0	0			+	0			48
Rose (1984)	Shapes	0	0	+	+	+	+																					72
Summary: Significant − left hand		0	0	1	1	1	1	1	1	2	1	0		3	1	1	0	3	2	2	0	3	3	2	0	3	1	
Total		1	1	1	1	1	1	1	1	2	2	1	1	6	4	2	2	6	6	4	2	4	5	2	2	5	3	

Note. M − male; F − female. + − significant left-hand superiority; 0 − nonsignificant hand superiority. − = significant right-hand superiority.

tained with shapes of concrete objects, tactile exploration of letters may be subject to verbal mediation, thereby interfering with the spatial processing requirements of the task. This interpretation predicts that a right-hand advantage should emerge as the stimuli become more amenable to verbal mediation. There is some support for this prediction.

Coiffi and Kandel (1979) extended the single-letter task to include bigrams and two-letter words. The linguistic stimuli were compared to nonsense forms. They observed the usual left-hand–right-hemisphere advantage for the nonsense shapes. For bigrams, the boys showed a left-hand superiority, but the girls showed no lateral asymmetries until age 13 when the performance of the right hand surpassed the left hand. Both boys and girls showed a right-hand advantage for recognizing tactually presented words. These results indicate that tactile–spatial stimuli that cannot be easily verbalized may be processed by the right hemisphere, and stimuli that can be easily verbalized may be better processed by the left hemisphere in children of both sexes. Sex differences may emerge with stimuli that can be processed spatially and verbally. More research is needed to determine whether this effect is due to sex differences in cerebral organization or cognitive strategies.

In summary, a left-hand superiority for manual exploration of shapes varies with age, sex, and stimuli, but no consistent pattern of results has emerged. The adult pattern of hemispheric specialization for tactile–spatial exploration was observed by age 2. A few studies observed developmental changes in the processing of spatial stimuli, with a right-hemisphere superiority appearing around age 11. This effect was observed when the results were controlled for the overall increase in performance with increasing age, and it was confirmed when the proportion of children showing a superior left-hand performance was considered. Sex differences were observed, but the influence of cognitive strategies remains to be delineated.

Somatosensory Identification

Somatosensory sensitivity studies with children yield conflicting results (see Table 8). Some studies reported developmental changes and sex differences in the perception of somatosensory stimulation. Ghent (1961) examined single-point pressure sensitivity of the thumbs in 5-, 6-, 7-, 8-, 9-, and 11-year-old children. Sex differences were observed. For the girls, the right thumb was significantly more sensitive than the left thumb at age 5. The adult pattern of greater sensitivity of the left thumb appeared at age 6 and became significant in the 7- and 9-year-old girls. For the boys, a lower tactual threshold (greater sensitivity) of the left thumb was significant only in the 11-year-old group. Using the same procedure, Kimura (1963) tested 5-to-9-year-olds. Greater sensitivity of the left thumb first appeared at age 6, but it did not reach significance until age 11. Sex differences were noted, with the girls, but not the boys, showing a lower threshold at age 11. Both studies concluded that developmental changes in tactual sensitivity occur and that these changes differ between boys and girls.

A third study found no sex differences in the perception of

tactile stimulation. Moreau and Milner (1981) examined lateral differences in the perception of tactile pressure applied to the hands in 5-year-old children. Boys and girls were significantly more accurate in perceiving stimuli applied to the left hand than to the right hand, suggesting that the adult pattern of right-hemisphere superiority for perceiving somesthetic threshold may be present by age 5. The discrepancies between this study and the studies using single-point pressure sensitivity could be due to methodological differences. Ghent included several left-handed subjects (13%) unevenly distributed across age and sex. All three studies used different procedures to determine the threshold level. Moreau et al. applied pressure to the center dorsum of each hand and measured number of omissions, whereas Ghent and Kimura applied pressure to the thumbs and measured stimulus perception. In addition, Ghent and Kimura's findings of sex differences disagree sharply with several studies showing either no sex differences (Coiffi et al., 1979; Etaugh & Levy, 1981; Klein & Rosenfield, 1980; Rose, 1984) or that boys develop left-hand advantage before girls (Affleck & Joyce, 1979; Coiffi et al., 1976; Hatta et al., 1981; Rudel, Denckla, & Hirsch, 1977; Rudel, Denckla, & Spalten, 1974; Witelson, 1976).

Two studies examined lateral differences in somatosensory sensitivity with the finger localization and fingertip writing techniques (Finlayson & Reitan, 1976; Reitan, 1971). No lateral asymmetries or sex differences were observed in 6-to-14-year-old children. The performance of both hands was equivalent, suggesting that the finger localization and fingertip writing techniques may be inappropriate for studying cerebral asymmetries in normal children. The results indicated that each hemisphere processes finger localization and fingertip writing stimulation when presented to the contralateral side of the body.

Tactual identification of individual braille letters has also been examined. Braille provides a unique combination of somatosensory and spatial information (i.e., different configurations of raised dots). Blind children and adults typically use their left hand to read braille (Hermelin & O'Connor, 1971). Children with normal eyesight show age and sex differences in their ability to recognize individual braille letters (Rudel et al., 1974, 1977). In both studies, the boys developed a left-hand superiority between the ages of 10 and 12. Sex differences were noted. The girls developed a significant left-hand advantage only by age 14. No age or sex differences were observed in the 10-year-old children, but sex differences were observed in the 8-year-olds. Eight-year-old girls were better able to recognize braille letters with their right hand, whereas the boys showed no hand superiority (Rudel et al., 1974).

With one exception (Moreau & Milner, 1981), the results from the studies using somatosensory stimulation suggest that developmental changes occur in the right hemisphere. However, there are marked disagreements concerning sex differences. Some studies found that girls developed the ability to make somatosensory discriminations earlier than boys (Ghent, 1961; Kimura, 1963), whereas other studies found the opposite effect (Rudel et al., 1974, 1977). These sex differences are confounded with the type of stimulus used. The girls showed an earlier development of single-point pressure sensitivity, whereas the boys developed the ability to discriminate stimuli with somatosensory and spatial characteristics earlier than the girls.

Interestingly, for the boys, the left-hand superiority appeared at around age 11 for tactile and somatosensory-spatial stimuli. Two studies that were discussed in the previous section used tactile-spatial stimuli and obtained similar results. Boys developed a left-hand superiority for the identification of shapes of concrete objects between 10 and 12 years of age and for the identification of nonsense shapes by age 11 (Flanery & Balling, 1979; Hatta et al., 1981).

Methodological Criticisms

The methodological limitations of the tactile-perceptual paradigm have not been systematically investigated. This is curious in light of Witelson's (1974) early warning about the influence of attentional factors in the manual exploration task. Two studies reported attentional biases in manual asymmetries. Witelson (1974) obtained a left-hand superiority for nonsense shapes only when the shapes were presented before the letter stimuli. LaBreche et al. (1977) found a right-hand advantage for letters only when the letters were presented prior to the nonsense forms. Most studies avoid this bias by presenting linguistic and nonlinguistic stimuli in a counterbalanced order. Sex differences in tactile sensitivity, information processing, motor control, and environmental and sociological factors have been proposed to account for the observed sex differences in tactile perceptual asymmetries (Klein & Rosenfield, 1980; Rose, 1984; Witelson, 1977). These factors, along with the reliability of the tactile perceptual task, need to be investigated.

Conclusions

Age and sex differences in cerebral lateralization of function are important for theorists hypothesizing about the developmental course of cerebral representation of cognitive functions (Maccoby & Jacklin, 1974; McGee, 1979). The following discussion will attempt to integrate the findings from five lines of research used to examine age and sex differences in normal, right-handed children. The results from studies investigating the specialization of the left and right hemispheres will be considered separately.

For the functions thought to be lateralized in the left hemisphere, consensual validation from dichotic listening, tachistoscopic viewing, electrophysiological evoked potentials, manual discrimination, and somatosensory sensitivity experimental paradigms supports the hypotheses that (a) the left hemisphere is specialized for the processing of linguistic stimuli, (b) this specialization is constant through childhood, and (c) consistent sex differences do not exist (e.g., G. Berlin et al., 1973; Kinsbourne & Hiscock, 1977; Saxby & Bryden, 1984). Lenneberg's progressive lateralization model that the left hemisphere's ability to process linguistic information develops with age received only tentative support. The paucity of studies with infants less than 3 months of age, the lack of longitudinal studies, and the inconsistent results of the published studies prevent definitive conclusions from being drawn. However, Kinsbourne's invariant lateralization model was more strongly supported.

The results from the studies assessing the developmental course of the functional specialization of the right hemisphere indicate that certain abilities are lateralized from birth, whereas other abilities develop with age. These effects depend on the sen-

Table 8
Age and Sex Differences in Left-Hand Superiority for Somatosensory Sensitivity

		\multicolumn{20}{c	}{Age group and sex}	
		5		6		7		8		9		10		11		12		13		14	
Study	Stimulus	M	F	M	F	M	F	M	F	M	F	M	F	M	F	M	F	M	F	M	F	N
Rudel, Denckla, & Spalten (1974)	Braille							0	−			0	0			+	0			+	+	80
Rudel, Denckla, & Hirsch (1977)	Braille							0	0			0	0			+	0			+	+	96
Ghent (1961)	S-P-P-S (thumb)	0	−	0	+	0	+			0	+			+	0							105
Finlayson & Reitan (1976)	Finger localization			0	0	0	0	0	0							0	0	0	0	0	0	120
	Fingertip writing			0	0	0	0	0	0							0	0	0	0	0	0	120
Moreau & Milner (1981)	Hand	+	+																			31
Summary: Significant — left hand / Total		1/3	1/3	0/4	1/4	0/4	1/4	0/5	0/5	0/2	2/2	0/2	0/2	1/1	0/1	2/4	0/4	0/2	0/2	2/4	2/4	

Note. M = male; F = female. + = significant left-hand superiority; 0 = nonsignificant hand superiority. − = significant right-hand superiority.

sory modality being tested. The results from the dichotic listening and electroencephalography paradigms indicated that the right hemisphere is specialized from birth for the processing of nonlinguistic stimuli. Both paradigms delivered stimuli via the auditory modality. The results from studies presenting stimuli via the somatosensory modality suggested that some developmental changes may occur in the right hemisphere's ability to process spatial information. A left-hand superiority appeared only around age 11 for identifying individual braille letters and shapes of concrete objects and for the manual exploration and the manual recognition of nonsense shapes.

The studies that found developmental changes in the right hemisphere disagree with studies that found a left-hand advantage across several age groups for manual exploration of shapes (Etaugh & Levy, 1981; Rose, 1984). An absence of a statistically significant hand superiority at a particular age does not imply that hemispheric specialization is absent at that age or that one hemisphere does not possess the neural substrate capable of subserving a given function. Similar to the conclusions reached for the left hemisphere, the results from dichotic listening and tachistoscopic viewing studies suggest that factors other than structural asymmetries affect age differences in perceptual asymmetries. The marked absence of studies with infants precludes reaching firm conclusions about either the progressive or invariant lateralization models.

With regard to sex differences in cerebral lateralization of function in children, the data indicate that neither the male brain nor the female brain is more asymmetrically organized. Some studies found the male brain to be more asymmetrically organized than the female brain, whereas other studies found the female brain to be more asymmetrically organized than the male brain. But in most cases, the data showed that sex differences do not exist. These results disagree with McGlone's (1980) conclusions based on the adult literature that the male brain is more asymmetrically organized than the female brain.

Although developmental studies did not assess children beyond age 15, it is unlikely that sex differences develop between the ages of 15 and 18.

Throughout this review, several factors extrinsic to hemispheric specialization were found to affect behavioral asymmetries. These factors can be classified into two broad categories: stimulus specific and psychological factors.

The dichotic listening and tachistoscopic viewing paradigms are most susceptible to variations in stimulus presentation. In dichotic listening, both the intensity and the signal-to-noise ratio vary from study to study and between the linguistic and nonlinguistic stimuli within the same study. The studies measuring AEP demonstrated that very subtle variations of the stimulus produce lateral asymmetries. As a general rule, future dichotic listening studies should report the acoustic characteristics of the stimuli used to investigate lateral asymmetries.

In tachistoscopic viewing, the intensity, duration, and visual angle of the stimulus are usually the same for right and left visual field projections. However, each hemisphere differs in its ability to extract information depending on the overall energy level and perceived acuity of the visual display. Stimulus intensity, duration, and visual angle vary from study to study. Basic research is needed on the effect of stimulus characteristics on lateral asymmetries.

Psychological factors, such as attention, memory duration, and reporting biases, also affect lateral asymmetries. Their influence is more pronounced when sex differences are examined. This indicates that behavioral asymmetries are a relatively fragile effect and suggests that individual differences exceed left versus right and male versus female differences.

Although there is no doubt that differences exist between the left and right hemispheres, the uncritical acceptance of the results from dichotic listening, tachistoscopic viewing, haptic exploration, and somatosensory sensitivity seems unwarranted. Theoretical formulations of the developmental course of hemispheric specialization need to consider a host of variables that affect behavioral asymmetries.

Throughout this survey, several lines of research were suggested, and these will not be reiterated here. The verbal-nonverbal dichotomy is only one dimension in which cerebral asymmetries are found. Future research should address two global issues. First, the verbal-nonverbal dichotomy is descriptive, and it says nothing about the more basic characteristics of the information-processing abilities of each hemisphere. Molfese and his colleagues have begun to examine subtle differences in hemispheric processing that could be extended to other experimental paradigms. Second, there is some indication from the tachistoscopic studies that the retinal location of the stimulus projection affects lateral asymmetries. Further research on the characteristics of the stimulus and stimulus presentation will provide valuable information concerning cerebral lateralization of function beyond the verbal-nonverbal dichotomy.

References

Affleck, G., & Joyce, P. (1979). Sex differences in the association of cerebral hemisphere specialization of spatial function with conservation task performance. *Journal of Genetic Psychology, 134,* 271-280.

Anstis, S. M. (1974). A chart demonstrating variations in acuity with retinal position. *Vision Research, 14,* 589-592.

Bakker, D. J., Hoefkens, M., & Van der Vlugt, H. (1979). Hemispheric specialization in children. *Cortex, 15,* 619-625.

Bakker, D. J., Van der Vlugt, H., & Claushuis, M. (1978). The reliability of dichotic ear asymmetry in normal children. *Neuropsychologia, 16,* 753-758.

Basser, L. S. (1962). Hemiplegia of early onset and the faculty of speech with special reference to the effect of hemispherectomy. *Brain, 85,* 427-460.

Bener, A. (1980). Sex differences: Asymmetry in dermatoglyphics and brain. *Behavioral and Brain Sciences, 3,* 228-229.

Benninger, C., Matthis, P., & Scheffner, D. (1984). EEG development of healthy boys and girls. Results of a longitudinal study. *Electroencephalography and Clinical Neurophysiology, 57,* 1-12.

Berlin, C. I., & Cullen, J. K. (1977). Acoustic problems in dichotic listening tasks. In S. J. Segalowitz & F. A. Gruber (Eds.), *Language development and neurological theory* (pp. 75-88). New York: Academic Press.

Berlin, G., Hughes, L., Lowel-Bell, S., & Berlin, H. (1973). Dichotic right ear advantage in children 5 to 13. *Cortex, 9,* 394-402.

Best, C. T., Hoffman, H., & Glanville, B. B. (1982). Development of infant ear asymmetry for speech and music. *Perception and Psychophysics, 31,* 75-85.

Bigum, H. B., Dustman, R. E., & Beck, E. C. (1970). Visual and somatosensory evoked responses from mongoloid and normal children. *Electroencephalography and Clinical Neurophysiology, 28,* 576-585.

Blumstein, S., Goodglass, H., & Tartter, V. (1975). The reliability of ear advantage in dichotic listening. *Brain and Language, 2,* 226-236.

Borowy, T., & Goebel, R. (1976). Cerebral lateralization of speech: The effect of age, sex, race, and socioeconomic class. *Neuropsychologia, 14,* 363-370.

Bradshaw, G. J., Hicks, R. E., & Rose, B. (1979). Lexical discrimination and letter string identification in the two visual fields. *Brain and Language, 8,* 10-18.

Bradshaw, J. L., & Nettleton, N. C. (1981). The nature of hemispheric specialization in man. *Behavioral and Brain Sciences, 4,* 51-91.

Brinkman, J., & Kuypers, H. G. (1972). Split-brain monkeys: Cerebral control of ipsilateral arm, hand and finger movements. *Science, 176,* 536-539.

Broman, M. (1978). Reaction time differences between the left and right hemispheres for face and letter discrimination in children and adults. *Cortex, 14,* 578-591.

Bryden, M. P. (1970). Laterality effects in dichotic listening: Relations with handedness and reading ability in children. *Neuropsychologia, 8,* 443-450.

Bryden, M. P., & Allard, F. (1981). Do auditory perceptual asymmetries develop? *Cortex, 17,* 313-318.

Burden, V., Bradshaw, J. L., Nettleton, N. C., & Wilson, L. (1985). Hand and hemispace effects in tactual tasks in children. *Neuropsychologia, 23,* 515-525.

Caplan, B., & Kinsbourne, M. (1981). Cerebral lateralization, preferred cognitive mode, and reading ability in normal children. *Brain and Language, 14,* 349-370.

Carmon, A., Nachson, I., & Starinsky, R. (1976). Developmental aspects of visual hemifield differences in perception of verbal material. *Brain and Language, 3,* 463-469.

Carter, G. L., & Kinsbourne, M. (1979). The ontogeny of cerebral lateralization of spatial mental set. *Developmental Psychology, 15,* 241-255.

Coiffi, J., & Kandel, G. (1979). Laterality of stereognostic accuracy of children for words, shapes, and bigrams: Sex differences for bigrams. *Science, 204,* 1432-1434.

Crowell, D. J., Jones, R. H., Kapuniai, L. E., & Nakagawa, J. K. (1973). Unilateral cortical activity in newborn humans: An early index of cerebral dominance? *Science, 180,* 205-208.

Davis, A. E., & Wada, J. A. (1977). Hemispheric asymmetries in human infants: Spectral analysis of flash and click evoked potentials. *Brain and Language, 4,* 23-31.

Denenberg, V. H. (1980). Some principles for interpreting laterality differences. *Behavioral and Brain Sciences, 3,* 232-233.

Dustman, R. E., & Beck, E. C. (1963). Long-term stability of visually evoked potentials in man. *Science, 142,* 1480-1481.

Entus, A. (1977). Hemispheric asymmetry in processing of dichotically presented speech and nonspeech stimuli by infants. In S. J. Segalowitz & F. A. Gruber (Eds.), *Language development and neurological theory* (pp. 64-73). New York: Academic Press.

Etaugh, C., & Levy, R. B. (1981). Hemispheric specialization for tactile-spatial processing in preschool children. *Perceptual and Motor Skills, 53,* 621-622.

Fairweather, H. (1980). Sex differences still being dressed in the emperor's new clothes. *Behavioral and Brain Sciences, 3,* 234-235.

Finlayson, M. A. J., & Reitan, R. M. (1976). Handedness in relation to measure of motor and tactile-perceptual functions in normal children. *Perceptual and Motor Skills, 43,* 475-481.

Flanery, R. C., & Balling, J. D. (1979). Developmental changes in hemispheric specialization for tactile spatial ability. *Developmental Psychology, 15,* 364-372.

Forgays, D. G. (1953). The development of differential word recognition. *Journal of Experimental Psychology, 45,* 165-168.

Gardiner, M. F., & Walter, D. O. (1976). Evidence of hemispheric specialization from infant EEG. In S. Harnad, R. W. Doty, & L. Goldstien (Eds.), *Lateralization in the nervous system* (pp. 481-500). New York: Academic Press.

Geffen, G. (1978). The development of the right ear advantage in dichotic listening with focused attention. *Cortex, 14,* 169-177.

Geffen, G., & Wale, J. (1979). Development of selective listening in hemispheric asymmetry. *Developmental Psychology, 15,* 138-146.

Geffner, D., & Dorman, M. (1976). Hemispheric specialization for speech perception in four year old children from low and middle socio-economic classes. *Cortex, 12,* 71-73.

Geffner, D. S., & Hochberg, I. (1971). Ear laterality performance of children from low and middle socioeconomic levels on verbal dichotic listening task. *Cortex, 7,* 193-203.

Geschwind, N., & Levitsky, W. (1968). Human brain: Left-right asymmetries in temporal speech region. *Science, 161,* 186-187.

Ghent, L. (1961). Developmental changes in tactual thresholds on dominant and non-dominant sides. *Journal of Comparative and Physiological Psychology, 54,* 670-673.

Glanville, B. B., Best, C. T., & Levenson, R. A. (1977). A cardiac measure of cerebral asymmetries in infant auditory perception. *Developmental Psychology, 13,* 54-59.

Gordon, D. P. (1983). The influence of sex on the development of lateralization of speech. *Neuropsychologia, 21,* 139-146.

Harris, L. J. (1981). Sex related variations in spatial skills. In L. S. Liben, A. H. Patterson, & N. Newcombe (Eds.), *Spatial representation and behavior across the life span: Theory and applications* (pp. 83-125). New York: Academic Press.

Hatta, T., Yamamoto, M., Kawabata, Y., & Tsutui, K. (1981). Development of hemispheric specialization for tactile recognition in normal children. *Cortex, 17,* 611-616.

Hecaen, H. (1976). Acquired aphasia in children and the ontogenesis of hemispherical functional specialization. *Brain and Language, 3,* 114-134.

Hellige, J. B. (1980). Effects of perceptual quality and visual fields of probe stimulus presentation on memory search for letters. *Journal of Experimental Psychology, 6,* 639-651.

Hermelin, B., & O'Connor, N. (1971). Functional asymmetry in the reading of Braille. *Neuropsychologia, 9,* 431-435.

Herron, J. (Ed.). (1980). *Neuropsychology of left-handedness.* New York: Academic Press.

Hiscock, M., & Bergstrom, K. J. (1982). The lengthy persistence of priming effects in dichotic listening. *Neuropsychologia, 20,* 43-53.

Hiscock, M., & Kinsbourne, M. (1977). Selective listening asymmetry in preschool children. *Developmental Psychology, 13,* 217-224.

Hiscock, M., & Kinsbourne, M. (1978). Ontogeny of cerebral dominance: Evidence from time-sharing asymmetry in children. *Developmental Psychology, 14,* 321-329.

Hynd, G., & Obrzut, J. (1977). Effects of grade level and sex on magnitude of the dichotic ear advantage. *Neuropsychologia, 15,* 689-692.

Inglis, J., & Sykes, D. H. (1967). Some sources of variation in dichotic listening performance in children. *Journal of Experimental Child Psychology, 5,* 480-488.

Ingram, D. (1975). Cerebral speech lateralization in young children. *Neuropsychologia, 13,* 103-105.

Jones, B., & Anuza, T. (1982). Sex differences in cerebral lateralization in 3- and 4-year-old children. *Neuropsychologia, 20,* 347-350.

Kimura, D. (1963). Speech lateralization in young children determined by an auditory test. *Journal of Comparative and Physiological Psychology, 56,* 899-902.

Kimura, D. (1967). Functional asymmetry in the brain in dichotic listening. *Cortex, 3,* 163-178.

Kinsbourne, M. (1975). The ontogeny of cerebral dominance. *Annals of the New York Academy of Science, 263,* 244-250.

Kinsbourne, M., & Hiscock, M. (1977). Does cerebral dominance develop? In S. J. Segalowitz & F. A. Gruber (Eds.), *Language development and neurological theory* (pp. 169-191). New York: Academic Press.

Klein, S. P., & Rosenfield, W. D. (1980). The hemispheric specialization for linguistic and nonlinguistic tactile stimuli in third grade children. *Cortex, 16,* 205-212.

Knox, C., & Kimura, D. (1970). Cerebral processing of nonverbal sounds in boys and girls. *Neuropsychologia, 8,* 227-237.

Kraft, R. H. (1982). Relationship of ear specialization to degree of task difficulty, sex, and lateral preference. *Perceptual and Motor Skills, 54,* 703-714.

Kroon, J. N., Rijsdijk, J. P., & Van der Wildt, G. J. (1980). Peripheral contrast sensitivity for sine-wave gratings and single periods. *Vision Research, 20,* 243-252.

LaBreche, T. M., Manning, A. A., Goble, W., & Markman, R. (1977). Hemispheric specialization for linguistic and nonlinguistic tactual perception in a congenitally deaf population. *Cortex, 13,* 184-194.

Lenneberg, E. H. (1967). *Biological foundations of language.* New York: Wiley.

Lewandowski, L. L. (1982). Hemispheric asymmetry in children. *Perceptual and Motor Skills, 54,* 1011-1019.

Lewkowicz, D. J., & Turkewitz, G. (1983). Relationship between processing and motor asymmetries in early development. In G. Young, S. J. Segalowitz, C. M. Corter, & S. E. Trehub (Eds.), *Manual specialization and the developing brain* (pp. 375-393). New York: Academic Press.

Lokker, R., & Morais, J. (1985). Ear differences in children at two years of age. *Neuropsychologia, 23,* 127-129.

Maccoby, E., & Jacklin, C. (1974). *The psychology of sex differences.* Stanford, CA: Stanford University Press.

Marcel, T., Katz, L., & Smith, M. (1974). Laterality and reading proficiency. *Neuropsychologia, 12,* 131-139.

Marcel, T., & Rajan, P. (1975). Lateral specialization for recognition of words and faces in good and poor readers. *Neuropsychologia, 13,* 489-497.

Marsh, G. R. (1978). Asymmetry of electrophysiological phenomena and its relation to behavior in humans. In M. Kinsbourne (Ed.), *Asymmetrical function of the brain* (pp. 292-317). New York: Cambridge University Press.

McGee, M. G. (1979). Human spatial abilities: Psychometric studies and environmental, genetic, hormonal, and neurological influences. *Psychological Bulletin, 86,* 889-910.

McGlone, J. (1980). Sex differences in human brain asymmetry: A critical review. *Behavioral and Brain Sciences, 3,* 215-227.

Miller, L. K., & Turner, S. (1973). Development of hemifield differences in word recognition. *Journal of Educational Psychology, 65,* 172-176.

Mirabile, P. J., Porter, R. J., Hughes, L. F., & Berlin, C. I. (1978). Dichotic lag effect in children 7 to 15. *Developmental Psychology, 14,* 277-285.

Molfese, D. L. (1973). Central asymmetry in infants, children, and adults: Auditory evoked responses to speech and music. *Journal of the Acoustical Society of America, 53,* 363.

Molfese, D. L. (1977). Infant cerebral asymmetries. In S. J. Segalowitz & F. A. Gruber (Eds.), *Language development and neurological theory* (pp. 22-35). New York: Academic Press.

Molfese, D. L. (1978). Left and right hemisphere involvement in speech perception: Electrophysiological correlates. *Perception and Psychophysics, 23,* 237-243.

Molfese, D. L., Freeman, R. B., & Palermo, D. S. (1975). The ontogeny of brain lateralization for speech and nonspeech stimuli. *Brain and Language, 2,* 356-368.

Molfese, D. L., & Hess, T. M. (1978). Hemispheric specialization for VOT perception in preschool children. *Journal of Experimental Child Psychology, 26,* 71-84.

Molfese, D. L., & Molfese, V. J. (1979). Hemisphere and stimulus differences as reflected in the cortical responses of newborn infants to speech stimuli. *Developmental Psychology, 15,* 505-511.

Molfese, D. L., & Molfese, V. J. (1980). Cortical response of preterm infants to phonetic and nonphonetic speech stimuli. *Developmental Psychology, 16,* 574-581.

Molfese, D. L., & Molfese, V. J. (1985). Electrophysiological indices of auditory discrimination in newborn infants: The bases for predicting later language development? *Infant Behavior and Development, 8,* 197-211.

Moreau, T., & Milner, P. (1981). Lateral differences in the detection of touched body parts in young children. *Developmental Psychology, 17,* 351-356.

Nagafuchi, M. (1970). Development of dichotic and monaural hearing abilities in young children. *Acta Otolaryngologia, 69,* 409-414.

Newcombe, N., & Bandura, M. M. (1983). Effect of age at puberty on spatial ability in girls: A question of mechanism. *Developmental Psychology, 19,* 215-224.

Olson, M. E. (1973). Laterality differences in tachistoscopic word recognition in normal and delayed readers in elementary school. *Neuropsychologia, 11,* 343-350.

Peters, J. F., Varner, J. L., & Ellingson, R. J. (1981). Interhemispheric amplitude symmetry in the EEG of normal full term, low risk premature, and trisomi-21 infants. *Electroencephalography and Clinical Neurophysiology, 51,* 165-169.

Piazza, D. (1977). Cerebral lateralization in young children as measured by dichotic listening and finger tapping tasks. *Neuropsychologia, 15,* 417-429.

Pizzamiglio, L., & Checchine, M. (1971). Development of the hemispheric dominance in children from 5 to 10 years of age and their relations with development of cognitive processes. *Brain Research, 31,* 363-364.

Porter, R. J., & Berlin, C. I. (1975). On interpreting developmental changes in the dichotic right ear advantage. *Brain and Language, 2,* 186-200.

Pring, T. R. (1980). The effects of stimulus size and exposure duration on visual field asymmetries. *Cortex, 17,* 227-240.

Ramsay, D. S., & Willis, M. P. (1984). Organization and lateralization of reaching in infants: An extension of Bresson et al. *Neuropsychologia, 22,* 639-641.

Reitan, R. M. (1971). Sensorimotor functions in brain damaged and normal children of early school age. *Perceptual and Motor Skills, 33,* 655-664.

Reynolds, D. M. Q., & Jeeves, M. A. (1978). A developmental study of hemisphere specialization for alphabetical stimuli. *Cortex, 14,* 259-267.

Rhodes, L. E., Dustman, R. E., & Beck, E. C. (1969). The visual evoked response: A comparison of bright and dull children. *Electroencephalography and Clinical Neurophysiology, 27,* 364-372.

Richlin, M., Weisinger, M., Weinstein, S., Giannini, M., & Morganstern, M. (1971). Interhemispheric asymmetries of evoked cortical responses in retarded and normal children. *Cortex, 7,* 98-105.

Rose, S. (1984). Developmental changes in hemispheric specialization for tactual processing in very young children: Evidence from crossmodal transfer. *Developmental Psychology, 20,* 568-574.

Rosenzweig, M. R. (1951). Representation of the two ears at the auditory cortex. *The American Journal of Physiology, 167,* 147-158.

Rudel, R., Denckla, M., & Hirsch, S. (1977). The development of left hand superiority for discriminating braille configurations. *Neurology, 27,* 160-164.

Rudel, R., Denckla, M., & Spalten, E. (1974). The functional asymmetry of braille letter learning in normal sighted children. *Neurology, 24,* 733-738.

Saxby, L., & Bryden, M. P. (1984). Left-ear superiority in children for processing of auditory emotional material. *Developmental Psychology, 20,* 72-80.

Schulman-Galambos, C. (1977). Dichotic listening performance in elementary and college students. *Neuropsychologia, 15,* 577-584.

Segalowitz, S. J., & Chapman, J. S. (1980). Cerebral asymmetry for speech in neonates: A behavioral measure. *Brain and Language, 9,* 281-288.

Sergent, J. (1983). Role of the input in visual hemispheric asymmetries. *Psychological Bulletin, 93,* 481-512.

Sexton, M. A., & Geffen, G. (1979). Development of three strategies of attention in dichotic monitoring. *Developmental Psychology, 15,* 299-310.

Springer, S. P., & Searleman, A. (1978). The ontogeny of hemispheric specialization: Evidence from dichotic listening in twins. *Neuropsychologia, 16,* 269-281.

Tomlinson-Keasey, C., Kelly, R., & Burton, J. (1978). Hemispheric changes in information processing during development. *Developmental Psychology, 14,* 214-223.

Treisman, A., & Geffen, G. (1968). Selective attention and cerebral dominance in perceiving and responding to speech messages. *Quarterly Journal of Experimental Psychology, 20,* 139-150.

Turkewitz, G., & Ross-Kossak, P. (1984). Multiple modes of right hemisphere information processing: Age and sex differences in facial recognition. *Developmental Psychology, 20,* 95-103.

Vargha-Khadem, F., & Corballis, M. (1979). Cerebral asymmetry in infants. *Brain and Language, 8,* 1-9.

Vargha-Khadem, F., & Watters, G. W. (1985). Development of speech and language following bilateral frontal lesions. *Brain and Language, 25,* 167-183.

Witelson, S. F. (1974). Hemispheric specialization for linguistic and nonlinguistic tactual perception using a dichotomous stimulation technique. *Cortex, 10,* 3-17.

Witelson, S. F. (1976). Sex and single hemisphere: Right hemisphere specialization for spatial processing. *Science, 193,* 425-427.

Witelson, S. F. (1977). Developmental dyslexia: Two right hemispheres and none left. *Science, 195,* 309-311.

Yeni-Komshian, G., Isenberg, D., & Goldberg, H. (1975). Cerebral dominance and reading disability: Left visual field deficit in poor readers. *Neuropsychologia, 13,* 83-94.

Young, A. W., & Bion, P. J. (1980). Absence of any developmental trend in right hemisphere superiority for face recognition. *Cortex, 16,* 113-221.

Young, A. W., & Bion, P. J. (1981). Accuracy of naming laterally presented known faces by children and adults. *Cortex, 17,* 97-106.

Young, A. W., & Ellis, H. D. (1976). An experimental investigation of developmental differences in ability to recognize faces presented to the left and right cerebral hemispheres. *Neuropsychologia, 14,* 495-498.

Received March 17, 1986
Revision received August 13, 1986 ■

Sex Equality in Intrahemispheric Language Organization

ANDREW KERTESZ

Department of Clinical Neurological Sciences, Research Institute of St. Joseph's Hospital, University of Western Ontario, London, Canada

AND

THOMAS BENKE

Department of Neurology, University Clinic, Innsbruck, Austria

Sex differences in inter- and intrahemispheric cerebral organization, found in previous studies, have been used to explain sex differences in cognitive abilities. This study highlights data to contradict such widely held beliefs. Intrahemispheric language organization was examined by determining the location of lesions causing aphasia by computed tomography. No sex differences in the incidence of anterior, posterior, or central lesions was found. The distribution of left-hemisphere lesions in stroke patients, with or without aphasia, was also equal among the sexes. This study does not support the postulated gender difference in intrahemispheric cerebral organization. © 1989 Academic Press, Inc.

There has been evidence for group differences between normal males and females in verbal abilities and visuospatial skills for some time (Wechsler, 1955; Macoby & Jacklin, 1974). Generally, the verbal differences are small, mathematical differences are larger, and visuospatial differences are the largest (Halpern, 1986). Nevertheless, a substantial number of males show high verbal ability and, conversely, many females have higher than average mathematical and spatial ability. Whether the slightly better performance of females in verbal tasks and males on visuospatial and mathematical tasks can be attributed to differences in maturation and cerebral organization or to social causes remains hotly debated (Macoby & Jacklin, 1974).

The concept of sex differences in interhemispheric organization of

Address correspondence to Andrew Kertesz, M.D., Department of Clinical Neurological Sciences, Research Institute of St. Joseph's Hospital, University of Western Ontario, London, Ontario, Canada N6A 4V2.

language was originally suggested on the basis of more severe impairment of verbal intelligence in males following left temporal lobectomy (Lansdell, 1962; Lansdell & Urbach, 1965). Sex differences in cerebral processing of visual tasks have been suspected on the basis of more impaired Block Designs or Raven's Coloured Progressive Matrices scores in males with right-hemisphere lesions when compared to females (McGlone & Kertesz, 1973). The same study, however, showed no significant difference for aphasia scores between the sexes. Further sex differences in the effect of unilateral acquired lesion on verbal and spatial intelligence scores have been observed (McGlone, 1977; Inglis & Lawson, 1981). It was also suggested that females may become aphasic less often with left-hemisphere lesions on the basis of a small sample of patients (McGlone, 1977). However, an epidemiologic study of aphasic and cognitive impairments following stroke suggested that a higher male-to-female ratio in aphasic populations was related to the distribution of cerebral infarcts rather than to the sex differences in cerebral organization (Kertesz & Sheppard, 1981). Females became aphasic as often with left-hemisphere lesions as males when the ratio was corrected for sex differences in the incidence of infarcts and females did not show an increased incidence of aphasia from right-hemisphere lesion as one would expect if they had more bilateral distribution of language (Kertesz & Sheppard, 1981).

Another study proposed that females less often became aphasic following left posterior damage than males and that some functions dependent on left posterior speech systems in males may be subserved by left anterior region in females (Kimura, 1983). This study utilized a mixed population of tumors and vascular disease, with the males having a higher incidence of strokes and the females a higher incidence of tumors. The presence of aphasia was based on clinical judgment or a partial aphasia test; lesion localization was based on EEG and/or clinical data in many instances, and no radiological criteria were given for the location of anterior or posterior lesions. Only 2 of the 10 aphasic females had posterior lesions, but the distribution of nonaphasic lesions was similar to the males. A subsample in a small series with global aphasia showed that all eight anterior lesion were females, while all three posterior lesions were males, and tentatively supported the hypothesis of sex differences in anterior–posterior cerebral organization (Vignolo et al., 1986). Other evidence suggests that the incidence of Wernicke's and transcortical aphasia and neologistic jargon with posterior localization in females is no different from that of males (Kertesz & Sheppard, 1981; Kertesz, 1982a). Other studies using careful anatomical localization also found that given a lesion in the same location, males and females develop similar deficits in speech and language (Tranel & Damasio, 1987). The present study provides further information concerning intrahemispheric organization of cerebral functions by reviewing the sex incidences of anterior and posterior lesions in aphasic and nonaphasic left-hemisphere-damaged patients.

METHODS

(a) Subjects. Subjects were selected by two methods in order to lessen the selection bias that might occur if only the method of selecting patients referred for aphasia was used. This could possibly bias the results toward ignoring the lesions that did not cause aphasia in one gender or the other.

(1) Patients were selected from an aphasic stroke population on the basis of a computer tomography (CT) localized left-hemisphere lesion and aphasia on a standardized examination. One hundred twenty-eight patients, 71 males and 57 females, who performed below the cut-off point for aphasia on the Western Aphasia Battery (WAB) (Kertesz, 1982b) were included. Each patient was evaluated in the acute phase between 10 and 45 days after stroke.

(2) The second population was a sample of 88 unilateral lesions, coded left hemisphere positive by the radiology department during the previous 2 years. The clinical files of these patients were reviewed and those with dementia, obtundation, coma, lack of language data, or multiple events were excluded. This population allowed us to look at unselected lesions of the left hemisphere, including those that did not cause aphasia.

(3) Thirty-one patients who were selected through the scan reviews (method 2) were also added, increasing the total aphasic population to $n = 159$: males = 89; females = 70. This population from Southern Ontario has an average education of Grade IX and represents a fairly uniform, basically literate, socioeconomic background, with presumably average, evenly distributed premorbid language capacities.

(b) Lesion location. All CT scans in both groups were reviewed by two neurologists, blind to the sex of the patient, who classified the lesion location as mostly anterior, central, or mostly posterior with respect to the location of the central sulcus and Sylvian fissure. Patients with bilateral or multiple lesions were excluded. The central sulcus was identified on some basal cuts, and its location was estimated on the higher cuts using Matsui and Hirano's CT Atlas (Matsui & Hirano, 1978). In the plane of the third ventricle, a line 15° forward to the horizontal line perpendicular to the center of the ventricle was drawn. This forward angled line connects the genu of the internal capsule with the estimated position of the central sulcus, separating the anterior and posterior subcortical regions (Fig. 1). In the parietal cuts, the center of the crescent of the lateral ventricle was the dividing point from which a horizontal line perpendicular to the midsagittal line served as an antero-posterior boundary (Fig. 2). On higher cuts, 15° angulation posterior to the midline horizontal was used to reach the estimated position of the central sulcus on the surface.

RESULTS

(1) No significant sex differences between anterior, posterior, and central lesions were found in the total aphasic population, that included the 159 subjects selected by methods 1 and 2, on a χ^2 test (Table 1). Among the 89 males, 18 had predominantly anterior, 44 predominantly posterior, and 27 central lesions. In 70 females, 15 had predominantly anterior, 34 predominantly posterior, and 21 central lesions. In order to confirm the validity of the null hypothesis, a power analysis of n as a function of effect size, α, and power was performed. Power analysis of n for the χ^2 design, with a power of .80 and α of .05, results in an $n = 96$ with a medium observable effect. At higher power, .95, the medium effect yields a required sample size of 154 (Cohen, 1969).

(2) The distribution of lesions was analyzed in each aphasic group in

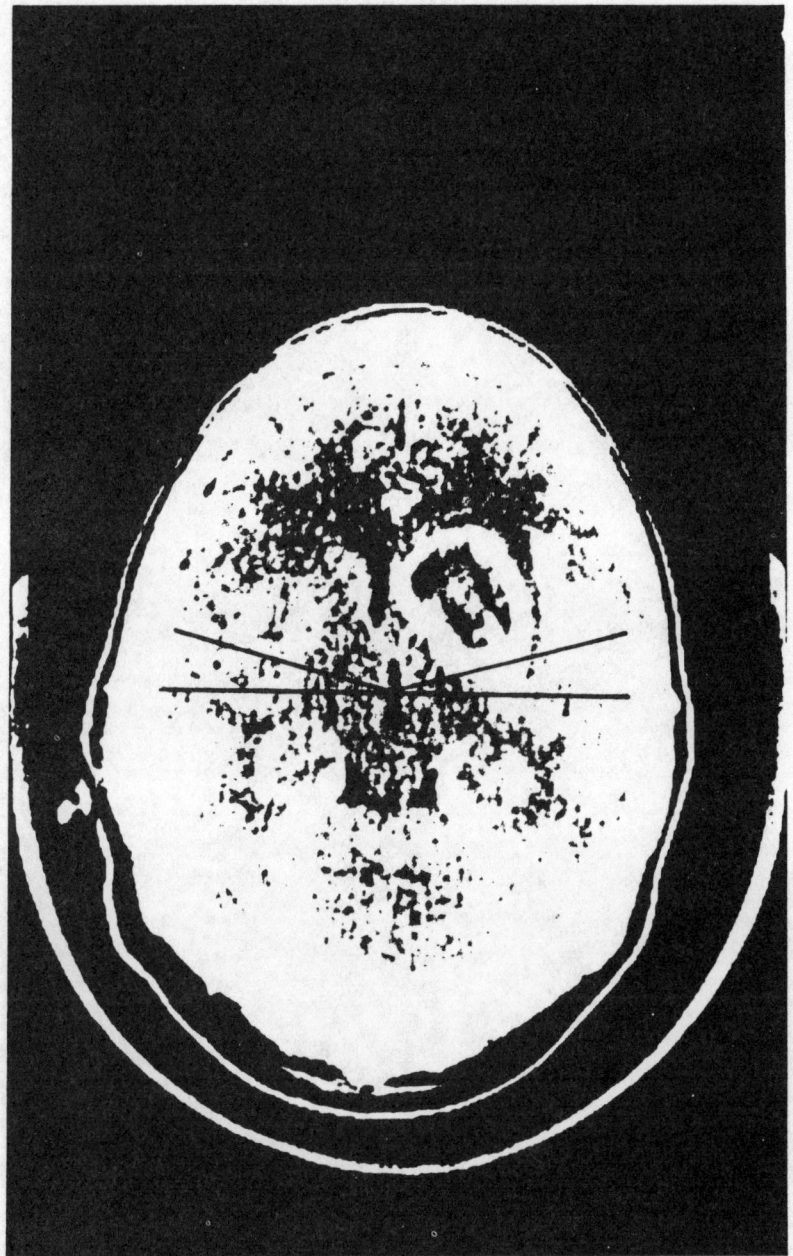

FIG. 1. This is a contrast enhanced CT of a male who had Broca's aphasia at the time of the CT scanning which evolved toward anomic aphasia 1 month later. The lesion is in the caudate at the anterior internal capsule and anterior putamen with the interior portion of the insula enhancing also. A 15° forward angulation from the horizontal line perpendicular to the middle of the third ventricle connects the estimated position of the central sulcus with the center point and, in this case, determines a lesion as anterior. The patient's left hemisphere is on the right side of the image.

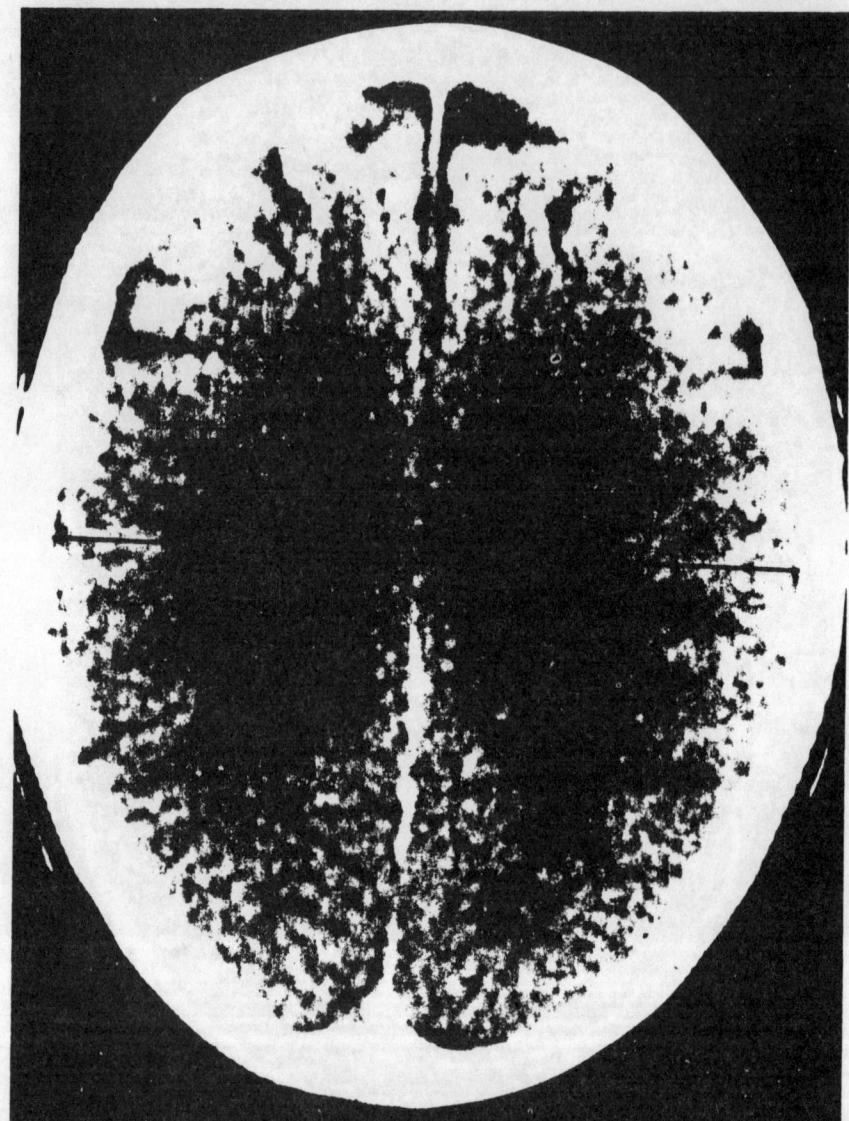

FIG. 2. This woman had Wernicke's aphasia with the lesion almost entirely behind the horizontal line positioned at the center of the crescent of the lateral ventricles. The left hemisphere is on the right side of the image.

population 1 ($n = 128$), defined by test scores obtained on the WAB (Kertesz, 1982b). In none of these groups was the sex difference in the location of lesions found to be significant on χ^2 test (Table 2). Wernicke's (22), anomic (34), and conduction aphasics (12) had mostly posterior lesions and there was no significant sex difference in their distribution.

TABLE 1
Stroke Lesions of Acute Aphasics

		Ant.	Post.	Central
Males	89	18	44	27
Females	70	15	34	21
Total	159	33	78	48

Note. $\chi^2 = 0.0348$; $p = 0.98$.

A second analysis was performed by excluding the central group, including only the anterior and posterior lesions, and, again, no significant sex differences were found.

(3) The CT scan selected population of 57 left-hemisphere lesions was also reviewed for the incidence of aphasia (population 2). The aphasic ($n = 31$) and nonaphasic ($n = 26$) groups were analyzed separately. Left-hemisphere lesions with aphasia showed a trend of slightly more anterior lesions in males than females, which did not reach statistical significance (Table 3). This trend is in the direction opposite to Kimura's (1983). Left-hemisphere lesions without aphasia were evenly split for gender (Table 3).

(4) The severity of aphasia was compared across the sexes and various locations where the complete WAB scores were available ($n = 128$) with a two-way ANOVA (Table 4). The results showed a significant difference for location but not for sex or sex by location interaction. In other words, the mean Aphasia Quotients (AQ) representing the severity of aphasia were the lowest in the central location (most severe deficits) and the highest in the posterior group (mildest aphasia). The posterior group was significantly different on the Newman–Keuls test ($p = .05$). However, there was no difference in the severity of aphasia between the sexes overall or between the sexes by location.

TABLE 2
Location by Sex in Aphasic Groups

| Type | Sex | Location | | | p |
		Ant.	Post.	Central	
Global	M	3	3	8	0.9
(29)	F	4	3	8	
Broca	M	2	7	7	0.3
(27)	F	4	4	3	
Wernicke	M	0	11	5	0.7
(23)	F	0	5	2	
Conduction	M	0	5	0	0.8
(12)	F	1	6	0	
Anomic	M	3	12	5	0.5
(37)	F	2	8	7	

TABLE 3
LEFT-HEMISPHERE LESIONS

	n	Ant.	Post.	Central
		Aphasics[a]		
Males	19	10	4	5
Females	12	4	7	1
		Nonaphasics[b]		
Males	12	3	8	1
Females	14	3	8	3

[a] $\chi^2 = 4.716; p = 0.094$
[b] $\chi^2 = 0.851; p = 0.653$

DISCUSSION

These results indicate no significant sex differences in intrahemispheric organization of language function, based on the incidence of left-hemispheric lesions and aphasia. Although sex differences in visuospatial and verbal abilities have been established in large group studies of normals, postulated inter- and intrahemispheric differences in cerebral organization remain more controversial. In particular, no convincing anatomical or physiological evidence indicates that anterior cerebral regions in females subserve functions that are carried out by posterior areas in males.

Many reasons can be suggested why a small series of posterior lesions, such as were used in previous studies, would not include aphasics. Substantial recovery may have taken place by the time the patient was examined. Tumors and arteriovenous malformations often cause few or no symptoms despite considerable size. Thus a population controlled for lesion etiology as well as lesion localization is more reliable than a small mixed group where selection factors can produce significant differences. Finally, there is the problem of what constitutes anterior or posterior lesions in the brain. EEG and clinical evidence is less reliable than CT scan evidence that is carefully evaluated, using anatomical templates,

TABLE 4
APHASIA SEVERITY: SEX AND LOCATION (MEAN APHASIA QUOTIENTS)

	Male		Female	
	$\bar{x}$	SD	$\bar{x}$	SD
Ant.	42.1	(38.9)	36.8	(29.3)
Central	34.8	(30.4)	33.3	(34.9)
Post.*	53.1	(25.5)	57.5	(38.8)

Note. Anova: Location, $p = 0.02$; sex, $p = 0.88$; sex by location, $p = 0.80$.
*$p = .05$ on Newman–Keuls.

such as in this study. Even with the CT scans or MRI's, it is often difficult to tell where the central sulcus divides the frontal and parietal lobes and much variability is introduced by the angle of the scan. Correlation with anatomical templates and determining the extent of the lesion requires experience. We attempted to standardize the judgment and increase the accuracy by using two evaluations.

Sex differences in performance or laterality may be related to anatomical, physiological, endocrine, and acquired psychological differences. It is unlikely that sex differences in the anterior–posterior cerebral organization account for the subtle yet significant differences in normal performance. If there are any sex differences in cerebral organization, a more complex relationship at a physiological or psychological level must be sought instead of an anatomical division to anterior and posterior structures. This study, using a rigorous method of localization of lesions and aphasia examination, presents substantial evidence against an intrahemispheric sex difference.

REFERENCES

Cohen, J. 1969. *Statistical power for the behavioral sciences.* New York: Academic Press.
Halpern, D. 1986. *Sex differences in cognitive abilities.* Hillsdale, NJ: Erlbaum.
Inglis, J., & Lawson, J. S. 1981. Sex differences in the effects of unilateral brain damage on intelligence. *Science,* 212, 693–694.
Kertesz, A. 1982a. Sex distribution in aphasia. *The Behavioural and Brain Sciences,* 5(2), 310.
Kertesz, A. 1982b. *The Western Aphasia Battery.* New York: Grune & Stratton.
Kertesz, A., & Sheppard, A. 1981. The epidemiology of aphasic and cognitive impairment in stroke—Age, sex, aphasia type and laterality differences. *Brain,* 104, 117–128.
Kimura, A. 1983. Sex differences in cerebral organization for speech and praxic functions. *Canadian Journal of Psychology,* 27(1), 19–25.
Lansdell, H. 1962. The effect of neurosurgery on design preference. *Nature (London),* 194, 852–854.
Lansdell, H., & Urbach, N. 1965. Sex differences in personality measures related to size and side of temporal lobe ablations. *Proceedings of the American Psychological Association,* 73, 113–114.
Macoby, E. E., & Jacklin, C. N. 1974. *The psychology of sex differences.* Stanford: Stanford Univ. Press.
Matsui, T., & Hirano, A. 1978. *An atlas of the human brain for computerized tomography.* Tokyo: Igaku-Shoin.
McGlone, J. 1977. Sex differences in the cerebral organization of verbal functions in patients with unilateral lesions. *Brain,* 100, 775–793.
McGlone, J., & Kertesz, A. 1973. Sex differences in cerebral processing of visuospatial tasks. *Cortex,* 9, 313–320.
Tranel, D., & Damasio, H. 1987. The role of gender in aphasia following focal cerebral lesions. Presented at Academy of Aphasia, Phoenix, Az, October 25–27, 1987.
Vignolo, L. A., Boccardi, E., & Caverni, L. 1986. Unexpected CT-scan findings in global aphasia. *Cortex,* 22, 55–69.
Wechsler, D. 1955. *Manual for the Wechsler Adult Intelligence Scale.* New York: Psychological Corp.

[18]

ARE MEN'S AND WOMEN'S BRAINS REALLY DIFFERENT?

DOREEN KIMURA
University of Western Ontario

ABSTRACT

Sex hormones have been shown to determine basic sexual differentiation *in utero*, and to influence the level of certain cognitive abilities. Sex differences in brain morphology are known to be present and to undergo systematic changes throughout the prenatal period. In the adult, brain organization for basic speech and related motor praxic function is found to be more focally organized within the left hemisphere in women than in men. Such functions are particularly dependent on the left anterior region in women, and are not less asymmetrically organized than in men. Some verbal intelligence functions less specifically tied to speech mechanisms may be more bilaterally organized in women, but no such statement can be made for all verbal or indeed nonverbal functions. Adult cognitive sex differences may to some extent reflect pre- and peri-natal sexual dimorphism in brain organization at critical stages of development. Possible evolutionary bases for sex differences in brain organization are discussed.

The simple answer to the question posed in my title is, yes, of course. It would be amazing if men's and women's brains were not different, given the gross morphological and often striking behavioural differences between men and women, which are not restricted to their different roles in parenting and reproductive behaviour. So the real questions are: how different are they, how did the differences come about, and how significant are such differences for our everyday lives and the choices we make? I will concentrate here on what are called intellectual differences between men and women, by which we usually mean those behaviours related to problem-solving, communication, cognitive style, and so on.

The Role of Hormones

Sex Hormones and Abilities

First let me just remind you of some of the intellectual differences that one finds, on average, between men and women. Men, on the whole, do better on certain spatial tests, on perceptual disembedding tasks, and on mathematical reasoning tests than do women. Women, on average, are better on articulatory and verbal fluency tasks, on manual dexterity, and in perceptual speed. The popular view among social scientists used to be that these differences are due largely to the way in which males and females are reared. I am not contesting that experience contributes to these intellectual differences, but my interest here is going to be in the biological base upon which such experience acts.

There is now good evidence that there is a hormonal contribution to the development of such abilities. For example, men who are deficient in androgen from birth or early life are inferior to normal men on certain spatial tasks, and also inferior to men who˙suffer from androgen deficiency later in life. In verbal ability, however, the early-androgen-deficient men are not poorer than their normal counterparts. The spatial ability of androgen-deficient men is positively correlated with testicular size, a finding suggesting a fairly close association between the peripheral and central effects of the androgens. However, there is no simple linear relation between androgens and spatial ability: normal men who are less "masculine" in appearance, or who have demonstrably lower levels of testosterone, actually perform better on spatial tasks than more masculine men; and normal women with higher levels of testosterone perform better than those with lower levels. These facts taken together suggest that, for spatial ability, there is an optimal level of androgens, or an optimal androgen/estrogen bal-

---

An invited talk given at the annual meeting of the Canadian Pyschological Association in Toronto, June 1986, in connection with the 1985 award for Distinguished Contributions to Psychology as a Science. The research was supported by grants from the Medical Research Council and the Natural Sciences and Engineering Research Council. I would like to thank Neil Watson for his help in compiling and analysing much of the data.

Requests for reprints should be sent to the author, Department of Psychology, University of Western Ontario, London, Ontario N6A 5C2.

TABLE 1
Human sexual differentiation: Clinical syndromes

Syndrome	Genotype	Disorder	External genitalia	"Stereotypic" behaviour
Testicular feminization	XY (male)	Androgen insensitivity	Female	Female
Congenital adrenal hyperplasia	XX (female)	Overproduction of androgens prenatally	Increased masculinization	If treated early, only "tomboyishness"
Dominican Republic cases	XY	5-alpha reductase deficiency (reduced dihydro-testosterone)	Ambiguous or female	Female until puberty? At puberty, take on male role.

ance, that is slightly below that of the average male and above that of the average female.

That high estrogen levels may not be conducive to good spatial ability has been suggested in the past by studies on fluctuations throughout the menstrual cycle in females. Some spatial tasks, like disembedding a hidden figure, have been found to be less well performed at the high estrogen point in the cycle. This finding has been confirmed recently in my laboratory for the rod-and-frame task, by Elizabeth Hampson. We thought that high estrogen levels might work rather differently on those skills at which females excel, in contrast to those at which males excel. Therefore, it was decided to sample some verbal-fluency, perceptual-speed, and motor-skill tasks. The interesting result was that, on motor skill at least, women performed *better* during the high-estrogen/progesterone period, even though at this same period they performed worse on the spatially demanding rod-and-frame task.

Hormones and Sexual Differentiation

To understand the role of hormones in mediating male/female ability differences, and their probable brain mechanisms, we need to know something about their paramount importance in sexual differentiation. The sex hormones are essential not just to maintaining appropriate reproductive behaviours: they are the basic determinants of almost every feature of an individual that makes him or her male or female. Whereas we used to think of sex determination as being simply genetically determined by whether the 23rd pair of chromosomes was XX or XY, we now know that the story is not so simple. In mammals, experimental work has shown that *the basic form is female* and, no matter what the genetic make-up, a female organism is formed unless male hormones are present in the first few weeks of foetal life. If there are no androgens, or the tissue is insensitive to androgens, a female is formed.

Most of the definitive work on sexual differentiation has been done on non-human animals, especially rodents, since they have a shorter developmental period, which allows one to see the effects of early hormonal environments in a shorter space of time. This work suggests that, not only is the genital morphology under unequivocal hormonal control, but so is the sex-appropriate *behaviour*. Thus, the undifferentiated brain is also female, and will exhibit typical female behaviour under appropriate conditions. Since genital and brain differentiation do not necessarily occur at the same time, one can in theory have an organism that is genitally one sex and behaviourally another sex. It happens that in rats, brain differentiation occurs just after birth, although the genitalia are already differentiated by then. This discrepancy means that hormonal manipulations right after birth in a male rat, for example, can result in the appearance in adulthood of the lordosis behaviour pattern typical of females in heat. This finding obviously has some interesting implications for the origins of variations in sexual preference in human beings.

There are some clinical syndromes that suggest that this basic mechanism of sexual differentiation operates in human beings as well. They are summarized in Table 1.

Hormones and Brain Organization

Although it must be obvious from the behavioural data that brain organization is affected by hormones, information on visible *structural* influence is only beginning to emerge. The best evidence to date, as one might expect, is for hypothalamic structures, since they control sex-specific behaviours. Roger Gorski and his co-workers have shown that there is an area of the hypothalamus (dubbed the "sexually dimorphic nucleus") that is larger in the male rat than in the female, and that its size is under the regulation of androgens. The size is reduced if androgens are decreased, and it can be enlarged in females if androgens are administered. Recent studies from the same laboratory have shown that there are sexually dimorphic areas in the human hypothalamus as well.

There is, however, every reason to think that structures outside the hypothalamus are also affected by hormones. We know from Marian Diamond's work that the cortex of the right hemisphere is thicker than the left in male rats but not in female rats; she has also demonstrated that relative thickness is altered by early hormonal manipulation.

Sex Differences in Human Brain Organization

Clearly, if hormones are having an effect on human behaviour, they must operate through the brain. Some of the possible neural mechanisms for sexual differentiation of the human brain might be:

— Differential specialization of the two hemispheres in males and females. Such specialization includes the possibility that some functions may be more asymmetrically organized in one sex, other functions more asymmetrically organized in the other sex.

— Differential allotment of total brain space to some abilities, regardless of hemisphere. For example, spatial abilities might occupy more neuronal space in males, verbal functions more in females.

— Differential intrahemispheric or cortical/subcortical organization. This is the same principle as hemispheric specialization, but the divisions are different.

— Neural systems essentially the same in males and females, but hormonal influences somehow selectively activating one system rather than another.

— Finally, any or all of these mechanisms.

Brain Asymmetry

Consider first the possibility of sexual dimorphism in brain asymmetry — that is, in the degree to which the left and right hemispheres are specialized for different functions. If male and female brains were not equivalently asymmetric, the differences could possibly be advantageous to some abilities and disadvantageous to others. Because many people think of brain asymmetry as a specifically human organization, tied to the development of human language, it may be worthwhile to review some basic facts about brain asymmetry.

First, brain asymmetry is not specifically human. There is a wealth of evidence now that animals other than humans have brains that look and function asymmetrically, from birds to chimpanzees. Nor is brain asymmetry inevitably tied to any uniquely human abilities. Moreover, asymmetry is a *general* feature of organisms, not specific to neural tissue. In fact, it is quite possible that brain asymmetry is a consequence of some more general somatic asymmetry, and perhaps specifically the asymmetric growth and development of the gonads, which produce sex hormones. There is evidence from human hermaphrodites that ovarian development slightly favours the left side, and testes the right. (This difference is also true in birds.) There is also good evidence for a gonadal-hypothalamic axis, such that the gonads exert a strong influence on the hypothalamic brain structures of the same side.

One might therefore expect some asymmetry to be present in hypothalamic function, and this does appear to be the case. Not only do the left and right hypothalamus appear to function differently, but there is a sex difference in the nature of the asymmetry. In rats at least, the right hypothalamus appears to be more critical for mediating male sexual behaviour, and the left for mediating female sexual behaviour. That fact raises the interesting question whether the tendency for the entire right hemisphere cortex to be thicker than the left in male rats is related to the hypothalamic function. However, although the rodent data provide us with strong reasons for

TABLE 2
Effect of left and right lesions on Performance IQ

	Left-hemisphere lesions (including aphasics)				Right-hemisphere lesions				
	N	Age	Perf. IQ	(SD)	N	Age	Perf. IQ	(SD)	L-R
Males	144	47.7	96.4	(14.1)	134	45.7	92.5	(17.4)	3.9
Females	92	46.8	98.8	(14.0)	100	40.9	93.1	(15.5)	5.7

TABLE 3
Effect of left and right lesions on constructional tasks
(mean scaled scores and SDs)

	Block Design			Object Assembly		
	L lesion	R lesion	L-R	L lesion	R lesion	L-R
Males	8.2 (3.2)	7.7 (4.1)	.5	8.0 (3.0)	7.2 (3.5)	.8
Females	8.6 (3.1)	8.1 (3.8)	.5	8.6 (3.1)	7.7 (3.2)	.9

expecting to see sex differences in human brain asymmetry, the human data are still equivocal.

Human Brain Asymmetry

The idea has been around for some time that androgens somehow favour the growth of the right hemisphere. This idea carries with it certain implicit predictions. One is that the preferential or earlier growth of the right hemisphere in males gives rise to a higher incidence of left-handedness (due to the crossed organization of the motor systems). Although the incidence of left-handedness is generally reported to be higher in males, its determinants are still unknown.

Another prediction that has been made from the suggestion that androgens favour right-hemisphere development is that it is this influence that gives rise to the male superiority on certain spatial tasks. Thus, one would expect nonverbal or spatial ability to be more right-hemisphere-dependent in males than in females. One common measure of nonverbal/spatial ability is the Performance IQ of the Wechsler Adult Intelligence Scale. If the hypothesis of greater right-hemisphere dependence in males were correct, one would expect to see the relative decrement in Performance IQ after right- as compared to left-hemisphere damage to be greater in males than in females. However, when we actually look at our data in patients with unilateral damage to left or right hemisphere, there is really no difference between men and women in this regard, as can be seen in Table 2.

If we look specifically at the visuoconstructional subtests of the Performance IQ (Block Design and Object Assembly), in these same subjects we again find no evidence that performance depends more on the right hemisphere in men than in women. It should be noted that aphasic patients are included in the left-hemisphere group in both of these comparisons, since the tasks are not verbal.

One might legitimately argue that the Performance IQ subtests of the WAIS are complex and are not the purest measures of spatial ability, in particular of abilities that yield sex differences. Unfortunately there is little or no information concerning the brain organization for tests such as disembedding or spatial rotation tasks, which do yield sex differences. Nevertheless, the lack of any sex difference on the comparisons just described should at least encourage us to keep in mind alternative mechanisms for the appearance of sex differences in abilities — for example, the possibility that greater ability may be related to wider representation in the brain, or some difference in organization other than that of asymmetry.

What, then, is the evidence in favour of differing degrees of hemispheric specialization in males and females? There are two main sources. The first is perceptual asymmetry studies.

TABLE 4
Incidence of aphasia in right-handers with right-hemisphere damage

	Total N	Aphasics n	(%)
Males	105	2	(1.9)
Females	84	1	(1.2)

Because the control of sensory and motor systems from the brain is primarily crossed, we can get some ideas about the nature of specialization of the hemispheres through studying perceptual and motor asymmetries. Stimuli coming into left and right visual fields, or left and right ears, send impulses first to the opposite cerebral hemisphere. As a consequence, when words, for example, are presented to the two ears simutaneously, those words arriving at the right ear are better perceived than words at the left ear, because the right ear has the stronger connection with the left hemisphere, which is important for language processing. When differences are found in degree of asymmetry between males and females, males tend to show more asymmetry. The simplest interpretation of these findings, although other interpretations are certainly possible, is that male brains are more asymmetrically organized than female brains.

The other chief source of information about sex differences in brain organization is the effect of damage to one hemisphere on appropriate verbal or nonverbal tasks. It has been reported, and we confirm from our large series of cases, that women less often suffer from speech disorders or aphasia, after left-hemisphere damage, than do men. The reasonable conclusion initially drawn from this finding is that speech is less critically dependent on the left hemisphere in women than in men. The difference has been presumed to be due to more bilateral or diffuse organization for speech functions in women than in men.

There are, however, some problems with this attractive but simple explanation. One problem is that the higher incidence of left-handedness in men than in women does not easily fit the idea that men's brains are generally more asymmetric than women's. Even within right-handers, women appear to be more consistently right-handed than men, and that would suggest that left-hemisphere dependence for some kinds of manual control is, if anything, greater in women than in men.

Another difficulty is that, if speech functions were more dependent on the right hemisphere in women, one might expect to see a higher incidence of aphasia after right-hemisphere lesions in women, but this does not happen. As Table 4 indicates, we find an extremely low incidence of aphasia after right-hemisphere lesions in right-handers (1 to 2%); and there is no difference between men and women in this respect.

Brain Organization for Speech

I would now like to describe some of the research I have done on brain organization for speech and related functions, which I hope adds a significant piece to the puzzle of sex differences in brain organization. The patients I studied were all cases of damage to one hemisphere of the brain. About two-thirds of the patients had vascular problems of various kinds, primarily strokes. The remainder were largely tumor cases. Fewer than 10% of the total were seizure cases. The only screening of these patients that took place was to ensure that they had unilateral damage. Only data for right-handers are shown.

First, we confirmed that aphasia was less common after left-hemisphere damage in women than in men. However, the surprising finding occurred when we broke down the unilaterally damaged groups into those with lesions restricted to the anterior or to the posterior parts of the left hemisphere, using the Rolandic sulcus as the dividing line. A quite different pattern of incidence of aphasia emerged in men and women. I would like to interject here that in order to do this kind of study, one needs to have a very large pool of patients. Although it is fairly easy to accumulate cases with hemisphere-wide damage (since the vascular supply is so organized), selecting cases with damage restricted to any subdivision of the brain sharply reduces the sample sizes. Restricted lesions occur in fewer than 50% of our cases with unilateral damage. The sample size for anterior damage is especially small.

One typically refers to two major cortical speech areas, the anterior and posterior, shown in Figure 1. What I found, however, was that, in women, aphasia was much more common after anterior lesions than after posterior; whereas in men, asphasia was slightly more common after posterior lesions; and the distribution of aphasic cases was more equal across the two regions (Figure 2). This finding is still compatible with a

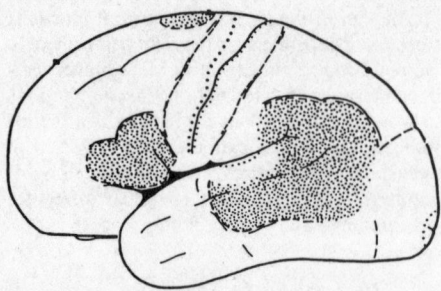

FIGURE 1
Major cortical speech areas as traditionally defined

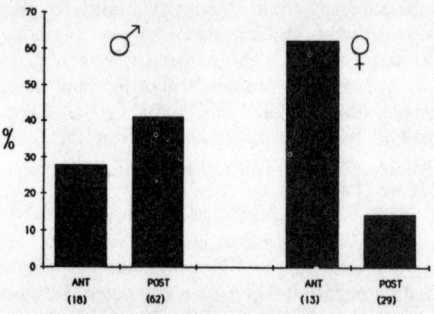

FIGURE 2
Incidence of aphasia after anterior or posterior lesions in males (left) and females (right)

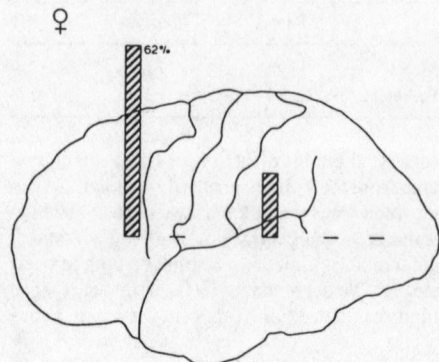

FIGURE 3
Incidence of aphasia after anterior, central, temporal, parietal, and occipital lesions, in females (top) and males (bottom)

lower incidence of aphasia overall in women, because the sample sizes for anterior lesions are quite small.

If we break down these locations still further, we see that, in men, speech is more diffusely organized in the left hemisphere than in women. In men, aphasia might result from damage to anterior, central, temporal, parietal, or (rarely) occipital lesions. In women, it is very much dependent on the anterior region, with a small incidence of aphasia also in the temporal region. Of course, the sample sizes become even smaller as we do these breakdowns, with the smallest subsamples in the left parietal group (males = 8, females = 6). (See Figure 3.)

These are rather startling data, and one wonders why such findings have not been previously reported. One reason is that, if one selects cases for study on the basis of a disorder, one cannot get a very good picture of frequency related to locus, because all the negative cases (those which do not show the disorder) have been omitted. An important feature of our study was that it was a consecutive series of cases selected only for unilateral damage, not for any particular symptom.

One would naturally like some corroboration from other laboratories, although current *replication* of a study like this, which covers a 10-year span, is out of the question. There are, however, two indirect sources of corroboration. One is concerned with the effect of cortical stimulation on speech, by Katy Mateer. She found, in her sample, that naming disorders did not occur

Are Men's and Women's Brains Different?

in women when stimulated in the posterior parietal region, whereas they were common in men when stimulated in this area. In fact, Mateer's data in general support the suggestion that speech is more diffusely organized within the left hemisphere in males than in females.

Luigi Vignolo and his co-workers in Italy also found a sex difference in the cortical distribution of global aphasia. Global aphasia refers to a severe generalized form of aphasia that affects both comprehension and production of speech to a significant degree. It is typically a consequence of quite severe or widespread damage to the hemisphere, but it can sometimes occur with restricted damage. They found that all cases in whom damage was restricted to the anterior part of the left hemisphere were women, whereas all posterior cases were men.

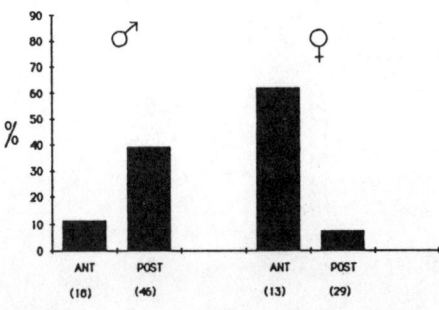

FIGURE 4
Incidence of manual apraxia after anterior or posterior lesions in males (left) and females (right)

Brain Organization for Manual Apraxia

Much of my past research has been concerned with uncovering the relationship between the control of speech and the control of other motor functions. I think it is now established that the left hemisphere is in fact specialized for motor programming, which contributes significantly to its capacity to mediate language, but that it is not specifically specialized for language. This is a huge topic, and I cannot adequately cover it here; but for example, we know that defects in reproducing speech after cerebral damage are very closely tied to defects in producing nonspeech oral movements. Furthermore, we see similar deficits in the control of hand and arm movements after damage to the regions that overlap with speech areas. Findings like these suggest that there is a general motor programming function vested in the left hemisphere.

The defects in motor programming of the limbs, called "manual apraxia," are usually tested in the neurological examination by having patients demonstrate how to use an object, to command. Since many such patients are also aphasic, we employed a simpler method of testing for this disorder that requires only that they imitate a series of unfamiliar movements. Because there is no linguistic content to these movements, performance is presumably not contaminated by verbal processing. When we administer this movement-copying task to unilaterally damaged patients, we find that difficulties occur almost exclusively after left-hemisphere damage, as does aphasia. Moreover, the difficulties are present in both hands: so what we are sampling is not the primarily crossed corticospinal systems, but rather a programming system in the left hemisphere antecedent to it. This programming system clearly has bilateral control functions (although it may be slightly more available to corticospinal systems in the same hemisphere, perhaps a source of our greater skill with the right hand).

If we compare the effects of anterior and posterior lesions in the left hemisphere, we see similar but even sharper sex differences in brain organization than we did for speech, as indicated in Figure 4. A more detailed localization analysis shows that in men, again, there is a tendency for manual apraxia to occur with lesions throughout the left hemisphere (but with far greater dependence on the parietal region); whereas in women, manual apraxia after restricted damage occurs only with anterior lesions (Figure 5). Note that the slight tendency for temporal-lobe lesions to produce aphasia in women is not seen here for manual apraxia. In men, manual apraxia is also rarer than is aphasia, after temporal-lobe lesions. This finding probably reflects the role of the temporal lobe in mediating some *auditory* control of speech, a function not needed in manual control.

Visuoconstructional Skills

There is another kind of disorder, called constructional apraxia, that may occur after damage to the left or right hemisphere. It includes difficulties in drawing, in moving blocks or sticks to

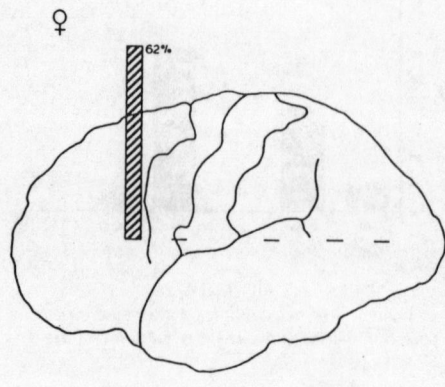

INCIDENCE OF MANUAL APRAXIA
LOCALIZED LESIONS - LEFT HEMISPHERE

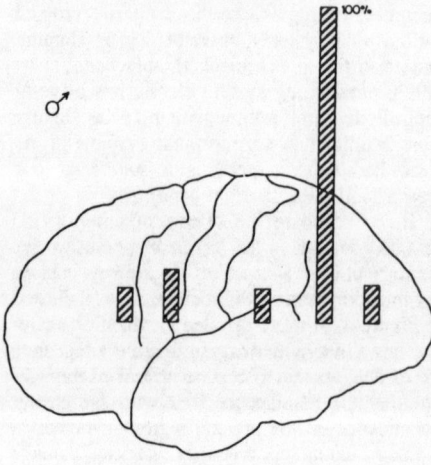

FIGURE 5
Incidence of manual apraxia after anterior, central, temporal, parietal, and occipital lesions, in females (top) and males (bottom)

make a designated pattern, and the like. When constructional apraxia occurs after left-hemisphere damage, it is very closely tied to manual apraxia. Thus, it shows the same pattern of sex differences as does manual apraxia, and the data will therefore not be shown here. However, it was of some interest to look at how anterior or posterior locus of lesion in the *right* hemisphere might interact with sex. Table 5 shows, not incidence of disorders, but the actual performance scores on a variety of tasks.

One sees, again, a sharp dependence of constructional skills on the right *anterior* region in females. The fact that there is no impairment on the movement copying task, which measures manual praxis, indicates that the constructional deficit in the right-hemisphere-damaged groups is not related to praxic difficulties. In men, the deficits on the constructional tasks show a tendency to be greater after posterior damage, though the trend is strong only for the Object Assembly test ($p < .10$).

Thus, men and women are showing differing patterns of brain organization in the right hemisphere, parelleling those in the left. The patients with right-hemisphere damage are, of course, a totally different group from the patients shown earlier with left-hemisphere damage.

Conclusions about Basic Speech and Motor Function

We see no evidence in the clinical findings of a more diffuse or bilateral organization for speech and related praxic function in women. On the contrary, the evidence suggests that these functions are more focally organized within the left hemisphere in women than in men. The critical systems for the control of speech and praxis appear to differ between sexes, with the anterior regions of paramount importance in women. In men, both anterior and posterior regions contribute, but there is a trend for more dependence on posterior regions, and for manual praxis the parietal lobe is of crucial importance.

No morphological sex differences parallelling these functional differences have yet been reported for the adult. However, Christine deLacoste reports sex differences in foetal brains as early as the first trimester. In females, the left frontal region is relatively large in the first two trimesters, though the patterns of development change for both males and females throughout the prenatal period. It may therefore be that the functional organization in the adult reflects an organization determined at a critical stage prenatally. A possible sexual dimorphism in the corpus callosum will be discussed later.

It is tempting to speculate that the concentrated focus for praxis and speech control in women may be related to their earlier development of speech. It may also be related to their better dexterity, since it is reasonable to think that some advantage might accrue from having

TABLE 5
Manual constructional praxis in right-hemisphere lesions

Locus of lesion	N	Perf. IQ	Manual praxis (max = 24)	Block Design (max = 48)	Object Assembly (max = 44)
Males					
right anterior	12	100.4	18.3	27.8	28.2
right posterior	18	95.3	17.7	25.8	21.3
Females					
right anterior	12	89.4	19.4	20.8	20.5
right posterior	22	98.5	19.5	29.6	26.7

the (anterior) programming regions synaptically closer to motor cortex. I will return to this point later.

Other Verbal Skills

When we turn to other more abstract or conceptual verbal abilities, in the realm of "language," the picture changes. Verbal intelligence does, of course, require abilities beyond those needed to produce clear articulate speech quickly, and much of the processing requires reference to experiences that may be stored in modes other than speech. One would therefore not expect the left hemisphere alone to be involved in such processing.

Verbal IQ. The WAIS Verbal IQ provides several different measures of verbal function, in which verbal conceptualization is tapped. Several previous studies by McGlone, Inglis, myself, and others have suggested that, for these measures, there is evidence of more bilateral organization in women than in men. However, some of these claims are based on smaller reductions in verbal IQ after left-hemisphere lesions in women; and since we now know about the importance of anterior systems in women, we need to accept these conclusions with caution. The lesser changes in verbal IQ could simply be an artifact of the low frequency of anterior lesions. A more convincing finding would be the demonstration of a depressed Verbal IQ after right-hemisphere lesions in women, but the problem here is the choice of an appropriate comparison group. Young healthy subjects not in hospital are not very good controls for people in their fifties who have had a stroke, are hospitalized, and are often not feeling in the peak of health.

We therefore decided to compare our unilaterally damaged groups with a control group of other patients who had had vascular problems of a transient kind but had no residual neurological signs nor any demonstrable lesion on a CT scan. These patients (18 male, 18 female) had all been screened for carotid endarterectomy, and some of them subsequently underwent surgery. The mean age of the males was 63.2, and of the females 64.8 The mean IQ of the males was 103.8, and of the females 102.2. Because the two groups were not exactly matched for age, age-corrected scale scores were used to compare them. In the graphs in Figure 6 a line is drawn to indicate performance that is half a standard deviation below the mean of the control group. This was the most representative measure of when a significant deficit occurred in the restricted-lesion groups. On these Verbal IQ subtests, only non-aphasic patients were considered, for the obvious reason that aphasics would be unable to express themselves adequately. (While this is a necessary exclusion, it must be kept in mind.) Comparisons between lesioned and control groups were always made between same-sex groups, since males and females may differ somewhat in their base level on particular subtests.

Consider first the subtest Digit Span. This is one test on which the findings best fit a pattern suggesting a more diffuse organization in women, since all female groups (left and right anterior, left and right posterior) show performance below the deficit line, while males show impairment only after left-hemisphere damage. The Vocabulary subtest is not shown, but it has a similar pattern. In contrast to the pattern for Digit Span, the Comprehension subtest (which requires verbalization of a solution to common situations) indicates significant impairment only

IMPAIRMENT ON AGE-CORRECTED SCORES

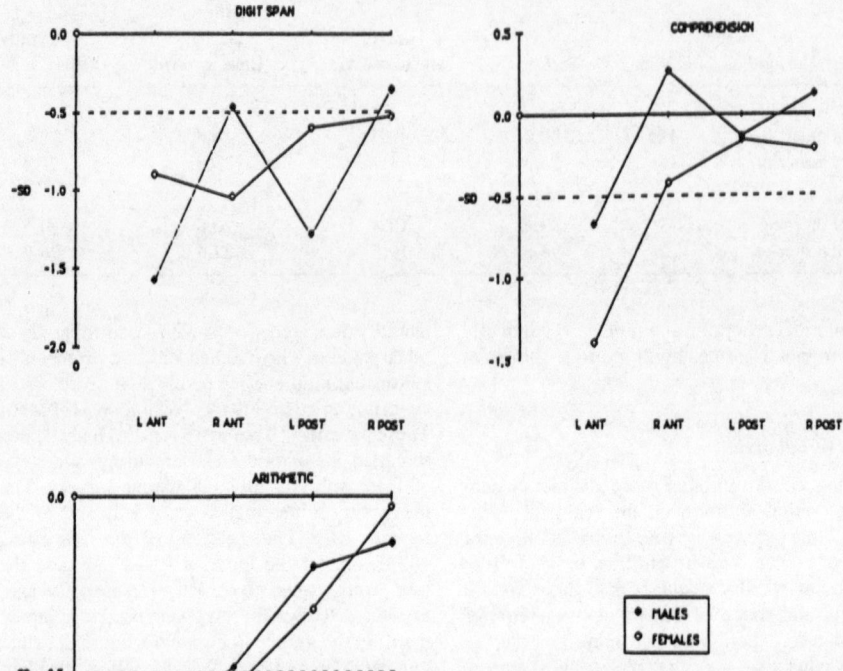

FIGURE 6
Performance on age-corrected Verbal IQ subtests after restricted damage, compared to same-sex controls

after left anterior damage, and the pattern is similar for men and women. The Arithmetic subtest shows yet another pattern, with both males and females showing greater impairment after anterior than after posterior lesions.

It is apparent that there is no one pattern of sexual dimorphism in brain organization that fits all of these "verbal" tasks. In women, the importance of the left anterior region is still evident, but the right anterior also contributes substantially to some of the verbal subtests. This pattern of function is quite unlike the control of basic speech and praxic function, where no effect of right anterior damage was seen in women. In men, there is generally greater dependence on the left hemisphere for the Verbal IQ subtests, but the degree of dependence varies with the particular subtest and with the locus of damage within the left hemisphere.

The fact that no one pattern of organization holds across all the verbal subtests may be due to two possible factors. One may be that each subtest samples substantially different functions that are organized differently in the brain. The other is that the subtests themselves are not pure — that is, each samples several more basic functions, which tap different brain systems to differing degrees, and therefore we just see a different composite pattern from test to test. In either case, the inference to be made is that classifying

IMPAIRMENT ON AGE-CORRECTED SCORES

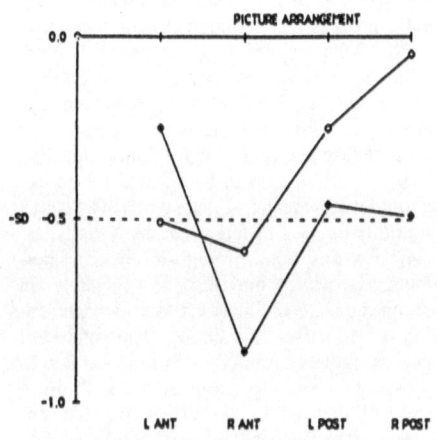

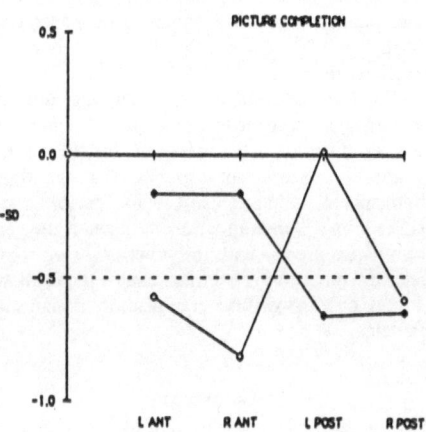

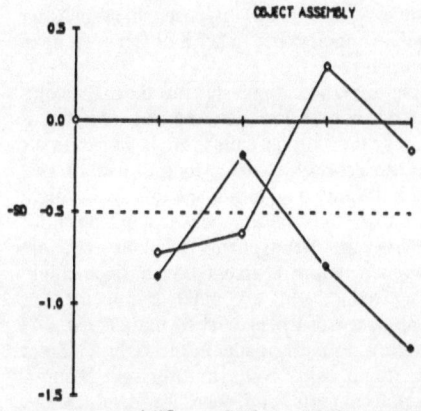

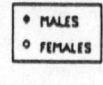

FIGURE 7
Performance on age-corrected Performance IQ subtests after restricted damage, compared to same-sex controls

a test as "verbal" does not in any simple way predict its representation in the brain, for men or women.

Performance IQ. If impurity is characteristic of the Verbal subtests, it is even more apparent on subtests of the Performance IQ. Nevertheless, there is the expectation in the neuropsychological literature that the Performance IQ will be depressed by right-hemisphere lesions, and it is implicit in this assumption that the subtests have something in common. The results are depicted in Figure 7 for three of the subtests. In Picture Arrangement, a set of pictures is presented in scrambled order, and the subject is required to arrange them in a sensible order. This subtest shows the best fit to the expectation that males are affected by right-hemisphere damage but not by left. Note, however, that the greatest contribution in males appears to come from the right anterior region. Also note that the pattern is not very different in males and females.

One might expect the other pictorial task, Picture Completion, to show the same pattern as Picture Arrangement. In Picture Completion, the task is to point out the missing feature. However, the pattern of impairment is quite different. On this task, women show a sharper impairment after right-hemisphere lesions than do men. Men appear to be affected by posterior lesions of either hemisphere. Finally, if we map

Object Assembly, we see that there is a sharp dependence on the anterior regions in women and on the posterior regions in men. (Note that in data reported in Table 3, aphasics were included in the left-hemisphere group; here they are excluded.)

For the Performance IQ, then, the anterior lesions again appear to cause greater deficits in women than do posterior lesions; but there is no suggestion, across all subtests, that the right hemisphere is more critical for performance skills in males than in females. Instead, the pattern varies greatly with the function being studied, and no general statement can be made about a more or a less diffuse organization in males or females.

Comment

Brain Organization

In discussing the data, I will concentrate on speech, related praxic functions, and verbal functions, because we know most about these. It seems quite clear that there is a difference between men and women in the organization of basic speech function, in that speech is more dependent on the anterior than the posterior region in women, whereas in men it is more equally distributed between these regions. The same may be said for manual praxis, and praxis appears to involve somewhat more restricted areas in the left hemisphere than does speech, for both men and women. It is probable that the lower incidence of aphasia in women after left-hemisphere damage is related to this concentration of function within a hemisphere. That is, if one limited region is paramount for a function, then randomly occurring lesions have a smaller chance of affecting it than they would if several areas subserved that function, regardless of the aetiology of the lesion. In strokes, when pathology is not hemisphere-wide (the most common situation), the most probable area to suffer lasting pathology is the posterior part of the hemisphere. This pattern again reduces the probability of aphasia in women, since speech is so anteriorly represented.

When we consider language functions not so tightly dependent on speech/motor programming, we see a picture rather different from the one just described. Thus, with Verbal IQ subtests, we see greater right-hemisphere participation in both men and women than is the case for speech/praxic function. This finding is consistent with the split-brain literature, which suggests that the right hemisphere is capable of substantial semantic processing, although it cannot produce speech. This capability is somewhat more marked for women than for men, but only on specific subtests. Findings from verbal conceptual tests suggest that there is no one pattern of representation that holds for all abilities labelled "verbal." The lesson to be learned for neuropsychological research is to treat all such tests as potentially tapping different neural systems.

The sex differences found in degree of perceptual asymmetry may also be explicable, in part, on the basis of anterior/posterior representation of function. Assuming that right-field visual or right-ear auditory superiority is due to processing in speech-related areas, such areas might well be synaptically further from the sensory input in women and the perceptual asymmetry would thus be reduced. The lesser perceptual asymmetry need not in this case indicate a lesser brain asymmetry, but rather a different *locus* of asymmetry.

It has also been suggested that the major commissural connection between the two hemispheres, the corpus callosum, is larger in its posterior aspect in women than in men. Translated into functional terms, the difference might mean that transmission between the posterior parts of the hemispheres is more efficient in women. More efficient transmission might further reduce the perceptual asymmetry. For example, a word presented to the left ear, and activating primarily paths in the right temporal lobe, might enjoy better transmission of information to the left hemisphere for identification, in women than in men. This advantage would reduce the difference in accuracy of report between the two ears, without necessarily implying a difference in functional brain asymmetry.

These considerations lead us to expect that if we looked at a kind of function that is less dependent on posterior regions for control or processing, then asymmetry might be as sharp in women as in men. One obvious asymmetry of this kind is the motor asymmetry manifested as hand preference, with the right hand being able to perform a variety of skilled acts. We know that the motor programming for many movements is sharply dependent on the left anterior region in women, and this region is synaptically close to the motor cortex, which is required for the movements to occur. The literature indicates, as one might expect from the argument above, that women show, if anything, greater motor asymmetry than do men. They have a higher incidence of right-hand preference (or a lower incidence of left-handedness), and right-handed women tend to be more right-handed than right-handed men.

The general finding after restricted lesions is that deficits tend to be severe after anterior damage in women, but we do not find striking deficits after posterior damage. This pattern of deficit tends to be true regardless of whether the task is verbal or nonverbal. Since it is highly unlikely that the posterior areas of the brain serve no current function, two possible explanations for the absence of deficit after damage must be entertained. One is that the left and right posterior regions share more functions in women than in men — that is, they overlap more. A unilateral lesion would therefore be less likely to cause a striking impairment. The overlap might be achieved by greater duplication of systems between posterior regions (which seems a little unlikely) or by greater sharing of functions. If the latter, one might expect stronger commissural connections between the hemispheres. The claim that the posterior third of the callosum is somewhat larger in women than in men makes the function-sharing mechanism more probable.

A second possible explanation (not incompatible with the above) is that we are not adequately sampling the functions of the posterior regions in women because we are not using the correct measures. In searching for what the posterior areas might do in women, it might be reasonable, rather than looking primarily at IQ tests, to measure abilities at which women excel. Some candidates for measurement are functions such as perceptual speed or retention of incidental information. I am not aware of any studies that have employed such measures in the study of sex differences in brain organization.

Evolutionary Determinants of Brain Organization?

We must keep in mind that the brain organization we enjoy today was probably present in its basic form as long ago as half a million years, and for some functions probably longer. It was thus determined in an environment very different from the present one. Just as an illustration, abilities such as reading and writing and operating any kind of machine or advanced technology were non-existent. In that environment, all signs indicate that the division of labour between men and women was fairly similar to that seen in many preliterate societies today. That is, women were concerned with activities in and near the home base, while men engaged in hunting and foraging at a distance, bringing food back. Typical "female" activities would include grinding and preparing food, gathering plants and seed for food, making clothing, making pots, and, of course, tending children. Note that none of these activities except food-gathering requires significant route-finding ability: the food-gathering could be done near the home base and within view of it. Typical "male" activities would include weapon manufacture, fishing, hunting, boat-building, trapping, warfare, and the like.

What distinctive kinds of abilities would be selected for in a female under these conditions? One set of abilities might be fine manual skills, but particularly within personal space, or within arm's reach, such as food and clothing preparation and child care. These would not require much integration of motor activity with distant information. Another might be fine perceptual discrimination and rapid scanning, in order to detect minimal changes in infants' appearance, and in order to pick out edible from inedible food. This ability would include good colour discrimination and identification. A third ability that might also aid detection of minimal changes in the environment would be the ability to note "irrelevant" or incidental perceptual information.

What kinds of abilities would be selected for in males? One would be orientation ability, or the capacity to correct for turns made when walking from a camp or home base to another location. This would be required in hunting and long-distance foraging. A second important ability would be the capacity to coordinate body movements vis-à-vis external objects, as in throwing or aiming a missile.

How can we relate all this to sex differences in anterior/posterior representation of praxic control or motor programming? In women, specialization of motor skills might be considered in the domain of movements that could be executed with the body as framework. There would be a lesser need for integration of movements with visual and auditory receptor systems that bring information from a distance. (But one might expect more integration with somesthetic input). Thus motor programming might be more advantageously located close to direct downstream motor systems, that is, near the motor cortex. In men, in contrast, motor programming systems would need to encompass both the body as framework and extrapersonal space. Coordination of movement vis-à-vis external and often moving objects would require arm control coordinated with visual tracking, and therefore a more posterior-based system.

One puzzle is why speech should develop earlier, and some say better, in women. It should be noted that most of the verbal skills at which women excel are related to speed and precision of production, and fluency — that is, to the motor aspects of speech. Some have argued that communication skills are important for interpersonal interactions with the family, and particularly with infants. However, others have proposed that speech itself is a relatively late evolutionary development, and that a manual communication system antedated speech by over a million years. Speech might, therefore, have built onto a praxic system already developed for other functions, such as manual communication and manipulation of tools. In that case, better speaking skills might simply be a by-product in women of better fine motor skills.

Relevance for Modern Everyday Life

What information we have suggests that brain organization is not simply coded on the X or Y chromosome, but is dependent on a much more dynamic hormonal environment early in life. Such a mechanism permits a much larger variation in brain organization within "masculine" and "feminine" brains than would be possible with a fixed pre-wired mechanism. Despite the distinctive composite patterns in brain organization I have described, the so-called "typical" male or female is an abstraction. Fairly broad variations in intra-uterine hormonal environment could result in wide variations within each sex, in brain organization and in behaviour. Similarly, assuming that intellectual function can tell us something about brain organization, the population differences in abilities that we see between men and women do not have a high predictive value for the individual. As a means of screening for admission to occupations or life activities, genital sex is a very poor instrument. As psychologists, we have, I hope, developed much better measuring instruments than that.

Most activities that people engage in are complex, and employ a number of basic abilities. This complexity means that there is scope for widely differing brain organizations to solve problems in different ways. Human beings are obviously very well able to adapt abilities developed in a different environment hundreds of thousands of years ago to the demands of a modern environment. We should not be surprised that women now have interests and capacities other than housekeeping and child care, any more than that men are able to read, write, and work computers rather than be limited to hunting and fishing.

Moreover, there is reason to think that brain organization is dynamic to some degree throughout the lifespan of the individual. It is probably true that hormones organize the brain early in life, and also true that we see typically distinct patterns of brain organization in adult men and women for speech and motor function. But the fact of menstrual-cycle fluctuations in abilities must mean that current hormonal environments also have an influence. (Change over time may be true for men as well, since they undergo diurnal and lifespan changes in androgen levels.) It is probable that some of the life-cycle changes in interests and activities are hormonally influenced, and it is reasonable to consider that intellectual functions can undergo the same changes. We might, therefore, expect differences between men and women to increase or decrease as these hormonal influences undergo change throughout life.

A final caution is that sex is but one of several individual-difference variables that can affect brain organization. For example, another potent predictor of brain organization is hand preference. Some recent data of Richard Harshman's suggest that yet another is intelligence level. Harshman's research also suggests that all these variables — sex, hand preference, and intelligence level — are *interactive*. That is, one's particular profile of abilities is dependent not only on whether one is male or female, but whether one is a left- or a right-handed male or female, and whether one has high or low reasoning ability. The sex of an individual is thus just one factor that helps to determine brain organization, and it interacts with other factors to produce the particular brain organization that is unique to one individual.

Are Men's and Women's Brains Different?

RÉSUMÉ

On a démontré que les hormones sexuelles déterminent la différenciation sexuelle fondamentale *in utero* et influent sur le niveau de certaines aptitudes cognitives. On sait qu'il y a des différences sexuelles de la morphologie cérébrale et que celles-ci subissent des changements systématiques tout au long de la période prénatale. Chez l'adulte, l'organisation du cerveau pour la fonction fondamentale de la parole et pour la fonction motrice praxique connexe est organisée de manière plus focalisée dans l'hémisphère gauche des femmes que des hommes. Ces fonctions sont particulièrement dépendantes de la région antérieure gauche chez les femmes, et ne sont pas moins asymétriquement organisées que chez les hommes. Il se peut que certaines fonctions d'intelligence verbale moins spécifiquement liées aux mécanismes de la parole soient plus bilatéralement organisées chez la femme, mais on ne peut pas faire une telle affirmation pour toutes les fonctions verbales, voire même non verbales. Dans une certaine mesure, des différences sexuellement cognitives chez les adultes pourraient refléter le dimorphisme sexuel prénatal et périnatal de l'organisation cérébrale, à des stades critiques du développement. On a discuté des bases évolutionnaires possibles des différences sexuelles de l'organisation cérébrale.

Suggested Further Reading

Bryden, M.P. (1982). *Laterality: Functional asymmetry in the intact brain*. New York: Academic Press.

Daly, M., & Wilson, M. (1983). *Sex, evolution and behavior*. Boston: Willard Grant Press.

deLacoste, M.C., Holloway, R.L., & Woodward, J. (1986). Sex differences in the fetal human corpus callosum. *Human Neurobiology*, 5, 93–96.

Diamond, M.C., Dowling, G.A., & Johnson, R.E. (1981). Morphological cerebral cortical asymmetry in male and female rats. *Experimental Neurology*, 71, 261–268.

Harshman, R.A., Hampson, E., & Berenbaum, S.A. (1983). Individual differences in cognitive abilities and brain organization. Part I: Sex and handedness differences in ability. *Canadian Journal of Psychology*, 37, 144–192.

Hines, M. (1982). Prenatal gonadal hormones and sex differences in human behavior. *Psychological Bulletin*, 92, 56–80.

Kimura, D. (1983). Sex differences in cerebral organization for speech and praxic functions. *Canadian Journal of Psychology*, 37, 19–35.

Mateer, C., Polen, S.B., & Ojemann, G.A. (1982). Sexual variation in cortical localization of naming as determined by stimulation mapping. *Behavioral and Brain Sciences*, 5, 310–311.

McGlone, J. (1980). Sex differences in human brain asymmetry: A critical survey. *Behavioral and Brain Sciences*, 5, 215–264.

Nicholson, J. (1984). *Men and women. How different are they?* Oxford: Oxford University Press.

Robinson, T.E., Becker, J.B., Camp, D.M., & Mansour, A. (1985). Variation in the pattern of behavioral and brain asymmetries due to sex differences. In S.D. Glick (Ed.), *Cerebral lateralization in nonhuman species*. New York: Academic Press.

Vignolo, L.A., Boccardi, E., & Caverni, L. (1986). Unexpected CT-scan findings in global aphasia. *Cortex*, 22, 55–69.

Intrahemispheric Sex Differences in the Functional Representation of Language and Praxic Functions in Normal Individuals

RICHARD S. LEWIS AND LOIS CHRISTIANSEN

Pomona College, Claremont, California

Kimura (1980, *The Behavioral and Brain Sciences*, 3, 240–241; 1983, *Canadian Journal of Psychology*, 37, 19–35; 1987, *Canadian Psychology*, 28, 133–147) recently proposed that there are intrahemispheric sex differences in the organization of particular language and praxic functions such that in females these functions are more focally represented. This hypothesis, as well as supporting data, was derived from research with brain-injured subjects. The purpose of the present study was to test the utility of using dual-task methodology for investigating sex-related variation in intrahemispheric functional organization in normal individuals. Women were found to show greater interference than men on concurrent tasks of language and right-hand finger tapping. In support of Kimura's model, the present findings yielded evidence suggestive of intrahemispheric sex differences in the "functional distance" between language and praxic functions within the left hemisphere of normal individuals. © 1989 Academic Press, Inc.

Variation in the lateral representation of cognitive functions has been the focus of much attention in neuropsychology and has been associated with the subject characteristics of sex (see McGlone, 1980) and handedness (see Herron, 1980). Kimura (1980, 1983, 1987) has recently stressed that the anterior–posterior direction may also be an important dimension of variation in functional brain organization, and reported sex differences in the intrahemispheric representation of language and praxic functions. She studied a group of right-handed patients with unilateral brain damage that was localized anterior to or posterior to the Rolandic fissure of the left hemisphere. Kimura found that women suffered from aphasia and apraxia more often after left anterior lesions than after left posterior lesions. Men showed a different pattern of results with no significant

---

We express our appreciation to William P. Banks, Ph.D., for his valuable comments on an earlier draft, and Julie A. Lindberg for her artistry. Requests for reprints should be addressed to Richard S. Lewis, Department of Psychology, Pomona College, Claremont, CA 91711.

difference in frequency of aphasia and apraxia after either anterior or posterior left hemisphere lesions. Kimura concluded that particular language and praxic functions may be more diffusely represented within the left hemisphere of males.

Mateer, Polen, and Ojemann (1982) reported supporting evidence for Kimura's claims that women show a more restricted representation of language functions. They found that men demonstrated naming errors after stimulation to the frontal and parietal lobes, but that women did not show naming errors after posterior parietal stimulation.

In a study of global aphasia, Vignolo, Boccardi, and Caverni (1986) reported that all cases of global aphasia (in their sample) after lesions restricted to the left posterior hemisphere (as judged from CT scans) were in men, whereas all cases of global aphasia after lesions restricted to the anterior left hemisphere were in women.

Although all three of these studies report converging evidence for Kimura's hypothesis of intrahemispheric sex differences, their conclusions must be cautiously interpreted because all of these studies used brain-injured individuals. These findings would be strengthened if converging data were also found in studies of normal subjects.

Techniques such as visual half-field and dichotic listening that have been used to study lateralization of cognitive functions in normal individuals are not useful in studying the representation of functions along the anterior–posterior dimension. Dual task methodology, however, holds promise for investigating intrahemispheric functional organization.

Kinsbourne and Hiscock (1983) proposed the cerebral functional distance model to account for experimental findings utilizing divided attention tasks. This principle states that the closer the *functional* distance between the representation of two functions, the greater the interference when the two functions are concurrently activated. Kinsbourne and Hiscock defined functional distance in terms of the degree of neural connectivity between two functional areas, rather than in terms of physical distance. Therefore, if we assume that the two cerebral hemispheres represent relatively independent attentional resources, then the functional distance principle would predict that more interference should be present when performing two functions represented within the left hemisphere, such as concurrently performing a verbal fluency task while tapping with the right hand, than when performing two functions represented within separate hemispheres, such as concurrently performing a verbal fluency task while finger tapping with the left hand, a finding supported by the majority of studies (Kinsbourne & Hiscock, 1983). This presumably occurs because of the greater degree of neural connectivity between areas represented within a hemisphere than usually found between hemispheres (except in the case of the extensive connections between complementary cortical areas). This principle should also hold for investigations of the functional distance within a cerebral hemisphere. If two functional areas within a hemisphere are more extensively connected than are two other functional areas within a hemisphere, we would expect to find greater interference when concurrently performing activities represented with the former two functions than when concurrently performing activities represented by the latter two functions.

Dual task methodology, therefore, offers a useful technique for investigating variations in the intrahemispheric representation of cognitive functions. The present study was designed to test the utility of this method for investigating sex differences in the functional distance of language and praxic functions. It was hypothesized that if intrahemispheric sex differences in the representation of language and praxic functions exist, then there would most likely be a sex difference in the degree of neural connectivity between these two functions, resulting in a sex difference in their functional distance. Therefore, if Kimura's model is correct, we would expect to find a sex difference in the degree of interference when simultaneously performing a language and right-hand praxic task.

METHODS

Subjects. Fourteen undergraduate men and 14 undergraduate women, age 18 to 21 years, participated in this experiment. All of the subjects were self-reported right-handers. Handedness was verified by having the subjects demonstrate which hand they use during writing. This variable was selected because handwriting has been shown to have the highest loading on handedness factors (e.g. Orsini, Satz, Soper, & Light, 1985; Williams, 1986).

Materials and apparatus. Finger tapping was performed on a four-button apparatus connected to a digital counter that registered each time a sequence of four buttons was depressed. During the reading condition, subjects were asked to read aloud from five passages of an introductory psychology text, independently judged to be of similar difficulty. For the verbal fluency condition, subjects were instructed to generate words beginning with a target letter [F, A, S, C, and L, selected from Borkowski, Benton, & Spreen's (1967) norms].

Procedure. First, subjects were familiarized with the finger tapping apparatus. They were then instructed to depress the buttons in a sequence using four fingers, starting from the index finger and progressing toward the little finger. Each subject was given two trials of 30 sec each with each hand, one for practice, and the other to calculate a baseline finger tapping rate.

Two verbal tasks were administered to each subject, one of which was verbal fluency. This task involved generating as many words as possible starting with one of the target letters. Prior to the concurrent finger tapping–verbal fluency condition, subjects were given a practice trial of 30 sec with one of five letters (F, A, S, C, L). The practice trial was followed by the concurrent finger tapping–verbal fluency conditions. Two trials of tapping with each hand were presented. The number of complete sequences of finger tapping was recorded.

The other verbal task was reading text passages aloud. Again subjects were presented with a practice trial during which they were asked to read aloud as many words as possible. This was followed by four 30-sec concurrent task trials, finger tapping and reading, two with each hand. As in the previous conditions, the number of complete finger tapping sequences was recorded.

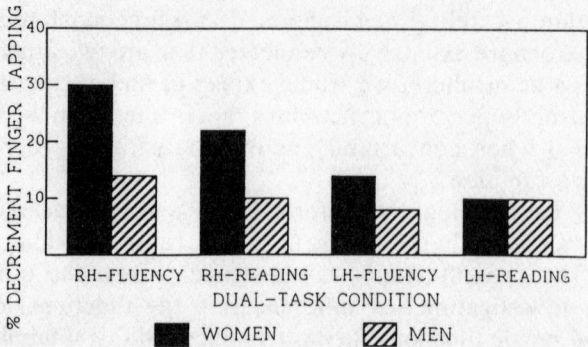

FIG. 1. Percentage decrement in finger tapping as a function of sex and tapping hand for the verbal fluency and reading aloud conditions.

The order of hand tapping, the verbal tasks, and the stimuli within the verbal tasks (i.e., the letters and reading passages) were randomly presented.

RESULTS

The number of finger tapping sequences was collapsed across the trials for each condition. The percentage decrement in finger tapping was calculated for each of the concurrent task conditions [(baseline tapping − concurrent tapping)/baseline tapping] × 100, and then entered into a multivariate analysis with the concurrent tasks and tapping hand the within-subject factors, and sex the between-subjects factor.

No three-way interaction was found between the effects of the tasks, tapping hand, and sex of the subject. A two-way interaction, however, was found between sex of the subject and tapping hand, $F(1, 26) = 5.84$, $p = .023$. As depicted in Fig. 1, for the right-hand condition, the women showed a significantly greater percentage decrement in finger tapping than the men, $t(26) = 4.29$, $p < .001$, but for the left-hand condition, there was no significant sex difference in finger tapping decrement, $t(26) = 1.46$, NS. A two-way interaction was not found between either the effects of tapping hand and task, or the effects of task and sex of subject.

In addition, there was (1) a main effect for the concurrent task condition, $F(1, 26) = 5.94$, $p = .022$, with greater finger tapping decrements occurring for the verbal fluency concurrent task; (2) a main effect for tapping hand, $F(1, 26) = 15.02$, $p = .001$, with a greater decrement in tapping occurring for the right-hand; and (3) a main effect for sex, $F(1, 26) = 12.96$, $p = .001$, with females showing greater tapping decrements.

DISCUSSION

The results of the present study, with normal subjects, are consistent with previous reports of intrahemispheric sex differences in the representation of particular language and praxic functions found in brain-injured subjects (Kimura, 1980, 1983, 1987; Mateer et al., 1982; Vignolo et al., 1986). Evidence was found suggesting that for the right-hand (left hemisphere) condition females, relative to males, show less functional distance between the language and praxic functions examined in this study. This sex difference in intrahemispheric functional representation was not found for the left-hand (right hemisphere) condition.

Previous research from brain-damaged samples suggested that certain language and praxic functions were found to be more focally represented within the left hemisphere of females. Together with the present study, this suggests that the smaller functional distance (i.e., increased interference) between language and praxic functions found for women results from their more focal representation of these functions within the left hemisphere.

The main effect of tapping hand is consistent with the majority of data finding greater interference in the right-hand (left hemisphere) condition for verbal concurrent tasks (see Kinsbourne & Hiscock, 1983) and supports the suggestion that the verbal tasks are interfering to a greater degree with left hemisphere functions.

The main effect of task, with greater interference in the finger tapping–verbal fluency condition relative to the finger tapping–reading aloud condition, suggests that the two former functions are functionally closer than reading and finger tapping, and is consistent with other studies finding similar results for these types of tasks (see Kinsbourne & Hiscock, 1983). It is important to note that the present results suggest that dual task methodology may be limited in its usefulness for investigating variation in *inter*hemispheric representation of function (at least for sex differences). Figure 1 shows that the percentage decrement of finger tapping between the left- and right-hand conditions is smaller for males than females. A laterality index derived from these finger tapping values would usually be interpreted as reflecting greater hemispheric asymmetry for the females (or greater symmetrical representation for males), results at odds with the majority of evidence regarding sex differences in cerebral lateralization (see, e.g., McGlone, 1980). The present results, therefore, suggest that such an interpretation could be very misleading because the degree of interference may be due to functional differences in *intra*hemispheric variation as well.

In summary, the results of the present study support the presence of intrahemispheric sex differences in the representation of language and praxic functions in a normal sample. As such, these results support previous research using brain-damaged samples which find a sex difference in the intrahemispheric representation of these functions. Together with Kimura's data this study suggests that the greater functional distance found for males is related to their more diffuse representation of language and praxic functions within the left hemisphere. This study has also demonstrated how dual-task methodology can be productively used to investigate variations in the intrahemispheric representation of cerebral functions and could be extended to other potential sources of variation such as hand preference. Furthermore, future studies using concurrent tasks to investigate variation in cerebral lateralization will need to take into account the influence of variation in the intrahemispheric representation of cognitive functions, especially on the outcome of lateralization indices.

REFERENCES

Borkowski, J. G., Benton, A. L., & Spreen, O. 1967. Word fluency and brain damage. *Neuropsychologia*, **5**, 135–140.

Herron, J. 1980. *Neuropsychology of left-handedness.* New York: Academic Press.

Kimura, D. 1980. Sex differences in intrahemispheric organization of speech. *The Behavioral and Brain Sciences*, **3**, 240–241.

Kimura, D. 1983. Sex differences in cerebral organization for speech and praxic functions. *Canadian Journal of Psychology*, **37**, 19–35.

Kimura, D. 1987. Are men's and women's brains really different? *Canadian Psychology*, **28**, 133–147.

Kinsbourne, M., & Hiscock, M. 1983. Asymmetries of dual-task performance. In J. B. Hellige (Ed.), *Cerebral hemisphere asymmetry; Method, theory, and application.* New York: Praeger.

Mateer, C. A., Polen, S. B., & Ojemann, G. A. 1982. Sexual variation in cortical localization of naming as determined by stimulation mapping. *The Behavioral and Brain Sciences*, **5**, 310–311.

McGlone, J. 1980. Sex differences in human brain asymmetry: A critical survey. *The Behavioral and Brain Sciences*, **3**, 215–264.

Orsini, D. L., Satz, P., Soper, H. V., & Light, R. K. (1985). The role of familial sinistrality in cerebral organization. *Neuropsychologia*, **23**, 223–232.

Vignolo, L. A., Boccardi, E., & Caverni, L. (1986). Unexpected CT-scan findings in global aphasia. *Cortex*, **22**, 55–69.

Williams, S. M. 1986. Factor analysis of the Edinburgh Handedness Inventory. *Cortex*, **22**, 325–326.

Sex differences in human brain asymmetry: a critical survey

Jeannette McGlone
Department of Psychological Services, University Hospital, London, Ontario, Canada N6A 5A5

Abstract: Dual functional brain asymmetry refers to the notion that in most individuals the left cerebral hemisphere is specialized for language functions, whereas the right cerebral hemisphere is more important than the left for the perception, construction, and recall of stimuli that are difficult to verbalize. In the last twenty years there have been scattered reports of sex differences in degree of hemispheric specialization. This review provides a critical framework within which two related topics are discussed: Do meaningful sex differences in verbal or spatial cerebral lateralization exist? and, if so, Is the brain of one sex more symmetrically organized than the other? Data gathered on right-handed adults are examined from clinical studies of patients with unilateral brain lesions; from dichotic listening, tachistoscopic, and sensorimotor studies of functional asymmetries in non-brain-damaged subjects; from anatomical and electrophysiological investigations, as well as from the developmental literature. Retrospective and descriptive findings predominate over prospective and experimental methodologies. Nevertheless, there is an impressive accumulation of evidence suggesting that the male brain may be more asymmetrically organized than the female brain, both for verbal and nonverbal functions. These trends are rarely found in childhood but are often significant in the mature organism.

Keywords: asymmetry; human brain; sex differences

> It would appear that the tendency to symmetry in the two halves of the cerebrum is stronger in women than in men.
> J. Crichton-Browne, *Brain*, 1880.

Introduction

The notion that the structure or function of the human brain may be sexually dimorphic is not entirely new. Previous work in nonhuman species clearly links the difference between male and female patterns of reproductive behaviour to sex differences in neural control centres (Goy 1970; Levine 1966; Reinisch 1974). A fresh approach to this topic, however, is reflected in recent publications suggesting that nonreproductive functions in humans may also be organized differently in male and female brains. Thus, it has been suggested that the cerebral representation of cognitive functions such as linguistic and visuospatial abilities may vary according to sex (Lansdell 1961; McGlone 1977b; 1978; McGlone and Kertesz 1973).

Functional brain asymmetry refers to the idea that, for most individuals, the left cerebral hemisphere is specialized for language functions as well as for the execution of learned manual activities. By comparison, the right cerebral hemisphere is less involved in subserving speech functions but more critical than the left hemisphere for the perception, construction, and recall of stimuli that are difficult to verbalize (Kimura 1973; Milner 1971). Recently, the possibility of sexual variation in the degree of brain lateralization has attracted attention from researchers investigating sex differences in overall psychological abilities. According to many psychologists, there are reliable group differences between males and females in those functions that have previously been described as being represented in opposite sides of the brain. Males, particularly after puberty, surpass females in visuospatial skill, such as the alignment of a rod to the vertical, left-right discrimination, disembedding figures, mental rotation, and point localization (Bakan and Putnam 1974; Sandström 1953; Stafford 1961; Thurstone 1938; Witkin 1949). In contrast, there appears to be a female advantage in certain executive speech tasks such as speed of articulation, fluency, and grammar, but not in other language tasks such as verbal reasoning (Hutt 1972). Several authors have speculated that these sex differences in overall cognitive patterning may be biologically influenced by underlying differences in lateralized brain organization (Harris 1978; Hutt 1972; McGee 1979; Maccoby and Jacklin 1974; Sherman 1974).

The 1970s produced several reviews dealing with the topic of sex differences and functional brain asymmetry (Bryden 1979; Buffery and Gray 1972; Fairweather 1976; Harris 1978; Harshman and Remington 1974; Hutt 1979; McGlone 1977a). Consensus has been reached on at least two points: First, there has been an inadequate data base on which to form conclusions. This is because most normative studies have tended to ignore the sex of the subject in the data analysis, and clinical investigations of psychological deficits after unilateral brain damage contain predominantly male patients, thus precluding cross-sex comparisons. The second point of agreement is that findings accruing from immature organisms must be considered separately from those derived from adults.

Opinions are more divergent regarding the existence of meaningful sex differences in the cerebral lateralization of verbal and spatial functions, and, if such differences exist, regarding whether the brain of one sex is more symmetrically organized than the other. Two opposing points of view have emerged with respect to the latter question. Buffery and Gray (1972) posit that the male brain is more symmetrically organized than the female brain for both speech and spatial representation. Most reviewers find very little support for this model and instead favour just the reverse pattern, albeit with reservations. That is, the adult male brain is more asymmetrically organized than the female brain for verbal functions (Harshman et al. 1974; McGlone 1977b), spatial functions (Harris 1978; McGee 1979; Witelson 1976; 1977b), or both verbal and spatial functions (Bryden 1979; Harshman and Remington 1974; Hier 1979; Hutt 1979; McGlone 1977a; 1978). Fairweather (1976) stands apart by arguing that there exist no convincing sex differences either in cerebral lateralization or in cognitive abilities.

The purpose of this review is twofold: to provide a critical framework from which future publications on the topic of sex differences and asymmetric brain organization can be evaluated, and to update and expand the literature, particularly of brain-lesioned patients. Adult studies (clinical, normative, anatomical, and physiological) are dealt with before developmental and animal data. Throughout this paper, emphasis is placed upon right-handed samples, since the atypical speech lateralization present in approximately one third of non-right handers (Branch et al. 1964; Zangwill 1960) may confound or entirely override whatever sex effects exist. Furthermore, it was felt that studies containing only one sex de facto precluded meaningful comparisons of sex effects; hence, investigations were selected only if they included both males and females.

Clinical Studies

The assumption underlying clinical research on unilaterally brain-damaged patients is that deficits observed after localized lesions provide a valid source of information regarding the functioning of the affected region in the healthy brain. Thus, patterns of psychological impairment observed after left and right hemisphere lesions have been compared to determine which functions appear more dependent on one side of the brain than the other. However, the sex composition of neurological patient samples has traditionally been biased by the inclusion of a greater proportion of males. It is only in the last twenty years that female patients have been studied separately from males.

One way to examine sexual variation in cerebral asymmetry is to contrast residual verbal skills with residual nonverbal skills after left and right brain damage. Lansdell and Urbach (1965) compared verbal/nonverbal ratio scores based on four of the verbal subtests from the Wechsler-Bellevue Scale of Intelligence (Information, Comprehension, Similarities, and Vocabulary) and the remaining seven subtests, two of which require verbal responses (Digit Span and Arithmetic) and five of which do not (Picture Completion, Block Design, Object Assembly, Picture Arrangement and Digit Symbol). Men with left temporal lobectomies showed relatively impaired verbal to "nonverbal" skills, a pattern significantly different from men with right temporal lobectomies, who showed relatively impaired "nonverbal" to verbal skills. In women there were no significant differences in verbal/nonverbal ratio scores between left and right temporal lobe groups.

Similar laterality by sex interactions were found by McGlone (1978) on a sample of adults with strokes and tumors confined to one cerebral hemisphere. Only right-handers were tested in this study, and IQ scores were calculated on the basis of six Verbal subtests of the Wechsler Adult Intelligence Scale (Wechsler 1955) and four of the five Performance subtests (i.e., all but Digit Symbol). In males, a significant discrepancy between Verbal and Performance scores was found after left-sided lesions (Verbal minus Performance IQ = −11.2), and a significant Performance decrement was found after right-sided lesions (Verbal minus Performance IQ = +13.5). In females, Verbal and Performance IQ scores were not significantly discrepant after left or right hemisphere damage. Patients whose cerebral hemispheres have been disconnected surgically also demonstrate significant sex differences in verbal/nonverbal ratio scores (Bogen et al. 1972). When a verbal response was demanded both for linguistic (Similarities) and spatial tasks (Street Figure-Completion), thus limiting the response to the dominant (i.e. left) hemisphere, adult males showed poorer spatial skills relative to verbal ones than did the commissurotomized females. Taken together, these three studies support the hypothesis of greater hemispheric specialization in males than in females, but they fail to indicate which function (verbal, nonverbal, or both) may be represented more asymmetrically in the male brain. In order to clarify this issue, the effects of unilateral lesions upon verbal functions must be studied separately from their effects on nonverbal functions.

Verbal functions. Although the typology of aphasic disorders (fluent, nonfluent, etc.) has not been examined for possible sex differences, the incidence of severe speech disorders has been reported to differ between men and women. In a sample of acute-stroke victims, Brust et al. (1976) found that the aphasic group contained more males than females, whereas the nonaphasic group contained more females than males, but these trends were not significant. Messerli et al. (1976) also observed a preponderance of male aphasics in an outpatient speech-therapy program (M/F:4.9/1). Edwards et al. (1976) reported that residual speech disorders were significantly worse in males than in females. McGlone and Kertesz (1973) indicated that after left hemisphere lesions the performance of males on a composite aphasia battery was slightly worse that that of females, but after right hemisphere lesions, females appeared slightly more impaired than males. The trends were not significant when analyzed statistically.

Language deficits other than aphasia also manifest sex differences according to which hemisphere has been compromised. Without giving details, Lansdell (1961) suggested that proverb interpretation was disturbed by left temporal lobe lesions in men, but not in women. Similar sex-dependent asymmetries were reported on a word-association test after left thalamotomies, but not after left or right temporal lobectomies (Lansdell 1973). The extent of the left temporal lobe excision in one study was negatively correlated with Wechsler's Verbal IQ scores in men, but not in women (Lansdell 1968a). Though not explicitly stated by Lansdell, these findings, with various language measures, suggest greater left hemisphere control of verbal functions in men than in women. Exceptions have been reported in Lansdell's own series. For example, on Atwell and Well's multiple choice vocabulary test (Lansdell 1968b) and on the verbal subtests of the Differential Aptitude Test (such as Verbal Reasoning, Clerical Speed, Spelling, and Sentences, (Lansdell 1968c), no significant sex-by-laterality interactions were found. The discrepancy between these and the previous positive studies may be related to the nature of the verbal task, or, more specifically, to whether or not overt speech production is required. The probability of obtaining significant sex by side-of-lesion interactions appears to decrease if a response mode other than expressive speech is permitted. However, these observations are speculative at best and may not be applicable to cases other than temporal lobectomy.

Nonverbal functions. It appears that perceptual tasks involving form or pattern recognition show no systematic or lasting interactions between sex and side of brain damage. Lansdell's data (1968b) on the Mooney Closure Task implied more bilateral representation in males than in females. In contrast, results from the Graves Design Judgment Task implied greater right hemisphere dependence in men, compared to greater left hemisphere dependence in women, though the significance of these findings was limited to the immediate postoperative period (Lansdell 1962). Other studies, using Raven's Coloured Progressive Matrices (Edwards et al. 1976; McGlone and Kertesz, 1973) and

McGlone: Sex differences in brain asymmetry

line-orientation tasks (Benton et al. 1975), showed no obvious sex differences after lateralized brain lesions.

When nonverbal tasks require constructional praxis in addition to perceptual discrimination, a more consistent pattern emerges. With right hemisphere lesions, greater dysfunction has been found in males than in females (Lansdell 1968a; McGlone 1977b). However, these trends are not always statistically significant (McGlone and Kertesz 1973) and may be entirely absent (Mack and Levine 1978). In some studies sex effects further interact with the underlying neuropathology. For example, in McGlone's (1977b) paper, only the vascular cases showed significant sex-by-laterality interactions on visuospatial tasks, whereas the tumour group did not (see Table 1). These data suggest that the etiology of the lesion may be an important control factor, particularly when sex differences in *spatial* asymmetries are being examined.

Limitations of clinical studies. Comparisons among the various clinical studies, which have thus far looked at the effects of lateralized brain lesions as a function of sex, are problematic for a number of reasons. First of all, more than one author has simply failed to publish the data on which his conclusions were based, thus preventing further evaluation of the claims (Bakan 1971; Eisenson 1967; Lansdell 1961; Levita and Riklan 1965a; 1965b; McFie 1975).

Secondly, the lateralization of the cerebral lesion site is unclear in most studies. Lesions are not unilateral when patient selection is based upon neurological deficits affecting one hemisphere *more* than the other (Lansdell 1968a; 1968b; 1973). The finding of more male than female aphasics (Brust et al. 1976; Edwards et al. 1976; Messerli et al. 1976) reflects nothing more than the known male bias in neurological samples, unless there is further documentation of the side of the lesion. Inclusion of cases with potentially bilateral lesions and cases of known atypical speech representation (Lansdell 1962) can mask or perhaps distort the effects of sex on hemispheric specialization.

Cross-study comparisons are also made difficult because the patient samples differ in central nervous system pathologies (i.e., temporal lobectomy, thalamotomy, infarcts, neoplasms, etc.). For example, Taylor (1976) found that the etiology of temporal lobe lesions (i.e., alien tissue versus mesial temporal lobe sclerosis) interacted with the sex of the subject and the side of the lesion in determining overall intellectual scores. Variations in pathology often result in systematic variations in extent and locus of the lesion, age of the patient at onset of pathology and age at time of testing, surgical intervention, recovery period, and medications. These factors, in turn, are known to alter performance on psychological tests (Matarazzo 1972; Meyer and Jones 1957). With few exceptions (e.g., McGlone 1977b; 1978) little attempt has been made to match sex and laterality groups for extent and locus of lesions, age, education, hand preference, or familial sinistrality.

Therefore, one must examine carefully whether earlier reports on sex differences in lesion effects may be attributable to systematic differences between the sexes in the uncontrolled variables mentioned above. For example, in Lansdell's series the mean number of months after surgery was higher in women with left temporal lobectomies than in any other group (Lansdell 1968a; 1968b), and left-sided excisions were smaller than right-sided excisions, particularly in the women (Lansdell 1968b; Lansdell and Urbach 1965). Hence, it is possible that smaller lesions and longer postoperative recovery periods in females than in males with left temporal lobectomies may account for the former's relative lack of verbal deficits. Similarly, reports of significant correlations between extent of left temporal lobe removal and Verbal IQ in males, but not in females, may be related to the attenuated range of scores obtained by the female group (Lansdell 1968a).

In 1973 I initiated a prospective study to systematically examine sexual variations in functional brain asymmetry using right-handed adults admitted to University Hospital in London, Ontario with strictly unilateral brain lesions (vascular or neoplastic). The incidence of aphasia after left hemisphere lesions was found to be at least three times as great in men as in women (McGlone 1977b). When aphasics were removed from the sample, only males continued to show the expected pattern of depressed verbal intelligence and verbal memory loss after left hemisphere damage compared to males with right hemisphere damage. No significant differences in these verbal scores appeared between females with left- and right-sided brain damage. However, both female lesion groups were significantly impaired on age-

Table 1. *Spatial results in nonaphasic vascular and tumour cases*

	Vascular			Tumour		
	Left hemisphere lesions	Right hemisphere lesions	Two-tailed t-test	Left hemisphere lesions	Right hemisphere lesions	Two-tailed t-test
WAIS block design (age-corrected scores)	(N)	(N)		(N)	(N)	
males	(11) 8.7	(13) 6.2	$p<.20$	(9) 7.0	(9) 7.3	ns
females	(9) 7.0	(14) 7.6	ns	(8) 8.9	(3) 5.3	ns
Mental rotation (max. = 12)						
males	(11) 10.7	(11) 8.3	$p<.01$	(8) 9.1	(10) 8.3	ns
females	(9) 8.4	(14) 8.6	ns	(8) 10.3	(2) 11.0	ns
Memory for photographed faces (max. = 12)						
males	(8) 9.0	(11) 6.8	$p<.05$	(7) 9.3	(8) 8.3	ns
females	(7) 9.6	(11) 8.7	ns	(8) 10.3	(2) 12.0	ns

Source: McGlone 1977b.

corrected Verbal IQ scores relative to non-brain-damaged controls. These sex differences were not explicable on the basis of age, education, etiology, length of illness, neurological signs (hemiparesis and/or visual field deficits), locus or severity of the lesion, familial sinistrality, or generalized intellectual deterioration. Table 2 presents additional Verbal IQ and verbal memory data on patients tested from June 1976 to June 1978. This replication study yields results similar to those obtained in the previous sample (McGlone 1977b), in so far as the males demonstrate verbal deficits subsequent to left-sided lesions, whereas females do not. Thus, at least with respect to verbal asymmetries, the findings are quite robust.

These data suggest that male right-handers may be more homogeneous than female right-handers with respect to left hemisphere dominance for speech functions (McGlone 1977b). Impaired Verbal IQ scores in right-hemisphere-damaged females further raise the possibility that some degree of bilateral speech representation may be more common in adult females than in males. However, the absence of aphasic disorders, per se, in right-hemisphere-damaged women implies that strict right hemisphere speech dominance may not show a female preponderance. These predictions are not contradicted by the limited clinical information available from sodium amytal studies and single-case illustrations of crossed aphasia.

The injection of sodium amytal directly into the internal carotid artery pharmacologically inactivates one hemisphere for a brief period and has been used to determine speech lateralization in humans. Unfortunately, the incidence of transient aphasic disturbances after left- and right-sided injections has not been compared between men and women (Milner 1975; Serafetinides et al. 1965; Wada and Rasmussen 1960). However, Lansdell et al. (1963) found that when low doses of the drug (125-130 mg) were injected into the *left* common carotid artery, men made slightly, but not significantly, more speech errors than women. However, the effective dosage would have been greater in women, given their smaller brain size compared to men. Thus, the reported sex differences in misnaming after left-sided injections would probably be enhanced if dosages were based upon brain proportions. It is likely that a good number of Lansdell's patients were left-handers; hence, conclusions specific to sex differences in right-handers cannot be made.

According to Milner's (1975) extensive series of amytal injections, evidence for bilateral speech representation has

Table 2. *Verbal intelligence and verbal memory after unilateral brain damage according to sex and side of lesion (1976-1978 sample)*

	Left hemisphere lesion	Right hemisphere lesion	Two-tailed t	p
Males				
(N)	(9)	(5)		
Age	37.7 yrs.	51.8 yrs.	not analyzed	
WAIS Verbal IQ				
(age-corrected)	95.2	105.6	1.73	< .10
Delayed Verbal	7.7	12.6	2.36	< .05
Females				
(N)	(5)	(6)		
Age	50.0 yrs.	40.7 yrs.	not analyzed	
WAIS Verbal IQ				
(age-corrected)	106.4	97.0	1.71	ns
Delayed Verbal	10.6	12.1	.86	ns

Table 3. *Reports of crossed aphasia in adult male and female right-handers*

Author (year)	Sex of patient
Angelerques et al. (1962)	female
Barraquer-Bordas et al. (1963)	female
Botez and Wertheim (1959)	male
Brown and Wilson (1973)	female
Clarke and Zangwill (1965)	2 females
Denes and Caviezel (1979)	male
Ettlinger et al. (1955)	male
Foroglou et al. (1975)	male
Hécaen et al. (1971)	male
Homes and Sadoff (1966)	male
Kennedy (1916)	2 females, 1 male
Marinesco et al. (1938)	male
Milner, Branch, and Rasmussen (1964)	
case D.R.	male
Solomon and Taylor (1979)	male
Stone (1934)	male
Urbain et al. (1978)	female
Wechsler (1976)	female
Weisenberg and McBride (1935)	
case 20	male
Total males = 12	
Total females = 9	

never been found in right-handed patients without early damage to the left hemisphere. These data appear to be incompatible with McGlone's (1977b) suggestion that some degree of bilateral language representation is more common in right-handed females than males. However, amytal testing has focused exclusively on expressive speech skills, whose disruption results in aphasic errors (e.g., dysnomia, impaired sequencing, perseveration, and misarticulation exclusive of dysarthria). In contrast, McGlone's right-hemisphere-damaged females showed depressed verbal intelligence scores, but not dysphasia.

The suggestion that right hemisphere *dominance* for speech function is not more common in females than in males is also compatible with, but not demonstrated by, scattered reports of crossed aphasia – i.e., aphasic disorders resulting from brain lesions ipsilateral to the preferred hand. Table 3 summarizes 18 previously published articles containing a total of 21 cases. Aphasia subsequent to right hemisphere lesions in right-handers was not more common in women compared to men, though selection bias in favour of males has not been controlled in these data, nor is it known what role the left hemisphere played in speech representation. In conclusion, the available amytal, crossed aphasia, and lesion data are not necessarily contradictory but may in fact be complementary.

Questions arise, however, about the nature of the language impairment found in females with damage to the right hemisphere, particularly if the defect is not related to aphasia. One possibility is that the underlying impairment simply limits the full expression of "higher"-level linguistic skill. For example, impoverished fluency would reduce the number of words or ideas that could be generated in a specified period of time, thus indirectly lowering verbal intelligence scores. However, Table 4 indicates that oral fluency scores (i.e., the number of words beginning with "d" produced in one minute) are not depressed in right-hemisphere-damaged females. Nor is there a significant correlation between Verbal IQ and oral-fluency scores in the female patient groups (Table 4). Hence, it appears unlikely

Table 4. *Verbal IQ and Oral Fluency scores and their correlations in nonaphasic patients and old-age control groups*

Age		(N)	Verbal IQ (age-corrected)	(N)	Oral Fluency	(N)	
48.0	Left hemisphere lesioned males	(23)	88.7	(19)	5.5	(19)	.519[a]
45.8	Left hemisphere lesioned females	(16)	103.6	(14)	13.2	(14)	−.096
45.8	Right hemisphere lesioned males	(23)	109.0	(19)	11.6	(19)	.606[b]
44.3	Right hemisphere lesioned females	(17)	101.1	(15)	13.0	(15)	−.096
68.8	Old age control males	(6)	111.5	(6)	11.7	(6)	.312
67.5	Old age control females	(11)	113.9	(11)	11.3	(11)	.247

[a] $p < .01$ [b] $p < .003$.

that verbal-fluency deficits account for the mild verbal intellectual impairments seen in women with right hemisphere lesions. Similarly, language-comprehension deficits were not significantly worse in females than males with right hemisphere lesions (McGlone 1977b). Obviously more research is needed to solve this puzzle, and explanations other than bilateral speech should be entertained (see Anatomical Studies section).

Based on the notion of greater bilateral language representation in female than male brains, McGlone (1977b) hypothesized that recovery from dysphasia should proceed more quickly in female than in male right-handers. Indirect support for this prediction is provided by Edwards et al. (1976), who administered two standardized tests of language production and comprehension to patients whose aphasia had lasted for at least three months after the onset of symptoms. Residual speech disorders were significantly worse in males than in females. In contrast, Kertesz and McCabe (1977) reported no significant differences between 23 male and 13 female aphasics in rate of recovery of language skills over an initial three-month period. However, both of these studies failed to control for sex differences in age, initial aphasia scores, typology of aphasia, hand preference, and laterality of the lesion; therefore, definitive conclusions are not warranted at this time.

At this stage the clinical literature tells us more about sex differences in cerebral dominance for language than for visuospatial skill (although just the reverse situation was true only five years ago). For right-handed men the predominant role of the left hemisphere in speech and language production remains unquestioned. Cerebral insult almost invariably results in some verbal deficit in male samples, but less consistently so in female samples. The role of the right hemisphere in subserving language processes in females is less clear. There is no evidence of more frequent right hemisphere dominance for basic speech functions in women than in men. Some degree of bilateral speech representation (but not necessarily equal representation) in an unknown percentage of right-handed females would explain McGlone's observation (1977b and Table 2) of impaired Verbal IQ scores after right hemisphere lesions in women. These arguments are attractive but require further investigation.

Regardless of sex, right hemisphere dominance for visuospatial processing is more difficult to demonstrate than left hemisphere dominance for speech functions in right-handed, brain-lesioned populations (Piercy 1964). Similarly, differences between left- and right-handed patients in spatial asymmetries are less marked than verbal asymmetries (Hécaen and Sauget 1971). From this perspective it is noteworthy that a small number of clinical studies finds males to be more right-hemisphere-dependent than females on certain visuospatial tasks. However, studies that control across sex for age, etiology, and extent and locus of lesion have yet to be published; thus any conclusions must remain tentative.

Very little has been said regarding sex differences in left hemisphere spatial analysis. This issue is complicated because "spatial" processing may be influenced by both verbal and nonverbal systems (McGlone and Kertesz 1973), hence the pressing need to design experiments that will dissociate these factors. Lastly, it is probably accurate to say that the incidence and severity of apraxia (oral or manual), unilateral paresis, incoordination, sensory loss, and neglect resulting from left and right brain damage have not been studied for possible sex differences. To summarize, the adult clinical literature on verbal and nonverbal functions offers support for the hypothesis that functional brain asymmetry is less marked in the female than the male population. This notion is further strengthened by several recent normative studies employing dichotic listening and tachistoscopic techniques.

Normative studies

Dichotic listening. Special techniques have made it possible to study some aspects of functional brain asymmetry in non-brain-damaged subjects. Dichotic listening tasks, in which different auditory stimuli are presented simultaneously to the two ears, have revealed consistent right-ear advantages in right-handers for verbal material such as digits, words, and consonant-vowel (CV) syllables (Darwin 1971; Kimura 1961; 1967; Shankweiler and Studdert-Kennedy 1967). Conversely, a left-ear advantage has been obtained for the recognition of nonverbal sounds (Curry 1967; Kimura 1964; Knox and Kimura 1970; Spreen et al. 1970). The advantage of one ear over the other in identifying auditory stimuli has been interpreted as reflecting specialization for that function in the contralateral hemisphere (Kimura 1961; 1967). Unfortunately, the majority of dichotic listening studies either failed to specify the sex of the subjects or failed to report whether sex differences were observed or analyzed (for reviews, see Fairweather 1976; Harshman and Remington 1974; Lake and Bryden 1976).

A retrospective look at fourteen previously published articles that included both men and women in the experimental design and also analyzed for possible interactions between sex and ear asymmetry revealed nine dichotic investigations reporting that the sex of the subject did not significantly relate to the degree fo right-ear advantage for verbal material (Briggs and Nebes 1976; Bryden 1965; 1975, as reanalyzed by Bryden 1979; Bryden 1979; Carr 1969; Demarest and Demarest 1979; McGlone and Davidson 1973; McKeever and Van Deventer 1977; Scott et al. 1979). One study found that the right-ear effect for CV syllables was significantly larger in ten right-handed women than in ten right-handed men (Dorman and Porter 1975). These investigations focused primarily on the mean difference between left- and right-ear scores, used relatively small samples, and all but three (Bryden 1975; Dorman and Porter 1975; Scott et al. 1979) required the recall of short sequences of items.

In contrast to the above findings, Lake and Bryden (1976) indicated that right-handed men had significantly greater right-ear superiorities than right-handed women on single dichotic CV syllables. In this study 94% of the men compared with only 69% of the women showed a right-ear advantage. In a re-analysis of earlier work (Bryden 1965), 75% of 112 men and 58% of 60 women showed right-ear effects on digit recognition (cited by Bryden 1979). Thistle (1975) also found trends for a greater right-ear advantage in males than females, though not significantly so. After combining data from three independent samples of right-handers, Harshman et al. (1974) found that the right-ear advantage for CV sounds was significantly stronger and occurred significantly more often in males than in females. Springer and Searleman (1978) discovered similar sex-by-ear interactions in a large sample of twins. Studies finding significantly greater asymmetries in males tended to use single pairs rather than **multiple sequences of stimuli, and the samples contained over fifty subjects.**

Nonverbal auditory tasks have not been as extensively investigated as verbal ones for sex differences in laterality effects. However, King (1970) reported that a left-ear superiority for the perception of hummed melodic patterns and vocal nonspeech sounds did not vary according to sex.

Tachistoscopic studies. In the visual modality the differential recognition of material presented tachistoscopically to the left or to the right of a central fixation point depends upon the verbal-nonverbal nature of the stimuli in a manner consistent with dichotic laterality effects. A right visual field advantage has been demonstrated for the identification of words and letters (Bryden 1965; 1973; Kimura 1966; Mishkin and Forgays 1952). In contrast, nonverbal stimuli yield left visual field superiorities for location of a dot in space (Kimura 1969), enumeration of scattered stimuli (Kimura 1966; McGlone and Davidson 1973), identification of line orientation (Kimura and Durnford 1974), and depth perception (Durnford and Kimura 1971).

Many recent tachistoscopic studies have indicated that laterality effects for both verbal and nonverbal material differ significantly between sexes. For alphabetic material the magnitude of the right field effect was markedly greater in right-handed males than in right-handed females (Bradshaw and Gates 1978; Bradshaw et al. 1977; Bryden 1965, cited by Bryden 1979; Ehrlichman 1971; Hannay and Malone 1976; Kail and Siegel 1978; Levy and Reid 1976; Marshall and Holmes 1974). Of four additional studies that have examined specifically for sex-by-laterality interactions on verbal tasks, two found none (Hannay and Boyer 1978; Leehey et al. 1978) and two were unable to replicate their initial results (McKeever et al. 1976; McKeever and Van Deventer 1977).

Tachistoscopically presented nonverbal material often yields significantly stronger left field advantages in men than in women: for perception of photographed faces (Berlucchi et al. 1976; Perez et al., 1975; Rizzolatti and Buchtel 1977; Umiltà et al. 1976); for the detection, localization, or enumeration of scattered dots (Davidoff 1977; Kimura 1969; Levy et al. 1976; McGlone and Davidson 1973); and for line orientation (Sasanuma and Kobayashi 1978; Walter et al. 1976; but not Durnford 1970). Three tachistoscopic studies that have specifically examined differences in field effects according to sex, but failed to find any, were also unable to replicate an overall left field advantage for the perception of nonverbal material (Bryden 1976; Ehrlichman 1971; Kail and Siegel 1978). Two studies claimed that there were no laterality effects related to sex in face recognition, but the data base and subsequent analysis were not published (Leehey et al. 1978; Sasanuma et al. 1977). Left field superiorities in the perception of schematic faces, depth perception, and hue discrimination appear to show no obvious sex differences (Durnford 1970; Fromm 1977; Patterson and Bradshaw 1975; Pennal 1977).

Limitations of dichotic and tachistoscopic studies. The possibility that sex differences in peripheral auditory thresholds may contribute to trends for greater right-ear superiority on dichotic listening experiments in men than women cannot be overlooked. In a review of five large-scale hearing surveys, Kannan and Lipscomb (1974) compared the median hearing thresholds for the left and right ears in middle- and high-frequency bands. The right-ear threshold was significantly lower than the left in 30 male samples and 8 female samples. In contrast, lower left- than right-ear thresholds were reported in 4 male and 9 female samples. This sex-by-ear-superiority interaction is highly significant (x^2 = 10.0, $p < .005$). Thus, auditory thresholds may be slightly lower on the right than the left ear in large male groups, but no obvious female bias exists. If similar sex effects were present in a dichotic listening paradigm, they might systematically enhance right-ear scores in men, but not in women. However, Cullen et al. (1974) demonstrated that the magnitude of the right-ear superiority for speech stimuli (CV pairs) presented dichotically could survive an intensity difference of 10 decibels between ears. Nevertheless, without audiometric screening and control nonverbal dichotic stimuli, a larger right-ear advantage in males than in females for verbal material cannot be accepted as unquestionably reflecting the asymmetrical cerebral representation of speech functions.

A well-controlled study prospectively examining the effect of sex on dichotic asymmetries has yet to be published, although several reviewers have speculated on currently available information. The fact that only large-scale dichotic studies tend to uncover significant sex-by-ear-asymmetry scores suggests that within-sex variation may be greater than variation between males and females (Harshman et al. 1974). Harshman also pointed out that failure to find sex differences in dichotic laterality effects may be associated with the presence of a significant memory load in the task – i.e., the use of multiple pairs of stimuli instead of a single pair. Dichotic paradigms that place verbal short-term memory demands on the subject are said to enhance the right-ear advantage (Broadbent 1958; Yeni-Komshian and Gordon 1974) and thus have the potential to minimize the already weak sex effect in ear asymmetry. However, memory factors cannot be the only explanation, since at least one tachistoscopic task showed enhanced sex differences as the length of the retention interval increased (Hannay and Malone 1976).

Bryden (1978; 1979) has argued that sex-related differences in ear- or visual-field effects may reflect strategy differences rather than differences in hemispheric functioning. For example, women may prefer verbal mediation in spatial problem-solving because their language skills are presumed to be better developed. In contrast, men are believed to depend less upon verbal analysis than purely spatial analysis. While it has been demonstrated that, for tachistoscopic word recognition, men responded faster when instructed in imaging strategies and women responded faster when instructed in verbal strategies, visual-field asymmetry patterns were similar in men and women regardless of strategy instructions (Metzger and Antes 1976). Furthermore, Harshman et al. (1974) have pointed out that a female tendency to use verbal mediation in spatial analysis should not reduce the right-ear or right-field advantage for verbal stimuli. If strategies or cognitive style totally accounted for sex differences in perceptual asymmetries, one would have to postulate the improbable situation in which women prefer to verbalize spatial analyses but that they prefer nonverbal processing for linguistic analyses! A more parsimonious explanation of the available normative literature would be that functional brain asymmetry is less marked in females than in males.

Manual asymmetries. We now turn to the sensorimotor system in order to compare and contrast these results with earlier reports of sex differences in verbal or visuospatial asymmetries. The incidence of left-handedness or mixed hand preference is often higher in male than in female adult samples (Annett 1973; Bakan 1971; Burt 1958; Bryden 1977; Hécaen and Ajuriaguerra 1964; Heim and Watts 1976; Hicks and Kinsbourne 1976; Hicks et al. 1978; Newcombe et al. 1975; Oldfield 1971; Silverberg et al. 1979; Teng et al. 1976; Thompson and Marsh 1976; Wile 1934). Annett (1972) interprets these figures as demonstrating the greater preponderance of right-hand preference in females than males. Others find no significant differences between men and women in hand-preference ratios (Annett 1967; 1970; Briggs and Nebes 1975; Fleminger et al. 1977; Hécaen and Ajuriaguerra 1964; Silverberg et al. 1979).

If frequency of hand usage over several activities is scaled, and the difference between hands is taken as a laterality index, females show a more pronounced dextrality than do males (Annett 1972; Barnsley and Rabinovitch 1970; Searleman et al. 1979; Tiffin and Asher 1948). Presumably, this sex effect is related to the greater proportion of right-handed females in undifferentiated samples, although Searleman's study (1979) contained only self-classified right-handers. Bryden (1977) claimed that in rating hand usage, females were more likely than males to endorse extreme items. Thus, strength of right-handedness in women may be somewhat inflated in studies that rely entirely on questionnaire-derived information. If unimanual motor skill is measured directly on tasks of speeded coordination, strength, or individual finger flexion, no significant sex differences in left-right asymmetry have been found in right-handed adults (Gardner 1942; Kimura and Davidson 1975; Kimura and Vanderwolf 1970; McGlone 1970; 1972). Therefore, hemispheric control over basic motor skills of the contralateral limb or facial musculature (Chaurasia and Goswami 1975) is not more asymmetrical in one sex compared to the other, at least in adult samples.

Manual tasks have also been used to examine the relative involvement of the left and right hemisphere in language representation. For example, it is known that speaking interacts selectively with right- but not left-hand performance (Hicks et al. 1975; Kinsbourne and Cook 1971; McGlone 1972). In addition, Lomas and Kimura (1976) reported that significant right-hand decrements in dowel balancing (from silent to concurrent speaking conditions) occurred only in male, not in female right-handers. It is difficult to interpret Low and Rebert's (1978) finding that manual reaction times on a verbal discrimination task were shorter in the left than the right hand for females, but shorter in the right than the left hand for males. Strictly speaking, this was not a case of functional competition (i.e. simultaneous movement and verbalization); therefore, whether the asymmetries reflect interference or enhancement effects is unclear.

Somatosensory asymmetries. Weinstein (1968) has studied two-point discrimination, pressure sensitivity, and point localization on each side of the body in right-handed men and women. In general, the left side tended to have lower thresholds than the right side, but no clear sex differences in laterality effects emerged. Pain thresholds are lower on the left side, but sex differences have not yet been investigated (Haslam 1970).

The tactual modality has also been used to present complex spatial material. A left-hand superiority has been reported for both sexes in shape recognition (Dodds 1978). Line-orientation judgments showed a left-hand advantage for men, but not for women, when the presentation was unimanual (Benton et al. 1978). But "dihaptic" tasks (simultaneous presentation to both hands) revealed a left-hand advantage in line orientation that did not interact with the sex of the subject (Oscar-Berman et al. 1978). Braille consists of a series of raised dot patterns that vary in spatial configuration, each pattern representing a letter of the alphabet. The reading of Braille by blind adults shows a left-hand advantage (Hermelin and O'Connor 1971), but sex differences in this asymmetry have not yet been investigated in adults.

To summarize, asymmetries in basic sensorimotor functions (pressure sensitivity, two-point discrimination, strength, coordination) appear to be equivalent in adult male and female right-handers. However, if tactile or motor systems are used to present verbal or spatial stimuli, sex differences analogous to those reported in the auditory and visual modalities have been found that favour greater asymmetry of function in men than in women. But if the stimuli have both verbal *and* spatial properties (e.g. Braille), no clear sex differences in asymmetry patterns have been found in adults. The higher incidence of right-hand preference for females compared to males in some samples is difficult to interpret solely on the basis of neural asymmetries because cultural, environmental, and response strategies play a prominent role in the development of an individual's stated hand preference (Bryden 1977; Dennis 1958).

Anatomical studies

Neural asymmetries. It has been argued that anatomical asymmetries between the left and the right halves of the brain may be the basis for the development of functional hemispheric specialization. If this is so, it would be important to note any sexual variation in structural asymmetries. These issues were studied intensively in the late 1800s and then again 100 years later.

In 32 post-mortem specimens, Crichton-Browne (1880) found that weight differences between the left and right hemispheres were less marked in females than in males. After viewing photographs of male and female brains, he was of the opinion that, ". . . the superior symmetry of the female brain (is) due to its comparative poverty in secondary gyri." (Crichton-Browne 1892, p. 950). No data were presented to support this conclusion. However, Rubens et al. (1976) published diagrams indicating that the shape of the Sylvian fissure in right-handers is symmetrical in a greater percentage of female (50% or 4/8) than male brains (31% or 5/16), though these differences are not statistically significant (see Fig. 1).

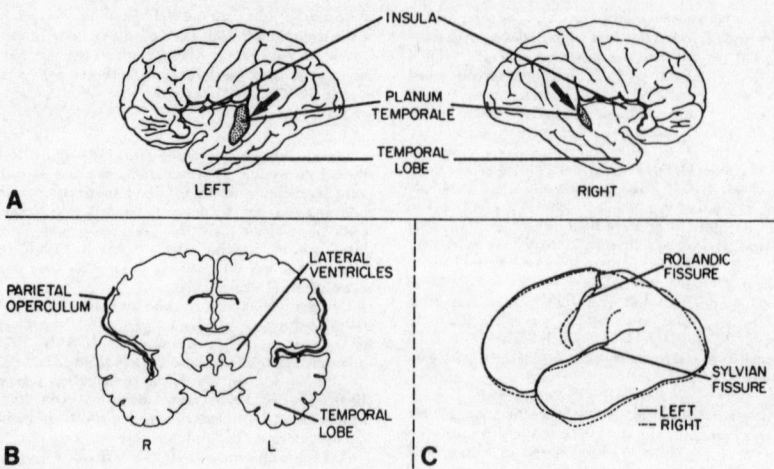

Figure 1. Anatomical asymmetries of the human brain.
A. Cytoarchitectonic delineation of the planum temporale. Note the left-right asymmetry (see Galaburda et al. 1978).
B. Coronal section of the brain through the insula. The blood vessels leave the ends of the Sylvian fissure at a lower level on the left because of greater opercularization on that side (see LeMay and Culebras 1972).
C. Composite tracing of the hemispheric sulci and lateral fissures (see Rubens et al. 1976).

At autopsy, Heschl (1878) observed that an elbow-like formation between the anterior transverse temporal gyrus and the superior temporal gyrus was present more commonly on the left than the right side, and in males (14.4% of 632 male specimens) more often than in females (4.2% of 455 female specimens). However, the ratio of left to right occurrence of the elbow formation was equivalent in men (17:1) and women (19:1). The superior surface of the temporal lobe posterior to Heschl's gyrus – i.e. the planum temporale – is believed to subserve auditory speech functions and is reported to be larger on the left side than on the right in the majority of both sexes (Chi et al. 1977; Geschwind and Levitsky 1968; Teszner et al. 1972; Wada et al. 1975; Witelson and Pallie 1973; Yeni-Komshian and Benson 1976). However, this anatomical asymmetry is attenuated in adult females, because significantly more female than male specimens showed the reverse asymmetry pattern – i.e., a larger right than left planum temporale (Wada et al. 1975).

Unfortunately, most recent studies searching for anatomical asymmetries in gyral configuration or planimetric units have not analyzed for sex differences (Akesson et al. 1975; Geschwind and Levitsky 1968; Kertesz and Geschwind 1971; LeMay 1977; LeMay and Kido 1978; McRae et al. 1968; Teszner et al. 1972; Yeni-Komshian and Benson 1976). Wada et al. (1975) found that the frontal opercular regions showed asymmetry patterns that were similar in men and women – i.e., larger on the right than the left side. Wada (1976) also reported sex-dependent anatomical asymmetries in the medial aspects of the occipital lobe – i.e. the cuneus. In a preliminary analysis of 24 adult specimens, females tended to have larger right than left cuneate areas, whereas in males the left side was larger.

Computerized axial tomography measures differences in density across brain structures. Gyldensted (1977) examined parts of the ventricular system of 100 normal adult brains, 50 of each sex. Left-right comparisons in linear measurements of the anterior horn and of the body of the lateral ventricles varied significantly according to sex, but interpretation of these asymmetries with reference to size or shape of adjacent neural structures is unclear.

The cerebral commissures, connecting one side of the brain with the other, may be involved in the establishment of speech lateralization (Selnes 1974). They may also be important pathways whereby an acute focal lesion in one hemisphere could inhibit function in the opposite side (i.e. diaschisis). Unfortunately, little is known about variation between men and women in the anatomy of interhemispheric systems. Rabl (1958; cited by Lansdell and Davie 1972) reported that the massa intermedia, a band of neural tissue connecting the thalami, was absent from the brain in about a third of the men and a quarter of the women undergoing pneumoencephalography for suspected neurological disease. Lansdell and Davie (1972) further reported that the presence of the massa intermedia resulted in relatively poorer nonverbal than verbal skills in men, but no such effect was present in women. The possibility that males and females differ in interhemispheric connections should not be overlooked.

Vascular Asymmetries. If sex differences are present premorbidly in the vascular system, or if there are systematic biases in the localization of vascular pathology according to sex, then differences in functional asymmetry between males and females might be related more to extracerebral factors than to neural organization. This would be an important distinction to make.

Variation in the relative diameters of the three major veins draining blood from the convexity of each cerebral hemisphere may be predictive of speech lateralization (Di Chiro 1972). However, Hochberg and LeMay (1975) reported that these venous asymmetries occur equally often in men and women. Matsubara (1960) found that the majority of atypical drainage patterns occurred in the right hemisphere in females 10- to 19-years old and in males 20- to 29-years old. The functional significance of Matsubara's data is unknown, but Lansdell's (1964) interpretation that ". . . the right vein of

Trolard is larger than the left in girls, but not in boys" seems overly inclusive. There are no sex differences in the angle at which the middle cerebral artery leaves the Sylvian fissure in the region of the parietal operculum; each sex shows a wider angle on the right side (Hochberg and LeMay 1975; LeMay and Culebras 1972).

The incidence of cerebrovascular disease may differ between males and females in side and vessel site. In general, arteries feeding the left side of the brain are occluded more often than those on the right side, although this trend is not significant in every investigation and may further depend upon the particular artery being studied (Hutchinson and Acheson 1975; Kaste and Waltimo 1976; Sindermann et al. 1969; 1970). Data from at least three independent surveys of patients undergoing angiography suggest that the preponderance of left-sided vascular lesions was equal in magnitude across male and female samples (Hutchinson and Acheson 1975; Kaste and Waltimo 1976; Sindermann et al. 1970). However, sex differences were found in patients with recurrent (i.e. more than one) vascular episodes, whereby the side of first episode was significantly more often the left in males, but the right in females (Hutchinson and Acheson 1975).

The site of occlusion within a cerebral vessel also appears to differ between the sexes, with males tending toward occlusions in the proximal (larger) vessels, whereas females tend more toward occlusions in the distal (smaller) vessels. Thus, relatively more males than females suffer occlusions in the internal carotid artery than in the middle cerebral artery (Sindermann et al. 1970), and relatively more males than females suffer occlusions in the trunk of the middle cerebral artery than in one or more of its branches (Kaste and Waltimo 1976). However, sex differences in the site of middle cerebral artery occlusion (i.e. trunk versus branch), when further analyzed by side, were significant only on the left, not on the right side (Kaste and Waltimo 1976).

If occlusions in the distal portion of an artery result in less ischemic damage (i.e. tissue damage due to an inadequate blood supply) than proximally occurring occlusions, then female stroke patients should demonstrate less extensive ischemic damage than males, particularly on the left side. It might follow that functional deficits subsequent to left hemisphere ischemia may also be less marked in females than in males. However, because of collateral circulation, occlusion of a vessel does not necessarily result in ischemic damage to all brain tissue in the territory beyond the site of blockage (Vander Eeken 1959). Thus, one must bear in mind that the type, severity, and recovery of focal neurological deficits such as hemiparesis, visual-field defects, and aphasia, are not systematically related to site or degree of occlusion in any particular artery (Dyken et al. 1974; Lascelles and Burrows 1965; Sindermann et al. 1969; Waltimo et al. 1976; Yarnell et al. 1976). Whether this lack of correlation between site of vessel damage and extent of dysfunction also holds true for less focally represented functions (i.e. intelligence and memory) is unknown.

Limitations of anatomical studies. The tacit assumption underlying much of the anatomical research is that cerebral specialization may arise when one region of the brain is larger than its contralateral homologue. A mechanism relating size (volume, density, weight, number of neurons) to function has not been elaborated, and other interpretations are possible (Galaburda et al. 1978; Rubens 1977). Moreover, until it is clear that surface linear measurements of the brain accurately predict the total number of neurons in a functional region, the relevance of partial measures is in doubt. Thus, it is still an open question whether asymmetric morphology forms the basis of subsequent functional specialization or whether it merely reflects balanced accommodation for an irregularly expanding cortical mantle.

The 19th-century reports of sex differences in anatomical asymmetries were based on postmortem examinations of patients who died in insane asylums, many with neurological disorders. Methodologies were primitive, and no statistical analyses were performed. Therefore, these studies must be viewed with a healthy degree of skepticism. Similarly, vascular asymmetries must be interpreted with caution, given that the data are not derived from healthy individuals, but rather from hospitalized patients undergoing neuroradiological investigation because of suspected central nervous system disorders. Support for Crichton-Browne's (1880) notion that the female brain may be more symmetrically structured than the male brain comes from only a few scattered reports (Rubens et al. 1976; Wada et al. 1975). Other anatomical studies do not find that one sex is more symmetrical, just differently structured (Gyldensted 1977; LeMay 1977; LeMay and Kido 1978; Wada 1976). However, since most investigations have overlooked the possibility of sex differences in morphological asymmetries, it is premature to make definitive conclusions at this time.

Even less known of sex differences in the blood supply to the left and right hemispheres, in health or disease. Some preliminary work would suggest that, under certain physiological conditions (i.e. hypertension), vessel occlusion may cause more pronounced ischemic changes in the brains of male than female rats (Nakatomi et al. 1979). The elastic properties of the arteries are greater in the human female than in the male under age forty (Cope and Roach 1977), and anticoagulants (aspirin) have been reported to significantly reduce the risk of continuing ischemic attack, stroke, or death in men but not in women (The Canadian Co-operative Study Group, 1978). These suggestions of greater vulnerability of the male than the female brain toward ischemic damage must be borne in mind when reviewing lesion and recovery studies in neurological populations. For example, clinical reports of greater cognitive impairment in males compared to females would be suspect if based only on vascular etiologies, unless the sexes were well matched for extent of the cerebral lesion. Moreover, if it could be demonstrated that the female brain was more susceptible than the male brain to the bilateral effects of diaschisis after a unilateral lesion, then the hypothesis of less *functional* asymmetry in the female brain need not be invoked. The author is unaware of any data that would support or reject this suggestion.

Electrophysiological studies and their limitations. Electrographic recordings of brain wave activity have also been used to investigate hemispheric specialization in normal humans. Language stimuli elicit asymmetric electrographic patterns favouring the left hemisphere, whereas nonlanguage stimuli elicit lateralized patterns favouring the right hemisphere (Cohn 1971; Molfese et al. 1975). Interpretation of these results in terms of functional brain asymmetry depends on the assumption that a difference in level or in pattern of electrical activity between left and right sides reflects the extent to which each hemisphere of the brain is actively involved in processing the stimuli.

To date, the few electrophysiological studies looking at degree of lateralized brain activation during verbal and nonverbal tasks are inconsistent regarding which, if either, sex may be the more asymmetrically organized. In adults, evoked potential recording over the temporal region yielded no obvious sex differences in the response of the left hemisphere to verbal stimuli presented auditorily (Molfese 1978). Nor are there significant sex differences in the amount of alpha activity of the left and right sides at temporal, parietal, or occipital sites during vocabulary or visuospatial tasks (Tucker 1976).

However, verbal/nonverbal ratios or difference scores

between the left and right hemisphere in alpha-wave activity have been related to the sex of the subject. Davidson et al. (1976) and Rebert and Mahoney (1978) claimed greater asymmetry in hemispheric activation in females, as opposed to others who claimed greater hemispheric asymmetry in males (Ray et al. 1976; Tucker 1976; Wogan et al. 1979).

Inconsistencies in sex effects among the studies may be due to the use of different types of "verbal" or "nonverbal" tasks, to differences in the modality of presentation (auditory versus visual), to differences in task demands (overt versus covert), or simply to different electrode-placement sites (occipital, temporal, central, or frontal). At present, there is no way to decide which study is most accurate in its conclusions, since so many of these variables were uncontrolled (see Donchin et al. 1977).

Furthermore, electroencephalographic (EEG) recordings may reflect the degree to which there is asymmetrical control of body movements (Gevins et al. 1979). Although investigators are aware of, and hence eliminate, artifacts associated with gross body movement, more subtle limb, eye, and tongue movements have not been monitored. Males and females may, however, differ in amount and direction of such task-related movement (Beveridge and Hicks 1976; Gur and Gur 1977; Weiten and Etaugh 1974). Thus, EEG asymmetries that differ between males and females may be monitoring asymmetrical cerebral control of movement rather than the cerebral lateralization of verbal and non-verbal functions per se. This would be an important distinction to make, even if the underlying mechanisms controlling movement and cognitive functions are subserved by the same hemisphere.

Bearing in mind earlier reports of sex differences in anatomical asymmetries, the interpretation of scalp EEG recordings becomes even more ambiguous. For example, electrode placements over homologous regions on the skull may, in fact, be less homologous for one sex than the other, due to sexual variations in underlying brain structures. Thus, findings of sex differences in EEG asymmetry may be structurally rather than functionally based (Davis and Wada 1978).

Developmental studies

Anatomical and electrophysiological. Anatomical asymmetries of frontal or temporal lobe regions have been found in large-scale studies on infants, but these asymmetries did not vary between males and females (Chi et al. 1977; Wada et al. 1975). On the basis of only five brains of each sex, Witelson and Pallie (1973) reported that the increased size of the left planum temporale was significant in female infants, but not in age-matched males. For a slightly older sample of nine male infants, the left planum was significantly larger than the right; hence no meaningful sex differences in structural asymmetries of the infant brain have been found.

Auditory-evoked potentials recorded from the temporal lobes in response to stop-consonants differing in voice-onset time reflect sex differences in the right but not the left hemisphere (Molfese and Hess 1978). Right hemisphere differences between males and females have not been found in adults but are significant in neonates, infants, and preschool-age children. The factor that distinguished boys from girls in Molfese's study is one that makes fine distinctions both within and between phoneme categories (i.e., sounds with unique verbal labels – /p/ versus /b/ – and sounds without such labels). The data suggest that auditory discrimination processes in the right hemisphere may be more finely tuned in young females than in young males.

Verbal functions. Few clinical studies have examined the effects of strictly unilateral brain lesions in childhood, and even fewer report the data separately for girls and boys. Woods and Teuber (1978) retrospectively examined the incidence and severity of acquired aphasia and its recovery in 34 boys and 31 girls according to the side of the lesion. Subsequent examination of the right-handed sample reveals no obvious sex differences. A preliminary analysis by Lansdell based on a small sample of seven-year-old children whose lesions dated from the first year of life yielded no statistically significant laterality effects or sex-by-laterality interactions on verbal intelligence, reading, or spelling (Lansdell 1976). However, locus and extent of perinatal brain injury, hand preference, and side of speech representation were not controlled across girls and boys.

There appears to be some controversy in the dichotic literature with respect to the effects of sex on degree of speech lateralization in right-handed children. Kimura (1967) tested five- to eight-year-olds and found a significant right-ear effect in each group except five-year-old boys. Seven- to eleven-year-old girls with reading disabilities (dyslexia) showed significant right-ear effects for verbal material, but dyslexic boys of the same age did not (Taylor 1962). From these two studies, Buffery and Gray (1972) inferred that left hemisphere speech lateralization occurred earlier in females than in males, and this sex difference was accentuated in children with reading difficulties.

The association of dyslexia with attenuation of the right-ear advantage in boys, however, has been contradicted recently by Witelson (1977a). In her sample, 85 dyslexic and 156 nondyslexic boys ranging from six to fourteen years of age showed equally significant right-ear effects for the perception of digits. Buffery and Gray's conclusions are also inconsistent with more recent dichotic studies, which yielded significant right-ear effects in both sexes as early as age three (Ingram 1975a; Kinsbourne and Hiscock 1977; Nagafuchi 1970), and even in infants (Entus 1977).

Table 5 contains a summary of seven dichotic studies in three- to nine-year-old right-handed, nondyslexic children. These studies were selected because, at every age tested, the statistical significance of the right-ear effect was calculated separately for each sex. Significant right-ear effects appeared slightly more often in boys (21/26 times) than in girls (15/26 times) – a trend most clearly seen in the four-year-old samples. Bryden (1970) indicated that the proportion of right-handed boys with higher right-ear scores increased steadily from grades 2 to 6, but this trend was more variable in girls. These data do not convincingly demonstrate greater left hemisphere specialization for speech in boys compared to girls, but the inconsistency of the right-ear advantage in girls tested at various ages is curious. Ingram (1975a) has suggested that such apparent fluctuations in the right-ear effect across age groups could be related to developmental periods of cerebral re-organization, but this idea is speculative at present and requires further longitudinal rather than cross-sample investigations.

Other dichotic listening studies examining the effects of age and sex on right-ear superiority for verbal material have not provided enough information to be included in Table 5. The majority reported no significant interactions of sex with ear superiority (e.g. Berlin et al. 1973; Borowy and Goebel 1976; Geffner and Hochberg 1971; Hynd and Obrzut 1977; Kinsbourne and Hiscock 1977; Knox and Kimura 1970; Satz et al. 1975; Schulman-Galambos 1977).

Tachistoscopic procedures employing alphabetical material to determine degree of speech lateralization are precluded in very young children who lack the necessary reading skills. Presumably, prereaders identify letter material through visual-visual matching, rather than visual-phonetic matching. The degree to which letter symbols are phonetically coded affects the direction and magnitude of the right visual field effect (Cohen 1972; Geffen et al. 1972).

Table 5. *The incidence of a significant right-ear superiority on verbal dichotic listening tasks as a function of age and sex*

Study	3 years		4 years		5 years		6 years		7 years		8 years		9 years	
	boys	girls	boys	girls	boys	girls	boys	girls	boys	girls	boys	girls	boys	girls
Nagafuchi (1970) 2 syllables	+	0	0	0	+	0	+	0						
Nagafuchi (1970) 3 syllables	+	+	+	0	0	+	+	0						
Ingram (1975a) digits	+	+	+	0	+	+								
Kimura (1963) digits			+	+	+	+	+	+	+	0	+	+	+	0
Kimura (1967) digits					0	+	+	+	+	+	+	+		
Geffner and Dorman (1976) syllables			+	0										
Piazza (1977) words	0	+	+	0	+	+								
Pizzamiglio and Checchine (1971) words					0	+								

Note: + = significant right-ear superiority reported by author. 0 = right-ear superiority not statistically significant at the $p < .05$ level.

Thus, tachistoscopic word recognition is influenced by reading proficiency, which, in turn, is generally advanced in girls compared to boys (for review, see Maccoby and Jacklin 1974). When boys and girls are matched for chronological age and have average or above average reading skills, tachistoscopic studies of verbal asymmetries in right-handers have failed to show significant effects of sex on visual-field scores (Marcel and Rajan 1975; Yeni-Komshian et al. 1975). One study found that the right field advantage was significantly greater in boys than in girls, although longer exposure times for males than females may have influenced these results (Marcel et al. 1974).

Spatial, somatosensory, and motor functions. Very few investigators have examined the influence of sex on nonverbal auditory or visual spatial asymmetries in children, but those who have found no significant interactions of sex with laterality effects (Davidoff 1977; Knox and Kimura 1970; Lansdell 1976; Marcel and Rajan 1975; Piazza 1977).

However, tactual and tactual-spatial asymmetries may differ between boys and girls as a function of age. A left-hand superiority in right-handed children has been reported for single-point-pressure sensitivity (Ghent 1961; Kimura 1963), for the identification of unfamiliar shapes (Affleck and Joyce 1979; Cioffi and Kandel 1979; Witelson 1976), and for Braille letter learning (Rudel et al. 1974; 1977). On thumb sensitivity, girls showed the laterality effect at an earlier age than boys (Ghent 1961). Witelson's (1976) initial report that boys showed a left-hand preference for the dihaptic identification of nonsense shapes earlier than did girls was not replicated by Cioffi and Kandel (1979). The left-hand superiority in Braille letter learning is apparent earlier in boys than in girls (Rudel et al. 1974; 1977). These findings have been interpreted as reflecting a sex difference in right hemisphere dominance for spatial functions (Witelson 1976; 1977b). Alternatively, the less-marked left-hand superiority in girls may be related to greater left hemisphere participation in the task via verbal mediation. If girls tended to identify ambiguous shapes with verbal labels, this kind of approach might favour a right-hand advantage or at least reduce the left-hand superiority. Indeed, Cioffi and Kandel (1979) reported that the tactile identification of nonword bigrams (i.e. letter pairs) showed a right-hand (i.e. left hemisphere) superiority for girls and a left-hand (i.e. right hemisphere) superiority for boys, whereas two-letter words showed a significant right-hand advantage across both sexes. It is also possible that the left hemisphere's control over the right limb, which tends to be more marked in girls than boys, may reduce the influence of the right hemisphere in those tactual-spatial tasks that specifically require movement. Whatever the explanation, it is clear that by the age of puberty, sex differences in tactile asymmetries have disappeared (Ghent 1961; Rudel et al. 1974; 1977; Witelson 1976) and do not reappear in adult samples.

Most children prefer the right hand for writing and other skilled motor acts, but there are more right-handed girls than boys (Annett 1970; Jones 1947) and more left-handed boys than girls (Heim and Watts 1976; Hildreth 1949; Teng et al. 1979; Peters and Pedersen 1978). Moreover, among right-handers, girls show more consistent preferences for the right side and greater relative right-hand superiority in strength and dexterity than do boys (Annett 1970; Buffery and Gray 1972; Denckla 1973; Ingram 1975b; Jones 1947; Rosenblum 1978). The latter findings, taken with Ghent's (1961) somatosensory data, raise the possibility that rudimentary sensory and motor systems may be more asymmetrically organized in young females than in young males. However, these trends (excluding hand-*preference* data, per se) are not present in previously reviewed adult studies; hence, girls fail to maintain a pattern of enhanced left-right sensorimotor asymmetries relative to boys as a function of age, just as boys lose their lateralized advantage relative to girls on complex tactual spatial tasks.

Limitations of developmental studies. Buffery and Gray (1972) recognized that "... sex differences in children are difficult to interpret when there is an advantage in favour of girls, since this may be due to their general maturational advance over boys" (p. 131). Harshman et al. (1974) further point out that similar confounding effects may complicate comparisons of degree of cerebral lateralization between boys and girls. In fact, the degree of ear advantage on dichotic verbal tasks has been linked with rate of sexual maturation during puberty. Between the ages of thirteen and sixteen, early maturers showed a less marked right-ear superiority than did late maturers (Waber 1976; 1977). Moreover, when boys and girls were matched for rate of sexual maturation, rather than for chronological age, no sex differences in ear asymmetries were found (Waber 1977).

Previous criticisms directed at clinical, normative, and anatomical investigations of adult populations are equally applicable to children and need not be reiterated. The interpretation of developmental studies is further limited by difficulties in obtaining reliable data from youngsters whose comprehension, motivation, and behaviour can vary considerably from task to task and from session to session. The effects of physical, mental, and cerebral maturational level on sex differences in overall skill further reduce the likelihood of uncovering simple relationships between laterality effects and sex. For these reasons, perhaps, one should not expect to find exact parallels between adult and developmental studies, although interactions of age and sex with brain asymmetry are interesting in their own right. The relative paucity of developmental studies indicating sex differences in functional brain asymmetry further suggests that such differences are not marked until some stage after puberty. If this is true, the release of sexual hormones under genetic control may be an important influence in the degree to which brain asymmetry evolves. For example, high concentrations of testosterone in the male fetus may prime the brain as well as the genitalia into a masculine template that is not fully realized until full sexual maturation. Or, perhaps, the regular cyclicity of estrogen/progesterone levels unique to the brains of females throughout their reproductive lives may somehow alter brain specialization. If nothing more, these speculations suggest that individual differences in degree of cerebral asymmetry may have several origins. Thus, factors that underly brain organizational differences between males and females may not necessarily account for differences between left- and right-handers.

Animal studies

Anatomical asymmetries akin to those reported of the human brain have recently been found in nonhuman primates. For example, the planum temporale is significantly larger on the left than the right side of the brain, though this asymmetry is less marked than that found in humans (LeMay and Geschwind 1975; Yeni-Komshian and Benson 1976). The cerebral cortex in male rats appears to be thicker on the right than the left side (Diamond et al. 1975). Functional asymmetries roughly analogous to those reported in humans may also be present in other primates. A left hemisphere dominance in processing species-specific vocalizations (Petersen et al. 1978) and auditory temporal patterns (Dewson 1977) has been found in monkeys. In addition, there is some evidence, albeit disputed, for hemispheric specialization of visual discrimination in the cat (Gazzaniga 1963; Hamilton 1977; Webster 1972). Unfortunately, sex differences were not studied in any of the above publications.

Motor asymmetries such as paw preference are found in the mouse, rat, cat, rhesus monkey, and chimpanzee, but there is no species shift toward a right-paw preference (Collins 1975; Finch 1941; Peterson 1931; Warren et al. 1967; Webster 1972). On a food-reaching task, however, Collins (1975) observed that adult female mice were more strongly lateralized than males for both left and right preferences. Sex differences in turning behaviour and in the lateralization of dopamine content have been reported in the rat (Robinson, Becker, and Ramirez, unpublished manuscript). Thus, certain motor and biochemical asymmetries in rodents, though not specific to direction, suggest that the female is more lateralized than the male. One cannot help but wonder if this might be a phylogenetic predisposition that becomes unidirectional in higher primates.

Sex and laterality effects are found in vocal-control areas of certain songbirds. Female canaries and zebra finches do not usually display complex song patterns unless they are given early injections of testosterone. In these species, vocal-control areas in the brain are strikingly larger in males than in unandrogenized females. However, anatomical differences between the right and left cerebral vocal areas are not found in either sex (Nottebohm and Arnold 1976). In males, however, there appears to be a functional dominance of the left hemisphere for control over complex song patterns (Nottebohm 1977; Nottebohm and Nottebohm 1976). It would be interesting to know if the early administration of testosterone had an affect not only on later song development but also on the establishment of functional hemispheric dominance for song.

From this brief summary it is clear that sex differences in brain asymmetry have hardly been studied in animal populations. This is an understandable omission, given the general impression that functional and anatomical brain specialization is much less striking in species other than *Homo sapiens*. Nevertheless, if sexual hormones play a role in the structure and function of the central nervous system (see Reinisch 1974; 1976), hormonally influenced variation in functional brain asymmetry could be studied more readily in nonhuman than in human species.

Conclusions

Individual differences in lateral brain specialization are interesting in their own right and important for theorists hypothesizing relationships between brain organization and behaviour. This review offers a growing body of evidence that sex differences in brain asymmetry exist, particularly in adulthood. The following discussion will attempt to identify and integrate some emerging trends, while avoiding the temptation to relate sex differences in brain organization to sex differences in overall cognitive skill.

Very little support indeed has accrued for Buffery and Gray's (1972) model that male brains are more symmetrically organized than female brains. Neither do the data overwhelmingly confirm that male brains show greater functional asymmetry than female brains. However, when sex differences are found, the vast majority are compatible with the latter hypothesis. Consensual validation from clinical, dichotic listening, and tachistoscopic studies in adults further strengthens this proposal. However, when statistically analyzed, sex-by-laterality interactions often tend to be weaker than the main effect of laterality, and they are easily altered by other factors, such as age, etiology of the lesion, strategies, and test procedures. Thus, one must not overlook perhaps the most obvious conclusion, which is that basic patterns of male and female brain asymmetry seem to be more similar than they are different. Nevertheless, it is only by focusing on those differences that our knowledge of brain function will expand.

At this stage, more is known of sex differences in language representation than those in spatial representation. Verbal asymmetries suggesting left hemisphere dominance appear to be more common and more marked in male than in female adult right-handers across several dichotic listening and tachistoscopic studies. Complementary results provided by the clinical literature further indicate greater dependence in men than in women on the left hemisphere for speech functions. In addition, there is evidence for some degree of right hemisphere speech representation in women, which is not found in men. Less satisfactory evidence is currently available on the issue of sexual variation in the cerebral representation of nonverbal functions because of the methodological inadequacies in clinical publications and the absence of relevant dichotic studies. Nevertheless, some tachistoscopic investigations, when considered with the available clinical data, suggest the possibility of greater right hemisphere dominance for "nonverbal" material in males than in females. In conclusion, enough data have accumulated to take seriously the notion of sexual variation in brain asymmetry. Questions such as "Why?" or "Does it matter?" remain unanswered.

ACKNOWLEDGMENTS
I am grateful to Dr. Doreen Kimura for her incisive comments on previous manuscripts, and to Ms. Jody Bain for her helpful assistance. The preparation of this paper was supported by a grant to the author from the Ontario Mental Health Foundation #752-78/80, and by grants to Dr. Kimura from the Medical Research Council and The National Research Council, Ottawa, Canada

BRAIN STEM ELECTRICAL RESPONSES OF STUTTERERS AND NORMALS BY SEX, EARS, AND RECOVERY

PARLEY W. NEWMAN, KARIN BUNDERSON,
and ROBERT H. BREY
Brigham Young University
Provo, Utah

Auditory brainstem electrical responses (BSER) of right and left ears of active stutterers, recovered stutterers, and nonstutterers, both male and female adults, were obtained at click rates of 11.1 and 71.1/sec. Latency intervals of waves I, III, and V were measured. The auditory systems of subjects were stressed using a rapid rate of 71.1 clicks/sec. The latency of wave V was used as the measure of the stress condition.

Analysis of variance was used to determine statistical significances of main effects and interactions of mean BSER (waves I, III, V, and wave V in stress condition) of left and right ears of male stutterers (active and recovered), female stutterers (active and recovered), and male and female nonstutterers.

With one exception, all main effects and all higher order interactions were nonsignificant. The one main effect that was significant was gender. Females have significantly faster rates of neural transmission than do males. The question was raised, does this finding contribute toward an explanation of the sex ratio in stuttering?

INTRODUCTION

Hannley and Dorman (1982) reviewed the literature on auditory functions as they relate to stuttering. In general, their conclusions were that stuttering had no significant relation to peripheral auditory function, to cerebral dominance in auditory processing, or to temporal lobe function. On the basis of data available from tests of brainstem function, using the Synthetic Sentence Identification Test with Ipsilateral Competing Message (SSI-ICM), Hannley and Dorman were unwilling to accept auditory brainstem dysfunction as contributing to the problem of stuttering. However, they did suggest that the more recently developed procedures of measuring brainstem electrical response (BSER) showed promise in displaying subtle differences in brainstem function between stutterers and normal speakers. This investigation followed that suggestion.

Address correspondence to Parley W. Newman, Ph.D., 135 John Taylor Building, Brigham Young University, Provo, UT 84602.

P. W. NEWMAN, K. BUNDERSON, and R. H. BREY

The purpose of the study was to compare BSER of stutterers and normal speakers. BSERs were obtained from right and left ears of active stutterers, recovered stutterers, and normal speakers, both male and female. Click repetition rates were varied, and latency intervals between waves I, III and V were measured. Also, the auditory processing systems of subjects were stressed and the effects of the stress condition were recorded. The rate of transmission of wave V was used as the measure of the stress condition.

SUBJECTS

A total of 68 persons served as subjects. There were 22 male stutterers, of which 16 were active stutterers and 6 were recovered stutterers, and 12 female stutterers, of which 7 were active stutterers and 5 were recovered stutterers. Controls consisted of 22 normal speaking males and 12 normal speaking females. The age range of the active stuttering males was 23–48 yr (mean, 29.8 yr). The age range of the recovered stuttering males was 20–48 yr (mean, 32.5 yr). The age range of the active stuttering females was 21–53 yr (mean, 30.1 yr). The age range of the recovered stuttering females was 19–29 yr (mean, 23.8 yr). The age range of the normal males was 20–30 yr (mean, 24.8 yr). The age range of the normal females was 18–26 yr (mean, 21.3 yr). See Table 1 for subject information.

Subjects who stuttered were located through advertising for research subjects in the university student newspaper, reviewing recent clinic files, inviting volunteers, and drawing from current clients. The classifications of recovered stutterers versus active stutterers were based on replies to brief questionnaires found in Appendix A and B. The categorization of a person as a recovered stutterer is tenuous. Of the 11 subjects who considered themselves recovered stutterers and who were so classified, 10

Table 1. Subjects by Age, Sex, and Nature of Speech Condition

	n	Age range (yr)	Mean age (yr)
Male stutterers			
All	22	20–48	30.5
Recovered	6	20–48	32.5
Active	16	23–48	29.8
Normal males	22	20–30	24.8
Female stutterers			
All	12	19–53	27.5
Recovered	5	19–29	23.8
Active	7	21–53	30.1
Normal females	12	18–26	21.3
Total	68		

reported some residual stuttering. Five indicated that they consider themselves to be normal speakers who stutter occasionally. Four others indicated that they stutter rarely, i.e., once or twice per year, and one recovered stutterer said that sometimes in front of groups or when making specific points in arguments he ". . . sometimes gets hung up on words." Only one of the "recovered" stutterers reported that he no longer stutters. In reply to the question, "Do you consider yourself a normal speaker who stutters rarely, i.e., once or twice a year?", he replied, "No, I virtually never stutter now unless I want to." These reports are consistent with other studies of recovery in stuttering in which minimal, residual stuttering usually remains (Wingate, 1964; Shearer and Williams, 1965).

PROCEDURES

Subjects were relaxed or lightly sleeping in a reclining chair. The electrode configuration for obtaining BSERs follows. The active electrode was located on the vertex and referenced to the mastoid of the stimulated ear, with the opposite mastoid as common. Electrode impedance was monitored and maintained below 5000 ohms. A 100-μsec condensation click was delivered to the subjects through a TDH-39 earphone mounted in an MX41/AR cushion. Click repetition rates of 11.1 and 71.1/sec were presented monaurally to each ear at 70 dB re normal hearing threshold level. The click repetition rate of 71.1 was used to stress the system. A 150-1500 Hz bandpass filter was utilized to filter the raw EEG which contains the BSER signal, which was amplified 100,000 times. All data were collected using an artifact reject mode. The raw signal was summed using a Nicolet 1170 signal averager, which was set to measure a 10.24-msec time window following the stimulus onset. Responses to 1024 clicks were summed with each trial and replicated at least once to ensure reproducibility. Waveforms were recorded on a Hewlett Packard (HP 7015B) X-Y plotter, and latencies were measured using the cursor on the Nicolet 1170 signal averager.

BSERs are measured in milliseconds. These are measures of latencies between the onset of the stimulus and what is believed to be the electrical activity of the auditory pathway. In typical BSER testing, only latencies of waves I, III, and V are reported, for these provide the most reliable measures.

RESULTS

Means and SD of all measures are given in Table 2. These same data are depicted graphically in Figures 1 through 4. Analysis of variance (ANOVA) was used to determine statistical significances of main effects and interactions of mean BSERs (waves I, III, V, and wave V in stress condition) of left and right ears of male stutterers (active and recovered),

Table 2. Means and SD of all BSER Measures

Type of subject	n		Wave I ears		Wave III ears		Wave V ears		Wave V stress ears	
			Right	Left	Right	Left	Right	Left	Right	Left
All male stutterers	22	X̄	2.057	2.063	4.137	4.171	5.987	6.022	6.531	6.561
		SD	0.183	0.288	0.237	0.293	0.258	0.242	0.470	0.371
Active male stutterers	16	X̄	2.051	2.066	4.123	4.200	5.986	6.039	6.534	6.583
		SD	0.201	0.326	0.268	0.309	0.260	0.271	0.538	0.411
Recovered male stutterers	6	X̄	2.073	2.053	4.173	4.093	5.990	5.976	6.521	6.505
		SD	0.137	0.172	0.137	0.250	0.277	0.148	0.241	0.256
Normal males	22	X̄	1.996	2.027	4.001	4.080	5.823	5.920	6.425	6.430
		SD	0.145	0.162	0.156	0.283	0.230	0.203	0.235	0.273
All female stutterers	12	X̄	1.953	1.952	3.941	3.914	5.755	5.746	6.193	6.146
		SD	0.104	0.122	0.190	0.192	0.192	0.182	0.271	0.211
Active female stutterers	7	X̄	1.961	1.957	4.007	3.973	5.786	5.786	6.270	6.180
		SD	0.131	0.156	0.226	0.222	0.214	0.225	0.309	0.255
Recovered female stutterers	5	X̄	1.940	1.944	3.848	3.832	5.712	5.690	6.084	6.098
		SD	0.059	0.064	0.059	0.114	0.171	0.092	0.184	0.139
Normal females	12	X̄	1.931	2.003	3.865	3.877	5.786	5.832	6.252	6.246
		SD	0.075	0.180	0.189	0.240	0.086	0.127	0.169	0.232

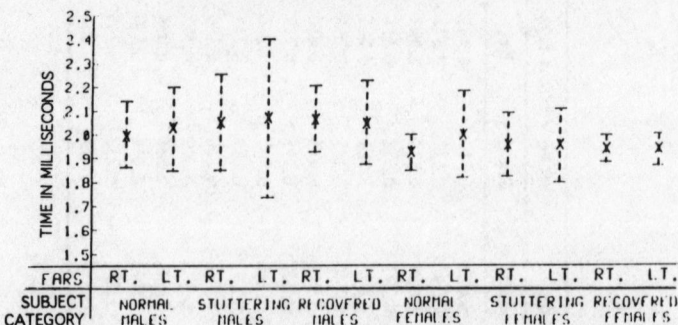

Figure 1. Means and SD of BSER latencies for wave I for right and left ears of all categories of subjects.

female stutterers (active and recovered), and normal male and female speakers. Because the number of subjects in the various cells was unequal a nonorthogonal ANOVA was utilized in the analysis of the data.

Stutterers did not differ significantly from nonstutterers. Recovered stutterers did not differ significantly from active stutterers, and differences between ears were not significant. With one exception, all main effects and all higher order interactions were not significant. The one main effect that was significant was sex. Females had significantly faster rates of neural transmission than males. Means and SD comparing gender are presented in Table 3. These data are depicted graphically in Figure 5. For wave I the difference between sexes was significant ($F = 4.00$, $p = 0.05$). For waves III and V, and wave V in the stress condition, differences between sexes were significant, wave III ($F = 14.06$, $p < 0.01$), wave V ($F = 11.99$, $p < 0.01$), and wave V in the stress condition ($F = 14.84$, p

Figure 2. Means and SD of BSER latencies for wave III for right and left ears of all categories of subjects.

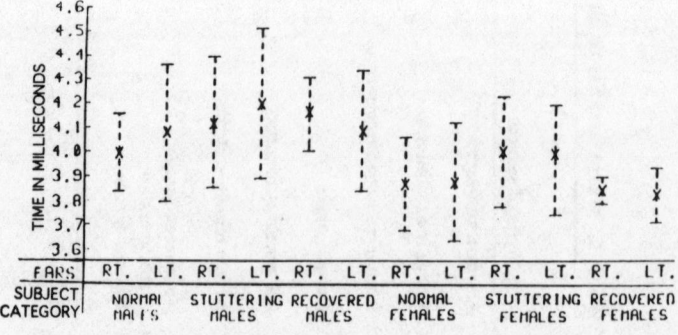

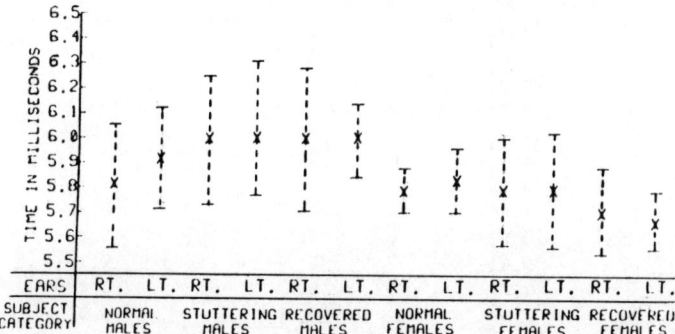

Figure 3. Means and SD of BSER latencies for wave V for right and left ears of all categories of subjects.

< 0.01). A gender difference in rates of neural transmission between normal subjects has been reported previously (Jerger and Hall, 1980).

DISCUSSION

One of the facts of stuttering is the high male/female ratio. Male stutterers outnumber female stutterers by 3 or 4:1. This well known fact has yet to be explained. The explanation for the sex ratio is probably accounted for in terms of some unidentified physiologic difference between males and females.

There are obvious physical differences between males and females. The primary and secondary male–female characteristics, such as distribution of body hair or muscle and bone mass have never caught the attention

Figure 4. Means and SD of BSER latencies for wave V in stress condition for right and left ears of all categories of subjects.

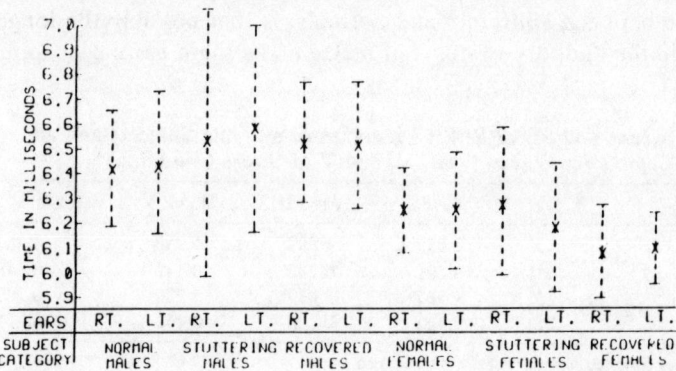

BRAIN STEM RESPONSES

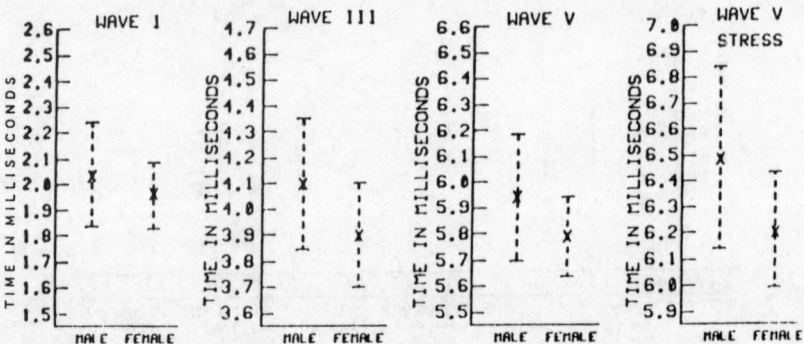

Figure 5. Means and SD of BSER latencies for waves I, III, and V in the stress condition comparing all male subjects with all female subjects.

of the researcher interested in explaining the sex ratio in stuttering. It would seem that the reason for this is simply that these types of differences are so far removed from the speech act that they have not merited attention.

The auditory system, however, is intimately connected with speaking. Hearing the speech of others and hearing one's own speech is fundamental to learning to speak. Also, speech production is related to auditory feedback. The influence of delayed auditory feedback (DAF) on speaking has established this as a fact. The results of this study reveal clearly differences in the auditory systems between sexes that is both physiologic and intimately related to speaking.

Perhaps the next question to consider is how does a slower rate of neural transmission in the auditory system of the male relate to stuttering? The answer to this question is made more difficult by the finding that there are no significant differences in rate of neural transmission between stutterers and normal speakers. A speculative answer to the question, which takes into account the difficulty raised by the finding of nonsignificance between stutterers and normals, is that possibly the longer latencies in the auditory systems of males make them more susceptible to

Table 3. Means and SD of BSER Latencies of all Male Subjects and all Female Subjects for Waves I, III, V, and V of Stress Conditions*

Sex	n		Wave I	Wave III	Wave V	Wave V stress
Males	44	$\bar{X}$	2.035	4.097	5.938	6.487
		SD	0.201	0.252	0.242	0.349
Females	24	$\bar{X}$	1.960	3.899	5.780	6.209
		SD	0.125	0.200	0.152	0.221

* Measures from left and right ears are combined.

stuttering. The gender difference observed in this investigation may contribute toward an explanation of the male/female ratio in stuttering. The primal causes of stuttering, however, are yet to be delineated.

REFERENCES

Hannley, M. and Dorman, M.F. Some observations on auditory function and stuttering. *Journal of Fluency Disorders*, 1982, 7, 93–108.

Jerger, J. and Hall, J. Effects of age and sex on auditory brainstem response. *Archives of Otolaryngology*, 1980, 106, 387–391.

Shearer, W.M. and Williams, J.D. Self-recovery from stuttering. *Journal of Speech and Hearing Disorders*, 1965, 30, 288–290.

Wingate, M.E. Recovery from stuttering. *Journal of Speech and Hearing Disorders*, 1964, 29, 312–321.

Appendix A. Interview to Identify Those Who Are Active Stutterers

1. Rate the severity of your present stuttering:
   MILD   MODERATE   SEVERE
2. At any time in the past was your stuttering different than it is now? If different in the past, was it:
   MILD   MODERATE   SEVERE

Survey to determine if person actively stutters who is fluent during the interview

1. Do you consider yourself to be a stutterer?
2. When you stutter, do you experience:
   Stoppings/Repetitions of syllables/Prolongation of sounds/Tremors/Tension/Other
3. At this time do others, such as parents, teachers, or friends consider you a stutterer?
4. Do you ever avoid certain sounds, words, or phrases to keep from stuttering?
5. Do you ever avoid any speaking situations to save yourself from the embarrassment of stuttering?
6. Do you ever feel that speech is a difficult task?
7. Are you highly self-conscious of your stuttering?

Appendix B. Questionnaire to Identify Persons Recovered from Stuttering

1. Do you consider yourself a normal speaker who stutters occasionally?
2. Do you consider yourself a normal speaker who stutters rarely, i.e., once or twice a year?
3. Do you consider yourself to be a normal speaker with no stuttering at all except for normal hesitations and repetitions?
4. When you used to stutter, what did you experience:
   Stoppings/Repetitions/Prolongation of sounds/Tremors/Tensions/Other
5. Did you consider yourself a stutterer at that time?
6. At that time did others, such as parents, teachers, or friends consider you a stutterer?

BRAIN STEM RESPONSES

7. Did you ever avoid certain sounds, words, or phrases to keep from stuttering?
8. Did you ever avoid any speaking situations to keep from stuttering?
9. Did you ever feel that speech was a difficult task?
10. Were you highly self-conscious of your stuttering?
11. What was the level of your stuttering at its worst:
    MILD   MODERATE   SEVERE
12. Have you received any formal speech therapy?
13. Was the therapy beneficial?
14. How much have you improved?
15. To what do you attribute your improvement or recovery:
    Slowing down/Relaxing/Speaking more/Improved self-concept/Speech therapy/Don't know/Other
16. Based on your experience as a stutterer, what advice would you give to a stutterer:
    Speak slowly/Think before speaking/Relax/Talk more/Seek therapy/Don't know/Other
17. How much fear of stuttering do you have at the present time?
    NONE   SOME   VERY MUCH

Evidence for Sex Differences in Brain Organization in Recovery in Aphasia

L. PIZZAMIGLIO AND A. MAMMUCARI

Università di Roma, Rome, Italy

AND

C. RAZZANO

Clinica S. Lucia, Rome, Italy

Ninety-one adult aphasics of both sexes were studied before and after a 3-month period of language therapy. Although no initial sex difference was found in severity of language disorders, females within the global aphasic group showed significantly greater improvement in three tests of language comprehension. It is suggested that more bilateral representation of language functions in the female brain may account for this greater improvement. © 1985 Academic Press, Inc.

In the literature sex differences in brain organization have been discussed from several viewpoints. A number of studies suggest that in normal subjects there are greater laterality differences in males than in females over a variety of cognitive tasks (see McGlone, 1980).

This view is supported by anatomical studies: Wada, Clarke, and Hamm (1975) and Le May and Geschwind (1978) found a higher percentage of males with left-hemisphere specialization for language function. In recent years the problem of sex differences has been studied in patients with left- and right-hemisphere lesions. In the Block Design subtest, McGlone and Kertesz (1973) found males with right-side lesions to be more impaired than females. McGlone (1977) compared the verbal and performance IQs in two groups of left- and right-damaged patients of both sexes. Males with right lesions showed lower performance IQ scores while nonaphasics

This research has been partially supported by a grant from CNR and by an exchange program with the Western Psychiatric Institute and Clinic, University of Pittsburgh. The authors thank Dr. A. L. Holland and Dr. A. W. Gordon for their useful comments on the manuscript. Send requests for reprints to L. Pizzamiglio, Dipartimento di Psicologia Università di Roma, Via del Castro Pretorio 20, 00185 Rome, Italy.

with left lesions had lower verbal IQ performance scores than females. In addition, only 2 out of 16 aphasics of the left group were females.

These data were interpreted to mean that there is a greater degree of differential specialization of the two hemispheres in males than in females for spatial and verbal abilities. A corollary of McGlone's hypothesis is that a more bilateral speech representation in females leads to a lower incidence of aphasia in left lesions as compared to males.

Early data by Lansdell and Urbach (1965), showing lower verbal scores in males than in females with left-temporal-lobe removal, can be similarly interpretated. Comparing male and female aphasics, McGlone (1977) found a smaller incidence of aphasia in the latter group; this conclusion seems very tentative since the sample used in the study was too small to test such a hypothesis. More systematic studies have been carried out by De Renzi, Faglioni, and Ferrari (1980), Kertesz and Sheppard (1981), and Miceli et al. (1981).

However, when the absolute frequency of aphasia in the populations was adjusted to reflect the higher ratio of men suffering strokes, no sex differences were found for the incidence of language disorders, including the severity and type of aphasia in both sexes, thus disproving this hypothesis. These findings are based on very large numbers of unselected patients and, therefore, conclusively reject the hypothesis of sex differences in the incidence of aphasia. Holland (1980) described another sample of chronic aphasics where incidence and type of aphasia did not differ in males and females. She did, however, find an interaction between severity of aphasia, sex, and institutionalization of the patients: Aphasic disorders were more severe for females living in institutions.

There is some additional support for this in a study which showed greater cognitive deterioration in institutionalized females (Kasl & Rosenfield, 1980). Therefore, the observed results may be considered the consequence of different adjustments of the two sexes to the environmental situation or by a cultural tendency to institutionalize males with lesser amounts of disturbance.

Since there appears to be no difference in frequency and severity of pathology, the notion that there is a different language representation in males and females is not supported. However, before completely rejecting this hypothesis it is necessary (a) to reformulate more accurately what is meant by lateralization of language representation and (b) to check the hypothesis in different clinical settings.

The statement that verbal functions are more lateralized in the left hemisphere is too broad and does not correspond with what is actually known about a variety of linguistic processes. A very good illustration of this concept comes from the studies on disconnected hemisphere and on hemispherectomy. Zaidel (1978) showed that the isolated right hemisphere has little or no speech, very reduced phonetic analysis, very rudimentary syntax, and poor comprehension of long nonredundant sentences for reduced short-term memory. Nevertheless, the right hemisphere does show a "substantial visual vocabulary and surprisingly rich auditory lexicon."

Similar abilities have also been shown in left-hemidecorticated patients although their ability to handle large units of texture structure were clearly poorer than the right-hemispherectomized ones (Dennis & Whitaker, 1976). It seems therefore that some linguistic functions have quite definite or absolute lateralization while others show more bilateral representation. It may also be that there are qualitative as well as quantitative differences between the two hemispheres. It seems more appropriate therefore to look for sex differences as a consequence of the degree of functional differentiation and to focus attention on the linguistic capacities which show a bilateral representation instead of considering them together with an absolute representation in one hemisphere.

Therefore in this research quantitative measures of phonemic, semantic, and syntactic oral comprehension, together with the Token test, were given to aphasics within 2 months of a stroke. It seems interesting to stress the need not only for extensive but also quantitative testing of these abilities since previous studies used only ordinal scales, such as "severe–moderate–mild" (Kertesz & Sheppard, 1981; Miceli et al., 1981). Although the number of subjects was adequate, the small range of the scale may have decreased the sensitivity of the comparison.

Thus far, the test of the hypothesis of differential language specialization in the two sexes has been discussed with reference to incidence, severity, and type of aphasia. Another important contribution can be made by comparing the degree of recovery in males and females. This approach is not only necessary, but it has the statistical advantage of comparing repeated measures on the same subjects after a given interval of time, thus increasing the power of the test.

In this regard Kertesz and McCabe (1977) did not find any sex difference in amount of recovery of a small group of aphasics, while Edwards, Ellams, and Thomson (1976) described a male subgroup in their study as more severely impaired after several months. Basso, Capitani, and Moraschini (1982) found a significantly greater improvement in females' oral expression, but not in their verbal comprehension. However, since females in their study were less severely impaired than males following the stroke, the authors suggested that either the right or the spared left areas could account for the recovery.

The second purpose of this research is to test the hypothesis that language functions have different localizations in the two sexes by measuring the severity of impairment before and after treatment using quantitatively wider scaling and controlling for etiology, age, education, and time from onset.

MATERIALS AND METHODS

Subjects

Eighty-nine brain-damaged patients with aphasia (48 males and 41 females) admitted to a rehabilitation clinic between January 1980 and December 1981 were selected for this study based on the following criteria:

(a) unilateral brain damage;
(b) cerebrovascular pathology;
(c) right-handedness;
(d) age (70 years of age maximum);
(e) first testing within 3 months of the stroke; and
(f) language rehabilitation for 3 consecutive months, with a frequency of at least four sessions per week.

The unilateral lesions were assessed by means of clinical examination, EEG, and neuroradiological examination, including the CT scan when available. No patient with a history of multiple strokes was included.

Assessment of Aphasia

All patients were tested using a battery for language disorders which included subtests for naming objects (score: 0–4), for repetition (score: 0–20), for comprehension of phonemic discrimination (score: 0–27), of semantic discrimination (score: 0–27), and of syntactic comprehension (score: 0–60) (Pizzamigilio & Parisi, 1970). The battery also included the fifth part of the modified "token test" (score: 0–35) (Appicciafuoco, Pizzamiglio, & Razzano, 1976), a subtest of written word naming (score: 0–20), and a subtest of written word comprehension (score: 0–20). The standard battery was first given to the patients within 3 months of the stroke and prior to rehabilitation, followed by a restest 3 months later.

The patients were classified, following Goodglass and Kaplan (1972), as fluent, nonfluent, and global aphasics. The characteristics of the population are summarized in Table 1.

Statistical Analysis

Raw scores of each subtest of the aphasia battery were treated separately by a covariate analysis of variance: sex, type of aphasia, and test–retest (before and after rehabilitation as repeated measures) were independent variables; age and education were covariates.

TABLE 1
SEX, AGE, EDUCATION, AND TYPE OF APHASIA

	Type of aphasia		
	Nonfluent	Fluent	Global
Males			
n	19	10	19
Age	56.36 ± 9.37	62.60 ± 6.14	61.26 ± 8.79
Education	7.16 ± 4.44	9.00 ± 5.31	6.95 ± 3.85
Females			
n	14	12	15
Age	65.35 ± 8.46	66.25 ± 6.77	62.53 ± 9.20
Education	4.43 ± 1.40	4.58 ± 1.83	4.87 ± 1.85

Note. Values for age and education are $\overline{X}$ ± SD.

RESULTS

A summary of the mean scores in each subtest, adjusted for age and education, is presented in Table 2. The outcomes of the nine covariance analyses are shown in Table 3. The significant results can be summarized in three main points:

(a) Principal effects for type of aphasia and for test–retest, but not for sex, wee highly significant in all tests.

(b) Significant interactions (test–retest × type of aphasia) were found for naming and repetition subtests: in the former a post hoc comparison with the Duncan's test indicated that fluent and nonfluent, but not global, aphasics show significant improvement in the second test. In the latter comparison the nonfluents showed greater improvement in the second test than the global aphasics.

(c) The major finding consisted of a pattern of interactions for the three tests of verbal comprehension: rehabilitation × type of aphasia for the phonemic ($p < .06$), the semantic, and the syntactic comprehension

TABLE 2
MEAN SCORES ADJUSTED BY AGE AND EDUCATION

		Nonfluent		Fluent		Global	
		Males	Females	Males	Females	Males	Females
Naming	1[a]	1.41	0.61	0.36	1.46	0.17	0.08
	2	6.15	1.54	0.86	5.36	0.04	0.08
Repetition	1	3.92	3.85	5.12	6.90	0.30	0.30
	2	7.61	6.78	6.45	9.07	0.82	0.76
Phonemic discrimination	1	21.16	19.44	17.12	24.62	10.02	7.50
	2	24.58	22.44	21.79	20.62	14.60	16.44
Semantic discrimination	1	17.06	14.99	12.97	14.87	7.57	5.44
	2	21.54	18.42	19.57	18.14	11.15	14.54
Syntactic comprehension	1	42.86	39.31	34.57	38.07	27.45	19.70
	2	46.38	41.98	40.87	40.53	30.8	34.2
Token	1	3.93	3.02	2.58	3.11	0.14	0.13
	2	7.41	3.72	4.29	4.81	0.53	0.36
Writing	1	1.41	0.61	0.36	1.46	0.17	0.08
	2	6.15	1.54	0.86	5.36	0.04	0.08
Reading	1	11.94	14.22	8.26	15.19	0.41	2.02
	2	17.20	18.43	13.51	21.37	9.28	6.33

[a] 1 = first test; 2 = second test

TABLE 3
Summary of the Analysis of Covariance for the Nine Tests

Test	Type of aphasia*	Test-retest*	Type of aphasia × test-retest	Sex × type of aphasia × test-retest
Naming	$F(2, 78) = 16.58$	$F(1, 80) = 56.86$	$F(2, 80) = 6.23*$	—
Repetition	$F(2, 78) = 13.03$	$F(1, 80) = 32.90$	$F(2, 80) = 7.49*$	—
Phonemic	$F(2, 81) = 20.40$	$F(1, 83) = 9.72$	$F(2, 83) = 2.81$ ($p < .06$)	$F(2, 82) = 2.73$ ($p < .07$)
Semantic	$F(2, 80) = 28.46$	$F(1, 82) = 36.52$	$F(2, 82) = 2.48$ ($p < .06$)	$F(2, 82) = 8.78*$
Syntactic	$F(2, 75) = 18.27$	$F(1, 77) = 41.82$	$F(2, 77) = 4.93*$	$F(2, 77) = 7.68*$
Token	$F(2, 71) = 11.50$	$F(1, 73) = 17.61$	$F(2, 73) = 3.32**$	—
Writing	$F(2, 77) = 4.83$	$F(1, 79) = 15.54$	—	—
Reading	$F(2, 73) = 18.99$	$F(1, 75) = 31.75$	—	—

Note. Independent variables were sex, type of aphasia, and test-retest; covariates were age and education.

* $p < .01$.
** $p < .05$.

tests; test-retest × type of aphasia × sex for the phonemic ($p < .07$), the semantic, and the syntactic tests.

In all cases a Duncan's post hoc comparison showed greater improvement for the global group and for the female group. Looking at the data in Table 2, it is clear that all groups of aphasics improved in the retest; however, the fluent and nonfluent groups do not show greater changes in females than in males. The pattern is different for global aphasics since improvement is not only numerically greater; and females, who already started from lower performances, ended up with better scores following treatment. These results on verbal comprehension in the global aphasics warrant further analysis and discussion.

Before accepting these data it is necessary to make sure that the male and female global groups do not differ in any characteristics which might affect degree of recovery. The post onset time of the initial language testing is, respectively, 54.33 ($SD = 17.51$) days for males and 70.53 ($SD = 20.26$) for females. If spontaneous recovery were to account for improvement after 3 months, then the small difference would be in favor of the male group. The etiology was cerebral hemorrhage or thrombosis in 14 males and 9 females, embolism in 4 males and 5 females, and aneurysm in 1 patient in each group.

The degree of motor impairment was evaluated on a 4-point scale: 0 indicated no impairment, and 3 indicated complete paralysis. Both groups showed severe motor impairments: upper limbs for males $x = 2.58$, $SD = 0.30$, and for females $x = 2.80$, $SD = 0.15$; lower limbs for males $x = 1.98$, $SD = 0.40$, and for females $x = 2.25$, $SD = 0.35$. Similarly, sensory loss was evaluated on a 4-point scale: upper limbs for males $x = 2.20$, $SD = 0.28$, and for females $x = 2.35$, $SD = 0.33$; lower limbs for males $x = 1.90$, $SD = 0.45$, and for females $x = 2.01$, $SD = 0.41$.

Nine males and seven females showed clear signs of visual-field defects. Among the social aspects which may interfere with recovery are two male and one female global patients who were not married, all of the patients had supportive families except for two males and three females, and one patient in each group had a history of chronic alcoholism.

Therefore these data indicate that observed differences in the rate of recovery cannot be accounted for by differences in this set of variables. In fact, slight variations among the two genders were in the direction of favoring males' greater recovery.

Going back to the data from the verbal comprehension test, the difference in the improvement between fluent, nonfluent, and global groups may simply be due to the fact that the latter group started with a very low performance in the first observation; thus, even a very small change in linguistic competence could produce an apparently greater numerical variation as compared to the other group, with greater performance level in the first observation. Nevertheless, the variations in the mean scores of the global group (Table 2) are quite substantial and correspond to clinically relevant changes.

A second argument against the "floor effect" interpretation is that, even though there were no detectable differences between the two sexes on first observation, the female group showed a significantly greater improvement than the male group, which would not be expected if the reason for this change was simply the low starting score. We decided to split the global groups into two subgroups with relatively low and high scores on the first observation to see whether improvement is present only in the former or in both subgroups. A Duncan's test comparison showed a significant ($p < .01$) improvement for the three tests of verbal comprehension and for both higher and lower subgroups of global aphasics. Furthermore, a floor effect could be expected on all other subtests of the battery, including naming and repetition. However, no such pattern between sexes resulted in those cases, emphasizing the specificity of this differential improvement within the global group only for these three tests of oral comprehension.

Another interpretation could be that of a ceiling effect, or it could be speculated that fluent and nonfluent aphasics fall into a range of scores in which the rate of improvement is lower as compared with the rate of recovery in the lower range of the global patients. None of the results obtained by the fluent and nonfluent groups really approach the maximum scores of each test (see methodology); but more than that, such an interpretation could not explain the "pattern" observed in the global group, where the female scores were higher than male scores, although the former started from a lower performance level.

The fourth test of verbal comprehension, a modified version of the Token test, does not follow the trend of the other three tests: the reason may be that the 22 items used are very complex and sensitive in detecting very subtle comprehension disorders. Therefore, the performances of the global aphasics, even following partial improvement, are still too low to show differences in such a task.

DISCUSSION

The systematic differences between the first and second testing in all oral and written subtests can either be interpreted as a specific effect of the language treatment given to all patients or to the replication of the testing procedure over a 3-month period; the design of this research was not intended to test the impact of rehabilitation on different linguistic domains and therefore no claim can be made for this.

The most interesting finding concerns the results observed in the two tasks of verbal output (naming and repetition) and in the three out of four tests of verbal comprehension. After 3 months of treatment, naming improved in both fluent and nonfluent aphasics, but not in the global group; repetition improved in the fluent group and not in the others.

Other findings concern the significantly greater improvement of global aphasics as compared to fluent and nonfluent aphasics and the greater recovery of female patients in the global group on the tests of phonemic, semantic, and syntactic comprehension. This improvement can hardly be considered as purely numerical and corresponds to clinically perceivable improvement; i,e., global aphasics are perceived as substantially improved in their ability to communicate in everyday living. As a matter of fact the level of comprehension on the three tests shifts from an almost chance level to a performance similar to that of fluent aphasics during the first testing. The interpretation of this finding in terms of the floor effect can be ruled out considering that:

(a) female global aphasics improve significantly more than males, even though they do not differ in their initial performance;

(b) splitting the global group into relatively higher and lower performance before treatment does not change the degree of the improvement present in each group.

Furthermore, the ceiling effect cannot account for the results, since what is most important is the different "pattern" of recovery between sexes and not so much the degree of improvement. In no case can either

SEX DIFFERENCES

the floor or ceiling effect account for the specificity of the greater improvement of female global aphasic performance in these three tasks of oral comprehension, while in all other linguistic tasks the recovery was similar for both sexes.

What do the results say about differential language impairment and language representation in the two sexes? In line with previous findings (Miceli et al., 1981; De Renzi et al., 1980; Kertesz & McCabe, 1977), no sex difference was found in the initial severity of linguistic disorders or any aspect of aphasia, including comprehension and verbal expression.

In contrast to this, female global aphasics improve more than males in verbal comprehension. It is not that females show greater recovery in all language functions, but only in verbal comprehension. Two hypotheses can be advanced: (a) females may have easier access to the linguistic competence of the right hemisphere, and (b) females may have larger representation of language functions in the left hemisphere (Kinsbourne, 1980) and, therefore, the left hemisphere would produce different recovery of functions in the two sexes. Before discussing these hypotheses, it must be pointed out that sex differences in recovery do not appear in the fluent and nonfluent groups; that is, only when the language capacities of the patients are functionally eliminated can such differential recovery be found. Since it has been shown that in vascular patients global aphasia is correlated with the size of the lesion (Basso et al., 1980), it can be speculated that extensive damage in the territory of the middle cerebral artery is the condition under which differential recovery can take place. Moscovitch (1981) suggests that any functional language in the left hemisphere produces an interference within the linguistic competence of the opposite hemisphere; therefore no compensatory language activity can be performed by the right hemisphere until some spared area in the left side is effective. It is only under the circumstances of no functional language that the two alternative interpretations can be compared. The greater verbal comprehension recovery in female global aphasics may be compatible with the hypothesis of a more diffuse representation of language function within the left hemisphere only if this assumption is restricted to decoding processing; i.e., if "females have more diffuse and redundant cognitive representation within a hemisphere than males" (Kinsbourne, 1980), one would expect to find greater improvement for all language functions and not just for oral comprehension, as in the present condition.

The good lexical and syntax comprehension of the isolated right hemisphere, reported earlier, may account for the observed results. Furthermore, although computerized tomography did not show significant morphological asymmetry between the two sexes (Le May, 1980), a larger right than left planum temporalis was found more often in the female than in the male brain (Wada et al., 1975). This information, together with the present data, supports the idea that a differential interhemispheric representation of language is still a useful concept to account for observed clinical data. The finding of a specific clinical ground on which observed sex differences can be investigated offers the possibility of empirically testing whether the greater plasticity of the female brain is due to a difference in language representation within the left hemisphere or as due to a more bilateral control of language functions. A longitudinal study of the activation of spared areas of the brain, using metabolic or blood flow measures, in relation to the presence or absence of functional language recovery, could provide an explanation for this yet unsolved but intriguing problem.

REFERENCES

Appicciafuoco, A., Pizzamiglio, L., & Razzano, C. 1976. A new version of the "token test" for aphasics: A concrete objects form. *Journal of Communication Disorders*, 9(1), 1–5.

Basso, A., Capitani, E., Laiacona, M., & Luzzatti, C. 1980. Factors influencing type and severity of aphasia. *Cortex*, 16, 631–636.

Basso, A., Capitani, E., & Moraschini, S. 1982. Sex differences in recovery from aphasia. *Cortex*, 18, 469–475.

Dennis, M., & Whitaker, H. 1976. Language acquisition following hemidecortication: Linguistic superiority of the left over the right hemisphere. *Brain and Language*, 3, 403–433.

De Renzi, E., Faglioni, P., & Ferrari, P. 1980. The influence of sex and age on the incidence and type of aphasia. *Cortex*, 16, 627–630.

Edwards, S., Ellams, J., & Thomson, J. 1976. Language and intelligence in dysphasia: Are they related? *British Journal of Disorders of Communication*, 11, 83–94.

Goodglass, H., & Kaplan, E. 1972. *The assessment of aphasia and related disorders*. Philadelphia: Lea & Febiger.

Holland, A. L. 1980. *Communicative ability in daily living*. Baltimore: Univ. Park Press.

Kasl, S. V., & Rosenfield, S. 1980. The residential environment and its impact on the mental health of the aged. In J. E. Birren & R. B. Sloane (Eds.), *Handbook of mental health and aging*. Englewood Cliffs, NJ: Prentice-Hall.

Kertesz, A., & McCabe, P. 1977. Recovery patterns and prognosis in aphasia. *Brain*, 100, 1–18.

Kertesz, A., & Sheppard, A. 1981. The epidemiology of aphasic and cognitive impairment in stroke. *Brain*, 104, 117–128.

Kinsbourne, M. 1980. If sex differences in the brain lateralization exist, they have to be discovered. *Behavioural and Brain Science*, 3, 241–242.

Lansdell, H., & Urbach, N. 1965. Sex differences in personality measures related to size and side of temporal lobe ablation. *Proceedings of the American Psychological Association*, 113–114.

Le May, M. 1980. Sex differences in the human brain morphology. *Behavioural and Brain Science*, 3, 242.

Le May, M., & Geschwind, N. 1978. Asymmetries of the human cerebral hemisphere. In A. Caramazza & E. B. Zurif (Eds.), *Language acquisition and language breakdown*. Baltimore: Johns Hopkins Univ. Press.

McGlone, J. 1977. Sex differences in the cerebral organization of verbal functions in patients with unilateral brain lesions. *Brain*, 100, 775–793.

McGlone, J. 1980. Sex differences in human brain asymmetry: A critical survey. *Behavioural and Brain Science,* **3,** 215-263.

McGlone, J., & Kertesz, A. 1973. Sex differences in cerebral processing of visuo-spatial tasks. *Cortex,* **9,** 313-320.

Miceli, G., Caltagirone, C., Gainotti, G., Masullo, C., Silveri, M. C., & Villa, G. 1981. Influence of age, sex, literacy and pathologic lesion on incidence, severity and type of aphasia. *Acta Neurologica Scandinavica,* **64,** 370-382.

Moscovitch, M. 1981. Right hemisphere language. *Topics in Language Disorders,* 1(4), 41-61.

Pizzamiglio, L., & Parisi, D. 1970. Studies on verbal comprehension in aphasia. In G. B. Flores d'Arcais & W. J. Levelt (Eds.), *Advances in psycholinguistics.* Amsterdam: North-Holland.

Wada, J., Clarke, R., & Hamm, A. 1975. Cerebral hemispheric asymmetry in humans. *Archives of Neurology,* **32,** 239-246.

Zaidel, E. 1978. Lexical organization in the right hemisphere. In P. A. Buser & A. Rougeul-Buser (Eds.), *Cerebral correlates of conscious experience.* New York: North-Holland/Elsevier.

Gender and Recovery from Aphasia after Stroke

MARTHA TAYLOR SARNO, M.D.HC., ANTONIA BUONAGURO, ED.D., AND ERIC LEVITA, PH.D.[1]

Moderate and severely impaired poststroke aphasic patients followed in a rehabilitation medicine program were systematically examined initially between 4 and 6 months poststroke and again between one and 2½ years postonset. No gender differences were found on ratings of everyday communication function or certain measures of language, specifically auditory comprehension and the spontaneous generation of spoken words.

A relatively limited literature addresses the impact of specific variables on recovery from aphasia after stroke. The most frequently studied variables—age, etiology, size and site of lesion, neuroradiological findings, type and severity of aphasia, recovery patterns, recovery of linguistic rules, psychosocial factors, time since onset, and educational level—have been reviewed by several aphasiologists (Darley, 1972; Eisenson, 1973; Sarno, 1981; Vignolo, 1964).

It is not surprising that gender and recovery did not engage the attention of investigators until the advent of the women's liberation movement. In the past decade, it has been postulated that language is more strongly lateralized among males (McGlone, 1980) and that they present aphasic impairment more often than females after left hemisphere strokes (McGlone, 1977). The reported interaction between sex and aphasia type (Brown and Grober, 1983) may introduce a measure of variability in a gender and recovery study (Basso et al., 1982). Some have concluded that sex was not a factor in the rate or degree of recovery (Gloning et al., 1976; Kertesz and McCabe, 1977; Rose et al., 1976).

Recently, Basso and her colleagues (Basso et al., 1982) at the Aphasia Unit of the Clinic for Nervous Diseases of Milan University reported the first study that specifically addressed sex differences in recovery from aphasia. In a group of 385 patients (264 males and 121 females) with aphasia due to mixed etiology, patients with vascular pathology comprised the majority of cases (78% of the males, 84% of the females). Patients were administered tests of oral expression and auditory comprehension at intervals greater than 6 months. Over 50% of the females and 55% of the males were less than 2 months post onset at the time of the first test, and 23% of the females and 19% of the males were more than 6 months postonset. Using scales that rated auditory comprehension and speech production from 0 to 4, patients were assigned to moderate and severe groups. Patients were considered treated if they received treatment for no less than 6 months at a rate of three times weekly.

Basso et al. (1982) concluded that females recover significantly more than males in oral expression but not in auditory verbal comprehension, and hypothesized a difference in cerebral organization in males and females.

The present study examines male-female differences in recovery from aphasia after stroke in a sample of patients typical of a rehabilitation medicine setting associated with a large metropolitan teaching hospital.

Methods

Subjects

A group of 23 females and 37 males who received comprehensive rehabilitation services, including intensive speech therapy at the Rusk Institute of Rehabilitation Medicine, New York University Medical Center, provided the data for this study. These patients were selected from among those already admitted to the Rehabilitation Medicine Program on the basis of their candidacy for rehabilitation management. In other words, they were beyond the point of needing acute medical care and were considered sufficiently free of organic mental symptoms (i.e., cognitive deficits, memory deficits) to participate in a treatment program.

Patients were selected for study who were aphasic on the basis of cerebrovascular lesions of the left hemisphere confirmed by neuroradiological studies. The subjects were right-handed, literate, and native speakers of English, with normal hearing thresholds (30 dB) across the speech frequencies (500, 1000, and 2000 Hz).

Patients were excluded from the study if they presented a history of alcohol or drug abuse, preexisting speech disorder, psychiatric disease, previous cerebrovascular accident, neoplasm, equivocal handedness,

---

[1] Department of Rehabilitation Medicine, New York University Medical Center, 400 East 34th Street, New York, New York 10016. Send reprint requests to Dr. Sarno.

This work was supported by Grant G008300039 from the National Institute of Handicapped Research, United States Department of Education.

The authors wish to thank Dr. John E. Sarno for his constructive comments.

previous head injury, or evidence of right hemisphere pathology. Patients who were not alert or who seemed otherwise unable to cope with testing because of illness, fatigue, severity of cognitive and/or aphasic deficits, or symptoms associated with senile dementia were also excluded. The rationales for controlling for these variables have been frequently pointed out (Darley, 1972; Sarno, 1981; Vignolo, 1964).

Group characteristics are shown in Table 1, illustrating that the two groups may be equated in terms of demographic variables (i.e. age, education, etc.).

Type Classification

The selected study subjects were assigned to three diagnostic groups according to the classification scheme of Benson (1967), Geschwind (1971), and Goodglass and Kaplan (1983): fluent, nonfluent, or global groups.

Aphasia type was determined by a consensus of clinical impressions combined with an analysis of linguistic deficits obtained on tests of language performance (i.e., relationship of speech proficiency to auditory comprehension). Judgments of fluency were made according to the guidelines elaborated by Goodglass and Kaplan (1983), that is, a judgment of speech production during extended conversation and free narrative was the basis for assigning a subject to the fluent or nonfluent group.

Fluent aphasia, characterized by impaired auditory comprehension of fluently articulated speech, is usually associated with a lesion in the vicinity of the posterior portion of the first temporal gyrus of the left hemisphere (Goodglass and Kaplan, 1983). In fluent aphasia, the melody and rate of speech are generally normal in all respects. In severe fluent aphasia, word and sound substitutions may be of such magnitude and frequency that speech is virtually meaningless.

Nonfluent aphasia is characterized by awkward articulation, limited vocabulary, hesitant slow speech output, restricted use of grammatical forms, and a relative preservation of auditory comprehension. The syndrome is associated with anterior lesions usually involving the third frontal convolution of the left hemisphere (Goodglass and Kaplan, 1983).

The category global aphasia, sometimes referred to as total aphasia (Mohr et al., 1973), is characterized by an evenness of severe dysfunction across all modalities and a severely limited residual use of all communication modes for oral-aural interactions (Boller, 1981; Kertesz and McCabe, 1977; Sarno and Levita, 1981; Yarnell et al., 1976). Global aphasia has been cited by several investigators as the most common type of aphasia in patients referred for speech rehabilitation services (Prins et al., 1978; Sarno, 1970). Their recovery timetable appears to differ from those of the nonfluent and fluent aphasia patient categories (Sarno and Levita, 1979, 1981).

Therapy Schedule

Patients received speech therapy ranging from three to five individual and/or group sessions weekly. Speech/language pathologists administered speech therapy without knowledge of which patients were being studied. As can be seen in Table 1, the mean length of speech therapy for each group was 10 months.

Test Schedule

The first test (T_1) was administered between 4 and 6 months postonset, and the second (T_2) between 1 and 2½ years postonset. Median time since onset for the first test was 25 weeks for the men and 26 weeks for the women, and was 65 weeks for the men and 53 weeks for the women on the follow-up examination.

Test Measures

The Functional Communication Profile (FCP) (Sarno, 1969; Taylor-Sarno, 1965) and the Word Fluency (WF) and Token Test (TT) subtests of the Neurosensory Center Comprehensive Examination for Aphasia (NCCEA) (Spreen and Benton, 1977) were administered to all subjects.

The FCP is an assessment tool which was specifically designed to measure communication perform-

TABLE 1
Group Characteristics

	Median Age (yrs)	Median Education (yrs)	Physical Disability[a]	Type of Aphasia[b]	Severity	Mean Length of Therapy (mos)	Employment	Occupation
Male ($N = 37$)	60 (28–76)	16 (7–20)	34 RH 3 None	12 F 11 NF 14 G	8 Moderate 29 Marked	10	31 Employed 6 Retired 0 Student	33 Professional 4 Skilled laborer 0 Student
Female ($N = 23$)	59 (22–73)	12 (8–16)	22 RH 1 None	4 F 10 NF 9 G	8 Moderate 15 Marked	10	12 Employed 2 Retired 8 Housewife 1 Student	10 Professional 4 Skilled laborer 8 Housewife 1 Student

[a] RH, right hemiplegia.
[b] F, fluent; NF, nonfluent; G, global.

ance in aphasic patients in terms of the natural use of language. It has been shown to tap a dimension of performance which traditional language tasks do not generally measure (Lesser, 1978) by attempting to quantify the communication behaviors a patient actually uses rather than the verbal behavior elicited in formal language tests (Lesser, 1978; Sarno, 1969; Taylor-Sarno, 1965). The scoring, rationale, reliability, and validity of this instrument have been elaborated elsewhere (Sarno, 1969; Taylor-Sarno, 1965). This scale was never intended to distinguish types of aphasia (Sarno, 1969).

The WF and TT subtests of the NCCEA are generally acknowledged by students of aphasia as sensitive detectors of linguistic processing deficits. The justification for the use of these measures as well as their sensitivity to aphasic deficits were elaborated by Spreen and Risser (1981) in their review of assessment of aphasia. The WF task is considered by some to be a "highly sensitive measure of residual dysfunction when many other aspects of language show near complete recovery" (Lomas and Kertesz, 1978, p. 399). In this regard, it may be similar to other demanding verbal abilities, such as verbal memory. The TT is well known for its sensitivity and discriminative power in the measurement of auditory comprehension as well as its reliability (Boller and Dennis, 1979; DeRenzi and Vignolo, 1962; Hartje et al., 1973; Orgass and Poeck, 1966).

Results

The study findings were remarkable in their uniformity and consistency. The .01 level of significance was chosen as a criterion to minimize the likelihood of a significant finding which could be attributed to chance when 32 Mann-Whitney and 15 Wilcoxon tests were used in the present context. Generally, the demographic differences were limited to the area of education where women had less formal education than men. There was a median difference of 4 years, which reached significance beyond the .008 level (Mann-Whitney z of -2.65). This agrees with the characteristics of the group studied by Basso et al. (1982). However, in contrast to the Basso study, there were no significant age differences between men and women (Mann-Whitney z of .56; $p = .58$).

A listing of the initial group medians is shown in Table 2. For the purpose of general information, comparison scores for T_1 and T_2 within groups are provided in Table 3. Comparisons of changes over time within patient groups have been reported previously (Sarno and Levita, 1979).

Comparisons between initial and follow-up evaluations, regardless of gender, all revealed differences significant at or beyond the .0003 level (by two-tailed test). Specifically, Wilcoxon z values were as follows: FCP overall $= -6.38$, FCP speaking $= -5.47$, FCP understanding $= -5.12$, WF $= -4.26$, TT $= -3.59$. Such findings can be taken to indicate continuing recovery for the period under study. As a result, recovery could not be considered terminated 4 to 6 months postonset.

Comparisons between men and women regardless of severity yielded no significant differences on any of the tests used initially (T_1) or on follow-up (T_2). Specific results are shown in Table 4. Since outcome is a function of severity, we divided the groups according to ratings obtained on the Boston Diagnostic Aphasia Examination (BDAE) (Goodglass and Kaplan, 1983). Our patients fell into two severity categories: moderate severity (2 to 4) and marked severity (0 to 1). It is noteworthy that no patient fell into the mild (5) category. There were eight men and eight

TABLE 2
Initial Group Medians

	Male	Female
FCP overall	42.9%	42.1%
FCP speaking	32%	21%
FCP understanding	57%	48%
WF	36%	22%
TT	40%	37%

TABLE 3
Wilcoxon Values for Males and Females Reflecting Changes over Time[a]

	Male	Female
FCP overall	$T = 25$*	$T = 2$*
FCP speaking	$z = -4.01$*	$T = 10.5$*
FCP understanding	$z = -4.04$*	$T = 33$*
WF	$T = 38$*	$T = 8$*
TT	$z = -2.90$*	$T = 20.5$**

[a] T, Wilcoxon T value; z, z transformation value.
* Significant beyond the .01 level (two-tailed test); ** significant at .05 level (two-tailed test).

TABLE 4
Mann-Whitney (MW) Values for Differences between Males and Females for Entire Group[a]

	MW z	p
T_1		
FCP overall	$-.22$	.83
FCP speaking	$-.28$	.78
FCP understanding	$-.13$	.90
WF	$-.22$	.83
TT	$-.30$	.76
T_2		
FCP overall	$-.64$	.52
FCP speaking	$-.31$	.76
FCP understanding	$-.24$	.81
WF	$-.05$	.96
TT	$-.20$	.84

[a] T_1, first test; T_2, follow-up test. None of the MW values was significant at the .01 level (two-tailed test).

TABLE 5
Mann-Whitney (MW) Values for Differences between Male and Female Severity Groups[a]

	Moderate		Marked	
	MW U	p	MW z	p
T_1				
FCP overall	8	.01*	−.004	1.00
FCP speaking	21	.28	−.077	.94
FCP understanding	11	.03**	−.710	.48
WF	18	.16	−.004	1.00
TT	29	.80	−.042	.97
T_2				
FCP overall	21	.28	−.007	.99
FCP speaking	29	.80	−.388	.70
FCP understanding	21	.28	−.233	.82
WF	27	.65	−.211	.83
TT	32	1.04	−.699	.50

[a] T_1, first test; T_2, follow-up test.
* Significant at .01 level (two-tailed test); ** significant at .03 level (two-tailed test).

women in the moderate severity category and 29 men and 15 women in the marked severity group.

The Moderate Severity Group

An initial examination (T_1) revealed no significant changes, with the exception of a lower FCP overall score among women than men (Mann-Whitney U of 8 with $p = .01$, two-tailed test) and a lower FCP understanding score (Mann-Whitney U of 11 with p .03, two-tailed test). Follow-up (T_2) testing failed to reveal any gender differences (see Table 5).

The Marked Severity Group

In this group, no significant differences at the .01 level were found between men and women on any of the tasks at any time (see Table 5).

Discussion

In contrast to the findings of Basso et al. (1982), we found that only women in the moderate group tended to have more severe aphasic impairment than men. Generally, our outcome results showed that women and men reached the same level by 1 to 2½ years poststroke.

Since the women who began with a moderate degree of severity had to make greater gains than the men, it is tempting to invoke the observation that women are more resilient biologically and perhaps have a greater capacity to maximize residuals through compensatory mechanisms. We should not overlook recovery in the marked severity groups where men and women did not differ initially or on outcomes.

While this study and the report of Basso et al. (1982) might seem related, there are methodological differences which preclude comparison. Some of the differences in findings may relate to sampling differences.

Our samples were more restricted and homogeneous, as we did not include trauma or neoplasm. Also patients who are referred for treatment to rehabilitation centers tend to be more severely affected than those seen in general hospitals and neurology services. In fact, few fluent aphasia patients are referred to rehabilitation medicine centers because they usually lack physical disabilities. This may account for the small number of aphasic females in this study. Furthermore, in contrast to Basso's study, none of our aphasic patients had normal comprehension.

Conclusions

Definitive conclusions concerning the existence of gender differences in recovery from poststroke aphasia must await repetitions with many more samples reflecting different severities of impairment at different points in the recovery continuum. The increasing importance of the problems associated with advancing age make studies of recovery particularly relevant.

Essentially no differences in recovery from aphasia were found as a function of gender in this study.

References

Basso A, Capitani E, Moraschini S (1982) Sex differences in recovery from aphasia. *Cortex* 18:469–475.
Benson DF (1967) Fluency in aphasia: Correlation with radioactive scan localization. *Cortex* 8:373–394.
Boller F (1981) Strokes and behavior: Disorders of higher cortical functions following cerebral disease—Disorders of language and related functions. *Stroke* 12:532–534.
Boller F, Dennis M (Eds) (1979) *Auditory comprehension: Clinical and experimental studies with the token test.* New York: Academic Press.
Brown JW, Grober E (1983) Age, sex and aphasia type: Evidence for a regional cerebral growth process underlying lateralization. *J Nerv Ment Dis* 171:431–434.
Darley F (1972) The efficacy of language rehabilitation in aphasia. *J Speech Hear Disord* 37:3–21.
DeRenzi E, Vignolo LA (1962) The token test: A sensitive test to detect receptive disturbance in aphasics. *Brain* 85:665–678.
Eisenson J (1973) *Adult aphasia: Assessment and treatment.* Englewood Cliffs NJ: Prentice-Hall.
Geschwind N (1971) Current concepts: Aphasia. *N Engl J Med* 284:654–656.
Gloning K, Trappl R, Heiss W, et al (1976) Prognosis and speech therapy in aphasia. In Y Lebrun, R Hoops (Eds), *Recovery in aphasics* (pp 57–64). Amsterdam: Swets and Zeitlinger.
Goodglass H, Kaplan E (1983) *The assessment of aphasia and related disorders* (2nd ed). Philadelphia: Lea & Febiger.
Hartje W, Kerschensteiner M, Poeck K, et al (1973) A cross validation study on the token test. *Neuropsychologia* 7:119–121.
Kertesz A., McCabe P (1977) Recovery patterns and prognosis in aphasia. *Brain* 100:1–18.
Lesser R (1978) *Linguistic investigations of aphasia.* New York: Elsevier.
Lomas J, Kertesz A (1978) Patterns of spontaneous recovery in aphasic groups: A Study of adult stroke patients. *Brain Lang* 5:388–401.
McGlone J (1977) Sex differences in the cerebral organization of verbal functions in patients with unilateral brain lesions. *Brain* 100:775–793.
McGlone J (1980) Sex differences in human brain asymmetry: A critical survey. *Behav Brain Sci* 3:215–263.

Mohr JP, Sidman M, Stoddard LT, et al (1973) Evaluation of the deficit in total aphasia. *Neurology* 23:1302–1312.

Orgass B, Poeck K (1966) Clinical validation of a new test for aphasia: An experimental study on the token test. *Cortex* 2:222–243.

Prins R, Snow C, Wagenaar E (1978) Recovery from aphasia: Spontaneous speech versus language comprehension. *Brain Lang* 6:192–211.

Rose C, Boby V, Capildeo R (1976) A retrospective survey of speech disorders following stroke, with a particular reference to the value of speech therapy. In Y Lebrun, R Hoops (Eds), *Recovery in aphasics* (pp 189–197). Amsterdam: Swets and Zeitlinger.

Sarno MT (1969) *The functional communication profile.* New York: Rusk Institute of Rehabilitation Medicine, New York University Medical Center.

Sarno MT (1970) A survey of 100 aphasic medicare patients in a speech pathology program. *J Am Geriatr Soc* 18:471–480.

Sarno MT (1981) Recovery and rehabilitation in aphasia. In MT Sarno (Ed), *Acquired aphasia* (pp 485–529). New York: Academic Press.

Sarno MT, Levita E (1979) Recovery in treated aphasia during the first year post stroke. *Stroke* 10:663–670.

Sarno MT, Levita E (1981) Some observations on the nature of recovery in global aphasia after stroke. *Brain Lang* 13:1–12.

Spreen O, Benton A (1977) *Neurosensory center comprehensive examination for aphasia* (rev ed). Victoria BC Canada: University of Victoria.

Spreen O, Risser A (1981) Assessment of aphasia. In MT Sarno (Ed), *Acquired aphasia* (pp 67–127). New York: Academic Press.

Taylor-Sarno M (1965) A measurement of functional communication in aphasia. *Arch Phys Med Rehabil* 46:101–107.

Vignolo LA (1964) Evolution of aphasia and language rehabilitation: A retrospective exploratory study. *Cortex* 1:344–367.

Yarnell P, Monroe P, Sobel L (1976) Aphasia outcome in stroke: A clinical-neuroradiological correlation. *Stroke* 7:514–522.

Sex-Related Differences in Hemispheric Lateralization: A Function of Physical Maturation

Mirna I. Vrbancic
University of Waterloo

James L. Mosley
University of Calgary

> The patterns of perceptual asymmetry on three dichotic listening tasks were evaluated to assess the hypothesis that late-maturing individuals have more clearly lateralized cerebral functions. A total of 64 right-handed prepubescent ($n = 32$) and postpubescent ($n = 32$) males and females, classified by physical exams as early or later maturers, were given dichotic listening tasks of consonant-vowel syllables (CVs), simple square-wave tones (STs), and complex square-wave tones (CTs). Partial support was obtained for the maturation hypothesis, but in unexpected directions. There were no significant differences between early and late maturers in the magnitude of the dichotic right-ear advantage (REA) for CVs, in either the prepubescent or postpubescent group. Only the postpubescent group obtained a significant REA, regardless of sex or maturation rate. In contrast, maturation rate was related to dichotic ST and CT tone performance. Late maturers demonstrated a stronger left-ear advantage (LEA) in the prepubescent group, and early maturers demonstrated a stronger LEA in the postpubescent group, regardless of sex. These results suggest that maturation rate may contribute independently to left-hemisphere and right-hemisphere lateralization.

Of all the putative sex-related differences, that favoring males in spatial ability has probably received the most attention (Linn & Peterson, 1985). Of particular interest and debate is the underlying cause of these differences (Vandenberg & Kuse, 1978) and the age of onset for such differences (Linn

---

Requests for reprints should be sent to Mirna I. Vrbancic, Department of Psychology, University of Waterloo, Waterloo, Ontario, N2L 3G1, Canada.

& Petersen, 1985; Waber, 1976, 1977). Waber (1976) advanced the hypothesis that the male advantage in spatial ability is related to the later onset of puberty in males (by about 2 years) relative to females. She examined the effect of maturation rate by comparing young (10-year-old girls and 13-year-old boys) early and late maturers and older (13-year-old girls and 16-year-old boys) early and later maturers. The chronological age difference between the sexes was intended to reflect the sex difference in the onset of peak height velocity. Employing the scale of physical development devised by Tanner (1962, 1978) to classify individuals' pubertal status and maturation rate, Waber found that later maturers, irrespective of age and sex, scored significantly better on the spatial tasks relative to the verbal one, in contrast to early maturers. The groups (younger, older) did not differ in verbal skills, and sex-related differences, although not statistically significant, were in the expected direction.

A number of investigators have subsequently attempted to replicate these findings, but with mixed success. In accordance with the findings of Waber, most studies have not found an association between maturational rate and verbal ability (Diamond, Carey, & Back, 1983; Meyer-Bahlburg et al., 1985; Petersen, 1976; Rierdan & Koff, 1984; Sanders & Soares, 1986; Strauss & Kinsbourne, 1981). The only exception is a clinical study by Rovet (1983). In contrast, a number of studies have, in part, supported the association between spatial ability and maturation rate, in both clinical (Meyer-Bahlburg et al., 1985; cf. Hines & Shipley, 1984; Rovet, 1983) and nonclinical samples (Diamond et al., 1983; Newcombe & Bandura, 1983; Ray, Newcombe, Semon, & Cole, 1981; Sanders & Soares, 1986; Waber, Bauermeister, Cohen, Ferber, & Wolff, 1981; cf. Berenbaum & Resnick, 1982; Petersen, 1976; Rierdan & Koff, 1984; Strauss & Kinsbourne, 1981; Waber, Mann, Merola, & Moylan, 1985).

As such, the data at present support an association of maturation rate with spatial ability, but not with verbal or fluent production ability. However, Waber's suggestion that hemispheric lateralization may be the mechanism accounting for this effect has not been replicated by the few investigators that have attempted to do so (Meyer-Bahlburg et al., 1985; Rovet, 1983; Waber et al., 1985). For example, Meyer-Bahlburg et al. (1985) administered monotic word discrimination and dichotic consonant-vowel syllable (CV) discrimination listening tests to 12 idiopathic precocious puberty (IPP) adult females and their matched controls. The IPP group did not differ significantly from the matched controls in monotic word or dichotic CV discrimination. Rovet (1983) also assessed IPP individuals and their matched controls, as well as delayed-puberty children and their matched controls, with a dichotic CV discrimination task. The only group differing from controls was the delayed-developing males, who demonstrated stronger lateral asymmetries. These results directly contrast with those reported by Waber (1976). Most recently, Waber et al. (1985) conducted a longitudinal study to assess 78 girls and 67 boys both before puberty and 2 years later. At the later time, children who could be classified into extreme groups of early and late maturers were reassessed on a battery of cognitive measures and a dichotic CV discrimination task. As in her previous study (Waber, 1977), Waber failed to obtain a maturational effect for laterality scores in children with a similar chronological age range (120 to 140 months old). In her earlier study, Waber (1977) had found that only the later maturers in the older age grouping (midadolescent)—not in the younger age grouping—showed a stronger right-ear advantage (REA) for CVs in comparison to early maturers of the same age. She interpreted those findings as indicating greater hemispheric lateralization for speech perception in late maturers regardless of sex.

There are a number of explanations possible for the pattern of ear advantages found by Waber (1977). First, hemispheric lateralization may increase with age and not fully develop until puberty. This possibility seems unlikely because several dichotic listening studies have demonstrated the existence of a significant REA for speech in both sexes in childhood, and there seems to be no developmental increase in the magnitude of the REA (Bryden & Saxby, 1986). Second, hemispheric lateralization may be present during childhood but be disrupted by the onset of puberty at which time cerebral functions undergo reorganization. This second possibility has recently received some support from a study of the development of face encoding ability (Diamond et al., 1983). This study found that actively pubescent girls were significantly poorer at face encoding than prepubescent and postpubescent controls. The pattern of results was reversed for a spatial measure, the Embedded Figures Test. The association between maturation rate and spatial ability and the lack of an association between maturation and hemispheric lateralization have led a number of investigators to suggest that hemispheric lateralization and spatial ability may be independently related to maturation rate, but not to each other. Newcombe and Bandura (1983) suggested the possibility that pubertal disruptions may obscure a relationship of maturation rate to hemispheric organization.

Our study provides a further examination of the association between maturation rate and hemispheric lateralization. It differs from previous work in that it was designed to assess the lateralization of both left- and right-hemisphere functions. The few studies that have examined the relationship between maturation rate and hemispheric lateralization have employed a verbal dichotic-listening procedure, ostensibly a left-hemisphere task. Yet the most consistent association between maturation rate and cognitive performance has been for spatial ability, which is described as right-hemisphere function. We are aware of only one study that has examined right-hemisphere lateralization and its relation to maturation rate. Newcombe and Bandura (1983) used a dichaptic test (Witelson, 1977) to assess eighty-five 11-year-old girls who were classified as early and late maturers and found a nonsignificant correlation between dichaptic task performance and (a) timing of puberty and (b) spatial ability as assessed by the Primary Abilities Test and by the Block Design subtest of the Wechsler Intelligence Scale for Children. However, dichaptic tests typically present relatively few trials and are therefore not highly stable.

To address the association of maturation rate and right- and left-hemisphere lateralization, we employed a dichotic listening procedure. The stimuli chosen for presentation were CVs—in an attempt to replicate and permit comparison with previous studies—and two sets of complex tones, simple square-wave tones (STs) and complex square-wave tones (CTs). The task termed ST in this study was developed by Sidtis (1981), and demonstrated to yield a reliable and robust left-ear advantage (LEA; right-hemisphere processing) equal in magnitude to the REA obtained for dichotic CVs. The CT task in this study was developed by imposing a random square wave on the ST wave form to eliminate the regularity of the ST stimulus and create a more complex, irregular, and novel stimulus that should require the specialization of the right hemisphere for processing. The two sets of tones were chosen in preference to visual or dichaptic tasks to maintain equivalent procedures for assessing right- and left-hemisphere lateralization.

Participants chosen for this study were an equal number of right-handed males and females who were either prepubescent (early and late maturers) or postpubescent (early and late maturers) as assessed by physical examinations. The choice of this sample was dictated by the following issues. First, we wished to determine if maturation rate (early, late) or maturation status (prepubescent, postpubescent) is associated with hemispheric lateralization. Second, we wished to determine if adolescents who are just entering puberty, at which time sex-hormone levels are on the increase and may lead to a disruption or reorganization of hemispheric function, demonstrate the same pattern of hemispheric lateralization as adolescents who are just completing puberty, with a consequent decrease and stabilization in sex-hormone levels. If maturational status rather than rate is involved in the association between physical maturation and hemispheric lateralization, then the association should not emerge in the postpubescent sample where both the early and late maturers have attained almost complete adult status, but should emerge in the prepubescent sample just entering puberty.

METHOD

Participants

The prepubescent sample (girls and boys in Grades 5 and 6) and the postpubescent sample (girls in Grades 10 to 11, boys in Grades 11 to 12) were selected from the separate school system in the city of Calgary. They were of average verbal ability or above as determined by the Peabody Picture Vocabulary Test (PPVT) mental age equivalent scores. They were selected from middle- and upper-middle-class schools. Informed consent was obtained from parents/guardians and the participants themselves. The voluntary aspect of the study and the confidentiality of the data were emphasized and maintained.

Physical staging criteria. The physical stage criteria for females (breast stages, pubic hair stages) and males (genitalia stages, pubic hair stages) proposed by Tanner (1978) and Marshall and Tanner (1969, 1970) were employed to assess the stage of pubertal physical maturation of the participants in this study. In addition, measurements of height and weight were also obtained. The physical examinations were undertaken by the same medical practitioner from the Health Sciences Centre at the University of Calgary. The examinations were conducted in a private room within the schools. From the physical examination protocol, females and males who demonstrated the appropriate Stage 1 prepubescent pubertal status or Stage 5 postpubertal status were selected. Of importance for inclusion was evidence of secondary sexual development in the prepubescent sample, but not yet Stage 2 development, and almost complete attainment of Stage 5 development for the postpubescent sample. By these criteria, it was possible to obtain an estimate of how long each individual would remain at a particular stage in pubertal development. Although all individuals were mainly prepubescent or postpubescent, each pubertal status group was composed of chronologically younger and older individuals. Therefore, it was possible to differentiate by age the early and late maturers within each pubertal status group. Consequently, the chronologically younger individuals within each pubertal status group were classified as *early maturers,* and the chronologically older individuals within each pubertal status group were classified as *late maturers.*

Laterality. The laterality criteria included the demonstrated use of the right hand for writing and brushing one's teeth, the use of the right foot in kicking a ball, and the use of the right eye to sight a target through a small hole in a piece of cardboard, from an arm's length, as it is gradually moved in toward the face.

To aid in the pubertal-rate screening process, teachers from the appropriate grade levels assisted in identifying students who appeared to be maturing earlier or later than their classmates. The re-screening resulted in 77 individuals being assessed for the study. Of the 42 prepubescent volunteers, 2 individuals did not meet the criteria for laterality (hand, foot, and eye) and 8 individuals were in Stage 2 or State 3 of physical development. Of the postpubescent group, 3 of the 35 volunteers did not meet the laterality criteria. The remaining 32 individuals were all assessed by the physical exams to be mainly in Stage 5 of physical development.

Apparatus

Auditory sensitivity test. Auditory sensitivity was assessed with a diagnostic audiometer (Maico MA22) at frequencies of 500 Hz, 1000 Hz, 2000 Hz, 3000 Hz, and 4000 Hz. Air conduction audiometry was used and audiograms were constructed showing the threshold (in decibels) for each participant's left and right ear at each of the above frequencies. Participants demonstrating left-ear or right-ear differences of 6 dB or greater at an intensity level of no greater than 25 dB above standard detection threshold were excluded from the study.

Dichotic listening tasks. A Sony (Model FC-FX44) dual-cassette stereophonic tape recorder and Superior SP-40 earphones were used to present the dichotic stimuli. All stimuli were recorded on Sony UCX-S low-noise magnetic tape cassettes and presented at a mean intensity of approximately 65 dB as measured by a Bruel and Kjaer sound-level meter (Model 2218) and filter (Model 1613). The dichotic stimuli consisted of spoken pairs of CVs, pairs of STs, and pairs of CTs. Onset alignment and regular spacing of the dichotic pairs and the probes on Channels 1 and 2 was achieved using a digitizing program (speech editor) with a VAX 11/730 computer.

For each type of stimulus (CV, ST, CT) a dichotic-probe stimulus technique was employed where half the probes were the same as one member of the dichotic pair (distributed randomly and equally to each channel), and half were different to allow for the assessment of guessing. In all cases, the intertrial interval was 4 sec.

The spoken CV pairs were chosen from among the syllables /ba da ga pa ta ka/. All syllables were produced by a female speaker and had a duration of 200 msec. All possible paired combinations of the six CV stimuli were produced yielding 30 dichotic stimulus pairs. The 30 dichotic stimulus pairs were then repeated three times and were randomized to yield a total of 120 stimulus pairs. Each CV pair was followed at 500 msec by the CV probe.

STs having frequencies corresponding to the six notes in the octave between C4 and C5 on the major scale—D (297 Hz), E (330 Hz), F (352 Hz), G (396 Hz), A (440 Hz), B (495 Hz)—were generated by a PDP 11/23 plus computer which also controlled the duration of each dichotic and probe tone (200 msec). The six possible combinations of the STs were generated, repeated three times, and randomized to yield 120 dichotic stimulus pairs. Each ST pair was followed at 500 msec by the ST probe. The generation of these tones was prompted by the findings of Sidtis (1981), who demonstrated that these simple square-wave tones produced an LEA equal in magnitude to the REA for CVs.

The CTs (also generated by the PDP 11/23 plus computer) were constructed by adding to the ST a second square-wave tone whose frequency randomly varied between +50 Hz and −50 Hz of the STs every half period. The six possible combinations of the CTs were generated, repeated three times, and randomized to yield 120 dichotic stimulus pairs. Each CT pair was followed at 500 msec by the CT probe.

The simple and complex tones each had a 3 msec rise/fall time shaped according to a raised cosine function.

Procedure

Participants, having given informed consent, were seen in school for a brief physical examination by the medical practitioner. Those meeting the criteria specified by prepubescent and postpubescent were then seen in school individually for three sessions each separated by 1 week. In Session 1 (30 min), the Auditory Sensitivity Test and the PPVT were administered. The assessment of laterality (hand, foot, eye) was also undertaken.

The dichotic listening tasks were administered in a quiet but not soundproof room in the following two sessions. Half the participants received the CV dichotic pairs in Session 2 (15 min) followed by the two types of tones in Session 3 (30 min). The remainder of each group received the reverse order. During the dichotic-tone session, half the participants received the STs first followed by the CTs, and half received the reverse order. This resulted in four task orders (i.e., CV–ST–CT, CV–CT–ST, CT–ST–CV, ST–CT–CV), which were counterbalanced across and within subjects. Headphones were reversed after each participant to compensate for a potential mechanical laterality influence.

In the CV pair–CV probe condition, participants were instructed to verbally report whether the CV probe was the same as one of the two dichotic CV inputs or different from both. In the total stimulus conditions, they were asked to motorically indicate with the left hand by depressing one of two keys on a response panel whether the dichotic tones were the same or different.

Prior to the presentation of the 120 dichotic pair–probe stimulus trials for each of the CVs, the STs, and the CTs, 30 stimulus-appropriate binaural practice trials were given. The practice trials consisted of 75% of the probes being the same and 25% being different. Participants were required to achieve 100% accuracy on these trials before proceeding with the dichotic pair–probe trials.

RESULTS

All statistical analyses were executed employing the Biomedical Computer Programs–P and D series (BMDP) software. For all within-subject effects with more than 1 df, the Greenhouse–Geisser adjustment to the degrees of freedom are reported. An alpha level of $p < .05$ was maintained for all tests of significance. Interaction effects were analyzed employing simple main-effect or simple interaction-effect analyses where appropriate.

Participant Characteristics

Each of the participant characteristic scores (age, PPVT, height, weight) was subjected to a separate 2 (Status: Prepubescent–Postpubescent) × 2 (Maturation Rate: Early–Late) × 2 (Sex) analysis of variance (ANOVA). Means and standard deviations are presented in Table 1.

As planned in forming the pubertal status and maturation rate groups, the prepubescent sample was significantly younger than the postpubescent sample, $F(1, 56) = 2602.90$, $p < .0001$, with females being significantly younger than the males regardless of pubertal status, $F(1, 56) = 109.63$, $p < .0001$, reflecting the sex difference in pubertal onset. In addition, early maturers regardless of pubertal status or sex were significantly younger than later maturers, $F(1, 56) = 72.02$, $p < .0001$. Within pubertal status groups, the Sex × Maturation Rate interactions were nonsignificant ($p > .08$), indicating that any Sex × Maturation Rate interactions obtained for the dichotic listening tests are not confounded by age.

Analysis of the PPVT mental-age equivalent scores indicated that the postpubescent group had scored significantly higher than the prepubescent group, $F(1, 56) = 33.91$, $p < .0001$. In the prepubescent group, females obtained significantly higher scores than the males, $F(1, 56) = 8.76$, $p = .0045$, and males in the postpubescent group obtained significantly higher PPVT scores than the females, $F(1, 56) = 11.07$, $p = .0016$. It is again important to note that within pubertal status groups, the Sex × Maturation Rate interactions were nonsignificant ($p > .08$).

TABLE 1
Means and Standard Deviations of Participant Characteristics

	Early Maturers		Late Maturers		Total	
Group	M	SD	M	SD	M	SD
Prepubescent						
Female						
Age	10.19	0.25	10.80	0.38	10.50	0.32
PPVT[a]	14.19	5.88	10.18	0.52	12.19	0.32
Weight (kg)	33.71	6.98	32.91	7.52	33.31	7.25
Height (cm)	142.83	5.05	139.21	9.78	141.02	7.42
Male						
Age	10.77	0.46	11.63	0.14	11.20	0.30
PPVT	10.29	1.00	11.51	1.34	10.90	1.17
Weight (kg)	31.35	3.72	39.55	6.43	35.45	5.08
Height (cm)	139.64	2.54	146.45	9.36	143.05	5.95
Postpubescent						
Female						
Age	15.38	0.26	16.30	0.61	15.84	0.44
PPVT	15.46	2.84	14.95	1.86	15.21	2.35
Weight (kg)	59.30	5.92	56.73	9.12	58.02	7.52
Height (cm)	163.38	4.18	158.63	5.67	161.01	4.93
Male						
Age	16.78	0.29	18.27	0.85	17.53	0.57
PPVT	19.14	6.28	21.18	7.33	20.16	0.57
Weight (kg)	67.35	6.60	70.55	12.79	68.95	9.70
Height (cm)	175.31	4.67	178.31	7.29	176.81	5.98

[a]Mental-age equivalent scores.

Although it had been anticipated that early maturers, regardless of pubertal status or sex, would also be taller and heavier, this was true only for early-maturing females. Early-maturing females were both taller and heavier than late-maturing females. In contrast, late-maturing males were significantly taller and heavier than early-maturing males, $F(1, 56) = 34.13, p < .0001$.

Hemispheric Lateralization

Prior to analyzing correct "same" dichotic listening responses the total correct "different" responses were analyzed to rule out guessing as a factor in performance. The 2 (Status) × 2 (Maturation Rate) × 2 (Sex) × 3 (Stimulus Type) ANOVA with stimulus type (CV, ST, and CT) as the repeated measure revealed no significant main effects or interactions. The overall accuracy was 73.5% for the prepubescent group and 72.5% for the postpubescent group. These percentages suggest that the three dichotic listening tasks were not constrained by floor or ceiling effects.

Consequently, the number of correctly reported "same" responses were subjected to a 2 (Status) × 2 (Maturation Rate) × 2 (Sex) × 3 (Stimulus Type) × 2 (Ear: Right–Left) ANOVA with stimulus type and ear as repeated measures. The analysis indicated a significant main effect for pubertal status, $F(1, 56) = 4.06$, $p < .05$. Examination of the means indicated that the prepubescent group ($M = 19.18$, $SD = 4.12$) was significantly less accurate than the postpubescent group ($M = 20.59$, $SD = 4.79$).

To correct for any possible effects resulting from the differing levels of accuracy between the pubertal status groups, a laterality coefficient developed by Bryden and Sprott (1981) was employed for all subsequent analyses. This laterality coefficient, termed *lambda*, is the difference between the log likelihood of identifying a right-ear item correctly and the log likelihood of identifying a left-ear item correctly. This coefficient,

TABLE 2
Means and Standard Deviations of Stimulus Lambdas

Group	Early Maturers		Late Maturers		Total	
	M	SD	M	SD	M	SD
Prepubescent						
Female						
CV	0.02	0.38	0.03	0.69	0.02	0.54
ST	0.01	0.32	−0.11	0.20	−0.05	0.27
CT	−0.02	0.24	−0.08	0.22	−0.05	0.23
Male						
CV	0.20	0.79	−0.09	0.47	0.06	0.65
ST	0.06	0.34	−0.14	0.47	−0.04	0.41
CT	−0.07	0.26	−0.30	0.28	−0.18	0.29
Total						
CV	0.11	0.61	−0.03	0.57	0.04	0.59
ST	0.03	0.32	−0.13	0.35	−0.05	0.34
CT	−0.05	0.24	−0.19	0.27	−0.12	0.26
Postpubescent						
Female						
CV	0.21	0.55	0.23	0.78	0.22	0.65
ST	−0.27	0.21	−0.11	0.34	−0.19	0.28
CT	−0.18	0.21	−0.05	0.41	−0.11	0.32
Male						
CV	0.29	0.61	0.34	0.39	0.31	0.50
ST	−0.28	0.39	0.09	0.37	−0.10	0.41
CT	−0.30	0.36	−0.11	0.39	−0.21	0.37
Total						
CV	0.25	0.56	0.28	0.60	0.27	0.57
ST	−0.27	0.30	−0.01	0.36	0.14	0.35
CT	−0.24	0.29	−0.08	0.39	0.16	0.35

therefore, indicates both the magnitude and the direction of the ear advantages. For present purposes, lambda for each of the stimulus types (CV, ST, and CT) was computed by obtaining the natural logarithm of [(correct right-ear score × incorrect left-ear score)/(correct left-ear score × incorrect right-ear score)]. Separate 2 (Status) × 2 (Maturation Rate) × 2 (Sex) ANOVAs were conducted for each CV, ST, and CT stimulus lambda. The lambda means and standard deviations for each pubertal status and maturation rate groups are presented in Table 2.

Analysis of lambda for CV stimuli indicated a significant REA, $F(1, 56) = 4.17$, $p < .05$. No other main or interaction effects were significant. Simple effects analysis indicated that there was a significant laterality effect in the postpubescent group but not in the prepubescent group, $F(1, 56) = 4.35$, $p < .05$ (see Figure 1).

As expected, a significant LEA was revealed by the analysis of lambda for ST stimuli, $F(1, 56) = 4.01$, $p < .04$. The only other significant effect was a Pubertal Status × Maturation Rate interaction, $F(1, 56) = 6.26$, $p < .02$. This interaction indicated that later maturers were more lateralized in the prepubescent group, whereas early maturers were more lateralized in the postpubescent group. Simple interaction effects analysis indicated postpubescent early maturers were significantly more lateralized than prepubescent early maturers, $F(1, 56) = 6.59$, $p < .02$. As with CV stimuli, the postpubescent group as a whole showed a significant laterality effect, in this case demonstrating an LEA for ST stimuli, $F(1, 56) = 5.52$, $p < .03$. Within the postpubescent group, early-maturing males demonstrated a

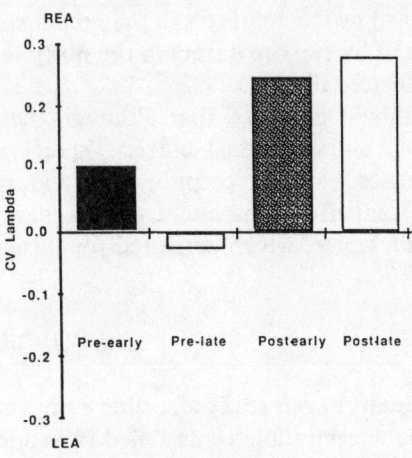

FIGURE 1 CV stimulus lambdas for prepubescent and postpubescent, early and late maturers. REA = right-ear advantage; LEA = left-ear advantage.

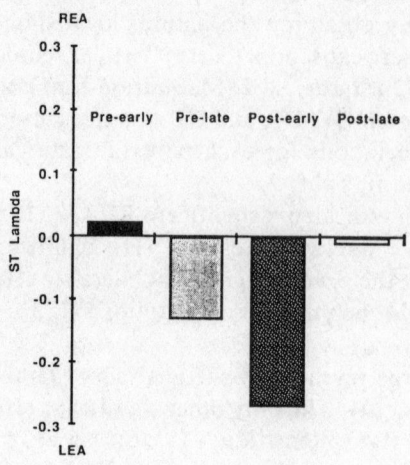

FIGURE 2   ST stimulus lambdas for prepubescent and postpubescent, early and late maturers. REA = right-ear advantage; LEA = left-ear advantage.

significantly stronger LEA relative to late-maturing males, $F(1, 56) = 4.83$, $p < .04$. The Pubertal Status × Maturation Rate interaction is illustrated in Figure 2.

Analysis of the CT stimulus lambda also indicated the presence of a significant LEA, $F(1, 56) = 13.24$, $p = .0006$. The analysis also revealed a Pubertal Status × Maturation Rate interaction that was marginally significant, $F(1, 56) = 3.79$, $p = .057$. No other main or interaction effects emerged as significant. Simple interaction effects analyses indicated a pattern of results similar to that obtained with ST. Significant LEAs were obtained by late maturers in the prepubescent group, $F(1, 56) = 6.12$, $p < .02$, and by early maturers in the postpubescent group, $F(1, 56) = 9.68$, $p < .003$ (see Figure 3).

It should be noted that although the initial analysis of variance, employing untransformed correct "same" responses indicated an accuracy difference between prepubescent and postpubescent groups, the same significant effects and interactions were revealed by the analyses of stimulus lambda scores, which corrected for this accuracy difference.

DISCUSSION

The results of our study assessing early and late maturing prepubescent and postpubescent adolescents failed to support Waber's (1976, 1977) hypothesis that late maturers, regardless of sex, should demonstrate stronger

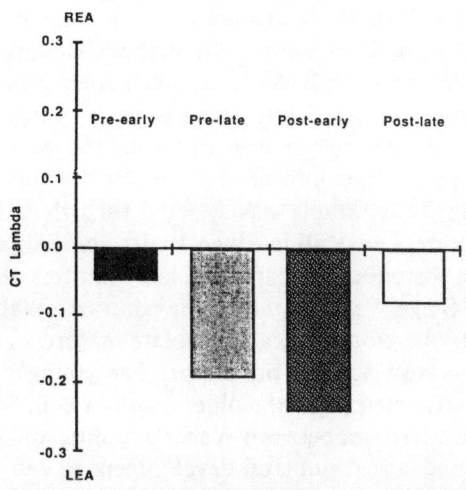

FIGURE 3   CT stimulus lambdas for prepubescent and postpubescent, early and late maturers. REA = right-ear advantage; LEA = left-ear advantage.

hemispheric lateralization than a comparable group of early maturers. In accordance with previous studies, this study has not found an association between maturation rate and left-hemisphere lateralization for dichotic CV discrimination. Only the postpubescent group demonstrated a significant REA for CVs, irrespective of maturation rate. In contrast, maturation rate was associated with right-hemisphere lateralization for dichotic tone discrimination.

It is important to note that Waber found support for the maturation–hemispheric lateralization hypothesis only in the older age group employing dichotic CV stimuli. She proposed that the lack of an effect in the younger age group may have been due to the onset of puberty, which may in turn have led to disruption of functional hemispheric lateralization. Our results for CV discrimination are in accordance with this hypothesis. The postpubescent sample demonstrated a significant REA but the prepubescent sample did not, suggesting that following a pubertal disruption, hemispheric lateralization reemerges and is detectable in a midadolescent (Waber, 1977) and late-pubescent sample of adolescents. A similar pattern of results was obtained by Diamond et al. (1983) for face-encoding ability: actively pubescent girls were significantly poorer at face encoding than prepubescent and postpubescent controls. These results suggest that pubertal onset may lead to a disruption of a variety of functions the nature of which has yet to be determined. An alternative explanation for our results may be the suggestion by Newcombe and

Bandura (1983) that pubertal disruptions may obscure a relationship of maturation rate to hemispheric organization.

The lack of a maturation effect in the present postpubescent sample for CV stimuli, in contrast to Waber's finding may be due in part to sample differences. Puberty is a continuous process; as such, it is difficult to determine accurately the extent of time an adolescent has been in a particular stage of development, and when they will proceed to the next stage of development. To control for this variation in pubertal development, our sample was selected such that the prepubescent early and late maturers were all in Stage 1 with some signs of Stage 2 development, and the postpubescent early and late maturers all in Stage 5 with still some signs of Stage 4 development. In contrast, Waber's sample was composed of extreme groups of early and late maturers (1 *SD* below or above the norm) who were actively pubescent. The younger group was in Stages 2 to 3 of development, and the older group was in Stages 3 to 5 of development. If the difference between Waber's finding and our finding can be attributed to the advanced pubertal development of our older sample, it would suggest that left-hemisphere lateralization is associated with pubertal *status* rather than pubertal *rate*. If pubertal rate is the determining factor, then late maturers, although late adolescent or adult, should be more lateralized than a comparable group of early maturers. This is, in fact, an assumption inherent in investigations examining the association of maturation rate, hemispheric lateralization, and spatial ability by use of retrospective data of pubertal onset. The studies that have been successful in demonstrating an association of maturation and spatial ability, such as Waber's (1977), employed extreme groups of early and late maturers (Sanders & Soares, 1986) in contrast to the relatively homogeneous sample of early and late maturers in our study. These studies, like ours, have failed to demonstrate an association between maturation and left-hemisphere lateralization in the directions predicted by Waber (see Meyer-Bahlburg et al., 1985; Rovet, 1983).

In contrast to left-hemisphere lateralization, right-hemisphere lateralization does appear to be sensitive to maturation rate as assessed by dichotic tones in our study. A very similar pattern emerged for both types of tones. Late maturers were more lateralized in the prepubescent group, and early maturers were more lateralized in the postpubescent group. These results suggest that late-maturing adolescents who demonstrate a strong right-hemisphere lateralization for tones at the beginning of puberty will show a weaker LEA at the completion of puberty. In contrast, early-maturing adolescents who are weakly lateralized prepubescents will desmonstrate a strong LEA at the completion of puberty. These results also suggest that the relation between timing of puberty and right-hemisphere lateralization is not linear. Examination of the exact nature of this relationship would entail assessment of adolescents going through puberty employing pubertal markers, such as the stages of pubertal development devised by Tanner (1962), to determine assessment periods. Ideally, at these various pubertal stages, hormonal assays should be obtained to complement the behavioral measures. Due to the time and cost-effectiveness of such an examination, it is unlikely that it will be carried out in the near future, although there is an obvious need for such extensive research in this area.

Considering that no other studies have examined the relation between pubertal onset and right-hemisphere lateralization employing the dichotic listening procedure, further research is needed to confirm our observations. In addition, these results suggest that left-hemisphere and right-hemisphere lateralization may be independently influenced by maturational rate. Others have also found the association of maturation rate and visuospatial ability (right-hemisphere function) to be independent of its association with left-hemisphere lateralization (Meyer-Bahlburg et al., 1985).

In summary, we assessed Waber's (1977) maturation rate–hemispheric lateralization hypothesis in a sample of prepubescent and postpubescent early and late maturing males and females. The results suggest that maturational status rather than rate may be associated with left-hemisphere lateralization. In contrast, maturation rate was associated with right-hemisphere lateralization. These findings suggest, therefore, that maturation rate may independently influence left-hemisphere lateralization and right-hemisphere lateralization. Clearly what is needed to elucidate the relationship of maturation, cognitive abilities, and hemispheric specialization is longitudinal developmental research. Assessment of these relationships should be undertaken at various pubertal stages and corroborated with hormonal assays. Future investigations should employ several different measures of spatial and verbal functioning, assessing both cognitive abilities and hemispheric specialization, by use of lateralized presentation to a number of sensory modalities, and their relation to maturation.

ACKNOWLEDGMENTS

We gratefully acknowledge the technical assistance of Mike Procter, David Naugler, and Tim Holt. A special acknowledgment is due Dr. Harvey Black for his medical expertise and the time he devoted to this research. Without his participation, this study would not have been possible. We also acknowledge the assistance and cooperation of Dr. Joseph Quinn, assistant superintendent of student services, Calgary Catholic Board of Education; Dennis Gruenwald, principal, St. Mary's Community High School; Dennis Maguire, principal, St. Vincent de Paul Elementary School; Erv Hickey, principal, Mother Teresa of Calcutta Elementary School; John Early, principal, St. Thomas Aquinas Elementary School; and the staff and students who voluntarily gave of their time to participate in this research. Finally, we thank Drs. Philip Bryden and Runa Steenhuis for their constructive commentary on earlier drafts of this article.

REFERENCES

Berenbaum, S. A., & Resnick, S. (1982). Somatic androgyny and cognitive abilities. *Developmental Psychology, 18,* 418-423.

Bryden, M. P., & Saxby, L. (1986). Developmental aspects of cerebral lateralization. In J. E. Obrzut & G. W. Hynd (Eds.), *Child neuropsychology: Vol. 1. Theory and research* (pp. 73-94). Orlando, FL: Academic.

Bryden, M. P., & Sprott, D. A. (1981). Statistical determination of degree of laterality. *Neuropsychologia, 19,* 571-581.

Diamond, R., Carey, S., & Back, K. J. (1983). Genetic influences on the development of spatial skills during early adolescence. *Cognition, 13,* 167-185.

Hines, M., & Shipley, C. (1984). Prenatal exposure to diethylstibestrol (DES) and the development of sexually dimorphic cognitive abilities and cerebral lateralization. *Developmental Psychology, 20,* 81-94.

Linn, M. C., & Petersen, A. C. (1985). Emergence and characterization of sex differences in spatial ability: A meta-analysis. *Child Development, 56,* 1479-1498.

Marshall, W. A., & Tanner, J. M. (1969). Variations in the pattern of pubertal changes in girls. *Archives of Disease in Childhood, 44,* 291-303.

Marshall, W. A., & Turner, J. M. (1970). Variations in the patterns of pubertal changes in boys. *Archives of Disease in Childhood, 45,* 13-22.

Meyer-Bahlburg, H. F. L., Bruder, G. E., Feldman, J. F., Ehrhardt, A. A., Healey, J. M., & Bell, J. (1985). Cognitive abilities and hemispheric lateralization in females following idiopathic precocious puberty. *Developmental Psychology, 21,* 878-887.

Newcombe, N., & Bandura, M. M. (1983). Effect of age at puberty on spatial ability in girls: A question of mechanism. *Developmental Psychology, 19,* 215-224.

Petersen, A. C. (1976). Physical androgyny and cognitive functioning in adolescence. *Developmental Psychology, 12,* 524-533.

Ray, W. J., Newcombe, N., Semon, J., & Cole, P. M. (1981). Spatial abilities, sex differences and EEG functioning. *Neuropsychologia, 19,* 719-722.

Rierdan, J., & Koff, E. (1984). Age at menarche and cognitive functioning. *Bulletin of the Psychonomic Society, 22,* 174-176.

Rovet, J. (1983). Cognitive and neuropsychological test performance of persons with abnormalities of adolescent development: A test of Waber's hypothesis. *Child Development, 54,* 941-950.

Sanders, B., & Soares, M. P. (1986). Sexual maturation and spatial ability in college students. *Developmental Psychology, 22,* 199-203.

Sidtis, J. J. (1981). The complex tone test: Implications for the assessment of auditory laterality effects. *Neuropsychologia, 19,* 103-112.

Strauss, E., & Kinsbourne, M. (1981). Does age of menarche affect the ultimate level of verbal and spatial skills? *Cortex, 17,* 323-326.

Tanner, J. M. (1962). *Growth at adolescence* (2nd ed.). Oxford, England: Blackwell.

Tanner, J. M. (1978). *Fetus into man: Physical growth from conception to maturity.* Cambridge, MA: Harvard University Press.

Vandenberg, S. G., & Kuse, A. R. (1978). Mental rotations: A group test of three-dimensional spatial visualizations. *Perceptual and Motor Skills, 47,* 599-604.

Waber, D. P. (1976). Sex differences in cognition: A function of maturation rate? *Science, 192,* 572-574.

Waber, D. P. (1977). Sex differences in mental abilities, hemispheric lateralization, and rate of physical growth at adolescence. *Developmental Psychology, 13,* 29-38.

Waber, D. P., Bauermeister, M., Cohen, C., Ferber, R., & Wolff, P. H. (1981). Behavioral correlates of physical and neuromotor maturity in adolescents. *Psychobiology, 14,* 513-522.

Waber, D. P., Mann, M. B., Merola, J., & Moylan, P. M. (1985). Physical maturation rate and cognitive performance in early adolescence: A longitudinal examination. *Developmental Psychology, 21,* 666-681.

Witelson, S. F. (1977). Early hemisphere specialization and interhemisphere plasticity: An empirical and theoretical review. In F. A. Gruber & S. J. Segalowitz (Eds.), *Language development and neurological theory* (pp. 213-287). New York: Academic.

Part IV
Maturation and Motor Development

A Craniofacial Growth Maturity Gradient for Males and Females Between 4 and 16 Years of Age

PETER H. BUSCHANG, ROBERT M. BAUME, AND G. GISELA NASS
Department of Orthodontics, School of Dental Medicine, University of Connecticut Health Center, Farmington, Connecticut 06032 (P.H.B., R.M.B.) and University of Maryland, Far East Division, F.P.O. San Francisco 96651 (G.G.N.)

KEY WORDS   Craniofacial, Maturity, Growth, Gradient

ABSTRACT   Differential growth of the craniofacial complex implies variation in ontogenetic patterns of development. This investigation quantifies the relative maturity—as defined by percent adult status—of nine cephalometric dimensions and stature. Analysis is based on 663 lateral cephalograms from a mixed longitudinal sample of 26 males and 25 females between 4 and 16 years of age. Graphic comparison of maturity status across the age range shows that variation is intergraded between the neural and somatic growth maturity patterns, as described by head height and stature, respectively. The maturity gradient moves from head height through anterior cranial base, posterior cranial base and maxillary length, upper facial height, corpus length, and ramus height to stature. After 9 years of age ramus height is less mature than stature. Anterior maxillary and mandibular heights diminish during transitional dentition and thereafter exhibit maturity patterns that compare to corpus length. Although females are consistently more mature than males, the gradient of variation between dimensions is sex independent.

Developmental gradients imply a continuous range of variation in activity and thereby reveal systematization (Weiss, 1969). Initially applied to studies of regeneration and reconstitution (Child, 1915), the gradient concept has been extended to growth and maturation. Embryologically established, axial patterns of development are described by the anteroposterior, dorsoventral, and mediolateral gradients (Arey, 1954). Secondary gradients show ontogenetic coordination within specific anatomical regions and/or tissues. Human growth maturity gradients are defined for the extremities and trunk, and regions of the brain (Tanner, 1962). They provide one means of further understanding growth's organization (Tanner, 1978).

The ontogenetic organization of the craniofacial complex remains poorly understood. Thus far, attempts toward simplification have applied Scammon's typology (1930) for organ growth, relating craniofacial growth and maturity to either the skeletal or neural curve. Based on the presence or absence of the adolescent growth spurt, it is accepted that the splanchnocranium and neurocranium follow the skeletal and neural growth curves, respectively; cranial base is considered a composite of neural and skeletal growth (Nanda, 1955). Dichotomization of craniofacial growth patterns is an oversimplification. Baughan and coworkers (1979) have recently identified three distinct skeletal growth patterns: a cranial pattern for the cranial vault and base, a facial pattern for the maxilla and mandible, and a general pattern for the long bones of the body. Moving from the cranial to the general type of pattern, component parts exhibit greater relative growth and more intense pubertal spurts. Although categorized for descriptive purposes, a continuous pattern of relative growth between facial dimensions is suggested.

Assuming a continuous pattern of variation in relative growth, a craniofacial maturity gradient is implied. The less-mature dimensions would be expected to grow relatively the most.

Received October 15, 1982; accepted March 1, 1983.

P.H. BUSCHANG, R.M. BAUME, AND G.G. NASS

To examine whether craniofacial dimensions follow discrete or continuous patterns of variation in maturity, this investigation describes and compares the percent adult craniofacial status of males and females between 4 and 16 years of age.

MATERIALS AND METHODS

The data for this analysis are derived from 663 cephalograms of 51 individuals, including 26 males and 25 females, taken by the Child Research Council, Denver, Colorado. All subjects were born in Denver and are of Northern European extraction. Socioeconomically, the sample may be described as upper middle-class. Subjects for this investigation were chosen on the basis of available examinations, including any cephalograms taken at roughly yearly intervals between 4 and 16 years of age, and an additional cephalogram representing adult status. For any subject a minimum of nine to a maximum of 13 cephalograms are available (mean = 11). Table 1 shows the sample size for males and females at each age. Since this was not an orthodontic study, occlusal relationships were not selected for. As evaluated by an experienced orthodontist, four of the 26 males (15.4%) and six of the 25 females (24.0%) are rated as Angle Class II. The remaining subjects are classified as Angle Class I.

Lateral head films were taken using conventional cephalometric procedures (McDowell, 1941; Nanda, 1956). This produces a 4% enlargement factor, for which no corrections were necessary in this analysis. Each of the radiographs was traced and digitized by a single technician. Where right and left images exist, the midline was followed. Eighteen landmarks were identified on each tracing from which digitized coordinates were read into a computer by means of a "Scriptographic" digitizer. Twelve of the 18 landmarks are including in this investigation. Their positions are shown in Figure 1 and they are defined as follows:

1. Sella (S): center of sella turcica as defined by inspection.
2. Basion (B): middle point of anterior edge of foramen magnum.
3. Nasion (N): most anterior point of the frontonasal suture.
4. Anterior nasal spine (ANS): most anterior point of the nasal spine.
5. Posterior nasal spine (PNS): most posterior point of the nasal spine.
6. Prosthion (Pr): lowest point on the bony septum between the upper central incisors.
7. Infradentale (In): highest point on the bony septum between the lower central incisors.
8. Gnathion (Gn): point where the curvature of the anterior mandible is confluent with the base.
9. Menton (M): lowest point on the symphyseal shadow.
10. Gonion (Go): point on the bone defined by the bisected angle formed by the tangent to the ramus and mandibular planes.
11. Articulare (Ar): intersection point of the dorsal edge of the mandibular ramus with the temporal bone.
12. Bregma (Br): highest point on the cranium as identified by the coronal suture.

The following measurements were derived from the 12 landmarks: basion-bregma (head height), sella-nasion (anterior cranial base), sella-basion (posterior cranial base), nasion-anterior nasal spine (upper facial height), anterior nasal spine-posterior nasal spine (maxillary length), anterior nasal spine-prosthion (ante-

TABLE 1. *Number of radiographs measured at each age from a longitudinal sample of 26 males and 25 females*

Males		Females	
Mean age	No.	Mean age	No.
4.6	13	4.7	13
5.5	17	5.6	21
6.5	21	6.6	24
7.5	25	7.6	21
8.5	21	8.6	24
9.5	26	9.6	25
10.5	27	10.6	24
11.5	24	11.6	22
12.5	25	12.5	17
13.5	23	13.6	22
14.6	15	14.5	15
15.5	11	15.1	13
22.4	27	21.0	25

Abbreviations

ANS, anterior nasal plane
Ar, articulare
B, basion
Br, bregma
Go, gonion
Gn, gnathion
In, infradentale
M, menton
N, nasion
PNS, posterior nasal plane
Pr, prosthion
S, sella

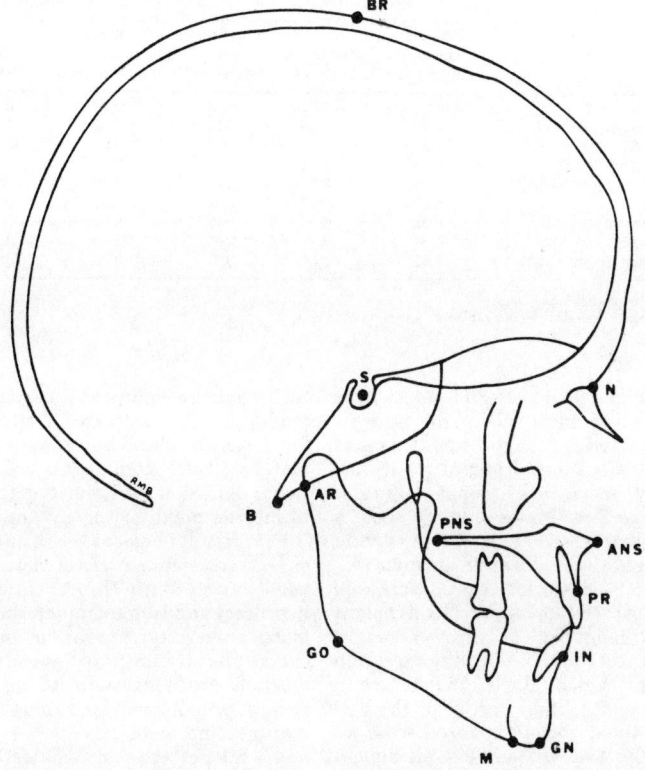

Fig. 1. Positions of cephalometric landmarks.

rior maxillary height), infradentale-menton (anterior mandibular height), gonion-gnathion (corpus length), and articulare-gonion (ramus height).

To increase the reliability of the cephalometric procedures, care was taken to reduce and identify the technical errors. Intraobserver error for tracing is greatest for maxillary length. Posterior nasal spine, gonion, and basion are the most difficult landmarks to identify (Table 2). Mean absolute differences of tracing replicates range from 0.51 mm to 1.43 mm; coefficients of variation show 1–2% error for most dimensions. Digitizing error—less than 0.6 mm or 1.5%—is small and consistent.

The sex-specific relative size of each dimension is computed as the percentage of adult status completed at each age. Percent adult status provides a maturity measure that effectively controls for differences in scale, allowing graphic comparison of patterns (Tanner, 1962). For purposes of comparison, it is assumed that head height and stature best represent the neural and skeletal growth maturity patterns, respectively.

RESULTS

Tables 3 and 4 present statistics describing the proportions of adult status completed by males and females between 4 and 16 years of age. Note should be taken of the sample size

TABLE 2. Intraexaminer replicate analysis

Measurement	Tracing error (n = 39)			Digitizing error (n = 37)		
	Mean absolute difference (mm)	Technical error[1]	Coefficient of variation[2]	Mean absolute difference (mm)	Technical error[1]	Coefficient of variation[2]
Anterior cranial base (S-N)	0.51	0.53	.008	0.28	0.27	.004
Posterior cranial base (S-B)	1.13	0.95	.023	0.32	0.48	.012
Upper facial height (N-ANS)	0.63	0.72	.015	0.23	0.24	.005
Maxillary length (ANS-PNS)	1.43	1.51	.031	0.25	0.28	.006
Anterior maxillary height (ANS-Pr)	0.66	0.61	.040	0.26	0.23	.015
Head height (B-Br)	1.12	0.97	.007	0.29	0.45	.003
Ramus height (Ar-Go)	1.02	1.04	.025	0.31	0.59	.015
Corpus length (Go-Gn)	0.94	0.91	.014	0.20	0.22	.003
Anterior mandibular height (In-Me)	0.62	0.58	.020	0.23	0.24	.009

[1]Technical error = $\sqrt{\text{mean difference}^2/2n}$.
[2]Coefficient of variation = technical error/mean size.

fluctuations at the youngest and oldest ages (Table 1). Absolute adult size of the nine dimensions, corrected for magnification, is provided for the estimation of immature status. Mean maturity scores are compared graphically in Figures 2–4. Males (Fig. 2) show a maturity gradient at 4.5 years of age moving from head height (91%), through anterior cranial base (86.5%), posterior cranial base and maxillary length (80%), upper facial height (73%), corpus length (70%), ramus height (66.5%), and stature (60%). With the exception of ramus height, which falls behind stature in maturity status after the ninth year, the pattern is maintained though reduced with increasing age. By 15.5 years of age all dimensions except ramus height have attained 96% to 99% of their adult size. Ramus height remains 90% complete, in part due to the unrepresentative sample size. Female dimensions show the same general maturity pattern (Fig. 3). Although the gradient between dimensions is comparable, females are more mature than males at all ages. There is also more overlap of pattern than observed for males. This might reflect technical error and/or sample size fluctuation. Nevertheless, the variation is minor and the general growth maturity gradient identified for males is preserved.

The relative adult status of anterior maxillary and mandibular heights are presented separately (Fig. 4) due to their decrease in relative size between 5 and 8 years of age. This represents smaller absolute size. Anterior maxillary height, having attained over 100% of its adult size at 5.5 years of age, decreases to approximately 80% in both males and females with the replacement of deciduous by permanent dentition. Subsequently, the maturity pattern compares to corpus length of the mandible. The decrease in adult proportions for anterior mandibular height is approximately 5% for both sexes. Following transitional dentition its maturity pattern compares to anterior maxillary height and corpus length.

For most dimensions the results show a more or less consistent pattern of maturation through adolescence. With the exception of anterior maxillary and mandibular heights, yearly maturation rates appear to maintain or decrease slightly until adolescence, when accelerations are suggested. Adolescent acceleration is pronounced for ramus height, which matures approximately 7% per year for males and 7.5% per year for females. The timing of the acceleration compares to statural growth, which shows an increase of about 5% per year during adolescence.

DISCUSSION

As described by traditional cephalometric measures, the total pattern of craniofacial maturity intergrades between the neural and skeletal patterns. Delineation of such descrete categories would be arbitrary. The gradient identified is consistent for both males and females. This is in agreement with Goldstein's (1936) anthropometric analysis of relative craniofacial growth, in which it was also shown that the graded range of variation is dependent upon anatomical location and axis of orientation. Goldstein's comparable data also show a similar range and pattern of variation. Similarly, the radiographic evaluation of relative facial growth of French-Canadian females (Baughan et al., 1979) is comparable in most instances. Ramus height (by 4–5%) and anterior cranial base (by 1–2%) are systematically

TABLE 3. Means (M) and standard deviations (sd) for relative adult proportions and adult size of males

Age	Stature M	sd	S-N M	sd	S-B M	sd	N-ANS M	sd	ANS-PNS M	sd	ANS-Pr M	sd	B-Br M	sd	Ar-Go M	sd	Go-Gn M	sd	In-Me M	sd
4.6	.60	.015	.86	.024	.78	.059	.73	.039	.80	.103	.98	.162	.91	.016	.66	.052	.70	.028	.80	.040
5.5	.63	.018	.87	.034	.81	.057	.75	.038	.81	.113	1.01	.141	.92	.019	.67	.049	.74	.025	.81	.054
6.5	.67	.016	.88	.026	.84	.048	.79	.042	.84	.115	.93	.164	.93	.018	.70	.046	.76	.032	.76	.056
7.5	.70	.018	.89	.026	.85	.055	.81	.041	.84	.076	.82	.185	.94	.017	.74	.038	.78	.029	.75	.051
8.5	.74	.017	.91	.027	.87	.048	.84	.045	.89	.100	.80	.093	.95	.018	.75	.045	.81	.027	.78	.059
9.5	.76	.018	.92	.029	.89	.051	.86	.046	.88	.106	.83	.083	.96	.016	.76	.038	.83	.030	.80	.051
10.5	.79	.021	.93	.024	.90	.049	.88	.046	.90	.099	.86	.088	.96	.013	.77	.048	.85	.037	.83	.049
11.5	.82	.022	.94	.026	.92	.050	.90	.042	.93	.110	.88	.077	.97	.016	.79	.043	.86	.033	.84	.051
12.5	.85	.027	.95	.023	.94	.043	.91	.038	.92	.097	.90	.062	.97	.014	.80	.048	.88	.033	.86	.043
13.5	.89	.037	.96	.029	.95	.053	.94	.039	.95	.097	.93	.082	.98	.016	.83	.048	.90	.049	.89	.045
14.6	.94	.037	.97	.025	.97	.035	.97	.027	.99	.086	.94	.065	.99	.015	.90	.060	.94	.045	.94	.038
15.5	.96	.033	.97	.031	.99	.033	.98	.044	1.01	.098	.95	.058	.99	.010	.90	.059	.97	.041	.94	.065
Adult[1] size	180.68	5.772	71.30	3.629	45.00	3.618	54.20	3.711	52.70	4.580	17.40	3.118	144.30	4.370	52.10	3.651	77.50	3.450	33.30	2.681

[1]Stature in cm, craniofacial dimensions (corrected for magnification) in mm.

TABLE 4. Means (M) and standard deviations (sd) for relative adult proportions and adult size of females

Age	Stature M	sd	S-N M	sd	S-B M	sd	N-ANS M	sd	ANS-PNS M	sd	ANS-Pr M	sd	B-Br M	sd	Ar-Go M	sd	Go-Gn M	sd	In-Me M	sd
4.7	.64	.020	.87	.025	.84	.053	.74	.049	.80	.078	1.00	.086	.93	.020	.71	.055	.76	.029	.87	.034
5.6	.68	.019	.89	.021	.85	.046	.80	.039	.85	.084	1.01	.093	.94	.014	.75	.072	.80	.030	.86	.085
6.6	.72	.021	.91	.023	.89	.054	.84	.042	.88	.085	.89	.187	.95	.013	.78	.053	.82	.037	.81	.061
7.6	.76	.019	.92	.020	.92	.045	.87	.046	.90	.088	.81	.176	.96	.011	.79	.051	.85	.027	.82	.054
8.6	.79	.024	.94	.017	.93	.053	.88	.049	.92	.090	.82	.066	.97	.015	.82	.055	.87	.034	.84	.044
9.6	.83	.029	.95	.019	.94	.048	.90	.048	.94	.099	.85	.065	.97	.014	.83	.051	.89	.028	.86	.046
10.6	.86	.032	.96	.017	.96	.040	.93	.042	.95	.083	.89	.066	.98	.020	.85	.043	.91	.030	.89	.047
11.6	.90	.030	.97	.019	.97	.045	.94	.041	.96	.087	.89	.077	.98	.014	.87	.047	.94	.029	.91	.048
12.5	.92	.031	.98	.019	.99	.037	.96	.034	.94	.065	.92	.072	.99	.015	.88	.049	.95	.026	.93	.037
13.6	.97	.023	.99	.021	.99	.053	.97	.041	1.02	.086	.96	.063	.99	.016	.96	.062	.97	.033	.95	.038
14.5	.98	.011	1.00	.018	1.00	.040	1.00	.029	1.01	.041	.94	.051	1.00	.012	.96	.042	.98	.018	.97	.034
15.1	.99	.007	.99	.010	1.00	.026	.99	.035	1.02	.076	.96	.051	1.00	.007	.97	.034	.99	.022	.99	.037
Adult[1] Size	169.85	5.501	66.30	2.915	42.00	2.338	49.60	2.674	47.20	4.364	15.90	2.200	137.00	3.963	45.60	3.623	71.50	5.057	29.20	2.037

[1]Stature in cm, craniofacial dimensions (corrected for magnification) in mm.

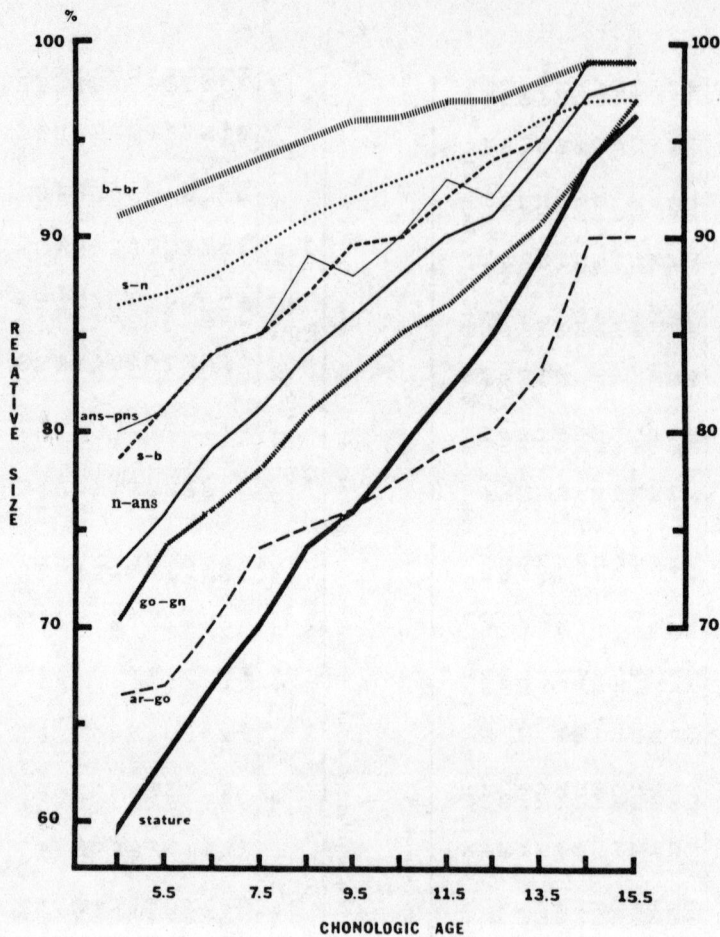

Fig. 2. Percent adult status of seven craniofacial dimensions and stature for males.

more mature in the French-Canadian sample. The variation in ramus height is due to the use of age 15 as the standard for relative size comparisons. Denver females have achieved only 97% of their adult ramus height at 15 years of age, suggesting a 3% underestimation for the French-Canadians. The other measures, having completed 99–100% of their adult status by 15 years of age, are comparable. Our results verify that the pattern of facial growth is intermediate between the neural and skeletal patterns (Baughan et al., 1979) and substantiate the intergraded nature of the variation.

The growth maturity gradient described provides quantitative support for prevailing conceptions of craniofacial development. It reflects the differential growth of the craniofacial complex; the greatest relative growth is expected for the mandible, followed by the maxilla, upper face, cranial base, and head height. Since the craniofacial complex shows negative allometry with total body size increase (Buschang et al., 1982), the more mature dimensions

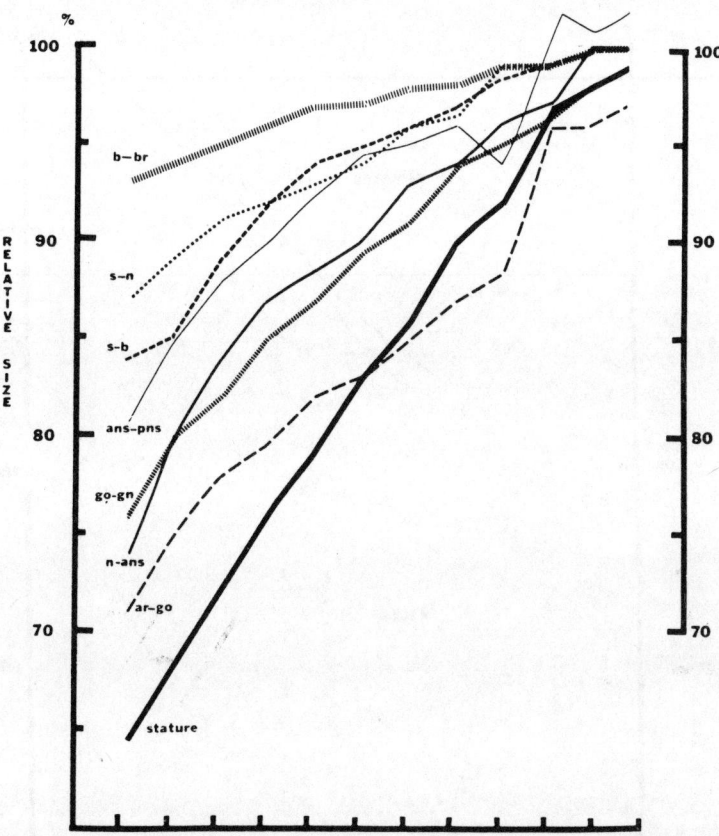

Fig. 3. Percent adult status of seven craniofacial dimensions and stature for females.

growing relatively the least show the greatest proportional reduction. Thus, the face apparently undergoes an unfolding process with growth (Hellman, 1935). Statistical descriptions of relative facial growth (Baughan et al., 1979; Goldstein, 1936), as well as the early graphic comparisons (Holl, 1898; Welcker, 1866), substantiate a differential pattern of growth and maturity.

As originally conceived, the gradient concept applies to centers of developmental activity or growth fields, suggesting operative physiological agents (Child, 1915; Tanner, 1962) or less specific morphological potentials (Waddington, 1966). A variety of growth fields have been suggested for the craniofacial complex (Enlow, 1982; van der Klaauw, 1945). The functional capacity of the various fields establishes a "priority plan" which determines the patterns of relative growth and maturation of the facial regions and parts (Enlow, 1982). Variation in growth and maturity might be expected within and between growth fields. Moreover, conventional cephalometric measurements do not describe fields or functional spaces (Enlow and Moyers, 1971). They depend on landmarks chosen for convenience and practical utility. Given the potential number of functionally variable growth fields and the arbitrary nature of cephalometric description, a craniofacial growth

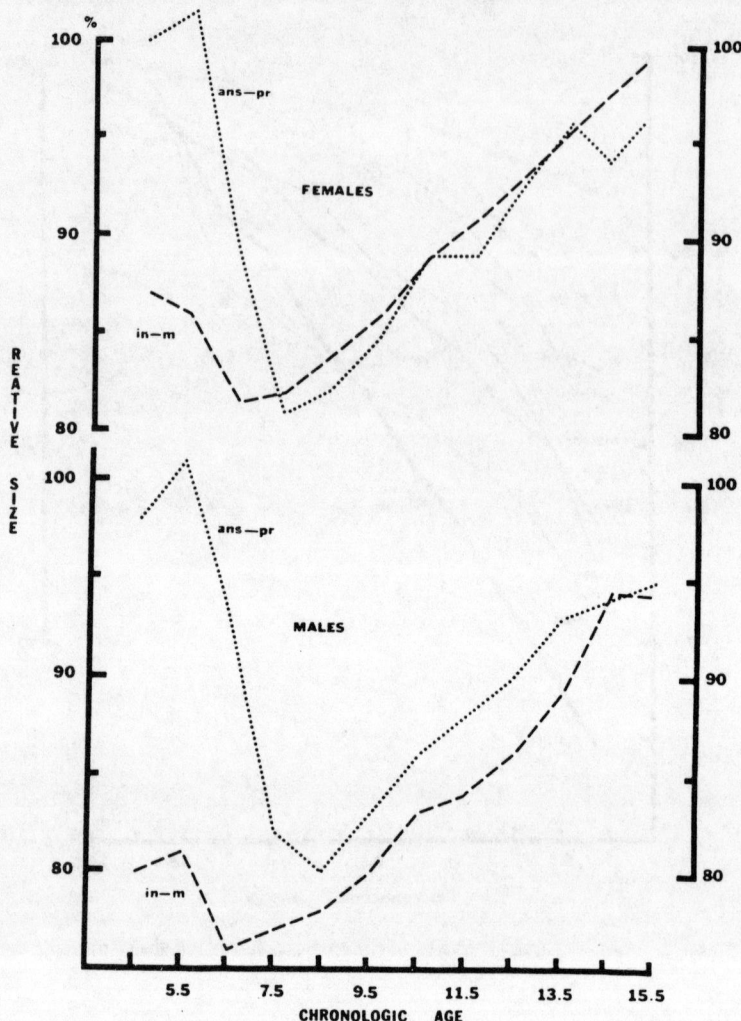

Fig. 4. Percent adult status of maxillary (ANS-pr) and mandibular (In-Me) heights for males and females.

maturity gradient might be expected. It describes the statistical intergradation of the various parts. As expressed by van der Klaauw (1945), craniofacial form performs many functions which inevitably results in compromise.

ACKNOWLEDGMENTS

This research is supported by NIDR grant #T-32-DEO7047. We extend our thanks to Dr. Sam Weinstein for his constructive comments and to Dr. Robert W. McCammon for use of the Denver material. The cephalograms were traced by Nicholas Bellintoni and digitized by Dr. Bruce Goldin.

LITERATURE CITED

Arey, LB (1954) Developmental Anatomy. Philadelphia: W. B. Saunders.

Baughan, B, Demirjian, A, Levesque, GY, and Lampalme-Chaput, L (1979) The pattern of facial growth before and during puberty, as shown by French-Canadian girls. Ann. Hum. Biol. 6:59–76.

Buschang, PH, Baume, RM, and Nass, GG (1982) Relative maturity and size increase of nine craniofacial dimensions during growth. Am. J. Phys. Anthropol. 57:174.

Child, CM (1915) Individuality in Organisms. Chicago: University of Chicago Press.

Enlow, DH (1982) Handbook of Facial Growth, 2nd Ed. Philadelphia: W. B. Saunders.

Enlow, DH, and Moyers, RE (1971) Growth and architecture of the face. J. Am. Dent. Assoc. 82:763–774.

Goldstein, MS (1936) Changes in dimensions and form of the face and head with age. Am. J. Phys. Anthropol. 22:37–89.

Hellman, M (1935) The face in its developmental career. Dent. Cosmos 77:685–699, 777–787.

Holl, M (1898) Über gesichsbildung. Mitt. Anthropol. Ges. Wien 28:57–100.

Klaauw, CJ van der (1945) Cerebral skull and facial skull: A contribution to the knowledge of skull structure. Arch. Neerl. Zool. 7:16–37.

McDowell, RM (1941) The use of lateral head radiographs for evaluating orthodontic results as distinguished from growth changes. Part I. Techniques and statement of problem. Am. J. Orthod. Oral Surg. 27:59–74.

Nanda, RS (1955) The rates of growth of several components measured from serial cephaometric roentgenograms. Am. J. Orthod. 41:658–673.

Nanda, RS (1956) Cephalometric study of the human face from serial roentgenograms. Ergebnisse der Anatomie und Entwicklungs-geschichte 35:358–419.

Scammon, RE (1930) The measurement of the body in childhood. In JA Harris, CM Jackson, DG Patterson, and RE Scammon (eds): The Measurement of Man. Minneapolis: University of Minnesota Press.

Tanner, JM (1962) Growth at Adolescence. Oxford: Blackwell Scientific Publications.

Tanner, JM (1978) Fetus Into Man. Cambridge: Harvard University Press.

Waddington, CH (1966) Fields and Gradients. In M Locke (ed): Major problems in Developmental Biology. New York: Academic Press.

Weiss, P (1969) Principles of Development. New York: Hafner Publ. Co.

Welcker, H (1866) Kraniologische Mitteilungen. Arch. Anthropol. 1:89–160.

Growth in Head Size During Infancy: Implications for Sound Localization

Rachel K. Clifton
University of Massachusetts, Amherst

Marsha G. Clarkson
University of Massachusetts, Amherst

Jane Gwiazda and Joseph A. Bauer
Massachusetts Institute of Technology, Infant Vision Laboratory

Richard M. Held
Massachusetts Institute of Technology, Infant Vision Laboratory

We measured head circumference and interaural distance in infants between birth and 22 weeks of age. A small sample of preschool children and adults were measured for comparison over the life span. We used these data to calculate changing interaural time differences across ages. Large shifts in this important binaural cue suggest that an ongoing developmental process recalibrates the association between interaural time differences and spatial location. These new data confirmed the sex differences in head circumference described in the Berkeley Growth Study (Eichorn & Bailey, 1962) and found no secular trend in this measure in the 60 years since the earlier data were collected.

Growth of the head during gestation and early infancy is a significant index of normal development. Head circumference at birth reflects prenatal brain growth (Dekaban, 1970; Winick & Rosso, 1969), and postnatal patterns of growth have been related to neurological functioning and cognitive performance (Eckerman, Sturm, & Gross, 1985). Measurements of growth in head circumference from birth through adulthood have been obtained on several longitudinal samples. One of the best known is the Berkeley Growth Study (Eichorn & Bayley, 1962) in which measurements of head circumference were obtained at monthly intervals from birth through 1 year of age and at longer intervals thereafter to young adulthood. Head circumference increased an average of 21.8 cm between birth and 25 years of age, a 62% increase over birth measurements.

Increasing head size, especially during infancy when growth is most rapid, carries implications for perceptual functioning. Aslin, Pisoni, & Jusczyk (1983) suggested that infants' smaller heads may bias their sound localization toward higher frequencies and reduce the effectiveness of time cues, because the magnitude of interaural differences would be less. In terms of the visual system, Banks (1988) elaborated the need for recalibration because of growth of the eye and increasing interocular distance. He diagrammed the distortions produced in the visual field by ocular growth (Figure 3.5, p. 153, in Banks, 1988), noting that the optical projection of points in the visual field onto the retina changes dramatically from birth to adulthood. Such recalibration may also be required with regard to auditory localization, to the extent that the infant's map of auditory space is sufficiently fine-grained at an age when head size is still rapidly changing.

Although newborns orient their heads correctly to lateral sounds (Muir & Field, 1979), they may be making only a hemifield distinction (because responses are judged correct if the infant turns off midline in the direction of the sound). More precise localization has been measured, in studies of developmental changes in minimal audible angle (MAA), using threshold procedures to determine the smallest displacement of sound off midline that can be reliably detected. Three recent studies have yielded estimates for 6-month-old infants ranging from 19° (Ashmead, Clifton, & Perris, 1987) to 14.5° (Ashmead, LeRoy, Whalen, & Odom, 1987) and 12° (Morrongiello, 1988). The latter two studies reported progressive improvement in MAA with age: At 12 months infants' MAA was estimated at 9.4° (Ashmead, LeRoy, et al., 1987) and at 8° (Morrongiello, 1988). By 18 months infants' MAA reached 4° (Morrongiello, 1988), very close to adults' performance of 1° for broad-band sounds (Mills, 1972). Although we know of no data testing MAA under 5 months of age, Bundy (1980) demonstrated that 16-week-olds could detect a binaural intensity difference of 6 dB and a time difference of 300 μs, when these cues were independently manipulated over earphones. Eight-week-olds responded to the temporal cue but not the intensity cue; however, Clifton, Morrongiello, Kulig, and Dowd (1981) pointed out that lack of habituation in the younger group may have obscured their sensitivity to the intensity cue. These data, along with the MAA re-

---

This research was supported by Grants BNS 8304419 from the National Science Foundation and NS23771 from NIH to Rachel Clifton and Marsha Clarkson, by Grant MH 00332 from the National Institute of Mental Health to Rachel Clifton, and by Grant EY 01191 to Richard Held.

We thank Irina Swain for helping with data collection and William Dietz of the Department of Nutrition and Food Science at MIT for the loan of the anthropometer. We are very grateful to Daniel Ashmead for many discussions of the data and his valuable insights into interpretative issues. We greatly benefited by comments from Martin Banks and from anonymous reviewers on a draft of this article.

Correspondence concerning this article should be addressed to Rachel Clifton, Department of Psychology, University of Massachusetts, Amherst, Massachusetts 01003.

sults on older infants, lead one to conclude that (a) infants as young as 2 months show some sensitivity to binaural time differences and (b) precision in localization improves substantially during infancy, reaching near-adult levels by 18 months of age. Head circumference at 18 months averages 48.9 cm, compared with adult head circumference of 56.9 cm (Eichorn & Bayley, 1962). If a stable relation between binaural cues and spatial location is to be maintained, some recalibration appears to be necessary.

Before considering how changes in head size might affect binaural cues, let us briefly review how time and intensity differences at the ears are used in sound localization (for fuller presentations, see Aslin et al., 1983; Mills, 1972). Although numerous cues, both monaural and binaural, have been identified (Blauert, 1983; Lewis, 1983), interaural time differences (ITD) and interaural intensity differences (IID) have been studied most often. Sound presented off-midline arrives first at the "near" ear, producing a time-of-arrival difference between the ears. In addition, pure tones produce usable differences in phase at low frequencies. The head also acts as a sound shield, so that higher intensities are received by the near ear. The intensity drop at the "far" ear can be as high as 20 dB for high frequencies (Moore, 1982, p. 151). Neither ITD nor IID gives rise to unambiguous locations for a sound, because diffraction of sound around the head varies with frequency. For example, the same ITD may result from different azimuthal locations, depending on the frequency (see Figure 8 in Kuhn, 1977, and Figure 3 in Roth, Kochhar, & Hind, 1980). Likewise, the same IID is not unique to a particular location in space (Figures 6 and 7 in Kuhn, 1977). The exception to these ambiguities is sound from the midline, which produces an interaural time difference of zero. Recent neurophysiological evidence suggests that spatial mapping of sound localization takes frequency into account. Jenkins and Merzenich (1984) found that they could limit cats' sound localization deficits to narrow frequency bands if only the cortical areas representing those frequencies were lesioned. They concluded that "sound-location representation is organized by frequency channel in the auditory forebrain" (p. 819). Such cortical mapping of space in terms of frequency would be a powerful way to disambiguate the cues associated with ITD and IID. The developmental issue in this complex picture is how changing head size might affect the basic auditory input for this map.

There are few studies that have directly measured how auditory input changes as a function of age. Moore and Irvine (1979) measured IID in cats of three ages, 35 days, 97 days, and adult. Compared with the older age groups, the youngest kittens had their maximum IID at higher frequencies, particularly at greater lateral azimuths. The authors had predicted this, because the smaller head size was expected to raise the frequency at which head shadowing would begin to be a significant factor. Moore and Irvine (1979) discussed the problem of developmental changes in neural mechanisms that code IID, but did not resolve how this was accomplished. No comparable measurements have been made for ITD across ages, but excellent estimates can be made, on the basis of Woodworth's model (1938), using head circumference. In the present study we calculated ITDs between birth and adulthood in order to estimate the magnitude of change in binaural time differences to which the infant is exposed as a consequence of growth. We measured head circumference and interaural distance at short intervals between birth and 22 weeks of age, the period of most rapid postnatal growth. We also measured preschool children and adults in order to compare rates of growth for head circumference and interaural distance over the life span. This comparison may reveal whether changes in head shape produce more or less deviation from a sphere during early infancy compared with older ages.

Method

Subjects

Longitudinal sample. Twenty-three infants (14 boys and 9 girls) participating in a study of the development of binocular vision and binaural audition were measured at biweekly intervals from 8 to 22 weeks of age. Postterm ages are reported in this article: For example, an infant born after 38 weeks instead of the full 40 weeks' gestation and measured at 10 weeks after birth was considered to be 8 weeks old. All of the infants were born within 2.5 weeks before or after their due date. Infants were recruited through letters to parents whose names were obtained from central files of birth certificates in Cambridge, Massachusetts. Responses to the letters that resulted in participation in the study averaged 10%. Parents received $5 per visit as well as a bonus at the end of the study if they had maintained biweekly appointments.

Cross-sectional samples. We selected 28 healthy newborn infants (12 boys and 16 girls) from a well-baby nursery in Northampton, Massachusetts. All of these infants were born within 2 weeks before or after their due date (M gestation = 39.55 weeks). They were tested between 6 and 59 hours after birth (M = 28.41 hr). We tested 14 of these infants (7 boys and 7 girls) again in their homes 4 weeks later (M postterm age = 3.6 weeks).

Fourteen children (5 boys and 9 girls), 3 to 6 years of age (M = 4.7 years), and 12 adults (5 men and 7 women), 27 to 54 years of age (M = 39 years), also participated in the study.

Apparatus and Procedure

A plastic tape measure graduated in millimeters was used to measure head circumference of the 8- to 22-week-old longitudinal sample, the children, and the adults. Disposable, paper tape measures were used with neonates in the hospital. The tape measure was placed around the head, over the inion in the back and across the forehead in the front, and read to the nearest millimeter. For all subjects, interaural distance (IAD) was measured with a set of custom-built calipers. A 1-in. piece of hard plastic was shaped into a curve, one side of which contained a small plastic tip that fit comfortably on one tragus (the prominence in front of the external opening of the ear). A plastic bar calibrated in millimeters was attached to the other end of the curved plastic. This bar was fitted with a plastic tip on its inside end and could be moved toward the subject's head until the tip met the opposite tragus. These calipers were calibrated to an anthropometer (Martin Type, Model 104). We obtained the interaural distance data by fitting the calipers on the tragi and reading the distance between those points to the nearest millimeter.

Infants were measured while lying supine on a changing table or in a crib. The older children and adults were seated comfortably in a chair facing the experimenter. Jane Gwiazda, who was experienced in testing infants and children, made all measurements except for the newborn and 1-month data, which were obtained by Rachel Clifton and Marsha Clarkson.

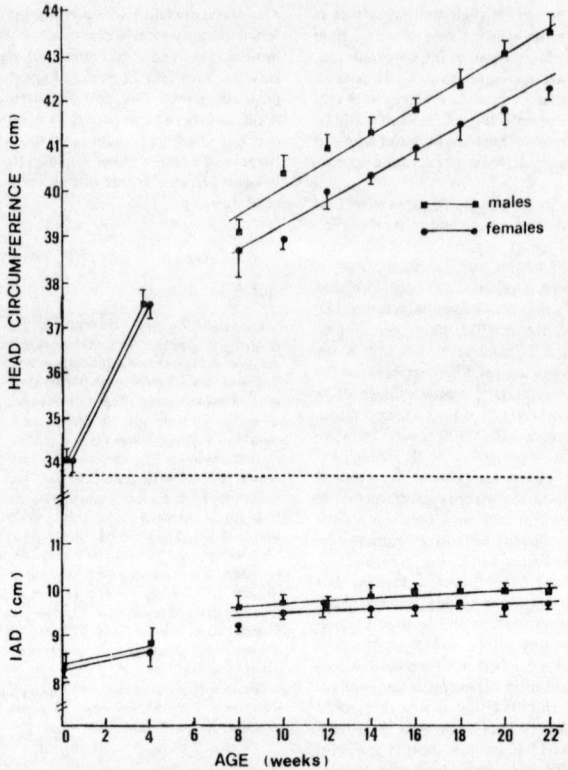

Figure 1. Head circumference and interaural distance for infants from birth to 22 weeks of age. (Data at birth and 1 month are from the infant cross-sectional sample; the remaining data points are from the longitudinal sample.)

Results and Discussion

Growth in Head Circumference and Interaural Distance

Head circumference (HC) data for infants are plotted in the top half of Figure 1. The most rapid period of growth was between birth and 1 month, a finding also reported in the Berkeley Growth Study (Eichorn & Bayley, 1962). The bottom half of Figure 1 displays IAD across age for these infants. The fastest rate of growth for this measure was also in the early weeks after birth, with IAD leveling off after 8 weeks.

The rate of growth was analyzed for the longitudinal sample measured between 8 and 22 weeks of age. Two questions were addressed in this analysis: Were there significant sex differences and was the rate of growth similar for the two measures of head size? We expected boys to have larger heads than girls, reflecting their greater birth weight and length (Tanner, 1970), but rate of growth could be similar for both sexes. An analysis of covariance (ANCOVA) for the comparison of the regression lines of IAD on age for boys and girls revealed that boys had a larger mean IAD, $F(1, 13) = 7.48$, $p < .05$, whereas the slopes of the regression lines (rate of growth) were not different for the two sexes (Snedecor & Cochran, 1967). A similar ANCOVA for comparing the regression lines of HC on age showed that boys had a larger mean HC, $F(1, 13) = 121.62$, $p < .001$. Again, the rate of growth of HC was not significantly different for boys and girls.

The second question concerning relative rate of growth for the two measures is related to changing head shape. If the head were a perfect sphere, HC and IAD would be related by π, that is, HC = π (IAD). The slope of the curve for IAD on age is 0.024, and the slope for HC on age is 0.26. An ANCOVA was performed to compare these slopes of the regression lines, with

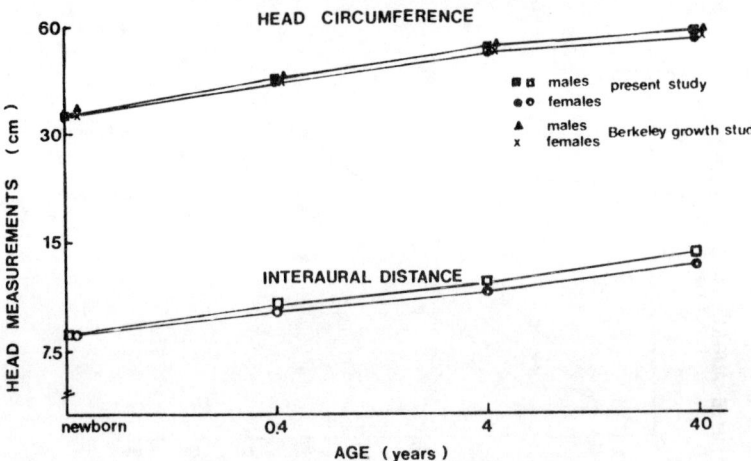

Figure 2. Head circumference and interaural distance from the newborn period to adulthood. (The Berkeley Growth Study data on HC are from Eichorn & Bayley, 1962, and are included for comparison with our samples.)

boys and girls combined. Results showed a significant difference between the rates of development of the two measurements, $F(1, 12) = 46.8$, $p < .01$: Head shape is changing so that the distance from forehead to inion is increasing at a faster rate than the distance between the ears.

Head circumference and IAD cross-sectional data from birth through adulthood are shown in Figure 2, plotted on a log-log scale. Comparisons across the life span deemphasize the first few weeks of rapid growth, so the rate of growth of HC is not significantly different from that of IAD in the birth-to-adult data. The points at 0.4 years are taken from the longitudinal data reported above. HC data from the Berkeley Growth Study (Eichorn & Bayley, 1962) are plotted at each age for comparison. Larger head size for boys was also present in this earlier study. The agreement between the HC measurements for infants and children in our data and the Berkeley Growth Study are noteworthy because 57 years separate the two data-collection periods. Infants in the Berkeley study were born in 1928–1929, whereas infants in our study were born in 1985–1986. Roche (1979) noted that secular trends in weight and height increases had leveled off for upper-socioeconomic groups during the period from the 1930s to 1960s, although they continued for less privileged groups. Our data indicate that head circumference, too, has shown no secular trend for approximately the past 60 years.

Implications of Head Growth for Changes in Sound Localization

The central implication of these data is the effect that changing head size may have on sound localization. As head size changes, ITDs also change. But how do these time differences translate into hypothetical spatial locations? A plot of theoretical interaural time differences for sound sources located between midline (0°) and 90° is shown for three ages in Figure 3. These calculations were based on Woodworth's (1938) classic formula in which the difference in path length at the two ears is derived from the following equation: $\Delta d = r(\Theta + \sin \Theta)$, where r is the radius of the head and Θ is the angle (in radians) at which sound is located. Dividing r by the speed of sound (34,000 cm/s, see Green, 1976, p. 202) gives the time of arrival difference. Thus, the equation for time of arrival difference at the ears is: $\Delta t = $ radius (in cm)$/34,000(\Theta + \sin \Theta)$. Woodworth's formula assumes a spherical head, so we calculated r from our measured head circumference at each age. If the actual interaural distance were used in the equation, head circumference would be substantially underestimated at *every* age and the calculated ITD would be too low. Actual measurements of time of arrival differences, using clicks, show excellent agreement with ITDs estimated using Woodworth's formula (Feddersen, Sandel, Teas, & Jeffress, 1957), a finding confirmed more recently by Kuhn (1977). These empirical confirmations of Woodworth's spherical model allow us to assume that the adult curve in Figure 3 is a good theoretical approximation of ITDs for clicks. The infant curves should also approximate their ITDs, because the ratio of interaural distance to head circumference remains virtually the same over the life span (see Figure 2).

A comparison of the curves in Figure 3 illustrates rather dramatically that increasing head size during infancy and childhood necessitates changing associations between a sound's spatial location in the horizontal plane and a particular interaural

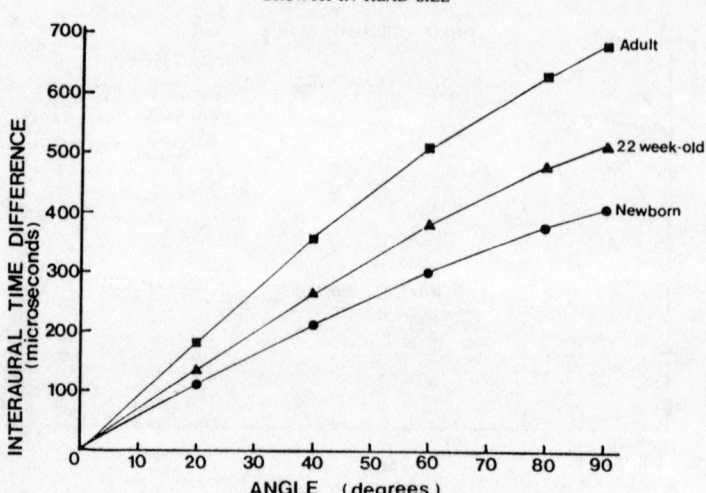

Figure 3. Estimates of interaural time differences for angles between midline and 90° horizontal eccentricity at three ages.

time difference. For example, an ITD of 411 μs may be produced by a sound source at 90° for the newborn, whereas this time difference would be produced by a sound source near 65° for the 22-week-old and 47° for the adult. This amount of change in ITD over the life span suggests that the child must update the map of auditory space through learned associations or some intrinsic adjustment throughout development.

What sort of evidence can be mustered in support of recalibration? Let us take an extreme view and postulate that no recalibration occurs during infancy. That is, imagine the adult's spatial map is prewired in the young organism and does not change from the adult curve shown in Figure 3. If that were true, one would predict that infants of 5 to 6 months of age would not accurately localize sounds beyond eccentricities of 60° to 70° because their maximum ITD of about 500 μs corresponds to this location in the adult. In other words, the infant's smaller head prevents auditory input of 660 μs from any location. Another prediction is that there would be a systematic tendency at all ages in infancy to underestimate (rather than overestimate) the eccentricity of the sound's location. The data needed to test these predictions are some measure of the organism's ability to identify a sound's spatial location. This is a different question from that posed by the MAA research referred to earlier, because MAA is detection of a *change* in location; the subject does not ever specify any particular location for the sound in this task.

Perrot, Ambarsoom, and Tucker (1987) argued that head orientation toward sound is a biologically relevant response in which the subject makes an absolute judgment about the sound's direction. Accurate head orientations would imply some sort of map, because the auditory input has been translated into an external spatial response system. How accurate are infants' head orientations when faced with an array of loudspeakers? Morrongiello (in press) presented infants between 6 and 18 months of age with loudspeakers located at 18°, 36°, 54°, 72°, and 90° in the horizontal plane. If no recalibration occurred, head turns toward the two extreme positions would show gross errors of underestimation, as suggested above. In fact, Morrongiello (in press) found that 6-month-olds did make some accurate head orientations toward sounds located at the extremes. Although error rates were greater for extreme positions, head orientations toward sounds at 72° and 90° were correct within 6° on 32% and 22% of trials, respectively (see Table 1, in Morrongiello, in press). Infants of all ages made more "overshoot" errors for sounds at 18° and 36° locations and more "undershoot" errors at the remaining locations. Neither finding supports the "no recalibration" hypothesis, therefore, the conservative conclusion is that recalibration is not refuted.

In fact, Morrongiello's pattern of errors fits adult data using the head orienting response. Perrot et al. (1987) asked adults to turn and face sounds from hidden loudspeakers at 10°, 30°, and 60°. Responses were very accurate at 10° and 30°, with a tendency toward overestimating the angle nearer midline. At 60° errors were large underestimates of the sound's position, with best performance averaging 7.7° misalignments for 500 Hz tones and 24.3° for 2000 Hz tones. Surprisingly, these adults performed more poorly than Morrongiello's infants. At the 54° location 18-month-olds were accurate within 6° on 92% of trials; at younger ages accuracy decreased so that 6-month-olds were correct on only 31% of trials (see Table 1 in Morrongiello, in press). The infants' superior head alignments may have been due to the sound of white noise bursts, which are easier to localize than the tone pulses used by Perrot et al. (1987).

The process by which the young organism adjusts its perceptual input to its sensory motor output has received a great deal of attention for the visual system (see Hirsch, 1985, for review), but much less is known about adjustments in the auditory system. Flexibility in spatial coding for sounds has been demonstrated in guinea pigs (Kelly, 1986) and owls (Knudsen and Knudsen, 1985) by measuring young animals' adjustment to ear blocks that decrease intensity in one ear relative to the other. For owls the role of vision proved critical in adjustment of auditory localization errors. Owls who had their eyes covered after earplug removal did not adjust their auditory errors. Knudsen and Knudsen (1985) also reported that adult owls maintained their auditory localization errors even with correct visual feedback. In this regard, humans may show more plasticity. Held (1955) showed that adults were able to make corrections for erroneous auditory input. He exposed adults to shifted ITDs by outfitting their heads with pseudophones, a device that substituted microphones for the outer ears to pick up environmental sounds, which were then fed to earphones. The microphones were mounted on a bar that could be rotated in relation to the interaural axis. By placing the left microphone in front of the left ear and the right microphone in back of the right ear, the aural axis was displaced by 22°. After 1 hr of exposure adults partially corrected the errors in localization induced by the experience. Held emphasized the role of translational head movements in adapting to the displaced localization. This work revealed the plasticity still available to adults and suggested mechanisms by which the infant may be able to adjust to changing binaural input. Gray and Jahrsdoefer (1986) tested patients with congenital aural atresia (absence of external ear canal and abnormal middle-ear ossicles) before and after surgery was performed to restore hearing in the damaged ear. Binaural tasks involving localization of single-source and precedence-effect sounds revealed that younger patients improved more following surgery than older patients, particularly on the precedence effect. These data, although supporting the plasticity found by Held, place limits on changes in binaural functioning when new auditory input becomes available.

In summary, increasing head size during infancy and childhood presents the child with a potential problem of maintaining accurate sound localization in the face of changing ITDs. Because head growth occurs slowly, increasing ITDs would be accompanied by rich visual and sensorimotor experience. Ample opportunities to correct errors would be present in the everyday environment. Thus, there is no reason to postulate that children with normal binaural hearing would experience difficulties in sound localization because of changing auditory input. Rather, these considerations offer a striking example of the nervous system's plasticity, which enables developing organisms to solve sensorimotor problems associated with physical growth.

References

Ashmead, D. H., Clifton, R. K., & Perris, E. E. (1987). Precision of auditory localization in human infants. *Developmental Psychology, 23,* 641–647.

Ashmead, D. H., LeRoy, D., Whalen, T., & Odom, R. (1987, April) *Precision of horizontal auditory localization.* Paper presented at the biennial meetings of the Society for Research in Child Development, Baltimore, MD.

Aslin, R., Pisoni, D., & Jusczyk, P. (1983) Auditory development and speech perception in infancy. In P. H. Mussen (Series Ed.) and M. M. Haith & J. J. Campos (Vol. Eds.), *Handbook of child psychology* (4th ed., Vol. 2, pp. 573–687). New York: Wiley.

Banks, M. S. (1988) Visual recalibration and the development of contrast and optical flow perception. In A. Yonas (Ed.), *The Minnesota Symposia on Child Psychology* (Vol. 20, pp. 145–196). Hillsdale, NJ: Erlbaum.

Blauert, J. (1983). *Spatial hearing.* Cambridge, MA: MIT Press.

Bundy, R. (1980) Discrimination of sound localization in young infants. *Child Development, 51,* 292–294.

Clifton, R. K., Morrongiello, B. A., Kulig, J. W., & Dowd, J. M. (1981) Developmental changes in auditory localization in infancy. In R. Aslin, J. Alberts, & M. Petersen (Eds.), *The development of perception: Psychobiological perspectives: Vol. 1. Audition, somatic perception, and the chemical senses* (pp. 141–160). New York: Academic Press.

Dekaban, A. (1970) *Neurology of early childhood,* New York: Williams & Wilkins.

Eckerman, C. O., Sturm, L. A., & Gross, S. J. (1985) Different developmental courses for very-low-birthweight infants differing in early head growth. *Developmental Psychology, 21,* 813–827.

Eichorn, D. H., & Bayley, N. (1962) Growth in head circumference from birth through young adulthood. *Child Development, 33,* 257–271.

Feddersen, W. E., Sandel, T. T., Teas, D. C., & Jeffress, L. A. (1957). Localization of high frequency tones. *Journal of Acoustical Society of America, 29,* 988–991.

Gray, L. C., & Jarhsdoefer, R. A. (1986) Effects of congenital aural atresia on the ability to localize sounds. *Otolaryngology Head and Neck Surgery, 94*(August Special Issue), 46.

Green, D. (1976) *An introduction to hearing.* Hillsdale, New Jersey: Erlbaum.

Held, R. (1955) Shifts in binaural localization after prolonged exposures to atypical combinations of stimuli. *The American Journal of Psychology, 68,* 526–548.

Hirsch, H. V. B. (1985) The tunable seer: Activity-dependent development of vision. In E. M. Blass (Ed.), *Handbook of behavioral neurobiology* (Vol. 8., pp. 237–295). New York: Plenum.

Jenkins, W. M., & Merzenich, M. M. (1984) Role of cat primary auditory cortex for sound-localization behavior. *Journal of Neurophysiology, 52,* 819–847.

Kelly, J. B. (1986) The development of sound localization of auditory processing in mammals. In R. N. Aslin (Ed.), *Advances in neural and behavioral development* (Vol. 2, pp. 202–234). Norwood, NJ: Ablex.

Knudsen, E. I., & Knudsen, P. F. (1985) Vision guides the adjustment of auditory localization in young barn owls. *Science, 230,* 545–548.

Kuhn, G. F. (1977) Model for the interaural time differences in the azimuthal plane. *Journal of Acoustical Society of America, 62,* 157–167.

Lewis, B. (1983) Directional cues for auditory localization. In B. Lewis (Ed.), *Bioacoustics: A comparative approach* (pp. 233–257). New York: Academic Press.

Mills, A. W. (1972) Auditory localization. In J. V. Tobias (Ed.), *Foundations of modern auditory theory* (Vol. 2, pp. 301–348). New York: Academic Press.

Moore, B. C. J. (1982) *An introduction to the psychology of hearing.* New York: Academic Press.

Moore, D. R., & Irvine, D. R. F. (1979) A developmental study of the sound pressure transformation by the head of the cat. *Acta Otolaryngologica, 87,* 434–440.

Morrongiello, B. A. (1988) Infants' localization of sounds along the horizontal axis: Estimates of minimal audible angle. *Developmental Psychology, 24*, 8–13.

Morrongiello, B. A. (in press) Infants' localization of sounds along two spatial dimensions: Horizontal and vertical axes. *Infant Behavior and Development.*

Muir, D., & Field, J. (1979) Newborn infants orient to sounds. *Child Development, 50*, 431–436.

Perrot, D. R., Ambarsoom, H., & Tucker, J. (1987) Changes in head position as a measure of auditory localization performance: Auditory psychomotor coordination under monaural and binaural listening conditions. *Journal of the Acoustical Society of America, 82*, 1637–1645.

Roche, A. F. (1979) Secular trends in human growth, maturation, and development, *Monographs of the Society for Research in Child Development, 44* (Serial No. 179, pp. 3–27).

Roth, G. L., Kochhar, R. K., & Hind, J. E. (1980) Interaural time differences: Implications regarding the neurophysiology of sound localization. *Journal of the Acoustical Society of America, 68*, 1643–1651.

Snedecor, G. W., & Cochran, W. G. (1967) *Statistical methods* (6th ed., pp. 432–435). Ames, IA: Iowa State University Press.

Tanner, J. M. (1970) Physical growth. In P. H. Mussen (Ed.), *Carmichael's manual of child psychology* (3rd ed., pp. 77–155). New York: Wiley.

Winick, M., & Rosso, P. (1969) Head circumference and cellular growth of the brain in normal and marasmic children. *Journal of Pediatrics, 74*, 774–778.

Woodworth, R. S. (1938). *Experimental psychology.* New York: Holt.

Received July 2, 1987
Revision received January 13, 1988
Accepted January 20, 1988 ■

Gender Differences Across Age in Motor Performance: A Meta-Analysis

Jerry R. Thomas
Departments of Physical Education
and Psychology
Louisiana State University

Karen E. French
Department of Physical Education
Louisiana State University

A meta-analysis was conducted to examine gender differences in motor performance during childhood and adolescence. Data were 64 studies yielding 702 effect sizes based on 31,444 subjects. Age was regressed on effect size, and the relation was significant for 12 of 20 tasks. Several types of age-related curves were found; the curve for a throwing task was the most distinctive. Five of the tasks followed a typical curve of gender differences across age. For eight tasks, gender differences were not related to age, and effect sizes were small. Results are discussed relating the development of gender differences to biological and environmental sources.

Across the childhood and adolescent years, gender differences have been reported in performance for many motor tasks. A typical description is one in which female and male performance differences are slight but favor males in early childhood. Performance rapidly accelerates linearly across childhood, with boys maintaining a slight but increasing advantage. At puberty, female performance levels off, whereas male performance continues to improve and may even accelerate.

How large are gender differences in motor performance? Can their rate of development be estimated from literature that are basically cross-sectional in nature? If a description of one or more gender difference curves across age is developed, can the sources of the differences be inferred from descriptive data? The purpose of this article is to evaluate by meta-analysis the gender differences in motor performance across childhood and adolescence and to suggest possible sources of the differences. The obvious potential sources of explanation are biology, environment, and their interaction.

Anastasi (1981) indicated that to progress from merely describing sex differences to explaining them the function of heredity and environment (nature–nurture, biology–culture) had to be considered. For example, she suggested that the biological acceleration of girls is the mechanism to explain girls' more rapid acquisition of language skills. Anastasi noted girls' physical acceleration, but seemed to imply that boys' advantage in gross motor skills during infancy and childhood has some biological basis (p. 198). Why would girls not perform gross motor skills more effectively than boys if they are physically and psychologically accelerated? Given the small size of the prepubertal gender differences in most motor performance tasks, are environmental factors a more likely source?

Why are Gender Differences in Motor Performance Present?

Biology

The physical characteristics of boys and girls are very similar prior to puberty. In fact, gender sameness rather than difference is a more appropriate descriptor of biological characteristics such as body type, body composition, strength, and limb lengths (Malina, 1984). Thus, biology seems to offer little explanation for motor performance differences prior to puberty.

Girls have their peak growth spurt approximately 2 years earlier than boys. Ultimately, this results in the termination of long bone growth earlier, which causes girls, on the average, to be shorter than boys (Espenschade &

Karen E. French is now at the Department of Physical Education, University of South Carolina, Columbia.

Requests for reprints should be sent to Jerry R. Thomas, School of Health, Physical Education, Recreation, and Dance, Louisiana State University, Baton Rouge, Louisiana 70803.

Eckert, 1980). Also, boys during and after puberty produce increasing amounts of testosterone, which is closely associated with increased muscle tissue. The ratio of muscle to fat is similar for boys and girls prepuberty. However, after puberty, this ratio remains approximately the same for females but doubles for males (Malina & Johnson, 1967). On the average, boys become taller and heavier than girls after puberty (National Center for Health Statistics, 1977). Boys have more lean body mass and less fat (Burmeister, 1965), greater arm and calf circumference (Roche & Malina, 1983), broader shoulders and narrower hips (Roche & Malina, 1983), and greater midarm muscle circumference and smaller triceps skinfold (Frisancho, 1981). Thus, in any motor task for which size and strength are an advantage, adolescent boys will have a biological advantage in performance when compared with adolescent girls because boys are larger and have more muscle.

Environment

An important potential source of environmental influence on gender differences in motor performance is the child's perception, which evolves over time, of the appropriate gender role (Greendorfer, 1980). In particular, the child's family, peers, teachers, and coaches are potential sources for learning a gender role regarding motor skill performance. The process of gender-role identification has been attributed to three sources: imitation, socialization, and self-socialization (Maccoby & Jacklin, 1974).

Several studies have reported that, during preschool years, both parents tend to emphasize the development of gross motor behavior in boys more than girls (for a brief review, see Maccoby & Jacklin, 1974, pp. 307–311). This included the fathers engaging in more rough play with boys and treating girls as more fragile. In particular, both parents (but especially fathers) reacted more negatively when boys chose to play with dolls than when girls chose "rough and tumble" games (Fling & Manosevitz, 1972; Lansky, 1967), a fact which seems pertinent to the development of gender differences in motor skills during early childhood. This early gender difference in motor performance may also be influenced by parents' subtle messages that gross motor activities and some types of toys are more appropriate for boys than girls (Fagot, 1978). Thus, the gender differences in motor performance that are present as children enter elementary school may be largely socialized by parents, either by subtle coercion or by the children modeling what is perceived as sex-appropriate behavior.

If Sherif and Rattray (1976) are correct, physical education teachers and coaches in organized sport programs have treated the gender differences in motor performance exhibited in early childhood as naturally evolving biological factors. Even professional organizations such as the American Alliance for Health, Physical Education, Recreation and Dance (AAPHER) may contribute to gender differences by publishing separate norms for elementary school boys and girls for their physical fitness tests (AAHPER, 1976). This may lead to different expectations for boys and girls by teachers, coaches, parents, and the children themselves. As previously suggested, these motor performance differences are generally not large by the time children enter kindergarten or first grade and are most likely created by social factors. The treatment of differences as natural and biological may serve to increase them in many motor performance tasks during the elementary school years. Greendorfer (1980) and Housner (1981) provided interesting reviews and speculations about the role of physical educators and coaches in the development of gender differences in motor performance.

At puberty, gender differences in motor performance appear to be influenced by both biological and environmental factors. Although we must acknowledge the importance of biological changes as being closely associated with increasingly larger gender differences in many motor performance tasks, environmental factors may assume even greater importance at and following puberty. Boys are expected to be more masculine and girls more feminine, whereas in prepuberty some "tomboy" type behavior may have been socially acceptable in girls (Maccoby & Jacklin, 1974). Because of social pressures to conform, girls may be less inclined to participate in athletic activities and less motivated to perform well on motor tasks they do attempt. Thus, true gender differences may be overestimated.

A summary suggests that prior to puberty most gender differences in motor performance are socially induced by parents, peers, teachers, and coaches, although differences are by no means uniform and may include some type of gender-related predisposition toward certain motor tasks (a view originally suggested by Maccoby & Jacklin, 1974, pp. 363-364, as a framework to evaluate sex differences in psychological factors). Even though environmental pressures may be greater after puberty, biology plays an important role in the development of gender differences in many motor performance tasks, specifically those for which size and force production are important.

Gender Difference Inferences

We believe that quantifying the gender differences across age levels from early childhood to late adolescence provides a basis for theorizing about environmental and biological causes of any observed differences. If gender differences are small (even though reliable) across early childhood but begin to increase during the elementary school years, environment seems the more likely cause. This is particularly true if a remedial program eliminates most of the gender differences. The basis for this explanation is the previously presented evidence that parents and peers influence the early development of motor skills around sex-role models. These differences may be viewed as natural by teachers and coaches, who continue to contribute to their gradual increase during the elementary school years.

Biological factors seem to be implicated if large gender differences are noted during early childhood, particularly if these differences can be corroborated by cross-cultural findings and are difficult to reduce by training. However, even differences in biology seem to be subject to environmental reinforcement and enhancement. This is evident when a large difference noted in early childhood continues to increase during the elementary school years.

The influence of biology may also be evident in many motor tasks at puberty when male performance accelerates while female performance levels off, especially if task performance is enhanced by increased strength and size. But more likely a biology–environment interaction is involved, as social pressures are intense to conform to the feminine or masculine sex role.

"For obvious ethical and practical reasons, research on human subjects cannot expose individuals to drastic and long-lasting variations in living conditions" (Anastasi, 1981, p. 188). Thus, we are forced to use relations found in large bodies of developmental data to infer cause–effect. This methodology is essentially the same as cross-cultural research; the source of the variation is simply vertical (across time) rather than horizontal (over cultures). However, the reader should be aware that these data are only correlational, making cause–effect conclusions tenuous.

Use of Meta-Analysis

Meta-analysis (Glass, McGaw, & Smith, 1981; Hedges & Olkin, 1985) offers an objective way to evaluate the large body of literature in which gender comparisons of motor performance are reported during childhood and adolescence. In many studies, motor performance may be measured in slightly different ways. For example, running speed may be tested over varying distances. If we express male–female differences in a standard metric (standard deviation units) effect size, these studies may be combined quantitatively in a meaningful way. Thus, running speed and its development can be analyzed as a concept rather than having to consider the individual measures of running speed.

Effect size provides a way of judging the size and meaningfulness of gender differences in motor performance. Because effect size is in standard deviation units, the size of the differences and degree of overlap between the distributions can be estimated. Cohen (1969) provided a means by which to judge effect sizes: 0.20 = small, 0.50 = medium, and 0.80 = large.

The use of meta-analysis eliminates two methodological problems. First, meta-analysis overcomes the problem (Jacklin, 1981) of doing regressions within gender and then inferring between-gender differences when predictors are entered in one gender's prediction equation but not the other. The differences between genders are directly calculated as effect sizes prior to regressing age and study characteristics on them. Second, meta-analysis allows the quantitative integration of a large number of cross-sectional and longitudinal studies of gender differences in motor performance. We believe that having a large number of effect sizes of gender differences in motor performance at a specific age provides the best available estimate for any true differences that may exist.

Thus, we believe that this meta-analysis of age-related changes in gender differences in motor performance provides the means to integrate and describe a large data set. In addition, it has considerable potential to further define theory about the development of sex differences, as well as to overcome some of the related methodological issues. In the following section, we have provided the details the reader needs for evaluating our work.

Method

Selection of the Data

Data were from studies that reported gender differences on motor performance during childhood and adolescence. Motor performance is defined as the outcome of movement (e.g., how fast a subject runs, how far a subject throws). In this study, motor performance was delimited to include (a) fundamental skills such as throwing, catching, running, striking, and jumping; (b) basic abilities such as balance and fine eye-motor coordination; (c) motor fitness items such as agility, arm strength, grip strength, flexibility, shuttle run, and sit-ups; and (d) information-processing responses such as reaction time, pursuit rotor tracking, and anticipation timing. The variables selected for study are those generally reported in studies and summaries in the motor-development literature (e.g., Corbin, 1980; Ridenour, 1978; Thomas, 1984; Wickstrom, 1983). Specifically excluded from the motor performance definition were cardiovascular fitness measures such as distance runs, step tests, and laboratory tests (treadmill walking and cycle ergometer riding).

Within the constraints of this definition of motor performance, a literature search was conducted using two computer bases—Educational Resources Information Center (ERIC) and PsycINFO. Health, Physical Education, and Recreation (HPER) Microform Publications (dissertations and theses) were searched by hand, as were eight journals identified as being likely to contain appropriate research reports: *Child Development, Developmental Psychology, Journal of Experimental Child Psychology, Journal of Human Movement Studies, Journal of Motor Behavior, Journal of Sport Psychology, Perceptual and Motor Skills,* and *Research Quarterly for Exercise and Sport*. The first study located was conducted in 1899, and the literature was searched through 1983.

From this search 176 studies were identified for initial consideration. Of these, 40 (23%) were from unpublished sources, mostly theses and dissertations. Only 64 (36%) of the studies could be included in the meta-analysis. (The Appendix provides citations for each of these articles.) Of the 112 (64%) studies excluded (a list can be obtained from the first author), 32 (18%) had collapsed the design and data across age levels of more than 3 years, 45 (26%) had used both girls and boys but had not provided specific information about gender ratios, 31 (18%) did not provide the minimal information necessary to calculate effect size, and 4 (2%) were eliminated because the tasks were dropped. To be included a study had to provide male–female comparisons within the childhood and adolescent years.

Data Coded From Each Study

Effect sizes (ESs) were calculated for all male–female comparisons at each age level for motor performance tasks reported. An ES was obtained for a given task at a specific age by subtracting the mean for girls from the mean for boys and dividing by the standard deviation (Glass et al., 1981; Hedges & Olkin, 1985). When the mean for boys represented better performance, the ES was positive. When the girls averaged a better performance, the ES was negative.

To calculate ES, a pooled estimate of the standard deviation (weighted for sample size) was used (Hedges & Olkin, 1985). When means and standard deviations were provided, these techniques were used to estimate ES. When complete data are not available, ES can be estimated given some minimal statistical information. These procedures were applied to estimate ES when possible (Glass et al., 1981; Hedges & Olkin, 1985).

A common practice in gender difference research is to collapse the design across gender if the test of gender is not significant. Frequently, when this is done neither the means and standard deviations nor F ratios are provided. The author could be contacted and asked to provide the information, but this technique has proved unsuccessful in the past (Hyde, 1981). The ES of interest could be discarded, but this tends to bias the data to studies reporting significant gender differences. Finally, an ES as 0 could be used because by definition the statistical test is evaluating the null hypothesis of no reliable difference between the means. The data reported are with 0 ES included because the difference with and without was trivial.

Some studies included boys and girls in the sample but did not test the gender effect or report means and standard deviations by gender. These articles were excluded because there is no way to estimate an ES.

Effect size is still a biased estimator when sample sizes are small. Hedges (1981) and Hedges and Olkin (1985) provided a correction factor for small ESs. This factor— $c = 1 - 3/\{4(n^m + n^f - 2) - 1\}$, where n^m = number of boys and n^f = number of girls—is multiplied by the ES, thereby correcting overestimation of ES with a small sample size. All ESs (now labeled ES') in this study were corrected for bias using this formula.

In addition to ES', omega-squared (ω^2) was calculated for each boy-girl comparison using the formula provided by Tolson (1980). The use of ω^2 allows an estimate of the percent of variance accounted for by gender in the dependent measure. Or ω^2 estimates how well a specific motor performance task can be predicted if the gender of the subject is known. Thomas and Nelson (1985) discussed the need for considering the magnitude of the difference

(ω^2) as well as the reliability (significance) of the difference.

Our major interest was to relate the ES' for gender differences in 20 motor performance tasks to age. However, five additional characteristics of each study were coded, and their relation to ES' was calculated.

1. *Internal validity* was coded as high, average, or low, using qualities of the study such as representativeness of the sample, quality of the motor performance test selected, and appropriateness of the measurement schedule.

2. *Gender of the first author* was used, based on literature suggesting that the gender of the experimenter is sometimes related to gender differences in motor performance (Rikli, 1976). This assumes that the first author is the experimenter, an assumption that may be incorrect in some instances. Thus, any relations found should be treated with caution.

3. *Type of manuscript* refers to published versus unpublished articles. Theses/dissertations were considered unpublished. If a thesis/dissertation was later published, it was coded as published and eliminated from the unpublished list.

4. *Year published* was coded as studies published before 1970 or 1970 and later. This date was selected because considerable change in sex roles occurred in the 1960s and 1970s (Anastasi, 1981, p. 202). More specifically, Title IX was passed in 1972. Thus, we wanted to see if changes in sex roles and opportunities were reflected in gender differences in motor performance.

5. *Number of male and female subjects in each study* was coded.

Characteristics of the Data

Sixty-four studies were included in the analysis. Several of the studies tested the subjects on more than one motor performance task: 16 studies had data on each subject for more than three motor tasks; 8 had three tasks; 14 had two tasks; and 26 had only one task. To some extent, when more than one measure is taken on each subject, task performance is correlated. However, these correlations are generally low for the tasks included, so we treated the tasks as if they were independent. We believe this is a valid assumption. The correlation of tests of the same characteristic (e.g., balance) are generally low (Johnson & Nelson, 1979). The specificity hypothesis (Henry, 1968) indicates that motor abilities are task specific, and that two similar tasks (e.g., throwing a football and a baseball) tend to have a correlation of zero. This is because the abilities underlying these tasks are different. Thus, correlations among different motor performance tasks (e.g., throwing and running) are expected to be low, and evidence generally supports this hypothesis (Schmidt, 1982, p. 401).

The 64 studies included 31,444 subjects of which 15,926 were boys and 15,518 were girls. Of the 64 studies included, 24 used fewer than 100 subjects, 33 used between 101 and 600 subjects, 6 used between 601 and 1,000 subjects, and 1 used more than 9,000 subjects. Several studies measured subjects on more than one motor performance task. Table 1 shows the number of measurements made for boys and girls by age level for the 64 studies.

Combining Effect Sizes

Hedges (1981) and Hedges and Olkin (1985) showed that, because of the way ES' is distributed, the variance (s^2) of each ES' can be calculated directly, and they provided the formula. From this formula, the observation can be made that the accuracy of ES' is a function of sample size and ES'. Because the accuracy varies with this function, each ES' should be weighted by the reciprocal of its variance prior to combining ES' (Hedges, 1982; Hedges & Olkin, 1983, 1985). Thus, studies based on larger samples should be more precise estimators of true gender differences and, therefore, are given greater weight in the averaging of ES'. An overall or weighted mean estimate can be obtained by the formula provided by Hedges and Olkin (1985). An estimate of the variance for the weighted mean ES' is obtained from the bottom half of the same formula. These formulas were used in combining and estimating the variance of the $\overline{ES'}$.

Results

We calculated the weighted mean of ES' for each gender comparison for all tasks. Then we examined the number of ES's for each task for all studies. When the number of studies was less than three, the task was eliminated, with one exception: Several tasks—hole punching, peg shifting, manual dexterity, tracing, and turning a screw (called speed prehension)—were combined and called fine eye–hand coordination. Table 2 lists those tasks that met the criteria for retention and those that were eliminated. Table 3 contains the number of measurements made on male and female subjects for each of the 20 tasks that were retained for the analysis.

Table 1
Number of Measurements for Boys and Girls by Age Level Included in the Meta-Analysis

Age (years)	No. for boys	No. for girls	Total
3	316	259	575
4	863	805	1,668
5	1,855	1,816	3,671
6	1,980	1,733	3,713
7	6,325	5,808	12,133
8	3,378	3,578	6,956
9	2,374	2,332	4,706
10	4,256	4,054	8,310
11	6,371	6,012	12,383
12	4,696	4,892	9,588
13	5,221	5,447	10,668
14	3,021	3,108	6,129
15	3,369	3,112	6,481
16	3,256	3,162	6,418
17	3,647	2,865	6,512
20	142	142	284
Totals	51,070	49,125	100,195

Table 2
Motor Performance Tasks Included and Excluded

Task	No. studies	No. ES's	Task	No. studies	No. ES's
Included			*Included (continued)*		
Agility	9	19	Throw velocity	5	13
Anticipation timing	3	23	Vertical jump	5	20
Arm hang	3	16	Wall volley	4	32
Balance	14	71	*Excluded*		
Catching	4	25			
Dash	19	82	Choice RT	2	10
Fine eye–hand	5	30	Dribble	1	2
Flexibility	5	13	8 choice RT	2	21
Grip strength	4	42	4 choice RT	2	21
Long jump	19	85	Free throw	1	4
Pursuit rotor	5	14	Hurdle jump	2	7
Reaction time	6	42	Leg torque	1	5
Shuttle run	7	33	Movement time	2	11
Sit-ups	7	36	Pull-ups	2	13
Tapping	4	34	Push-ups	2	7
Throw accuracy	5	14	Squat thrust	1	8
Throw distance	11	58	Striking	2	15
			2 choice RT	2	21

Note. RT = reaction time. Total number of studies included = 144; this is more than the total number of studies because some contained more than one task. Number of ES's for studies included = 702. Total number of studies excluded = 22. Total number of ES's for studies excluded = 145.

The first issue is to test if ES' has homogeneity within each task (Hedges & Olkin, 1985). This test (H statistic) is the total sum of squares tested as a χ^2 using the number of ES's minus 1 as the degree of freedom. This test was significant ($p < .05$) for 9 of the 20 tasks (balance, grip strength, shuttle run, throw for velocity, vertical jump, dash, long jump, sit-ups, and throw for distance). However, we hypothesized a priori that a major source of this lack of homogeneity would be the large age range in the data. Other possible sources of a lack of homogeneity are outliers and study characteristics. Therefore, we used a weighted regression as outlined by Hedges and Olkin (1983, 1985, chap. 8) to examine the correlation of ES' to age within each task. We allowed the fit of the regression line to be linear (age), quadratic (age^2), or cubic (age^3).

Tasks in Which Gender Differences in Motor Performance and Age Were Related

The first step was to identify which tasks had ES's for gender that were age related. Table 4 provides a summary of the regression statistics for the 12 tasks (out of 20) that correlated significantly with age. (The H statistic for these 12 tasks is the sum of the χ^2 for the regression plus the χ^2 for within tested against the sum of the degrees of freedom for each.)

Table 3
Number of Measurements by Gender for the 20 Motor Performance Tasks

Task	No. for boys	No. for girls	Total
Agility	1,869	1,643	3,512
Anticipation timing	303	433	736
Arm hang	268	234	502
Balance	2,269	2,122	4,391
Catching	742	698	1,440
Dash	8,191	7,830	16,021
Fine eye–hand	1,035	982	2,017
Flexibility	1,074	995	2,069
Grip strength	1,446	1,338	2,784
Long jump	9,406	8,953	18,359
Pursuit rotor	245	237	482
Reaction time	1,478	1,597	3,075
Shuttle run	5,953	5,714	11,667
Sit-ups	5,805	5,545	11,350
Tapping	759	706	1,465
Throw accuracy	688	624	1,312
Throw distance	7,754	7,558	15,312
Throw velocity	480	465	945
Vertical jump	384	423	807
Wall volley	921	1,028	1,949

Hedges and Olkin (1983, 1985) argued that the typical way of interpreting this regression is inappropriate. They indicated that the first step is to determine if the regression is significant by treating the sum of squares for the regression as a χ^2 with the degrees of freedom associated with the regression (model). Note in Table 4 that the column labeled χ^2_{reg} is this test with its associated degrees of freedom.

Once the regression is declared significant, a test should be made to determine if the model is correctly specified. "The test for model specification provides a basis for deciding whether the variation in effect magnitude is accounted for by the explanatory variables in the model" (Hedges & Olkin, 1983, p. 137). Hedges and Olkin (1983, 1985) indicated that the sum of squares for within (error) is the appropriate test of model specification.

This sum of squares is treated as a χ^2, with the degrees of freedom associated with the within factor (see Table 4, column labeled χ^2_{wi}). Note in Table 4 that we have placed the eight tasks (balance, catching, grip strength, pursuit rotor, shuttle run, tapping, throwing velocity, and vertical jump) where the model is correctly specified in the top part of the table and the four tasks (dash, long jump, sit-ups, and distance throw) where the model is incorrectly specified at the bottom of the table. The fact that the data do not fit the model means that the results should be viewed with caution.

As indicated by the data in Table 4, the line of best fit is linear (see column labeled Age where the top value is the beta and the bottom value is the z score of the beta, all corrected according to procedures indicated by Hedges & Olkin, 1985) for balance, pursuit rotor, tapping, throwing velocity, and throwing distance. The best fit was quadratic (column labeled Age^2) for catching, grip strength, shuttle run, vertical jump, dash, long jump, and sit-ups.

For the figures that follow, the weighted $\overline{ES}'$ is bounded by a 95% confidence interval for the 12 tasks in which gender differences are related to age. Clearly, throwing for either velocity or distance (Figure 1) is very different from the other 10 motor performance tasks. Boys exceed girls in throwing velocity by 1.5 standard deviation units as early as 4 to 7 years of age. This difference rapidly increases so that by 12 years of age (last age with sufficient data for a comparison) the boys' performance exceeds the girls' performance by 3.5 standard deviation units. Throwing for distance, which to a large extent is dependent on the velocity of the throw, follows a similar pattern. The boys exceed the girls by 1.5 standard deviation units as early as 2 to 4 years of age. The increase is linear through puberty to 17 years of age when male performance is 3 standard deviation units better than female performance. The weighted $\overline{ES}'$ collapsed over age is 1.98 standard deviation units for throwing velocity and 2.18 for throwing distance. These data indicate that there is very little overlap in the distribution of throwing performance for boys and girls.

Balance, pursuit rotor tracking, and tapping (Figure 2) seem to have similar patterns. Basically, the gender difference is zero until puberty (10 to 13 years of age) when the male performance becomes better than female performance: Weighted $\overline{ES}'$ for balance is about 1 standard deviation unit, about 0.75 for pursuit rotor tracking, and about 0.50 for tapping. However, when averaged across age, the weighted $\overline{ES}$'s are relatively small: 0.09 for balance, 0.11 for pursuit rotor tracking, and 0.13 for tapping.

Five of the remaining tasks follow what has become regarded as the typical pattern for a motor performance task across childhood and adolescence. The weighted $\overline{ES}$'s are slightly in favor of the boys in early childhood by 0.25 to 0.50 standard deviation units. This difference increases somewhat during middle childhood to 0.50 to 1.00 standard deviation units. The difference increases to between 1.00 and 2.00 standard deviation units after puberty. The tasks following this pattern are the dash and situps (Figure 3) and the long jump, grip strength, and shuttle run (Figure 4).

For the vertical jump (Figure 5) the weighted $\overline{ES}'$ is essentially zero until puberty, when it increases to more than 1 standard deviation unit in favor of boys. Catching (Figure 5) follows a U-shaped pattern; boys perform about 0.75 standard deviation units better than girls during preschool. Then the differences become smaller, dropping to 0.25 units until postpuberty, when they again go up to 0.75 units. We have no data points after 13 years of age.

The model was not correctly specified for the shuttle run (Table 4) until three additional variables were included to reduce the within-

Table 4
Age-Related Studies: Regression Summary for ES'

Task	No. studies	No. ES'	$\overline{ES'}$	χ^2_{reg}	χ^2_{wi}	Age	Age^2	Validity of study	Year pub.	Gender of 1st author	Type article
						Studies for which model is correctly specified					
Balance	14	67	0.09	42.9** 1 df	76.0 65 df	0.067** 6.55 z					
Catching	4	23	0.43	13.4** 2 df	15.6 20 df	−0.226* 1.96 z	0.019** 2.62 z				
Grip strength	4	37	0.66	78.4** 2 df	45.2 34 df	−0.419** 5.24 z	0.024** 6.43 z				
Pursuit rotor	5	14	0.11	5.0* 1 df	4.5 12 df	0.125* 2.23 z					
Shuttle run	7	28	0.32	673.4** 5 df	29.6 22 df	−0.002 0.034 z	0.006** 2.39 z	1.40** 14.22 z		−1.96** 9.40 z	1.91** 11.44 z
Tapping	4	34	0.13	11.0** 1 df	21.5 32 df	0.080** 3.31 z					
Throw velocity	5	12	2.18	42.2** 1 df	11.3 10 df	0.454** 6.49 z					
Vertical jump	5	20	0.18	62.3** 1 df	16.6 17 df	−0.607 1.95	0.042** 2.62				
						Studies for which model is incorrectly specified					
Dash	19	66	0.63	1061** 3 df	103** 62 df	−0.298** 8.42 z	0.021** 2.91 z				0.383** 7.42 z
Long jump	19	68	0.54	1212** 2 df	123** 65 df	−0.337** 4.95 z	0.023** 16.45 z				
Sit-ups	7	29	0.64	697** 4 df	79** 24 df	0.799** 2.87 z	−0.022** 4.89 z		−0.975** 10.0 z	−0.127** 5.80 z	
Throw distance	11	47	1.98	433** 1 df	87** 45 df	0.153** 20.8 z					

Note. ES = effect size. Year pub. = published before 1970 or not. Type article = published/unpublished article. z = z score.
* $p < .05$. ** $p < .01$.

sum of squares: the validity of the study (column labeled Validity in Table 4), gender of the first author, and type of article (published or unpublished). An interpretation of these characteristics is that larger weighted $\overline{ES}$'s for gender (better male performance) were associated

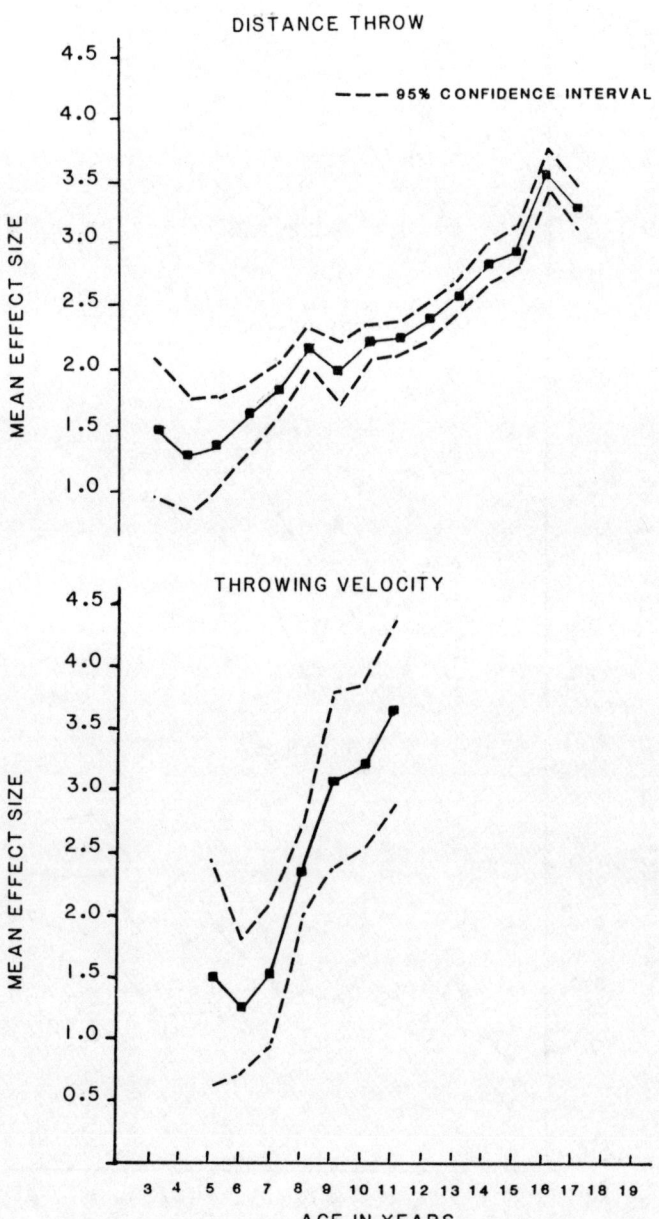

Figure 1. $\overline{ES'}$ by age and gender for throwing for velocity and distance.

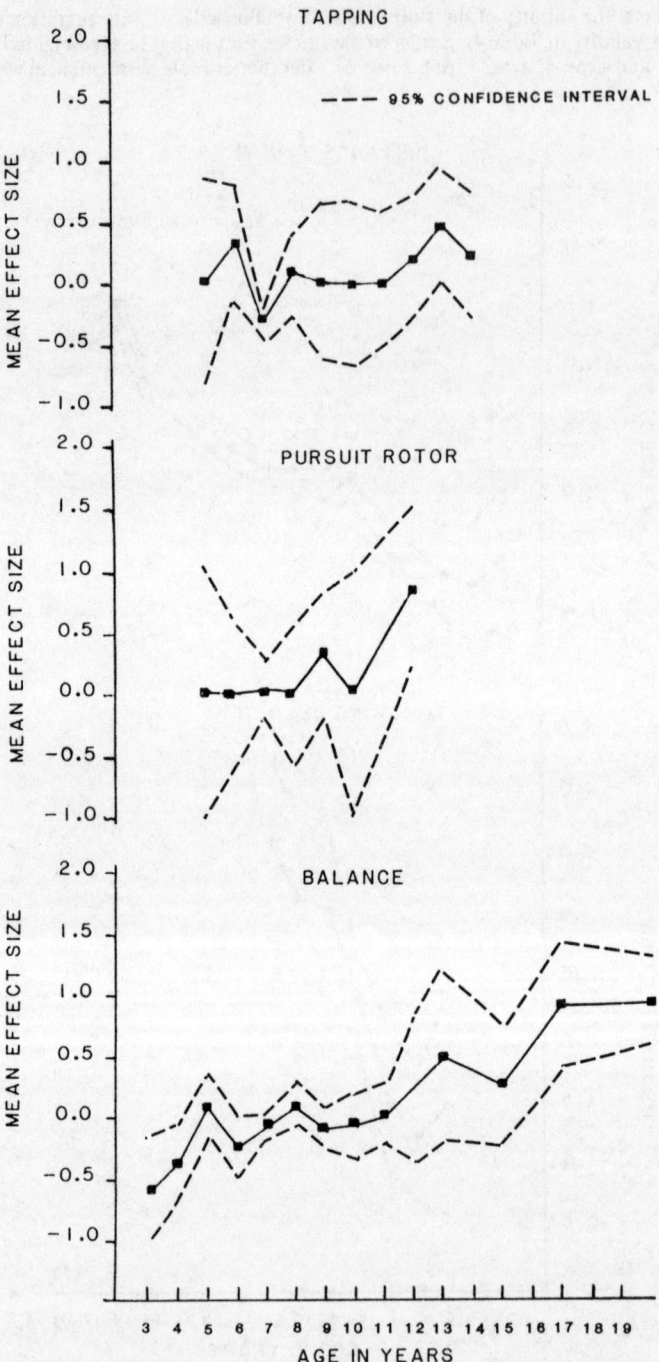

Figure 2. $\overline{\mathrm{ES}}'$ by age and gender for balance, pursuit rotor tracking, and tapping.

with studies published since 1970, having higher internal validity, and women as first author.

For the tasks in which the model was not correctly specified, a significant amount of variance was accounted for by some of the coded characteristics in addition to age. Sit-ups had larger weighted $\overline{ES}$'s associated with studies published before 1970 and studies in which women were first author. The dash had

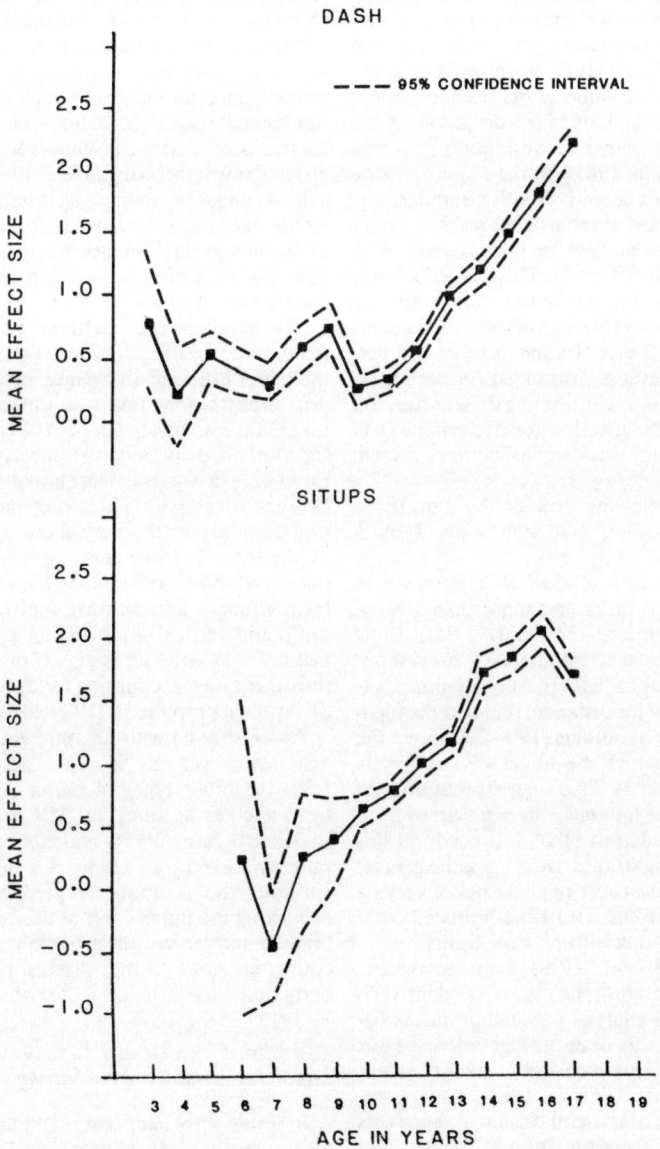

Figure 3. $\overline{ES'}$ by age and gender for dash and sit-ups

larger weighted $\overline{ES}$'s associated with published as opposed to unpublished articles.

In any data set, outliers (extreme and unrepresentative values) are likely to exist, even when data points are ES's rather than individual performances. Outliers are particularly likely in data sets including young children (Thomas, 1984). An appropriate way to test for outliers in a meta-analysis using regression is to output the residuals from the regression, take the absolute value of the residual, calculate the mean and standard deviation of the residuals, and change the residuals to z scores (Hedges & Olkin, 1985). By definition (because the mean of a z score is 0 with a standard deviation of 1) any standardized residual larger than 2 is an outlier because it falls outside 95% of the score distribution. This procedure was used to identify outliers in the age-related data set. The data in Table 4 have the outliers eliminated. Table 5 includes the number and percentages of outliers eliminated for each task. An upper limit of eliminating 20% of the data was set and the criterion for declaring a data point an outlier was established as a z score of 2.

Although allowing 20% of the data to be declared as outliers may seem high, Table 5 shows that half of the tasks (6 of 12) actually had less than 10% of the ES's eliminated as outliers, only 4 tasks had more than 15% of the ES's eliminated, and only 1 task (long jump) actually reached the 20% maximum. Note that the four tasks (dash, long jump, sit-ups, and throw for distance) that had the highest percentage of outliers (19%–20%) were the same four for which the model was incorrectly specified (Table 4). This suggests that ES's for gender for these four tasks are not derived from the same population of ES's. Procedural differences among studies using the same general tasks may be the cause (e.g., dashes of varying lengths and sit-ups with time limits as compared with sit-ups with no time limits).

Hedges and Olkin (1985) believed the use of omega-squared (ω^2) as the dependent variable in a meta-analysis was inappropriate because the direction of the gender difference was not specified. However, the procedure is not without precedent (Hyde, 1981), and we believe analyzing ω^2 is useful because it represents the strength of the association between gender and the various motor performance tasks. Table 6 has a summary of the results of a standard regression analysis of age on ω^2. We have included the 12 tasks that were related to age in the earlier analysis of the weighted ES'. This table provides data for each task in which ω^2s were significantly related to age in a linear (shuttle run, sit-ups, throwing distance, and throwing velocity) or quadratic (balance, catching, dash, grip strength, long jump, pursuit rotor, and vertical jump) manner, or in one instance (tapping) in which the task was not related to age. The ω^2 for gender accounted for the most variance (averaged across age levels) in the two throwing tasks: 51% in throwing velocity and 47% in throwing distance. In other words, at any age about one half of the variance in throwing performance between boys and girls can be estimated by knowing the performer's gender.

The developmental patterns for ω^2 are similar to those for ES'. Thus, we have not included them. For example, in balance, catching, dash, grip strength, long jump, sit-ups, and vertical jump, little variance ($\omega^2 < .10$) is accounted for until about puberty. At puberty, there is a rapid rise in variance accounted for with ω^2 between .20 and .65. Thus, knowing the gender of the subject postpuberty allows a reasonable prediction of performance, especially in speed (dash and shuttle run), strength and endurance (grip strength and sit-ups), and power (long jump and vertical jump) motor performance tasks. The shuttle run is slightly different from the other tasks, accounting for a great amount of variance prepuberty (10%–20%).

As we showed with ES', throwing for either distance or velocity is clearly very different from the other types of motor performance tasks. Gender accounts for 35% to 60% of the variance before puberty and 60% to 70% after puberty. Given that gender is a dichotomous variable, the postpuberty prediction is approaching the upper limit of this relation. For tapping and pursuit rotor tracking, gender accounts for none of the variance prior to puberty and very little ($\omega^2 < .15$) after puberty.

Tasks for Which Gender Differences in Motor Performance Were Not Age Related

In Table 7 the summary data are reported for the motor performance tasks (8 of 20) for which gender differences were not related to

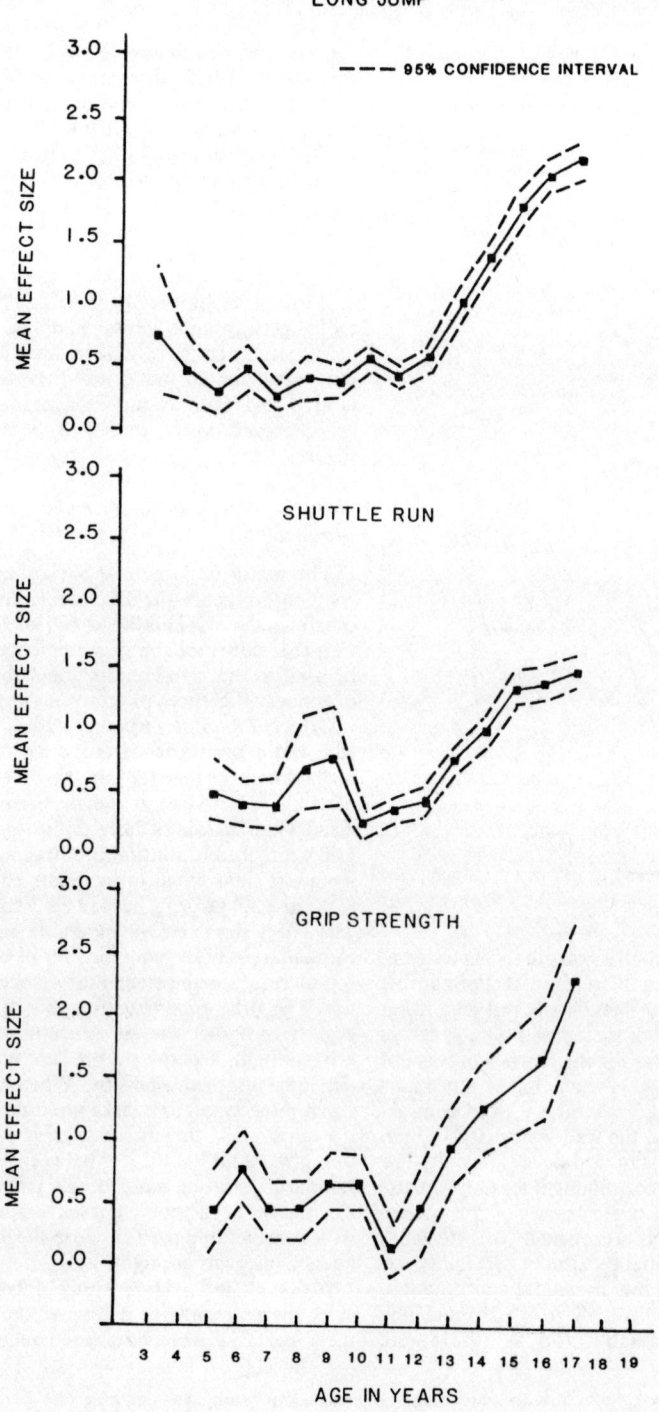

two tasks at which female performance was consistently better than male performance. The variance accounted for by gender in these five tasks was small ($\omega^2 < .08$). The arm hang showed no meaningful difference in $\overline{ES}'$ (0.01) or in variance accounted for ($\omega^2 = .01$).

Discussion

These data do not support the notion of uniform development of gender differences in motor performance across childhood and adolescence. Effect sizes were related to age in only 12 of the 20 (60%) motor performance tasks. These relations can be placed into several groups based on the shapes of the curves in Figures 1 to 5.

Tasks for Which Age and Gender Are Related

The major issue is how biology and environment influence the development of gender differences across childhood and adolescence. Can the nature of the developmental curves be used to make inferences about the causes of gender differences in motor performance?

Typical motor performance curve. If a typical motor performance curve exists (as described earlier) that reflects the development of gender differences, it is depicted in Figures 3 and 4 for the tasks of dash, sit-ups, long jump, grip strength, and shuttle run. In general these five tasks show small to moderate effect sizes (0.20 to 0.50) favoring boys in early childhood. The effect sizes remain moderate across the elementary school years for four of the tasks, but increase during elementary school for sit-ups. The girls, upon reaching puberty, appear slightly to reduce the difference on the dash, grip strength, and the shuttle run, but not in the long jump and sit-ups. When the boys reach puberty, all five tasks are influenced in the same way—they increase their advantage over girls rapidly until it is between 1.5 and 2 standard deviation units at 17 years of age. The nature of these five curves can be viewed with considerable trust because the 95% confidence intervals are tight.

Although girls on reaching puberty may close the performance difference on some of these five tasks, when boys reach puberty their

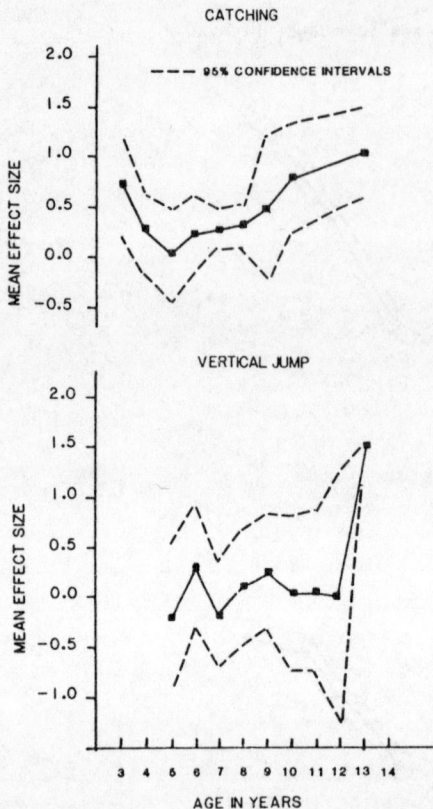

Figure 5. $\overline{ES}'$ by age and gender for vertical jump and catching.

age. The homogeneity statistic (H) is tested as a χ^2 with degrees of freedom as the number of ES's minus 1. The H was not significant ($p > .05$) for any of these tasks. The χ^2 test of the sum of squares for the regression was not significant ($p > .05$) for any of the 8 tasks.

The weighted $\overline{ES}'$ was large for throwing accuracy (0.96) and the wall volley (0.83), both being close to 1 standard deviation unit. The percent of variance accounted for (ω^2) by these two tasks was also the largest of this group. The weighted $\overline{ES}$'s were small (0.18 to 0.38) for agility, anticipation timing, flexibility, reaction time, and fine eye–hand coordination. Note that flexibility ($\overline{ES}' = -0.29$) and fine eye–motor coordination ($\overline{ES}' = -0.21$) were

Figure 4. $\overline{ES}'$ by age and gender for long jump, grip strength, and shuttle run.

Table 5
Number and Percentage of Outliers by Task

Task	No. studies	No. ES's	No. ES's lost as outliners	No. ES's kept	% of ES's lost
Balance	14	71	4	67	5.6
Catching	4	25	2	23	8.0
Dash	19	82	16	66	19.5
Grip strength	4	42	5	37	13.5
Long jump	19	85	17	68	20.0
Pursuit rotor	5	14	0	14	0.0
Shuttle run	7	33	5	28	15.0
Sit-ups	7	36	7	29	19.0
Tapping	4	34	0	34	0.0
Throw distance	11	58	11	47	19.0
Throw velocity	5	13	1	12	8.0
Vertical jump	5	20	0	20	0.0

increase in size and muscle tissue is dramatically reflected in better performance across all five tasks. The average performance of boys and girls of 2 standard deviation units apart at age 17 shows that there is little overlap between the two distributions. This is an expected finding for tasks in which speed, power, muscular strength, and endurance are important.

The differences prior to puberty are more moderate and, we believe, more likely to reflect environmental influences. When differences between the mean performances of boys and girls are less than 0.50 standard deviation units, many of the girls are performing better than many of the boys. If equal expectations, encouragement, and practice opportunities were provided by parents, teachers, and coaches, differences of this size could probably be eliminated. Opportunities and encouragement to practice may be the key issue; Halverson, Roberton, and Langendorfer (1982) reported that seventh-grade boys remembered practicing throwing more over the years than did seventh-grade girls.

Several authors (Greendorfer, 1980; Housner, 1981; Sherif & Rattray, 1976) suggested that teachers and coaches take as biological the gender differences evident in motor performance when children begin elementary school. The implication is that these differences are maintained or increased because teachers and coaches have different expectations for boys than for girls. Although these data cannot speak directly to expectations, the differences

Table 6
Summary Data for Regression Using ω^2

Task	Age	Age^2	$\bar{\omega}^2$	R^2
Balance	$F(1, 64) = 22.24**$	$F(1, 64) = 44.41**$	.03	.63
Catching	$F(1, 20) = 12.37**$	$F(1, 20) = 25.79**$	.05	.81
Dash	$F(1, 63) = 38.01**$	$F(1, 63) = 72.89**$	.10	.79
Grip strength	$F(1, 34) = 26.48**$	$F(1, 34) = 41.28**$	.10	.74
Long jump	$F(1, 65) = 73.63**$	$F(1, 65) = 127.19**$	.08	.81
Pursuit rotor	ns	$F(1, 11) = 7.38*$	.02	.70
Shuttle run	$F(1, 26) = 46.36**$	ns	.12	.64
Sit-ups	$F(1, 27) = 22.93**$	ns	.14	.46
Tapping	ns	ns	.01	.04
Throw distance	$F(1, 45) = 31.72**$	ns	.47	.41
Throw velocity	$F(1, 10) = 30.89**$	ns	.51	.75
Vertical jump	$F(1, 17) = 13.61**$	$F(1, 17) = 17.47**$	.03	.64

* $p < .05$. ** $p < .01$.

Table 7
Summary Data for Motor Performance Tasks Where Gender Differences Were Not Related to Age

Task	Age range (years)	No. ES's	No. studies	H[a]	$\overline{ES'}$	s^2	$\tilde{\omega}^2$
Agility	3–17	19	9	27.15	0.21	.0019	.04
Anticipation timing	7–20	23	3	18.43	0.38	.0066	.07
Arm hang	3–12	16	3	7.86	0.01	.0100	.01
Fine eye-motor	3–10	30	5	35.82	−0.21	.0022	.04
Flexibility	5–10	13	5	19.01	−0.29	.0023	.02
Reaction time	5–20	42	6	38.90	0.18	.0013	.02
Throw accuracy	6–11	14	5	12.81	0.96	.0041	.24
Wall volley	7–13	32	4	21.31	0.83	.0023	.15

[a]H statistic is treated as a χ^2 with df equal to the number of ES's − 1. None of these are significant at $p < .05$.

present in these five tasks when children begin elementary school are maintained or increased.

Other motor performance curves. A second group of tasks (Figure 2)—balance, pursuit rotor tracking, and tapping—is similar in nature. Gender differences are not present during the elementary school years but increase to a moderate level ($\overline{ES'} = 0.50$) favoring boys at about 11 to 12 years of age. In our opinion, this small an increase is more likely to reflect increasing environmental pressures rather than any biological factor related to puberty. These three tasks do not seem to be related to the strength, endurance, and size increases noted in boys at puberty. The finding is particularly interesting for balance because balance is a task in which girls have been reported as performing better than boys (Roberton, 1984). Although girls do have a slight advantage in early childhood (3 to 4 years of age), the gender difference is essentially zero until puberty, when male performance is moderately better.

The vertical jump (Figure 5) is similar to balance, pursuit rotor tracking, and tapping in that there are no gender differences until puberty. At puberty boys show a large increase in performance so that they are more than 1 standard deviation unit better than girls. The lack of prepuberty gender differences favoring boys is unexpected. We expected that vertical jump performance would be similar to performance in the long jump, dash, and the shuttle run as reported in previous reviews (DeOreo & Keogh, 1980; Espenschade & Eckert, 1974; Wickstrom, 1983). We are hesitant to offer an explanation for this unexpected result because the 95% confidence intervals are very large prior to puberty, indicating that effect sizes show large variations about the mean.

The curve for catching (Figure 5) is different from all the others. Boys' performance exceeds girls' performance in early childhood (3 years of age), but the differences are reduced to zero by 5 years of age. Boys' performance increasingly exceeds the girls' during elementary school until the difference is 1 standard deviation unit by age 13. These differences are likely environmental due to boys having more practice. The effect sizes are also likely to be underestimated because the ball is generally projected with little velocity in the tests reported.

In our opinion, any gender differences in performance prior to puberty on these 10 tasks (balance, catching, dash, grip strength, long jump, pursuit rotor tracking, shuttle run, sit-ups, tapping, and vertical jump) are mostly environmentally induced. The attitudes, expectations, and actions of parents, teachers, peers, and age-group coaches either produce or reinforce the differences. This is reflected by the increased opportunity and encouragement to practice these tasks afforded to boys. We believe that differences this small ($\overline{ES'} < 0.50$) could easily be eliminated if girls and boys were treated similarly.

Six tasks (dash, long jump, sit-ups, grip strength, shuttle run, and vertical jump) show postpuberty changes that are probably related to biological development, even though environmental factors continue to be important. Although equal encouragement and opportunity to practice would probably reduce gender differences after puberty, boys would still, on the average, perform better than girls. For balance, pursuit rotor tracking, and tapping, the biological changes associated with puberty do not seem to be the cause of the slight increase observed. We suspect that environmentally related variables such as competitive motivation and sex-role expectations that become increasingly significant for boys and girls create these differences. The differences in catching skills after puberty are probably not a good estimate of the true difference in sports in which the ball is projected with velocity (e.g., baseball, softball).

Throwing is different. Even a casual glance at Figure 1 indicates that throwing for velocity and distance are different from the other 10 tasks. The differences are 1.5 standard deviation units at 3 years of age. These differences increase substantially during the elementary school years. We only have data points through 12 years of age for throwing velocity, but the boys' throwing velocity is already between 3.5 and 4 standard deviation units higher than the girls'. The acceleration of gender differences is not so rapid for distance thrown but is above 2 standard deviation units at age 12 and above 3 standard deviation units after age 16. The 95% confidence intervals are moderately tight on throwing velocity and very tight on throwing for distance. Thus, we have considerable confidence in these developmental curves.

Although Maccoby and Jacklin (1974) discussed some differences in the treatment of boys and girls in early childhood, differences as large as 1.5 standard deviation units at age 3 are unlikely to be completely environmentally caused. A substantial amount of throwing practice for boys would be needed to produce a difference this large. However, the fact that this relatively large gender difference continues to increase in childhood and adolescence is probably a combination of biology and environment.

Malina (1984) reported that prepubescent boys have slightly more total lean body mass and less fat in both an absolute and relative sense than girls. In addition, sex differences in somatotypes during early childhood have been reported (Walker, 1962). Over 50% of girls have a larger endomorphic component in body type (as compared with ectomorphic and mesomorphic), whereas over 50% of boys have a larger mesomorphic component. Malina (1975) believed these sex differences were of genetic origin. These total body differences are also present specifically in the arm. Boys have a greater midarm circumference and a smaller triceps skinfold (i.e., more muscle tissue) than girls. Haubenstricker and Sapp (1980) reported that boys' forearms are 6 mm (on the average) longer than girls by 5.5 years, and that the differences continue throughout childhood. In addition, boys show an increasing advantage in late childhood in the biacromial/bicristal (shoulder/hip) ratio (Malina, 1984). Although each of these biological differences is small, taken together they may account for a portion of the gender difference in throwing performance. That biology is a factor in the differences is further confirmed by the fact that training in throwing has had little effect in reducing male-female performance differences in young children (Dusenberry, 1952; Halverson, Roberton, Safrit, & Roberts, 1977).

The increasing advantage boys gain over girls in throwing performance during elementary school is also partially attributable to environment. Both data (Halverson et al., 1982) and observation at playing fields indicate that elementary-age boys practice throwing skills much more than girls.

Thus, although gender differences in throwing velocity and throwing for distance can probably be reduced by providing equal encouragement and practice for girls, we believe that biological factors will not allow, on the average at least, their elimination. Therefore, prior to puberty, careful groupings by skill level should be made if boys and girls are to participate jointly in sports and skill drills in which throwing is important. This suggestion is reinforced by looking at the catching difference between boys and girls. The boys catch better during the elementary school years. The catching difference is most likely minimized by the low ball velocity reported in most tests of catching.

Of the 12 tasks that were age related, sports and skill drills involving throwing (or catching throws of high velocity) are the only ones for which biology appears to play an important role in the development of gender differences prior to puberty. Given the documented differences in expectations and treatment of boys and girls, the differences before puberty in the other 10 tasks are probably environmentally induced. After puberty, the importance of biology and environment are confounded in many motor tasks, but especially in tasks requiring size, strength and endurance, and power.

Tasks Where Differences Were Not Age Related

Effect sizes for gender in 8 of the 20 (40%) motor performance tasks were not related to age. Thus, performance on these tasks did not change in any systematic way across childhood and adolescence. The gender differences favored boys and were low (0.01 to 0.38) for four of the tasks: agility, anticipation timing, arm hang, and reaction time. The differences were low and favored girls for fine eye–motor coordination (−0.21) and flexibility (−0.29). We see little reason to suspect that any of these small differences have a biological basis. The only difference of any substantial size—anticipation timing ($\overline{ES}' = 0.38$)—is likely to be a result of boys, more often than girls, practicing sports (e.g., baseball, football) that require this skill.

The effect size of throwing for accuracy ($\overline{ES}' = 0.96$), even though large, probably reflects more practice by boys rather than any biological differences. The difference in male and female performance is not developmental. The nature of the tests for throwing accuracy (i.e., the performer is a short distance from the target) is such that throwing velocity is not a factor.

The wall volley (batting an inflated ball repeatedly against a wall with the hands) also has a large effect size favoring boys. We suspect this reflects greater amounts of practice for the boys as well as their advantage in anticipation timing skills.

We see little reason to suspect that gender differences in performance on any of these eight tasks reflect anything but environmental factors. If biology were involved in the differences, we would expect them to be larger, especially after puberty.

Tasks in Which Characteristics Coded From Studies Were Important

In 3 of the 12 tasks in which gender differences were related to age, effect sizes were also related to other characteristics coded about the study. Both the shuttle run and sit-ups were negatively related to the gender of the first author. Thus, effect sizes were larger (favored boys) when the first author was female. If, in fact, the first author and the experimenter are the same person (not always true), the finding is consistent with Rikli's (1976) report that experimenters of the opposite gender cause larger gender differences in motor performance for tasks in which more effort results in better performance.

Effect sizes in the shuttle run and the dash were both positively related to whether the article was published or not, being larger in those published. This finding may reflect journals' bias toward publishing articles in which differences are significant.

Effect sizes in the shuttle run were also positively related to the validity of the study; more valid studies showed larger differences favoring boys. Sit-ups were negatively related to the year published, indicating that differences were larger in studies published before 1970. This may reflect the increasing standardization of sit-up tests. Earlier tests involved the number of sit-ups the performer could do; more recent tests typically have either a time limit (usually 30 s to 60 s) or a maximum number (50 to 100). Thus, differences between boys and girls would be reduced in more recent tests.

Issues That Remain Unaddressed

There are a number of important points that we have not considered here. First, motor performance is only the outcome of the movement. Although the outcome reflects the movement process, it does not do so perfectly and does not describe this process. Even a casual observer notes that individuals may run or throw in different ways, yet obtain similar outcomes or, conversely, run or throw in similar ways and obtain different outcomes. Thus, whether the development of gender differences across age exists in the quality of the movement cannot be determined by this meta-analysis, although work has been done in this area (see Roberton, 1984, for a summary). Roberton (1982) suggested that the form of the movement was not different between girls and boys, just that girls lag behind boys in the development of "good" form. This suggests that the nature of the underlying motor control mechanisms do not differ by gender. Although this view is consistent with most of the motor performance tasks evaluated in this study (at least prior to puberty), it could be inconsistent with the large gender differences noted in throwing and in some of the other tasks after puberty.

A second point that remains unaddressed is the ethnicity and socioeconomic status of the subjects. We estimate that most subjects in the 64 studies included are white and of middle socioeconomic status. However, that information is not generally provided in the studies, particularly in the earlier ones. These issues may be of considerable importance because ethnic variation in rearing has been suggested as a factor in motor performance variation. Yet, ethnicity and socioeconomic status are confounded with gender in this report.

Third, the role of genetics (and its interaction with environment) cannot be evaluated from this data base. However, studies of twins and siblings suggest sex differences in the heritability of motor performance.

Last, an important issue is whether longitudinal and cross-sectional data points estimate gender differences in motor performance equally well at any given age. These data do not include enough longitudinal data points for any specific motor performance task to provide a fair test of this question. However, meta-analysis offers an interesting approach to this issue, if a task could be found in which a sufficient number of longitudinal and cross-sectional data points were available.

Conclusions

We believe the gender differences prior to puberty in 15 of the 20 tasks (agility, anticipation timing, arm hang, balance, dash, grip strength, fine eye–motor coordination, flexibility, long jump, pursuit rotor tracking, reaction time, shuttle run, sit-ups, tapping, vertical jump) studied are environmentally induced. This conclusion is based on the small effect sizes, usually less than 0.50 of a standard deviation unit, as well as documented observations that treatment, expectations, and practice opportunities differ by gender. If one single factor is of importance, it is that boys are involved in more competitive games than girls and generally participate in games of longer duration (Lever, 1976).

The effect sizes for 6 of the previously mentioned 15 tasks (dash, grip strength, long jump, shuttle run, sit-ups, vertical jump) show rapid increases at puberty that are probably associated with the increase in boys' size and strength. However, the same environmental variables discussed previously inflate these gender differences beyond biological explanations.

The differences in effect sizes for throwing (velocity or distance) seem to begin with biological differences (1.5 standard deviation units at 3 years of age), but are increased by more practice opportunities for boys. The effect size for throwing accuracy is also large and may have some biological basis. However, given that the throwing-accuracy tests usually require minimal force, we suspect this gender difference in performance is also the result of boys practicing more than girls.

These findings of gender differences in motor performance are generally consistent with recent theories about sex-role development. Robinson and Green (1981) suggested that both cognitive-developmental (Kohlberg & Ullian, 1974) and transcendence (Hefner, Rebecca, & Oleshansky, 1975) views of sex-role development indicate that early development is strongly influenced by parents and peers. As children enter elementary school, teachers, peers, and parents influence sex stereotyping. Finally, as adults, men and women choose the type of sex role that fits their natures. However, biology does appear to play a greater role in gender differences for throwing at all ages and postpuberty in tasks for which size, strength, and power are important. This at least limits complete choice postpuberty in cross-sex, high-level competition for sports involving size, strength, and power. We are not suggesting that women cannot become skillful performers in these types of sports, just that some levels of joint sport participation remain constrained by the biology of gender differences.

References

American Alliance for Health, Physical Education, Recreation and Dance. (1976). *Youth fitness test manual*. Washington, DC: Author.
Anastasi, A. (1981). Sex differences: Historical perspectives and methodological implications. *Developmental Review, 1*, 187–206.
Burmeister, W. (1965). Body cell mass as the basis of allometric growth functions. *Annales Paediatrici, 204*, 65–72.

Cohen, J. (1969). *Statistical power analysis for the behavioral sciences*. New York: Academic Press.

Corbin, C. B. (Ed.). (1980). *A textbook of motor development* (2nd ed.). Dubuque, IA: Brown.

DeOreo, K., & Keogh, J. (1980). Performance of fundamental motor tasks. In C. B. Corbin (Ed.), *A textbook of motor development* (2nd ed., pp. 76–91). Dubuque, IA: Brown.

Dusenberry, L. M. (1952). A study of the effects of training in ball throwing by children ages three to seven. *Research Quarterly, 23*, 9–14.

Espenschade, A., & Eckert, H. (1974). Motor development. In W. R. Johnson & E. R. Buskirk (Eds.), *Science and medicine in exercise and sport* (2nd ed., pp. 322–333). New York: Harper & Row.

Espenschade, A. S., & Eckert, H. M. (1980). *Motor development* (2nd ed.). Columbus, OH: Merrill.

Fagot, B. I. (1978). The influence of sex of child on parental reaction to toddler children. *Child Development, 49*, 459–465.

Fling, S., & Manosevitz, M. (1972). Sex typing in nursery school children's play interest. *Developmental Psychology, 7*, 146–152.

Frisancho, A. R. (1981). New norms of upper limb fat and muscle areas for assessment of nutritional status and weight. *American Journal of Clinical Nutrition, 34*, 2540–2545.

Glass, G. V., McGaw, B., & Smith, M. L. (1981). *Meta-analysis in social research*. Beverly Hills, CA: Sage.

Greendorfer, S. L. (1980). Gender differences in physical activity. *Motor Skills: Theory into Practice, 4*, 83–90.

Halverson, L. E., Roberton, M. A., & Langendorfer, S. (1982). Development of the overarm throw: Movement and ball velocity changes by seventh grade. *Research Quarterly for Exercise and Sport, 53*, 198–205.

Halverson, L. E., Roberton, M. A., Safrit, M. J., & Roberts, T. W. (1977). Effect of guided practice on overhand-throw ball velocities of kindergarten children. *Research Quarterly, 48*, 311–318.

Haubenstricker, J., & Sapp, M. (1980, April). *A longitudinal look at physical growth and motor performance: Implications for elementary and middle school activity programs*. Paper presented at the meeting of the American Alliance for Health, Physical Education, Recreation and Dance, Detroit, MI.

Hedges, L. V. (1981). Distribution theory for Glass's estimator of effect size and related estimators. *Journal of Educational Statistics, 6*, 107–128.

Hedges, L. V. (1982). Fitting categorical models to effect sizes from a series of experiments. *Journal of Educational Statistics, 7*, 119–137.

Hedges, L. V., & Olkin, I. (1983). Regression models in research synthesis. *American Statistician, 37*, 137–140.

Hedges, L. V., & Olkin, I. (1985). *Statistical methods for meta-analysis*. New York: Academic Press.

Hefner, R., Rebecca, M., & Oleshansky, B. (1975). Development of sex-role transcendence. *Human Development, 18*, 143–158.

Henry, F. M. (1968). Specificity vs. generality in learning motor skill. In R. C. Brown & G. S. Kenyon (Eds.), *Classical studies on physical activity* (pp. 328–331). Englewood Cliffs, NJ: Prentice-Hall.

Housner, L. D. (1981). Sex-role stereotyping: Implications for teaching elementary physical education. *Motor Skills: Theory into Practice, 5*, 107–116.

Hyde, J. S. (1981). How large are cognitive gender differences? A meta-analysis using ω^2 and d. *American Psychologist, 36*, 892–901.

Jacklin, C. N. (1981). Methodological issues in the study of sex-related differences. *Developmental Review, 1*, 266–273.

Johnson, B. L., & Nelson, J. K. (1979). *Practical measurement for evaluation in physical education* (3rd ed.). Minneapolis, MN: Burgess.

Kohlberg, L., & Ullian, D. Z. (1974). Stages in the development of psychosexual concepts and attitudes. In R. C. Friedman, R. M. Richart, & R. L. Vande Wiele (Eds.), *Sex differences in behavior* (pp. 209–222). New York: Wiley.

Lansky, L. M. (1967). The family structure also affects the model: Sex-role attitudes in parents of preschool children. *Merrill-Palmer Quarterly, 13*, 139–150.

Lever, J. (1976). Sex differences in the games children play. *Social Problems, 23*, 478–487.

Maccoby, E. E., & Jacklin, C. N. (1974). *The psychology of sex differences*. Stanford, CA: Stanford University Press.

Malina, R. M. (1975). *Growth and development: The first twenty years in man*. Minneapolis, MN: Burgess.

Malina, R. M. (1984). Physical growth and maturation. In J. R. Thomas (Ed.), *Motor development during childhood and adolescence* (pp. 2–26). Minneapolis, MN: Burgess.

Malina, R. M., & Johnson, F. E. (1967). Significance of age, sex, and maturity differences in upper arm composition. *Research Quarterly, 38*, 219–230.

National Center for Health Statistics. (1977). NCHS growth curves for children, birth–18 years, United States. *Vital and Health Statistics*, Series 11, No. 165.

Ridenour, M. V. (Ed.). (1978). *Motor development: Issues and applications*. Princeton, NJ: Princeton Book.

Rikli, R. (1976). Physical performance scores as a function of experimenter sex and experimenter bias. *Research Quarterly, 47*, 776–782.

Roberton, M. A. (1982). Describing "stages" within and across motor tasks. In J. A. S. Kelso & J. E. Clark (Eds.), *The development of movement control and coordination* (pp. 293–307). New York: Wiley.

Roberton, M. A. (1984). Changing motor patterns during childhood. In J. R. Thomas (Ed.), *Motor development during childhood and adolescence* (pp. 48–90). Minneapolis, MN: Burgess.

Robinson, B. E., & Green, M. G. (1981). Beyond androgyny: The emergence of sex-role transcendence as a theoretical construct. *Developmental Review, 1*, 247–265.

Roche, A. F., & Malina, R. M. (Eds.). (1983). *Manual of physical status and performance in childhood* (Vol. 1). New York: Plenum.

Schmidt, R. A. (1982). *Motor control and learning*. Champaign, IL: Human Kinetics.

Sherif, C. W., & Rattray, G. D. (1976). Psychological development and activity in middle childhood. In J. G. Albinson & G. M. Andrew (Eds.), *Child in sport and physical activity* (pp. 97–132). Baltimore: University Park.

Thomas, J. R. (Ed.). (1984). *Motor development during childhood and adolescence*. Minneapolis, MN: Burgess.

Thomas, J. R., & Nelson, J. K. (1985). *Introduction to research in HPERD*. Champaign, IL: Human Kinetics.

Tolson, H. (1980). An adjunct to statistical significance: ω^2. *Research Quarterly for Exercise and Sport, 51*, 580–584.

Walker, R. M. (1962). Body build and behavior in young children: I. Body build and nursery school teachers' ratings. *Monographs of the Society for Research in Child Development, 27* (3, Serial No. 34).

Wickstrom, R. L. (1983). *Fundamental motor patterns* (3rd ed.). Philadelphia: Lea & Febiger.

Appendix

Studies Included in the Meta-Analysis ($N = 64$)

Bachman, J. C. (1961). Motor learning and performance as related to age and sex in two measures of balance coordination. *Research Quarterly, 32*, 123–137.

Boley, E. H. (1975). *Generality and specificity of motor performance of children as related to age and sex*. Unpublished master's thesis, Louisiana State University, Baton Rouge, LA.

Broekhoff, J. (1978). Longitudinal comparison of the growth, physical fitness, and motor performance of suburban and inner city elementary school children. In F. Landry & W. A. R. Orban (Eds.) *Motor learning, sport psychology, pedagogy, and didactics of physical activity* (pp. 203–210). Miami, FL: Symposia Specialists.

Caskey, S. R. (1968). Effects of motivation on standing broad jump performance of children. *Research Quarterly, 39*, 54–59.

Cowgill, S. (1978). *Nebraska physical fitness norms: Grades 1–12*. Unpublished master's thesis, Colorado State University, Fort Collins, CO.

Davol, S. H., & Breakell, S. L. (1968). Sex differences in rotary pursuit performance of young children: A follow-up. *Perceptual and Motor Skills, 26*, 1199–1202.

Davol, S. H., Hastings, M. L., & Klein, D. A. (1965). Effect of age, sex, and speed of rotation on rotary pursuit performance by young children. *Perceptual and Motor Skills, 21*, 351–357.

Dohrman, P. (1964). Throwing and kicking ability of 8-year-old boys and girls. *Research Quarterly, 35*, 464–471.

Dunham, P., Jr. (1977). Age, sex, speed, and practice in coincidence-anticipation performance of children. *Perceptual and Motor Skills, 45*, 187–193.

Eckert, H. M. (1970). Visual-motor tasks at 3 and 4 years of age. *Perceptual and Motor Skills, 31*, 560.

Eckert, H. M. (1974). Variability in skill acquisition. *Child Development, 45*, 487–489.

Eckert, H. M., & Eichorn, D. H. (1974). Construct standard in skilled action. *Child Development, 45*, 439–445.

Eckert, H. M., & Eichorn, D. H. (1977). Developmental variability in reaction time. *Child Development, 48*, 452–458.

Eckert, H. M., & Rarick, G. L. (1976). Stabilometer performance of educable mentally retarded and normal children. *Research Quarterly, 47*, 619–623.

Espenschade, A. S., & Meleney, H. E. (1961). Motor performance of adolescent boys and girls of today in comparison with those of 24 years ago. *Research Quarterly, 32*, 186–189.

Finlayson, M. A. J., & Reitan, R. M. (1976). Handedness in relation to measures of motor and tactile-perceptual functions in normal children. *Perceptual and Motor Skills, 43*, 475–481.

Fitch, J. H. (1980). *An analysis of the factors on the North Carolina motor fitness battery test among students aged ten to seventeen*. Unpublished master's thesis, North Carolina Central, Durham, NC.

Gabbard, C., Kirby, T., & Patterson, R. (1979). Reliability of the straight-arm hang for testing muscular endurance among children 2 to 5. *Research Quarterly, 50*, 735–738.

Glassow, R. B., Halverson, L. E., & Rarick, G. L. (1965). *Improvement of motor development and physical fitness in elementary school children*. Unpublished manuscript, University of Wisconsin, Cooperative Research Project #696.

Glover, E. G. (1962). *Physical fitness test items for boys and girls in the first, second, and third grades*. Unpublished master's thesis, University of North Carolina, Chapel Hill, NC.

Govatos, L. A. (1959). Relationships and age differences in growth measures and motor skills. *Child Development, 30*, 333–340.

Green, J. M. (1973). *The relative effectiveness of a perceptual motor program, a movement education program, and a traditional program in the enhancement of motor performance of kindergarten children*. Unpublished master's thesis, University of Washington, Seattle, WA.

Greene, J. L. (1973). *Effects of a prescribed physical education program upon movement characteristics of 4-year-old boys and girls*. Unpublished doctoral dissertation, University of Utah, Salt Lake City, UT.

Halverson, L. E., Roberton, M. A., & Langendorfer, S. (1982). Development of the overarm throw: Movement and ball velocity changes by seventh grade. *Research Quarterly, 53,* 198–205.

Halverson, L. E., Roberton, M. A., Safrit, M. J., & Roberts, T. W. (1977). Effect of guided practice on overhand-throw ball velocities of kindergarten children. *Research Quarterly, 48,* 311–318.

Harper, C. J. (1975). *Movement responses of kindergarten children to a change of direction task—an analysis of selected measures.* Unpublished master's thesis, University of Wisconsin, Madison, WI.

Hartman, D. (1943). The hurdle jump as a measure of the motor proficiency of young children. *Child Development, 14,* 201–211.

Harvey, D. A. (1970). *The effects of level of aspiration and team competition as motivational techniques upon children's performances on selected sports skill tests.* Unpublished doctoral dissertation, Indiana University, Bloomington, IN.

Haywood, K. M., Greenwald, G., & Lewis, C. (1981). Contextual factors and age group differences in coincidence-anticipation performance. *Research Quarterly, 52,* 458–464.

Hunsicker, P. A. (1965). *A survey and comparison of youth fitness, 1958–1965.* Unpublished manuscript, University of Michigan, Cooperative Research Project #2418.

Ikeda, N. (1961). *A comparison of physical fitness of children in Iowa, USA and Tokyo, Japan.* Unpublished doctoral dissertation, State University of Iowa, Iowa City, IA.

Ingersoll, M. T. (1976). *The motor fitness of primary boys and girls.* Unpublished master's thesis, Ithaca College, Ithaca, NY.

Isaacs, L. D. (1980). Effects of ball size, ball color, and preferred color on catching by young children. *Perceptual and Motor Skills, 51,* 583–586.

Kane, R. J., & Meredith, H. V. (1952). Ability in the standing broad jump of elementary school children 7, 9, and 11 years of age. *Research Quarterly, 23,* 198–208.

Keating, D. P., & Bobbitt, B. L. (1978). Individual and developmental differences in cognitive-processing components of mental ability. *Child Development, 49,* 155–167.

Keogh, J. (1965). *Motor performance of elementary school children.* Unpublished manuscript, Department of Physical Education, University of California, Los Angeles. (Available through ERIC)

Knights, R. M., & Mouls, A. D. (1967). Normative and reliability data on finger and foot tapping in children. *Perceptual and Motor Skills, 25,* 717–720.

Latchaw, M. (1954). Measuring selected motor skills in fourth, fifth, and sixth grades. *Research Quarterly, 25,* 439–449.

Lee, A. M., Fant, H., Life, M. L., Lipe, L., & Carter, J. A. (1978). Field independence and performance on ball handling tasks. *Perceptual and Motor Skills, 46,* 439–442.

Maples, M. G. (1977). *Second grade children's performance on the overhand throw in relation to maternal and self preference for play activities.* Unpublished master's thesis, Purdue University, West Lafayette, IN.

McCaskill, C. L., & Wellman, B. L. (1938). A study of common motor achievements of the preschool ages. *Child Development, 9,* 141–149.

Miller, J. L. (1957). Effect of instruction on development of throwing accuracy of first grade children. *Research Quarterly, 28,* 132–137.

Milne, C., Seefeldt, V., & Reuschlein, P. (1976). Relationship between grade, sex, race, and motor performance in young children. *Research Quarterly, 47,* 726–730.

Miyashita, M., & Kanehisa, H. (1979). Dynamic peak torque related to age, sex, and performance. *Research Quarterly, 50,* 249–255.

Montpetit, R. R., Montoye, H. J., & Laeding, L. (1967). Grip strength of school children, Saginaw, Michigan: 1899 and 1964. *Research Quarterly, 38,* 231–240.

Morris, A. M., Williams, J. L., Atwater, A. E., & Wilmore, J. H. (1982). Age and sex differences in motor performance of 3 through 6-year-old children. *Research Quarterly, 53,* 214–221.

Nestroy, J. A. (1978). *Fitness levels of children taught by the physical education specialists and classroom teachers.* Unpublished master's thesis, Texas Woman's University, Denton, TX.

Pissanos, B. W., Moore, J. B., & Reeve, T. G. (1983). Age, sex, and body composition as predictors of children's performance on basic motor abilities and health-related fitness items. *Perceptual and Motor Skills, 56,* 71–77.

Pomeroy, J. E. (1938). The relation of reaction time of five-year-old children to various factors. *Child Development, 9,* 281–283.

Roberton, M. A., Halverson, L. E., Langendorfer, S., & Williams, K. (1979). Longitudinal changes in children's overarm throw ball velocities. *Research Quarterly, 50,* 256–264.

Ross, B. M. (1960). A study of the performance of boys and girls taught by the specialist and nonspecialist. *Research Quarterly, 31,* 199–207.

Seils, L. G. (1951). The relationship between measures of physical growth and gross motor performance of primary-grade school children. *Research Quarterly, 22,* 244–258.

Singer, R. N. (1969). Physical characteristic, perceptual-motor, and intelligence differences between third- and sixth-grade children. *Research Quarterly, 40,* 803–811.

Smith, J. (1956). Relation of certain physical traits and ability of motor learning in elementary children. *Research Quarterly, 27,* 221–228.

Smith, T. L. (1982). Self-concepts and movement skills of third grade children after physical education programs. *Perceptual and Motor skills, 54,* 1145–1146.

Smoll, F. L. (1966). *The influence of physical growth and muscular strength upon motor performances within and between year observations.* Unpublished master's thesis, University of Wisconsin, Madison, WI.

Stachnik, T. J. (1964). Cross-validation of psychomotor test for children. *Perceptual and Motor Skills, 18,* 913–916.

Taddonio, D. A. (1966). Effect of daily fifteen-minute periods of calisthenics upon the physical fitness of fifth grade boys and girls. *Research Quarterly, 37,* 276–281.

Thomas, J. R., Gallagher, J. D., & Purvis, G. J. (1981). Reaction time and anticipation time: Effects of development. *Research Quarterly, 52,* 359–367.

Torres, J. A. (1966). *The relationship between figure-ground perceptual ability and ball catching ability in ten and thirteen year old boys and girls.* Unpublished master's thesis, Purdue University, West Lafayette, IN.

Trussell, E. M. (1969). Relation of performance of selected physical skills to perceptual aspects of reading readiness in elementary school children. *Research Quarterly, 40,* 383–390.

Wilson, J. G., Silva, P. A., & Williams, S. M. (1981). An assessment of motor ability in seven year olds. *Journal of Human Movement Studies, 7,* 221–231.

Workman, D. J. (1979). Comparison of performance of children taught by the physical education specialist and by the classroom teacher. *Research Quarterly, 49,* 389–394.

Wright, E. J. (1967). Effects of light and heavy equipment on acquisition of sports-type skills by young children. *Research Quarterly, 38,* 705–714.

Received October 17, 1984
Revision received February 7, 1985 ∎

Quantifying Gender Differences in Physical Performance: A Developmental Perspective

Frank L. Smoll
University of Washington

Robert W. Schutz
University of British Columbia
Vancouver, British Columbia, Canada

The purpose was to quantify the contribution of anthropometric variables to gender differences in performance during childhood and adolescence. Measures of height, percentage body fat, and fat-free body weight were obtained for 2,142 students in Grades 3, 7, and 11 (ages 9, 13, and 17 years), and the subjects were tested on 6 motor tasks. Multivariate analysis of variance indicated that performance decrements resulting from greater adiposity affect boys and girls equally. Furthermore, this male–female similarity in the degree that fatness handicaps performance holds constant across grades. Percentage-variance analyses revealed that childhood gender differences are substantially influenced by anthropometric variables, with approximately 50% of between-gender variance being accounted for by fatness alone. Boys exhibited progressively greater performance superiority from Grade 3 to Grade 11. However, for specific tasks, there was an age-related decrease in the degree to which anthropometric variables contributed to these gender differences. This prompted the conclusion that with advancing age gender differences may become increasingly more a function of environmental factors.

The majority of motor development research has been devoted to describing age-related patterns of change and gender differences in mean achievement scores across childhood and adolescence. Studies have shown that, for most tasks, gender differences favoring boys become progressively greater with increasing age (see Eckert, 1987; Haubenstricker & Seefeldt, 1986; Haywood, 1986; Keogh & Sugden, 1985). Surprisingly, however, no specific theory has been advanced to explain the cause of gender differences in the psychomotor domain.

When one considers why gender differences in motor behavior develop, it seems likely that the potential sources of explanation would focus on the roles of biology, environment, and their interaction. Traditional biological models (e.g., Hutt, 1972; Wilson, 1975) have implicated hormonal, genetic, and physical factors as determinants of sex differences, whereas early social learning and experiences are at the core of environmental theories (Eagly, 1983; Maccoby & Jacklin, 1974; Mischel, 1966). Rather than perpetuating the nature versus nurture (either/or) debate, the prevailing tendency among many social scientists is to emphasize the interactive function of biology and environment as codeterminants of gender-related behaviors (e.g., Anastasi, 1981; Archer & Lloyd, 1985; Petersen, 1980).

What are the biological and environmental factors that contribute to gender differences in physical performance? Anthropometric characteristics have long been accepted as sources of variability in children's motor behavior. Malina's (1975) comprehensive review substantiates the negative effects of excessive body weight, fatness, and endomorphy on tasks involving movement of the entire body and the positive effects of body size on strength. With respect to gender differences, anthropometric measures are very similar for prepubescent boys and girls (Hansman, 1970; Malina, 1986; National Center for Health Statistics, 1977); but boys acquire considerably larger bodies than do girls as a result of differences in the timing and intensity of the pubescent growth spurt. Furthermore, in comparison with boys, girls possess greater absolute as well as relative amounts of adipose tissue at all ages, with the differences becoming accentuated during adolescence (Hansman, 1970; Malina, 1986; National Center for Health Statistics, 1972, 1974). It seems reasonable to assume that gender differences in physical performance emerge, in part, from these sources.

In addition to biological factors, cultural norms, expectations, and experience are generally held to play an important role in differentiation of performance between the sexes. Studies of gender differences in physical activity and play behavior have indicated that cultural conditioning for specific sex-associated roles begins very early in life. Moreover, the continued effects of sex role stereotyping have been shown in investigations of children's activity levels, their perceptions of sex-appropriate motor acts, and the influence of sex-typed labels on children's play preferences and styles (see Lewko & Greendorfer, 1982; Liss, 1983; Maccoby, 1988; Smith, 1986). Because of sex role stereotypes and resultant expectations held by parents, peers, teachers, and sport coaches, girls generally receive less encouragement to excel, less instruction, and less opportunity to practice than boys. This ultimately contributes to the development of gender differences in performance (Branta, Painter, & Kiger, 1987; Greendorfer, 1980; Housner, 1981; Malina, 1980).

Both authors contributed equally to this article; the order of authorship was determined by the flip of a coin.

We wish to thank three anonymous reviewers for their insightful comments on earlier drafts of the article.

Correspondence concerning this article should be addressed to Frank L. Smoll, Department of Psychology, NI-25, University of Washington, Seattle, Washington 98195.

Thomas and French (1985) conducted a meta-analysis to examine gender differences in performance during childhood and adolescence. The data were taken from 64 studies yielding 702 effect sizes based on 31,444 subjects. When age was regressed on effect size, the relation was significant for 12 of the 20 tasks studied. Thus, the notion of uniform development of gender differences was not supported. Differences between the mean scores of boys and girls during childhood were moderate and resulted in small effect sizes (usually less than 0.50 of a standard deviation unit). In light of this, Thomas and French suggested that prior to puberty, throwing (distance and velocity) was the only task with gender differences large enough to be attributable to biological variables. At puberty, however, the effect sizes for 6 of the 15 tasks showed rapid increases that are probably associated with the increase in boys' size and strength. Although Thomas and French acknowledged that biology plays a salient role in increasingly larger gender differences, they proposed that environmental factors assume even greater importance at and following puberty.

Because of the perceived importance of physical factors, several investigators have attempted to determine the specific role of anthropometric variables in gender differences in children's performance. Slaughter, Lohman, and Misner (1977, 1980) assessed the association of body size, somatotype, and body composition to performance in rather small samples of 7- to 12-year-old boys ($N = 68$) and girls ($N = 50$). Similarly, Hensley, East, and Stillwell (1982) investigated the relation between body fatness and selected motor tasks with a sample of elementary school boys and girls (Grades 1–4). Unfortunately, however, the studies did not include actual quantification/statistical testing of gender differences in the percentage of variance attributable to anthropometric variables. Furthermore, the investigators failed to account for age-related changes that might occur in relations between anthropometric dimensions and performance as a function of gender; that is, a developmental perspective was lacking in the designs and analyses. Thus, critical questions remain unanswered.

The purpose of the present study was to quantify the contribution of major anthropometric variables affecting gender differences in physical performance during childhood and adolescence. Specifically, we sought answers to the following questions:

1. Is the extent to which body fatness affects performance the same for boys as for girls?
2. What proportion of the gender differences in performance can be attributed to anthropometric differences between the sexes?
3. What is the influence of age on gender differences in performance as they relate to anthropometric variables? That is, are there age-related differences in the handicapping effects of body fatness on boys and girls, and to what extent do physically based gender differences vary as a function of age?

We noted earlier that gender differences in motor development are probably subject to the interactive functioning of biological and environmental forces. Yet no theory has been formulated to explicate the roles of potential causal factors and the nature of their influence across age. In this regard, the inductive process of theory construction may best proceed as a result of acquiring information about relevant variables that have an impact on gender differences. The present study quantified age-related changes in the effect of anthropometric variables on gender differences in performance. The work thus represents an initial attempt to provide an empirical basis for future theory generation.

Method

Sampling Procedures

The data were collected as part of a comprehensive study of the status of physical education in the province of British Columbia (Carre, Mosher, & Schutz, 1982). The sample was composed of approximately 3,000 students, 500 boys and 500 girls in each of Grades 3, 7, and 11. These grades were chosen as they represented the end of primary, intermediate, and secondary physical education programs in British Columbia.

The target size of 3,000 students was attained by sampling 1,150 students at each of the three grade levels. The sampling of schools was stratified on the basis of student enrollment in the six geographic zones in the province. This was done separately for each grade. Individual students were systematically sampled within the selected schools, with a random starting point, from a master list of eligible students. Approximately 30 students were sampled from each school. An eligible student was defined as an individual who participated fully in regular physical education classes; thus, students with educational or physical disabilities, or both, were excluded.

Subjects

The numbers of students for which complete data were obtained for all variables used in this study were as follows: Grade 3 = 492 boys, 467 girls; Grade 7 = 481 boys, 469 girls; and Grade 11 = 407 boys, 357 girls. To avoid the problem of nonorthogonality in the multivariate analyses of variance (MANOVAS), and to ensure that the sum of squares would be additive in the composite variance analyses, equal cell sizes were required. Complete data were available for 357 Grade-11 girls, which was the smallest cell size. Thus, all other grade–sex groups were reduced to this size through random deletion. Examination of means and standard deviations (initial student groups vs. final sample) for the variables of interest revealed that the final sample had not been biased by this procedure.

The median chronological ages for subjects in Grades 3, 7, and 11 were 8 years 11 months, 12 years 11 months, and 16 years 11 months, respectively. There were no between-sex differences in ages at any grade.

Data Collection Procedures

Each school's on-site field assessment was completed during a 3-hr morning session by one of six trained teams. A team consisted of six members (physical education graduate and undergraduate students), with each member undergoing an extensive 6-week training program. The training program included the conduct of pilot studies, which provided reliability data for all assessment procedures. During the 2-month data collection period, the six-person team remained together as a unit and the same person was responsible for the same test (e.g., skinfolds) throughout the testing period. Standardized instructions to the subjects were used by all testers.

Anthropometric Measures

In addition to obtaining measures of height and weight, skinfold thickness measurements (triceps and subscapular) were made with Harpenden calipers. Two measures were taken at each site, and a third was recorded in the presence of a discrepancy (i.e., more than 1 mm difference between the first two readings). Test–retest (intrarater) reliability coefficients obtained in pilot studies were above .95 for both sites, for both the male and female subjects, at all three grades.

In estimating percentage body fat, the methods proposed by Lohman (1986) were used. Lohman, and others, stressed the necessity of taking into consideration the changes in fat-free body composition during growth—primarily changes in water, mineral, and potassium content of the fat-free body. The following equation was used for both sexes: percentage fat = $1.35 x - 0.012 x^2$ – intercept. The intercept values were 3.4, 4.4, and 5.7 for the Grade 3, 7, and 11 boys, respectively, and 1.6, 2.8, and 4.0 for the girls, respectively. In each case, the independent variable (x) was the sum of the skinfolds at the two sites, triceps and subscapular. After determining the percentage fat, fat-free body weight was calculated as the weight of all tissues in the body (body weight) minus the extractable fat for each subject.

Our selection of anthropometric measures was limited to those previously described, partly because of the nature and scope of the parent project. Specifically, it involved an assessment of learning objectives in physical education on a provincewide basis. Recognizing that body size and composition constitute only a portion of the broad range of anthropometric parameters, it would have been desirable to examine additional measures (e.g., segment lengths, body diameters, and ratios). However, we wish to emphasize that the variables included in this study (i.e., height, percentage body fat, and fat-free body weight) are widely accepted as having a major impact on performance, and they would be expected to have important affects on gender-related performance differences as well.

Physical Performance Measures

Six performance variables were used in this study. Five of the tasks were among the motor performance items included in the meta-analysis study conducted by Thomas and French (1985). According to their classification, the standing long jump and wall pass are measures of the fundamental skills of jumping and catching, respectively, and the flexed arm hang, sit-ups, and side slide are motor fitness items. Cardiovascular fitness, which was not included in the Thomas and French study, is an important component of the broader domain of physical performance. We incorporated the timed run to measure this particular attribute. Because of the diverse nature of the six tasks in terms of their biomechanical and physiological characteristics, one might expect gender differences to be differentially affected by associated anthropometric variables. Thus, it seems reasonable that gender differences in tasks emphasizing support of body weight or body projection (flexed arm hang, standing long jump, and timed run) would be considerably affected by fatness. Conversely, gender differences in wall pass performance would be relatively unaffected by body fatness.

Test–retest reliabilities obtained in pilot studies ranged from a low of .83 (wall pass, Grade-3 girls) to a high of .95 (sit-ups, Grade-11 boys). A description of the performance measures follows.

Flexed arm hang. The student hung from a bar for as long a period of time as possible. A reverse grip (underhand) was used with thumbs around the bar, hands shoulder width apart, and eyes level with the bar. The score was the time, in seconds, from start to release or until the eyes dropped below the level of the bar.

Standing long jump. The student jumped as far as possible, using a two-foot takeoff. Four practice trials and two test trials were given. The score (in cm) was the best obtained from the two trials.

Timed run. The student ran or walked as far as possible around an oval track for a 9-min period for Grade 3, and a 12-min period for Grades 7 and 11. The scores were converted to meters per minute to allow for between-grade comparisons.

Sit-ups. As many bent-knee sit-ups as possible were performed in 1 min. The body position consisted of forearms crossed, hands on opposite shoulders, and knees bent so that the heels were situated 30 cm–46 cm from the buttocks. A partner sat on the student's feet in a position that ensured the student's feet maintained contact with the floor.

Side slide. Three parallel lines, 91 cm in length, were marked on a carpeted surface. The distance from the center line to each side line was 1.2 m. The starting position involved standing and straddling the center line, with the body's frontal plane perpendicular to the line. The student performed a series of lateral slide movements to the left side line, and then reversed direction going back across the center line to the right side line. The student did not cross feet and had to overstep each side line with a part of one foot. The object was to traverse as many lines as possible in a 10-s time period. Following a 5-s practice trial, two test trials were given, recording the total number of lines crossed in 10 s, including the center line. The final score was the best of the two trials.

Wall pass. A ball was thrown against a wall and caught on its return, as many times as possible in 15 s. A volleyball, junior-size basketball, and regulation basketball were used for Grades 3, 7, and 11, respectively. The student stood behind a restraining line marked 1.2 m from the wall for Grade 3, and 2.7 m from the wall for Grades 7 and 11. Following a 10-s practice trial, two test trials were given, recording the number of times the ball hit the wall without bouncing. The final score was the best of the two trials.

Results

Descriptive Statistics

Table 1 contains the means and standard deviations of the four anthropometric and six performance variables for the boys and girls at each grade level. For the anthropometric variables, the sample subjects were similar to those in most other studies. The boys and girls were approximately equal in height and weight at Grades 3 and 7, with the Grade-7 girls being slightly heavier than the boys. At Grade 11, there were large differences in body size between the sexes. With respect to body fat, the girls had a greater percentage fat at all grade levels, which was pronounced in Grade 11. The performance measures favored the boys at all grade levels, with two exceptions. The gender differences for the sit-ups and the side slide were negligible at Grade 3 and minimal at Grade 7.

Comparisons Among Group Means: MANOVA

In order to examine the nature of gender differences in performance, and how these varied as a function of grade and percentage fat, a MANOVA was conducted on the six performance variables. This analysis was performed on a 3 × 2 × 3 (Grade × Gender × Percentage Fat) complete factorial randomized design with the six dependent variables (see Table 2). The percentage fat factor consisted of three levels (low, medium, and high), with the cutoff points for classification into one of these levels being unique to each grade–gender condition. For example, the cutoff point for assigning a Grade-7 boy to the high-percentage fat level was based upon the distribution of percentage fat for the Grade-7 boys only. Consequently, the 66.7 and 33.3 percentiles of the Grade-7 boys' frequency distribution yielded the following values: High = greater than 17%, medium = 17.0% to 12.9%, and low = less than 12.9%. The corresponding values for the Grade-7 girls were as follows: greater than 23.6%, 23.6% to 18.8%, and less than 18.8%, respectively. The use of cutoff points specific to each grade–gender condition was necessary to

Table 1
Means and Standard Deviations of the Anthropometric and Physical Performance Variables

	Grade 3		Grade 7		Grade 11	
Variable	Boys	Girls	Boys	Girls	Boys	Girls
Height (cm)						
M	133.9	133.3	157.1	156.7	175.8	163.6
SD	6.4	6.3	8.1	7.1	6.5	6.3
Weight (kg)						
M	29.6	29.7	46.1	47.2	65.8	56.3
SD	4.9	5.2	8.8	9.1	8.7	7.7
Percentage fat						
M	14.4	20.2	16.1	21.8	14.0	24.0
SD	4.8	5.8	5.8	5.8	4.7	4.9
Fat-free body weight (kg)						
M	25.2	23.4	38.4	36.6	56.4	42.6
SD	3.3	3.0	6.1	5.6	6.3	4.7
Flexed arm hang (s)						
M	19.0	13.2	32.4	20.0	50.2	18.1
SD	12.9	8.7	20.5	15.8	20.6	11.8
Standing long jump (cm)						
M	133.9	129.1	171.6	159.6	221.1	171.4
SD	16.4	17.0	21.6	19.8	22.5	20.9
Timed run (m/min)						
M	160.2	141.5	186.7	157.3	215.8	165.0
SD	25.5	23.4	28.6	25.9	26.5	23.1
Sit-ups						
M	30.1	30.5	41.7	39.6	47.9	38.0
SD	9.5	9.0	9.4	10.0	8.6	10.6
Side slide						
M	11.6	11.5	15.6	15.1	19.8	16.5
SD	2.1	2.0	2.3	1.9	3.3	2.1
Wall pass						
M	11.9	10.5	10.6	9.7	13.7	10.6
SD	2.9	2.7	1.5	1.4	1.7	1.5
n	357	357	357	357	357	357

remove the confounding of percentage fat and gender, at each grade level. In effect, this procedure is based on the fact that a Grade-7 boy with 17% fat had the same relative fatness as did a Grade-7 girl with 23.6% fat (i.e., relative to the other Grade-7 boys and girls, respectively). The rationale for this procedure is the assumption that percentage fat differences in boys and girls are not only quantitatively different, but also qualitatively different. Because of gender differences in the manner in which fat is distributed throughout the body, it is not appropriate to use a common scale; 20% fat content does not mean the same in a Grade-7 boy as in a Grade-7 girl.

Grade and gender. The main effects were significant for grade, multivariate $F(12, 4238) = 409.1, p < .001$, and for gender, multivariate $F(6, 2119) = 293.4, p < .001$. All six univariate F ratios for each of these two main effects were significant ($p < .001$). Averaged over gender, there was an increase in performance on five performance variables from Grade 3 to Grade 7 to Grade 11. Wall pass performance declined from Grade 3 to Grade 7 and increased from Grade 7 to Grade 11 (mean values of 11.2, 10.2, and 12.2, respectively). The decrease from Grade 3 to Grade 7 can be attributed to the change in test conditions. With respect to gender, averaged over the three grades, the boys outperformed the girls. The significant Grade × Gender interaction, multivariate $F(12, 4238) = 61.7, p < .001$, indicates that the male-female difference in performance increased with age for all six variables ($p < .001$, for all univariate F ratios). For example, in the timed run, the boys ran approximately 19 m/min faster than the girls at Grade 3, 30 m/min faster at Grade 7, and 50 m/min faster by Grade 11.

Percentage fat. The significant percentage fat main effect, multivariate $F(12, 4238) = 36.7, p < .001$, indicates that, averaged over the levels of gender and grade, there was a difference in performance among the three levels of fat classifications. To examine the nature of this difference more closely, preplanned nonorthogonal contrasts were conducted on the percentage fat factor. The contrasts of interest were the low versus medium categories and the medium versus high categories. Because of the nonorthogonality of these contrasts, the level of significance was set at .01 for the multivariate tests of significance. The medium versus high contrast was significant, multivariate $F(6, 2119) = 38.5, p < .001$, and all univariate F ratios were significant ($p < .001$), except for the wall pass, $F(1, 2124) = 3.19, p = .074$. For the low versus medium contrast, multivariate $F(6, 2125) = 5.29, p < .001$, only the flexed arm hang, $F(1, 2130) = 19.2, p < .001$, and standing long jump, $F(1, 2130) = 9.39, p < .002$, were significant. In general, the medium versus high differences were much larger than the low versus medium contrasts; that is, the difference in performance attributed to percentage fat was primarily accounted for by the poor performance of the high-percentage fat subjects. For example, the

Table 2
*MANOVA Results: Flexed Arm Hang (FAH), Standing Long Jump (SLJ), Timed Run (TR),
Sit-Ups (SU), Side Slide (SS), and Wall Pass (WP)*

		Univariate p values					
Effect	Multivariate p	FAH	SLJ	TR	SU	SS	WP
Grade (Gr)	s	s	s	s	s	s	s
Gender (Ge)	s	s	s	s	s	s	s
Percentage fat (% Fat)	s	s	s	s	s	s	ns
Low vs. medium (L-M)	(s)	(s)	(s)	(.07)	(ns)	(ns)	(ns)
Medium vs. high (M-H)	(s)	(s)	(s)	(s)	(s)	(s)	(.07)
Gr × Ge	s	s	s	s	s	s	s
Gr × % Fat	s	s	s	s	s	ns	ns
Gr × % Fat (L-M)	(ns)	(-)	(-)	(-)	(-)	(-)	(-)
Gr × % Fat (M-H)	(.003)	(.006)	(s)	(.03)	(.01)	(-)	(-)
Ge × % Fat	ns	—	—	—	—	—	—
Ge × % Fat (L-M)	(ns)	(-)	(-)	(-)	(-)	(-)	(-)
Ge × % Fat (M-H)	(ns)	(-)	(-)	(-)	(-)	(-)	(-)
Gr × Ge × % Fat	.054	—	—	—	—	—	—
Gr × Ge × % Fat (L-M)	(ns)	(-)	(-)	(-)	(-)	(-)	(-)
Gr × Ge × % Fat (M-H)	(.09)	(-)	(-)	(-)	(-)	(-)	(-)

Note. s (significant) = $p < .002$; ns = $p > .10$. - = univariates that were not examined because the multivariate omnibus test was nonsignificant at $\alpha = .05$. MANOVA = multivariate analysis of variance.

high versus medium difference in the flexed arm hang was 8.2 s ($M_{high} = 18.7$, $M_{medium} = 26.9$); whereas, the medium versus low difference was only 4.0 s ($M_{low} = 30.9$).

Grade × Percentage Fat interaction. Because of the method by which the percentage fat level was established, this effect is virtually free of any confounding effects of gender. The significant Grade × Percentage Fat interaction, multivariate $F(24, 7394) = 2.69$, $p < .001$, was primarily due to the Grade-7 students, whose differences in performance among the levels of fat classification were considerably greater than they were for the Grade-3 or Grade-11 students. More specifically, the differences between the low and medium percentage fat groups were approximately the same at all three grade levels, but the Grade × Percentage Fat (medium vs. high) contrast was significant, multivariate $F(12, 4238) = 2.46$, $p = .003$. The side slide, $F(2, 2124) = 2.24$, $p = .106$, and the wall pass, $F(2, 2124) = .39$, $p = .677$, were the only nonsignificant variables. As mentioned earlier, these effects are relatively free of any gender influence; however, a substantive interpretation becomes difficult because the gender differences were so much larger at the higher grades that the *relative* contribution of percentage fat to performance actually decreased over grades. The interpretation of this interaction effect may therefore not be the most appropriate method by which to identify the relative contributions of gender, percentage fat, and age to the performance differences. The *percentage-variance* approach, which is presented later, does permit an adequate identification and interpretation of these effects.

Gender × Percentage Fat interactions. The nonsignificant Gender × Percentage Fat interaction, multivariate $F(12, 4238) = 1.30$, $p = .209$, indicates that differences in performance between subjects classified as low, medium, and high-percentage fat were similar for the boys and girls. That is, the detrimental effects of excessive adiposity were equally debilitating for both sexes. Furthermore, the lack of a significant three-way interaction, multivariate $F(24, 7394) = 1.50$, $p = .054$, indicates that this nonsignificant Gender × Percentage Fat interaction held true at each grade level.

Percentage Variance Analyses

Computational procedures. The previously reported analysis (MANOVA) is a traditional procedure that was necessary in order to permit statements about the significance of differences among marginal and cell means. Although it was helpful to identify which sources of variance contributed to variability in the subjects' performance, the technique suffers from two shortcomings. First, it does not permit a quantitative comparison of the magnitude of the main effects or interactions. For example, one cannot conclude that an effect that is significant at $p < .001$ is "larger" or "more important" than an effect that is significant at $p < .01$. Second, although the percentage-fat categorization procedure resulted in percentage-fat effects unconfounded by gender effects, interpretation of the relative contributions of gender and percentage fat to performance was still not possible. An additional analysis was therefore conducted that permitted the quantification, on an absolute as well as a relative basis, of both the gender and percentage-fat effects on physical performance. This was essentially a G study in the context of generalizability theory (Brennan, 1983), performed with an analysis of variance (ANOVA) and an analysis of covariance (ANCOVA) separately by grade on each of the six dependent variables. The covariate used was the raw-score (continuous scale) percentage-fat score, not the coded ordered-scaled score used in the MANOVA. Using the flexed arm hang as an example, the following steps were undertaken:

1. An ANOVA (one-way, gender being the only factor) was conducted on the Grade 3 sample.
2. Expected mean square values were derived from the BMDP8V program, based on a model in which subjects were

treated as a random factor and gender as a fixed effect. Variances due to subjects and gender were then computed.

3. The percentage variance due to gender was calculated, indicating the percentage of total variability in flexed arm hang performance that could be attributed to gender differences.

4. An ANCOVA (gender being the only factor, percentage fat the covariate) was conducted, and expected mean squares and percent variances were calculated, resulting in a measure of the variance due to gender controlling for (partialing out) any between-gender percentage-fat differences.

5. Using the results from Steps 3 and 4, we calculated the proportion of the percentage variance accounted for by gender that was accounted for by percentage fat. Specifically, this involved the following calculation: the Step 3 value minus the Step 4 value, divided by the Step 3 value.

6. Steps 4 and 5 were repeated using three anthropometric variables (percentage fat, fat-free body weight, height) as covariates.

This set of procedures was replicated for each of Grades 7 and 11 and then for all three grades for the remaining five dependent variables.

Findings. The results presented in Table 3 corroborate and quantify the Grade × Gender interaction reported in the MANOVA results. For all six performance measures, the percentage variance due to gender increased dramatically with increasing grades (see Table 3, row a for each variable). For example, for the timed run at Grade 3, only 23% of the variability in performance among all of the 714 subjects can be attributed to gender differences; the remaining 77% were due to true intraindividual differences and other unexplained factors. However, in the Grade-11 subjects, the majority (68%) of the between-subjects variability can be attributed to gender differences.

The values in rows b were derived from Step 3 of the computational procedures. They indicate that when the between-gender differences in percentage fat were controlled for, the percentage of variance in performance attributable to gender differences was considerably reduced. For example, for the timed run, the percentage variance due to gender dropped from 23% to 7% at Grade 3, and from 68% to 37% at Grade 11. This indicates that if there were *no* differences between the boys and girls in percentage fat, only 37% of the total variance in the Grade-11 timed run performance may still be attributed to gender differences.

The values in rows d are especially revealing and quantify the gender–fat–performance relation in a unique way (see Step 5 for the computational procedures). These values indicate that with increasing age, the detrimental effect of excessive body fat became *relatively* less important in accounting for the gender differences in performance for all of the variables except the wall pass. Given that there were no gender differences at Grade 3 for the variables sit-ups and side slide, and only very small differences at Grade 7, the effect is much less pronounced for these variables. However, for the three variables that were expected to be most affected by fatness, the effect is striking. Using the standing long jump, which gives the strongest example of this phenomenon, it can be seen at Grade 3 that 100% of the performance differences attributed to gender were due to the percentage-fat differences between the boys and girls. That is, although there were very small gender differences in the stand-

Table 3
Percentage Variance in Physical Performance Accounted for by Gender Differences

Measure	Grade 3	Grade 7	Grade 11
Flexed arm hang			
a. Gender	12	19	65
b. Gender (% FAT)	1	3	29
c. Gender (% FAT, FFBW, HT)	0	2	22
d. Proportion (a − b)/a	.92	.84	.55
e. Proportion (a − c)/a	1.00	.89	.66
Standing long jump			
a. Gender	4	14	72
b. Gender (% FAT)	0	1	42
c. Gender (% FAT, FFBW, HT)	0	0	15
d. Proportion (a − b)/a	1.00	.93	.42
e. fProportion (a − c)/a	1.00	1.00	.79
Timed run			
a. Gender	23	37	68
b. Gender (% FAT)	7	18	37
c. Gender (% FAT, FFBW, HT)	5	16	18
d. Proportion (a − b)/a	.70	.51	.46
e. Proportion (a − c)/a	.78	.57	.74
Sit-ups			
a. Gender	0	2	34
b. Gender (% FAT)	0	0	13
c. Gender (% FAT, FFBW, HT)	0	0	0
d. Proportion (a − b)/a	—	1.00	.62
e. Proportion (a − c)/a	—	1.00	1.00
Side slide			
a. Gender	0	2	41
b. Gender (% FAT)	0	0	14
c. Gender (% FAT, FFBW, HT)	0	0	3
d. Proportion (a − b)/a	—	1.00	.66
e. Proportion (a − c)/a	—	1.00	.93
Wall pass			
a. Gender	12	16	65
b. Gender (% FAT)	10	13	46
c. Gender (% FAT, FFBW, HT)	5	5	12
d. Proportion (a − b)/a	.17	.19	.29
e. Proportion (a − c)/a	.58	.69	.82

Note. Rows a present the percentage of variance in performance accounted for by gender differences (no covariates). Rows b present the percentage of variance in performance accounted for by gender differences, controlling for (covariate) between-gender differences in percentage fat (% FAT). Rows c present the percentage of variance in performance accounted for by gender differences, controlling for (covariates) between-gender differences in percentage fat (% FAT), fat-free body weight (FFBW), and height (HT). Rows d and e present the proportions of the gender effects (variance due to gender) that are accounted for by the anthropometric covariates; that is, d = (a − b)/a, and e = (a − c)/a.

ing long jump at the Grade-3 level (4% of the total between-subjects variance), all of this difference was related to the fact that the boys had lower percentage fat than did the girls. This proportion decreased slightly by Grade 7 (.93), and it was only .42 at Grade 11. In other words, of the very substantial differences in standing long jump performance between the boys and girls at Grade 11 (72% of the total variance being gender related), only 42% of this difference can be attributed to the fact that the girls had considerably greater amounts of fat than did the boys. The remaining 58% of between-gender differences was due to factors other than the percentage-fat differences.

Figure 1 provides a clear, graphic representation of this phenomenon for the variables flexed arm hang, standing long jump,

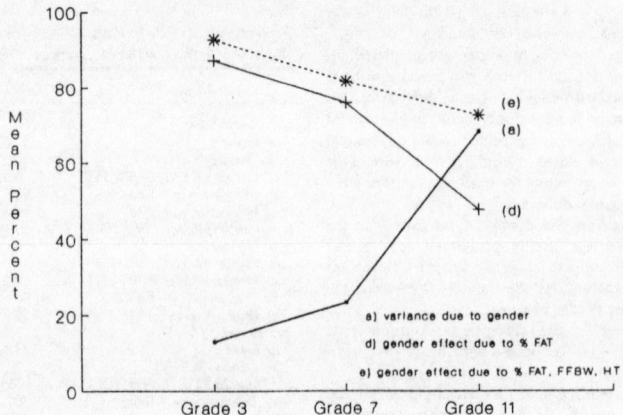

Figure 1. Variance in performance due to gender, and relative contribution of anthropometric indexes averaged over the variables flexed arm hang, standing long jump, and timed run.

and timed run. Line a, representing the variance due to gender, was derived by averaging the row a values for the three variables, separately for each grade. Line d, representing the proportion of the gender effect that can be accounted for by percentage fat, was derived by averaging the values of rows d. These average values show that the magnitude of the gender effect increased dramatically from Grade 7 to 11, but the relative degree to which percentage fat contributed to the gender effect was markedly reduced from Grade 7 to 11.

At this point, it is necessary to account for as much of the gender-related variance as possible. Consequently, the ANCOVAs and percentage-variance calculations were repeated with percentage fat, fat-free body weight, and height being used as covariates (i.e., Steps 4 and 6 of the computational procedures). The results, reported in rows c of Table 3, have a pattern of increasing (over grades) percentage variances accounted for by gender differences, which is similar to the case when only percentage fat was used as a covariate. However, the addition of fat-free body weight and height as covariates resulted in a considerable reduction in the percentage of the total variance that can be attributed to gender. Using the timed run as an example, it can be seen that adding fat-free body weight and height as covariates had little effect at Grades 3 and 7. Approximately 5% (Grade 3) and 16% (Grade 7) of the variability in timed run performance could be attributed to gender if percentage fat, fat-free body weight, and height were partialed out. These values differ only marginally from the situation in which percentage fat was the sole covariate, as there were minor fat-free body weight and height differences between the boys and girls at Grades 3 and 7. At Grade 11, however, the greater fat-free body weight and height of the boys contributed to the large between-gender differences in timed run performance, thus reducing the *anthropometric-free* variance due to gender to 18%.

The proportion of the gender effects that are accounted for by the three anthropometric variables are given in rows e of Table 3. The pattern is not as clear as in rows d, where percentage fat was the only covariate. The pattern of a reduced contribution, over grades, holds true only for the flexed arm hang and standing long jump; but it holds true, in general, when averaged over the three performance variables (see Figure 1, line e). This is not surprising, given that the flexed arm hang and standing long jump are our most most direct measures of weight support and body projection. However, it does weaken the generalization made above based only on rows d results.

Correlation Analysis

Zero-order correlations are presented in Table 4. Although we do not use these results in answering the specific questions posed, they are useful for descriptive purposes and to assist in interpreting the previously reported analyses. Percentage fat, the anthropometric variable with the strongest linear relation with performance, had a very consistent strength of association across five of the six performance variables (the wall pass again being the exception) over all three grades, and for both sexes. This corroborates the finding emanating from the nonsignificant Grade × Gender × Percentage Fat interaction in the MANOVA: The amount of decrement in performance resulting from excessive body fatness was similar for the boys and girls, and somewhat consistent over Grades 3, 7, and 11. It is interesting that the Grade 7s (especially the Grade-7 boys) had a stronger negative percentage fat–performance relation than did the other two grades. This effect, which was also revealed in the interpretation of the significant Grade × Percentage Fat interaction, can be attributed to the larger variability in percentage fat at Grade 7 (see Table 1).

As can be seen in Table 4, performance on the wall pass was virtually independent of percentage fat for both the boys and girls at all three grade levels. This underlies the nonsignificant

Table 4
Correlations Between Anthropometric and Physical Performance Variables

	Anthropometric variable					
	Height		Percentage fat		Fat-free body weight	
Performance variable	Boys	Girls	Boys	Girls	Boys	Girls
Flexed arm hang						
Grade 3	−.11	−.17	−.36	−.38	−.09	−.20
Grade 7	−.15	−.09	−.47	−.42	−.12	−.22
Grade 11	−.06	−.02	−.29	−.40	−.12	−.04
Standing long jump						
Grade 3	.09	−.01	−.29	−.27	.10	−.01
Grade 7	.20	.23	−.49	−.37	.22	.16
Grade 11	.11	.19	−.30	−.30	.22	.13
Timed run						
Grade 3	.06	−.01	−.24	−.34	.02	−.08
Grade 7	−.07	−.02	−.44	−.40	−.08	−.15
Grade 11	.02	.19	−.29	−.20	.08	.04
Sit-ups						
Grade 3	.06	−.03	−.16	−.19	.14	.01
Grade 7	−.10	.01	−.33	−.32	−.06	−.07
Grade 11	−.05	.08	−.17	−.07	.08	.14
Side slide						
Grade 3	.08	.06	−.04	−.15	.06	.04
Grade 7	−.10	.12	−.20	−.17	−.08	.07
Grade 11	.06	.12	−.19	−.15	.15	.04
Wall pass						
Grade 3	.22	.18	−.01	.07	.20	.16
Grade 7	.18	.19	−.06	−.01	.25	.22
Grade 11	.17	.23	−.06	.01	.36	.27

Note. r .01/2; 355 = .10.

percentage-fat effect in the MANOVA and in the exception noted in the results of the percentage-variance analyses.

Discussion

The purposes of the study were set in the framework of three questions, two dealing with gender-performance differences as they relate to anthropometric variables, and the third pertaining to whether the effects held constant over age. This section of the article contains a discussion of the results relative to each of the primary questions, with the age issue being integrated into the responses.

Is the extent to which body fatness affects performance the same for boys and girls? The question is based on the generally accepted assumption that excessive fatness is detrimental to performance, and it focuses on whether this phenomenon is equally valid for boys and girls. Before addressing the question, it was necessary to verify the assumption, and the results provided strong affirmative support. The significant percentage-fat effect and the negative percentage-fat–performance correlations clearly indicate that individuals with a high fat content were low achievers on performance tasks. Furthermore, the nonsignificant Gender × Percentage Fat interaction indicated that the differences in performance between high, medium, and low percentage fat boys were essentially equivalent to those differences in girls. This finding must be interpreted in light of the unique classification procedure, which when used resulted in a gender-free examination of the role of fatness in performance and permitted valid between-gender comparisons. In essence, male subjects with excessive fatness were disadvantaged in performance to the same degree as were female subjects. One may thus conclude that the performance decrement resulting from greater adiposity affects boys and girls similarly. Our discovery has an important practical implication. Specifically, with respect to achievement on physical performance tasks, excessive fatness is a critical issue for boys and girls alike. Consequently, members of both genders should receive sufficient attention in terms of preventative measures and remediation.

Contrary to the aforementioned, Hensley et al. (1982) reported that "among preadolescent children body fatness may have relatively different effects on the performance of boys and girls" (p. 139). However, because of several methodological differences between the present study and the work of Hensley et al., meaningful comparisons are unwarranted. Specifically, the Hensley et al. data were derived from a relatively small sample (563 children) and were inappropriately collapsed across Grades 1–4. Moreover, the atypical nature of the sample was shown by a nonsignificant gender difference in body fatness (sum of skinfold thicknesses at two sites). Finally, the data analysis was limited to a number of simple linear regression analyses (separately for boys and girls and for each performance variable), with no actual statistical testing of gender differences.

Turning to the age component of the main question, the male-female similarity in the degree that body fatness hindered performance did not vary with age. The nonsignificant Grade × Gender × Percentage Fat interaction indicated that the nature of the Gender × Percentage Fat interaction remained relatively stable over the three grade levels. We wish to emphasize that this does *not* imply that the effect of fatness on performance was independent of age. On the contrary, the effect became much more pronounced with increasing age (as evidenced by the significant Grade × Percentage Fat interaction). Therefore, we conclude that the negligible male–female differences in the degree to which excessive fatness affects performance is a fairly consistent effect over the ages 9 to 17 years.

What proportion of the gender differences in performance can be attributed to anthropometric differences between the sexes? The basic assumption of this question is that gender differences in performance do exist; the question is to what degree are anthropometric factors responsible for these differences? Our data verified the assumption, with gender accounting for up to 23% of the between-subjects variability in performance at Grade 3, and from 34% to 72% of the variability at Grade 11. In answer to the question, the extent to which these gender differences were related to differences in anthropometric factors was quite substantial, ranging from as high as 100% to as low as 17% for fatness alone. Thus, in a weight-supporting activity such as the flexed arm hang, even when there were relatively small gender differences (Grade 3), a large percentage (92%) of that difference could be accounted for by gender differences in fatness. When large gender differences were present in older children (e.g., standing long jump, Grade 11), only 42% of these differences could be accounted for by gender differences in fatness. However, the answer to the question does not generalize to all physical performance tasks, as the relative contribution of the three anthropometric variables varies from task to task. For example, with the flexed arm hang, the major proportion of the gender difference is accounted for by gender differences in percentage fat; whereas, for the timed run and wall pass, height and fat-free body weight add considerably in accounting for the between-gender differences. These data analyses and interpretations reinforce the position that simply viewing gender-related differences in performance as a function of percentage fat is incomplete; other anthropometric variables may or may not contribute as well.

As noted earlier, Thomas and French (1985) suggested that, with the exception of the fundamental skill of throwing, gender differences in performance prior to puberty are not large enough to be attributed to biological factors. But this particular notion was not supported by our data analyses. Rather, the results provided convincing evidence that some anthropometric variables have a significant impact on gender differences during childhood. Elaboration of this finding prompts consideration of two relevant issues, the first of which concerns the separability of biological factors from environmental ones. To reiterate, the results show that certain anthropometric variables greatly affect gender differences in performance. But environmental factors, such as physical activity and exercise, may contribute to gender differences in anthropometric variables, particularly body weight and fat. The extent to which this occurs and ultimately impacts on gender-related performance differences is not clearly understood at the present time. It does seem apparent, however, that future research and theory development should take biological-environmental interactions into account, rather than approaching gender differences from an either/or perspective. Furthermore, although it is virtually impossible to disentangle the effects of all potential factors, the dynamics of an interactive paradigm might be considered in terms of directional and bidirectional causal relations. Empirical evaluation of longitudinal data through structural equation modeling (Bentler, 1985; Jöreskog & Sörbom, 1984; Judd, Jessor, & Donovan, 1986) may be the most viable approach.

The second interpretive caveat pertains to a practical implication of the finding presented herein. When gender differences in physical performance are mistakenly viewed as solely biological in origin (i.e., as a naturally evolving phenomenon), parents, teachers, and coaches have different expectations for boys than for girls (Greendorfer, 1980; Housner, 1981; Sherif & Rattray, 1976). This fosters differential treatment in terms of encouragement, instruction, and practice opportunities, which serves to increase gender differences. Our results affirm that anthropometric factors have a substantial influence on gender differences during childhood. However, environmental factors also contribute to gender differences in performance prior to puberty. In addition, it is generally held that girls can benefit from various forms of intervention and efforts designed to enhance performance. Therefore, although physically based gender differences are real, there is no reason why girls should not receive equal treatment and opportunities relative to participation in physical activities and sports.

The extent to which the results varied with age was quite dramatic. As indicated in Figure 1, the gender differences in performance of three specific variables exhibited very marked increases with advancing age. What is most interesting, however, is the age-related *decrease* in the degree to which fatness contributed to these gender differences. Thus, the fatness differences between the boys and girls, although contributing substantially to the performance differences at all ages, were *relatively* less important at the older age levels. To a lesser degree, and only for activities that are predominantly weight supporting or body projection, this holds true for the combination of fatness, fat-free body weight, and height differences between boys and girls.

These findings and interpretations may run counter to common beliefs. In particular, it is generally acknowledged that gender differences in performance increase with age and that gender differences in anthropometric measures increase with age. A reasonable deduction from such facts is that increasing performance differences can be attributed to increasing anthropometric differences, and even become more dependent on them with advancing age. However, the findings of this study run counter to such an argument. Our results indicated that the age-related increase in male performance superiority could not be totally accounted for by changes in male–female differences in anthropometric characteristics. How can this be explained? Although other anthropometric variables could play a role, the three measures included in the present study were found to have a major impact on performance. In addition, the results substantiated that our variables significantly affect performance differences between the sexes. In accordance with the interactional perspective presented earlier, we reaffirm that both biological and environmental factors contribute to gender differences in performance. However, we conclude that, with advancing age, the gender-related differences in performance may become increasingly more a function of previously discussed environmental factors. Support for this position derives from the widely held premise that boys are more likely than girls to receive encouragement and reinforcement for sport participation, which differentially influences their physical activity behaviors and patterns (see Coakley, 1987; Greendorfer & Brundage, 1987; McPherson, 1986). With advancing age, the cumulative effect of society's gender-related norms and opportunities may thus exert a more powerful environmental force on gender differences in performance. Our conclusion reinforces Thomas and French's (1985) assertion that at puberty environmental factors "inflate these gender differences beyond biological explanations" (p. 278). We recognize, however, that our conclusion is less than definitive. Rather, it invites future empirical attention to quantification of the interactive functioning of biological and environmental factors that serve as codeterminants of gender differences in performance.

A final result pertaining to task specificity merits consideration. Unlike the performance measures that require considerable movement or support of body weight, the wall pass is primarily an eye–hand coordination task. As expected, there was a lack of association between wall pass performance and percentage fat for both sexes at all three grade levels. This finding, along with the task-specific results discussed earlier, emphasizes that the nature of the task is an important factor on which generalizability is partly dependent. Therefore, in addition to considering the bipolar (biological–environmental) determination paradigm, future empirical work and theorizing should aptly take account of the complex interplay among many factors, including the nature of the task and the manner in which specific tasks are affected by anthropometric variables. In this regard, adoption of a multidimensional perspective will best serve to advance understanding of gender-related performance differences.

References

Anastasi, A. (1981). Sex differences: Historical perspectives and methodological implications. *Developmental Review, 1,* 187-206.

Archer, J., & Lloyd, B. (1985). *Sex and gender.* New York: Cambridge University Press.

Bentler, P. M. (1985). *Theory and implementation of EQS: A structural equations program.* Los Angeles: BMDP Statistical Software.

Branta, C. F., Painter, M., & Kiger, J. E. (1987). Gender differences in play patterns and sport participation of North American youth. In D. Gould & M. R. Weiss (Eds.), *Advances in pediatric sport sciences: Vol. 2. Behavioral issues* (pp. 25-42). Champaign, IL: Human Kinetics.

Brennan, R. L. (1983). *Elements of generalizability theory.* Iowa City, IA: American College Testing Program.

Carre, F. A., Mosher, R. E., & Schutz, R. W. (1982). B. C. assessment of physical education. *Canadian Association for Health, Physical Education, and Recreation Journal, 48,* 7-10.

Coakley, J. (1987). Children and the sport socialization process. In D. Gould & M. R. Weiss (Eds.), *Advances in pediatric sport sciences: Vol. 2. Behavioral issues* (pp. 43-60). Champaign, IL: Human Kinetics.

Eagly, A. H. (1983). Gender and social influence: A social psychological analysis. *American Psychologist, 38,* 971-981.

Eckert, H. M. (1987). *Motor development* (3rd ed.). Indianapolis, IN: Benchmark Press.

Greendorfer, S. L. (1980). Gender differences in physical activity. *Motor Skills: Theory into Practice, 4,* 83-90.

Greendorfer, S. L., & Brundage, C. L. (1987). Sex differences in children's motor skills: Toward a cross-disciplinary perspective. In M. Adrian (Ed.), *Medicine and sport science: Sportswomen* (Vol. 24, pp. 125-137). Basel, Switzerland: Karger.

Hansman, C. (1970). Anthropometry and related data. In R. W. McCammon (Ed.), *Human growth and development* (pp. 101-154). Springfield, IL: Charles C Thomas.

Haubenstricker, J. L., & Seefeldt, V. (1986). Acquisition of motor skills during childhood. In V. Seefeldt (Ed.), *Physical activity and well-being* (pp. 41-102). Reston, VA: American Alliance for Health, Physical Education, Recreation, and Dance.

Haywood, K. M. (1986). *Life span motor development.* Champaign, IL: Human Kinetics.

Hensley, L. D., East, W. B., & Stillwell, J. L. (1982). Body fatness and motor performance during preadolescence. *Research Quarterly for Exercise and Sport, 53,* 133-140.

Housner, L. D. (1981). Sex-role stereotyping: Implications for teaching elementary physical education. *Motor Skills: Theory into Practice, 5,* 107-116.

Hutt, C. (1972). *Males and females.* Harmondsworth, Middlesex, England: Penguin.

Jöreskog, K. G., & Sörbom, D. (1984). *LISREL VI: Analysis of linear structural relationships by the method of maximum likelihood.* Mooresville, IN: Scientific Software.

Judd, C. M., Jessor, R., & Donovan, J. E. (1986). Structural equation models and personality research. *Journal of Personality, 54,* 149-198.

Keogh, J., & Sugden, D. (1985). *Movement skill development.* Englewood Cliffs, NJ: Prentice-Hall.

Lewko, J. H., & Greendorfer, S. L. (1982). Family influence and sex differences in children's socialization into sport: A review. In R. A. Magill, M. J. Ash, & F. L. Smoll (Eds.), *Children in sport* (2nd ed., pp. 279-293). Champaign, IL: Human Kinetics.

Liss, M. B. (1983). *Social and cognitive skills: Sex roles and children's play.* New York: Academic Press.

Lohman, T. G. (1986). Applicability of body composition techniques and constants for children and youths. *Exercise and Sport Sciences Reviews, 14,* 325-357.

Maccoby, E. E. (1988). Gender as a social category. *Developmental Psychology, 24,* 755-765.

Maccoby, E. E., & Jacklin, C. N. (1974). *The psychology of sex differences.* Stanford, CA: Stanford University Press.

Malina, R. M. (1975). Anthropometric correlates of strength and motor performance. *Exercise and Sport Sciences Reviews, 3,* 249-274.

Malina, R. M. (1980). Environmentally related correlates of motor development and performance during infancy and childhood. In C. B. Corbin (Ed.), *A textbook of motor development* (2nd ed., pp. 212-224). Dubuque, IA: Wm. C. Brown.

Malina, R. M. (1986). Physical growth and maturation. In V. Seefeldt (Ed.), *Physical activity and well-being* (pp. 3-38). Reston, VA: American Alliance for Health, Physical Education, Recreation, and Dance.

McPherson, B. D. (1986). Socialization theory and research: Toward a "new wave" of scholarly inquiry in a sport context. In C. R. Rees & A. W. Miracle (Eds.), *Sport and social theory* (pp. 111-134). Champaign, IL: Human Kinetics.

Mischel, W. (1966). A social-learning view of sex differences in behavior. In E. E. Maccoby (Ed.), *The development of sex differences* (pp. 56-81). Stanford, CA: Stanford University Press.

National Center for Health Statistics. (1972). *Skinfold thickness of children 6-11 years* (DHEW Publication No. HSM 73-1602). Washington, DC: U.S. Government Printing Office.

National Center for Health Statistics. (1974). *Skinfold thickness of youths 12-17 years* (DHEW Publication No. HRA 74-1614). Washington, DC: U.S. Government Printing Office.

National Center for Health Statistics. (1977). *NCHS growth curves for children birth-18 years* (DHEW Publication No. PHS 78-1650). Washington, DC: U.S. Government Printing Office.

Petersen, A. C. (1980). Biopsychosocial processes in the development of sex-related differences. In J. E. Parsons (Ed.), *The psychobiology of sex differences and sex roles* (pp. 31-55). Washington, DC: Hemisphere.

Sherif, C. W., & Rattray, G. D. (1976). Psychological development and activity in middle childhood. In J. G. Albinson & G. M. Andrew (Eds.), *Child in sport and physical activity* (pp. 97-132). Baltimore, MD: University Park.

Slaughter, M. H., Lohman, T. G., & Misner, J. E. (1977). Relationship of somatotype and body composition to physical performance in 7- to 12-year-old boys. *Research Quarterly, 48,* 159-168.

Slaughter, M. H., Lohman, T. G., & Misner, J. E. (1980). Association of somatotype and body composition to physical performance in 7-12 year-old girls. *Journal of Sports Medicine and Physical Fitness, 20,* 189-198.

Smith, P. K. (1986). Exploration, play and social development in boys and girls. In D. J. Hargreaves & A. M. Cooley (Eds.), *The psychology of sex roles* (pp. 118-141). London: Harper & Row.

Thomas, J. R., & French, K. E. (1985). Gender differences across age in motor performance: A meta-analysis. *Psychological Bulletin, 98,* 260-282.

Wilson, E. O. (1975). *Sociobiology: The new synthesis.* Cambridge, MA: Harvard University Press.

Received February 13, 1989
Revision received October 2, 1989
Accepted October 5, 1989 ∎

Sex Differences in Human Motor Activity Level

Warren O. Eaton and Lesley Reid Enns
University of Manitoba, Winnipeg, Manitoba, Canada

Motor activity level, or customary energy expenditure through movement, is a cornerstone dimension of temperament. In this article we address the unresolved question of sex differences in activity level (AL) by quantitatively integrating results from 90 citations encompassing 127 independent sex difference contrasts. Males are generally more active than females, $d = .49$, although the magnitude of the difference is associated with other features of the research investigation, such as participant age and situational characteristics. This AL result is judged a large effect within the context of established behavioral sex differences, and implications are discussed.

Activity level (AL) is a dimension of individual difference that appears as a primary component of most scales of infant and child temperament (Buss & Plomin, 1984; Hubert, Wachs, Peters-Martin, & Gandour, 1982; Thomas & Chess, 1977), in large measure because motor activity is a highly salient feature of child behavior. Although it is widely believed that males have higher motor AL than females, the question of AL sex differences has remained largely unresolved in the scientific literature. For example, in the most recent review of the issue, Maccoby and Jacklin (1974) failed to reach a firm conclusion. Research integration techniques have improved considerably since Maccoby and Jacklin's review, and our intent was to use such improvements to clarify the uncertainty about sex differences in AL. Should they exist, sex differences in AL may well be influential in the sex-differentiated experiences of males and females. For example, AL has been correlated with caregiver behavior during infancy (Campbell, Kuyek, Lang, & Partington, 1971; Fish & Crockenberg, 1981). If male and female infants systematically differ in AL, caregiver behavior might systematically differ for the sexes as a consequence.

Activity level has been operationalized and measured in a variety of ways, and to bring order to the diversity of measures, we define *activity level* as the individual's customary level of energy expenditure through movement. It is helpful to draw an analogy between one's AL and one's disposable income. Just as one's income can be spent for a variety of purposes and in a variety of ways, so too can one's motor energy be directed toward a variety of goals and in a variety of forms. Despite the diversity of expenditures, it remains possible to make generalizations about both one's customary energy expenditure and one's level of spending. From our perspective, a measure of behavior that reflects energy expenditure through movement is considered a measure of AL. Movement frequency, duration, amplitude, and type may all affect the amount of energy expended. In general, large, frequent, long-duration, or expansive movements require more energy than fine, infrequent, short-duration, or constricted ones. Therefore, acceptable measures of AL include measurements of movement type, frequency, duration, or amplitude, and encompass specific limb movements as well as whole body actions.

The diversity of AL measures used across studies makes it impossible to compare one study's raw scores directly with another's. In order to integrate study findings, we used a scale-independent index of effect size, d (Cohen, 1969), to summarize the results of a between-sexes comparison, and then aggregated ds across investigations with measures of AL. Using the effect size statistic also allowed us to estimate the magnitude of any sex difference found and to assess, through correlational analyses, a variety of developmental, situational, measurement, and investigator factors thought to be related to the AL sex difference magnitude.

Factors Related to Sex Differences in AL

Developmental Factors

Maccoby and Jacklin (1974) suggested that sex differences in AL are age-specific. They concluded that there was no evidence for AL sex differences in children under 12 months, but that the data for older children were more consistent in portraying boys as more active, at least during the preschool years. On this basis one would expect a positive correlation between age and d during childhood. Also, if AL sex differences are the product of sex-socialization processes, one would generally expect larger differences in older samples because such processes are thought to take time before their presence is felt. A positive correlation between age and effect size could, however, also result from other causes, such as puberty-related increases in sexual dimorphism.

Preliminary findings were reported both in a master's thesis by the second author under the supervision of the first, University of Manitoba, 1982, and in a paper presented to the Society for Research in Child Development, Detroit, 1983.

This work was supported by Social Sciences and Humanities Research Council of Canada grants 410-80-0123 and 410-81-0125 to Warren Eaton.

A special debt of gratitude is owed the many investigators who cooperated with requests for unpublished information. The hospitality of the Arizona State University Department of Psychology during a research study leave of the first author is also gratefully acknowledged, as are the contributions of Art Beaman and Solange Lagassé.

Correspondence concerning this article should be addressed to Warren Eaton, Department of Psychology, University of Manitoba, Winnipeg, Manitoba, Canada R3T 2N2.

As a component of temperament, AL is often presumed to be constitutional in origin. Although heritable characteristics are not necessarily manifest in early life, the early developmental appearance of variability on a temperamental dimension lends credibility to the contention that the variable has congenital or genetic origins while rendering less plausible a social-environmental explanation. Consequently, sex differences apparent at birth or in early infancy have interesting theoretical implications.

Even the neonate is subject to direct social-environmental influences, and a complete disentangling of social influences from the child's endogenous characteristics is impossible even in the first postnatal days. Socialization influences could, however, be discounted as the cause of AL sex differences if such differences exist prior to birth. An interesting feature of the AL construct is its amenability to measurement during fetal life. If sex differences in AL exist prior to birth, a congenital basis for AL sex differences becomes more plausible. To evaluate this possibility, we extended our consideration to studies of fetal activity level.

Situational Factors

Activity level sex differences may be situation-specific inasmuch as, in Maccoby and Jacklin's (1974) view, those studies with significant sex differences had involved situations with salient elicitors of activity for boys rather than for girls. For example, Maccoby and Jacklin (1974) hypothesized that under stress, girls freeze and become less active, whereas boys maintain more normal ALs. Thus, if the research situation is stressful, a sex difference may emerge when it would not otherwise. Little support has emerged, however, for the stress hypothesis. Maccoby and Jacklin (1973) found that one-year-old boys, who were generally more active than their female counterparts, showed greater activity reductions in response to a fear-arousing situation than did girls. Eaton and Keats (1982) found that in comparison with a triad condition, both sexes showed comparable activity reductions under the stress of being alone in a relatively novel setting. Other investigators have induced stress in young children by having the youngster's mother leave the room (Cox & Campbell, 1968; Gershaw & Schwarz, 1971; Routh, Walton, & Padan-Belkin, 1978), and have reported comparable reductions in AL for both boys and girls. Nevertheless, we hypothesized that the sex difference magnitude would positively correlate with level of stress.

Other aspects of the research setting may also influence the magnitude of the obtained sex difference. Novel or unfamiliar settings have been used in research with young children, and if, in comparison to girls, boys are more inclined to explore, the level of situational novelty for the setting should correlate positively with the magnitude of AL sex differences.

Situations also vary considerably in the degree to which motor activity is controlled. A child on a playground has greater choice in her or his selection of motor behavior than does the same child at a desk in school. Consequently, any sex-differentiated predispositions toward high or low AL should be more apparent in uncontrolled or unrestricted settings. Therefore, a negative correlation between restrictiveness and effect size was predicted.

The presence of same-sex peers may stimulate higher ALs in boys than in girls (Maccoby & Jacklin, 1974). If such a sex-related "contagion" effect is operative, the well-known tendency of children to select same-sex peers as playmates (Fagot & Patterson, 1969; Laosa & Brophy, 1972) could magnify existing sex differences. Boys choosing other boys as playmates would naturally tend to be more active than would girls choosing girls as playmates. Although Eaton and Keats (1982) found that peer presence had a powerful facilitating effect on motor activity level, it did not interact with sex. Consequently, we simply predicted greater AL sex differences for those situations in which peers were present than for those in which they were absent.

Measurement Factors

The AL measures fall into three general categories: instruments, ratings, and observations. Instruments designed to measure motor activity (see Tryon, 1984, for examples) do not depend directly on human judges and are the most objective of the three types of measures. Measures based on observational systems (e.g., counting the squares on a floor grid into which a child enters) are probably more susceptible to bias than instruments because observers have to make coding decisions within a social context. The gender of the subject is nearly always known and might influence coding decisions. Rating measures, which have typically required parents, caregivers, or other knowledgeable persons to rate a focal individual's AL, could be readily influenced by social stereotypes, and we saw ratings as the least objective class of measures. To the extent that AL sex differences are a product of social myths about sex differences, measurement objectivity should be negatively correlated with effect size, and the largest effect should be found with rating measures, the smallest with instrument measures.

We considered the inclusiveness of the AL measure, which could range from a very specific measure such as an arm movement to a broad, global measure encompassing many aspects of the individual's behavior. Measurement procedures also vary considerably in how obtrusive they are within the research setting. To explore the possibility that the level of obtrusiveness could covary with sex difference magnitude, we also assessed studies for degree of measure obtrusiveness. No hypotheses regarding measure inclusiveness or obtrusiveness were formulated.

Measurement reliability and sensitivity were two additional characteristics we thought might affect study outcomes. As Block (1976) and Epstein (1979) have cogently argued, failures to find coherence in research outcomes may result from the use of crude and unreliable measures. Error-ridden and insensitive measures are less likely to produce coherent findings than are more discriminating ones, and greater measurement reliability and sensitivity should be associated with AL sex differences of greater magnitude.

Investigator Factors

Of necessity, research reviews rely primarily on the published literature. Interpretive difficulties arise because it can be plausibly argued that published work is biased in favor of statistically significant findings and thus toward inflated effect size estimates. We found, for example, that the information necessary for the calculation of d scores was more often present in studies with significant findings. Other reviewers have addressed this problem by assuming a null effect ($d = 0.0$) when d cannot be calculated from available information. However, unpublished d scores may not average to a null effect, and we sought to test this directly by obtaining the necessary information from authors who had conducted an investigation with an acceptable measure of AL and who had not provided a significance test or adequate information for a d score calculation. The effect size so estimated from the unpublished sources represents a lower bound population effect size.

On the assumption that researchers tend to find that for which they are searching, we also expected that larger effect sizes would be found when sex differences were explicitly hypothesized by the investigator versus when they were examined incidentally.

Once taken for granted, sex differences have drawn increasingly skeptical scrutiny in recent years, and it seemed possible that year of publication would correlate negatively with effect size. In this vein, Hyde (1984) found an historical decline in the magnitude of gender differences in aggression. To consider this possibility, we looked at the association between year of publication and effect size magnitude.

Lastly, we considered sex of researcher as a potential source of influence. Eagly and Carli (1981) found that sex of researcher correlated with outcomes in studies of social influence. To investigate this possibility we chose to correlate the proportion of male authors for a given publication with the magnitude of the AL sex difference reported. Because the social desirability of high motor AL is somewhat ambiguous, we were uncertain about the direction researcher bias would take and consequently made no directional prediction.

Method

Literature Search

Study selection conventions. Studies selected for analysis were drawn from the English-language, empirical research literature. Because our goal was to evaluate AL sex differences in normal populations, subject samples with reported evidence of pathology (emotional, behavioral, physical, or mental problems) were excluded. Consequently most of the work on hyperactivity is not a part of the present review. The control groups used in hyperactivity studies, however, often fulfilled our selection criteria and were suitable for inclusion. We began our search with a free text search of the *Psychological Abstracts* data base using the following descriptors: rhythmicity, movement, activity level, mobility, restlessness, vigor in play, motoric activity, motor activity, tempo, locomotor activity, energy level, and change in activity. Additional studies were located through the standard bibliographic practice of following up references from pertinent studies. Finally, we found a number of studies simply by chance; for example, through colleagues who knew about our research and who, in the course of their own work, noticed studies with information on AL.

Appropriate measures. We selected measures for inclusion that, however crudely, reflected energy expenditure through movement. They included measures of movement type (gross vs. fine), frequency, duration, and amplitude, as well as ratings on personality descriptors such as "energetic," "active," and "vigorous." In cases in which a scale comprised multiple items, we examined the item content, and included the scale only if a majority of the constituent items were primarily concerned with motor activity. This criterion excluded scales such as the Conners (1969) hyperactivity factor, which has only one purely motor activity item out of eight. If information was presented on each item of a composite scale, only motor activity items were included in the analysis. These restrictions were designed to minimize the confounding of motor activity with correlated variables such as inattentiveness and aggressiveness.

Calculation of d scores. The index of effect size used was the d score, which is simply the difference between male and female means standardized by dividing by the pooled standard deviation. An unbiased estimator (Hedges, 1982, p. 492, Equations 4 and 5) was used to adjust the d scores. With this procedure, d scores based on large samples are weighted more heavily than are those drawn from small samples. Even though d scores can be derived from a number of commonly reported statistics, many studies did not provide the requisite information and so could not be included in a quantitative integration. We requested information for such studies from the authors of 45 post-1976 publications. If no reply was received after 6 weeks, we sent a second request. Twenty-five authors provided the necessary information. In several other cases we obtained unpublished data from preprints, correspondence, and archival sources (e.g., the Library of Congress).

Studies versus comparisons. Many studies used multiple, nonindependent measures of AL. Because quantitative research integration techniques typically assume independent observations, we found it necessary to distinguish between independent and nonindependent ds. Hereafter, we refer to independent d scores as *studies* and to nonindependent d scores as *comparisons*.

Sample. Inspection of the initial distribution of comparison d scores revealed a distribution with a few very large positive d scores. To better meet the assumption of normality, three comparisons with d scores larger than 2.0 were dropped from the analysis, leaving a sample of 205 comparisons from 127 studies. These studies were drawn from 90 citations.

Coding

We chose to code each comparison rather than each study because in many situations an investigation included several comparisons, each with a different AL measure. Averaging across measures in this situation would have meant the loss of much valuable information. In cases of multiple comparisons within a given report (e.g., several appropriate AL measures) the mean of comparison d scores was used as the study d score (all comparison d scores were first weighted using Hedges's procedure). Coded features of each comparison, such as novelty, stress, and the like, were not averaged when combined to create study variables. Rather, if the comparisons being combined to create a study value all had the same comparison value on a given variable, that value was used for the study. Otherwise the study value for the variable was omitted from analyses. Parallel analyses, one based on comparisons (nonindependent) and the other based on studies (independent) were consequently possible. The first 104 comparisons identified were coded separately by each author. Interrater reliabilities were estimated using Cohen's kappa (κ) for categorical codes and correlations (r) for continuously scored characteristics, and are reported in parentheses after the variable descriptions that follow. The kappa statistic is a stringent test because it corrects for chance agreements, which can be frequent when the number of coding categories is small. After reliability calculations, we decided on final codes for the 104 comparisons, discussing initial disagreements and revising codes until a mutually acceptable decision was reached. Subsequent coding was done by the first author.

Age ($r = .99$). For each comparison we coded the mean chronological age in months of the sample. If only an age range was given, the midpoint of the range was used. For some analyses four age groups were formed as follows: prenatal, infant (0–11 months), preschool (12–72 months), and older (73 months and greater).

Stress (κ = .47). The stressfulness of the situation for participants was coded on a 3-point scale. High stress (3) was assigned in settings in which the subject was being tested or timed, as well as in settings in which the apparatus was intrusive. Settings were low in stressfulness (1) if the subject was inferred to be comfortable and at ease, such as during free play at home. Unspecified school classrooms were typically assigned a moderate amount of stress (2) and unspecified home settings a low level of stress.

Novelty (κ = .71). We coded a frequently encountered setting as low in novelty (1), while coding a setting inferred to be totally unfamiliar to the subject as highly novel (3). A setting with which the subject was familiar but did not encounter frequently was rated as of medium novelty (2).

Restrictiveness (κ = .58). Restrictiveness was based on the degree of inferred movement restriction in the setting. Low restrictiveness (1) was assigned for settings in which behavior was relatively unfettered, such as outdoor free play. Medium restrictiveness (2) was assigned for settings such as school classrooms or structured preschool activities. High restrictiveness (3) was assigned when major setting restrictions were present, such as when the subject was seated in a chair while taking a test.

Peer presence (κ = .79). Comparisons were also classified as to whether peers were absent (1) or present (2).

Objectivity (κ = .88). The categories we used were ratings, observations, and instruments. The ratings category (1) included all measures based on subjective judgments of a focal individual's activity level. The rating could involve a specific judgment, such as "tends to wriggle in seat," or an inclusive one, such as "is a very active person." The observations category (2) comprised direct observation measures that used established scoring rules, such as counting grid crossings. These observation measures usually included some form of time-based sampling. The instruments category (3) included all types of automatic recording devices, such as mechanical, sonographic, and electronic instruments.

Reliability (r = .76). A number of studies presented some type of reliability coefficient, for example, interrater agreement, and we recorded these. When more than one reliability coefficient was available, we used the smallest, and presumably the most conservative, estimate.

Sensitivity (r = .47). We were only able to operationalize this variable for rating scale measures. Such ratings typically involved individual items, each with ordered scale points specifying varying levels of vigor, energy, activity, and so on. We assumed that more sensitive measures used more scale points per item, and consequently reasoned that a 3-point scale would be less sensitive to differences than a 7-point scale. In cases in which items were collapsed or eliminated for data analysis by the authors, we coded the number of scale points actually used in calculating the statistic on which *d* was based.

Inclusiveness (κ = .52). Low inclusiveness (1) was coded if a highly specific measure, such as an arm movement, was the measure of AL. Medium inclusiveness (2) was coded when several specific measures of AL were combined, and high inclusiveness (3) was inferred when a broad or global AL measure was used, such as a rating of general behavior.

Obtrusiveness (κ = .90). Obtrusiveness was judged as low (1) when AL was measured in some hidden or nonobvious fashion, as medium (2) when measurement procedures were apparent but mildly attention-getting, and as high (3) when highly salient procedures or apparatuses were used.

Hypothesis test (κ = .44). The hypothesis test was coded as a (1) if sex differences in AL were treated in an incidental fashion and as a (2) if the study description stated or implied an expectation of sex differences.

Percentage of male authors (r = .92). We coded the percentage of male authors without consideration of order of authorship. Because in several instances many comparisons came from a single publication, each publication was only considered once in the analyses for this investigation variable. To correlate effect size with percentage of male authors, we used the mean of all *d* scores for a given publication.

Publication status. This was coded as (1) if the necessary information for a *d* score calculation was available in a published source, and as (2) if the effect size information was obtained from an unpublished source. No reliability estimate was calculated for this variable.

Year of publication. As with sex of researcher, each publication was coded once for this variable, and the calendar year was used. No reliability estimate was calculated.

Results

Sample sizes ranged from 7 to 25,000, with a median of 68. The mean chronological age of the samples ranged from 2 months before birth to 30 years, with a median of 55.5 months. A variety of research settings were represented, with 25% of all comparisons done in home settings, 25% in preschool settings, 10% in laboratories, 9% in school classrooms, and 30% in a variety of other settings.

As Figure 1 shows, the frequency distribution of the *d*s from the 127 studies is roughly symmetrical, with a mean effect size of .49 and a standard deviation of .44. Testing the null hypothesis ($d = 0.0$) using Hedges's (1982, Equation 13) procedure, the null hypothesis was rejected, $z = 50.79$, $p < .001$. Translated into correlational terms, the obtained effect size represents a point-biserial correlation between sex and AL of .24, and the proportion of total AL variance associated with sex is about 5%. Expressed in yet another way, the average male subject (at the 50th percentile) is more active than 69% of the female subjects.

Unlocated studies with null findings are not included in the present analysis for obvious reasons. Using Orwin's (1983) procedure we estimated that 500 such undiscovered null studies were required to reduce the mean effect size to .10, a magnitude we judged to be trivial. The fail-safe sample size necessary to

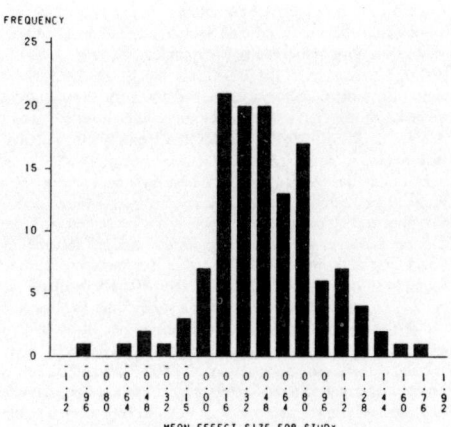

Figure 1. Frequency bar chart of mean study effect sizes ($n = 127$).

Table 1
Descriptive Statistics for Coded Variables

Coded variables	M	SD	Range	n
Developmental				
Chronological age (months)	75.4	64.9	-2-360	127
Situational				
Stress	1.22	0.46	1-3	107
Novelty	1.20	0.58	1-3	95
Restrictiveness	1.40	0.56	1-3	108
Peer presence	1.67	0.47	1-2	82
Measurement				
Objectivity	1.69	0.82	1-3	118
Reliability	.80	.13	.40-.98	54
Sensitivity	4.90	2.06	1-11	58
Inclusiveness	2.01	0.83	1-3	119
Obtrusiveness	1.38	0.57	1-3	117
Investigator				
Publication status	1.22	0.42	1-2	127
Hypothesis test	1.19	0.39	1-2	127
Percentage of male authors	54	42	0-100	81
Year	1971	14.9	1900-1983	88

Note. All statistics are based on studies, except for percentage of male authors and year, which are based on citations.

reduce the combined probability of our outcome to nonsignificance (Rosenthal, 1979) would be much larger. Moreover, our sample of 127 comprised 99 studies from published sources and 28 from unpublished ones. The mean effect size for the unpublished studies was .37 and differed significantly from zero, $z = 14.05, p < .001$. Thus, the findings of an AL sex difference are to be found in file drawers as well as in journal articles and books.

Hedges (1982) and others (e.g., Rosenthal & Rubin, 1982) have argued that the homogeneity of the sample needs to be considered to avoid, among other situations, a bimodal distribution of effect size. Whereas inspection of Figure 1 clearly rules out the possibility of bimodality, it is possible that not all observed effect sizes share a common population effect size. Hedges's test for homogeneity was significant, $\chi^2(126) = 937.7$, and thus we can reject the hypothesis that all observed effects reflect the same population value. We now turn to an analysis of variables associated with sex difference magnitude. A summary of the descriptive statistics for these variables is presented in Table 1.

In evaluating factors that may have influenced effect size magnitude, we first considered the correlations between coded variables and d, and these correlations are presented in Table 2. Four variables emerged as significant: age, restrictiveness, sensitivity, and inclusiveness. Greater sex differences were found in studies with older samples, in unrestricted situations, with more finely differentiated rating scales, and with specific rather than global measures. These results are illustrated in more detail in Table 3, which lists effect size statistics by study variable values. An examination of Table 3 also illustrates a problem common to many meta-analyses, namely that all levels of a given coding variable are often not well represented in the sample. For example, relatively few studies were scored as being medium or high on novelty. Thus, the coded variables are limited by imperfect reliability, coarse categorization, and nonnormal distributions, all factors that attenuate observed relations with effect size outcome.

Developmental Factors

In reevaluating the question of sex differences in the first year of life, we found that the mean effect size for the 14 infancy studies (mean ages of from 0 to 11 months), $d = .29$, differed significantly from zero, $z = 3.62, p < .001$. It would take 27 undiscovered null ($d = 0.0$) studies to reduce the obtained d to .10, and it seems likely that AL sex differences are present in infancy. The mean effect size for the 6 prenatal studies, $d = .33$, did not differ significantly from zero, $z = 1.39$, and fewer unrecovered null studies (14) would be needed to reduce the mean effect to .10. In contrast, for preschool and older subjects the data point unequivocally to an AL sex difference. The mean effects for these two older groups were large (mean ds of .44 and .64, respectively), were significantly different from zero (zs of 14.32 and 49.02), and were relatively immune to file drawer studies (fail-safe ns of 197 and 259).

Situational factors. In addition to being related to effect size magnitude, restrictiveness was positively correlated with stress, $r = .59, p < .0001$, and novelty, $r = .36, p < .001$. Novelty itself correlated negatively with peer presence, $r = -.76, p < .0001$. Though other situational variable intercorrelations were nonsignificant, the pattern of results suggested marked interdependence among the situational variables.

Measurement factors. Measurement factors were less strongly interrelated than were situational variables, though inclusiveness was related to objectivity, $r = -.44, p < .0001$. Objectivity, in turn, correlated positively with obtrusiveness, $r = -.71, p < .0001$, and sensitivity, $r = .28, p < .05$.

Table 2
Correlations of Coded Variables With Adjusted Effect Sizes

Coded variables	r	n
Developmental		
Chronological age	.26**	127
Situational		
Stress	-.13	107
Novelty	-.12	95
Restrictiveness	-.22*	108
Peer presence	.18	82
Measurement		
Objectivity	.02	118
Reliability	-.05	54
Sensitivity[a]	.33*	58
Inclusiveness	-.28**	119
Obtrusiveness	.05	117
Investigator		
Publication status[b]	-.15	127
Hypothesis test[c]	-.06	127
Percentage of male authors	.02[d]	81
Year	.00[d]	88

[a] Based on rating measures only. [b] Published = 1, unpublished = 2.
[c] Activity level (AL) sex difference hypothesized = 1, AL sex difference incidental = 2. [d] Based on citations rather than studies.
* $p < .05$. ** $p < .01$.

Table 3
Descriptive Statistics for Adjusted Effect Sizes by Coded Variables

Categorical variables	M	SE	n
Age group			
Prenatal	.33	.15	6
Infant	.29	.11	14
Preschool	.44	.06	58
Older	.64	.06	49
Stress			
Low	.55	.05	85
Medium	.37	.09	20
High	.52	.38	2
Novelty			
Low	.52	.05	84
Medium	.48	.17	3
High	.32	.21	8
Restrictiveness			
Low	.59	.06	69
Medium	.39	.07	35
High	.32	.31	4
Peer presence			
Absent	.44	.10	27
Present	.62	.06	55
Objectivity			
Rating	.50	.05	64
Observation	.47	.10	27
Instrument	.53	.08	27
Reliability			
<.70	.41	.07	12
.70–.84	.50	.07	22
>.84	.43	.09	22
Sensitivity (no. of rating categories)			
3 or fewer	.26	.08	20
4–6	.47	.06	25
7 or more	.58	.13	13
Inclusiveness			
Low	.71	.07	40
Medium	.38	.06	38
High	.41	.07	41
Obtrusiveness			
Low	.49	.05	7
Medium	.56	.08	35
High	.46	.15	5
Publication status			
Published	.53	.05	99
Unpublished	.37	.06	28
Hypothesis test			
No	.51	.04	103
Yes	.44	.10	24

Investigator factors. These factors—publication status and hypothesis test—were not significantly correlated, r = −.16.

Multiple Regression

Given the lack of orthogonality within the sets of study characteristics, we conducted a multiple regression analysis with d as the dependent variable. Significance tests were applied to four sets of predictors: chronological age, situational factors, measurement factors, and investigator factors. To avoid multicollinearity problems, novelty was deleted from the situation set; to avoid undue sample size shrinkage, reliability and sensitivity were deleted from the measurement set. The resulting model was significant, $F(9, 61) = 3.43$, $p < .01$, $R^2 = .34$, and detailed results are presented in Table 4. A parallel regression analysis confirmed with comparisons, $F(9, 116) = 4.55$, $p < .0001$, $R^2 = .26$, the pattern of results obtained with studies, though in the comparison case the larger sample sizes contribute to more highly significant outcomes. In general, then, the regression analyses indicate that larger magnitudes in AL sex differences are found with older participants whose behavior is assessed in familiar, nonstressful, unrestrictive surroundings in the presence of peers.

Discussion

In general we found that males were more active than females by roughly one-half a standard deviation, a difference that accounts for a little less than 5% of the variation in the AL distribution. This general conclusion is mediated by various features of the surveyed studies but is nonetheless quite robust; hundreds of null studies would be required to reduce the mean d to a magnitude of .10 standard deviations and thousands of null studies would be needed to render the outcome nonsignificant. Attaching a descriptive adjective to the overall mean effect size is a hazardous enterprise, but it is possible to compare the present findings with others in the literature. In the context of other sex difference meta-analyses, a difference of one-half a standard deviation is large for a behavioral variable. Indeed, Deaux (1984) has surmised that 5% of explained variance in a specific social or cognitive variable is an upper boundary for sex differences. Differences of this boundary magnitude and their mean effect sizes include: spatial ability, .45 (Hyde, 1981); aggression, .50 (Hyde, 1984); mathematical reasoning, .44 (Rossi, 1983); and proportional reasoning, .48 (Meehan, 1984). Within this context, it can be concluded that sex differences in AL, $d = .49$,

Table 4
Multiple Regression Analyses of Activity Level Effect Size Magnitude

	Studies		Comparisons	
Coded variables	F^a	$t(69)$	F^b	$t(124)$
Developmental	5.79*		7.12**	
Chronological age		2.40*		2.67**
Situational	4.08*		8.18***	
Stress		−1.36		−1.25
Restrictiveness		−1.25		−2.52*
Peer presence		2.19*		2.14*
Measurement	1.21		2.33	
Objectivity		−0.22		0.25
Inclusiveness		−0.56		−0.82
Obtrusiveness		1.47		1.70
Investigator	2.25		1.35	
Pubication status		1.07		0.53
Hypothesis test		−1.59		−1.30

[a] df for numerator = number of variables in set; df for denominator = 61. [b] df for numerator = number of variables in set; df for denominator = 116.
* $p < .05$. ** $p < .01$. *** $p < .001$.

are well established, and Maccoby and Jacklin's (1974) equivocal conclusion about AL sex differences can be set aside.

Sex differences of this magnitude are probably more influential than one might think because small differences in means translate into large differences in the proportions of males and females beyond some extreme cutoff point (Hyde, 1981; Rossi, 1983). Data to illustrate this point with an AL example come from a large British study of the children on the Isle of Wight (Schachar, Rutter, & Smith, 1981), in which the teachers and parents rated child activity on a 7-point scale. With a scale cutoff that identified 9% of the sample as hyperactive, the ratio of boys to girls was 2 to 1. This 2-to-1 ratio at the extreme was generated by a difference of .25 SDs at the means. Such inequalities in male-to-female ratios can appear in other domains; for example, 15 DSM-III (American Psychiatric Association, 1980) categories make explicit reference to abnormally low or high levels of overt motor activity (Tryon, 1984). Insofar as AL is important for such diagnoses, unequal numbers of males and females are likely to appear in these diagnostic categories. In a more materialistic application, we would note that a gambler would do well to always bet that the most active child in a group will be a boy. For example, in a group of 20 children the odds would be 2 to 1 in the gambler's favor, assuming $d = .40$.

Sex ratios at the extremes may play a more commonplace role because AL is a likely candidate for what Hasher and Zacks (1984) characterize as automatic encoding. They argue that individuals are extremely sensitive to frequency of occurrence information. We would suggest that, as a highly visible characteristic, AL beyond some threshold is a likely candidate for such encoding. Thus, even though a rater might not be aware of the AL difference for the average boy and girl, the frequencies with which boys or girls appear at the extremes of the AL distribution might be automatically encoded and very accessible to retrieval, thus contributing to the common belief that boys are the more motorically active of the sexes.

The general finding of a sex difference proved to be resistant to the expected influences of many research variables we thought important. Most surprising, in our view, was the absence of a correlation between measure objectivity and effect size. We had incorrectly anticipated that raters, under the influence of sex role stereotypes, would overestimate sex differences relative to more objective measures. The absence of an objectivity effect suggests AL sex differences are not solely in the minds of beholders. Furthermore, the absence of influence for the year of publication, the percentage of male authors, and the hypothesis test variables also provides useful information. Findings of AL sex differences were not limited only to those looking for them, only to the past, or only to investigators of a particular gender.

Situations certainly influence ALs (Carpenter & Huston-Stein, 1980; Eaton & Keats, 1982), and it is not surprising that situational factors also influence the magnitude of AL sex differences. Two hypotheses regarding the effect of stress and novelty were clearly not supported by the data, and the trend ran opposite to that expected. Greater effect sizes tended to be found in low- rather than high-stress situations and in familiar rather than novel settings. On the other hand, our expectations about peer presence and restrictiveness were supported because greater differences appeared when peers were present and when the situation was unrestricted. This overall pattern suggests that maximal sex differences in AL will be found in situations that offer a good deal of latitude for the expression of individual differences: a familiar, nonthreatening, unrestricted social setting.

Age emerged as an important mediating variable. Though evidence for age-specificity was not to be found in our sample of studies, increasing CAs were associated with increasing sex difference magnitude. Nonetheless, AL sex differences were apparent in infancy as well as at later stages. Because 90% of the studies were of samples with mean ages of 15 years or less, it must be emphasized that this relation between AL sex difference magnitude and age is primarily applicable from infancy to middle adolescence, and it would be hazardous to extrapolate beyond adolescence. Indeed, if motor AL declines across adulthood, the magnitude of sex differences might well diminish in later life.

The association between age and sex difference magnitude confirms Block's (1976) contention that age correlates positively with sexual differentiation. Such an association was likely, Block argued, because social influences take time, because some sex differences do not emerge until adolescence, and because assessments of young children are psychometrically less reliable. Block's analysis is only partly applicable because, in the present case, AL sex differences were present before adolescence, and study reliability was not correlated with effect size. Nevertheless, the view that social influences enlarge AL sex differences is quite compatible with our data. At the same time, the early appearance of sex differences is also compatible with the position that social influences magnify existing differences rather than create them.

It is unfortunate that more prenatal studies could not be found, because even though the mean effect for the prenatal studies is close to that for infancy investigations, its magnitude could be quickly altered by a very few new studies. Whether or not additional prenatal studies will converge on a nonzero effect size remains to be seen, and the theoretically interesting question of prenatal sex differences has yet to be conclusively answered.

References

American Psychiatric Association (1980). *Diagnostic and statistical manual of mental disorders* (3rd ed.). Washington, DC: Author.

Block, J. H. (1976). Issues, problems, and pitfalls in assessing sex differences: A critical review of *The psychology of sex differences*. *Merrill-Palmer Quarterly, 22*, 283–308.

Buss, A. H., & Plomin, R. (1984). *Temperament: Early developing personality traits.* Hillsdale, NJ: Erlbaum.

Campbell, D., Kuyek, J., Lang, E., & Partington, M. W. (1971). Motor activity in early life: II. Daily motor activity output in the neonatal period. *Biology of the Neonate, 18,* 108–120.

Carpenter, C. J., & Huston-Stein, A. (1980). Activity structure and sex-typed behavior in preschool children. *Child Development, 51,* 862–872.

Cohen, J. (1969). *Statistical power analyses for the behavioral sciences.* New York: Academic Press.

Conners, C. K. (1969). A teacher rating scale for use in drug studies with children. *American Journal of Psychiatry, 126,* 884–888.

Cox, F. N., & Campbell, D. (1968). Young children in a new situation with and without their mothers. *Child Development, 39,* 123–131.

Deaux, K. (1984). Analysis of a decade's research on gender. *American Psychologist, 39,* 105-116.

Eagly, A., & Carli, L. (1981). Sex of researchers and sex-typed communications as determinants of sex differences in influenceability: A meta-analysis of social influence studies. *Psychological Bulletin, 90,* 1-20.

Eaton, W. O., & Keats, J. G. (1982). Peer presence, stress, and sex differences in the motor activity levels of preschoolers. *Developmental Psychology, 18,* 534-540.

Epstein, S. (1979). The stability of behavior: I. On predicting most of the people much of the time. *Journal of Personality and Social Psychology, 37,* 1097-1126.

Fagot, B. I., & Patterson, G. R. (1969). An in vivo analysis of reinforcing contingencies for sex-role behaviors in the preschool child. *Developmental Psychology, 1,* 563-568.

Fish, M., & Crockenberg, S. (1981). Correlates and antecedents of nine-month infant behavior and mother-infant interaction. *Infant Behavior and Development, 4,* 64-81.

Gershaw, N. J., & Schwarz, J. C. (1971). The effects of a familiar toy and mother's presence on exploratory and attachment behaviors in young children. *Child Development, 42,* 1662-1666.

Hasher, L., & Zacks, R. T. (1984). Automatic processing of fundamental information: The case of frequency of occurrence. *American Psychologist, 39,* 1372-1388.

Hedges, L. V. (1982). Estimation of effect size from a series of independent experiments. *Psychological Bulletin, 92,* 490-499.

Hubert, N. C., Wachs, T. D., Peters-Martin, P., & Gandour, M. J. (1982). The study of early temperament: Measurement and conceptual issues. *Child Development, 53,* 571-600.

Hyde, J. S. (1981). How large are cognitive gender differences? *American Psychologist, 36,* 892-901.

Hyde, J. S. (1984). How large are gender differences in aggression? A developmental meta-analysis. *Developmental Psychology, 20,* 722-736.

Laosa, L. M., & Brophy, J. E. (1972). Effects of sex and birth order on sex-role development and intelligence among kindergarten children. *Developmental Psychology, 6,* 409-415.

Maccoby, E. E., & Jacklin, C. N. (1973). Stress, activity, and proximity seeking: Sex differences in the year-old child. *Child Development, 44,* 34-42.

Maccoby, E. E., & Jacklin, C. N. (1974). *The psychology of sex differences.* Stanford, CA: Stanford University Press.

Meehan, A. M. (1984). A meta-analysis of sex differences in formal operational thought. *Child Development, 55,* 1110-1124.

Orwin, R. G. (1983). A fail-safe n for effect size in meta-analysis. *Journal of Educational Statistics, 8,* 157-159.

Rosenthal, R. (1979). The "file drawer problem" and tolerance for null results. *Psychological Bulletin, 85,* 638-641.

Rosenthal, R., & Rubin, D. B. (1982). Comparing effect sizes of independent studies. *Psychological Bulletin, 92,* 500-504.

Rossi, J. S. (1983). Ratios exaggerate gender differences in mathematical ability. *American Psychologist, 38,* 348.

Routh, D. K., Walton, M. D., & Padan-Belkin, E. (1978). Development of activity level in children revisited: Effects of mother presence. *Developmental Psychology, 14,* 571-581.

Schachar, R., Rutter, M., & Smith, A. (1981). The characteristics of situationally and pervasively hyperactive children: Implications for syndrome definition. *Journal of Child Psychology and Psychiatry, 22,* 375-392.

Thomas, A., & Chess, S. (1977). *Temperament and development.* New York: Brunner/Mazel.

Tryon, W. W. (1984). Principles and methods of mechanically measuring motor activity. *Behavioral Assessment, 6,* 129-139.

Appendix

Citations Used in the Review

Achenbach, T. M. (1969). Cue learning, associative responding, and school performance in children. *Developmental Psychology, 1,* 717-725.

Battle, E. S., & Lacey, B. (1972). A context for hyperactivity in children, over time. *Child Development, 43,* 757-773.

Baumrind, D., & Black, A. E. (1967). Socialization practices associated with dimensions of competence in preschool boys and girls. *Child Development, 38,* 291-327.

Bell, R. Q., Weller, G. M., & Waldrop, M. F. (1971). Newborn and preschooler: Organization of behavior and relations between periods. *Monographs of the Society for Research in Child Development, 36*(1 and 2, Serial No. 142).

Bernard, J. (1964). Prediction from human fetal measures. *Child Development, 35,* 1243-1248.

Beth-Halachmy, S. (1980). Elementary school children's play behavior during school recess periods. In P. F. Wilkinson (Ed.), *In celebration of play* (pp. 135-142). London: Croom Held.

Billman, J. (1982). [Teacher ratings using the Preschool Temperament Inventory]. Unpublished summary data.

Billman, J., & McDevitt, S. C. (1980). Convergence of parent and observer ratings of temperament with observations of peer interaction in nursery school. *Child Development, 51,* 395-400.

Bjorklund, D. F., & Butter, E. J. (1973). Can cognitive impulsivity be predicted from classroom behavior? *Journal of Genetic Psychology, 123,* 185-194.

Blurton-Jones, N. G., & Konner, M. J. (1973). Sex differences in behaviour of London and Bushman children. In R. P. Michael & J. H. Crook (Eds.), *Comparative ecology and behaviour of primates* (pp. 690-741). London: Academic Press.

Brindley, C., Clarke, P., Hutt, C., Robinson, I., & Wethli, E. (1973). Sex differences in the activities and social interactions of nursery school children. In R. P. Michael & J. H. Crook (Eds.), *Comparative ecology and behaviour of primates* (pp. 799-828). London: Academic Press.

Bronson, W. C. (1966). Central orientations: A study of behavior organization from childhood to adolescence. *Child Development, 37,* 125-155.

Buss, D. M., Block, J. H., & Block, J. (1980). Preschool activity level: Personality correlates and developmental implications. *Child Development, 51,* 401-408.

Cohen, D. J., Dibble, E., & Grawe, J. M. (1977). Fathers' and mothers' perceptions of children's personality. *Archives of General Psychiatry, 34,* 480-487.

Crowther, J. H., Bond, L. A., & Rolf, J. E. (1981). The incidence, prevalence, and severity of behavior disorders among preschool-aged children in day care. *Journal of Abnormal Child Psychology, 9,* 23-42.

Dierker, L. J., Jr., Pillay, S. K., Sorokin, Y., & Rosen, M. G. (1982). Active and quiet periods in the preterm and term fetus. *Obstetrics and Gynecology, 60,* 65-70.

DiPietro, J. A. (1981). Rough and tumble play: A function of gender. *Developmental Psychology, 17,* 50-58.

Earls, F. E., & Richman, N. (1980). The prevalence of behaviour problems in the three-year-old children of West-Indies born parents. *Journal of Child Psychology and Psychiatry, 21,* 99–106.

Eaton, W. O. (1983). Measuring activity level with actometers: Reliability, validity, and arm length. *Child Development, 54,* 720–726.

Eaton, W. O., & Keats, J. G. (1982). Peer presence, stress, and sex differences in the motor activity levels of preschoolers. *Developmental Psychology, 18,* 534–540.

Elder, M. S. (1970). The effects of temperature and position on the sucking pressure of newborn infants. *Child Development, 41,* 95–102

Fales, E. (1937). A comparison of the vigorousness of play activities of preschool boys and girls. *Child Development, 8,* 144–158.

Feiring, C., & Lewis, M. (1980). Temperament: Sex differences and stability in vigor, activity, and persistence in the first three years of life. *Journal of Genetic Psychology, 136,* 65–75.

Feldman, J. F., Brody, N., & Miller, S. A. (1980). Sex differences in nonelicited neonatal behaviors. *Merrill-Palmer Quarterly, 26,* 63–73.

Fischel, J. E. (1982). The organization of human newborn sucking and movement during auditory stimulation. *Infant Behavior and Development, 5,* 45–61.

Fish, M., & Crockenberg, S. (1981). Correlates and antecedents of nine-month infant behavior and mother–infant interaction. *Infant Behavior and Development, 4,* 69–81.

Friedman, S. I., Jacobs, B. S., & Werthmann, M. W., Jr. (1982). Preterms of low medical risk: Spontaneous behaviors and soothability at expected date of birth. *Infant Behavior and Development, 5,* 3–10.

Garside, R. F., Birch, H., Scott, D. M., Chambers, S., Kolvin, I., Tweddle, E. G., & Barber, L. M. (1975). Dimensions of temperament in infant school children. *Journal of Child Psychology and Psychiatry, 16,* 219–231.

Goggin, J. E. (1975). Sex differences in the activity level of preschool children as a possible precursor of hyperactivity. *Journal of Genetic Psychology, 127,* 75–81.

Goldsmith, H. H., & Gottesman, I. I. (1981). Origins of variation in behavioral style: A longitudinal study of temperament in young twins. *Child Development, 52,* 91–103.

Goodenough, F. L. (1930). Inter-relationships in the behavior of young children. *Child Development, 1,* 29–47.

Guilford, J. S., Zimmerman, W. S., & Guilford, J. P. (1976). *The Guilford-Zimmerman Temperament Survey handbook.* San Diego, CA: EdITS.

Halverson, C. F., Jr., & Waldrop, M. F. (1973). The relations of mechanically recorded activity level to varieties of preschool play behavior. *Child Development, 44,* 678–681.

Harper, L. V., & Sanders, K. M. (1978). Preschool children's use of space: Sex differences in outdoor play. In M. S. Smart & R. C. Smart (Eds.), *Preschool children* (2nd ed., pp. 39–51). New York: MacMillan.

Harrison, R. (1941). Personal tempo and the inter-relationship of voluntary and maximal rates of movement. *Journal of General Psychology, 24,* 343–379.

Hart, H., & Olander, E. (1924). Sex differences in character as indicated by teachers' ratings. *School and Society, 20,* 381–382.

Hattwick, L. A. (1937). Sex differences in behavior of nursery school children. *Child Development, 8,* 343–355.

Hegvik, R., McDevitt, S., & Carey, W. (1982). The Middle Childhood Temperament Questionnaire. *Journal of Developmental and Behavioral Pediatrics, 3,* 197–200.

Holborow, P., Elkins, J., & Berry, P. (1981). The effect of the Feingold diet on 'normal' school children. *Journal of Learning Disabilities, 14,* 143–147.

Jacklin, C. N., Maccoby, E. E., & Halverson, C. F., Jr. (1980). Minor physical anomalies and preschool behavior. *Journal of Pediatric Psychology, 5,* 199–205.

Kaspar, J. C., Millichap, J. G., Backus, R., Child, D., & Schulman, J. L. (1971). A study of the relationship between neurological evidence of brain damage in children and activity and distractability. *Journal of Consulting and Clinical Psychology, 36,* 329–337.

Korner, A. F., Hutchinson, C. A., Koperski, J. A., Kraemer, H. C., & Schneider, P. A. (1981). Stability of individual differences of neonatal motor and crying patterns. *Child Development, 52,* 83–90.

Kurtz, R. M. (1969). Sex differences and variations in body attitudes. *Journal of Consulting and Clinical Psychology, 33,* 625–629.

Kurtz, R. M. (1971). Body attitude and self-esteem. *Proceedings of the 79th Annual Convention of the American Psychological Association, 8,* 467–468.

Lahey, B. B., Hammer, D., Crumrine, P. L., & Forehand, R. L. (1980). Birth Order × Sex interactions in child behavior problems. *Developmental Psychology, 16,* 608–615.

Lewis, M. (1972). State as an infant–environment interaction: An analysis of mother–infant interaction as a function of sex. *Merrill-Palmer Quarterly, 18,* 95–121.

Loo, C., & Wenar, C. (1971). Activity level and motor inhibition: Their relationship to intelligence-test performance in normal children. *Child Development, 42,* 967–971.

McFarlane, J. W., Allen, L., & Honzik, M. P. (1962). *A developmental study of the behavior problems of normal children between 21 months and 14 years.* Berkeley: University of California Press.

Matheny, A. P., Jr., & Dolan, A. B. (1980). A twin study of personality and temperament during middle childhood. *Journal of Research in Personality, 14,* 224–234.

McDowell, M. S. (1937). Frequency of choice of play materials by preschool children. *Child Development, 8,* 305–310.

McGhee, Z. (1900). A study in the play life of some South Carolina children. *Journal of Genetic Psychology, 7,* 459–478.

Melson, G. F. (1977). Sex differences in use of indoor space by preschool children. *Perceptual & Motor Skills, 44,* 207–213.

Messer, S. B., & Lewis, M. (1972). Social class and sex differences in the attachment and play behavior of the year-old infant. *Merrill-Palmer Quarterly, 18,* 295–306.

Moss, H. A. (1967). Sex, age, and state as determinants of mother–infant interaction. *Merrill-Palmer Quarterly, 13,* 19–36.

Nelson, J. (1931). *Personality and intelligence.* New York: Columbia Teachers College.

Partington, M. W., Lang, E., & Campbell, D. (1971). Motor activity in early life: I. Fries' congenital activity types. *Biology of the Neonate, 18,* 94–107.

Patrick, J., Campbell, K., Carmichael, L., Natale, R., & Richardson, B. (1982). Patterns of gross fetal body movements over 24-hour observation intervals during the last 10 weeks of pregnancy. *American Journal of Obstetrics and Gynecology, 142,* 363–371.

Patrick, J., Campbell, K., Carmichael, L., & Probert, C. (1982). Influence of maternal heart rate and gross fetal body movements on the daily pattern of fetal heart rate near term. *American Journal of Obstetrics and Gynecology, 144,* 533–538.

Paulsen, K., & Johnson, M. (1980). Impulsivity: A multidimensional concept with developmental aspects. *Journal of Abnormal Child Psychology, 8,* 269–277.

Persson-Blennow, I., & McNeil, T. F. (1979). A questionnaire for measurement of temperament in six-month-old infants: Development and standardization. *Journal of Child Psychology and Psychiatry, 20,* 1–13.

Phillips, S., King, S., & DuBois, L. (1978). Spontaneous activities of female vs. male newborns. *Child Development, 49,* 590–597.

Plomin, R., & Foch, T. T. (1980). A twin study of objectively assessed personality in childhood. *Journal of Personality and Social Psychology, 39,* 680–688.

Pressé, M. C. (1983). *The relationships among preschool activity level,* peer group status, and social interactions. Unpublished master's thesis, University of Manitoba, Winnipeg, Canada.

Pulaski, M. A. S. (1970). Play as a function of toy structure and fantasy predisposition. *Child Development, 41*, 531–537.

Richman, N., Stevenson, J. E., & Graham, P. J. (1975). Prevalence of behaviour problems in 3-year-old children: An epidemiological study in a London borough. *Journal of Child Psychology and Psychiatry, 16*, 277–287.

Robertson, S. S. (1982). Intrinsic temporal patterning in the spontaneous movement of awake neonates. *Child Development, 53*, 1016–1021.

Robertson, S. S., Dierker, L. J., Sorokin, Y., & Rosen, M. G. (1982). Human fetal movement: Spontaneous oscillations near one cycle per minute. *Science, 218*, 1327–1330.

Rose, H. E., & Mayer, J. (1968). Activity, calorie intake, fat storage, and the energy balance of infants. *Pediatrics, 41*, 18–29.

Routh, D. K., Walton, M. D., & Padan-Belkin, E. (1978). Development of activity level in children revisited: Effects of mother presence. *Developmental Psychology, 14*, 571–581.

Rowe, D. C., & Plomin, R. (1977). Temperament in early childhood. *Journal of Personality Assessment, 41*, 150–156.

Schachar, R., Rutter, M., & Smith, A. (1981). The characteristics of situationally and pervasively hyperactive children: Implications for syndrome definition. *Journal of Child Psychology and Psychiatry, 22*, 375–392.

Schulman, J. L., Kaspar, J. C., & Throne, F. M. (1965). *Brain damage and behavior: A clinical-experimental study.* Springfield, IL: Charles C Thomas.

Seifer, R., Sameroff, A. J., & Jones, F. (1981). Adaptive behavior in young children of emotionally disturbed women. *Journal of Applied Developmental Psychology, 1*, 251–276.

Simonds, J. F., & Simonds, M. P. (1982). Nursery school children's temperament related to sex, birth position, and socioeconomic status. *Journal of Pediatric Psychology, 7*, 49–59.

Smith, P. K., & Connolly, K. (1972). Patterns of play and social interaction in pre-school children. In N. Blurton-Jones (Ed.), *Ethological studies of child behaviour* (pp. 65–95). London: Cambridge University Press.

Smith, P. K., & Daglish, L. (1977). Sex differences in parent and infant behavior in the home. *Child Development, 48*, 1250–1254.

Sontag, L. W. (1963). [Unpublished data on sex differences in fetal movement]. (Cited in Bernard, 1964)

Spring, C., Blunden, D., Greenberg, L. M., & Yellin, A. M. (1977). Validity and norms of a hyperactivity rating scale. *Journal of Special Education, 11*, 313–321.

Stein, K. B., & Lenrow, P. (1970). Expressive styles and their measurement. *Journal of Personality and Social Psychology, 16*, 656–664.

Stone, F. B. (1981). Behavior problems of elementary-school children. *Journal of Abnormal Child Psychology, 9*, 407–418.

Tauber, M. A. (1979). Parental socialization techniques and sex differences in children's play. *Child Development, 50*, 225–234.

Torgerson, A. M. (1979, September). *Temperamental differences in infants and 6 year old children.* Paper presented at the International Conference on Temperament, Warsaw, Poland.

Vaughn, B. E., Crichton, L., & Egeland, B. (1982). Individual differences in qualities of caregiving during the first six months of life: Antecedents in maternal and infant behavior during the newborn period. *Infant Behavior and Development, 5*, 77–95.

Vlietstra, A. G. (1981). Full- versus half-day preschool attendance: Effects in young children as assessed by teacher ratings and behavioral observations. *Child Development, 52*, 603–610.

Walker, R. N. (1967). Some temperament traits in children as viewed by their peers, their teachers, and themselves. *Monographs of the Society for Research in Child Development, 32*(6, Serial No. 114).

Whyte, J. (1974). Behavioural styles and teachers' estimations of intelligence. *Irish Journal of Education, 8*, 62–76.

Wilkinson, P. W., Parkin, J. M., Pearlson, G., Strong, H., & Sykes, P. (1977). Energy intake and physical activity in obese children. *British Medical Journal, 1*, 756.

Willerman, L. (1973). Activity level and hyperactivity in twins. *Child Development, 44*, 288–293.

Willerman, L., & Plomin, R. (1973). Activity level in children and their parents. *Child Development, 44*, 854–858.

Wolfensberger, W. P., Miller, M. B., Foshee, J. G., & Cromwell, R. L. (1962). Rorschach correlates of activity level in high school children. *Journal of Consulting Psychology, 26*, 269–272.

Received September 5, 1985
Revision received November 7, 1985 ■

[30]

ADOLESCENT MEDICINE W. A. Daniel, Jr., *Editor*

Educational correlates of early and late sexual maturation in adolescence

From the National Health Examination Survey data, 5,735 Caucasian males and females, 12 to 17 years, were classified by age and stage of sexual maturation (Tanner). Early and late maturers were each compared to all other youth of comparable age and sex, in eight education-related categories: youth and parental aspirations and expectations concerning the level of education which would be achieved by the student, teacher reports of intellectual ability and academic achievement, and test scores (WISC and WRAT). Except at age 12, late maturing boys received significantly lower ratings than mid maturers in all these areas, and early maturing males received higher ratings. For females, no differences persisted across age groups. In advising male adolescents, physicians should be alert to the possibility that school functioning may be linked to maturational processes.

Paula M. Duke, M.D.,* J. Merrill Carlsmith, Ph.D.,

Dennis Jennings, Ph.D., John A. Martin, Ph.D.,

Sanford M. Dornbusch, Ph.D., Ruth T. Gross, M.D., and

Bryna Siegel-Gorelick, Ph.D., *Stanford, Calif.*

DURING ADOLESCENCE, school performance gains great importance in determining a youth's later educational and career attainments.[1] Does the fact that a youth matures early or late have an impact on his or her educational performance? Do parents and teachers respond differently to early and late maturers? In this study, data from a large national sample of adolescents were analyzed in an effort to address these questions.

Previous research has examined the hypothesis that certain behavioral characteristics may be more closely related to maturational age than to chronologic age during adolescence, since youth at the same chronologic age are often at very different levels of sexual maturation.[2,3] Despite the strong intuitive appeal of such a hypothesis, published data are contradictory. In a British study early maturing girls were reported to be "superior with better powers of concentration,"[4] whereas in a smaller 1930 study in the United States, they had below average scores in "prestige, popularity, and leadership."[5] Faust[6] demonstrated the complexity of the problem by noting that the interaction of maturational and chronologic age influences girls' popularity in junior high school.

There are fewer studies relating behavior and maturational rate in boys, probably because there are no easily measured male maturational markers comparable to menarche in girls. Jones and Bayley[7] found that for their small sample, early maturing boys were "more attractive to

---

Abbreviations used
WISC: Weschler Intelligence Scales for Children
WRAT: Wide Range Achievement Test

---

adults, with more social recognition and popularity"; intelligence test scores showed no difference between early and late maturing males.[8]

Douglas et al[9] demonstrated that early maturing girls and boys had a higher average academic test performance than late maturing young persons. His results are perhaps explained by the fact that these early maturing boys and girls came from smaller families, a clear educational advantage.

The present study examines data which provide an opportunity to relate chronologic age and sexual maturation to educational variables for both sexes in a representative national sample of adolescents.

From the Department of Pediatrics, Stanford University School of Medicine.

*Reprint address: Department of Pediatrics, Stanford University School of Medicine, Stanford, CA 94305.

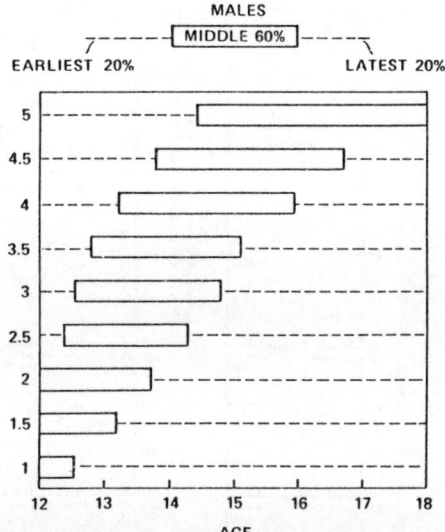

Fig. 1. Definition of early, late, and mid maturational groups for males by stage of sexual maturation and chronologic age.

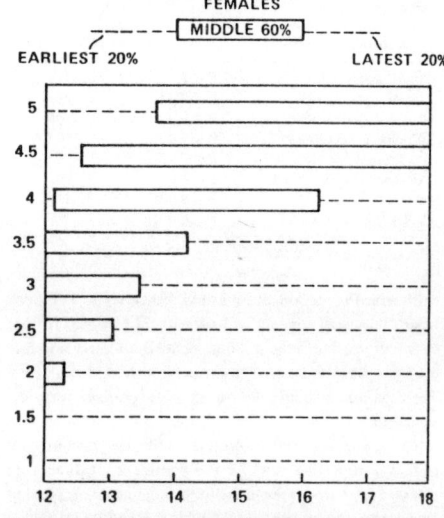

Fig. 2. Definition of early, late, and mid maturational groups for females by stage of sexual maturation and chronologic age.

METHODS

The National Health Examination Survey, Cycle III, drew a nationwide probability sample of the total population of 22.7 million noninstitutionalized youth of ages 12 to 17 years.[10] The sample consisted of 6,768 subjects examined between 1966 and 1970, and was appropriately stratified to represent the target population with respect to age, sex, race, region, population density, and population growth. Extensive information was obtained about each adolescent's physical and psychosocial status. These data are available on computer-readable tapes distributed by the National Center for Health Statistics. In this report, we will focus on descriptive information obtained separately from the youth and from their parents, from teacher ratings of each youth's intellectual ability, academic achievement, popularity, behavior, and adjustment to school, as well as test scores of intellectual ability and achievement, and physical examination, for white males and females. The number of subjects in other racial groups was too small for detailed analysis.

Tanner sexual maturation stages[11] were determined at the time of the physical examination. These stages, which correlate very well with other pubertal measures, provide an excellent noninvasive assessment of pubertal status. The correlation with bone age is 0.69 for males and 0.81 for females; the correlation with menarche is 0.74.[12] During the physical examination, each youth was compared with standard photographs (breast and pubic hair for females, and testes, penis and pubic hair for males) in order to assign a sexual maturity rating. In analyzing the data, we averaged the Tanner ratings for each youth, thus obtaining one sexual maturity score per youth. For each girl, the mean of the two Tanner ratings for each breast was averaged with the pubic hair rating. Each boy's score was derived by averaging his pubic hair and genitalia scores.

We then assigned each adolescent to one of three groups: an early developing group, a late developing group, and a mid developing group (for those who were neither early nor late developers). Early maturers were defined as those youth, for each sex and age group, who had achieved a level of sexual maturation above the eightieth percentile of their cohort. Late maturers were defined analogously as those who had achieved a level of sexual maturation below the twentieth percentile for that sex and age group (Figs. 1 and 2). Most of the youth defined as early or late maturers were, from a clinical perspective, well within the normal range.

These three groups were then compared on a variety of educational measures: youth and parental aspirations and expectations about the level of education which would eventually be achieved by the student, teachers' reports of intellectual ability and academic achievement, and scores

Table

Statistical analysis	Late vs mid	Mid vs early
Youth aspirations	P < 0.02	NS
Youth expectations	P < 0.02	NS
Parental aspirations	P < 0.02	0.05
Parental expectations	P < 0.02	0.02
Intellectual Development	P < 0.02	0.05
Academic Achievement	P < 0.02	0.05
WISC	P < 0.001	NS
WRAT	P < 0.001	NS

on standard achievement and intelligence tests. Teachers' reports on school conduct and adjustment provided further information about school adjustment. Both early and late maturers were compared separately with mid maturers. The Stouffer technique was used to determine statistical significance.[13]

Youth and parental aspirations and expectations concerning prospective level of the youth's education were obtained from responses to the following questions asked of both youth and parents: (1) Looking ahead, what would you like to do about school? (aspirations); (2) What do you think will happen about school? (expectations). Each question was answered separately with one of the following responses: (a) Quit school as soon as possible; (b) finish high school; (c) get some college or other training after high school; (d) finish college and get a college degree; or (e) finish college and take some further training. For analysis, we combined answers a, b, and c into one category (low aspirations or low expectations) and answers d and e into second category (high aspirations or high expectations).

Intellectual ability and academic achievement were assessed by each youth's teacher via the following questions: (1) In terms of intellectual ability, which of the following best describes this student: (a) above average; (b) average; (c) below average. (2) In terms of academic achievement, is this student: (a) in the upper third of his class; (b) in the middle third of his class; (c) in the lower third of his class.

The test scores reported were subtests of both the Weschler Intelligence Scales for Children and the Wide Range Achievement test.

A second set of variables reflected the teacher's evaluation of the student's conduct and adjustment. Included were questions about absenteeism, adjustment, need for disciplinary action, and popularity with other students.

RESULTS

In all eight education-related variables at all ages (except WISC and WRAT for 12-year-old subjects), late maturing white males were at a disadvantage compared to

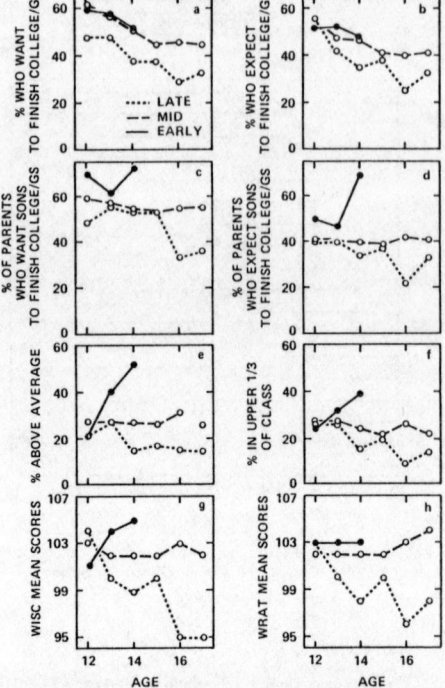

Fig. 3. Findings for the three maturational groups of white males. The average number of subjects per group is 52 late maturers, 378 mid maturers, and 63 early maturers.

the mid-maturers (Fig. 3 and Table). Late maturing males were less likely to want to complete college and less frequently expected to do so. The parents concurred in these lower expectations and aspirations. The teachers of late maturing males less often characterized them as above average in intellectual ability and less often ranked them in the upper third of their class in terms of academic achievement when compared with mid maturers or early maturers. The mean scores on the WISC and WRAT were also lower in this late maturation group, except for 12-year-old boys. In addition to these overall differences, the negative relation of late maturation to the educational variables was even more pronounced among the older males.

There were consistent differences between early and mid maturers among the white males, although smaller than for late versus mid maturers. With some exceptions at age 12, the early maturers were rated higher on the educational variables than were the mid maturers.

In order to determine whether these findings could be accounted for by differences in intelligence between the early, mid, and late maturers, an analysis of covariance was performed in which intelligence (as measured by WISC scores) was held constant. This analysis demonstrated that the above finding persists even when intelligence is partialled out of the relationship between educational achievement and sexual maturation.

The relationships between these educational variables and birth order as well as family size were neither strong nor consistent, and do not provide an explanation of our results. When controlling for socioeconomic status, the pattern of findings remains the same within the low and middle socioeconomic groups. Within the high socioeconomic status group, in which there are already high expectations for education, the rate of pubertal development does not predict these results.

The second set of variables considered in this report concerns school conduct. In contrast to our findings in the area of school achievement, there were no differences among the three maturation groups of white males in rate of absenteeism, degree of adjustment, or need for discipline or level of popularity with peers (as reported by teachers).

The observed relationships between stage of sexual maturation and educational achievement, aspirations, and expectations appear to be limited to males. Although there are some intriguing suggestions of differential effects at various ages for females, no easily described pattern exists, nor do these differences for females reach acceptable levels of statistical significance (these data are available upon request).

DISCUSSION

Our data indicate that in the United States in the late 1960s, late maturing white males scored lower in education related variables than mid maturers, and early maturers did somewhat better than late and mid maturers. There are several possible explanations for these findings. Although these cross-sectional data do not give information about adult height, the late maturing males were shorter and the early maturers taller than the other males at the time of examination. Physical size may affect one's self-esteem. In addition, boys smaller or larger than their age mates may evoke stereotypic responses from their parents and teachers about their capabilities. Cognitive delay or acceleration is an unlikely explanation of our findings, since the reported differences among maturation groups persist even after controlling for any differences in intelligence. These data do not allow differentiation among these explanations. It is clear, however, that late maturation in males may serve as a marker of potential or actual difficulty in academic performance as well as lowered parental and youth aspirations and expectations concerning their educational achievements, whether or not these perceptions are well founded.

Another important observation from the present study was the interaction between chronologic age and stage of sexual maturation. Whatever phenomena are contributing to the associations between late maturation and lower ratings on the educational variables, they are weaker at age 12 and more powerful at older ages, when the late maturing boys are more obviously out of synchrony with their age mates.

Teacher judgments are, of course, influenced by the overall level of performance in the particular school. However, the congruence of the results of teacher ratings with the objective measures such as WISC and WRAT suggest that this is not a serious difficulty. Furthermore, analyses controlling for social class show a consistent pattern across social classes.

It is puzzling that the associations reported in this paper appear only among the boys. The absence of consistent and statistically significant differences for girls in the present study fails to elucidate the pattern of results found in previously published studies.

CLINICAL IMPLICATIONS

Physicians are often called upon to give advice about the adjustment and well-being of adolescents. In advising male adolescents, they should be alert to the possibility that school functioning may be linked to maturational processes. In view of the abundant evidence that educational attainment has a strong impact on adult functioning, being out of synchrony with one's age mates in terms of physical maturation during adolescence may have disadvantageous effects in later life.

REFERENCES

1. Blau PM, and Duncan OD: The American occupational structure, New York, 1967, John Wiley & Sons, Inc.
2. Jones M, Bayley N, Macfarlane J, et al, editors: The course of human development, Toronto, 1971, John Wiley & Sons, Inc.
3. Gross RT, and Duke PM: The effect of early versus late physical maturation on adolescent behavior, Pediatr Clin North Am. 27:1, 1980.
4. Douglas J: The home and the school, London, 1964, Macgilbon & Kee.
5. Everett E: Behavioral characteristics of early and late maturing girls, unpublished doctoral dissertation, quoted by Eichorn D: Biological correlates of behavior, in Stevenson H, Kagan J, and Spilser C, editors: Child psychology, Chicago, 1963, University of Chicago Press.
6. Faust M: Developmental maturity as a determinant in prestige of adolescent girls, Child Dev. 31:173, 1960.

7. Jones M, and Bayley N: Physical maturing among boys as related to behavior, J Educ Psychol **41:**129, 1950.
8. Jones MC: Psychological correlates of somatic development, Child Dev, **36:**911, 1965.
9. Douglas JWB, Ross JM, and Simpson HR: All our future: A longitudinal study of secondary education, London, 1968, Peter Davies, Ltd.
10. Plan and Operation of a Health Examination Survey of United States Youths 12-17 Years of Age, National Center for Health Statistics, **1:**8, 1969.
11. Tanner JM: Growth at adolescence, ed 2, Oxford, 1962, Blackwell Scientific Publications, p 32.
12. Tanner JM: Growth at adolescence, ed 2, Oxford, 1962, Blackwell Scientific Publications, p 79.
13. Mosteller F, and Bush RR: Selected quantitative techniques, Lindzey G. handbook of social psychology (I), Reading, Mass., 1954, Addison-Wesley Publishing Co., Inc.

Longitudinal Correlation Analysis of Standing Height and Intelligence

Lloyd G. Humphreys, Timothy C. Davey, and Randolph K. Park
University of Illinois at Urbana-Champaign

> HUMPHREYS, LLOYD G.; DAVEY, TIMOTHY C.; and PARK, RANDOLPH K. *Longitudinal Correlation Analysis of Standing Height and Intelligence.* CHILD DEVELOPMENT, 1985, **56**, 1465–1478. Intercorrelations of 10 successive years of measurement of height and intelligence are presented for separate samples of girls and boys. These correlations are based on data originally gathered and published by Dearborn, Rothney, and Shuttleworth as the Harvard Growth Study. Sample size varies from correlation to correlation, but most of those for girls are based on samples of 500–700 and those for boys on samples of 400–500. The intercorrelations of each of the 2 variables over 10 occasions do not differ appreciably by sex, but there are significant differences between the sexes in the cross-correlations. For the sample of girls there is clear evidence that individual differences in height at 8 and 9 anticipate later individual differences in intelligence. Correlations of early height with intelligence at 11 and 12 are especially high (.40). There is little evidence for similar anticipation of intelligence by height for boys. Correlates for both height and intelligence are found in socioeconomic status, ethnicity, and age of first menstruation for girls. Only the last of these contributes to the explanation of the changes in the cross-correlations with age. Analyses of sitting-height correlations with intelligence indicate that length of the long bones of the legs is also related to the observed pattern of correlations.

There have been numerous correlations reported between height and intelligence as well as correlations of height with variables that are themselves correlates of intelligence. These include academic grades, occupation, social class status, and class mobility. Tanner (1966) has reviewed this literature. Correlations are small (around .20) but consistently positive. Jensen (1980) also discussed the correlation between height and intelligence. He suggested that there might be a between-family genetic basis for the small relationship even though a within-family basis could be rejected.

A within-family genetic basis is ruled out on two lines of evidence. Laycock and Caylor (1964), whose research was summarized by Jensen, compared the height and intelligence of siblings of an intellectually superior group. The within-family genetic hypothesis required the siblings of the gifted group to regress toward the mean on both measures. The expected regression occurred at a statistically significant level for intelligence but not for height. Husen (1959) compared within-twin and between-twin correlations for height and intelligence for monozygotic and dizygotic male twins. If the covariation between two traits is 100% heritable, the ratio of between-twin to within-twin correlations for monozygotes is 1.0, and for dizygotes in the absence of assortative mating it is .5. The presence of environmental variance in the covariance of the two traits will reduce the 1.0 and can increase the .5. Assortative mating increases the .5 somewhat, but absence of any difference between these ratios for the two types of twins allows one to reject any within-family genetic contribution to the covariation. In Husen's data both ratios are slightly less than unity, and in the sample the one for dizygotes is actually slightly larger.

There is, however, assortative mating for height and intelligence when each is considered separately, and joint assortative mating might produce the correlation of .2 between height and intelligence, as Jensen hypothesized. He accepted a father-mother correlation of .5 for intelligence and .3 for height and assumed that there might be sufficient joint selection to produce a correlation of .2 between these measures in successive generations. To the best of our knowledge no one has reported correlations between father's

---

This research was supported by grant no. MH23612-06 from the National Institute of Mental Health and by the Research Board, Urbana-Champaign Campus, University of Illinois. Requests for reprints should be addressed to Lloyd G. Humphreys, Department of Psychology, 603 East Daniel, Champaign, IL 61820.

height and mother's intelligence or vice versa, but it seems reasonable to conclude that these correlations are positive but no greater than .2.

Husen, in contrast to Jensen, did not consider the possibility of a between-family genetic explanation for the correlation between height and intelligence. He suggested that the common intrauterine environment was the causal factor. In formulating this hypothesis he was influenced by the mean deficits for both types of twins in height, weight, and intelligence relative to the population of single-birth individuals.

No investigator or theorist has considered the possibility that the generally accepted correlation of .2 might not be constant during development. That the cross-correlations between the two measures might change in interesting ways is supported by the substantial changes in the intercorrelations of height and intelligence over occasions when considered independently. For both traits one finds high correlations of their measures between adjacent occasions, but stability over extended time spans is much lower. These statements are as true for height as for intelligence. Both sets of intercorrelations over occasions follow approximately the pattern expected in data involving either learning or maturation. Such R matrices are frequently called quasi simplexes. With the rank-order of individuals within age groups changing from year to year, it seems highly improbable that the correlations between height and intelligence would remain constant over time.

We had no a priori hypothesis concerning how these correlations would change other than that change was highly likely. We did believe that the change we anticipated would be of interest to theorists concerned with either environmental or genetic explanations for the covariation among human traits. We also strongly defend a research strategy that attempts to form theory after empirical relationships become dependable.

The Harvard Growth Study.—At one point in the history of developmental psychology there was widespread interest in physical development. There are numerous reports, for example, in the earliest volumes of the Monographs of the Society for Research in Child Development. Among these is one by Dearborn, Rothney, and Shuttleworth (1938) that included measurements on the entire sample of children for height as well as several other measures of physique and intelligence. The samples were quite large, especially between 8 and 17, but there are appreciable numbers of cases at 7 and 18 as well. Indices of social class and ethnic background were also reported along with age of first menstruation for the girls. It is not surprising, however, that the large number of correlations that could have been computed for 10 variables measured in many cases on 12 occasions do not appear in a 1938 research monograph. It is feasible today to make these computations. Correlations of intelligence with other measures of physique have been computed, but those involving standing height and intelligence are highest. There has also been more attention paid to standing height in the literature. Therefore we focus on this measure of physique in this report.

The children were obtained from the schools of Medford, Revere, and Beverly, all in the Boston area. A largely successful attempt was made to obtain all measurements on the same day. Occasionally the intelligence testing was delayed by a week but rarely by a month. Because rapid physical and mental growth occurs in the age range covered, these cases introduce additional attenuation into the cross-correlations between measures of physique and intelligence beyond that produced by random measurement error. Annual measurements were not obtained on the precise anniversary of those taken the year before, but the variation from year to year was small.

The data presented in the monograph represented those examinees whose data were most complete. The presumption, therefore, is that there should be relatively little bias produced by selective attrition. We have checked this presumption against the ethnic and socioeconomic constitution of the sample. Because of missing data, there is some degree of variation from year to year, but when early, middle, and late years are aggregated, some small trends are evident. There is approximately a 1% increase in the proportion of boys in the lowest SES category, but the only change for girls is in the third decimal place. For both boys and girls there is an increase in children of northwest European ethnic heritage of about 1.5%, and the decrease in those of Italian heritage reaches 3% for girls. Note, however, that this last change was not accompanied by a socioeconomic shift. Selective attrition appears to be a minor factor in interpreting the correlations between measures of physique and intelligence.

There are other deficiencies in these data to which attention should be called. Every child was not measured on each occasion. We

TABLE 1
Correlations for Height and Intelligence for Girls 8–17

	8	9	10	11	12	13	14	15	16	17
8		67	64	70	69	64	64	64	63	54
9	99		65	68	73	73	69	61	61	61
10	97	98		78	78	73	73	73	69	59
11	93	95	98		88	80	79	80	80	75
12	90	92	95	98		85	84	79	79	77
13	89	91	93	94	97		85	75	77	79
14	89	90	90	88	89	96		81	77	75
15	86	87	85	80	80	87	97		90	79
16	82	83	81	75	74	81	93	98		87
17	80	81	78	72	69	78	90	97	99	

NOTE.—Correlations for intelligence are above, and correlations for height are below the diagonal.

decided that we would lose more by restricting the computations of correlations to a sample of constant size than by using the maximum N available. This decision has the effect of making certain statistical computations only approximate. These include the t test for a difference in correlations computed in a single sample and the use of partial correlations.

The intelligence tests administered to the children were group tests constructed by a variety of authors, containing somewhat different content, and normed in various ways. The tests and their ordering are listed in the Appendix. It is seen that two different tests were administered in most years, but sample sizes were smaller for the second test. Both sets of correlations were obtained, and the results are similar but will not be presented here. There also is not a one-to-one correspondence between the year of the research and the age of the child, but there are relatively few exceptions. Because mental ages were reported, the units of measurement for the several tests are roughly comparable. Any error in norms represents the equivalent of measurement error in its effect on correlations.

Results

Table 1 presents the intercorrelations over 10 occasions for height and intelligence for the sample of girls. Correlations for the former are below the diagonal, for the latter above. As noted earlier, each correlation is based on a slightly different N with a range from 495 to 693. The intercorrelations of height and intelligence over the same 10 occasions are presented in Table 2 for the sample of boys. Data for height are below the diagonal, for intelligence above. The range in size of samples for these correlations is from 391 to 511. Although correlations for 7 and 18 were also computed, these are omitted from the tables. Sample sizes were smaller for the extreme ages, and the methodology used to estimate the reliabilities required at a later stage of the analysis did not produce unique estimates at these ages.

Table 3 contains the cross-correlations between intelligence and standing height for

TABLE 2
Correlations for Height and Intelligence for Boys 8–17

	8	9	10	11	12	13	14	15	16	17
8		60	63	67	64	59	60	62	62	53
9	99		74	70	68	68	68	59	60	57
10	98	99		79	77	70	75	71	71	60
11	97	98	99		87	78	75	79	81	75
12	95	95	97	98		84	79	77	80	76
13	89	90	92	94	97		85	77	77	77
14	85	86	88	90	92	96		84	80	75
15	84	85	87	88	89	88	95		88	78
16	86	87	88	89	88	78	85	95		85
17	84	85	87	87	84	71	75	87	97	

NOTE.—Correlations for intelligence are above, and correlations for height are below the diagonal.

TABLE 3

SAMPLE SIZES AND CROSS-CORRELATIONS BETWEEN HEIGHT AND INTELLIGENCE FOR GIRLS 8–17

	8	9	10	11	12	13	14	15	16	17
8	31 (605)	31 (596)	35 (589)	38 (600)	41 (585)	33 (596)	32 (601)	34 (610)	32 (566)	25 (484)
9	30 (642)	32 (685)	34 (656)	38 (667)	40 (656)	35 (661)	33 (666)	35 (671)	32 (628)	25 (540)
10	29 (640)	31 (680)	33 (689)	37 (684)	39 (670)	33 (676)	32 (685)	33 (688)	32 (644)	25 (557)
11	27 (649)	29 (687)	31 (682)	35 (724)	38 (690)	32 (692)	30 (700)	32 (703)	32 (659)	25 (569)
12	28 (636)	29 (671)	29 (666)	33 (687)	37 (706)	32 (688)	30 (688)	32 (693)	31 (651)	25 (559)
13	27 (646)	29 (673)	28 (668)	31 (688)	34 (685)	31 (712)	29 (694)	30 (696)	30 (652)	23 (560)
14	25 (661)	27 (696)	26 (691)	30 (710)	33 (701)	29 (711)	28 (726)	28 (720)	27 (676)	24 (581)
15	22 (650)	25 (687)	22 (678)	29 (698)	31 (690)	27 (695)	26 (705)	26 (732)	24 (682)	23 (585)
16	20 (601)	24 (637)	21 (631)	27 (647)	30 (641)	25 (645)	24 (660)	23 (678)	22 (685)	22 (579)
17	17 (523)	21 (554)	16 (552)	23 (565)	25 (559)	21 (561)	19 (572)	18 (591)	18 (592)	21 (589)

NOTE.—Height defines the rows and intelligence defines the columns; sample size appears in parentheses beneath each correlation.

the sample of girls. Because large numbers of statistical tests are required, the sample size for each correlation is reported as well. This allows independent verification and extension of our analyses if desired. It also allows omission of the several tables of t ratios that otherwise would be required.

Although there is only a little evidence for selective attrition, there is an appreciable drop in sample size from 16 to 17. There is also, generally, a larger difference in the size of correlations from 16 to 17 than elsewhere in the matrix. We shall therefore concentrate on the first nine columns and rows.

The largest correlations in the matrix are found between early height and intelligence. Correlations gradually decrease down the columns defined by intelligence. Across the rows there is a gradual increase to age 12 followed by a decrease in size to 16 and 17. The highest correlations are those involving height at 8, 9, and 10 with intelligence at 12. These are substantially higher than the expected .20, but the latter figure is closely approximated by the near-adult correlations in the lower-right-hand corner of the matrix.

The confidence to be placed in the preceding description of the sample data requires several different statistical tests. Among the 30 correlations in the first three rows, 26 differ from a population value of .20, with $p < .01$. One has an accompanying $p < .05$. Only the correlations involving intelligence at 17 fail to differ significantly from .20. Down the columns and across the rows we used the standard t test for comparisons, entering the smallest of the three N's on which the required three correlations were based. Down the columns there are very large numbers of highly significant differences. Also, for most of these comparisons, the N's do not differ sufficiently to explain the significant differences on grounds of nonoverlapping samples.

Correlations are, of course, attenuated by measurement error. Comparisons down the columns, however, all involve constant reliability of the measure of intelligence with only height varying. On a priori grounds one would expect standing height to be measured with high reliability with little variability from year to year. We also have in this sample measures of sternal height that were obtained in an independent measurement operation. Correlations with standing height vary from .98 to .99.

TABLE 4
SAMPLE SIZES AND CROSS-CORRELATIONS BETWEEN HEIGHT AND INTELLIGENCE FOR BOYS 8–17

	8	9	10	11	12	13	14	15	16	17
8	21 (441)	17 (424)	28 (438)	24 (440)	25 (444)	19 (444)	19 (448)	21 (448)	20 (433)	14 (386)
9	20 (472)	21 (511)	29 (487)	26 (487)	27 (483)	24 (488)	23 (492)	24 (491)	24 (478)	16 (420)
10	20 (468)	20 (479)	27 (511)	24 (499)	27 (496)	24 (502)	22 (504)	22 (505)	23 (493)	15 (442)
11	19 (478)	20 (487)	27 (511)	25 (518)	28 (507)	25 (515)	23 (515)	24 (518)	24 (503)	18 (452)
12	19 (476)	20 (486)	26 (507)	25 (510)	28 (515)	25 (512)	22 (513)	25 (516)	24 (503)	17 (452)
13	19 (481)	20 (490)	26 (514)	24 (515)	29 (511)	24 (527)	21 (522)	25 (523)	22 (510)	17 (458)
14	20 (484)	20 (493)	26 (516)	24 (517)	28 (514)	25 (523)	21 (527)	24 (526)	22 (512)	18 (460)
15	18 (480)	20 (489)	26 (511)	25 (513)	28 (509)	25 (520)	22 (519)	25 (529)	23 (511)	18 (459)
16	16 (461)	19 (470)	27 (493)	25 (494)	28 (494)	26 (501)	23 (501)	25 (508)	24 (512)	18 (459)
17	13 (412)	16 (419)	25 (444)	24 (443)	28 (445)	26 (451)	22 (451)	23 (457)	22 (460)	18 (459)

NOTE.—Height defines the rows and intelligence defines the columns; sample size appears in parentheses beneath each correlation.

In contrast there is reason to expect lower reliability of scores on a group test of intelligence in the earlier years, but reliability would be expected to stabilize by 11 or 12. For the moment, therefore, we shall compare correlations in the middle years of intelligence with those involving intelligence at 16. Using the same statistical test as before, there are indeed significant differences involving intelligence at 11 and 12 with intelligence at 16. If the decrease in correlations between 16 and 17 is not due to some unknown selective attrition factor, there are many additional decreases of the correlations in the population from early to late intelligence.

The boys' cross-correlations between intelligence and height are in Table 4. Again the individual N's are presented with each correlation. Other than the fact that the near-adult correlations are highly similar to those for the girls, one's impression is that the results are quite different.

In the first three rows of the matrix there is only one correlation greater than .20 at the .05 level. Only the column of intelligence at 8 has a significant decrease in size of correlations from early to late height, but from 8 to 16 the p value is barely less than .05. The larger drop from 8 to 17 involves less overlap of the samples. Across the rows, also, the only significant decrease for largely overlapping samples is from intelligence at 10 to intelligence at 16, with $p < .05$.

The preceding analyses support the impression that there is a sex difference in the pattern of correlations between height and intelligence, but there is a more direct test available. This test, furthermore, is independent of the changing sample sizes from year to year. When the z transformations of the first three rows of Table 3 are compared to those of the first three rows of Table 4, the distribution of critical ratios supports a sex difference. There are 30 critical ratios in all with a range from .92 to 2.86, all in the same direction. There are 16 in the distribution with p values less than .05, and 27 with less than .10. The one of 2.86 is well beyond the level required for $p = .01$. In contrast the average sex difference in the last three rows of both tables is approximately zero.

Possible confounding factors.—The problem of differential reliability of measurement from year to year was avoided earlier for height on the basis of indirect evidence for nearly constant reliability and for intelligence

1470 Child Development

by looking for the moment only at the middle and later years. A more detailed look is required. A second factor requiring analysis is chronological age, controlled in Tables 1–4 only within ± 6 months. Age in months was recorded, however, and can be controlled statistically. Obtaining estimates of reliabilities is more difficult. Reliabilities published in test manuals are not adequate for samples from different populations tested in a particular research or operational context, but there is a feasible approach to the problem.

These matrices in Tables 1 and 2 resemble the simplex in which all $r_{ik \cdot j}$ among true scores are equal to zero in the population (subscripts designate the order of occasions; adjacent occasions are not required). This suggests the possibility of obtaining estimates of the reliabilities in these samples of the various intelligence tests used during the children's development by fitting a simplex matrix to the intercorrelations.

In this process reliabilities are uniquely determined for all occasions other than the first and the last. As a first step, we decided to apply the methodology to the 12 × 12 matrices for intelligence extending from age 7 through age 18 for both boys and girls. This allowed us to determine reliabilities for the 10 intermediate ages for which we have been reporting data. In order to make certain that our smaller samples at 7 and 18 were not systematically affecting the estimates, we also dropped those ages in a second cycle. This allowed us to compare two estimates for ages 9–16 and to find that the omission of 7 and 18 had little effect.

For the second cycle the chi square for the fit of the model to the girls' intercorrelations of intelligence, after making a conservative estimate of N, is 184 with 28 df. The corresponding chi square for boys is 203 with the same df. Obviously the model must be rejected for these data. On the other side of the coin, however, the lack of a constant N is known to decrease the goodness of fit. The residuals, although many are too large, are seemingly scattered at random in the 10 × 10 matrix. In the light of the successes in fitting the simplex model to more nearly equivalent measures of intellectual development from grade 5 through grade 11 in a sample of constant size (Humphreys & Parsons, 1979; Humphreys, Parsons, & Park, 1979), we suggest that the present lack of fit may be attributable, in addition to the varying N, to the lack of parallel measures of intelligence in the data. This interpretation is reinforced by a later success in obtaining good fits to correlations based on individual tests of intelligence from preschool to age 15 (Humphreys & Davey, 1985).

We also, for comparative purposes, tried to fit the simplex model to the measures of height that are clearly parallel to each other from age to age. The chi squares are 603 and 396 with 28 df for girls and boys, respectively, and the residuals show a clear pattern. Large residuals of the same sign occur for the years of the adolescent growth spurt. Both the residuals and the growth spurt occur later for boys than for girls. There are systematic effects on the growth of height at the time of sexual maturation that produce a break in the simplex pattern.

The intelligence correlations, in spite of the different tests represented, show descriptively better fits to the model. In our judgment it is useful to estimate the effects of measurement error on our sample correlations using the reliabilities for the intelligence measurements generated by this methodology. The reliabilities obtained in this way are, in effect, means of multiple estimates that form a distribution with greater variance than would be true if the fit of the model to the observations were closer.

There are some minor problems in making use of the data concerning variability of chronological age within annual age groups. The children in the original study were not measured at precisely annual intervals. Thus an individual age had to be determined for each measurement occasion. Complete 10 × 10 tables of cross-correlations of the age score with both height and intelligence were obtained. In the absence of bias there should be only random variability from one age score to another of the correlations with height and intelligence at each annual measurement occasion. Finding this to be true, we obtained the mean correlation with age score for each age group.

Table 5 contains the reliability estimates for intelligence and the mean correlations with the age score for each age group for both variables. The reliability estimates vary but overall appear to be quite reasonable. Reliabilities are relatively low in the earliest years, as expected, although the reliability at 9 may be too low. For one thing, it is not expected to be lower than the one at 8. We also applied an independent test of reasonableness. A diagonal factor at 9 cannot be identified after identification of one at 8.

We have corrected the observed correlations reported in Tables 1–4 for attenuation,

TABLE 5

ESTIMATED RELIABILITIES OF THE INTELLIGENCE MEASUREMENTS AND CORRELATIONS WITH AGE WITHIN AGE GROUPS FOR BOTH HEIGHT AND INTELLIGENCE

	ESTIMATED RELIABILITIES: INTELLIGENCE		CORRELATIONS WITH AGE WITHIN AGE GROUPS			
			Intelligence		Height	
AGE	Males	Females	Males	Females	Males	Females
8	71	76	20	21	22	23
9	65	69	00	09	19	22
10	80	72	16	16	16	20
11	88	86	09	13	15	18
12	90	91	08	07	16	16
13	84	84	−06	03	19	13
14	85	84	01	04	21	08
15	87	89	10	14	18	06
16	92	94	09	10	11	05
17	92	88	−04	00	00	06

realizing that we were probably overcorrecting correlations involving intelligence at 9, but these corrected coefficients do not make enough difference in outcomes to justify the space required to report them. The corrected year-to-year stabilities are somewhat variable but overall are quite reasonable. The important finding is that the pattern of correlations between height and intelligence in the girls' data and the differences between boys and girls in these patterns are not modified appreciably in the corrected correlations.

The correlations of height with age variability in months decrease quite regularly with increase in the age at which height was measured. Even the largest of these correlations have trivial effects on the intercorrelations of height over occasions. The correlations of the age variable with intelligence are smaller and change less smoothly from year to year. Again these have trivial effects on the intercorrelations of intelligence over occasions. With respect to the cross-correlations between height and intelligence, only those involving intelligence at 8 are reduced in more than trivial fashion by holding the age score constant. If the correlations of intelligence at 8 were corrected for both unreliability and age variability, the two corrections would approximately balance each other.

Correlates of height and intelligence.—Information was also recorded by the original investigators that may furnish insight into the interpretation of the correlations between height and intelligence. Three measures were reported for many girls, and two for many boys, that are highly appropriate for this purpose.

Occupation of the parent could be reasonably categorized into three levels. Ethnic heritage was reported in six categories, but the two that largely determine the relationships with height and intelligence are northwestern and southern Europeans. There were few blacks in the Boston area in the twenties. For girls the age of first menstruation was also available. This was reported in five categories, starting with "not before 11."

The roots of the correlation ratios for these variables with height and intelligence appear in Table 6. These correlations capitalize on chance a good deal more than product-moment correlations with the amount being a function of the number of categories. Because these correlations are nonlinear, they cannot be used directly in partial correlations, but we can assume that they represent the maximum amount of common variance. This maximum could be achieved with dummy coding and by holding constant the dummy variables in partial correlations. The amount by which the numerator of the partial correlation between height and intelligence would be reduced by holding SES constant varies from about .03 to .05 for boys and from about .03 to .04 for girls. For ethnicity the correction would be larger. The product for boys varies from about .06 to .08, for girls from about .10 to .12. Ethnicity and SES are themselves correlated so that holding both constant would add little to the amount of variance held constant by ethnicity alone.

TABLE 6

Relationships (Etas) of Socioeconomic Status,[a] Ethnicity,[b] and Girls' Age[c] of First Menstruation with Height and Intelligence

	Height						Intelligence				
	Boys		Girls				Boys		Girls		
Age	SES	Ethnicity	SES	Ethnicity	Menstruation		SES	Ethnicity	SES	Ethnicity	Menstruation
8	18	32	13	32	16		22	22	24	29	12
9	20	31	12	33	20		16	22	23	31	10
10	20	30	12	31	30		23	27	24	32	22
11	20	30	12	28	34		24	28	24	33	21
12	19	27	09	26	38		26	27	32	34	20
13	19	25	09	28	32		27	27	25	34	21
14	18	24	12	34	22		24	32	27	37	20
15	18	25	14	38	13		24	29	21	30	29
16	18	28	15	39	10		23	27	21	29	34
17	20	33	15	34	12		25	29	19	23	23

[a] Three categories.
[b] Six categories.
[c] Five categories.

Two important conclusions can be drawn from these approximations to partial correlations. Holding constant SES and ethnicity would not reduce the correlations between height and intelligence to zero. More important, because there is relatively little variation in the size of the relationships involving these correlates from year to year, holding constant SES and ethnicity would not account for the trends from age to age, especially those in the girls' data, in the cross-correlations between height and intelligence. Socioeconomic status and ethnicity, however, do have common variance with adult height and intelligence. They do not suggest any explanation for the larger correlations in the earlier years.

The nonlinear correlations for SES and ethnicity are based on very similar rank orders of the categories from one year to another. This is not the case for age of first menstruation. The regression of height on menstrual age group from 8 to 12 is generally monotonic with the youngest group being tallest. The two youngest groups become about equal at 13. Thereafter the regression is an inverted U.

The highest correlations between height and intelligence involve height at 8 and 9, but, at these ages, correlations between height and menstrual age are low. As the latter correlations increase, the former decrease. Individual differences in the age of sexual maturation attenuate the relationship between height and intelligence obtained in earlier years. The attenuation increases as the regression becomes the inverted U. Height that is not confounded with age of sexual maturation is the variable that has the maximum relationship with intelligence.

The prime physical correlate.—As described earlier, the Harvard Growth Study included other measures of physique in addition to standing height. One of these in particular provides a hint about where to look for causal influences on the correlation between standing height and intelligence. This is sitting height. It shows a similar pattern of correlations with intelligence but at a lower level. The difference between standing and sitting height represents the length of the long bones of the legs.

In order to conserve space the comparison of correlations involving the two measures of height have been summarized in two ways. In the first place we computed the difference in the size of the separate correlations with intelligence. As the next step we obtained means of these differences along both rows and columns of the 10 × 10 matrices for both boys and girls. These summaries appear in Table 7.

Because all differences in the correlations were signed, the trend is toward higher correlations of standing height with intelligence. As a matter of fact, there are only two differences in the 200 for the two sexes that are negative and these only in the third decimal place. It also appears that the differences for girls are larger than those for boys. We checked the statistical significance of some of the differences between differences for height at 8, 9, and 10 with intelligence at 10, 11, and 12 and found that the null hypothesis could be rejected at $p < .05$. These differences did represent the largest differences between standing and sitting height correlations with intelligence, but these ages also represent those that one would select knowing only the correlations reported in Tables 3 and 4.

Interpretations of partial correlations based on samples that are not constant from one zero-order correlation to another are a little hazardous, especially when one is inter-

TABLE 7

MEAN DIFFERENCES BETWEEN CORRELATIONS OF INTELLIGENCE WITH STANDING AND SITTING HEIGHT, RESPECTIVELY, FOR BOYS AND GIRLS

	8	9	10	11	12	13	14	15	16	17
Measurement of the two heights:										
Girls	.10	.10	.09	.08	.07	.07	.06	.04	.03	.05
Boys	.06	.05	.06	.06	.06	.05	.04	.03	.03	.02
Measurement of intelligence:										
Girls	.03	.06	.08	.10	.09	.06	.08	.09	.06	.04
Boys	.05	.04	.06	.06	.05	.04	.03	.04	.06	.03

TABLE 8

EFFECT OF A DIFFERENCE IN STABILITY OF TRUE SCORES ON CROSS-LAGGED DIFFERENCES

	X_1	X_2	Y_1	Y_2	X_1	X_2	Y_1	Y_2
X_1		.950	.500	.450		.950	.488	.462
X_2			.475	.496			.463	.498
Y_1				.900				.900
Y_2								

ested in statistical significance; but these are, nonetheless, suggestive. In the years previously mentioned, controlling sitting height in the correlations between standing height and intelligence has relatively little effect in the girls' sample, but controlling standing height in the correlations involving sitting height results in seemingly significant negative correlations. For girls at these ages length of trunk, which makes the major contribution to variance of sitting height, is negatively correlated with intelligence. In this sample the same correlation for boys is essentially zero.

A cross-lagged analysis.—Following the publication of Rogosa's (1980) critique of the cross-lagged correlation (CLC) methodology, the burgeoning interest in the technique came to a screeching halt. This was unfortunate. Rogosa's sweeping recommendation that further development of CLC be dropped was not supported by his analyses. He did show in detail what Humphreys and Parsons (1979) had illustrated earlier, that is, that true-score stabilities of the two measures being analyzed had to be known before any direct or indirect causal interpretation could be made. Correcting for uniqueness alone was indeed inadequate.

The importance of stability is illustrated in the two true-score correlation matrices in Table 8 in which the subscripts to X and Y indicate the occasion of measurement. There is a cross-lagged difference in the left-hand matrix of .025 that is reduced to nearly zero at the right. There is no causal influence on the left, but there is on the right.

The basis for this conclusion can be seen by computing multiple regression weights for X_1 and Y_1 as predictors of X_2 and Y_2. In the left-hand matrix in Table 8, X_1 has zero regression weight in predicting Y_2, and Y_1 has a zero weight in predicting X_2. In the right-hand matrix, Y_1 still has a zero weight in predicting X_2, but X_1 has a positive regression weight in predicting Y_2. The general principle is that, in the absence of either direct or indirect causal influence, the less stable measure will appear to anticipate (to use the descriptive term adopted by Humphreys & Parsons) the more stable.

It also follows that the appearance of a cross-lagged difference in which the true-score correlation between the more stable and the less stable is higher than the reverse combination allows one to conclude that individual differences on the more stable do anticipate later individual differences on the less stable. It is only necessary to have acceptable estimates of reliabilities so that correlations can be corrected for attenuation before evaluating cross-lagged differences. That evaluation must consider the stabilities of the two measures, as well as the cross-lagged correlations, following correction.

When the evidence for anticipation is not spuriously determined by a difference in the true-score stabilities, several causal models are possible: a direct influence from X to Y or from Y to X; an influence on both X and Y arising from Z; or an influence on both arising from a complex of determinants, $Z_1, Z_2, \ldots, Z_n$. When there is evidence for anticipation, and when the causal influence is indirect, as it almost certainly is with intelligence and height, one of the two variables is affected earlier than the other by the unknown determinant or complex of determinants.

During the earliest years of the 10-year period represented by the correlations in Tables 3 and 4, the true scores in height are more stable than the true scores in intelligence. If early height predicts intelligence more highly than the reverse, there is nothing spurious in a conclusion that height is anticipating changes in intelligence.

Table 9 presents the full set of cross-lagged differences between the correlations corrected for measurement error in intelligence of height and intelligence. Differences for girls are above, for boys below, the diagonal. A positive sign indicates that the prediction of intelligence from height is higher than the reverse. There are many posi-

TABLE 9

CROSS-LAGGED TRUE-SCORE CORRELATION DIFFERENCES FOR HEIGHT AND INTELLIGENCE AT ALL AGES BETWEEN 8 AND 17

	8	9	10	11	12	13	14	15	16	17
8		04	08	10	11	06	06	11	11	07
9	-02		03	06	07	03	04	07	04	02
10	08	08		04	07	04	05	09	11	07
11	04	03	-04		05	01	01	04	04	01
12	04	04	00	03		-01	-02	01	00	00
13	-02	01	-02	01	-03		00	02	04	02
14	-03	-01	-05	-01	-06	-04		02	02	06
15	01	00	-06	-01	-03	-01	02		01	06
16	01	02	-07	-02	-05	-05	-01	-03		05
17	-01	-04	-12	-08	-12	-10	-05	-06	-04	

NOTE.—A positive sign indicates that height predicts intelligence more accurately than intelligence predicts height. Correlations for girls are above, and correlations for boys are below the diagonal.

tive differences above the diagonal, many quite substantial in size. The largest ones are for the early years of height when the stability of true scores for the two measures favors a difference of opposite sign. Individual differences in height around 8–10 anticipate individual differences in intelligence in later years for these girls.

For the boys there are more negative differences overall than positive, but there is a small cluster of small positive differences for height at 8 and 9 with intelligence from 10 to 12. Elsewhere, the largest differences are negative and associated with intelligence at intermediate ages and later height. There are very few similarities in the cross-lagged differences for the two sexes, but for ages 8 and 9, when height anticipates later intelligence for girls, there may be a similar tendency in the data for boys.

Discussion

The first issue to be discussed concerns the possible sex differences in these data. The differences appear to be superimposed on similar growth patterns. Intercorrelations of height and intelligence over occasions are highly similar, with the exception that relative instability of individual differences in height occurs at a later age for the boys. Individual differences in age of growth spurts within groups combined with the mean difference between groups produce the one difference. Correlations within each sex of height and intelligence with age variability in months, SES, and ethnic origin are also highly similar. Estimated reliabilities and stabilities seemingly differ only randomly.

When attention is turned to the cross-correlations, there are many differences. The girls show large differences down the columns defined by age of measurement of intelligence and across the rows defined by the age of measurement of height. Girls have many correlations in the early years that differ substantially from a hypothetical population value of .20, the accepted figure for the adult relationship, but boys do not. When individual correlations for the two sexes are compared directly with each other, there are many differences in size that allow one to reject the null hypothesis at the .05 level or beyond.

A difference in the pattern of cross-correlations is reinforced by the differences in size of correlations with intelligence of standing and sitting height. Because the two height measurements are highly correlated, the a priori expectation would be for similar patterns of cross-correlations with intelligence. Instead the data indicate that leg length makes the primary contribution to the standing height correlations with intelligence in the early years, while length of the trunk has negative correlations with intelligence during the same period.

The primary contribution to the pattern of the cross-correlations is from age of sexual maturation. Some tall, intelligent girls mature early and stop increasing in height, but their intelligence continues to grow. Some short girls of lower intelligence mature late with continuing increases in height. Their intelligence continues to grow, but they do not show an intellectual spurt.

The cross-lagged analysis for girls indicates strongly that individual differences in height at 8, 9, and 10 anticipate individual differences in intelligence several years later. Height is very stable from year to year during

1476 Child Development

these early years. Our corrections for measurement error in the stabilities of intelligence produce somewhat lower values. This difference in stability biases the cross-lagged differences in the opposite direction. Even if our reliabilities are too high, the use of lower reliabilities would not abolish the cross-lagged differences. True-score stabilities cannot be greater than unity. Thus the data suggest a causal mechanism in girls that affects individual differences in height earlier than in intelligence.

On the basis of this summary it is tempting to conclude that the observed sex differences characterize the populations from which our samples were drawn. A sex difference in the relationship between height and intelligence has also been found by at least one other group of investigators (Brucefors et al., 1974) and recently brought to our attention. These authors compared two groups of children within each sex who were tested at frequent intervals from 1 month to 8 years of age. Height and weight were also measured. One group was selected on the basis of large positive correlations between test occasion and development or intelligence quotient. The other had large negative correlations between the same measures. After the first few months those who were gaining became taller and heavier than those who were losing. The differences were appreciably greater in the samples for girls than for boys. Note that the methodology insured that the gainers would be relatively high in intelligence at 8 and the losers relatively low.

An important drawback to a conclusion that the sex differences are real is that we do not have any hypothesis to account for the differences. We are forced to defer to those more familiar with growth patterns of boys and girls than we are the task of explaining the differences. On the other hand, if sex differences are rejected on the grounds of sampling fluke, an ever-present possibility in all research, the most reasonable estimate of population correlations is obtained by averaging the obtained value for the two sexes. The girls' sample is larger, and the z transformation gives greater weight to the higher correlations for girls in the early years. Thus the combined correlations presented in Table 10 are more similar to those in Table 3 than in Table 4.

The degrees of freedom available for hypothesis testing are $N_1 - 3$ plus $N_2 - 3$ for the hypothesis that the population correlation is .20 throughout. There are many correlations in the table, especially in the early years, for which the hypothesis can be rejected. It is also noteworthy that the value of .2 is highly congruent with the mean obtained correlation for a 2×2 or a 3×3 block in the lower-right-hand corner of the table. The ages for these blocks represent near adulthood.

There are differences in correlations along the rows and down the columns, but it is probably unwise to apply statistical tests of differences. These tests would require matrices of mean cross-correlations between height and intelligence over occasions, but the two sexes have different patterns of stability for height. The discrepancies between correlations of intelligence with standing and sitting height remain prominent in the combined samples. The partial correlations that served

TABLE 10

MEAN CROSS-CORRELATIONS BETWEEN HEIGHT AND INTELLIGENCE

	8	9	10	11	12	13	14	15	16	17
8	27	25	32	32	34	27	27	29	27	20
9	26	28	32	33	35	31	29	31	29	21
10	25	27	31	32	34	29	28	29	28	21
11	24	25	29	31	34	29	32	29	29	22
12	24	25	28	30	33	29	27	29	28	22
13	24	25	27	28	32	28	26	28	27	20
14	23	24	26	28	31	27	25	26	24	21
15	20	23	24	27	30	26	24	26	24	21
16	18	22	24	26	29	25	24	24	23	20
17	15	19	20	24	26	23	20	20	20	20

NOTE.—Height defines the rows and intelligence defines the columns.

as the basis for positive relationships between leg length and intelligence, on the one hand, and the negative relationship involving trunk length, on the other, are smaller but remain statistically significant. The cross-lagged differences in the early years also remain. Even a zero cross-lagged difference when there is a difference in stability is suggestive of an underlying causal process.

What are the relationships of these data to Jensen's and Husen's explanations for the adult correlation between height and intelligence? Both of these researchers rejected a within-family genetic basis for the correlations but suggested genetic and environmental explanations, respectively. Jensen hypothesized that it represented a between-family genetic phenomenon resulting from assortative mating. Husen suggested a prenatal environmental explanation.

The between-family genetic explanation for the adult correlation of .20 must cope with a correlation of .41 in girls, or a correlation of .36 in the combined groups, between height at 8 and intelligence at 12. Selection of the mate is based on the phenotypic traits observable at the time of mating. Ethnicity and SES are involved in mate selection, height, and intelligence, but the measures of these demographic variables available in our data do not account for the changing size of the height-intelligence correlation.

If one accepts the sex differences in cross-correlations as real, an environmental hypothesis is at least awkward. If one accepts instead the data in Table 10, a nutritional hypothesis is attractive. Similar data for height and intelligence are required for the years prior to 8, however, before one could push a nutritional hypothesis back to the prenatal period that Husen suggested. This hypothesis also becomes complex because it must account for differences in nutrition having more substantial effects on the long bones of the legs than on the trunk. On the other hand, an association of diet with SES and ethnicity would be no problem.

The anticipation of individual differences in intelligence by individual differences in stature, however, is not a major problem for either Jensen or Husen. Changes in biological functioning, whatever the causes may be, are not expected to have an immediate effect on intelligent behaviors. The intelligence measured by a standard test is a behavioral repertoire that is acquired over time. A biological deficit of less than traumatic proportions could affect future acquisitions but not the current repertoire. Thus intelligence would lag behind growth. Humphreys (1971, 1979) has discussed the nature of intelligence in this fashion.

Appendix

Group Tests of Intelligence on Which the Longitudinal Correlations were Based

First Year

Dearborn Group Test of Intelligence, General Examination A, also B in some instances.

Second Year

Dearborn Group Test of Intelligence, General Examination A.

Third Year

Dearborn Group Test of Intelligence, General Examination A.
Otis Primary Intelligence Test, Form A.

Fourth Year

Dearborn Group Test of Intelligence, General Examination A.
Otis Primary Intelligence Test, Form A.

Fifth Year

Dearborn Group Test of Intelligence, General Examination C.
Otis Self-administering Test of Mental Ability, Form A.

Sixth Year

Dearborn Group Test of Intelligence, General Examination C.
Otis Self-administering Test of Mental Ability, Form B.

Seventh Year

Haggerty Intelligence Test, Delta 2.
Dearborn Group Test of Intelligence, General Examination C.

Eighth Year

Terman Group Test of Mental Ability, Form A or B.
Haggerty Intelligence Examination, Delta 2.

Ninth Year

Terman Group Test of Mental Ability, Form B (to grades 7 and above).
Kuhlmann-Anderson Intelligence Tests (grade 9 to maturity).

Tenth Year

Kuhlmann-Anderson Intelligence Test (grade 9 to maturity).
Detroit Advanced Intelligence Test (Form V).

1478 Child Development

Eleventh Year

Detroit Advanced Intelligence Test (Form W).
Revised Alpha Examination (Form VII).

Twelfth Year

Kuhlmann-Anderson Intelligence Test (grade 9 to maturity).
Revised Alpha Examination (Form V).

References

Brucefors, A., Johannesson, I., Karlberg, P., Klackenberg-Larsson, I., Lichenstein, H., & Svenberg, I. (1974). Trends in development of abilities related to somatic growth. *Human Development*, 17, 152–159.

Dearborn, W. F., Rothney, J. W. M., & Shuttleworth, F. K. (1938). Data on the growth of public school children. *Monographs of the Society for Research on Child Development*, 3(1, Serial No. 14).

Humphreys, L. G. (1971). Theory of intelligence. In R. Cancro (Ed.), *Intelligence: Genetic and environmental influences* (pp. 31–42). New York: Grune & Stratton.

Humphreys, L. G. (1979). The construct of general intelligence. *Intelligence*, 3, 105–120.

Humphreys, L. G., & Davey, T. C. (1985). Continuity in the development of intelligence from one year to 17. Unpublished manuscript.

Humphreys, L. G., & Parson, C. K. (1979). A simplex process model for describing differences between cross-lagged correlations. *Psychological Bulletin*, 86, 325–334.

Humphreys, L. G., Parsons, C. K., & Park, R. K. (1979). Application of a simplex model to six years of cognitive development in four demographic groups. *Applied Psychological Measurement*, 3, 51–64.

Husen, T. (1959). *Psychological twin research*. New York: Free Press.

Jensen, A. R. (1980). *Bias in mental testing*. New York: Free Press.

Laycock, F., & Caylor, J. S. (1964). Physiques of gifted children and their less gifted siblings. *Child Development*, 35, 63–74.

Rogosa, D. (1980). A critique of cross-lagged correlation. *Psychological Bulletin*, 88, 245–258.

Tanner, J. M. (1966). Galtonian eugenics and the study of growth: The relation of body size, intelligence test score, and social circumstances in children and adults. *Eugenics Review*, 58, 122–135.

Influence of social background on psychomotor development in the first year of life and its correlation with later intellectual capacity: a prospective cohort study

Paula Rantakallio *, L. von Wendt and Helena Mäkinen

Departments of Public Health Science and Paediatrics, University of Oulu, Oulu, Finland

Accepted for publication 16 December 1984

Summary

The effect of the sex of the child, somatic growth and five family background variables upon psychomotor development during the first year of life was studied by regression analysis in a Northern Finland birth cohort ($n = 12058$) for 1966. Children with mental retardation and cerebral palsy were excluded from the series. The significant explanatory variables for the age of learning to stand and to walk without support were gestational age, birth weight, sex and maternal age. The girls and children of young mothers revealed a faster pattern of development. Urban residence enhanced learning to walk with support, an ability which was attained at the same age in both sexes. Female sex was the most powerful explanatory variable for early development of speech, the other significant variable being height at one year, birth weight, low parity of the mother and urban place of the residence. The social class and marital status of the mother proved insignificant for the developmental milestones studied here. The fast learners during their first year of life were superior to the others in their educational capacity at the age of 14 years. The prognosis in this respect was independent of social class.

psychomotor development; social class; intellectual capacity

---

* *To whom correspondence should be addressed:* University of Oulu, Department of Public Health Science, Kajaanintie 46 E, 90220 Oulu 22, Finland.

0378-3782/85/$03.30 © 1985 Elsevier Science Publishers B.V. (Biomedical Division)

Introduction

Various measures of ability in school-age children (reading, school performance, etc.) have been shown to be associated with social class, position of family, family size, etc. [3,4,13], and similar associations have also been demonstrated for psychomotor development in the first year [7,22], even though these are obviously less marked. It has been assumed that improved environmental conditions in infancy may prevent the development of the social-class differential at school age [17,19] and in this respect any early signs of social deprivation would be important.

The present paper records developmental milestones of the first year of life in a birth cohort of 12000 children in Northern Finland which was followed up until the age of 14 years. The social background factors for each child were collected prospectively during pregnancy [10,11] and the effect of these factors on the psychomotor development of the children was evaluated. The predictive value of delayed psychomotor development during the first year with respect to mental subnormality and educational problems at the age of 14 years was also studied by social classes.

Series and Method

The birth cohort comprises a total of 12058 live-born children, representing 96% of all children born in 1966 in the northern-most provinces of Finland, Lapland and Oulu [10]. The investigation was started at the sixth or seventh month of pregnancy in the antenatal clinics, when biological characteristics of the mother and the social standing of the family were recorded. Developmental data obtained during the children's visits to the welfare centres were supplemented with information obtained in a special examination performed by public nurses at the age of one for research purposes [14]. The mean number of contacts with a children's welfare centre during the first year was 9.9 [8,9].

Data on the age for learning to stand without support and to walk with and without support and the number of words spoken by the child at 12 months were obtained for 91% of the children alive at 1 year ($n = 11870$), and in 95% of these cases the information was collected at an age of at least 11.5 months. When calculating the cumulative indices for reaching the above developmental levels at the age of 11 or 12 months (Table I), those children whose sheets had been filled in prior to this age and who had not reached the actual level of development until the age of completing the sheet were assumed to develop in a similar manner to those who had been observed until the age of 12 months. In other events only cases with data collected at a minimum age of 11 months and 3 weeks were accepted. Of the background variables used in the regression analysis (Tables III and IV), height and weight at the age of one were unknown in less than 6% of cases, the gestational age was unknown in 3.4% and the other variables in less than 1%. Any missing variables were assigned the value for the next case. All the measurements of height and weight for one year of age were corrected to that age exactly [14]. The classification by social class was based on the prestige of the father's occupation [12,18]. Children born to unmarried mothers and those with missing data (< 5%) were allocated to social class IV. In the regression analyses the farmers with a minimum of 8 hectares of arable land were placed in class III and the others in class IV.

Children with mental retardation, IQ below 70, and with cerebral palsy [16,24] were excluded from the study. The methods of data collection for mental retardation, subnormality and educational problems at the age of 14 years are presented in detail in an earlier study [16].

Results

The cumulative percentage of children having learned to walk with and without support and to stand without support up to the age of 12 months are presented in Table I. The girls were ahead in learning to stand without support after 7 months of age whereas the boys were ahead in learning to walk with and without support. Social class seemed to influence the pattern of development in that the children belonging to social classes I + II tended to develop at a faster rate than the others, whereas the children of the farmers had the slowest development. This trend was regular only for standing without support, whereas the children in social class III were no slower in learning to walk than those in classes I and II.

The percentages of children with early and late speech development are presented separately for the boys and the girls by social classes in Table II. The sex differences are very clear, the girls being superior in each social class, but the effect of social class differences is also marked, as the children in class IV and the farmers' group are clearly slower in their speech development. The children in class III, however, were ahead of those in classes I and II.

Social classes may differ not only in the economic standing of the family but also in many demographic characteristics applying to the mother and the family, such by

TABLE I

The Northern Finland birth cohort for 1966 [a]

Age in full months	Walking with support	Standing without support	Walking without support
6	1.5	0.2	0
7	11.5	1.6	0
8	32.6	7.0	0.7
9	56.3	21.0	5.4
10	79.3	43.8	19.8
11	93.0	70.0	44.4
12	96.9	82.7	64.3

[a] Cumulative percentage of standing without support ($n = 10377$), walking with support ($n = 10268$) and walking without support ($n = 10343$).

TABLE II

The Northern Finland birth cohort for 1966 [a]

Social class	Speech (No. of words)					
	< 3 words		≥ 3 words		Total	
	Boys (%)	Girls (%)	Boys (%)	Girls (%)	Boys (%)	Girls (%)
I + II ($n = 2422$)	46.8	39.4	53.2	60.6	100.0	100.0
III ($n = 3395$)	46.3	36.0	53.6	64.0	100.0	100.0
IV ($n = 2760$)	50.0	42.3	50.0	57.7	100.0	100.0
Farmers ($n = 1950$)	51.3	46.2	48.7	53.9	100.0	100.0
Total ($n = 10527$)	48.3	40.4	51.7	59.7	100.0	100.0

[a] Speech at one year of age among boys and girls by social class.

the number of children in the family, maternal age, etc. The classes are also unevenly distributed in the urban and rural areas [6]. All these factors may affect the development of the child during the first year of life, and also the child's somatic

TABLE III

Regression analysis on age of learning to walk unsupported with 10 explanatory variables ($n = 9053$) (MCS = 0.031 [a])

Explanatory variable	Standard coefficient	t-value	2-tail significance
Gestational age	−0.094	−8.260	0.0000
Birth weight	−0.095	−7.612	0.0000
Maternal age	−0.072	4.933	0.0000
Sex of the child	−0.022	−2.070	0.0385
Height at 1 year	−0.021	−1.537	0.1243
Place of residence	0.017	1.517	0.1294
Marital status	0.011	1.067	0.2859
Weight at 1 year	−0.009	−0.672	0.5016
Parity of the mother	−0.007	−0.452	0.6514
Social class	−0.003	−0.228	0.8195

[a] MCS = multiple correlation squared (giving the total variance in age of learning to walk unsupported accounted for by all the explanatory variables introduced into the analysis).

TABLE IV

Regression analysis on the number of words at the age of one with 10 explanatory variables ($n = 10473$) (MCS = 0.023 [a])

Explanatory variable	Standard coefficient	t-value	2-tail significance
Sex of the child	0.113	11.191	0.0000
Height at 1 year	0.058	4.658	0.0000
Parity of the mother	−0.065	−4.653	0.0000
Place of residence	−0.049	−4.651	0.0000
Birth weight	0.026	2.178	0.0294
Marital status	−0.018	−1.793	0.0731
Gestational age	0.018	1.724	0.0848
Maternal age	−0.012	0.911	0.3623
Weight at 1 year	0.006	0.514	0.6071
Social class	−0.004	−0.366	0.7142

[a] MCS = multiple correlation squared (giving the total variance in number of words accounted for by all the explanatory variables introduced into the analysis).

growth. Four regression analyses were therefore performed in which each of the variables measuring the child's psychomotor development was used as the dependent variable in turn, and the following factors as explanatory variables: gestational age, birth weight, height and weight at the age of one, sex of the child, maternal age, parity and marital status, place of residence (town, village, remote village) and social class of the family according to the father's occupation.

The results of the regression analysis with respect to the age for learning to walk without support as the dependent variable is seen in Table III. The significant explanatory variables were length of gestation, birth weight, maternal age and sex of the child, in this order of importance. Younger age of the mother and female sex of the child accelerated the development. The same explanatory variables were significant for the age of learning to stand unsupported, but for the age of walking with support the sex of the child was unimportant, whereas weight at one year was significant and urban residence accelerated the development significantly.

The results of the analysis which took the number of words at the age of one year as the depending variable are presented in Table IV. The sex of the child was the most important explanatory variable, the girls being superior, and other significant variables were height at one year of age, parity of the mother, place of residence (low parity and urban residence tending to promote development), and birth weight. Social class was not a significant explanatory variable in any of the 4 analyses performed.

In order to study the correlation between psychomotor development during the first year and the child's educational capacity at the age of 14 years, the children were divided into three groups according to their ability at one year of age.
- Early learners, children who were able both to walk unsupported and to speak at least three words, 3 641 children, 1 728 boys and 1 913 girls.

146

TABLE V

Distribution of children in a lower class at school than appropriate at 14 years (306) or with an IQ of 71–85 (133) by psychomotor development during the first year (early, late and medium learners, see text), and by social class

Social class	Psychomotor development during 1st year							
	Early learners ($n = 3641$)		Medium learners ($n = 5911$)		Late learners ($n = 733$)		Total ($n = 10285$)	
	No.	%	No	%	No.	%	No.	%
I+II ($n = 2356$)	16	13.9	33	12.3	6	10.9	55	12.5
III ($n = 3327$)	36	31.3	82	30.5	19	34.6	137	31.2
IV ($n = 2687$)	48	41.8	112	41.6	23	41.8	183	41.7
Farmers ($n = 1915$)	15	13.0	42	15.6	7	12.7	64	14.6
Total ($n = 20285$)	115	100.0	269	100.0	55	100.0	439	100.0

– Late learners, those who were unable either to speak or to walk, 733 children, 439 boys and 294 girls.
– Medium learners, children who could walk and speak at the most two words, and children who could not walk but spoke, 5 911 children, 3 045 boys and 2 866 girls.

133 children, 94 boys and 39 girls, with known psychomotor development at the age of one year had a later IQ measurement of 71–85, and similarly the number of children who later went to an ordinary school but were in a lower class than was appropriate for their age, although not known to have an IQ < 86, was 306 (208 boys and 98 girls).

As expected, there was a significant difference in subsequent school performance between the early and late learners, 24.4 per 1 000 of the former and 47.7 per 1 000 of the latter having educational problems (P = 0.000), the corresponding prevalences for IQ 71–85 being 7.1 per 1 000 and 27.3 per 1 000 (P = 0.000). The children with an IQ 71–85 together with the children with delayed school performance, divided into early, late and medium learners according to their psychomotor development during the first year, are presented by social class in Table V. The proportion of each social class remains fairly constant in the early, late and medium learners' groups, so that there cannot be said to be any trend for the late learners in the lowest social classes to be overrepresented among the educationally subnormal children.

Discussion

There are quite large variations between countries in the ages at which the various milestones of motor development are achieved [5]. The mode of motor development in this Northern Finland series (Table I) seems to represent a rather early type as compared with series from other countries [1,5,20,21]. A large number of these differences are obviously caused by variations in the requirements for each performance in different countries. Intra-national variations, on the other hand, can be expected to be minimized in a country like Finland in which psychomotor milestones are continuously recorded for all children, especially where the mean number of contacts per child with a health centre during the first year is as high as 10 [8,9].

When only one background variable was cross-tabulated with the milestones of psychomotor development, a correlation was found with social class, this being highest for speech development (Table II). The children in social class III were similar or faster learners than those in class I + II, a finding which corresponds to that of Neligan and Prudham [7]. When the effect of social class was studied simultaneously using four other family background factors, four variables measuring somatic growth of the child and the sex of the child by regression analysis (Tables III and IV), social class came out as an insignificant explanatory variable for each of the four milestones studied here. The variables related to somatic growth were the most important explanatory variables for early standing and walking, whereas female sex had the same impact on speech development (Tables 3 and 4). Connections between somatic growth and psychomotor development have rarely been studied, but faster development by girls in speech has been reported by Touwen [20]. Contrary to Touwen's results [20], however, our series also connected the female sex with faster development in standing and walking without support.

Theoretically, multiple regression analysis gives the effect of each explanatory variable on the dependent variable in such a manner that the other variables can be regarded as standardized. Thus the effect of social class on the number of words at the age of one in Table IV, for example, represents a situation in which all the children were of the same size at birth and at one year, had had the same duration of gestation, represented the same sex, and had mothers of the same parity, same age and marital status and similar place of residence. The fact that social class was unimportant in this situation (Table IV) even though it showed a clear correlation when studied separately (Table II) means that some of the explanatory variables (Table IV), e.g. size of the child, parity of the mother and/or place of residence, are unevenly divided between the social classes.

In all four regression analyses either low parity or young age of the mother was significantly associated with rapid development in the child. This is in good agreement with the findings of Bryant and Davies [2], who report some evidence for the first-born child developing faster during the first year of life.

There was a clear correlation between late psychomotor development during the first year and later educational problems, similar to the correlation with mental retardation described earlier in this series [23]. This correlation was about the same in each social class, so that late psychomotor development during the first year did not mean a worse prognosis in the lowest social classes.

References

1. Bhandari, A. and Ghosh, B.N. (1979): A longitudinal study on gross motor development of the children from birth to one year of age in an urban community. Indian J. Med. Res. 70, 58–69.
2. Bryant, G.M. and Davies, K.J. (1974): The effect of sex, social class and parity on achievement of Denver Developmental Screening Test items in the first year of life. Dev. Med. Child Neurol. 16, 485–493.
3. Davie, R., Butler, N. and Goldstein, H. (1972): From Birth to Seven. Lowe & Brydone Ltd., Norfolk.
4. Douglas, J.W.B. (1976): The Home and the School. Panther Books, London.
5. Hindley, C.B., Filliozat, A.M., Klackenberg, G., Nicolet-Meister, D. and Sand, E.A. (1966): Differences in age of walking in five European longitudinal samples. Hum. Biol. 38, 364–379.
6. Krause, U., Krause, K. and Rantakallio, P. (1978): Regional differences in the use of opthalmological services during the pre-school period. Nordic Council Arct. Med. Res. Rep. 23, 20–25.
7. Neligan, G. and Prudham, D. (1969): Norms for four standard developmental milestones by sex, social class and place in family. Dev. Med. Child Neurol. 11, 413–422.
8. Public Health and Medical Care (1968): The Official Statistics of Finland, Helsinki.
9. Public Health and Medical Care (1971): The Official Statistics of Finland, Helsinki.
10. Rantakallio, P. (1969): Groups at risk in low birth weight infants and perinatal mortality. Acta Paediatr. Scand. Suppl. 193, 1–71.
11. Rantakallio, P. (1973): The assessment of small-for-dates infants and associated socio-biological factors. Ann. Chir. Gynaecol. Fenn. 62, 1–47.
12. Rantakallio, P. (1979): Social background of mothers who smoke during pregnancy and influence of these factors on offspring. Soc. Sci. Med. 13A, 423–429.
13. Rantakallio, P. (1983): A follow-up study up to the age of 14 of children whose mothers smoked during pregnancy. Acta Paediatr. Scand. 72, 747–753.
14. Rantakallio, P. and Mäkinen, H. (1983): The effect of maternal smoking on the timing of deciduous tooth eruption. Growth 47, 122–128.
15. Rantakallio, P. and Mäkinen, H. (1984): Number of teeth at the age of one year in relation to maternal smoking. Ann. Hum. Biol. 11, 45–52.
16. Rantakallio, P. and von Wendt, L. (1984): Mental retardation and subnormality in a birth cohort of 12000 children in Northern Finland, a prospective study. In press.
17. Sameroff, A.J. (1975): Early influences on development: fact or fancy? Merril-Palmer Q. 21, 267–294.
18. Sosiaaliryhmitys (1954): Helsingin Kaupungin Tilastotoimisto, Helsinki.
19. Stratton, P.M. (1977): Criteria for assessing the influence of obstetric circumstances on later development. In: Benefits and Hazards of The New Obstetrics, pp. 139–156. Editors: T. Chard and M. Richards, Lavenham Press Ltd., Lavenham, U.K.
20. Touwen, B. (1976): Neurological development in infancy. Clinics in Developmental Medicine, No 58. Spastics International Medical Publications. William Heinemann Medical Books Ltd., London.
21. Ueda, R. (1978): Child development in Okinawa compared with Tokyo and Denver, and the implications for developmental screening. Dev. Med. Child Neurol. 20, 657–663.
22. Werner, E.E., Honzik, M.P. and Smith, R.S. (1968): Prediction of intelligence and achievement at ten years from twenty months pediatric and psychologic examinations. Child Dev. 39, 1063–1075.
23. Von Wendt, L., Mäkinen H. and Rantakallio, P. (1984): Psychomotor development in the first year and mental retardation – a prospective study. J. Ment. Defic. Res. 28, 219–225.
24. Von Wendt, L., Rantakallio, P., Saukkonen, A.-L., Tuisku, M. and Mäkinen, H. (1984): Cerebral palsy and additional handicaps in a one-year birth cohort from Northern Finland – a prospective follow-up study to the age of 14 years. In press.

Physical Maturation Rate and Cognitive Performance in Early Adolescence: A Longitudinal Examination

Deborah P. Waber, Madeline B. Mann, James Merola, and Patricia M. Moylan
Department of Psychiatry and Mental Retardation Center
Children's Hospital, Boston, Massachusetts

A longitudinal study was undertaken to examine (a) the development of the relationship between physical maturation rate and cognitive performance as children become adolescent and (b) the specific components of cognitive processing that are most closely linked to physical maturation rate. Seventy-eight girls and 67 boys were examined prepubertally on a battery of cognitive ability and perceptual asymmetry measures and reexamined 2 years later when secondary sex characteristics could be evaluated as a measure of pubertal status. At that time, extreme groups of early and late maturers were selected for examination on a more detailed battery designed to assess specific components of cognitive processing. Although there were no maturation-related differences in performance on the cognitive ability tasks, differences were detected on the cognitive process tasks. Implications of these findings are discussed.

Given the central role of sex hormones in the development of sex-related behaviors in nonhuman mammalian species (Goy & McEwen, 1982), it is not unreasonable to suspect that these hormones are involved in the development of sex-related behaviors among humans as well. Examining the relationship of hormonal factors to the development of these behaviors is important not only because of what it can tell us about the etiology of the sex differences themselves, but also because sex-related behaviors provide an ideal vehicle for the investigation of more basic issues concerning the role of biological processes in human behavorial development (Waber, 1979).

The evidence that can be brought to bear on these questions is necessarily indirect. One strategy that has been employed is to establish systematic associations between achievement levels on tasks whose performance is known to be sex-related and morphological characteristics presumed to be induced by sex hormones. Typically, females excel at verbal abilities and males at visuospatial ones (Maccoby & Jacklin, 1974).[1] Several years ago, I examined the relationship of these cognitive abilities to rate of physical maturation, as measured by secondary sexual development in early adolescence (Waber, 1977). Because girls generally undergo physical maturation earlier than do boys, I reasoned, an association between maturation rate and cognitive ability patterns could give rise to the typically reported difference between the sexes in ability patterns. If so, early maturers of both sexes should outperform late maturers of the same sex on measures of verbal ability, and the opposite should be the case for measures of visuospatial ability.

In fact, late maturing children did outperform early maturers of the same age on visuospatial tasks independent of sex. Cor-

---

This research was supported by Research Grants MH31308 from the National Institute of Mental Health and BNS-7817751 from the National Science Foundation as well as Research Scientist Development Award MH00287 to Deborah P. Waber and in part by U.S. Public Health Service/National Institute of Child Health and Human Development Grant HD-06276 to the Mental Retardation Center.

The authors gratefully acknowledge the cheerful cooperation of the students, staff, and parents of the public school systems of Weston and Wellesley, Massachusetts as well as the assistance of Ann Sattler and Walt Karniski, who administered the physical examinations.

Requests for reprints should be sent to Deborah P. Waber, Department of Psychiatry, Children's Hospital, 300 Longwood Avenue, Boston, Massachusetts 02115.

[1] Recent literature reviews, however, indicate that this pattern is by no means fixed. It is interesting that, the more recent the study, the less likely it is that a sex difference is reported (Rosenthal & Rubin, 1982).

roboration for this finding comes from studies that relate cognitive performance not only to secondary sexual development (Diamond, Carey, & Back, 1983; Waber, Bauermeister, Cohen, Ferber, & Wolff, 1981) and menarcheal age (Petersen, 1981) but also to physical androgyny (Broverman, Broverman, Vogel, & Klaiber, 1964; Petersen, 1976) and body composition (Carey & Diamond, 1980; Newcombe & Bandura, 1983; Waber, 1981), indicators that may themselves be derivative of maturation rate (Broverman et al., 1964; Frisch, 1974).

In the same study, the early and late maturers who were in the older age groups (13-year-old girls and 16-year-old boys) also performed differently on a dichotic listening task, which measures asymmetries of information processing in the auditory system. Because of the hypothesized relationship between lateralization and spatial abilities (Levy, 1969), this finding seemed to support the claim that the maturation-related differences in cognitive performance are a function of biological processes involving the central nervous system rather than social influences associated with maturation rate. Further support for this assertion comes from a study by Newcombe and Bandura (1983), who found the association of spatial ability with maturation rate to be independent of its association with sex-related personality characteristics and sex role perception. (It should be noted, however, that these investigators found no association between their maturational index, body composition, and a tactile measure of lateralization.)

Even though the association between maturation rate and cognitive abilities has now been demonstrated repeatedly, its significance is not well understood. One issue that remains to be resolved concerns its developmental antecedents. The emergence of sexually differentiated behaviors at puberty in nonhuman mammalian species seems to be dependent on the presence of sex hormones during early periods of development (Goy & McEwen, 1982; see, per contra, however, Emery & Sachs, 1975). Thus, although these associations have been demonstrated only among adolescents, the possibility that the relationship is a manifestation of developmental processes originating in the early postnatal or even the prenatal period merits consideration (Berenbaum & Resnick, 1982; Levy & Reid, 1978; Netley & Rovet, 1982; Waber, 1977). Yet little is known about the natural history of this relationship. If the association were indeed a consequence of events occurring prior to adolescence, then the specific behavioral differences that characterize early and late maturing adolescents might be evident among preadolescent children who later emerge as early or late maturers.

Another area that merits further investigation is the nature of the specific cognitive processes that are related to the biological indicators. In previous studies, the behavioral outcome has generally been measured by psychometric test instruments that yield summary ability scores. With rare exceptions (Rovet & Netley, 1982), the relationship of these cognitive processes to maturation rate or other associated physiological indicators has not been examined. Neurological function, however, is likely to be more closely linked to specific component operations underlying task performance than to summary outcome scores per se (Allen, 1983; Lashley, 1937; Marshall, 1973), and so it is important to examine maturation rate in relation to these specific operations as well.

The present study, therefore, had as its primary focus two questions: (a) can a relationship between maturation rate and cognitive performance be demonstrated prior to adolescence, and (b) what specific aspects of cognitive processing are related to maturation rate? To address these questions, we undertook a short-term longitudinal investigation. Prepubertal children unselected for physical growth characteristics were examined on the test battery previously applied by Waber (1977) to extreme groups of early and late maturers. The same children were reexamined 2 years later when maturational status could be specified in terms of the development of secondary sexual characteristics. In the context of this design, we could determine whether the association between cognitive performance and maturation rate is present prior to adolescence or whether it emerges concurrent with the physiological changes of puberty. The existence of differences prior to the onset of puberty would suggest that the association observed in adolescence is indeed part of a more long-term developmental process.

The second question, that is, which aspects of cognitive processing are associated with maturation rate, was addressed by administering a series of experimental tasks to groups of extremely early and late maturing children selected on the basis of the physical examinations administered at the time of the follow-up testing. The purpose of administering these tasks was to examine in greater detail cognitive processes presumed to be involved in performance of the psychometric tests for which differences had been demonstrated previously.

Method

Design

The initial sample was composed of third-grade girls and fifth-grade boys because it was assumed that within these age ranges, none of the children would yet have entered puberty. Their performance was assessed on the battery of standardized ability tests used previously (Waber, 1977), on two dichotic listening measures, and on the Peabody Picture Vocabulary Test (PPVT). Height and weight were measured at this time. Two years later when the girls were in the fifth grade and boys were in the seventh, the same test battery (excluding the PPVT) was once again administered to all the children along with several supplementary visuospatial tasks. At that time, each child also received a physical examination whose purpose was to assess maturational status as measured by the development of secondary sexual characteristics. In the context of this design, cognitive performance could be evaluated retrospectively in relation to adolescent maturational status. Sex differences could be examined by comparing boys' and girls' fifth-grade performance (Time 1 for boys and Time 2 for girls).

The findings from the physical examination at Time 2 were used to identify extreme groups of 10 early- and 10 late-maturing children within each sex. The additional battery of experimental tasks designed to detect differences in cognitive processing was administered to these children only. Although it would have been desirable to administer this battery to all participants, time constraints precluded this possibility.

Subjects

Third-grade girls and fifth-grade boys from the public school systems of two adjacent middle to upper middle-class towns near Boston (called here Towns A and B) were contacted by letter in December 1978. The sample was limited to right-handed (by self-report) white children not identified by the school as learning disabled. All boys and girls in the designated grade levels who met these criteria were solicited. Of the families contacted, the compliance rate was as follows: Town A girls, 73%; Town A boys, 56%; Town B girls, 52%; Town B boys, 50%.

The initial sample included 95 girls and 90 boys. Of these, 78 girls (Town A, $N = 18$; Town B, $N = 60$) and 67 boys (Town A, $N = 18$; Town B, $N = 49$) were available for follow-up testing. Dropout rates were as follows: Town A girls, 28%; Town A boys, 28%; Town B girls, 10%; Town B boys, 25%. Those who dropped out did so either because the family had moved out of the area or because the child had enrolled in a private school in the interim. The data to be reported here pertain only to those children who completed both phases of testing.

The mean age in months was 104.71 (range: 95 to 112) at Time 1 and 127.41 (range: 120 to 134) at Time 2 for girls, and 130.69 (range: 122 to 140) at Time 1 and 153.4 (range: 145 to 162) at Time 2 for boys. Mean IQ measured by the PPVT at Time 1 was 116.54 (range: 86 to 146) for girls and 123.3 (range: 97 to 146) for boys.

Previous studies (Waber et al., 1981; Waber, 1981) indicated that socioeconomic status (SES) can play an important modifying role in this relationship, the effect of maturation rate appearing for children from middle- but not lower-class backgrounds. The father's occupation was therefore ascertained for as many participants as possible so that a variable estimating SES could be included in the analysis. The occupations were rated according to the Hollingshead system (1965). Of the 90% of the girls for whom parental occupation was known, 93% were classified as upper to upper middle class (1 or 2). Similarly, for the boys, of the 91% for whom parental occupation was known, 89% were classified as upper to upper middle class.

Measurement

The measurement schedule is displayed in Table 1, and the measures are described in detail below.

Physical growth. Height and weight were assessed at both testing times so that rate of growth during the 2-year interval could be estimated. At Time 2, the children were also classified by physical examination according to Tanner's (1962) system for rating secondary sexual development. The 40 children (10 early and 10 late-maturing boys and girls) who had the most deviant maturation scores relative to their chronological age were designated as belonging to the extreme groups.

Cognitive abilities. The cognitive ability battery applied in the previous study (Waber, 1977) was applied here so that associations between performance on these tests and maturation rate could be assessed prior to and at adolescence. It included the following measures: Stroop Color–Word Interference Test, Wechsler Intelligence Scale for Children–Revised (WISC–R) Coding Subtest, Word Fluency, a short form of the Embedded Figures Test (EFT), WISC–R Block Design, and Primary Mental Abilities (PMA) Spatial Test. A detailed description of the measures and their administration appears in Waber (1977).

There were, however, several relatively minor deviations from the procedure used previously. First, the entire Stroop test, including Word Naming and Interference, was given rather than just the Color Naming subtest. Second, the Wechsler subtests were taken from the WISC–R rather than from the WISC. Finally, because the standard adult EFT stimuli were too difficult for the third-grade girls, a new perceptual disembedding task,

Table 1
Measurement Schedule

Type of measure	Time 1	Time 2
Physical growth	Height Weight	Height Weight Tanner stage
IQ	PPVT	
Cognitive abilities	Stroop Color–Word Interference WISC–R Coding PMA Word Fluency Embedded Figures Test WISC–R Block Design PMA Mental Rotation	Stroop Color–Word Interference WISC–R Coding PMA Word Fluency Embedded Figures Test WISC–R Block Design PMA Mental Rotation
Dichotic listening	Phonemes Words	Phonemes Words
Supplementary visuospatial		Rey–Osterrieth Mooney
Experimental tasks (Extreme groups)		Selective Attention Mental Rotation Block Design

Note. WISC–R = Wechsler Intelligence Scale for Children–Revised, PMA = Primary Mental Abilities Test, PPVT = Peabody Picture Vocabulary Test.

designed so that its demand characteristics would be more similar to those of the adult version of the EFT than the standard children's version (CEFT), was introduced for this group. This task was adapted from the EFT included in Benton and Spreen's Neuropsychological Test Battery (Benton & Spreen, 1969). Twelve items demonstrated by pretesting to show adequate variability in this age range were used. For each item, the child looked at a complex design for 10 s and then at a simple figure for 10 s. The simple figure was then taken away, and using a pencil, the child was given 1 min to trace the complex design. The score for each item was time to correct solution. Failed items were assigned a score of 60 s. The total score was the sum of the times for the 12 items. Prior administration of this task to 46 third graders, divided equally by sex, indicated that its performance was in fact related to performance on the standard CEFT for both girls, $r = .44$, $p < .01$, and boys, $r = .63$, $p < .01$ (Waber, Davies, & Mann, 1982).

Dichotic listening. Because of the previous finding that dichotic listening asymmetries are related to maturation rate (Waber, 1977), it was of interest to ascertain whether early and late maturers would show different asymmetry patterns prior to adolescence. Further, because laterality patterns are thought to vary for different levels of linguistic processing (Porter & Berlin, 1975), an association with maturation rate might emerge for one type of linguistic stimulus but not for another. Therefore, two dichotic listening tests were administered, one involving phonemic stimuli and the other monosyllabic concrete nouns.

1. Phonemes: This task, a longer version of which was applied in the previous study (Waber, 1977), entailed presentation of single pairs of phonemes and, therefore, measured perceptual asymmetries independent of cognitive factors such as semantic encoding and memory capacity. Sixty pairs of the six phonemes—/ba/, /da/, /ga/, /pa/, /ta/, and /ka/—were presented dichotically with a 5-s interval between trials and a 10-s interval after every 10 trials. Headphones were reversed after the first 30 trials to control for possible confounding effects of chennel. Order of channel to ear presentation was counterbalanced across children. The children were instructed to write down for each trial a consonant letter indicating the sound that they had heard. Practice included 12 binaural trials and 5 dichotic ones. The children were told that the latter might be more difficult to understand but were not informed that two different stimuli were to be presented simultaneously. The test was scored for number of stimuli correctly reported from each ear. A laterality coefficient was computed according to the formula recommended by Marshall, Caplan, and Holmes (1975), which is intended to be independent of accuracy level. In addition, because of the controversy surrounding the use of such coefficients (Jones, 1983), absolute difference scores were evaluated as well. It was predicted that late maturers would exhibit a greater degree of asymmetry than would early maturers. In addition, given their hypothesized advantage at verbal skills, it was predicted that early maturers would report stimuli more accurately (Fennell, Satz, & Morris, 1983).

The dichotic listening procedure can elicit individual differences not only in terms of accuracy and laterality but also in the rate of perception of fusions, combinations of features of the two dichotically presented stimuli to yield yet a third. On phoneme tasks of this type, phonetic feature-fusion errors (Cutting, 1976) can occur. These errors represent a combination of features of the phonemic stimuli presented to the two ears. For example, fusion of the unvoiced labial /pa/ with the voiced alveolar /ga/ yields either the voiced labial /ba/ or the unvoiced alveolar /ka/. Because the phonemes /ta/ and /da/ could not have been perceived by such a process, they are not classified as fusions. All errors were therefore classified as fusion or nonfusion. Because the previous study indicated that early maturers exhibited less lateralization than did late maturers, it was expected that their processing of these stimuli would be less well differentiated and that they would therefore commit a higher proportion of these fusion errors. Thus performance on this task was analyzed in terms of (a) accuracy, (b) absolute difference between ears, (c) laterality coefficient, and (d) proportion of errors that were fusions.

2. Monosyllabic concrete nouns: This task included 30 trials, each consisting of dichotic presentation of three pairs of monosyllabic nouns (Schulman-Galambos, 1977). It was chosen because it involves cognitive, in addition to perceptual, aspects of language processing and because normative data exist for children (Schulman-Galambos, 1977). The child was instructed to report as many words as possible in a free-recall format for each trial. Order of channel to ear presentation was counterbalanced across children, and the headphones were reversed after the first 15 trials to control for channel effects. The test was scored for number of stimuli correctly reported from each ear. Laterality coefficients were generated using the formula recommended by Marshall, Caplan, and Holmes (1975) as were absolute difference scores. In addition, the ear from which the child reported the first stimulus word was noted and a laterality coefficient (R–L/30) derived in order to ascertain lateral bias independent of memory load. Because of the nature of the stimuli, analysis of fusion errors was not appropriate for this task. Again, it was predicted that late maturers would exhibit a greater degree of asymmetry and early maturers would report the words more accurately. Performance on this task was analyzed in terms of (a) accuracy, (b) absolute difference between ears, (c) laterality coefficient, and (d) first report coefficient.

Supplementary visuospatial measures. To expand the range of visuospatial skills measured, two tasks were added to the battery and administered to all children at Time 2.

1. Rey–Osterrieth Complex Figure Copying Test: This test (Osterrieth, 1946), in which the child is required to copy, freehand, a complex abstract design (see Figure 1), measures visuoconstructive skills. Five colored pencils were provided in a predetermined sequence for 30-s intervals as the child copied the figure. Erasures were not permitted. Using this color-coded method, it is possible to obtain information not only about the child's skill at copying the design but also about strategies used to do so. The reproductions are scored for two parameters: goodness of organization and copying style (configurational or part-oriented) using a rating system based on the presence or absence of criterial features of the design (Waber & Holmes, in press). It was predicted that late maturers would produce better organized copy productions than would early maturers and that they would reproduce the design in a more configurational manner.

2. Mooney Faces Test: This task, which requires that the child categorize incomplete depictions of faces, measures synthetic visuospatial perception (Lansdell, 1968; Mooney, 1957). The 48 stimulus cards are sorted according to six categories: boy, girl, grownup man, grownup woman, old man, and old woman. The test was administered in this study with a 7-min time limit and scored for the number of items correctly classified. It was predicted that late maturers would outperform early maturers.

Experimental cognitive measures. These measures were intended to assess in greater detail cognitive functions presumed to play a role in the performance of some of the visuospatial tasks on which early and late maturers had been previously demonstrated to differ.

1. Selective attention: An auditory central-incidental learning task (Conroy & Weener, 1976; Hagen, 1967) was administered to assess selective attention in early and late maturers. Selective attention was measured in order to examine the possibility that the advantage displayed by late maturing children on certain visuospatial tasks reflects an ability to effectively deploy attention. The auditory version of this task was chosen to determine whether such a difference, if demonstrated, would extend beyond the visual modality. This particular paradigm also permits analysis of serial-order effects, which are indicative of specific processes involved in memory, such as cumulative rehearsal and immediate storage (Atkinson & Shiffrin, 1968; Conroy & Weener, 1976).

Ten stimulus trials, each of which consisted of five pairs of monosyllabic names of animals and household items (e.g., fish–lamp, horse–bed), were presented over headphones by tape recorder at a rate of one pair per second. A total of 10 pairs was used, each pair being presented once in each position in the course of the 10 trials. After each trial, the child was asked to report the ordinal position in which a particular animal name had occurred. There were two such probes for each of ten trials. After completion of these 10 central learning trials, incidental learning was assessed by asking the child to name the household item that had been paired with each animal name. It was predicted that late maturers would exhibit a greater capacity for selective attention than would early maturers.

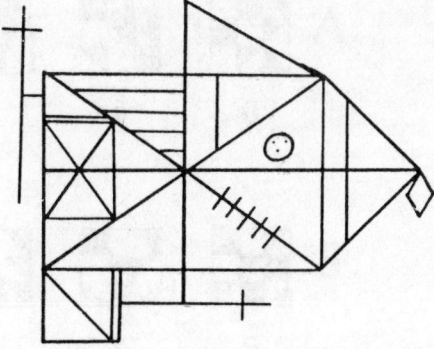

Figure 1. The Rey–Osterrieth Complex Figure (from Osterrieth, 1946).

2. Mental rotation: Because maturation-related differences have been demonstrated for rotational ability (Waber, 1977), a tachistoscopic reaction-time paradigm was used to examine cognitive processes involved in the performance of mental rotation (Childs & Polich, 1979; Cooper & Shepard, 1973; Waber, Carlson, & Mann, 1982). On each trial, one of the four uppercase letters, R, F, G, or J, is presented briefly (for 1 s) at one of four orientations, 0°, 60°, 120°, and 180°. The child determines whether the letter is forward or backward and responds by depressing a response key. After completing 32 trials of this no information (NI) condition, an advance information (AI) condition is introduced in which the child first sees a clue letter indicating the identity and orientation of the test letter and then the test letter itself. This task (described in detail in Waber et al., 1982) yields accuracy and response-time scores at each of four orientations in the two conditions.

Of particular interest is the relation in individuals between performances in the NI and AI conditions. In the NI condition, response time typically increases and accuracy decreases as the angle of rotation increases from 0° to 180°. In the AI condition, however, there is more variation between individuals. A response curve shaped like that seen in the NI condition indicates the child is performing a mental rotation of the test letter despite the presence of the clue letter and, therefore, that the clue letter is not being used as a visual image. A flat response curve indicates the child is not rotating the test letter and can, therefore, be assumed to be comparing a visual image of the clue letter with the test letter (Cooper & Shepard, 1973). It was, therefore, predicted that late maturers would show greater differentiation between the NI and AI conditions than would early maturers.

3. Block design: To examine block-design performance in greater detail, we administered a Kohs-type block-design task in which stimulus parameters are systematically varied (Royer & Weitzel, 1977; Waber, 1983). The time required to copy these designs increases as a function of its perceptual cohesiveness as measured by the number of adjacent same-color sides. When the test is given in the cued version, that is, with the grid superimposed to demarcate the block outlines, the relationship between copying time and cohesiveness disappears. By inference, then, the difference between performance times in the uncued and cued conditions represents the time required to decompose the design into component subunits. The primary reason for using this task, therefore, was to determine whether early and late maturers differed in the ability to fractionate the Gestalt.

The series of five nine-block designs shown in Figure 2 was constructed so that the number of adjacent red sides would increase systematically from 0 through 4, 8, 12, and 16 (Waber, 1983). To increase the probability that these response times would reflect perceptual rather than motor aspects of the task, flat tiles from the Wechsler Preschool and Primary Scale of Intelligence (WPPSI) Block Design subtest were used rather than the standard WISC blocks. These were presented in three piles: solid red, solid white, and diagonal, so that the desired surface could be located easily and manipulation time, therefore, minimized. A 180-s time limit was imposed for each item. Testing was begun with the item with 0 adjacent sides, and the rest of the items were then administered in order until the child failed to complete two successive items within the time limit or all five items were completed. A cued series with the grid superimposed was then administered in the same fashion. The score for each item was time to completion. Designs reproduced inaccurately but completed within the time limit were assigned the maximum score of 180 s. It was predicted, therefore, that as the number of adjacent same-color sides increased, early maturers' response times would increase more steeply than would those of late maturers.

Procedure

All children were tested individually in school. At each testing time, the cognitive testing was carried out in two sessions lasting approximately 45 min each. The early and late maturers participated in a third session lasting

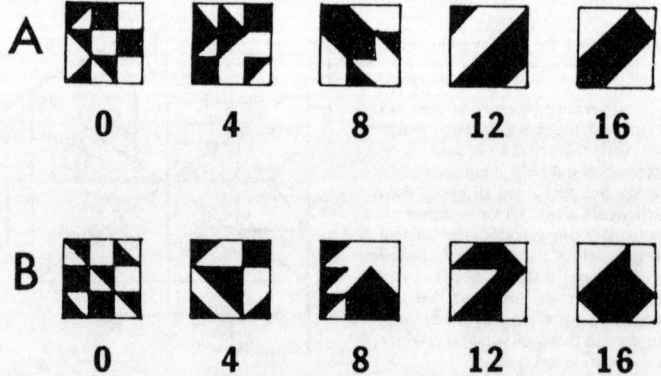

Figure 2. Block design stimuli.

approximately 1 hr at Time 2. Maturation status was established in the course of a well-child physical examination administered by a physician of the same sex as the child in the school nurse's office.

Results

The initial predictions of the study and actual outcomes are summarized in Table 2. These results are described in detail below.

Physical Growth

Means and standard deviations for the physical growth measures for the entire sample and for the extreme groups of early and late maturers appear in Table 3. Because of the sex differences in physical growth and body size, heights and weights were converted to standardized percentile scores (NCHS, 1976) prior to analysis. A 2 (sex) × 2 (maturation) × 2 (test time) mixed analysis of variance (ANOVA) confirmed ($p < .01$) that early maturers were taller and heavier than late maturers even at the first testing time. Interactions between maturation group and test time for both height and weight indicated that the size disparity increased during the two intervening years, with the early maturers growing more rapidly.

Test–Retest Reliability

Test–retest correlations for the repeated measures appear in Table 4. Reliability of the ability measures was high. The correlation for the EFT was as strong for the girls, for whom the actual tasks differed between the two testing times, as it was for the boys, who were given the same task twice. Performance was considerably more stable for the dichotic word task than it was for the phoneme task.

Sex Effects

Sex differences were examined for the six cognitive ability measures by comparing the performance of boys and girls when they were tested in the fifth grade (see Table 5). Girls outperformed boys on the WISC-R Coding subtest, and boys outperformed girls on the WISC-R Block Design subtest, the PMA Spatial Ability Test, and the PMA Word Fluency Test, and boys outperformed girls on the WISC-R Block Design subtest, the PMA Spatial Ability Test, and the PMA Word Fluency Test. Analyses of covariance (AN-COVAs) controlling for possible sex-related differences in age and IQ yielded the same result. Apart from the boys' superiority on word fluency, the results were consistent with the typically reported male advantage for spatial ability and female advantage for verbal and sequencing abilities (Maccoby & Jacklin, 1974). There were no sex differences for any of the dichotic listening variables.

Town Effects

There were no town-related differences in level of physical maturity, as measured by Tanner ratings, nor was there a difference in the distribution of SES ratings. Performance differences on the ability measures did emerge, however, for girls from the two towns. Girls from Town B outperformed those from Town A on the word fluency Time 1, $t(76) = 3.5$, $p < .001$; Time 2, $t(47.7) = 2.58$, $p < .02$, and coding tests, Time 1, $t(74) = 2.19$, $p < .05$; Time 2, $t(75) = 2.51$, $p = .014$. Girls from Town A outperformed those from Town B on the EFT, $t(48.5) = 2.81$, $p < .01$.

Maturation and Cognitive Performance

Cognitive abilities. Of greatest interest was the relation between physical maturity as measured at Time 2 and cognitive abilities measured at both times. To assess these relationships, each ability test (as measured at each testing time) was regressed hierarchically on (a) age and IQ and (b) the Tanner rating scores, entered in two successive steps. This regression analysis revealed no association between the maturation variables and any of the cognitive ability measures. Entering estimates of body composition, based on height and weight measurements (Mellits & Cheek, 1970), and percent increase in height and weight as predictor variables yielded similar results.

Repeated measures ANOVAs computed for the extreme groups also failed to reveal a

Table 2
Predictions and Outcomes for Behavioral Measures Based on Hypothesis of Study

	Predictions	Outcomes
Cognitive abilities		
	Early maturers will outperform late maturers at verbal and sequencing abilities and late maturers will outperform early maturers at spatial abilities.	0
	This difference will be present prior to the onset of puberty.	0
Dichotic listening		
	Late maturers will exhibit greater asymmetry than will early maturers.	0
	Early maturers will perceive linguistic stimuli more accurately than will late maturers.	+ (phonemes only)
	Early maturers will perceive a higher proportion of phonetic feature fusions than will late maturers.	+
Supplementary visuospatial		
	Late maturers will outperform early maturers on the Mooney Faces Test.	0
	Late maturers will produce better organized copy productions of the Rey–Osterrich Complex Figure than will early maturers.	+
	Late maturers will reproduce the design in a more configural manner than will early maturers.	0
Experimental tasks		
	Late maturers will exhibit a greater capacity to attend selectively than will early maturers (selective attention task)	0
	Late maturers will be more likely to use advance information as a visual image than will early maturers.	+
	Early maturers will require more time to copy uncued block designs (fractionate the Gestalt) as the number of same-color sides increases than will late maturers.	0

Note. + = Confirmed. 0 = No difference.

Table 3
Physical Growth Characteristics of Study Sample and Early and Late Maturing Subgroups

Growth characteristics	Whole sample		Early		Late	
	M	SD	M	SD	M	SD
Girls (N = 78)						
Time 1						
Height (in.)	51.85	2.16	53.41	2.08	51.87	2.54
Weight (lb)	61.92	8.66	69.17	12.91	58.12	6.86
Time 2						
Height (in.)	55.87	2.48	58.74	2.42	55.67	2.62
Weight (lb)	75.93	10.92	88.11	12.91	69.85	11.33
Breasts[a]	3.06	1.69	6.00	1.40	1.00	0
Pubic hair[a]	2.54	1.79	5.80	1.20	1.00	0
Age (months)	104.70	3.97	127.50	1.13	126.00	3.50
Boys (N = 67)						
Time 1						
Height (in.)	56.47	3.23	57.71	3.70	54.72	3.96
Weight (lb)	82.77	14.77	88.99	21.49	71.21	11.00
Time 2						
Height (in.)	61.53	3.83	64.19	3.67	58.66	4.36
Weight (lb)	102.42	22.70	116.14	8.71	83.60	15.69
Genitals[a]	4.47	1.92	7.20	0.63	2.60	0.84
Pubic hair[a]	3.79	2.09	6.80	0.63	1.00	0
Age (months)	130.69	4.64	152.00	3.59	151.00	4.60

[a] Tanner (1962) described a 5-point scale. This, however, was converted to an 11-point scale to permit physicians to more confidently rate those cases in which they had difficulty deciding between two stages. Thus Stage 1 = 1, Stage 1–2 = 2, Stage 2 = 3, and so forth.

Table 4
Test–Retest Reliability for Repeated Measures

Measures	Girls	Boys
Ability measures		
Stroop word	.698*	.743*
Stroop color	.725*	.823*
Stroop interference	.636*	.650*
Coding (scaled score)	.655*	.635*
Word fluency	.633*	.577*
Block design (scaled score)	.711*	.648*
Primary Mental Ability	.495*	.644*
Embedded Figures Test	.471*	.464*
Dichotic listening		
Phonemes—laterality	.134	.147
Phonemes—accuracy	.102	.182
Phonemes—% fusion error	.448*	.170
Words—laterality	.534*	.649*
Words—accuracy	.569*	.599*

* $p < .001$.

maturation effect. To rule out the possibility that the absence of an effect was due to the inclusion in the sample of low SES children, who had been found previously not to show the rate of maturation effect (Waber, 1981; Waber et al., 1981), the regression analyses were computed excluding the scores of those children whose SES ratings were below 2. The results were unchanged.

Analysis of the data separately by town, however, revealed the predicted associations among the 18 girls from Town A. Simple correlations of the Tanner ratings at Time 2 and percent increase in height and weight with performance on the ability tests at both testing times appear in Table 6. At Time 2, the breast development ratings are the best predictor of cognitive ability test performance. Every correlation is in the predicted direction, and their magnitude attains acceptable levels of statistical significance for three measures: Coding, Block Design, and the EFT. Repeating the hierarchial regression analyses described above for this group alone indicated that the correlations could not be attributed to confounding effects of age or IQ. Given the magnitude of these correlations and their consistency with previous findings, it is un-

Table 5
Differences in Abilities According to Sex

	Girls ($N = 78$)		Boys ($N = 67$)			
Ability measure	M	SD	M	SD	t(2-tail)	p
Stroop word	51.69	8.04	52.10	7.69	−0.31	ns
Stroop color	74.32	11.53	77.46	13.94	−1.48	ns
Stroop interference	142.0	31.92	148.85	27.23	−1.38	ns
Coding (scaled score)	14.19	2.27	12.97	2.48	3.09	.002
Word fluency	34.98	10.20	40.98	10.43	−3.6	.0001
Block design (scaled score)	12.72	2.92	14.43	3.02	−3.44	.001
PMA	22.24	7.6	26.08	7.8	−3.00	.003
EFT	384.39	221.14	369.42	207.58	0.42	ns
PPVT IQ	116.53	13.19	123.28	12.03	−3.2	.002

Note. PMA = Primary Mental Abilities, EFT = Embedded Figures Test, PPVT = Peabody Picture Vocabulary Test.

Table 6
Simple Correlations of Maturational Indicators With Cognitive Ability Measures for Town A Girls

Ability measure	Time 1				Time 2			
	Δ Height	Δ Weight	Breast	Pubic hair	Δ Height	Δ Weight	Breast	Pubic hair
Stroop word	.47	.33	.03	−.09	.40	.29	−.17	.13
Stroop color	.35	−.05	−.30	−.19	.45	.07	−.34	−.32
Stroop interference	.20	.08	−.32	−.40	.38	.24	−.16	−.35
Coding	−.19	−.13	.10	.32	−.31	−.23	.56*	.31
Fluency	.01	−.13	−.11	.01	−.08	−.12	.37	.08
Block design	−.18	−.04	−.42	.18	.14	.15	−.53*	.15
PMA spatial	−.15	.21	−.14	.44	.02	.31	−.12	.10
EFT	−.14	.003	.38	−.15	−.04	.09	.74**	.04

Note. PMA = Primary Mental Abilities, EFT = Embedded Figures Test.
* $p < .05$. ** $p < .001$.

likely that these associations represent a chance occurrence in a relatively small sample.

To summarize, the predicted association between maturation rate, specifically, secondary sexual development, and cognitive abilities could not be detected for the sample as a whole. It did, however, emerge among a subsample of the girls.

Dichotic listening. Dichotic listening performance was examined in relation to physical maturity by the hierarchical regression procedure described above. Physical maturity did not effectively predict any of the dichotic listening outcome measures, nor did examination of the data separately by town reveal meaningful associations.

The dichotic listening data for the extreme groups were submitted to a 2 (sex) × 2 (maturation) × 2 (time of testing) × 2 (ear) ANOVA on the number of items reported correctly from each ear. For the phonemes task, several aspects of performance were related to maturation: Early maturers reported more stimuli accurately than did late maturers, $F(1, 36) = 6.66, p = .015$, and they committed a higher proportion of fusion errors, $F(1, 36) = 6.14, p = .019$. All children were more accurate on the second testing than the first, $F(1, 36) = 9.19, p = .005$. The absence of higher order interactions involving maturation indicated that these differences were present for both sexes at both testing times.

A similar analysis for the word task revealed that (a) boys reported more items correctly than did girls, $F(1, 36) = 4.28, p = .046$ (an effect that may be a function of age in this design), (b) the group as a whole reported more words correctly on the second testing than on the first, $F(1, 36) = 125.5, p < .001$, and (c) children reported more words correctly from the right ear than the left, $F(1, 36) = 13.88, p < .001$. There were no main effects or interactions involving maturation.

Supplementary visuospatial tests. Neither the hierarchical regression procedure nor ANOVA on the extreme groups revealed any relation between physical maturity and performance on the Mooney test.

Performance on the Rey–Osterrieth test, was, however, systematically related to maturation rate. Although the hierarchical regression analysis did not reveal an association, a 2 (sex) × 2 (maturation) ANOVA on the scores of the extreme groups confirmed the predicted advantage for late maturers, who produced better organized designs, $F(1, 36) = 4.36, p < .05$. There was no interaction with sex.

This difference presumably reflected the relatively greater skill of the late maturers at perceiving the logical organization of the configuration and using it to plan their execution of the design. To determine empirically whether this was in fact the case, we ascertained how many of the 12 segments that comprise the base rectangle were executed at the outset (i.e., in the first color), because it is this rectangle that provides the structural basis for the overall organization of the design (see Figure 1). As predicted, the late maturers of both sexes produced more base rectangle segments in the first color ($M = 6.6$) than did early maturers ($M = 5.0$), $t(38) = 1.98$, $p < .05$.

Because style ratings (configurational or part-oriented) are systematically related to organizational level (Waber & Holmes, in press) and because there was a maturation-related difference in organization, the effect of maturation on the style parameter was analyzed by a 2 (sex) × 2 (maturation) AN-COVA with organization as the covariate. There were no effects of either sex or maturation.

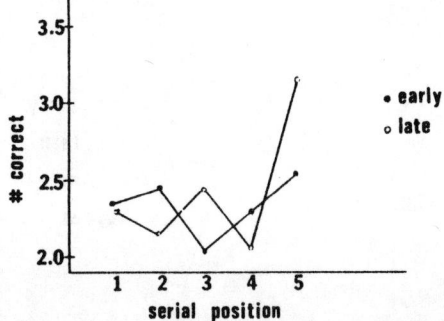

Figure 3. Number of stimuli correctly reported at each serial position by early and late maturers on the selective attention task.

Experimental Cognitive Measures

The analysis of performance on these tasks is described below. All findings that are reported are significant at least at the 5% probability level.

1. Selective attention: The attentional component of the selective attention task was analyzed by a 2 (sex) × 2 (maturation) × 2 (Condition) mixed ANOVA on the percentage of central and incidental items correctly reported. Children performed better on the central than the incidental part of the task. A Sex × Condition interaction was attributable to the fact that boys showed an advantage of central over incidental items (65% vs. 40%), whereas girls did not (53% vs. 52%). Because the disparity between central and incidental recall generally increases in adolescence, this difference presumably reflects the fact that in this study the boys were 2 years older than the girls. There were no main effects of or interactions with maturation.

A 2 (sex) × 2 (maturation) × 5 (position) mixed ANOVA on the number of stimuli correctly reported at each position did reveal, in addition to a main effect of serial position, an interaction between maturation group and position (see Figure 3). Analysis of the simple effects of this interaction indicated that the late maturers showed an effect of position, but early maturers did not. This difference was presumably due to a recency effect among the late maturers, who reported stimuli in the final position more accurately than did early maturers. Finally, there was an interaction between sex and position, with boys reporting more items correctly than girls in the initial position. Again, this difference may well be attributable to age, because primacy effects are believed to be indicative of rehearsal strategies, which children apply with increasing frequency as they grow older (Conroy & Weener, 1976). There were no interactions involving both sex and maturation.

2. Mental rotation: The mental rotation data were analyzed by a 2 (sex) × 2 (maturation) × 2 (condition) × 4 (rotation) mixed ANOVA on both accuracy and response time. Consistent with previous findings (Waber et al., 1982), analysis of the *accuracy* scores revealed effects of both condition and rotation, as well as a Condition × Rotation interaction. Of greter interest, however, was the three-way, Maturation × Condition × Rotation interaction (see Figure 4). Decomposition of this interaction indicated that when stimuli were rotated 180°, late maturers performed more accurately in the AI than in the NI condition, but early maturers were equally accurate in both conditions. Early and late maturers did not, however, differ in their performance on either the NI or AI items at 180°. This finding is consistent with the prediction that late maturers would exhibit more differentiation between conditions as well as with previous studies indicating that individual differences emerge most clearly at the 180° rotation (Cooper & Shepard, 1973; Waber et al., 1982).

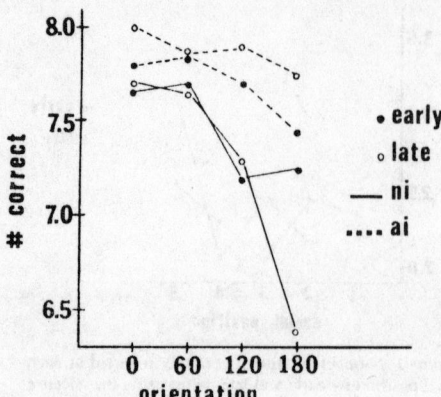

Figure 4. Number of stimuli correctly reported in the NI and AI conditions by early and late maturers at each orientation on the mental rotation task.

Analysis of the response time scores indicated that boys responded more quickly (presumably a function of the age difference). There were also main effects of condition and rotation, as well as a Condition × Rotation interaction. There was no main effect of or interaction with maturation for response time.

3. Block design: The response time data from the block-design task were analyzed by a 2 (sex) × 2 (maturation) × 2 (condition) × 5 (cohesiveness) mixed ANOVA. As was the case for the mental rotation task, the boys, who were older, performed faster. There were also main effects of condition, cued designs being executed faster than uncued ones, and of cohesiveness, designs with a greater degree of cohesiveness taking longer to execute, as well as a Condition × Cohesiveness interaction. In addition, there was a three-way, Sex × Condition × Cohesiveness interaction; in the uncued condition, girls' scores showed a marked increase in response times with increasing contiguity, whereas boys' scores did not. Again, however, because of the confounding of sex with age in this design, these data cannot be viewed as evidence for a true sex difference.

To summarize, the results of the experimental tasks indicated that early and late maturing children showed differences in serial memory on the selective attention task and use of advance visual information on a mental rotation task. These differences distinguished early and late maturers of both sexes. There were no maturation-related differences for performance on the block-design task.

Discussion

This study was undertaken to address two questions. The first was whether systematic associations between maturation rate and cognitive performance exist prior to adolescence. Because, as we discuss in detail below, the predicted effects of maturation on cognitive ability test performance were not observed at puberty in these children, this question must remain unanswered by these data.

The second question concerned the relationship of specific aspects of cognitive processing to maturation rate. Here, there were a number of instances of maturation-related differences. First, in performing mental rotations, early and late maturers used advance visual information differently. Second, late maturers constructed better organized copies of the Rey–Osterrieth Complex Figure than did early maturers. Third, early and late maturers exhibited differences in phonemic perception. Early maturers reported phonemes more accurately than did late maturers, and they also reported a higher proportion of phonemic feature fusions. Finally, late maturers showed a recency effect on the serial memory task that was absent among early maturers.

For several reasons, it seems unlikely that these are chance findings. First, in every case in which a difference appeared, it emerged consistently for both sexes. In addition, the nature of the differences observed is in keeping with the original hypothesis: The superiority of the early maturers on phonemic perception is consistent with their hypothesized verbal advantage (Fennell et al., 1983) and the superiority of the late maturers in the organization of visuospatial constructions and use of advance visual information with their hypothesized visuospatial advantage. Moreover, the finding that early maturers reported more phonemic feature fusions was predicted on the basis of the earlier finding of differences in performance asymmetries related to maturation rate. The serial position effect, which was not predicted at the outset, may reflect a maturation-related difference in immediate memory (Atkinson & Shiffrin, 1968).

The Maturation Effect

In contrast to the results from previous studies cited in the introduction of this article, maturation rate was unrelated to performance on both the cognitive-ability test battery and the dichotic measures of laterality in this study. Although the absence of an effect for the laterality scores can be reconciled with the results of the previous study (Waber, 1977), in which no relationship emerged for children in the chronological age range examined in this study, the results obtained for the cognitive-ability measures are at variance with the previous finding and thus merit more detailed consideration.

Although this study is not the only instance of a failure to confirm the predicted effect (Petersen, 1976), given the repeated demonstrations of it by ourselves and others, it would seem precipitous to dismiss the previous finding (Waber, 1977) as a chance event. Thus the question that needs to be addressed here is not *whether* such an association exists but rather *under what circumstances* it does or does not appear.

One parsimonious explanation for the present finding is sampling bias. The consent rate for the Town A girls, who did show the predicted effect, was 73%, whereas for the rest of the sample, it was closer to 50%. Unfortunately, the data we collected provide little insight into what the nature of such a bias might be. In carrying out the study, however, we noted what we felt to be an unusual number of children with neuropsychological profiles consistent with learning difficulties. Conceivably, parents of children with such problems were more eager to be participants than were parents of children who did not have such concerns.

Another approach to understanding these findings is to examine the data themselves for clues as to what differentiates this sample from others in which the effect did appear. Because the present study was designed to be congruent with the previous one (Waber, 1977), it was possible to compare the raw data from the two studies directly in order to specify the ways in which the performance of this sample differed from the previous one. WISC Block Design scores were selected for this comparison for several reasons: First, children's performance on this test was systematically associated with their maturational status in the previous study but showed no such association in the present one; second, the test has proven reliability; and third, its standardization permits valid comparisons across chronological age groupings.

Figure 5 displays distributions of the (scaled) scores for the children seen in 1974 and the comparable distributions for those tested in 1980. In both samples and for both sexes, the distribution of the late maturers' scores suggests that there exists a small group of late maturing children who exhibit unusually poor spatial ability. Although the distribution of the early maturers' scores is continuous, that of the late maturers shows an unexpected absence of scores in the middle ranges (10-11 in 1974 and 12-13 in 1980), which suggests that the scores of this group are not normally distributed. To the extent that these "low spatial" late maturers are represented in a particular sample, the overall performance level of that group is likely to be depressed. In fact, the 1980 sample included a higher proportion of late maturers whose scores fell below the gap (35%) than did the 1974 sample (15%).

Of apparently greater consequence, however, is the performance of the early maturers. Their scores were considerably higher (an average of nearly 5 scaled points) in the 1980 than in the 1974 sample, whereas those of the late maturers were equivalent for both groups. This pattern raises the question of the role of experiential influences in the differential performance of the 1974 and 1980 samples. As was suggested at the outset, biological factors, like maturational rate, are likely to express themselves more clearly in the processes of cognition than in their products (Lashley, 1937). Such variation may in turn influence choices of strategy in more complex problem-solving situations (Hunt, Frost, & Lunneborg, 1973); and these strategies, moreover, may be differentially efficient. If so, level of performance on the more complex tasks will bear a systematic relation to the biological factors in question.

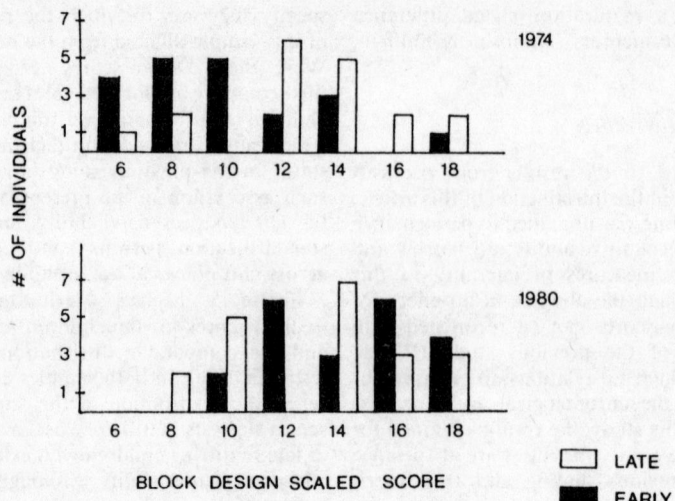

Figure 5. Distribution of Wechsler Intelligence Scale for Children Block Design Scores (6 = 6 + 7, 8 = 8 + 9, etc.) for early and late maturers in the present study (1980 cohort) and the previous one (1974 cohort). Mean scores are 10.5 (early) and 13.5 (late) for the 1974 cohort and 14.7 (early) and 14.0 (late) for the 1980 cohort.

Choice of strategies can also be influenced, however, by specific kinds of experience or instruction. The performance of children whose (biologically induced) preferred strategies are relatively efficient (in this case the late maturers) would be expected to be affected by the same experiential influences to a relatively lesser degree than would that of children whose preferred strategies are less effective (in this case the early maturers). If so, the biological contribution to variation in final outcome scores could be minimized or eliminated. Selective effects of this type have in fact been documented for tasks like those applied in this study (Connor, Schackman, & Serbin, 1978; Goldstein & Chance, 1965). Females, who generally perform more poorly than do males on embedded figure tasks, exhibit more marked improvement in response to training, leading to an elimination of the sex difference.[2]

Specifying the aspects of experience that may have affected the performance of the early maturers in this study would be of considerable theoretical interest. It may be significant that school personnel characterized the families in the communities in which the study was carried out as being intensely concerned with academic achievement. In such a context, children may well have learned compensatory strategies, thus masking biologically induced differences.

In sum, reliable maturation-related differences emerged for tasks designed to assess discrete components of cognitive processing but were absent for more complex problem-solving tasks (for which success or failure is the only metric). These findings are most consistent with the thesis that relatively minor behavioral variations induced by biological processes can in the course of development be either amplified or obscured, depending on the experiential context (Harris, 1978).

The Maturation Hypothesis Reconsidered

As stated at the outset, investigation of the relationship of hormonal factors to sex-related behaviors provides a basis for understanding

---

[2] This pattern does not appear invariably in training studies. Stericker and LeVesconte (1982) reported that both sexes benefited from training. The trained females, however, performed only as well as untrained males.

the etiology of the sex differences themselves as well as a vehicle for addressing more fundamental questions concerning the role of biological processes in human behavioral development. The data generated by this study are best evaluated in view of these two goals.

The extent to which sex-related differences in performance can be attributed to maturational factors, as originally hypothesized (Waber, 1977), is problematic. Even though cognitive ability test scores were unrelated to maturation rate in this study, sex differences nevertheless emerged quite clearly for the same measures. Moreover, where systematic maturation-related performance differences appeared, as in phonemic perception, sex differences were absent. The inference that sex differences in cognitive abilities are attributable to the sex-related variation in maturation rate, therefore, should be viewed with some caution pending further study.

It is with respect to the second goal, that is, understanding the role of biological processes in human behavioral development, that these data can make a contribution. Although the actual amount of variance in cognitive performance accounted for by maturation is, in general, relatively small (Diamond et al., 1983; Newcombe, 1982), it is, nevertheless, of considerable interest that such a regular association appears at all. We have suggested here that the proximal effect of maturation rate (or, to be more precise, of its physiological correlates) is to induce behavioral variation at a fairly molecular level whose expression in terms of more complex functions is determined, in part, by the experiential context. These findings, therefore, may provide a model for understanding the nature of the contribution of biological processes to complex cognitive functions. Further research is needed, however, to establish the reliability of the maturation-related differences in specific components of cognitive processing observed here as well as the nature of the hypothesized link between these specific component processes and more complex problem-solving skills.

References

Allen, M. (1983). Models of hemispheric specialization. *Psychological Bulletin, 93,* 73–104.

Atkinson, R. C., & Shiffrin, R. M. (1968). Human memory: a proposed system and its control processes. In K. W. Spence & J. T. Spence (Eds.), *The psychology of learning and motivation: advances in research and theory* (Vol. 2, pp. 90–191). New York: Academic Press.

Benton, A. L., & Spreen, O. (1969). *Embedded figure test: Manual of instructions and norms.* Neuropsychology Laboratory, Department of Psychology, University of Victoria.

Berenbaum, S. A., & Resnick, S. (1982). Somatic androgyny and cognitive abilities. *Developmental Psychology,* 418–423.

Broverman, D. M., Broverman, I. K., Vogel, W., & Klaiber, E. L. (1964). The automatization cognitive style and physical development. *Child Development, 35,* 1343–1359.

Carey, S., & Diamond, R. (1980). Maturational determination of the developmental course of face encoding. In D. Caplan (Ed.), *Biological studies of mental processes* (pp. 60–93). Cambridge, MA: MIT Press.

Childs, M. K., & Polich, J. M. (1979). Developmental differences in mental rotation. *Journal of Experimental Child Psychology, 27,* 339–351.

Connor, J. M., Schackman, M., & Serbin, L. (1978). Sex related differences in response to practice on a visual-spatial test and generalization to a related test. *Child Development, 49,* 24–29.

Conroy, R. L., & Weener, P. (1976). The development of visual and auditory selective attention using the central-incidental paradigm. *Journal of Experimental Child Psychology, 22,* 400–407.

Cooper, L. A., & Shepard, R. N. (1973). Chronometric studies of the rotation of mental images. In W. G. Chase (Ed.), *Visual information processing* (pp. 95–176). New York: Academic Press.

Cutting, J. E. (1976). Auditory and linguistic processes in speech perception: Inferences from six fusions in dichotic listening. *Psychological Review, 83,* 114–140.

Diamond, R., Carey, S., & Back, K. (1983). Genetic influences on the development of spatial skills during early adolescence. *Cognition, 13,* 167–185.

Emery, D. E., & Sachs, B. D. (1975). Ejaculatory pattern in female rats without androgen treatment. *Science, 190,* 484–485.

Fennell, E. B., Satz, P., & Morris, R. (1983). The development of handedness and dichotic ear listening asymmetries in relation to school achievement: A longitudinal study. *Journal of Experimental Child Psychology, 35,* 248–262.

Frisch, R. E. (1974). A method of prediction of age of menarche from height and weight at ages 9 through 13 years. *Pediatrics,* 384–390.

Goldstein, A. G., & Chance, J. E. (1965). Effects of practice on sex-related differences in performance on embedded figures. *Psychonomic Science, 3,* 361–362.

Goy, R. W., & McEwen, B. S. (1982). *Sexual differentiation of the brain.* Cambridge, MA: MIT Press.

Hagen, J. W. (1967). The effect of distraction on selective attention. *Child Development, 38,* 685–694.

Harris, L. J. (1978). Sex differences in spatial ability: Possible environmental, genetic and neurological factors. In M. Kinsbourne (Ed.), *Asymmetrical function of the brain* (pp. 405–521). Cambridge, MA: Cambridge University Press.

Hollingshead, A. B. (1965). *Two-factor index of social position.* Unpublished manuscript, Yale Station, New Haven.

Hunt, E., Frost, N., & Lunneborg, C. (1973). Individual differences in cognition: A new approach to intelligence. In A. Brown (Ed.), *The psychology of learning and motivation: Advances in research and theory* (Vol. 7, pp. 87–122). New York: Academic Press.

Jones, B. (1983). Measuring degree of cerebral lateralization in children as a function of age. *Developmental Psychology, 19,* 237–242.

Lansdell, H. (1968). Effect of extent of temporal lobe ablations on two lateralized deficits. *Physiology and Behavior, 3,* 271–273.

Lashley, K. S. (1937). Functional determinants of cerebral localization. *Archives of Neurology and Psychiatry, 38,* 371–387.

Levy, J. (1969). Possible basis for the evolution of lateral specialization of the human brain. *Nature, 224,* 614–615.

Levy, J., & Reid, M. (1978). Variations in cerebral organization as a function of handedness, hand posture in writing and sex. *Journal of Experimental Psychology, 107,* 119–144.

Maccoby, E. E., & Jacklin, C. N. (1974). *The psychology of sex differences.* Stanford, CA: Stanford University Press.

Marshall, J. C. (1973). Some problems and paradoxes associated with recent accounts of hemispheric specialization. *Neuropsychologia, 11,* 463–470.

Marshall, J., Caplan, D., & Holmes, J. (1975). The measure of laterality. *Neuropsychologia, 13,* 315–321.

Mellits, B. D., & Cheek, D. G. (1970). Assessment of body water and fatness from infancy to childhood. *Monographs of the Society for Research in Child Development, 35*(7, Serial No. 140), 12–26.

Mooney, C. M. (1957). Age in the development of closure ability in children. *Canadian Journal of Psychology, 11,* 219–226.

National Center for Health Statistics. (1976). *NCHS Growth Charts, 1976.* Monthly Vital Statistics Report (Vol. 25, No. 3, Supplement HRA 76-1120).

Netley, C., & Rovet, J. (1982). Relationships among brain organization, maturation rate and the development of verbal and nonverbal ability. In S. Segalowitz (Ed.), *Language functions and brain organization* (pp. 245–266). New York: Academic Press.

Newcombe, N. (1982). Sex related differences in spatial ability: Problems and gaps in current approaches. In M. Potegal (Ed.), *Spatial ability* (pp. 223–250). New York: Academic Press.

Newcombe, N., & Bandura, M. M. (1983). The effect of age at puberty on spatial ability in girls: a question of mechanism. *Developmental Psychology, 19,* 215–224.

Osterrieth, P. A. (1946). Le test de copie d'une figure complexe. *Les Archives de Psychologie, 31,* 206–356.

Petersen, A. C. (1976). Physical androgeny and cognitive functioning in adolescence. *Developmental Psychology, 12,* 524–533.

Petersen, A. C. (1981). Sex differences in performance on spatial tasks: biopsychosocial influences. In A. Ansara, N. Geschwind, A. Galaburda, M. Albert, & N. Gertrell (Eds.), *Sex differences in dyslexia* (pp. 41–54). Towson, MD: Orton Society.

Porter, R., & Berlin, C. I. (1975). On interpreting developmental changes in the dichotic right ear advantage. *Brain and Language, 2,* 186–200.

Rosenthal, R., & Rubin, D. B. (1982). Further meta-analytic procedures for assessing cognitive gender differences. *Journal of Educational Psychology, 74,* 708–712.

Rovet, J., & Netley, C. (1982). Processing deficits in Turner's Syndrome. *Developmental Psychology, 18,* 77–94.

Royer, F. L., & Weitzel, K. E. (1977). Effect of perceptual cohesiveness on pattern recoding in the block design task. *Perception and Psychophysics, 21,* 39–46.

Schulman-Galambos, C. (1977). Dichotic listening performance in elementary and college students. *Neuropsychologia, 15,* 577–584.

Stericker, A., & LeVesconte, S. (1982). Effect of brief training on sex-related differences in visual-spatial skill. *Journal of Personality and Social Psychology, 43,* 1018–1029.

Tanner, J. M. (1962). *Growth at adolescence.* Oxford, England: Blackwell Scientific Publications.

Waber, D. P. (1977). Sex differences in mental abilities, hemispheric lateralization, and rate of physical growth in adolescence. *Developmental Psychology, 13,* 29–38.

Waber, D. P. (1979). The meaning of sex-related variations in maturation rate. In J. E. Gullahorn (Ed.), *Psychology and women: In transition* (pp. 37–59). Washington, DC: Winston.

Waber, D. P. (1981). [Maturation rate and cognitive functions in girls from different socioeconomic backgrounds]. Unpublished raw data.

Waber, D.P. (1983, April). *A neuropsychological analysis of SES-related differences in children's cognitive performance.* Paper presented at the meeting of the Society for Research in Child Development, Detroit.

Waber, D. P., Bauermeister, M., Cohen, C., Ferber, R., & Wolff, P. H. (1981). Behavioral correlates of physical and neuromotor maturity in adolescents from different environments. *Developmental Psychobiology, 14,* 513–522.

Waber, D. P., Carlson, D., & Mann, M. (1982). Developmental and differential aspects of mental rotation in early adolescence. *Child Development, 53,* 1614–1621.

Waber, D. P., Davies, M., & Mann, M. B. (1982). *Are there sex differences in spatial processing prior to adolescence.* Unpublished manuscript.

Waber, D. P., & Holmes, J. M. (in press). Assessing children's copy productions of the Rey-Osterrieth Complex Figure. *Journal of Experimental and Clinical Neuropsychology.*

Received December 13, 1983
Revision received February 13, 1984 ∎

Part V
Hormones and Behaviour

[34]
A Window for the Study of Prenatal Sex Hormone Influences on Postnatal Development

JO-ANNE FINEGAN
Department of Psychology
The Hospital for Sick Children, Toronto

BETTY BARTLEMAN
Faculty of Medicine
Queen's University

P. Y. WONG
Department of Biochemistry
Toronto General Hospital

ABSTRACT. In humans, the influence of prenatal sex hormones on the fetal brain and subsequent postnatal development has had limited study because of the apparent inaccessibility of hormone levels in normal fetuses. We propose that amniotic fluid obtained via midtrimester amniocentesis can be assayed for fetal hormone levels during the period thought to be important for sexual differentiation of the brain. Amniotic fluid samples from midgestation ($N = 70$) were assayed for levels of testosterone and follicle-stimulating hormone, and significant sex differences were observed ($ps < .001$), with some degree of overlap between the sexes. The possibility of applying hormone levels obtained from amniotic fluid to the study of postnatal development is discussed.

PRENATAL HORMONES play an important role in postnatal behaviour, as indicated by studies with animals (Goy & McEwen, 1980). In humans, it has been proposed that sex hormones acting on the fetal brain are one influence on sex-related differences in postnatal development, but this hypothesis has had limited study because of the inaccessibility of information on the hormonal status of normal fetuses. The central purpose of the present paper is to alert behavioral researchers to the possibility of using hormone levels from amniotic fluid in midgestation for studies of postnatal development.

Past Approaches

Currently, most of the available information about the relation between fetal sex hormone levels and postnatal development in humans comes from studies of atypical populations (e.g., Ehrhardt & Meyer-Bahlburg, 1981), which do not necessarily provide information on normal processes. For example, studies of the development of individuals with genetic conditions associated with altered prenatal hormone levels are difficult to interpret because it is not possible to separate the effects of the hormone from those of the gene. Another problematic approach involves the study of individuals exposed to exogenous hormones *in utero*. In studying fetuses exposed to synthetic sex hormones (e.g., diethylstilbestrol) for treatment of maternal obstetrical problems, it is difficult to disentangle the effects of the maternal condition, the effects of the drug, and the joint effects of both variables. Despite the aforementioned problems, the findings from studies on atypical human populations converge with the results of experiments with animals to suggest that prenatal sex hormones have an important influence on postnatal behaviour (for reviews see De Vries, De Bruin, Uylings & Corner, 1984; Ehrhardt & Meyer-Bahlburg, 1981; Hines, 1982; Meyer-Bahlburg & Ehrhardt, 1980; Quadagno, Briscoe, & Quadagno, 1977; Reinisch, Gandelman, & Spiegel, 1979).

Hormonal influences on the development of normal infants have been investigated by studying the relation between perinatal sex hormones from cord blood samples (Maccoby, Doering, Jacklin, & Kraemer, 1979) and postnatal variables such as timidity (Jacklin, Maccoby, & Doering, 1983), muscle strength (Jacklin, Maccoby, Doering, & King, 1984) and mood (Marcus, Maccoby, Jacklin, & Doering, 1985). The effects of hormones during the prenatal period have not yet been studied because there has not been a way to obtain information about fetal hormonal status that could be related to subsequent postnatal development. Current hypotheses about hormone action on the fetal brain are based on mechanisms of fetal gonadal differentiation.

Hormones and Fetal Development

It is well known that male and female embryos have undifferentiated gonads until the 6th week of gestation, when testes develop in fetuses with XY chro-

---

Financial support was provided by the physicians of Ontario through the Physicians' Services Incorporated Foundation. Jo-Anne Finegan was supported by the Laidlaw Foundation and the Ontario Mental Health Foundation.

Sherri MacKay-Soroka, Susan Goldberg, Helen Hughes, Charles Netley, and Kenneth Zucker made helpful comments on earlier versions of this manuscript.

Requests for reprints should be sent to Jo-Anne Finegan, Department of Psychology, The Hospital for Sick Children, 555 University Avenue, Toronto, Canada M5G 1X8.

mosomes. Between 9 and 18 weeks of fetal age, high levels of androgens secreted by the fetal testes differentiate the fetus as male. The fetus differentiates as female when exposed to lower levels of androgens during this period. Thus, it is the influence of androgens on undifferentiated fetal tissues during a "critical period" for phenotypic differentiation that results in male development. (For more detailed discussions of fetal gonadal differentiation, see Smail, Reyes, Winter, & Faiman, 1981; Wilson, Griffin, George, & Leshin, 1981; Wilson, Griffin, Leshin, & George, 1981).

Hormonal influences on fetal brain development and postnatal behavior have been studied extensively in animals. This work has shown that higher levels of androgens act on undifferentiated brain tissue during a maximally sensitive period to organize the brain for masculine postnatal behavior; lower levels of androgens during this sensitive period lead to brain organization for feminine postnatal behavior (Gorski & Jacobson, 1981; Goy & McEwen, 1980; McEwen, 1983).

The developmental period for fetal central nervous system sensitivity to hormones differs among species. In humans it is presumed to occur in early or midgestation (Abramovich & Rowe, 1973; Hines, 1982; Money & Ehrhardt, 1971; Reinisch et al., 1979; Reinisch & Sanders, 1984), which corresponds closely to the critical period when hormonal effects induce phenotypic or gonadal differentiation. Because androgen levels in the male fetus remain high for at least two weeks following the development of the genitalia, it has been proposed that this may be the period for sexual differentiation of the brain (Abramovich, 1974, 1981; Reinisch & Sanders, 1984). Support for the hypothesis that fetal brain differentiation closely follows fetal gonadal differentiation comes from a study of aborted fetuses demonstrating that the fetal hypothalamus takes up radioactivity from labelled testosterone between 14 and 18 weeks and does so most markedly at 16 weeks (Abramovich & Rowe, 1973). Support is also provided by evidence that the fetal brain is able to metabolize testosterone during this period (Jenkins & Hall, 1977). In a recent study, however, androgen receptors could not be found in the midtrimester fetal brain (Abramovich, Davidson, Longstaff, & Pearson, 1985), but the implications for sexual differentiation of the brain are not yet clear.

Information about the utility of midtrimester amniotic fluid samples as a source of data on fetal hormone levels has surfaced in the medical literature. For example, in several studies it has been demonstrated that fetal sex can be predicted with a high degree of accuracy from levels of testosterone and follicle-stimulating hormone in amniotic fluid (Abeliovich, Leibermann, Teuerstein, & Levy, 1984; Belisle, Fencl, & Tulchinsky, 1977; Bremme, Eneroth, & Nilsson, 1982; Doran, Wong, Allen, & Falk, 1980; Ketupanya & Weist, 1978; Mennuti, Wu, Mellman, & Mikhail, 1977). Behavioral researchers have not yet availed themselves of the opportunity to use this method to study prenatal hormone influences on postnatal development.

Here, we replicate the findings of sex differences in amniotic fluid hormones for fetuses who are available for postnatal study.

Method

Subjects

Amniotic fluid samples ($N = 70$) obtained between 14 and 20 weeks from the date of the last menstrual period were available from women 35 to 40 years old, who were eligible for amniocentesis because their age (≥ 35 years) increased the risk of a fetal chromosome abnormality. The women were in good health and took no medications except vitamins during pregnancy. Women from the upper social classes were overrepresented (additional information is presented in Finegan et al., 1984). Five amniotic fluid samples were discarded because four had traces of blood and one was from a fetus subsequently born with a major congenital malformation. Thus, the final sample consisted of amniotic fluid from 32 male and 33 female fetuses. Fourteen males (42%) and 9 females (28%) were first born, $\chi^2_1 = 0.69$, ns. The karyotypes of amniotic fluid cells showed that all fetuses had the expected number of chromosomes (46,XX or 46,XY) without structural rearrangements. Fetal sex was confirmed on physical examination of the newborns. All infants were the predicted sex, and none had external genital abnormalities that would have suggested perturbation of prenatal sex hormone levels.

Procedure

On average, 20 ml of amniotic fluid was obtained by amniocentesis. Of this, 15 ml was used for cell culture for chromosome analysis, and 2 ml was used in a biochemical test for fetal neural tube defects. The remainder of this latter aliquot was stored at $-20°C$ and assayed for testosterone and FSH. Amniotic fluid testosterone was measured by the modified radioimmunoassay technique developed by Wong, Wood, and Johnson (1975). The amniotic fluid FSH level was determined with Amerlex FSH radioimmunoassay kits (Amersham Corporation).

Results

Levels of testosterone in amniotic fluid samples from male and female fetuses were compared using t tests. Because first-born infants have been found to have higher levels of testosterone in cord blood samples (Maccoby et al., 1979), birth-order effects in levels of testosterone in amniotic fluid were tested with 2×2 (Birth Order: first born, later born × Sex) analyses of variance (ANOVAs).

Mean values for testosterone and FSH are presented in Table 1. Significant sex differences were observed for levels of testosterone, $t(64) = 10.74$, $p < .001$, but 25% of the males and 9% of the females had testosterone levels that fell within the range of overlap between the sexes (23.1 to 28.8 ng/dl). Birth-order effects were not observed.

FSH levels are undetectable in many amniotic fluid samples (i.e., ≤ 1 mIU/ml), especially in males; in the present study 59% of the samples from males and 9% from females were in this category. Therefore, sex differences were tested with the Mann-Whitney U Test. Significant sex differences were observed for levels of FSH: $U = 87.00, z = -5.87, p < .001$.

Discussion

The finding of significant sex differences in levels of testosterone and FSH in amniotic fluid samples suggests that amniocentesis may be a means of obtaining information on hormonal events in midgestation. In the case of testosterone, however, 25% of the males and 9% of the females had levels in the overlap range, indicating that hormone levels were not entirely determined by fetal sex. This finding of within- and between-sex variability in prenatal hormone levels may be related to diversity in postnatal behaviour. This hypothesis now may be tested.

For the purpose of postnatal studies, direct measures of circulating hormone levels in fetuses cannot be obtained for obvious reasons. Information on hormone levels at various points in gestation are available from studies of aborted fetuses, however. In the following section, levels of testosterone and FSH in fetal tissues are described briefly to permit the reader to evaluate the utility of amniotic fluid hormone levels in midgestation as markers of fetal exposure to hormones.

TABLE 1
Mean Concentration of Testosterone and FSH in Amniotic Fluid Samples

Hormone	Male ($n = 32$)	Female ($n = 33$)
Testosterone		
M (ng/dl)	38.75[a]	16.84[a]
SD	10.92	4.16
FSH		
M (mIU/L)	1.04[b]	7.75[b]
SD	1.57	6.75

Note. Means with the same superscript differ at $p < .001$.

Testosterone

Peak concentrations of testosterone are found in fetal testes at 11 to 15 weeks (Reyes, Winter, & Faiman, 1973; Siiteri & Wilson, 1974; Tapanainen, Kellokumpu-Lehtinen, Pelliniemi, & Huhtaniemi, 1981). By 14 to 16 weeks, peak concentrations are observed in fetal serum, although the levels begin to decline by 17 weeks (Abramovich, 1974; Reyes, Boroditsky, Winter, & Faiman, 1974), and there is little change in levels between 27 and 37 weeks (Tapanainen, 1983). By term, there is considerable overlap in values in cord blood samples from males and females, and significant sex differences are reported inconsistently (Abramovich, 1974; Abramovich et al., 1985; Abramovich & Rowe, 1973; Dawood & Saxena, 1977; Forest & Cathiard, 1975; Forest, Ances, Tapper, & Migeon, 1971; Forest, Sizonenko, Cathiard, & Bertrand, 1974; Maccoby et al., 1979; Mathur, Landgrebe, Moody, Powell, & Williamson, 1980; Pang et al., 1979; Rivarola, Forest, & Migeon, 1968; Takagi et al., 1977; Warne, Faiman, Reyes, & Winter, 1977; Winter, Hughes, Reyes, & Faiman, 1976).

In amniotic fluid there are significant sex differences in levels of testosterone at many points in gestation, but maximal differences are observed between 12 and 18 weeks (Kunzig, Meyer, Schmitz-Roeckerath & Broer, 1977; Nagamani, McDonough, Ellegood, & Mahesh, 1979; Warne et al., 1977), coinciding with peak levels in fetal serum from 14 to 16 weeks (Abramovich, 1974; Reyes et al., 1974); however, sex differences are not observed at term (Kunzig et al., 1977; Robinson, Judd, Young, Jones, & Yen, 1977).

FSH

The role of testosterone in male phenotypic differentiation is more clearly understood than the role of FSH in the development of the female. FSH is thought to influence the growth and maintenance of the fetal gonads. A role in ovarian development is suggested because peak levels are observed in the pituitary and serum of female fetuses during the period of follicular development (Kaplan & Grumbach, 1976; Reyes, Faiman, & Winter, 1981).

FSH is found in the pituitary glands in both sexes by 10 weeks gestation (Kaplan & Grumbach, 1976). The concentration increases dramatically and significantly in females between 12 and 20 weeks. The peak level and significant sex difference in FSH is reflected in both fetal serum and amniotic fluid (Clements, Reyes, Winter, & Faiman, 1976). Levels begin to decline sharply in female pituitaries by 24 to 28 weeks, and there is a corresponding decrease in serum and amniotic fluid levels. By term, there is no sex difference in FSH levels in either cord serum or amniotic fluid (Abeliovich et al., 1984; Belisle & Tulchinsky, 1980; Belisle et al., 1977; Faiman et al., 1974; Levina, 1968,

1972; Mennuti et al., 1977; Reyes et al., 1981; Siler-Kodhr & Kodhr, 1980; Tapanainen et al., 1984).

In summary, for both testosterone and FSH, peak levels and maximal sex differences are observed in midgestation when levels of these hormones in amniotic fluid can be obtained via amniocentesis.

Relationship Between Amniotic Fluid and Fetal Hormone Levels

In considering the utility of amniotic fluid hormone levels for studies of postnatal development, information is needed on the relation between hormone levels in amniotic fluid and levels circulating in the fetus. It is generally believed that these hormones enter the amniotic fluid via diffusion through the fetal skin in early pregnancy and from fetal urination later in pregnancy (Klopper, 1970; Nagamani et al., 1979; Robinson et al., 1977). The mother apparently contributes little to hormone levels in amniotic fluid because there is no correlation between levels in maternal blood and amniotic fluid (Dawood & Saxena, 1977; Glass & Klein, 1981, Nagamani et al., 1979; Rodeck, Gill, Rosenberg, & Collins, 1985).

A careful search of the literature uncovered no reports on the correlation between levels of testosterone in fetal serum and amniotic fluid during the period of their peak concentrations. Rodeck et al. (1985) found no significant correlations at 18 to 20 weeks gestation. Testosterone levels decline after 17 weeks, however, and may alter the relation between levels in amniotic fluid and fetal serum in this post-peak period.

There is some assurance that the level of FSH in amniotic fluid provides a good estimate of fetal circulating levels because levels in fetal tissues are related to levels in amniotic fluid between 12 and 20 weeks gestation. For example, FSH levels in amniotic fluid are significantly correlated (all $ps < .001$) with levels in fetal serum, $r(27) = .87$, pituitary concentration, $r(23) = .78$, and pituitary content, $r(23) = .95$ (Clements et al., 1976).

Considerations for Postnatal Studies

Data on hormone levels in amniotic fluid obtained by amniocentesis holds promise for studies of postnatal development, but certain considerations constrain the use of this method. Amniocentesis obviously cannot be undertaken simply for developmental studies because this invasive intrauterine procedure is not free of risk (Finegan et al., 1984, 1985). Thus, hormone assays must be conducted incidentally on the fluid available when amniocentesis is undertaken for accepted indications, such as increased risk for a fetal abnormality. Moreover, investigators need to be aware of potential sampling biases. The population of women who avail themselves of amniocentesis tends to be upwardly skewed with regard to both age and social class (Bannerman, Gillick,

Van Coevering, Knobloch, & Ingall, 1977), and the influence that these variables may exert on the independent and dependent variables must be given consideration. Nevertheless, although the mothers may be relatively older, it is unlikely that age influences the fetal levels of testosterone because, as mentioned above, the data show no correlation between maternal and fetal testosterone levels.

Future research will need to be concerned with determination of the direct relation between testosterone levels in amniotic fluid and fetal blood. Information also is needed on the stability of amniotic fluid hormone levels, but such data depends on repeat amniocenteses, which are precluded because of fetal risk. The hormones assayed in the present study by no means exhaust those showing sex differences in midgestation, as sex differences in other androgenic steroids have been reported (Forest et al., 1980; Nagamani et al., 1979; Robinson et al., 1977). We hope that the present report will stimulate others to conduct further studies in this area.

In summary, amniocentesis provides an opportunity to gain information on hormone levels in normal fetuses who will be available for study postnatally. Significant sex differences in testosterone and FSH can be observed in amniotic fluid samples from midgestation, the period hypothesized to be important for sexual differentiation of the fetal brain. Amniocentesis permits access to the fetal hormonal milieu and provides a window for the study of prenatal hormone influences on postnatal development in normal humans.

REFERENCES

Abeliovich, D., Leibermann, J. R., Teuerstein, I., & Levy, J. (1984). Prenatal sex diagnosis: Testosterone and FSH in midtrimester amniotic fluids. *Prenatal Diagnosis, 4*, 347–353.

Abramovich, D. R. (1974). Human sexual differentiation—*In utero* influences. *The Journal of Obstetrics and Gynaecology for the British Commonwealth, 81*, 448–453.

Abramovich, D. R. (1981). Interrelation of fetus and amniotic fluid. *Obstetrics and Gynecology Annual, 10*, 27–43.

Abramovich, D. R., Davidson, I. A., Longstaff, A., & Pearson, C. K. (1985). When does sexual differentiation of the human brain occur? In C. T. Jones & P. W. Nathanielz (Eds.), *The physiological development of the fetus and newborn* (pp. 659–662). London: Academic Press.

Abramovich, D. R., & Rowe, P. (1973). Foetal plasma testosterone levels at midpregnancy and at term: Relationship to foetal sex. *Journal of Endocrinology, 56*, 621–622.

Bannerman, R. M., Gillick, D., Van Coevering, R., Knobloch, N. L., & Ingall, G. B. (1977). Amniocentesis and educational attainment. *New England Journal of Medicine, 297*, 449.

Belisle, S., & Tulchinsky, D. (1980). Amniotic fluid hormones. In D. Tulchinsky & K. J. Ryan (Eds.), *Maternal-fetal endocrinology* (pp. 169–262). Philadelphia: W. B. Saunders.

Belisle, S., Fencl, M. de M., & Tulchinsky, D. (1977). Amniotic fluid testosterone and follicle-stimulating hormone in the determination of fetal sex. *American Journal of Obstetrics and Gynecology, 128,* 514–519.

Bremme, K., Eneroth, P., & Nilsson, B. (1982). Hormone levels in amniotic fluid and fetal sex. *Gynecologic and Obstetric Investigation, 14,* 245–262.

Clements, J. A., Reyes, F. I., Winter, J. S. D., & Faiman, C. (1976). Studies on human sexual development: III. Fetal pituitary and serum, and amniotic fluid concentrations of LH, CG, and FSH. *Journal of Clinical Endocrinology and Metabolism, 42,* 9–19.

Dawood, M. Y., & Saxena, B. B. (1977). Testosterone and dihydrotestosterone in maternal and cord blood and in amniotic fluid. *American Journal of Obstetrics and Gynecology, 129,* 37–42.

De Vries, G. J., De Bruin, J. P. C., Uylings, H. B. M., & Corner, M. A. (Eds.). (1984). *Progress in brain research: Vol. 61. Sex differences in the brain.* Amsterdam: Elsevier.

Doran, T. A., Wong, P. Y., Allen, L. C., & Falk, M. (1980). Amniotic fluid testosterone and follicle-stimulating hormone assay in the prenatal determination of fetal sex. *American Journal of Obstetrics and Gynecology, 36,* 309–312.

Ehrhardt, A. A., & Meyer-Bahlburg, H. F. L. (1981). Effects of prenatal sex hormones on gender-related behavior. *Science, 211,* 1312–1318.

Faiman, C., Reyes, R. I., & Winter, J. S. (1974). Serum gonadotropin patterns during the perinatal period in man and in the chimpanzee. In M. G. Forest & J. Bertrand (Eds.), *Endocrinologie sexuelle de la période périnatal* (pp. 281–297). Paris: INSERM.

Finegan, J. K., Quarrington, B. J., Hughes, H. E., Rudd, N. L., Stevens, L. J., Weksberg, R., & Doran, T. A. (1984). Midtrimester amniocentesis: Obstetric outcome and neonatal neurobehavioral status. *American Journal of Obstetrics and Gynecology, 150,* 989–997.

Finegan, J. K., Quarrington, B. J., Hughes, H. E., Rudd, N. L., Stevens, L. J., Weksberg, R., & Doran, T. A. (1985). Infant outcome following mid-trimester amniocentesis: Development and physical status of age six months. *British Journal of Obstetrics and Gynaecology, 92,* 1015–1023.

Forest, M. G., Ances, I. G., Tapper, A. J., & Migeon, C. J., (1971). Percentage binding of testosterone, androstenedione and dehydroisoandrosterone in plasma at the time of delivery. *Journal of Clinical Endocrinology and Metabolism, 32,* 417–425.

Forest, M. G., & Cathiard, A. M. (1975). Pattern of plasma testosterone and Δ^4-androstenedione in normal newborns: Evidence for testicular activity at birth. *Journal of Endocrinology, 41,* 977–980.

Forest, M. G., de Peretti, E., Lecoq, A., Cadillon, E., Zabot, M. T., & Thoulon, J. M. (1980). Concentration of 14 steroid hormones in human amniotic fluid of midpregnancy. *Journal of Clinical Endocrinology and Metabolism, 51,* 816–822.

Forest, M. G., Sizonenko, P. C., Cathiard, A. M., & Bertrand, J. (1974). Hypophyso-gonadal function in humans during the first year of life. *Journal of Clinical Investigation, 53,* 819–828.

Glass, A. R., & Klein, T. (1981). Changes in maternal serum total and free androgen levels in early pregnancy: Lack of correlation with fetal sex. *American Journal Obstetrics and Gynecology, 140,* 656–660.

Gorski, R. A., & Jacobson, C. D. (1981). Sexual differentiation of the brain. In S. J. Kogan & E. S. E. Hafez (Eds.), *Pediatric andrology* (pp. 109–134). The Hague: Martinus Nijhoff.

Goy, R. W., & McEwen, B. S. (1980). *Sexual differentiation of the brain.* Cambridge, MA: The MIT Press.
Hines, M. (1982). Prenatal gonadal hormones and sex differences in human behavior. *Psychological Bulletin, 92,* 56–80.
Jacklin, C. N., Maccoby, E. E., & Doering, C. H. (1983). Neonatal sex-steroid hormones and timidity in 16–18-month-old boys and girls. *Developmental Psychobiology, 16,* 163–168.
Jacklin, C. N., Maccoby, E. E., Doering, C. H., & King, D. R. (1984). Neonatal sex-steroid hormones and muscular strength of boys and girls in the first three years. *Developmental Psychobiology, 17,* 301–310.
Jenkins, J. S., & Hall, C. J. (1977). Metabolism of [^{14}C] testosterone by human foetal and adult brain tissue. *Journal of Endocrinology, 74,* 425–429.
Kaplan, S. L., & Grumbach, M. M. (1976). The ontogenesis of human foetal hormones: I. Luteinizing hormone (LH) and follicle-stimulating hormone (FSH). *Acta Endocrinologica, 81,* 808–829.
Ketupanya, A., & Weist, W. G. (1978). Amniotic fluid testosterone concentration as an index of fetal sex. *Pediatric Research, 12,* 708–710.
Klopper, A. (1970). Steroids in amniotic fluid. *Annals of Clinical Research, 2,* 289–299.
Kunzig, H. J., Meyer, U., Schmitz-Roeckerath, B., & Broer, K. H. (1977). Influence of fetal sex on the concentration of amniotic fluid testosterone: Antenatal sex determination? *Archiv fur Gynäkologie, 223,* 75–84.
Levina, S. E. (1968). Endocrine features of human hypothalamus, hypophysis, and placenta. *General and Comparative Endocrinology, 11,* 151–159.
Levina, S. E. (1972). Times of appearance of LH and FSH activities in human fetal circulation. *General and Comparative Endocrinology, 19,* 242–246.
Maccoby, E. E., Doering, C. H., Jacklin, C. N., & Kraemer, H. (1979). Concentrations of sex hormones in umbilical cord blood: Their relation to sex and birth order of infants. *Child Development, 50,* 632–642.
Marcus, J., Maccoby, E. E., Jacklin, C. N., & Doering, C. H. (1985). Individual differences in mood in early childhood: Their relation to gender and neonatal sex steroids. *Developmental Psychobiology, 18,* 327–340.
Mathur, R. S., Landgrebe, S., Moody, L. O., Powell, S., & Williamson, H. O. (1980). Plasma steroid concentrations in maternal and umbilical circulation after spontaneous onset of labour. *Journal of Clinical Endocrinology and Metabolism, 51,* 1235–1238.
McEwen, B. S. (1983). Gonadal steroid influences on brain development and sexual differentiation. *International Review of Physiology IV. Reproductive Physiology, 27,* 99–145.
Mennuti, M. T., Wu, C. H., Mellman, W. J., & Mikhail, G. (1977). Amniotic fluid testosterone and follicle-stimulating hormone levels as indicators of fetal sex during mid-pregnancy. *American Journal of Medical Genetics, 1,* 211–216.
Meyer-Bahlburg, H. F. L., & Ehrhardt, A. A. (1980). Neurobehavioral effects of prenatal origin: Sex hormones. In R. A. Schwarz & S. J. Yaffe (Eds.), *Drug and chemical risks to the fetus and newborn* (pp. 93–107). New York: Alan R. Liss.
Money, J., & Ehrhardt, A. A. (1971). Fetal hormones and the brain: Effect on sexual dimorphism of behaviour—A review. *Archives of Sexual Behavior, 1,* 241–262.
Nagamani, M., McDonough, P. G., Ellegood, J. O., & Mahesh, V. B. (1979). Maternal and amniotic fluid steroids throughout human pregnancy. *American Journal of Obstetrics and Gynecology, 134,* 674–680.
Pang, S., Levine, L. S., Chow, D., Sagiani, F., Saenger, P., & New, M. I. (1979).

Dihydrotestosterone and its relationship to testosterone in infancy and childhood. *Journal of Clinical Endocrinology and Metabolism, 48,* 821–826.

Quadagno, D. M., Briscoe, R., & Quadagno, J. S. (1977). Effect of perinatal gonadal hormones on selected nonsexual behavior patterns: A critical assessment of the nonhuman and human literature. *Psychological Bulletin, 84,* 62–80.

Reinisch, J. M., Gandelman, R., & Spiegel, F. S. (1979). Prenatal influences on cognitive abilities: Data from experimental animals and human genetic and endocrine syndromes. In M. A. Wittig & A. C. Petersen (Eds.), *Sex-related differences in cognitive functioning* (pp. 215–239). New York: Academic Press.

Reinisch, J. M., & Sanders, S. A. (1984). Prenatal gonadal steroidal influences on gender-related behavior. In G. J. De Vries, J. P. C. De Bruin, H. B. M. Uylings, & M. A. Corner (Eds.), *Progress in brain research: Vol. 61. Sex differences in the brain* (pp. 407–416). Amsterdam: Elsevier.

Reyes, F. I., Boroditsky, R. S., Winter, J. S. D., & Faiman, G. (1974). Studies on human sexual development: II. Fetal and maternal serum gonadotropin and sex steroid concentrations. *Journal of Clinical Endocrinology and Metabolism, 38,* 612–617.

Reyes, F. I., Faiman, C., & Winter, J. D. S. (1981). Development of the regulatory mechanisms of the hypothalamic-pituitary-gonadal system in the human fetus: The chorionic-hypothalamic-pituitary-gonadal axis. In M. J. Novy & J. A. Resko (Eds.), *Fetal endocrinology* (pp. 285–302). New York: Academic Press.

Reyes, F. I., Winter, J. S. D., & Faiman, C. (1973). Studies on human sexual development: I. Fetal gonadal and adrenal sex steroids. *Journal of Clinical Endocrinology and Metabolism, 37,* 74–78.

Rivarola, M. A., Forest, M. G., & Migeon, C. J. (1968). Testosterone, androstenedione and dihydroepiandrosterone in plasma during pregnancy and at delivery: Concentrations and protein binding. *Journal of Clinical Endocrinology and Metabolism, 28,* 34–40.

Robinson, J. D., Judd, H. L., Young, P. E., Jones, D. W., & Yen, S. S. C. (1977). Amniotic fluid androgens and estrogens in midgestation. *Journal of Clinical Endocrinology, 45,* 755–761.

Rodeck, C. H., Gill, D., Rosenberg, D. A., & Collins, W. P. (1985). Testosterone levels in midtrimester maternal and fetal plasma and amniotic fluid. *Prenatal Diagnosis, 5,* 175–181.

Siiteri, P. K., & Wilson, J. D. (1974). Testosterone formation and metabolism during male sexual differentiation in the human embryo. *Journal of Clinical Endocrinology and Metabolism, 38,* 113–125.

Siler-Khodr, T. M., & Kodhr, G. (1980). Studies in human fetal endocrinology: II. LH and FSH content and concentration in the pituitary. *Obstetrics and Gynecology, 56,* 176–187.

Smail, P. J., Reyes, F. I., Winter, J. S. D., & Faiman, C. (1981). The fetal gonadal environment and its effect on the morphogenesis of the genital system. In S. J. Kogan & E. S. E. Hafez (Eds.), *Pediatric andrology* (pp. 9–19). The Hague: Martinius Nijhoff.

Takagi, S., Yoshida, T., Tsubata, K., Ozaki, H., Fujii, T. K., Namura, Y., & Sawada, M. (1977). Sex differences in fetal gonadotropins and androgens. *Journal of Steroid Biochemistry, 8,* 609–620.

Tapanainen, J. (1983). Hormonal changes during the perinatal period: Serum testosterone, some of its precursors, and FSH and prolactin in preterm and fullterm male infant cord blood and during the first week of life. *Journal of Steroid Biochemistry, 19,* 13–18.

Tapanainen, J., Huhtaniemi, I., Koivisto, M., Kujansuu, E., Tuimala, R., & Vihko, R. (1984). Hormonal changes during the perinatal period: FSH, prolactin and some steroid hormones in the cord blood and peripheral serum of preterm and fullterm female infants. *Journal of Steroid Biochemistry, 20,* 1153–1156.

Tapanainen, J., Kellokumpa-Lehtinen, P., Pelliniemi, L., & Huhtaniemi, I. (1981). Age-related changes in endogenous steroiods of human fetal testes during early and midpregnancy. *Journal of Clinical Endocrinology and Metabolism, 52,* 98–102.

Warne, G. L., Faiman, C., Reyes, F. I., & Winter, J. S. D. (1977). Studies on human sexual development: V. Concentrations of testosterone, 17-hydroxyprogesterone and progesterone in human amniotic fluid throughout gestation. *Journal of Clinical Endocrinology and Metabolism, 44,* 934–938.

Wilson, J. D., Griffin, J. E., George, F. W., & Leshin, M. (1981). The role of gonadal steroids in sexual differentiation. *Recent Progress in Hormone Research, 37,* 1–39.

Wilson, J. D., Griffin, J. E., Leshin, M., & George, F. W. (1981). Role of gonadal hormones in development of the sexual phenotypes. *Human Genetics, 58,* 78–84.

Winter, J. S. D., Hughes, I. A., Reyes, F. I., & Faiman, C. (1976). Pituitary-gonadal relations in infancy: 2. Patterns of serum gonadal steroid concentrations in man from birth to two years of age. *Journal of Clinical Endocrinology and Metabolism, 42,* 679–686.

Wong, P. Y., Wood, D. E., & Johnson, T. (1975). Routine radioimmunoassay of plasma testosterone, and results for various endocrine disorders. *Clinical Chemistry, 21,* 206–210.

Received April 11, 1988

[35]

Excerpt from *Gender and the Life Course*, 81–96

5

The Psychobiology of Gender

ANKE A. EHRHARDT
College of Physicians and Surgeons
Columbia University

Introduction

Two changes have recently occurred in our thinking about human development. One is a change in focus from childhood and adolescence to the study of the entire life course. The other is the inclusion of biological aspects in the analysis of behavior and the exploration of the interplay between various factors—biological, sociological, psychological, and historical. To take such an interdisciplinary approach has not been popular in the past. Every discipline has perfected its argument to justify field-specific blinders. Sociologists and psychologists often shy away from biological variables out of fear of misuse: Once you consider biological aspects in the study of human behavior, the ghost of "biology is destiny" looms large. On the other hand, endocrinologists, biochemists, and geneticists are reticent to consider psychological and sociological aspects that they may consider to be imprecise and speculative. However, if progress is to be made in the comprehensive analysis of behavior, we cannot responsibly continue to hone in on the evidence presented by one discipline alone and thus neglect important new knowledge from other fields.

Models of Development

This chapter focuses on gender-related behavior, a field in which evidence of various prenatal and postnatal influences is rapidly accumulating. One of the roadblocks to progress lies in the interpretation of the data regarding the relative contribution of constitutional vs. environmental or innate vs. learned factors.

The difficulties begin with terminology. The dichotomies of nature vs. nurture, constitutional vs. acquired, and heredity vs. environment reflect outdated thinking of a bipolarity that does not exist. As John Money (1982, 504) succinctly puts it: "To polarize biology against social learning puts the latter unscientifically on a par with the occult." Money is referring to the fact that both kinds of influences exist in the brain, irrespective of how they gained entry—whether internally by way of genetics or externally by way of stimuli transmitted through the senses from the environment. He argues that learning and memory are just as much biology as the process of DNA replication. The bipolarity of these issues is thus a false one because social influences are not taking place outside the central nervous system.

This is important because the distinction is often drawn in order to divide the different classes of influences into immutable (i.e., biologic) and modifiable (i.e., learned) categories. This presents another false dichotomy, since *all effects* are more or less modifiable. A particular chain of events can modify conception itself. The range of hormonal variations from the mother and the fetus may also affect the development of the central nervous system which, in turn, may receive totally different stimuli postnatally during early parent–child bonding and later in sibling and peer relations, with different social reinforcers for specific behaviors.

Even without the false bipolarity of biology vs. environment, different models that help integrate all the information, prenatal or postnatal, must be considered. Three models come to mind that apply to both gender behavior and developmental disorders in general (discussed in detail in Samaroff & Chandler, 1975).

Main-Effect Model

The model most often applied is the *main-effect model*, which postulates that *one* factor determines or predominantly influences a particular behavioral outcome. A defect in the constitution, such as an abnormality in the prenatal or postnatal hormonal makeup of a person, produces a specific gender identity or gender disorder, irrespective of the social environment the individual grows up in. Conversely, a pathogenic environment will produce a disorder in gender behavior, no matter what the individual's genes, hormones, and sex organs are. This model has the advantage of being simple, practical for the researcher, and conclusive. Researchers typically hone in on one event that is taken to be the most important determinant of the behavior, and they are often ready to discard all knowledge of other relevant factors. The problem with the main-effect model is that many cases do not fit such a one-factor model. Therefore, we are particularly vulnerable to going from one new discovery to the next in the hope of finding a better explanation of the behavior under study.

Interactional Model

The second model is the *interactional model*. This model considers a variety of constitutional and social environmental factors to explain and, more importantly, to predict an individual's behavior. Basically two-dimensional, the interactional model predicts the individual's behavior outcome from any combination of two factors. As Samaroff and Chandler state, children with constitutional problems (e.g., with genetic or hormonal problems) raised in a deviant environment would be predicted to have poor outcome. Children with hormonal abnormalities with the good fortune to be raised in supportive environments and children without problems raised in deviant environments would have better outcomes. The best outcome, of course, is found among children with no hormonal or genetic problems who were raised in supportive environments. Certainly, this interactive model substantially increases the general efficiency of the main-effect model because it takes more influences into consideration. The major disadvantage of the model in this narrow version is that it presupposes the constancy of social environment and constitutional factors. The characteristics of children and their environment change, however, and, more importantly, they can modify each other at any point during development. The child can alter the response of the environment and is in turn altered by this changed world.

It is crucial then to move from a static interactional model to a more dynamic concept of development which posits a continual and progressive interplay between the organism and its environment.

Transactional Model

Such a dynamic model may be called a *transactional model*, which assumes that a variety of influences may have their source at different points in development, either in the constitution or in the outside world, exerting influence on the central nervous system. All these factors actively participate and interact with each other and are, therefore, plastic modifiers. The constants in development are not a set of genetic or hormonal traits, on the one hand, and the environmental reaction to these traits, on the other, but rather the processes by which these traits are maintained in the transactions between organism and environment. A deviant development, according to the transactional model, is not to be seen as an inborn inability to respond appropriately to a specific environment but rather a continuous malfunction in the organism–environment transaction across time that prevents the child from organizing his or her self-image and behavior adaptively. The deviant environment is not one traumatic event but rather continuous environmental responses to the child with a vulnerability that must operate throughout development. The transactional model does not assume directionality in development, that is, a greater etiological importance of one particular factor. Rather, the model stresses that the intensity of a deviant factor, be it social–environmental or constitutional, may have a *relatively* greater effect.

The outcome of development in a transactional model may consist of many different options, but regarding one aspect of psychosexual differentiation—gender identity development—there are surprisingly few possibilities. Gender identity may be unambiguously female, male, or ambiguous with no fixed anchor point in one or the other. Since the outcome is usually in accordance with expectations at birth, it appears that the human organism may produce normal developmental outcomes under seemingly all but the most adverse conditions.

Gender Identity

The definitions of gender identity vary; most of them infer a person's sense of belonging to one sex or the other, male or female. Until about 30 years ago, scientists and clinicians did not use the term *gender* but spoke of *sex*. Sex was determined by biology, and at that time biology meant the structure of the gonads, testicular or ovarian. If a person's sex was in doubt, as in babies with ambiguous genitalia, an exploratory laporotomy and a histologic examination of the gonads determined the sex of rearing. The underlying assumption was that the gonads represented the *true* sex and also determined a person's feelings of identity. Several examples exist of people with tragic lives of obscurity because they could not identify with their declared gonadal sex. Many were not allowed to get a valid birth certificate or to get married because no physician would verify their gender identity if it differed from their gonadal sex. In particular, this applied to genetic males with an extreme degree of microphallus who identified as females or to genetic females totally virilized during pre- and postnatal development who identified as males.

In 1945, Albert Ellis published a review article based on 84 cases of hermaphrodites, stating that the sex role in such cases "accords primarily not with his or her internal or external somatic characteristics, but rather with his or her masculine or feminine upbringing (p. 120)." The breakthrough, however, came in 1955 when John Money, in co-authorship with John and Joan Hampson (1955a,b) formulated a new theory of the determinants of sex, using for the first time the terms *gender role* and *gender identity*. The introduction of gender role and gender identity as new terms was critical because it meant having a term not bound to biologic sex that included other than sexual behaviors related to masculinity and femininity. The most important scientific advance of the proposed theory, though, was that sex was determined by a number of variables rather than one, including psychologic and social sex. Not until 1981 did the twenty-sixth edition of *Dorland's Illustrated Medical Dictionary* include "social sex" as one of the defining aspects under the entry on "sex."

The theory of John Money and his colleagues that the determination of sex depends on a number of variables, like links in a chain, was pioneering and may be considered a major contribution to our knowledge of psychosexual differentiation. It led to a major change in the traditional policy regarding the sex of rearing of intersex babies. Money and the Hampsons added a new criterion for sex assignment, namely, the prognosis of sexual functioning of the individual. They justified this by formulating a new theory of gender development based on their unique and rich clinical case material. Their theory stated that the best "prognosticator" of a satisfactory gender identity is the sex of assignment and rearing, and they added a critical time dimension to their model, that is, that aspects of gender identity are typically formed by two-and-a-half years of age. Money and the Hampsons had observed gender change at a later point in development but warned there was increased risk of psychopathology for the individual in such cases. Ambiguity of gender identity had been observed by them and was identified as a sequela of ambiguity in rearing. Clinicians were advised, therefore, to minimize such ambiguities by rapid decision making, counseling the parents, and surgically correcting the appearance of the external genitalia to accord with the assigned sex. Under Money and his medical collaborators and with the support of a prestigious institution such as the Johns Hopkins Hospital, sex of assignment on the basis of future social and sexual functioning became an adopted policy on a worldwide basis.

The model of gender identity development continued to be useful even when prenatal sex hormones and their effects on gender-related behavior came under study. Based on their findings, researchers generally agreed that variations of prenatal sex hormones may predispose and affect temperament in the direction of a certain pattern of sex dimorphic behavior, but they do not appear to have a major influence on the acquisition of gender identity unless coupled with a highly deviant environment (Money & Ehrhardt, 1972).

For a while, the theory that gender is determined by a number of variables interacting with each other seemed to be on solid ground. It came as a surprise, then, that the model was newly questioned and debated because of a radically different position espoused by Imperato-McGinley and co-workers beginning in 1974 based on their study of a newly diagnosed syndrome:

> It appears that the extent of androgen (i.e., testosterone) exposure of the brain in utero, during the early postnatal period and at puberty has more effect in determining male-gender identity than does sex of rearing. This experiment of nature emphasizes the importance of androgens, which act as inducers (in utero and neonatally) and as activators (at puberty) in the evolution of male-gender identity. (1979, p. 1236)

The theory has resulted in controversy, the debate is still ongoing and has had grave consequences because of its impact on clinical management of many patients with intersexuality. There is nothing wrong with a proposed new theory if it is based on new knowledge. What is startling, however, is that the Imperato-McGinley theory caused this controversy in the first place, considering the poor quality of its observational basis and what had already been learned from prior research.

The Imperato-McGinley observations are based on a group of people in the Dominican Republic who were genetic male pseudohermaphrodites due to an enzyme deficiency of 5α-reductase which decreases prenatal production of dihydrotestosterone. This results in severe ambiguity in the external genitalia in the male fetus. At birth, the subjects have a bifid scrotum which appears labia-like and a very small phallus. There is a urogenital sinus with a blind-ending vaginal pouch. The testes are in the abdomen, inguinal canal, or scrotum. In the past, these individuals were raised as girls. At puberty, under the influence of their own testosterone, these individuals undergo definite virilization with deepening of the voice, phallic growth, and masculine development. Their testes descend if they had not done so earlier. Of the original 18 subjects on which interview data exist, 17 are said to have changed their gender identity and 16 their gender role at puberty from female to male. Of the two exceptions, one kept the female gender identity and gender role, the other switched to a male gender identity but continued to dress as a female.

Most of the individuals who show this syndrome in the Dominican Republic appeared to change their gender identity during adolescence to that of a man. Before one concludes that this is due to testosterone, one needs to ask whether they really had a female gender identity in childhood and whether the rearing experience was unambiguously female. Unfortunately, the information on rearing and the concept of the parents regarding the sex of their child is very scanty in the existing publications. Some critical questions must be raised, similar to those in publications by Rubin, Reinisch, and Haskett (1981), and by Meyer-Bahlburg (1982). Perhaps the villagers and the parents of these individuals recognized some ambiguity in the children's genitalia from birth which may have given these children a special status. Imperato-McGinley suggests that after the initial observation of the pubertal change, the children became known as "penis at 12," making it likely that they were not unambiguously raised as girls. It is also likely that long before puberty, the affected individuals noted the ambiguity of their own genitalia, especially since boys play in the nude until age 7 or 8 in the Dominican village, whereas girls wear underpants after they are toilet trained. Imperato-McGinley argues that the children became slowly aware from about age 7 that their true sex was male, which certainly supports the hypothesis that the affected individuals knew themselves to be different from other girls long before puberty.

One also has to consider the specific cultural conditions in which these individuals grew up. Strict segregation of play behavior allows more freedom for boys to romp and play, whereas girls are encouraged to stay with their mothers near the house. Their prenatal androgen status might have influenced the affected individuals to have a temperamental makeup of physically energetic play behavior which would have made them happy-go-lucky tomboys in Western society. In the Dominican Republic, it might have increased their feelings of being different from other girls.

Lastly, a rural village in the Dominican Republic prescribes a dramatic status difference for men and women. To lead the life of an infertile woman with no breasts and ambiguous male genitalia probably means considerable hardship, no chance of having a normal marriage, and little possibility of supporting oneself. The gender change, on the other hand, meant joining the higher male status and attaining greater economic advantage.

Nonetheless, the example of these villagers *does* illustrate that human beings are capable of changing their gender relatively late in life under specific circumstances. That, however, was known from several earlier reports by Money and the Hampsons. In fact, Money (1968) published cases of gender change in adolescence by outlining the various roots of ambiguity in the person's development in great detail. It therefore comes as a surprise that a theory of determination of gender identity by pre- and postnatal hormones should be attractive, especially based on scanty evidence that does not explain many other existing phenomena. Women with untreated congenital adrenal hyperplasia, for instance, heavily virilized before and after birth, still usually do not want to change their gender to become male if brought up as a female. Consider the phenomenon of male transsexualism. If male gender identity is determined by prenatal androgens and pubertal hormonal activation, as Imperato-McGinley argues, shouldn't males who have normal male genitals at birth who get assigned to the male sex (even if they sometimes have ambiguous rearing experiences), and often have a totally normal male puberty, get the determining signals of testosterone to identify with the male gender? For a male child with gender ambiguity in childhood, the prognosis would be that his dilemma will definitely be solved during adolescence, and parents of effeminate boys would be reassured that everything will change in puberty, since the brain will get the message to identify with the male gender. In reality, the opposite is true—the dilemma of male transsexuals intensifies in adolescence.

Nonetheless, while the scientific debate continues, many clinicians have become insecure and now seriously suggest assigning genetic males with 5α-reductase deficiency to the male sex, despite the fact that they will grow up severely demasculinized and with ambiguous genitalia. Such clinicians believe that by puberty everything will be all right. The alternative suggested by some clinicians, to raise these children first as females and then switch them in adulthood to males, is equally naive and simple-minded considering the complexities of social events in the child's and the parents' lives.

The recent controversy on the determinants of gender identity shows how tempted researchers and clinicians are to believe in a simple truth rather than a complex interaction that may vary, be modified, and be mutable from case to case. However, simple models will not yield answers to complex pheonomena.

Sex Differences of Behavior

Gender identity, as a complex and specifically human phenomenon, may not be the most suitable aspect of gender on which to examine the interaction between biological and psychological variables. Sex-dimorphic behavior, encompassing those aspects of personality, play behavior, and temperament in which boys and girls and subsequently men and women differ, may be a more appropriate focus.

In the area of gender-related behavior, of all the constitutional variables to consider, sex hormones are of particular importance. Therefore, it is the field of behavioral endocrinology with its focus on the interplay between hormones and behavior that needs to be singled out for this discussion. Since behavioral endocrinology has made rapid advances over the past several decades, I will present a very brief discourse into some of the new knowledge that is relevant to the future study of human gender-related behavior.

Behavioral Endocrinology and Neuroendocrinology

In a recent historical overview, Frank Beach (1981) divides the field of behavioral endocrinology into three phases: The predisciplinary era (1850–1900), the formative era (1900 to the decade between 1950 and 1960), and the modern era (the post-1960 period, when the development of new methodology resulted in an increase in the amount of empirical evidence available). Within behavioral endocrinology, the research on mammalian sexual differentiation is the most exciting area for the study of human gender-related behavior. The emerging evidence is predominantly based on the study of rats, mice, guinea pigs, and nonhuman primates. The methodology of studying the relationship of hormones and behavior in nonhuman mammalian sexual differentiation has become highly sophisticated, including an increase in the number of species studied, the expansion of the type of behavioral patterns investigated, the multiplication of the types of hormones studied, and particularly the biochemical techniques for measuring and controlling endocrine variables.

In addition, there has been major progress in the area of neuroendocrinology. Over the last 100 years, it has been believed that hormonal effects have to be mediated via the central nervous system (CNS). In the modern era, our knowledge has been advanced in a number of different aspects, including the localization of structural sex differences in the brain, the identification of steroid-receptive cells, and the determination of effects of behaviorally significant hormones on neuronal metabolism. According to Beach, behavioral endocrinology is clearly on the way to an independent, mature discipline and will be established as such in the next 25 years or so.

Psychoendocrinology

Our knowledge of the psychoendocrinology of human gender-related behavior is much more fragmentary. Therefore, it is imperative that the knowledge gained on the basis of hormone-behavior relations in other species be taken as hypothesis-generating at most. Findings from such animal studies will then have to be put to a scrupulous test in human psychoendocrine studies and will most certainly have to match the sophisticated methodology used in the recent animal experimental work.

One of the important facts of psychoendocrinology is that there are distinct phases in development during which dramatic gender-specific hormonal changes occur. In the area of sexual differentiation in animals, we know most about the prenatal/neonatal phase and the time of sexual maturation, analogous to fetal development and puberty in the human life course. Animal experimentalists have paid much less attention to later phases of development; therefore, we have much less information to inspire research on the middle years or the aging process in human subjects.

The original so-called "central hypothesis" focused on the prominent role of androgens and particularly of testosterone as the most potent of all androgens. It was found that the presence of testosterone during a critical time of development is crucial for male sexual differentiation, whereas female sexual differentiation ensues in the absence of androgens. This principle was established in the study of normal animals and by hormonal modification of male and female animals: For instance, if you deprive a genetic male of androgen by castration or by treatment with an antagonist to testosterone (a so-called antiandrogen), the development of the reproductive tract proceeds along female lines. Conversely, if you provide the female fetus with androgen by injection during the critical time of differentiation, the genitals will become masculinized. Behavior differentiation has been shown to be controlled by the same principle in several subhuman species. The behaviors that have been measured in nonhuman mammals include both sexual behavior and nonreproductive behavior such as aggressive play fighting, activity, maze learning, sensitivity to taste and pain, and other sexually dimorphic behavior traits. Different sets of behavior were modified differentially so that different types of change were distinguished as "defeminization" and "masculinization." Beach, Kuehn, Sprague, and Anisko (1972) define these terms as follows:

> *Masculinization* of the female refers to the induction of anatomical, physiological or behavioral characters or traits which normally are well developed in males but lacking or poorly developed in females. *Defeminization* signifies partial or complete inhibition of traits normally well developed in females but absent or weakly developed in males. (p. 159)

The importance of distinguishing between so-called masculinization and defeminization became clear when it was found that hormones could modify different behavior sets, that is, so-called masculine behavior sets could be augmented in females by the exposure to androgens without cancelling out behavior patterns typical for females and vice versa.

The central hypothesis of organization also implies a *critical time phase* during which sex hormones can alter CNS differentiation during development. In lower mammals, this phase has been established as prenatal or neonatal, while in nonhuman primates it is limited to the prenatal developmental phase.

More recently, our knowledge has been advanced in terms of the way testosterone exerts its influence on the brain and of the importance of other sex hormones. From the work of experimental neuroendocrinologists, we now know that testosterone exerts its effects upon the developing brain in the rat through two pathways: The first is by being transformed into estrogen and by binding to specific estrogen receptors, a process called *aromatization*; the second pathway is by so-called 5 α-reductase through the reduction of testosterone to nonaromatizible androgens which bind to different androgen receptors (McEwen, 1983).

We have also learned that the modification of different behaviors is under the influence of different actions on the brain level and that the various sex hormones can antagonize each other; for instance, progesterone can act as an antiandrogen if injected at certain times in development and at certain dose levels.

While the role of sex hormones during prenatal/neonatal times has been described as *organizational* (which means they influence CNS differentiation permanently), sex hormones during adulthood have been labeled as *activational*, suggesting that they can activate behavior that was preorganized during an earlier phase of development. Sex hormones in adulthood have a facilitative effect on sex-related responses. In other words (e.g., in the rat) androgen is needed for the expression of male behavior and will occur if the normal output of testosterone from the animal's testes occurs or if castrated in adulthood and injected with androgen. However, this effect will only occur if the male fetus and neonate was not deprived of androgen at the critical time of CNS differentiation. The hormonal effect in adulthood, therefore, has been termed *temporary* and *reversible*, in contrast to the permanent and developmental action of the same hormone during fetal differentiation.

Another important principle that has been added through the study of mammalian sexual differentiation is the interactional or reciprocal aspect of hormone–environment relations. This principle encompasses the fact that environmental conditions can affect hormonal levels as seen, for instance, in the fact that testosterone decreases if a male monkey loses a dominant position in a hierarchy of social relations. This is analogous to the research on human behavior that suggests that physical or psychological stress lowers testosterone values temporarily. Another example is the well-known observation that women's menstrual cycle is affected by travel, nutrition, and even by living with other females in a dormitory situation (McClintock, 1971).

Now let us examine what is known about the application of these principles to the study of human gender-related behavior. We know that one cannot generalize from one species to the next, since rats and monkeys already differ in some important ways from each other. The question is rather whether one should include any of these established principles of hormones and behavior in nonhuman mammals as researchable hypotheses in the study of human gender-related behavior. I would suggest that one has to pay attention to hormonal variables in order to explain important developmental sequences provided, of course, that (1) one does not generalize from animal behavior but puts the observation to vigorous tests of human behavior; (2) one is not seduced by a main-effect model but applies transactional thinking; and (3) one uses the sophisticated methods developed by behavioral endocrinologists for measuring hormones in animal behavior. We also must focus on clearly defined behavior units rather than global and complex units, and we must never forget that biological markers are as modifiable as learned behavior.

What do we know so far about the roles of hormones in human sexual differentiation? Endocrine research has established that the role of sex hormones on the differentiation of reproductive and sex organs follows much the same principles as in lower mammals, that is, the male fetus is exposed to much higher levels of androgens from the output of his own testes. The basic structures of the sex organs are bipotential. If anything interferes with the action of androgens during human fetal development, a genetic male will be born with female-looking external genitalia, and if a genetic female is exposed to high levels of androgens either by maternal drugs or from her own overactive adrenal glands, she will be born with a more or less developed penis and an empty scrotum. The critical time seems to be the second trimester of pregnancy. These facts are reasonably well established.

However, the information on hormonal effects on the human CNS is speculative at this point. Up to now, all we can go by is the suggestive evidence mostly based on clinical groups of girls and boys who have a documented history of abnormal levels of sex hormones during prenatal development and whose gender-related behavior was studied at different age levels and compared with normal controls. The main findings of that research can be stated as follows (see reviews by Ehrhardt & Meyer-Bahlburg, 1981; Money & Ehrhardt, 1972): Girls who were exposed to unusually high levels of androgen during their prenatal development were found to show high levels of physically energetic outdoor play behavior and low levels of nurturant behavior in terms of parenting rehearsal. They were significantly different in these respects from matched normal controls and, in a separate study, from their endocrinologically normal sisters. The behavior was long term and could not be solely explained by the various social and environmental factors assessed. In a number of separate studies, prenatal exposure to pharmacological doses of estrogen and progesterone was assessed, and it was found that those sex hormones were associated with the expected opposite effect, namely, relatively less physically energetic play behavior and an increase in more nurturant behavior as exhibited in doll play and infant care in girls and in less aggressive play behavior in boys. This finding could be interpreted as an antiandrogenic effect of some of the estrogen/progesterone compounds, analogous to some of the actions of these hormones demonstrated in animal experiments.

The behavior differences between the samples of girls and boys exposed to abnormal levels of sex hormones during gestation and normal control groups happen to be those that are believed to be the cornerstone of so-called masculine and feminine behavior of normal females and males, as suggested in the review by Maccoby and Jacklin (1974). Therefore, it is customary to speak in terms of behavior masculinization and feminization by the exposure to androgens and other sex hormones. As is well known, the behavior of human males and females is largely overlapping, and when we refer to sex differences, we are referring to mean differences between groups. The terms *masculine* and *feminine* are unfortunate, since they are often erroneously taken to be a true dichotomy, which does not exist. The terminology is similarly misleading when we divide the major sex hormones into so-called male and female hormones. Androgens, estrogens, and progesterone occur in both sexes, albeit in different quantities and different ratios.

The behavior variation within one gender is often wider than between the genders. Therefore, it may well be that the studies on clinical populations may ultimately point to more interesting relationships between levels of sex hormones and temperamental differences *within* rather than *between* gender.

Hormonal and Social Interaction

Rather than examining in more detail the evidence on psychoendocrine relations in the development of human sex differences, we can suggest the ways in which hormones might interact with social and environmental stimuli. For instance, if high levels of prenatal androgens are indeed associated with physical, energetic, rough-and-tumble play in normal children, what conclusion can be drawn from such a contingency? It certainly does not mean that prenatal androgens *determine* this particular play behavior independent of the social environment in which a child grow up. Rather, it may mean a predisposition to learn certain behaviors more readily.

If, for instance, the child is a boy and has been exposed to relatively high levels of prenatal androgen from his own testicular production during prenatal differentiation, and if he then meets strong cultural reinforcements from his parents, peers, and school that reward physically active play behavior and athletic pursuits, the probability of the expression of that behavior is greatly increased. If the child is a girl who has a history of relatively high levels of prenatal androgens (although within the normal range for females), she may therefore have a predisposition to physically energetic play behavior, but if she grows up in a family where this kind of behavior is not reinforced or is even suppressed, she is less likely to exhibit rough-and-tumble play. Traditionally, Western society has reinforced rough-and-tumble play in boys and doll play and infant care in girls, but this socialization process may not be the most opportune for our changing society.

The model suggested by Alice Rossi (1977) regarding parenting and nurturant behavior, may also apply to physical, energetic play behavior. Rossi suggested that it might be more advantageous for a society such as ours, in which both men and women share most occupational roles, to provide equal preparation for family roles. One might even institute the opposite social reinforcement approach, namely, to expose boys more to nurturant situations than girls in a pattern Rossi calls "compensatory learning." The end result might be that both sexes would be equally adept in both parental and work roles. Regarding the predisposition for physically energetic rough-and-tumble play, one may follow the same reasoning, namely, active play behavior such that sports and athletics would be more encouraged and reinforced in girls than in boys. In fact, there are more opportunities today for girls to participate in athletics and highly competitive sports than in the past, and the gap between the sexes in some areas of sports is narrowing. To continue in our developmental sequence, a predisposition toward physical, energetic play augmented by prenatal androgen and reinforced by society for participation in competitive sports has much wider implications for behavior development than just a proficiency in that particular athletic pursuit. Being part of a team, learning to compete, and having experience in both winning and losing enhances qualities that may develop competence and assertiveness in adult occupational and family roles.

Thus, a hormonal factor at one point in development is surely not the determinant of a complex behavior at a much later point in the life course. However, it may present one of the links in a long chain of events leading to the expression of a specific trait. But even if that kind of developmental sequence can be analyzed for a specific behavior set, it clearly does not mean that there is only one pathway for the expression of the same behavior. For instance, while prenatal androgen may predispose to rough-and-tumble play, it requires special social environmental reinforcement for the behavior expression to occur. The same behavior pattern may be developed in an individual with a relatively low level of prenatal androgens with a different, more strongly reinforcing social environment. The pliability of the human organism is such that *many* pathways during the life course lead to similar behavior sets.

One of the crucial developmental crossroads is puberty. At this developmental point, we do not know what the relationship is between variations in levels of prenatal hormones and pubertal hormones within the same person. For instance, it is unknown whether females with relatively high levels of prenatal androgen also secret relatively high levels of androgen in adulthood. Therefore, if a correlation between a hormonal factor and adult behavior is found, we do not know whether this relationship had hormonal precursors early in the development of that individual. Equally, we do not know whether the behavior affects the hormone levels or whether the hormonal factors precede the behavior, since the interaction between hormones and behavior is reciprocal. A good example of this point is the recent observation that testosterone is correlated with the occupational status of women. In a careful study of 55 normal females, Purifoy and Koopmans (1980) assessed their serum androstenedione, testosterone, testosterone-binding globulin, and free testosterone. These hormones are all different androgens. To measure more than one of these hormones increases the accuracy of assessment. The authors found that, independent of age, women in professional, managerial, and technical occupations had higher levels of all androgens, (i.e., androstenedione, testosterone, and free-testosterone) than women clerical workers and housewives.

Within the framework of old simple minded, now outdated, thinking, one might assume a simple cause-and-effect model stating that high levels of androgen in women determine their job status. Within a more sophisticated biosocial framework, one might instead hypothesize that the observed relationship is an indication of a complex interplay of hormones and behavior over time. For some of these women, it may reflect a developmental sequence that started in prenatal life with a relatively high level of androgen that predisposes them to learn to expend high levels of physical energy in play and sports. They may have been fortunate to live in a social environment that fostered this predisposition. Within a larger societal context, such women grew up at a time when full-time professional careers for women were permissible and socially reinforced, and they might have had a family and school environment that fostered their interest in such occupational roles. At puberty, these women might or might not have started to produce relatively high levels of androgen during their menstrual cycle, and eventually they might have excelled in a professional career. On the other hand, some or all of these women might not have had a particular hormonal pattern during prenatal or pubertal development at all but underwent a developmental sequence that was strongly influenced by social reinforcement for professional careers. Ultimately, fulfilling such an occupational status might have increased their androgen production via a feedback effect of their work upon their endocrine system. The point is that hormonal factors can play different roles in a complex interplay of many variables within a particular developmental sequence. Hence, a correlation between a specific hormone level and a particular behavior pattern has to be seen as a contingency that may signal a whole network of different transactions that vary from one individual to another.

The Purifoy and Koopmans study demonstrates several features that reflect more sophisticated thinking in human psychoendocrinology. Not only did they measure more than *one* androgen and apply up-to-date and sophisticated biochemical methodology, but their interpretation allowed for the various possibilities of transactions between hormones and behavior. Furthermore, not only did they take occupational status as *one* behavior variable, but they attempted to classify the different careers and found that different androgens seem to be associated with different types of jobs. For instance, androestenedione and free testosterone were associated with the degree of job complexity in relation to *people*, whereas testosterone significantly correlated with the degree of job complexity in relation to *things*. It is too early to draw any conclusions from this finding, but it does point to a very important rule to follow in modern psychoendocrine studies. Endocrinologists have become more and more sophisticated in breaking down the specific sex hormones they measure, but they must also be very specific regarding the behavioral units they assess.

The history of psychoendocrinology is full of dead-end investigations because the behavior under study was too complex and, therefore, different studies came up with contradictory findings. Mood changes in relation to the menstrual cycle in women is a good example. Older studies assessed mood changes in women, correlated them with the various sex hormones over their menstrual cycle, and disregarded what else went on in the lives of the women at the same time. A more sophisticated study that exemplifies the transactional approach was conducted by Alice and Peter Rossi (1977), who looked at mood patterns in relationship to two time dimensions—body time (as indexed by the female menstrual cycle) and social time (as measured by the calendar week). The complexity of their study enabled them to demonstrate individual variations of mood in relation to personality factors, phase of the menstrual cycle, and whether a specific phase of the cycle fell on week days or the weekend.

Conclusion

The study of gender requires a biosocial approach that includes knowledge from various disciplines. Behavior needs to be viewed as the end product of a complex interplay of many variables that interact with each other. Such transactional thinking may shed light on long-term developmental sequences in the areas of sex-dimorphic behavior and sexuality. It may also advance our knowledge of the etiological roots of sexual orientation and preference, and it may give us insight into change of behavior over time. If this new approach is followed, we may look forward to an exciting era in psychoendocrinology, developmental psychology, and the sociology of the life course.

References

Beach, F. A. Historical origins of modern research on hormones and behavior. *Hormones and behavior*, 1981, *15*, 325–376.

Beach, F. A., Kuehn, R. E., Sprague, R. H., & Anisko, J. J. Coital behavior in dogs—XI. Effects of androgenic stimulation during development on masculine mating responses in females. *Hormones and Behavior*, 1972, *3*, 143–168.

Ehrhardt, A. A., & Meyer-Bahlburg, H. F. L. Effects of prenatal sex hormones on gender-related behavior. *Science*, 1981, *211*, 1312–1318.

Ellis, A. The sexual psychology of human hermaphrodites. *Psychosomatic Medicine*, 1945, *7*, 108–125.

Imperato-McGinley, J., Peterson, R. E., Gautier, T., & Sturla, E. Androgens and the evolution of male-gender identity among male pseudohermaphrodites with 5α-reductase deficiency. *The New England Journal of Medicine*, 1979, *300*, 1233–1237.

McClintock, M. K. Menstrual synchrony and suppression. *Nature*, 1971, *229*, 244–245.

Maccoby, E. E., & Jacklin, C. N. *The psychology of sex differences*. Stanford: Stanford University Press, 1974.

McEwen, B. S. Gonadal steroidal influences in brain development and sexual differentiation. In R. O. Greep (Ed.), *Reproductive physiology IV. International review of physiology* (Vol. 27). Baltimore: University Park Press, 1983, pp. 99–145.

Meyer-Bahlburg, H. F. L. Hormones and psychosexual differentiation: Implications for the management of intersexuality, homosexuality and transsexuality. *Clinics in Endocrinology and Metabolism*, 1982, *11*, 681–701.

Money, J. Psychologic approach to psychosexual misidentity with elective mutism: Sex reassignment in two cases of hyperadrenocortical hermaphroditism. *Clinical Pediatrics*, 1968, *7*, 331–339.

Money, J. Search for the causes of sexual preference. *Contemporary Psychology*, 1982, *27*, 503–505.

Money, J., & Ehrhardt, A. A. *Man & woman, boy & girl*. Baltimore, Maryland: Johns Hopkins University Press, 1972.

Money, J., Hampson, J. G., & Hampson, J. L. An examination of some basic sexual concepts: The evidence of human hermaphroditism. *Bulletin of The Johns Hopkins Hospital*, 1955, 97, 301–319. (a)

Money, J., Hampson, J. G., & Hampson, J. L. Hermaphroditism: Recommendations concerning assignment of sex, change of sex, and psychologic management. *Bulletin of The Johns Hopkins Hospital*, 1955, 97, 284–300. (b)

Purifoy, F. E., & Koopmans, L. H. Androstenedione, T and free T concentrations in women of various occupations. *Social Biology*, 1980, 26, 179–188.

Rossi, A. S. A biosocial perspective on parenting. *Daedalus, Journal of the American Academy of Arts and Sciences*, 1977, 106, 1–31.

Rossi, A. S., & Rossi, P. E. Body time and social time: Mood patterns by menstrual cycle phase and day of week. *Social Science Research*, 1977, 6, 273–308.

Rubin, R. T., Reinisch, J. M., & Haskett, R. F. Postnatal gonadal steroid effects on human behavior. *Science*, 1981, 211, 1318–1324.

Samaroff, A. J., & Chandler, M. J. Reproductive risk and the continuum of caretaking causality. In F. D. Horowitz (Ed.), *Review of child development research* (Vol. 4). Chicago: The University of Chicago Press, 1975, pp. 187–244.

[36]
Neonatal Sex-Steroid Hormones and Cognitive Abilities at Six Years

CAROL NAGY JACKLIN
KAREN THOMPSON WILCOX
Department of Psychology
University of Southern California
Los Angeles, California

ELEANOR E. MACCOBY
Department of Psychology
Stanford University
Stanford, California

Five sex-steroid hormones (testosterone, androstenedione, estradiol, estrone, and progesterone) were assayed in umbilical cord blood. Cognitive abilities were assessed as a part of a 6-year follow-up laboratory visit. Four subtests were given: reading, numbers, listening, and spatial ability. There were no significant differences between boys and girls in cognitive ability scores. Higher levels of perinatal androgens (testosterone and androstenedione) were significantly associated with low age-6 spatial ability in girls. Multiple regression analyses revealed a significant proportion of the variance in cognitive abilities in girls could be accounted for by testosterone and androstenedione. No significant predictions were found for boys. The finding of a stable inverse association between sex and effect of hormones on abilities is discussed.

Whether sex-steroid hormones are associated with cognitive abilities in boys and girls has been an intriguing question. There are both sex-related differences in cognitive abilities and in circulating sex-steroid hormones beginning in adolescence. However, when one tries to find a causal link, either in associations between hormonal measures and concurrent cognitive abilities or early hormonal and later cognitive abilities, the relationship is not clear.

Hormones may have the greatest effect early in fetal development when levels of the sex-steroid hormones are quite high (Faiman, Reyes, & Winter, 1974). The theoretical argument is that these sex-steroid hormones change the fetal brain even though behavioral effects may not be seen for years. The

---

Reprint requests should be sent to Carol Nagy Jacklin, Ph.D., Department of Psychology, University of Southern California, Los Angeles, CA 90089-1061, U.S.A.

Received for publication 6 February 1987
Revised for publication 28 September 1987
Accepted at Wiley 24 March 1988

Developmental Psychobiology, 21(6):567–574 (1988)
© 1988 by John Wiley & Sons, Inc.   CCC 0012-1630/88/060567-08$04.00

theory is better instantiated with animal than human studies. (See Hines, 1982, for a review.)

Several studies have tried to assess the effects of prenatal hormones and later intellectual behaviors in humans, but the picture is incomplete. With populations of fetally androgenized girls, Ehrhardt and Money (1967) reported higher intelligence test scores than would have been expected for the general population. However, it was later found that although fetally androgenized girls did have higher-than-average IQ scores, so too did their sisters who had not been fetally androgenized (Erhardt & Baker, 1973). Similar findings are reviewed by Ehrhardt and Meyer-Bahlburg (1979). The Ehrhardt and Money findings, then, might well have reflected a selection of subjects from more advantaged segments of the population. However, a recent study of females with congenital adrenal hyperplasia (CAH), an autosomal recessive disorder associated with elevated adrenal androgen, found that CAH females, as compared with unaffected female relatives, showed significantly enhanced performance on three tests of spatial ability (Resnick, Berenbaum, & Gottesman, 1986).

Other investigations of prenatal exposure to hormones find relationships between the exposure and later development. In one study, both boys and girls who received large dosages of progesterone in utero, had higher general aptitude than matched controls at seven years of age, as reported by their teachers (Dalton, 1968). These children are more likely to enter University, and they leave school with higher grades than their non-progesterone-treated controls (Dalton, 1976). However, other work has not replicated this finding with lower dosages of progesterone (Meyer-Bahlburg & Ehrhardt, 1977).

No difference in intelligence test results were found in groups prenatally treated with estrogen, progestins or combinations compared to untreated sibling controls (Reinisch & Karrow, 1977). Women given the synthetic estrogen, diethylstilbestrol (DES) prenatally did not differ from their nontreated sisters in cognitive test scores (Hines, 1984). Similarly, men given estrogens prenatally did not have different cognitive test scores than matched controls (Kester, Green, Finch, & Williams, 1980).

Unfortunately, in addition to being equivocal, the majority of the work cited above on prenatal hormone associations with later cognitive ability has been with exogenous hormones. That is, for therapeutic reasons, hormones were administered to the pregnant mother and the children's abilities were later tested. These exogenous hormones differ in quantity and quality from the circulating hormones of the placenta and fetus. Work has not thus far been reported for endogenous hormones in a normal population.

The present study addresses the following issues: (1) Are there sex differences in cognitive abilities at 6 years of age?; and (2) are cognitive abilities at 6 years of age related to nenonatal sex-steroid hormones in boys and girls in a normal population.

Method

Sample

The sample of children were a part of the Stanford Longitudinal Study. Ninety-six of the children, who were initially seen by the experimenters at birth, were recontacted and tested at 6 years of age as a part of a longitudinal follow-up. Cohort I, II, and III, from the original study, will be combined for the present paper. Of the original cohorts, cohort I and II comprised all the children born in a university hospital and a general hospital during the summer of 1973 and winter and spring of 1974, and cohort III was comprised of the children born in the general hospital in the fall of 1975, who met the specific criteria, viz: (1) no complications of pregnancy or delivery, (2) a 5-min Apgar score of 7 and above, (3) 15 cubic centimeters (cc) of umbilical cord blood taken at birth (by the delivery room nurses), and (4) permission obtained from the parents for the family to participate in the longitudinal study.

The birth hormone measures of all of the children in the original sample does not differ from the smaller sample that was recontacted and tested at 6 yr of age.

Procedure

Hormones

At the time of each infant's birth, at least 15 cc. of blood were taken from the umbilical cord as soon as it was severed. The blood was predominantly venous, with relatively smaller amounts from the cord artery. The blood was allowed to clot in a refrigerator and the serum was stored frozen at $-25°F$ until assay. On the day following the infant's birth, the mother was asked for permission to include the infant in the longitudinal study. For the infants so enrolled (a large majority of those eligible) the frozen serum samples were subsequently analyzed for five hormones. Androstenedione (4-androsten-3, 17-dione), testosterone (17B-hydroxy-4-androsten-3-one), estrone (3-hydroxy-1,3,5(10)-estratrien-17-one), and estradiol (1,3,5(10)-estratriene-3, 17B-diol) were estimated by radioimmunoassay methods. Progesterone (4-pregnen-3, 20-dione) was assayed by a competitive protein binding method.

It should be noted that the birth concentrations of testosterone were greater in males than females. The other four hormones did not differ significantly by sex. Further details of the assays and hormone relationships are described in Maccoby, Doering, Jacklin, and Kraemer (1979).

Cognitive Testing

At age $6\frac{1}{2}$, each child was given a cognitive test by a trained experimenter as a part of the 6-yr laboratory visit. The cognitive testing was done after an initial warm-up game played by the parents and child. The test consisted of four subtests. The first three subtests (reading, numbers and listening were taken from the kindergarten and first grade versions of the Metropolitan Instructional Tests (1979). The fourth subtest, spatial ability, was taken from the kindergarten and first grade versions of the Primary Mental Abilities Test.

The scores of the subtests were positively correlated in both boys and girls, thus summary scores were constructed. The first summary score or Total Academic Cognitive Score is a summed score of the four subtests. In addition, a principal components analysis was done of the four subtests, with two components emerging. The first principal component was a general academic cognitive cluster accounting for .585 proportion of the variance. This is called the General Academic Component. A second principal component was a spatial cluster and it accounted for .180 proportion of the variance. This is referred to as the Spatial Component.

TABLE 1. *Cognitive Ability Scores for Boys and Girls at 6½ Years.*

	Boys (n = 53)	Girls (n = 43)	t	Two-Tail Probability
TAC	396.58	404.85	−1.35	.18
GAC	−.18	.23	−1.33	.19
SC	−.03	.04	−0.38	.70

* TAC = Total Academic Cognitive Score, GAC = General Academic Component, SC = Spatial Component.

Results

Cognitive scores for boys and girls are presented in Table 1. There are no significant differences in the Total Academic Cognitive Score, General Academic Component, or Spatial Component.

The strength of association between the five sex-steroid hormones assayed at birth and the cognitive measures was examined using a Pearson correlation coefficient. Results are presented in Table 2. The male hormones, testosterone and androstenedione, are negatively and significantly associated with the Spatial Component in girls ($r = -.34$ & $r = -.37$; $p = .05$). No other significant associations are seen. A consistent pattern of opposite hormone/cognitive associations for boys and girls is found with the hormones testosterone, estradiol, and progesterone and the Total Academic Cognitive Score and General Academic Component. All correlations are in the negative direction for boys, while for girls all correlations are in the positive direction.

The neonatal hormone scores are intercorrelated. In psychological correlational research on individual differences, a common method of dealing with cor-

TABLE 2. *Correlations of Hormones and Cognitive Ability Scores.*

	TAC	GAC	SC
		Testosterone	
Boys	−.028	−.025	−.085
Girls	.264	.264	−.337*
		Androstenedione	
Boys	−.190	−.184	−.190
Girls	−.260	−.251	−.366*
		Estradiol	
Boys	−.152	−.145	−.236
Girls	.019	.031	−.152
		Estrone	
Boys	−.267	−.262	−.260
Girls	−.138	−.137	−.149
		Progesterone	
Boys	−.117	−.119	−.151
Girls	.005	.001	−.072

* $p = .05$. TAC = Total Academic Cognitive Score, GAC = General Academic Component, SC = Spatial Component.

HORMONES AND COGNITIVE ABILITIES

relations among predictive variables is to identify the component that they have in common, determine the effect of this component, and then determine whether the individual variables have any predictive power that is independent of the common component. Principal component analysis was used to identify the shared component of the five sex-steroid hormones (see Marcus, Maccoby, & Jacklin, 1985, for further details of the hormone analysis). The analysis revealed a primary component that accounted for 59% of the variance in hormone levels and is called the "all hormone" component. All hormones had substantial and significant loadings, of about equal magnitude, on this component. A second component, accounting for 18% of the variance, had positive loadings on androstenedione and testosterone, and a negative loading on progesterone. The second component is labeled the "androgen" component. Two hormone component scores were derived for each child by weighing each individual's hormone scores by the loading of each hormone in the principal component analysis. Sex differences were found in the two hormone component scores. The mean scores for male neonates is significantly higher than for females on both components ($p = .01$ "all hormone" component; and $p = .001$ "androgen" component).

First-order correlations between the hormone component scores and the cognitive ability scores are reported in Table 3. There is no significant relationship between the Total Academic Cognitive Score or General Academic factor and the hormone components. There is a significant negative association between the Spatial factor in girls and the androgen component score ($p = .01$).

Stepwise multiple regression analyses were performed for all hormone scores and all cognitive ability measures to examine to what extent particular neonatal sex-steroid hormones could predict cognitive ability in boys and girls at 6 years of age. For boys, estrone and estradiol accounted for approximately 10% of the variance in the Total Academic Cognitive Score, General Academic Component, and Spatial Component. F tests on the coefficient of determination (r squared) were nonsignificant for all cognitive ability measures. The contributions of progesterone, testosterone, and androstenedione were negligible to any prediction of cognitive ability measures in boys.

For girls, approximately 20% of the variance in Total Academic Cognitive Score, General Academic Component, and Spatial Component, was accounted for by testosterone and androstenedione. F tests for all three cognitive measures were significant with $p = .025$. Progesterone contributed slightly to the prediction,

TABLE 3. Correlations of Hormone Component Scores and Cognitive Ability Scores by Sex.

	All Hormone Component		Androgen Component	
	Boys	Girls	Boys	Girls
TAC	−.207	−.073	.027	.032
GAC	−.202	−.072	.030	.040
SC	−.245	−.256	.029	−.398**

** $p = .01$. TAC = Total Academic Cognitive Score, GAC = General Academic Component, SC = Spatial Component.

with estrone and estradiol having a negligible effect. A multiple regression with sex, androgen component score and the interaction of sex × androgen component as predictors of the Spatial Factor was performed to test for significant interactions between these variables. The test was nonsignificant at the $p = .05$ level.

Discussion

In this study, no significant differences were found in cognitive abilities between males and females tested at 6 years. However, boys and girls show systematic differences in the pattern of relationships between their 6 years abilities and their neonatal sex-steroid hormones. For three of the hormones: testosterone, estradiol, and progesterone, correlations were in opposite directions for boys and girls. These findings echo previous findings between hormones and behaviors found by Jacklin, Maccoby, and Doering, (1983) and Jacklin, Maccoby, Doering, and King (1984). In examining the relationships between hormones and strength, and hormones and timidity in boys and girls the following different directions in associations were found. In boys, neonatal progesterone levels were positively related to strength measures and inversely related to timidity; whereas in girls, progesterone was negatively related to strength and unrelated to timidity. In the present study, there was a significant relationship between male hormones and spatial abilities in girls. An inverse association between sex and effect of hormones seems to exist.

While systematic associations of direction were found between hormones and cognitive abilities for boys and girls, the correlations were only significant for testosterone and androstenedione and spatial abilities in girls. These findings are contrary to previous research on hormones and spatial abilities which found a positive relationship between androgens and spatial abilities in females (Resnick et al., 1986). In this study, a negative association was found.

These inconsistencies in the literature lead to the larger question of how to study hormone-behavior relationships in humans. One approach has been to study "atypical" populations, such as the effect of prenatal exposure to exogenous hormones used for the treatment of at-risk pregnancies (Hines & Shipley, 1984) or individuals with autosomal disorder, such as CAH. These "experiments in nature" are important in human subjects where other experimentation is impossible. However, an obvious problem with this research is that the findings concern atypical populations and may not be generalizable to normal populations. A methodology that utilized a "normal" population entails taking samples of cord blood from infants at the time of delivery, such as was done in the present study. Sex hormone levels are then ascertained from the cord blood samples. While this method circumvents the problem of using an atypical sample, it is not without other problems.

First, it is not clear how the onset of labor and the stress of labor and delivery affect the levels of hormones found in cord blood (Fuchs & Fuchs, 1984). Second, the hormones present at labor and delivery may not be representative of the hormone levels present in the fetus during the time of maximum sensitivity for brain exposure to hormones. In humans, this time of maximum sensitivity has not been specified, although, it is believed to be in early or midgestation (Hines, 1982; Reinsich & Sanders, 1984). Further clarification of the sensitizing effects of endogenous hormones in normal humans may have to wait until safe methods are devised to measure sex-steroid hormones in the fetus during the midgestational period.

HORMONES AND COGNITIVE ABILITIES

The repeated findings of differential effects of sex-steroids on males and females is curious. This has been reported in our work with very young children and recently with concurrent hormones in older children (Susman, Inoff-Germain, Nottelman, Loriaux, Cutler, & Chrousos, 1987). Sometimes effects are only found in one sex and sometimes opposite effects are found for the same hormone in boys and girls. We cannot explain this phenomenon at present. The explanation may have to await understanding the mechanism linking hormones and brain organization (Crockett & Petersen, 1984).

However, one plausible hypothesis is that the ranges of hormone sensitivity may be different for the sexes. That is, what is too much or too little hormone may be different for the developing girl or boy. A given amount of progesterone then, for example, could effect the sexes differently as has been demonstrated (Jacklin et al., 1984). Or, as in the present study, having a given amount of male hormone may be deleterious to females, but not affect males in their behavior at all. Looking at the actual range of hormone scores is one mechanism that could serve to separate the endogenous hormones studies from exogenous hormone studies. Unfortunately, exogenous hormones differ at present from endogenous hormones in both quantity and quality.

Additional studies need to be carried out with perinatal endogenous hormone samples in order to understand the complex picture of the hormone-behavior phenomenon. Hopefully, it will soon also be possible to safely study prenatal endogenous hormones. While research with both normal and atypical populations support the hypothesis that differential hormone level or exposure influences later patterns of cognitive behavior, it is not yet clear what direction this contribution may take and how large an influence hormones have on later behavior.

References

Dalton, K. (1968). Ante-natal progesterone and intelligence. *Br. J. Psychiatry, 129:* 438–442.
Dalton, K. (1976). Prenatal progesterone and educational attainments. *Br. J. Psychiatry, 129:* 438–442.
Ehrhardt, A. A., and Baker, S. W. (1974). Fetal androgens, human central nervous system differentiation, and behavior sex differences. In R. C. Friedman, R. Richart, and R. Vande Wiele (Eds.), *Sex Differences in Behavior.* New York: Wiley.
Ehrhardt, A. A., and Meyer-Bahlberg, J. F. L. (1979). Prenatal sex hormones and the developing brain: Effects on psychosocial differentiation and cognitive function. *Ann. Rev. Med., 30:* 417–430.
Ehrhardt, A. A., and Money, J. (1967). Progestin-induced hemaphroditism: IQ and psychosexual identity in a study of ten girls. *J. Sex Res., 3:* 83–100.
Faiman, C., Reyes, F. I., and Winter, J. S. D. (1974). Serum gonadotropin patterns during the perinatal period in man and chimpanzee. In M. G. Forest and J. Bertrand (Eds.), *Endocrinologie sexuelle de la periode perinatale.* Paris: Inserm.
Fuchs, A. R., and Fuchs, F. (1984). Endocrinology of human parturition: A review. *Bri. J. Obstet. & Gynaecol., 91:* 948–967.
Hines, M. (1982). Prenatal gonadal hormones and sex differences in human behavior. *Psychol. Bull., 92:* 56–80.
Hines, M., and Shipley, C. (1984). Prenatal exposure to diethylstilbestrol (DES) and the development of sexually-dimorphic cognitive abilities and cerebral lateralization. *Dev. Psychol., 20:* 81–94.
Jacklin, C. N., Maccoby, E. E., and Doering, C. H. (1983). Neonatal sex-steroid hormones and timidity in 6-18 month-old boys and girls. *Dev. Psychobiol., 16:* 163–168.
Jacklin, C. N., Maccoby, E. E., Doering, C. H., and King, D. (1984). Neonatal sex-steroid hormones and muscular strength of boys and girls in the first three years. *Dev. Psychobiol., 17:* 301–310.
Kester, P., Green, R., Finch, S. J., and Williams, K. (1980). Prenatal "female hormone" administration and psychosexual development in human males. *Psychoendocrinology, 5:* 269–285.

Maccoby, E. E., Doering, C. H., Jacklin, C. N., and Kraemer, H. (1979). Concentrations of sex hormones in umbilical cord blood: Their relation to sex and birth order of infants. *Child Dev., 50:* 632–642.

Metropolitan Instructional Tests. (1979). New York: Harcourt, Brace, & Javanovich, Inc.

Meyer-Bahlburg, H. F., and Ehrhardt, A. A. (1977). Effects of prenatal hormone treatment on mental abilities. In R. Gemme & C. C. Wheeler (Eds.), *Progress in Sexology.* New York: Plenum.

Reinisch, J. M., and Karrow, W. G. (1977). Prenatal exposure to synthetic progestine and estrogens: Effects of human development. *Arch. Sexual Behav., 6:* 257–288.

Reinisch, J. M., and Sanders, S. A. (1984). Prenatal gonadal steroidal influences on gender-related behavior. In G. J. De Vries, J. P. C. DeBruin, H. B. M. Ulyings, and M. A. Corner (Eds.). *Progress in brain research. Vol. 61: Sex Differences in the Brain* (pp. 407–416). Amsterdam: Elsevier.

Resnick, S. M., Berenbaum, S. A., Gottesman, I. I., and Bouchard, T. J. (1986). Early hormonal influences on cognitive functioning in congenital adrenal hyperplasia. *Dev. Psychol., 22:* 191–198.

Susman, E. J., Inoff-Germain, G., Nottelmann, E. D., Loriaux, L., Cutler, G. B., and Chrousos, G. P. (1987). Hormones emotional dispositions, and aggressive attributes in young children. *Dev. Psychol., 58:* 1114–1134.

[37]

Hormones, Emotional Dispositions, and Aggressive Attributes in Young Adolescents

Elizabeth J. Susman, Gale Inoff-Germain, and Editha D. Nottelmann
National Institute of Mental Health

D. Lynn Loriaux, Gordon B. Cutler, Jr., and George P. Chrousos
National Institute of Child Health and Human Development

SUSMAN, ELIZABETH J.; INOFF-GERMAIN, GALE; NOTTELMANN, EDITHA D.; LORIAUX, D. LYNN; CUTLER, GORDON B., JR.; and CHROUSOS, GEORGE P. *Hormones, Emotional Dispositions, and Aggressive Attributes in Young Adolescents.* CHILD DEVELOPMENT, 1987, 58, 1114–1134. Relations among hormone levels, emotional dispositions, and aggressive attributes were examined in 56 boys and 52 girls, age 9 to 14 years. The adolescents represented all 5 stages of pubertal development. Serum levels of gonadotropins, gonadal steroids, adrenal androgens, and testosterone-estradiol binding globulin were assessed. Levels of these hormones were related to stage of pubertal development and were assumed to represent relatively stable biological characteristics. The emotional dispositions assessed were adolescent self-reported anger, nervousness, sadness, and impulse control. The aggressive attributes assessed were mother-reported acting out and aggressive behavior problems and rebellious and nasty characteristics. Hormone levels were related to emotional dispositions and aggressive attributes for boys but not for girls. For example, higher levels of androstenedione in boys were related to higher levels of acting-out behavior problems. Level of testosterone-estradiol binding globulin was negatively related to sad affect and acting out behavior.

Puberty is a period of physical development accompanied by dramatic increases in the circulating levels of many hormones (Sizonenko, 1978; Williams, 1981). Puberty also is a period of psychological development characterized by increases in aggressive and rebellious behavior in most cultures (Weisfeld & Berger, 1983). How these two sets of changes relate to each other is the focus of the present study.

At a folk-wisdom level, hormonal changes are associated with behavior change in adolescents. The empirical evidence confirming this link is almost nonexistent. It is known that the rapid hormone changes at puberty include increases in androgens, which are presumed to be linked to aggressive behavior. In many species studied, aggression also increases at puberty, most clearly for males (Weisfeld & Berger, 1983).

The link between androgen levels and aggressive behavior in animals has been found consistently for males and sometimes for females (Bouissou, 1983; Eleftheriou & Sprott, 1975; also see Ellis, 1982). Furthermore, increases in androgen levels in males are implicated in the increases in aggression at puberty. In elegantly designed studies of aggression in mice, Cairns, MacCombie, and Hood (1983) found that at early sexual maturity, aggression began to rise in male mice. In humans, similar but less consistent androgen-aggression relations have been reported in adult males (Mazur & Lamb, 1980) and in late pubertal male adolescents (Olweus, Mattsson, Schalling, & Low, 1980). Females are less frequently studied than males with regard to hormonal influences on aggression.

The extensive animal literature demonstrating the role of hormones in aggression (e.g., Adams, 1983; Bouissou, 1983; Brain, 1977) and the growing psychoneuroendocrinology literature demonstrating the influence of hormones on the behavior of humans (e.g., Rose & Sachar, 1981; Sachar, 1980) provide the basis for the hypothesis that hormone levels are related to aggression in human adolescents. This study simultaneously examines hormone levels, emotions theoretically related to aggression, and aggression in a sample of male and female young adolescents.

The authors would like to thank Marian Radke-Yarrow for her support for all aspects of this project. Requests for reprints should be sent to Elizabeth J. Susman, Laboratory of Developmental Psychology, NIMH, Building 15K, 9000 Rockville Pike, Bethesda, MD 20892.

[Child Development, 1987, 58, 1114–1134. Copyright is not claimed for this article.]

Emotions and aggression.—An unanswered question is, What are the mechanisms whereby the effects of hormones become exhibited in aggressive behavior? One approach to answering this question involves emotional states in the hormone-aggressive behavior pathway. The emotions predisposing adolescents to overt aggressive behavior include rage (Berkowitz, 1964; Fonberg, 1979), sadness (Doering, Brodie, Kraemer, Moos, Becker, & Hamburg, 1975), and fear or anxiety (Bouissou, 1983; Ehrenkranz, Bliss, & Sheard, 1974; Frodi, Macaulay, & Thome, 1977; Leshner, 1983). Fear can have activating as well as inhibitory effects on aggression, depending on the circumstances. Emotions that can have inhibitory or antagonistic effects on the expression of aggression also include happiness or elation (Alpert, Cohen, Shaywitz, & Piccirillo, 1981; Fonberg, 1979). Aggression probably is motivated by multiple emotions that may or may not be experienced consciously by the aggressor.

The mechanisms whereby hormones influence emotions and behavior have been conceptualized in terms of the organizing and activating influences of hormones (Hays, 1981; Phoenix, Goy, Gerall, & Young, 1959; Tieger, 1980). Organizational influences stem from prenatal and perinatal hormone exposure, which affects the structure or functioning of the central nervous system such that development and functioning are altered. Activational influences stem from contemporaneous effects of hormones on behavior. Gonadal steroids are involved prenatally and perinatally in the organization of the central nervous system; during and after puberty, they serve primarily an activating function (Rubin, Reinisch, & Haskett, 1981; Young, Goy, & Phoenix, 1964). The organizing and activating influences of hormones may result in differences among groups, such as those found between the sexes as well as differences among individuals.

The organizing influence of hormones, as reflected in the degree of prenatal and perinatal exposure to gonadal steroids, may sensitize individuals in such a way that they differ with respect to their readiness for certain types of emotional responding (Marcus, Maccoby, Jacklin, & Doering, 1985). Individual differences in early hormone exposure were thought to account for sex differences in frequency, intensity, and age patterns of emotional behaviors, such as girls showing more fearfulness than boys and boys showing more anger and frustration reactions than girls. Links between neonatal hormone levels and predominant mood states in early childhood have been reported (Marcus et al., 1985). In most cases, hormones are presumed to be involved in emotions in children but are not examined.

Hormone links to emotions in adults also have been reported. Although not all the evidence has been consistent, findings indicate hormone links to both emotional states (Bardwick, 1976; de Lignieres & Vincens, 1982; Mazur & Lamb, 1980) and traits (Doering et al., 1975; Houser, 1979). Relations between changes in hormone levels and depression and other affective disorders (e.g., see Anisman & LaPierre, 1982; Puig-Antich, 1986) and premenstrual or menopausal symptoms (e.g., see Bardwick, 1976; de Lignieres & Vincens, 1982; Floody, 1983) also have been examined. Additionally, the bidirectional influence of hormone levels affecting behavior and behavior or experience (e.g., defeat) affecting hormone levels is well recognized in psychobiological research (Leshner, 1983). The pathway involving hormonal influences on behavior was the theoretical focus of this study.

In young adolescents, emotional states may undergo major perturbations as a sequelae of the rise in hormone levels at puberty. The activating influences of hormones may be reflected in the emotions of adolescents because neural tissues are target tissues for some puberty-related hormones. Disturbances in emotions also may reflect disequilibrium in biological processes that may stem from the rapidity of change in hormone levels. In our cross-sectional sample of young adolescents, hormone levels had not yet reached adult levels, even for the adolescents in the later stages of puberty. Therefore, the adolescents still may have been experiencing emotional perturbations related to increases in hormone levels.

In this study, four aspects of emotion were examined: anger, nervousness, sadness, and impulsivity. These aspects of emotion are referred to as "emotional dispositions." Rather than describing specific emotional states, they describe traits or dimensions of behavior similar to temperament or the behaviors examined in the Stanford Longitudinal Study (Maccoby, Doering, Jacklin, & Kraemer, 1979; Marcus et al., 1985). Impulsivity is not usually labeled an emotion, but it is considered to reflect characteristics of temperament. Impulsivity also is thought to link hormones and aggression (Olweus et al., 1980; Schlain, 1976).

While hormones may affect both positive and negative emotions, it is negative emotions that are implicated in aggression. If negative emotions are expressed in behavior, they are likely to be expressed as irritability, talking back, or some other similar negative attribute. It is this form of aggression that was investigated in the present study. Irritability and rebellious behaviors are more likely expressions of aggression in normal adolescents than physical attack. As in the case of emotions, the measures of aggression describe traits. They are referred to as "aggressive attributes."

We examined relations among (a) hormones and emotional dispositions, (b) hormones and aggressive attributes, and (c) hormones and emotional dispositions together and aggressive attributes. If the activational influences of hormones at puberty are reflected in emotional dispositions and emotional dispositions are reflected in aggressive attributes, then prediction of aggressive attribute scores should be improved by using both hormones and emotional dispositions, rather than hormones alone.

Sex differences.—Sex differences in the expression of aggression are reported for most species, but the degree and pattern of differences depend on the species and type of aggression being considered (Cummings, Hollenbeck, Iannotti, Radke-Yarrow, & Zahn-Waxler, 1986; Floody, 1983; Frodi et al., 1977). The most marked sex differences are seen in rank-related aggression (Brain, 1977). In most species, males tend to be more aggressive than females (Maccoby & Jacklin, 1974, 1980). Sex differences in socialization practices (Friedman, Richart, & Vande Wiele, 1974) and, as mentioned earlier, the organizing and activating influences of hormones (Gandelman, 1980; Hays, 1981; Tieger, 1980; van de Poll, Smeets, & van der Zwan, 1982) are viewed as important factors in sex differences in the expression of aggression.

State versus trait characteristics.—In addition to short-term variations within individuals, hormone levels also vary across individuals. In adolescents, a major source of the variation in hormone levels across individuals is associated with stage of pubertal development. The hormones examined in this study correlate with stage of pubertal development using Tanner criteria (Marshall & Tanner, 1969, 1970). Therefore, for adolescents progressing through puberty, the hormone levels represent the hormone analogue of psychological traits. In this study, individual differences in hormone levels were examined in relation to individual differences in typical or average behavior, that is, to psychological traits. The traits were the emotional dispositions and aggressive attributes. For human males, individual differences in testosterone level have related to the traits of aggressiveness, assertiveness, and impulsiveness, especially where provocation and threat were involved (Doering et al., 1975; Ehrenkranz et al., 1974; Houser, 1979; Mattsson, Schalling, Olweus, Low, & Svensson, 1980; Olweus et al., 1980; Persky, Smith, & Basu, 1971; Scaramella & Brown, 1978). Thus, in this study, both the hormone and behavior measures were assumed to assess traits.

Hormone-behavior specificity.—The literature on aggression provides few empirical findings relevant to developing hypotheses about which particular hormones should be related to aggression in healthy human young adolescents under normal conditions. In the Olweus et al. study (1980), testosterone levels related to certain aspects of aggression in adolescent males in the later stages of puberty. Hormone-aggression findings generally are based on studies of experimentally induced changes in hormone level (e.g., Bouissou, 1983), pathological conditions (Hines, 1982; Kelly, 1981; Siris, Siris, Van Kammen, Docherty, Alexander, & Bunney, 1980), unusual or prison samples (e.g., Ehrenkranz et al., 1974; Mattsson et al., 1980), or infrahumans (e.g., Bouissou, 1983; Rose, Bernstein, Gordon, & Lindsley, 1978). Whether these findings can be generalized to normal adolescents of both sexes is an open question.

The groups of hormones examined in this study were: gonadotropins (luteinizing hormone and follicle stimulating hormone), gonadal steroids (testosterone and estradiol), and adrenal androgens (dehydroepiandrosterone, dehydroepiandrosterone sulphate, and androstenedione). Testosterone-estradiol binding globulin also was measured. These hormones were chosen because of their contribution to sexual development (Sizonenko, 1978; Williams, 1981) and because of assumed links between sexual maturation and aggression (Cairns et al., 1983). Along with testosterone, it was hypothesized that higher levels of adrenal androgens would be related to higher levels of aggression. The adrenal glands are a major source of androgens during early puberty for boys and girls and throughout puberty for girls. It also was hypothesized that estrogen would be negatively related to aggression. Estrogen may inhibit aggression, especially in females. Estrogen levels are high during ovulation and pregnancy (Fregly

& Luttge, 1982), periods of the reproductive cycle during which aggression may be antithetical to species survival. Gonadotropins were included as measures to provide preliminary findings on their relation to emotions and aggression (see Lloyd, 1975; Rubin et al., 1981). To summarize, our hypothesis was that hormone levels, particularly androgen levels, would be positively related to negative emotional dispositions and aggressive attributes.

Method

Participants

Ten- to 14-year-old boys ($N = 56$) and 9–14-year-old girls ($N = 52$) and their parents were the participants in the study. The adolescents were assessed three times on both biological and psychological measures at 6-month intervals over 1 year. Information provided by the adolescents and their mothers at the first time of assessment was used in this report. Adolescents at all five stages of pubertal development, based on Tanner criteria (Marshall & Tanner, 1969, 1970), were included in the sample. There were at least seven adolescents of each sex at each stage of pubertal development. The wider age range of girls was necessary in order to include girls in all five stages of pubertal development. The adolescents were from intact families, although the parents were not necessarily the biological parents. The majority of the families were middle to upper middle class (Hollingshead, 1975).

Recruitment of participants was done mainly through notices distributed at churches, health clinics, community centers, and parent-teacher association and scout troop meetings. Families who contacted the project laboratory were sent a written explanation of the study. The project staff then contacted the family to determine if the family wished to participate. If the decision was positive, two appointments were scheduled: (a) a 4-hour visit for mother, father, and adolescent at a home-like laboratory, where most of the behavioral data were collected, and (b) a 2-hour visit for the adolescent and one parent at an outpatient clinic in a research hospital, where the biological data were collected. Mother and adolescent also made mood ratings at home during the week following the laboratory and clinic visits.

Procedure

Behavioral measures.—The adolescent, mother, and father were given a battery of standardized tests and interviews to assess various aspects of the adolescent's social, emotional, and cognitive development as well as family relationships. Measures for the present analyses were selected from the larger battery of tests based on the following criteria: (1) The measures had to be relevant to the theoretical perspective of the study. For the emotional dispositions, the following variables were included: (a) angry mood (angry-friendly), (b) anxious or fearful mood (nervous-calm), (c) sad mood (happy-sad and emotional tone), and (d) impulse control, which could affect whether or not aggressive tendencies are expressed as aggressive behavior. For the aggressive attributes, variables tapping delinquent (acting out), aggressive, rebellious, and "nasty" behavior were included. (2) The measures needed to be limited in number. The hormone levels, emotional dispositions, and aggressive attributes were analyzed using multiple regression. Therefore, the total number of variables selected was limited to take into account constraints related to number of variables and number of participants.

Angry-friendly, nervous-calm, and happy-sad.—The adolescents were instructed to complete a series of self-ratings at home at the end of every day for 5 consecutive days during the week following the laboratory and clinic visits. These self-ratings included angry-friendly, nervous-calm, and happy-sad. Ratings were made using five-point scales. Scores of 5 represented feeling very friendly to others, feeling very calm, and feeling very sad, respectively. For example, for angry-friendly, 1 = very angry, 2 = angry, 3 = neither angry nor friendly, 4 = friendly, and 5 = very friendly. Scores used in analyses are comprised of means across 5 days of self-ratings.

Stabilities for each of these ratings were assessed by correlating the mean of the scores for the odd days (days 1, 3, and 5) with the mean of the scores for the even days (days 2 and 4). For angry-friendly, nervous-calm, and happy-sad, the respective r's were .55, $p \leq .001$, .55, $p \leq .001$, and .33, $p \leq .05$, for boys and .32, $p \leq .05$, .26, $p \leq .10$, and .48, $p \leq .001$, for girls. Because these self-ratings reflected emotions, it was expected that there would be considerable day-to-day variability. The stability coefficients supported this expectation. In addition to intraindividual variability in emotions, there also was interindividual variability in emotions, which was reflected in the mean scores across 5 days of self ratings. Thus, means for angry-friendly, nervous-calm, and happy-sad were used as indices of emotional dispositions.

1118 Child Development

Emotional tone and impulse control.—Emotional tone and impulse control are subscales from the Offer Self-Image Questionnaire for Adolescents (Offer, Ostrov, & Howard, 1977). Wording of the items was modified for use with younger adolescents. Statements were rated by the adolescent on a six-point scale (1 = describes me very well; 6 = describes me not at all). Cronbach's alphas for the emotional tone and impulse control subscales, based on this sample, were .81 and .65, respectively. Examples of items from the emotional tone subscale are: "Most of the time I am happy" (negative weight) and "I often feel sad." Examples of items from the impulse control subscale are: "I rarely lose my temper (rarely get mad)" (negative weight) and "I get wild if I don't get my way." High scores on emotional tone indicate high levels of sadness. High scores on impulse control indicate problems with impulse control. The Offer Self-Image Questionnaire has been used on more than 120 samples, including younger and older teenagers. It differentiates among groups of normal, delinquent, and psychiatrically disturbed youths (Offer, Ostrov, & Howard, 1984).

Delinquent and aggressive.—The delinquent and aggressive measures are two subscales from the Child Behavior Checklist (CBC) (Achenbach & Edelbrock, 1979). The CBC consists of 113 behavior problems rated on a scale of 0 (not true of my child) to 2 (very true or often true of my child). The items are grouped into nine subscales for boys and eight subscales for girls. Mothers completed the checklist during the evening visit to the laboratory. While these two subscales do not include exactly the same items for boys and girls, they are very similar for both sexes. Examples of items (common to boys and girls) on the delinquent subscale are: disobeys at school, lies and cheats, steals at home, steals outside the home, and poor schoolwork. Examples of items (common to boys and girls) on the aggressive subscale are: argues, demands attention, sulks, stubborn, cruel to others, temper tantrums, and threatens people.

The CBC is a widely used instrument for which reliability and validity data are available (see Achenbach & Edelbrock, 1983). One-week test-retest reliabilities for the delinquent and aggressive subscales have ranged from .94 to .97 and .87 to .95, respectively. These subscales are highly correlated with scales from other instruments assessing similar dimensions. Ninety-eight percent of the items on the scale differentiate clinically referred from nonreferred but demographically similar children. (While the CBC subscale aggressive was actually labelled "aggressive," the variables delinquent, rebellious, and nasty also were assumed to index aspects of aggression.)

Rebellious.—The mother of each adolescent was instructed to rate her child on 28 items at the end of every day for 5 consecutive days during the week following the laboratory and clinic visits. The items consisted of adjectives (or verbs) that have been used in mood and behavior checklists and rating scales with established reliability and validity (e.g., the Multiple Affect Adjective Check List; Zuckerman & Lubin, 1965). The items were chosen on the basis of hypothesized relevance to emotional states and behaviors of adolescents. Mothers were instructed to rate each item on a seven-point scale (1 = not at all; 7 = very much) in terms of how it described their adolescent's mood or behavior that day. Mean scores across the 5 days of ratings were used in a varimax rotation of a principal components factor analysis. The rebellious attribute is the second of four factors derived from this analysis. High-loading items (with loadings given in parentheses) on the rebellious factor are: rebellious (.88), talks back (.88), sulks (.68), irritable (.64), irresponsible (.52), agreeable (−.52), cries (.51), and assertive (.51). Initial factor analyses were done separately for boys and girls. A four-factor solution identified in these analyses was highly similar for boys and girls. Factor scores used in the regression analyses reported here are based on the combined sample. The factor replicated across two independent samples: The correlation for the factor loadings for boys and girls was $r = .88$. Thus, the rebellious factor was viewed as representing a reliable structure.

Nasty.—Mothers rated their adolescents on 20 items modified from the Adolescent Q-Set (Block, 1971). The ratings were made during the evening visit to the laboratory. Using a seven-point scale (1 = not at all true; 7 = extremely true), each mother rated the degree to which each of the items was descriptive of her adolescent. The nasty attribute measure was the first of two factors derived from a varimax rotation of a principal components analysis. High-loading variables (with factor loadings given in parentheses) on the nasty factor are: tries to see how much he/she can get away with (.75), blames others for things (.71), tries to take advantage of others (.69), is jealous of others (.67), is stubborn (.65), is moody (.63), gets upset when he/she has to wait for things (.62), is obedient and well-behaved (−.58), and gets upset even at unimportant things (.57). Initial factor analyses were done separately for boys and girls. A two-factor solution in these analyses was highly similar for boys and girls. Factor scores used in the regression analyses are based on the combined sample. The factor replicated across two independent samples: The correlation for the factor loadings for boys and girls was $r = .89$. Thus, the nasty factor was viewed as representing a reliable structure.

Biological measures.—The biological measures were obtained during a 2-hour visit at an outpatient clinic. The clinic visit was scheduled within a mean number of 2.3 days from the behavioral measures assessment. The biological measures were obtained by a pediatric nurse practitioner or by an endocrinologist. For this report, pubertal stage was based on genital development for boys and breast development for girls (Marshall & Tanner, 1969, 1970). Interexaminer agreement for pubertal stage for boys and girls was $r = .99$ and 1.00, respectively.

Hormone levels may exhibit many types of variation that are relevant to the interpretation of findings: (1) diurnal variations, (2) minute-to-minute fluctuations because of the pulsatile release of some hormones, (3) variations related to stress responses to the experimental situation, (4) variations with age, (5) variations because of illness or other unusual circumstances such as pregnancy, (6) variations related to the menstrual cycle, and (7) other interindividual variations related to constitutional or genetic characteristics.

To minimize the effects of diurnal variations, blood samples were collected between the hours of 8:00 and 10:00 A.M. To minimize the effects of minute-to-minute fluctuations due to pulsatile release of hormones, three blood samples were drawn at 0, 20, and 40 min. Mean values for the three samples were used in statistical analyses. One sample of testosterone-estradiol binding globulin was obtained at Time 0 only. There were significant differences among the three samples for only one measure—testosterone in boys. Testosterone level decreased across the three samples, but the post hoc tests were not significant. Use of the mean hormone levels based on three samples also minimized the effects of stress on our results. Adolescents may vary in the timing of their physiological stress responses to the phlebotomy procedure. Some adolescents may have heightened physiological responses prior to the venipuncture as a result of anticipatory anxiety. Others may not respond until they actually experience the venipuncture itself. Therefore, no one sample was viewed, a priori, as more reliable than any other sample.

Hormones also vary with age as a result of timing and rate of maturation. The decision regarding whether or not to control for age in statistical analyses was complicated by the fact that developmental phenomena are of interest in this study. For that reason, statistical analyses were done controlling for age as well as without controlling for age. Variations in hormone levels due to unusual circumstances such as illness or disease were minimized by excluding adolescents with a history of major health problems that could have affected hormone levels (e.g., adolescents with diabetes). The adolescents had no known chronic illnesses or major health problems at the time of study.

Menstrual cycle–related variations in hormone levels in females were not controlled in this study. In the sample of 52 girls, 34 (65%) were premenarcheal and 18 (35%) were menarcheal. The probability of a regular cycle of increases and decreases in hormone levels related to ovulation varies with gynecological age (duration of time since first menses) (Vihko & Apter, 1980). However, menarche does not absolutely differentiate girls who show hormone cycles from those who do not. Menarche merely is the culmination of a long series of endocrine changes that are occurring at least 2 years prior to menarche (Apter & Vihko, 1985). Thus, variations in hormone levels in both the premenarcheal and menarcheal girls may introduce error in the data to an unknown extent.

Finally, no attempts were made to control for interindividual variations related to constitutional or genetic characteristics.

Radioimmunoassays were performed according to the following techniques: luteinizing hormone (Odell, Ross, & Rayford, 1967); follicle stimulating hormone (Cargille & Rayford, 1970); testosterone (Nieschlag & Loriaux, 1972); estradiol (Abraham, Buster, Lucas, Corrales, & Teller, 1972); and dehydroepiandrosterone, dehydroepiandrosterone sulfate, and androstenedione (Cutler, Glenn, Bush, Hodgen, Graham, & Loriaux, 1978). Testosterone-estradiol binding globulin, a glycoprotein produced by the liver that serves in binding and transporting gonadal steroids, was measured by a competitive binding assay (Dunn, Nisula, & Rodbard, 1981). The serum concentrations of this glycoprotein change

1120 Child Development

during puberty in boys (Cunningham, Loughlin, Culliton, & McKenna, 1984). Testosterone-estradiol binding globulin influences the fraction of testosterone that is free (unbound) and active. Findings involving testosterone-estradiol binding globulin indirectly may provide information about the effects of free testosterone. The testosterone to estradiol ratio also was computed and used in the analyses. Interassay and intraassay coefficients of variation and assay detection limits appear elsewhere (Nottelmann et al. 1987b).

Results

Mean Levels and Sex Differences

Behavioral measures.—Means and standard deviations for the behavioral variables for boys and girls appear in the top half of Table 1. Analysis of variance for sex differences was conducted for seven of the nine behavioral variables. There were no significant mean level differences between boys and girls. The two Child Behavior Checklist subscales, delinquent and aggressive behavior problems, are highly similar for boys and girls, but some of the items are different for the sexes. Therefore, tests for sex differences were not conducted for these two variables.

Hormone levels.—Means and standard deviations for the hormone levels for boys and girls appear in the bottom half of Table 1. The means and standard deviations by pubertal stage appear elsewhere (Nottelmann et al., 1987b). Analysis of variance for sex differences was conducted for the nine hormone measures (see Table 1). Boys were significantly higher than girls for level of testosterone, the testosterone to estradiol ratio, and dehydroepiandrosterone sulphate. Girls were significantly higher than boys for level of luteinizing hormone, follicle stimulating hormone, estradiol, and androstenedione. There were no significant group differences between boys and girls for dehydroepiandrosterone or testosterone-estradiol binding globulin.

Intercorrelations

Behavioral variables.—Intercorrelations among the behavioral measures for boys and girls appear in Table 2. In general, the behav-

TABLE 1

MEANS, STANDARD DEVIATIONS, AND F RATIOS FOR SEX DIFFERENCES FOR BEHAVIORAL MEASURES AND HORMONE LEVELS FOR BOYS AND GIRLS

	Boys			Girls			
	$\bar{X}$	SD	N	$\bar{X}$	SD	N	F
Behavioral measures:							
Angry-friendly............	3.50	.61	52	3.50	.64	49	.00
Nervous-calm............	3.51	.68	52	3.29	.67	48	2.84
Happy-sad	2.17	.40	53	2.15	.67	49	.02
Emotional tone	2.22	.68	55	2.22	.73	52	.00
Impulse control...........	2.86	.68	55	2.91	.57	52	.12
Delinquent...............	57.80	4.05	55	58.33	4.73	52	...
Aggressive	58.65	6.17	55	58.50	5.86	52	...
Rebellious	−.11	.86	53	.12	1.13	48	1.31
Nasty	−.04	1.11	56	.05	.88	52	.22
Hormone levels:							
LH (mIU/ml).............	5.66	3.74	54	7.58	5.68	51	4.26*
FSH (mIU/ml)...........	6.97	4.74	54	9.12	4.98	51	5.16*
T (ng/dl)................	214.65	204.35	55	19.25	9.24	52	47.43***
E_2 (pg/ml)..............	12.79	8.19	48	44.99	49.61	50	19.70***
T/E_2 (ng/l)..............	158.10	142.95	48	9.01	8.64	50	54.21***
TeBG (ug/dl)	1.91	1.29	42	1.87	1.16	34	.02
DHEA (ng/dl)	256.01	139.86	54	240.48	162.46	50	.27
DHEAS (ug/dl)	104.57	51.08	55	71.98	41.79	52	12.96***
Δ4-A (ng/dl)	62.27	41.14	52	87.18	54.25	51	6.91**

NOTE.—LH = luteinizing hormone, FSH = follicle stimulating hormone, T = testosterone, E_2 = estradiol, T/E_2 = testosterone to estradiol ratio, TeBG = testosterone-estradiol binding globulin, DHEA = dehydroepiandrosterone, DHEAS = dehydroepiandrosterone sulphate, Δ4-A = androstenedione.

* $p \leq .05$.
** $p \leq .01$.
*** $p \leq .001$.

TABLE 2

INTERCORRELATIONS OF BEHAVIORAL MEASURES FOR BOYS AND GIRLS

	1	2	3	4	5	6	7	8	9
1. Angry-friendly		.59***	−.48***	−.28	−.15	.03	.06	−.09	.19
2. Nervous-calm	.41**		−.20	−.28	−.14	−.06	−.08	−.12	.01
3. Happy-sad	−.39***	−.08		.28	.35**	.04	.15	.16	.10
4. Emotional tone	−.24	−.07	.14		.57***	−.07	.00	.02	.01
5. Impulse control	−.21	−.17	.10	.60***		.02	.15	.03	.05
6. Delinquent	−.24	−.38**	.04	.20	.30*		.70***	.45***	.49***
7. Aggressive	−.12	−.20	−.13	.07	.27*	.61***		.62***	.72***
8. Rebellious	−.16	.13	.24	.06	.00	−.05	.14		.56***
9. Nasty	−.22	−.21	−.01	.07	.23	.56***	.65***	.27*	

NOTE.—The correlation coefficients below the diagonal are for boys; those above the diagonal are for girls. N's range from 52 to 56 for boys and from 47 to 52 for girls.

* $p \leq .05$.
** $p \leq .01$.
*** $p \leq .001$.

ioral measures showed only minimal to moderate intercorrelations. The strongest relations were among the measures of aggression, although, even there, there was considerable independence of each measure.

Hormone levels.—Intercorrelations of the hormone levels for boys and girls appear in Table 3. There were moderate to high intercorrelations among the hormone levels.

Correlations with Age

Behavioral measures.—Only one of the behavioral measures was significantly correlated with age, emotional tone ($r = .36$, $p \leq .01$), for males only. High scores on emotional tone denote sad affect.

Hormone levels.—For boys, there were significant positive correlations between age and luteinizing hormone ($r = .46$, $p \leq .001$), follicle stimulating hormone ($r = .40$, $p \leq .01$), testosterone ($r = .54$, $p \leq .001$), the testosterone to estradiol ratio ($r = .56$, $p \leq .001$), dehydroepiandrosterone ($r = .29$, $p \leq .05$), and androstenedione ($r = .32$, $p \leq .05$). There was a significant negative correlation between age and testosterone-estradiol binding globulin ($r = -.40$, $p \leq .01$). Estradiol and dehydroepiandrosterone sulphate were not significantly correlated with age. For girls, there were significant positive correlations between age and luteinizing hormone ($r = .52$, $p \leq .001$), follicle stimulating hormone ($r = .40$, $p \leq .01$), testosterone ($r = .56$, $p \leq .001$), estradiol ($r = .52$, $p \leq .001$), dehydroepiandrosterone ($r = .40$, $p \leq .01$), dehydroepiandrosterone sulphate ($r = .53$, $p \leq .001$), and androstenedione ($r = .65$, $p \leq .001$). There was a significant negative correlation between age and the testosterone to estradiol ratio ($r = -.44$, $p \leq .001$). Testosterone-estradiol binding globulin was not significantly correlated with age.

Regression Analyses

Findings are reported for three separate sets of regression analyses: (*a*) the hormones as predictors of emotional dispositions, (*b*) the hormones as predictors of aggressive attributes, and (*c*) both hormones and emotional dispositions as predictors of aggressive attributes. In the reporting of findings, the terms predictor, dependent variable, and independent variable are used for their statistical meaning and not to imply causality. The zero-order correlations between the hormones and the behavioral variables appear in Table 4.

Both the hormones and the emotional dispositions were entered into the regression equations as sets of independent variables. The hormones were entered as a set into the regression equations because they appear to act in synchrony in bringing about maturation during puberty. The exact mechanisms regulating pituitary, gonadal, and adrenal functioning and, thus, the relative levels of these hormones under various circumstances are currently being examined extensively. What is known is that some combination of these hormones is responsible for normal pubertal maturation. Therefore, the set of hormones was entered into regression equations. There was only a moderate degree of multicollinearity among the hormones.

The emotional dispositions also were entered as a set into the regression equations because they were assumed collectively to reflect important aspects of the emotional development of adolescents. By treating the hormones or the behaviors as sets in terms of how they relate to the dependent variables, the set is effectively reduced to a single variable (Cohen & Cohen, 1975). In each multiple regression analysis, the overall F test for each equation is tested for its statistical significance. The individual variables within the set also are tested for their significance by a standard t test, such that the partial contribution of each individual independent variable is assessed (Cohen & Cohen, 1975). The partial contribution of each individual independent variable to the overall result is reflected in its beta weight. In the analyses reported here, all significant results are reported, but findings involving significant betas should be interpreted with caution if the overall F is not also significant.

Hormones and emotional dispositions.—The hormone values (luteinizing hormone, follicle stimulating hormone, testosterone, estradiol, the testosterone to estradiol ratio, testosterone-estradiol binding globulin, dehydroepiandrosterone, dehydroepiandrosterone sulphate, and androstenedione) were entered into the regression equations as a set of independent variables with adolescent emotional dispositions as the dependent variables (angry-friendly, nervous-calm, happy-sad, emotional tone, and impulse control). For each dependent variable, the betas and overall R, R^2, and F ratio appear in Table 5. The findings shown are for boys only. There were no significant findings for girls.

Emotional tone was the only emotional disposition that was related to chronological age. Therefore, for multiple regression to emotional tone, age was entered into the equation first, so as to control for the relation between age and emotional tone before the

TABLE 3

INTERCORRELATIONS OF HORMONE LEVELS AND PUBERTAL STAGE FOR BOYS AND GIRLS

	LH	FSH	T	E_2	T/E_2	TeBG	DHEA	DHEAS	Δ4-A	Pubertal Stage
LH		.63***	.47***	.49***	-.32*	-.16	.24	.41**	.57***	.56***
FSH	.51***		.47***	.20	-.20	-.23	.22	.26	.39**	.34*
T	.61***	.60***		.43**	-.08	.25	.29*	.42***	.62***	.48***
E_2	.41**	.43**	.63***		-.51***	.16	.33*	.35**	.76***	.55***
T/E_2	.41**	.44**	.68***	.01		-.07	-.21	-.21	-.38*	-.47***
TeBG	-.31*	-.30*	-.45**	-.35*	-.34*		-.02	-.23	.03	.02
DHEA	.26	.39**	.39**	.26	.31*	-.31*		.53***	.60***	.37**
DHEAS	.14	.20	.13	.16	-.01	-.25	.59***		.57***	.46***
Δ4-A	.27	.42**	.50***	.49***	.41**	-.36*	.56***	.31*		.61***
Pubertal stage[a]	.60***	.53***	.82***	.46***	.69***	-.57***	.38**	.14	.53***	

SOURCE.—Nottelmann et al., 1987b.
NOTE.—LH = luteinizing hormone, FSH = follicle stimulating hormone, T = testosterone, E_2 = estradiol, T/E_2 = testosterone to estradiol ratio, TeBG = testosterone-estradiol binding globulin, DHEA = dehydroepiandrosterone, DHEAS = dehydroepiandrosterone sulphate, Δ4-A = androstenedione. Correlations below the diagonal are for boys; correlations above the diagonal are for girls. N's range from 42 to 55 for boys and 34 to 52 for girls.

[a] Pubertal stage is represented by genital development for boys and breast development for girls.
* $p \leq .05$.
** $p \leq .01$.
*** $p \leq .001$.

TABLE 4

Zero-Order Correlations of Behavioral Measures with Hormone Levels

Behavioral Measures	\multicolumn{9}{c}{Hormones}								
	LH	FSH	T	E_2	T/E_2	TeBG	DHEA	DHEAS	Δ4-A
Boys:									
Angry-friendly	-.06	.05	-.05	-.04	-.07	.08	-.20	-.08	-.16
Nervous-calm	.25	-.05	.10	.25	-.09	-.17	-.07	-.14	-.01
Happy-sad	.17	.12	.13	.32*	-.07	-.15	.35**	.22	.23
Emotional tone	.06	.18	-.07	.11	-.13	-.31*	.10	.03	.28*
Impulse control	-.11	.06	-.13	-.04	-.10	-.26	.19	-.05	.20
Delinquent	.01	.17	.10	-.11	.22	-.21	.19	-.02	.41**
Aggressive	-.08	-.07	.06	-.12	.15	-.21	.06	-.12	.16
Rebellious	.32*	-.15	-.01	.03	-.04	-.24	.28*	.22	-.03
Nasty	.01	-.21	.02	-.15	.10	-.06	.02	-.14	.15
Girls:									
Angry-friendly	.06	-.18	.08	.17	.09	.24	-.01	.17	.08
Nervous-calm	.22	-.04	.18	.08	.14	.20	-.01	.29*	.12
Happy-sad	.19	.21	.02	.17	-.22	-.06	.13	-.01	.10
Emotional tone	.16	.20	.02	.13	-.09	.15	.10	.06	.14
Impulse control	.27*	.29*	-.05	.15	-.26	-.17	.09	.06	.21
Delinquent	-.08	-.02	-.15	.00	-.04	.07	-.11	-.17	-.11
Aggressive	-.03	-.05	-.21	-.10	.04	-.01	-.26	-.33*	-.22
Rebellious	-.13	-.14	-.27	-.09	-.01	-.08	-.20	-.24	-.20
Nasty	-.26	-.28*	-.19	-.14	.14	.18	-.12	-.34**	-.27*

Note.—LH = luteinizing hormone, FSH = follicle stimulating hormone, T = testosterone, E_2 = estradiol, T/E_2 = testosterone to estradiol ratio, TeBG = testosterone-estradiol binding globulin, DHEA = dehydroepiandrosterone, DHEAS = dehydroepiandrosterone sulfate, Δ4-A = androstenedione. For boys, N's range from 40 to 55; for girls, N's range from 30 to 52.

* $p \leq .05$.
** $p \leq .01$.

TABLE 5

MULTIPLE REGRESSION OF HORMONE LEVELS TO EMOTIONAL DISPOSITIONS FOR BOYS: BETA WEIGHT FOR EACH HORMONE MEASURE, MULTIPLE R, R^2, AND F RATIO

EMOTIONAL DISPOSITIONS	AGE	LH	FSH	T	E_2	T/E_2	TeBG	DHEA	DHEAS	Δ4-A	R	R^2	F^a
Angry-friendly	...	-.09	.22	.06	-.01	-.03	.03	-.22	.06	-.12	.28	.08	.25
Nervous-calm	...	.34	-.23	-.04	.21	-.17	-.20	.04	-.23	-.04	.47	.22	.87
Happy-sad	...	.14	-.07	-.27	.37	-.03	-.03	.39	-.03	-.03	.48	.23	.88
Emotional tone	.59***	.02	.28	-.15	-.40	-.82**	-.35*	-.04	-.23	.54**	.77	.59	3.74**
Impulse control	...	-.04	.20	.08	-.53	-.65	-.45*	.35	-.46*	.40	.62	.38	1.87

NOTE.—LH = luteinizing hormone, FSH = follicle stimulating hormone, T = testosterone, E_2 = estradiol, T/E_2 = testosterone to estradiol ratio, TeBG = testosterone-estradiol binding globulin, DHEA = dehydroepiandrosterone, DHEAS = dehydroepiandrosterone sulfate, Δ4-A = androstenedione. Results presented are for boys only. There were no significant findings for girls.

[a] Df's were 9,27 for all measures except emotional tone, for which df was 10,26.
* $p \leq .05$.
** $p \leq .01$.
*** $p \leq .001$.

1126 Child Development

relation between the set of hormones and emotional tone was assessed. Higher emotional tone, indicating sad affect, was related to older age. The set of hormones was significantly related to emotional tone. Higher emotional tone was related to lower testosterone to estradiol ratios, lower levels of testosterone-estradiol binding globulin, and higher levels of androstenedione. Difficulty with impulse control also was related to lower levels of testosterone-estradiol binding globulin and lower levels of dehydroepiandrosterone sulphate, but the overall F was not significant.

Hormones and aggressive attributes.—The same hormones were entered into the regression equations as a set of independent variables with aggressive attributes as the dependent variables (delinquent, aggressive, rebellious, and nasty behavior). For each independent variable, the betas and overall R, R^2, and F ratio appear in Table 6. These results are for boys only. The set of hormones was significantly related to delinquent and rebellious behavior problems. There were no significant findings for girls. Higher scores on delinquent behavior problems were related to lower levels of estradiol and higher levels of androstenedione. Higher scores on the rebellious attribute were related to higher levels of luteinizing hormone, lower levels of follicle stimulating hormone, and higher levels of dehydroepiandrosterone. Higher scores on the nasty factor also were related to higher levels of androstenedione, but the overall F was not significant.

Hormones, emotional dispositions, and the aggressive attributes.—The hormones were entered into the regression equations as a set, followed by the emotional dispositions as a second set of independent variables predicting the aggressive attributes. The hormones were entered into the equation first because they were assumed to be causally prior to the emotional dispositions and aggressive attributes. Emotional dispositions and aggressive behaviors also may affect hormone levels. However, it is unlikely that emotions and aggressive behaviors are totally responsible for the rapid increases in hormones during puberty, and that changes in the emotions and behavior of adolescents during puberty are totally unaffected by these hormone changes. Emotional dispositions were entered into the regression equations second. Therefore, the variance accounted for by emotional dispositions is the increment that is added after controlling for the variance accounted for by the hormones.

For each dependent variable, the betas and overall R, R^2, and F ratio appear in Table 7. The findings shown are for boys only. There were no significant findings for girls. Hormones and emotional dispositions, jointly, were significantly related to delinquent behavior problems in boys. For delinquent behavior problems, three additional single hormones and one emotional disposition became significant when the emotional dispositions were added to the equation. Higher scores on delinquent behavior problems were related to lower testosterone to estradiol ratios, lower levels of testosterone-estradiol binding globulin, lower levels of dehydroepiandrosterone sulphate, and lower levels of calm disposition (higher nervousness), in addition to lower levels of estradiol and higher levels of androstenedione. Further, the multiple R for delinquent behavior problems increased from .66 to .76 as a function of adding the emotional dispositions to the regression equation. The overall F for rebellious attributes became nonsignificant when the additional variables were added. Similarly, the betas for follicle stimulating hormone and dehydroepiandrosterone in predicting rebellious attributes became nonsignificant.

Age, Hormones, Emotional Dispositions, and Aggressive Attributes

As mentioned previously, age was correlated with only one behavioral variable, emotional tone. For the regression analysis predicting to emotional tone, age was entered first into the equation, and the beta for age was significant. Although age was not related to the other behavioral variables, age was related to most hormone levels. Therefore, the relations between hormones and the other behavioral variables were examined when age was controlled for by entering it first into the regression equations. Analyses parallel to those described above were conducted. Including age in the regression equations did not affect the pattern of findings.

Pubertal stage.—For boys, pubertal stage was significantly related to luteinizing hormone, follicle stimulating hormone, testosterone, estradiol, the testosterone to estradiol ratio, testosterone-estradiol binding globulin (negative relation), dehydroepiandrosterone, and androstenedione (see Table 3). Pubertal stage did not relate to dehydroepiandrosterone sulphate. For girls, pubertal stage was significantly related to luteinizing hormone, follicle stimulating hormone, testosterone, estradiol, the testosterone to estradiol ratio (negative relation), dehydroepiandrosterone, dehydroepiandrosterone sulphate, and an-

TABLE 6

MULTIPLE REGRESSION OF HORMONE LEVELS TO AGGRESSIVE ATTRIBUTES FOR BOYS: BETA WEIGHT FOR EACH HORMONE MEASURE, MULTIPLE R, R^2, AND F RATIO

AGGRESSIVE ATTRIBUTES	HORMONES									R	R^2	F^a
	LH	FSH	T	E_2	T/E_2	TeBG	DHEA	DHEAS	$\Delta 4$-A			
Delinquent	−.02	.19	.56	−.95***	−.64	−.25	.03	−.30	.77**	.66	.43	2.28*
Aggressive	−.11	−.11	.60	−.67	−.44	−.31	.09	−.31	.37	.49	.24	.93
Rebellious	.57**	−.44*	−.38	.14	.04	−.25	.46*	−.00	−.23	.67	.45	2.44*
Nasty	.15	−.36	.65	−.73	−.53	−.14	.07	−.30	.51*	.53	.28	1.16

NOTE.—LH = luteinizing hormone, FSH = follicle stimulating hormone, T = testosterone, E_2 = estradiol, T/E_2 = testosterone to estradiol ratio, TeBG = testosterone-estradiol binding globulin, DHEA = dehydroepiandrosterone, DHEAS = dehydroepiandrosterone sulfate, $\Delta 4$-A = androstenedione. Results are for boys only. There were no significant findings for girls.
[a] Df's were 9,27.
* $p \leq .05$.
** $p \leq .01$.
*** $p \leq .001$.

TABLE 7

MULTIPLE REGRESSION OF HORMONE LEVELS AND EMOTIONAL DISPOSITIONS TO AGGRESSIVE ATTRIBUTES FOR BOYS

AGGRESSIVE ATTRIBUTES	HORMONES								
	LH	FSH	T	E_2	T/E_2	TeBG	DHEA	DHEAS	Δ4-A
Delinquent	.15	.16	.52	−.95**	−.85*	−.44*	.06	−.46*	.86**
Aggressive	.04	−.15	.50	−.56	−.54	−.42	.12	−.38	.41
Rebellious	.57*	−.43	−.35	.07	−.03	−.30	.48	−.06	−.21
Nasty	.28	−.41	.60	−.65	−.59	−.21	.05	−.35	.52

	EMOTIONAL DISPOSITIONS							
	Angry-Friendly	Nervous-Calm	Happy-Sad	Emotional Tone	Impulse Control	R	R^2	F^a
Delinquent	−.04	−.43*	−.02	−.19	−.04	.76	.58	2.21*
Aggressive	−.01	−.30	−.16	−.19	.11	.57	.33	.76
Rebellious	−.01	−.06	.06	.04	−.13	.68	.46	1.35
Nasty	−.03	−.31	−.03	−.14	.11	.61	.37	.93

NOTE.—LH = luteinizing hormone, FSH = follicle stimulating hormone, T = testosterone, E_2 = estradiol, T/E_2 = testosterone to estradiol ratio, TeBG = testosterone-estradiol binding globulin, DHEA = dehydroepiandrosterone, DHEAS = dehydroepiandrosterone sulfate, Δ4-A = androstenedione. Results are for boys only. There were no significant findings for girls.
^a Df's were 14,22.
* $p \leq .05$.
** $p \leq .01$.
*** $p \leq .001$.

drostenedione. Pubertal stage did not relate to testosterone-estradiol binding globulin.

To determine whether the relations among hormone levels, emotional dispositions, and aggressive attributes were changed by including pubertal stage in the equation, the following regression analyses were conducted: (a) The hormones as a set were entered into the equation first, followed by pubertal stage, in predicting each of the emotional dispositions and aggressive attributes. (b) The hormones as a set were entered into the equation first, followed by pubertal stage, followed by the emotional dispositions as a set, in predicting each of the aggressive attributes. (c) Pubertal stage was entered into the equation first, followed by the emotional dispositions as a set, in predicting each of the aggressive attributes. In all cases, entering pubertal stage into the equations did not change the previous results.

Discussion

Hormone levels were related to both emotional dispositions and aggressive attributes for boys, but not for girls. For the emotional dispositions, the strongest relations were between hormones and sad affect (based on the emotional tone subscale) and anxious affect. For the aggressive attributes, the strongest relations were between hormones and delinquent (acting-out) and rebellious behavior.

Our expectations regarding specific hormone-behavior relations were confirmed in some cases but not in others. The expectation that serum testosterone levels (which include bound and unbound testosterone) would be related to negative emotional dispositions and aggressive attributes was not supported directly. Olweus et al. (1980) reported associations between testosterone and a specific type of aggression, response to provocation and threat and lack of frustration tolerance. Testosterone was not associated with many of the items that also were expected to index aggressive behavior. Our sample of adolescents differed from the Olweus et al. sample. While the Olweus et al. sample was limited to male adolescents in the later stages of puberty, adolescents from each of the five pubertal stages were included in our sample. Thus, the testosterone levels in the Olweus et al. adolescents were likely to be close to reaching adult levels for many of the adolescents, while the testosterone levels in our adolescents had not yet reached adult levels for the majority of adolescents.

Although testosterone levels and aggression were not directly related, there was some evidence linking testosterone and emotional dispositions and aggressive attributes in males. The level of testosterone-estradiol binding globulin, a carrier protein which serves in binding and transporting of gonadal steroids, was negatively related to sad affect. Furthermore, when both hormones and emotional dispositions were used to predict aggressive attributes, testosterone-estradiol binding globulin level was negatively related to delinquent behavior problems. As total testosterone and testosterone-estradiol binding globulin are negatively correlated, these relations between testosterone-estradiol binding globulin in males and the behavioral variables are consistent with our prediction for total testosterone. The pattern of findings for adrenal androgens, androstenedione and, to a lesser degree, dehydroepiandrosterone, in males, was consistent with what was expected for androgens of gonadal origin. Higher levels were related to sad affect and delinquent and rebellious behavior problems. Higher levels of adrenal androgens and higher degrees of negative behavior is a pattern that we have identified in other aspects of our larger study (Nottelmann et al., 1987a). While little is known about the influences of adrenal androgens on behavior, it may be speculated that their effects parallel those of androgens of gonadal origin.

The findings relating specific hormones and emotional dispositions and aggressive attributes should be interpreted with caution. Two factors should be considered. First, the significant beta weights may be affected by the nature of the distribution of each hormone and behavioral variable in the equation. Therefore, the significant betas may reflect random rather than true associations between specific hormones and specific emotional dispositions and aggressive attributes. Thus, a conservative interpretation of our findings is that some linear combination of hormones relates to emotional dispositions and aggressive attributes in boys. Second, a particular relation cannot be interpreted as meaning that that specific hormone is the active metabolic ingredient associated with an emotion or behavior. The hormones that we measured are metabolized into other substances which may, in turn, act on neural tissue. For instance, testosterone may be aromatized into estradiol. Estradiol is generally hypothesized to be the active metabolic substance affecting central nervous system functioning, which in turn may influence the expression of aggression (Clark & Nowell, 1979). Experimental

1130 Child Development

studies or experiments in nature (e.g., with hypogonadal males) are the preferred method for determining the causal role of specific hormones on behavior.

The assumption that emotional states are involved in the hormone-aggressive behavior pathway received only moderate support. The addition of emotional dispositions to the hormones in the regression equations improved the multiple R of the hormones in predicting delinquent behavior problems in boys so as to account for an additional 15% of the variance. In the case of rebellious attributes, the multiple R became nonsignificant when additional variables were added to the equation.

Nervous-calm, an index of anxiety, was the emotional disposition significantly related to delinquent behavior problems in the regression equation in which both hormones and emotions were entered. Higher anxiety was related to more delinquent behavior problems in boys. The role of fear or anxiety in mediating the expression of aggressive behavior has been examined in animals and, to a lesser extent, in humans (Ehrenkranz et al., 1974; Frodi et al., 1977). Determining the specific mechanisms whereby anxiety affects aggression is complicated by the fact that anxiety may have inhibitory as well as activating effects on the expression of aggression. As with the other relations, our cross-sectional findings do not allow us to assign a causal link between anxiety and aggression.

Sad affect also was related to hormone levels. These findings are consistent with research on the psychoneuroendocrinology of emotions in adults. Disturbances in hypothalamic-pituitary-adrenal (Chrousos, Schuermeyer, Oldfield, Doppman, Schulte, Gold, & Loriaux, 1985; Gold & Chrousos, 1985) and hypothalamic-pituitary-gonadal (Rubinow, Roy-Byrne, & Hoban, 1985) axes functioning have been reported in individuals with clinical depression. The findings relating sad affect to specific hormones among boys should be interpreted with caution for the reasons mentioned earlier. However, the question of whether changes in hormone levels are causal factors in the appearance of depressive symptoms in adolescents is an important one. Kandel and Davies (1986) reported that feelings of dysphoria in adolescence predicted similar feelings in adulthood as well as use of habit-forming substances and problems in peer and family relationships. A question for future research is whether the degree of sensitivity to changes in hormones during puberty, when hormone changes are most dramatic, predicts affective disorders or other emotional characteristics later in the lifespan.

Pubertal stage did not relate to the emotional dispositions or the aggressive attributes. Similarly, Olweus and colleagues (1980) failed to find relations between pubertal stage and aggression. Pubertal stage was related to cognitive abilities as well as characteristics of parent-child interactions in previous studies of adolescents (Steinberg, 1981; Steinberg & Hill, 1978). In recent studies, external indices of pubertal status generally have not related to many behaviors during adolescence. When such relations are found, they tend to be small in number and inconsistent across domains of behavior (Susman et al., in press).

The complete absence of relations between hormone level and both emotional dispositions and aggressive attributes for girls was striking. One explanation for this lack of findings involves the error introduced by menstrual cycle–related variations in hormone levels. While only 35% of the girls had reached menarche, these girls were in various phases of the menstrual cycle when they participated in the study. Considerable controversy exists in the literature regarding the validity and reliability of relations between phase of the menstrual cycle and behavioral variability (Rubinow & Roy-Byrne, 1984). If phase of the menstrual cycle influences emotions and aggression, then our findings might have been influenced to an unknown extent by the variations in behavior related to phase of the menstrual cycle. Hormone-level variability even in the girls who were premenarcheal also may have affected our findings to an unknown extent. For example, level of follicle stimulating hormone shows an increase in girls as young as 7 (see Apter & Vihko, 1985, for a comprehensive longitudinal study of hormone level variations in 7–17-year-old girls).

The possibility that error is introduced by menstrual cycle–related variations in hormone levels did not negate the value of measuring hormone levels in girls. Correlations between hormone levels and pubertal stage were similar in boys and girls in this study. Furthermore, in other aspects of our larger study, hormone levels were related to behavioral measures in our sample of girls. For example, girls who were earlier maturers based on hormone levels were found to be higher on sad affect and to spend less time with peers than did later maturers (Susman et al., 1985). However, relations between hormones and behaviors were much stronger and more consistent for boys than for girls for the behaviors that we have examined. The less consistent pattern of findings for girls is also consistent with previous studies by other investigators. Marcus and colleagues (1985) found many of the correlations between neonatal sex steroid levels and behavior in early childhood for girls to be lower and nonsignificant or opposite in sign from the correlations for boys.

Our aggressive attributes failed to discriminate between males and females in level of aggression. There were no differences between males and females on rebellious and nasty attributes, the two attributes for which we could test for sex differences. Males generally are reported to be more aggressive than females (Maccoby & Jacklin, 1980), although sex differences in aggression tend to be greater in younger rather than in older children (Hyde, 1984). Females can be highly aggressive under certain circumstances, for example, those involving defense of one's young (Rose, Bernstein, Gordon, & Catlin, 1974) or those in which aggression is positively sanctioned. For many species, hormonal abnormalities or treatments also can increase aggressive behavior in females (Floody, 1983). In addition to there being no mean level difference between boys and girls on the behavioral measures, the behavioral measures were not related to hormone levels in females. Thus, we are unable to discern whether the measures were inadequate to assess aggression in females or whether aggression in females is unaffected by changes in hormone levels at puberty. It may be that levels of aggressive behavior and dominance shown by females are influenced more by social interactions and relationships than by hormonal changes (Floody, 1983; Marcus et al., 1985). Thus, males and females could show comparable overall levels of aggression but have different correlates of aggression.

In conclusion, relations between hormones and some emotional dispositions and aggressive attributes were found for boys but not for girls. This pattern of findings indicates that puberty-related hormone changes may not be as important in the development of aggression in adolescents as previously speculated. These findings, including the lack of findings for girls, need to be replicated, and future studies need to be extended to include other age groups. The influences of culture, family, and peers as moderators of hormone-aggression links also remain to be explored. Nevertheless, hormones responsible for physical and sexual development during puberty were related to emotions and the expression of aggression in early adolescent boys. These findings suggest the need for consideration of hormonal processes in future studies of the behavioral development of adolescents.

References

Abraham, G. E., Buster, J. E., Lucas, L. A., Corrales, P. C., & Teller, R. C. (1972). Chromatographic separation of steroid hormones for use in radioimmunoassay. *Analytical Letters*, 5, 509–517.

Achenbach, T. M., & Edelbrock, C. S. (1979). The Child Behavior Profile: 2. Boys aged 12–16 and girls aged 6–11 and 12–16. *Journal of Consulting and Clinical Psychology*, 47, 223–233.

Achenbach, T. M., & Edelbrock, C. S. (1983). *Manual for the Child Behavior Checklist and Revised Child Behavior Profile*. Burlington: Department of Psychiatry, University of Vermont.

Adams, D. B. (1983). Hormone-brain interactions and their influence on agonistic behavior. In B. B. Svare (Ed.), *Hormones and aggressive behavior* (pp. 223–245). New York: Plenum.

Alpert, J. E., Cohen, D. J., Shaywitz, B. A., & Piccirillo, M. (1981). Neurochemical and behavioral organization: Disorders of attention, activity, and aggression. In D. O. Lewis (Ed.), *Vulnerabilities to delinquency* (pp. 109–171). New York: Spectrum.

Anisman, H., & LaPierre, Y. D. (1982). Neurochemical aspects of stress and depression: Formulations and caveats. In R. W. Neufeld (Ed.), *Psychological stress and psychopathology* (pp. 179–217). New York: McGraw-Hill.

Apter, D., & Vihko, R. (1985). Hormonal patterns of the first menstrual cycles. In S. Venturoli, C. Flamigni, & J. R. Givens (Eds.), *Adolescence in females* (pp. 215–238). Chicago: Year Book Medical Publishers.

Bardwick, J. M. (1976). Psychological correlates of the menstrual cycle and oral contraceptive medication. In E. J. Sachar (Ed.), *Hormones, behavior, and psychopathology* (pp. 95–103). New York: Raven.

Berkowitz, L. (1964). Aggressive cues in aggressive behavior and hostility catharsis. *Psychological Review*, 71, 104–122.

Block, J. (1971). *Lives through time*. Berkeley, CA: Bancroft.

Bouissou, M. F. (1983). Androgens, aggressive behavior and social relationships in higher mammals. *Hormone Research*, 18, 43–61.

Brain, P. F. (Ed.). (1977). *Hormones and aggression: Vol. 1. Annual research review*. Montreal: Eden.

Cairns, R. B., MacCombie, D. J., & Hood, K. E. (1983). A developmental-genetic analysis of aggressive behavior in mice: I. Behavioral outcomes. *Journal of Comparative Psychology,* 97, 69–89.

Cargille, C. M., & Rayford, P. L. (1970). Characterization of antisera for follicle-stimulating hormone radioimmunoassay. *Journal of Laboratory and Clinical Medicine,* 75, 1030–1040.

Chrousos, G. P., Schuermeyer, T., Oldfield, E., Doppman, J., Schulte, H. M., Gold, P. W., & Loriaux, D. L. (1985). Clinical applications of corticotropin releasing factor. *Annals of Internal Medicine,* 102, 344–358.

Clark, C. R., & Nowell, N. W. (1979). The effect of the antiestrogen CI-628 on androgen-induced aggressive behavior in castrated male mice. *Hormones and Behavior,* 12, 205–210.

Cohen, J., & Cohen, P. (1975). *Applied multiple regression/correlation analysis for the behavioral sciences.* Hillsdale, NJ: Erlbaum.

Cummings, E. M., Hollenbeck, B., Iannotti, R. J., Radke-Yarrow, M., & Zahn-Waxler, C. (1986). Early organization of altruism and aggression: Developmental patterns and individual differences. In C. Zahn-Waxler, E. M. Cummings, & R. J. Iannotti (Eds.), *Altruism and aggression: Social and biological origins* (pp. 165–188). New York: Cambridge University Press.

Cunningham, S. K., Loughlin, T., Culliton, M., & McKenna, T. J. (1984). Plasma sex hormone–binding globulin levels decrease during the second decade of life irrespective of pubertal status. *Journal of Clinical Endocrinology and Metabolism,* 58, 915–918.

Cutler, G. B., Jr., Glenn, M., Bush, M., Hodgen, G., Graham, C. E., & Loriaux, D. L. (1978). Adrenarche: A survey of rodents, domestic animals and primates. *Endocrinology,* 103, 2112–2118.

de Lignieres, B., & Vincens, M. (1982). Differential effects of exogenous oestradiol and progesterone on mood in post-menopausal women: Individual dose/effect relationship. *Maturitas,* 4, 67–72.

Doering, C. H., Brodie, K. H., Kraemer, H. C., Moos, R. H., Becker, H. B., & Hamburg, D. A. (1975). Negative affect and plasma testosterone: A longitudinal human study. *Psychosomatic Medicine,* 37, 484–491.

Dunn, J. F., Nisula, B. C., & Rodbard, D. (1981). Transport of steroid hormones: Binding of 21 endogenous steroids to both testosterone-binding globulin and corticosteroid-binding globulin in human plasma. *Journal of Clinical Endocrinology and Metabolism,* 53, 58–67.

Ehrenkranz, J., Bliss, E., & Sheard, M. H. (1974). Plasma testosterone: Correlation with aggressive behavior and social dominance in man. *Psychosomatic Medicine,* 36, 469–475.

Eleftheriou, B. E., & Sprott, R. L. (1975). *Hormonal correlates of behavior: Vol. 1. A lifespan view.* New York: Plenum.

Ellis, L. (1982). Developmental androgen fluctuations and the five dimensions of the mammalian sex (with emphasis upon the behavioral dimension and the human species). *Endocrinology and Sociobiology,* 3, 171–197.

Floody, O. R. (1983). Hormones and aggression in female mammals. In B. B. Svare (Ed.), *Hormones and aggressive behavior* (pp. 39–89). New York: Plenum.

Fonberg, E. (1979). Physiological mechanisms of emotional and instrumental aggression. In S. Feshbach & A. Fraczek (Eds.), *Aggression and behavior change: Biological and social processes* (pp. 6–53). New York: Praeger.

Fregly, M. J., & Luttge, W. G. (1982). *Human endocrinology: An interactive text.* New York: Elsevier Biomedical.

Friedman, R. C., Richart, R. M., & Vande Wiele, R. L. (Eds.). (1974). *Sex differences in behavior.* New York: Wiley.

Frodi, A., Macaulay, J., & Thome, P. R. (1977). Are women always less aggressive than men? A review of the experimental literature. *Psychological Bulletin,* 84, 634–660.

Gandelman, R. (1980). Gonadal hormones and the induction of intraspecific fighting in mice. *Neuroscience & Biobehavioral Reviews,* 4, 133–140.

Gold, P. W., & Chrousos, G. P. (1985). Clinical studies with corticotropin releasing factor: Implications for the diagnosis and pathophysiology of depression, Cushing's disease and adrenal insufficiency. *Psychoneuroendocrinology,* 10, 401–419.

Hays, S. (1981). The psychoendocrinology of puberty and adolescent aggression. In D. A. Hamburg & M. B. Trudeau (Eds.), *Biobehavioral aspects of aggression* (pp. 107–119). New York: Liss.

Hines, M. (1982). Prenatal gonadal hormones and sex differences in human behavior. *Psychological Bulletin,* 92, 56–80.

Hollingshead, A. B. (1975). *Four-factor index of social status.* New Haven, CT: Yale University.

Houser, B. B. (1979). An investigation of the correlation between hormonal levels in males and mood, behavior, and physical discomfort. *Hormones and Behavior,* 12, 185–197.

Hyde, J. S. (1984). How large are gender differences in aggression? A developmental meta-analysis. *Developmental Psychology,* 20, 722–736.

Kandel, D., & Davies, M. (1986). Adult sequelae of adolescent depressive symptoms. *Archives of General Psychiatry,* 43, 255–262.

Kelly, D. D. (1981). Sexual differentiation of the nervous system. In E. R. Kandel & T. H.

Schwartz (Eds.), *Principles of neural science* (pp. 533–546). North Holland: Elsevier.

Leshner, A. I. (1983). Pituitary-adrenocortical effects on internale agonistic behavior. In B. B. Svare (Ed.), *Hormones and aggressive behavior* (pp. 27–38). New York: Plenum.

Lloyd, J. A. (1975). Social behavior and hormones. In B. E. Eleftheriou & R. L. Sprott (Eds.), *Hormonal correlates of behavior: Vol. 1. A lifespan view* (pp. 185–197). New York: Plenum.

Maccoby, E. E., Doering, C. H., Jacklin, C. N., & Kraemer. H. (1979). Concentrations of sex hormones in umbilical-cord blood: Their relation to sex and birth order of infants. *Child Development*, 50, 632–642.

Maccoby, E. E., & Jacklin, C. N. (1974). *The psychology of sex differences*. Stanford, CA: Stanford University Press.

Maccoby, E. E., & Jacklin, C. N. (1980). Sex differences in aggression: A rejoinder and reprise. *Child Development*, 51, 964–980.

Marcus, J., Maccoby, E. E., Jacklin, C. N., & Doering, C. H. (1985). Individual differences in mood in early childhood: Their relation to gender and neonatal sex steroids. *Developmental Psychobiology*, 18, 327–340.

Marshall, W. A., & Tanner, J. M. (1969). Variations in the pattern of pubertal changes in girls. *Archives of Disease in Childhood*, 44, 291–303.

Marshall, W. A., & Tanner, J. M. (1970). Variations in the pattern of pubertal changes in boys. *Archives of Disease in Childhood*, 45, 13–23.

Mattsson, A., Schalling, D., Olweus, D., Low, H., & Svensson, J. (1980). Plasma testosterone, aggressive behavior, and personality dimensions in young male delinquents. *Journal of the American Academy of Child Psychiatry*, 19, 476–490.

Mazur, A., & Lamb, T. A. (1980). Testosterone, status and mood in human males. *Hormones and Behavior*, 14, 236–246.

Nieschlag, E., & Loriaux, D. L. (1972). Radioimmunoassay for plasma testosterone. *Zeitschrift fuer Klinische Chemie und Klinische Biochemie*, 10, 164–168.

Nottelmann, E. D., Susman, E. J., Blue, J. H., Inoff-Germain, G., Dorn, L. D., Loriaux, D. L., Cutler, G. B., Jr., & Chrousos, G. P. (1987a). Gonadal and adrenal hormone correlates of adjustment in early adolescence. In R. M. Lerner & T. T. Foch (Eds.), *Biological-psychosocial interactions in early adolescence: A life-span perspective*. Hillsdale, NJ: Erlbaum.

Nottelmann, E. D., Susman, E. J., Dorn, L. D., Inoff-Germain, G., Loriaux, D. L., Cutler, G. B., Jr., & Chrousos, G. P. (1987b). Developmental processes in early adolescence: Relations among chronologic age, pubertal stage, height, weight, and serum levels of gonadotropins, sex steroids, and adrenal androgens. *Journal of Adolescent Health Care*, 8, 35–48.

Odell, W. D., Ross, G. T., & Rayford, P. L. (1967). Radioimmunoassay for luteinizing hormone in human plasma or serum: Physiological studies. *Journal of Clinical Investigation*, 46, 248–255.

Offer, D., Ostrov, E., & Howard, K. I. (1977). *The Offer Self-Image Questionnaire for Adolescents: A manual*. Chicago: Michael Reese Hospital.

Offer, D., Ostrov, E., & Howard, K. I. (1984). The self-image of normal adolescents. *New Directions for Mental Health Services*, 22, 5–17.

Olweus, D., Mattsson, A., Schalling, D., & Low, H. (1980). Testosterone, aggression, physical, and personality dimensions in normal adolescent males. *Psychosomatic Medicine*, 42, 253–269.

Persky, H., Smith, K. D., & Basu, G. K. (1971). Relation of psychologic measures of aggression and hostility to testosterone production in man. *Psychosomatic Medicine*, 33, 265–277.

Phoenix, C. H., Goy, R. W., Gerall, A. A., & Young, W. C. (1959). Organizing actions of prenatally administered testosterone propionate on the tissues mediating mating behavior in the female guinea pig. *Endocrinology*, 65, 369–382.

Puig-Antich, J. (1986). Psychological markers: Effects of age and puberty. In M. Rutter, C. E. Izard, & P. B. Read (Eds.), *Depression in young people: Developmental and clinical perspectives* (pp. 341–381). New York: Guilford.

Rose, R., & Sachar, E. (1981). Psychoendocrinology. In R. H. Williams (Ed.), *Textbook of endocrinology* (pp. 646–669). Philadelphia: Saunders.

Rose, R., Bernstein, I. S., Gordon, T. P., & Catlin, S. F. (1974). Androgens and aggression: A review and recent findings in perspective. In R. L. Holloway (Ed.), *Primate aggression, territoriality, and xenophobia: A comparative perspective*. New York: Academic Press.

Rose, R. M., Bernstein, I. S., Gordon, T. P., & Lindsley, J. G. (1978). Changes in testosterone and behavior during adolescence in the male Rhesus monkey. *Psychosomatic Medicine*, 40, 60–70.

Rubin, R. T., Reinisch, J. M., & Haskett, R. F. (1981). Postnatal gonadal steroid effects on human behavior. *Science*, 211, 1318–1324.

Rubinow, D. R., & Roy-Byrne, P. (1984). Premenstrual syndromes: Overview from a methodologic perspective. *American Journal of Psychiatry*, 141, 163–172.

Rubinow, D. R., Roy-Byrne, P., & Hoban, M. C. (1985). Menstrually related mood disorders: Methodological and conceptual issues. In M. Y. Dalwood, J. L. McGuire, & L. M. Demers (Eds.), *Premenstrual syndrome and dysmenorrhea* (pp. 27–40). Baltimore: Urban & Schwartzenberg.

1134 Child Development

Sachar, E. J. (Ed.). (1980). Advances in psychoneuroendocrinology. *Psychiatric Clinics of North America*, 3, 203–368.

Scaramella, T. J., & Brown, W. A. (1978). Serum testosterone and aggressiveness in hockey players. *Psychosomatic Medicine*, 40, 262–265.

Schlain, E. A. (1976). A factor analytic study of three aspects of aggression: Assertiveness, hostility, and self-control. *Dissertation Abstracts International*, 37(2-B), 961–962.

Siris, S. G., Siris, E. S., Van Kammen, D. P., Docherty, J. P., Alexander, P. E., & Bunney, W. E., Jr. (1980). Effects of dopamine blockade on gonadotropins and testosterone in men. *American Journal of Psychiatry*, 137, 211–214.

Sizonenko, P. C. (1978). Endocrinology in preadolescents and adolescents: I. Hormonal changes during normal puberty. *American Journal of Diseases of Childhood*, 132, 704–712.

Steinberg, L. D. (1981). Transformations in family relations at puberty. *Developmental Psychology*, 17, 833–840.

Steinberg, L. W., & Hill, J. P. (1978). Patterns of family interaction as a function of age, the onset of puberty, and formal thinking. *Developmental Psychology*, 14, 683–684.

Susman, E. J., Nottelmann, E. D., Inoff, G. E., Dorn, L. D., Cutler, C. B., Jr., Loriaux, D. L., & Chrousos, G. P. (1985). The relation of relative hormonal levels and physical development and social-emotional behavior in young adolescents. *Journal of Youth and Adolescence*, 14, 245–264.

Susman, E. J., Nottelmann, E. D., Inoff-Germain, G., Dorn, L. D., & Chrousos, G. P. (in press). Hormonal influences on aspects of psychological development during adolescence. *Journal of Adolescent Health Care*.

Tieger, T. (1980). On the biological basis of sex differences in aggression. *Child Development*, 51, 943–963.

Van de Poll, N. E., Smeets, J., Van Oyen, H. G., & van der Zwan, S. M. (1982). Behavioral consequences of agonistic experience in rats: Sex differences and the effects of testosterone. *Journal of Comparative and Physiological Psychology*, 96, 893–903.

Vihko, R., & Apter, D. (1980). The role of androgens in adolescent cycles. *Journal of Steroid Biochemistry*, 12, 369–373.

Weisfeld, G. E., & Berger, J. M. (1983). Some features of human adolescence viewed in evolutionary perspective. *Human Development*, 26, 121–133.

Williams, R. H. (Ed.). (1981). *Textbook of Endocrinology*. Philadelphia: Saunders.

Young, W. C., Goy, R. W., & Phoenix, C. H. (1964). Hormones and sexual behavior. *Science*, 143, 212–218.

Zuckerman, M., & Lubin B. (1965). *Multiple Affect Adjective Check List, Today Form*. San Diego: Educational and Industrial Testing Service.

The Relation of Relative Hormonal Levels and Physical Development and Social-Emotional Behavior in Young Adolescents

E. J. Susman,[1,3] E. D. Nottelmann,[1] G. E. Inoff-Germain,[1] L. D. Dorn,[1] G. B. Cutler, Jr.,[2] D. L. Loriaux,[2] and G. P. Chrousos[2]

The study examined the relation between timing of physical maturation and problems of adjustment and peer relations. The participants were 9–14-year-old boys (N = 56) and girls (N = 52). Assessments of physical maturation consisted of pubertal staging according to Tanner criteria and serum determinations of luteinizing hormone, follicle stimulating hormone, testosterone, estradiol, dehydroepiandrosterone, dehydroepiandrosterone sulfate, and androstenedione. There was approximately an equal number of boys and girls in each pubertal stage. The psychological measures were the Psychopathology and Emotional Tone subscales from the Offer Self-Image Questionnaire for Adolescents and interview questions to assess interactions with peers. Psychopathology and emotional tone (sad effect) scores were higher for boys with high-for-age adrenal androgens and lower for boys with high-for-age sex steroids. Behavioral manifestations of sexuality, interest in dating, was higher for boys with high-for-age adrenal androgens. Dating and spending time with friends were higher for boys with high-for-age gonadotropins. Psychopathology and emotional tone were higher for girls with high-for-age gonadotropins. The results indicate that high-for-age hormone level or early timing of puberty generally was related to adverse psychological consequences for boys and girls, with relations being stronger for boys than for girls.

---

[1]National Institute of Mental Health
[2]National Institute of Child Health and Human Development.
[3]Correspondence should be sent to Elizabeth J. Susman, Laboratory of Developmental Psychology, National Institute of Mental Health, Building 15K, 9000 Rockville Pike, Bethesda, Maryland 20892.

INTRODUCTION

Timing of maturation, or whether or not an adolescent progresses through the stages of puberty early or late relative to other same-aged adolescents, is believed to influence aspects of social and emotional development. The specific effects depend on (a) whether adolescents are male or female, (b) whether they are early or late maturers relative to their peers, (c) how "early" and "late" are defined, and (d) the behavior under study. Early maturing girls in early adolescence tend to report less general happiness (Peskin and Livson, 1972) and have more problems in school (Simmons et al., 1983) than late maturing girls. Yet early maturing girls have been found to have high social prestige (Faust, 1960) and self-confidence (Clausen, 1975). Early maturing boys are reported to be poised, relaxed, and respected in their peer group (Blyth et al., 1981), but they also have been reported to possess undesirable attributes such as being submissive, somber, and anxious (Peskin, 1967). Similarly, late maturing boys are reported to possess both positive and negative attributes: to be expressive, dynamic and buoyant, yet tense and concerned with physical self (Blyth et al., 1981). Thus, neither early nor late maturation is an entirely positive or negative experience for either boys or girls.

A wide variety of indices of physical development have been used to define physical maturity. They include height and weight (Blyth et al., 1981), onset of menarche (Blyth et al., this issue), skeletal age (Jones and Bayley, 1950), pubertal stage (Waber, 1977; Petersen and Crockett, this issue), and total body water as a percentage of body weight (Frisch et al., 1973; Waber, 1977; Newcombe and Bandura, 1983). The assumption underlying the incorporation of the anthropomorphic measures and secondary sexual characteristics of relative maturity in the study of psychological development is that the external changes of physical development have a significant effect on behavior because they signal to adults and peers and to adolescents themselves that the adolescents are more mature and that their behavior should change to fit their new status.

Inconsistent findings from previous studies appear to reflect both the advantages and disadvantages conferred by early and late maturation. That is, earlier maturation is thought to have positive effects on psychosocial development because accelerated physical development tends to enhance popularity with peers, particularly among boys who participate in sports. It also has detrimental effects because it reduces the time children need to prepare emotionally for pubertal changes and their new status and responsibilities. Conversely, while later maturation may facilitate emotional preparation for pubertal and social status change, prepubertal appearance and short stature tend to be disadvantageous in the peer culture. Most previous research concerned with timing of maturation has focused on the effect of such relative differences in physical development on adolescent behavior, the exception being the studies using skeletal age. To our knowledge, no extant studies of healthy children have used endocrine status to assess adolescent maturational status. Endocrine status may produce results different from those of previous studies for several reasons: (a) Endocrine changes are not directly observable. Previous studies have related the behavior of adolescents to observable changes in physical development. (b) Hormones may be related to different aspects of behavior than are previously used measures of pubertal status. The animal literature links aggression and sexual behavior to hormone levels. (c) There are no perfect correspondences between any of the measures of pubertal status. Variability is great in the levels of hormones within each pubertal stage (Nottelmann *et al.*, 1985), and secondary sex characteristics and height and weight develop at different rates.

The purpose of this study was to investigate the effect of timing of maturation on psychosocial adjustment and interest in same- and opposite-sex peers through assessment of endocrine status (i.e., level of gonadotropins, sex steroids, and adrenal androgens). The degree of earlier or later timing of maturation was determined by assessing the maturational status of each adolescent relative to his/her peers in the study.

Many family and social environmental factors foster behavior changes during adolescence, but the importance of endocrine changes in influencing social and emotional development during early adolescence should not be understated. An extensive body of literature links aspects of animal and human behavior to changes in hormones. For example, distinct patterns of steroid hormone binding have been found in the brain of many subhuman species. Estrogens and androgens appear to be accumulated by specific hypothalamic and limbic nerve cells (Pfaff, 1980). Changes in levels of these hormones have been found to affect a variety of behaviors of all animals studied. Therefore, it is not unreasonable to assume that variations in hormone level also may affect emotions and behaviors (e.g., aggression) in human adolescents. In the few existing studies of hormone-behavior relations in healthy adolescents, high levels of testosterone were related to high levels of aggression (Olweus *et al.*, 1980). The adolescents in the Olweus *et al.* study were males in the late stages of puberty, and it is unclear whether timing of maturation played a role in influencing the testosterone-aggression relation.

Sex steroids and possibly gonadotropins are the hormones generally thought to be responsible for changes in sexual behavior and adjustment during puberty. These hormones are implicated in the intensification of sex drive and sexual activity (Ehrhardt and Meyer-Bahlburg, 1975) and changes in social rank and dominance (Lloyd, 1975). The influence of adrenal androgens on behavior during puberty is unknown, but androgens have been implicated in psychiatric disorders in adults (Erb *et al.*, 1981; Brambilla *et al.*, 1978). Thus, while animal studies and studies of humans in other age groups link some hormones to behaviors, the mechanisms whereby hormones affect the brain and, in turn, the behavior of adolescents or humans in general are unknown.

The study of hormones as a measure of maturational timing is important for several reasons. First, hormone levels may indicate the degree to which brain and other target tissue is exposed and likely to be affected by particular hormones. Second, hormone levels allow early detection of puberty, well in advance of the external manifestations of puberty that are obvious to adolescents themselves and to their parents and peers. Nocturnal pulsatile releases of luteinizing hormones are the first endocrine event of puberty (Boyer *et al.*, 1972). These nocturnal releases and the subsequent rise in the production of sex steroids occur well before any external manifestations of puberty begin to appear. Thus, hormone-dependent changes in behavior prior to the appearance of the external changes are less likely to be confounded with the psychosocial events of pubertal development.

How hormone levels and the psychosocial events of earlier or later maturation interact is unknown. Hormone level may affect behavior differentially depending on whether it is higher or lower, earlier or later, than is typical in pubertal development. For instance, a relative high-for-age level of hormones may have a greater impact on earlier than later maturing adolescents. Earlier maturers may be less prepared to cope with hormone-related emotional changes than late maturers, just as they may be less prepared to adapt to physical change. While hormone levels may affect behavior differentially depending on the age of the adolescent, hormone levels within age groups may be a better index of timing of maturation than absolute hormone levels. Adolescents with levels high for their age may be especially unprepared to deal with the emotional and behavioral upheaval related to hormones, especially if most of their same-age peers are not experiencing similar turmoil. Our first hypothesis is that hormones will be related to behavior differentially, depending on whether levels are higher or lower within one's age group (level-for-age hypothesis). According to the level-for-age hypothesis, having a higher level of a hormone relative to one's age-mates defines an earlier maturer. Conversely, having a lower level relative to one's age-mates defines a later maturer. Alternatively, it could be argued that hormone level, *per se,* will be related to behavior, regardless of whether the adolescent is an earlier or later maturer. Also, higher hormone levels are generally presumed to be related to more aberrant behavior, regardless of timing, than lower levels. Thus, our second hypothesis is that hormone levels, regardless of age, will be related to problems of adjustment (level hypothesis).

Pubertal stage also was used to assess timing of maturation. We expected similarities between findings based on hormone level and findings based on pubertal stage as indices of timing of maturation, although we know of no other studies comparing the two. Similarities are especially likely because hormone changes are reflected in changes such as increased height and weight and changes in secondary sex characteristics. However, interindividual variation in hormone levels within pubertal stage may render the correspondence of findings across type of assessment far from perfect.

Our exploration of links between timing of maturation, assessed by hormone level and stage of puberty, and social and emotional development focused on the development of adjustment problems for two reasons: First, there exists the belief that hormone changes in adolescents lead to emotional upheaval. Adjustment problems ranging from irritability to serious psychiatric problems have been attributed to hormone changes during adolescence. There also is evidence that psychiatric disorders are related to atypical hormone levels in adults (e.g., Gold and Chrousos, in press). However, to date, few studies have examined the relation between psychiatric disorders and hormone levels during puberty. Second, adolescent delinquency has been linked to elevated testosterone level (Mattsson *et al.,* 1980). We expected that adjustment problems would be more prevalent in adolescents with high-for-age hormone levels.

Another aspect of emotional development that may be related to hormone levels and, in turn, predispose adolescents to adjustment problems is intensification of interest in same- and opposite-sex peers. Peer relationships can provide an important source of support and self-esteem for adolescents, but problems in peer relationships can have profound detrimental effects. Peer relationships also can serve as a major source of conflict between parents and adolescents. Interest in peers is influenced by many cultural as well as biological factors. However, evidence of the effect of hormones on sexual behavior is abundant in the animal literature. Similarly, human female sexual behavior reportedly varies with hormonally regulated phases of the menstrual cycle (Bancroft *et al.,* 1983). While no one-to-one correspondence between sexual behavior and interest may exist, interest in same- and opposite-sex peer relationships may be related to hormone levels, regardless of the timing of maturation. However, there are many family and peer pressures to conform to social conventions regarding expression of interest in the opposite sex, given a certain level of physical maturity. For this reason, stage of pubertal development also may play a role in determining the nature of interactions with peers, given that such changes are observable.

METHOD

Participants

The participants were 56 boys ranging in age from 10 to 14 years and 52 girls ranging in age from 9 to 14 years. These adolescents represented all five stages of pubertal development as described by Tanner (Marshall and Tanner, 1969, 1970). Table I shows the number of participants and the mean and standard deviation for age of participants in each pubertal stage group. The wider age range of females was necessary in order to include females in all five stages of pubertal development. The adolescents were from intact

Table I. Number of Participants and Means and Standard Deviations for Age (in Years) of Participants by Pubertal Stage[a]

Pubertal stage	n	Age[b] M	S.D.
Boys			
1	11	10.91	0.84
2	14	12.75	0.98
3	10	12.88	0.69
4	7	13.44	0.90
5	13	13.82	0.88
Girls			
1	10	9.90	0.74
2	10	11.31	0.99
3	13	12.10	1.08
4	10	12.80	0.71
5	9	13.86	0.69

[a] Pubertal stage is based on genital stage for boys and breast stage for girls.
[b] Age and stage are not independent. The correlation between age and stage was 0.70 ($p < 0.001$) for boys and 0.83 ($p < 0.001$) for girls.

families. The majority of the adolescents had middle to upper middle class backgrounds (Hollingshead, 1975). The adolescents were healthy and free from any chronic or acute illness at the time of the study.

Recruitment of participants was done mainly through fliers placed on bulletin boards in churches, health clinics, and community centers and through fliers distributed at parent-teacher association and scout troop meetings. Families who contacted the project laboratory were sent the informed consent form, which provided a written description of the study. The project staff then contacted the family to determine if the family wished to participate. If the decision was positive, the family was scheduled for two appointments: (a) a four-hour visit for mother, father, and adolescent at a home-like laboratory where the behavioral measures were administered and (b) a two-hour visit for the adolescent and one parent at an outpatient clinic in a research hospital where the biological data were collected.

Procedure

Behavioral Measures. Adolescent, mother, and father were given a battery of standardized tests and interview schedules to assess various aspects of the adolescent's social, emotional, and cognitive development as well as family relationships. The interactions of the family members also were videotaped in structured and unstructured situations. Measures from this battery of tests which were hypothesized to be related to timing of maturation are reported in this paper: (a) the Psychopathology and Emotional Tone subscales from the Offer Self-Image Questionnaire for Adolescents (OSIQ; Offer *et al.*, 1977) and (b) interview questions designed to assess interest in same- and opposite-sex peers. The OSIQ is a questionnaire on which adolescents rate themselves on items designed to assess adjustment and family and social relationships on a scale of 1 to 6 ("describes me very well" to "describes me not at all"). The Psychopathology subscale consists of items designed to tap emotional problems ranging from anxiety to psychotic thinking. The Emotional Tone subscale consists of items designed to tap emotions such as sad affect. High scores on the Emotional Tone subscale denote sad affect. In our sample, the reliabilities for the two subscales using Cronbach's alpha were 0.81 and 0.72, respectively. The interview items consisted of questions about interest in dating (rated on a 5-point scale) and number of dates, number of friends, and number of hours spent with friends per week.

Biological Measures. The physical maturity and endocrine status measures were obtained during a two-hour visit at an outpatient clinic. The clinic visit was scheduled within a mean number of 2.26 days from the behavioral measures assessment. The biological measures were obtained by an endocrinologist or by a pediatric nurse practitioner. Girls who had reached menarche were in various phases of their menstrual cycle.

Blood samples were collected between the hours of 8 A.M. and 10 A.M. to minimize possible diurnal variations in the hormones being assessed. Samples of blood were drawn at 0, 20, and 40 minutes. Three samples were drawn to minimize the measurement error that may result from the minute-to-minute fluctuations in serum concentration of some hormones. The blood samples were obtained from the antecubital vein of the adolescents. The mean value of the three samples is the value used in all analyses. Radioimmunoassays were performed according to the following techniques: luteinizing hormone (LH) (Odell *et al.*, 1967); follicle stimulating hormone (FSH) (Cargille and Rayford, 1970); testosterone (T) (Nieschlag and Loriaux, 1972); estradiol (E_2) (Abraham *et al.*, 1972); and dehydroepiandrosterone (DHEA), dehydroepiandrosterone sulfate (DHEAS) and androstenedione (ΔA) (Cutler *et al.*, 1978). The testosterone-to-estradiol ratio also was computed (T/E_2). There were no differences between the three samples.

During the period of blood sampling, height, weight, and head circumference were measured. After the blood samples were drawn, a physical examination was done to determine the stage of pubertal development according to the criteria of Tanner (Marshall and Tanner, 1969, 1970). For girls, breast development and pubic hair growth were assessed; for boys, genital development and pubic hair growth were evaluated. Interexaminer agreement for stage of pubertal development was as follows(r): girls, breast stage = 1.00, pubic hair stage = 1.00; boys, genital stage = .99, pubic hair stage = 1.00.

RESULTS

The first step in the analysis was the conversion of hormone values to z scores. This standardization procedure was done to put all values on a comparable scale. Hormones are measured in units that range from mIU per milliliter to micrograms per deciliter. The mean levels and standard errors for the hormones by Tanner stage are reported elsewhere (Nottelmann *et al.*, 1985).

Sex Differences

There were no mean sex differences between boys and girls on any of the behavioral variables. Girls were significantly higher than boys on mean level of LH, FSH, E_2 and ΔA; boys were significantly higher than girls on mean level of T and DHEAS.

Level-for-Age Hypothesis

To test the level-for-age hypothesis, hormone values were standardized within chronological age groups by sex. Maturational status was defined by the level of a hormone within each age group. Forward regression analysis was used to test the relationship between maturational status and the behavioral variables. The standardized LH, FSH, T, E_2, T/E_2, DHEA, DHEAS, and ΔA hormone values were used as predictors of each behavioral variable. These hormones were given equal weight because no theoretical reason exists for assuming that one of the hormones is more predictive of the behaviors under consideration than any of the other hormones. Table II shows the bivariate correlations between the behavioral variables and each hormone. Table III and the text below provide the R, R^2, B, and F ratio for hormones that were entered into the regression equation for each behavioral variable. The criterion for entry into the equation was significance at the $p \leq 0.05$ level. For this set of analyses, positive B values indicate higher-for-age hormone levels and earlier maturational status; negative B values indicate lower-for-age hormone values and later maturational status. The mean level for each hormone for relatively early, on-time, and late maturers appears in Table IV. Within each age group, the 25% of the adolescents with the highest levels of each hormone were considered early, the 25% with the lowest levels were considered late, and the remaining 50% were considered on time.

Psychopathology. For boys, psychopathology scores were lower for high-for-age E_2 and T/E_2 and higher for high-for-age ΔA. For girls, psychopathology scores were higher for high-for-age FSH and lower for high-for-age DHEAS.

Emotional Tone. For boys, emotional tone scores were lower for high-for-age E_2 and T/E_2 and higher for high-for-age ΔA. For girls, emotional tone scores were higher for high-for-age FSH.

Interest in Dating. For boys, interest in dating was lower for high-for-age DHEA ($R = 0.28$, $R^2 = 0.08$, $B = -0.43$, $F(2, 32) = 5.32$, $p < 0.05$). Since this was the only significant finding for DHEA for boys or girls, it was considered likely to be a chance finding. Interest in dating was higher for boys with high-for-age ΔA ($R = 0.42$, $R^2 = 0.18$, $B = 0.51$, $F(1, 32) = 6.74$, $p < 0.01$).

Number of Dates. For boys, number of dates was higher for high-for-age FSH ($R = 0.33$, $R^2 = 0.11$, $B = 0.31$, $F(1, 41) = 5.12$, $p < 0.05$) and low-for-age E_2 ($R = 0.28$, $R^2 = 0.08$, $B = -0.28$, $F(2, 41) = 4.59$, $p < 0.05$).

Table II. Correlations Between Adjustment and Hormone Levels Standardized by Age and Sex for Boys and Girls

Adjustment	LH	FSH	T	E_2	T/E_2	DHEA	DHEAS	ΔA
Boys								
Psychopathology	-0.16	0.01	-0.25	-0.17	-0.36[a]	0.05	0.12	0.31[a]
Emotional tone	-0.09	-0.08	-0.27	-0.08	-0.34[a]	-0.02	-0.03	0.27
Interest in dating	0.15	0.01	0.19	0.15	-0.05	-0.01	0.20	0.42[b]
Number of dates	0.06	0.33[a]	-0.07	-0.20	0.08	0.11	0.10	0.17
Number of hours spent with friends	0.09	0.34[a]	0.07	-0.03	0.03	0.11	0.26	0.27
Girls								
Psychopathology	0.20	0.46[b]	0.11	0.10	-0.19	0.01	-0.28	0.18
Emotional tone	0.14	0.44[b]	0.11	0.22	-0.16	-0.07	0.23	0.11
Interest in dating	-0.04	0.06	-0.01	0.06	0.03	0.17	0.27	0.16
Number of dates	-0.03	-0.09	-0.16	-0.10	0.10	0.17	-0.08	-0.27
Number of hours spent with friends	-0.41[b]	0.01	0.05	0.24	0.17	-0.05	-0.12	0.09

[a] $p \le 0.05$.
[b] $p \le 0.01$.

Table III. Regression Statistics for Adjustment Showing Variance Explained by Hormone Level Standardized by Age and Sex and by Sex for Boys and Girls[a]

Variable	Gonadotropins: FSH[b]	Sex steroids			Adrenal androgens		Age	Total
		E_2	T/E_2		DHEAS	ΔA		
Psychopathology								
Boys								
R	—	(0.12_3)	(0.09_3)	(0.12_1)	—	(0.10_2)	—	0.64 (0.62)
R^2	(0.08_1)	0.12₃	(-0.25)	(-0.30)	—	(0.24)	—	0.41 (0.39)
B	(0.24)	-0.27	(4.80^c)	(3.32^c)	—	(4.08^c)	—	
F	(5.26^d)	9.19^c						
Girls								
R	.21₁	—	—	—	(0.08_2)	—	(0.13_1)	0.53 (0.45)
R^2	.29	—	—	—	(-0.20)	—	(0.01)	0.28 (0.21)
B	9.74^d	—	—	—	7.16^d	—	(5.71^c)	
F					(4.78^c)			
Emotional tone								
Boys								
R	—	0.06_3	(0.11_1)	(0.14_2)	—	(0.12_2)	(0.17_1)	0.54 (0.52)
R^2	—	-0.19	-0.26	-0.34	—	0.28	(0.02)	0.29 (0.27)
B	—	5.31^d	5.26^c	(8.91^d)	—	6.15^c	(8.32^d)	
F						(7.78^c)		
Girls								
R	0.20	—	—	—	—	—	—	0.45
R^2	0.37	—	—	—	—	—	—	0.20
B	9.08^d	—	—	—	—	—	—	—
F	—							—

[a] The statistics for data standardized by sex alone appear in parentheses. Boys' df = 42; Girls' df = 38; dfs reflect missing data for some of the hormones. Age was entered first into the regression equations for the standardization by sex analyses. Subscripts denote order of entry of the hormones into the regression equations.

[b] LH, T, and DHEA were omitted because there were no significant findings for LH and T and there was only one significant finding for DHEA.

[c] $p \leq 0.05$.
[d] $p \leq 0.01$.
[e] $p \leq 0.001$.

Table IV. Mean Hormone Values of Early, On-Time, and Late Maturers for Males and Females by Age[a]

Hormone and age	Early M		On time M		Late M	
Boys						
LH (mIU/ml)						
10-11	7.17	(4)	2.35	(9)	1.37	(4)
12-13	12.73	(6)	6.04	(13)	2.38	(6)
14	9.77	(2)	6.76	(6)	4.20	(2)
FSH (mIU/ml)						
10-11	10.12	(4)	4.43	(9)	2.56	(4)
12-13	14.66	(6)	6.00	(12)	2.95	(7)
14	14.04	(3)	7.74	(5)	4.00	(2)
T (ng/dl)						
10-11	355.75	(4)	25.60	(8)	12.06	(5)
12-13	480.31	(7)	175.61	(13)	39.97	(6)
14	610.50	(2)	381.47	(6)	136.27	(2)
E_2 (pg/ml)						
10-11	22.80	(4)	10.01	(8)	6.35	(4)
12-13	16.03	(6)	9.81	(11)	6.60	(5)
14	33.35	(2)	14.41	(4)	8.78	(2)
T/E_2 (ng/l)						
10-11	197.06	(4)	27.14	(8)	11.56	(4)
12-13	315.11	(5)	138.98	(12)	44.51	(5)
14	395.45	(2)	272.31	(4)	72.97	(2)
DHEA (ng/dl)						
10-11	326.17	(4)	199.30	(9)	73.85	(4)
12-13	456.64	(6)	278.23	(11)	123.64	(7)
14	558.34	(2)	343.67	(4)	121.48	(3)
DHEAS (µg/dl)						
10-11	173.58	(4)	93.1	(8)	38.43	(4)
12-13	179.61	(6)	96.84	(14)	44.86	(6)
14	147.11	(3)	113.86	(5)	46.57	(2)
ΔA (ng/dl)						
10-11	107.16	(4)	39.39	(8)	17.35	(4)
12-13	99.06	(7)	52.50	(12)	25.80	(6)
14	166.17	(2)	80.67	(6)	28.50	(2)
Girls						
LH (mIU/ml)						
9-10	6.66	(3)	2.65	(7)	1.86	(3)
11-12	14.02	(5)	7.37	(10)	1.80	(6)
13-14	22.80	(2)	11.72	(6)	3.67	(2)
FSH (mIU/ml)						
9-10	11.64	(3)	4.14	(6)	2.31	(4)
11-12	17.03	(5)	10.27	(11)	3.96	(5)
13-14	13.71	(2)	11.49	(5)	7.61	(3)
T (ng/dl)						
9-10	19.07	(4)	11.12	(6)	5.91	(4)
11-12	32.31	(6)	18.15	(10)	11.37	(5)
13-14	29.59	(3)	19.12	(6)	11.59	(2)
E_2 (pg/ml)						
9-10	19.55	(3)	8.34	(8)	4.16	(3)
11-12	100.64	(5)	40.00	(11)	12.36	(5)
13-14	200.34	(2)	43.62	(4)	10.40	(2)

Table IV. Continued

Hormone and age	Early M		On time M		Late M	
Girls						
T/E_2 (ng/l)						
9-10	29.80	(3)	11.75	(8)	6.91	(3)
11-12	19.45	(4)	5.98	(12)	1.82	(4)
13-14	16.20	(2)	5.63	(4)	.97	(2)
DHEA (ng/dl)						
9-10	226.06	(3)	137.26	(7)	73.62	(3)
11-12	400.92	(4)	209.12	(11)	118.02	(4)
13-14	595.50	(2)	288.00	(5)	104.77	(3)
DHEAS (µg/dl)						
9-10	83.67	(3)	41.39	(6)	18.39	(4)
11-12	120.84	(5)	57.12	(11)	30.30	(5)
13-14	169.67	(3)	111.88	(6)	58.24	(2)
ΔA (ng/dl)						
9-10	52.94	(4)	35.93	(7)	22.51	(3)
11-12	146.93	(5)	85.71	(10)	41.06	(5)
13-14	216.44	(3)	103.37	(5)	52.19	(2)

*a*The adolescents were designated by their hormone level as early, on-time, or late maturers as follows: early, 25% of the adolescents with the highest levels; on time, 50% of the adolescents with middle levels; late, 25% of the adolescents with the lowest levels. The *n*s for each group are given in parentheses.

Number of Friends. There were no associations between endocrine status and number of friends for this set of analyses.

Number of Hours Spent with Friends. For boys, the number of hours spent with friends was higher for high-for-age FSH ($R = 0.35$, $R^2 = 0.12$, $B = 0.61$, $F(1, 43) = 5.57$, $p < 0.05$). For girls, the number of hours spent with friends was lower for high-for-age LH ($R = 0.41$, $R^2 = 0.17$, $B = -0.50$, $F(1, 38) = 7.64$, $p < 0.01$) and FSH ($R = 0.24$, $R^2 = 0.06$, $B = -0.67$, $F(2, 38) = 5.49$, $p < 0.01$).

Level Hypothesis

To test the level hypothesis, hormone values were standardized separately by sex. Forward regression analysis was used to test the relations between maturational status and the behavioral variables. Chronological age and the standardized hormone values for LH, FSH, T, E_2, T/E_2, DHEA, DHEAS, and ΔA were used as predictors of each behavioral variable. Age was entered first into the equations in order to remove the proportion of the variance accounted for by age before the relation between the hormone level and behavior was calculated. Table III and the text below provided (in parentheses) the R, R^2, B, and F ratio for each hormone entered into each regression equation.

The findings for this analysis were similar to the level-for-age analysis with the following exceptions: For boys, psychopathology scores were higher for higher levels of FSH ($R = 0.28$, $R^2 = 0.08$, $B = 0.24$, $F(5, 42) = 5.26$, $p < 0.01$). For girls, numbers of dates was lower for higher levels of ΔA ($R = 0.33$, $R^2 = 0.11$, $B = -0.33$, $F(2, 38) = 3.93$, $p < 0.05$). For boys, relations between emotional tone and E_2 and interest in dating and DHEA did not emerge as in the level-for-age analysis.

For girls, relations between psychopathology and emotional tone and FSH and between time spent with friends and LH and FSH did not emerge as in the level-for-age analysis.

Pubertal Status

To examine whether timing of maturation as assessed by Tanner stage of pubertal development is related to adjustment and peer relations, the following analyses were carried out. Chronological age was standardized using z scores within each pubertal stage, separately for boys and girls. The z scores represent the degree to which the adolescent is younger or older relative to his/her peers within his/her pubertal stage. In forward regression analyses, age was regressed against each behavioral variable. For this analysis, positive B weights indicate later maturational status and negative B weights indicate earlier maturational status. Older boys within each pubertal stage had higher emotional tone scores than younger boys ($R = 0.33$, $R^2 = 0.11$, $B = 0.24$, $F(1, 54) = 6.87$, $p = 0.01$).

DISCUSSION

Two hypotheses involving hormone level were tested: (a) High- or low-for-age hormone level and (b) hormone level, regardless of age, will be related to the adjustment of adolescents. Both hypotheses received some support, and the similarities between the two sets of findings are more striking than their differences. The findings for hormone level for age will be discussed in detail because they generally summarize both sets of results. Earlier maturation, whether assessed by hormone level for age or simply by level itself, generally was associated with more negative consequences than later maturation, but the specific effects of timing of maturation depended on the hormone under consideration. For boys, earlier maturation as assessed by FSH was associated with more dates and more hours spent with friends than later maturation. Also for boys, earlier maturation as assessed by adrenal androgen level was associated with higher psychopathology and emotional tone scores and more interest in dating. Adjustment problems as reflected in the psychopathology and emotional tone scores indicate negative or disequilibrating consequences of earlier maturation. Issues of dating and spending time with friends frequently are a source of conflict between parents and their adolescents. If dating and spending a lot of time with friends occur at a younger age for early maturers than for the majority of adolescents, then early maturers may have even more conflicts over these issues than adolescents who are on-time or late maturers. Furthermore, earlier maturers who begin to date and engage in heterosexual social activities earlier than their peers also are less likely to be prepared for successful negotiation of relationships.

The relations between hormones and our indices of maladjustment were stronger than those between hormones and our measures of peer relations. There is evidence of the effects of gonadotropins on maladjustment of adults. Abnormalities in gonadotropin secretion (LH and FSH) have been found in chronic schizophrenics (Ferrier *et al.*, 1982) and in depressed patients (Brambilla *et al.*, 1978). Furthermore, in a study of normal males, FSH was correlated with negative affect (Houser, 1979). The relationship that emerged for our adolescent girls was similar; high-for-age FSH, but not LH, was related to sad affect. In general, there were fewer relations between LH and behavior than between FSH and behavior. Although studies have indicated that many neurotransmitters may affect secretion of LH in animals (Gallo, 1980), there may be fewer such effects in adult humans (Johnstone and Ferrier, 1980). The role of LH in adolescent behavior is relatively unknown.

In our sample of boys, timing of maturation as assessed by sex steroids yielded an unanticipated pattern of findings. Based on the literature on testosterone and aggression, we had anticipated that earlier maturational status on T would be associated with negative behavioral characteristics. For boys, the T/E_2 ratio increases across the stages of puberty. There is a faster increase in level of T than there is in level of E_2. One, therefore, might also expect high T/E_2 ratios to relate to negative behavioral characteristics. However, we found virtually no associations between level of T, examined as a single hormone, and behavior; and high-for-age levels of E_2 and T/E_2 were related to positive aspects of behavior. Earlier maturational status as assessed by E_2 and by T/E_2 was related to lower psychopathology and emotional tone scores. Part of the difficulty of interpreting the meaning of T and E_2 as single hormones is that T can be aromatized to form estrogen. Thus, it is difficult to determine whether levels of T or E_2 relate to behavior. Our findings indicate that levels of both E_2 and T/E_2 may have important implications for the behavior of boys. The T/E_2 ratio may be a more integrated measure of the effects of sex steroids on the brain than either T or E_2 alone. To interpret the precise meaning of the T/E_2 ratio and its role on behavior is premature at this point in our study and, perhaps, in psychoneuroendocrinology in general. However, E_2 may be more important as a moderator of behavior than previously assumed. Estradiol receptor sites have been identified in the brain and appear to exert a direct effect on the dopamine-producing neurons of the tuberoinfundibular system and incertohypothalamic system (Sar, 1984). Dopamine may function as the neurotransmitter that mediates the relation between level of E_2 and affect and behavior. For instance, E_2 may have a positive influence on behavior which may moderate the negative influence of increases of T during puberty. Estradiol given in moderate doses has been shown to induce feelings of well-being in women (DeLignieres and Vincens, 1982). The speculation is that E_2 decreases plasma monoamine oxydase activities which may have a natural anti-depressive effect (Broverman et al., 1968). Thus, the relation between T and behavior may be far more complex than previously recognized. Part of this complexity may be related to processes involving E_2.

The relations between adrenal androgens and behavior of adolescents have not been explored in previous research. Adrenal androgens may influence brain functioning in a manner similar to androgens from other sources such as the gonads. With regard to androgens in general, we speculate that because the male brain is exposed to large doses of androgens prenatally (Reyes et al., 1973, 1974) and during the first 6 months of life (Forest et al., 1973, 1974), it may develop greater sensitivity to androgens during puberty. Thus, the male brain may be exquisitely sensitive to the rise in androgens during puberty. Our finding that ΔA, but not T, was related to adjustment was unanticipated. However, adolescents in our sample were exposed to increasing levels of ΔA since the onset of adrenarche at approximately age 7 (Collu and Ducharme, 1978). Testosterone levels do not begin to increase until a few years later. Therefore, the brains of early adolescents may be sensitive to adrenal androgens as well as to sex steroids.

For girls, earlier maturation assessed by level-for-age gonadotropin's was related to higher psychopathology and emotional tone scores than was later maturation. These negative aspects of earlier maturation are consistent with previous findings (Peskin and Livson, 1972; Simmons et al., 1983). What was unanticipated was the far fewer relations between timing of maturation and behavior for girls than for boys. One hypothesis for explaining the findings is that girls are under more severe socialization pressures to suppress the possible energizing influence of changing hormone levels than are boys. This hypothesis will be explored in future analyses.

Another possible explanation for the fewer findings in girls is based on research from two areas of study: (1) research on human stress responses, with males becoming more behaviorally active and females becoming more behaviorally inhibited when stressed (Inoff and Halverson, 1977; Hamburg and Inoff, 1982), and (2) research on sex differences in aggression, fear, submission, and reaction to novel or aversive stimuli, done primarily on rodents (van de Poll *et al.*, 1982; Gray and Buffery, 1971).

The argument examined by van de Poll *et al.* (1982) involves the stimulation of agonistic behaviors by T and susceptibility for inhibition of aggression and the development of submissive behaviors as a result of outcomes of conflict. This susceptibility is hypothesized to be differentially activated depending upon the sex of the organism. Furthermore, this sex difference is presumed to be tied to sex differences in organizational actions of hormones during development. In van de Poll *et al.*'s data (1982), male rats demonstrated behavioral inhibition after defeat; and, based on a large body of findings, it was concluded that the behavioral inhibition after defeat was a specific characteristic of the male rat's agonistic repertoire.

Our findings of more or stronger relations between hormones and behavior for boys than girls may also reflect sex differences in susceptibility for inhibition of behavior, with human females assumed to be able to inhibit behavior better than males. If both males and females are activated or motivated by hormones, but females are better able to inhibit their behavioral responses, hormone-behavior relations would be stronger for males than for females. In the van de Poll *et al.* (1982) data, T appeared to be critical for differential reactions to agonistic experiences, but the effects of estrogens were not examined. In our sample, T was important only in conjunction with E_2 (i.e., the ratio of T/E_2).

In summary, based on hormonal indices of maturation, earlier maturers generally exhibited more negative effects of maturation than did later maturers. This was true for both boys and girls. However, the consequences of earlier maturation were more dramatic for boys than for girls. The negative behavioral aspects of earlier maturation for boys may be partially attributable to relative hypersensitivity to androgens in males. Socialization influences and biological factors may enable girls to inhibit the activating influence of hormones.

Caution is advised in formulating conclusions about relations between hormones and behaviors. The cross-sectional findings do not allow us to infer causal relations between hormones and behavior. Moreover, reciprocal relations exist between hormones and behavior; that is, hormone levels may affect behavior and, conversely, behavior may affect hormone levels. For instance, depression often activates hypothalamic-pituitary-adrenal function, and higher levels of adrenal androgens may sometimes be the consequence rather than the cause of depression. Thus, our findings should not necessarily be taken to imply the direction of influence between hormones and behavior. Hypotheses about the specific effects of gonadotropins, sex steroids, and adrenal androgens need to be tested experimentally. Finally, there are few empirical findings with humans or animals to guide the formulation of hypotheses about the effects of specific hormones on specific behaviors, with the exception of testosterone and aggression. Our study represents an effort to begin to clarify the relations between hormones and behavior during early adolescence.

ACKNOWLEDGMENT

The authors would like to thank Marian Radke-Yarrow for her support for all aspects of this project.

REFERENCES

Abraham, G. E., Busler, G. E., Lucas, L. A., Corrales, P. C., and Teller, R. C. (1972). Chromatographic separation of steroid hormones for use in radioimmunoassay. *Analyt. Letters* 5: 509-517.
Bancroft, J., Sanders, D., Davidson, D., and Warner, P. (1983). Mood, sexuality, hormones, and the menstrual cycle. III. Sexuality and the role of androgens. *Psychosom. Med.* 45: 509-516.
Blyth, D. A., Simmons, R. G., Bulcroft, R., Felt, D., Van Cleave, E. F., and Bush, D. M. (1981). The effects of physical development on self-esteem and satisfaction with body-image for early adolescent males. *Res. Commun. Ment. Hlth.* 2: 43-73.
Boyer, R. Finkelstein, J., and Roffwang, H. (1972). Synchronization of augmented luteinizing hormone secretion with sleep during puberty. *New Eng. J. Med.* 287: 582-586.
Brambilla, F., Smeraldi, E., Sacchetti, E., Negri, F., Cocchi, D., and Muller, E. E. (1978). Deranged anterior pituitary responsiveness to hypothalamic hormones in depressed patients. *Arch. Gen. Psychiat.* 35: 1231-1238.
Broverman, D. M., Klaiber, E. L., Kobayashi, Y., and Vogel, W. (1968). Roles of activation and inhibition in sex differences in cognitive abilities. *Psych. Rev.* 75: 23-50.
Cargille, C. M., and Rayford, P. L. (1970). Characterization of antisera for follicle-stimulating hormone radioimmunoassay. *J. Lab. Clin. Med.* 75: 1030-1040.
Clausen, J. A. (1975). The social meaning of differential physical and sexual maturation. In Dragastin, S. E., and Elder, G. H., Jr. (eds.), *Adolescence in the Life Cycle: Psychological Change and Social Context*, Hemisphere, Washington, D.C.
Collu, R., and Ducharme, J. R. (1978). Role of adrenal steroids in the initiation of pubertal mechanisms. In James, V. H. T., Serio, M., Giusti, G., and Martini, L. (eds.), *The Endocrine Function of the Human Adrenal Cortex*, Academic Press, London.
Cutler, G. B., Jr., Glenn, M., Bush, M., Hodgen, G., Graham, C. E., and Loriaux, D. L. (1978). Adrenarche: A survey of rodents, domestic animals and primates. *Endocrinology* 103: 2112-2118.
DeLignieres, B., and Vincens, M. (1982). Differential effects of exogenous oestradiol and progesterone on mood in post-menopausal women: Individual dose/effect relationship. *Maturitas* 4: 67-72.
Ehrhardt, A., and Meyer-Bahlburg, H. (1975). Psychosocial correlates of abnormal pubertal development. *Clin. Endocrinol. Metab.* 4: 207-222.
Erb, J. L. Kadane, J. B., Tourney, G., Mickelsen, D., Szabo, R., and David, V. (1981). Discrimination between schizophrenic and control subjects by means of plasma dehydroepiandrosterone measurements. *J. Clin. Endocrinol. Metab.* 52: 181-186.

Faust, M. S. (1960). Developmental maturity as a determinant in prestige of adolescent girls. *Child Dev.* 31: 173-184.
Ferrier, I. N., Cotes, P. M., Crow, T. J., and Johnstone, E. C. (1982). Gonadotropin secretion abnormalities in chronic schizophrenia. *Psychol. Med.* 12: 263-273.
Forest, M. G., Cathiard, A. M., and Bertrand, J. A. (1973). Evidence of testicular activity in early infancy. *J. Clin. Endocrinol. Metab.* 37: 148-151.
Forest, M. G., Simonenko, P. C., Cathiard, A. M., and Bertrand, J. A. (1974). Hypophysogonadal function in humans during the first year of life. *J. Clin. Investig.* 53: 819-828.
Frisch, R. E., Revelle, R., and Cook, S. (1973). Components of weight at menarche and the initiation of the adolescent growth spurt in girls: Estimated total water, lean body weight and fat. *Hum. Biol.* 45: 469-483.
Gallo, R. V. (1980). Futher studies on dopamine-induced supression of pulsatile LH release in ovariectomized rats. *Neuroendocrinology* 32: 187-192.
Gold, P. W., and Chrousos, G. P. (In press). Clinical studies with corticotropin releasing factor: Implications for the diagnosis and pathophysiology of depression, Cushing's disease and adrenal insufficiency. *Psychoneuroendocrinology.*
Gray, J. A., and Buffery, A. W. H. (1971). Sex differences in emotional and cognitive behavior in mammals including man: Adaptive and neural bases. *Acta Psychologica* 35: 89-111.
Hamburg, B. A., and Inoff, G. E. (1982). Relationships between behavioral factors and diabetic control in children and adolescents: A camp study. *Psychosoma. Med.* 44: 321-339.
Hollingshead, A. B. (1975). *Four Factor Index of Social Status,* New Haven, Conn., Yale University.
Houser, B. B. (1979). An investigation of the correlation between hormonal levels in males and mood, behavior, and physical discomfort. *Hormones Behav.* 12: 185-197.
Inoff, G. E., and Halverson, C. F., Jr. (1977). Behavioral disposition of child and caretaker-child interaction. *Dev. Psychol.* 13: 274-281.
Johnstone, E. C., and Ferrier, I. N. (1980). Neuroendocrine markers of CNS drug effects. *Br. J. Clin. Pharmacol.* 10: 5-21.
Jones, M. C., and Bayley, N. (1950). Physical maturing among boys as related to behavior. *J. Educ. Psychol.* 41: 129-148.
Lloyd, J. A. (1975). Social behavior and hormones. In Eleftheriou, B. E., and Sprott, R. L. (eds.), *Hormonal Correlates of Behavior: A Lifespan View,* Vol. 1, New York, Plenum Press, pp. 185-204.
Marshall, W. A., and Tanner, J. M. (1969). Variations in the pattern of pubertal changes in girls. *Arch. Dis. Childhood* 44: 291-303.
Marshall, W. A., and Tanner, J. M. (1970). Variations in the pattern of pubertal changes in boys. *Arch. Dis. Childhood* 45: 13-23.
Mattsson, A., Schalling, D., Olweus, D., Low, H., and Svensson, J. (1980). Plasma testosterone, aggressive behavior, and personality dimensions in young male delinquents. *J. Am. Acad. Child Psychiat.* 19: 476-490.
Newcombe, N., and Bandura, M. M. (1983). Effect of age at puberty on spatial ability in girls: A question of mechanism. *Dev. Psychol.* 19: 215-224.
Nieschlag, E., and Loriaux, D. L. (1972). Radioimmunoassay for plasma testosterone. *Z. Klin. Chem. Klin. Biochem.* 10: 164-168.
Nottelmann, E. D., Susman, E. J., Dorn, L. D., Inoff-Germain, G. E., Loriaux, D. J., Cutler, G. B. Jr., and Chrouses, G. P. (1985). Developmental processes in early adolescence: I. Relations among chronological age, pubertal stage, height, weight and serum levels of gonadotropins, sex steroids, and adrenal androgens. Manuscript submitted for publication.
Odell, W. D., Ross, G. T., and Rayford, P. L. (1967). Radioimmunoassay for luteinizing hormone in human plasma or serum: Physiological studies. *J. Clin. Investig.* 46: 248-255.
Offer, D., Ostrov, E., and Howard, K. I. (1977). *The Offer Self-Image Questionnaire for Adolescents. A Manual,* Chicago, Micheal Reese Hospital.
Olweus, D., Mattsson, A., Schalling, D., and Low, H. (1980). Testosterone aggression, physical, and personality dimensions in normal adolescent males. *Psychosom. Med.* 42: 253-269.
Peskin, H. (1967). Pubertal onset and ego functioning: A psychoanalytic approach. *J. Abnorm. Psychol.* 72: 1-15.

Peskin, H., and Livson, N. (1972). Pre- and post-pubertal personality and adult psychological functioning. *Seminars Psychiat.* 4: 343-353.
Pfaff, D. W. (1980). *Estrogens and Brain Function,* New York, Springer-Verlag.
Reyes, F. I., Winter, J. S. D., and Faiman, C. (1973). Studies on human sexual development. I. Fetal gonadal and adrenal sex steroids. *J. Clin. Endocrinol.* 37: 74-78.
Reyes, F. I., Boroditsky, R. S., Winter, J. S. D., and Fairron, C. (1974). Studies on human sexual development. II. Fetal and maternal serum gonadotropins and sex steroid concentration. *J. Clin. Endocrinol.* 38: 612-617.
Sar, M. (1984). Estradiol is concentrated in tyrosine-hydroxylase-containing neurons of the hypothalamus. *Science* 223: 938-940.
Simmons, R. G., Blyth, D. A., and McKinney, K. L. (1983). The social and psychological effects of puberty on White females. In Brooks-Gunn, J., and Perterson, A. C. (eds.), *Girls at Puberty,* New York, Plenum.
van de Poll, N. E., Smeets, J., van Oyen, H. G., and van der Zwan, S. M. (1982). Behavioral consequences of agonistic experience in rats: Sex differences and the effects of testosterone. *J. Compar. Physiol. Psychol.* 96: 893-903.
Waber, D. P. (1977). Sex differences in mental abilities, hemispheric lateralization and rate of physical growth at adolescence. *Dev. Psychol.* 13: 29-38.

Biological and Social Contributions to Negative Affect in Young Adolescent Girls

J. Brooks-Gunn
Educational Testing Service

Michelle P. Warren
St. Luke's-Roosevelt Hospital Center, Columbia College of Physicians and Surgeons

BROOKS-GUNN, J., and WARREN, MICHELLE P. *Biological and Social Contributions to Negative Affect in Young Adolescent Girls.* CHILD DEVELOPMENT, 1989, 60, 40–55. This study is a preliminary attempt to investigate whether internal or external pubertal changes and whether social or biological factors are more likely to be associated with negative affect. About 100 white girls aged 10–14 years were given a physical examination, had blood drawn, and filled out the Youth Behavior Profile and a life-events checklist. Negative affect increased during the most rapid rises in hormone levels; however, hormones accounted for only 4% of the variance in negative affect. Pubertal status and timing were not associated with negative affect. In contrast, social factors accounted for more variance than hormonal pubertal factors alone (8%–18%), as did the interaction of negative life events and pubertal factors (9%–15%). Results are discussed in terms of what hormonal activation effects are most likely to be found, the meaning of such effects for subsequent behavior, and the interaction of biological and social events.

"Storm and stress" is one of the appellations frequently applied to the early adolescent life phase, since emotional expression is believed to become more intense, labile, and negative at this time compared to late childhood (Blos, 1979; Deutsch, 1944; Hall, 1904). The emotionality and moodiness of the young adolescent are often considered typical of the life phase rather than an indicator of clinical dysfunction (Offer, 1987). While considered normative, considerable interindividual variation in emotional expression exists, even though on the average increases are seen between childhood and adolescence (Larson, Csikszentmihalyi, & Graef, 1980; Rutter, Graham, Chadwick, & Yule, 1976; Simmons, Rosenberg, & Rosenberg, 1973). Sex differences in emotional expression and clinical disorders also often emerge in early to middle adolescence (depression and eating behavior, either in their mild or severe forms, are more characteristic of young women than young men; Crisp, 1984; Garner & Garfinkel, 1985; Rutter et al., 1976; Rutter, Izard, & Read, 1986).

Hormonal factors have been postulated to account in part for the rise in negative emotions as well as their links with gender; given the tantalizing associations (regrettably based on few studies) between hormone levels and certain behavioral-affective clusters in primates and human adults, it is possible that changes in hormone levels during early adolescence may have activating effects on such behavioral-affective clusters (Beach, 1975; Coe, 1988; Tieger, 1980). Hormonal activation may influence behavior directly or indirectly. With few exceptions (sexual and aggressive behavior), hormones are thought to influence behavior indirectly, via excitability, arousal, or emotionality, which in turn may influence how individuals behave. The present study focuses on negative emotional expression, specifically depressive and aggressive affect, in the early adolescent period (ages 10–14) when large biological changes occur.

Clinical disorders are not addressed in this normative study, even though hormonal

---

The research reported in this paper was funded by the National Institutes of Health and the W. T. Grant Foundation; we appreciate their support. We wish to thank all of those who contributed their time and energy to the Adolescent Study Program; J. Gargiulo, D. Friedman, L. Ferrington, and M. Samelson for collecting the data; L. Yen and E. Ewen for conducting the assays; J. Rosso and R. Fox for analyzing the data; L. Lissemore and R. Deibler for preparing the manuscript; the schools and the families for participating in the study. Portions of this paper were presented at the Society for Research in Child Development meetings, Baltimore, April 1987. Reprint requests may be addressed to Dr. J. Brooks-Gunn, Educational Testing Service, Princeton, NJ 08541.

[*Child Development*, 1989, 60, 40–55. © 1989 by the Society for Research in Child Development, Inc. All rights reserved. 0009-3920/89/6001-0013$01.00]

associations have been postulated in adult women (depression and estrogen; Klaiber, Broverman, Vogel, & Kobayashi, 1979; Oppenheim, 1983; Strober, 1985) and adult men (conduct disorders/aggression and testosterone in studies of criminality; Rubin, Reinisch, & Hasket, 1981), and increases in certain clinical disorders occur postpubertally (but typically not pubertally; Crisp, 1984; Garner & Garfinkel, 1985; Rutter et al., 1976, 1986). It is our premise that associations between negative emotional expression and hormonal changes will occur when the endocrine system is being "turned on," in the sense of moving from prepubertal to postpubertal levels. Three questions are being addressed in this study: (a) whether and how hormone levels are related to depressive and aggressive affect; (b) whether internal or external pubertal changes are more likely to be associated with depressive and aggressive affect; and (c) whether pubertal or social factors account for more variance in self-reports of depressive and aggressive affect.

First, hormone-affect associations were expected. Whether these are linear or nonlinear will be tested. Although previous investigators have examined only linear relations (Olweus, Mattsson, Schalling, & Low, 1980; Susman et al., 1987; Udry, Billy, Morris, Groff, & Raj, 1985), we believe that negative emotional expression is more likely to increase at the time of the most rapid hormone increases, when the endocrine system is beginning to function, than later, after the early hormonal rises have taken place. Individuals may be more sensitive to hormonal level rises when the endocrine system is undergoing early changes than when the system is undergoing later changes and is beginning to stabilize at more adult levels (or, for females, with adult patterns of cyclic fluctuations). Additionally, the role of various hormones in emotional expression will be explored. Given previous research, estrogens and androgens are likely candidates. Changes in estradiol levels may be associated with depressive affect and well-being in adult women, testosterone with sexual arousal, and adrenal androgens with stressful events (Klaiber et al., 1979; Melges & Hamburg, 1977; Parker, Levin, & Lifrak, 1985; Udry et al., 1985; Zipser et al., 1981). However, the endocrine system, being integrated, may not be amenable to efforts to "partial out" variance (Cohen & Cohen, 1975). Hormone-affect associations, if they are activational, may be due to general rises in gonadal and hypothalamic-pituitary hormones rather than to any one hormone in particular. To examine specific and general hormonal influences, regressions with individual hormones and hormonal groupings will be constructed.

Second, while few studies have directly addressed possible activation effects of hormones during early adolescence, evidence is accumulating on relations between behavior and the obvious manifestations of pubertal processes (the growth spurt, secondary sexual characteristic development, and menarche; Brooks-Gunn, Petersen, & Eichorn, 1985; Gunnar & Collins, 1988; Hill, 1982; Lerner & Foch, 1987). However, these changes are not only biological but also carry psychological meaning to the young person experiencing them and have social stimulus value to others. For example, girls alter their self-definitions at the time of menarche and the onset of breast growth (Brooks-Gunn & Warren, 1988; Ruble & Brooks-Gunn, 1982), and parents and peers respond differently to girls as a function of pubertal status (Blyth, Simmons, & Zakin, 1985; Hill, 1988; Hill, Holmbeck, Marlow, Green, & Lynch, 1985; Simmons & Blyth, 1987; Steinberg, 1987). Most of this research addresses relationships with others and aspects of self-image and self-esteem rather than emotional expression (see, for exceptions, Brooks-Gunn & Warren, 1985; Petersen & Crockett, 1985; Susman et al., 1987). Emotionality may be more likely to be associated with hormonal changes than other domains of behavior, which are more dependent on social interactions for their emergence and maintenance. We need to ask, then, in what circumstances may behavior-affective clusters be influenced by biological factors and in what ones may effects be mediated by the social stimulus value of physical changes, which are themselves influenced by hormonal factors? In order to separate these possible influences, we are able to take advantage of the fact that the levels of circulating gonadal hormones do not show a one-to-one correspondence with secondary sexual characteristics, in part because of individual differences in sensitivity to hormones and in what gonadal-releasing hormones influence which secondary changes (Faiman & Winter, 1974). It is expected that hormonal changes will be more strongly associated with emotional expression than will physical changes of puberty.

Third, given that social events have been shown to play a role in emotional expression in adolescents and adults (Compas, 1987; Kaplan, 1983; Thoits, 1983), the relative influence of pubertal and social factors must be considered. It is expected that social events

42 Child Development

will explain more variance in emotional expression than pubertal events, given the large effect sizes seen in the life events literature and the small effect sizes seen in the admittedly sparse hormone literature cited earlier.

To summarize, three issues were examined in the present study, having to do with possible hormone/affect links occurring in the early adolescent period. It is expected that depressive and aggressive affect will rise at the time when the endocrine system is first changing (pre- to mid-puberty), that greater effects will be found for gonadal hormones than external physical changes, and that social events will account for more variance than biological ones. A nonclinical sample of young adolescent girls was chosen given our focus on the normative course of emotional expression rather than on clinical or severe emotional disorders.

Method

Subjects

One hundred and three white girls who were 10–14 years of age (mean age, 12.13; SD, .80) and in the fifth to seventh grades were seen at the end of the school year. The girls attended one of several private day schools in New York City, where private school attendance is common for middle- to upper-middle-class families who have not moved to the suburbs. These schools are academically oriented, and most of their students attend college, like most samples drawn from suburban school systems (see Brooks-Gunn et al., 1985; Hill, 1982). The girls' parents were well-educated; four-fifths of the mothers had graduated from college. Two-thirds of the mothers were working full-time or part-time. No demographic differences were found in relation to grade-in-school or school attended.

Procedure

Girls were recruited from a large cross-sectional study of female adolescent biopsychosocial development. Families were invited to participate in a longitudinal study involving one yearly visit to a hospital laboratory where physical, hormonal, nutritional, and social aspects of development would be assessed. Sixty-seven percent of the families contacted participated. Nonparticipation was due to (a) the family moving from the metropolitan area, the adolescent's attendance at boarding school, or scheduling conflicts due to the adolescent's school activities or summer vacations (17%); and (b) the adolescent's reluctance to have a physical examination or have blood drawn (16%). The families who participated in the longitudinal study did not differ from those who did not participate on maternal education, maternal employment, birth order, social class, initial physical development, and selected aspects of psychological development (as measured by the nine subscales of the Self-Image Questionnaire for Young Adolescents; Petersen, Schulenberg, Abramowitz, Offer, & Jarcho, 1984). All girls were seen in the late spring and summer of 1983. The data were gathered in a physical examination, by questionnaire, and by interview. Girls were paid for their laboratory visit.

Measures

Self-report scales were chosen to measure depressive and aggressive affect as well as life events. Pubertal status was measured via physical examination, and hormonal status via blood sample.

Affective expression.—The Youth Behavior Profile, developed by Achenbach and Edelbrock (1983, 1987) from their Child Behavior Checklist, was used to assess two emotional states—depressed-withdrawal and aggressive affect. These dimensions are moderately reliable across instruments and studies; moreover, they discriminate between children referred for psychosocial problems and nonreferred children (Achenbach & Edelbrock, 1981, 1983; Boyle & Jones, 1985). Girls indicated whether items were not at all true, somewhat true, or very true of themselves (3-point Likert scale); sum scores were used in the analyses. Alpha coefficients were .68 for the depressive-withdrawal and .82 for the aggressive affect scales. Item inclusion procedures were used for girls over 12 (even though some of our girls were younger). These scores may not be used to identify girls with clinical depression or conduct disorders.

Life events.—A list of possible significant life events was generated using earlier scales designed for adolescents (Coddington, 1972; Johnson & McCutcheon, 1980) and open-ended responses to questions about significant events obtained in an earlier cross-sectional study. Given previous research indicating that undesirable life events are more likely to be related to psychological and physical problems than desirable ones (Compas, 1987; Johnson, 1982) and that 12–14-year-olds typically use only the appraisal of desirability to distinguish life events (rather than multiple dimensions, including impact and specificity of cause; Davis & Compas, 1986), events were classified as positive or negative. Classifications were based on previous research (Davis & Compas, 1986; Johnson & McCutcheon, 1980). Twelve positive and 19 negative life events were included from the three contexts in which the young adolescent operates—family, friend, and school. Girls were asked to indicate if any of the events had occurred in the past 6 months.

Pubertal development.—Each girl was given a physical examination, at which time Tanner ratings were obtained; pubic hair growth and breast development were rated on a five-point scale, from prepubertal to postpubertal (Marshall & Tanner, 1969; Reynolds & Wines, 1948). The examinations were conducted by the second author or by a nurse practitioner. Interobserver reliabilities between the two were obtained by an independent assessment of 10 girls; agreement was 100% on pubic hair and 90% on breast development. Questions were asked about menarcheal age; such reports are quite accurate, even for this age group (Brooks-Gunn, Warren, Rosso, & Gargiulo, 1987; Damon, Damon, Reed, & Valadian, 1969). The percentage of girls in each Tanner breast stage (pubic hair stage) were as follows: 20% (17%) in Stage 1; 35% (25%) in Stage 2; 28% (25%) in Stage 3; 15% (23%) in Stage 4; 2% (10%) in Stage 5. The correlation between the two was .65.

Girls were classified as early, on-time, or late maturers by Tanner ratings, using National Health Examination Survey norms (Duke et al., 1982). Girls in the highest and lowest twentieth percentiles of Tanner staging for their age were classified as early and later, respectively, while those in the middle 60% were classified as on time.[1]

Hormonal assessment.—Measurements of serum FSH (follicle stimulating hormone), LH (luteinizing hormone), estradiol, DHEAS (dehydroepiandosterone sulfate), and testosterone by specific RIA were made. Assays for LH and FSH were performed as previously described (Warren, 1980). Estradiol was measured by a Serono Diagnostics kit that employs a standard double antibody radioimmunoassay technique. All samples were determined in duplicate to decrease intraassay error, with a mean difference between duplicates of 2%. Interassay coefficient of variation ranged between 2% and 4%. Intraassay coefficient of variation ranged between 1% and 2% (Abraham, Manlimos, & Gargu, 1977). DHEAS was measured by a Diagnostic Products kit that employs antibody-coated tubes for a radioimmunoassay in which 125 I-labeled DHEA-SO4 competes with DHEA-SO4. Separation of bond from free is achieved by decanting. Cross-reaction antibody with other steroids is low, and the assay may differentiate 2.1 μg/dl from zero.

TABLE 1

MEAN LEVELS OF SERUM HORMONES[a]

Hormone	Mean	SD
Estradiol (pg/ml)	44.59	42.44
LH (ng/ml) LER907	28.74	16.11
FSH (ng/ml) LER907	142.04	49.51
Testosterone (ng/ml)	.44	.21
DHEAS (ug/dl)	111.25	56.02

[a] $N = 103$ early adolescent girls, mean age, 12.13.

Blood was taken at the same time of the day for all girls to reduce the chance of possible interindividual diurnal variations in hormonal levels. Late afternoon rather than morning assays were taken, given school and family schedules (as this is a school-based, not medical clinic-based, sample). Following previous research, one blood sample was drawn (Udry et al., 1985); intraindividual variation was minimal in the one study using a time technique to collect blood three times over 60 min (Nottelmann et al., 1987). Twenty percent of the girls had begun to menstruate, all but one in the past 6 months; only one of these girls was reporting regular cycles, making it likely that many of them were experiencing anovulatory cycles. The mean levels of the five hormones are presented in Table 1. The values are comparable to other studies of young adolescent girls (Nottelmann et al., 1987).

In order to test the premise that depressive and aggressive affect will increase during the most rapid endocrine system changes, hormonal categories were derived. Estradiol was used (*a*) because it is the principal gonadal hormone in girls; (*b*) because it exhibits the most dramatic increases during puberty (serum estradiol increases approxi-

---

[1] At age 11, a girl was classified early if her combined Tanner rating for breast and pubic hair development was between 3.5 and 5.0, as on time if she was between 1.5 and 3.0, and late if she was 1.0. At age 12, a girl was classified as early if her Tanner rating was between 4.0 and 5.0, as on time if she was between 2.0 and 3.5, and late if she was between 1.0 and 1.5. At age 13, an early maturer's Tanner rating was between 4.5 and 5.0, an on-time maturer between 3.0 and 4.0, and a late maturer between 1.0 and 2.5. At age 14, early maturation was a rating of 4.5 or 5.0, on-time maturation a rating of 3.5 or 4.0, and late maturation as a rating of 1.0 to 3.0.

44 Child Development

mately 8 to 10-fold, testosterone 5-fold, and DHEAS, LH, and FSH 2 to 4-fold; Apter, 1980; Apter & Vihko, 1977; Faiman & Winter, 1974; Grumbach, 1980); (c) because the rises occur principally between Tanner Stage 1–4, which corresponds to our sample's status; and (d) because estradiol is associated with many of the physical changes of puberty. The four groupings were 2–25, 26–50, 51–74, and 75 and higher of estradiol (pg/ml). Levels of less than 25 pg/ml are generally known to have minimal effect. Levels of 25–50 pg/ml generally have early visible physiological effects such as secondary sexual development, and effects on the vagina estrogens at this level are generally not significant enough to cause proliferation of the endometrium and withdrawal bleeding with a progesterone challenge. Levels of 50–75 pg/ml typically are commensurate with mid or late puberty and early follicular levels in menstruating girls. These levels have significant effects on endometrial growth and other organs such as the breast. Girls with levels in this range would generally experience withdrawal bleeding to progesterone and/or have spontaneous periods. Levels greater than 75 pg/ml are associated with cyclicity in women (Gold & Iosimovich, 1980; Grumbach & Sizonenko, 1986). Using these groupings also took into account LH levels, as almost no overlap in LH levels across the estradiol groupings was found.

Results

Zero-Order Correlations

Zero-order correlations among hormones, Tanner stages, age, and negative affect are presented in Table 2. As can be seen, hormonal levels were positively associated with each other, although the magnitude of the relation was often modest. Those of moderate magnitude (i.e., r's over .50) were estradiol and LH, LH and FSH, LH and testosterone, and testosterone and DHEAS. Associations with Tanner breast and pubic hair stages were moderate for estradiol and LH, modest for testosterone and DHEAS, and not significant for FSH. Age was moderately associated with Tanner stages and with estradiol; correlations were smaller in magnitude with the other four hormones.

Associations with Hormonal Levels

Associations between biological status and negative affect were tested via three different sets of analyses. The first is the most common method for assessing hormonal effects; it assumes linear and unique effects of individual hormones. Ordinary least-squares (OLS) regressions were performed, entering age and five hormones (FSH, LH, estradiol, testosterone, and DHEAS) as possible predictors. These were conducted in order to compare our findings with those of other researchers. The nonsignificant multiple R for depressive affect was .22 for all six variables entered; none of the individual variables had significant beta weights; and no significant associations for the zero-order correlations were found (Table 2). The multiple R for aggression of .24 also was not significant; however, DHEAS was negatively associated with aggression in the zero-order correlations (see Table 2), and in the OLS regression (beta = $-.21$, $p < .08$).

The second set of analyses tests linear and nonlinear effects; we entered gonadal and adrenal hormones in this equation—estradiol, testosterone, and DHEAS. The square of each hormone also was entered as a test for nonlinear associations (Cohen & Cohen, 1975). In this regression, the variables were entered hierarchically: (a) age was entered first (as a "control");[2] (b) estradiol was entered second, given the postulated links between estrogen and depressive affect and the fact that estradiol is the main gonadal hormone showing large increases in pubertal girls; and (c) testosterone and DHEAS were entered last (other analyses found no linear or nonlinear effects for LH and FSH). The findings, presented in Table 3, indicate a nonlinear effect of estradiol for depressive affect. No other hormone effects, linear or nonlinear, entered the equation. As seen in Table 3, a linear effect of DHEAS was found for aggression.

Given the existence of nonlinear effects for estradiol, we proceeded to test our premise about rises in affect only occurring during the most rapid rise in hormones. Girls were divided into four categories, as described earlier. The mean depressive affect scores were found to differ as a function of estradiol cate-

---

[a] Age was entered as a factor separate from the biological ones in all analyses (Susman et al., 1987; Udry et al., 1985). This was done since age is associated with social as well as maturational change in puberty and since one of our aims was to examine relative effects of biological and social factors. However, rerunning all regressions with age entered last rather than first did not alter any of the findings reported here.

TABLE 2

ZERO-ORDER CORRELATIONS BETWEEN HORMONAL LEVELS, AGE, PUBERTAL STATUS, AND EMOTIONAL EXPRESSION

	Depressive Withdrawal Affect	Aggressive Affect	Estradiol	LH	FSH	Testosterone	DHEAS	Tanner Breast	Tanner Pubic Hair
Age	.10	−.04	.46**	.33*	.21	.29*	.36*	.58**	.48*
Depressive-withdrawal		.60**	.03	.05	.11	−.02	−.03	−.07	−.01
Aggressive affect			−.15	−.07	−.02	−.12	−.20*	−.00	.04
Estradiol				.54**	.34*	.39*	.21	.59**	.62**
LH					.60**	.54**	.39**	.54**	.60**
FSH						.31*	.16	.28*	.30*
Testosterone							.52	.45**	.47**
DHEAS								.36*	.43*
Tanner breast									.65**

* $p < .05$.
** $p < .01$.

46 Child Development

TABLE 3
POSSIBLE LINEAR AND NONLINEAR HORMONAL RELATIONS WITH DEPRESSIVE AFFECT AND AGGRESSIVE AFFECT

Step	Variable	Depressive Affect			Aggressive Affect		
		Multiple R	R^2 Change	Beta[a]	Multiple R	R^2 Change	Beta
1	Age	.07	.01	.07	.04	.00	−.04
2	Estradiol	.08	.00	.02	.15	.02	−.16
3	Estradiol^2	.22	.04**	−.62	.17	.01	−.27
4	DHEAS	.24	.01	−.09	.26	.04*	−.20
5	DHEAS^2	.24	.00	−.04	.26	.00	.14
6	Testosterone	.26	.01	−.15	.24	.00	−.02
7	Testosterone^2	.27	.00	−.19	.27	.01	.31

* $p < .05$.
** $p < .001$.

gory, with the relation being curvilinear and the quadratic function being significant, even after controlling for age (see Table 4): depressive affect increased between the first and third category and decreased between the third and fourth category. A series of hierarchical analyses were performed in order to control for other possible hormone relations in contributing to this last finding. Variables were entered in the following order: (a) age; (b) estradiol; (c) estradiol^2 (given the nonlinear effect just shown); (d) LH and (e) FSH; and testosterone and DHEAS. Only the nonlinear effect of estradiol reached significance in the equation.

For aggressive affect, a similar but nonsignificant quadratic trend ($p < .07$) was found: aggressive affect increased between the first and third category but not thereafter.

The nonlinear effect of estradiol did not reach significance in the hierarchical regression. However, DHEAS entered the equation (multiple $R = .26$, R^2 change $= .03$, $p < .10$, beta weight $= -.21$). When DHEAS was entered second (given the earlier results), the R^2 change was significant at the .05 level.

Biological Factors With and Without Social Signal Value

Our second issue concerned the relative effects of biological factors with and without social signal value. Following others (Susman et al., 1987; Udry et al., 1985), OLS regressions were conducted in which secondary sexual characteristic development (Tanner breast and pubic hair stage), maturational timing, and menarcheal status were entered as well as age and the five hormones. For depressive affect, the multiple R was not signifi-

TABLE 4
MEAN SCORES FOR DEPRESSIVE AND AGGRESSIVE AFFECT BY AGE AND ESTRADIOL LEVEL

	Depressive Affect[b]		Aggressive Affect[c]		
	Mean	SD	Mean	SD	N
Estradiol:[a]					
One (2–25)	5.88	3.05	10.91	4.62	44
Two (26–50)	6.96	3.47	13.00	7.32	24
Three (51–74)	8.07	2.84	10.93	4.37	16
Four (75–100)	5.94	2.77	9.16	5.92	21
Age:					
10½	6.75	3.89	12.36	8.92	43
11½	6.21	2.90	10.80	5.26	24
12½	6.63	3.19	10.96	5.56	15
13½	6.58	3.29	10.06	4.57	18

[a] Estradiol (pg/ml).
[b] Quadratic trend, $p < .05$.
[c] Quadratic trend, $p < .10$.

cant, as were none of the individual beta weights for any of the biological factors. Given our finding of a nonlinear effect of estradiol, a hierarchical regression was performed in which age, estradiol, estradiol^2, physical status (menarche, breast and pubic hair stages), and timing of maturation were entered. Only the nonlinear effect of estradiol was significant (multiple R for that step was .23, R^2 change was .04, $p < .05$, beta weight $= -.62$; the overall multiple R for the entire equation was .24, suggesting that, in the case of depressive affect, hormonal but not physical changes were associated with affective expression.

For aggressive affect, the multiple R in the OLS regression was not significant. In a hierarchical regression entering estradiol and physical status measurements, no pubertal index entered the equation. Entering DHEAS and physical status measurements resulted in DHEAS significantly entering the equation.

The Contribution of Biological and Social Events

To examine the relative role of social and biological events in emotional expression, two sets of hierarchical regressions were performed, one in which external physical status measures were entered and one in which hormonal measures were entered. In the first set, the following factors were entered: (a) age; (b) pubertal status (menarche, breast and pubic hair development, and maturational timing); (c) negative life events; (d) positive life events; and (e) interaction of negative life events and pubertal processes. (Given earlier findings that the interactions of positive life events and pubertal processes were not significant, they were not entered here.) As can be seen in Table 5, age and physical pubertal processes were not associated with depressive affect. However, negative but not positive life events were. A significant interaction was found between negative events and pubertal processes; the occurrence of negative events was more likely to be associated with depressive affect in premenarcheal than postmenarcheal girls, while in girls for whom no negative events occurred, depressive affect was somewhat higher postmenarcheally than premenarcheally. (The same was true using Tanner breast and pubic hair stages combined and breast stage separately but not pubic hair separately.) The interaction did not reach significance for aggressive affect.

A similar set of hierarchical regressions was conducted entering estradiol^2 (given the nonlinear effect found in earlier analyses) as well as negative and positive social events (see Table 6). Hormonal status did not enter the equation, while negative life events did. Unlike the earlier analyses, no interaction between hormonal status and negative life events was found. For aggressive affect, a hierarchical regression was run with DHEAS, given the results of earlier analyses (see Table 7). DHEAS as well as negative life events entered the equation, as did the interaction between hormonal status and negative life events (see Fig. 1). For girls with relatively low levels of DHEAS (median split), girls who experienced negative friend events had higher aggressive affect scores than those who had not had negative events occur; for the girls with higher levels of DHEAS, this relation was not found.

Discussion

While hormonal effects were found in the present study, they must be considered relative to other factors. Age alone was not associated with an increase in negative affect. While increases in negative affect from childhood to adolescence have been reported, results are mixed as to age-related differences within the early adolescent life phase (Achenbach & Edelbrock, 1981; Brooks-Gunn, Rock, & Warren, 1989; Simmons et al., 1973; Susman et al., 1987). Our findings suggest that when increases are reported within this life phase, they may be associated more with hormonal functioning than age per se, which may in part explain previous disparate findings. The endocrine system factors that were related to affect, however, accounted for no more than 4% of the variance in negative emotional expression. In the few studies of adolescent boys and girls and of normally cycling women, the hormone-affect associations, when found, also are small (Melges & Hamburg, 1977; Susman et al., 1987; Udry et al., 1985). No direct effects of pubertal status were found.

In contrast, social factors accounted for more variance (8% and 18% for depressive and aggressive affect, respectively) than biological factors. Thus, hormonal activation effects in humans may not be large (i.e., may account for a small portion of the variance in a particular behavior) and may be overshadowed by environmental events. We know the hypothalamic-pituitary-gonadal system is exquisitely sensitive to environmental conditions. For example, when weight loss is large (as in the case of anorexia nervosa), levels of gonadotropin secretions are suppressed in women, with the most obvious manifestation being amenorrhea and anovu-

TABLE 5

IMPACT OF PHYSICAL AND SOCIAL EVENTS ON DEPRESSIVE AFFECT AND AGGRESSIVE AFFECT

STEP	DOMAIN	VARIABLE	DEPRESSIVE AFFECT			AGGRESSIVE AFFECT		
			Multiple R	R^2 Change	Beta	Multiple R	R^2 Change	Beta
1	Age	Age	.10	.01	.10	.02	.00	−.13
2	Puberty	Timing	.13	.01	−.06	.06	.00	−.78
		Menarche			.02			−.43
		Tanner			.13			−.58
3	Negative events	Family	.30	.08*	.20	.43	.18**	1.69
		Friend			−.11			.94
		School			.18			1.46
4	Positive events	Family	.32	.01	.09	.46	.02	.35
		Friend			.07			−.07
		School			.01			−.74
5	Negative events by puberty	Family	.44	.09**	−.99	.48	.02	−.00
		Friend			−.18			.42
		School			−.32			−1.08

* $p < .05$.
** $p < .01$.

TABLE 6
RELATION OF HORMONAL STATUS AND SOCIAL EVENTS TO DEPRESSIVE AFFECT

Step	Domain	Variable	Multiple R	R^2 Change	Beta
1	Age	Age	.10	.01	.10
2	Estradiol^2	Estradiol^2	.12	.01	−.05
3	Negative events	Family	.31	.08*	.20
		Friend			−.12
		School			.18
4	Positive events	Family	.32	.01	.08
		Friend			.06
		School			−.00
5	Negative events by estradiol^2	Family	.33	.01	.03
		Friend			−.19
		School			.15

* $p < .05$.

TABLE 7
RELATION OF HORMONAL STATUS AND SOCIAL EVENTS TO AGGRESSIVE AFFECT

Step	Domain	Variable	Multiple R	R^2 Change	Beta
1	Age	Age	.04	.00	−.04
2	DHEAS	DHEAS	.20	.04*	−.21
3	Negative events	Family	.47	.18**	.35
		Friend			.16
		School			.21
4	Positive events	Family	.49	.02	−.03
		Friend			−.03
		School			−.15
5	Negative events by DHEAS	Family	.63	.15**	.25
		Friend			1.26
		School			−.19

* $p < .05$.
** $p < .01$.

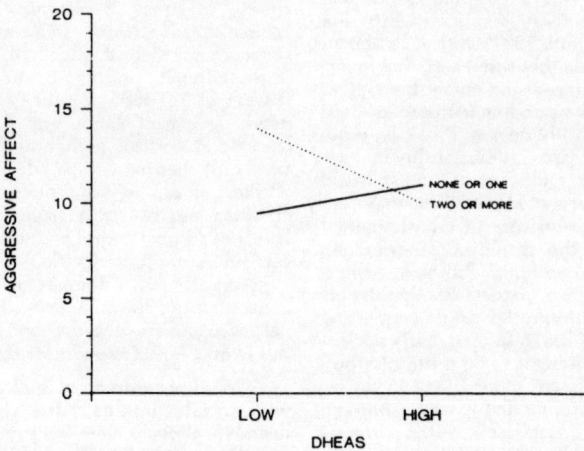

FIG. 1.—Relation between levels of DHEAS and negative friend events

latory cycles (Vigersky & Loriaux, 1977; Warren, 1985). In some adolescents with anorexia nervosa or exercise-induced weight loss, a reversion to the prepubertal pattern of low LH secretion, lowered amplitude secretion, and nocturnal LH spiking occurs (Boyar et al., 1972, 1974). These changes are reversible with weight gain. Also, the genetic program for the timing of puberty may be partially overridden through environmental factors such as nutritional intake, weight, and intensity and extensiveness of exercise (Brooks-Gunn, 1988; Malina, 1983). When interpreting the findings of this study, the relative influence of biological and social factors on emotionality must be considered.

With regard to hormonal contributions, no linear hormonal-depressive affect relations were found, although a curvilinear one was, such that depressive affect increased as the endocrine system was undergoing its greatest change (first three estradiol categories). These data fit our premise that activational effects may be greatest when the endocrine system is being turned on. Negative emotionality may reach an apex during the initiation of various endocrine functioning, as has been implied for other behaviors in the use of the term perturbation (Hill, 1988; Hill et al., 1985). Whether the nonlinear relation found for depressive affect and, to a lesser extent, for aggressive affect is specific to estradiol or is more generally related to the changes throughout the system may not be answered by the present study. Inferentially, evidence for a specific estradiol effect may be forthcoming from the few relevant animal and human studies linking activity levels and estradiol (Melges & Hamburg, 1977). Although speculative, it is possible that when estradiol levels rise for the first time, as the endocrine system is activated, a corresponding increase in excitability or arousability occurs. Possibly, emotionality also increases, as excitability may result in more rapid and/or more intense mood fluctuations (Larson et al., 1980) or may render a girl more sensitive to environmental conditions with the result of experiencing more negative emotions following interchanges with peers or parents or other events that could be interpreted as discomforting (Miller & Eccles, 1987). Indeed, early adolescence has been thought to be a life phase in which individuals are more likely to be influenced by environmental events, although this premise has not been tested directly (Brooks-Gunn, 1988). By late puberty, individuals may have adapted to the higher estradiol levels, in which case hormonal associations with emotionality may change. In adult women, lower estrogen levels may be associated with negative depressive affect and moderate levels with positive affect (deLignieres & Vincens, 1982; Melges & Hamburg, 1977; Southam & Gonzaga, 1965), although methodological problems in the menstrual, pregnancy, and menopause literature make these findings suggestive but not conclusive (Miller & Eccles, 1987; Parlee, 1973; Ruble & Brooks-Gunn, 1979). Our curvilinear findings (i.e., the drop in depressive affect in the fourth estradiol category) might be indicative of associations such as those reported for adult women.

At the same time, general endocrine system changes may not be ruled out as an explanation for the curvilinear association. The rapid changes throughout the endocrine system may be represented by the gonadal hormonal changes, so that the effects are not specific to estradiol. That similar findings emerged for aggressive affect would be supporting evidence for the general system premise. We hasten to add that causal inferences must be made with caution, or not at all, regardless of whether regression analyses or clustering of subjects by hormone profiles is used. Rises in hormonal levels and negative affective expression co-occur; only longitudinal analyses will allow for testing of directionality.

The possible role of adrenal androgens in emotional expression is intriguing. While adrenal androgens function in part like androgens from other sources (i.e., the gonads), they also may be indicative of adrenal response to stress (Sassenrath, 1970). In response to a stressor such as illness, adrenocortical steroid metabolism may shift from adrenal androgens toward cortisol (Parker et al., 1985; Zipser et al., 1981). Indeed, levels of DHA and DHEAS were lower and cortisol higher in a group of severely ill men as compared to healthy men (Parker et al., 1985). Young women with anorexia nervosa also have relatively low levels of adrenal androgens and high levels of cortisol (Zumoff et al., 1983). Environmental stressors also may influence adrenal androgen concentration; the interaction between adrenal androgens and negative (and possibly stressful) events lends support for this possibility.

No direct effects of biological changes with social stimulus value were found for negative affect. Other behaviors have been found to be associated with observable, physical changes, such as body image, self-consciousness, dating, and self-esteem (Blyth et al., 1985; Gargiulo, Attie, Brooks-Gunn, &

Warren, 1987; Ruble & Brooks-Gunn, 1982; Simmons, Blyth, & McKinney, 1983). Clearly, more work needs to be done to distinguish between behavior and affect associated with biological changes with and without psychological meaning. Emotional expression and sexual behavior seem likely candidates for direct hormonal associations, as in our findings and those of our colleagues (Olweus et al., 1980; Susman et al., 1987; Udry et al., 1985). Much more work needs to focus on possible direct and mediated effects. For example, levels of testosterone are related to sexual activity in boys, independent of secondary sexual development (Udry et al., 1985). However, whether engagement in sexual intercourse increases androgen levels or androgen levels influence sexual behavior is not known. Additionally, contextual effects, if entered into the equation, might account for more of the variation in sexual activity than hormonal levels. Initiation of sexuality is highly associated with what is normative in one's peer group (Furstenberg, Moore, & Peterson, 1986), so it is likely that while very early sexual initiations may in part be hormonally influenced, by the time the behavior is normative, social factors may account for sexual initiation (see Gargiulo et al., 1987, for a similar argument about dating behavior). Thus, even if hormonal effects are demonstrated, they must be evaluated relative to contextual effects and relative to interactive effects before assuming a direct relation between hormones and behavior.

Social factors and interactions accounted for more variance than pubertal factors in emotionality. Specifically, the combination of negative life events (8%) and the interaction of negative life events with the pubertal status measures and with social stimulus value (menarcheal status and breast growth, 9%) accounted for 17% of the variance in depressive affect. Even higher amounts of variance were explained for aggressive affect—18% by negative life events and 15% by the interaction of negative events and DHEAS. Many studies find stronger effects of pubertal status on behavior when interactions between biological and social factors are considered (Gargiulo et al., 1987; Magnusson, Stattin, & Allen, 1985; Simmons et al., 1983; Simmons & Blyth, 1987) or combinations of both types of factors are taken into account (Simmons, Burgeson, Carlton-Ford, & Blyth, 1987). For example, early-maturing girls with older friends were more likely to exhibit deviant behavior for their age group than were early maturers without older friends; also, early maturers had more older friends than later maturers (Magnusson et al., 1985). The present study extends previous work by focusing on affect and by including hormonal measures.

Limitations of this study include sampling of hormones at one point in time, which raises questions about stability, particularly with regard to diurnal variation and monthly cyclicity. In our study, diurnal variation was minimized by collecting samples at the same time of day across girls. Whether collection at another point in the day (i.e., early morning) or multiple samples across 24 hours would alter the hormone-affect associations reported here is unknown. With regard to hormonal levels, short-term changes (i.e., day-to-day lability) may be associated with mood fluctuations reported by adolescents (Larson et al., 1980); however, no study to date has examined this interesting issue. Monthly fluctuations were in part controlled by the fact that the few postmenarcheal girls all had begun to menstruate in the last 6 months and, with one exception, still had irregular cycles; also, examination of the LH and FSH levels suggested that no premenarcheal girls were exhibiting a LH surge prior to menarche (which has been reported in some clinical studies). Cyclic fluctuations in hormone concentrations do not stabilize in most girls for several years postmenarche (Winter & Faiman, 1973). Since most of our postmenarcheal girls had just begun to menstruate, we suspect that few girls were experiencing normal cycles. However, given the fact that girls with estradiol levels under 75 pg/ml (estradiol groups 1–3 in our analyses) typically do not exhibit cyclic hormonal variations (Grumbach & Sizonenko, 1986), the findings for the first three hormonal groups might be interpreted with more confidence than the findings for the fourth group (i.e., the rise in depressive affect from groups 1–3 may be more robust than the decline from group 3 to group 4).

Single-time blood draws may be more appropriate for examining general increases for the endocrine system than for individual hormones. Indeed, the hormone groupings were derived to test the hypothesis that hormone-negative affect associations, if found, would be most likely to be linked to general, early increases in endocrine system functioning than specific hormonal levels. This study was not designed to examine day-to-day fluctuations in affect or hormones but to examine possible increases in negative affect as a function of increases in endocrine output over the pubertal period.

Another possible limitation is that level of testosterone-estradiol binding globulin, a

52 Child Development

carrier protein perhaps more indicative of active testosterone, was not measured; however, in the one study in which it was, no relation to girls' self-reports of emotionality was found, although associations were reported for boys (Susman et al., 1987). This may be because variation in this binding globulin is less systematic in girls than boys, perhaps making it a better hormonal measure for the latter group (Cunningham, Loughlin, Culliton, & McKenna, 1984).

From the behavioral viewpoint, the Youth Behavior Profile, as used in this study, provides an indicator of negative affect; it is not a substitute for scales specifically designed to identify severe depression or conduct disorder. Finally, the findings of this study may not be generalized to other groups, such as boys or minority adolescent girls. Interactions between social and pubertal factors may be quite different for other groups, given the cross-cultural, ethnic, and gender variations in the meaning of pubertal change to the child in responses of others to a child's growth. Given the few studies examining hormone-behavior associations in adolescents, the expense, the invasive nature of obtaining hormone data, the reliance on clinical rather than school-based samples, and the use of single-point-in-time measures of behavior in most developmental studies, we feel that our data make a contribution over and above these limitations. However, we also see this study as a first step in elucidating hormone-behavior associations.

References

Abraham, G. E., Manlimos, F. S. H., & Gargu, R. (1977). Radioimmunoassay of steroids. In G. E. Abraham (Ed.), *Handbook of radioimmunoassay* (pp. 591–656). New York: Dekker.

Achenbach, T. M., & Edelbrock, C. S. (1981). Behavioral problems and competencies reported by the parents of normal and disturbed children aged 4 through 16. *Monographs of the Society for Research in Child Development*, 46(1, Serial No. 188).

Achenbach, T. M., & Edelbrock, C. (1983). *Manual for the Child Behavior Checklist and Revised Child Behavior Profile*. Burlington, VT: Queen City Printers.

Achenbach, T. M., & Edelbrock, C. (1987). *Manual for the Youth Self-Report Checklist and Profile*. Burlington: University of Vermont.

Apter, D. (1980). Serum steroids and pituitary hormone in female puberty: A partly longitudinal study. *Clinical Endocrinology*, 12, 107–120.

Apter, D., & Vihko, R. (1977). Serum pregnenolone, progesterone, 17-hydroxy-progesterone, testosterone and 5a-dihydrotestosterone during female puberty. *Journal of Clinical Endocrinology and Metabolism*, 45, 1039–1048.

Beach, F. A. (1975). Behavioral endocrinology: An emerging discipline. *American Scientist*, 63, 178–187.

Blos, P. (1979). *The adolescent passage*. New York: International Universities Press.

Blyth, D. A., Simmons, R. G., & Zakin, D. F. (1985). Satisfaction with body image for early adolescent females: The impact of pubertal timing within different school environments. *Journal of Youth and Adolescence*, 14, 207–225.

Boyar, R. M., Finkelstein, J., Roffwarg, H., Kapan, S., Wertzman, E., & Hellman, L. (1972). Synchronization of augmented luteinizing hormone secretion with sleep during puberty. *New England Journal of Medicine*, 287, 582–586.

Boyar, R. M., Katz, J., Finkelstein, J. W., Kapen, S., Weiner, H., Weitzman, E. D., & Hellman, L. (1974). Anorexia nervosa: Immaturity of the 24-hour luteinizing hormone secretory pattern. *New England Journal of Medicine*, 291, 861–865.

Boyle, M. H., & Jones, S. C. (1985). Selecting measures of emotional and behavioral disorders of childhood for use in general populations. *Journal of Child Psychology and Psychiatry*, 20, 137–159.

Brooks-Gunn, J. (1988). Transition to early adolescence. In M. Gunnar (Ed.), *Development during transition to adolescence. Minnesota symposia on child psychology* (Vol. 21, pp. 189–208). Hillsdale, NJ: Erlbaum.

Brooks-Gunn, J. (1988). Antecedents and consequences of variations in girls' maturational timing. *Journal of Adolescent Health Care*, 9(5), 1–9.

Brooks-Gunn, J., Petersen, A. C., & Eichorn, D. (1985). Special issue: The study of maturational timing effects in adolescence. *Journal of Youth and Adolescence*, 14, Vols. 3 & 4.

Brooks-Gunn, J., Rock, D., & Warren, M. P. (1989). Comparability of constructs across the adolescent years. *Developmental Psychology*, 25(1).

Brooks-Gunn, J., & Warren, M. P. (1985). Effects of delayed menarche in different contexts: Dance and nondance students. *Journal of Youth and Adolescence*, 14, 285–300.

Brooks-Gunn, J., & Warren, M. P. (1988). The psychological significance of secondary sexual characteristics in 9- to 11-year-old girls. *Child Development*, 59, 161–169.

Brooks-Gunn, J., Warren, M. P., Rosso, J., & Gargiulo, J. (1987). Validity of self-report measures of girls' pubertal status. *Child Development*, 58, 829–841.

Coddington, R. D. (1972). The significance of life events as etiologic factors in the diseases of children: A survey of professional workers. *Journal of Psychosomatic Research*, 16, 7–18.

Coe, C. (1988). The role of gonadal hormones in the pubertal transition: Activation or concatenation. In M. Gunnar & W. A. Collins (Eds.), *Minnesota symposia on child development* (Vol. 21, pp. 17–41). Hillsdale, NJ: Erlbaum.

Cohen, J., & Cohen, P. (1975). *Applied multiple regression/correlation analysis for the behavioral sciences*. Hillsdale, NJ: Erlbaum.

Compas, B. E. (1987). Coping with stress during childhood and adolescence. *Psychological Bulletin*, 101, 1–11.

Crisp, A. H. (1984). The psychopathology of anorexia nervosa: Getting the "heat" out of the system. In A. J. Stunkard & E. Stellar (Eds.), *Eating and its disorders* (pp. 209–234). New York: Raven.

Cunningham, S. K., Loughlin, T., Culliton, M., & McKenna, T. G. (1984). Plasma sex hormone-binding globulin levels decrease during the second decade of life irrespective of pubertal status. *Journal of Clinical Endocrinology and Metabolism*, 58, 915–918.

Damon, A., Damon, S. T., Reed, R. B., & Valadian, I. (1969). Age at menarche of mothers and daughters with a note of accuracy of recall. *Human Biology*, 41, 161–175.

Davis, G. E., & Compas, B. E. (1986). Cognitive appraisal of major and daily stressful events during adolescence: A multidimensional scaling analysis. *Journal of Youth and Adolescence*, 15, 377–388.

deLignieres, B., & Vincens, M. (1982). Differential effects of exogenous oestradiol and progesterone on mood in post-menopausal women: Individual dose/effect relationship. *Maturitas*, 4, 67–72.

Deutsch, H. (1944). *The psychology of women*. Vol. 1. New York: Grune & Stratton.

Duke, P. M., Carlsmith, J. M., Jennings, D., Martin, J. A., Dornbusch, S. M., Siegel-Gorelick, B., & Gross, R. T. (1982). Educational correlates of early and late sexual maturation in adolescence. *Journal of Pediatrics*, 100, 633–637.

Faiman, C., & Winter, J. S. D. (1974). Gonadotropins and sex hormone patterns in puberty: Clinical data. In M. M. Grumbach, G. D. Grave, & F. E. Mayer (Eds.), *Control of the onset of puberty* (pp. 32–61). New York: Wiley.

Furstenberg, F. F., Jr., Moore, K. A., & Peterson, J. L. (1986). Sex education and sexual experience among adolescents. *American Journal of Public Health*, 75(11), 1331–1332.

Gargiulo, J., Attie, I., Brooks-Gunn, J., & Warren, M. P. (1987). Dating in middle school girls: Effects of social context, maturation, and grade. *Developmental Psychology*, 23(5), 730–737.

Garner, D. M., & Garfinkel, P. E. (1985). *Handbook of psychotherapy for anorexia nervosa and bulimia*. New York: Guilford.

Gold, J. J., & Iosimovich, J. (1980). *Gynecologic endocrinology*. New York: Harper & Row.

Grumbach, M. M. (1980). The neuroendocrinology of puberty. In D. T. Krieger & J. C. Hughes (Eds.), *Neuroendocrinology* (pp. 249–258). Sunderland, MA: Sinauer.

Grumbach, M. M., & Sizonenko, P. C. (Eds.). (1986). *Control of the onset of puberty II*. New York: Academic Press.

Gunnar, M., & Collins, W. A. (Eds.). (1988). *Minnesota symposia on child development*. Vol. 21. Hillsdale, NJ: Erlbaum.

Hall, G. S. (1904). *Adolescence: Its psychology and its relations to physiology, anthropology, sociology, sex, crime, religion and education*. Englewood Cliffs, NJ: Prentice-Hall.

Hill, J. P. (Ed.). (1982). Special issue: Early adolescence. *Child Development*, 53(6).

Hill, J. P. (1988). The role of conflict in familial adaptation to biological change. In M. Gunnar & W. A. Collins (Eds.), *Minnesota symposia on child development* (Vol. 21, pp. 43–77). Hillsdale, NJ: Erlbaum.

Hill, J. P., Holmbeck, G. N., Marlow, L., Green, T. M., & Lynch, M. E. (1985). Menarcheal status and parent-child relations in families of seventh-grade girls. *Journal of Youth and Adolescence*, 14, 301–316.

Johnson, J. H. (1982). Life events as stressors in childhood and adolescence. In B. B. Lahey & A. E. Kazdin (Eds.), *Advances in clinical child psychology* (Vol. 5, pp. 219–253). New York: Plenum.

Johnson, J. H., & McCutcheon, S. M. (1980). Assessing life stress in older children and adolescents: Preliminary findings with the Life Events Checklist. In I. G. Sarason & C. D. Sprelberger (Eds.), *Stress and anxiety* (Vol. 7, pp. 111–125). Washington, DC: Hemisphere.

Kaplan, H. P. (1983). *Psychosocial stress: Trends in theory and research*. New York: Academic Press.

Klaiber, E. L., Broverman, D. M., Vogel, W., & Kobayashi, Y. (1979, May). Estrogen therapy for severe persistent depressions in women. *Archives of General Psychiatry*, 36, 550–554.

Larson, R., Csikszentmihalyi, M., & Graef, R. (1980). Mood variability and the psychosocial adjustment of adolescents. *Journal of Youth and Adolescence*, 9, 469–490.

Lerner, R. M., & Foch, T. T. (Eds.). (1987). *Biological-psychosocial interactions in early adolescence: A life span perspective*. Hillsdale, NJ: Erlbaum.

Magnusson, D., Stattin, H., & Allen, V. L. (1985). Biological maturation and social development: A longitudinal study of some adjustment processes from mid-adolescence to adulthood. *Journal of Youth and Adolescence*, 14, 267–283.

Malina, R. M. (1983). Menarche in athletes: A synthesis and hypothesis. *Annals of Human Biology*, 10, 1–24.

54 Child Development

Marshall, W. A., & Tanner, J. M. (1969). Variations in pattern of pubertal changes in girls. *Archives of Diseases in Childhood,* 44, 291–303.

Melges, F., & Hamburg, D. (1977). Psychological effects of hormonal changes in women. In F. A. Beach (Ed.), *Human sexuality in four perspectives* (pp. 269–295). Baltimore: Johns Hopkins University Press.

Miller, C. L., & Eccles, J. S. (1987). *Evidence for relationships between hormones and behavior at early adolescence.* Unpublished manuscript, University of Michigan.

Nottelmann, E. D., Susman, E. J., Blue, J. H., Inoff-Germain, G., Dorn, L. D., Loriaux, D. L., Cutler, G. B., Jr., & Chrousos, G. P. (1987). Gonadal and adrenal hormone correlates of adjustment in early adolescence. In R. M. Lerner & T. T. Foch (Eds.), *Biological-psychosocial interactions in early adolescence* (pp. 303–324). Hillsdale, NJ: Erlbaum.

Offer, D. (1987). In defense of adolescents. *Journal of the American Medical Association,* 257(24), 3407–3408.

Olweus, D., Mattsson, A., Schalling, D., & Low, H. (1980). Testosterone, aggression, physical, and personality dimensions in normal adolescent males. *Psychosomatic Medicine,* 42, 253–269.

Oppenheim, G. (1983). Estrogen in the treatment of depression: Neuropharmacological mechanisms. *Biological Psychiatry,* 18, 721–725.

Parker, L. N., Levin, E. R., & Lifrak, E. T. (1985). Evidence for adrenocortical adaptation to severe illness. *Journal of Clinical Endocrinology and Metabolism,* 60, 947–952.

Parlee, M. B. (1973). The premenstrual syndrome. *Psychology Bulletin,* 80, 454–465.

Petersen, A. C., & Crockett, L. (1985). Pubertal timing and grade effects on adjustment. *Journal of Youth and Adolescence,* 14, 191–206.

Petersen, A. C., Schulenberg, J. E., Abramowitz, R. H., Offer, D., & Jarcho, H. D. (1984). A Self-Image Questionnaire for Young Adolescents (SIQYA): Reliability and validity studies. *Journal of Youth and Adolescence,* 13, 93–111.

Reynolds, E. L., & Wines, J. V. (1948). Individual differences in physical changes associated with adolescence in girls. *American Journal of Diseases in Childhood,* 75, 329–350.

Rubin, R. T., Reinisch, J. M., & Hasket, R. F. (1981). Postnatal gonadal steroid effects on human behavior. *Science,* 211(20), 1318–1324.

Ruble, D. N., & Brooks-Gunn, J. (1979). Menstrual symptoms: A social cognitive analysis. *Journal of Behavioral Medicine,* 2, 171–194.

Ruble, D. N., & Brooks-Gunn, J. (1982). The experience of menarche. *Child Development,* 53, 1557–1566.

Rutter, M., Graham, P., Chadwick, O. F. D., & Yule, W. (1976). Adolescent turmoil: Fact or fiction? *Journal of Child Psychology and Psychiatry,* 17, 35–56.

Rutter, M., Izard, C. E., & Read, P. B. (Eds.). (1986). *Depression in young people: Developmental and clinical perspectives.* New York: Guilford.

Sassenrath, E. N. (1970). Increased adrenal responsiveness related to social stress in Rhesus monkeys. *Hormones and Behavior,* 1, 283–298.

Simmons, R. G., & Blyth, D. A. (1987). *Moving into adolescence: The impact of pubertal change and school context.* New York: Aldine.

Simmons, R. G., Blyth, D. A., & McKinney, K. L. (1983). The social and psychological effects of puberty on white females. In J. Brooks-Gunn & A. C. Petersen (Eds.), *Girls at puberty: Biological and psychosocial perspectives* (pp. 229–272). New York: Plenum.

Simmons, R. G., Burgeson, R., Carlton-Ford, S., & Blyth, D. A. (1987). The impact of cumulative change in early adolescence. *Child Development,* 58, 1220–1234.

Simmons, R. G., Rosenberg, F., & Rosenberg, M. (1973). Disturbance in the self-image at adolescence. *American Sociological Review,* 38, 553–568.

Southam, A. L., & Gonzaga, F. P. (1965). Systemic changes during the menstrual cycle. *American Journal of Obstetrics and Gynecology,* 91, 142–165.

Steinberg, L. (1987). The impact of puberty on family relations: Effects of pubertal status and pubertal timing. *Developmental Psychology,* 23, 451–460.

Strober, M. (1985). Depressive illness in adolescence. *Psychiatric Annals,* 15, 375–378.

Susman, E. J., Inoff-Germain, G., & Nottelmann, E. D., Loriaux, D. L., Cutler, G. B., Jr., & Chrousos, G. P. (1987). Hormones, emotional dispositions, and aggressive attributes in young adolescents. *Child Development,* 58, 1114–1134.

Thoits, P. A. (1983). Dimensions of life events that influence psychological distress: An evaluation and synthesis of the literature. In H. P. Kaplan (Ed.), *Psychosocial stress: Trends in theory and research* (pp. 33–103). New York: Academic Press.

Tieger, T. (1980). On the biological basis of sex differences in aggression. *Child Development,* 5, 943–963.

Udry, J. R., Billy, J. O. G., Morris, N. M., Groff, T. R., & Raj, M. H. (1985). Serum androgenic hormones motivate sexual behavior in boys. *Fertility and Sterility,* 43, 90–94.

Vigersky, R. A., & Loriaux, D. (1977). Anorexia nervosa as a model of hypothalamic dysfunction. In R. Vigersky (Ed.), *Anorexia nervosa* (pp. 109–121). New York: Raven.

Warren, M. P. (1980). The effects of exercise on pubertal progression and reproductive function

in girls. *Journal of Clinical Endocrinology Metabolism, 51,* 1150–1157.
Warren, M. P. (1985). When weight loss accompanies amenorrhea. *Contemporary Obstetrics and Gynecology, 28,* 588–597.
Winter, J. S. P., & Faiman, C. (1973). Pituitary-gonadal relations in female children and adolescents. *Pediatric Research, 7,* 948–953.
Zipser, R. O., Davenport, M. W., Martin, K. L., Tuck, M. L., Warner, N. E., Swinney, R. R., Davis, C. L., & Horton, R. (1981). Hyperreninemic hypoaldosteronism in the critically ill: A new entity. *Journal of Clinical Endocrinology and Metabolism, 53,* 867–870.
Zumoff, B., Walsh, B. T., Katz, J. L., Levin, J., Rosenfeld, B. S., Kream, J., & Weiner, H. (1983). Subnormal plasma dehydroisoandrosterone to cortisol ratio in anorexia nervosa: A secondary hormonal parameter of ontogenic regression. *Journal of Clinical Endocrinology and Metabolism, 56,* 668–670.

Mood and Behavior at Adolescence: Evidence for Hormonal Factors*

MICHELLE P. WARREN AND J. BROOKS-GUNN

Departments of Obstetrics and Gynecology, Medicine, and Pediatrics, St. Luke's-Roosevelt Hospital, and Columbia College of Physicians and Surgeons, New York, New York 10019; and the Educational Testing Service, Princeton, New Jersey 08541

ABSTRACT. We studied the relationship among behavior, mood, pubertal development, hormonal levels, and psychological functioning in 100 adolescent white girls between the ages of 10.6–13.3 yr.

The girls were grouped by pubertal breast stages and four stages of estradiol secretion. No significant mood or behavior changes were found as a function of pubertal stages, controlling for age effects, except for a decrease in interest in sports. The hormonal stages revealed a significant curvilinear trend for depressive affect (increase, then decrease; $P < 0.01$), impulse control (decrease, then increase; $P < 0.04$), and psychopathology (increase, then decrease; $P < 0.03$) scales, indicating significant changes in these behaviors during times of rapid increases in hormone levels. These data suggest that hormonal changes may be more important than the physical changes as determinants of certain mood and behavior patterns at adolescence. (*J Clin Endocrinol Metab* **69**: 77, 1989)

MOODINESS and associated behavioral changes are common at the time of puberty (1–4). Certain behaviors, such as depressive affect, are relatively rare before adolescence (2), yet occur with relative frequency at puberty, with as much as a 4-fold increase in the 10–15 yr age group, predominantly in girls (5). Despite the high incidence of depression during the pubertal years, the possible hormonal determinants of depression and other behavior patterns at this time have not been examined. Early adolescence also seems to be a time when impulse control decreases, and aggression, delinquency, and other externalizing behavior as well as depressive affect/anxiety may increase (1–4). Although sex hormone-mediated behavior changes are well documented in animals (6–8), and some behavior patterns, specifically aggression and sexuality, have been correlated with hormone levels in boys (9–12), few hormonally related behavior patterns have been described in girls. Since a significant number of the health problems in adolescence may be linked to behavioral changes, the hormonal determinants of behavior, if any, are of great interest.

This study was designed to examine behavior during puberty in girls within a standard hormonal framework as well as within the standards of physical pubertal change. Since the etiology of behavioral changes in adolescence is probably multifactorial, an attempt was made to separate the changes due to exogenous social forces, *i.e.* the change in attitudes of the society which perceives the physical change in the adolescent, from those that may be linked to endogenous forces brought about by rapid hormonal changes.

Materials and Methods

Subjects

We studied 100 adolescent white girls with a mean age of 12.1 yr (range, 10.6–13.3) who were in grades 5–7 of school. These girls represented the entire spectrum of physical development: 41 in stage 1, 24 in stage 2, 15 in stage 3, and 20 in stages 4 and 5 of breast development (Tanner).

These girls were recruited from a larger group of girls participating in a large cross-sectional study of female adolescent biopsychosocial development. They and their families were invited to participate in a study involving one visit to a hospital where physical, hormonal, nutritional, and social aspects of development would be assessed. Sixty-seven percent of the families contacted chose to participate.

The girls were from well educated, middle to upper middle class families. They attended one of four private day schools in a large city; parental education and family social class were similar in this sample to those in affluent suburban school systems. Virtually all (96%) of the families were in the two highest of the five Hollingshead social classes (13); 85% of the mothers had graduated from college, and 60% of the mothers were working part or full time. No demographic differences

Received August 16, 1988.
Address all correspondence and requests for reprints to: Michelle P. Warren, M.D., St. Luke's-Roosevelt Hospital, Antennucci Building, 428 West 59th Street, New York, New York 10019.
* This work was supported by the W. T. Grant Foundation and NIH Grant R01-HD-18508.

were found for age or grade in school. A consent form describing the psychological and medial aspects of the study was approved by the Institutional Review Board and was signed by all participants and their parents. One hundred and four girls volunteered for the study.

Measures

The data were gathered by physical examination, questionnaire, and interview.

Physical measures

The girls were examined in the laboratory by a nurse practitioner or a physician who took a short medical history and evaluated pubertal development according to the classification of Marshall and Tanner (14). A detailed menstrual history was obtained from the postmenarcheal girls. A blood sample was drawn for hormonal assays, and the psychological tests were taken at the same time. The girls were paid for their visits. None was taking any hormonal medications, and all were in good health and of normal weight. Four girls were eliminated from the study because of medication (1), the presence of a gonadal dysgenesis (1), and weight greater than 120% of ideal (2). All but 19 of the patients were premenarcheal. Among the postmenarcheal girls, 18 were in the first 6 months postmenarche and 1 was in the second year.

Hormonal studies

All blood samples for hormonal studies were drawn in the midafternoon. Serum LH and FSH were measured in duplicate as previously described (15). Serum PRL was measured in serum by RIA using kits obtained from Diagnostic Products (Los Angeles, CA). The assay was standardized in terms of the WHO First International PRL Reference Preparation (1st IRP 75/504). The cross-reactivity of the antiserum with GH was less than 0.01%, and the sensitivity was such that 1.4 μg/L could be detected from zero. Intra- and interassay coefficients of variation were 2.8–4.4% and 6.3–8.6%, respectively.

Estradiol and testosterone were measured in duplicate in dried ethyl acetate and hexane extracts of serum by RIA using kits obtained from Serono Diagnostics (Braintree, MA). The intra- and interassay coefficients of variation ranged from 4–10% and 2.7–4.7%, respectively, for estradiol and 3–7% and 5–10% for testosterone. The sensitivity was such that 5.1 pmol/L could be differentiated from zero for estradiol and 0.38 nmol/L for testosterone.

Serum dehydroepiandrosterone sulfate (DHEAS) was measured in serum by RIA using kits obtained from Diagnostic Products. The cross-reactivity with DHEA was low (<5%), and the sensitivity of the assay was 0.57 nmol/L. Intra- and interassay coefficients of variation were 3.9–4.7% and 4.6–7.0%, respectively.

Psychological measures

The girls filled out standard self-report scales chosen to examine five domains: psychopathology (emotional and mental health), behavior problems, mastery/competence, relations with others, body image, and interest in sports. Three scales were used.

The Youth Behavior Profile (YBP), developed by Achenbach and Edelbrock from their Child Behavior Checklist (17), consists of scales that reflect internalizing (withdrawal) and externalizing (acting out) behavior identified in most studies of developmental psychopathology (18). These dimensions are moderately reliable across instruments and studies (19) and discriminate between children referred for psychosocial problems and nonreferred children (17, 20, 21). The girls indicated whether individual items were not at all true, somewhat true, or very true of themselves (three-point Likert scale); sum scores were used in analyses. The scales in this study specifically tapped depressive affect (α coefficient[1], 0.65), aggressive behavior (α coefficient, 0.82), delinquent behavior (α coefficient, 0.73), and immature hyperactive behavior (α coefficient, 0.57). These scores may not be used to identify girls with clinical depression or conduct disorders.

The Self Image Questionnaire for Young Adolescents (SIQYA) is an adaptation of the Offer Self Image Scale (22, 23). The girls were asked to rate how well 78 items described them on a 6-point scale (not at all true of me to very true of me). Nine scales were constructed; high internal consistency for each scale has been reported for sixth and seventh graders (α coefficients, >0.80) (24). The scales have been labeled emotional tone ("I feel nervous most of the time"), impulse control ("I become violent if I don't get my way"), body image ("Most of the time I am happy with the way I look"), peer relationships ("I think that other people just do not like me"), parent relationships ("I can count on my parents most of the time"), mastery and coping ("When I decide to do something, I do it"), educational goals ("A job well done gives me pleasure"), psychopathology/emotional dysfunction ("When I am with people, I am afraid that someone will make fun of me"), and superior adjustment ("I am a leader in school"). All scales had at least 8 items, including both positive and negative items, with the exception of psychopathology (all negative) and superior adjustment (all positive). The α coefficients were high (0.74–0.81), short term stability has been demonstrated, and these measures are comparable throughout the adolescent period (25).

Interest in sports

Given our interest in possible behavioral changes as a function of puberty, we constructed a scale for interest and participation in sports. Six items rated on the same six-point scale as the SIQYA were included ("Doing well in sports is important to me"). The α coefficient was 0.81.

Measurement of depressive mood perceived by mothers

Depressive mood also was assessed by asking the mothers how often their daughters had been bothered or troubled by six emotional states with the past 6 months (three-point scale). The scale is reliable, and valid high scores are indicative of severe depression (26).

---

[1] The α coefficient is a reliability coefficient that measures the internal consistency of this scale and other possible similar item scales measuring the same thing.

Data analysis

The girls were divided according to their stages of physical development and hormonal development in the following way. Physical development was characterized using the well known Marshall and Tanner (14) stages of breast development; four groups were identified, breast stages 1, 2, and 3, with stages 4 and 5 considered together. To assess behavior within a standard hormonal framework, serum estradiol levels were used to categorize the girls into four hormonal stages: less than 0–25, 25–50, 50–75, and greater than 75 pg/mL or less than 92, 93–184, 184–275, and 275 pmol/L (hormonal stages I, II, III, and IV, respectively). Serum estradiol was used because 1) it is the principal gonadal hormone in girls; 2) it increases the most (8-fold) during puberty (27–29), in contrast with other hormones such as DHEAS (30), LH, and FSH (29, 31), which increase 2.5- to 3-fold; and 3) the rises occur principally between breast stages 1–4, which correspond to those in our study group. Specifically, serum estradiol levels less than 92 pmol/L have minimal biological effects, and girls with such levels are physiologically prepubertal (32) and do not respond to progesterone with withdrawal bleeding (33). Girls with serum estradiol levels of 92–184 pmol/L generally have early sexual development, including breast development, effects on the vagina, and uterine growth (34, 35); such levels are generally not sufficient to cause proliferation of the endometrium and withdrawal bleeding after progesterone administration (33, 36). Serum estradiol levels of 184–275 pmol/L are commensurate with mid- or late puberty and early follicular phase levels in menstruating women, and those with levels in this range generally have progesterone withdrawal bleeding and/or spontaneous periods. Levels greater than 275 pmol/L are associated with cyclic menstrual function in women (33, 37). According to multiple studies of maturation of cyclic pituitary-gonadal function in adolescent girls, hormonal stages I and IV are distinct from one another, while stages II, III, and IV overlap (28, 37, 38).

One-way analyses of variance were performed for each scale to determine whether there were differences among the hormonal stages as well as the Tanner stages. Multiple comparisons among means were made using the Student-Newman-Keuls test. Tests for polynomial trends were performed with linear and quadratic components extracted. To control for the effects of age, analyses of covariance were performed on each scale, with age entered as a covariate. To compare our data with those of others, least square regressions were performed, entering age and five hormones (FSH, LH, estradiol, testosterone, and DHEAS) as possible predictors of behavior. Pearson correlations were calculated between scales and hormone values. Partial correlation controlling for age were also calculated between scales and hormone values. $P < 0.05$ was considered significant.

Results

Serum estradiol levels correlated with the physical stages of development (Tanner breast stages) as reported by others (28, 29) (Fig. 1). When the girls were divided according to their serum estradiol levels (Fig. 2), the largest increments in serum LH, FSH, testosterone, and

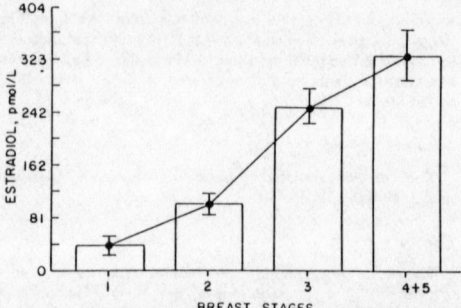

FIG. 1. Relationship between estradiol levels and Tanner breast stages of female pubertal development ($r = 0.58$, $P < 0.01$). *Points and brackets represent the mean ± SE*.

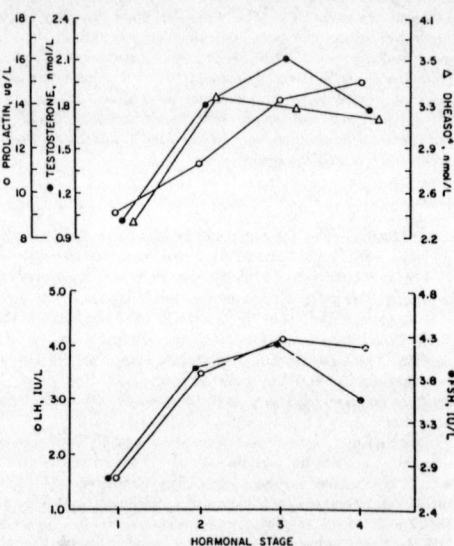

FIG. 2. PRL, testosterone, and DHEAS in relation to hormonal (estradiol) categories. *Lower panel*, LH and FSH in relation to hormonal (estradiol) categories.

DHEAS occurred between hormonal (estradiol) stages I and II. Thus, the transition from hormonal stage I to II represented the time of most rapid hormonal change.

The girls in the first physical and hormonal stages were younger, but age or grade level did not differ for breast and hormonal stages II, III, and IV. The 19 postmenarcheal girls were all in hormonal stages II (6), III (3), and IV (10).

The mean scores for depression, impulse control, and

psychopathology differed significantly as a function of hormonal stage, even after controlling for age; in fact, removal of the effects of age enhanced the hormonal effects (Fig. 3 and Table 1). These relationships were curvilinear, with an increase in the middle two hormonal stages followed by a decline for depression ($P < 0.01$) and psychopathology ($P < 0.03$). Impulse control ($P < 0.04$) showed a curvilinear change that was almost a inverted image of the change in psychopathology. Although the trend for aggression was not significant, the increase in the middle hormonal stages suggested a rise (Fig. 3), which approached significance with the removal of the effects of age ($P < 0.07$; Table 1).

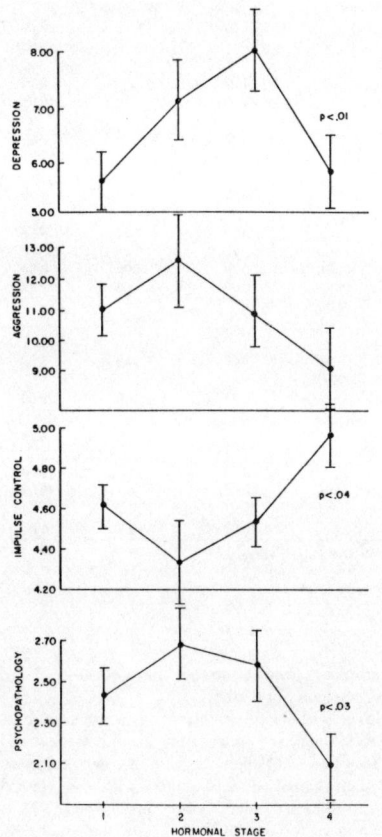

FIG. 3. Relationship among depression (determined by YBP), aggression (YBP), impulse control (YBP), and psychological (YBP) and hormonal (estradiol) stages.

When the data were analyzed for physical (breast) stages of development, only educational goals and impulse control were related to pubertal stages, but the relationships were not significant when age effects were controlled (Fig. 4 and Table 1). Interest in sports decreased at midpuberty whether measured by hormonal or physical stages, even after controlling for age (Fig. 5 and Table 1). There was no correlation between the mother's rating of depression with the depressive scales for the girls, indicating that the depressive affect perceived by the girls as a depressive mood was not noticed by the mothers.

No differences were found between pubertal stages or hormonal stages and the psychological measures using analyses of variance, except for interest in sports, which was higher in hormonal stage I than in hormonal stage III. No significant correlations were found, except for aggression, which correlated negatively with serum DHEAS ($r = -0.21$; $P < 0.04$), and interest in sports, which correlated negatively with serum DHEAS ($r = -0.24$; $P < 0.04$) and testosterone ($r = -0.38$; $P < 0.001$). However, after controlling for the effect of age, only interest in sports correlated significantly with serum DHEAS ($r = -0.24$; $P < 0.02$) and testosterone ($r = -0.34$; $P < 0.001$).

Discussion

Behavior at adolescence has been widely studied, but to date no patterns have been consistently related to hormonal changes in girls. Our data suggest that there are significant changes in behavior associated with the rapid changes in hormones during midpuberty. After controlling for age, these behavior patterns were not correlated to visible physical changes, specifically breast development, despite the high correlation of this variable to hormonal levels. These findings are consistent with those of others who found that the external indices of pubertal status were not related to behavior during midpuberty, or if relations do exist, they tend to be infrequent or limited to certain domains of behavior (11, 12).

The increase in depressive affect with increased hormonal stage suggests that depressive affect in particular is related to the rapid hormonal changes that occur during puberty. Hormonal events may explain in part the large increase in depression reported at puberty by others, particularly in girls in whom as much as a 4-fold increase may occur (2, 5). These effects may not be large and may be overridden by environmental effects; thus, they are difficult to identify. Grouping subjects using a hormonal framework circumvents some of the problems in addressing these questions and provides a background for examining behavior during times of rapid hormonal change. The lack of correlation of the behavior patterns

TABLE 1. Psychological measures and their relation to physical and hormone stages in adolescence

	Mean Score for stage[a]				F values (P value)		F values (P value) adjusted for age	
	I	II	III	IV	Linear	Quadratic	Linear	Quadratic
Behavior problems								
Impulse control[b]								
Hormone	4.62	4.33	4.53	4.96		4.45 (0.04)[c]		6.57 (0.012)[c]
Breast	4.36	4.56	4.68	4.90	4.98 (.03)[c]	0.002	1.76	0.01
Depression[d]								
Hormone	5.73	7.14	8.07	5.94		6.78 (0.01)[c]		7.85 (0.006)[c]
Aggression[d]								
Hormone	10.93	12.50	10.93	9.16		1.89		3.29 (0.07)
Psychopathology[b]								
Hormone	2.43	2.69	2.59	2.10		4.73 (0.03)[c]		5.72 (0.019)[c]
Emotional tone[b]								
Hormone	4.54	4.48	4.42	4.51		0.33		0.59
Competent behavior								
Mastery[d]								
Hormone	4.98	5.12	4.85	5.13		0.29	0.03	0.53
Adjustment[d]								
Hormone	4.47	4.65	4.42	4.80		0.56	0.92	0.68
Educational goals[d]								
Hormone	4.89	5.05	5.01	5.12	1.01	0.02	0.01	0.09
Breast	4.59	5.16	5.01	5.17	5.33 (0.02)[c]	2.03	0.66	1.79
Relationships								
Peer (social)[d]								
Hormone	4.84	4.92	4.58	4.82		0.26	0.58	0.62
Family (parent)[d]								
Hormone	4.87	4.59	4.58	4.70		1.53	2.66	2.68
Body image[d]								
Hormone	4.57	4.45	4.35	4.54		1.00	0.38	1.28
Interest in sports[e]								
Hormone	3.98	3.53	3.21	7.78		6.25 (0.01)[c]		5.16 (0.03)[c]
Breast	4.02	3.62	3.32	3.90	1.69	9.22 (0.003)[c]		8.82 (0.004)[c]

[a] Hormone, <92, 93–184, 184–275, and <275 pmol/L estradiol. Breast, Marshall and Tanner stage.
[b] Determined by SIQYA (six-point scale).
[c] Significant P value.
[d] Determined by Achenbach (three-point scale).
[e] Six point scale.

studied with physical maturity at puberty is surprising and suggests that the hormonal changes at puberty may be more important than physical changes in the development of behavior patterns during adolescence.

Previous investigators also have attempted to correlate hormonal levels with behavior patterns using regression analysis (11, 12). Our analyses of this type did not reveal any significant correlations between hormones and behavior, in agreement with previous reports. Analysis of data using hormonal groups provides a physiological framework that groups subjects in the various stages of development and compares them to subjects who are more hormonally mature.

Hormone-behavior relationships exist in animals, and the relationship of androgen levels and aggressive behavior is well established. In humans, serum testosterone has been related to sexual activity in boys, regardless of the extent of secondary sexual development (9). In boys, serum testosterone (39) and adrenal androgens (40) have been related to high levels of aggression, and a high for age serum FSH level has been related to sad affect in girls (40). Psychopathology and emotional tone (sad af-

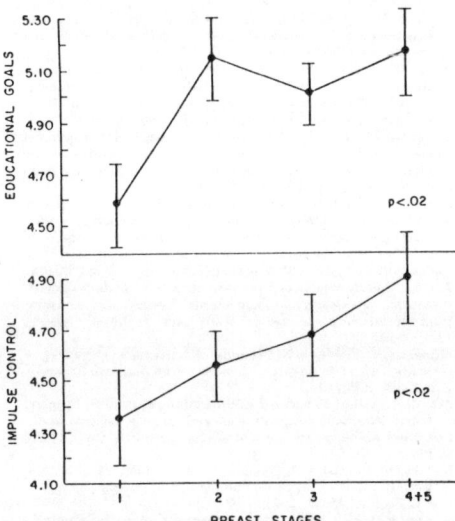

FIG. 4. Relationship between educational goals (determined by SIQYA) and impulse control (SIQYA) and hormonal stages.

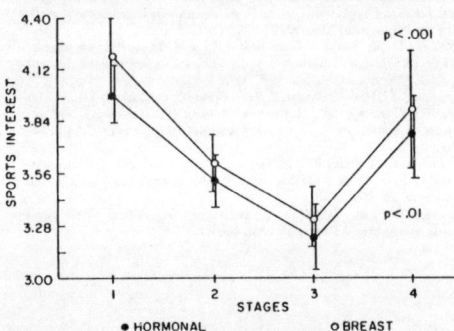

FIG. 5. Relationship between interest in sports and physical (Tanner Breast) stages and hormonal (estradiol) stages.

fect) are found in boys who have high for age serum DHEAS values and lower in boys who have lower sex hormone-binding globulin levels. The negative relationship between serum DHEAS and testosterone levels and interest in sports in the girls we studied is puzzling, although negative relationships between serum androgens and subscales of aggressive attributes and emotional dispositions have been reported by others (10).

This study suggests that certain behaviors change in midpuberty and that the changes may be biologically mediated. The return to the values found in the earliest hormonal stage as the girls mature in some of these measures also suggests that certain behaviors, such as depression and psychopathology, may reflect adolescent "turmoil." These data also suggest that adolescent girls may be more vulnerable to depressive affect at certain stages of puberty. Depression in puberty may have important clinical consequences. Several investigators have suggested that drug use in adolescence may be an inadvertent form of self-medication for depression (41, 42).

The limitations of this study include single hormone measurements; however, in one study the results of three measurements at 20-min intervals in adolescent girls and boys were very similar (12). Another limitation is that the study was cross-sectional, and the study subjects were relatively homogeneous in regard to their social and economic backgrounds.

In conclusion, these findings suggest that some behavioral patterns in adolescence may be due to biological rather than social factors. A time of vulnerability appears to occur during time of rapid hormonal change. The endocrine mechanisms underlying this behavior and the value of intervention merit further research.

Acknowledgments

We are very grateful to the girls who participated in this study as well as their families and their schools, with special thanks to the teachers who gave time and energy to the project. We are also grateful to Richard Fox for performing the statistics, Linda Ferington for the medical evaluation, Denise Newman for the psychological studies, Lily Toniolo for the hormonal studies, and Catherine Hendershot who helped organize the project.

References

1. Offer D, Offer JB. From teenage to young manhood. New York: Basic Books; 1975.
2. Rutter M, Graham P, Chadwick OFD, Yule W. Adolescent turmoil: fact or fiction? J Child Psychol Psychiatry. 1976;17:35–56.
3. Creydanus DE. Depression in adolescence. J Adolescent Health Care. 1986;7:1095–205.
4. Daniel WAJ. Adolescent growth and development. Update Semin Adolesc Med. 1985;1:1–96.
5. Kandel DB, Davies M. Epidemiology of depressive mood in adolescence. Arch Gen Psychiatry. 1982;39:1205–12.
6. Bouissou MF. Androgens, aggressive behavior and social relationships in higher mammals. Horm Res. 1983;18:43–61.
7. Cairns RB, Maccombie DJ, Hood KE. A developmental-genetic analysis of aggressive behavior in mice. I. Behavioral Outcomes. J Comp Psychol. 1983;97:69–89.
8. Brain PF, ed. Hormones and aggression. Montreal: Eden Press; 1977;1.
9. Udry RR, Billy JOG, Morris NM, Groff TR, Raj MH. Serum androgenic hormones motivate sexual behavior in boys. Fertil Steril. 1985;43:90–4.
10. Susman EJ, Inoff-Germain G, Nottelmann ED, Loriaux DL, Cutler Jr GB, Chrousos GP. Hormones, emotional disparitions, and aggressive attitudes with early adolescents. Child Dev. 1987;58:1114–34.
11. Susman EJ, Nottelmann ED, Inoff GE, et al. The relation of relative hormonal levels and physical development and social-emotional behavior in young adolescents. J Youth Adoles. 1985;14:245–64.

12. Nottelmann ED, Susman EJ, Blue JH, et al. Gonadal and adrenal hormone correlates of adjustment in early adolescence. In: Lerner RM, Fochs TT, eds. Biological-psychosocial interactions in early adolescence: a life-span perspective. Hillsdale: Erlbaum, 1987;303-23.
13. Hollingshead AB, Redlich FC. Social class and mental illness: a community study. New York: Wiley and Sons; 1958.
14. Marshall WA, Tanner JM. Variations in the pattern of pubertal changes in girls. Arch Dis Child. 1969;44:291-303.
15. Warren MP, Siris ES, Petrovich C. The influence of severe illness on gonadotropin secretion in the postmenopausal female. J Clin Endocrinol Metab. 1977;45:99-104.
16. Abraham GE, Manlimos FSH, Garga R. Radioimmunoassay for steroids. In: Abraham GE, ed. Handbook of radioimmunoassay. New York: Dekker; 1977;591-656
17. Achenbach TM, Edelbrock C. Manual for the child behavior checklist and revised child behavior profile. Burlington: Queen City Printers; 1979.
18. Quay HC. Classification. In: Quay HC, Werry JS, eds. Psychopathological disorders of childhood. New York: Wiley and Sons; 1979;1-42.
19. Achenbach TM, Edelbrock CS. The classification of child psychopathology: a review and analysis of empirical efforts. Psychol Bull. 1978;85:1275-1301.
20. Boyle MH, Jones SC. Selecting measures of emotional and behavioral disorders of childhood for use in general populations. J Child Psychol Psychiatry. 1985;20:137-59.
21. Achenbach TM, Edelbrock CS. Behavioral problems and competencies reported by the parents of normal and disturbed children aged 4 through 16. Monogr of the Soc for Res in Child Dev. 1981;46.
22. Offer D, Ostrov E, Howard KI. The Offer Self-Image Questionnaire for Adolescents: a manual, 3rd ed. Chicago: Michael Reese Hospital; 1982.
23. Offer D. In defense of adolescents. JAMA. 1987;254:3407-8.
24. Petersen AC, Schulenberg JE, Abromowitz RH, Offer D, Jarcho HD. A self-image questionnaire for young adults (SIQYA): reliability and validity studies. J Youth Adolesc. 1984;13:93-111.
25. Brooks-Gunn J, Rock D, Warren MP. Comparability of constructs across the adolescent years. Dev Psychol. 1989;25:51-60.
26. Kandel DB, Davis M. Epidemiology of adolescent depressive mood. Arch Gen Psychiatry. 1982;39:1205-12.
27. Lee P, Xenakis T, Winner J, Matsenbaugh S. Puberty in girls: correlation of serum levels of gonadotrophins, prolactin, androgens, estrogens and progestins. J Clin Endocrinol Metab. 1976;43:775.
28. Apter D. Serum steroids and pituitary hormones in female puberty: a partly longitudinal study. Clin Endocrinol (Oxf). 1980;12:107.
29. Jenner MR, Helch RP, Kaplan SL, Grumbach MM. Hormonal changes in puberty. IV. Plasma estradiol, LH, and FSH in prepubertal children, pubertal females, and in precocious puberty, premature thelarche, hypogonadism, and in a child with a feminizing ovarian tumor. Clin Endocrinol (Oxf). 1972;34:521.
30. Reiter EO, Fuldauer UG, Root AW. Secretion of the adrenal androgen, dehydroepiandrosterone sulfate during normal infancy, childhood and adolescence, in sick infants and in children with endocrinologic abnormalities. J Pediatr. 1977;90:766-70.
31. Sizonenko PC, Burr IM, Kaplan SL, Grumbach MM. Hormonal changes in puberty. II. Correlation of serum luteinizing hormone and follicle stimulating hormone with stages of puberty and bone age in normal girls. Pediatr Res. 1970;4:36-45.
32. Comite F, Cutler Jr GB, Rivier J, Vale WW, Loriaux DL, Crowley WF. Short-term treatment of idiopathic precocious puberty with a long-acting analogue of luteinizing hormone-releasing hormone. N Engl J Med. 1981;305:1546-50.
33. Kletzky OA, Davajan V, Makamura RN, Thorneycroft JH, Mishell Jr DR. Clinical categorization of patients with secondary amenorrhea using progesterone-induced uterine bleeding and measurement of serum gonad-otropin levels. Am J Obstet Gynecol. 1975;121:695.
34. Schneider V, Friedrich E, Schindler AE. Hormonal cytology: a correlation with plasma estradiol, measured by radioimmunoassay. Acta Cytol. 1977;21:37.
35. Salardi S, Orsini LF, Cacciari E, Bovicelli L, Tassoni P, Reggiani A. Pelvic ultrasonography in premenarcheal girls: relation to puberty and sex hormone concentrations. Arch Dis Child. 1985;60:120-5.
36. Kletsky OA, Davajan V, Makamura RN, Mishell DR. Classification of secondary amenorrhea based on distinct hormonal patterns. J Clin Endocrinol Metab. 1975;41:660.
37. Winter JSD, Faiman C. The development of cyclic pituitary-gonadal function in adolescent females. J Clin Endocrinol Metab. 1973;37:7148.
38. Lemarchand-Beraud T, Zuffery MM, Reymond M, Rey I. Maturation of the hypothalmo-pituitary-ovarian axis in adolescent girls. J Clin Endocrinol Metab. 1982;54:241-6.
39. Olweus D, Mattsson A, Schalling D, Low H. Testosterone, aggression, physical and personality dimensions in normal adolescent males. Psychosomat Med. 1980;42:253-69.
40. Susman EJ, Inoff-Germain G, Nottelmann ED, Loriaux DL, Cutler Jr GB, Chrousos GP. Hormones, emotional dispositions, and aggressive attributes in young adolescents. Child Dev. 1987;58:1114-34.
41. Kandel DB, Kessler RC, Marguiles RZ. Antecedents of adolescent initiation into stages of drug use: a developmental analysis. J Youth Adolesc. 1979;7:13-39.
42. Deykin EY, Levy JC, Wells V. Adolescent depression, alcohol and drug abuse. Am J Public Health. 1987;77:178.

Biological Basis of the Sex Differential in Longevity

William R. Hazzard, MD

That women outlive men is a fundamental truth in all societies. Nowhere is this more evident than in the practice of geriatric medicine, wherein the physician cares preponderantly for women. This phenomenon becomes all the more pervasive with the increasing average age of patients in the physician's practice and, on a societal level, with the increasing proportion and number of elderly in our society, especially the "old old." This treatise will review selectively the extant literature on the topic of the sex differential in longevity, drawing most heavily upon the author's principal areas of experience: lipoprotein metabolism, atherogenesis, and "preventive gerontology."[1]

As evident in Figure 1, the pyramidal distribution of the population by age characteristic of developing nations (eg, Mexico) is notable for its symmetry by gender across the age spectrum. By contrast, with the full rectangularization of the population distribution by age which accompanies societal maturation and will reach steady state in the United States in approximately 2030, this symmetry is lost, resulting in a preponderant survival of women over men beyond age 75. The stages in this evolutionary pattern are also apparent in Figure 2, in which the increasing average longevity from birth and beyond age 65 has selectively favored women, females enjoying greater longevity both beyond age 65 and, especially, from birth pari passu with socioeconomic development of the American society over the past 150 years. A by-product of this selective survival of women is the far greater preponderance of widows than widowers among the elderly in our society. Whereas nearly 80% of men over age 65 in this nation are married, this holds true for only half that percentage of women. This disproportion grows ever greater with increasing survival and is thus progressively skewed toward women in their 70s, 80s, and 90s. The sociologic and health care ramifications of their selective survival are clear; given the primacy of home (and spouse) support for maintenance of the frail and dependent elderly outside of institutions, widowhood represents a major risk factor for institutionalization in our society. Thus, were a mechanism discovered whereby the longevity of men and women could be equalized (obviously preferably via selective prolongation of male longevity), the benefits to society would be enormous. These would accrue both to society, given the aggregate cost of long-term care among the elderly, and also to persons of both sexes and their families, since the loneliness of widowhood (currently averaging nearly ten years in duration) represents a major negative attribute of increased longevity.

The biological basis of this sex differential and, specifically, its exaggeration simultaneous with socioeconomic development and greater average longevity for both sexes is clearly complex. The premature deaths that are most obviously eliminated with such development are concentrated in the first years of life, notably those from infectious diseases attributable largely to malnutrition, overcrowding, inadequate immunization, poor hygiene, and poor sanitation. Social science might suggest that girls in underdeveloped societies are especially subject to discrimination, eg, in competition for limited food supplies. Hence socioeconomic advances might especially benefit girls, allowing a yet greater increase in the proportion of those born to survive childhood than boys in the same era of societal progress. More obviously, great reductions in childbearing-associated mortality among women have occurred in recent generations. This reflects not only enhanced hygiene, nutrition, housing, and related concomitants of socioeconomic development but

---

From the Department of Medicine, The Johns Hopkins University School of Medicine, Baltimore, Maryland.
Address correspondence and reprint requests to Dr. William R. Hazzard: Department of Medicine, Bowman Gray School of Medicine, 300 South Hawthorne Road, Winston-Salem, NC 27103

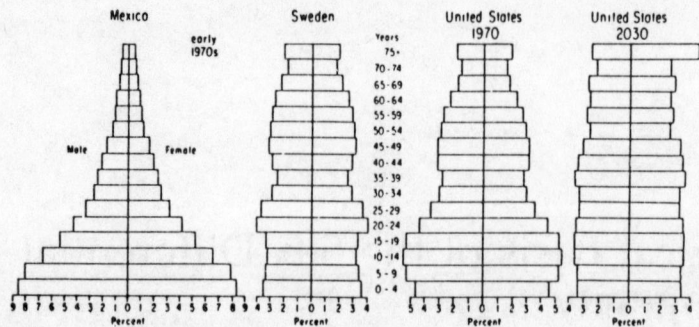

FIGURE 1. *Comparative population profiles: age and sex distribution. Reprinted with permission from Bureau of the Census, National Center for Health Statistics and United Nations Demographic Yearbook, from Somers AR: The high cost of health care for the elderly: Diagnosis, prognosis, and some suggestions for therapy. Journal of Health Politics, Policy and Law 3:163–180, 1978. Copyright, Department of Health Administration, Duke University, Durham, NC.*

also the relatively greater stature accorded women in industrialized societies, and their access to better health care, notably prenatal and obstetric care.

Another phenomenon that parallels socioeconomic development also requires examination; namely, the increased entry of women into the work force. The effect of this trend upon mortality is not dramatic in either direction. What is dramatic, however, is its effect upon morbidity as reflected in physician visits and related use of the health care system. Traditionally women have used health care resources more than men until old age, attributable to health care needs related to childbearing. However, such use is remarkably less among employed than nonemployed women, more closely resembling that of their male counterparts.[2] Thus, the traditionally greater number of physician visits and hospitalizations for women from childbearing age through the age of normal retirement from work appears in part an artifact of the historically different employment status of women versus men. Whether or not this apparent benefit of employment will carry over into even greater survival of (formerly employed) women beyond retirement and into old age remains to be seen. However, this possibility remains one of the fundamental mechanisms wherein the sex differential in longevity may grow yet larger as our society approaches economic and employment parity for women in the latter portions of this century. This is, of course, in direct contrast to the popular theory (sometimes called "They'll get theirs" by male sexual chauvinists), wherein job-related "stress" (possibly mediated by proxies such as cigarette smoking) is held to be a major contributor to premature male mortality in Western society. Suffice it to say here that this theory is largely unfounded in experience to date, suggesting either: 1) that it is fundamentally flawed and premature male mortality is not attributable to job-related stress, 2) that women manage such stress with fewer adverse health consequences than do their male counterparts, or 3) that it is simply too early to determine whether changing employment patterns will narrow, have no effect upon, or widen the current sex differential in mortality. In any event there is little objective evidence to support the contention that the increased entry of women into the work force will adversely affect their health or longevity.

A most popular and controversial treatise on pres-

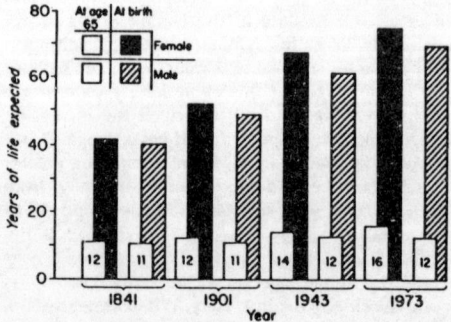

FIGURE 2. *Life expectancies of males and females at birth and at age 65. Reprinted with permission from Coni N, Davison W, Webster S: Lecture Notes on Geriatrics. Oxford, England, Blackwell Scientific Publications, 1977.*

ent and future trends in morbidity and mortality was advanced by Fries[3] in an engaging article entitled, "Aging, Natural Death, and the Compression of Morbidity." Although this lyrical statement has stirred much controversy and drawn strong rebuttal,[4,5] the clear elements of truth in its argument continue to attract followers. An important subthesis within that argument is the assumed elimination of the sex differential in mortality such that a single, narrow Gaussian curve would describe the histogram of mortality (at 85 ± 4 years) in the milennium projected by Fries to occur by the middle of the next century (Figure 3). A more sobering and more realistic depiction of the distribution of ages of death, confined here to whites succumbing of cardiovascular disease, is shown in Figure 4. Note that the distributions in this figure are quite different by sex. Among white women the majority might already be said to be dying of forces related to (primary) aging ("natural death" in the parlance of Fries), a smaller proportion succumbing "early" to potentially reversible or delayable causes, prevention of which might shift them into the right hand mode with its median age at death of approximately 85 years. Perhaps discouragingly, however, in this construct not only is the distribution among males broader and the modal longevity lower (by more than a decade), but also the proportion of early and hence potentially preventable mortality among white men is lower than among white women. Therefore, ac-

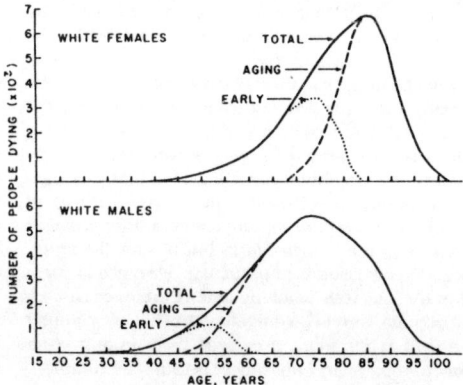

FIGURE 4. *Deaths in US cohorts, at the 1966 rate, from arteriorsclerotic heart disease. Plotted from US Vital Statistics, 1966, in Kohn RR: Heart and cardiovascular system, in Finch CE, Hayflick L (eds): Handbook of the Biology of Aging. New York, Van Nostrand-Reinhold, 1977.*

cording to this more realistic estimate (and the experience of other cultures more mature than our own), further societal maturation in the United States will be accompanied by an even greater average sex differential in longevity than at present (currently approximately 7.4 years, stemming from average life expectancy at birth among men of 70.7 years and among women of 78.1 years.[6]) Thus, the gender gap in age-specific annual death rates in the United States has grown progressively in the last four decades in each segment of the adult age span. However, the sex differential in mortality rates is far greater in young adulthood and middle age than in old age and especially in the old old (over 85 years; Figure 5). Thus, perhaps encouragingly, the sex differential in remaining longevity narrows progressively beyond middle age, specifically declining from 4.9 years at age 60 to only 1.3 years at age 85.[6] Although it is possible that this narrowing of the gender gap in longevity is more apparent than real (confounded by the possible survival of an especially hardy group of men into their 80s and 90s compared with their more average surviving female counterparts), it would appear most likely that the major basis of the sex differential in longevity lies not in old age once achieved but before old age.[7] This conclusion underlies much of the strategy outlined for possible interventions whereby premature male mortality might be attenuated and hence the sex differential in longevity narrowed.

Related importantly to that strategy has been the sex differential in cigarette smoking behavior in this nation since smoking became popular shortly after

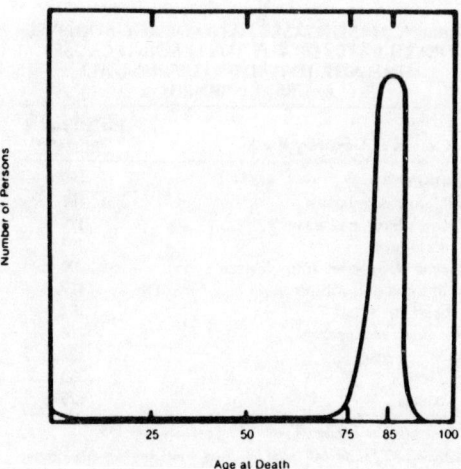

FIGURE 3. *Mortality according to age, in the absence of premature death. Reprinted with permission from Fries J: Aging, natural death, and the compression of morbidity. New England Journal of Medicine 303:130–135, 1980.*

the turn of the 20th century. This topic has been the recent source of major controversy, sparked by the report of a retrospective, community-based mortality survey claiming that the sex differential in cigarette smoking behavior was sufficient to account for the entire sex differential in mortality in that study. However, a more balanced estimate arising from the rebuttal to this argument has suggested that this cigarette smoking sex differential may account for up to four of the more than seven years sex differential in longevity in the United States but not for the entire margin.[8] This issue is of particular relevance at present in that cigarette smoking among younger women has become roughly equivalent to that in younger men and is far more prevalent than among older women. Moreover, lung cancer became the commonest malignancy among women in 1985, presumably reflecting their equal susceptibility to the adverse sequelae of cigarette smoking and their increased average cigarette smoking in recent decades. Thus, should the current equivalence in cigarette smoking between the sexes among young adults persist as this cohort ages, a narrowing of the sex differential in mortality might occur in the future. That cigarette smoking is more common among employed than nonemployed women is also pertinent to the discussion above relating to the future projections of the sex differential in longevity in a society in which female employment will be yet more prevalent than in the current era. However, given the tradition of health conscious and risk-aversive behavior in women and the reinforcement of such behavior among more educated, higher socioeconomic classes, this observer predicts that cigarette smoking will decline at least as dramatically in women, especially beyond age 35, as it has among men, preserving their relative immunity to premature mortality in other spheres.

These higher rates of mortality among men than women in adult life span the spectrum from heart disease and malignancies through pneumonia and chronic obstructive pulmonary disease (also perhaps related to the sex differential in cigarette smoking) to those attributes of male behavior more related to their generally greater predilection to risk-taking and violence-related behavior (Table 1).[6] However, despite this long list of causes of premature mortality in which rates for men exceed those for women, the aggregate impact of atherosclerosis and its clinical sequelae far outweigh that of all other causes combined (Table 2). Thus, were the process of atherosclerosis amenable to major attenuation via alterations in behavior, an attractive hypothesis, fully 11 years might be added to average human longevity in American society. This would allow a greater proportion of men to survive to an age at which the sex differential in remaining longevity has greatly narrowed (and allow average longevity to achieve the figure of 85 years in both sexes popularized by Fries).

Given the author's long-standing fascination with atherogenesis, however, it is important to introduce an element of balance in the argument. For example (Figure 6), it seems unlikely that the greater average longevity of female over male houseflies is attributable to less atherosclerosis in the female of that species! Furthermore, the greater mortality rates of males over females in old- and middle-age extends back to birth and even to conception, when atherogenesis has clearly not yet begun (Figure 7). It would appear that

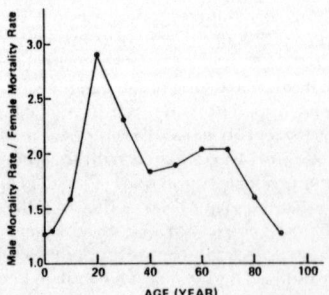

FIGURE 5. *Sex mortality ratio, US, 1976. Compiled from data presented in Gee EM, Veevers JE: Accelerating sex differentials in mortality: An analysis of contributing factors. Social Biology 30:75–85, 1984.*

TABLE 1. MALE/FEMALE RATIO OF AGE-ADJUSTED DEATH RATE FOR THE TEN LEADING CAUSES OF DEATH, UNITED STATES, 1980, ALL RACES COMBINED*

Causes of Death by Rank	Male/Female Ratio (%)
Heart disease	199
Malignant neoplasms	151
Cerebrovascular diseases	119
All accidents	293
Chronic obstructive lung disease	293
Pneumonia and influenza	177
Diabetes mellitus†	102
Chronic liver disease	216
Atherosclerosis	132
Suicide	333
All causes	179

*Rank based on number of deaths from each cause in 1980.[5]

†Among blacks, the M/F ratio for diabetes mellitus was 80%, among whites, 109%. The greater number of pregnancies in black women partly cause this sex reversal between the two races.

Reprinted with permission from Wylie CM: Contrasts in the health of elderly men and women: An analysis of recent data for whites in the United States. J Am Geriatr Soc 32:670, 1984.

TABLE 2. GAIN IN LIFE EXPECTANCY FROM ELIMINATING SPECIFIED CAUSES OF DEATH AND CHANCE OF EVENTUALLY DYING FROM THESE CAUSES: 1969-71

Causes of Death	Gain in Life Expectancy (yrs)		Chance of Eventually Dying	
	At Birth	At Age 65	At Birth	At Age 65
Major cardiovascular and renal diseases	11.8	11.4	.588	.672
Diseases of the heart	5.9	5.1	.412	.460
Cerebrovascular diseases	1.2	1.2	.122	.149
Malignant neoplasms*	2.5	1.4	.163	.145
Motor vehicle accidents	0.7	0.1	.020	.006
All other accidents	0.6	0.1	.026	.018
Influenza and pneumonia	0.5	0.2	.034	.037
Diabetes mellitus	0.2	0.2	.020	.021
Infective and parasitic disease	0.2	0.1	.007	.005

*Including neoplasms of lymphatic and hematopoietic tissues.

Reprinted with permission from Brock DB, Brody JA: Statistical and epidemiological characteristics, in Andres R, Bierman E, Hazzard W (eds): Principles of Geriatric Medicine. New York, McGraw-Hill, 1984.

the only clear point of advantage occurring to the male over the female of the human species is at the point of fertilization: various estimates have placed the male:female sex ratio at conception to as high as 170:100. In the first trimester of pregnancy, the point at which the earliest secure estimates of sex ratios can be ascertained, the sex ratio has already diminished to almost 130:100, with a further decline throughout fetal life to a sex ratio at birth of 106:100.[9] Before adulthood the greater mortality of male infants and children than girls of comparable age is largely attributable to infections and accidents. Parity in numbers between the sexes is accomplished at about the time of adolescence, the gap thereafter continually widening to favor female over male survival throughout the remainder of the human lifespan. In pursuing the mechanism of the sex differential in longevity,

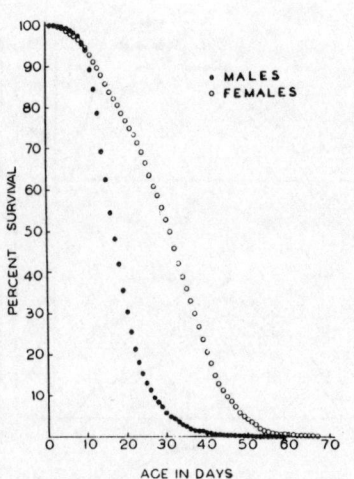

FIGURE 6. Survival curves for male and female houseflies. Reprinted with permission from Rockstein M, Lieberman HM: A life table for the common house fly, Musca domestica. Gerontologia 3:23-36, 1959.

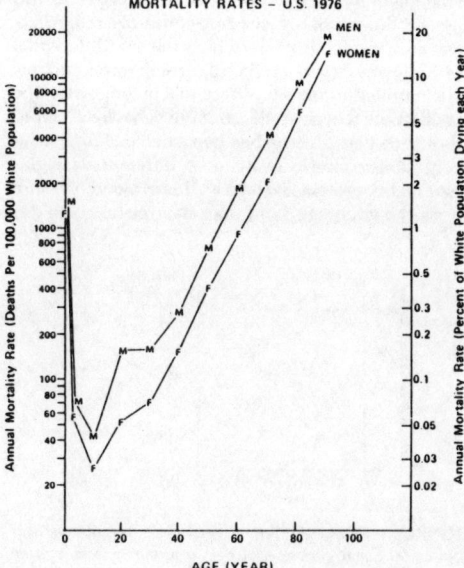

FIGURE 7. Mortality rates by sex, US, 1976. Compiled with data presented in Gee EM, Veevers JE: Accelerating sex differentials in mortality: An analysis of contributing factors. Social Biology 30:75-85, 1984.

therefore, it may prove instructive to examine those attributes of predilection to infection and violence-related deaths to which males are especially disposed. In this regard further research into the sex differential in immune response as well as in behavior may prove fruitful.[10] The potential importance of this avenue of investigation is clear. It is well known, for instance, that females carry a higher risk of almost all kinds of autoimmune disease (and a strain of mice in which systemic lupus erythematosus is endemic is a notable exception to the greater longevity of males over females throughout the animal kingdom).[11] However, the aggregate impact of all forms of autoimmune disease upon human longevity would appear negligible. On the other hand, might there accrue some benefits to females in immune response, proceeding from a sex steroid-mediated difference in isoimmunity, which would account for their lower rates of death from infection and most malignancies? This could conceivably extend to their lesser susceptibility to atherogenesis, if that also has a component of an immune basis.[12] Moreover, the risk-taking behavior characteristic of males in our culture is evident in homocide, suicide, and vehicle accident statistics. Is this behavior only culturally determined, or is there a biological (ie, hormonal) basis as well?

All of the above, however, is but an introduction to the major hypothesis of the present treatise; to wit: The sex differential in sex hormones (secretion, action, and metabolism) underlies the sex differential in atherogenesis and its clinical consequences and this in turn underlies the sex differential in longevity. The sex differential in cigarette smoking behavior as a contributor to that process has been noted. Other relatively subtle concerns relate to sex differentials in glucose and lipoprotein levels as well as in blood pressure across the adult age span that may relate to sex dif-

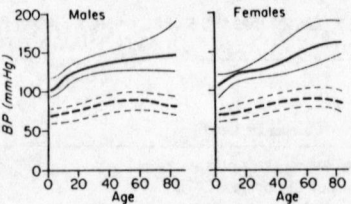

FIGURE 9. *Relationship between age and systolic (upper, solid lines) and diastolic blood pressure (BP) (lower, dashed lines) in men and women in an American community—Tecumseh, Michigan. Heavy lines are 50th percentile; light lines are 20th (lower) and 80th (upper) percentiles. (As per Smith, Bierman, and Robinson, see Figure 8.)*

ferentials in relative body weight (and in fat distribution). As can be seen in Figure 8, one hour after 100 g of oral glucose, blood concentrations in a population sample from Tecumseh demonstrate a greater age-related rise in males than females in young adulthood but an accelerated increase in females beyond middle-age, with a crossover at approximately the time of the menopause. (All of these age-related population data are cross-sectional in nature; these generalizations thus carry with them the appropriate ca-

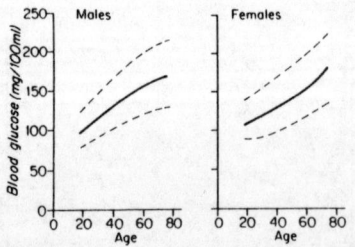

FIGURE 8. *Relationship between age and blood glucose one hour after a 100-g oral glucose challenge in men and women in an American community—Tecumseh, Michigan. Solid lines are 50th percentiles; dashed lines are 20th (lower) and 80th (upper) percentiles. Reprinted with permission from Smith D, Bierman E, Robinson N: The Biologic Aging of Man, 2nd ed. Philadelphia, Saunders, 1978, p 225.*

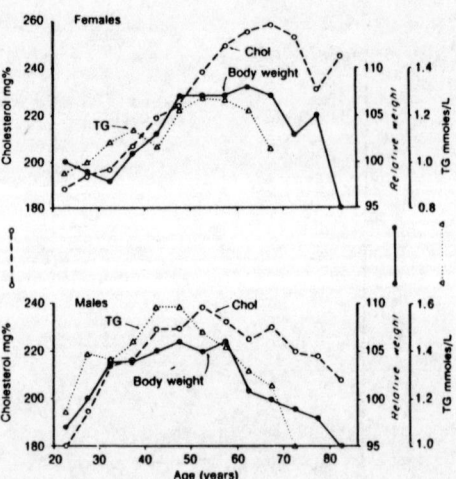

FIGURE 10. *Median plasma cholesterol (Chol), triglyceride (TG), and relative body weight values as a function of age in Tecumseh (cholesterol and relative weights) and Stockholm (TG) community studies. Reprinted with permission from Williams RH (ed): Textbook of Endocrinology, 5th ed. Philadelphia; Saunders, 1974.*

TABLE 3. COEFFICIENT FOR REGRESSION OF CORONARY HEART DISEASE INCIDENCE OF RISK FACTORS MEN AND WOMEN 50 TO 82 YEARS FRAMINGHAM STUDY

	Standardized Logistic Regression Coefficients			
	Univariate		Multivariate	
Risk Attributes	Men	Women	Men	Women
HDL cholesterol	−.488*	−.741	−.610*	−.650
LDL cholesterol	.288†	.303†	.332‡	.260†
Triglyceride	.048	.276‡	−.092	−.106
Systolic pressure	.323‡	.400‡	.327‡	.216
ECG-LVH	.279*	.207‡	.245‡	.159†
Relative weight	.029	.283†	−.016	.031
Diabetes	−.024	.474*	−.114	.390*

HDL = high-density lipoproteins; LDL = low-density lipoproteins; ECG-LVH = electrocardiogram-left ventricular hypertrophy.
*P = <.001; †P < .05; ‡P < .01.
Reprinted with permission from Kannel WB, Brand FN: Cardiovascular risk factors in the elderly, in Andres R, Bierman E, Hazzard W (eds): Principles of Geriatric Medicine. New York, McGraw-Hill, 1984.

veats.) Population blood pressure statistics (Figure 9) show somewhat similar trends, young females having lower median systolic and diastolic blood pressures than their male counterparts, those increasing to produce higher levels (among survivors), especially for systolic pressures, in women than men beyond middle age. Serum lipids (Figure 10) also show similar trends, with increases during young adulthood through middle-age in females lagging approximately a decade behind those of their male counterparts, a crossover in, notably, serum (and low-density lipoproteins [LDL]) cholesterol levels being evident beyond age 50 before a decline among both (surviving) females and males in old age. The close concordance among these graphs and patterns of relative body weight (Figure 10) has been pointed out by Bierman.[13] These trends have called attention to changing distributions of relative body weight across the adult lifespan, it being clear

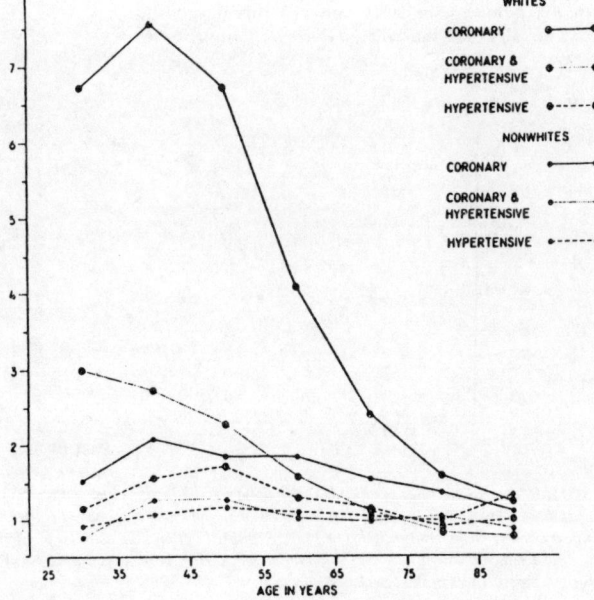

FIGURE 11. Linear sex ratio (M:F) in cardiovascular mortality, coronary and hypertensive, US, by age and race, 1955. From Furman RH: Coronary heart disease and the menopause, in Ryan KJ, Gibson DC (eds): Menopause and Aging. US Department of HEW, DHEW Publication No. [NIH] 73-319, 1973.

that relative body weight increases with age in both males and females but in women at a slower rate before age 50 than among men, average body mass indexes being lowered among survivors of both sexes beyond middle age. Thus, a sex differential in the rate at which body mass indexes change with age in adulthood might account for at least a portion of the sex differential in atherogenic risk, especially before age 50.[14] Moreover, recent research[15] has suggested that not all adiposity confers the same risk to atherosclerosis, specifically that above the umbilicus ("upper body"), characteristic of male adult weight gain, carrying substantially more risk than that below the waist, characteristic of female adult fat distribution.[14] These patterns are not only called "android" and "gynoid" according to their prototypic sex association but thought to be mediated by sex steroids.[15]

Despite the attractiveness of this line of inquiry, relative adiposity is not strongly predictive of atherosclerosis, especially that incident beyond middle age (Table 3),[16] and whether except with degrees of obesity that are uncommon in the population any excess net risk of all-cause mortality is conferred by adiposity is currently controversial.[17] Therefore, other avenues of investigation must be pursued. When focusing specifically upon ischemic cardiovascular disease, it becomes apparent that the sex differential in cardiovascular mortality is at its peak in young middle-age and declines progressively thereafter throughout the remainder of adult life (Figure 11). A more conventional depiction of these trends in semilog-linear terms (Figure 12, note the similarity between this figure and that for all-cause mortality, Figure 7) demonstrates approximately a decade lag in females relative to males in achieving comparable ischemic heart disease death rates from middle-age throughout the remainder of the lifespan. Of note, this gestalt is maintained even in the presence of a major, monogenically determined mechanism of increased risk, familial hypercholesterolemia (Figure 13): With LDL cholesterol levels increased to at least twice normal by virtue of a genetically determined approximately 50% reduction in LDL receptors, female siblings afflicted with this disorder do not achieve an incidence of ischemic vascular events comparable to that in their affected male siblings until approximately a decade later. In at least one pedigree this has correlated with the levels of high density lipoproteins (HDL) in individual family members, these in turn being affected by gender (higher in females). A clue to the hormonal basis of this differential is evident in age-adjusted ischemic vascular disease event rates in postmenopausal versus premenopausal women (Figure 14), rates in postmenopausal women being consistently higher than those in premenopausal women at a given age and more closely approximating those of men of equal age.

The primacy of lipoproteins in determining atherogenic risk in middle-through old-age is evident in the population-based studies from Framingham (Table 3). A hierarchy of risk factors to ischemic heart disease in participants ages 50 to 94 clearly demonstrates the powerful inverse association between HDL cholesterol levels and atherogenic risk. Low-density

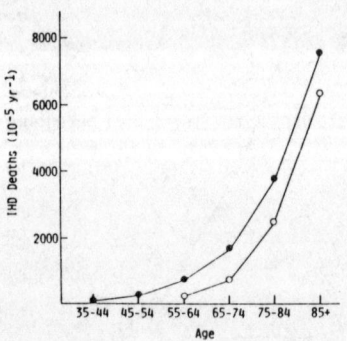

FIGURE 12. *Death rates per 100,000 population for ischemic heart disease by age in years in men (closed circles) and women (open circles) in the United States in 1976. Reprinted with permission from Sullivan JL: The sex differential in ischemic heart disease. Perspectives in Biology and Medicine 26:657–671, 1983.*

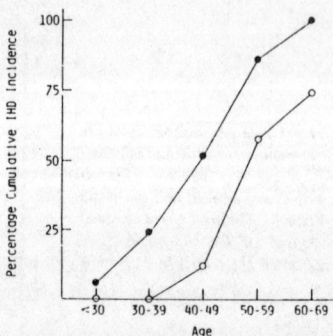

FIGURE 13. *Percentage cumulative incidence of first attack from ischemic heart disease by age in years in men (closed circles) and women (open circles) heterozygous for familial hypercholesterolemia (Fredrickson's type II hyperbetalipoproteinemia). Reprinted with permission from Sullivan JL: The sex differential in ischemic heart disease. Perspectives in Biology and Medicine 26:657–671, 1983.*

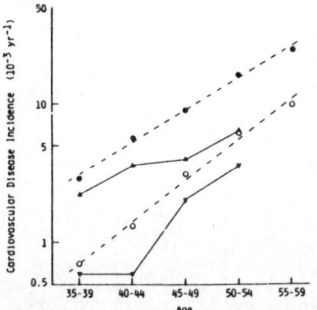

FIGURE 14. *Incidence of cardiovascular disease by age in years, sex, and menopausal status in the Framingham Study 20-year follow-up. Rates per 1000 per year are displayed for men (closed circles), all women (open circles), premenopausal women (downward arrowhead), and postmenopausal women (upward arrowhead). Rates for pre- and postmenopausal women "less than 40 years" are plotted with the 35 to 39 year group. (As per Sullivan, see Figure 12).*

lipoprotein cholesterol, blood pressure, and left ventricular hypertrophy on the other hand, continue to make positive, though less powerful contributions in old age than before that time. As noted, relative body weight, once its inverse relationship with HDL cholesterol is accounted for by multivariate analysis, fails to confer increased risk in either sex. Triglyceride levels (also inversely related to HDL cholesterol) behave in a similar fashion. Only diabetes mellitus places the female at selectively greater risk, a risk greater enough to overcome their relative immunity in other spheres. This represents an intriguing exception to the general rule and is as yet of undetermined explanation. A more in-depth analysis of the Framingham study suggests that the sex differential in total cholesterol/HDL ratio is sufficient to account for the sex differential in atherosclerosis only in the highest two quintiles of the distribution of this ratio (Figure 15). At intermediate and low levels, males at a given total LDL/HDL cholesterol ratio have approximately twice the incidence of cardiovascular disease as their female counterparts.

A more specific clue to the basis of this differential is obtained from population studies of median HDL and LDL cholesterol concentrations by age (and the LDL/HDL ratio, the currently preferred single index of lipoprotein-mediated atherogenic risk; Figure 16). Not shown, median population HDL and LDL levels are equivalent between the sexes until puberty.[18] Thereafter, HDL levels are higher in women than in men throughout the remainder of the human lifespan, with some tendency for the gap to narrow beyond age 50 (the average age of menopause in contemporary American culture). Low-density lipoprotein levels show a different trend. Whereas median population LDL cholesterol levels increase in both sexes between ages 20 and 50, they are significantly lower in women than men until the era of the menopause, at which time a crossover occurs, median female levels exceeding those of males throughout the remainder of the lifespan (a

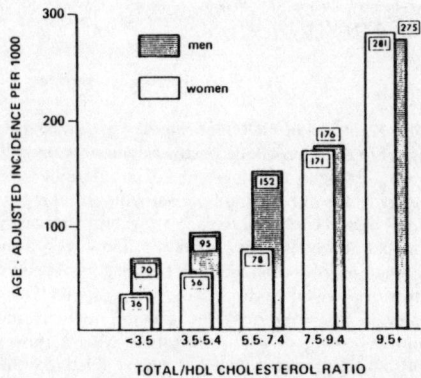

FIGURE 15. *Risk of coronary heart disease by total/HDL cholesterol. Framingham study: 26-year follow-up; subjects 50 to 90 years of age. Reprinted with permission from Kannel WB, Brand FN: Cardiovascular risk factors in the elderly, in Andres R, Bierman E, Hazzard W (eds): Principles of Geriatric Medicine. New York, McGraw-Hill, 1984*

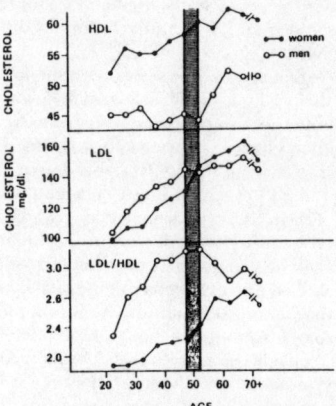

FIGURE 16. *Median North American population high-density lipoprotein (HDL) cholesterol, low-density lipoprotein (LDL) cholesterol, and the ratio between the two versus age in postadolescent white subjects. Data from Lipid Research Clinics Prevalence Survey.[18]*

phenomenon we have referred to as "the postmenopausal overshoot"). However, the magnitude of this overshoot is not sufficient to render the LDL/HDL cholesterol ratio higher in postmenopausal women than in men of comparable age. The continued lower level of HDL levels in men after adolescence would appear most likely attributable to the proponderant effect of androgens in determining HDL levels and their continued secretion in men throughout life. The crossover in LDL cholesterol concentrations at about the time of the menopause, however, suggests that the lower population cholesterol concentration in premenopausal women and the higher concentration in postmenopausal women are attributable to the secretion of estrogen before the menopause and its marked reduction postmenopausally.

Thus the observations which form the basis of the primary hypothesis of this work can be summarized as follows: 1) the male/female coronary risk ratio is greater than 1.0 at all ages, though it narrows progressively with age; and 2) the median female LDL-/HDL-cholesterol ratio is greater than 1.0 at all ages beyond puberty, but also narrows progressively with age (The median male LDL-cholesterol level is greater than the median female LDL-cholesterol from puberty to menopause, reversed after the menopause, and the median female HDL-cholesterol is greater than the median male HDL-cholesterol from puberty throughout adult life.

Proceeding from this hypothesis, the central theme of this article becomes clear: The sex differential in sex hormone levels gives rise to the sex differential in lipoprotein metabolism which in time (given our Occidental lifestyle) leads to the sex differential in atherosclerosis and this in turn to the sex differential in longevity.

If endogenous sex hormones account for the sex differential in lipoprotein levels, it follows that exogenous sex hormones should exaggerate that differential when given in pharmacologic doses. This prediction proves true in the data also drawn from the national Lipid Research Clinics' collaborative studies (Figure 17). In these studies median population LDL cholesterol levels were lower in postmenopausal women taking exogenous estrogens (predominantly conjugated equine estrogens in the usual therapeutic doses) than among their non-hormone-supplemented counterparts. Among premenopausal women taking combination oral contraceptives, however, median LDL cholesterol levels were higher than among non-oral contraceptive-taking subjects, suggesting that the progestational components of these contraceptives, most of which bear some androgenic properties, predominate in increasing LDL cholesterol concentrations. A different pattern emerged relative to HDL concentrations. Among the study subjects as a whole

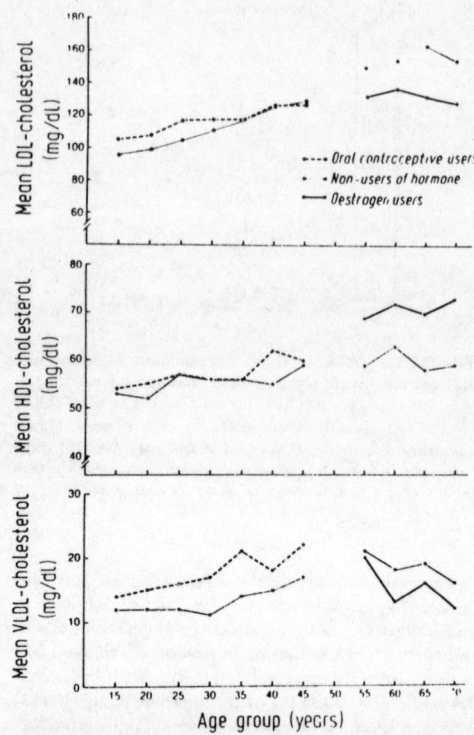

FIGURE 17. *Plasma lipoprotein cholesterol levels in users and nonusers of oral contraceptives and estrogens. Reprinted with permission from Wallace RB, et al: Altered plasma lipid and lipoprotein levels associated with oral contraceptive and oestrogen use. Lancet 2:111–114, 1979.*

concentrations of HDL cholesterol were substantially higher in estrogen-taking postmenopausal women than in non-estrogen-taking women of comparable age. By contrast, among premenopausal women taking combination oral contraceptives, no effect on median HDL cholesterol levels was apparent.[18] However, a more detailed examination of those subjects by type of oral contraceptive taken disclosed a heirarchy of HDL cholesterol concentrations, those being lowest among women taking oral contraceptives with a powerful androgenic progestational component relative to those taking weaker androgenic and predominantly the estrogenic combinations, in whom average HDL cholesterol levels were higher than among non-hormone-taking women.[19,20] The specific aspects of these effects have been further dissected by the Finnish workers, who have reported an HDL cholesterol-depressing effect of 19-nortestosterone-derived progestational agents, whereas those (notably medroxyprogesterone) not in the 19-nortestosterone series failed to affect HDL cholesterol concentrations.[21]

Perhaps the most intriguing (and still controversial) aspect of the studies reported from the Lipid Research Clinics' group was the major reduction in all-cause mortality associated with postmenopausal estrogen use in these free-living volunteers.[22] This was most evident in those with surgical menopause, in whom postmenopausal estrogen replacement was associated with reduced all-cause mortality of 88%. Cardiovascular mortality rates in all estrogen-taking women were as low as 33% of that among untreated subjects, a figure not unlike the risk ratio of 0.43 for cardiovascular disease incidence among estrogen-taking versus nonestrogen-taking women in a Southern California community under close surveillance by Ross et al.[23] Such dramatic reductions in all-cause and cardiovascular mortality and morbidity have not been uniformly observed, however,[24,25] and hence the prescription of estrogens for postmenopausal women to reduce atherogenic risk was not generally recommended at a recent consensus conference on postmenopausal estrogen replacement[26] and thus remains controversial.

Early studies in nonhuman species (notably chickens) were sufficiently impressive, however, to lead to trials of estrogens in the secondary prevention of cerebrovascular[27] and coronary heart disease, the latter in middle-aged men with previous myocardial infarction who participated in the Coronary Drug Project (CDP).[28] In the CDP, estrogen use after the onset of clinical atherosclerosis was associated with *increased*, not decreased, recurrent events, causing estrogen at both higher (5.0 mg conjugated equine estrogens per day[29]) and lower doses (2.5 mg/day[30]) to be withdrawn and that aspect of the trial terminated prematurely. This concern as to a paradoxical increase in atherogenic complications was underscored in a study of elderly male veterans with noninvasive prostatic carcinoma treated with high-dose estrogens.[31] In these subjects, despite a decrease in prostatic carcinoma deaths, overall mortality was increased in estrogen-taking subjects, the difference being attributable to a higher incidence of cardiovascular events. Finally, recent studies[32,33] have suggested higher circulating estrogen levels in men with premature coronary heart disease than in those without clinical atherosclerosis, consistent with (but not demonstrating) a cause-and-effect relationship between increased estrogen levels and atherogenic events. The mechanism of this potential association remains unclear but may relate to the known increase in various clotting factors (and decrease in anticlotting factors such as antithrombin III or thrombolytic factors) induced by estrogens.[34]

This side effect of estrogen appears most likely related to the increased risk of thromboembolism of the peripheral, pulmonary, and cerebral vasculature in women taking combination oral contraceptives.[35] Alternative explanations for these important epidemiologic phenomena relate to possible autoimmune responses to synthetic and endogenous estrogens,[36] with possible induced arterial endothelial injury. Such mechanisms, and especially increased thrombotic diathesis might also underlie the increased risk of cardiovascular mortality[37] and nonfatal myocardial infarction[38] in women taking combination oral contraceptives. These coronary complications are not clearly evident in postmenopausal women taking estrogens alone,[39] in whom a net reduction in cardiovascular disease seems likely.[24,25] The resolution of this paradox is far from at hand. However, to recall a cliché: "What is good for the goose may not be good for the gander"; endogenous estrogens secreted cyclically over a long period may confer benefits (and exogenous estrogens net benefits in postmenopausal and especially surgically postmenopausal women), whereas those same benefits may not accrue when given together with androgenic progestins in oral contraceptives or to males, especially when administered in pharmacologic doses to those with pre-existing cardiovascular disease for whom thrombosis may represent a more proximate risk than atherogenesis per se.

It would appear that these reports of adverse consequences of estrogen administration, particularly in men, have inhibited research on the effects of estrogen upon serum lipoproteins in humans. One study from the Finnish group reported the efficacy of exogenous estrogen (specifically estradiol valeranate) in reducing LDL cholesterol concentrations in "Type IIa" (hyperbetalipoproteinemic) women,[40] confirming studies conducted over two decades previously that had disclosed increases in HDL and decreases in LDL with estrogen.[41] These findings were in contrast, however, to those of Schaefer et al.[42] in which premenopausal women under careful metabolic control were administered ethinyl estradiol in a pharmacologic dose (0.1 mg per day). In these subjects, despite increases in HDL cholesterol concentrations, no decrease in LDL cholesterol levels was apparent (in five such subjects). Previous studies from our laboratories,[43] also of premenopausal women, had failed to disclose predictable or uniform changes in LDL cholesterol concentrations with similar estrogen treatment (although increases in HDL concentration and the principal HDL apolipoprotein A-I were consistently induced[44]; LDL results unpublished).

Undaunted by these findings, in recent preliminary studies[45] we sought to maximize the potential for demonstrating an important effect of exogenous estrogen upon LDL cholesterol levels by selecting six clearly postmenopausal women (57 ± 6 years of age). We challenged their ability to assimilate cholesterol by adding 900 mg per day of cholesterol (three large egg yolks) to a solid diet of constant composition consumed in a rotating menu every third day (with a constant polyunsaturated/saturated fatty acid ratio; P/S = .85) for an 84-day period. During the middle 28 days of this 84-day period, exogenous ethinyl estrodiol was taken in a dosage of 1 mg/kg per day (averaging 60 μg per day, a dose close to that in many oral contraceptives). Lipids, lipoproteins, apolipoproteins, and postheparin triglyceride lipolytic enzymes (hepatic and lipoprotein lipase) were measured at weekly intervals throughout and more frequently during periods of onset and offset of estrogen therapy. As anticipated, mean plasma triglyceride concentrations uniformly increased (by approximately 50%) during estrogen and returned rapidly to baseline levels after its discontinuation. Surprisingly, however, total (Table 4) and, specifically, LDL cholesterol levels decreased uniformly and abruptly during estrogen therapy, increasing to baseline levels promptly upon its discontinuation. High-density lipoprotein levels, on the other hand, increased more gradually (and also decreased more gradually after cessation of estrogen). The magnitude of these changes was impressive. The decreases in LDL cholesterol, for example, averaging 25%, compared favorably with changes in LDL cholesterol concentration induced by specific hypocholesterolemic drugs currently on the market. Within HDL the increases were confined to the more buoyant HDL_2 fraction, that subfraction most clearly inversely related to cardiovascular risk (and perhaps accounting for the entire inverse relationship between HDL cholesterol and ischemic cardiovascular disease).[46] Thus, the theoretical benefit of this intervention was magnified through concomitant reductions in LDL and increases in HDL (specifically HDL_2) levels.

Simultaneous measurement of carrier apolipoprotein concentrations demonstrated a modest, approximately 9% reduction in total plasma apolipoprotein B (the structural apolipoprotein within very low density lipoproteins [VLDL] and LDL) and a 33% reduction in mean apolipoprotein E (thought to represent the most powerful signal to VLDL remnant uptake by the liver[47]), while apo A-1 increased as predicted.

The metabolic mechanism (more likely, mechanisms) of these effects remain unclear. However, it seems likely that previous studies with estrogen in the uncommon disorder type III hyperlipoproteinemia (dysbetalipoproteinemia) might be relevant.[48,49] These demonstrated a paradoxical, hypolipidemic effect of estrogen (in contrast with the anticipated hypertriglyceridemic effect seen in normal and hypertriglyceridemic women with other disorders). Because one basis of type III hyperlipoproteinemia lies in the genetically determined homozygous inheritance of the lack of isoapolipoproteins E_3 and E_4, demonstrated to be necessary for the recognition of apo E-containing lipoproteins by fibroblasts and hepatic receptors, it seemed possible that estrogen might correct this deficiency. However, careful studies by Falko et al.[50] made it clear that estrogen treatment fails to correct this genetically determined deficiency. Alternatively, because LDL-receptors (which recognize apo B of hepatic origin as well as apo E_3 and apo E_4) are dramatically induced in nonhuman species by estrogens,[47] and estrogen enhances VLDL remnant uptake in the cholesterol-fed rabbit,[51] the uptake of VLDL remnants and LDL by the liver may be enhanced via increased activity of this receptor in the human liver as well (a possibility yet to be tested directly). Thus, the reduction in apo E levels seen with estrogen in these studies of normal postmenopausal women may reflect the enhanced clearance of VLDL remnants, whereas the less dramatic decrease in total apo B levels may reflect the selective reduction in LDL concentrations while VLDL (also containing apo B) may be simultaneously increased, as reflected in the higher

TABLE 4. MEAN CHOLESTEROL LEVEL CHANGES DURING A FIXED HIGH CHOLESTEROL DIET AND WITH THE ADDITION OF ESTROGEN IN POSTMENOPAUSAL WOMEN*

	Day	Cholesterol (mg/dL)					
		Total	VLDL	IDL + LDL	HDL	HDL_2	HDL_3
	0	256 ± 36	14 ± 6	172 ± 30	70 ± 8	33 ± 7	37 ± 3
†Estrogen	28	255 ± 35	14 ± 4	173 ± 22	68 ± 16	33 ± 11	35 ± 6
	56	225 ± 30‡	13 ± 5	130 ± 23†	82 ± 20	46 ± 17§	36 ± 7
	84	256 ± 41§	12 ± 8	169 ± 27†	76 ± 18	37 ± 12	39 ± 6

VLDL = very low-density lipoproteins; IDL = intermediate density lipoprotein; LDL = low-density lipoprotein; HDL = high-density lipoprotein.
*Statistics are for each period versus the previous one.
†P < .01; ‡P < .02; §P < .05.
From Applebaum-Bowden D, et al: Estrogen reduces LDL cholesterol on high cholesterol diet in post-menopausal women (abstract). Arteriosclerosis 2:415A, 1982.

triglyceride levels (and higher apo B concentrations and production rates previously demonstrated in the studies of premenopausal volunteers by Schaefer et al.[42]). This hypothesis, however, remains to be tested.

Possibly related to the mechanism of the changes in HDL with estrogen (and conceivably LDL as well) was the prompt, dramatic, and uniform decrease in postheparin hepatic triglyceride lipase (HTGL) levels in these subjects (while postheparin lipoprotein lipase levels remained unaltered), a phenomenon previously demonstrated in premenopausal volunteers.[43] The possible relevance of this finding to HDL metabolism was raised in studies that disclosed phospholipase activity versus HDL surface phospholipids in postheparin HTGL,[52] other workers suggesting that hepatic lipase accelerates HDL catabolism via this mechanism.[53,54] More directly relevant studies have demonstrated an increase in phospholipase and hepatic triglyceride lipase activities with androgens (specifically oxandrolone[55]) and androgenic progestational steroids,[56] although progestins lacking the androgenicity or the 19-nortestosterone series fail both to increase postheparin HTGL and to alter HDL concentrations.[56] Furthermore, the inverse relationship between postheparin HTGL levels and HDL (selectively HDL$_2$) concentrations has been demonstrated in specific subject groups[53] and a representative American population.[57] Thus, estrogens may raise HDL levels by inducing lower levels of HTGL (in hepatic tissue as well as in postheparin plasma in studies of rats from this laboratory[58]) which in turn retards HDL catabolism, a possibility thus far tested in but a single subject.

At the same time that our interest in the effects of

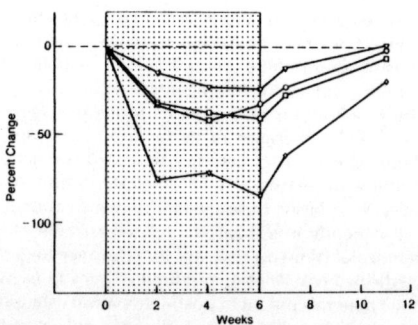

FIGURE 19. *Percent changes in mean plasma levels of HDL$_2$ cholesterol (diamonds) HDL$_3$ cholesterol (circles), apolipoprotein A-I (squares), and apolipoprotein A-II (arrowheads) during six weeks of stanozolol, 6 mg/per day (stippled area), and for five weeks after its discontinuation in ten postmenopausal osteoporotic women (as per Taggart et al, see Figure 18)*

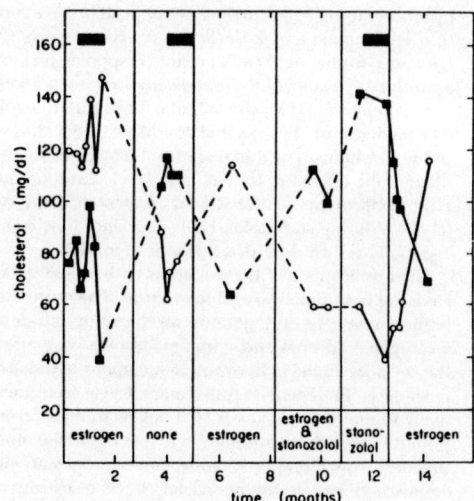

FIGURE 20. *High-density lipoprotein cholesterol (HDL-C, circles) and low-density lipoprotein cholesterol (LDL-C, squares) levels during treatment with estrogen (ethinyl estradiol, 0.06 mg/per day), stanozolol (6 mg/per day), both, or neither. Solid bars indicate timing of HDL turnover studies. The subject had been on cyclic estrogen therapy for several years when these studies were initiated. Reprinted with permission from Hazzard WR, et al: Preliminary report: Kinetic studies on the modulation of high-density lipoprotein, apolipoprotein, and subfraction metabolism by sex steroids in a postmenopausal woman. Metabolism 33:779–784, 1984.[66]*

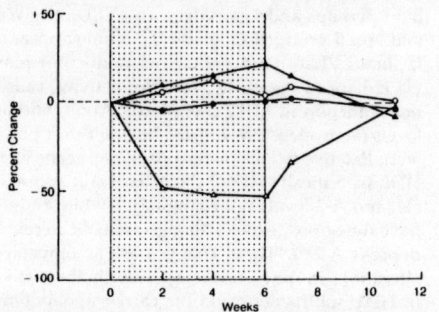

FIGURE 18. *Percent changes in mean plasma LDL-cholesterol (upward arrowhead), triglyceride (open circle), total cholesterol (closed circle), and HDL-cholesterol in ten postmenopausal steoporotic women during (stippled area) and after treatment with stanozolol, 6 mg/per day. Reprinted with permission from Taggart HMcA, et al: Reduction in high density lipoproteins by anabolic steroid (stanozolol) therapy for postmenopausal osteoporosis. Metabolism 31:1147, 1982.*

estrogen upon human lipoprotein concentrations was spurred, we became intrigued by the contrasting effects of oxandrolone, an androgenic anabolic steroid chosen as one of the four agents in a pharmacogenetic study of subjects with various forms of dyslipoproteinemia,[59,60] because of its reported hypotriglyceridemic effects. These studies disclosed dramatic and uniform decreases in HDL cholesterol and ApoA-I levels in subjects during oxandrolone treatment. We subsequently investigated a related anabolic steroid, stanozolol (Winstrol), of specific relevance to geriatric medicine because of its reported efficacy in *increasing* bone mineral content in postmenopausal osteoporotic women.[61] In subsequent studies of a subset of these same osteoporotic women it was demonstrated that stanozolol in the usual therapeutic dose of 6 mg per day induced uniform decreases in HDL cholesterol concentration that were equal and opposite to the increases in LDL cholesterol concentrations throughout the duration of stanozolol treatment, levels of both lipoproteins returning to baseline five weeks after cessation of the drug[62] (Figures 18 and 19). Perhaps yet more cogent to the issue of atherogenesis, stanozolol selectively decreased the HDL_2 concentration by an average of 85%, carrier apolipoproteins A-1 and, to a lesser extent, A-2 declining concominantly. Of relevance to the mechanism of this response, like oxandrolone,[55] stanozolol dramatically increased levels of postheparin HTGL, consistent with its putative role as a mediator of HDL catabolism. More direct studies of the mechanism of this response through measurement of the residence time of radiolabeled autologous HDL apoproteins demonstrated accelerated HDL catabolism during stanozolol, HDL_3 residence time being especially reduced by this anabolic steroid.[63]

The implications of these studies with anabolic steroids are both practical and theoretical. The more theoretical relate to endogenous mechanisms whereby androgenic adrenal and gonadal steroids may affect the sex differential in lipoprotein metabolism and atherogenesis. Endogenous testosterone levels seem most likely to mediate the lower HDL levels in males from puberty throughout adult life. Proceeding to the more practical considerations, androgenic progestational agents may negate the beneficial effects of estrogens upon lipoprotein levels in premenopausal women when given in combination oral contraceptives as well as in postmenopausal women in whom combination (or sequential) progestational therapy is contemplated to offset the carcinogenic effects of estrogens upon the endometrium. Yet more practical and more proximate are the profound effects that anabolic steroids have upon lipoproteins (and theoretical atherogenic risk) in postmenopausal osteoporotic women and, especially, power athletes consuming megapharmacologic doses. Such athletes, notably weight lifters, have exhibited profound decreases in HDL concentrations when taking testosterone and/or anabolic steroids.[64] Specific atherogenic risk has yet to be demonstrated, however, and some have suggested that the enhanced fibrinolysis and lower coagulation factor levels secondary to anabolic steroid administration might be sufficient to offset the putative enhanced atherogenesis during (eg, stanozolol) therapy.[65]

The contrasting effects of estrogens and anabolic steroids upon human lipoprotein metabolism were most clearly demonstrated in a postmenopausal volunteer who underwent sequential treatment with estrogens (ethinyl estradiol 1 μg/kg per day), stanozolol (6 mg per day), no sex steroid supplementation, and the combination of both (Figure 20).[66] This woman, who was hyperalphalipoproteinemic and hypobetalipoproteinemic when initially seen on estrogen alone, demonstrated exaggerated responses to the sex steroids, perhaps related to her native lipoprotein regulation. Nevertheless, during estrogens her HDL levels increased dramatically while LDL decreased; during stanozolol the opposite trends were evident; during treatment with both steroids, levels of LDL and HDL equal to those while off both agents were observed. Studies of the mechanism of this response confirmed the increased postheparin HTGL activity during stanozolol and decreased activity during estrogen treatment, whereas measurements of HDL apolipoprotein turnover demonstrated retarded A-1 and HDL-2 catabolism during estrogen and accelerated apo A-2 and HDL-3 catabolism during stanozolol.

Thus, investigations both of an epidemiologic and of clinical nature have demonstrated opposing effects of estrogens and androgens upon the regulation of human lipoprotein levels. Estogens appear to increase (and perhaps androgens decrease) VLDL triglyceride and apo-B production, at the same time appearing to facilitate VLDL (and perhaps chylomicron) removal via enhanced apo-B, $E_{3,4}$ receptor activity, causing a net reduction in LDL, cholesterol, ApoE, and apo-B levels (androgens presumably having the opposite effect). Relative to HDL metabolism, estrogens increase HDL (specifically HDL_2) cholesterol and apo A-1 levels (apo A-2 levels not changing),[67] while androgens have the opposite effect (though anabolic steroids also depress A-2[66]). These changes are accompanied by alterations in the turnover, specifically the catabolism of HDL subfractions and the carrier apolipoproteins in the predicted fashion, perhaps mediated by decreases in hepatic triglyceride lipase during estrogen use (and increases during androgen). These changes in lipolytic activity may also mediate redistributions between intermediate density lipoproteins (IDL, d 1.006–1.019) and within LDL (estrogens decreasing and androgens increasing the proportion of the denser, potentially more atherogenic subspecies[68]). Many of the mechanistic aspects of these studies remain conjectural and subject to confirmation in direct studies of both normal and dyslipoproteinemic volunteers.

Nevertheless, given the Occidental lifestyle currently prevalent in the United States and specifically its high intake of cholesterol and saturated fat, the hypothesis remains attractive that women adapt to this lifestyle more readily than do men by virtue of facilitated metabolism of these dietary constituents and hence less atherogenesis than their male counterparts. In the mode of preventive gerontology,[1] therefore, men have selectively more to gain (and their spouses will benefit indirectly) by adoption of a lifestyle designed to attenuate atherogenesis, including consumption of a diet relatively restricted in cholesterol (currently recommended as less than 300 mg per day) and total fat (to as low as 30%, equally distributed among saturated, monounsaturated, and polyunsaturated), avoidance of cigarette smoking, maintenance of an aerobically active exercise pattern, and optimal relative body weight (both should raise HDL cholesterol levels), and monitoring of blood pressure with early and continuous treatment of hypertension when present. For the foreseeable future it would seem that only through such voluntary, population-wide interventions throughout adult life is the prospect bright for narrowing the sex differential in longevity in America.

REFERENCES

1. Hazzard WR: Preventive gerontology: Strategies for healthy aging. Postgrad Med 74:279, 1983
2. Nathanson CA, Lorenz G: Women and health: The social dimensions of biomedical data, in Giele JZ (ed): Women in the Middle Years. New York, Wiley, 1982, pp 37-87
3. Fries J: Aging, natural death, and the compression of morbidity. N Engl J Med 303:130, 1980
4. Manton KG: Changing concepts of morbidity and mortality in the elderly population. Milbank Mem Fund Health Soc 60:183, 1982
5. Schneider EL, Brody JA: Aging, natural death, and the compression of morbidity: Another view. N Engl J Med 309:854, 1983
6. Wylie CM: Contrasts in the health of elderly men and women: An analysis of recent data for whites in the United States. J Am Geriatr Soc 32:670, 1984
7. Murphy EA: Genetics of longevity in man, in Schneider EL (ed): The Genetics of Aging. New York, Plenum, 1978, pp 261-302
8. Holden C: Can smoking explain the ultimate gender gap? Science 221:1034, 1983
9. McMillen MM: Differential mortality by sex in fatal and neonatal deaths. Science 204:89, 1971
10. Grossman CJ: Interactions between the gonadal steroids and the immune system. Science 227:257, 1985
11. Talal N: Disordered immunologic regulation and autoimmunity. Transplant Rev 31:240, 1976
12. Hazzard WR: Atherosclerotic cardiovascular disease: Differential prevention strategies across the lifespan, in Stout RW (ed): Arterial Disease in the Elderly. Edinburgh and New York, Churchill Livingston, 1984, pp 101-123.
13. Bierman E: Aging and atherosclerosis, in Stout RW (ed): Arterial Disease in the Elderly, Edinburgh, Churchill Livingston, 1984
14. Hazzard WR: The sex differential in longevity, in Andres R, Bierman E, Hazzard W (eds): Principles of Geriatric Medicine. New York, McGraw-Hill, 1984, pp 72-81
15. Kissebah AH, Nadarajen V, Murray R, et al: Relation of body fat distribution to metabolic complications of obesity. J Clin Endocrinol Metab 54:254, 1982
16. Kannel WB, Brand FN: Cardiovascular risk factors in the elderly, in Andres R, Bierman E, Hazzard W (eds): Principles of Geriatric Medicine. New York, McGraw-Hill, 1984
17. Andres R: Mortality and obesity: The rationale for age-specific height-weight tables, in Andres R, Bierman E, Hazzard W (eds): Principles of Geriatric Medicine. New York, McGraw-Hill, 1984
18. The Lipid Research Clinics: Population Studies Data Book. Volume 1. The Prevalence Study. NIH Pub No 80:1527, 1980. US Dept Health and Human Services, 1980
19. Wahl P, Walden C, Knopp R, et al: Effects of estrogen/progestin potency on lipid/lipoprotein cholesterol. N Engl J Med 308:862, 1983
20. Knopp RH, Walden CE, Wahl PW, et al: Oral contraceptive and postmenopausal estrogen effects on lipoprotein triglyceride and cholesterol in an adult female population: Relationships to estrogen and progestin potency. J Clin Endocrinol Metab 53:1123, 1981
21. Hiroven E, Malkonen M, Manninen V: Effects of different progestogens on lipoproteins during postmenopausal replacement therapy. N Engl J Med 304:560, 1981
22. Bush T, Cowan T, Barrett-Connor E, et al: Estrogen use and all-cause mortality: Preliminary results from the Lipid Research Clinics Program. J Am Med Assoc 249:903, 1983
23. Ross RK, Paganini-Hill A, Macke TM, et al: Menopausal estrogen therapy and protection from ischemic heart disease. Lancet 1:858, 1981
24. Gordon T, Kannel WB, Hjortland MC, et al: Menopause and coronary heart disease. The Framingham Study. Ann Int Med 89:157, 1978
25. Rosenberg L, Armstrong B, Jick HB: Myocardial infarction and estrogen therapy in post-menopausal women. N Engl J Med 294:1256, 1976
26. National Institutes of Health: Consensus Development Conference Estrogen Use and Postmenopausal Women, Vol 2, No 8, 1979
27. McDowell F, Louis S, McDevitt E: A clinical trail of premarin in cerebrovascular disease. J Chron Dis 20:679, 1967

28. Coronary Drug Project Research Group: The Coronary Drug Project: Design, methods, and baseline results. Circulation 47 (suppl 1):I-1, 1973
29. Coronary Drug Project Research Group: The Coronary Drug Project: Initial findings leading to modifications of research protocol. JAMA 214:1301, 1970
30. Coronary Drug Project Research Group: The Coronary Drug Project: Findings leading to discontinuation of the 2.5 mg/day estrogen group. JAMA 226:652, 1973
31. The Veteran Administration Co-operative Urological Research Group: Treatment and survival of patients with cancer of the prostrate. Surg Gynecol Obstet 124:1011, 1967
32. Phillips AB: Evidence for hyperoestrogenaemia as a risk factor for myocardial infarction in men. Lancet 2:14, 1976
33. Phillips GB: Relationship between serum sex-hormones and glucose, insulin, and lipid abnormalities in men with myocardial infarction. Proc Natl Acad Sci USA 74:1729, 1977
34. Dugdale M, Masi AT: Hormonal contraception and thromboembolic disease: Effects of the oral contraceptives on hemostatic mechanisms—Review of the literature. J Chron Dis 23:775, 1971
35. Inman WHW, Vessey MP, Westerholm B, et al: Thromboembolic disease and the steroidal content of oral contraceptives. A report to the Committee on Safety of Drugs. Br Med J 2:203, 1970
36. Beaumont JL, Lemort N, Lorenzelli-Edouard L, et al: Antiethinyloestradiol antibody activities in oral contraceptive users. Clin Exp Immunol 38:445, 1979
37. Mann JI, Inman WHW: Oral contraceptives and death from myocardial infarction. Br Med J 1:245, 1975
38. Mann JI, Vessey MP, Thorogood M, et al: Myocardial infarction in young women with special reference to oral contraceptive practice. Br Med J 1:241, 1975
39. Pfeffer RI, Shipple GH, Kurosaki TT, et al: Coronary risk and estrogen use in postmenopausal women. Am J Epidemiol 107:479, 1978
40. Tikkanen JJ, Nikkila EA, Vantiainen E. Natural estrogen as an effective treatment for type II hyperlipoproteinemia in post-menopausal women. Lancet 1:490, 1978
41. Russ EM, Eder HA, Barr DP: Influence of gonadal hormones on protein-lipid relationships in human plasma. Am J Med 19:4, 1955
42. Schaefer EJ, Foster DM, Zech LA, et al: The effects of estrogen administration on plasma lipoprotein metabolism in premenopausal females. J Clin Endocrinol Metab 57:262, 1983
43. Applebaum DM, Goldberg AP, Pykalisto OJ, et al: Effect of estrogen on post-heparin lipolytic activity: Selective decline in hepatic triglyceride lipase. J Clin Invest 59:601, 1977
44. Albers JJ, Wahl PW, Cabana VG, et al: Quantitation of apolipoprotein A-I of human plasma high density lipoprotein. Metabolism 25:633, 1976
45. Applebaum-Bowden D, Hazzard W, McLean P, et al: Estrogen reduces LDL cholesterol on high cholesterol diet in post-menopausal women (abstract). Arteriosclerosis 2:415A, 1982
46. Gidez LI, Eder HA: The clinical significance of plasma high-density lipoproteins, in Miller NE, Miller GJ (eds): Clinical and Metabolic Aspects of High-Density Lipoproteins. New York, (Elsevier), 1984, pp 415–450
47. Mahley RW, Hui DY, Innerarity TL, et al: Two independent lipoprotein receptors on hepatic membranes of the dog, swine, and man: The apo-E and apo-B,E receptors. J Clin Invest 68:1197, 1981
48. Kushwaha RS, Hazzard WR, Gagne C, et al: Type III hyperlipoproteinemia: Paradoxical hypolipidemic response to estrogen. Ann Intern Med 87:517, 1977
49. Chait A, Hazzard WR, Albers JJ, et al: Impaired very low density lipoprotein and triglyceride removal in broad beta disease: Comparison with endogenous hypertriglyceridemia. Metabolism 27:1055, 1978
50. Falko JM, Weidman SW, Witztum JL, et al: Effects of estrogen therapy on apolipoprotein E in type III hyperlipoproteinemia. Metabolism 28:1171, 1979
51. Iozzo RV, Kushwaha RS, Wight TN, et al: Cellular and subcellular distribution of I25-I-labeled very low density lipoproteins in the liver of normal and estrogen-treated rabbits. Am J Pathol 107:6, 1982
52. Musliner TA, Herbert PN, Kingston MJ: Lipoprotein substrates of lipoprotein lipase and hepatic triacylglycerol lipase from human post-heparin plasma. Biochim Biophys Acta 575:277, 1979
53. Kuusi T, Saarinen P, Nikkila EA: Evidence for the role of hepatic endothelial lipase in the metabolism of plasma high density lipoprotein$_2$ in man. Atherosclerosis 36:589, 1980
54. Nikkila EA, Kussi T, Taskinen M-R: Role of lipoprotein lipase and hepatic endothelial lipase in the metabolism of high density lipoproteins: A novel concept on cholesterol transport in HDL cycle, in Carlson LA, Pernon B (eds): Metabolic Risk Factors in Ischemic Cardiovascular Disease. New York, Raven Press, 1982, pp 205–215
55. Ehnholm C, Huttenen JK, Kinnunen PJ, et al: Effect of oxandrolone treatment on the activity of lipoprotein lipase, hepatic lipase and phospholipase A_1 of human postheparin plasma. N Engl J Med 292:1314, 1975
56. Tikkanen MJ, Nikkila EA, Kuusi T, et al: Reduction of plasma high density lipoprotein and cholesterol and increase of postheparin plasma hepatic lipase activity during progestin treatment. Clin Chim Acta 115:63, 1981
57. Applebaum-Bowden D, Haffner SM, Wahl PW, et al: Post-heparin plasma triglyceride lipase: Relationships with very low density lipoprotein triglyceride and high density lipoprotein$_2$ cholesterol. Arteriosclerosis 5:273, 1985
58. Applebaum-Bowden D, Hazzard WR: Ethinyl estradiol lowers liver levels of triglyceride lipase. Circulation 60:186, 1980
59. Cheung MC, Albers JJ, Wahl PW, et al: High density lipoproteins during hypolipidemic therapy: A comparative study of four drugs. Atherosclerosis 35:215, 1980

60. Hazzard WR, Wahl PW, Gagne C, et al: Plasma and lipoprotein lipid responses to four hypolipid drugs. Lipids 19:73, 1984
61. Chestnut CH III, Ivey JL, Gruber HE, et al: Stanozolol in postmenopausal osteoporosis: Therapeutic efficacy and possible mechanisms of action. Metabolism 32:571, 1983
62. Taggart H McA, Applebaum-Bowden D, Haffner S, et al: Reduction in high density lipoproteins by anabolic steroid (stanozolol) therapy for postmenopausal osteoporosis. Metabolism 31:1147, 1982
63. Haffner SM, Kushwaha RS, Foster DM, et al: Studies on the metabolic mechanism of reduced high density lipoproteins during anabolic steroid therapy. Metabolism 32:413, 1983
64. Hurley BF, Seals DR, Hagberg JM, et al: High density lipoprotein cholesterol in bodybuilders V. Powerlifters negative effects of androgen use. JAMA 252:507, 1984
65. Davidson JF, Lockhead M, McDonald GA, et al: Fibrinolytic enhancement by stanozolol: A double blind trial. Br J Haematol 22:543, 1972
66. Hazzard WR, Haffner SM, Kushwaha RS, et al: Preliminary report: Kinetic studies on the modulation of high-density lipoprotein, apolipoprotein, and subfraction metabolism by sex steroids in a postmenopausal woman. Metabolism 33:779, 1984
67. Cheung MC, Albers JJ: The measurement of apolipoprotein A-I and A-II levels in men and women by immunoassay. J Clin Invest 60:43, 1977
68. Krauss RM, Burke DJ: Identification of multiple subclasses of plasma low density ipoproteins in normal humans. J Lipid Res 23:97, 1982

Name Index

Aall, A. 50–52
Aarkrog, T. 136
Abeliovich, D. 445, 448
Abraham, G.E. 484, 507, 523
Abramovich, D.R. 445, 448
Abramowicz, H.K. 133, 157
Abramowitz, R.H. 522
Abramsky, O. 141
Aceto, H. Jr. 158
Achenbach, T.M. 483, 522, 527, 537
Acher 42
Acheson, E.J. 289
Adams, D.B. 479
Adelman, S. 259
Adelson, J. 115
Adinolfi, M. 139, 141, 147, 153, 155, 167, 171–4
Adkinson, C.D. 125
Adler, A. 35
Affleck, G. 243–5, 291
Agboola, A. 185
Agobe, J.T. 185
Ahern, F.M. 136–7
Ainsworth, M.D.S. 120
Ajuriaguerra, J. 287
Akesson, E. 288
Akesson, J.O. 134
Akiyama, Y. 202
Alaway, N.C. 134
Albon, S.D. 162, 164
Alexander, P.E. 481
Allan, T.M. 150
Allard, E. 235
Allen, L.C. 445
Allen, M. 426
Allen, V.L. 531
Allon, R. 133
Alpert, J.E. 480
Alsberg 45
Altmann, J. 162, 164
Altus, W.D. 144, 153
Alvesalo, L. 151
Ambarsoom, H. 352
Anastasi, Anne 73–4, 78, 80–85, 355, 357, 359, 378
Ances, I.G. 448
Anders, Thomas 219, 222–3

Anderson, E.P. 120
Anderson, M.M. 33
Anderson, R.E. 61
Andrews, P.W. 137, 142
Angst, J. 143–4, 169
Anisko, J.J. 463
Anisman, H. 480
Annett, M. 287, 291
Annito, J.E. 137
Anstis, S.M. 240
Antes, J. 287
Anuza, T. 238–40
Appicciafuoco, A. 306
Apter, D. 484, 495, 524
Archer, J. 378
Archer, S.J. 141
Arena, J.F.P. 159, 184
Arey, L.B. 339
Aries, Elizabeth J. 115
Armitage, P. 212
Arnold, A.P. 292
Asch, Solomon 95, 102–5
Ash, I.E. 58
Asher, E. 287
Ashmead, D.H. 348
Aslin, R. 348–9
Atkins, L. 158
Atkinson, J.W. 85
Atkinson, R.C. 429, 437
Attie, I. 530
August, G.J. 134
Aussage 63
Axworthy, D. 158
Aylward, G.P. 206, 216

Back, K.J. 320, 426
Badian, N. 137, 144
Bagg, H.J. 35
Bailey, D.W. 142
Bakan, P. 165, 281, 283, 287
Baker, S.W. 472
Bakke, J.L. 157
Bakker, D.J. 235–7
Bakketeig, L.S. 137
Baldwin, B.T. 56
Ballard, J.L. 207
Ballard, P.B. 49, 60

Balling, J.D. 243–5
Balzer, W. 165
Ban, P. 123
Banchieri, F. 52
Bancroft, J. 504
Bandura, M.M. 243–4, 320–22, 332, 426, 501
Banks, M.S. 348
Bannerman, R.M. 449
Banting, G. 163
Barclay, G. 164
Bardawil, W.A. 141, 157
Bardwick, J. 115–16, 480
Barlow, G.W. 161
Barnes, R.D. 139
Barnett, C.R. 123
Barnsley, R. 487
Bartko, J.J. 211
Bartleman, Betty 443
Basser, L.S. 233
Basso, A. 305, 311, 314, 316–17
Basu, G.K. 481
Bauer, Joseph A. 348
Bauermeister, M. 320, 426
Baughan, B. 339, 342, 344–5
Baume, Robert M. 339
Bayley, N. 348–51, 398, 501
Beach, F.A. 462–3, 520
Beal, M.F. 141
Beard, A.W. 134
Beatty, Patricia A. 148, 169, 173–4
Beatty, R.A. 150
Beatty, William W. 148, 169, 173–4
Beck, E.C. 241–3
Beck, J.S. 140
Beck, S.E. 139
Becker, H.B. 480
Becker, J. 292
Becker, P.T. 206, 217
Beer, A.E. 137–8, 140, 151–2, 157, 173
Behan, P. 145, 148, 151, 156, 159, 164–5, 174
Beik, A.K. 48
Beintema, D. 206
Beisler, J.M. 133–6
Belisle, S. 445, 448
Bell, R.D. 144
Bell, R.Q. 125–6, 201
Bell, S.M. 120
Belmont, L. 137, 144, 153, 169
Beltran, I.C. 184
Bem, Daryl 79
Bem, Sandra 79
Benbow, Camilla P. 148, 171
Bender, B. 158

Bener, A. 234
Benjamin, L.T. Jr. 73
Benke, Thomas 250
Bennett, J. 157
Benninger, C. 240
Ben-Porath, Y. 159, 171
Benson, D. 264, 288, 292, 315
Benson, R.C. 125
Bentler, P.M. 400
Benton, A.L. 277, 283, 287, 315, 428
Berenbaum, S.A. 320, 426, 472
Berendes, H. 138
Berg, K. 158
Berg, W.K. 125
Berger, J.M. 479
Berglin, Carl-Gustaf 148–9, 170
Bergman, A. 117
Bergstrom, K.J. 235, 237
Berkowitz, L. 480
Berlin, C. 290
Berlin, C.I. 234, 237, 428
Berlin, G. 235, 237, 245
Berlin, H. 235, 237
Berlin, L.J. 147
Berliner, A. 34
Berlucchi, C. 286
Bernard, O. 139, 145
Bernstein, I.S. 481, 496
Berry, J.W. 75
Berryman, P.L. 138
Bertrand, J. 448
Best, C.T. 234, 236
Bevard, K.H. 57
Beveridge, R. 290
Bianco, S. 143, 150
Bierman, E. 549
Bigum, H.B. 241–3
Billingham, R.E. 138–40, 151, 157
Billy, J.O.G. 521
Binet-Simon (scale) 25, 35, 39, 50, 56–7, 64, 80
Bion, P.J. 238–9
Birch, D. 85
Birns, B. 125–6
Birren, J.E. 86
Birtchnell, J. 142, 149
Bishop, D.V.M. 156
Bixler, Ray H. 149, 171
Biziere, K. 154
Blair, A.W. 206
Blair, E. 153, 170
Blauert, J. 349
Bleier, Ruth 94
Blessing, W.W. 141

Bliss, E. 480
Bloch, Iwan 43
Block, J. 75, 82, 389, 394, 483
Blos, P. 520
Blumstein, S. 236
Blyth, D.A. 501, 521, 530–31
Bobertag, O. 49, 56–7, 59, 61, 64
Boccardi, E. 276
Bockman, D.E. 151
Bodmer, J.G. 147
Bodmer, W.F. 147, 228–9
Boehme, D.I. 141
Bogen, J.E. 282
Bokert, E. 199
Boklage, Charles E. 150–51, 168, 170–71, 174
Boller, F. 315–16
Bonham, D.G. 132–4, 136, 140
Bonnar, J. 147
Bonner, J.J. 141
Bonser 5, 14–15, 53, 55
Book, W.F. 76
Borelli, J. 158
Boring, E.G. 27, 73
Borkowski, J.G. 277
Borland, R. 138
Born, G. 158
Boroditsky, R.S. 448
Borowy, T. 235, 290
Bouissou, M.F. 479–81
Bourgois, M. 158
Bowe, T. 222
Bowers, M.J. Jr. 158
Boyar, R.M. 530
Boyer, C. 286
Boyer, R. 503
Boyle, M.H. 522
Boyse, F.A. 137
Brackbill, Y. 219–20, 222, 225
Bradley, A.J. 154
Bradley, B.A. 137, 163
Bradshaw, G.J. 233–4, 238
Bradshaw, J. 286
Bradshaw, J.L. 165
Brain, P.F. 479, 481
Braithwaite, R.W. 154
Brambilla, F. 503, 514
Branch, C. 282
Brandal 61
Brandeis, L.D. 141
Branta, C.F. 378
Brazelton, T.B. 206, 210
Breland, H. 139, 145, 156, 159
Bremme, K. 445

Brennan, R.L. 382
Brent, L. 138, 140–41, 173
Breskey, P.A. 184
Bresler, J. 160
Bresnihan, B. 140
Breukink, H. 51, 55, 63, 68
Brey, Robert H. 294
Bridges, J.W. 24–5
Briggs, G. 165, 286–7
Brinkman, J. 243
Briscoe, R. 444
Broad, F.E. 158
Broadbent, D. 286
Brodie, K.H. 480
Broer, K.H. 448
Broman, M. 238–40
Bronson, R.T. 158
Brooks, J. 119–20, 125, 155
Brooks-Gunn, J. 520–23, 527, 530–31, 536
Brophy, J.E. 389
Broverman, D.M. 115, 426, 515, 521
Broverman, I.K. 115, 426
Brown, Byron W. Jr. 205
Brown, J.C. 52
Brown, J.W. 314
Brown, W.A. 481
Brown, William 13, 30
Brown, W.T. 155
Brucefors, A. 414
Brundage, C.L. 386
Bruno, L.A. 125
Brust, J.C.M. 282–3
Bryant, G.M. 423
Bryden, M.P. 235, 245, 281–2, 285–7, 290, 321, 328
Buchtel, H. 286
Buech 87
Buffery, A.W.H. 281, 290–92, 516
Bühler, E. 158
Bukovský, Antonin 151–2
Bunderson, Karin 294
Bundy, R. 348
Bunney, W.E. Jr. 481
Buonaguro, Antonia 314
Buravlev, V.M. 141
Burbach, D. 158
Burbaeva, G.S. 141
Burden, V. 234
Burdi, A.R. 154
Burgerstein, L. 48
Burgeson, R. 531
Burgio, G.R. 133
Burke, J. 137–9
Burley, N. 158

Burmeister, W. 356
Burnett, S.A. 165
Burns, R.B. 81
Burrows, E. 289
Burt, C. 46, 49–50, 53–5, 58–9, 65, 67, 287
Burton, J. 238–9
Buschang, Peter H. 339, 344
Bush, M. 484
Buss, A.H. 388
Buster, J.E. 484
Butler, N.R. 132–4, 136, 140, 166

Cadoret, R.J. 132, 158
Cain, C. 132, 158
Caine, A. 163
Cairns, R.B. 479, 481
Calfee, M. 49, 52
Callan, S. 158
Cambiaso, C.L. 138
Campbell, D. 388–9
Cannon-Spoor, E. 135
Capitani, E. 305
Caplan, B. 235
Caplan, D. 428–9
Carey, S. 320, 426
Cargille, C.M. 484, 507
Carli, L. 390
Carlsmith, J. Merrill 398
Carlson, D. 430
Carlström, G. 155
Carlton-Ford, S. 531
Carmon, A. 238, 240
Carpenter, W.T. 211
Carr, B. 286
Carre, F.A. 379
Carrington, P. 202
Carter, C.O. 136
Carter, G.L. 238
Carter, J. 136, 156
Carter-Saltzman, L. 160
Castle, Cora Sutton 20, 64
Cathiard, A.M. 448
Catlin, S.F. 496
Cattell, J. McK. 18–19, 64, 77
Cavalli-Sforza, L.L. 228–9
Caverni, L. 276
Caylor, J.S. 403
Cenac, P.L. 147
Chadwick, O.F.D. 520
Chaganti, R.S.K. 157
Chance, J.E. 438
Chandler, M.J. 456–7
Chang, R.J. 136
Chapman, J.S. 234

Chaptal, C. 153
Charnov, E.L. 158, 162
Chaurasia, B. 287
Checchine, M. 235
Cheek, D.G. 431
Chen, T.C. 132–3, 137, 145, 166
Chesley, L.C. 137
Chess, S. 388
Chi, J. 288, 290
Chik, L. 185
Child, C.M. 339, 345
Childs, B. 132
Childs, M.K. 430
Chodorow, N. 116–17
Christiansen, K.O. 136
Christiansen, Lois 275
Chrousos, George P. 477, 479, 495, 500, 504
Chuck, B. 194
Cicirelli, V. 164
Ciocco, A. 134
Clare, J.E. 159
Clark, C.R. 494
Clarke, B. 138
Clarke, F.M. 191
Clarke, R. 303
Clarke-Stewart, K.A. 119, 121, 123, 125
Clarkson, F.E. 115
Clarkson, Marsha G. 348–9
Clausen, J.A. 501
Claushuis, M. 236
Clemens, L.E. 136
Clements, J.A. 448–9
Clements, P.R. 157
Clifton, Rachel K. 348–9
Cloninger, C.R. 136
Clutton-Brock, T.H. 150, 162, 164
Coakley, J. 386
Coale, A. 164
Coates, B. 120
Cobb, J.A. 149
Cochran, W.G. 350
Coddington, R.D. 522
Coe, C. 520
Cohen, B.E. 136–7, 153
Cohen, B.H. 140
Cohen, C. 320, 426
Cohen, D.J. 480
Cohen, G. 290
Cohen, H. 199
Cohen, J. 224, 252, 357, 388, 487, 521, 524
Cohen, P. 224, 487, 521, 524
Cohen, P.A. 82
Cohen, W.R. 185
Cohn, J. 47, 49–51, 53–6, 58, 62–3, 68

Cohn, R. 289
Coiffi, J. 243–5, 291
Cole, P.M. 320
Coleman, M. 156
Collins, R. 292
Collins, W.A. 521
Collins, W.P. 449
Collu, R. 515
Compas, B.E. 521–2
Coney 162
Conners, C.K. 390
Connor, J.M. 438
Conroy, R.L. 429, 435
Constantinople, A. 79
Cook 153
Cook, J. 287
Coolidge, M.R. 65, 68
Cooper, L.A. 430, 435
Cope, D. 289
Corballis, M. 234
Corbett, J.A. 133
Corbin, C.B. 405
Coren, S. 165
Corner, M.A. 444
Corrales, P.C. 484
Cosgrove, R.A. 137
Costa, M. 141
Costeff, Hanan 136–7, 152–3, 169–73
Costello, N. 125
Couette, J.E. 149
Courtis, S.A. 31, 53, 55, 64
Coventry, A.K. 165
Cox, F.N. 389
Cravens, H. 73–4, 83
Crawford, M.L. 145
Crichton-Browne, J. 281, 287, 289
Crisp, A.H. 520–21
Crockenberg, S. 388
Crockett, L. 477, 501, 521
Cronbach 483, 506
Crouchly, R. 159
Crowell, D.J. 242
Csikszentmihalyi, M. 520
Culebras, A. 289
Cullen, J. 237, 286
Culler, A.J. 49, 52
Culliton, M. 485, 532
Cummings, E.M. 481
Cunningham, L. 158
Cunningham, S.K. 485, 532
Cunningham, W.R. 86
Curry, F. 285
Curto, F. 158
Cutler, Gordon B. Jr. 477, 479, 484, 500, 507

Cutting, J.E. 428

da Costa-Woodson, E.M. 224, 226
Daglish, L. 124
Dalakas, M.C. 141
Dalton, K. 472
Daly, M. 149, 154
Damasio, H. 251
Damon, A. 523
Damon, S.T. 523
Darley, F. 314–15
Darling, J.F. 201
Darlington, C.D. 138, 147
Darwin, Charles 17, 154, 161, 285
Davey, Timothy C. 403, 408
Davidoff, J. 291
Davidson, I.A. 445
Davidson, R. 290
Davidson, R.T. 146
Davidson, W. 286–7
Davie, C. 288
Davie, R. 166
Davies, K.J. 423
Davies, M. 428, 495
Davies, R.B. 159
Davis, A. 290
Davis, A.E. 240–42
Davis, G.E. 522
Dawkins, S.N. 162
Dawood, M.Y. 448–9
Dawson, D.M. 141
Dearborn, W.F. 403–4
Deaux, K. 393
De Bruin, J.P.C. 444
Decker, S.N. 135
DeFries, J.C. 134–6, 160
Dekaban, A.S. 134, 348
deLacoste, C. 266
Delalieuz, A. 158
de Lignieres, B. 480, 515, 530
Delint, J.E.E. 142
Delozier, T. 149
Demarest, J. 286
Demarest, L. 286
Dement, W.C. 202, 206
Denckla, M. 245–6, 291
Denenberg, V.H. 206, 234
Dennis, M. 305, 316
Dennis, W. 287
Densmore 45
DeOreo, K. 370
de Renzi, E. 304, 311, 316
Deutsch, H. 520
Deutschberger, J. 138

De Vries, G.J. 444
Dewald, G. 158
Dewson, J. 292
Deykin, E.Y. 143, 150, 170
Diamond, J.M. 154, 169
Diamond, Marian C. 153, 169, 172, 261, 292
Diamond, R. 320–21, 331, 426, 439
Di Bianco, P. 199
Di Chiro, G. 288
Dibb, G. 165
Dickermann 162
Dieffenbacher, J. 47, 49–51, 53–5, 58, 62–3, 68
Dinnerstein, Dorothy 102, 116
Dimiceli, Sue 219
Divale, W. 162
Dobbing, J. 151
Docherty, J.R. 481
Dodds, A. 287
Doering, C.H. 136, 159, 164, 444, 473, 476, 480–81
Doglia, S. 52
Doherty, P.D. 163
Domaniewski-Sobczak 157
Donahue, M. 119
Donchin, E. 290
Donovan, J.E. 386
Dontchos, S. 194
Doppman, J. 495
Doran, T.A. 445
Dorman, M. 234–5, 286, 294
Dorn, L.D. 500
Dornbusch, Sanford M. 398
Doughty, R.W. 138–40
Douglas, J.W.B. 398
Douvan, E. 115–16
Dowd, J.M. 348
Dowling, G.A. 153
Downey, Miss 39–40
Dratt, L.M. 165
Dreyfus-Brisac, C. 206, 216
Drillien, C.M. 136, 145
Driver, M. 207
Drolette, M. 134
DuBois, L. 126
Ducharme, J.R. 515
Duganzich, D.M. 158
Duke, Paula M. 398, 523
Dunn, J.F. 484
Durefee, J.J. 119
Durnford, M. 286
Dusenberry, L.M. 371
Dustman, R.E. 241–3
Dwyer, C.A. 86

Dwyer, D.H. 75
Dyken, M. 289

Eagly, A. 378, 390
East, W.B. 379
Eaton, Warren O. 388–9, 394
Ebbin, A.J. 141
Ebbinghaus 53, 73
Eccles, J.S. 530
Eckerman, C.O. 120, 348
Eckert, H.M. 356, 370, 378
Edelbrock, C.S. 483, 522, 527, 537
Edison, T.A. 4
Edwards, J. 158–9, 164
Edwards, S. 282–3, 285, 305
Ehrenkranz, J. 480–81, 495
Ehrhardt, Anke A. 444–5, 455, 459, 465, 472, 503
Ehrlichman, H. 286
Eicher, E.M. 163, 172
Eichorn, D.H. 348–51, 521
Eichwald, E.J. 157
Eidelman, A.I. 151
Eisenson, J. 283, 314
Eleftheriou, B.E. 479
Ellams, J. 305
Ellegood, J.O. 448
Ellingson, R.J. 240
Elliot 56
Ellis, Albert 458
Ellis, H. 5–8, 18, 43–4, 77, 238–9
Ellis, L. 479
Ellman, S. 199
Elston, R.C. 134, 136
Emde, R.N. 191
Emery, D.E. 426
Eneroth, P. 445
Engel, A.G. 158
Engel, R. 125, 143
Engel, W.K. 141
Enlow, D.H. 345
Enns, Lesley R. 388
Entus, A. 234, 290
Ephron, H.S. 202
Epstein, S. 389
Erb, J.L. 503
Erikson, E.H. 201
Ernst, C. 143–4, 169
Espenschade, A. 402, 417
Esscher, E. 167
Etaugh, C. 243–6, 290

Fabia, J. 134
Faglioni, P. 304

Fagot, B.I. 121, 124, 356, 389
Faiman, C. 445, 448, 471, 521, 524, 531
Fairweather, H. 233, 281–2, 285
Faktor, M.I. 141
Falek, A. 158
Falk, M. 445
Falko, J.M. 554
Farber, C. 138
Farrell, Elizabeth E. 35
Farrell, P.M. 184
Faulk, W.P. 157
Faust, M. 398, 501
Feagans, L. 133
Febres, F. 136
Fechheimer, N.S. 150
Feddersen, W.E. 351
Feig, K. 158
Feldman, S.S. 121
Fencl, M. de M. 445
Fennell, E.B. 428, 436
Ferber, R. 320, 426
Ferguson, Mark W.J. 154, 165, 169, 174
Ferguson-Smith, M.A. 163
Fernbach, Stephen A. 205
Ferrari, P. 304
Ferrier, I.N. 514
Festenstein, H. 137, 139
Fialkow, P.J. 145
Field, J. 348
Finch, G. 292
Finch, S.J. 472
Finch, S.M. 146
Finegan, Jo-Anne 443, 446, 449
Finlayson, M.A.J. 245–6
Finot, J. 65, 67–8
Fish, M. 388
Fishaut, M. 152
Fisher, C. 198–9
Fisher, C.R. 26
Fisher, P. 133
Fisher, R.A. 162
Fiss, H. 199
Fitzpatrick, J.L. 86
Flanery, R.C. 243–5
Fleminger, J. 287
Fling, S. 356
Floody, O.R. 480–81, 496
Flor-Henry, P. 133–4
Foch, T.T. 521
Fonberg, E. 480
Forest, M.G. 448, 450, 515
Forgays, D. 238, 286
Forrest, T. 206
Forssman, H. 134

Forsyth, C.H. 56
Foster, J.W. 141
Fox, W.A. 14, 55
Fraccaro, M. 158, 168
Frankel, J. 123, 126
Franken, A. 58
Fraser, F.C. 151, 174
Frederiksen, C.H. 81
Freeman, B.J. 136, 156
Freeman, R.B. 240–42
Fregly, M.J. 481
Freier, S. 151
French, J. 155
French, J.W. 81
French, K.E. 355, 379–80, 386
Freud, S. 46, 54, 106, 108
Friedman, E. 155, 184
Friedman, R.C. 481
Friedman, S. 125
Friedman, S.L. 125
Fries, J. 545–6
Frieze, I.H. 126
Frisancho, A.R. 356
Frisch, R.E. 426, 501
Frodi, A. 480–81, 495
Fromm, D. 286
Frost, N. 437
Fuchs, A.R. 476
Fuchs, F. 476
Funderburk, S.J. 136, 156
Fürst, Emma 41
Furstenberg, F.F. Jr. 531

Gaar, D.G. 147
Gadjusek, D.C. 141
Galaburda, A.M. 289
Gallo, R.V. 514
Galton, Francis 144
Gandelman, R. 134, 444, 481
Gandour, M.J. 388
Garai, J.E. 81, 83–4, 125–6
Garbanati, J. 207, 217
Gardiner, M.F. 241–2
Gardner, C.G. 135
Gardner, P. 287
Garfinkel, P.E. 520–21
Gargiulo, J. 523, 530–31
Gargu, R. 523
Garner, D.M. 520–21
Garside, R.F. 136
Gashweiler, J.S. 154
Gasser, D.L. 163, 172
Gates, A. 28–9, 33, 286
Gazzaniga, M. 292

Gebauer, J. 158
Gefen, L.B. 141
Geffen, G. 235, 237, 290
Geffner, D.S. 234–5, 290–91
Geiringer, E.R. 81
Gelsthorpe, K. 138–40
Geodakjan, V.A. 151
George, F.W. 445
Gerall, A.A. 480
Gerendai, I. 151
Gershaw, N.J. 389
Geschwind, N. 145, 148, 151, 156, 159, 164–5, 174, 234, 288, 292, 303, 315
Gesell, A. 84
Gestalt 97, 100, 103–6, 112
Gevins, A. 290
Ghent, L. 244–6, 291
Giannini, M. 241–2
Gibbs, C.J. 141
Giese, F. 63
Gilbertson, A.N. 61
Gilgenkrantz, S. 158
Gill, D. 449
Gillberg, C. 136, 155–6, 168, 171, 173
Gillberg, I.C. 136
Gillick, D. 449
Gilligan, C. 115
Gilmour, D. 158
Ginsborg, A. 158
Glanville, B.B. 234, 236
Glass, A.R. 449
Glass, G.V. 82–3, 357–8
Gleicher, N. 138, 142
Glenn, M. 484
Glithero, E. 134
Gloning, K. 314
Gloninger, M.F. 157
Glucksmann, A. 132
Goble, W. 243
Goddard, H.H. 31, 57, 64
Goebel, R. 235, 290
Gold, J.J. 524
Gold, P.W. 495, 504
Goldberg, E.H. 137
Goldberg, H. 239–40
Goldberg, S. 119–20, 123
Goldstein, A.G. 438
Goldstein, H. 166
Goldstein, M.S. 342, 345
Gomez, M.R. 158
Gondos, B. 136
Gonzaga, F.P. 530
Goodard, K.E. 222
Goodfellow, P.N. 137, 142, 163

Goodglass, H. 236, 306, 315–16
Goodkin, Donald E. 148, 169, 173
Gooler, D.D. 89
Gorczynski, Reginald M. 156, 169, 172–3
Gordon, D.P. 235
Gordon, J. 286
Gordon, M. 136–8, 144, 171
Gordon, T.P. 481, 496
Gorin, P.D. 141
Gorski, R.A. 261, 445
Goswami, H. 287
Gottesman, I.I. 136, 472
Gough, H.G. 88
Gould, S.J. 161
Goulmy, E. 137, 163, 172
Gove, W.R. 157
Goy, R.W. 281, 425–6, 443, 445, 480
Grabstein, R. 123
Graef, R. 520
Graham, C.E. 484
Graham, P. 135, 169, 520
Gray, E. 158
Gray, J. 281, 290–92
Gray, J.A. 516
Gray, L.C. 353
Green, D. 351
Green, M.G. 373
Green, R. 472
Green, T.M. 521
Greenberg, R.A. 159, 164
Greendorfer, S.L. 356, 369, 378, 386
Griffin, J.E. 445
Griffiths, S.J. 167
Grigor, R.R. 140
Grober, E. 314
Grobstein, R. 192–3
Groff, T.R. 521
Gross, J. 198
Gross, Ruth T. 398
Gross, S. 48
Gross, S.J. 348
Grotevant, H.D. 144
Grubb, P. 154
Grumbach, M.M. 448, 524, 531
Grutzner, P. 158
Gualtieri, Thomas 132–3, 135, 139–40, 145, 147–67, 171
Guerrero, R. 150
Guidasci, L. 206
Guildford, J.P. 80
Guildford-Zimmerman 79
Guillaumin, J.M. 154
Guinness, F.E. 164
Gunnar, M.G. 119, 521

Gur, R. 290
Gurwitz, S.B. 125
Gutmann, D. 116
Gwiazda, Jane 348–9
Gyldensted, C. 288–9

Haaken, Janice 93
Haas, W. 163
Haber, A. 206
Haberman, M. 158
Haddad, S.A. 139
Hafer, M. 157
Hagberg, B. 136
Hagberg, G. 136
Hagen, J.W. 429
Haggerty, M.E. 50, 53–4
Hahn, William Kerr 233
Hakola, H.P.A. 158
Halbrecht, I. 141, 157
Hall, C.J. 445
Hall, G.S. 520
Hall, J. 299
Hall, J.L. 157
Halpern, D. 250
Halverson, C.F. Jr. 516
Halverson, H.M. 191
Halverson, L.E. 369, 371
Hamburg, B.A. 516
Hamburg, D.A. 480, 521, 527, 530
Hamilton, C. 292
Hamilton, J.B. 154
Hamilton, R.S. 154
Hamm, A. 303
Hampson, E. 260
Hampson, Joan 458–9, 461
Hampson, John 458–9, 461
Hannay, H. 286
Hannley, M. 294
Hansman, C. 378
Hare, E.H. 142, 149
Harlap, S. 150
Harris, L.J. 233–4, 240, 281, 438
Harris, M. 162
Harris, R. 133
Harris, R.E. 141
Harrison, Frederic 18
Harshman, R.A. 259, 272, 281–2, 285–7, 291
Hartje, W. 316
Hartley, C.G. 65, 68
Hartung, J. 164
Hartup, W.W. 120
Hasher, L. 394
Haskett, R.F. 460, 480, 521
Haslam, D. 287

Hatta, T. 243–5
Haubenstricker, J.L. 371, 378
Hauser, S.L. 141
Hay, S. 184, 480–81
Hay, W. 150
Hayata, I. 150
Haywood, K.M. 378
Hazzard, William R. 543
Head, J.R. 152
Hecaen, H. 234, 285, 287
Hedges, L.V. 357–61, 366, 390–92
Hefner, R. 373
Heidbreder, E. 82
Heilbrun, A.B. 88
Heim, A. 287, 291
Held, Richard M. 348, 353
Hellige, J.B. 238
Hellman, M. 345
Hemminger, H. 158
Hengartner, H. 163
Henry, F.M. 359
Henry, Joseph 4
Hensley, L.D. 379, 385
Hentschel, M. 50
Hermelin, B. 245, 287
Herrmann, D.J. 165
Herron, J. 234, 275
Hertz 48
Heschl, R. 288
Hess, T.M. 240–41, 290
Hevey, C.M. 123
Heymans, G. 55–6, 59, 65–7
Hicks, Robert E. 132, 135–6, 139–50, 145, 147–67, 171, 238, 287, 290
Hier, D.B. 158, 282
Hildreth, G. 291
Hill, D.S. 57, 61
Hill, J.P. 495, 521–2, 530
Hind, J.E. 349
Hines, M. 320, 444–5, 472, 476, 481
Hirano, A. 252
Hirfeld 157
Hirsch, H.V.B. 353
Hirsch, S. 245–6
Hirvonen, T. 133, 136–8, 173
Hiscock, M. 233–7, 240, 245, 276, 290
Hoban, M.C. 495
Hochberg, F. 288–90
Hochberg, I. 234–5
Hodgen, G. 484
Hodson, W.A. 158
Hoefkens, M. 235, 237
Hoepfner, R. 80
Hoesch-Ernst 61

Hoffman, H. 236
Hoffman, L.W. 116
Holinka, C.F. 150–51
Holl, M. 345
Holland, A.L. 304
Hollenbeck, B. 481
Hollingshead, A.B. 427, 482, 506
Hollingsworth, F. 158
Hollingworth, Leta Stetter 3, 10–11, 24, 29, 32, 34–5, 60, 64–5, 77
Holmbeck, G.N. 521
Holmes, J. 286, 428–9, 435
Holmes, R.K. 141
Holub, M. 152
Holve, L.M. 141
Hood, Kathryn E. 163, 168–9, 170, 172, 174, 479
Hoppe, P.C. 147
Horner, M.S. 86
Houser, B.B. 480–81, 514
Housner, L.D. 356, 369, 378, 386
Howard, K.I. 483
Hoyenga, Katharine Blick 157–8, 168–74
Hoyenga, K.T. 157–8
Huber, E. 53
Hubert, N.C. 388
Huggins, M.H. 145
Hughes, G.R. 140
Hughes, I.A. 448
Hughes, L. 235, 237
Huhtaniemi, I. 448
Hull, H. 35
Humphreys, Lloyd G. 403, 408, 412
Humphries, J.R. 147
Hunt, E. 437
Hunt, E.B. 191
Hunt, W.A. 191
Hurt, K.V. 158
Husen, T. 403–4, 415
Huston-Stein, A. 394
Hutchinson, C.A. 222
Hutchinson, E. 289
Hutt, C. 134, 281–2, 392
Hyde, J.S. 81, 358, 367, 390, 393–4, 496
Hynd, G. 235, 290

Iannotti, R.J. 481
Iivanain, M. 158
Ikeuchi, T. 150
Immelmann, K. 161
Imperato-McGinley, J. 459–61
Ingall, G.B. 450
Inglis, J. 158, 237, 251, 267
Ingram, D. 234–5, 290–91

Ingram, T.T.S. 133–4
Inoff, G.E. 516
Inoff-Germain, Gale 477, 479, 500
Iosimovich, J. 524
Irvine, D.R.F. 349
Isenberg, D. 239–40
Izard, C.E. 520

Jacklin, Carol Nagy 75, 84, 117, 120, 125–6, 136, 159, 164, 184, 219–20, 222–3, 245, 250, 281, 291, 356–7, 371, 378, 388–9, 394, 425, 431, 444, 465, 471, 473, 475–7, 480–81, 496
Jackson, E. 138
Jacobs, B.S. 125
Jacobs, P.A. 155
Jacobson, C.D. 445
Jahrsdoefer, R.A. 353
James, D.A. 138
James, W.H. 148, 150, 158–9, 171
Jarcho, H.D. 522
Jastrow, J. 29, 36
Jatlow, P.I. 158
Jeeves, M.A. 238–9
Jeffress, L.A. 351
Jenkins, E.C. 155
Jenkins, J.S. 445
Jenkins, W.M. 349
Jennings, Dennis 398
Jensen, Arthur R. 159–60, 169, 174, 403–4, 415
Jerger, J. 299
Jessor, R. 386
Joanen, T. 154, 165, 174
Joffe, J.M. 136
Johansen, K. 137–9
Johnson, B.L. 359
Johnson, D.W. 82
Johnson, E.M. 141, 173
Johnson, F.E. 356
Johnson, J.H. 522
Johnson, L.L. 142
Johnson, P.B. 126
Johnson, R. 82
Johnson, R.C. 136–7
Johnson, R.E. 153
Johnson, Samuel 78
Johnson, T. 446
Johnstone, E.C. 514
Jones, B. 238–40, 428
Jones, D.A. 154
Jones, D.W. 448
Jones, G.E. 47
Jones, H. 283, 291

Jones, L.A. 158
Jones, M. 398
Jones, M.C. 501
Jones, R.H. 242
Jones, S.C. 522
Jones, W.R. 138, 142
Jordan, J.V. 116, 127
Jöreskog, K.G. 386
Jörges, M. 44
Joyce, P. 243–5, 291
Juberg, R.R. 147, 173
Judd, C.M. 386
Judd, H.L. 448
Juret, P. 149
Jusczyk, P. 348

Kadotani, T. 141
Kagan, J. 124, 126
Kail, R. 286
Kandel, D. 495
Kandel, G. 243–4, 291
Kannan, P. 286
Kaplan, E. 306, 315–16
Kaplan, H.P. 521
Kaplan, J.M. 141
Kaplan, S.L. 448
Kapuniai, L.E. 242
Karacan, I. 197
Karp, C.H. 158
Karrow, W.G. 472
Kasl, S.V. 304
Kaste, M. 289
Katz, L. 239–40
Katz, P.A. 123, 126
Kaufman, M.H. 150
Kawabata, Y. 243–4
Kay, D.W.K. 136
Kay, S.R. 158
Keats, J.G. 389, 394
Keener, M. 222
Kellokumpu-Lehtinen, P. 149–50, 448
Kelly, D.D. 481
Kelly, J.B. 353
Kelly, P. 123
Kelly, R. 238–9
Kempf, E.J. 50, 53–4
Kenny, D.A. 220
Kent 34
Keogh, J. 378, 417
Kerschensteiner 62
Kertesz, Andrew 250–51, 254, 281–3, 285, 288, 303–5, 311, 314–16
Kessler, D.L. 158
Kester, P. 472

Ketupanya, A. 445
Kevy, S.V. 141
Kido, D. 288–9
Kiger, J.E. 378
Killian, G.A. 121, 125
Kim, H.S. 138
Kimura, A. 251, 255
Kimura, Doreen 234–7, 244–5, 258, 275–7, 279, 281, 285–7, 290–91
King, D.R. 444, 476
King, L. 286
King, S. 126
Kinsbourne, M. 136, 165, 233–6, 238, 240, 245, 276, 279, 287, 290, 311, 320
Kirby, D.R.S. 138, 147, 171
Kirby, M.L. 151
Kirkpatrick 62
Kisch 43
Kiser, C.V. 159
Kitzmiller, J.L. 140
Klaiber, E.L. 426, 521
Kleckner, H. 136–7
Klein, G.S. 199
Klein, J. 152
Klein, R.P. 119
Klein, S.P. 243–5
Klein, T. 449
Klinkenberg, L.M. 56
Klopper, A. 449
Knobloch, N.L. 450
Knox, C. 234–7, 285, 290–91
Knudsen, E.I. 353
Knudsen, P.F. 353
Kobayashi, T. 136
Kobayashi, Y. 286, 521
Kochhar, R.K. 349
Kodhr, G. 449
Koenig, K.L. 191
Koff, E. 320
Kohlberg, L. 420
Köhler, Wolfgang 103
Kohno, S. 150
Kolata, J.B. 219
Kolyaskina, G.I. 141
Komlos, L. 141, 157
Koo, G.C. 137, 147
Koopmans, L.H. 467–8
Kopec, A.C. 157
Koperski, J.A. 222
Korner, A.F. 125–6, 184, 190–91, 193–4, 197, 202, 205–7, 209–10, 216, 219–20, 222
Kossmann, R. 43
Kraemer, H. 136, 159, 164, 184, 187–8, 219–20, 222, 224–6, 444, 473, 480

Kraft, R.H. 234, 236
Kramer, M. 133
Krco, C.J. 137
Krombiegel, E.R. 133
Kron, R.E. 222, 226
Kroon, J.N. 240
Kuehn, R.E. 463
Kuhn, G.F. 349, 351
Kulig, J.W. 348
Kulik, C.-L.C. 82
Kulik, J.A. 82
Kunzig, H.J. 448
Kuper, Gertrude 12, 60
Kurtzberg, D. 206
Kuse, A.R. 319
Kuyek, J. 388
Kuypers, H.G. 243

Labouvie, G.V. 87–8
LaBreche, T.M. 243, 245
Lafitte 18
Lake, D. 285–6
Lamb, T.A. 479–80
Landerholm, E. 123
Landgrebe, S. 448
Lane, D.M. 165
Lang, E. 388
Langendorfer, S. 416
Lanman, J.T. 150
Lansberg 163
Lansdell, H. 251, 281–4, 288, 290–91, 304, 429
Lansky, L.M. 356
Laosa, L.M. 389
Lapidus, G.W. 75
LaPierre, Y.D. 480
Laroche, J. 191, 197–8
Larson, R. 520, 530–31
Lascelles, R. 289
Lashley, K.S. 426, 437
LaVeck, B. 157
LaVeck, G.D. 157
Lawler, S.D. 140, 147, 173
Lawrence, N.L. 157
Lawson, J.S. 158, 251
Laycock, F. 403
Le May, M. 288–9, 292, 303, 311
LeBoeuf, B.J. 154
Lecours, A.R. 151
Lee, A.K. 154
Lee, C.-F. 159
Leehey, S. 286
Lehrich, J.R. 141
Lehrke, R.G. 132

Lehtovaara, R. 139, 142, 147
Leibermann, J.R. 445
Leiderman, P.H. 123, 126
Leifer, A.D. 123
Leiskomia, R.M. 140
Lem, M.H. 51
Lenneberg, E.H. 233–5
Lens, W. 85
Leplat, G. 149
Lerner, R.M. 163, 521
Lernhardt, W. 163
LeRoy, D. 348
Leshin, M. 445
Leshner, A.I. 480
Lesser, R. 316
Levenson, R.A. 234
Lever, J. 373
Levin, E.R. 521
Levina, S.E. 448
Levine, J. 124
Levine, R. 283
Levine, S. 281
Levita, Eric 283, 314–16
Levitsky, W. 234, 288
Levni, E. 145
Levy, J. 286, 426, 445
Levy, N. 125
Levy, R.B. 243–6
Lewandowski, L.L. 236, 238
Lewerth, A. 136
Lewine, R. 179
Lewis, B. 349
Lewis, Helen Block 96, 99, 110–11
Lewis, M. 119–20, 123, 125–6
Lewis, Richard S. 275
Lewitter, F.I. 134, 136
Lewko, J.H. 378
Lewkowicz, D.J. 234
Libby, W. 58
Lichtenstein, L.M. 141
Lifrak, E.T. 521
Light, R.K. 277
Lilienfield, A.M. 136
Linberg, V. 136
Lindenmayer, J.-P. 158
Lindsley, J.G. 481
Lindsten, J. 158
Linn, M.C. 319
Lints, C.V. 158
Lints, F.A. 158
Lipmann, F. 36, 58, 64
Lipscomb, D. 286
Lipsitt, L.P. 125
Lisalc, R.P. 141

Liss, M.B. 378
Litvin, Y. 141
Livson, N. 501, 515
Lloyd, B. 378
Lloyd, C.W. 136
Lloyd, J.A. 482, 503
Lo, E.M. 158
Lobsien, M. 42, 53–4
Loftus, R. 158
Lohman, T.G. 379–80
Loke, Y.W. 136–8, 140–41, 147, 160, 171–4
Lokker, R. 234
Lomas, J. 287, 316
Lombroso-Ferraro, G. 36
Longstaff, A. 445
Lord, C. 134
Lordon, R.E. 141
Loriaux, D. Lynn 479, 484, 495, 500, 507, 530
Loriaux, L. 477
Lotter, V. 134
Loughlin, T. 485, 532
Low, D. 287
Low, H. 479, 481, 521
Low, J.B. 154
Lowel-Bell, S. 235, 237
Lubin, B. 483
Lubotsky, J. 136
Lucas, L.A. 484
Lunneborg, C. 437
Luria, Z. 116
Lurton, F.E. 57
Luttge, W.G. 482
Lynch, M.E. 521
Lyon, M.F. 158

Macaulay, J. 480
Maccoby, E.E. 75, 84, 117, 120–21, 125–6, 136, 158, 164, 170, 184, 220, 222, 245, 250, 281, 291, 356–7, 371, 378, 388–9, 394, 425, 431, 444, 446, 448, 465, 471, 473, 475–6, 480–81, 496
MacCombie, D.J. 479
Machover, Karen 110
Maciak, B.J. 157
Mack, J. 283
Mack, T. 143, 150
Mackey, Wade C. 161–2, 169
MacLusky, J.J. 153–4
MacMahon, B. 143, 150, 170
Maddison, P.J. 167
Madge, N. 166
Magnusson, D. 531
Mahadevaiah, S. 154

Mahesh, V.B. 448
Mahler, M. 115, 117–22, 126
Mahoney, R. 290
Main, M. 161
Mäkelä, O. 139, 142, 147
Mäkinen, Helena 417
Malina, R.M. 355–6, 371, 378, 530
Malone, D. 286
Malinvaud, E. 159, 171
Mall, Dr. Franklin P. 38–9, 44
Malone, D. 286
Mammucari, A. 303
Mandard, A.M. 149
Manlimos, F.S.H. 523
Mann, Madeline B. 320, 425, 428, 430
Manniello, R.L. 184
Manning, A.A. 243
Manosevitz, M. 403
Marcel, T. 238–40, 291
Marcus, J. 444, 475, 480, 496
Markle, G.E. 159
Markman, R. 243
Marlow, L. 521
Marolla, F.A. 144, 153, 169
Marsh, H.D. 33
Marsh, J. 287
Marshall, J. 286, 426, 428–9
Marshall, W.A. 323, 481–2, 484, 505, 507, 523, 537–8
Martin, H.E. 34
Martin, John A. 398
Maruyama, G. 82
Mason-Brothers, A. 156
Masson, P.L. 138
Matarazzo, J.D. 270, 283
Mateer, C.A. 264–5, 276, 279
Mathur, R.S. 448
Matsubara, T. 288
Matsui, T. 252
Matsunaga, T. 163
Matthis, P. 240
Mattsson, A. 479, 481, 504, 521
Maurenbrecher, H. 68
Mayer, D.L. 145
Mayerovó, A. 158
Mayo, J.P. 139–40, 145, 171
Mazur, A. 479–80
McCabe, P. 285, 305, 311, 314–15
McCarthy 107
McClintock, M.K. 464
McClure, P.A. 155
McCracken, G.H. 141
McCutcheon, S.M. 522
McDonough, P.G. 448

McDowell, R.M. 340
McEwen, B.S. 153, 425–6, 443, 445, 464
McFarland, H.F. 141
McFie, J. 283
McGaw, B. 404
McGee, M.G. 233, 245, 281
McGlone, J. 134, 233, 243, 251, 267, 275, 279, 281–7, 303–4, 314
McKahanon, G.M. 141
McKeever, W. 286
McKenna, T.J. 485, 532
McKeown, T. 142
McKinney, D. 133
McKinney, K.L. 531
McKusick 151
McLaren, A. 142, 147, 159, 164, 173
McMillen, M.M. 133–4, 136, 138, 149, 153, 170–71, 184, 229
McPherson, B.D. 386
McPherson, C.F.C. 141
McRae, D. 288
McWhirter, K.G. 138, 147
Mead, C.D. 49
Mead, M. 75
Meadows, J.L. 76
Meckel 4
Medawar, P.B. 134, 139–40, 163, 167, 173
Mednick, B. 135
Mednick, M.T.S. 75
Mednick, S.A. 135, 174
Meehan, A.M. 393
Meijere, J.C.H. 47
Meikle, D.B. 164
Melges, F. 521, 527, 530
Mellits, B.D. 431
Mellitts, E.D. 140
Mellman, W.J. 445
Meltzer, H.Y. 158
Melville, A.H. 62
Melville, M.M. 155
Mendel 47
Mennuti, M.T. 445, 449
Mercy, J.A. 143
Merola, James 320, 425
Mertens 43
Merzenich, M.M. 349
Messer, S. 119, 123
Messerli, P. 282–3
Mestler, G.E. 154
Metrakos, J.D. 142
Metrakos, K. 142
Metzger, R. 287
Meyer, U. 448
Meyer, V. 283

Meyer-Bahlburg, H.F.L. 320, 332–3, 444, 460, 465, 472, 503
Meyers, Garry C. 12–13
Miceli, G. 304–5, 311
Michael, R.P. 158
Michaelis, R. 206, 216
Mickey, M.R. 139
Migeon, C.J. 448
Mikamo, K. 150
Mikhail, G. 445
Mikkelsen, M. 158
Miles, C.C. 79, 85
Miles, W.R. 56
Miller, C.L. 530
Miller, J.B. 116
Miller, L.K. 238
Miller, R.B. Jr. 225
Mills, A.W. 348–9
Mills, J.A. 141
Milner, B. 281, 284
Milner, P. 245–6
Milton, G.A. 85
Minton, C. 124
Mirabile, P.J. 235, 237
Mischel, W. 82, 378
Mishkin, M. 286
Misner, J.E. 379
Mitchell, A. 148
Mittwoch, U. 154
Mizuno, M. 136
Möbius 44
Mobraaten, L.E. 142
Mohr, J.P. 315
Molfese, D.L. 240–42, 247, 289–90
Molfese, V.J. 240–42
Money, John 162, 167, 169, 445, 455–6, 458–9, 461, 465, 472
Monod, N. 206
Monroe, W.S. 50, 57
Montgomery, I.N. 158
Moody, L.O. 448
Mooney, C.M. 429
Moore, B.C. 143–4, 349
Moore, D.R. 349
Moore, K.A. 531
Moore, K.C. 150
Moore, R.C. 46, 49–50, 53–5, 58–9, 65, 67
Moos, R.H. 480
Morais, J. 234
Moraschini, S. 305
Moreau, T. 245–6
Morgan, T.H. 47–8
Morganstern, L. 241–2
Mori, M. 150

Morris, N.M. 521
Morris, R. 428
Morrongiello, B.A. 348, 352
Moscovitch, M. 311
Mosher, R.E. 379
Mosley, James L. 319
Moss, H.A. 123, 125–6
Mourant, A.E. 157
Moxcey, M.E. 35
Moyers, R.E. 345
Moylan, Patricia M. 320, 425
Mozans, H.J. 64
Muir, D. 348
Mulhall, E.F. 33
Müller, U. 157–8, 168
Müller-Lyer 14, 68
Munro 163
Münsterberg, H. 68
Mura, E. 135
Murasawa, Y. 136
Murdock, G.P. 84
Murphy, J. 158
Muth, G. 62
Muzio, J.N. 202, 206
Myers, G.C. 50, 52, 55

Nabholz, M. 163
Nachson, I. 238
Naditch, Sheridan Fenwick 111
Naftaly, N. 184
Nagafuchi, M. 234–5, 290–91
Nagamani, M. 448–50
Nakagawa, J.K. 242
Nakamura, D. 158
Nakano, K.K. 132
Nakatomi, Y. 289
Nam, C.B. 159
Nanda, R.S. 339–40
Nanko, S. 158
Nass, G. Gisela 339
Naylor, F. 138
Nebes, R.D. 165, 286–7
Neligan, G. 423
Nelson, D. 82
Nelson, J.K. 358–9
Netley, C. 426
Nettleton, N.C. 165, 233
Newcombe, F. 287
Newcombe, N. 243–4, 320–22, 331, 426, 439, 501
Newman, Parley W. 294
Nichols, P.L. 132–3, 136–7, 145, 166
Nielsen, J. 158
Nieschlag, E. 484, 507

Nilsson, B. 445
Nisbett, R.E. 125
Nisula, B.C. 484
Niswander, K.R. 126, 136–8, 141, 144, 171, 184
Nottebohm, F. 292
Nottebohm, M. 292
Nottelmann, Editha D. 477, 479, 485, 494, 500, 502, 507, 523
Novak, K.K. 207
Novitski, E. 138, 144
Nowell, N.W. 494

Obara, Y. 150
Obrzut, J. 235, 290
O'Connor, N. 245, 287
Odell, W.D. 484, 507
Odom, R. 348
Offer, D. 483, 520, 522
Offir, C. 75
Offner, Max 42, 58
Ogra, P.L. 152
Ohno, Susumu 137, 162–3, 172–3
Ojemann, G.A. 276
Oldersnaw, P.J. 138
Oldfield, E. 495
Oldfield, R. 287
O'Leary, S.E. 123, 126
Oleshansky, B. 373
Oliver, M. 140
Olkin, I, 357–61, 366
Olson, J.P. 126
Olson, M.E. 238–9
Olver, Rose R. 115
Olweus, D. 479–81, 494–5, 502, 521, 531
Omaha, K. 141
O'Malley, P.M. 85
Opler, L.A. 158
Oppenheim, G. 521
Orgass, B. 316
Orsini, D.L. 277
Orwin, R.G. 391
Oscar-Berman, M. 287
Osterrieth, P.A. 429
Ostrov, E. 483
Ounsted, C. 132–4, 136, 138, 149, 155, 163, 165, 167, 173–4
Ounsted, M. 138, 153

Padan-Belkin, E. 361
Page, B.M. 184
Painter, M. 378
Palermo, D.S. 240–42
Pallie, W. 288, 290

Palmblad, J. 164
Palmer, S. 158
Pang, S. 448
Pappas, C.T.E. 153
Park, Randolph K. 403, 408
Parke, R.D. 123, 126
Parker, L.N. 521, 530
Parkes, A.S. 164
Parlee, M.B. 94, 530
Parmalee, A.H. Jr. 126, 145, 202, 206–7, 216–17
Parsons, C.K. 408, 412
Parsons, J.E. 126
Partington, M.W. 388
Pasamanick, B. 136
Paterson, D.G. 33
Patterson, G.R. 361
Patterson, K. 286
Pearson, C.K. 445
Pearson, J. 141
Pearson, Karl 4–5, 7
Pedersen, K. 291
Pelletier 45
Pelliniemi, L.S. 149–50, 448
Peltin, S. 134
Pennal, B. 286
Pennington, B.F. 134
Perez, E. 286
Perlo, V.P. 158
Perris, E.E. 348
Perrot, D.R. 352–3
Persky, H. 481
Peskin, H. 501, 515
Peters, J.F. 240
Peters, M. 291
Peters-Martin, P. 388
Petersen, Anne C. 163–4, 168–70, 172, 174, 319–20, 378, 426, 437, 477, 501, 521–2
Petersen, M. 292
Peterson, G. 292
Peterson, H.A. 158
Peterson, J.L. 531
Petrinovich, L. 161
Pfaff, D.W. 502
Phebus, C.K. 157
Phillips, B.A. 57
Phillips, F.M. 52–3, 55
Phillips, S. 126
Phoenix, C.H. 480
Piaget, J. 203
Piazza, D. 234–5, 237, 291
Piccirillo, M. 480
Pickles, A.R. 159
Piercy, M. 285

Pine, F. 117
Pinter, R. 33
Pisoni, D. 348
Pittinger, B.F. 29
Pizzamiglio, L. 235, 303, 306
Placek, P. 137
Plaut, M. 141
Pleasure, D.E. 141
Plomin, R. 160, 388
Poduslo, S.E. 141
Poeck, K. 316
Polen, S.B. 276
Polich, J.M. 430
Ponder, B.A.J. 152
Popper 156
Porac, C. 165
Porges, S.W. 125
Porter, R. 234–5, 237, 286, 428
Portin, P. 151
Potkin, S.G. 135
Povey, S. 163
Powell, S. 448
Prader, A. 158
Prechtl, H.F.R. 206
Presl, Jiři 151–2, 172–3
Pressey, L.W. 33, 76
Pressey, S.L. 33
Price, J.S. 142, 149
Pring, T.R. 238
Prins, R. 315
Propper, R.D. 141
Provenzano, F.J. 116
Prudham, D. 423
Puck, M. 158
Puig-Antich, J. 480
Purifoy, F.E. 467–8
Purtilo, D.T. 157, 172
Putnam, W. 281
Pyle, W.H. 47, 50–51, 53, 58

Quadagno, D.M. 444

Rabinovitch, A. 287
Rabl 288
Race, H.V. 35
Radke-Yarrow, M. 481
Raguthu, S. 155
Raj, M.H. 521
Rajan, P. 238, 240, 291
Ramirez, V. 292
Ramsay, D.S. 234
Rantakallio, Paula 417
Rasmussen, P. 136, 155–6
Rasmussen, T. 284

Ratcliffe, C.G. 155, 158
Rattray, G.D. 356, 369, 386
Ray, W.J. 290, 320
Rayford, P.L. 484, 507
Razzano, C. 303, 306
Read, P.B. 520
Reade, Elaine P. 205
Rebecca, M. 373
Rebert, C. 287, 290
Record, R.G. 142
Redman, C.W.G. 147, 173
Reed, E.W. 143–5, 149, 170
Reed, P. 165
Reed, P.B. 520
Reed, R.B. 523
Reed, S.G. 143–5, 149, 170
Reed, T.E. 160
Reeves, B.R. 140, 147
Reich, T. 136
Reid, M. 286, 426
Reinhold 53
Reinisch, J.M. 133–4, 281, 292, 444–5, 460, 476, 480, 521
Reitan, R.M. 245–6
Remington, R. 281–2, 285
Renkonen, K.O. 137, 139, 142, 147, 171
Renoux, G. 154
Renoux, M. 154
Resnick, S. 320, 426, 472, 476
Revicki, D. 134
Rex, A. 151
Reyes, F.I. 445, 448–9, 471, 515
Reynolds, D.M.Q. 238–9
Reynolds, E.L. 523
Rheingold, H. 120
Rho, J.M. 206
Rhodes, L.E. 241–3
Rhodes, P. 133, 136
Richardson, S.A. 157
Richart, R.M. 481
Richlin, M. 241–2
Ridenour, M.V. 358
Rierdan, J. 320
Rife, D.C. 151
Rijsdijk, J.P. 240
Riklan, M. 283
Rikli, R. 359, 372
Risser, A. 316
Ritvo, E.R. 156
Ritzén, E.M. 158
Rivarola, M.A. 448
Rizzolatti, G. 286
Roach, M. 289
Roberton, M.A. 369–72

Roberts, J. 143
Roberts, T.W. 371
Robertson, F.W. 184
Robinette, W.L. 154
Robins, L. 135
Robinson, A. 158
Robinson, B.E. 373
Robinson, J.D. 448–50
Robinson, R.G. 133
Robinson, S. 157
Robinson, T. 292
Robson, E.B. 137
Roche, A.F. 125, 351, 356
Rock, D. 135, 527
Rodbard, D. 484
Rodeck, C.H. 449
Roffwarg, H.P. 202, 206, 216
Rogosa, D. 412
Rojas, O.I. 150
Ropers, H.-H. 158, 163
Rorschach 106
Rosado, V. 158
Rosanoff, A.J. 34
Rosanoff, I.R. 34
Rose, B. 238
Rose, C. 314
Rose, R. 479, 481, 496
Rose, S. 243–6
Rosen, G. 199
Rosen, M.G. 185
Rosenberg, B.G. 86, 145
Rosenberg, D.A. 449
Rosenberg, F. 520
Rosenberg, M. 520
Rosenblum, D. 291
Rosenfield, S. 304
Rosenfield, W.D. 243–5
Rosenkrantz, P.S. 115
Rosenthal, D. 135
Rosenthal, Robert 109, 392
Rosenzweig, M.R. 234
Rosenzweig, S. 159
Ross, G.T. 484
Ross, R.K. 553
Rossi, Alice 466, 469
Rossi, J.S. 393–4
Rossi, Peter 469
Ross-Kossak, P. 238–9
Rosso, J. 523
Rosso, P. 348
Rostron, J. 158
Roszkowski, W. 141
Rote 151
Roth, G.L. 349

Rothney, J.W.M. 403–4
Roubinian, J. 158
Routh, D.K. 389
Rovet, J. 320, 332, 426
Rowe, P. 445, 448
Rowell, N.R. 140
Rowland 4
Roy-Bryne, P. 495
Royer, F.L. 430
Rubens, A. 287, 289
Rubenstein, A. 141
Rubin, D.B. 392
Rubin, J.Z. 116, 126
Rubin, R.T. 460, 480, 482, 521
Rubinow, D.R. 495
Ruble, D.N. 126, 521, 530–31
Rudel, R. 245–6, 291
Ruppel, E.M. 206
Rush, R.A. 141
Russell, B. 36
Rutter, M. 132–5, 166, 169–70, 172–4, 394, 520–21

Sabin, A.G. 133
Sach, Hans 62
Sachar, E. 479
Sachs, B.D. 426
Sachtleben, M.R. 184
Sadowsky, D. 134
Safrit, M.J. 418
Salbenblatt, J. 158
Salzmann, K.D. 173
Samaroff, A.J. 456–7
Samuels, H. 120
Samuels, L. 133
Sandel, T.T. 351
Sanders, B. 320, 332
Sanders, L. 138, 144
Sanders, S.A. 445, 476
Sandhu 153–4
Sandler, L. 138, 144
Sandström, C. 281
Sanford, J.P.K. 141
Sapp, M. 371
Sar, M. 515
Sarno, Martha T. 314–16
Sasaki, M. 150
Sasanuma, S. 286
Sassenrath, E.N. 530
Satz, P. 277, 290, 428
Sauget, J. 285
Saxby, L. 235, 245, 321
Saxena, B.B. 448–9
Scammon, R.E. 339

Scaramella, T.J. 481
Scarr, S. 144, 160
Schachar, R. 394
Schackman, M. 438
Schaefer, E.J. 553, 555
Shaffer, D. 133
Schaie, K.W. 87–8
Schalling, D. 479, 481, 521
Scheffé, H. 225
Scheffner, D. 240
Scheifler, H. 61
Scheinfeld, A. 81, 83–4, 125–6
Schiller, B. 78
Schlain, E.A. 480
Schlegel, A. 75
Schlesinger, E.R. 134
Schmidt, R.A. 406
Schmitz-Roeckerath, B. 448
Schneider, P. 206
Schneider, P.A. 222
Schoenbaum, S. 143, 150, 170
Schooler, C. 149
Schopler, E. 134
Schrag, H.L. 137, 144
Schramm, F. 51
Schreier, M.H. 163
Schuermeyer, T. 495
Schulenberg, J.E. 522
Schulman-Galambos, C. 235–7, 290, 429
Schulsinger, F. 135
Schulte, H.M. 495
Schultz, M. 202
Schupf, N. 141
Schuster, D.H. 158
Schuster, L. 158
Schutz, Robert W. 378–9
Schuyten 39
Schwarz, J.C. 389
Scott, J. 286
Scott, J.R. 137–8, 151, 173
Scott, J.S. 167, 172
Scott, O. 167
Scriven, G.A. 123
Searleman, Alan 164–5, 174, 236, 286–7
Seashore, M.J. 123
Seavey, C.A. 123, 126
Sedlis, A. 138
Seefeldt, V. 378
Segal, J. 124
Segalowitz, S.J. 234
Seidman, L.J. 158
Selander, R.K. 154
Seller, M.H. 139
Selnes, O. 288

Semon, J. 320
Serafetinides, E. 284
Serbin, L. 438
Sergent, J. 238, 240
Seward, G.H. 83–4
Sexton, M.A. 235, 237
Shankweiler, D. 285
Shapiro, A. 199
Shaywitz, B.A. 480
Sheard, M.H. 480
Shearer, M.L. 146
Shearer, W.M. 296
Sheer, D. 163
Sheldon, E.B. 89
Shepard, R.N. 430, 435
Shepher, J. 75
Sheppard, A. 251, 304–5
Sherif, C.W. 356, 369, 386
Sherman, J. 281
Shields, S.A. 73
Shiffrin, R.M. 429, 437
Shipley, C. 320, 476
Shoaff, B. 222
Shuttleworth, F.K. 403–4
Sidtis, J.J. 322, 325
Siegel, A. 286
Siegel, I. 138, 142
Siegel-Gorelick, Bryna 398
Sievel, J. 206
Siiteri, P.K. 136, 158, 448
Silberger, D.H. 141
Siler-Kodhr, T.M. 449
Silmser, C.R. 157
Silverberg, R. 287
Silvers, W.K. 138, 163, 172
Silvey, R.G. 154
Simmons, R.G. 287, 520–21, 527, 531
Simmons, R.L. 139
Simpson, E. 163
Sindermann, F. 289
Singer, J.E. 126, 133, 136, 141
Sio, J.O. 157
Siris, E.S. 481
Siris, S.G. 481
Sizonenko, P.C. 448, 479, 481, 524, 531
Skinner, R.P. 167
Skoff, R. 158
Skon, L. 82
Slater, E. 134
Slaughter, M.H. 379
Slavkin, H.C. 141
Sloane, D.M. 159
Smail, P.J. 445
Smeets, J. 481

Smith, A. 394
Smith, A.M.A. 154
Smith, D.W. 159, 184
Smith, G. 145
Smith, K.D. 481
Smith, L. 158
Smith, M. 239–40
Smith, M.L. 82, 357
Smith, P.K. 124, 378
Smith, S.D. 134
Smolen, J.S. 151
Smoll, Frank L. 378
Snedecor, G.W. 350
Snow, M.E. 126, 222
Snow, M.H.L. 155
Soares, M.P. 320, 332
Sobel, D.E. 135
Sokal, M.M. 73
Sokol, R.J. 185
Solomon, G.F. 157, 172
Soper, H.V. 277
Sörbom, D. 386
Sørenson, K. 158
Sotelo, J. 141
Southam, A.L. 530
Spalten, E. 245–6
Spector, W.S. 150
Spence, J.T. 86
Spiegel, F.S. 134, 444
Spiro, M.E. 75
Sprague, R.H. 463
Spreen, O. 277, 285, 315–16, 428
Springer, S. 236, 286
Sprott, D.A. 328
Sprott, R.L. 479
Stafford, R. 281
Stamps, L.E. 125
Stanford-Binet 79
Stanley, F. 153, 170
Stanley, J.C. 148
Stapleton, D.W. 163
Starch, D. 49, 56
Starinsky, R. 238
Stastny, P. 173
Stattin, H. 531
Stechler, G. 185
Steelman, L.C. 143
Stein, M. 222
Stein, Z.A. 137, 144
Steinberg, A.D. 151
Steinberg, L. 495, 521
Steitz, J.A. 167
Stern, E. 126, 202, 206, 216
Stern, W. 65, 67

Stevenson, David K. 205
Stewart, A.L. 155
Stewart, M.A. 134
Stillwell, J.L. 379
Stites, D. 136
Stockton, M.I. 60
Stojkov, J. 185
Stoll, J. 158
Stone 14, 55
Stone, D.F. 138
Stoto, M. 164
Strauss, E. 320
Strober, M. 521
Strock, B.D. 125
Strong, A.C. 57
Strong, E.K. Jr. 11–12, 26–7, 34, 60
Srother, C.R. 87
Strumpel, B. 89
Stubbs, E.G. 145, 156
Studdert-Kennedy, M. 285
Sturm, L.A. 348
Sugden, D. 378
Sullivan, J.L. 157, 172
Surrey, J.L. 116
Susman, E.J. 477, 479, 495, 500, 521, 526–7, 531–2
Susser, M.W. 144
Sutton-Smith, B. 86, 145
Svenson, B. 155
Svensson, J. 481
Swigar, M.E. 158
Sykes, D.H. 237
Symons 162
Szekely, G.A. 145

Takagi, S. 448
Talal, N. 158
Talbot, Marion 44
Tam, P.P.L. 155
Tammisalo, E. 151
Tandler, J. 48
Tanguay, P. 136, 156
Tanner, J.M. 320, 323, 333, 339, 341, 345, 350, 398–9, 403, 427, 481–2, 484, 505, 507, 513, 523, 526, 536–8
Tapanainen, J. 448–9
Tapper, A.J. 448
Tartter, V. 236
Tavris, C. 75
Taylor, C. 157
Taylor, D. 283
Taylor, D.C. 132–4, 149, 155, 163, 165, 167, 174
Taylor, Eric 166, 169–70, 172–4

Taylor, L. 290
Taylor, M.A. 133, 146, 171
Taylor, M.J. 165
Taylor, Pamela V. 166–7, 169, 171–3
Taylor-Sarno, M. 315–16
Tcheng, F.C.Y. 191, 197–8
Teas, D.C. 351
Teasdale, T.W. 135
Teitelbaum, M.S. 138, 147, 164, 171, 229
Teller, R.C. 484
Teng, E. 287, 291
Terasaki, P.I. 139, 141
Terman, L.M. 25–6, 30, 35, 79, 85
Termijtelen, A. 137, 163
Teszner, D. 288
Teuber, H.L. 290
Teuerstein, I. 445
Theodore, C. 152
Theorell, K. 206
Thistle, A. 286
Thoits, P.A. 521
Thom, Valerie A. 205
Thoman, E.B. 126, 184, 206, 210, 217, 220
Thomas, A. 388
Thomas, Jerry R. 355, 358, 366, 379–80, 386
Thome, P.R. 480
Thompson, A. 287
Thompson, Clara 108
Thompson, Helen Bradford 9, 39, 41–2, 44
Thompson, R. 141
Thomson, J. 305
Thorley, J.D. 141
Thorndike, E.L. 3–4, 6, 9, 14, 18, 20, 55, 59–60, 64–6, 77
Thurstone, L.L. 80–81, 281
Thurstone, T.G. 80
Tieger, T. 480–81, 520
Tierney, I. 158
Tiffin, J. 287
Tiger, L. 75
Tilford, B.L. 164
Timonen, S. 137, 147
Tips, R.L. 145
Tizard, J. 166, 169
Toivanen, P. 133, 136–8, 166, 173
Tolson, H. 358
Tomlinson-Keasey 238–40
Touwen, B. 423
Trabue, M.R. 25, 30
Tranel 251
Treisman, A. 237
Trevarthen, C. 151
Trites, R.L. 133
Trivers, R.L. 155, 162

Truog, W.E. 158
Trussel, J. 164
Tryon, W.W. 389, 394
Tsai, L.Y. 133–6
Tsao, Y.C. 165
Tsutui, K. 243–4
Tucker, D. 289–90
Tucker, J. 352
Tuffrey, M. 139
Tulchinsky, D. 445, 448
Turkewitz, G. 234, 238–9
Turner, S. 238
Tyler, L.E. 81, 83–4

Udry, J.R. 521, 523, 526–7, 531
Ukaejoofo, E.D. 140, 147
Ullian, D.Z. 373
Umiltà, C. 286
Upton 18
Urbach, N. 251, 282–3, 304
Urberg, K.A. 88
Uylings, H.B.M. 444

Valadian, I. 523
Van Arsdale, M. 157
Van Coevering, R. 450
Van Deventer, A. 286
Van Kammen, D.P. 481
Van Leeuwen 163
van Rood, J.J. 137, 163
van de Poll, N.E. 481, 516
van den Berghe, P.L. 162
Van der Klaauw, C.J. 345–6
Van der Vlugt 235–7
Van der Wildt, G.J. 240
van der Zwan, S.M. 481
Vande Wiele, R.L. 481
Vandenberg, S.G. 319
Vander Eeken, H. 289
Vander Stoep, L.P. 121, 125
Vanderwolf, C. 287
Vargha-Khadem, F. 234
Varner, J.L. 240
Varrela, J. 151
Venables, P.H. 135
Venier, M.C. 138–9
Vernhes, J.C. 149
Vertes, J. 50
Vessey, M.P. 134
Vessey, S.H. 164
Vietze, P. 125
Vigersky, R.A. 530
Vignolo, L.A. 251, 265, 276, 279, 314–16
Vihko, R. 484, 495, 524
Vincens, M. 480, 515, 530

Vogel, S. 115
Vogel, W. 426, 521
von Boehmer, H. 163
von Wendt, L. 417
Voss, R. 163
Vrbancic, Mirna I. 319
Vredevoe, D. 139

Waber, Deborah P. 291, 320–21, 330–33, 425–30, 433, 435, 437, 439, 501
Wachs, T.D. 388
Wachtel, G.M. 158
Wachtel, S.S. 137, 157–8
Wada, J.A. 240–42, 284, 288–90, 303, 312
Waddington, C.H. 345
Wagner, P.A. 62
Wahlström, J. 155
Waldenström, E. 155–6
Waldeyer 39
Waldrop, M.F. 126, 144
Wale, J. 235, 237
Walker, R.M. 371
Wallace, S.J. 145
Walter, D.O. 241–2
Walter, J. 286
Waltimo, O. 289
Walton, M.D. 389
Warburton, D. 138
Ward, W.F. 158
Warne, G.L. 448
Warren, J. 292
Warren, Michelle P. 520–21, 523, 527, 530–31, 536
Watters, G.W. 234
Watts, K. 287, 291
Webb, G.J.W. 154
Webster, W. 292
Wechsler, D. 250, 282
Weener, P. 429, 435
Weinberg, R.A. 144
Weinberg, W. 149
Weinberger, D.R. 135
Weiner, H.L. 141
Weininger 44
Weinraub, M. 123, 125–6
Weinstein, S. 241–2, 287
Weisfeld, G.E. 479
Weisinger, M. 241–2
Weiss, J. 43
Weiss, P. 339
Weiss, W. 138
Weist, W.F. 445
Weiten, W. 290
Weitzel, K.E. 430

Weizman, A. 145
Weizman, R. 145
Welch, F. 159, 171
Welcker, H. 345
Weller, G.M. 126
Weller, L.E. 136-7, 153
Wells, F.L. 10, 36, 39, 44-5, 50, 52-4
Wenner, W.H. 202
Wernicke 251, 254
Wertheimer, Max 103-4
West, S. 123, 126
Westlake, J.R. 136, 156
Westphal, M. 126, 136, 141
Westwood, J.H. 152
Weyerer, S. 133
Whalen, T. 348
Whitaker, H. 305
White, C. 159, 164
Whitmore, K. 166, 169
Whyte, M.K. 161
Wickstrom, R.L. 405, 417
Wiersma, E.D. 57, 66
Wigand, R. 133
Wijsenbeek, H. 145
Wilcox, Karen T. 471
Wile, I. 287
Willard, D.E. 155, 162
Wilkinson, M.M. 152
Williams, A.F. 151
Williams, C.A. 141
Williams, J.D. 296
Williams, K. 472
Williams, R.H. 479, 481
Williams, S.M. 277
Williamson, H.O. 448
Willis, M.P. 234
Wilson, E.O. 161, 378
Wilson, J.D. 445, 448
Wilson, L. 141, 234
Wilson, M. 149, 154
Wilson, M.G. 145
Winch, W.H. 40, 50
Wines, J.V. 523
Wing, L. 133-5
Wingate, M.E. 296
Winick, M. 348
Winter, J.S. 445, 448, 471, 521, 524, 531
Winter, S.T. 153
Wisniewski, K. 155
Wissler 9
Witelson, S.F. 239, 243-5, 281, 288, 290-91, 322
Witke, R. 75
Witkin, Herman 94-112, 281

Wittes, J.A. 137, 144
Wogan, M. 290
Wolf, T.H. 73, 75
Wolf, V. 137
Wolff, P.H. 125, 190-94, 196-7, 202-3, 210, 320, 426
Wolin, S.L. 167
Wolowitz, H. 116
Womer, F.B. 89
Wong, P.Y. 443, 445-6
Wood, C.B.S. 173
Wood, D.E. 446
Wood, M. 152
Woodrum, D.E. 158
Woods, B.T. 290
Woodson, R.H. 224, 226
Woodworth, R.S. 50, 349, 351
Woolf, C.M. 136, 144
Woolley, Helen Thompson 26, 30, 45-6, 77
Wrangham, R.W. 164
Wrenschner, A. 40-42, 65-7
Wu, C.H. 445
Wyatt, R.J. 135
Wyshak, G. 145

Yakovlev, P.I. 151
Yamamoto, M. 149-50, 243-4
Yamazaki, J.N. 139
Yarnell, P. 289, 315
Yen, S.S.C. 448
Yen, W.M. 81
Yeni-Komshian, G. 239-40, 286, 288, 291-2
Yerkes, R.M. 24-5
Yoakum, C.S. 52
Young, A.W. 238-9
Young, P.E. 448
Young, W.C. 480
Yule, W. 520

Zacks, R.T. 394
Zahn-Waxler, C. 481
Zaidel, E. 304
Zajonc, R.B. 144, 153, 166
Zakin, D.F. 521
Zalk, S.R. 123, 126
Zambie, M.F. 147
Zangwill, O. 282
Zborowski 157
Zeidner, L.P. 206
Zellman, G.L. 126
Zerssen, D.V. 133
Židovský, J. 152
Zigler, Edward 101
Zinkernagel, R.M. 163

Zipser, R.O. 521, 530
Zuch, J. 198
Zuckerman, M. 483

Zuffardi, O. 158
Zumoff, B. 530
Zybert, P. 144